OPERATING GRANTS for NONPROFIT ORGANIZATIONS 2012

7th Edition

Schoolhouse Partners LLC
West Lafayette, Indiana

Why 'Partners'? Partners work together as a team, with each person contributing different skills and expressing his or her individual interests and opinions to the unity and efficiency of the group in order to achieve common goals. Our aim is to make worthwhile resources available to you so that you and your institution or organization can and will achieve those goals.

Schoolhouse Partners, 1281 Win Hentschel Blvd, West Lafayette, IN 47906
www.schoolhousepartners.net
Published 1999, 7th edition 2011

Printed and bound in the United States of America

ISBN 978-0-9837622-1-8
0-9837622-1-X

Table of Contents

Introduction

For over three decades the GRANTS Database and its print directories, including the annual *Operating Grants for Nonprofit Organizations*, have provided the grant seeking community with funding sources to enrich or improve the lives of community residents. Funding in support of operating costs is one of the most difficult grants to find. Expenses may include overhead, salary support, administration, utilities, and other ongoing costs of an organization that are not related to a specific project. Since operating costs do not fund a specific goal or objective, the struggle to locate and fund ongoing expenses is fierce. This directory is a tool that can greatly assist with this difficult task.

Operating Grants for Nonprofit Organizations 2012

Operating Grants for Nonprofit Organizations 2012, now in its seventh edition, features more than 1,750 current funding programs that support some or all general operating expenses of nonprofits and other institutions. Listings in the main section of *Operating Grants* contain annotations describing each program's overall focuses and goals, program requirements explaining eligibility, funding amounts, deadlines for Application, restrictions, *Catalog of Federal Domestic Assistance* program number (for U.S. government programs only), samples of previously awarded grants, sponsor name and address, contact information, and the sponsor's Internet Web address. Grantseekers with access to the Internet can use the addresses to locate further information about the organizations and their application procedures. Internet addresses are also provided, when available, within listings. Some of the grant programs listed in the main section have geographic restrictions for applicants.

The following people have devoted a great deal of patience, hard work and thought to keep this project and the database an informative service for the user. It is especially important to mention the GrantSelect team – Louis S. Schafer, Ed.S., and Anita Schafer – for their diligent research, editorial work, development and assignment of index terms, and production – as well as all Schoolhouse Partners team of editors, which includes Susan Bales, Jeanne Winstead, and Marilyn Martin Zerbes, who contribute to the grants editorial effort on a daily basis.

Inclusion in the book indicates that each funder gives some form of operating support, has an active funding program that accepts unsolicited inquiries, and gives monetary awards. Funders' interests span a wide range of areas, including the arts, humanities, child development, social and human services, youth programs, economic development, education, environmental programs, health care, religious programs, community development, and more.

Indexes. The Subject Index of this *Funding Sources* lists all program titles—with accession numbers—under their applicable subject terms. Other indexes follow, including the Grants by Program Type Index, which lists a variety of program categories, such as Community Development, Cultural Outreach, Educational Programs, etc., with grants that fall within their scope; and the Geographic Index, which lists programs that have state, regional, or international focus. See How to Use This Directory on pages v-vii for sample index entries.

Using *Funding Sources* for Grantseeking

By using this edition of *Operating Grants for Nonprofit Organizations*, grantseekers can match the needs of their particular programs with those sponsors offering funding in the grantseekers' area of interest. The information listed here is meant to eliminate the costs incurred by both grantseekers and grantmakers when inappropriate proposals are submitted for a sponsor's funding program. However, because the GRANTS Database is updated on a daily basis, with program listings continually added, deleted, and revised, grantseekers using this edition of may also search the GRANTS database online through *GrantSelect* (www.grantselect.com).

All new and revised information within *Operating Grants* has been taken from (1) the sponsor's updated of previously published program statements included in earlier editions of GRANTS publications, (2) questionnaires sent to sponsors whose programs were not listed in previous editions, or (3) other materials published by the sponsor and furnished to Schoolhouse Partners. Updated information for U.S. government programs includes new and revised program information published in the *Federal Register*; the latest edition of the *Catalog of Federal Domestic Assistance*; the *NIH Guide*, published weekly by the National Institutes of Health; and the *NSF E-Bulletin*, a monthly publication of the National Science Foundation.

 Anyone having questions regarding the content, format, or any other aspect of the *Operating Grants for Nonprofit Organizations 2012*, GrantSelect, or the GRANTS Database should contact the Editors, GRANTS, Schoolhouse Partners or editor@schoolhousepartners.net.

How to Use This Directory

Operating Grants for Nonprofit Organizations 2012 is designed to allow the user quick and easy access to information regarding funding programs in a researcher's specific area of interest. This *Funding Sources* is composed of a main section, Grant Programs, which lists grant programs in alphabetical order, and three indexes: the Subject Index, the Grants by Program Type Index, and the Geographic Index.

GRANT PROGRAMS

Each listing in this section consists of the following elements: an annotation describing each program's focus and goals, requirements explaining eligibility, funding amounts, application and renewal dates, sponsor information, contact information, and Internet address.

GRANT TITLE	**Abbot and Dorothy H. Stevens Foundation Grants 18**	ACCESSION NUMBER
	The Abbot and Dorothy H. Stevens Foundation funds Massachusetts non-profits with a emphasis on the greater Lawrence/Merrimack Valley area. Giving primarily for the arts, education, conservation, and health and human services. Fields of interest include: arts; children/youth, services; crime/violence prevention, domestic violence; education; elderly; environment, natural resources; health care; health organizations, association; historic preservation/historical societies; humanities; human services; immigrants; medical school/education; museums. Types of support include: building/renovation; capital campaigns; continuing support; endowments; equipment; general/operating support; management development/capacity building; matching/challenge support; program-related investments/loans; program development; technical assistance.	GRANT DESCRIPTION
REQUIREMENTS	*Requirements:* Massachusetts 501(c)3 tax-exempt organizations serving the greater Lawrence and Merrimack Valley are eligible. There is no deadline date when applying for funding, nor is there a application form required. The Foundation will however accept the Associated Grantmakers Common Proposal Form. Applicants should submit a copy of their IRS Determination Letter and one copy of their proposal when applying for funding. The board meets and reviews proposals monthly except for the months of July and August.	
RESTRICTIONS	*Restrictions:* Grants do not support national organizations, state or federal agencies, individuals, annual campaigns, deficit financing, exchange programs, internships, professorships, scholarships, or fellowships.	
	Geographic Focus: Massachusetts	GEOGRAPHIC FOCUS
AMOUNT	*Amount:* 1,000 - 20,000 USD	
	Samples: Boston Childrens Museum, Boston, MA, $15,000 (2008); Boston Symphony Orchestra, Boston, MA, $10,000 (2008); Boston Ballet, Boston, MA, $5,000 (2008).	SAMPLES
	Contact: Josh Miner, Executive Director; (978) 688-7211; (978) 686-1620;	CONTACT
	grantprocess@stevensfoundation.com	INTERNET ADDRESS
SPONSOR INFORMATION	*Sponsor:* Abbot and Dorothy H. Suitevens Foundation P.O. Box 111 North Andover, MA 01845-7211	

SUBJECT INDEX

The most effective way to access specific funding programs is through the Subject Index. This index lists the subject terms with applicable grants program titles – and their accession numbers – alphabetically under each term. Terms were assigned to target the specific area of research designated in the description of each program. Cross-references are used to link subjects and assist the user in finding specific grant information.

Following are general guidelines that can make your search of this index more successful. First, check under the specific topic of interest rather than a more general term. For instance, if you are interested in chemical engineering, look under "Chemical Engineering" rather than "Engineering." Items indexed under "Engineering" indicate funding in broad areas of engineering.

Use general headings when you want grants covering broader areas or if you can't find a specific topic. For example, many grants list funding for humanities research, health programs, or science and technology. To find these grants use such headings as "Humanities," "Medical Programs," "Science," or "Technology." For additional grant information on more specific humanities research opportunities, such as in American History or Cultural Anthropology, also check under the topics "United States History" and "Anthropology, Cultural."

Grants concerning study of a particular country are listed under the name of the country. Grants concerning the history, literature, art and language of a country are listed under the name of the country also, e.g., "Chinese Art" and "Chinese Language/Literature."

SUBJECT TERM —— **Education**

A.L. Mailman Family Foundation Grants, 5
AAAS Science & Technology Policy Fellowships - Health, Education & Human Services, 22
AARP Andrus Foundation Grants, 104
Abbott Laboratories Fund Grants, 125
ACIE Host University Edmund S. Muskie/Freedom Support Act Graduate Fellowships, 156
ACT Awards, 189
Akonadi Foundation Anti-Racism Grants, 351 —— **PROGRAM TITLE**
Akron Community Foundation Grants, 352
Albert and Margaret Alkek Foundation Grants, 370
Albuquerque Community Foundation Grants, 379
Alcoa Foundation Grants, 380
Alcon Foundation Grants Program, 382

GEOGRAPHIC INDEX

This index lists programs that have state, regional, or international geographic focus. The Geographic Index is arranged by state, followed by Canadian programs, then by international programs by country, and lists grant program titles and their corresponding accession numbers.

COUNTRY —— **United States**

Alabama —— **STATE**

3M Fndn Grants, 2
Alabama Humanities Fndn Grants Program, 368
Arkema Inc. Fndn Science Teachers Program, 705
CDC Injury Control Research Centers Grants, 1198
PROGRAM TITLE —— DOE Experimental Program to Stimulate Competitive Research (EPSCoR), 1653
Hill Crest Fndn Grants, 2293
Linn-Henley Charitable Trust Grants, 2777
NOAA Community-Based Restoration Program (CRP) Grants, 3843
Southern Company's Longleaf Pine Reforestation Fund, 4726

PROGRAM TYPE INDEX

This index is broken into 43 categories according to the type of program funded:

- Adult Basic Education
- Adult/Family Literacy Training
- Awards/Prizes
- Basic Research
- Building Construction and/or Renovation
- Capital Campaigns
- Centers: Research/Demonstration/Service
- Citizenship Instruction
- Community Development
- Consulting/Visiting Personnel
- Cultural Outreach
- Curriculum Development/Teacher Training
- Demonstration Grants
- Development (Institutional/Departmental)
- Dissertation/Thesis Research Support
- Educational Programs
- Emergency Programs
- Endowments
- Environmental Programs
- Exchange Programs
- Exhibitions, Collections, Performances, Video/ Film Production
- Faculty/Professional Development
- Fellowships
- General Operating Support
- Graduate Assistantships
- Grants to Individuals
- International Exchange Programs
- International Grants
- Land Acquisition
- Matching/Challenge Funds
- Materials/Equipment Acquisition (Computers, Books, Tapes, etc.)
- Preservation/Restoration
- Professorships
- Publishing/Editing/Translating
- Religious Programs
- Scholarships
- Seed Grants
- Service Delivery Programs
- Symposia, Conferences, Workshops, Seminars
- Technical Assistance
- Training Programs/Internships
- Travel Grants
- Vocational Education

Government and Organization Acronyms

AAAAI	American Academy of Allergy Asthma and Immunology
AAAS	American Association for the Advancement of Science
AACAP	American Academy of Child and Adolescent Psychiatry
AACN	American Association of Critical Care Nurses
AACR	American Association of Cancer Research
AAFCS	American Association of Family and Consumer Sciences
AAFP	American Academy of Family Physicians Foundation
AAFPRS	American Academy of Facial Plastic and Reconstructive Surgery
AAR	American Academy in Rome
AAS	American Antiquarian Society
AASL	American Association of School Libraries
AAUW	American Association of University Women
ACC	Asian Cultural Council
ACLS	American Council of Learned Societies
ACM	Association for Computing Machinery
ACS	American Cancer Society
ADA	American Diabetes Association
ADHF	American Digestive Health Foundation
AF	Arthritis Foundation
AFAR	American Federation for Aging Research
AFOSR	Air Force Office of Scientific Research
AFUD	American Foundation for Urologic Disease
AFUW	Australian Federation of University Women
AGS	American Geriatrics Society
AHA	American Heart Association
AHAF	American Health Assistance Foundation
AFHMR	Alberta Heritage Foundation for Medical Research
AHRQ	Agency for Healthcare Research and Quality
AICR	American Institute for Cancer Research
AIIS	American Institute for Indian Studies
AJA	American Jewish Archives
ALA	American Library Association
ALISE	Association for Library and Information Science Education
AMNH	American Museum of Natural History
AMS	American Musicological Society
ANL	Argonne National Library
ANS	American Numismatic Society
AOA	American Osteopathic Association
APA	American Psychological Association
APSA	American Political Science Association
ARIT	American Research Institute in Turkey
ARO	Army Research Office
ASA	American Statistical Association
ASCSA	American School of Classical Studies at Athens
ASECS	American Society for Eighteenth-Century Studies
ASF	American-Scandinavian Foundation
ASHRAE	American Society of Heating, Refrigerating, and Air Conditioning Engineers
ASME	American Society of Mechanical Engineers
ASNS	American Society for Nutritional Sciences
ASPRS	American Society of Photogrammetry and Remote Sensing
AWU	Associated Western Universities
AWWA	American Water Works Association
BA	British Academy
BWF	Burroughs Wellcome Fund
CBIE	Canadian Bureau for International Education
CCFF	Canadian Cystic Fibrosis Foundation
CDC	Centers for Disease Control and Prevention
CES	Council for European Studies
CF	The Commonwealth Fund
CFF	Cystic Fibrosis Foundation
CFPC	College of Family Physicians of Canada
CFUW	Canadian Federation of University Women
CHEA	Canadian Home Economics Association
CIES	Council for International Exchange of Scholars
CIUS	Canadian Institute of Ukrainian Studies
CLA	Canadian Lung Association
CLF	Canadian Liver Foundation
CRI	Cancer Research Institute
DAAD	Deutscher Akademische Austauschdienst (German Academic Exchange Service)
DHHS	Department of Health and Human Services
DOA	Department of Agriculture
DOC	Department of Commerce
DOD	Department of Defense
DOE	Department of Energy
DOI	Department of the Interior
DOJ	Department of Justice
DOL	Department of Labor
DOS	Department of State
DOT	Department of Transportation
EFA	Epilepsy Foundation of America
EPA	Environmental Protection Agency
ESF	European Science Foundation
ETS	Educational Testing Service
FCAR	Formation de Chercheurs et L'Aide a la Recherche
FDA	Food and Drug Administration
FIC	Fogarty International Center
GAAC	German American Academic Council

GCA	Garden Club of America
HHMI	Howard Hughes Medical Institute
HRSA	Health Resources and Services Administration
HUD	Department of Housing and Urban Development
IRA	International Reading Association
IREX	International Research and Exchanges Board
IUCP	Indiana University Center on Philanthropy
JDF	Juvenile Diabetes Foundation International
JMO	John M. Olin Foundation
JSPS	Japan Society for the Promotion of Science
KFC	Kidney Foundation of Canada
LSA	Leukemia Society of America
MHRC	Manitoba Health Research Council
MLA	Medical Library Association
MMA	Metropolitan Museum of Art
MSSC	Multiple Sclerosis Society of Canada
NAACP	National Association for the Advancement of Colored People
NARSAD	National Alliance for Research on Schizophrenia and Depression
NASM	National Air and Space Museum
NATO	North Atlantic Treaty Organization
NCCAM	National Center for Complementary and Alternative Medicine
NCI	National Cancer Institute
NCIC	National Cancer Institute of Canada
NCRR	National Center for Research Resources
NEH	National Endowment for the Humanities
NEI	National Eye Institute
NFID	National Foundation for Infectious Diseases
NFWF	National Fish and Wildlife Foundation
NHGRI	National Human Genome Research Institute
NHLBI	National Heart, Lung and Blood Institute
NIA	National Institute on Aging
NIAAA	National Institute on Alcohol Abuse and Alcoholism
NIAF	National Italian American Foundation
NIAID	National Institute of Allergy and Infectious Diseases
NIAMS	National Institute of Arthritis and Musculoskeletal Skin Diseases
NICHD	National Institute of Child Health and Human Development
NIDA	National Institute on Drug Abuse
NIDCD	National Institute on Deafness and Other Communication Disorders
NIDCR	National Institute of Dental and Craniofacial Research
NIDDK	National Institute of Diabetes, and Digestive and Kidney Diseases
NIDRR	National Institute on Disability and Rehabilitation Research
NIEHS	National Institute of Environmental Health Sciences
NIGMS	National Institute of General Medical Sciences
NIH	National Institutes of Health
NIJ	National Institute of Justice
NIMH	National Institute of Mental Health
NINDS	National Institute of Neurological Disorders and Stroke
NINR	National Institute of Nursing Research
NIOSH	National Institute for Occupational Safety and Health
NIST	National Institute of Standards and Technology
NKF	National Kidney Foundation
NL	Newberry Library
NLM	National Library of Medicine
NMF	National Medical Fellowships, Inc.
NMSS	National Multiple Sclerosis Society
NOAA	National Oceanic and Atmospheric Administration
NRC	National Research Council
NSERC	Natural Sciences and Engineering Research Council of Canada
NSF	National Science Foundation
OAH	Organization of American Historians
ONF	Oncology Nursing Foundation
ONR	Office of Naval Research
OREF	Orthopaedic Research and Education Foundation
ORISE	Oak Ridge Institute for Science and Education
OSI	Open Society Institute
PDF	Parkinson's Disease Foundation
PhRMA	Pharmaceutical Research and Manufacturers of American Foundation
PHSC	The Photographic Historical Society of Canada
RCPSC	Royal College of Physicians and Surgeons of Canada
RSC	Royal Society of Canada
RWJF	Robert Wood Johnson Foundation
SLA	Special Libraries Association
SSHRC	Social Sciences and Humanities Research Council of Canada
SSRC	Social Science Research Council
STTI	Sigma Theta Tau International
USHMM	United States Holocaust Memorial Museum Research Institute
USIA	United States Information Agency
USIP	United States Institute of Peace
WAWH	Western Association of Woman Historians

How To Write A Winning Grant

by Louis S. Schafer, Ed.S.

A number of foundations and grant funders set aside large sums of money in support of a variety of programs. A successful grant proposal is one that is well-prepared, thoughtfully planned, and concisely packaged. In order to secure funding, a grant writer must submit a proposal written according to the specifications of the prospective funder. This involves profiling the organization, outlining the demographics of the target population, describing a significant need or opportunity, and proposing a program that meets the need or takes advantage of that opportunity.

Yet, grant writing involves a lot more than simply sitting down at a computer and composing a narrative. The process also includes a number of important considerations: strategic planning, research, preparing the proposal, building an evaluation plan, and follow-up. Because of the intense competition for funding, giving organizations publish specific deadlines, restrictions, and requirements about formatting, content and how to submit the proposal. These stipulations function as a type of preliminary screening device to be used when you have completed the writing process. Grants that do not follow the funder's specific directions usually do not make it into the boardroom, which is where they will be considered by top decision makers for final approval.

A well-designed funding request breaks down the proposed program into measurable evaluation goals that will be accomplished according to a specified schedule. Furthermore, a sound request should provide a detailed budget, outlining how the funds will be used. Typically, all of this vital information must be provided within two to ten pages, not including attachments.

Success in grant writing continues to gain importance in the economy of the nonprofit world. Expectations for knowing how to write grants and secure approval crosses all fields and ranks, and has become a unique skill in most areas. In fact, to some, grants represent the very lifeblood of an ongoing program and, without them, a great many of those programs would cease to exist.

Thus, each of the twelve steps highlighted below represents a cross-section of what experts, program officers, foundation staff, and others with grant writing experience have to say on gaining advantage in the highly competitive environment of the grant writer. By following these steps, nearly any grant can become a winning proposal.

Step 1: Know What Ingredients to Include
Grant writing must combine skillful and formulaic writing with customized language that leads the funder organization to conclude that the proposal will fulfill their philanthropic mission, and that the nonprofit organization has the capacity to actually accomplish what it is proposing. Whether a grant proposal is two pages or twenty pages long, it should contain an executive summary, a profile of the organization, the objectives of the proposal stated in terms of the beneficiaries or clients, specific steps that are attached to a time line by which the proposal will be achieved, a detailed program budget, a clearly described plan by which the organization will evaluate the proposal, and a plan of sustainability. In addition, the proposal should be prefaced by a carefully written cover letter. It can often also contain attachments such as the 501(c)3 designation letter and letters of endorsement from key constituents.

Step 2: Essential Tools of the Trade
You should begin by gathering together a number of grant writing tools that are essential to you as a writer. For example, if you are writing from a novice perspective, it makes sense to learn and understand the meanings of the vocabulary being used in grant guidelines or to access a glossary of common terms. Some sponsor guidelines will even provide just such a glossary unique to the particular sponsor.

If you have never written a grant proposal before do some research on the topic before you begin. The old adage "learning by doing" certainly can apply to the best means for an individual to learn how to write a grant proposal. Yet, numerous how to listings and guidelines offer insights to novice grant writers, and even those with experience. Much like texts on how-to write resumes, a wide variety of articles exist on the subject of writing grant proposals. You should always keep a few of these close at hand.

Finally, most novice or experienced grant writers working in a new area seek out copies of proposals that have been successful with a particular sponsor. Some federal agencies like the U.S. Department of Education may make winning proposals available or provide grant workshop participants with a copy of a successful proposal to aid new writers in understanding how the agency means or expects its proposals to be prepared for successful results.

Step 3: Proposal Uniqueness
Educators, program creators, and service providers generally seek funding from a variety of organizations that provide open competitions for funds to support projects complimentary to the organization's mission.

Before beginning the writing process, take some time to contact the right person within the funding organization office. It is best to do this by telephone, followed up by an email. Tell them a little about your project, and ask them if it sounds like something they might consider for funding. Be direct, concise, and forthcoming, and listen closely to their responses.

Never write from a "boiler-plate, one-size-fits-all" perspective. In fact, project development, application completion, and application submissions should concisely follow the unique guidelines provided by the funding organization. The funding organization will know if you have sent them a mass-mailing, and will likely reciprocate with a standard form letter without much rejection explanation.

Step 4: Write for the Reader
Any proposal should offer a concise plan to fill a need or solve a problem, and your reader will evaluate your plan according to how well your written presentation answers questions about what you are proposing, how you plan to do it, when you plan to do it, and how much it is going to cost.

Don't assume that the funder knows much about your subject area. Most grant readers and evaluators are generalists. They will probably know something about topics like Shakespeare, water pollution, and HIV/AIDS, but you should not assume that they are familiar with "Troilus and Cressida," taconite disposal methods or Kaposi's sarcoma. If your topic is complex, you might add an informative article or suggest some background reading.

Therefore, to present the information well, you should begin by ascertaining - not assuming - the level of knowledge that your audience possesses and take the positions of all your readers into account. You might also provide, for those outside of your specific area of expertise, an executive summary written in non-technical language, or you might include your own glossary of terms that explains technical language use in the body of the proposal. Don't take for granted that everyone who reads your proposal understands your jargon.

The most basic composition of a proposal, as with any other written document, is simple; it needs a beginning (the introduction), a middle (the body of material to be presented) and an end (the conclusion or recommendation).

Step 5: Research Your Perspective Funders
Research prospective grant funders using one of Schoolhouse Partners' nine directories, or by utilizing our online database known as *GrantSelect*. Thoroughly search for requests for proposals from grant funders that might match your proposed project. Both the hard copy and online versions of the database provide a wealth of information concerning how-to, when-to, who-to, and so on. Search there using vital keywords, such as "education," "elementary and secondary education" or "children and youth."

After you identify several potential funders, follow the funders' specifications for a first approach, which should be by an initial telephone contact, email, letter or the submission of a full request. Your goal is to pre-qualify your request and to learn the name of a person at the foundation to whom you can direct your final grant proposal. This is essential, so that your grant submission does not get lost in the shuffle of things.

Step 6: Profiling Your Organization
Grant writers should begin by profiling their organization using demographic information. In a couple short paragraphs explain exactly what it is you or your organization does, as well as why the grantor can trust you or your organization to handle the project and money appropriately. If the proposal is in support of an individual, you may focus on that person's stellar credit history and budgeting skills. If it is for an organization, you will want to add information showing a track record of successfully achieving goals and a governing body that is more than capable or carrying out the project being outlined.

Ideally you want to portray a pattern of growth and change over time (e.g. graduated high school and sought a college education to improve myself or the non-profit started as a small two-person operation and has now grown to include more than 20 volunteers). It is always best to show people helping people to accomplish something that they could not accomplish without the funding organization's assistance.

Step 7: The Problem or Needs Statement
This is the main part, or body, of your grant proposal. You want to convince the grantor that your project is vitally important, that your group can accomplish it, that it can be done within the budget parameters, and that no one else is meeting that need. Typically, unless you are applying to a government agency or targeted foundation, you should assume that the reader does not know very much about your organization, the issue, or the problems at hand.

Describe the problem or need in both factual and human interest terms, if possible. Providing sound data demonstrates that your organization is expert in the field. If there are no good data on your issue, consider doing your own research study, even if it is simple and short-term.

Outline your issue in as local a context as possible. If you want to educate people in your county about HIV/AIDS, tell the funder about the epidemic in your county — not in the United States as a whole.

Always describe a problem or need that is about the same size as your solution or target audience. Do not, under any circumstances, draw a dark picture of nuclear war, teen suicide and lethal air pollution if you are planning a modest neighborhood arts program for children. Make sure that the problem and solution are of similar scope and size.

List a precise estimate of how many individuals will be impacted by the funding, their socio-economic and ethnic information, and measurable statistics about their current situation and/or academics. In the first few lines of this section, identify the issue, opportunity or problem in terms of measurable evaluative benefits to your target group. This forms the executive summary section, which should be only one or two paragraphs in length.

Step 8: Overview of How You Will Solve the Problem
Next, you should offer some detail of precisely how you will take advantage of an opportunity or solve a serious problem for your target audience. Perhaps, if you are an educator, your school has a large problem with truancy, which you think you could combat by hiring a social worker to work with the families of students with histories of habitual truancy. After researching other schools that have had success using a similar approach, you decide to fund the salary of an additional social worker for one year through a grant.

Then, if your truancy rate shows improvement, you will request that the district fund the position permanently, which will pay for itself in state funds based on daily attendance rates. This plan provides the objectives section of your grant proposal, which should be a detailed single paragraph in length.

Step 9: Evaluation Plan
By now, you should have begun formulating exactly how you will evaluate your success. If you are attempting to reduce truancy at your school, state precisely what percentage of reduction you believe will occur; if you are sending a group a ten-year-olds to baseball camp, list the number that will be impacted and what they will gain from the experience; and if you plan to install a security system within a library, discuss the amount of savings that will occur from theft prevention measures. Don't hesitate to detail the evaluation of three or four goals that you have established.

Explain exactly what your organization plans to do about the problem. What are your overall goals and how will you measure reduction or eradication of the problem? You might say: "The goals of this project are to increase the understanding among Indianapolis middle school students about the impact of smoking on their health, and to reduce the number of students who smoke by at least ten percent"

Step 10: Timelines and Budgets
Next, take the time to break your plan down into specific steps that are tied to a specific, well-designed timeline. Each step should become one sentence in the methods section of your grant request, and should have measurable goals or outcomes aligned with it. The entire section should be one to two paragraphs. Follow this with both a narrative and detailed budget.

Don't support the budget need by outlining a problem as the *absence* of equipment. "We don't have enough beds in our battered women's shelter" is not the problem itself. The problem is increased levels of domestic violence and, therefore, more shelter beds is a solution.

Instead, the budget should be written in narrative format, with a specific explanation for each expenditure. For example: "We will hire one school social worker at an annual salary of $36,000 including benefits," then list the benefit costs. Format the same budget information as a chart using Excel or some other type of spreadsheet. This budget detail should be attached to the body of your grant proposal, and should be in the format requested by the funder.

Here the funder will further want to know if other organizations have committed funds to the project or have been asked to do so. Few funders want to be the sole support of any project. (This may not be true if the project cost is very small — less than $5,000, for example — or if a corporation is seeking public visibility by sponsoring the project.) Funders generally expect you to ask for support from more than one source. So make sure you identify and outline other funding sources. In this section, you can also describe the in-kind contributions (goods or services instead of cash) that people are giving to the project.

Step 11: Sustainability and Finishing Touches
Now ask yourself, if you continue this project in the future, how will it be supported? Most funders don't want to support the same set of projects forever. Many funders see their niche as funding innovation: supporting new approaches to old problems or finding solutions to new problems.

What the funder really wants to see is that you have a long-term vision and funding plan for the project, that the project is "sustainable," especially if it is a new activity. "We plan to offer free books to children by organizing a regular donation and distribution campaign."

Prior to forwarding your final submission, take the time to revise your grant proposal so that you can insert language that resonates with the funder. Make sure that you have followed the exact directions that the funder specified in its guidelines, and never, ever miss the deadline. The final section of the proposal should explain how you will communicate information about the program to your funder.

Have any participating agencies or constituents write a letter of support to your contact at the funding organization. Have the proposal reviewed by someone who has not read it before. Then revise it for spelling, punctuation, grammar and clarity. Always use 12-point font with 1-inch margins. Do not fold the proposal before forwarding.

Step 12: Forwarding the Proposal

Step away from the proposal for a few hours. Then come back and reread everything you have written to ensure there are no typos, everything is clear and concise, and that you have said everything that you had hoped to say. Make certain that: your sentence structure matches the intended message; that, if you wanted to create and keep momentum for an idea, you have utilized longer sentences; and, if there is a specific point you wanted to make, it is highlighted.

Now, read the request for proposal and make sure you understand exactly what the grantor wanted you to include. Some may require a list of your board members, a copy of your financial statement from the previous year, a cover letter from your CEO, a copy of your IRS tax free letter, or other information. Make sure you include all of these as attachments.

Reread the proposal guidelines to see how many copies you should forward. Some may require 3 or 5 copies. Also pay attention to the deadline. Check if it is postmark or delivery deadline and make sure that you get it there in time.

Conclusion

Writing and submitting grants can be both agonizing and fulfilling, but by following the above steps you will greatly enhance your chances of success..

Among the country's largest grantmakers, about one proposal in three is typically funded. You may find that you can get project money but not the operating money you need to keep your basic activities going. You may be surprised by funders' generosity, but you may also be surprised by their periodic changes in focus, especially if those changes leave you on the outside looking in.

But remember that the U.S. has an extraordinary fundraising climate. People from other countries envy the major corporations and large family foundations that form the backbone of many of our innovative social and cultural programs. Most funders have board and staff people who are thoughtful, careful, curious, well-educated about community issues and willing to help you. If you have a good project that has been carefully planned to meet some real needs, you will find people willing to talk with you and advise you on what you might do to move closer to success.

Grant Programs

1st Source Foundation Grants 1

Established in 1952 and administered by the 1st Source Bank, the Foundation supports community foundations, youth clubs and organizations involved with television, education, health, and human services. Giving is primarily centered in Indiana, and the major type of funding given is for general operating support. Since there are no specific applications forms required or deadlines with which to adhere, applicants should send a letter of request detailing the project and the amount of funding needed.
Requirements: Any 501(c)3 serving the residents of Indiana communities where 1st Source Banks are located are eligible to apply.
Geographic Focus: Indiana
Amount: 500 - 5,000 USD
Samples: South Bend Heritage Foundation, South Bend, Indiana, $5,000 - general operations support (2010); Boys and Girls Club of Street Joseph County, Mishawaka, Indiana, $5,000 - general operations support (2010); Indiana Academy, Indianapolis, Indiana, $5,000 - general operations support (2010).
Contact: Lee Morton, Trustee; (574) 235-2790
Sponsor: 1st Source Foundation
100 N Michigan Street
South Bend, IN 46601-1630

2COBS Private Charitable Foundation Grants 2

The Foundation, established in Colorado in 2005, supports a variety of causes, which include: health care; cancer services; community services; and local community foundations. Although giving is centered around the Durango, Colorado, region, it is not uncommon for support to be offered to 501(c)3 programs across the country. There are no specific application formats or deadlines with which to adhere, and applicants should send a letter of request outlining the program need and overall budget.
Geographic Focus: All U.S. States
Amount: 250 - 1,000 USD
Samples: St Vincent DePaul, Street Louis, Missouri, $750—for operating costs; Manna Soup Kitchen, Durango, Colorado, $500—for general operating costs.
Contact: Christopher J. O'Brien, Chairperson; (970) 247-7828
Sponsor: 2COBS Private Charitable Foundation
105 Rockridge Circle, P.O. Box 2565
Durango, CO 81301-6910

4-C's Foundation Grants 3

Established in Tennessee in 2004 by a donation from TAP Publishing, the 4-c's Foundation limits its grants to the Crossville, Tennessee region. Currently the Foundation supports organizations involved with education via funding for general operations and awards scholarships to graduates of Cumberland County High School and Stone Memorial High School.
Geographic Focus: Tennessee
Samples: Cumberland County Band Boosters, Crossville, Tennessee, $5,450 - band uniforms (2010); Forest J. Longway, Crossville, Tennessee, $1,000 - scholarship (2010).
Contact: Fran Young, President; (931) 484-8674
Sponsor: 4-C's Foundation
294 Cleveland Street
Crossville, TN 38555-4854

4:19 Foundation Grants 4

The 4:19 Foundation, established in Connecticut in 2002, offers general operating support to Lutheran faith-based organizations that provide services to poor and underprivileged communities as part of their mission's ministry work. Giving is primarily in the State of Maryland. There are no specific guidelines, application forms, or deadlines with which to adhere. Potential applicants should first contact the foundation in writing, outlining the need and overall operating budget.
Requirements: Protestant agencies and churches in Maryland are eligible to apply.
Restrictions: No grants are given to individuals
Geographic Focus: Maryland
Samples: Street Matthew Lutheran Church, Bel Air, Maryland, $12,000 - proclaiming the Gospel (2009); Hartford Christian School, Dublin, Maryland, $6,000 - Christian education (2009); John Carroll School, Bel Air, Maryland, $5,000 - Christian education (2009).
Contact: Blaise Sedney, President; (410) 893-0185
Sponsor: 4:19 Foundation
105 Colvard Court
Forest Hill, MD 21050-1531

5 51 5 Foundation Grants 5

The 5 51 5 Foundation, established in New York in 2007, offers funding in the way of general operating support of K-12 education, higher education, and community education programs. Its primary geographic focus is Maryland, Massachusetts, New Hampshire, and New York. There are no specific application guidelines or deadlines with which to adhere, and applicants should begin by contacting the Foundation directly.
Requirements: 501(c)3 organizations and educational facilities that either serve or are located in Maryland, Massachusetts, New Hampshire, and New York are eligible to apply.
Geographic Focus: Maryland, Massachusetts, New Hampshire, New York
Amount: 10,000 - 3,000,000 USD
Samples: Spence School, New York, New York, $100,000—for general operating purposes; John Hopkins Medicine, Baltimore, Maryland, $32,448—for general operating purposes; Dartmouth College, Hanover, New Hampshire, $3,000,000—for general operating purposes.
Contact: Richard Gold, Secretary; (203) 618-4623; (203) 302-3123
Sponsor: 5 51 5 Foundation
755 Fifth Avenue, Apt. 12B
New York, NY 10021

20th Century Trends Institute Grants 6

Classified as a private operating foundation in 1991 in both New York and Vermont, the 20th Century Trends Institute evolved into a private foundation in 2002. Currently, the Foundation offers funding to secondary education and higher education throughout Connecticut and New York. Support comes primarily in the form of general operations funding. There are no specific guidelines, application forms, or deadlines with which to adhere, and potential applicants should contact the office in writing, explaining their need and overall operating budget.
Geographic Focus: Connecticut, New York
Samples: New York University, New York, New York, $6,000 - general operating fund (2010); Choate Rosemary Hall, Wallingford, Connecticut, $20,500 - general operating fund (2010); Darien High School, Darien, Connecticut, $1,000 - general fund (2010).
Contact: Ward Frank Cleary, Vice President; (203) 324-6777, ext. 208; (203) 324-9621; cleary@curtisbb.com
Sponsor: 20th Century Trends Institute
666 Summer Street
Stamford, CT 06901-1401

80 / 20 Fund Grants 7

The 80-20 Fund supports and promotes various public charities and private operating foundations which are qualifying 501(c)3 organizations by annually making direct qualifying grants to such organizations. Giving is primarily in the Boston, Massachusetts, region. There are no specific applications, guidelines, or deadlines with which to adhere. Applicants an initial approach in writing, along with a copy of their IRS determination letter.
Restrictions: No grants to individuals.
Geographic Focus: Massachusetts
Contact: James E. Irwine, Treasurer; (210) 223-0875 or (210) 775-2370
Sponsor: 80 / 20 Fund
112 E Pecan Street, #555
San Antonio, TX 78205

100 Angels Charitable Foundation Grants 8

The Foundation, a furniture industry-based public charity, is spearheading projects to encourage all segments of the home furnishings industry to support human service programs across the country. Although grants are given throughout Florida, giving is primarily centered in and around the Pensacola area. Types of support include general support and operating support, as well as disaster relief efforts. There are no particular application formats or deadlines with which to adhere, and applicants should contact the Foundation directly via a letter of application.
Restrictions: Giving is primarily centered in and around Pensacola, Florida. Grants are not made to individuals.
Geographic Focus: Florida
Contact: Martin Libowsky, Chairman; (800) 643-0975 or (205) 368-4815; (850) 916-4550; mbigdaddy125@aol.com
Sponsor: 100 Angels Charitable Foundation
P.O. Box 1379
Gulf Breeze, FL 32562-1379

118 Foundation Grants 9

The mission of The 118 Foundation is to support organizations that play a key role in making communities better in the areas of housing, education, and health care. The foundation has also expanded its outreach internationally to support organizations that also fight poverty, create jobs, and transform lives. Giving is primarily to public charities that match the foundation's mission in the areas of child and youth development, affordable housing, and micro-finance and micro-enterprise development, in disadvantaged communities in both the U.S. and abroad.
Restrictions: No support is available for organizations lacking 501(c)3 status. No grants are given to individuals, or for endowments, capital campaigns, scholarships, or medical research.
Geographic Focus: All U.S. States
Amount: Up to 135,000 USD
Contact: Diane Tollefson, Executive Director; (703) 338-5948; the118foundation@mac.com or grants@webmethods.org
Sponsor: 118 Foundation
1350 Beverly Road, #115-325
McLean, VA 22101

1675 Foundation Grants 10

The foundation is a private family foundation dedicated to improving the quality of life for individuals and families through the support of non-profit organizations working in the areas of health, human services, education, the environment, and history. Priority is given to organizations serving Chester County, southeastern Pennsylvania, the Greater Boston area, and other geographic areas of interest to the Trustees. Grants are made for operating support, special projects, endowment, and capital. Grants range from $2,000 to $50,000 and are made twice a year at the discretion of the Trustees. Requests should be in writing and mailed to the executive director.
Requirements: 501(c)3 nonprofit organizations and public charities under IRS Code 509(a) are eligible.
Restrictions: The foundation does not make grants to individuals, nor are they made for political purposes.
Geographic Focus: Massachusetts, Pennsylvania
Date(s) Application is Due: Oct 1; Mar 1
Amount: 2,000 - 50,000 USD
Contact: Marge Brennan, Grants Manager; (610) 896-3868; (610) 896-3869; mbrennan@1675foundation.org
Internet: http://www.1675foundation.org/guidelines.htm
Sponsor: 1675 Foundation
16 East Lancaster Avenue, Suite 102
Ardmore, PA 19003-2228

1912 Charitable Foundation Grants 11

The Foundation, established in West Virginia in 1996, has as its priority to support both higher education and Protestant churches/agencies. The primary type of funding is in the form of general operations money, and the average grant ranging from $1,000 to $15,000. There are no specific deadlines, guidelines, or applications with which to adhere. Initial approach should be by letter.
Requirements: 501(c)3 organizations serving the residents of West Virginia are able to apply.
Restrictions: No grants are given to individuals.
Geographic Focus: West Virginia
Samples: Wade Center, Bluefield, West Virginia, $5,000—general operations; The Children's Home, Prnceton, West Virginia, $1,500—general operations.
Contact: Diana S. Coulthard, Secretary; (304) 325-7151; (304) 327-9663
Sponsor: 1912 Charitable Foundation
211 Federal Street, P.O. Box 950
Bluefield, WV 24701-0950

1988 Irrevocable Cochrane Memorial Trust Grants 12

The Trust, established in Minnesota in 1989 and placed under the supervision of the U.S. Bank, gives support primarily to organizations in the Washington, DC, area and throughout Maryland. Funding is primarily given to support Roman Catholic churches, schools, and their agencies. Fields of interest include: the environment, preservation of natural resources, community foundations, higher education, human services, and secondary schools. Applicants should forward a letter offering a detailed project description and the amount of funding requested. There are no deadlines.
Requirements: 501(c)3 organizations serving the residents of Washington, DC, and the State of Maryland are eligible to apply.
Geographic Focus: District of Columbia, Maryland
Amount: Up to 75,000 USD
Samples: American Chestnut Land Trust, Prince Frederick, Maryland, $50,000 - operating costs (2009); Bethlehem House, Washington, DC, $40,000 - general operations (2009); Catholic Campaign for Human Development, Washington, DC - annual support (2009).
Contact: John L. Jerry, (651) 466-8708 or (651) 466-8724
Sponsor: 1988 Irrevocable Cochrane Memorial Trust
101 East 5th Street, P.O. Box 64713
Saint Paul, MN 55164-0713

A.C. Ratshesky Foundation Grants 13

The foundation gives priority consideration to programs in education and training, and arts and culture. Support for programs that serve disadvantaged Jewish populations is also of special interest. Preference is given to small and medium-sized organizations. The foundation makes grants for operating support, start-up support/seed money, programs, and organizational capacity building or technical assistance. Contact office for application forms.
Requirements: Boston area nonprofits may apply.
Restrictions: Grants are not awarded to individuals or for continuing support, annual campaigns, general endowments, deficit financing, land acquisition, scientific or other research, publications, conferences, or loans.
Geographic Focus: Massachusetts
Date(s) Application is Due: Oct 1; Feb 1; Jul 1
Amount: 5,000 - 10,000 USD
Samples: Cambridge School Volunteers Inc., Cambridge, MA, $5,000—to train and deploy supportive adults to move low-income Cambridge public school students toward school success and access to higher education (2009); Centro Presente, Inc., Somerville, MA, $5,000—to support an award-winning arts education and leadership development program for 60 Latino immigrant youth in Cambridge and Somerville (2009); Charlestown Working Theater, Inc., Charlestown, MA, $5,000—to provide programming in acting, music, and visual arts for 350 children and youth in Charlestown (2009).
Contact: Yasmin Shah, Program Officer; (617) 391-3094 or (617) 426-7080; (617) 426-7087; yshah@gmafoundations.com
Internet: http://ratsheskyfoundation.grantsmanagement08.com/?page_id=5
Sponsor: A.C. Ratshesky Foundation
77 Summer Street, 8th Floor
Boston, MA 02110-1006

A.V. Hunter Trust Grants 14

The purpose of the foundation's grant program is to support Colorado nonprofit organizations that give direct aid, comfort, support, or assistance to children or aged persons or indigent adults. Types of support include program support and general operating support.
Requirements: Applications are considered from charitable 501(c)3 nonprofit Colorado-based organizations or projects or endeavors located in Colorado. The trust will consider only one request from an organization during any 12-month period.
Restrictions: The Foundation does not fund: new programs in their first three years of operation; grants or loans to individuals; developmental, pass-through or start-ups; research projects; publications, films or other media projects; capital campaigns or capital acquisitions, including construction and renovations; grants for education or scholarship aid; grants to cover deficits

or retirement of debt; purchase of tickets for fundraising benefits, special events or sponsorships; endowments; recruiting and training; or gathering and disseminating information.
Geographic Focus: Colorado
Date(s) Application is Due: Mar 1; Jun 1; Aug 1
Amount: 10,000 - 20,000 USD
Contact: Barbara L. Howie, Executive Director; (303) 399-5450; (303) 399-5499; barbarahowie@avhuntertrust.org
Internet: http://avhuntertrust.org
Sponsor: A.V. Hunter Trust
650 South Cherry Street, Suite 535
Glendale, CO 80246

Aaron Copland Fund for Music Performing Ensembles 15
The program's objective is to support organizations whose performances encourage and improve public knowledge and appreciation of serious contemporary American music. Funds are available for general operating support or project support to professional performing ensembles with a history of substantial commitment to contemporary American music and with plans to continue that commitment. Guidelines are available online.
Requirements: Applicants must meet the following requirements: nonprofit tax-exempt status; performance history of at least two years at the time of application; at least 20 percent of the ensemble's programming (in terms of duration) for the preceding two seasons consists of contemporary American music; and demonstrated commitment to contemporary American music.
Restrictions: Individuals, student ensembles, festivals, and presenters without a core ensemble are not eligible. Grants will not be made for the purpose of commissioning composers.
Geographic Focus: All U.S. States
Date(s) Application is Due: Jun 30
Amount: 1,000 - 20,000 USD
Contact: James M. Kendrick, Secretary; (212) 461-6956; (212) 810-4567; recording@coplandfund.org
Internet: http://www.coplandfund.org/ensembles.html
Sponsor: American Music Center
322 8th Avenue, Suite 1401
New York, NY 10001

Aaron Copland Fund for Music Supplemental Grants 16
The Program's objective is to support non-profit organizations that have a history of substantial commitment to contemporary American music. Applications may be submitted by non-profit organizations that have a history of substantial commitment to contemporary American music but whose needs are not addressed by the Fund's programs of support for performing organizations and recording projects, such as presenters and music service organizations. Applicants may request either general operating support or support for special projects. Applicants should be aware that support in one year does not imply continuation of that support. Special projects relating to a broad spectrum of American music will be viewed more favorably than those relating to a single work or to a single composer.
Requirements: Organizations must have been in existence for at least two years at the time of application. Presenters, or organizations that are otherwise involved with performances, must have presented two full seasons prior to the season for which support is requested.
Restrictions: Projects that are part of the curriculum of an educational institution are not eligible for support.
Geographic Focus: All U.S. States
Date(s) Application is Due: Sep 30
Contact: Jessica Rauch, Grants Manager; (212) 461-6956 or (212) 366-5260, ext. 29; (212) 810-4567; grantsmanager@coplandfund.org
Internet: https://grants.coplandfund.org/supplemental-program
Sponsor: Aaron Copland Fund for Music
254 West 31st Street, 15th Floor
New York, NY 10001

Aaron Copland Fund Supplemental Program Grants 17
The program's objective is to support nonprofit organizations that have a history of substantial commitment to contemporary American music. Applicants may request either general operating support or support for special projects. Special projects relating to contemporary American music generally will be viewed more favorably than those relating to an individual work or to an individual composer.
Requirements: Nonprofit organizations with a history of substantial commitment to contemporary American music that have been in existence for at least two years at the time of application are eligible.
Restrictions: No grants are made to individuals.
Geographic Focus: All U.S. States
Date(s) Application is Due: Sep 15
Amount: 1,000 - 20,000 USD
Contact: James M. Kendrick, Secretary; (212) 461-6956; (212) 810-4567; recording@coplandfund.org
Internet: http://www.coplandfund.org/supplemental.html
Sponsor: American Music Center
322 8th Avenue, Suite 1401
New York, NY 10001

Abbot and Dorothy H. Stevens Foundation Grants 18
The Abbot and Dorothy H. Stevens Foundation funds Massachusetts non-profits with a emphasis on the greater Lawrence/Merrimack Valley area. Giving primarily for the arts, education, conservation, and health and human services. Fields of interest include: arts; children/youth, services; crime/violence prevention, domestic violence; education; elderly; environment, natural resources; health care; health organizations, association; historic preservation/historical societies; humanities; human services; immigrants; medical school/education; museums. Types of support include: building/renovation; capital campaigns; continuing support; endowments; equipment; general/operating support; management development/capacity building; matching/challenge support; program-related investments/loans; program development; technical assistance.
Requirements: Massachusetts 501(c)3 tax-exempt organizations serving the greater Lawrence and Merrimack Valley are eligible. There is no deadline date when applying for funding, nor is there a application form required. The Foundation will however accept the Associated Grantmakers Common Proposal Form. Applicants should submit a copy of their IRS Determination Letter and one copy of their proposal when applying for funding. The board meets and reviews proposals monthly except for the months of July and August.
Restrictions: Grants do not support national organizations, state or federal agencies, individuals, annual campaigns, deficit financing, exchange programs, internships, professorships, scholarships, or fellowships.
Geographic Focus: Massachusetts
Amount: 1,000 - 20,000 USD
Samples: Boston Childrens Museum, Boston, MA, $15,000 (2008); Boston Symphony Orchestra, Boston, MA, $10,000 (2008); Boston Ballet, Boston, MA, $5,000 (2008).
Contact: Josh Miner, Executive Director; (978) 688-7211; (978) 686-1620; grantprocess@stevensfoundation.com
Sponsor: Abbot and Dorothy H. Suitevens Foundation
P.O. Box 111
North Andover, MA 01845-7211

Abbott Fund Access to Health Care Grants 19
Abbott's Access to Health Care programs seek innovative solutions to improve and expand access to health care services for disadvantaged populations. Specific areas of focus include cardiovascular health, diabetes, nutrition, maternal and child health and neonatal care. Many Abbott Fund programs are engaged in closing gaps in ethnic and minority communities, promoting health and nutrition education for families, training health workers, and improving delivery of health services.
Requirements: Grants are made to tax-exempt organizations supporting access to health care.
Restrictions: Contributions will not be made to individuals; for-profit entities; purely social organizations; political parties or candidates; sectarian religious organizations; advertising; symposia, conferences, and meetings; ticket purchases; memberships; business-related purposes; volunteer efforts of non-Abbott employees; or marketing sponsorships.
Geographic Focus: Arizona, California, Illinois, Kansas, Massachusetts, Michigan, New Jersey, New York, North Carolina, Ohio, Puerto Rico, Texas, Utah, Virginia
Amount: 20,000 - 10,000 USD
Contact: Cindy Schwab, Vice President; (847) 937-7075; (847) 935-5051; cindy.schwab@abbott.com
Internet: http://www.abbottfund.org/sections/what.html
Sponsor: Abbott Fund
100 Abbott Park Road, Department 379, Building 6D
Abbott Park, IL 60064-3500

Abbott Fund Community Vitality Grants 20

The Abbott Fund Community Vitality Grant program is active in communities around the world where Abbott has a significant presence. It pursues local partnerships and creative programs that address unmet needs of a community. Emphasis is placed on improving access to health care and promoting science education. The program also supports major civic, arts and other cultural institution programming, primarily in the Chicago metropolitan area where Abbott is headquartered.

Requirements: Grants are made to tax-exempt organizations supporting company operating areas in Arizona, California, Illinois, Kansas, Massachusetts, Michigan, New Jersey, New York, North Carolina, Ohio, Puerto Rico, Texas, and Virginia, and Utah. It also supports the communities of: Abingdon, England; Brockville, Canada; Campoverde, Italy; Clonmel, Ireland; Cootehill, Ireland; Delkenheim, Germany; Kanata, Canada; Katsuyama, Japan; Ludwigshafen, Germany; Queenborough, England; Rio de Janeiro, Brazil; Sligo, Ireland; and Zwolle, the Netherlands.

Restrictions: Contributions will not be made to individuals; for-profit entities; purely social organizations; political parties or candidates; sectarian religious organizations; advertising; symposia, conferences, and meetings; ticket purchases; memberships; business-related purposes; volunteer efforts of non-Abbott employees; or marketing sponsorships.

Geographic Focus: Arizona, California, Illinois, Kansas, Massachusetts, Michigan, New Jersey, New York, North Carolina, Ohio, Puerto Rico, Texas, Utah, Virginia

Amount: 10,000 USD

Contact: Cindy Schwab, Vice President; (847) 937-7075; (847) 935-5051; cindy.schwab@abbott.com

Internet: http://www.abbottfund.org/sections/what.html

Sponsor: Abbott Fund
100 Abbott Park Road, Department 379, Building 6D
Abbott Park, IL 60064-3500

Abbott Fund Global AIDS Care Grants 21

Abbott has been a significant contributor to the fight against HIV/AIDS for more than two decades. Since 2000, Abbott and the Abbott Fund have invested $225 million in grants and product donations targeted to resource poor countries most impacted by HIV/AIDS. The focus of these efforts includes expanding access to care, testing and treatment; strengthening HIV/AIDS health care systems; preventing mother-to-child transmission; and supporting children and families affected by HIV/AIDS. In addition, Abbott and the Abbott Fund have helped pioneer innovative model programs to combat the disease. For example, we helped build the Baylor International Pediatric AIDS Initiative's first pediatric outpatient clinic in Romania in 2001 that has served an average of 600 patients per year. The clinic has reduced pediatric HIV mortality rates by more than 90 percent. Today Baylor has replicated the Romania model in additional clinics throughout Africa and now serves nearly 60,000 children and young people with HIV – including those at two clinics built by and supported by the Abbott Fund in Malawi and Tanzania.

Requirements: Grants are made to tax-exempt organizations supporting global HIV/AIDS programs.

Restrictions: Contributions will not be made to individuals; for-profit entities; purely social organizations; political parties or candidates; sectarian religious organizations; advertising; symposia, conferences, and meetings; ticket purchases; memberships; business-related purposes; volunteer efforts of non-Abbott employees; or marketing sponsorships.

Geographic Focus: Arizona, California, Illinois, Kansas, Massachusetts, Michigan, New Jersey, New York, North Carolina, Ohio, Puerto Rico, Texas, Utah, Virginia

Amount: 10,000 - 100,000 USD

Contact: Cindy Schwab, Vice President; (847) 937-7075; (847) 935-5051; cindy.schwab@abbott.com

Internet: http://www.abbottfund.org/project/20/30/Helping-Children-and-Young-People-Living-with-HIV-AIDS

Sponsor: Abbott Fund
100 Abbott Park Road, Department 379, Building 6D
Abbott Park, IL 60064-3500

Abel and Sophia Sheng Charitable Foundation Grants 22

The foundation awards grants to nonprofit organizations in its areas of interest, including: fine arts, secondary education, higher education, museums, hospitals, and general charitable giving. Types of support include general operating support. There are no application forms or deadlines, and applicants should begin by contacting the office directly.

Geographic Focus: Massachusetts, New York, Rhode Island

Contact: Abel Sheng, (201) 784-0238 or (201) 567-5991; (201) 567-8862

Sponsor: Abel and Sophia Sheng Charitable Foundation
52 Rio Vista Drive, P.O. Box 1042
Alpine, NJ 07620-1042

Abelard Foundation East Grants 23

The Abelard Foundation is a family foundation, with offices on both the east and west coasts, which has been making grants in support of progressive social change since 1958. The foundation is committed to social change activities that expand and protect civil liberties and civil and human rights; increase opportunities for the poor, the disenfranchised, and people of color; and enhance and expand community involvement in, and control over, economic and environmental decisions affecting members of the community. Grants support activities such as community and grassroots organizing, action research, and advocacy. Seed grants, project, and/or general support grants are awarded for new projects or organizations addressing issues that traditional philanthropic sources might avoid. By supporting model efforts that can be duplicated elsewhere and that offer the potential for broader impact, the foundation encourages grantees to use these funds as leverage in gaining additional support. The foundation accepts proposals on a year-around basis.

Requirements: Eligible applicants must represent or be associated with a nonprofit, 501(c)3 tax-exempt organization. The foundation gives priority to projects that are in their first years of development and have budgets less than $300,000. Nonprofit organizations offering services east of the Mississippi are eligible. The foundation is not able to respond to phone inquiries. Inquiries should be made by mail or email.

Restrictions: The foundation does not support social service programs offering ongoing or direct delivery of service; medical, educational, or cultural institutions; capital expenditure, construction, or renovation programs; programs undertaken at government initiative; or scholarship funds or other aid to individuals.

Geographic Focus: Alabama, Arkansas, Connecticut, Delaware, District of Columbia, Florida, Georgia, Illinois, Indiana, Kentucky, Louisiana, Maine, Maryland, Massachusetts, Michigan, Minnesota, Mississippi, Missouri, New Hampshire, New Jersey, New York, North Carolina, Ohio, Pennsylvania, Rhode Island, South Carolina, Tennessee, Vermont, Virginia, West Virginia, Wisconsin

Date(s) Application is Due: Mar 15; Sep 15

Amount: Up to 10,000 USD

Samples: Alliance for Appalachia, Charleston, West Virginia, $10,000 - to support the organizing and advocacy efforts of this 13-member coalition to end mountaintop removal and to support a just, sustainable economy in Appalachia (2010); Queers for Economic Justice, New York, New York, $10,000 - to support its organizing among low-income queer people, particularly those who are homeless or receiving public assistance, to get public systems to embrace sexual and gender diversity (2009); Domestic Workers United, Bronx, New York, $10,000 - to support its organizing among largely Caribbean, Latina and African domestic workers to raise the level of respect for domestic work, establish fair labor standards, and build a national movement (2009).

Contact: Susan B. Collins, Vice President; eastabel@aol.com

Internet: http://foundationcenter.org/grantmaker/abelardeast/index.html

Sponsor: Abelard Foundation East
P.O. Box 148
Lincoln, MA 01773

Abelard Foundation West Grants 24

The foundation is committed to grassroots social change activities that expand and protect civil liberties and civil and human rights; increase opportunities for the poor, the disenfranchised, and people of color; and enhance and expand community involvement in, and control over, economic and environmental decisions affecting members of the community. Grants support activities such as community and grassroots organizing, action research, and advocacy. Seed grants, project, and/or general support grants are awarded for new projects or organizations addressing issues that traditional philanthropic sources might avoid. By supporting model efforts that can be duplicated elsewhere and that offer the potential for broader impact, the foundation encourages grantees to use funds as leverage in gaining additional support. Applicants located in the Northern Rockies, the Great Basin, the Northwest, the Southwest, or California should contact the office listed at the website. Deadlines for Letters of Inquiry are January 15th and June 15th (LOIs must be received by these dates) for Spring and Fall grant making meetings. Decisions usually take at least 4-6 months from the date of submittal.

Requirements: 501(c)3 organizations located in the Northern Rockies, the Great Basin, the Northwest, the Southwest, and California are eligible.
Restrictions: The foundation does not support social service programs offering ongoing or direct delivery of service; medical, educational, or cultural institutions; capital expenditure, construction, or renovation programs; programs undertaken at government initiative; or scholarship funds or other aid to individuals.
Geographic Focus: Arizona, California, Colorado, Idaho, Kansas, Montana, Nebraska, Nevada, North Dakota, Oklahoma, Oregon, South Dakota, Utah, Washington, Wyoming
Date(s) Application is Due: Jan 15; Jun 15
Amount: 6,000 - 20,000 USD
Samples: Alliance of Californians for Community Empowerment, Oakland, California, $10,000 - to support community organizing campaigns that seek to advance economic opportunity, promote bank accountability, and improve access to affordable public transportation for low-income residents in Oakland, California (2010); Common Counsel Foundation Grassroots Exchange Fund, Oakland, California, $20,000 - to support capacity building, networking and collaboration for grassroots social change and environmental justice organizations across the nation (2010); Filipino Advocates for Justice, Oakland, California, $10,834 - to support worker rights organizing among Filipino home-care workers (2010).
Contact: Patricia Street Onge, Interim Executive Director; (510) 834-2995; (510) 834-2998; info@commoncounsel.org
Internet: http://www.commoncounsel.org/Abelard%20Foundation%20West
Sponsor: Abelard Foundation West
678 13th Street, Suite 100
Oakland, CA 94612

Abeles Foundation Grants 25

The Abeles Foundation is an organization that provides general operating to the areas of elementary and secondary education, public foundations, higher education, and the performing arts in the Albuquerque and Santa Fe areas. The Foundation makes gifts to organizations in New Mexico based on their interactions living within the community.
Restrictions: No grants are made to individuals and applicant's organization must be a qualified 501(c)3 organization.
Geographic Focus: New Mexico
Contact: Richard A. Abeles, President; (505) 988-1115; (505) 984-2040; rick@abeles.net
Sponsor: Abeles Foundation
3730 Old Santa Fe Trail
Santa Fe, NM 87505-4573

Abel Foundation Grants 26

The foundation awards grants to eligible Nebraska nonprofit organizations in its areas of interest, including environmental programs and natural resource conservation, health care, higher education, Protestant religion and churches, and social services. Types of support include building construction/renovation, capital campaigns, general operating support, and program grants. Contact the office for application forms. Applications qualifying for review will be considered within 1 to 3 months of receipt.
Requirements: Nebraska nonprofit organizations are eligible. Preference is given to requests from Licoln, Nebraska, and the state's southeastern area.
Restrictions: The Foundation does not accept applications from organizations: that have had requests approved or declined in the past 12 months; or that are currently received payments for a multi-year grant.
Geographic Focus: Nebraska
Date(s) Application is Due: Apr 15; Jul 31; Oct 31
Amount: 50 - 40,000 USD
Contact: J. Ross McCown; (402) 434-1212; (402) 434-1799; rossm@nebcoinc.com
Internet: http://www.abelfoundation.org/grant.htm
Sponsor: Abel Foundation
1815 Y Street, P.O. Box 80268
Lincoln, NE 68501-0268

Abell-Hanger Foundation Grants 27

The foundation makes grants to nonprofit Texas organizations, other than private foundations, that are involved in such undertakings for the public/society benefit including arts, cultural, and humanities; education; health; human services; and religion. Types of support include general operating support, continuing support, annual campaigns, capital campaigns, building construction/renovation, equipment acquisition, endowment funds, program development, seed funds, scholarship funds, research grants, and matching funds. Block scholarship grants are made only to institutions of higher education located in Texas. Recipient colleges and universities are free to administer the grants. Education grants are limited generally to institutions of higher education, including religious institutions (Baptist, Christian, Lutheran, Methodist, and Presbyterian). Applicants must seek funding for the same proposal from various sources because sole sponsorship of programs is rarely undertaken. Grant requests are considered and awarded throughout each year. The trustees prefer to consider only one request per applicant each fiscal year. Unsuccessful proposals may not be resubmitted for at least 12 months. Applicant organizations that have never received funding from the foundation should request a preproposal questionnaire; the trustees will review the request to determine whether it warrants a complete proposal.
Requirements: Applicant organizations must be located in Texas and be 501(c)3 tax-exempt. National organizations with significant operations in, or providing material benefits to the citizens of, Texas will be considered based on the degree of operations/benefits within the state.
Restrictions: The foundation does not fund grants, scholarships, or fellowships for individuals.
Geographic Focus: Texas
Date(s) Application is Due: Feb 28; May 31; Sep 30; Nov 11
Amount: 20,000 - 50,000 USD
Samples: Church on Wheels, Inc. (Midland, TX), $36,000 for operating expenses; Rock the Desert Ministries, Inc. (Midland, TX), $15,000 for operating expenses for the 2006 Christian music rock concert to reach teenagers; Street Andrew's Presbyterian Mission (Midland, TX), $37,500 for the utility bill assistance program.
Contact: David L. Smith, Executive Director; (432) 684-6655; (432) 684-4474; ahf@abell-hanger.org
Internet: http://www.abell-hanger.org/GrantCriteria.htm
Sponsor: Abell-Hanger Foundation
P.O. Box 430
Midland, TX 79702-0430

Abell Foundation Arts and Culture Grants 28

In recognition of the overall economic health of a city, the Foundation seeks funding opportunities to strengthen existing cultural arts organizations and to support emerging arts groups that are providing programming in under-served neighborhoods. The Foundation looks for initiatives that help keep artists working and living in the metropolitan area; increase organizations' capacity to expand audiences; attract more cultural visitors; and stabilize and revitalize neighborhoods. The Foundation also supports pilot projects that seek to determine the outcomes of cultural arts curricula on overall student academic achievement while at the same time reinforcing the State's mandate to integrate the cultural arts into the K-12 educational programming.
Requirements: 501(c)3 organizations serving Maryland communities, especially in the Baltimore area, may apply. The foundation prefers grantees that show strong fiscal management, their project's benefit to the community, ability to achieve goals, unique work, and other sources of financial support.
Restrictions: Grants are not given to individuals, or for sponsorships, deficit financing, operating budgets, annual sustaining funds, travel, or loans. The foundation currently does not fund housing projects, hospitals, or medical research.
Geographic Focus: Maryland
Date(s) Application is Due: Jan 1; Mar 1; May 1; Aug 1; Sep 1; Nov 1
Amount: 5,000 - 50,000 USD
Contact: Robert C. Embry, Jr., President; (410) 547-1300; (410) 539-6579; embry@abell.org or abell@abell.org
Internet: http://www.abell.org/programareas/arts.html
Sponsor: Abell Foundation
111 S Calvert Street, Suite 2300
Baltimore, MD 21202-6174

Abell Foundation Community Development Grants 29

The Foundation recognizes the need to enhance the livability of neighborhoods and create desirable housing and commercial areas as a means to retain and attract both residents and jobs. By encouraging investment in redevelopment projects and housing renovations, leveraging of public and private capital, community planning and maximizing reuse of historic structures, the Foundation focuses on those initiatives that foster improvement of downtown and neighborhoods. It further seeks to promote cost-efficient delivery of municipal services, maximize Baltimore's use of competitive funding sources

and increase the tax base. The Foundation also encourages efforts to tie the health of the City to the region and state, through the support of housing mobility, regional planning and growth management.
Requirements: 501(c)3 organizations serving Maryland communities, especially in the Baltimore area, may apply. The foundation prefers grantees that show strong fiscal management, their project's benefit to the community, ability to achieve goals, unique work, and other sources of financial support.
Restrictions: Grants are not given to individuals, or for sponsorships, deficit financing, operating budgets, annual sustaining funds, travel, or loans. The foundation currently does not fund housing projects, hospitals, or medical research.
Geographic Focus: Maryland
Date(s) Application is Due: Jan 1; Mar 1; May 1; Aug 1; Sep 1; Nov 1
Amount: 5,000 - 50,000 USD
Contact: Tracey M. Barbour-Gillett, Program Officer; (410) 547-1300; (410) 539-6579; tbarbour@abell.org or abell@abell.org
Internet: http://www.abell.org/programareas/community.html
Sponsor: Abell Foundation
111 S Calvert Street, Suite 2300
Baltimore, MD 21202-6174

Abell Foundation Conservation and Environment Grants 30
The Foundation supports organizations that are working to protect and preserve Maryland's natural resources. Partnering with the public and private sectors, the Foundation places special emphasis on those initiatives supporting ecosystem-wide conservation programs, including forests, wetlands, agricultural lands, watersheds and air and water quality. The Foundation also focuses attention on local projects reinforcing Maryland's Smart Growth, Rural Legacy and Green Print initiatives. Areas of interest include: watershed, resource, and habitat protection; environmental education; advocacy for air and water protection; land acquisition; technical assistance for planning sustainable communities.
Requirements: 501(c)3 organizations serving Maryland communities, especially in the Baltimore area, may apply. The foundation prefers grantees that show strong fiscal management, their project's benefit to the community, ability to achieve goals, unique work, and other sources of financial support.
Restrictions: Grants are not given to individuals, or for sponsorships, deficit financing, operating budgets, annual sustaining funds, travel, or loans. The foundation currently does not fund housing projects, hospitals, or medical research.
Geographic Focus: Maryland
Date(s) Application is Due: Jan 1; Mar 1; May 1; Aug 1; Sep 1; Nov 1
Amount: 5,000 - 50,000 USD
Contact: Robert C. Embry, Jr., President; (410) 547-1300; (410) 539-6579; embry@abell.org or abell@abell.org
Internet: http://www.abell.org/programareas/conservation.html
Sponsor: Abell Foundation
111 S Calvert Street, Suite 2300
Baltimore, MD 21202-6174

Abell Foundation Criminal Justice and Addictions Grants 31
The Foundation seeks to increase access to substance abuse treatment and supportive services such as housing and job training for the uninsured and drug addicted individuals residing in Baltimore City. The Foundation works to increase the impact and effectiveness of treatment services through cutting edge research and support of innovative service models designed to reach under-served populations. The Foundation supports programs and initiatives that increase public safety and reduce recidivism with a special focus on initiatives that address the barriers facing the returning ex-offender. A particular emphasis is placed on initiatives that provide transitional housing and the necessary wraparound services to support a successful return to the community.
Requirements: 501(c)3 organizations serving Maryland communities, especially in the Baltimore area, may apply. The foundation prefers grantees that show strong fiscal management, their project's benefit to the community, ability to achieve goals, unique work, and other sources of financial support.
Restrictions: Grants are not given to individuals, or for sponsorships, deficit financing, operating budgets, annual sustaining funds, travel, or loans. The foundation currently does not fund housing projects, hospitals, or medical research.
Geographic Focus: Maryland
Date(s) Application is Due: Jan 1; Mar 1; May 1; Aug 1; Sep 1; Nov 1
Amount: 5,000 - 50,000 USD
Contact: Amanda Owens, Program Officer; (410) 547-1300; (410) 539-6579; aowens@abell.org or abell@abell.org
Internet: http://www.abell.org/programareas/criminal.html
Sponsor: Abell Foundation
111 S Calvert Street, Suite 2300
Baltimore, MD 21202-6174

Abell Foundation Health and Human Services Grants 32
Through grants awarded in this area, the Foundation seeks to address societal issues associated with family disintegration, family planning, child support, teenage parenting, domestic violence, children's health and well-being, child abuse and neglect, hunger, food self-sufficiency and homelessness. The Foundation also supports advocacy programs for better health care and social services for children and youth as well as for a comprehensive system of universal health care. Of particular concern is the support of efforts to combat childhood lead paint poisoning and mental health disorders. Furthermore, the Foundation continues to provide opportunities for low-income families to live in quality housing in good neighborhoods in the region. While the Foundation's primary focus is on the development of permanent housing, it also will consider emergency and transitional housing.
Requirements: 501(c)3 organizations serving Maryland communities, especially in the Baltimore area, may apply. The foundation prefers grantees that show strong fiscal management, their project's benefit to the community, ability to achieve goals, unique work, and other sources of financial support.
Restrictions: Grants are not given to individuals, or for sponsorships, deficit financing, operating budgets, annual sustaining funds, travel, or loans. The foundation currently does not fund housing projects, hospitals, or medical research.
Geographic Focus: Maryland
Date(s) Application is Due: Jan 1; Mar 1; May 1; Aug 1; Sep 1; Nov 1
Amount: 5,000 - 50,000 USD
Contact: Melanie Styles, Program Officer; (410) 547-1300; (410) 539-6579; styles@abell.org or abell@abell.org
Internet: http://www.abell.org/programareas/health.html
Sponsor: Abell Foundation
111 S Calvert Street, Suite 2300
Baltimore, MD 21202-6174

Able To Serve Grants 33
Able to Serve Inc. is a public charity, providing services and opportunities for persons with mental and physical disabilities. Able primarily serves Wake and Johnston counties in North Carolina with some services extended to surrounding counties when resources are available. There are currently four programs that cover the services Able fund within the local community; Local Ministry Network, Community Partnerships, Van Transportation Services, and Computer Learning/Donations.
Requirements: Able to Serve provides each service and program at no charge to the individual or family receiving services within the Wake and Johnston counties of North Carolina.
Geographic Focus: North Carolina
Contact: Carlton S. McDaniel, President; (919) 779-5545; carlton@abletoserve.com
Internet: www.abletoserve.com
Sponsor: Able To Serve
P.O. Box 334
Garner, NC 27529-0334

Able Trust Vocational Rehabilitation Grants for Agencies 34
The trust supports individuals and non-profit vocational rehabilitation programs throughout Florida with fund-raising, grant making and public awareness of disability issues. The program provides grant funds to Florida not-for-profit agencies and Floridians with disabilities for a wide array of projects leading to the employment of individuals with disabilities. To be considered for funding a proposal must address the employment of individuals with disabilities and priority is given to those projects with direct employment placement outcomes during the grant time period. Grants to organizations are typically around $45,000. Historically grants have been made between $5,000 and $200,000. The amount is relative to the scale, scope and complexity of the proposed employment project.
Requirements: Agency applicants must be a 501(c)3 organization serving the disability community in Florida and interested in providing employment services for individuals with disabilities. Any employment program that will provide direct placement in competitive employment, the transition from

school-to-work, transition from sheltered/work enclave settings to community-based employment, job skills training such as resume and interview assistance, computer skills, office skills and etiquette, transportation training to access work, and other research, public awareness and promotion that focuses on creating employment opportunities for individuals with disabilities. There are no deadlines. Guidelines, helpful tips and application forms can be found at the sponsor's website.
Restrictions: Grants funds may not be used to purchase: vehicles, property, building improvements, capital campaigns, endowments, fellowships, scholarships, travel grants, tuition where state and federal aid is available, lobbying, medical items, incurred debt, and program expenses prior to grant approval.
Geographic Focus: Florida
Amount: 5,000 - 200,000 USD
Contact: Guenevere Crum, Senior Vice President; (850) 224-4493; (850) 224-4496; guenevere@abletrust.org or info@abletrust.org
Internet: http://www.abletrust.org/grant/booklet.shtml
Sponsor: Able Trust
3320 Thomasville Road, Suite 200
Tallahassee, FL 32308

Abundance Foundation International Grants 35
The Abundance Foundation makes grants to organizations aligned with its mission to improve global health through education, economic empowerment and health systems strengthening. It is focused on programs that unlock the potential of local communities particularly in Africa, Central America and Haiti. Its grantee partners train, support and empower local leaders to create new capabilities that result in lasting improvement in quality of life. In addition to direct grant funding that allows for upscaling of successful existing programs, the Foundation raise awareness about local leaders whose vision and heroism are creating positive change in their communities.
Geographic Focus: All U.S. States, Haiti
Contact: Stephen Kahn, President; (510) 841-4123; (510) 841-4093; info@abundancefound.org
Internet: http://www.abundancefound.org/grants/
Sponsor: Abundance Foundation
127 University Avenue
Berkeley, CA 94710-1616

Achelis and Bodman Foundations Grants 36
Both Foundations concentrate their grant programs in New York City, although The Bodman Foundation also makes grants in northern New Jersey. Funding is concentrated in six program areas: Arts and Culture, Education, Employment, Health, Public Policy, and Youth and Families.
Requirements: Nonprofit organizations based in New York City and northern New Jersey that are tax-exempt under Section 501(c)3 of the Internal Revenue Code and fall within the program areas of the foundations are welcome to submit an inquiry or proposal letter by regular mail. Do not send initial inquiries by email or fax; also do not send CDs, DVDs, computer discs, video tapes, or proposals through the Internet or by facsimile. An initial inquiry to the foundations should include only the following items: (1) A proposal letter that briefly summarizes the history of the project, need, research, objectives, time period, key staff, project budget, and evaluation plan. (2) Latest annual report. (3) Latest complete audited financial statements. (4) IRS 501(c)3 tax-exemption letter. There are no deadlines and applications may be submitted at any time during the year. Each request is reviewed by staff and will usually receive a written response within thirty days. Those requests deemed consistent with the interests and resources of the Foundations will be evaluated further and more information will be requested. Staff may request a site visit, conference call, or meeting. All grants are reviewed and approved by the Trustees at one of their three board meetings in May, September, or December.
Restrictions: The foundations generally do not make grants for the following purposes or program areas: Nonprofit organizations outside of New York and New Jersey; Annual appeals, dinner functions, and fundraising events; Endowments and capital campaigns; Loans and deficit financing; Direct grants to individuals; Individual day-care and after-school programs; Housing; Organizations or projects based outside the U.S; Films or video projects; Small art, dance, music, and theater groups; Individual K-12 schools (except charter schools); National health and mental health organizations; Government agencies or nonprofit organizations significantly funded or reimbursed by government agencies. Limited resources prevent the foundations from funding the same organization on an ongoing annual basis.
Geographic Focus: New Jersey, New York
Samples: Foundation for Cultural Review - (Achelis, 2007) $35,000 toward the redesign of the website of the New Criterion magazine; High 5 Tickets to the Arts - (Bodman, 2006) $15,000 for the Take 5 Program for disadvantaged youth; Coalition for Educational Freedom - (Bodman, 2007) $50,000 toward the creation of a state-wide school choice organization in Connecticut; Center for Alternative Sentencing and Employment Services - (Achelis, 2007) $35,000 toward the Career Exploration Program for young ex-offenders in New York City; Jericho Project - (Achelis, 2007) $50,000 toward the Vocational and Educational Program for those with substance abuse or mental health problems; Brain Trauma Foundation - (Achelis, 2007) $50,000 for the Veterans Information Initiative; Children of Bellevue - (Bodman, 2007) $25,000 for the Frances L. Loeb Child Protection and Development Center at Bellevue Hospital Center
Contact: John B. Krieger, Executive Director; (212) 644-0322; (212) 759-6510; main@achelis-bodman-fnds.org
Internet: http://foundationcenter.org/grantmaker/achelis-bodman/guidelines.html
Sponsor: Achelis and Bodman Foundations
767 Third Avenue, 4th Floor
New York, NY 10017

Actuarial Foundation Advancing Student Achievement Grants 37
The foundation considers proposals for funding of mentoring programs that involve actuaries in supporting the teaching and learning of mathematics at all levels. Grants may be awarded to U.S. and Canadian local groups that can provide the support necessary to develop a network of mathematics mentors in the public and private school systems. Such groups include actuarial clubs and other education-oriented organizations. The programs can also encourage interest in mathematics applications in business and societal issues by students and teachers. Applicants will be given wide latitude in designing and organizing programs to best utilize local community resources. Preference is given to innovative programs that do not merely replicate existing grant programs. Grants support direct project overhead expenses.
Requirements: U.S. and Canadian local groups or organizations are eligible. Collaboration among school systems, local actuarial clubs, corporations, and other stakeholders in education is encouraged.
Geographic Focus: All U.S. States, Canada
Amount: Up to 25,000 USD
Contact: Grants Administrator; (847) 706-3535; (847) 706-3599; ASA@ActFdn.org
Internet: http://www.actuarialfoundation.org/grant/index.html
Sponsor: Actuarial Foundation
475 N Martingale Road, Suite 600
Schaumburg, IL 60173-2226

Adams County Community Foundation Grants 38
The Adams County Community Foundation was established in October of 2007 as a Pennsylvania corporation to succeed the Adams County Foundation which for 22 years had operated as a trust-based community foundation. The Foundation is a public charity that the IRS has determined to be a 501(c)3 organization. The purpose of this foundation is to inspire people and communities to build and distribute charitable funds for Good, for Adams County, forever. After one year of operation, the foundation had acquired nine funds established by individual people or families, members of the Foundation's Board of Directors, groups of business people, a local charity and by a visionary patriot from the 1700s. The Foundation's assets are managed by a professional investment company hired by the Board of Directors and overseen by the Foundation's Investment & Finance Committee. From these funds, distribution of grants is made to qualified, local charities who demonstrate that they are meeting community needs. With a 16 member Board of Directors, Adams County Community Foundation serves as a good steward of the monies of our donors and demonstrates accountability, transparency, confidentiality, compassion, inclusiveness and excellence in its work. The foundation gives to organizations that assist, promote and improve the moral, mental, social and physical well-being of area residents. Fields of interest include: arts; Christian agencies and churches; community and economic development; education; and health organizations.
Requirements: Applicants must serve residents living in Adams County, Pennsylvania.
Geographic Focus: Pennsylvania
Contact: Barbara Ernico, (717) 337-0060 or (717) 337-3353; (717) 337-1080; info@adamscountycf.org

Internet: http://www.adamscountycf.org/funds.html
Sponsor: Adams County Community Foundation
101 W Middle Street, P.O. Box 4565
Gettysburg, PA 17325-2109

Adams County Community Foundation Grants 39

The Adams County Community Foundation and supporting organization, John and Kay Boch, award numerous grants annually. Areas of primary interest include: children and youth; community and economic development; education; and parks and recreation. Money awarded from the various funds helps to enrich and enhance the quality of life throughout Adams County. Grants awarded annually help both businesses and the communities in which it serves.
Requirements: Must support businesses, educational programs, or residents of Adams County, Indiana.
Geographic Focus: Indiana
Date(s) Application is Due: Jan 2; Apr 2; Jul 2; Oct 2
Amount: 200 - 2,000 USD
Contact: Coni Mayer, Executive Director; (260) 724-3939; (260) 724-2299; accfoundation@earthlink.net
Internet: http://www.adamscountyfoundation.org/grant-info.aspx
Sponsor: Adams County Community Foundation
102 N Second Street
Decatur, IN 46733

Adams County Foundation Grants - Colorado 40

The Adams County Foundation is a non-profit organization focused on the success of programs that: support Workforce Development; enhance early care and education; promote community and neighborhood development; weave arts and culture into everyday lives; and nurture the independence and mobility of seniors. The Foundation keeps excellent programs and initiatives funded and in motion, allowing school districts, businesses, public and private agencies to work together to create amazing results they could not accomplish alone. Contact the office directly for application details and guidelines.
Requirements: Applicant organization must be either located in or serve the residents of Adams County, Colorado.
Geographic Focus: Colorado
Contact: Claire Mannato, Program Manager; (303) 654-6222; (303) 659-6821; info@acfco.org
Internet: http://www.acfco.org/about.html
Sponsor: Adams County Foundation
12200 Pecos Street
Westminster, CO 80234

Adams Family Foundation Grants 41

The Foundation, established in Minnesota in 2000, is most interested in supporting youth development, local libraries, and environmental awareness. Additionally, its fields of interest include higher education and the arts. The primary type of support in for general operations, Although there are no specific deadlines or applications with which to adhere, applicants should submit a detailed description of the proposed program, purposes of the organization, and budgetary needs.
Requirements: Nonprofit organizations within the northern and west central Minnesota regions may apply.
Geographic Focus: Minnesota
Amount: 500 - 2,000 USD
Samples: Center for the Arts, Fergus Falls, Minnesota, $1,800 - support for local arts (2010); Kaddatz Galary, Fergus Falls, Minnesota, $1,704 - general operations / support for the arts (2010); Otter Tail County Historical Society, Fergus Falls, Minnesota, $2,000 - general operations (2010).
Contact: Virginia S. Adams, President; (218) 736-4842
Sponsor: Adams Family Foundation
504 South Oak Street
Fergus Falls, MN 56537-2614

Adams Family Foundation Grants 42

The Foundation, established in Tennessee in 2006, provides grants to individuals for family services, cemetery/burial needs, and for the prevention of domestic violence in the Paris, Tennessee, region. There are no application forms or deadlines with which to adhere, and those in need should forward a letter of request directly to the Foundation office. Amounts range from $1,000 to $2,000.
Geographic Focus: Tennessee
Amount: 1,000 - 2,000 USD
Samples: Henry County Food Bank, Paris, Tennessee, $2,000 - general operations (2010); Damascus Road Homeless Shelter, Paris, Tennessee, $1,000 - general operations (2010); Tomorrow's Hope Pregnancy Care Center, Paris, Tennessee, $1,000 - general operations (2010).
Contact: David E. Sullivan, Director; (731) 642-2940 or (731) 642-2752
Sponsor: Adams Family Foundation
1101 East Wood Street, P.O. Box 909
Paris, TN 38242-0909

Adams Family Foundation I Grants 43

The Foundation, founded in 1993, offers support primarily in Tennessee and the southeastern portion of the United States. Its fields of interest include: the arts, children and youth services, Christian agencies and churches, elementary and secondary education programs, and human services. The primary type of funding is general operating support. There are no specific deadlines with which to adhere, and applicants should forward a request by letter outlining the project and a detailed budgetary need. Most grants are in the neighborhood of $500 to $10,000, though occasionally reach as high as $100,000.
Requirements: Any 501(c)3 that is located in, or offers support to, Tennessee or the southeastern portion of the United States is eligible to apply.
Geographic Focus: Tennessee
Amount: Up to 100,000 USD
Samples: Adams Memorial Public Library, Woodbury, Tennessee, $13,000 (2010); Children's Discovery House, Murfreesboro, Tennessee, $5,000 (2010); Middle Tennessee Medical School, Murfreesboro, Tennessee, $100,000 (2010).
Contact: Robert G. Adams, Treasurer; (615) 890-2020 or (615) 896-0374; (615) 890-0123
Sponsor: Adams Family Foundation I
2217 Battleground Drive
Murfreesboro, TN 37129-6006

Adams Family Foundation II Grants 44

The Foundation, established in 1993 by the founder of the Murfreesboro-based National HealthCare L.P. and National Health Investors, is primarily interested in supporting: boys and girls clubs; Boy Scouts of America; children and youth services; Christian agencies and churches; human service organizations; and secondary education. Funding is typically in the form of general operating support. Grants are usually in the $500 to $10,000 range, although occasionally somewhat higher. There are no particular deadlines, and applicants should approach the Foundation initially by letter describing their program and specifying an amount needed.
Geographic Focus: Tennessee
Amount: 100 - 200,000 USD
Contact: W. Andrew Adams, Treasurer; (615) 848-2638 or (615) 848-0171
Sponsor: Adams Family Foundation II
801 Mooreland Lane
Murfreesboro, TN 37128-4634

Adam Smith Institute Grants 45

The Institute is the United Kingdom's leading innovator of free-market economic and social policies. Politically independent and non-profit, the Institute promotes its ideas through grants, reports, briefings, events, media appearances, and its website and blog. Giving is primarily in London, England, and goes to general operating costs for museums. There are no specific deadlines or application forms with which to adhere.
Geographic Focus: All U.S. States, United Kingdom
Contact: Grants Manager; (301) 770-3750
Internet: http://www.adamsmith.org/
Sponsor: Adam Smith Institute
6163 Executive Boulevard
Rockville, MD 20852-3901

Adolph Coors Foundation Grants 46

The foundation's grant program supports programs in the area of health that are preventive in nature, promote wellness and/or can demonstrate a reduction in health-care costs. The support in education is directed to institutions and programs that foster excellence in the knowledge of free enterprise, science, technology and ethics. The Foundation is generally supportive of community and human services agencies that assist the disadvantaged in their efforts to be self-sufficient and productive and that nurture the development of integrity and leadership. Civic and cultural programs attracting the Foundation's attention

are typically those that enhance our culture and heritage, demonstrate our creativity as a people and are likely to be of economic benefit to and broadly used by the communities they serve. Past grants have supported boys and girls clubs and inner-city health programs. Types of support include building funds, general operating budgets, seed money, and special projects. Application guidelines are available from the foundation; there is no formal application form. Applications are not accepted by fax or email.
Requirements: Only tax-exempt, nonprofit organizations in or benefiting Colorado that do not also receive tax money are eligible to apply.
Restrictions: Individuals are ineligible. The foundation does not support preschools or day-care centers.
Geographic Focus: Colorado
Samples: Colorado College (Colorado Springs, CO)—to renovate Palmer Hall, an academic building that was constructed in 1904, $400,000.
Contact: Jeanne Bistranin, Program Officer; (303) 388-1636; generalinfo@acoorsfdn.org
Internet: http://www.coorsfoundation.org/guidelines.html
Sponsor: Adolph Coors Foundation
4100 E Mississippi Avenue, Suite 1850
Denver, CO 80246

Advance Auto Parts Corporate Giving Grants 47

The Advance Auto Parts Corporate Giving program was founded on the belief that good business is more than just selling merchandise. Since the company was founded in 1932, it has been guided by the following principles, known as the Advance Values: inspire and build the self-confidence and success of every Team Member; serve customers better than anyone else and help them succeed; and grow the business and profitability with integrity. While the corporation understands that there are a variety of worthy causes in every community, to maximize its giving and make the greatest possible impact, Advance has chosen to focus its charitable efforts on serving those in need through support of the following four impact areas: health – improving the health and well-being of others; education – helping people reach their potential by providing educational opportunities; at-risk children and families – helping children and families to assure their critical needs are met through comprehensive, community-based programs; and disaster relief – providing timely support to those impacted by disasters such as earthquakes, hurricanes, floods and other natural disasters.
Geographic Focus: All U.S. States
Contact: Grants Manager; (540) 362-4911; (540) 561-1448
Internet: http://corp.advanceautoparts.com/english/about/public.asp
Sponsor: Advance Auto Parts Corporate Giving
5008 Airport Road
Roanoke, VA 24012

Advent Software Corporate Giving Grants 48

Advent Software makes charitable contributions to nonprofit organizations to nonprofit organizations involved with education and low-performing K-12 schools. The primary field of interest is elementary and secondary education, and comes in the form of general operation funds. Advent Software will also leverage Community Involvement to support Advent's business strategy, streamline program operations, and support employees and the company.
Requirements: Giving is primarily restricted to areas of company operations in California, Massachusetts, and New York, as well as in China, Denmark, India, the Netherlands, Norway, Singapore, Sweden, Switzerland, and the United Kingdom.
Geographic Focus: California, Massachusetts, New York, China, Denmark, India, Netherlands, Norway, Singapore, Sweden, Switzerland, United Kingdom
Contact: Director of Grants; (415) 543-7696; (415) 543-5070; nfo@advent.com
Internet: http://www.advent.com/about/community-involvement
Sponsor: Advent Software Corporation
600 Townsend Street
San Francisco, CA 94103

AEC Trust Grants 49

The AEC Trust is a private foundation established in 1980 as a philanthropic, grantmaking organization. The trust awards grants to eligible nonprofits in Colorado, Florida, Georgia, Massachusetts, and Wisconsin in its areas of interest, including AIDS, arts and culture, community development, elementary education, the environment, health care, higher education, social services, and women. Types of support include building construction/renovation, capital campaigns, challenge/matching grants, equipment acquisition, general operating support, land acquisition, project support, and publications. Request guidelines in writing.
Requirements: 501(c)3 nonprofit organizations in the communities of Boulder, Colorado, Gainesville, Florida, Atlanta, Georgia, Amherst, Massachusetts, and Green Bay, Wisconsin, are eligible.
Restrictions: Grants do not support individuals, international organizations, political organizations, religious organizations, school districts, special events/benefit dinners, state and local government agencies, United Way agencies, national public charities, endowments, sponsorships, or annual fund campaigns.
Geographic Focus: Colorado, Florida, Georgia, Massachusetts, Wisconsin
Date(s) Application is Due: Apr 1; Sep 1
Amount: 10,000 - 50,000 USD
Contact: Julia Beisel, (800) 839-1754 or (401) 881-3409; requests@foundationsource.com
Internet: https://online.foundationsource.com/public/home/aec
Sponsor: AEC Trust
191 Peachtree Street, Suite 2300
Atlanta, GA 30309-7676

AED New Voices Fellowships 50

The program seeks to strengthen small nonprofit organizations by supporting resident fellows who can bring a new voice to an organization and its field of work. Applications are reviewed under one of the following categories: foreign policy, peace and security; HIV/AIDS; international economic policy international human rights; migrant and refugee rights; racial justice and civil rights; and women's and reproductive rights. Awards include support for fellow's salary, fringe benefits, and to purchase a computer. Preference is given to nonprofits with budgets between $100,000 and $2 million. Applications are prepared jointly by an organization and its proposed fellow.
Requirements: 501(c)3 nonprofit organizations that reflect diverse educational, cultural, and experiential backgrounds are eligible. Potential fellows should have completed an undergraduate or graduate degree or have comparable education, skills, and relevant experience.
Restrictions: Groups with budgets of more than $5 million are not eligible.
Geographic Focus: All U.S. States
Date(s) Application is Due: Jan 10
Amount: 100,000 USD
Contact: Program Officer; (202) 884-8607; (202) 884-8400; newvoice@aed.org
Internet: http://www.aed.org/newvoices
Sponsor: Academy for Educational Development
1825 Connecticut Avenue NW, Suite 744
Washington, DC 20009-5721

AEGON Transamerica Foundation Grants 51

The foundation supports organizations involved with arts and culture, education, cancer, ALS research, hunger, human services, and the disabled. Giving on a national basis in areas of company operations, with some emphasis on Little Rock, Arkansas, California, Atlanta, Georgia, Cedar Rapids, Iowa, Louisville, Kentucky, Baltimore, Maryland, Charlotte, North Carolina, New York, Pennsylvania, and Fort Worth, Texas.
Requirements: Grant recipient must be a 501(c)3 organization.
Restrictions: Grants are not awarded to individuals. Unsolicited proposals not accepted.
Geographic Focus: Arkansas, California, Georgia, Iowa, Kentucky, Maryland, New York, North Carolina, Pennsylvania, Texas
Amount: 50 - 2,500,000 USD
Samples: Johns Hopkins University, Baltimore, MD, $2,500,000 (2008); United Way of Central Carolinas, Charlotte, NC, $46,676 (2008); Theater Cedar Rapids, Cedar Rapids, IA, $150,000 (2008).
Contact: Grants Administrator; (319) 398-8935
Sponsor: AEGON Transamerica Foundation
4333 Edgewood Road, NE
Cedar Rapids, IA 52499-3210

AFG Industries Grants 52

The corporation awards general operating grants to nonprofits in its headquarters area in the categories of arts and humanities, civic and public affairs, education at all levels, health care, and social services. There are no application deadlines. Submit a brief letter of inquiry.
Requirements: Tennessee nonprofits are eligible.

Geographic Focus: Tennessee
Amount: 100,000 - 250,000 USD
Contact: Human Resources; (800) 251-0441 or (423) 229-7200; (423) 229-7459
Internet: http://www.afgglass.com
Sponsor: AFG Industries
P.O. Box 929
Kingsport, TN 37662

African American Fund of New Jersey Grants 53
The fund concentrates on providing significant funding to New Jersey's African American communities to promote and enhance human services delivery and community empowerment. Program areas that will receive primary funding consideration are in the areas of pre-school through high school education initiatives, technology-oriented initiatives, health-related programs, community issues, and building wealth. Programs that emphasize positive family values, traditions, social customs, and family practices that have contributed to the survival of the African American family are encouraged. Types of support include general operating grants, program development grants, and technical assistance. Proposals must demonstrate the intention to commit the necessary financial and human resources to a program that is well coordinated with related human services within the respective communities. All applicants will be notified of approval or disapproval of their proposals. Annual deadline dates may vary; contact program staff for exact dates.
Requirements: New Jersey 501(c)3 nonprofit, tax-exempt agencies, community-based organizations, and schools are eligible.
Geographic Focus: New Jersey
Amount: 1,000 - 5,000 USD
Samples: Hudson County Child Abuse Prevention Center - grant recipient; Link Community School - grant recipient; Newark Literacy Campaign, Inc. - grant recipient; Young Science Achievers, Inc. - grant recipient.
Contact: Sondra Clark, President; (973) 676-5283; (973) 672-5030; sclark@aafnj.org
Internet: http://www.aafnj.org/HBW_Grants.htm
Sponsor: African American Fund of New Jersey
132 S Harrison Street
East Orange, NJ 07018

African American Heritage Grants 54
Grants are awarded to assist organizations in the preservation and promotion of historic African American properties and sites in Indiana. Awards are made on a four-to-one matching basis, funding 80% of the total project cost up to $2,500, whichever is less.
Requirements: Civic groups, schools, libraries, historical societies, and other nonprofit agencies are eligible to apply for grants for organizational assistance, studies assisting in or leading to the preservation of a historic African American place, and programs promoting the preservation, interpretation, and/or visitation of a historic African American place. Contact the regional community preservation specialist that serves your community (see website for list of regional offices or contact the state headquarters office) for guidelines and forms.
Restrictions: Properties must be located in Indiana.
Geographic Focus: Indiana
Amount: 500 - 2,500 USD
Samples: Historic Eleutherian College Inc. - $2,500 to pay for a comprehensive master restoration and conservation plan for the c.1850 former African American college, which is now a National Historic Landmark.
Contact: Carla Jones, Receptionist, State Headquarters; (317) 639-4534; (317) 639-6734; info@historiclandmarks.org
Internet: http://www.historiclandmarks.org/help/grants.html
Sponsor: Historic Landmarks Foundation of Indiana
340 W Michigan Street
Indianapolis, IN 46202

Agnes Gund Foundation Grants 55
The foundation awards general operating grants in its areas of interest, including health organizations, higher education, and performing arts (dance, music). There are no application deadlines or forms. Submit a letter of inquiry.
Requirements: Although there are no funding restrictions there is a focus on New York City.
Restrictions: Applicants must be a tax-exempt organization.
Geographic Focus: New York
Amount: 5,000 - 100,000 USD
Samples: Museum of Modern Art (New York, NY)—for general operating support, $1 million; Cleveland Museum of Art (OH)—for general operating support, $200,000; Virginia Museum of Fine Arts (Richmond, VA)—for general operating support, $100,000; Creative Capital Foundation (New York, NY)—for general operating support, $75,000.
Contact: Program Director; (330) 385-3400
Sponsor: Agnes Gund Foundation
517 Broadway, 3rd Floor
East Liverpool, OH 43920

AHFMR Establishment and Independent Establishment Grants 56
The two types of grants available include: Establishment Grants—AHFMR provides funds to assist reseachers (newly recruited to Alberta) in the start-up of their laboratories and/or research projects; and Independent Establishment Grants—open to new Alberta Investigators who are not candidates for Heritage personnel awards (it is understood that these investigators will commit much of their time to medical or health research). Those sponsoring investigators for these awards must notify the Foundation of their intent to do so at least four months in advance of the application deadline, and request a determination of the eligibility of the candidate. The Foundation will not accept applications for which advanced notice has not been received. There are two categories of grant funding: Operating Funds and Major Equipment Funds.
Requirements: Eligibility to apply for these grants is restricted to applicants recruited to leadership positions (such as Department Head or Director of a centre, institute or division), where the recruitment is expected to stimulate the development of research in a field or discipline of interest to the Foundation.
Geographic Focus: Canada
Date(s) Application is Due: Sep 15
Contact: Pamela Valentine, Director of Grants and Awards; (780) 423-5727; (780) 429-3509; pamela.valentine@ahfmr.ab.ca
Internet: http://www.ahfmr.ab.ca/grants/EstabIndep.php
Sponsor: Alberta Heritage Foundation for Medical Research
10104-103 Avenue, Suite 1500
Edmonton, AB T5J 4A7 Canada

Air Products and Chemicals Grants 57
The foundation supports nonprofit organizations in company-operating areas in the fields of precollege and higher education; fitness, health, and welfare; community and economic development, arts and culture; and the environment and safety. Types of support include capital grants, employee matching gifts, general operating support, multiyear-continuing grants, project grants, seed grants, fellowships, employee-related scholarships, and donated equipment. There are no application forms; requests must be in writing. Guidelines are available online.
Requirements: 501(c)3 nonprofit organizations in company-operating areas are eligible.
Restrictions: Grants are not made to/for individuals, sectarian or denominational organizations, political candidates or activities, veterans organizations, organizations receiving United Way support, labor groups, elementary or secondary schools, capital campaigns of national organizations, hospital operating expenses, national health organizations, or goodwill advertising.
Geographic Focus: All U.S. States
Contact: Kassie Hilgert, Program Manager; hilgerk@airproducts.com
Internet: http://www.airproducts.com/Responsibility/SocialResponsibility
Sponsor: Air Products and Chemicals Corporation
7201 Hamilton Boulevard
Allentown, PA 18195-1501

Akonadi Foundation Anti-Racism Grants 58
The foundation's mission is to work with others to eliminate racism, with a particular focus on structural and institutional racism. Grants have supported programmatic approaches including research, policy work, advocacy, litigation, organizing, media, arts, diversity training, education, and other tools in their anti-racism work. The foundation awards general operating grants and project grants. Grants are made to organizations in the San Francisco Bay area and to national organizations with national reach. Letters of interest will be accepted year round. Full proposals should only be submitted upon request.
Geographic Focus: California
Date(s) Application is Due: Feb 18
Amount: 10,000 - 50,000 USD
Samples: Asian Pacific Environmental Network (Oakland, CA)—to involve Asian-Pacific Islanders in grassroots organizing to fight environmental racism, $20,000; Ctr for Third World Organizing (Oakland, CA)—for general

support, $30,000; Leadership Excellence (Oakland, CA)—for leadership development for black youths and for critical analysis of racism, $25,000; Poverty and Race Research Action Council (Washington DC)—to support a civil-rights teaching curriculum, institutes on civil rights, and teacher workshops, $25,000.
Contact: Grants Administrator; (510) 663-3867; info@akonadi.org
Internet: http://www.akonadi.org/application_guidelines.html
Sponsor: Akonadi Foundation
469 9th Street, Suite 210
Oakland, CA 94607

Alabama Power Foundation Grants 59
The foundation's mission is to improve the lives and circumstances of Alabama residents and to strengthen the communities in which they live. It supports programs that will improve education (by supporting innovative programs and assisting teachers in their crucial responsibilities), strengthen communities, promote arts and culture or restore and enhance the environment. The project must meet several of the guidelines to be considered. The majority of grants are made to support targeted efforts with specific objectives. The foundation also provides general operating assistance to organizations, capital grants for endowment and building, and scholarship funds. Applications should be sent to the local Alabama Power Company office for review and recommendation to the foundation. The amount of the request determines the review frequency.
Requirements: Applications are accepted from Alabama nonprofit organizations whose programs fall within foundation guidelines.
Restrictions: Grants are not made to individuals, for sectarian religious purposes, or for political activities.
Geographic Focus: Alabama
Date(s) Application is Due: Feb 1; May 1; Aug 1; Nov 1
Amount: 1,000 - 100,000 USD
Contact: William Johnson, President; (205) 257-2508; (205) 257-1860
Internet: http://www.alabamapower.com/foundation/grantsandinitiatives.asp
Sponsor: Alabama Power Foundation
600 N 18th Street, P.O. Box 2641
Birmingham, AL 35291-0011

Alabama State Council on the Arts Community Arts Operating Support Grants 60
Larger local arts councils and arts centers that have developed a successful track record of diverse programs and services in the community and region may qualify for general operating assistance. It is expected that strong cooperation will exist with local government entities. All organizations receiving operating support from the Council will be required to match the grant with an equal amount in local government contributions of either cash or cash and in-kind support.
Requirements: To be eligible for funding under this category, organizations must have been incorporated and recognized as having non-profit tax exempt status by the Internal Revenue Service for at least three years prior to application, or have been an agency of a city or county government for that length of time. To qualify, a Local Arts Council or Arts Center must have an actual three-year average cash income of at least $300,000. Organizations receiving operating support must also have a full time administrative staff responsible for overall functions of the organization and have an annual audit conducted by an independent Certified Public Accountant.
Restrictions: The Council does not fund: projects not available to the general public; activities and performances planned solely for fund raising purposes; food, beverages or other refreshments; interest on loans, fines, penalties, and/or litigation costs; expenses incurred prior to October 1 or after September 30 of the current grant year; investments of any kind; projects which have sectarian or religious purposes (however, such institutions may apply on behalf of the community for arts activities or programming where artistic expression is a primary focus); or indirect costs.
Geographic Focus: Alabama
Date(s) Application is Due: Jun 1
Contact: Randy Shoults, Community Arts Program Manager; (334) 242-4076, ext. 224; (334) 240-3269; randy.shoults@arts.alabama.gov or staff@arts.alabama.gov
Internet: http://arts.state.al.us/grants/index-grants.html
Sponsor: Alabama State Council on the Arts
201 Monroe Street, Suite 110
Montgomery, AL 36130-1800

Alabama State Council on the Arts Operating Support Grants 61
These grants are designed to provide support and stability to large arts organizations with far-reaching cultural impact, to promote general program development and stimulate private and other public funding. Eligible groups are expected to show a high level of professionalism, both artistically and administratively, strong community service and educational outreach, and well-established, ongoing fund raising efforts.
Requirements: An organization is eligible to apply for funding support of arts activities taking place in Alabama if the organization is legally domiciled in Alabama, and meets either of the following qualifications: the organization is non-profit with a determination letter from the Internal Revenue Service declaring the organization exempt from federal income tax under Section 501(c)3 of the Internal Revenue Code; or the organization is a public or private educational institution (such as an elementary or secondary school), a school board, a local or county governmental agency or a college or university. Private educational institutions must be non-profit and meet the tax-exempt requirements described above.
Restrictions: Organizations receiving operating support may not submit more than two (2) applications per deadline or more than three (3) per year, including the operating support request. The Council does not fund: projects not available to the general public; activities and performances planned solely for fund raising purposes; food, beverages or other refreshments; interest on loans, fines, penalties, and/or litigation costs; expenses incurred prior to October 1 or after September 30 of the current grant year; investments of any kind; projects which have sectarian or religious purposes (however, such institutions may apply on behalf of the community for arts activities or programming where artistic expression is a primary focus); or indirect costs.
Geographic Focus: Alabama
Date(s) Application is Due: Jun 1
Amount: 5,000 - 7,500 USD
Samples: Central Baldwin Middle School (Robertsdale, AL)—for the Arts in Education program, $9,924; Red Mountain Chamber Orchestra (Birmingham, AL)—project grant, $1,500.
Contact: Albert B. Head, Executive Director; (334) 242-4076, ext. 245; (334) 240-3269; al.head@arts.alabama.gov or staff@arts.alabama.gov
Internet: http://arts.state.al.us/grants/index-grants.html
Sponsor: Alabama State Council on the Arts
201 Monroe Street, Suite 110
Montgomery, AL 36130-1800

Alabama State Council on the Arts Program Development Grants 62
Requests may be submitted to fund establishment of permanent staff, existing staff development, program specialists, consultants, and general operating costs. Applicants will be expected to describe how this assistance will upgrade organizational programs. Programming development support is limited to three years, based on the assumption that the organization will be strong enough to sustain more advanced operations by that time. Generally, organizations that have a proven track record of programming for three years can be considered. All applications in this category must be submitted by June 1 for the full year.
Requirements: Grants must be matched dollar-for-dollar in cash or a combination of cash and in-kind support. An organization is eligible to apply for funding support of arts activities taking place in Alabama if the organization is legally domiciled in Alabama, and meets either of the following qualifications: the organization is non-profit with a determination letter from the Internal Revenue Service declaring the organization exempt from federal income tax under Section 501(c)3 of the Internal Revenue Code; or the organization is a public or private educational institution (such as an elementary or secondary school), a school board, a local or county governmental agency or a college or university. Private educational institutions must be non-profit and meet the tax-exempt requirements described above.
Restrictions: Large cultural institutions receiving operating support and non-arts organizations such as cities, schools, universities and civic groups are not eligible to apply. The Council does not fund: projects not available to the general public; activities and performances planned solely for fund raising purposes; food, beverages or other refreshments; interest on loans, fines, penalties, and/or litigation costs; expenses incurred prior to October 1 or after September 30 of the current grant year; investments of any kind; projects which have sectarian or religious purposes (however, such institutions may apply on behalf of the community for arts activities or programming where artistic expression is a primary focus); or indirect costs.
Geographic Focus: Alabama
Date(s) Application is Due: Jun 1

Contact: Albert B. Head, Executive Director; (334) 242-4076, ext. 245; (334) 240-3269; al.head@arts.alabama.gov or staff@arts.alabama.gov
Internet: http://arts.state.al.us/grants/index-grants.html
Sponsor: Alabama State Council on the Arts
201 Monroe Street, Suite 110
Montgomery, AL 36130-1800

Aladdin Industries Foundation Grants 63

The foundation awards grants, primarily in Tennessee, in its areas of interest, including arts and culture, youth services, health and human services, education, business, drug abuse, and the elderly. Types of support include general operating support, seed grants, and employee-related scholarships. Proposals are reviewed quarterly.
Requirements: Most grants are awarded in Tennessee. Proposals are reviewed quarterly.
Geographic Focus: Tennessee
Contact: L.B. Jenkins, Secretary & Treasurer; (615) 748-3360
Sponsor: Aladdin Industries Foundation
703 Murfreesboro Road
Nashville, TN 37210-4521

Alaska Conservation Foundation Operating Support Grants 64

ACF awards operating support grants to in-state, Alaska-based conservation organizations focused on effective conservation advocacy. Operating support grants are used at the discretion of the recipients, within the limits of laws governing the use of ACF funds. These funds can be used to cover administrative and/or program costs including salaries, facilities, travel, equipment, supplies, training, membership, fundraising, and specific program activities.
Requirements: Applicant organizations must be engaged in environmental advocacy, incorporated as a nonprofit corporation, a 501(c)3 or (c)4 organization for at least three years from application date, and have a dues-paying membership of more than 300. Applicants must first send a letter of inquiry to the program officer.
Restrictions: Proposals received via fax or email will not be accepted.
Geographic Focus: Alaska
Date(s) Application is Due: Dec 1
Amount: Up to 15,000 USD
Samples: Chickaloon Village Traditional Council (AK)—for the tribal school's wind/solar project, $25,000; Alaska Youth for Environmental Action (AK)—for a summer youth gathering, $1000.
Contact: Polly Carr, Program Officer; (907) 276-1917; (907) 274-4145; pcarr@alaskaconservation.org or grants@akcf.org
Internet: http://alaskaconservation.org/_pages/grants_amp_awards/types_of_grants/operating_support.php
Sponsor: Alaska Conservation Foundation
441 West Fifth Avenue, Suite 402
Anchorage, AK 99501-2340

Alaska State Council on the Arts Operating Support Grants 65

Grants assist with a portion of an organization's ongoing artistic and administrative functions. These may include, but are not limited to, salaries, travel, promotion, and production costs of an entire program or a majority of the organization's yearly activities. The council funds applications in all areas of the arts: dance, visual arts, literature, music, theater, media arts, and traditional Native arts. Applications that promote and develop the cultural heritage of Alaska and the creation of new works by Alaskan artists are encouraged.
Requirements: The council awards funds only to Alaskan nonprofit organizations, schools, or government agencies. Eligible organizations must: be involved in producing, presenting, or undertaking a series of events or ongoing arts programs; provide proof of 501(c)3 status; be at least three years from the date of incorporation; and have a cash budget of at least $50,000. A maximum award amount is not set; however, applicants must provide matching funds, and grants will not exceed 50 percent of the total cash expenses.
Geographic Focus: Alaska
Date(s) Application is Due: Mar 1
Amount: Up to 21,000 USD
Contact: Andrea Noble, Grant Administrator; (907) 269-6605 or (888) 278-7424; (907) 269-6601; andrea.noble@alaska.gov
Internet: http://www.eed.state.ak.us/aksca/grants2.htm#osla
Sponsor: Alaska State Council on the Arts
411 W Fourth Avenue, Suite 1E
Anchorage, AK 99501-2343

Alberta Law Foundation Grants 66

The objectives of the foundation are to conduct research into and recommend reform of law and the administration of justice; establish, maintain, and operate law libraries; contribute to the legal education and knowledge of the people of Alberta and provide programs and facilities for those purposes; provide assistance to native people's legal programs, student legal aid programs, and programs of like nature; and contribute to the costs incurred by the Legal Aid Society of Alberta to administer a plan to provide legal aid. To be considered for funding, programs or projects must fall within these objectives. Operating grants and project grants are awarded. The application process begins with a discussing the program or project idea with the executive director. This will be followed by an exchange of drafts during the development of the application.
Restrictions: Grants will not be made to individuals or for support of a commercial venture. Funds are not available for bursaries, fellowships, sabbaticals, endowments, etc.
Geographic Focus: Canada
Contact: David Aucoin, Executive Director; (403) 264-4701; (403) 294-9238; contact@albertalawfoundation.org
Internet: http://www.albertalawfoundation.org/Apply/general.html
Sponsor: Alberta Law Foundation
407 8th Avenue SW, Suite 300
Calgary, AB T2P 1E5 Canada

Albert and Bessie Mae Kronkosky Charitable Foundation Grants 67

The charitable foundation supports efforts to improve the quality of life in San Antonio-area counties for the elderly and those with disabilities; programs encouraging character and leadership development of youth; efforts to free children from abuse and neglect; cultural activities and broadening public participation in museums and libraries; improvement of public parks, zoos, and wildlife sanctuaries; prevention of cruelty to animals; and assistance for victims of public disasters in Texas. The foundation also supports a computer resources program that is designed to build the capacity of nonprofit organizations. Eligible organizations may submit proposals for computer resources for administrative purposes, such as office administration, program evaluation, donor management, and client tracking. Letters of inquiry be submitted at any time. The distribution committee will meet bi-monthly in January, March, May, July, September and November.
Requirements: Nonprofits in Texas counties Bandera, Bexar, Comal, and Kendall, are eligible to receive grant support.
Restrictions: Grants do not support economic development, annual fund and fundraising event sponsorships, political or lobbying activities, or religious organizations for sectarian purposes.
Geographic Focus: Texas
Amount: 550 - 1,000,000 USD
Samples: Operations grant of $132,450 to enable Street Paul Lutheran Child Development Center to continue is parenting education program; operations grant of $57,300 to Street Peter the Apostle Catholic Church to continue its parenting education program.
Contact: Grants Administrator; (888) 309-9001 or (210) 475-9000; (210) 354-2204; kronfndn@kronkosky.org
Internet: http://www.kronkosky.org
Sponsor: Albert and Bessie Mae Kronkosky Charitable Foundation
112 E Pecan Street, Suite 830
San Antonio, TX 78205

Alberto Culver Corporate Contributions Grants 68

The company prefers to make small donations to a large number of organizations rather than substantial contributions to a few institutions. Major areas of support are civic and community programs, health and welfare, education, culture and art, and youth activities. Special consideration is given to proposals that benefit a large number of people; directly or indirectly assist women's groups or other purchasers or potential customers of Alberto-Culver products; are involved in programs that rehabilitate, train, teach skills or employ the underprivileged, handicapped or minorities; have received support from Alberto-Culver in the past; and received matching grants for donations. Grants are awarded for one year and may be renewed.
Requirements: Only 501(c)3 organizations are eligible. Requests should be in writing on organization letterhead and should state amount requested, and whether the donation will be used for operating funds, capital expansion, supplies or special projects. The objectives and programs of the organization should be clearly defined.

Restrictions: Grants are not awarded to support United Way affiliates, religious groups, preschools, K-12 schools, tax-supported colleges, projects that duplicate other efforts, and multiyear commitments.
Geographic Focus: All U.S. States
Contact: V. James Marino, Director; (708) 450-3000; (708) 450-3435
Internet: http://www.alberto.com
Sponsor: Alberto Culver
2525 Armitage Avenue
Melrose Park, IL 60160

Albert Pick Jr. Fund Grants 69

The fund contributes to organizations in the following categories: culture, education, health and human services, civic and community organizations. The fund will consider assistance to new and creative programs within these areas and to operating support. Support will be given to requests from organizations that conduct their programs in Chicago, IL, only. The fund functions on a calendar year; applications are considered four times a year based on dates of board meetings. The fund prefers that prospective grantees call or write for guidelines prior to sending their proposals.
Requirements: Only Illinois organizations may apply.
Restrictions: Funds will not be provided for reduction or liquidation of debts, religious purposes, endowments, long-term commitments, building programs, individuals, political purposes, or advertising/program books.
Geographic Focus: Illinois
Date(s) Application is Due: Jan 21; Apr 1; Jul 1; Oct 1
Amount: 3,000 USD
Samples: Children First Fund/CPS Foundation (Gale Academy Links to Literacy Program) $6900; Art Resources in Teaching (Chicago, IL)—for general operating support, $7500; Chicago Academy of Sciences/Peggy Notebaert Nature Museum (Chicago, IL)—for general operating support, $10,000; Chicago Opera Theater (Chicago, IL)—for general operating support, $10,000.
Contact: Cleopatra Alexander, Executive Director; (312) 236-1192; cleopatra@albertpickjrfund.org
Internet: http://www.albertpickjrfund.org
Sponsor: Albert Pick Jr. Fund
30 N Michigan Avenue, Suite 1002
Chicago, IL 60602

Albertson's Charitable Giving Grants 70

Albertson's Inc invests in its operating communities and makes corporate contributions to support nonprofits. Areas of charitable giving include health and hunger relief—food banks, churches, and other community-based relief groups; health and nutrition—medical services, flu shots, health screening for diseases such as diabetes and heart disease; and education and development of youth—academic excellence or nurturing efforts. Submit requests in writing and include information about the organization's goals, accomplishments, evaluation plans, leadership, and finances. Requests are accepted throughout the year.
Requirements: Tax-exempt organizations in company locations are eligible. Applicants must pass an online eligibility test. Preference will be given to requests that offer volunteerism opportunities.
Restrictions: Contributions cannot be made to churches or religious organizations for purposes of religious advocacy.
Geographic Focus: Arizona, Arkansas, California, Colorado, Delaware, Florida, Georgia, Idaho, Illinois, Indiana, Iowa, Kansas, Louisiana, Maine, Maryland, Massachusetts, Michigan, Minnesota, Mississippi, Missouri, Montana, Nebraska, Nevada, New Hampshire, New Jersey, New Mexico, North Dakota, Oklahoma, Oregon, Pennsylvania, South Dakota, Tennessee, Texas, Utah, Vermont, Washington, Wisconsin, Wyoming
Contact: Community Relations Manager; (877) 932-7948 or (208) 395-6200; (208) 395-4382; albertsonscustomercare@albertsons.com
Internet: http://www.albertsons.com/abs_inthecommunity
Sponsor: Albertson's
250 E Parkcenter Boulevard
Boise, ID 83706

Albert W. Cherne Foundation Grants 71

The foundation awards grants to nonprofit organizations, primarily in Minnesota, for general operating support, continuing support, and annual campaigns in its areas of interest, which include adult basic education and literacy, children and youth services, services for the disabled, and human services.
Requirements: Grants support nonprofit organizations primarily in the five-county metropolitan area of Minneapolis and Saint Paul, MN.
Restrictions: Grants do not support veterans, fraternal, or labor organizations; religious purposes; conduit organizations; civil rights/social action groups; mental health counseling; specific-disease organizations; housing programs; individuals; capital improvements; or endowment funds.
Geographic Focus: Minnesota
Amount: 1,000 - 55,000 USD
Samples: Planned Parenthood of Minnesota (Saint Paul, MN)—to support a high-risk youth program, $5000; Loring Nicollet-Bethlehem Community Ctrs (Minneapolis, MN)—to support adult education and literacy programs, $12,000; YMCA, Greater Lake County Family (Waukegan, IL)—for a dining hall, $75,000.
Contact: Sara Ribbens, President; (952) 944-4378; (952) 944-3070; sararibbens@awchernefoundation.org
Sponsor: Albert W. Cherne Foundation
P.O. Box 975
Minneapolis, MN 55440

Albuquerque Community Foundation Grants 72

The foundation seeks to improve the quality of life in the greater Albuquerque, New Mexico, area by providing support for projects and organizations that serve the community in arts and culture, education, environmental and historic preservation, children and youth, and health and human services. Through its grant program, the foundation supports projects that are innovative, meet the needs of underserved segments of the community, encourage matching funds or additional gifts, promote cooperation among agencies, empower the disadvantaged and disabled, and enhance the effectiveness of local charitable organizations. Types of support include continuing support, general operating support, program development, publication, seed grants, scholarships funds and scholarships to individuals, and technical assistance.
Requirements: IRS 501(c)3 organizations based in Albuquerque, NM, are eligible. Proposals are reviewed on the basis of the following priorities: impact, innovation, leverage, management, and nonduplication.
Restrictions: Grants are generally not made to or for individuals, political or religious purposes, debt retirement, payment of interest or taxes, annual campaigns, endowments, emergency funding, to influence legislation or elections, scholarships, awards, or to private foundations and other grantmaking organizations.
Geographic Focus: New Mexico
Date(s) Application is Due: Apr 16; Aug 15
Amount: Up to 10,000 USD
Contact: R. Randall Royster, Executive Director; (505) 883-6240; (505) 883-3629; rroyster@albuquerquefoundation.org
Internet: http://www.albuquerquefoundation.org/grants/grant-home.htm
Sponsor: Albuquerque Community Foundation
P.O. Box 36960
Albuquerque, NM 87176-6960

Alcatel-Lucent Technologies Foundation Grants 73

The Alcatel-Lucent Foundation is the philanthropic arm of Alcatel-Lucent and it leads the company's charitable activities. With a focus on volunteerism, the Foundation's mission is to support the commitment of Alcatel-Lucent to social responsibility by serving and enhancing the communities where its employees and customers live and work. To accomplish its mission, the Foundation manages grants and employee volunteerism on a global level. It receives its income from the corporation - Alcatel-Lucent - whose name it bears. However, legally the Foundation is an independent, charitable, non-profit and private entity and is governed by its own board of trustees that is separate from the corporate board of directors. Global Foundation grants are dedicated to the main focus areas of the Foundation and are managed by the Foundation.
Requirements: Giving is on an international basis.
Geographic Focus: All U.S. States
Amount: 500 - 5,000 USD
Contact: Michele Donato, Manager; (908) 582-7906; (908) 508-2576; foundation@alcatel-lucent.com
Internet: http://www.alcatel-lucent.com/wps/portal/foundation
Sponsor: Alcatel-Lucent Technologies Foundation
600 Mountain Avenue, Room 6F4
Murray Hill, NJ 07974-2008

Alcoa Foundation Grants 74

General priorities of the foundation include safe and healthy children and families—ensuring that children and their families have the tools, the knowledge and the services to remain healthy and safe at home, in the community and in the workplace; conservation and sustainability—educating young leaders on conservation issues, protecting forests, promoting sound public policy research, and understanding the linkages between business and the environment; skills today for tomorrow—providing individuals with critical skills and services to be economically connected, workplace-ready, and productive in a changing economy; business and community partnerships—strengthening the nonprofit sector and developing meaningful partnerships among nonprofits, the private sector, and local government; and global education in science, engineering, technology and business—broadening student participation in areas central to Alcoa to prepare a diverse cross-section of our communities for a global workplace. Types of support include capital grants, building funds, challenge grants, matching gifts, general support, research grants, scholarships, and seed money. Initial contact should be a letter of inquiry.

Requirements: The foundation awards grants to nonprofit public charities in communities where Alcoa has a presence. Local Alcoans work within their communities to evaluate organizations and make recommendations for funding to Alcoa Foundation. Nonprofit organizations that serve localized communities should find the Alcoa facility nearest to them and write a one-page letter describing their mission, nature of request, connection to the areas of excellence and offering contact information. If interested, the Alcoa location contact will notify the requesting organization and invite them to submit more information. Areas of operation include western Pennsylvania; Davenport, Iowa; Evansville, Indiana; Massena, New York; New Jersey; Cleveland, Ohio; Knoxville, Tennessee; and Rockdale, Texas.

Restrictions: The foundation does not make gifts to local projects other than those near Alcoa plant or office locations; endowment funds, deficit reduction, or operating reserves; hospital capital campaign programs unless the hospital presents a comprehensive area analysis that justifies, on a regional rather than an individual institutional basis, the need for the capital improvement; individuals, except for the scholarship program for children of Alcoa employees; tickets and other promotional activities; trips, tours, or student exchange programs; or documentaries and videos.

Geographic Focus: All U.S. States

Amount: 1,000 - 50,000 USD

Contact: Meg McDonald, President and Treasurer; (412) 553-2348; (412) 553-4498; alcoa.foundation@alcoa.com

Internet: http://www.alcoa.com/global/en/community/foundation.asp

Sponsor: Alcoa Foundation
201 Isabella Street
Pittsburgh, PA 15212-5858

Alcon Foundation Grants 75

The foundation supports organizations in the fields of health care, leadership programs, research, education and community responsibility. Programs that advance the education and skill levels of eye care professionals are given special consideration. General operating grants to organizations and institutions improving education and research in the areas of specialization of Alcon Laboratories—ophthalmology and vision care. Grants are also awarded to community activities that benefit company employees. Applications may be submitted at any time.

Requirements: Grants are not made for building programs.

Restrictions: Non 501(c)3organizations, individuals and scholarship programs, religious, veterans or fraternal organizations, political causes, capital campaigns, matching gifts, trips, tournaments and tours, and endowments are not supported.

Geographic Focus: All U.S. States

Amount: 100 - 50,000 USD

Samples: National Sjogrens Syndrome Assoc (Phoenix, AZ)—for general operating support, $2500.

Contact: Mary Dulle, Chair; (817) 293-0450; Mary.Dulle@Alconlabs.com

Internet: http://www.alconlabs.com/corporate-responsibility/alcon-foundation.asp

Sponsor: Alcon Foundation
6201 S Freeway
Fort Worth, TX 76134

Alexander & Baldwin Foundation Hawaiian and Pacific Island Grants 76

The foundation awards grants to eligible Hawaii nonprofit organizations in its areas of interest, including health and human services, education, the community, culture and arts, the maritime arena and the environment. Grant preferences are given to organizations and projects that address significant community needs, have the active support of A&B employees, are preventive in nature, and have demonstrated support of the community. Start-up, general operating and special project needs, as well as major and minor capital requests are considered. Deadlines listed are for organizations in Hawaii and the Pacific Islands. Although the majority of grants range between $1,000 and $5,000, the Foundation considers request upward of $20,000.

Requirements: The foundation gives funding to community-based projects and organizations that qualify with 501(c)3 status.

Restrictions: Grants are not awarded to support United Way agencies for operating support, individuals, events, travel expenses, or scholarships.

Geographic Focus: Hawaii

Date(s) Application is Due: Dec 1; Feb 1; Apr 1; Jun 1; Aug 1; Oct 1

Amount: 1,000 - 5,000 USD

Contact: Nami Nielipinski, (808) 525-6641; (808) 525-6677; nnielipinski@abinc.com

Internet: http://www.alexanderbaldwinfoundation.org/appguide.htm

Sponsor: Alexander and Baldwin Foundation
P.O. Box 3440
Honolulu, HI 96801-3440

Alexander & Baldwin Foundation Mainland Grants 77

The foundation awards grants to eligible U.S. nonprofit organizations in its areas of interest, including health and human services, education, the community, culture and arts, the maritime arena and the environment. Grant preferences are given to organizations and projects that address significant community needs, have the active support of A&B employees, are preventive in nature, and have demonstrated support of the community. Start-up, general operating and special project needs, as well as major and minor capital requests are considered. Although the majority of grants range between $1,000 and $5,000, the Foundation considers request upward of $20,000.

Requirements: The foundation gives funding to community-based projects and organizations that qualify with 501(c)3 status.

Restrictions: Grants are not awarded to support United Way agencies for operating support, individuals, events, travel expenses, or scholarships.

Geographic Focus: All U.S. States

Date(s) Application is Due: Jan 1; Feb 1; Mar 1; Apr 1; May 1; Jun 1; Jul 1; Aug 1; Sep 1; Oct 1; Nov 1; Dec 1

Amount: 1,000 - 5,000 USD

Contact: Paul Merwin, (707) 421-8121; (707) 421-1835; plmifm@aol.com

Internet: http://www.alexanderbaldwinfoundation.org/appguide.htm

Sponsor: Alexander and Baldwin Foundation
555 12th Street
Oakland, CA 94607

Alexander Eastman Foundation Grants 78

The purposes of the Alexander Eastman Foundation are served through grant support to organizations awarded in response to proposals and special initiative commitments planned collaboratively by the Foundation with local service providers. Grants are awarded to support the capital, special projects and operations needs of qualifying organizations. In considering proposals, priority is given to funding activity which serves the Foundation's priority interests. The Alexander Eastman Foundation supports: Education - provide information and community education to improve the health and well-being of residents of the greater Derry area; address goals for healthy individuals and families through a long-term commitment to prevention, health promotion and education of consumers and providers; foster individual responsibility, independence, self-care and healthy life-style choices; Family Systems - strengthen families as the critical unit for community health and well-being; recognize the changing nature of families and provide resources and assistance to reduce stress on families and improve family function; Access - expand access to quality health care and prevention services for people with financial need. Applications are available at the Foundations website.

Requirements: Nonprofit organizations serving Derry, Londonderry, Windham, Chester, Hampstead, and Sandown, NH, are eligible.

Restrictions: Grants are made neither to individuals nor to qualifying organizations to support the cost of services to particular individuals, except through the Alexander Eastman Scholarship Program.

Geographic Focus: New Hampshire

Date(s) Application is Due: Apr 1; Oct 1

Samples: Community Caregivers of Greater Derry, Derry, NH, $10,000 - to support the volunteer-driven program of quality client care in the greater

Derry community (2009); The Upper Room, A Family Resource Center, Derry, NH, $28,000 - to support prevention and intervention for families at risk of having a child placed in foster care (2009); Child and Family Services of New Hampshire, Manchester, NH, $19,760 - to support services to twelve non-Medicaid-eligible teens in the Healthy Family Home Visiting program, to support tuition assistance for low-income, at risk greater Derry area youth to attend a session of residential summer camp at Camp Spaulding (2009).
Contact: Amy Lockwood, Director of Grants; (888) 228-1821, ext. 80; alockwood@alexandereastman.org
Internet: http://www.alexandereastman.org/02grants.html
Sponsor: Alexander Eastman Foundation
26 South Main Street, PMB 250
Concord, NH 03301

Alexander H. Bright Charitable Trust Grants 79
The trust operates in Massachusetts and awards general operating grants to nonprofit organizations in its areas of interest, including wildlife and environmental conservation, children and youth, education, and social services. There are no application forms. The board meets in March, June, September, and December.
Requirements: Northeast U.S. nonprofits are eligible. Preference is given to requests from Massachusetts.
Geographic Focus: Connecticut, Maine, Massachusetts, New Hampshire, Rhode Island, Vermont
Amount: 100 - 75,000 USD
Contact: Administrator, c/o Boston Family Office; (617) 227-2676 or (617) 624-0800
Sponsor: Alexander H. Bright Charitable Trust
88 Broad Street
Boston, MA 02110

Alex Brown and Sons Charitable Foundation Grants 80
The foundation awards one-year renewable grants to U.S. nonprofit organizations in its areas of interest, including arts and culture, community affairs, education, medicine, and science. Types of support include annual campaigns, capital grants, endowment funds, general operating grants, program development grants, and scholarship funds. Applicants should submit a letter of intent that briefly outlines the purpose of the grant.
Requirements: 501(c)3 tax-exempt organizations in Maryland are eligible.
Restrictions: No support for private schools or churches. Grants are not made to individuals.
Geographic Focus: Maryland
Amount: 1,000 - 100,000 USD
Samples: Baltimore Symphony Orchestra (MD)—for discretionary use, $1 million; Johns Hopkins Hospital (Baltimore, MD)—for discretionary use, $1 million; Baltimore Zoo (MD)—for discretionary use, $1 million.
Contact: Margaret Preston, Secretary, c/o Deutsche Bank Alex Brown Inc
Sponsor: Alex Brown and Sons Charitable Foundation
P.O. Box 2257
Baltimore, MD 21203

Alex Stern Family Foundation Grants 81
The foundation awards grants to North Dakota and Minnesota nonprofits in its areas of interest, including arts and culture, child welfare, the elderly, alcohol abuse, community funds, family and social services, education, minorities, hospices, and cancer research. Types of support include general operating support, continuing support, annual campaigns, building construction/renovation, equipment acquisition, emergency funds, program development, scholarship funds, research, and matching funds. Applications are reviewed in June and November.
Requirements: Moorhead, MN, and Fargo, ND, nonprofit organizations are eligible.
Restrictions: Grants are not awarded to individuals or for endowments.
Geographic Focus: Minnesota, North Dakota
Date(s) Application is Due: Mar 31; Aug 31
Amount: 1,000 - 50,000 USD
Contact: Donald Scott, Executive Director; (701) 237-0170
Sponsor: Alex Suitern Family Foundation
609 1/2 1st Avenue N, Suite 205
Fargo, ND 58102

Alfred C. and Ersa S. Arbogast Foundation Grants 82
The Alfred C. and Ersa S. Arbogast Foundation, established in Indiana, supports organizations and programs throughout the State of Indiana, as well as a few throughout the United States. The Foundation's primary fields of interest include: animal/wildlife preservation and protection; human service programs; and United Ways and federated programs. The major type of support being offered is general operations funding. There are no particular deadlines or application formats with which to adhere, and applicants should submit the following: copy of IRS determination letter; and a detailed description of the project, with the amount of funding requested.
Requirements: 501(c)3 organizations located in, or supporting the residents of, Indiana can apply, as well as non-profits whose goals are aligned with the Arbogast Foundation's.
Geographic Focus: All U.S. States
Samples: Truck of Love, Rock Hill, South Carolina, $2,500 - general operations (2010); Colorado Music Festival, Lafayette, Colorado, $1,500 - general operations funding (2010); Goshen Community Chorale, Goshen, Indiana, $1,000, - general operating funds (2010).
Contact: Michelle Kindler, Bank Trustee; (260) 428-5009 or (574) 267-9187
Sponsor: Alfred C. and Ersa S. Arbogast Foundation
114 E. Market Street, P.O. 1387
Warsaw, IN 46580

Alfred I. DuPont Foundation Grants 83
Grants are awarded primarily to elderly adults requiring health, economic, or educational assistance. Support is also given for higher education and medical research. All grants to the elderly are made to individuals in the southeastern United States. General operating support and grants to individuals are awarded. An application form is required. Applications are accepted at any time and are dealt with promptly.
Requirements: Nonprofit organizations in the southeastern U.S. are eligible. Preference is given to those in Florida.
Geographic Focus: Florida
Amount: 1,000 - 35,000 USD
Samples: Gulf Coast Community College Fdn (Panama City, FL)—for operating support, $50,000; Dreams Come True of Jacksonville (Jacksonville, FL)—for operating support, $10,000.
Contact: Rosemary Cusimano Wills, Secretary; (904) 232-4123
Sponsor: Alfred I. DuPont Foundation
4600 Touchton Road E, Building 200, Suite 120
Jacksonville, FL 32246

Alfred P. Sloan Foundation Civic Program Grants 84
The goal of the Program is to make a contribution to the Foundation's home area, New York City. There are two directions to the Program: to respond to special opportunities in New York City; and to fund high-leverage projects in New York City that are related to other parts of our program. Interested readers should refer to the descriptions of other program areas in the Foundation website. Grant requests can be made at any time for support of activities related to Foundation program areas and interests. The Foundation is generally limited to supporting tax-exempt organizations.
Requirements: Concise, well-organized proposals are preferred. In no case should the body of the proposal exceed 20 double-spaced pages.
Restrictions: The Foundation's activities do not normally extend to religion, the creative or performing arts, elementary or secondary education, medical research or health care, the humanities or to activities outside the United States. Grants are not made for endowments or for buildings or equipment.
Geographic Focus: New York
Samples: City U of New York system (NY) and George Mason U (NY)—for the September 11 Digital Archives, $700,000 jointly.
Contact: Ted Greenwood, Program Director; (212) 649-1645 or (212) 649-1649; (212) 757-5117; greenwood@sloan.org
Internet: http://www.sloan.org/program/31
Sponsor: Alfred P. Sloan Foundation
630 Fifth Avenue, Suite 2550
New York, NY 10111-0242

Alfred P. Sloan Foundation Professional Science Masters Grants 85
The long period required to earn a Ph.D. in much of science, and doubts about the suitability of present graduate training for non-academic jobs suggest that graduate schools might consider a different kind of graduate degree in addition to the Ph.D. In this program, the Foundation makes grants that encourage and promote the development of the Professional Science Master's degree, a

two-year degree, heavily oriented toward coursework that provides a sound basis for work outside academia in scientific and technical fields.
Requirements: Concise, well-organized proposals are preferred. In no case should the body of the proposal exceed 20 double-spaced pages.
Restrictions: The Foundation's activities do not normally extend to religion, the creative or performing arts, elementary or secondary education, medical research or health care, the humanities or to activities outside the United States. Grants are not made for endowments or for buildings or equipment.
Geographic Focus: All U.S. States
Samples: Rutgers University, New Brunswick, NJ—start-up support for university-wide Professional Science Master's Initiative; State University of New York, Oswego, NY—to implement professional science master's degrees on many SUNY campuses; National Academy of Sciences, Washington, DC—for support of an expert committee and report on enhancing master's-level graduate education in the Sciences.
Contact: Drive Michael S. Teitelbaum, Program Director; (212) 649-1630 or (212) 649-1649; (212) 757-5117; teitelbaum@sloan.org
Internet: http://www.sloan.org/program/15
Sponsor: Alfred P. Sloan Foundation
630 Fifth Avenue, Suite 2550
New York, NY 10111-0242

A Little Hope Grants 86

A Little Hope is a not-for-profit publicly supported charitable foundation, recognized by the IRS under 501(c)3, which grants funds to organizations that provide bereavement support services and grief counseling to children and teens who have experienced the death of a parent, sibling or loved one. Strong preference is given to applicants who demonstrate a commitment to the use of community trained volunteers, whose programs demonstrate multicultural competence in addressing children and adolescent's bereavement needs, and whose programs are likely to be replicable in other communities. Grant applications are by invitation only and are processed during the last quarter of each year. To be considered, email (no telephone calls): the name of your program, your website address, the name of your executive director, and the name of the program director, including their credentials. No other information is needed or will be processed. Do not send letters of inquiry or any other materials unless they have been requested by A Little Hope. No other organizations are authorized to solicit RFP's or information on our behalf.
Geographic Focus: All U.S. States
Contact: Tanhya Vancho, Vice President and Secretary; granting@alittlehope.org
Internet: http://www.alittlehope.org/granting/applicants.aspx
Sponsor: A Little Hope
810 Seventh Avenue, 37th Floor
New York, NY 10019

Allegheny Foundation Grants 87

The foundation awards general operating grants, seed grants, and grants for projects and programs to nonprofit organizations in western Pennsylvania in the areas of education, historic preservation, and civic development. There are no application forms or deadlines. The foundation generally considers grants at an annual meeting held in November; however, requests may be submitted at any time and will be reviewed as soon as possible.
Requirements: Initial inquiries should be in letter form signed by the organization's president, or authorized representative, and have the approval of the board of directors. The letter should include a concise description of the specific program for which funds are requested. Additional information must include a budget for the program and for the organization, the latest audited financial statement, an annual report, and a board of director's list. A copy of the organization's 501(c)3 letter is required. Only Pennsylvania residents may apply.
Restrictions: Grants are not made to individuals.
Geographic Focus: Pennsylvania
Amount: 1,000 - 100,000 USD
Samples: Allegheny Institute for Public Policy—$100,000; The Extra Mile Education Foundation, Inc.—$100,000; Beginning with Books, Inc.—$25,000; Historical Society of Carnegie Pennsylvania—$10,000.
Contact: Matthew Groll, Executive Director; (412) 392-2900
Internet: http://www.scaife.com/alleghen.html
Sponsor: Allegheny Foundation
1 Oxford Center, 301 Grant Street, Suite 3900
Pittsburgh, PA 15219-6401

Allegheny Technologies Charitable Trust 88

The corporation awards one-year renewable grants to nonprofit organizations to enhance the quality of life for people in company operating locations. Areas of interest include arts and culture, civic and public affairs, education, health, and social services. Types of support include capital grants, general operating grants, program development grants, and employee matching gifts. Applicants should submit a letter of inquiry that describes the organization, purpose of grants, and funds sought. No particular form or information is required. Potential applicants are requested to provide proof of exempt public charity status. There are no deadlines.
Requirements: 501(c)3 tax-exempt organizations in company-operating areas are eligible.
Restrictions: Contributions are made only to public charities. Individuals and private foundations are excluded.
Geographic Focus: Pennsylvania
Amount: 1,000 - 35,000 USD
Samples: Pittsburgh Symphony Society (Pittsburgh, PA)—grant recipient, $55,000.
Contact: Jon D. Walton, Jr., Trustee; (412) 394-2800; (412) 394-3034
Internet: http://www.alleghenytechnologies.com
Sponsor: Allegheny Technologies
1000 Six PPG Place
Pittsburgh, PA 15222

Allen Hilles Fund Grants 89

The fund awards grants to support education, women's issues, economic development in disadvantaged communities, activities of the Religious Society of Friends, and organizations with annual budgets of less than $2 million. Types of support include project grants, seed money, and operating support for small organizations.
Requirements: Philadelphia-area and Wilmington, DE, nonprofit organizations are eligible.
Restrictions: Funding requests for endowments, scholarships, capital expenditures, political purposes, or agency promotion (i.e., marketing, development, publication of annual reports, or fundraising events) are denied.
Geographic Focus: Delaware, Pennsylvania
Date(s) Application is Due: Feb 1; May 1; Oct 1
Amount: 3,000 - 10,000 USD
Samples: Fellowship Farm (Pottstown, PA)—to support the Peace and Unity summer camp, $3000; Fair Hill Burial Ground Corporation (Philadelphia, PA)— to support children's educational programming, $2000; Women's Law Project (Philadelphia, PA)—for operating support, $3000; Simpson United Memorial United Methodist Church (Philadelphia, PA)—to support an after-school program, $3000.
Contact: Judith L. Bardes, Manager; (610) 828-8145; (610) 834-8175; hilles@grants-info.org or judy1@aol.com
Internet: http://www.grants-info.org/hilles
Sponsor: Allen Hilles Fund
P.O. Box 540
Plymouth Meeting, PA 19462

Alletta Morris McBean Charitable Trust Grants 90

The foundation awards grants in the areas of historic preservation and land preservation/conservation to organizations located in and around Newport, RI. Grant requests are considered two times each year when the trustees meet. Types of programs to receive support include capital construction; environmental programs; exhibitions, collections, and performances; general operations; seed funds; materials/equipment acquisition; preservation/restoration; matching/challenge grants; and capital campaigns.
Requirements: Rhode Island tax-exempt organizations in Newport and Aquidneck Island are eligible.
Geographic Focus: Rhode Island
Date(s) Application is Due: Feb 28; Jul 31
Amount: 50,000 - 100,000 USD
Samples: Foundation for Newport (RI)—for general operating support, $70,000; Preservation Society of Newport County (RI)—$500,000.
Contact: Charlene Kleiner, (650) 558-8480; (650) 558-8481; McBeanproperties@worldnet.att.net
Sponsor: Alletta Morris McBean Charitable Trust
400 S El Camino Real, Suite 777
San Mateo, CA 94402-1724

Allstate Corporate Hometown Commitment Grants 91

Allstate takes a special interest in the greater Chicagoland community, the company's hometown for more than 75 years. The corporation is particularly invested in this community because it recognizes that a thriving hometown is critical to Allstate's success. The company recruits local talent, relies on local infrastructure, and depends on the city's vibrancy to ensure that its associates have a rich quality of life. By supporting organizations that build strong Chicagoland communities, the company contributes to the city's position as a center of global culture, education and business.

Requirements: The Allstate Corporation makes grants to Chicago area nonprofit, tax-exempt groups under Section 501(c)3 of the Internal Revenue Code.

Geographic Focus: Illinois, Indiana

Samples: Chicago Children's Museum, Chicago, Illinois, $15,000,000 (2008).

Contact: Executive Director; (847) 402-5000 or (847) 402-5502; (847) 326-7517; allfound@allstate.com

Internet: http://www.allstate.com/social-responsibility/corporate/corporate-giving.aspx

Sponsor: Allstate Corporation
2775 Sanders Road, Suite F4
Northbrook, IL 60062

Alpine Winter Foundation Grants 92

Established in California in 1963, the Alpine Winter Foundation's primary purpose is to support alpine safety, health programs, and education within the Tahoe-Donner, California, region. Applications should be in the form of a written request, and should include the specific purpose and history of the requesting organization. There are no specific deadlines with which to adhere.

Requirements: Giving is limited to organizations described in Section 170(b)(1)(a) and Section 501(c)3(a) that promote alpine safety, heath, and education within the Tahoe-Donner area of California,

Geographic Focus: California

Amount: Up to 40,000 USD

Samples: Donner Trail School, Soda Springs, California, $1,500—for winter survival training programs (2008); Sugar Bowl Ski Team Foundation, Norden, California, $37,500—for need-based scholarships and a building fund *2008).

Contact: Mary S. Tilden, President; (415) 221-7762

Sponsor: Alpine Winter Foundation
3863 Jackson Street, P.O. Box 591659
San Francisco, CA 94118-1610

Altman Foundation Arts and Culture Grants 93

The Foundation mission is to support programs and institutions that enrich the quality of life in New York City, with a particular focus on initiatives that help individuals, families and communities benefit from the services and opportunities that will enable them to achieve their full potential. The Foundation has had a longstanding interest in the arts, reflecting not only Benjamin Altman's personal commitment, but also the Foundation's recognition of the value of the arts in enriching the lives of New Yorkers and the city as a whole. In this program area, the Foundation seeks: to promote positive youth development through arts and cultural programming; to promote the acquisition of pre-professional arts skills among under-served youth; and to promote access to the arts for under-served populations.

Requirements: IRS 501(c)3 organizations in New York are eligible.

Restrictions: Grants are not awarded to individuals. As a general rule, the foundation does not consider requests for bricks and mortar funds or the purchase of capital equipment.

Geographic Focus: New York

Amount: 10,000 - 100,000 USD

Samples: Brooklyn Botanic Garden Corporation—to help support the Garden Apprentice Program for middle and high school youth, $40,000; Figure Skating in Harlem—to help support the after-school skating and health program, $25,000; Rocking the Boat—to help support the Job Skills Program, $50,000.

Contact: Karen L. Rosa, Vice President and Executive Director; (212) 682-0970; krosa@altman.org

Internet: http://www.altmanfoundation.org/guide.html

Sponsor: Altman Foundation
521 Fifth Avenue, 35th Floor
New York, NY 10175

Altman Foundation Strengthening Communities Grants 94

The Foundation mission is to support programs and institutions that enrich the quality of life in New York City, with a particular focus on initiatives that help individuals, families and communities benefit from the services and opportunities that will enable them to achieve their full potential. The Foundation has an historic interest in ensuring that individuals and families living in the city have access to the services and resources they need to pursue and sustain successful lives. The Foundation has chosen to focus on efforts that: build and preserve economic security and independence among lowincome individuals and families; and promote and sustain the availability of, and equitable access to, essential community resources needed to support stable, healthy communities.

Requirements: IRS 501(c)3 organizations in New York are eligible.

Restrictions: Grants are not awarded to individuals. As a general rule, the foundation does not consider requests for bricks and mortar funds or the purchase of capital equipment.

Geographic Focus: New York

Amount: 10,000 - 100,000 USD

Contact: Karen L. Rosa, Vice President and Executive Director; (212) 682-0970; krosa@altman.org

Internet: http://www.altmanfoundation.org/guide.html

Sponsor: Altman Foundation
521 Fifth Avenue, 35th Floor
New York, NY 10175

Altria Group Arts and Culture Grants 95

For more than 50 years, Altria Group has been a strong supporter of both the visual and performing arts. The Group champions organizations that inspire and reflect the qualities it values in its business operations – creativity, diversity, excellence and innovation. Altria supports arts and cultural initiatives in Richmond, Virginia, Washington, D.C., and other communities where its companies operate. The Group's arts and culture grants are focused on: innovative programs to develop new audiences and increase access to the arts; major sponsorships that bring thought-provoking, world-class cultural experiences to our communities; and arts education programs that enhance the overall performance and development of middle school students, primarily in the public schools of Greater Richmond, Virginia.

Requirements: Unsolicited applications are generally not accepted. The company utilizes an invitation process for giving, which is the result of a letter of inquiry.

Geographic Focus: District of Columbia, Virginia

Date(s) Application is Due: Jan 30

Amount: 15,000 - 1,000,000 USD

Contact: Grants Administrator; (804) 274-2200

Internet: http://www.altria.com/en/cms/Responsibility/investing-in-communities/programs/arts-and-culture/default.aspx

Sponsor: Altria Group
6601 West Broad Street
Richmond, VA 23230-1723

Altria Group Education Grants 96

Quality education is the bedrock of our children's success and our country's continued progress. Yet, recent studies have shown that American students are lagging their international peers in important measures of performance and success. The Group supports organizations working to improve educational outcomes for underserved youth, while also addressing the demand for a diverse, highly skilled workforce. Altria and its companies focus their education contributions in four areas: middle-and high-school enrichment programs for urban public schools, particularly those that contribute to everyday student success, math and science excellence, and access to and preparation for higher education; technical education at community colleges and universities, including agricultural studies programs at select land-grant institutions; strengthening management skills among school leaders; and higher education and scholarship support. The Group's contributions are primarily focused in Central Virginia, with some donations in other geographies where Altria's companies operate. Altria also supports major national scholarship organizations and colleges and universities where we recruit future employees.

Requirements: Unsolicited applications are generally not accepted. The company utilizes an invitation process for giving, which is the result of a letter of inquiry.

Geographic Focus: All U.S. States

Amount: 1,000 - 75,000 USD

Contact: Program Manager; (804) 274-2200
Internet: http://www.altria.com/en/cms/Responsibility/investing-in-communities/programs/education/default.aspx
Sponsor: Altria Group
6601 West Broad Street
Richmond, VA 23230-1723

Altria Group Positive Youth Development Grants **97**
Philip Morris U.S. A has had a focus on positive youth development since the creation of its Youth Smoking Prevention department in 1998. Today that program has evolved to Underage Tobacco Prevention, and Altria's tobacco operating companies invest in a range of programs to support its goals of helping reduce underage tobacco use. As part of these efforts, the Group's tobacco operating companies have become a leading funder of positive youth development in the U.S. These investments focus on organizations and programs that emphasize kids' strengths, promote positive behaviors, connect youth with caring adults and enhance community-based resources for kids. These programs are designed to help kids develop the confidence and skills they need to avoid risky behaviors, such as underage tobacco use. The Group's tobacco companies also support adolescent tobacco cessation programs. Its tobacco operating companies' funding supports organizations that: provide evidence-based programs for kids like mentoring, life skills education and substance abuse prevention curricula; help national youth-serving organizations reach more young people, improve program quality and better measure their impact; help community leaders align youth programs and policies; and conduct research on effective positive youth development programs.
Requirements: Unsolicited applications are generally not accepted. The company utilizes an invitation process for giving, which is the result of a letter of inquiry.
Geographic Focus: All U.S. States
Date(s) Application is Due: Feb 20
Amount: 10,000 - 75,000 USD
Contact: Grants Administrator; (804) 274-2200
Internet: http://www.altria.com/en/cms/Responsibility/investing-in-communities/programs/positive_youth_development/default.aspx
Sponsor: Altria Group
6601 West Broad Street
Richmond, VA 23230-1723

Alvin and Fanny Blaustein Thalheimer Foundation Grants **98**
The foundation makes grants that strengthen the lives of individuals, families, and communities in the Baltimore region. Program areas include economic opportunity—technical and business entrepreneurship training, and asset-building strategies; health and human services—improve quality of service, and advocacy and policy initiatives; arts and culture—strengthening education and outreach programs that link arts institutions with communities and schools; and strengthening Jewish communities—renewal and development of communities in Eastern Europe and the Former Soviet Union; and addressing threats of anti-Semitism. Guidelines are available online.
Requirements: Only Maryland organizations are eligible to apply.
Restrictions: Grants are not made to individuals.
Geographic Focus: Maryland
Samples: Bon Secours of Maryland Foundation, $135,000 over three years for Our Money Place, a financial service center for the low-income communities of West Baltimore; Caroline Center, $40,000 over two years for occupational training programs designed to help economically disadvantaged women become self- sufficient; CASA of Maryland, $70,000 over two years for the Financial Empowerment Program at the Baltimore Worker's Rights Center; Center for Fathers, Families, and Workforce Development, $50,000 over two years (all 2005).
Contact: Betsy Ringel, Executive Director; (410) 347-7103; (410) 347-7210; info@blaufund.org
Internet: http://www.blaufund.org/foundations/alvinandfanny_f.html
Sponsor: Alvin and Fanny Blaustein Thalheimer Foundation
10 E Baltimore Street, Suite 1111
Baltimore, MD 21202

AMA Foundation Fund for Better Health Grants **99**
The philosophy of the AMA Foundation Fund for Better Health begins with the idea that local communities and organizations have great knowledge and insight into their community's health care issues. Based on this thought, the AMA Foundation, with support from the AMA Alliance, created the Fund for Better Health. Through this program, the AMA Foundation provides seed grants for grassroots, public health projects in communities throughout America. Over the years, the fund has provided over 200 grants totaling nearly $300,000 to projects that address healthy lifestyles, domestic violence prevention, substance abuse prevention, health literacy, patient safety and care for the uninsured. A maximum of $5,000 will be distributed to each grant recipient. The number of grant recipients will be determined by the AMA Foundation after all applications have been received. Typically, the number of grants awarded does not exceed twenty.
Requirements: Organizations are eligible to apply for grants which further the charitable and educational purposes of the AMA Foundation. Grants made in 2009 support programs addressing the issue of healthy lifestyles in the areas of nutrition and physical fitness, alcohol, substance abuse and smoking prevention (and cessation), and violence prevention. The three types of organizations eligible to apply are organizations with annual operating budgets of $1 million or less; new organizations begun in the last 5 years; or established organizations starting a new service or expanding a current service to an underserved population.
Restrictions: None of the funds awarded are to pay for staff salary or overhead expenses.
Geographic Focus: All U.S. States
Date(s) Application is Due: Jul 15
Amount: Up to 5,000 USD
Contact: Dina Lindenberg, Program Officer; (312) 464-4193; (312) 464-5973; dina.lindenberg@ama-assn.org or amafoundation@ama-assn.org
Internet: http://www.ama-assn.org/ama/pub/about-ama/ama-foundation/our-programs/public-health/fund-better-health.shtml
Sponsor: American Medical Association Foundation
515 N State Street
Chicago, IL 60654

Ameren Corporation Community Grants **100**
The corporation awards grants in AmerenUE and AmerenCIPS service areas to programs in arts and culture, civic affairs, housing, higher education, services for youth and the elderly, and the environment. Types of support include annual campaigns, building construction/renovation, capital campaigns, challenge/matching grants, conferences and seminars, equipment acquisition, federated giving, general operating support, multiyear support, project development, seed money, and sponsorships. Applicants should provide the following information on the nonprofit's letterhead: organization's mission and how the project addresses its mission; program description and expected outcomes; fundraising goal and current funding status; the organization's budget and audited financial statements; tax status determination letter; roster of governing board and executive staff; and specific amount requested. Nonprofits in the Saint Louis, MO, metropolitan area should send applications to AmerenUE Corporate Contributions at the office listed. Nonprofits in the Springfield, IL, metropolitan area should send applications to AmerenCIPS Public Affairs, 607 E Adams St/C1301, Springfield, IL 62739.
Requirements: Illinois and Missouri tax-exempt organizations in AmerenUE and AmerenCIPS service areas are eligible. Applicants from Missouri should address inquiries to the address above. Applicants from Illinois should address: Corporate Contributions, Ameren, 300 Liberty Street, Peoria, IL 61602-1404. 1-877-4AMEREN. Ext. 75001.
Restrictions: Grants do not support individuals or political, religious, fraternal, veteran, social, or similar groups. Ameren cannot donate electric or natural gas service.
Geographic Focus: Illinois, Missouri
Amount: 5,000 - 75,000 USD
Contact: Otis Cowan, Manager of Community Relations; (314) 554-4740; (314) 554-2888; ocowan@ameren.com
Internet: http://www.ameren.com/source/Community/Documents/ADC_BrochureCharitableGivingGuidelines.pdf
Sponsor: Ameren Corporation
P.O. Box 66149, MC 100
Saint Louis, MO 63166-6149

American Chemical Society Green Chemistry Grants **101**
The American Chemical Society Green Chemistry Institute sponsors a green chemistry grant program by promoting funding, increasing opportunities, and developing information on the benefits of green chemistry. Its efforts span the spectrum from theory and basic research through application and commercialization of science and technology. The program also sponsors a

number of research fellowships and scientific exchanges through its grants programs.
Geographic Focus: All U.S. States
Contact: Gayle Peterman, Finance and Grants Manager; (202) 872-6092 or (202) 872-4481; (202) 872-6319; g_peterman@acs.org
Internet: http://portal.acs.org/portal/acs/corg/content?_nfpb=true&_pageLabel=PP_TRANSITIONMAIN&node_id=1456&use_sec=false&sec_url_var=region1&__uuid=c14e3223-89d3-4263-8072-51ccffe52007
Sponsor: American Chemical Society
1155 Sixteenth Street, NW
Washington, DC 20036-4801

American Eagle Outfitters Foundation Grants 102
The foundation directs financial and volunteer contributions toward projects that try to improve the quality of life in American Eagle communities. The foundation supports Jumpstart, Big Brothers Big Sisters, The Student Conservation Association (SCA) and commuunity initiatives. Supporting and mentoring preschool children, volunteering with kids, high school and college students with conservation service internships and volunteer opportunities are all supported. Applicants and programs must fall within the scope of the foundation's mission statement; creatively involve AE business unit and/or employees in projects; provide regular reports of financial and program activities; direct at least 70 percent of the money raised toward beneficiaries; be willing to provide documentation to AE verifying financial donations; be in a community where AE operates business; significantly affect the surrounding community; and be inclusive in policies and practices involving all genders, races, ages, ethnic origin, sexual orientation, or creed. Funding guidelines and procedures are available online. Requests are considered at quarterly meetings.
Requirements: 501(c)3 public charities are eligible.
Restrictions: The foundation will not contribute to: fashion shows or other requests for clothing donations except for occasions where the company may provide disaster-related support to communities resulting from acts of nature (i.e., floods, tornadoes, hurricanes, fires, etc.); organizations that discriminate based on race, creed, color, sex, age, national origin, veteran status, or physical or mental disabilities; individual religious organizations; political organizations, campaigns, or candidates for political office; lobbying groups; medical or health-related causes; veteran or fraternal organizations; individuals; goodwill advertising in journals or program books; capital campaigns such as building grants; organizations that spend more than 30 percent of their total budget on fundraising efforts; or programs in communities without AE stores.
Geographic Focus: All U.S. States
Amount: 1,000 - 25,000 USD
Contact: Foundation Administrator; (877) 409-9587
Internet: http://www.ae.com/web/corp/foundation.htm
Sponsor: American Eagle Outfitters Foundation
150 Thorn Hill Drive
Warrendale, PA 15086

American Express Foundation Community Service Grants 103
Whether it is feeding the hungry, mentoring students, building homes for the homeless or cleaning up the environment, tens of thousands of American Express employees serve their communities through volunteerism and personal financial contributions, and the Foundation views this activity as an extension of the service ethic that lies at the heart of its business. It encourages good citizenship by supporting organizations that cultivate meaningful opportunities for civic engagement by employees and members of the community. The Foundation also serves its communities by supporting immediate and long-term relief and recovery efforts to help victims of natural disasters. Funding also goes to support preparedness programs that allow relief agencies to be better equipped in responding to emergencies as they occur.
Requirements: Eligible organizations must: certify tax-exempt status under Section 501(c)3 and 509(a)(1), (2) or (3) of the U.S. Internal Revenue Code. Organizations outside the U.S. must be able to document not-for-profit status.
Restrictions: The program does not fund: individual needs, including scholarships, sponsorships and other forms of financial aid; fund-raising activities, such as galas, benefits, dinners and sporting events; goodwill advertising, souvenir journals or dinner programs; travel for individuals or groups; sectarian activities of religious organizations; political causes, candidates, organizations or campaigns; or books, magazines or articles in professional journals.
Geographic Focus: All U.S. States
Samples: Arizona Foundation for Women, Phoenix, AZ; The Points of Light & Hands On Network, Washington, DC.
Contact: Philanthropic Programs Manager; (212) 640-5661; (212) 693-1033
Internet: http://home3.americanexpress.com/corp/gb/comm_serv.asp
Sponsor: American Express Foundation
3 World Financial Center, MC 01-48-04
New York, NY 10285-4804

American Express Foundation Cultural Heritage Grants 104
The funding supports organizations and projects that preserve or rediscover important cultural works and major historic sites in order to provide ongoing access and enjoyment for current and future audiences. The types of programs supported include a broad range of arts and culture: from historic landmarks and public spaces to dance, theater, music, film and the visual arts. The Foundation emphasizes preserving works that represent a range of diverse cultures. Supported programs must embrace preservation and enable ongoing public access and exposure through one or more of the following: ensuring public engagement with a restored work of art or historic site; producing or presenting a new interpretation of a work that is in danger of being lost; or preserving significant cultural traditions.
Requirements: Eligible organizations must: certify tax-exempt status under Section 501(c)3 and 509(a)(1), (2) or (3) of the U.S. Internal Revenue Code. Organizations outside the U.S. must be able to document not-for-profit status.
Restrictions: The program does not fund: individual needs, including scholarships, sponsorships and other forms of financial aid; fund-raising activities, such as galas, benefits, dinners and sporting events; goodwill advertising, souvenir journals or dinner programs; travel for individuals or groups; sectarian activities of religious organizations; political causes, candidates, organizations or campaigns; or books, magazines or articles in professional journals.
Geographic Focus: All U.S. States
Amount: Up to 100,000,000 USD
Samples: National Trust for Historic Preservation (Washington, DC) and World Monuments Fund (New York, NY)—to assist restoration and reconstruction measures in the wake of Hurricane Katrina that respect the historic and cultural assets of New Orleans and the Gulf Coast, $200,000 jointly; International Federation of the Red Cross and Red Crescent Societies (Geneva)—for relief efforts in South Asia and Africa, $1 million.
Contact: Philanthropic Programs Manager; (212) 640-5661; (212) 693-1033
Internet: http://home3.americanexpress.com/corp/gb/cult_her.asp
Sponsor: American Express Foundation
3 World Financial Center, MC 01-48-04
New York, NY 10285-4804

American Foodservice Charitable Trust Grants 105
American Foodservice Charitable Trust provides funding in the following areas of interest: Christian agencies & churches; community/economic development; higher education; hospitals (general) and; youth development. The types of support available are: general/operating support; program development; scholarship funds. Giving is primarily available in the areas of: King of Prussia, Pennsylvania; Thomasville, Georgia; and Fort Worth, Texas.
Requirements: Qualifying IRA 501(c)3 nonprofit organizations are eligible to apply. There's no application form nor is there a deadline date to adhere to when submitting a proposal to the Foundation.
Restrictions: No grants to individuals.
Geographic Focus: Georgia, Pennsylvania, Texas
Amount: 200 - 8,000 USD
Samples: Catholic Social Services, West Chester, PA, $200—social services grant (2008); American Red Cross, Philadelphia, PA, $1,000—disaster relief grant (2008); Police Atheletic League, Philadelphia, PA, $2,000—youth program grant (2008).
Contact: Richard S. Downs, Trustee; (610) 933-9792
Sponsor: American Foodservice Charitable Trust
860 First Avenue, Suite 9A
King of Prussia, PA 19406-1404

American Foundation Grants 106
The foundation is a public charity that helps individuals, families, and corporations create foundations that give financial support to their favorite charities. The foundation's primary focus is helping charities become more efficient and successful by supporting efforts in the following areas: governance and organization (structure)—efforts made to create, strengthen, and reinforce

the mission statement of an organization; human resources—staff recruitment for competence and expertise; and operations—access to high technology and leading-edge equipment and procedures. The foundation favors organizations with the following characteristics: competent management, clearly defined missions, organizational ethos, a multiplying and continuing impact, providing needed service, and fiscally responsible. Application and guidelines are available online.
Requirements: 501(c)3, 509(a)1, and 509(a)2 public charities are eligible.
Restrictions: Funding will not be considered for the following requests: organizations without tax-exempt 501(c)3, 509(a)1 or 509(a)2 public charity status; general endowment funds; direct aid to individuals; or governmental or quasi-governmental entities or activities other than colleges or universities.
Geographic Focus: All U.S. States
Contact: Grants Administrator; (602) 955-4770; (602) 955-4707; grantinfo@americanfoundation.org
Internet: http://www.americanfoundation.org
Sponsor: American Foundation
4518 N 32nd Street
Phoenix, AZ 85018

American Honda Foundation Grants **107**
American Honda Foundation seek out those programs and organizations with a well-defined sense of purpose, demonstrated commitment to making the best use of available resources and a reputation for accomplishing their objectives. Grants are provided in the fields of youth education and science education to the following: educational institutions, K-12; accredited higher education institutions (colleges and universities); community colleges and vocational or trade schools; scholarship and fellowship programs at selected colleges and/or universities or through selected non-profit organizations; other scientific and education-related, non-profit, tax-exempt organizations; gifted student programs; media concerning youth education and/or scientific education; private, non-profit scientific and/or youth education projects; other non-profit, tax-exempt, institutions in the fields of youth education and scientific education; and programs pertaining to academic or curriculum development that emphasize innovative educational methods and techniques.
Requirements: An applicant must be a nonprofit, tax-exempt educational organization.
Restrictions: The foundation does not consider proposals for service clubs, arts and culture, health and welfare issues, research papers, social issues, medical or educational research, trips, attempts to influence legislation, advocacy, annual funds, hospital operating funds, student exchanges, marathons, sponsorships, political activities, conferences, or fundraising events. An organization may submit only one proposal per year.
Geographic Focus: All U.S. States
Date(s) Application is Due: Feb 1; May 1; Aug 1; Nov 1
Amount: 10,000 - 100,000 USD
Samples: National Aquarium in Baltimore, Baltimore, MA, $75,000—for the Aquarium on Wheels program, giving underserved students in grades 9-12 from Baltimore City and County schools an opportunity to work year-round alongside scientists, conducting research on marine biology and conservation issues (2009); Detroit Educational Television Foundation, Wixom, MI, $100,000—supports the Think Squad project that was designed to increase science literacy and inspire children ages 10-14 to consider future careers in the science field (2009); The Tech Museum of Innovation, San Jose, CA, $35,008—supports the Tech Challenge program, which is a team-driven competition for students in grades 5-12 who are encouraged to build, document, and present a solution to a real-world problem (2009).
Contact: Kathryn A. Carey, Grants Manager; (310) 781-4090; (310) 781-4270; kathryn_carey@ahm.honda.com
Internet: http://corporate.honda.com/america/philanthropy.aspx?id=ahf
Sponsor: American Honda Foundation
1919 Torrence Boulevard, 100-1W-5A
Torrance, CA 90501-2746

American Humane Association Hearing Dog Grants **108**
The program awards grants to support agencies that provide hearing and assistance dog services. Grants are awarded for capital expenditures, general operating funds, scholarships, training, program development, material or curriculum development, and especially, efforts that involve collaboration among agencies. Application and guidelines are available online.
Requirements: An applicant agency must be a nonprofit or public animal welfare agency located and operating within the United States of America or its territories; be a 501(c)3 organization; provide a hearing dog program as its central focus or one of its primary services; and be an agency associate member of American Humane.
Geographic Focus: All U.S. States
Date(s) Application is Due: Jun 30
Amount: 3,000 - 7,000 USD
Contact: Grants Administrator; (800) 227-4645 or (303) 792-9900; (303) 792-5333; info@americanhumane.org
Internet: http://www.americanhumane.org/site/PageServer?pagename=pa_shelter_services_grant_hearing_dog
Sponsor: American Humane Association
63 Inverness Drive E
Englewood, CO 80112

American Humane Hearing Dog Grants **109**
The association awards grants to eligible organizations that provide hearing and assistance dog services. Grants, made possible by the Irene Jokisch Trust, are awarded for capital expenditures, general operating funds, scholarships, training, program development, material or curriculum development, and efforts that involve collaboration among agencies. Projects funded through the grant typically must be completed within one year. Application and guidelines are available online.
Requirements: The applicant agency must be a 501(c)3 nonprofit or public animal welfare agency located and operating within the United States or its territories; provide a hearing dog program as its central focus or one of its primary services; and be an Agency Associate member of American Humane.
Geographic Focus: All U.S. States
Date(s) Application is Due: Jun 30
Amount: 500 - 7,000 USD
Contact: Grants Administrator; (303) 792-9900; (303) 792-5333; info@americanhumane.org
Internet: http://www.americanhumane.org/site/PageServer?pagename=pa_shelter_services_grant_hearing_dog
Sponsor: American Humane Association
63 Inverness Drive E
Englewood, CO 80112

Amerigroup Foundation Grants **110**
Helping to create healthy communities is the cornerstone of the Amerigroup Foundation's mission. The objective is to serve as a national resource that fosters an environment where there is a continuum of education, access and care, all of which improve the health and well-being of the financially vulnerable and uninsured Americans. Support is available in the states of: Delaware; District of Columbia; Florida; Georgia; Nevada; New Mexico; New York; Ohio; South Carolina; Tennessee; Texas and; Virginia. The Foundation primarily provides grants is the form of general support but program development and, sponsorships are also available to qualified non-profit organizations.
Requirements: 501(c)3 non-profits are eligible to apply from the following states: Delaware; District of Columbia; Florida; Georgia; Nevada; New Mexico; New York; Ohio; South Carolina; Tennessee; Texas and; Virginia.
Restrictions: Funding is unavailable for: projects or organizations that offer a direct benefit to the trustees of the Foundation or to employees or directors of Amerigroup; projects or organizations that might in any way pose a conflict with Amerigroup's mission, goals, programs, products or employees; projects or organizations that do not benefit a broad cross section of the community; individuals; political parties, candidates or lobbying activities; benefits, raffles, souvenir programs, trips, tours or similar events; for-profit entities, including start-up businesses.
Geographic Focus: Delaware, District of Columbia, Florida, Georgia, Nevada, New Mexico, New York, Ohio, South Carolina, Tennessee, Texas, Virginia
Amount: 500 - 10,000 USD
Contact: Amy Sheyer, Grants Manager; (757) 490-6900; (757) 222-2360
Internet: http://www.realsolutions.com/company/pages/Foundation.aspx
Sponsor: Amerigroup Foundation
4425 Corporation Lane
Virginia Beach, VA 23462-3103

AMERIND Community Service Project Grants **111**
AMERIND Risk Management Corporation's Community Outreach program seeks to advance the community aspect of AMERIND's vision to Protect Tribal Families First. Funding limitations for small community service projects include: housing fairs will receive a standard $500 per event; youth activities, including graffiti paint-outs, community clean-up, meth awareness will range from $100 (less than 100 participants) to $250 (more than 100

participants); and health fairs will receive a standard $250. The AMERIND Outreach Committee meets once every month to discuss funding requests received by organizations.
Requirements: Requests for AMERIND contributions must meet of the following criteria; the project must address a demonstrated need in a Native American community in which AMERIND has a presence; the project must provide an opportunity for Native Americans to make learning about fire safety and home safety fun; or the project must support a project or program involving fire safety and/or home safety, business related or other related area to expand, improve and protect the lifestyles of Native Americans and their families.
Restrictions: Powwows and Rodeos are considered advertising and are not funded. AMERIND does not contribute to: individual requests; trip expenses; organizations that charge a fee or dues; lobbying organizations; or political organizations.
Geographic Focus: All U.S. States
Contact: Mike Jennings, Chief Financial Officer; (505) 404-5000 or (800) 352-3496; (505) 404-5001; outreach@amerind-corp.org
Internet: http://www.amerind-corp.org/grants.shtml
Sponsor: AMERIND Risk Management Corporation
502 Cedar Drive
Santa Ana, NM 87004

AMERIND Housing Development Capacity Building Grants 112
The corporation, National American Indian Housing Council, and the Enterprise Foundation award these grants to encourage small tribes and tribally designated housing entities representing small tribes to access new resources or subsidy financing toward developing a housing project or program. Grants can be used to cover the costs of staff, consultant, financing fees, training, travel, software, or other costs needed to learn about, apply for, or access new forms of financing. Complete guidelines and applications are available at the website.
Restrictions: AMERIND does not contribute to: individual requests; trip expenses; organizations that charge a fee or dues; lobbying organizations; or political organizations.
Geographic Focus: All U.S. States
Amount: 30,000 USD
Contact: Mike Jennings, Chief Financial Officer; (505) 404-5000 or (800) 352-3496; (505) 404-5001; outreach@amerind-corp.org
Internet: http://www.amerind-corp.org/Community/ServiceProjects.aspx
Sponsor: AMERIND Risk Management Corporation
502 Cedar Drive
Santa Ana, NM 87004

AmerUs Group Charitable Foundation 113
The foundation awards general support grants to nonprofits in the metropolitan areas of Des Moines, Indianapolis, Topeka, Boston, and Long Island; in the areas of arts and culture, civic and community, education, health and human services, United Way, and new initiatives. Guidelines and application are available online.
Requirements: Nonprofit organizations in metro Des Moines, Indianapolis, Topeka, and Boston, and Long Island, New York, are eligible to apply.
Restrictions: Grants do not support athletic organizations, conferences, goodwill advertising, endowments, fellowships, festival participation, fraternal organizations, hospital or health care facilities, individual K-12 schools, political parties, religious groups for religious programs, social organizations, and trade or professional associations.
Geographic Focus: Indiana, Iowa, Massachusetts, New York
Date(s) Application is Due: Feb 9; May 4; Aug 3
Amount: Up to 150,000 USD
Samples: American Institute of Business (Des Moines, IA)—$5000; Children and Families of Iowa (Des Moines, IA)—$18,000,; Iowa National Heritage Foundation (IA)—$2500; Young Women's Resource Ctr (IA)—$2500.
Contact: D'Arcy Reinhard, (515) 557-3917
Internet: http://www.avivausa.com
Sponsor: Aviva World
699 Walnut Street, Suite 2000
Des Moines, IA 50309

Ametek Foundation Grants 114
Corporate contributions are made through the foundation to nonprofit organizations in company-operating areas. The foundation supports programs and projects in the categories of health, education, and social services, with education being the largest area of support. Under the category of health, grants are awarded to hospitals, health care facilities, and for medical research. Support for education is given to colleges and universities and technical schools, as well as scholarship funds. Welfare funding supports philanthropic organizations, including the United Way. Arts groups, museums, and civic groups also receive support. Types of support include general operating support, annual campaigns, building construction/renovation, equipment acquisition, endowment funds, scholarship funds, research, technical assistance, and matching funds. Annual application deadline dates may vary; contact the office for specific dates. The board meets in November and May to consider requests.
Requirements: IRS 501(c)3 organizations are eligible.
Restrictions: Grants are not made to individuals or to political, fraternal, or veterans organizations.
Geographic Focus: All U.S. States
Date(s) Application is Due: Feb 28; Sep 1
Amount: 1,000 - 25,000 USD
Samples: Rochester City School District (Rochester, NY)—grant recipient, $116, 231; Gnaden Huetten Memorial Hospital (Lehighton, PA)—grant recipient, $1000; Abilities, Inc of Florida (Clearwater, FL)—grant recipient, $15,000.
Contact: Kathryn Londra, (610) 647-2121; (610) 296-3412
Sponsor: Ametek Foundation
37 N Valley Road, Building 4, P.O. Box 1764
Paoli, PA 19301-0801

Amgen Foundation Grants 115
Amgen seeks to: advance science education, improve quality of care and access for patients, and support resources that create sound communities where Amgen staff members live and work. Requests must be received at least 90 days in advance of the desired contribution date. Guidelines are available online.
Requirements: 501(c)3 tax-exempt organizations located in Amgen communities are eligible. Eligible grantees may include public elementary and secondary schools, as well as public colleges and universities, public libraries and public hospitals.
Restrictions: In general, Amgen does not consider requests for the following: support to individuals, fundraising or sports-related events, corporate sponsorship requests, religious organizations unless the program is secular in nature and benefits a broad range of the community, political organization or lobbying activity, labor unions, fraternal, service or veterans' organizations, private foundations, or organizations that are discriminatory.
Geographic Focus: All U.S. States
Samples: California State U (Camarillo, CA)—for scientific equipment, $950,000; Institute for Systems Biology (Seattle, WA)—for the endowment and operations, $3 million; International Federation of the Red Cross and Red Crescent Societies (Geneva)—for relief efforts in South Asia and Africa, $1 million.
Contact: Program Contact; (805) 447-4056 or (805) 447-1000; (805) 447-1010
Internet: http://wwwext.amgen.com/citizenship/apply_for_grant.html
Sponsor: Amgen Foundation
1 Amgen Center Drive, MS 38-3-B
Thousand Oaks, CA 91320-1799

AMI Semiconductors Corporate Grants 116
The company makes grants to nonprofit organizations in support of the performing arts, economic development, business education, health cost containment, and social services for senior citizens. Types of support include conferences and seminars, general operating support, matching grants, multiyear grants, professorships, research, and scholarships. There are no application deadlines. Submit a letter of inquiry that includes a description of the organization and program, amount of funds requested, purpose of the request, recently audited financial statement, and proof of tax-exempt status. Contact office for grant availability.
Restrictions: The company does not support political or lobbying groups.
Geographic Focus: All U.S. States
Amount: 1,000 - 2,500 USD
Contact: Tamera Drake, (208) 234-6890; (208) 234-6795; tamera_Drake@amis.com
Internet: http://www.amis.com/about
Sponsor: AMI Semiconductors
2300 Buckskin Road
Pocatello, ID 83201

Amon G. Carter Foundation Grants 117

The foundation awards grants that support benevolent, charitable, and educational purposes with emphasis on the arts and humanities. Other areas supported include education, health and medical services, human and social services, programs benefiting the youth and elderly, civic and community endeavors that enhance quality of life, religion, and visual and performing arts. Types of support include general operating support, continuing support, annual campaigns, capital campaigns, building construction/renovation, equipment acquisition, endowment funds, emergency funds, program development, professorships, seed money, research, and matching funds. The foundation's primary focus is directed to the Fort Worth/Tarrant County area of Texas, although the directors occasionally award a grant outside the Texas area. Proposals must be in writing, briefly giving background information on the requesting organization, specifically stating the purpose of the request and the amount being requested. A current copy of the organization's IRS determination letter must be furnished. Applications are accepted at any time for consideration during the April, September, and December board meetings.
Restrictions: Grants, loans, or scholarships are not made to individuals. Online applications are not accepted.
Geographic Focus: All U.S. States
Amount: 1,000 - 250,000 USD
Samples: Amon Carter Museum (TX)—program support, $5.57 million; Meals on Wheels (TX)—program support, $35,000; J.L. West Presbyterian Special Care—capital campaign support, $50,000.
Contact: Terry Woodfin, Program Contact; (817) 332-2783; (817) 332-2787; terry@agcf.org
Internet: http://www.agcf.org
Sponsor: Amon G. Carter Foundation
P.O. Box 1036
Fort Worth, TX 76101-1036

Andersen Corporate Foundation 118

The Foundation contributes to: organizations that enhance self-sufficiency for people living in poverty, senior citizens, and people with disabilities; organizations that promote safe and healthy environments, as well as organizations that seek to improve health through prevention and education programs, primarily for young people, senior citizens, and people in vulnerable situations; organizations that offer intellectual and social opportunities with a focus primarily on young people, senior citizens, and people with disabilities; and support that builds, promotes, and preserves communities. Complete guidelines are available online.
Requirements: All grant recipients must meet these giving guidelines: the organization's programs and services are consistent with Andersen Corporate Foundation's mission and values; the organization's purpose and programs fit within Andersen Corporate Foundation's defined program focus areas; the organization can demonstrate sound fiscal management and effective delivery of services; nonprofit corporation is registered under section 501(c)3 of the IRS Code in the United States or for Canadian Charities with the Canadian Revenue Agency.
Restrictions: The Foundation avoids making grants in organizations that are in competition with each other to provide the same service to the community. The Foundation does not support endowments or make grants to individuals. Funding is not granted to national research organizations.
Geographic Focus: Iowa, Minnesota, Virginia, Wisconsin, Canada
Date(s) Application is Due: Apr 15; Jul 15; Oct 15; Dec 15
Contact: Program Director; (888) 439-9508 or (651) 439-1557; (651) 439-9480; andersencorpfdn@srinc.biz
Internet: https://www.srinc.biz/bp/index.html
Sponsor: Andersen Corporate Foundation
342 5th Avenue N
Bayport, MN 55003

Andre Agassi Charitable Foundation Grants 119

The foundation awards grants to at-risk youth programs targeting education and recreation in the Las Vegas area. There are no application forms or deadlines. Submitted requests will be considered for funding in the following calendar year. Detailed guidelines are available online.
Requirements: Nevada 501(c)3 nonprofits serving the Las Vegas metropolitan area are eligible.
Restrictions: Grants do not support organizations or projects outside the Las Vegas community, organizations that discriminate, individuals, advertising, religious or sectarian organizations for religious purposes, or political organizations and programs designed to influence legislation or elect candidates to public office.
Geographic Focus: Nevada
Samples: Las Vegas Philharmonic, Las Vegas, NV, $10,000—art program for underprivileged youths; Boys and Girls Club of Nevada, Las Vegas, NV, $334,403—after school program; Center for Independent Living, Las Vegas., NV, $5,000—residential treatment for adolescents.
Contact: Julie Pippenger, Chief Operating Officer; (702) 227-5700; (702) 866-2928; info@agassi.net
Internet: http://www.agassifoundation.org
Sponsor: Andre Agassi Charitable Foundation
3960 Howard Hughes Parkway, Suite 750
Las Vegas, NV 89169

Andrew Family Foundation Grants 120

The Andrew Family Foundation is a private, philanthropic organization that will consider proposals from public, non-profit organizations under IRS Section 501(c)3 to support projects and organizations that foster individual growth and enhance communities through education, humanitarian efforts, and the arts. Funding primarily in the Illinois with a special interest in the Cook County region. The types of support available include: annual campaigns; building/renovation; capital campaigns; general/operating support; scholarship funds. There is no deadline date when applying for funding. Qualified grant proposals will be reviewed by the Andrew Family Foundation Grant Making Committee prior to quarterly board meetings. The committee will make a recommendation to the Board of Directors of the Foundation.
Requirements: 501(c)3 tax-exempt organizations are eligible to apply for funding. To begin the application process, take the Eligibility Quiz to confirm that you qualify for a grant from the foundation. Upon successful completion of the Eligibility Quiz, you will be invited to complete an online Letter of Inquiry. The Board will review your Letter of Inquiry and may invite you to submit a Full Application for review. Generally, the Board meets in February, May, August and November of each year.
Restrictions: The foundation does not provide funds: to individuals; taxable corporations; religious programs; political organizations; and other private foundations.
Geographic Focus: Illinois
Contact: Connor Humphrey, Grants Administrator; (708) 460-1288 or (602) 828-8471; (602) 385-3267; aff@inlignwealth.com or Connor.Humphrey@GenSpring.com
Internet: https://online.foundationsource.com/andrew/board2.htm
Sponsor: Andrew Family Foundation
14628 John Humphrey Drive
Orland Park, IL 60462

Anheuser-Busch Foundation Grants 121

Support is provided almost exclusively to causes that are located in communities in which the company has manufacturing facilities. Contributions are made for education, health, social services, minorities and youth, cultural enrichment, and environmental protection programs. Types of support include capital grants, employee matching gifts, equipment and material acquisition, general support, and donated products. Full proposals are accepted throughout the year. At the website, click on Guidelines for Charitable Giving.
Requirements: 501(c)3 tax-exempt organizations in Street Louis, MO; Baldwinsville, N.Y; Cartersvile, Ga; Columbus, Oh; Fairfield, Ca; Fort Collins, Co; Houston, Tx; Jacksonville, Fl; Los Angeles, Ca; Merrimack, N.H; Newark, N.J; Williamsburg, Va., Orlando, Fl; Tampa, Fl; San Antonio, Tx; San Diego, Tx.
Restrictions: Grants are not made to individuals; political, social, fraternal, religious, or athletic organizations; or hospitals for operating funds.
Geographic Focus: California, Colorado, Florida, Georgia, Missouri, New Hampshire, New Jersey, New York, Ohio, Texas, Virginia
Amount: 25,000 - 100,000 USD
Contact: Assistant Manager; (314) 577-2453; (314) 557-3251
Internet: http://www.anheuser-busch.com/CharitableGivingIndex.html
Sponsor: Anheuser-Busch Foundation
One Busch Place
Saint Louis, MO 63118-1852

Animal Welfare Trust Grants 122

Animal Welfare Trust's grant program seeks to assist organizations whose work can help alleviate animal suffering and/or raise public consciousness toward giving animals the respect they so need and deserve. Although general

organizational funding will be considered, preference will be given to well-defined projects with clear goals and objectives. Capital projects will not be considered. Areas of priority include farm animal welfare, vegetarianism and humane education. Grants will generally be made in the $2,500 to $20,000 range, although requests outside either end of this range will be considered. Grant requests can be for a single or multi-year period, depending on the nature of the project. Animal Welfare Trust anticipates giving out 10 to 15 grants per year.
Requirements: Grants will be made largely to organizations classified as public charities under section 501(c)3 of the IRS code. Under certain circumstances grants will be considered outside the boundaries of public charities, including organizations outside the United States that can meet appropriate legal standards.
Geographic Focus: All U.S. States
Amount: 5,000 - 75,000 USD
Samples: Heart Animal Rescue, Canutillo, Texas, $75,000 - General Support for humane education program (2010); Action for Animals, Seattle, Washington, $10,000 - 2010 Vans Warped Tour vegan outreach (2010); Center for Expansion of Fundamental Rights, Miami, Florida, $22,500 - Non human Rights Project (2010).
Contact: Brad Goldberg, President and Director; (914) 381-6177; (914) 381-6176; email@animalwelfaretrust.org
Internet: http://fdncenter.org/grantmaker/awt/prog.html
Sponsor: Animal Welfare Trust
141 Halstead Avenue, Suite 301, P.O. Box 737
Mamaroneck, NY 10543

ANLAF International Fund for Sexual Minorities Grants 123

Astraea's primary purpose is to advance the economic, political, educational, and cultural well-being of lesbians. Astraea raises and distributes funds to organizations, individuals, and projects that promote a feminist perspective advancing the social, political, economic, educational, and cultural well-being of lesbians and all women and girls. Programs and policies will be supported that actively work to eliminate those forms of oppression based on sexual orientation, class, race, age, physical and mental ability, religious affiliation, and all other factors that affect lesbians and gay men in the United States and internationally. Organizations may apply for general support or project support. Deadlines are the beginning of June and the beginning of November; contact program staff for exact dates.
Requirements: Groups must be based in Latin America, the Caribbean, Asia, the Pacific, Eastern Europe, the former Soviet Republics, the Middle East, and Africa.
Restrictions: Astraea Foundation generally does not fund government agencies or organizations with budgets above $500,000.
Geographic Focus: All U.S. States
Date(s) Application is Due: Mar 15; Oct 15
Amount: Up to 10,000 USD
Samples: Audre Lorde Project (Brooklyn, NY)—for the LBTST Women of Color Organizing Initiative, $4000; Triangle Project (Cape Town, Africa)—for expansion of services to the lesbian/gay/bisexual/transsexual communities in rural areas of the Western Cape, $4000.
Contact: Namita Chad, Grants Administrator; (212) 529-8021; (212) 982-3321; namita@astraeafoundation.org or grants@astraeafoundation.org
Internet: http://www.astraea.org/PHP/Grants/Main.php4
Sponsor: Astraea Lesbian Foundation for Justice
116 E 16th Street, 7th Floor
New York, NY 10003

Ann Jackson Family Foundation Grants 124

The foundation awards grants to eligible nonprofit organizations in its areas of interest, including secondary education, healthcare, child welfare, animal welfare, and the disabled. Types of support include building construction/renovation, capital campaigns, and general operating grants. Most grants are awarded to nonprofits in Santa Barbara, California. There are no application forms or deadlines. Contact the foundation for document attachments required.
Geographic Focus: California
Amount: 5,000 - 50,000 USD
Samples: All Saints By the Sea Episcopal Church, Santa Barbara, CA, $14,000—general purposes grant (2008); Bowl Foundation of Santa Barbara, Santa Barbara, CA, $20,000—building project grant (2008); Dunn School, Los Olivos, CA, $50,000—faculty housing grant (2008).
Contact: Palmer Jackson, President; (805) 969-2258
Sponsor: Ann Jackson Family Foundation
P.O. Box 5580
Santa Barbara, CA 93150-5580

Ann Peppers Foundation Grants 125

The foundation awards grants to eligible California nonprofit organizations in its areas of interest, including arts and cultural programs, disabled, elderly, health care, private education, and social services. Types of support include capital grants, general operating grants on a temporary basis, matching grants, scholarships, and research grants. Grants are initiated by the foundation manager. There are no application deadlines; the board meets quarterly to consider requests.
Requirements: Southern California 501(c)3 nonprofits, colleges, and universities are eligible. Preference is given to requests from Los Angeles County.
Geographic Focus: California
Amount: 2,000 - 50,000 USD
Samples: Boys Republic (Chino Hills, CA)—for kitchen renovation at residential facility , $5,000; Pepperdine University (Malibu, CA)—for scholarships, $25,000; Huntington Medical Research Institute (Pasadena, CA)—to purchase imaging technology for preclinical breast cancer, $5,000; Marymount College (Rancho Palos Verdes, CA)—for scholarships, $10,000.
Contact: Jack Alexander, Secretary; (626) 449-0793
Sponsor: Ann Peppers Foundation
625 S Fair Oaks Avenue
South Pasadena, CA 91030

Anschutz Family Foundation Grants 126

The foundation makes grants in Colorado's rural and urban communities, to assist the elderly, the young, and the economically disadvantaged. Support is given to programs and projects that strengthen families and enable individuals to become productive and responsible citizens of society. Religious organizations, including Christian, Lutheran, Presbyterian, Roman Catholic, and the Salvation Army, also are eligible for funding. Types of support include special projects, general operating budgets, continuing support, seed money, emergency funds, technical assistance, and publications.
Requirements: Nonprofit organizations in Colorado may apply.
Restrictions: Grants are not awarded to individuals, programs outside of Colorado, graduate and post-graduate research, religious organizations for religious purposes, special events, promotions or conferences, candidates for political office, endowments, debt reduction, multi-year grants, and capital campaigns.
Geographic Focus: Colorado
Date(s) Application is Due: Jan 15; Aug 1
Amount: 2,500 - 10,000 USD
Samples: The Center for Hearing, Speech, and Language (Denver, CO)—to support Kidscreen, a vision, hearing, speech and language developmental screening service for low-income families, $5,000; The Learning Source for Adults and Families (Denver, CO)—general operating support for neighborhood literacy programs for adults and families, $7,500; Seniors Resource Center (Denver, CO)—for general operating support for programs that maximize seniors' independence and dignity, $5000; Women's Resource Center (Durango, CO)—To support the resource and referral program, $5,000.
Contact: Sue Anschutz-Rodgers, President & Executive Director; (303) 293-2338; (303) 299-1235; info@anschutzfamilyfoundation.org
Internet: http://www.anschutzfamilyfoundation.org/info.htm
Sponsor: Anschutz Family Foundation
555 17th Street, Suite 2400
Denver, CO 80202

Anthony R. Abraham Foundation Grants 127

For more than 30 years, the Anthony R. Abraham Foundation mission has been to help non-profit organizations worldwide. The foundations strives to: provide programs and services to help people around the world become self-productive and give back to their communities; ensure that no child is denied medical treatment due to a lack of insurance; provide education that breaks barriers; guarantee that research into the cure of catastrophic diseases continues; help raise the quality of life. It's been a privilege for the Foundation to be able to help ease poverty, raise hospitals, build orphanages and further medical research and the Foundation looks forward to doing even more. Some of the organizations helped include: Domestic organizations -Street Jude Children's Research Hospital; Camillus House; Miami Rescue Mission;

Habitat for Humanity of Greater Miami; America's Second Harvest; Miami Children's Hospital; Jackson Memorial Hospital; Florida Heart Research Institute; Big Brothers/Big Sisters; Alonzo Mourning Charities; Honey Shine Mentoring Program; Cancer Link; The Miami Lighthouse for the Blind; Overtown Youth Center. International organizations: Brothers of the Good Shepherd; School for the Blind, Lebanon; Rene Moawad Foundation; Haitian Foundation; Children's International Network; Doctors without Borders; Little Sisters of Nazareth; Maronite Order of the Holy Family.
Requirements: Non-profit 501(c)3 organization requesting funding should fill out a funds-request form and submit it at the Foundation's website. The Foundation will contact you, if your organization qualifies under the Foundation's guidelines and the law.
Restrictions: Grants are not made to individuals.
Geographic Focus: All U.S. States
Amount: 100 - 50,000 USD
Contact: Anthony R. Abraham, Chairman; (305) 665-2222
Internet: http://www.abrahamfoundation.com/about
Sponsor: Anthony R. Abraham Foundation
1320 S Dixie Highway, Suite 241
Coral Gables, FL 33146-2937

Antone & Edene Vidinha Charitable Trust Grants **128**

The trust provides partial support to programs and projects of tax-exempt, public charities in Hawaii to improve the quality of life in the state, particularly the island of Kauai. Grants of one year's duration are awarded in categories of interest to the trust, including: churches on Kauai; hospitals; health organizations which benefit the people of Kauai; educational scholarships to colleges and universities in the State of Hawaii for deserving students from the Island of Kauai. Types of support include building/renovation; equipment; general/operating support; program development; scholarship funds. Grants average from $2,000 - $80,000.
Requirements: 501(c)3 nonprofit organizations in Hawaii are eligible to apply. The Trust places a special emphasis on the island of Kauai. Contact Paula Boyce to acquire the cover sheet/application forms and any additional guidelines required to begin the application process. Proposals must be submitted by December 1st.
Restrictions: No grants to/for: individuals; endowments; multi-year pledges.
Geographic Focus: Hawaii
Date(s) Application is Due: Dec 1
Amount: 2,000 - 80,000 USD
Samples: Lihue Missionary Church, Lihue, HI, $19,800—equipment acquisition/program support grant (2008); University of Hawaii Foundation, Honolulu, HI, $80,000—scholarship funds (2008); Christ Memorial Episcopal Church, Kilauea, HI, $30,000—parish hall restoration (2008).
Contact: Paula Boyce; (808) 538-4944; (808) 538-4647; pboyce@boh.com
Internet: http://www.hawaiicommunityfoundation.org/index.php?id=290
Sponsor: Antone and Edene Vidinha Charitable Trust
Bank of Hawai'i, Foundation Administration Department 758
Honolulu, HI 96802-3170

Aragona Family Foundation Grants **129**

Giving primarily in Austin, Texas, the Aragona Family Foundation provides general operating support grants in the following areas of interest: animals/wildlife, preservation/protection; cancer; children/youth, services; community/economic development; education; food banks; hospitals (general); philanthropy/voluntarism; protestant agencies & churches. Grants range from $2,000 - $100,000.
Requirements: Qualifying 501(c)3 organizations are eligible to apply for funding. There is no: application form required; deadline date to adhere to.
Geographic Focus: Texas
Amount: 2,000 - 100,000 USD
Samples: Street Stephens Episcopal School, Austin, TX, $100,000—to further the organizations charitable mission (2008); Harvard University, Cambridge, MA, $533,300—to further the organizations charitable mission (2008).
Contact: Joseph C. Aragona, President; (512) 328-2178
Sponsor: Aragona Family Foundation
3311 Westlake Drive
Austin, TX 78746-1901

Aratani Foundation Grants **130**

The foundation awards grants to nonprofits in its areas of interest, including education, health care, museums, recreation, and religion. Preference is given to Japanese-American cultural organizations. Types of support include annual campaigns, building construction/renovation, capital campaigns, conferences and seminars, continuing support, curriculum development, endowments, exchange programs, fellowships, general operating support, program development, scholarship funds, and seed grants.
Requirements: The Foundation gives primarily in the state of California but funding is also available in the states of: New York; District of Columbia; Washington; Florida; Rhode Island; Oregon. Application forms are not required, but application outlines are available. Contact the Foundation directly for additional guidelines. Applications maybe submitted in English and Japanese. There are no application deadline dates.
Restrictions: Grants are not made to individuals.
Geographic Focus: California, District of Columbia, Florida, New York, Oregon, Rhode Island, Washington
Amount: 1,000 - 150,000 USD
Samples: Asian Pacific American Legal Center of South California, Los Angeles, CA, $50,000 (2008); Asian Pacific American Institute for Congressional Studies, Washington, DC, $10,000 (2008); Buddhist Churches of America, San Francisco, CA, $200,000 (2008).
Contact: George Aratani, President; (310) 530-9900
Sponsor: Aratani Foundation
23505 Crenshaw Boulevard, North 230
Hollywood, CA 90505

Arbor Day Foundation Grants **131**

The mission of the National Tree Trust continues through the Arbor Day Foundation, a nonprofit, environmental education organization with a mission of inspiring people to plant, nurture, and celebrate trees. The Program provides appropriate support and resources to urban and community forestry and conservation nonprofit organizations working to engage the members of their community in urban and community forestry. The programs of the Foundation are Seeds—technology, general office equipment and supplies, rent for office space, salaries and wages, general printing and postage, and professional contract services; Roots—education, involvement of underserved communities, tree planting and maintenance, community nursery, and service learning; and Branches—community outreach. Guidelines are available online.
Requirements: Eligible organizations will include qualified 501(c)3 nonprofits that have been in existence for two years, and are either an urban and community forestry organization or a conservation-focused organization working on urban and community forestry projects.
Geographic Focus: All U.S. States
Contact: Mark Derowitsch, Public Relations Manager; (888) 448-7337; mderowitsch@arborday.org
Internet: http://www.arborday.org/programs/
Sponsor: Arbor Day Foundation
100 Arbor Avenue
Nebraska City, NE 68410

Arcadia Foundation Grants **132**

The foundation awards grants to Pennsylvania nonprofit organizations to improve the quality of life. Areas of interest include hospitals and hospital building funds, health agencies and services, nursing, hospices, early childhood, adult and higher education, libraries, child development and welfare agencies, youth organizations, and social service and general welfare agencies, including care of the handicapped, aged, and hungry. Also supported are family services, environment and conservation, wildlife and animal welfare, religious organizations, historical preservation, and music organizations. Types of support include general operating support, continuing support, annual campaigns, capital campaigns, building construction/renovation, equipment acquisition, endowment funds, program development, scholarship funds, and research. Applications are accepted between September 1 and November 1.
Requirements: Eastern Pennsylvania organizations whose addresses have zip codes of 18000-19000 are eligible. Application form not required. The initial approach should be a letter or proposal—not exceeding two pages.
Restrictions: Grants are not awarded to support individuals, deficit financing, land acquisition, fellowships, demonstration projects, publications, or conferences.
Geographic Focus: Pennsylvania
Date(s) Application is Due: Nov 1
Contact: Marilyn Lee Steinbright, President; (610) 275-8460
Sponsor: Arcadia Foundation
105 E Logan Street
Norristown, PA 19401

Arca Foundation Grants 133

The Arca Foundation believes that access to knowledge, vigorous public education and citizen engagement are essential to democracy. However, there exist structures and private interests that serve to limit the transparency of our government, stifle public debate on critical issues, and foster an environment where government is not effectively serving the interests of its citizens. In order to promote greater social equity and justice at home and abroad, the foundation supports organizations and projects that work to advance transparent, accountable, and just policies. They support strategic initiatives that work to directly affect policies by: Developing and advocating for innovative ideas; Promoting transparency and access to information; Fostering greater public debate on critical issues; Educating key stakeholders; Engaging citizens in strategic organizing and advocacy that builds power and drives change.

Requirements: Domestically, in the current sociopolitical climate, the foundation is concerned about the promotion of a more equitable, accountable, and transparent economic recovery. They are considering proposals that work to advance more just policies on this and other critical issues. Internationally, the foundation has a long history of working to promote greater dialogue between the U.S. and Cuba. They are considering proposals that advance policies that further normalized U.S. -Cuban relations, as well as proposals that work to foster more just policies on a range of international issues. The Arca Foundation has two deadlines annually, on March 1 and September 1 of every year, for consideration in June and December respectively. When deadline dates fall on a weekend, the deadline is effective on the next weekday. The foundation will not respond to letters of inquiry, but will accept complete proposals submitted according to the application guidelines on regular grant deadlines.

Restrictions: The foundation does not fund organizations that provide direct social services, scholarship funds or scholarly research, capital projects or endowments, individuals, or government programs. Proposals received via fax or email will not be considered. Late proposals will not be considered, and extensions are not available for any reason.

Geographic Focus: All U.S. States

Date(s) Application is Due: Mar 1; Sep 1

Amount: 50,000 USD

Samples: Catholics in Alliance for the Common Good (Washington, DC) $50,000 to support 'A Campaign for the Common Good' and related civic participation activities; Consumer Watchdog (Santa Monica, CA) $75,000 to support OilWatchdog.org, a company-by-company comprehensive watchdog of the oil industry; Medical Education Cooperation with Cuba (Decatur, GA) $30,000 to support continuing and expanding MEDICC's journalism internship program; Independent Media Institute (San Francisco, CA) $50,000 to support AlterNet and its news and information coverage of strategic issues

Contact: Emily Casteel, Program Associate; (202) 822-9193; (202) 785-1446; grants@arcafoundation.org

Internet: http://www.arcafoundation.org/howtoapply.htm

Sponsor: Arca Foundation
1308 19th Street NW
Washington, DC 20036

ARCO Foundation Education Grants 134

The foundation will concentrate its aid to education in support of the following: precollege programs to improve the quality of teaching and learning in urban public education; programs aimed at decreasing attrition rates among low-income and minority students; programs to motivate low-income and minority students to succeed in college, especially in mathematics-based careers of engineering, science, and business; support for laboratory renovation and scientific equipment in academic disciplines of interest at major research universities; programs to retain the most talented young faculty in academic careers in selected disciplines; selected liberal arts programs at colleges and universities of interest; state associations of private colleges in the states where the company has interests; academic programs relevant to energy interests at regional universities and colleges; and national education associations and organizations that seek to improve education in public high schools and at higher academic levels. Grants are awarded for operating budgets, seed money, equipment, land acquisition, matching funds, employee matching gifts, employee related scholarships, special projects, and technical assistance. Applications are accepted at any time; annual report should be obtained prior to submitting a formal proposal.

Requirements: The foundation is a regional organization funding nonprofit organizations in states where ARCO has facilities and personnel, including Alaska, Arizona, California, Colorado, Nevada, Texas, and Washington. Requests from those states and those nearby should be addressed to the local community affairs managers.

Restrictions: The foundation discourages applications from the following: programs not focused on promoting self-sufficiency and economic development of minority populations; historic preservation or urban development projects not tied to neighborhood economic revitalization; proposals from religious organizations; or funding requests from federal, state, county, and municipal agencies, including school districts. The foundation does not generally consider support of hospital building or endowment campaigns, medical equipment, medical research programs, single-issue health organizations, or health services not directed at low-income people.

Geographic Focus: Alaska, Arizona, California, Colorado, Nevada, Texas, Washington

Amount: 1,500 - 360,000 USD

Samples: U of Montana (Butte, MT)—to help retain and graduate minority students pursuing engineering degrees, $16,500; U of California (Davis, CA)—to help retain and graduate minority students pursuing engineering degrees, $47,000.

Contact: Virginia Victorin, Grants Administrator; (213) 486-3342; (213) 486-0113

Internet: http://www.ntlf.com/html/grants/5977.htm

Sponsor: ARCO Foundation
151 South Flower Street
Los Angeles, CA 90071

Arcus Foundation Fund Grants 135

The Arcus Foundation is a private grantmaking foundation that supports organizations around the world working in two areas - lesbian, gay, bisexual, and transgender (LGBT) human rights; and conservation of the world's great apes. In the former area, the Foundation supports organizations that are working to achieve social justice that is inclusive of sexual orientation, gender identity and race. In the latter area, it supports organizations seeking to ensure respect and survival of great apes and their natural habitat. Specifically, the Arcus Fund supports efforts within Michigan to improve the quality of life for the gay, lesbian, bisexual and transgender (GLBT) community. Areas of special interest include social equity, public awareness and understanding, health and safety, and scientific inquiry. Types of support include: annual campaigns; building/renovation; capital campaigns; conferences and seminars; consulting services; continuing support; curriculum development; employee matching gifts; endowments; general operating support; matching/challenge support; program development; program evaluation; program-related investments/loans; publication; and technical assistance.

Requirements: Nonprofit organizations are eligible.

Restrictions: No grants to are given to individuals, or for religious or political activities, medical research or film/video production.

Geographic Focus: Michigan

Amount: 1,000 - 50,000 USD

Contact: Myron Cobbs, Program Assistant; (269) 373-4373, ext. 110; (269) 373-0277; myron@arcusfoundation.org or info@arcusfoundation.org

Internet: http://www.arcusfoundation.org/pages_2/home.cfm

Sponsor: Arcus Foundation
402 East Michigan Avenue
Kalamazoo, MI 49007

Arie and Ida Crown Memorial Grants 136

The program supports programs that offer opportunities to the disadvantaged, strengthens the bond of families, and improves the quality of people's lives. As a general rule, the Foundation funds organizations that serve the greater Chicago area as well as organizations that serve the broader Jewish community. Most grants are awarded to organizations within the city of Chicago. Organizations are supported in the areas of arts and culture (concentrating on educational and enrichment programs for youth), civic affairs, education, health (stressing access to services, hospice and health promotion), and human service (focusing on programs which offer assistance for children and families).

Requirements: Nonprofit organizations in Chicago and Cook County, IL, may apply for grant support.

Restrictions: Grants are not made to support individuals, conference expenses, film projects, government programs (50 percent government funded), or research projects.

Geographic Focus: Illinois

Date(s) Application is Due: Jan 31; Jul 31

Amount: 1,000 - 200,000 USD

Contact: Susan Crown, President; (312) 236-6300; (312) 984-1499; AICM@crown-Chicago.com
Internet: http://www.crownmemorial.org/
Sponsor: Arie and Ida Crown Memorial
222 N LaSalle Street, Suite 2000
Chicago, IL 60601

Arizona Commission on the Arts Local Aid **137**
The program is designed to provide general operating support to local arts agencies with adjusted gross operating income in excess of $500,000. A maximum of 5 percent of the audited, adjusted operating income will be provided.
Requirements: The applicant must be an Arizona 501(c)3 nonprofit or a division of an Arizona city government for a minimum of five years and must be the officially designated (city or county) local arts agency; have a full-time paid professional management and evidence of sound management practices; show evidence of long-range planning for the effective use of resources and development of the goals for the organization; and submit an education plan approved by its board that designates financial resources to support the plan.
Restrictions: Funding excludes public art in private development, Percent for Art project costs, and public funds other than city or county (federal or state).
Geographic Focus: Arizona
Date(s) Application is Due: Mar 24
Contact: Patrick Demers, Director; (602) 229-8221; (602) 256-0282; pdemers@ArizonaArts.org
Internet: http://www.arizonaarts.org/guide/gos_local_arts.htm
Sponsor: Arizona Commission on the Arts
417 W Roosevelt Street
Phoenix, AZ 85003

Arizona Commission on the Arts Organization Development Program I Grants **138**
Grants are designed to assist arts organizations with annual operating budgets of generally less than $50,000. Grants may be used for part-time management or artistic salaries, outside consultant services, achieving nonprofit legal status, or marketing projects. Applicants are eligible for awards of up to 10 percent of the organization's current operating budget. Annual deadline dates vary; contact program staff for exact dates.
Requirements: Arizona 501(c)3 tax-exempt organizations, schools, or units of government may apply. An unincorporated Arizona organization may apply through a 501(c)3 fiscal agent or a government organization. Applicants must have at least a one-year track record of ongoing arts programming.
Geographic Focus: Arizona
Date(s) Application is Due: Mar 24
Contact: Shelley Cohn, Executive Director; (602) 255-5882; (602) 256-0282; scohn@ArizonaArts.org
Internet: http://www.arizonaarts.org/guide/gos_level_I.htm
Sponsor: Arizona Commission on the Arts
417 W Roosevelt Street
Phoenix, AZ 85003

Arizona Commission on the Arts Organization Development Program II Grants **139**
Grants are designed for arts organizations that have or intend to hire a professional full-time manager. Applicants are eligible to apply for support of up to 50 percent of the managing director's salary. Annual deadline dates vary; contact program staff for exact dates.
Requirements: Arizona 501(c)3 nonprofits, schools, or units of government may apply. The organization must commit to provide full financial support of a permanent full-time managerial position. A minimum of two years of fiscal and administrative stability must be demonstrated.
Geographic Focus: Arizona
Date(s) Application is Due: Feb 4
Contact: Jo Kobert, (602) 255-5882 or (800) 842-4681; (602) 256-0282; jkobert@ArizonaArts.org
Internet: http://www.arizonaarts.org/guide/gos_level_II.htm
Sponsor: Arizona Commission on the Arts
417 W Roosevelt Street
Phoenix, AZ 85003

Arizona Commission on the Arts Tribal Museum Assessment Program Grants **140**
The program is designed for tribal museums that have or intend to hire a professional, full-time managing director. Applicants are eligible to apply for up to 50 percent of the managing director's salary.
Requirements: Arizona 501(c)3 tax-exempt organizations, schools, and units of tribal government may apply.
Geographic Focus: Arizona
Date(s) Application is Due: Feb 10
Contact: Shelley Cohn, Executive Director; (602) 255-5882; (602) 256-0282; scohn@ArizonaArts.org or info@arizonaarts.org
Internet: http://www.arizonaarts.org/guide/gos_tribal.htm
Sponsor: Arizona Commission on the Arts
417 W Roosevelt Street
Phoenix, AZ 85003

Arizona Community Foundation Grants **141**
The foundation focuses on areas that bring together donor interests with community needs, best practices and respected research to influence long-term systemic change. The foundation's goal is to improve conditions, circumstances and opportunities for people across Arizona and beyond. The foundation focus areas include: arts in the schools; arts in the communities; children, youth and families; campaign for working families; community development; communities for all ages; capacity building; alliance of Arizona nonprofits; strategic partnerships; Hispanics in partnership; and the tapestry community fund. Types of support include general operating support, continuing support, building construction/renovation, equipment acquisition, emergency funds, program development, publication, seed money, scholarship funds, research, technical assistance, and matching funds. For a complete list of criteria, visit the website.
Requirements: Arizona 501(c)3 organizations are eligible as well as public schools, Native American tribes and their component agencies, and selected public programs.
Restrictions: Grants will not be made to individuals; for deficit financing; endowment funds; employee matching gifts; basic research; conferences and seminars; religious organizations for religious purposes; direct lobbying or influencing of elections; tax-supported governmental functions or programs; fund-raising campaigns and expenses; telephone and/or mail solicitation, capital campaigns; or support of veteran, fraternal, and labor organizations.
Geographic Focus: Arizona
Date(s) Application is Due: Apr 1; Oct 1
Contact: Alice McKinney, Grants Administrator; (602) 381-1400 or (800) 222-8221; (602) 381-1575; amckinney@azfoundation.org
Internet: http://www.azfoundation.org/File/static/grant_seekers/initiatives.shtml
Sponsor: Arizona Community Foundation
2201 E Camelback Road, Suite 202
Phoenix, AZ 85016

Arizona Diamondbacks Charities Grants **142**
The major-league baseball franchise awards grants in Arizona to support as wide as possible a variety of charitable causes. Priority will to be given to organizations that fall under the foundation's focus areas of health care for the indigent, homelessness and youth education. Types of support include general support, project grants, donated equipment, employee matching gifts, corporate sponsorships, and speakers. Organizations wishing to apply for a grant can fax a request to the community affairs department.
Requirements: Applicants must be 501(c)3 Arizona-based organizations committed to spending grant proceeds in Arizona.
Geographic Focus: Arizona
Samples: Arizona's Children (Phoenix, AZ)—for a program to provide behavioral health services to children and their families; Golden Gate Community Ctr (Phoenix, AZ)—to help replace evaporative coolers in the center's gymnasium; Make Way for Books (Tucson, AZ)—to promote early literacy in low-income area preschools.
Contact: Program Contact; (602) 462-6500; (602) 462-6575
Internet: http://arizona.diamondbacks.mlb.com/ari/community/foundation.jsp
Sponsor: Arizona Diamondbacks
P.O. Box 2095
Phoenix, AZ 85001

Arizona Foundation for Legal Services and Education Grants 143

The foundation awards general support grants to nonprofit organizations providing legal aid to the poor in Arizona. Application guidelines are available online in the Fall. Initial contact should be letter of inquiry; telephone calls also are welcome.
Requirements: Arizona nonprofits are eligible.
Geographic Focus: Arizona
Amount: 2,000 - 200,000 USD
Samples: Advocates For The Disabled (AZ)—$22,000; Florence Immigrant and Refugee Rights Project (AZ)—$105,000; The Justice Project (AZ)—$6000; William E. Morris Institute for Justice (AZ)—$85,000.
Contact: Lara Slifko, (602) 252-4804; (602) 271-4930; Lara.Slifko@azflse.org
Internet: http://www.azflse.org/AZFLSE/legalservices/ioltagrants.cfm
Sponsor: Arizona Foundation for Legal Services and Education
111 W Monroe, Suite 1800
Phoenix, AZ 85003-1742

Arizona Public Service Corporate Giving Program Grants 144

Grants are awarded to support Arizona nonprofit organizations in the areas of health and human services, community development, arts and culture, education, and environment. The foundation awards support for project grants, capital building funds, research, employee matching gifts, in-kind services, conferences and seminars, and operating support. Applications are accepted on an ongoing basis.
Requirements: Arizona 501(c)3 nonprofits are eligible.
Restrictions: APS Corporate Giving does not fund individual request, charter or private schools, religious, political fraternal, legislative or lobbying efforts to organizations, travel-related or hotel expenses, private or family foundation, private non-profit organizations, salaries and/or debt reduction.
Geographic Focus: Arizona
Samples: Hospice of the Valley (Phoenix, AZ)—for operating support, $10,000; Arizona Bridge to Independent Living (Phoenix, AZ)—for program support, $3000; Arizona Wolf Trap—to sponsor a series of field trips for children to visit performing arts centers.
Contact: Cindy Slick, Manager; (602) 250-4707; (602) 250-2113; Cindy.Slick@aps.com
Internet: http://www.aps.com/main/community/dev/default.html
Sponsor: Arizona Public Service Corporation
P.O. Box 53999, MS 8010
Phoenix, AZ 85072-3999

Arizona Republic Foundation Grants 145

The foundation awards grants in Arizona, with emphasis on the Phoenix metropolitan area, in its focus areas, including arts and culture, children, hunger, homelessness, the elderly, neighborhoods, victims of domestic violence, literacy, and community-based education programs. Support is given for general support, operating expenses, project grants, in-kind services, and donated products. Contact office for deadlines and availability.
Requirements: Arizona nonprofits may apply.
Geographic Focus: Arizona
Samples: Aunt Rita's Foundation (Phoenix, AZ)—AIDS assistance program; East Valley Child Crisis Center (Phoenix, AZ); Valley Citizen's League (Phoenix, AZ); Kids Voting Arizona (Phoenix, AZ).
Contact: Gene D'Adamo, Vice President; (602) 444-8202
Internet: http://www.azcentral.com/arizonarepublic/relations/initiatives.html
Sponsor: Arizona Republic Foundation
200 E Van Buren
Phoenix, AZ 85004

Arizona Republic Newspaper Corporate Contributions Grants 146

The corporation awards grants in Arizona, primarily in the Phoenix metropolitan area, for programs in its areas of interest, including child abuse prevention, domestic violence prevention, education and literacy, arts, drowning prevention, community leadership, regional community building, diversity and cultural awareness. Initiatives focus on the basic needs of individuals, with children as a primary focus. Priority is given to agencies that serve low-income and under-served families and children. Application materials and proposal guidelines are available from the office. Annual deadline dates may vary; contact program staff for exact dates.
Requirements: Arizona nonprofits may apply.
Geographic Focus: Arizona
Amount: 10,000 - 20,000 USD
Samples: Downtown Neighborhood Learning Ctr (Phoenix, AZ)—for general support, $15,000; Area Agency on Aging (Phoenix, AZ)—to support an elderly abuse prevention program, $20,000.
Contact: Laura McBride, Grants Manager; (602) 444-8071; (602) 444-8242
Internet: http://www.azcentral.com/arizonarepublic/relations
Sponsor: Arizona Republic Newspaper
200 E Van Buren
Phoenix, AZ 85004

Arkansas Arts Council Expansion Arts Grants 147

The Expansion Arts program is designed to assist qualified emerging arts organizations in developing increased organizational capacity by helping them acquire or maintain professional administrative personnel.
Requirements: Local arts agencies or single discipline arts organizations exempt from federal income tax under section 501(c)3 of the IRS code. Applicant organizations must have existed for one year prior to application and must produce or present community cultural programming. Entails a maximum three-year commitment. The next three year funding cycle will begin in 2012. Matching funds are to be increased to 2:1 in Year 3 (FY08) in overall organizational expenditures. The cash used for match must be from sources other than the Arkansas Arts Council, the Mid-America Arts Alliance, or the National Endowment for the Arts. Other portions of the proposal not involved in the specific arts council request and its match may be funded by government sources.
Restrictions: Arts Council funds may be spent only to support all or part of the salary of the organization's Executive Director. Expansion Arts grant funds may not be used for other administrative expenses, for artistic or technical staff, or for contracted administrative or artistic costs.
Geographic Focus: Arkansas
Date(s) Application is Due: Feb 16
Amount: 15,000 USD
Contact: Janet Harney, Expansion Arts Program Manager; (501) 324-9782; janet@arkansasheritage.org
Internet: http://www.arkansasarts.com/grants/#4
Sponsor: Arkansas Arts Council
323 Center Street, 1500 Tower Building
Little Rock, AR 72201-2606

Arkansas Arts Council General Operating Support Grants 148

Designed for established, professionally managed not-for-profit organizations whose primary purpose is the production or presentation of the arts. Funds must be spent for non-program activities including salaries of staff, rent, utilities, maintenance of facilities, staff travel and other expenses associated with the operations of the organization.
Requirements: Local arts agencies or single discipline arts organizations with a total operating budget equal to or greater than $50,000 that are exempt from federal income tax under section 501(c)3 of the IRS code. Applicant organizations must have existed for one year prior to application, must produce or present community cultural programming and must have a full- or part-time salaried director on staff. Potential new GOS applicants must send a Letter of Intent to apply. Organizations seeking to become eligible to apply for a General Operating Support grant must first consult with the Arts Council's Grantss Manager for further instructions.
Restrictions: Funding is not available for deficits or start-up costs for new organizations; contingency funds; contributions and donations to other organizations or individuals; building renovations or capital expenditures for facilities; entertainment expenses; tuition for academic study or any form of scholarship or student financial aid; faculty salaries; lobbying expenses; interest and other financial costs.
Geographic Focus: Arkansas
Date(s) Application is Due: Jan 29
Contact: Jess Anthony, Grantss Manager; (501) 324-9768; jess@arkansasheritage.org
Internet: http://www.arkansasarts.com/grants/#8
Sponsor: Arkansas Arts Council
323 Center Street, 1500 Tower Building
Little Rock, AR 72201-2606

Arkansas Arts Council Major Arts Partner (MAP) Grants 149

This grant program is designed for eligible not-for-profit art organizations with three-year budget averages equal to or greater then $1 million. The MAP program is divided into three categories: MAP General Operating

Support, MAP Arts in Education and MAP Major Arts Initiative Laboratory (MAIL).
Requirements: Local arts agencies or single discipline arts organizations with a total operating budget equal to or greater than $1 million that are exempt from federal income tax under section 501(c)3 of the IRS code. Applicant organizations must have received MAP General Operating Support in the previous year or must file a Letter of Intent with the Arkansas Arts Council and receive approval to apply for MAP funding. Specific match requirements are noted in the instructions for each grant category.
Restrictions: Funding is not available for deficits or start-up costs for new organizations; contingency funds; contributions and donations to other organizations or individuals; building renovations or capital expenditures for facilities; entertainment expenses; tuition for academic study or any form of scholarship or student financial aid; faculty salaries; lobbying expenses; interest and other financial costs.
Geographic Focus: Arkansas
Date(s) Application is Due: Jan 29; Feb 5
Amount: 10,000 - 100,000 USD
Contact: Jess Anthony, Grantss Manager; (501) 324-9768; jess@arkansasheritage.org
Internet: http://www.arkansasarts.com/grants/#8
Sponsor: Arkansas Arts Council
323 Center Street, 1500 Tower Building
Little Rock, AR 72201-2606

Arkell Hall Foundation Grants **150**
The primary mission of the foundation is the operation and maintenance of a home for elderly women. Funds that may become available above the needs of the home may be distributed annually to tax-exempt organizations providing services in the target community—Western Montgomery County, NY—with preference given to those active in service to senior citizens, education (higher education, medical education, adult basic education and literacy), religion (Christian, Christian Reformed Church, Lutheran, Methodist, Roman Catholic, the Salvation Army, and United Methodist), and health care. Types of support include capital, challenge, endowment, general support, matching, and seed money grants. Grants are made on a single-year basis and are awarded annually in October or November. It is recommended that requests be submitted between July 1 and September 15. Initial review of requests is performed upon receipt. Results are forwarded to the applicant within one month.
Requirements: IRS 501(c)3 organizations directly impacting the Western Montgomery County, NY, community are eligible.
Restrictions: Requests that do not include written proof of 501(c)3 status will not be considered. Projects or organizations with large service areas, such as national or regional, will not qualify for funding, nor will projects in which the target community is not the primary area of focus.
Geographic Focus: New York
Date(s) Application is Due: Oct 1
Amount: 1,000 - 50,000 USD
Samples: Cornell University, College of Human Ecology (Ithaca, NY)—for general support, $20,000; College of Saint Rose (Albany, NY)—to support scholarships for single mothers, $3000.
Contact: Joseph Santangelo, Vice President; (518) 673-5417; (518) 673-5493
Sponsor: Arkell Hall Foundation
68 Front Street, P.O. Box 240
Canajoharie, NY 13317-0240

Arlington Community Foundation Grants **151**
The foundation awards grants in Arlington to educators and nonprofit organizations for innovative projects that supplement and enrich the learning environment for preschool to adult students. The focus is curriculum enrichment, the arts (musical, dramatic, visual), pursuit of higher education, vocational education, after school and summer programs, life-long learning, environmental issues, parent involvement, and community involvement. The community enhancement grants support arts and humanities, children & families, community improvement, health, housing/homeless & hunger, legal, social services, and senior enrichment. The purpose of the Prompt Response Fund is to enable nonprofit groups in Arlington respond quickly to unanticipated opportunities or unexpected, urgent community needs. Deadlines may vary. Guidelines and applications are available online.
Requirements: Organizations and individuals with projects designed to meet educational needs of Arlington residents are encouraged to apply.
Restrictions: The foundation does not make grants for endowments, capital campaigns, religious purposes, individual debts, or political lobbying.
Geographic Focus: Virginia
Contact: Wanda L. Pierce; (703) 243-4785; (703) 243-4796; info@arlcf.org
Internet: http://www.arlcf.org/grants.html
Sponsor: Arlington Community Foundation
2525 Wilson Boulevard
Arlington, VA 22201

Armstrong McDonald Foundation Grants **152**
The foundation awards grants to eligible nonprofit organizations in its areas of interest, including animal welfare, children and youth, education, special needs, health, and relief and social.
Requirements: 510(c)3 nonprofit organizations, colleges and universities, schools, and school districts are eligible. Application must be downloaded from website.
Restrictions: Grants do not support advocacy organizations, individuals, international organizations, political organizations, or state and local government agencies. The foundation does not fund capital campaigns, salaries/stipends, and multi-year projects. Organization must have received a grant from the foundation within the last five years unless it is located within the states of Arizona or Nebraska. No organization east of the Mississippi is eligible for a grant.
Geographic Focus: All U.S. States
Date(s) Application is Due: Sep 30
Amount: 1,000 - 80,000 USD
Samples: San Diego Zoo (San Diego, CA) $40,000; Tucson Children's Museum (Tucson, AZ) $20,000; Omaha Street School (Omaha, NE) $17,500; UofA Found for Steele Children (Tucson, AZ) $72,900; Saddlebrook Community Outreach (Tucson, AZ) $10,000; Canine Co-Pilots (Flagstaff, AZ) $10,000; NW School for Hearing Impaired (Seattle, WA) $7,500.
Contact: Laurie Bouchard, Vice President; (520) 878-9627; info@ArmstrongMcDonaldFoundation.org
Internet: http://www.armstrongmcdonaldfoundation.org/
Sponsor: Armstrong McDonald Foundation
P.O. Box 70110
Tucson, AZ 85737.01

Arronson Foundation Grants **153**
The foundation supports nonprofit organizations in the areas of religion, including churches (Baptist, Christian, Jewish, Roman Catholic, and Salvation Army) and religious education, higher education, health care, hospices, Jewish welfare, international ministries/missions, and youth. The foundation awards grants primarily in New York, NY; Philadelphia, PA; and Israel. Types of support include endowment funds, general operating support grants, research, scholarships, and seed money grants. Applicants should submit a brief letter of inquiry and include information on the organization and its work. There are no application deadlines.
Requirements: Nonprofit organizations in Pennsylvania, with emphasis on the Philadelphia area, are eligible to apply.
Geographic Focus: Pennsylvania
Amount: 200 - 25,000 USD
Samples: Federation of Allied Jewish Appeal (Philadelphia, PA)—for operating support, $100,000.
Contact: Joseph Kohn, President; (215) 238-1700 or (215) 238-1968; jkohn@kohnswift.com
Sponsor: Arronson Foundation
1 S Broad Street, Suite 2100
Philadelphia, PA 19107

Arthur and Rochelle Belfer Foundation Grants **154**
The foundation awards grants to nonprofit organizations of the Jewish faith, with a focus on New York. Grants are targeted toward programs supporting the elderly and women; education/higher education; institutions such as seminaries, synagogues, and temples; hospitals; Jewish welfare; and medical centers. Types of support include general support grants and fellowships. There are no application deadlines. Applicants should send a brief letter of inquiry describing the program.
Restrictions: Grants are not made to individuals.
Geographic Focus: New York
Amount: 1,000 - 100,000 USD
Samples: Joan S. Brugge, PhD, chair, Department of Cell Biology, arvard Medical School—for breast cancer studies; Dana-Farber Cancer Institute

(Boston, MA)—for general support, $1 million; Anti-Defamation League of B'nai B'rith (New York, NY)—for operating support, $22,000; American Friends of Israel Museum (New York, NY)—for operating support, $5000.
Contact: Robert Belfer, President; (212) 508-6020
Sponsor: Arthur and Rochelle Belfer Foundation
767 Fifth Avenue, 46th Floor
New York, NY 10153-0002

Arthur F. and Alice E. Adams Charitable Foundation Grants 155

The Foundation, managed by a board of governors with the Wachovia Bank acting as corporate governor, offers support in the arts. Primary fields of interest include: performing arts centers and opera. Grants range from $1,000 to $100,000 on average, with giving in both Florida and Tennessee. There are no deadlines, though board members meet in May and November. Applicants should forward a letter describing their need and budget.
Geographic Focus: Florida, Tennessee
Amount: 1,000 - 100,000 USD
Samples: Florida Grand Opera, Miami, Florida, $75,000; New World Symphony, Miami Beach, Florida, $20,000; Opera Memphis, Memphis, Tennessee, $60,000.
Contact: Susan Best, Trust Officer; (305) 789-4615
Sponsor: Arthur F. and Alice E. Adams Charitable Foundation
200 S Biscayne Boulevard, 14th Floor
Miami, FL 33131

Artist Trust GAP Grants 156

The mission of the trust is to support individual artists working in all disciplines in order to enrich community life throughout the state of Washington. Grants for Artist Projects (GAP) provide support for artist-generated projects, which can include but are not limited to the development, completion, or presentation of new work. Projects created in all disciplines are eligible. A multidisciplinary panel of artists and arts professionals from around Washington State select GAP recipients. Applications/guidelines are available online only to Artist Trust members. Non-members may visit Artist Trust's office to pick up guidelines or request paper guidelines by sending a self-addressed, stamped, business-sized envelope to Artist Trust Office: Attn: GAP, 1835 12th Avenue, Seattle, WA, 98122-2437
Requirements: The applicant must be a practicing artist and submit only one application per year; be 18 years of age or older by the application deadline; and be a resident of the state of Washington at the time of application and when the award is granted. Applications must be made in the name of an individual artist.
Restrictions: The applicant must not be a graduate or undergraduate matriculated student enrolled in any degree program. Applications made in the name of collectives, companies, bands, groups, and ensembles will not be accepted.
Geographic Focus: Washington
Date(s) Application is Due: Jun 25
Amount: 1,500 USD
Samples: Heather Dew, Oaksen, Seattle, WA, $1,500— to go towards production costs for a location shooting of interviews throughout the State for the feature documentary, It's About Time (2009); Jason Skipper, Tacoma, WA, $1,500—to help defray the cost of living during, while Jason works on his short story (2009); Alma Garcia, Seattle, WA, $1,500— to fund childcare, allowing the author to transform a short story collection into a novel (2009).
Contact: Monica Miller, Director of Programs; (206) 467-8734, ext. 10; (206) 467-9633; info@artisttrust.org
Internet: http://www.artisttrust.org/grants
Sponsor: Artist Trust
1835 12th Avenue
Seattle, WA 98122-2437

Arts and Science Council Grants 157

The council administers a number of grant programs, allocating funds to affiliate organizations, schools, artists, and arts, science, history, and heritage organizations based on a competitive application process. Types of grants offered are fellowships, basic operating grants, Community Cultural Connections grants, education grants, Grassroots Grants, and the Regional Artist Project Grants. Application forms are available on the website.
Requirements: Artists and organizations in North Carolina's Mecklenburg County, and the City of Charlotte are eligible.
Geographic Focus: North Carolina
Amount: Up to 13,000,000 USD
Contact: Cathy Switalski, Grants Officer; (704) 372-9667, ext. 246; (704) 372-8210; cathy.switalski@artsandscience.org
Internet: http://www.artsandscience.org/index.asp?fuseaction=GrantsServices.GrantPrograms
Sponsor: Arts and Science Council - Charlotte/Mecklenburg
227 W Trade Street, Suite 250
Charlotte, NC 28202

Arts Council of Winston-Salem and Forsyth County Organizational Support Grants 158

The council awards a variety of grants to area organizations and individuals. The Organizational Support Grant is an evaluative program that rewards organizations demonstrating artistic and organizational excellence with financial support for operating and administrative costs. To apply for an Grant, whether a new applicant or current Funded Partner, applicants must attend one of two mandatory information sessions scheduled each year.
Requirements: Only members of The Arts Council of Winston-Salem and Forsyth County with an individual 501(c)3 IRS designation are eligible to apply.
Geographic Focus: North Carolina
Date(s) Application is Due: May 2
Contact: Chris Koenig, Director of Partner & Grantss; (336) 722-2585, ext. 121; (336) 761-8286; ckoenig@intothearts.org
Internet: http://www.intothearts.org/grants/available.asp
Sponsor: Arts Council of Winston-Salem and Forsyth County
226 North Marshall Street
Winston-Salem, NC 27101

ArvinMeritor Foundation Health Grants 159

The foundation provides grants primarily in company-operating locations in the areas of education and training, civic and health, youth organizations, and arts and culture. In the area of Health, the foundation supports programs designed to promote health research, treatment, education, and awareness; and reduce the cost of illness. Types of support include general operating budgets, building funds, continuing support, equipment, and projects. The committee foundation meets every six to eight weeks to review grant requests. Contact program staff for current guidelines.
Requirements: Nonprofit 501(c)3 organizations should submit a one- to two-page letter outlining the purpose and needs of the program, its budget, duration, goals, leadership, and amount requested.
Restrictions: Ineligibility applies to individuals; organizations that limit participation or services based on race, gender, religion, color, creed, age, or national origin; projects without ties to a community that is home to an ArvinMeritor facility; organizations that pose any conflict with the goals and mission of ArvinMeritor, its employees, communities, or products; operating expenses for United Way local agencies, except through the foundation's support of annual United Way campaigns; sponsorships of fund raising activities by individuals (i.e., walk-a-thons); requests for loans or debt retirement; religious or sectarian programs for religious purposes; labor, political, or veterans organizations; fraternal, athletic, or social clubs; or seminars, conferences, trips, and tours.
Geographic Focus: All U.S. States
Contact: Jerry Rush, Senior Director; (248) 435-7907; (248) 245-1031; jerry.rush@arvinmeritor.com
Internet: http://www.arvinmeritor.com/community/community.asp
Sponsor: ArvinMeritor Foundation
2135 W Maple Road
Troy, MI 48084

ArvinMeritor Foundation Human Services Grants 160

The foundation provides grants primarily in company-operating locations in the areas of education and training, civic and health, youth organizations, and arts and culture. In the area of Human Services, the foundation supports programs designed to provide emergency help and critical support toward promoting self-sufficiency. Types of support include general operating budgets, building funds, continuing support, equipment, and projects. The committee foundation meets every six to eight weeks to review grant requests. Contact program staff for current guidelines.
Requirements: Nonprofit 501(c)3 organizations should submit a one- to two-page letter outlining the purpose and needs of the program, its budget, duration, goals, leadership, and amount requested.
Restrictions: Ineligibility applies to individuals; organizations that limit participation or services based on race, gender, religion, color, creed, age,

or national origin; projects without ties to a community that is home to an ArvinMeritor facility; organizations that pose any conflict with the goals and mission of ArvinMeritor, its employees, communities, or products; operating expenses for United Way local agencies, except through the foundation's support of annual United Way campaigns; sponsorships of fund raising activities by individuals (i.e., walk-a-thons); requests for loans or debt retirement; religious or sectarian programs for religious purposes; labor, political, or veterans organizations; fraternal, athletic, or social clubs; or seminars, conferences, trips, and tours.
Geographic Focus: All U.S. States
Contact: Jerry Rush, Senior Director; (248) 435-7907; (248) 245-1031; jerry.rush@arvinmeritor.com
Internet: http://www.arvinmeritor.com/community/community.asp
Sponsor: ArvinMeritor Foundation
2135 W Maple Road
Troy, MI 48084

ASCO State Affiliate Grants **161**
The Program is designed to enable State/Regional Affiliates to engage in activities that will have an overall benefit to their members, ASCO members, other state societies, and the oncology community at-large. The purpose of the Program is to provide financial support to State/Regional Affiliates, which will assist them in implementing specific activities. The grant Program allows ASCO to utilize its strength and expertise in raising funds, taking advantage of resources not available on the state level, and demonstrates ASCO's commitment to strengthening state societies. Possible projects include, but are not limited to, conducting an educational meeting, developing an informational brochure or newsletter, creating a state clinical trials network, taking part in a quality cancer care initiative, or collaborating with a patient advocacy group on an awareness campaign.
Requirements: Grant applicants must be either the current President of Administrator/Executive Director of a state society that is formally affiliated with ASCO. Applications must illustrate a commitment by society leadership in carrying out the requested activities.
Restrictions: Funds should not be used for general operating costs of the state society. Grants will also not be provided for State/Regional Affiliates to carry out lobbying activities.
Geographic Focus: All U.S. States
Date(s) Application is Due: Nov 17
Amount: 10,000 USD
Samples: Denali (Alaska) Oncology Group, $10,000 (2009); Georgia Society of Clinical Oncology, $10,000 (2009); Maryland/DC Society of Clinical Oncology, $10,000 (2009); New York State Society of Medical Oncologists & Hematologists, $10,000 (2009); Northern New England Society of Clinical Oncology, $10,000 (2009).
Contact: Nancy R. Daly, Executive Director; (571) 483-1432; dalyn@asco.org
Internet: http://www.ascocancerfoundation.org/TACF/Professional+Education+and+Support/Cancer+Policy
Sponsor: American Society of Clinical Oncology
1900 Duke Street, Suite 200
Alexandria, VA 22314

Aspen Community Foundation Grants **162**
The foundation awards grants to 501(c)3 nonprofits that serve the residents of Pitkin, Garfield, and west Eagle Counties of Colorado in its areas of interest, including: health and human services (particularly with respect to children and families); education programs that develop thoughtful, self-sufficient citizens who contribute to their communities; and strengthening community to promote positive community integration, inter-ethnic understanding, citizen responsibility, volunteerism, and the capacity of communities to solve problems. Types of support include technical assistance, capital grants, general operating support, continuing support, program development, seed grants, and matching funds. Organizations applying for projects that have not previously received funds from the foundation should review their proposals with the program director in advance of submission.
Requirements: The foundation supports 501(c)3 organizations that enhance the quality of life in Pitkin, Garfield, and west Eagle Counties of Colorado.
Restrictions: The foundation does not consider grants for projects that have been completed or that will be held prior to the allocations decisions; deficits, retirement of debt, or endowments; religious purposes; political campaigns or organizations that publicly take political positions; medical research; organizations primarily supported by tax-derived funding; or conduit organizations. The foundation does not give priority to applications for hospital equipment; conferences; sports/recreational groups; civic, environmental, or media projects; or arts and culture groups.
Geographic Focus: Colorado
Date(s) Application is Due: Mar 3; Oct 6
Amount: 1,000 - 100,000 USD
Contact: Tamara Tormohlen, Executive Director; (970) 925-9300; (970) 920-2892; info@aspencommunityfoundation.org
Internet: http://www.aspencommunityfoundation.org/sitepages/pid25.php
Sponsor: Aspen Community Foundation
110 East Hallam Street, Suite 126
Aspen, CO 81611

AT&T Arts and Culture Grants **163**
The program supports innovative artistic projects by nationally and internationally recognized arts and cultural institutions. The foundation actively collaborates with local AT&T regional offices both to identify and develop proposals that reflect the central interests of AT&T and the AT&T Foundation. These interests include assisting in the creation, production, and presentation of new artistic work; bringing the work of women and artists of diverse cultures to a wider public; and mobilizing new technologies to promote artistic innovation and to increase access to the arts. Guidelines and application are available online.
Requirements: To qualify for consideration, organizations must have been professionally managed for at least five years and must compensate both artistic and managerial personnel.
Restrictions: Grants generally do not support student or amateur groups; arts education programs; individual artists; artistic training or scholarships; film and media productions; competitions; arts programs designed primarily for rehabilitation or therapy; public radio and television stations for unrestricted purposes, equipment acquisition, or program underwriting; science museums or science/technology exhibitions, except through the AT&T:NEAT (New Experiments in Art & Technology) initiative; and the purchase of equipment.
Geographic Focus: All U.S. States
Samples: Arena State (Washington, DC), Children's Theatre Co (Minneapolis, MN), Goodman Theatre (Chicago, IL), Lincoln Ctr Theater (New York, NY), Magic Theatre (San Francisco, CA), and Wilma Theater (Philadelphia, PA)—to support the production of new plays at these theaters and provide related support for the artists and playwrights, $3425,000.
Contact: Program Contact; (212) 387-4801; (212) 387-4882
Internet: http://www.att.com/foundation/guidelines.html#arts
Sponsor: AT&T Foundation
32 Avenue of the Americas, 24th Floor
New York, NY 10013

Atherton Family Foundation Grants **164**
The foundation supports the establishment, maintenance, or promotion of such religious, charitable, educational, benevolent, scientific, or other like purposes in Hawaii. Types of support include general operating grants, equipment acquisition, capital fund projects, seed grants, and theology scholarships to children of ministers in the state. The grant period generally is one year, though some multiyear grants will be awarded. Applications are due one month prior to board meetings. Contact the office for application procedures.
Requirements: Hawaii nonprofit organizations are eligible.
Restrictions: Requests for annual operating support or mature programs, an organization that has already received a grant in the same calendar year (with some exceptions), individuals or for the benefit of specific individuals, loans, grants to endowment funds, private foundations, purpose of lobbying, conferences, festivals and one-time events, re-granting, or individual Department of Education schools not typically funded.
Geographic Focus: Hawaii
Date(s) Application is Due: Feb 1; Apr 1; Aug 1; Oct 1; Dec 1
Amount: 2,000 - 75,000 USD
Samples: La Pietra-Hawaii School for Girls (Honolulu, HI)—for capital campaign, $112,000; Le Jardin Academy (HI)—to purchase computer network equipment, $5000; Hawaii State Committee on Family Violence (HI)—for general operating support, $4000.
Contact: Grant Coordinator; (808) 566-5524 or (888) 731-3863, ext. 524; (808) 521-6286; foundations@hcf-hawaii.org
Internet: http://www.Athertonfamilyfoundation.org
Sponsor: Atherton Family Foundation
1164 Bishop Street, Suite 800
Honolulu, HI 96813

Athwin Foundation Grants 165

Established in 1956, the Athwin Foundation serves the Minneapolis, Street Paul, Bloomington, Minnesota, Wisconsin area. Primary areas of interest include: arts and culture, church related projects, education, and social services. Providing support in the form of: capital campaigns, general/operating support and, program development. Contact the Foundation by submitting a Letter of Inquiry, if they are interested in your project, a formal request will be made & then a proposal maybe submitted.

Requirements: IRS 501(c)3 non-profit organizations are eligible to apply. The foundation prefers applicants to use the Minnesota Common Grant Application Form that can be obtained by calling the Minnesota Council on foundations (612) 338-1989 or by visiting their web site.

Restrictions: Grants do not support: individuals, scholarships, fellowships, or loans.

Geographic Focus: Minnesota, Wisconsin

Date(s) Application is Due: Mar 1

Amount: 2,000 - 100,000 USD

Samples: Foundation of Childrens Hospitals and Clinics of Minnesota, Roseville, MN, $100,000— for general operating support (2008); Neighborhood Involvement Program, Minneapolis, MN, $15,000—for general operating support (2008); Jungle Theater, Minneapolis, MN, $2,000—for general operating support (2008).

Contact: Bruce Bean, Trustee; (952) 915-6165

Sponsor: Athwin Foundation

5200 Wilson Road, Suite 307

Minneapolis, MN 55424-1344

Atkinson Foundation Community Grants 166

Community grants are awarded to agencies located within San Mateo County, CA, or serving residents of the county, with primary emphasis on the North County and Coastside areas. International grants are awarded to nonprofits in Latin America. The goals of the program are to provide opportunities for people to reach their highest potential and to improve the quality of their lives; and to foster the efforts of individuals and families to become socially, economically, and physically self-sufficient. Program priorities are to support nonprofit agencies that serve children, youth, and families; the elderly and the ill; immigrants; the disadvantaged, needy, and homeless; the mentally and physically disabled; and those suffering from drug, alcohol, or physical abuse. Priority also will be given to programs that provide basic human social, physical, and economic services; secondary, vocational, and higher education; adult literacy and basic skills; planning and health education; respite and child care; rehabilitation and job training; counseling; and community enrichment, including environmental conservation. Types of support include general operating support, continuing support, program development, seed grants, scholarship funds, and technical assistance. It is suggested that organizations contact the foundation by phone prior to submission of a grant request to ascertain whether or not the request is within current guidelines.

Requirements: International grants are awarded to organizations working in the Caribbean, Central America, and Mexico; domestic grants are awarded in San Mateo County, CA. 501(c)3 tax-exempt organizations are eligible but those serving residents of San Mateo County, CA, are given preference.

Restrictions: The fund does not make grants to organizations without proof of tax-exempt status; grants to organizations chartered outside the United States; grants, scholarships, or loans to individuals; grants designed to influence legislation; grants for doctoral study or research; grants for travel to conferences or events; grants for media presentations; donations to annual campaigns or special fund-raising events; sponsorship of sports groups; or grants to national or statewide umbrella organizations.

Geographic Focus: California, Antigua & Barbuda, Bahamas, Barbados, Belize, Costa Rica, Cuba, Dominica, Dominican Republic, El Salvador, Grenada, Guatemala, Haiti, Honduras, Jamaica, Mexico, Nicaragua

Date(s) Application is Due: Feb 1; May 1; Aug 1; Nov 1

Amount: 5,000 - 15,000 USD

Contact: Elizabeth Curtis, Administrator; (650) 357-1101; atkinfdn@aol.com

Internet: http://www.atkinsonfdn.org/guidelines.html

Sponsor: Atkinson Foundation

1720 South Amphlett Boulevard, Suite 100

San Mateo, CA 94402-2710

Atlanta Foundation Grants 167

Grants are awarded to assist Georgia charitable and educational institutions to improve the quality of life in Fulton and DeKalb Counties. Primary areas of interest include education, cultural programs, housing, and other charitable giving. Additional areas of support include adult basic education and literacy training; higher education; health care organizations; recreation; and youth, family, and human services. The board meets in August to consider requests.

Requirements: Nonprofit organizations in Georgia's DeKalb and Fulton Counties may apply for grant support.

Restrictions: Funding does not support individuals, scholarships, fellowships, or loans.

Geographic Focus: Georgia

Date(s) Application is Due: Mar 1; Sep 1

Amount: 2,500 - 50,000 USD

Contact: Trustee, c/o Wachovia Bank of Georgia NA; grantinquiriesga@wachovia.com

Internet: http://www.wachovia.com/corp_inst/charitable_services/0,,4269_3296,00.html

Sponsor: Atlanta Foundation

3414 Peachtree Road, 5th Floor, MC GA8023

Atlanta, GA 30326

Atlanta Women's Foundation Grants 168

The foundation awards grants to southern nonprofits to encourage projects that empower women and girls. The foundation supports efforts to promote economic justice, end all forms of violence, and develop alternatives to homelessness and other effects of poverty. Types of support include start-up and operating costs, conferences, fund-raising efforts that show a significant return, films, and small equipment.

Requirements: Southern nonprofits serving one or more of the following counties: Barrow, Bartow, Butts, Carroll, Cherokee, Clayton, Cobb, Cowetta, DeKalb, Douglas, Fayette, Forsyth, Fulton, Gwinnett, Hall, Henry, Newton, Paulding, Pickens, Rockdale, Spalding, and/or Walton are eligible.

Restrictions: Grants are not awarded for endowments, debt reduction, religious groups, building funds, or large equipment (e.g., vehicles).

Geographic Focus: Georgia

Amount: 5,000 - 25,000 USD

Samples: Alternate Life Paths (Atlanta, GA)—for support services and emergency, transitional, and group housing for homeless girls, $15,000; Flint Circuit Council on Family Violence (McDonough, GA)—to provide mental-health services, shelter, and job-placement and relocation assistance to women experiencing domestic violence, $15,000; Fulton County Juvenile Justice Fund (Atlanta, GA)—for an emergency safe house for girls and teenagers who are victims of sexual exploitation, $20,000; International Women's House (Decatur, GA)—to provide emergency housing and mental-health services to refugee and immigrant battered women, $10,000.

Contact: DiShonda Hughes, Program Contact; (404) 577-5000, ext. 104; (404) 589-0000; dhughes@atlantawomen.org or info@atlantawomen.org

Internet: http://awf.techbridge.org/grants/grants.asp

Sponsor: Atlanta Women's Foundation

50 Hurt Plaza, Suite 401

Atlanta, GA 30303

Atran Foundation Grants 169

The foundation supports Jewish nonprofits with a focus on New York and Israel in the areas of higher education, Jewish education, religious education, community services, Jewish welfare, temples, international ministries and missions, temples, medical centers, and women's affairs. Types of support include conferences and seminars, endowment funds, general support, matching funds, multiyear/continuing support, project support, research, scholarships, and seed money grants. The foundation requires that proposals be in writing. Proposals should include the nature of the project, its objectives and significance, time estimate, and budget.

Requirements: 501(c)3 tax-exempt Jewish organizations are eligible.

Restrictions: Grants are not made to individuals.

Geographic Focus: All U.S. States

Date(s) Application is Due: Sep 30

Amount: 250 - 100,000 USD

Samples: Yivo Institute for Jewish Research (New York, NY)—for project support, $90,000; Brandeis University (Waltham, MA)—for operating support, $28,000; Folksbiene Yiddish Theater (New York, NY)—for operating support, $15,000.

Contact: Diane Fischer, President; (212) 505-9677

Sponsor: Atran Foundation

23-25 E 21st Street, 3rd Floor

New York, NY 10010

ATR Foundation One-Year Basic Grants 170

ATR is a public foundation that supports groups in Idaho, Montana, Oregon, Washington, and Wyoming actively working to make institutions and society more democratic, equitable, and just for all. ATR seeks to support projects that bring people together to work for social change and to confront the fundamental problems of American society. Grants support specific projects or general operating expenses.
Geographic Focus: Idaho, Montana, Oregon, Washington, Wyoming
Date(s) Application is Due: Apr 9
Amount: 7,500 USD
Samples: Idaho Rural Council (Boise, ID)—for general support to preserve Idaho's rural way of life by protecting the environment and promoting a more just agricultural economy through organizing, education, and policy development, $12,000.
Contact: Scot Nakagawa, Grants Manager; (503) 267-0515; scot@socialjusticefund.org
Internet: http://www.atrfoundation.org/grants/Default.htm
Sponsor: A Territory Resource Foundation
603 Stewart Street, Suite 1007
Seattle, WA 98101-1264

ATR Foundation Three-Year Support Grants 171

ATR is a public foundation that supports groups in Idaho, Montana, Oregon, Washington, and Wyoming actively working to make institutions and society more democratic, equitable, and just for all. ATR seeks to support projects that bring people together to work for social change and to confront the fundamental problems of American society. Grants are announced in May and may support specific projects or general operating expenses of established organizations. Check website or call for information.
Requirements: Only organizations in Idaho, Montana, Oregon, Washington, and Wyoming may apply. To be eligible for these grants, organizations must have received a spring, fall, major, or one-year basic grant from ATR within the last five years.
Geographic Focus: Idaho, Montana, Oregon, Washington, Wyoming
Date(s) Application is Due: Jan 22
Amount: 15,000 USD
Samples: Chaya (Seattle, WA)—for grassroots organizing and leadership-development activities dealing with violence among immigrants and refugees from South Asia, $45,000 over three years; Environmental Justice Action Group (Portland, OR)—for community-based organizing activities that address air pollution and its effects on the health of Portland residents, $45,000 over three years; Powder River Basin Resource Council (Douglas, WY)—for community-based efforts to conserve Wyoming's land, mineral, and water resources and to protect air quality in the state, $45,000 over three years; VOZ: Worker's Rights Education Project (Portland, OR)—to promote the rights of immigrant workers, particularly day laborers, through organizing, leadership development, and community education, $45,000 over three years.
Contact: Scot Nakaqawa, Grants & Program Director; (503) 206-4919; scot@socialjusticefund.org
Internet: http://www.atrfoundation.org/grants/Default.htm
Sponsor: A Territory Resource Foundation
603 Stewart Street, Suite 1007
Seattle, WA 98101-1264

Auburn Foundation Grants 172

The purpose of the Foundation is to stimulate giving and cooperative leadership among the citizens of Auburn; help improve the lives of all community residents, especially those who are most vulnerable; and enrich the cultural environment and community life. Of special interest are projects that bring together all ages and sections of the town, or that contribute to healthy, active living. Application is available online.
Requirements: Any nonprofit organization that serves residents of Auburn is invited to apply.
Restrictions: Grants will not be awarded to for-profit businesses or expenses already incurred by the applicant.
Geographic Focus: Massachusetts
Date(s) Application is Due: Apr 15
Amount: 5,000 USD
Samples: Bancroft School (Worcester, MA)—for general support, $45,000; New England Science Ctr, Rutland House (Worcester, MA)—for repairs, $20,000; Tower Hill Botanic Garden (Boylston, MA)—for general support, $30,000.
Contact: Lois Smith, Senior Program Officer; (508) 755-0980, ext. 107; lsmith@greaterworcester.org
Internet: http://www.greaterworcester.org/grants/Auburn.htm
Sponsor: Auburn Foundation
370 Main Street, Suite 650
Worcester, MA 01608-1738

Audrey and Sydney Irmas Charitable Foundation Grants 173

The foundation awards grants to eligible nonprofit organizations in its areas of interest, including arts and culture, higher education, homeless and urban issues, hospitals, and Jewish welfare. Grants support long-term, nonrenewable pledges and general operating grants. Most grants are made to Los Angeles County, CA, nonprofits.
Requirements: 501(c)3 nonprofit organizations are eligible.
Geographic Focus: California
Amount: 1,000 - 75,000 USD
Samples: Childrens Hospital of Los Angeles (Los Angeles, CA)—$2810.65; Jewish Family Services (Los Angeles, CA)—$500; Downtown Womens Center (Los Angeles, CA)—$200; Carnegie Museum of Art (Pittsburg, PA)—$25,000.
Contact: Robert Irmas, Administrator; (818) 382-3313; (818) 382-3315; robirm@aol.com
Sponsor: Audrey and Sydney Irmas Charitable Foundation
16830 Ventura Boulevard, Suite 364
Encino, CA 91436-2797

Avon Foundation Speak Out Against Domestic Violence Grants 174

The Foundation is committed to helping end the cycle of domestic violence with the launch of the Speak Out Against Domestic Violence program in 2004. Since launching the program, more than $4 million has been awarded to domestic violence organizations across the U.S. . Speak Out supports awareness, education, direct services and prevention programs.
Requirements: To be considered for funding, you must complete an application and submit it by May 1.
Restrictions: Proposals must come from from non-profit organizations (501(c)3 organizations) and agencies that assist children who have been exposed to domestic violence.
Geographic Focus: All U.S. States
Amount: 10,000 - 50,000 USD
Contact: Christine Jaworsky, (866) 505-2866 or (212) 282-5519; info@avonfoundation.org
Internet: http://www.avoncompany.com/women/speakout/index.html
Sponsor: Avon Foundation
505 Eighth Avenue, Suite 1601
New York, NY 10018-6505

Avon Products Foundation Grants 175

The foundation's two-fold focus is to support education, community and social services, and arts organizations and programs that provide economic opportunities for women and girls; and to support breast cancer and other women's health organizations and programs. The foundation awards grants in cities and regions with a large concentration of representatives and business operations, with the majority of funds going to U.S. -based institutions. National, international, and New York metropolitan area programs are administered through the foundation's headquarters in New York. For regional funding support, refer to the Avon Foundation website.
Requirements: Applying organizations must be tax-exempt; national and municipal organizations are eligible. Request the guidelines brochure prior to submitting a formal proposal.
Restrictions: Grants do not support individuals; memberships; lobbying organizations; political activities and organizations; religious, veteran, or fraternal organizations; fundraising events; and journal advertisements.
Geographic Focus: All U.S. States
Amount: Up to 23,000,000 USD
Contact: Grants Administrator; (866) 505-2866; info@avonfoundation.org
Internet: http://www.avoncompany.com/women/avonfoundation
Sponsor: Avon Products Foundation
1345 Avenue of the Americas
New York, NY 10105

Azadoutioun Foundation Grants 176

The foundation provides general operating and project support for programs and activities in its areas of interest, including adult basic education and

literacy, reading, the environment, human services, and international economic development. Types of support include general operating support and program development. Application forms are not required; initial approach should be by letter. Letters of application are accepted at any time. Grants to support Ammenia's attempt to educate it's citizens in the fields of agriculture and ecology. The foundation operates a farm to assist in educating individuals in the field of agriculture to enable them to operate farms for the benefit of citizens.
Restrictions: Grants are not made to individuals.
Geographic Focus: All U.S. States
Amount: 5,000 - 50,000 USD
Contact: Laurie LeBlanc, (978) 374-5504; lleblanc9498C@aol.com
Sponsor: Azadoutioun Foundation
160 2nd Street
Cambridge, MA 02142

Bacon Family Foundation Grants 177

The foundation awards grants to Colorado nonprofit organizations in its areas of interest, including arts and culture, community development, disabilities, economic development, education, food distribution, environment, health care, historic preservation, homelessness, housing, literacy, recreation/parks, religion, social services, and youth. Types of support include capital campaigns, challenge/matching grants, equipment acquisition, general operating support, project grants, and seed grants. A letter should outline the project or program in brief but sufficient detail for the Foundation to initially evaluate the proposal. There are no application deadlines. The Bacon Family Foundation meets quarterly to consider applications.
Requirements: Colorado nonprofit organizations are eligible. Preference will be given to requests from western Colorado.
Restrictions: No grants are made to individuals.
Geographic Focus: Colorado
Contact: Linda Simpson, (970) 243-3767; lsimpson@wc-cf.org
Internet: http://www.wc-cf.org/bacon.htm
Sponsor: Bacon Family Foundation
P.O. Box 4570
Grand Junction, CO 81502-4570

Bailey-Fischer and Porter Grants 178

The company awards general support grants in its headquarters area in support of education at all levels, the arts, and civic and public affairs. There are no application deadlines. Applicants should submit a brief letter of inquiry.
Requirements: Philadelphia nonprofits are eligible.
Geographic Focus: Pennsylvania
Contact: Maria Novak, (215) 674-6000; (215) 674-7183
Sponsor: Bailey-Fischer and Porter
125 E County Line Road
Warminster, PA 18974

Ball Brothers Foundation Grants 179

The foundation seeks to build and sustain a high quality of life in Indiana by awarding grants to nonprofit organizations in broad subject areas, including elementary, secondary, higher, and adult basic education and literacy skills; cultural activities; community betterment; and health and human services. Usually Muncie and Delaware Counties receive a higher priority for funding than requests from within East Central Indiana or across the state. Types of support include general operations, annual campaigns, capital campaigns, building construction/renovation, program development, conferences and seminars, professorships, publication, curriculum development, research, fellowships, matching funds, seed grants, and technical assistance. Preference will be given to catalytic grants that will stimulate others to participate in problem solving or in matching fund programs and to innovative approaches for addressing either traditional or emerging community needs. Applications are reviewed by the board of directors in January, May, and September of each calendar year. Proposals are encouraged to be submitted from February to May. Grant seekers may send a preliminary proposal, complete proposal, or ask for a personal visit to discuss a potential grant request.
Requirements: Indiana nonprofit institutions and organizations are eligible.
Restrictions: The Foundation will not support: direct assistance to individuals or scholarships; applications coming from outside of Indiana; booster organizations; on-going salary requests of staff personnel to support an organization; services that the community-at-large should normally underwrite (i.e. roads, bus transportation, etc.); capital building projects; research projects (except for philanthropic studies); or unsolicited proposals (all requests must begin with a preliminary proposal).
Geographic Focus: Indiana
Samples: Muncie Center for the Arts (Muncie, IN)—for general operating support, $15,000; Ball State U (Muncie, IN)—for the university's museum, $2 million and artwork valued at $8 million; Minnetrista Cultural Foundation (IN)—for general support, $2.6 million.
Contact: Donna Munchel, (765) 741-5500; (765) 741-5518; donna.munchel@ballfdn.org
Internet: http://www.ballfdn.org
Sponsor: Ball Brothers Foundation
222 South Mulberry Street
Muncie, IN 47305

Ball Brothers Foundation Rapid Grants 180

Ball Brothers Foundation offers funding opportunities for a limited number of Ball Rapid Grants that are designed to provide funding to organizations requiring immediate funding for the following types of needs, but not limited too: continue a project; provide professional development; buy equipment or materials for a project; travel to meet representatives to advance ideas for a current or future project; to formulate a project idea; to carry out a mandated law or event; or for seed money to begin a new project. Generally requests up to $5,000 are considered. Ball Rapid Grants do not fall within the normal granting period. Requests may be submitted at any time between February 1 and November 30; decisions will be made within four business days and awards sent within 7 to 10 business days.
Requirements: Ball Brothers Foundation is restricted by its charter to grants to nonprofit institutions and organizations within Indiana.
Restrictions: The Foundation will not support: direct assistance to individuals or scholarships; applications coming from outside of Indiana; booster organizations; on-going salary requests of staff personnel to support an organization; services that the community-at-large should normally underwrite (i.e. roads, bus transportation, etc.0; capital building projects; research projects (except for philanthropic studies); or unsolicited proposals (all requests must begin with a preliminary proposal).
Geographic Focus: Indiana
Date(s) Application is Due: Nov 30
Amount: 5,000 USD
Contact: Donna Munchel, (765) 741-5500; (765) 741-5518; donna.munchel@ballfdn.org
Internet: http://www.ballfdn.org/index/staff/generalinfo.asp
Sponsor: Ball Brothers Foundation
222 South Mulberry Street
Muncie, IN 47305

BAML Albert W. Rice Charitable Foundation Grants 181

The Albert W. Rice Charitable Foundation was established in 1959 to support and promote quality educational, human-services, and health-care programming for underserved populations. In the area of education, the foundation supports academic access, enrichment, and remedial programming for children, youth, adults, and senior citizens that focuses on preparing individuals to achieve while in school and beyond. In the area of health care, the foundation supports programming that improves access to primary care for traditionally underserved individuals, health education initiatives and programming that impact at-risk populations, and medical research. In the area of human services the foundation tries to meet evolving needs of communities. Currently the foundation's focus is on (but is not limited to) youth development, violence prevention, employment, life-skills attainment, and food programs. Grant requests for general operating support are strongly encouraged. Program support and occasional capital support will also be considered. Special consideration is given to charitable organizations that serve the people of Worcester, Massachusetts, and its surrounding communities. The majority of grants from the Rice Foundation are one year in duration; on occasion, multi-year support is awarded. Applicants must apply online at the grant website. Applicants are strongly encouraged to do the following before applying: review the downloadable state application procedures for additional helpful information and clarifications; review the downloadable online-application guidelines at the grant website; review the foundation's funding history (link is available from the grant website); review the online application questions in advance; and review the list of required attachments. These will generally include: a list of board members, financial statements (audited, reviewed, or compiled by independent auditor); an organization summary; a list of other funding sources; an IRS Determination letter; and

other required documents. All attachments must be uploaded in the online application as PDF, Word, or Excel files. The application deadline for the Albert W. Rice Charitable Foundation is 11:59 p.m. on July 1. Applicants will be notified of grant decisions before September 30.
Requirements: Applicants must have 501(c)3 tax-exempt status.
Restrictions: The foundation does not support requests from individuals, organizations attempting to influence policy through direct lobbying, or any political campaigns.
Geographic Focus: Massachusetts
Date(s) Application is Due: Jul 1
Samples: Big Brothers, Big Sisters of Central Massacusetts Metrowest, Worcester, Massachusetts, $30,000, program development (2010); Youth Opportunities Upheld, Worcester, Massachusetts, $20,000, Dynamic Youth Academy (2010); Legal Assistance Corporation of Central Massachusetts, Worcester, Massachusetts, $20,000 (2010).
Contact: Michealle Larkins, Vice President; (866) 778-6859; michealle.larkins@baml.com
Internet: https://www.bankofamerica.com/philanthropic/fn_search.action
Sponsor: Albert W. Rice Charitable Foundation
225 Franklin Street, 4th Floor, MA1-225-04-02
Boston, MA 02110

BAML Alfred and Tillie Shemanski Testamentary Trust Grants 182

Alfred Shemanski was an immigrant from Poland with little formal education. He understood the struggles of being a stranger in a strange land and became a champion for both Jewish and secular education. His successes never blinded him to the plight of those less fortunate. Mr. Shemanski exercised philanthropy in the purest definition of the word — love of mankind. The Alfred & Tillie Shemanski Trust was established in 1974 to: improve the capacity of and cooperation among Jewish congregations in the City of Seattle, Washington; support interfaith tolerance and understanding; provide scholarship assistance, primarily to the University of Washington and Seattle University; and support and promote quality educational, human-services, and health-care programming for economically disadvantaged individuals and families. Grant requests for general operating support, start-up funding, and prizes or awards are encouraged. Grants from the Shemanski Trust are one year in duration. Application materials are available for download at the grant website. Applicants are strongly encouraged to review the state application guidelines for additional helpful information and clarifications before applying. Applicants are also encouraged to review the trust's funding history (link is available from the grant website). The application deadline for the Shemanski Trust is October 15. Applicants will be notified of grant decisions before November 30.
Requirements: Applicants must serve residents of the Seattle and Puget Sound area.
Restrictions: Requests for fundraising events or sponsorship opportunities will not be considered. The trust does not support requests from individuals, organizations attempting to influence policy through direct lobbying, or any political campaigns.
Geographic Focus: Washington
Date(s) Application is Due: Oct 15
Samples: Seattle University, Seattle, Washington, $45,000, for Schemanski Scholarship Fund (2010); College Success Foundation, Issaquah, Washington, $10,000, scholarship funds (2010); Temple De Hirsch Sinai, Seattle, Washington, $35,000, education initiative (2010); Mockingbird Society, Seattle, Washington, $10,000, Mockingbird Network (foster-youth-led program)(2010).
Contact: Nancy Atkinson, Vice President; (800) 848-7177; nancy.l.atkinson@baml.com
Internet: https://www.bankofamerica.com/philanthropic/fn_search.action
Sponsor: Alfred and Tillie Shemanski Testamentary Trust
800 5th Avenue, WA1-501-33-23
Seattle, WA 98104

BAML Alfred Bersted Foundation Grants 183

The Alfred Bersted Foundation was established in 1972 to support and promote quality educational, human services, and health care programming for underserved populations. The Foundation specifically serves the people of DeKalb, DuPage, Kane, and McHenry counties in Illinois. Application materials are available for download at the grant website. Applicants are strongly encouraged to review the state application guidelines for additional helpful information and clarifications before applying. Applicants are also encouraged to review the foundation's funding history (link is available from the grant website). The foundation has a rolling application deadline. In general, applicants will be notified of grant decisions three to four months after proposal submission.
Requirements: Applicant organizations must have 501(c)3 tax-exempt status and a physical presence in one of the following counties: DeKalb, DuPage, Kane, or McHenry.
Restrictions: The Alfred Bersted Foundation does not make grants to degree-conferring institutions of higher education, religious houses of worship, or organizations testing for public safety. In general, grant requests for endowment campaigns will not be considered.
Geographic Focus: Illinois
Contact: Debra Grand, Senior Vice President; (312) 828-4154; ilgrantmaking@bankofamerica.com
Internet: https://www.bankofamerica.com/philanthropic/fn_search.action
Sponsor: Alfred Bersted Foundation
231 South LaSalle Street, IL1-231-13-32
Chicago, IL 60604

BAML Alfred E. Chase Charitable Foundation Grants 184

The Alfred E. Chase Charitable Foundation was established in 1956 to support and promote quality educational, human-services, and health-care programming for underserved populations. Special consideration is given to charitable organizations that serve the people of the city of Lynn and the North Shore of Massachusetts. The foundation is a generous supporter of the Associated Grant Makers (AGM) Summer Fund which provides operating support for summer camps serving low-income urban youth from Boston, Cambridge, Chelsea, and Somerville. Excluding the grant to the AGM Summer Fund, the typical grant range is $10,000 to $30,000. In the area of education the foundation supports academic access, enrichment, and remedial programming for children, youth, adults, and senior citizens that focuses on preparing individuals to achieve while in school and beyond. In the area of human services the foundation supports organizations meeting the basic needs of all individuals to include but not limited to youth development, violence prevention, employment, life skills attainment, and food programs. In the area of health care, the foundation supports programming that improves access to primary care for traditionally underserved individuals, as well as supporting health education initiatives and programs that impact at-risk populations. Grant requests for general operating support are strongly encouraged. Program support will also be considered. Small, program-related capital expenses may be included in general operating or program requests. The majority of grants from the Chase Charitable Foundation are one year in duration. On occasion, multi-year support is awarded. Applicants must apply online at the grant website. Applicants are strongly encouraged to do the following before applying: review the downloadable Massachusetts state application procedures for additional helpful information and clarifications; review the downloadable online-application guidelines at the grant website; review the foundation's funding history (link is available from the grant website); review the online application questions in advance; and review the list of required attachments. These will generally include: a list of board members, financial statements (audited, reviewed, or compiled by independent auditor); an organization summary; a list of other funding sources; an IRS Determination letter; and other required documents. All attachments must be uploaded in the online application as PDF, Word, or Excel files. The application deadline is 11:59 p.m. on April 1. Applicants will be notified of grant decisions before June 30.
Requirements: Applicants must have 501(c)3 tax-exempt status.
Restrictions: The foundation does not support requests from individuals, organizations attempting to influence policy through direct lobbying, or any political campaigns.
Geographic Focus: Massachusetts
Date(s) Application is Due: Apr 1
Amount: 10,000 - 30,000 USD
Samples: Uphams Corner Community Center, Dorchester, Massachusetts, $15,000 (2010); Massachusetts Advocates for Children, Boston, Massachusetts, $20,000 (2010); Union Social Action Foundation, Cambridge, Massachusetts, $15,000 (2009).
Contact: Miki C. Akimoto, Vice President; (866) 778-6859; miki.akimoto@baml.com
Internet: https://www.bankofamerica.com/philanthropic/fn_search.action
Sponsor: Alfred E. Chase Charitable Foundation
225 Franklin Street, 4th Floor, MA1-225-04-02
Boston, MA 02110

BAML Amelia Sillman Rockwell and Carlos Perry Rockwell Charities Fund Grants 185

The Amelia Sillman Rockwell and Carlos Perry Rockwell Charities Fund was established in 1962 to support and promote quality educational, human-services, and health-care programming for underserved populations. Special consideration is given to charitable organizations that serve children or the elderly. Grant requests for general operating support are strongly encouraged. Program support will also be considered. Small, program-related capital expenses may be included in general operating or program requests. The majority of grants from the Rockwell Charities Fund are one year in duration; on occasion, multi-year support is awarded. Applicants must apply online at the grant website. Applicants are strongly encouraged to do the following before applying: review the downloadable state application procedures for additional helpful information and clarifications; review the downloadable online-application guidelines at the grant website; review the foundation's funding history (link is available from the grant website); review the online application questions in advance; and review the list of required attachments. These will generally include: a list of board members, financial statements (audited, reviewed, or compiled by independent auditor); an organization summary; a list of other funding sources; an IRS Determination letter; and other required documents. All attachments must be uploaded in the online application as PDF, Word, or Excel files. The application deadline for the Rockwell Charities Fund is 11:59 p.m. on February 1. Applicants will be notified of grant decisions before May 31.
Requirements: Applicants must have 501(c)3 tax-exempt status.
Restrictions: The trust does not support requests from individuals, organizations attempting to influence policy through direct lobbying, or any political campaigns.
Geographic Focus: Massachusetts
Date(s) Application is Due: Feb 1
Samples: Elizabeth Stone House, Jamaica Plains, Massachusetts, $10,000, general operating support (2010); First Congregational Church, South Windsor, Connecticut, $1,000, for favored charity of Rockwell (2010); Rogerson Communities, Boston, Massachusetts, $10,000, Adult Day Health Programs (2010).
Contact: Miki C. Akimoto, Vice President; (866) 778-6859; miki.akimoto@baml.com
Internet: https://www.bankofamerica.com/philanthropic/fn_search.action
Sponsor: Amelia Sillman Rockwell and Carlos Perry Rockwell Charities Fund
225 Franklin Street, 4th Floor, MA1-225-04-02
Boston, MA 02110

BAML Anne J. Caudal Foundation Grants 186

The Anne J. Caudal Foundation was established in 2007 to benefit disabled veterans of any time or of any branch of the United States armed forces and to perpetuate the recognition or memory of their accomplishments or sacrifice in time of war or otherwise. Special consideration is given to organizations that serve disabled veterans in New Jersey. Grant requests for general operating support are strongly encouraged. Program support will also be considered. Small, program-related capital expenses may be included in general operating or program requests. The majority of grants from the Caudal Foundation are one year in duration. On occasion, multi-year support is awarded. Application materials are available for download from the grant website. The application deadline for the Anne J. Caudal Foundation is July 1. Applicants are encouraged to review the state application guidelines for additional helpful information and clarification before applying. Applicants are also encouraged to view the foundation's funding history (link is available at the grant website). Applicants will be notified of grant decisions before August 15.
Requirements: Applicants must have 501(c)3 tax-exempt status.
Restrictions: The foundation does not support requests from individuals, organizations attempting to influence policy through direct lobbying, or any political campaigns.
Geographic Focus: All U.S. States
Date(s) Application is Due: Jul 1
Samples: United States Wounded Soldiers Foundation, Dallas, Texas, $12,500 (2010); Our Military Kids, McLean, Virginia, $12,500 (2010); Jewish Family Service of New Jersey, Wayne, New Jersey, $12,500 (2010).
Contact: Maryann Clemente, Vice President; (646) 855-0786; maryann.clemente@baml.com
Internet: https://www.bankofamerica.com/philanthropic/fn_search.action
Sponsor: Anne J. Caudal Foundation
One Bryant Park, NY1-100-28-05
New York, NY 10036

BAML Ann L. and Carol Green Rhodes Charitable Trust 187

Ann Rhodes and her mother Carol Green Rhodes were both very supportive of the local arts throughout their lives. Their charitable trust was established in 2010 to honor their love of theater and the local community. Ann was also an animal-lover who fed the wild animals that came into her backyard each night. The Ann L. and Carol Green Rhodes Charitable Trust supports charitable organizations focused on the arts, museums open to the public, theaters and other performing arts organizations, organizations whose primary purpose is to support the arts, organizations providing human services; and occasional support for animal-related charitable organizations. Ms. Rhodes requested that preference be given to organizations that she supported in her lifetime. Applicants must apply online at the grant website. Applicants are strongly encouraged to do the following before applying: review the downloadable state application procedures for additional helpful information and clarifications; review the downloadable online-application guidelines at the grant website; review the trust's funding history (link is available from the grant website); review the online application questions in advance; and review the list of required attachments. These will generally include: a list of board members, financial statements (audited, reviewed, or compiled by independent auditor); an organization summary; a list of other funding sources; an IRS Determination letter; and other required documents. All attachments must be uploaded in the online application as PDF, Word, or Excel files. This trust has bi-annual application deadlines of March 31 and September 30. Applications must be submitted by 11:59 p.m. on the deadline dates.
Requirements: Applicants must have 501(c)3 tax-exempt status.
Restrictions: This trust is restricted to Tarrant County. The trust does not support requests from individuals, organizations attempting to influence policy through direct lobbying, or any political campaigns.
Geographic Focus: Texas
Date(s) Application is Due: Mar 31; Sep 30
Amount: 3,000 - 25,000 USD
Samples: Casa Manana Musicals, Fort Worth, Texas, $75,000, general operating support (2010); Imagination Celebration of Fort Worth, Fort Worth, Texas, $10,000, to fund arts education programming for youth (2010); Amphibian Productions, Fort Worth, Texas, $45,500, to underwrite production of "Wittenberg" (2010).
Contact: Mark J. Smith, Philanthropic Relationship Manager; (817) 390-6028; tx.philanthropic@baml.com
Internet: https://www.bankofamerica.com/philanthropic/fn_search.action
Sponsor: Ann L. and Carol Green Rhodes Charitable Trust
500 West 7th Street, 15th Floor, TX1-497-15-08
Fort Worth, TX 76102-1700

BAML Carl R. Hendrickson Family Foundation Grants 188

The Carl R. Hendrickson Family Foundation was established in 1991 to support and promote quality educational, human-services, and health-care programming for underserved populations. Carl R. Hendrickson was a Chicago entrepreneur who, along with his father and brothers, built the Hendrickson Trucking Company. Carl and his wife, Agnes, had one child, Virginia. Virginia followed in her father's footsteps by leading the family business and by serving as President of the Hendrickson Foundation. Virginia died in 1995, leaving no heirs. The Hendricksons prided themselves on their entrepreneurial spirit, having been in the forefront of the trucking business by inventing the tandem truck. Reflecting the Hendrickson family's strong Christian faith, special consideration is given to charitable organizations that help individuals meet their basic needs while also addressing their spiritual needs. Preference is given to organizations or programs that approach their mission from an entrepreneurial perspective. The majority of grants from the Hendrickson Family Foundation are one year in duration. Application guidelines as well as a link to the downloadable application are given at the grant website. Applicants are also encouraged to review the Illinois state application guidelines and the foundation's funding history before applying (links are available from the grant website). The deadline for application to the Carl R. Hendrickson Family Foundation is July 31. Grant decisions will be made by December 31.
Requirements: Applicants must have 501(c)3 tax-exempt status. Applications must be mailed.
Restrictions: In general, grant requests for individuals, endowment campaigns or capital projects will not be considered. The foundation does not support requests from individuals, organizations attempting to influence policy through direct lobbying, or any political campaigns.
Geographic Focus: Illinois
Date(s) Application is Due: Jul 31

Samples: WorldVenture, Littleton, Colorado, $10,000 (2010); Chicago Lighthouse for People Who Are Blind or Visually Impaired, Chicago, Illinois, $10,000 (2010); Erie Family Health Network, Chicago, Illinois, $10,000 (2010).
Contact: Debra Grand, Senior Vice President; (312) 828-4154; ilgrantmaking@bankofamerica.com
Internet: https://www.bankofamerica.com/philanthropic/fn_search.action
Sponsor: Carl R. Hendrickson Family Foundation
231 South LaSalle Street, IL1-231-13-32
Chicago, IL 60604

BAML Charles H. Farnsworth Trust Grants **189**

The Charles H. Farnsworth Trust was established in 1930 to assist older adults to live in dignity and with independence. In describing the purpose of his legacy, Mr. Farnsworth made clear his interest in supporting housing, particularly in developing affordable housing options, and in providing support services to older adults. Program interests include: development of housing, especially housing with support services; services for elderly persons (i.e. health care, homemaker assistance, and nutritional support to enable the elderly to continue living in the community); and research, planning, and communication to better inform individuals, institutions, and the community at large on ways to improve the quality and quantity of housing and support services for seniors. Capital grants related to construction or renovation of housing for older adults is of particular interest. While general operating grants are provided, requests for support for new or special projects/programs are preferred. Planning grants investigating strategies for the development of supportive housing for the elderly are encouraged. Capital grants generally range between $25,000 and $250,000. General operating grants are usually no more than $10,000. Applicants must apply online at the grant website. Applicants are strongly encouraged to do the following before applying: review the downloadable state application procedures for additional helpful information and clarifications; review the downloadable online-application guidelines at the grant website; review the trust's funding history (link is available from the grant website); review the online application questions in advance; and review the list of required attachments. These will generally include: a list of board members, financial statements (audited, reviewed, or compiled by independent auditor); an organization summary; a list of other funding sources; an IRS Determination letter; and other required documents. All attachments must be uploaded in the online application as PDF, Word, or Excel files. The Farnsworth Trust has biannual deadlines of February 1 and October 15. Applications must be submitted by 11:59 p.m. on the deadline dates. Grant applicants for the February deadline will be notified of grant decisions by May 31 and applicants for the October deadline will be notified of grant decisions by December 31.
Restrictions: Grant oportunities are restricted to the Greater Boston area.
Geographic Focus: Massachusetts
Date(s) Application is Due: Feb 1; Oct 15
Amount: 10,000 - 250,000 USD
Samples: Hearth, Boston, Massachusetts, $100,000 (2010); Greater Boston Chinese Golden Age Center, Boston, Massachusetts, $289,346 (2010); Friends of Saint Josephs Food Pantry, Salem, Massachusetts, $10,000 (2010).
Contact: Michealle Larkins, Vice President; (866) 778-6859; michealle.larkins@baml.com
Internet: https://www.bankofamerica.com/philanthropic/fn_search.action
Sponsor: Charles H. Farnsworth Trust
225 Franklin Street, 4th Floor, MA1-225-04-02
Boston, MA 02110

BAML Charles H. Pearson Foundation Grants **190**

The Charles H. Pearson Foundation Fund was established in 1922 to support and promote quality educational, human-services, and health-care programming for underserved populations. In the area of education, the fund supports academic access, enrichment, and remedial programming for children, youth, adults, and senior citizens that focuses on preparing individuals to achieve while in school and beyond. In the area of health care, the fund supports programming that improves access to primary care for traditionally underserved individuals, health education initiatives and programming that impact at-risk populations, and medical research. In the area of human services the fund tries to meet evolving needs of communities. Currently the fund's focus is on (but is not limited to) youth development, violence prevention, employment, life-skills attainment, and food programs. Grant requests for general operating support are strongly encouraged. Program support will also be considered. Small, program-related capital expenses may be included in general operating or program requests. The majority of grants from the Pearson Fund are one year in duration; on occasion, multi-year support is awarded. Applicants must apply online at the grant website. Applicants are strongly encouraged to do the following before applying: review the downloadable state application procedures for additional helpful information and clarifications; review the downloadable online-application guidelines at the grant website; review the foundation's funding history (link is available from the grant website); review the online application questions in advance; and review the list of required attachments. These will generally include: a list of board members, financial statements (audited, reviewed, or compiled by independent auditor); an organization summary; a list of other funding sources; an IRS Determination letter; and other required documents. All attachments must be uploaded in the online application as PDF, Word, or Excel files. The application deadline for the Charles H. Pearson Foundation Fund is 11:59 p.m. on July 1. Applicants will be notified of grant decisions before September 30.
Requirements: Applicants must have 501(c)3 tax-exempt status.
Restrictions: In general, capital requests are not advised. The fund does not support endowment campaigns, events such as galas or award ceremonies, and costs of fundraising events. The fund does not support requests from individuals, organizations attempting to influence policy through direct lobbying, or any political campaigns.
Geographic Focus: Massachusetts
Date(s) Application is Due: Jul 1
Samples: United Way of Massachusetts Bay, Boston, Massachusetts, $36,000, (2010); Berklee College of Music, Boston, Massachusetts, $25,000, Berklee City Music Faculty Outreach Program to help underserved youth in the Boston Public Schools (2010); Community Legal Services and Counseling Center, Cambridge, Massachusetts, general operating support to provide free legal services and affordable mental health services to underserved families and individuals (2010).
Contact: Michealle Larkins, Vice President; (866) 778-6859; michealle.larkins@baml.com
Internet: https://www.bankofamerica.com/philanthropic/fn_search.action
Sponsor: Charles H. Pearson Foundation Fund
225 Franklin Street, 4th Floor, MA1-225-04-02
Boston, MA 02110

BAML Charles Nelson Robinson Fund Grants **191**

The Charles Nelson Robinson Fund was established in 1970 to support and promote quality educational, human-services, and health-care programming for underserved populations in Hartford, Connecticut. Preference is given to organizations that provide human services programming to underserved adults. Grants from the Robinson Fund are one year in duration. Applicants must apply online at the grant website. Applicants are strongly encouraged to do the following before applying: review the downloadable state application procedures for additional helpful information and clarifications; review the downloadable online-application guidelines at the grant website; review the foundation's funding history (link is available from the grant website); review the online application questions in advance; and review the list of required attachments. These will generally include: a list of board members, financial statements (audited, reviewed, or compiled by independent auditor); an organization summary; a list of other funding sources; an IRS Determination letter; and other required documents. All attachments must be uploaded in the online application as PDF, Word, or Excel files. The Charles Nelson Robinson Fund has an annual deadline of 11:59 p.m. on February 15. Applicants will be notified of grant decisions by letter within two to three months of the proposal deadline.
Requirements: Applicant organizations must have 501(c)3 tax-exempt status and have a principal office located in the city of Hartford, Connecticut.
Restrictions: Grant requests for capital projects will not be considered. Applicants will not be awarded a grant for more than three consecutive years. The fund does not support requests from individuals, organizations attempting to influence policy through direct lobbying, or any political campaigns.
Geographic Focus: Connecticut
Date(s) Application is Due: Feb 15
Samples: Hartford Interval House, Hartford, Connecticut, $5,000, general operating support (2010); Loaves and Fishes Ministries, Hartford, Connecticut, $4,000, general operating support (2010); Bulkeley High School, Hartford, Connecticut, $3,000, VOAG Horse Care Program (2011).
Contact: Carmen Britt, Senior Foundation Officer; (860) 657-7019; carmen.britt@baml.com
Internet: https://www.bankofamerica.com/philanthropic/fn_search.action

Sponsor: Charles Nelson Robinson Fund
200 Glastonbury Boulevard, Suite # 200, CT2-545-02-05
Glastonbury, CT 06033-4056

BAML Christine and Katharina Pauly Charitable Trust Grants 192

The Christine and Katharina Pauly Charitable Trust was established in 1985 to support and promote quality educational, health, and human-services programming for underserved populations. Special consideration is given to charitable organizations that serve the needs of children or older adults. The majority of grants from the Pauly Trust are one year in duration. Applicants must apply online at the grant website. Applicants are strongly encouraged to do the following before applying: review the downloadable state application procedures for additional helpful information and clarifications; review the downloadable online-application guidelines at the grant website; review the trust's funding history (link is available from the grant website); review the online application questions in advance; and review the list of required attachments. These will generally include: a list of board members, financial statements (audited, reviewed, or compiled by independent auditor); an organization summary; a list of other funding sources; an IRS Determination letter; and other required documents. All attachments must be uploaded in the online application as PDF, Word, or Excel files. The application deadline for the Christine and Katharina Pauly Charitable Trust is 11:59 p.m. on September 1. Applicants will be notified of grant decisions by December 31. The Christine and Katharina Pauly Charitable Trust was created under the wills of Ms. Hazel Katharina Pauly and Ms. Frieda Christine Oleta Pauly.
Requirements: Applicants must have 501(c)3 tax-exempt status.
Restrictions: In general, grant requests for individuals, endowment campaigns, or capital projects will not be considered. The Fund will consider requests for general operating support only if the organization's operating budget is less than $1 million. The trust does not support requests from individuals, organizations attempting to influence policy through direct lobbying, or any political campaigns.
Geographic Focus: Missouri
Date(s) Application is Due: Sep 1
Contact: George Thorn; (312) 828-4154; ilgrantmaking@bankofamerica.com
Internet: https://www.bankofamerica.com/philanthropic/fn_search.action
Sponsor: Christine and Katharina Pauly Charitable Trust
231 South LaSalle Street, IL1-231-13-32
Chicago, IL 60604

BAML Clara Blackford Smith and W. Aubrey Smith Charitable Foundation Grants 193

The Clara Blackford Smith & W. Aubrey Smith Charitable Foundation was established in 1978. Mrs. Smith was a well-known benefactor of health care. The foundation was established under her will to support and promote quality education, health-care, and human-services programming for underserved populations. Special consideration is given to charitable organizations that serve the people of Grayson County, Texas. The foundation makes an annual grant to Denison High School in Denison, Texas to provide college scholarship assistance for deserving graduates. The majority of grants from the Smith Charitable Foundation are one year in duration; on occasion, multi-year support is awarded. Applicants must apply online at the grant website. Applicants are strongly encouraged to do the following before applying: review the downloadable state application procedures for additional helpful information and clarifications; review the downloadable online-application guidelines at the grant website; review the foundation's funding history (link is available from the grant website); review the online application questions in advance; and review the list of required attachments. These will generally include: a list of board members, financial statements (audited, reviewed, or compiled by independent auditor); an organization summary; a list of other funding sources; an IRS Determination letter; and other required documents. All attachments must be uploaded in the online application as PDF, Word, or Excel files. The Clara Blackford Smith & W. Aubrey Smith Charitable Foundation has four deadlines annually: March 1, June 1, September 1, and December 1. Applications must be submitted by 11:59 p.m. on the deadline dates. Grant applicants are notified as follows: March deadline applicants will be notified of grant decisions by June 30; June applicants will be notified by September 30; September applicants will be notified by December 31; and December applicants will be notified by March 31 of the following year.
Requirements: Applicants must have 501(c)3 tax-exempt status.
Restrictions: The foundation does not support requests from individuals, organizations attempting to influence policy through direct lobbying, or any political campaigns.
Geographic Focus: Texas
Date(s) Application is Due: Mar 1; Jun 1; Sep 1; Dec 1
Samples: Denison Independent School District, Denison, Texas, $55,000, for Smart Boards for DISD classrooms (2011); Loy Park Improvement Association, Denison, Texas, $36,000, installation of ceiling fans in the Major Arena (2011); Grayson County Shelter, Denison, Texas, $50,000, general operating support (2011).
Contact: David Ross, Senior Vice President; tx.philanthropic@baml.com
Internet: https://www.bankofamerica.com/philanthropic/fn_search.action
Sponsor: Clara Blackford Smith and W. Aubrey Smith Charitable Foundation
901 Main Street, 19th Floor, TX1-492-19-11
Dallas, TX 75202-3714

BAML Clark and Ruby Baker Foundation Grants 194

The Clark and Ruby Baker Foundation was established to address a number of charitable concerns. The Baker family cared deeply about the Methodist Church and founded the Foundation to support Methodist affiliated, higher educational institutions in rural or small towns; charitable organizations that serve infirm, deserving, and aged ministers; economically disadvantaged and deserving children; and orphans and orphanages. The Foundation also provides support to charitable organizations that extend financial aid to the sick and infirm receiving medical treatment in any hospital or clinic in the state of Georgia. Capital support may be considered for the following purposes: for construction of educational facilities at a college or university; for clinics and hospitals; for libraries; and for any building with a charitable use. Grants from the Clark and Ruby Baker Foundation are primarily one year in duration; on occasion, multi-year support is awarded. Applicants must apply online at the grant website. Applicants are strongly encouraged to do the following before applying: review the downloadable state application procedures for additional helpful information and clarifications; review the downloadable online-application guidelines at the grant website; review the foundation's funding history (link is available from the grant website); review the online application questions in advance; and review the list of required attachments. These will generally include: a list of board members, financial statements (audited, reviewed, or compiled by independent auditor); an organization summary; a list of other funding sources; an IRS Determination letter; and other required documents. All attachments must be uploaded in the online application as PDF, Word, or Excel files. The Clark and Ruby Baker Foundation application deadline is 11:59 p.m. on June 1. Applicants will be notified of grant decisions by letter within one to two months after the deadline.
Requirements: Applicants must have 501(c)3 tax-exempt status.
Restrictions: The foundation does not support requests from individuals, organizations attempting to influence policy through direct lobbying, or any political campaigns.
Geographic Focus: Georgia
Date(s) Application is Due: Jun 1
Samples: LaGrange College, LaGrange, Georgia, $8,750 (2010); United Methodist Childrens Home, Decatur, Georgia, $18,000, continuing support (2010); Collins Memorial United Methodist Church, Atlanta, Georgia, $10,000, continuing support (2010).
Contact: Quanda Allen, Vice President; (404) 264-1377; quanda.allen@baml.com
Internet: https://www.bankofamerica.com/philanthropic/fn_search.action
Sponsor: Clark and Ruby Baker Foundation
3414 Peachtree Road, N.E., Suite 1475, GA7-813-14-04
Atlanta, GA 30326-1113

BAML Deborah Munroe Noonan Memorial Fund Grants 195

The Deborah Munroe Noonan Memorial Fund was established in 1949 by her son, Walter Noonan, to support and promote quality educational, human-services, and health-care programming for underserved populations. Grant requests for general operating support are strongly encouraged. Program support will also be considered. Small, program-related capital expenses may be included in general operating or program requests. To better support the capacity of nonprofit organizations, multi-year funding requests are strongly encouraged. Applicants must apply online at the grant website. Applicants are strongly encouraged to do the following before applying: review the downloadable state application procedures for additional helpful information and clarifications; review the downloadable online-application guidelines at the grant website; review the foundation's funding history (link is available from the grant website); review the online application questions in advance; and review the list of required attachments. These will generally include: a list of board members, financial statements (audited, reviewed, or compiled by independent auditor); an organization summary; a list of other funding sources; an IRS Determination letter; and other required documents. All attachments must be uploaded in the online application as PDF, Word, or Excel files. The application deadline for the Deborah Munroe Noonan Memorial Fund is 11:59 p.m. on July 1. Applicants will be notified of grant decisions before September 30.

Requirements: Applicants must have 501(c)3 tax-exempt status and serve the people of Greater Boston.

Restrictions: The fund does not support requests from individuals, organizations attempting to influence policy through direct lobbying, or any political campaigns.

Geographic Focus: Massachusetts

Date(s) Application is Due: Jul 1

Samples: Community Music Center of Boston, Boston, Massachusetts, $21,000, general operating support of CMCB's 100th anniversary and to support a continuum of music education programs and music therapy for children, teens, adults (2010); Family and Childrens Services of Greater Lynn, Lynn, Massachusetts, $25,000, capacity-building for program services that promote early literacy (2010); Brockton Neighborhood Health Center, Brockton, Massachusetts, $29,000, Certified Medical Interpreter Program (2010).

Contact: Miki C. Akimoto, Vice President; (866) 778-6859; miki.akimoto@baml.com

Internet: https://www.bankofamerica.com/philanthropic/fn_search.action

Sponsor: Deborah Munroe Noonan Memorial Fund
225 Franklin Street, 4th Floor, MA1-225-04-02
Boston, MA 02110

BAML Doree Taylor Charitable Foundation **196**

The mission of the Doree Taylor Charitable Foundation is to support charitable organizations that: provide relief to people the form of basic needs (including the provision of food, housing, shelter); promote the humane care of animals; provide health-care services for the underserved; and conduct Public radio or television. Occasional support will also be provided to colleges and universities as well as to environmental charitable organizations in Maine. The foundation will make grants throughout Maine, but has a priority for charitable organizations or projects located in the areas of Boothbay Harbor, Southport, and Brunswick. From time to time, the foundation may support organizations with a national scope. Grant requests for general operating support or program support are strongly encouraged and preferred; however, small capital requests may also be considered. The majority of grants from the Taylor Foundation are one year in duration; on occasion, multi-year support is awarded. Applicants must apply online at the grant website. Applicants are strongly encouraged to do the following before applying: review the downloadable state application procedures for additional helpful information and clarifications; review the downloadable online-application guidelines at the grant website; review the foundation's funding history (link is available from the grant website); review the online application questions in advance; and review the list of required attachments. These will generally include: a list of board members, financial statements (audited, reviewed, or compiled by independent auditor); an organization summary; a list of other funding sources; an IRS Determination letter; and other required documents. All attachments must be uploaded in the online application as PDF, Word, or Excel files. The application deadline for the Doree Taylor Charitable Foundation is 11:59 p.m. on April 1. Applicants will be notified of grant decisions before August 31.

Requirements: 501(c)3 charitable organizations and municipalities which meet the mission criteria are eligible to apply.

Restrictions: The foundation will not contribute to endowments or consider grant requests from individuals, organizations attempting to influence policy through direct lobbying, or political campaigns.

Geographic Focus: Maine

Date(s) Application is Due: Apr 1

Contact: Miki C. Akimoto, Vice President; (866) 778-6859; miki.akimoto@baml.com

Internet: https://www.bankofamerica.com/philanthropic/fn_search.action

Sponsor: Doree Taylor Charitable Foundation
225 Franklin Street, 4th Floor, MA1-225-04-02
Boston, MA 02110

BAML Edward and Ellen Roche Relief Foundation Grants **197**

The Edward & Ellen Roche Relief Foundation was established in 1953 to support organizations serving disadvantaged women and children. Recognizing the diverse array of programs that serve these populations, the Roche Relief Foundation has chosen to focus its limited resources on programs that address one or more of the following: housing needs of women and families; economic security of low-income women; violence against women; and child welfare. Grant requests for general operating support or program/project support are strongly encouraged. Applicants must apply online at the grant website. Applicants are strongly encouraged to do the following before applying: review the downloadable state application procedures for additional helpful information and clarifications; review the downloadable online-application guidelines at the grant website; review the foundation's funding history (link is available from the grant website); review the online application questions in advance; and review the list of required attachments. These will generally include: a list of board members, financial statements (audited, reviewed, or compiled by independent auditor); an organization summary; a list of other funding sources; an IRS Determination letter; and other required documents. All attachments must be uploaded in the online application as PDF, Word, or Excel files. The application deadline for the Edward & Ellen Roche Relief Foundation is 11:59 p.m. on July 31. Grant decisions will be made by December 31.

Requirements: Applicants must have 501(c)3 tax-exempt status and serve the residents of New York City.

Restrictions: The Roche Relief Foundation generally does not provide funding for projects in the areas of health care or disabilities, to individual schools or child care centers; or to organizations with annual budgets in excess of $10 million. In general, grant requests for endowment campaigns, capital projects, or research will not be considered. The foundation does not support requests from individuals, organizations attempting to influence policy through direct lobbying, or any political campaigns.

Geographic Focus: All U.S. States

Date(s) Application is Due: Jul 31

Samples: Global Partnerships, Seattle, Washington, $20,000, pilot program to use microfinance institutions as a delivery channel to provide essential health services to poor women and girls in Latin America (2010); Hot Bread Kitchen, Brooklyn, New York, $20,000, for programs to train and build the long-term economic security of immigrant women in New York City; Good Shepherd Services, New York, New York, $15,000, Safe Homes Project (2010).

Contact: Sara Rosen, Assistant Vice President; (646) 743-0425; sara.rosen@baml.com

Internet: https://www.bankofamerica.com/philanthropic/fn_search.action

Sponsor: Edward and Ellen Roche Relief Foundation
One Bryant Park, NY1-100-28-05
New York, NY 10036

BAML Edward N. and Della L. Thome Memorial Foundation Direct Services Grants **198**

The Edward N. and Della L. Thome Memorial Foundation was established in 2002 by Robert P. Thome to honor the memory of his parents, Edward and Della Thome. The mission of the foundation is twofold: to advance the health of older adults through (1) the support of direct service projects and (2) medical research on diseases and disorders affecting older adults. The goal of the foundation's direct services program is to support organizations in Maryland and Michigan that provide direct services addressing one or more of the following critical issues facing older adults: health care, housing, family services, neighborhood involvement, workforce opportunities, and aging with dignity at home. Grant requests for general operating support are strongly encouraged. Program support will also be considered. Program-related capital expenses may be included in general operating or program requests. To better support the capacity of nonprofit organizations, multi-year funding requests are encouraged. Applicants must apply online at the direct-services grant website above. Applicants are strongly encouraged to do the following before applying: review the downloadable state application procedures for additional helpful information and clarifications; review the downloadable online-application guidelines at the grant website; review the foundation's funding history (link is available from the grant website); review the online application questions in advance; and review the list of required attachments. These will generally include: a list of board members, financial statements (audited, reviewed, or compiled by independent auditor); an organization summary; a list of other funding sources; an IRS Determination letter; and other required documents. All attachments must be uploaded in the online application as PDF, Word, or Excel files. There is a rolling deadline for organizations applying for a

direct services grant from the Thome Foundation. Applicants will generally be notified of grant decisions within six months of proposal submission. The research aspect of the foundation's mission is managed by the Medical Foundation, a Division of Health Resources in Action (HRIA). Applicants interested in applying for research funding through the Edward N. and Della L. Thome Memorial Foundation's research program will find application information at the Medical Foundation's website.
Requirements: The Thome Foundation direct services program is most interested in expanding services for older adults. Requests should clearly state how many previously-unserved older adults will now be served as a result of funding from the Thome Foundation. Applicants must have 501(c)3 tax-exempt status.
Restrictions: The foundation does not support requests from individuals, organizations attempting to influence policy through direct lobbying, or any political campaigns.
Geographic Focus: Maryland, Michigan
Contact: George Thorn; (312) 828-4154; ilgrantmaking@bankofamerica.com
Internet: https://www.bankofamerica.com/philanthropic/fn_search.action
Sponsor: Edward N. and Della L. Thome Memorial Foundation
231 South LaSalle Street, IL1-231-13-32
Chicago, IL 60604

BAML Elizabeth Morse Genius Charitable Trust Grants **199**
Established in 1992, the Elizabeth Morse Genius Charitable Trust honors the memory of Elizabeth Morse Genius, the daughter of Charles Hosmer Morse, a nineteenth century Chicago financier, industrialist, and land developer. The trust supports and promotes charitable organizations that: encourage the principles of individual self-reliance, self-sacrifice, thrift, industry, and humility; relieve human suffering through scientific research and education regarding disease; provide assistance to youths with troubled childhoods and emotional disorders; attend to the care of the elderly; provide assistance to humankind during times of natural and man-made disasters; foster individual self-worth and dignity, with a broad emphasis on the classical fine arts; develop physical health and spiritual well-being through vigorous athletic activity; and promote world peace and understanding through the improvement of national and international means of travel by air, rail, and sea. The majority of grants from the Genius Charitable Trust are one year in duration; on occasion, multi-year support is awarded. Applicants must first submit a letter of inquiry. Downloadable application guidelines are available at the Sponsor's website by clicking on the "Grant Application Process Button", or prospective applicants may also call the second phone number given to obtain application information. A synopsis of the grant, contact information, and a link to the trust's giving history is available at the grant website. The Elizabeth Morse Genius Charitable Trust has a rolling application deadline. In general, applicants will be notified of grant decisions three to four months after proposal submission.
Requirements: Nonprofit organizations serving Chicago and Cook County are eligible.
Restrictions: The trust generally does not fund individuals; organizations outside the metropolitan Chicago city area; organizations attempting to influence policy through direct lobbying; capital campaigns; endowment campaigns; or political campaigns.
Geographic Focus: Illinois
Amount: 10,000 - 300,000 USD
Samples: WTTW Channel 11, Chicago, Illinois, $145,400 (2010); Chicago High School for the Arts, Chicago, Illinois, $125,000 (2010); Chicago Community Trust, Chicago, Illinois, $50,000 (2010).
Contact: Kristin Carlson Vogen, Senior Vice President; (312) 828-5554 or (312) 828-1029; ilgrantmaking@bankofamerica.com
Internet: https://www.bankofamerica.com/philanthropic/fn_search.action
Sponsor: Elizabeth Morse Genius Charitable Trust
231 South LaSalle Street, IL1-231-13-32
Chicago, IL 60604

BAML Florian O. Bartlett Trust Grants **200**
The Florian O. Bartlett Trust was established in 1937 to support and promote quality educational, human services, and health care programming for underserved populations. The application deadline for the Florian O. Bartlett Trust is April 1. Applicants will be notified of grant decisions before June 30. Grant requests for general operating support are strongly encouraged. Program support will also be considered. Small, program-related capital expenses may be included in general operating or program requests. The majority of grants from the Bartlett Trust are 1 year in duration. On occasion, multi-year support is awarded.
Geographic Focus: Massachusetts
Date(s) Application is Due: Apr 1
Contact: Michealle Larkins; (866) 778-6859; michealle.larkins@baml.com
Internet: https://www.bankofamerica.com/philanthropic/fn_search.action
Sponsor: Florian O. Bartlett Trust
225 Franklin Street, 4th Floor, MA1-225-04-02
Boston, MA 02110

BAML Frank B. Hazard General Charity Fund **201**
The Frank B. Hazard General Charity Fund was established in 1924 to support charitable organizations that work to improve the lives of "the poor, or the poor sick." Organizations receiving support from the fund must be managed and/or governed by individuals a majority of whom are of the Protestant religious faith. Grant requests for general operating support or program support are strongly encouraged. The majority of grants from the Hazard General Charity Fund are one year in duration. Applicants must apply online at the grant website. Applicants are strongly encouraged to do the following before applying: review the downloadable state application procedures for additional helpful information and clarifications; review the downloadable online-application guidelines at the grant website; review the trust's funding history (link is available from the grant website); review the online application questions in advance; and review the list of required attachments. These will generally include: a list of board members, financial statements (audited, reviewed, or compiled by independent auditor); an organization summary; a list of other funding sources; an IRS Determination letter; and other required documents. All attachments must be uploaded in the online application as PDF, Word, or Excel files. The application deadline for the Frank B. Hazard General Charity Fund is 11:59 p.m. on December 1. Applicants will be notified of grant decisions before January 31 of the following year.
Requirements: Applicants must have 501(c)3 tax-exempt status.
Restrictions: The Hazard General Charity Fund specifically supports charitable organizations that serve the people of Providence, Rhode Island. The fund does not support requests from individuals, organizations attempting to influence policy through direct lobbying, or any political campaigns.
Geographic Focus: Rhode Island
Date(s) Application is Due: Dec 1
Samples: Family Service, Providence, Rhode Island, $10,000 (2010); Community Preparatory School, Providence, Rhode Island, $17,000 (2010); Rhode Island Free Clinic, Providence, Rhode Island, $10,000 (2010).
Contact: Emma Greene, Director; (617) 434-0329; emma.m.greene@baml.com
Internet: https://www.bankofamerica.com/philanthropic/fn_search.action
Sponsor: Frank B. Hazard General Charity Fund
225 Franklin Street, 4th Floor, MA1-225-04-02
Boston, MA 02110

BAML Frank Reed and Margaret Jane Peters Memorial Fund I Grants **202**
The Frank Reed & Margaret Jane Peters Memorial Fund I was established in 1935 to support and promote quality educational, human-services, and health-care programming for underserved populations. Special consideration is given to charitable organizations that serve youth and children. The Peters Memorial Fund I is a generous supporter of the Associated Grant Makers (AGM) Summer Fund. The AGM Summer Fund is a collaborative group of donors that provides operating support for summer camps serving low-income urban youth from Boston, Cambridge, Chelsea, and Somerville. Excluding the grant made to the AGM Summer Fund, the typical grant range is $10,000 to $40,000. Grant requests for general operating support are strongly encouraged. Program support will also be considered. Small, program-related capital expenses may be included in general operating or program requests. The majority of grants from the Peters Memorial Fund I are one year in duration; on occasion, multi-year support is awarded. Applicants must apply online at the grant website. Applicants are strongly encouraged to do the following before applying: review the downloadable state application procedures for additional helpful information and clarifications; review the downloadable online-application guidelines at the grant website; review the foundation's funding history (link is available from the grant website); review the online application questions in advance; and review the list of required attachments. These will generally include: a list of board members, financial statements (audited, reviewed, or compiled by independent auditor); an organization summary; a list of other funding sources; an IRS Determination letter; and other required documents. All attachments must be uploaded in the online application as PDF, Word,

or Excel files. The application deadline for the Frank Reed & Margaret Jane Peters Memorial Fund I is 11:59 p.m. on September 1. Applicants will be notified of grant decisions before November 30.
Requirements: Applicants must have 501(c)3 tax-exempt status.
Restrictions: The fund does not support requests from individuals, organizations attempting to influence policy through direct lobbying, or any political campaigns.
Geographic Focus: Massachusetts
Date(s) Application is Due: Sep 1
Amount: 10,000 - 40,000 USD
Samples: Generations, Inc., Boston, Massachusetts, $20,000, general operating support (2010); Boston Scholars Program, Boston, Massachusetts, $15,000, general operating support (2010); Family Service, Lawrence, Massachusetts, $15,000, Youth Mentoring Department program development (2010).
Contact: Miki C. Akimoto, Vice; (866) 778-6859; miki.akimoto@baml.com
Internet: https://www.bankofamerica.com/philanthropic/fn_search.action
Sponsor: Frank Reed and Margaret Jane Peters Memorial Fund I
225 Franklin Street, 4th Floor, MA1-225-04-02
Boston, MA 02110

BAML Frank Reed and Margaret Jane Peters Memorial Fund II Grants 203
The Frank Reed & Margaret Jane Peters Memorial Fund II was established in 1935 to support and promote quality educational, human-services, and health-care programming for underserved populations. In the area of education, the fund supports academic access, enrichment, and remedial programming for children, youth, adults, and senior citizens that focuses on preparing individuals to achieve while in school and beyond. In the area of health care, the fund supports programming that improves access to primary care for traditionally underserved individuals, health education initiatives and programming that impact at-risk populations, and medical research. In the area of human services the fund tries to meet evolving needs of communities. Currently the fund's focus is on (but is not limited to) youth development, violence prevention, employment, life-skills attainment, and food programs. Grant requests for general operating support are strongly encouraged. Program support will also be considered. Small, program-related capital expenses may be included in general operating or program requests. The majority of grants from the Peters Memorial Fund II are one year in duration; on occasion, multi-year support is awarded. Applicants must apply online at the grant website. Applicants are strongly encouraged to do the following before applying: review the downloadable state application procedures for additional helpful information and clarifications; review the downloadable online-application guidelines at the grant website; review the foundation's funding history (link is available from the grant website); review the online application questions in advance; and review the list of required attachments. These will generally include: a list of board members, financial statements (audited, reviewed, or compiled by independent auditor); an organization summary; a list of other funding sources; an IRS Determination letter; and other required documents. All attachments must be uploaded in the online application as PDF, Word, or Excel files. The application deadline for the Frank Reed & Margaret Jane Peters Memorial Fund II is 11:59 p.m. on July 1. Applicants will be notified of grant decisions before September 30.
Requirements: Applicants must have 501(c)3 tax-exempt status.
Restrictions: In general, capital requests are not advised. The fund does not support endowment campaigns, events such as galas or award ceremonies, and costs of fundraising events. The fund does not support requests from individuals, organizations attempting to influence policy through direct lobbying, or any political campaigns.
Geographic Focus: Massachusetts
Date(s) Application is Due: Jul 1
Samples: Epiphany School, Dorchester, Massachusetts, $20,000, general operating support (2010); Esther R. Sanger Center for Compassion, Wollaston, Massachusetts, $15,000, for general operating support (2010); Boston Learning Center, Boston, Massachusetts, $20,000, general operating support (2010).
Contact: Michealle Larkins, Vice President; (866) 778-6859; michealle.larkins@baml.com
Internet: https://www.bankofamerica.com/philanthropic/fn_search.action
Sponsor: Frank Reed and Margaret Jane Peters Memorial Fund II
225 Franklin Street, 4th Floor, MA1-225-04-02
Boston, MA 02110

BAML Frank W. and Carl S. Adams Memorial Fund Grants 204
The Frank W. and Carl S. Adams Memorial Fund was established in 1925 to support and promote quality educational, human services, and health care programming for underserved populations. Annual gifts are also awarded to the Harvard University Medical School and the Massachusetts Institute of Technology for student scholarships. Grant requests for general operating support are strongly encouraged. Program support will also be considered. Small, program-related capital expenses may be included in general operating or program requests. To better support the capacity of nonprofit organizations, multi-year funding requests are strongly encouraged. The application deadline is February 1. Applicants will be notified of grant decisions before May 31.
Requirements: 501(c)3 organizations serving the residents of Massachusetts are eligible to apply.
Geographic Focus: Massachusetts
Date(s) Application is Due: Feb 1
Contact: Miki C. Akimoto, Vice President; (866) 778-6859; miki.akimoto@baml.com
Internet: https://www.bankofamerica.com/philanthropic/fn_search.action
Sponsor: Frank W. and Carl S. Adams Memorial Fund
225 Franklin Street, 4th Floor, MA1-225-04-02
Boston, MA 02110

BAML Fred & Gretel Biel Charitable Trust 205
The Fred & Gretel Biel Charitable Trust was established in 2004 to support and promote quality educational, human-services, and health-care programming for underserved populations. Special consideration is given to organizations that provide food and clothing to low-income individuals and families. Consideration is also given to organizations that serve the economically disadvantaged through the provision of housing, legal assistance, or day-care services. Grant requests for general operating and capital support are encouraged. Grants from the Biel Charitable Trust are one year in duration. Application materials are available for download at the grant website. Applicants are strongly encouraged to review the state application guidelines for additional helpful information and clarifications before applying. Applicants are also encouraged to review the trust's funding history (link is available from the grant website). The application deadline for the Biel Charitable Trust is May 1. Applicants will be notified of grant decisions by June 30.
Requirements: The Biel Charitable Trust typically supports organizations serving the people of King and Snohomish Counties in the Puget Sound region of Washington. Occasionally grants will be made outside of the Puget Sound area. Applicant organizations must have 501(c)3 tax-exempt status.
Restrictions: Requests to assist with debt retirement or to correct an operating deficit will not be considered. Applicants who have received a grant for three consecutive years must wait two years before reapplying to the trust. The trust does not support requests from individuals, organizations attempting to influence policy through direct lobbying, or any political campaigns.
Geographic Focus: Washington
Date(s) Application is Due: May 1
Samples: Edmonds School District, Lynnwood, Washington, $2,500 (2010); Haller Lake Christian Health Clinic, Seattle, Washington, $5,000 (2010); North Helpline, Seattle, Washington, $2,500 (2010).
Contact: Nancy Atkinson, Vice President; (800) 848-7177 or (206) 358-0912; nancy.l.atkinson@baml.com
Internet: https://www.bankofamerica.com/philanthropic/fn_search.action
Sponsor: Fred & Gretel Biel Charitable Trust
800 5th Avenue
Seattle, WA 98104

BAML Frederick McDonald Trust Grants 206
The Frederick McDonald Trust was established in 1950 to support and promote quality educational, human-services, and health-care programming for underserved populations. Grant requests for general operating support, program, project and capital support will be considered. The majority of grants from the McDonald Trust are one year in duration. On occasion, multi-year support is awarded. Applicants must apply online at the grant website. Applicants are strongly encouraged to do the following before applying: review the downloadable state application procedures for additional helpful information and clarifications; review the downloadable online-application guidelines at the grant website; review the trust's funding history (link is available from the grant website); review the online application questions in advance; and review the list of required attachments. These will generally include: a list of board members, financial statements (audited, reviewed, or

compiled by independent auditor); an organization summary; a list of other funding sources; an IRS Determination letter; and other required documents. All attachments must be uploaded in the online application as PDF, Word, or Excel files. The application deadline for the Frederick McDonald Trust is 11:59 p.m. on May 1. Applicants will be notified of grant decisions before August 31.
Requirements: Applicants must have 501(c)3 tax-exempt status.
Restrictions: Grants are made only to those organizations located in, or serving the people of Albany City. The trust does not support requests from individuals, organizations attempting to influence policy through direct lobbying, or any political campaigns.
Geographic Focus: New York
Date(s) Application is Due: May 1
Samples: Equinox, Albany, New York, $15,000 (2010); Albany Center for Economic Success, Albany, New York, $10,000 (2010); Girls, Inc. of the Greater Capital Region, Schenectady, New York, $15,000 (2010).
Contact: Christine O'Donnell, Vice President; (646) 855-1011; christine.l.o'donnell@baml.com
Internet: https://www.bankofamerica.com/philanthropic/fn_search.action
Sponsor: Frederick McDonald Trust
One Bryant Park, NY1-100-28-05
New York, NY 10036

BAML George E. Hatcher, Jr. and Ann Williams Hatcher Foundation Grants 207

The George E. Hatcher and Ann Williams Hatcher Foundation was created to support charitable organizations that provide for the relief of diseased people and the relief of human suffering which is due to disease, ill health, physical weakness, physical disability and/or physical injury. In addition, the foundation supports organizations that aid in the promotion and prolongation of life and that support the principle of dying with dignity. Grants from George E. Hatcher and Ann Williams Hatcher Foundation are primarily one year in duration; on occasion, multi-year support is awarded. Applicants must apply online at the grant website. Applicants are strongly encouraged to do the following before applying: review the downloadable state application procedures for additional helpful information and clarifications; review the downloadable online-application guidelines at the grant website; review the foundation's funding history (link is available from the grant website); review the online application questions in advance; and review the list of required attachments. These will generally include: a list of board members, financial statements (audited, reviewed, or compiled by independent auditor); an organization summary; a list of other funding sources; an IRS Determination letter; and other required documents. All attachments must be uploaded in the online application as PDF, Word, or Excel files. The George E. Hatcher and Ann Williams Hatcher Foundation application deadline is 11:59 p.m. on May 31. Applicants will be notified of grant decisions by letter within one to two months after the deadline.
Requirements: Disbursements are authorized to institutions or organizations located in the Middle Georgia area (Bibb County & surrounding communities) which provide health care and/or shelter for individuals (especially children) who cannot otherwise obtain such services due to circumstances beyond their control. A breakdown of number/percentage of people served by specific counties is required on the online application.
Restrictions: The foundation does not support requests from individuals, organizations attempting to influence policy through direct lobbying, or any political campaigns.
Geographic Focus: Georgia
Date(s) Application is Due: May 31
Samples: Macon Volunteer Clinic, Macon, Georgia, $25,000 (2010); Rebuilding Macon, Macon, Georgia, $25,000 (2010); Methodist Home of the South Georgia Conference, Macon, Georgia, $10,000 (2010).
Contact: Quanda Allen, Vice President; (404) 264-1377; quanda.allen@baml.com
Internet: https://www.bankofamerica.com/philanthropic/fn_search.action
Sponsor: George E. Hatcher, Jr. and Ann Williams Hatcher Foundation
3414 Peachtree Road, N.E., Suite 1475, GA7-813-14-04
Atlanta, GA 30326-1113

BAML George J. and Effie L. Seay Foundation Grants 208

The George J. & Effie L. Seay Foundation was established in 1957 to support and promote programs and services provided by qualifying charitable organizations in the Commonwealth of Virginia. Grants from the Seay Foundation are one year in duration. Application materials are available for download at the grant website. Applicants are strongly encouraged to review the state application guidelines for additional helpful information and clarifications before applying. Applicants are also encouraged to review the trust's funding history (link is available from the grant website). The George J. & Effie L. Seay Foundation has biannual deadlines of May 1 and November 1. Applicants for the May deadline will be notified of grant decisions by June 30. Applicants for the November deadline will be notified by February 28 of the following year.
Requirements: Applications must be mailed. Applicants must be classified by the Internal Revenue Service (IRS) as a 501(c)3 public charity.
Restrictions: Because requests for support usually exceed available resources, organizations are advised to apply to either the Morgan Trust or the Seay Foundation. An organization normally will not be considered for a subsequent grant from either the Morgan Trust or the Seay Foundation until at least 3 years after the date of the last grant payment. The Seay Foundation makes grants primarily for programs and projects designed to provide specific services or training. Requests for general operating grants will not be considered. The foundation does not support requests from individuals, organizations attempting to influence policy through direct lobbying, or any political campaigns.
Geographic Focus: Virginia
Date(s) Application is Due: May 1; Nov 1
Samples: Black History Museum and Cultural Center, Richmond, Virginia, $10,000, for exhibition guides and teacher workshops (2010); School of the Performing Arts, Richmond, Virginia, $15,000 (2009); Virginia Historical Society, Richmond, Virginia, $20,000 (2009).
Contact: Sarah Kay, Vice President; (804) 788-2673; sarah.kay@baml.com
Internet: https://www.bankofamerica.com/philanthropic/fn_search.action
Sponsor: George J. and Effie L. Seay Foundation
1111 E. Main Street, VA2-300-12-92
Richmond, VA 23219

BAML George W. Wells Foundation Grants 209

The George W. Wells Foundation was established in 1934 to support and promote quality educational, human-services, and health-care programming for underserved populations. In the area of education, the fund supports academic access, enrichment, and remedial programming for children, youth, adults, and senior citizens that focuses on preparing individuals to achieve while in school and beyond. In the area of health care, the fund supports programming that improves access to primary care for traditionally underserved individuals, health education initiatives and programming that impact at-risk populations, and medical research. In the area of human services the fund tries to meet evolving needs of communities. Currently the foundation's focus is on (but is not limited to) youth development, violence prevention, employment, life-skills attainment, and food programs. Special consideration is given to charitable organizations that serve the people of Southbridge, Massachusetts, and its surrounding communities. Grant requests for general operating support are strongly encouraged. Program support will also be considered. Small, program-related capital expenses may be included in general operating or program requests. The majority of grants from the Wells Foundation are one year in duration; on occasion, multi-year support is awarded. Applicants must apply online at the grant website. Applicants are strongly encouraged to do the following before applying: review the downloadable state application procedures for additional helpful information and clarifications; review the downloadable online-application guidelines at the grant website; review the foundation's funding history (link is available from the grant website); review the online application questions in advance; and review the list of required attachments. These will generally include: a list of board members, financial statements (audited, reviewed, or compiled by independent auditor); an organization summary; a list of other funding sources; an IRS Determination letter; and other required documents. All attachments must be uploaded in the online application as PDF, Word, or Excel files. The application deadline for the George W. Wells Foundation is 11:59 p.m. on October 15. Applicants will be notified of grant decisions before December 31.
Requirements: Applicants must have 501(c)3 tax-exempt status.
Restrictions: The foundation does not support requests from individuals, organizations attempting to influence policy through direct lobbying, or any political campaigns.
Geographic Focus: Massachusetts
Date(s) Application is Due: Oct 15
Samples: Southern Worcester County Rehabilitation Center, Webster, Massachusetts, $20,000, Assistance to establish a ceramics and crockery business as adjunct to current day support and vocational program options

(2010); Youth Opportunities Upheld, Worcester, Massachusetts, $18,500, Pregnant and Parenting Teens Program (2010); Family Health and Social Service Center, Worcester, Massachusetts, $25,000, for Oral Health Services for low-income residents in the Southbridge Area (2010).
Contact: Miki C. Akimoto, Vice President; (866) 778-6859; miki.akimoto@baml.com
Internet: https://www.bankofamerica.com/philanthropic/fn_search.action
Sponsor: George W. Wells Foundation
225 Franklin Street, 4th Floor, MA1-225-04-02
Boston, MA 02110

BAML Grace Bersted Foundation Grants **210**
The Grace Bersted Foundation was established in 1986 to support and promote quality educational, human services, and health care programming for underserved populations. Special consideration is given to charitable organizations that serve the needs of children or the disabled. Applicants must apply online at the grant website. Applicants are strongly encouraged to do the following before applying: review the downloadable state application procedures for additional helpful information and clarifications; review the downloadable online-application guidelines at the grant website; review the foundation's funding history (link is available from the grant website); review the online application questions in advance; and review the list of required attachments. These will generally include: a list of board members, financial statements (audited, reviewed, or compiled by independent auditor); an organization summary; a list of other funding sources; an IRS Determination letter; and other required documents. All attachments must be uploaded in the online application as PDF, Word, or Excel files. The deadline for application to the Foundation is 11:59 p.m. on September 1, and grant decisions will be made by December 31.
Requirements: Applicant organizations must have 501(c)3 tax-exempt status and an office located in one of the following counties: DuPage, Kane, Lake, or McHenry.
Restrictions: The foundation does not support requests from individuals, organizations attempting to influence policy through direct lobbying, or any political campaigns.
Geographic Focus: Illinois
Date(s) Application is Due: Sep 1
Contact: Debra Grand, Senior Vice President; (312) 828-4154; ilgrantmaking@bankofamerica.com
Internet: https://www.bankofamerica.com/philanthropic/fn_search.action
Sponsor: Grace Bersted Foundation
231 South LaSalle Street, IL1-231-13-32
Chicago, IL 60604

BAML Guy I. Bromley Trust Grants **211**
The Guy I. Bromley Trust was established in 1964 to support and promote quality educational, cultural, human-services, and health-care programming. In the area of education the trust supports programming that: promotes effective teaching; improves the academic achievement of, or expands educational opportunities for disadvantaged students; improves governance and management; strengthens nonprofit organizations, school leadership, and teaching; and bolsters strategic initiatives of area colleges and universities. In the area of culture the trust supports programming that: fosters the enjoyment and appreciation of the visual and performing arts; strengthens humanities and arts-related education programs; provides affordable access; enhances artistic elements in communities; and nurtures a new generation of artists. In the area of human services, the trust supports programming that: strengthens agencies that deliver critical human services and maintains the community's safety net; and helps agencies respond to federal, state, and local public policy changes. In the area of health the trust supports programming that: improves the delivery of health care to the indigent, uninsured, and other vulnerable populations; and addresses health and health-care problems that intersect with social factors. Grant requests for general operating support and program support will be considered. Grants from the trust are one year in duration. There are no application deadlines for the Bromley Trust. Proposals are reviewed on an ongoing basis. Downloadable application materials are available at the grant website. Applicants are encouraged to review the downloadable state guidelines at the grant website for further information and clarification before applying. Applicants are also encouraged to view the trust's funding history (link is available at the grant website).
Requirements: Applicants must have 501(c)3 tax-exempt status and serve the residents of Atchison, Kansas and the Greater Kansas City Metropolitan area. Applications must be mailed.
Restrictions: Grant requests for capital support will not be considered. The trust does not support requests from individuals, organizations attempting to influence policy through direct lobbying, or any political campaigns.
Geographic Focus: All U.S. States
Samples: Humane Society of Atchison, Atchison, Kansas, $5,000 (2010); Benedictine College, Atchison, Kansas, $30,000 (2010); Community of Christ, Independence, Missouri, $30,000 (2010).
Contact: Spence Heddens, Market President; (816) 292-4301; Spence.heddens@baml.com
Internet: https://www.bankofamerica.com/philanthropic/fn_search.action
Sponsor: Guy I. Bromley Trust
1200 Main Street, 14th Floor, P.O. Box 219119
Kansas City, MO 64121-9119

BAML Hahl Proctor Charitable Trust Grants **212**
Before moving to Midland, Hahl Proctor studied voice in a Chicago school of music. Although very active in the ranching industry, she continued to pursue her music interests through her church and other civic organizations. In addition to her vocation and avocation, Hahl was an attractive, popular, and generous woman who loved to entertain. She established a trust in her will to provide a continuous source of financial assistance to worthwhile charities. The trust focuses on charitable organizations dedicated to children and families, the arts, and education. Applicants must apply online at the grant website. Applicants are strongly encouraged to do the following before applying: review the downloadable state application procedures for additional helpful information and clarifications; review the downloadable online-application guidelines at the grant website; review the trust's funding history (link is available from the grant website); review the online application questions in advance; and review the list of required attachments. These will generally include: a list of board members, financial statements (audited, reviewed, or compiled by independent auditor); an organization summary; a list of other funding sources; an IRS Determination letter; and other required documents. All attachments must be uploaded in the online application as PDF, Word, or Excel files. The application deadline is 11:59 p.m. on May 15.
Requirements: Applicants must have 501(c)3 tax-exempt status and serve residents of the Permian Basin Area.
Restrictions: The trust does not support requests from individuals, organizations attempting to influence policy through direct lobbying, or any political campaigns.
Geographic Focus: Texas
Date(s) Application is Due: May 15
Amount: 2,000 - 20,000 USD
Samples: Midland Festival Ballet, Midland, Texas, $10,000, for season performances and program opportunities (2011); Safe Place of the Permian Basin, Midland, Texas, $10,000, for emergency shelter operations (2011); Texas FLOW Youth Ministry, Midland, Texas, $10,000, general operating support (2011).
Contact: Mark J. Smith, Philanthropic Relationship Manager; (817) 390-6028; tx.philanthropic@baml.com
Internet: https://www.bankofamerica.com/philanthropic/fn_search.action
Sponsor: Hahl Proctor Charitable Trust
500 West 7th Street, 15th Floor, TX1-497-15-08
Fort Worth, TX 76102-4700

BAML Harry S. Black and Allon Fuller Fund Grants **213**
The Harry S. Black & Allon Fuller Fund was established in 1930 to support quality health-care and human-services programming for underserved populations. The grantmaking focus is in the areas of health care and physical disabilities. The fund supports access to health care; health education; health/wellness promotion and disease prevention; health policy analysis and advocacy; access programs for physically disabled individuals; disability policy analysis and advocacy; workforce development programs; and programs that improve quality of life for the disabled. Emphasis will be placed on programs serving low-income communities. Grant requests for general operating support or program/project support are strongly encouraged. Applicants must apply online at the grant website. Applicants are strongly encouraged to do the following before applying: review the downloadable state application procedures at the grant website; review the downloadable online-application guidelines at the grant website; review the foundation's funding history (link is available from the grant website); review the online application questions in advance; and review the list of required attachments. These will generally include: a list of board members, financial statements (audited, reviewed, or compiled by independent auditor); an organization summary; a list of other

funding sources; an IRS Determination letter; and other required documents. All attachments must be uploaded in the online application as PDF, Word, or Excel files. The Harry S. Black & Allon Fuller Fund has a deadline of July 31. Grant decisions will be made by December 31.
Requirements: Nonprofit organizations must be geographically located within the city limits of New York City or Chicago to be eligible to apply.
Restrictions: The fund generally does not support the following: projects in the areas of health care specific to medical/academic research; organizations or programs that primarily provide mental health services; programs that primarily provide services to either the mentally or developmentally disabled; endowment campaigns; and capital projects. The fund does not support requests from individuals, organizations attempting to influence policy through direct lobbying, or any political campaigns.
Geographic Focus: Illinois, New York
Date(s) Application is Due: Jul 31
Samples: Saint Bernard Hospital and Health Care Center, Chicago, Illinois, $6,250 (2010); American Civil Liberties Union Foundation, New York, New York, $15,000 (2010); Theater Development Fund, New York, New York, $10,000 (2010).
Contact: Christine O'Donnell, Vice President; (646) 855-1011; christine.l.o'donnell@baml.com
Internet: https://www.bankofamerica.com/philanthropic/fn_search.action
Sponsor: Harry S. Black and Allon Fuller Fund
One Bryant Park, NY1-100-28-05
New York, NY 10036

BAML Helen Pumphrey Denit Charitable Trust Grants 214

The Helen Pumphrey Denit Trust for Charitable and Educational Purposes was established in 1988 to support charitable organizations that promote quality education, culture, human service, health service and arts opportunities. The grants are primarily made to organizations in the Baltimore region. Special consideration is given to the following three organizations: Montgomery General Hospital in Onley, Maryland; The George Washington University in Washington, D.C; and The Wesley Theological Seminary in Washington, D.C. Grants for capital and program support are encouraged. Requests for general operating support will be received, but they will be given lower priority than other grants that have more specific purposes. Grants are primarily one year in duration. On occasion, multi-year grants will be awarded. Applicants must apply online at the grant website. Applicants are strongly encouraged to do the following before applying: review the downloadable state application procedures for additional helpful information and clarifications; review the downloadable online-application guidelines at the grant website; review the trust's funding history (link is available from the grant website); review the online application questions in advance; and review the list of required attachments. These will generally include: a list of board members, financial statements (audited, reviewed, or compiled by independent auditor); an organization summary; a list of other funding sources; an IRS Determination letter; and other required documents. All attachments must be uploaded in the online application as PDF, Word, or Excel files. The Helen Pumphrey Denit Trust has an application deadline of 11:59 p.m. on February 1. The applicants will be notified of grant decisions by June 30.
Requirements: Applicants must have 501(c)3 tax-exempt status and serve residents of Baltimore and surrounding communities.
Restrictions: The trust does not support requests from individuals, organizations attempting to influence policy through direct lobbying, or any political campaigns.
Geographic Focus: Maryland
Date(s) Application is Due: Feb 1
Samples: George Washington University, Washington, D.C., $50,000 (2010); Walters Art Museum, Baltimore, Maryland, $20,000 (2010); Montgomery General Hospital, Olney, Maryland, $50,000 (2010).
Contact: Sarah Kay, Vice President; (804) 788-2673; sarah.kay@baml.com
Internet: https://www.bankofamerica.com/philanthropic/fn_search.action
Sponsor: Helen Pumphrey Denit Charitable Trust
1111 E. Main Street, VA2-300-12-92
Richmond, VA 23219

BAML Herbert A. and Adrian W. Woods Foundation Grants 215

The Herbert A. and Adrian W. Woods Foundation was established on June 9, 1999 upon the death of Mrs. Adrian W. Woods. Mrs. Woods had a long history of charitable giving in the Street Louis community and wanted to establish this foundation to continue that legacy of giving. The Foundation supports charitable organizations primarily in the greater Street Louis, Missouri area. The Trustees will consider the donor's past giving history and any special needs of any of the charities she has given to in the past. The Trustees will also consider requests from charitable organizations that fall into one or more of the following categories: abused, neglected, or troubled children; the poor; the Episcopal Church and affiliates, including outreach programs; arts and culture in the Metropolitan Street Louis area; animal welfare (in Missouri); and victims of illness or disability, including research in this area. The following types of requests may be submitted: special projects; capital campaign requests (capital grants are awarded only as a source of support among a broad community of funders); challenge or matching grants; and general operation funding. Applicants must apply online at the grant website. Applicants are strongly encouraged to do the following before applying: review the downloadable state application procedures for additional helpful information and clarifications; review the downloadable online-application guidelines at the grant website; review the foundation's funding history (link is available from the grant website); review the online application questions in advance; and review the list of required attachments. These will generally include: a list of board members, financial statements (audited, reviewed, or compiled by independent auditor); an organization summary; a list of other funding sources; an IRS Determination letter; and other required documents. All attachments must be uploaded in the online application as PDF, Word, or Excel files. The application deadline for this foundation is 11:59 p.m. on September 1. Final decisions about grant rewards will be made by November 30.
Requirements: Applicants must have 501(c)3 tax-exempt status.
Restrictions: The fund will not consider requests for multi-year grants (pledges) or endowment creation and funding. The fund does not support requests from individuals, organizations attempting to influence policy through direct lobbying, or any political campaigns.
Geographic Focus: Missouri
Date(s) Application is Due: Sep 1
Samples: Grace Hill Settlement House, Saint Louis, Missouri, $20,000 (2008); Humane Society of Missouri, Saint Louis, Missouri, $15,000 (2008); Central Institute for the Deaf, Saint Louis, Missouri, $5,000 (2008).
Contact: Shanise Evans, Vice President; (314) 466-8027; shanise.evans@baml.com
Internet: https://www.bankofamerica.com/philanthropic/fn_search.action
Sponsor: Herbert A. and Adrian W. Woods Foundation
100 North Broadway MO2-100-07-15
Saint Louis, MO 63102-2728

BAML Horace Moses Charitable Foundation Grants 216

The Horace Moses Charitable Foundation was established in 1923 to support and promote quality educational, human-services, and health-care programming for underserved populations. Special consideration is given to charitable organizations that serve the community of Springfield and its surrounding communities. Grant requests for general operating support are strongly encouraged. Program support will also be considered. Small, program-related capital expenses may be included in general operating or program requests. The majority of grants from the Moses Charitable Foundation are one year in duration; on occasion, multi-year support is awarded. Applicants must apply online at the grant website. Applicants are strongly encouraged to do the following before applying: review the downloadable state application procedures for additional helpful information and clarifications; review the downloadable online-application guidelines at the grant website; review the foundation's funding history (link is available from the grant website); review the online application questions in advance; and review the list of required attachments. These will generally include: a list of board members, financial statements (audited, reviewed, or compiled by independent auditor); an organization summary; a list of other funding sources; an IRS Determination letter; and other required documents. All attachments must be uploaded in the online application as PDF, Word, or Excel files. The application deadline for the Horace Moses Charitable Foundation is 11:59 p.m. on April 1. Applicants will be notified of grant decisions before June 30.
Requirements: Applicants must have 501(c)3 tax-exempt status.
Restrictions: The foundation does not support requests from individuals, organizations attempting to influence policy through direct lobbying, or any political campaigns.
Geographic Focus: Massachusetts
Date(s) Application is Due: Apr 1
Samples: Big Brothers Big Sisters of Hampden County, Springfield, Massachusetts, $15,000, Continuing Support (2010); Open Pantry Community Services, Springfield, Massachusetts, $10,000, for Loaves and

Fishes Community Kitchen (2010); Drama Studio, Springfield, Massachusetts, $2,500, Acting Training and Community Outreach Program (2010).
Contact: Michealle Larkins, Vice President; (866) 778-6859; michealle.larkins@baml.com
Internet: https://www.bankofamerica.com/philanthropic/fn_search.action
Sponsor: Horace Moses Charitable Foundation
225 Franklin Street, 4th Floor, MA1-225-04-02
Boston, MA 02110

BAML Ida S. Barter Trust Grants **217**
The Ida S. Barter Trust was established in 1953 to support and promote quality educational, human services, and health care programming for underserved populations. Grant requests for general operating support are strongly encouraged. Program support will also be considered. Small, program-related capital expenses may be included in general operating or program requests. The application deadline is April 1, and applicants will be notified of grant decisions before June 30. The majority of grants from the Barter Trust are 1 year in duration. On occasion, multi-year support is awarded.
Geographic Focus: Massachusetts
Date(s) Application is Due: Apr 1
Contact: Michealle Larkins, Vice President; (866) 778-6859; michealle.larkins@baml.com
Internet: https://www.bankofamerica.com/philanthropic/fn_search.action
Sponsor: Ida S. Barter Trust
225 Franklin Street, 4th Floor, MA1-225-04-02
Boston, MA 02110

BAML John D. and Katherine A. Johnston Foundation Grants **218**
The John D. and Katherine A. Johnston Foundation was established in 1928 to support charitable organizations that work to improve the lives of physically disabled children and adults. Special consideration is given to organizations that serve low-income individuals. Preference is given to charitable organizations that serve the people of Newport, Rhode Island. Capital requests that fund handicapped assistive devices (wheelchairs, walkers, etc.) or adaptive equipment (lift installation, ramp installation, etc.) are strongly encouraged. Grant requests for general operating or program support will also be considered. The majority of grants from the Johnston Foundation are one year in duration. The Johnston Foundation shares a mission and grantmaking focus with the Vigneron Memorial Fund. Both foundations have the same proposal deadline date of 11:59 p.m. on April 1. Applicants will be notified of grant decisions before May 31. Applicants must apply online at the grant website. Applicants are strongly encouraged to do the following before applying: review the downloadable state application procedures for additional helpful information and clarifications; review the downloadable online-application guidelines at the grant website; review the foundation's funding history (link is available from the grant website); review the online application questions in advance; and review the list of required attachments. These will generally include: a list of board members, financial statements (audited, reviewed, or compiled by independent auditor); an organization summary; a list of other funding sources; an IRS Determination letter; and other required documents. All attachments must be uploaded in the online application as PDF, Word, or Excel files.
Requirements: Applicants must have 501(c)3 tax-exempt status.
Restrictions: The foundation does not support requests from individuals, organizations attempting to influence policy through direct lobbying, or any political campaigns.
Geographic Focus: Rhode Island
Date(s) Application is Due: Apr 1
Samples: Rhode Island Hospital Foundation, Providence, Rhode Island, $7,500 (2010); CranstonArc, Cranston, Rhode Island, $4,000 (2010); Meals on Wheels of Rhode Island, Providence, Rhode Island, $3,500 (2010).
Contact: Emma Greene, Director; (617) 434-0329; emma.m.greene@baml.com
Internet: https://www.bankofamerica.com/philanthropic/fn_search.action
Sponsor: John D. and Katherine A. Johnston Foundation
225 Franklin Street, 4th Floor, MA1-225-04-02
Boston, MA 02110

BAML John W. Boynton Fund Grants **219**
The John W. Boynton Fund was established in 1952 by Dora Carter Boynton in memory of her husband. He had a thriving business in tinware in Templeton, MA, and later in his life was a resident of Athol, MA. In her will, Mrs. Boynton asked that "organizations which benefit poor, needy, and deserving persons and particularly those of advanced years and gentility" be considered. She also expressed a desire that special consideration be given to charitable organizations serving the Town of Athol. Grant requests for new or special programs and capital projects are preferred. General operating support also will be considered. In come cases, general operating grants are made to make up for a temporary loss of public or private funding. A typical grant is $5,000. Applicants must apply online at the grant website. Applicants are strongly encouraged to do the following before applying: review the downloadable state application procedures for additional helpful information and clarifications at the grant website; review the downloadable online-application guidelines at the grant website; review the foundation's funding history (link is available from the grant website); review the online application questions in advance; and review the list of required attachments. These will generally include: a list of board members, financial statements (audited, reviewed, or compiled by independent auditor); an organization summary; a list of other funding sources; an IRS Determination letter; and other required documents. All attachments must be uploaded in the online application as PDF, Word, or Excel files. The application deadline is 11:59 p.m. on July 15. Applicants will be notified of decisions by the end of September.
Requirements: Applicants must have 501(c)3 tax-exempt status and serve the residents of Greater Boston.
Restrictions: The fund does not support requests from individuals, organizations attempting to influence policy through direct lobbying, or any political campaigns.
Geographic Focus: Massachusetts
Date(s) Application is Due: Jul 15
Amount: 2,500 - 25,000 USD
Samples: Friends of the Athol Council on Aging, Athol, Massachusetts, $60,000 (2010); Associated Grant Makers, Boston, Massachusetts, $5,000 (2010); Womens Lunch Place, Boston, Massachusetts, $3,000 (2010).
Contact: Michealle Larkins; (866) 778-6859; michealle.larkins@baml.com
Internet: https://www.bankofamerica.com/philanthropic/fn_search.action
Sponsor: John W. Boynton Fund
225 Franklin Street, 4th Floor, MA1-225-04-02
Boston, MA 02110

BAML John W. Speas and Effie E. Speas Memorial Trust Grants **220**
The John W. Speas & Effie E. Speas Memorial Trust was established in 1943 to support and promote quality educational, cultural, human-services, and health-care programming. In the area of arts, culture, and humanities, the trust supports programming that: fosters the enjoyment and appreciation of the visual and performing arts; strengthens humanities and arts-related education programs; provides affordable access; enhances artistic elements in communities; and nurtures a new generation of artists. In the area of education, the trust supports programming that: promotes effective teaching; improves the academic achievement of, or expands educational opportunities for, disadvantaged students; improves governance and management; strengthens nonprofit organizations, school leadership, and teaching; and bolsters strategic initiatives of area colleges and universities. In the area of health, the trust supports programming that improves the delivery of health care to the indigent, uninsured, and other vulnerable populations and addresses health and health-care problems that intersect with social factors. In the area of human services, the trust funds programming that: strengthens agencies that deliver critical human services and maintains the community's safety net and helps agencies respond to federal, state, and local public policy changes. In the area of community improvement, the trust funds capacity-building and infrastructure-development projects including: assessments, planning, and implementation of technology for management and programmatic functions within an organization; technical assistance on wide-ranging topics, including grant writing, strategic planning, financial management services, business development, board and volunteer management, and marketing; and mergers, affiliations, or other restructuring efforts. Grant requests for general operating support and program support will be considered. Grants from the foundation are one year in duration. Application materials are available for download at the grant website. Applicants are strongly encouraged to review the state application guidelines for additional helpful information and clarifications before applying. Applicants are also encouraged to review the foundation's funding history (link is available from the grant website). There are no application deadlines for the Speas Memorial Trust. Proposals are reviewed on an ongoing basis.
Requirements: Applicants must have 501(c)3 tax-exempt status and serve the residents of the Greater Kansas City Metropolitan area. Applications must be mailed.

Restrictions: Grant requests for capital support will not be considered. The trust does not support requests from individuals, organizations attempting to influence policy through direct lobbying, or any political campaigns.
Geographic Focus: Missouri
Samples: TLC for Children and Families, Olathe, Kansas, $25,000, Technology Capacity Building Project (2010); Truman Medical Center Charitable Foundation, Kansas City, Missouri, $200,000, joint venture between Truman and Children's Mercy in support of Don Chisholm Hospital Hill Center (2010); Mid-America Regional Council Community Services Corporation, Kansas City, Missouri, $100,000, Kansas City Bi-State Health Information Exchange (2010).
Contact: Spence Heddens; (816) 292-4301; Spence.heddens@baml.com
Internet: https://www.bankofamerica.com/philanthropic/fn_search.action
Sponsor: John W. Speas and Effie E. Speas Memorial Trust
1200 Main Street, 14th Floor, P.O. Box 219119
Kansas City, MO 64121-9119

BAML Joseph S. Stackpole Charitable Trust Grants **221**

The Joseph S. Stackpole Charitable Trust was established in 1957 to support and promote quality educational and human-services programming for underserved populations. Preference is given to charitable organizations that serve the people of Hartford County, Connecticut. The Stackpole Charitable Trust makes approximately 10-15 grants each year. The grant range is $1000-$1500 and grants are one year in duration. Applicants must apply online at the grant website. Applicants are strongly encouraged to do the following before applying: review the downloadable state application procedures for additional helpful information and clarifications; review the downloadable online-application guidelines at the grant website; review the trust's funding history (link is available from the grant website); review the online application questions in advance; and review the list of required attachments. These will generally include: a list of board members, financial statements (audited, reviewed, or compiled by independent auditor); an organization summary; a list of other funding sources; an IRS Determination letter; and other required documents. All attachments must be uploaded in the online application as PDF, Word, or Excel files. The deadline for application to the Joseph S. Stackpole Charitable Trust is 11:59 p.m. on August 15. Applicants will be notified of grant decisions by letter within two to three months after the proposal deadline.
Requirements: First time applicants are asked to contact the Program Officer before applying to the Stackpole Charitable Trust. Applicants must be classified by the Internal Revenue Service (IRS) as a 501(c)3 public charity.
Restrictions: Grant requests for capital projects will not be considered. Applicants will not be awarded a grant for more than 3 consecutive years. The trust does not support requests from individuals, organizations attempting to influence policy through direct lobbying, or any political campaigns.
Geographic Focus: Connecticut
Date(s) Application is Due: Aug 15
Amount: 1,000 - 1,500 USD
Samples: Hartford Areas Rally Together, Hartford, Connecticut, $1,500, HOME Program (to create successful homeowners by educating individuals about the process of home purchase and home ownership) (2010); ConnectiKids, Hartford, Connecticut, $1,500, Tutoring/Mentoring and Arts/Enrichment programs (general operations) (2010); Bridge Family Center, West Hartford, Connecticut, $1,000, for youth shelters/short-term assessment and respite (STAR) homes (2010).
Contact: Kate Kerchaert; (860) 657-7016; kate.kerchaert@baml.com
Internet: https://www.bankofamerica.com/philanthropic/fn_search.action
Sponsor: Joseph S. Stackpole Charitable Trust
200 Glastonbury Boulevard, Suite # 200, CT2-545-02-05
Glastonbury, CT 06033-4056

BAML Katharine Matthies Foundation Grants **222**

The Katharine Matthies Foundation was established in 1987 to support and promote quality educational, human-services, and health-care programming for underserved populations. Special consideration is given to organizations that work to prevent cruelty to children and animals. The majority of grants from the Matthies Foundation are one year in duration; on occasion, multi-year support is awarded. Applicants must apply online at the grant website. Applicants are strongly encouraged to do the following before applying: review the downloadable state application procedures for additional helpful information and clarifications; review the downloadable online-application guidelines at the grant website; review the foundation's funding history (link is available from the grant website); review the online application questions in advance; and review the list of required attachments. These will generally include: a list of board members, financial statements (audited, reviewed, or compiled by independent auditor); an organization summary; a list of other funding sources; an IRS Determination letter; and other required documents. All attachments must be uploaded in the online application as PDF, Word, or Excel files. The deadline for application to the Katherine Matthies Foundation is 11:59 p.m. on May 1. Applicants will be notified of grant decisions by letter within three to four months after the proposal deadline.
Requirements: Applicant organizations must have 501(c)3 tax-exempt status and serve the people of the following Connecticut towns: Seymour, Ansonia, Derby, Oxford, Shelton, or Beacon Falls. A breakdown of number/percentage of people served by specific towns will be required in the online application. Special consideration will be given to organizations that serve the people of Seymour, Connecticut.
Restrictions: The Matthies Foundation specifically serves people of the Lower Naugatuck Valley. The foundation does not support requests from individuals, organizations attempting to influence policy through direct lobbying, or any political campaigns.
Geographic Focus: Connecticut
Date(s) Application is Due: May 1
Samples: Town of Seymour, Seymour, Connecticut, $22,000 (2010); Griffin Health Services Corporation, Derby, Connecticut, $66,000 (2010); Connecticut Hurricanes, Derby, Connecticut, $17,540 (2010).
Contact: Amy Lynch, Senior Foundation Manager; (860) 657-7015; amy.r.lynch@baml.com
Internet: https://www.bankofamerica.com/philanthropic/fn_search.action
Sponsor: Katharine Matthies Foundation
200 Glastonbury Boulevard, Suite # 200
Glastonbury, CT 06033-4056

BAML Kawabe Memorial Fund Grants **223**

The Kawabe Memorial Fund was established in 1971 to support and promote quality human-services programming for the economically disadvantaged, children and the elderly. The Fund also provides capital grants to churches as well as scholarships to support teachers and the clergy. The Kawabe Memorial Fund typically supports organizations serving the people of the Puget Sound area. Grant requests for general operating support are strongly encouraged. Program support will also be considered. Small, program-related capital expenses may be included in general operating or program requests. Grants from the Kawabe Memorial Fund are one year in duration. Application materials are available for download at the grant website. Applicants are strongly encouraged to review the state application guidelines for additional helpful information and clarifications before applying. Applicants are also encouraged to review the foundation's funding history (link is available from the grant website). Applications to the Kawabe Memorial Fund are due on the first Friday in February, May or September. Proposals must be post-marked on or before the application deadline and mailed to the address given in the downloadable state guidelines document. In general, applicants will be notified of grant decisions 3 to 4 months after proposal submission.
Geographic Focus: Washington
Samples: Asian Counseling and Referral Service, Seattle, Washington, $3,000 (2010); Buddhist Churches of America, Tacoma, Washington, $9,950 (2010); Shalom Zone Nonprofit Association, Seattle, Washington, $2,000 (2010).
Contact: Nancy Atkinson; (800) 848-7177; nancy.l.atkinson@baml.com
Internet: https://www.bankofamerica.com/philanthropic/fn_search.action
Sponsor: Kawabe Memorial Fund
800 5th Avenue, WA1-501-33-23
Seattle, WA 98104

BAML Lena Benas Memorial Fund Grants **224**

The Lena Benas Memorial Fund was established in 1986 to provide for the health, human services, and housing needs of underserved people living in Litchfield, Connecticut, and its surrounding communities. The deadline for application to the Fund is November 1, and applicants will be notified of grant decisions by letter within 2 months after the proposal deadline. Special consideration is given to organizations that provide housing maintenance and human services programming to needy populations.
Requirements: Preference is given to organizations serving the people of Litchfield, Connecticut. Organizations serving the towns contiguous to Litchfield, including Cornwall, Goshen, Harwinton, Morris, Thomaston, Torrington, Warren, Washington, and Watertown will also be considered.
Restrictions: Grants from the Benas Memorial Fund are 1 year in duration.
Geographic Focus: Connecticut

Date(s) Application is Due: Nov 1
Contact: Kate Kerchaert; (860) 657-7016; kate.kerchaert@baml.com
Internet: https://www.bankofamerica.com/philanthropic/fn_search.action
Sponsor: Lena Benas Memorial Fund
200 Glastonbury Boulevard, Suite #200, CT2-545-02-05
Glastonbury, CT 06033-4056

BAML Lewis H. Humphreys Charitable Trust Grants 225

The Lewis H. Humphreys Charitable Trust was established in 2004 to support and promote quality educational, cultural, human-services, and health-care programming for underserved and disadvantaged populations. In the area of arts, culture, and humanities, the trust supports programming that: fosters the enjoyment and appreciation of the visual and performing arts; strengthens humanities and arts-related education programs; provides affordable access; enhances artistic elements in communities; and nurtures a new generation of artists. In the area of education, the trust supports programming that: promotes effective teaching; improves the academic achievement of, or expands educational opportunities for, disadvantaged students; improves governance and management; strengthens nonprofit organizations, school leadership, and teaching; and bolsters strategic initiatives of area colleges and universities. In the area of health, the trust supports programming that improves the delivery of health care to the indigent, uninsured, and other vulnerable populations and addresses health and health-care problems that intersect with social factors. In the area of human services, the trust funds programming that: strengthens agencies that deliver critical human services and maintains the community's safety net and helps agencies respond to federal, state, and local public policy changes. In the area of community improvement, the trust funds capacity-building and infrastructure-development projects including: assessments, planning, and implementation of technology for management and programmatic functions within an organization; technical assistance on wide-ranging topics, including grant writing, strategic planning, financial management services, business development, board and volunteer management, and marketing; and mergers, affiliations, or other restructuring efforts. Grant requests for general operating support, program support, and capital support will be considered. Grant requests for capital support, such as for buildings, land, and major equipment should meet a compelling community need and offer a broad social benefit. Grants from the trust are one year in duration. Application materials are available for download at the grant website. Applicants are strongly encouraged to review the state application guidelines for additional helpful information and clarifications before applying. Applicants are also encouraged to review the trust's funding history (link is available from the grant website). Grant applications can be submitted between August 1 and September 30. Applicants will be notified of grant decisions by November 30.
Requirements: Applicants must have 501(c)3 tax-exempt status and serve the residents of Kansas. Grant application materials must be mailed.
Restrictions: The trust does not support requests from individuals, organizations attempting to influence policy through direct lobbying, or any political campaigns.
Geographic Focus: Kansas
Date(s) Application is Due: Sep 30
Samples: Kansas Childrens Discovery Center, Topeka, Kansas, $50,000 (2010); Hetlinger Developmental Services, Emporia, Kansas, $50,000 (2010); Boy Scouts of America, Topeka, Kansas, $75,000 (2010).
Contact: James Mueth, Vice President; (816) 292-4342; james.mueth@baml.com
Internet: https://www.bankofamerica.com/philanthropic/fn_search.action
Sponsor: Lewis H. Humphreys Charitable Trust
1200 Main Street, 14th Floor, P.O. Box 219119
Kansas City, MO 64121-9119

BAML Lloyd G. Balfour Foundation Educational Grants 226

The Lloyd G. Balfour Foundation was established in 1973. The Foundation's 3 primary focus areas reflect Mr. Balfour's strong affinity for the employees of the Balfour Company; his commitment to the city of Attleboro, Massachusetts; and his lifelong interest in education. The Foundation funds educational organizations, especially those that promote college readiness, access, and success for underserved populations. There is a rolling deadline for organizations applying for a general education grant from the Balfour Foundation. Educational organizations are strongly encouraged to submit grant requests for general operating support. Program support will also be considered. Small, program-related capital expenses may be included in general operating or program requests. To better support the capacity of nonprofit organizations, multi-year funding requests are strongly encouraged.
Geographic Focus: Connecticut, Maine, Massachusetts, New Hampshire, Rhode Island, Vermont
Contact: Miki C. Akimoto, Vice President; (866) 778-6859; miki.akimoto@baml.co
Internet: https://www.bankofamerica.com/philanthropic/fn_search.action
Sponsor: Lloyd G. Balfour Foundation
225 Franklin Street, 4th Floor, MA1-225-04-02
Boston, MA 02110

BAML Louis & Elizabeth Nave Flarsheim Charitable Foundation Grants 227

The Louis & Elizabeth Nave Flarsheim Charitable Foundation was established to support and promote quality educational, cultural, human-services, and health-care programming. In the area of arts, culture, and humanities, the foundation supports programming that: fosters the enjoyment and appreciation of the visual and performing arts; strengthens humanities and arts-related education programs; provides affordable access; enhances artistic elements in communities; and nurtures a new generation of artists. In the area of education, the foundation supports programming that: promotes effective teaching; improves the academic achievement of, or expands educational opportunities for, disadvantaged students; improves governance and management; strengthens nonprofit organizations, school leadership, and teaching; and bolsters strategic initiatives of area colleges and universities. In the area of health, the foundation supports programming that improves the delivery of health care to the indigent, uninsured, and other vulnerable populations and addresses health and health-care problems that intersect with social factors. In the area of human services, the foundation funds programming that: strengthens agencies that deliver critical human services and maintains the community's safety net and helps agencies respond to federal, state, and local public policy changes. In the area of community improvement, the foundation funds capacity-building and infrastructure-development projects including: assessments, planning, and implementation of technology for management and programmatic functions within an organization; technical assistance on wide-ranging topics, including grant writing, strategic planning, financial management services, business development, board and volunteer management, and marketing; and mergers, affiliations, or other restructuring efforts. Grant requests for general operating support and program support will be considered. Grants from the foundation are one year in duration. Application materials are available for download at the grant website. Applicants are strongly encouraged to review the state application guidelines for additional helpful information and clarifications before applying. Applicants are also encouraged to review the foundation's funding history (link is available from the grant website). There are no application deadlines for the Flarsheim Charitable Foundation. Proposals are reviewed on an ongoing basis.
Requirements: The Flarsheim Foundation supports organizations that serve the residents of Kansas City, Missouri. Applications must be mailed.
Restrictions: Grant requests for capital support will not be considered.
Geographic Focus: Missouri
Samples: Paul Mesner Puppets, Kansas City, Missouri, $10,000 (2010); Kansas City Chorale, Kansas City, Missouri, $5,000 (2010); Jewish Community Center Charitable Supporting Foundation, Overland Park, Kansas, $2,500 (2009).
Contact: Spence Heddens, Market President; (816) 292-4301; Spence.heddens@baml.com
Internet: https://www.bankofamerica.com/philanthropic/fn_search.action
Sponsor: Louis & Elizabeth Nave Flarsheim Charitable Foundation
1200 Main Street, 14th Floor, P.O. Box 219119
Kansas City, 64121-9119

BAML Lucy Downing Nisbet Charitable Fund Grants 228

The Lucy Downing Nisbet Charitable Fund was established in 2002 to support and promote educational, health-and-human-services, and arts programming for underserved populations. The Foundation specifically serves organizations located in and serving the people of Vermont. Special consideration is given to organizations in the area of healthcare/nursing, domestic violence awareness, heart disease, and endangered species, and organizations located in and serving the people of Morrisville, Vermont. Grants are one year in duration. Applicants must apply online at the grant website. Applicants are strongly encouraged to do the following before applying: review the downloadable state application procedures for additional helpful information and clarifications; review the downloadable online-application guidelines at the grant website;

review the foundation's funding history (link is available from the grant website); review the online application questions in advance; and review the list of required attachments. These will generally include: a list of board members, financial statements (audited, reviewed, or compiled by independent auditor); an organization summary; a list of other funding sources; an IRS Determination letter; and other required documents. All attachments must be uploaded in the online application as PDF, Word, or Excel files. The Lucy Downing Nisbet Charitable Fund application deadline is 11:59 p.m. on January 15. Applicants will be notified of grant decisions by letter within two to three months of the deadline.
Requirements: The foundation specifically serves organizations located in and serving the people of Vermont. Applicants must have 501(c)3 tax-exempt status.
Restrictions: The trustees do not make grants for deficit financing, annual giving, endowments or capital projects. The fund does not support requests from individuals, organizations attempting to influence policy through direct lobbying, or any political campaigns.
Geographic Focus: Vermont
Date(s) Application is Due: Jan 15
Amount: 5,000 - 20,000 USD
Samples: Copley Health Systems, Morrisville, Vermont, $58,400, to provide computerized Physician's Order Entry component of Electronic Medical Record Software and to fund Nursing Education (2010); Vermont Foodbank, South Barre Vermont, $20,000, for USDA Summer Food Service Program in high-poverty and extremely rural area (2010); River Arts of Morrisville, Morrisville, Vermont, $8,000, Arts for Everyone archive (2010).
Contact: Amy Lynch, Senior Foundation Manager; (860) 657-7015; amy.r.lynch@baml.com
Internet: https://www.bankofamerica.com/philanthropic/fn_search.action
Sponsor: Lucy Downing Nisbet Charitable Fund
200 Glastonbury Boulevard, Suite # 200, CT2-545-02-05
Glastonbury, CT 06033-4056

BAML Lydia deForest Charitable Trust Grants **229**

The Lydia Collins deForest Charitable Trust was established in 2002. The deForest Charitable Trust specifically supports: organizations that provide services to those who are visually limited; churches and organizations affiliated with the Protestant Episcopal Church in the United States and other religious organizations in union with or recognized by the Episcopal Church; and organizations that provide services to those who are homeless, unemployed, or substance-dependent. Special consideration is given to the following 3 organizations: The Lighthouse, Inc., in New York, New York; the Calvary Episcopal Church of Summit, New Jersey; and the Salvation Army in Union, New Jersey. Grant requests for general operating support are strongly encouraged. Program support will also be considered. Small, program-related capital expenses may be included in general operating or program requests. To better support the capacity of nonprofit organizations, multi-year funding requests are encouraged. Applicants must apply online at the grant website. Applicants are strongly encouraged to do the following before applying: review the downloadable state application procedures for additional helpful information and clarifications; review the downloadable online-application guidelines at the grant website; review the trust's funding history (link is available from the grant website); review the online application questions in advance; and review the list of required attachments. These will generally include: a list of board members, financial statements (audited, reviewed, or compiled by independent auditor); an organization summary; a list of other funding sources; an IRS Determination letter; and other required documents. All attachments must be uploaded in the online application as PDF, Word, or Excel files. The application deadline for the deForest Charitable Trust is 11:59 p.m., November 30. Applicants will be notified of grant decisions before February 28 of the following year.
Requirements: Applicants must have 501(c)3 tax-exempt status and serve the people of New Jersey. Occasional support is given to organizations within the Metro New York City area.
Restrictions: The trust does not support requests from individuals, organizations attempting to influence policy through direct lobbying, or any political campaigns.
Geographic Focus: New Jersey
Date(s) Application is Due: Nov 30
Samples: Family Promise, Summit, New Jersey, $40,000; Saint Philips Academy, Newark, New Jersey, $40,000; Salvation Army New Jersey Divisional Headquarters, Union, New Jersey, $40,000 (2010).
Contact: Ken Goody, Senior Vice President; (646) 855-0956; kenneth.l.goody@baml.com
Internet: https://www.bankofamerica.com/philanthropic/fn_search.action
Sponsor: Lydia Collins deForest Charitable Trust
One Bryant Park, NY1-100-28-05
New York, NY 10036

BAML Mabel A. Horne Trust Grants **230**

The Mabel A. Horne Trust was established in 1957 to support and promote quality educational, human-services, and health-care programming for underserved populations. Grant requests for general operating support are strongly encouraged. Program support will also be considered. Small, program-related capital expenses may be included in general operating or program requests. The majority of grants from the Horne Trust are one year in duration; on occasion, multi-year support is awarded. Applicants must apply online at the grant website. Applicants are strongly encouraged to do the following before applying: review the downloadable state application procedures for additional helpful information and clarifications; review the downloadable online-application guidelines at the grant website; review the trust's funding history (link is available from the grant website); review the online application questions in advance; and review the list of required attachments. These will generally include: a list of board members, financial statements (audited, reviewed, or compiled by independent auditor); an organization summary; a list of other funding sources; an IRS Determination letter; and other required documents. All attachments must be uploaded in the online application as PDF, Word, or Excel files. The application deadline for the Mabel A. Horne Trust is 11:59 p.m. on February 1. Applicants will be notified of grant decisions before May 31.
Requirements: Applicants must have 501(c)3 tax-exempt status.
Restrictions: The trust does not support requests from individuals, organizations attempting to influence policy through direct lobbying, or any political campaigns.
Geographic Focus: Massachusetts
Date(s) Application is Due: Feb 1
Samples: Casa Myrna Vasquez, Boston, Massachusetts, $20,000 (2010); Boston Ten Point Coalition, Boston, Massachusetts, $40,000 (2010); Asian Task Force Against Domestic Violence, Boston, Massachusetts, $25,000 (2010).
Contact: Miki C. Akimoto, Vice President; (866) 778-6859; miki.akimoto@baml.com
Internet: https://www.bankofamerica.com/philanthropic/fn_search.action
Sponsor: Mabel A. Horne Trust
225 Franklin Street, 4th Floor, MA1-225-04-02
Boston, MA 02110

BAML Marion and Miriam Rose Fund Grants **231**

The Marion and Miriam Rose Fund was established to support childcare facilities serving dependent, neglected, indigent, and emotionally disturbed children, and children in foster care. The Marion and Miriam Rose Fund was created under the wills of Mr. George B. Rose and Mrs. Marion Rose. The majority of grants from the Rose Fund are one year in duration. Applicants must apply online at the grant website. Applicants are strongly encouraged to do the following before applying: review the downloadable state application procedures for additional helpful information and clarifications; review the downloadable online-application guidelines at the grant website; review the foundation's funding history (link is available from the grant website); review the online application questions in advance; and review the list of required attachments. These will generally include: a list of board members, financial statements (audited, reviewed, or compiled by independent auditor); an organization summary; a list of other funding sources; an IRS Determination letter; and other required documents. All attachments must be uploaded in the online application as PDF, Word, or Excel files. The application deadline for the Marion and Miriam Rose Fund is 11:59 p.m. on February 1. Applicants will be notified of grant decisions by June 30.
Requirements: Organizations must be located in, or serve the children of Little Rock, Arkansas.
Restrictions: The Fund will consider requests for general operating support only if the organization's operating budget is less than $1 million. In general, grant requests for individuals, endowment campaigns, or capital projects will not be considered.
Geographic Focus: Arkansas
Date(s) Application is Due: Feb 1
Contact: George Thorn, Vice President; (312) 828-4154; ilgrantmaking@bankofamerica.com

Internet: https://www.bankofamerica.com/philanthropic/fn_search.action
Sponsor: Marion and Miriam Rose Fund
231 South LaSalle Street, IL1-231-13-32
Chicago, IL 60604

BAML Marion Gardner Jackson Charitable Trust Grants 232

The Marion Gardner Jackson Charitable Trust was established by Marion Gardner Jackson, the granddaughter of local industrialist, Robert W. Gardner, founder of the Gardner-Denver Company. Before her death in 1976, Mrs. Jackson set up a perpetual trust to aid religious, charitable, scientific, literary, and educational organizations in the Quincy, Illinois area and surrounding communities in Adams County. The trust supports capital, program, and operating grants. Applicants may apply for one- to five-year grants to support capital projects. Projects must support the mission of the organization and/or the stated outcome of a program or project. Applicants with organizational budgets of $1 million or less may apply for grants of up to $25,000 per year, for up to three years, for program or general operating support. Applicants must apply online at the grant website. Applicants are strongly encouraged to do the following before applying: review the downloadable state application procedures for additional helpful information and clarifications; review the downloadable online-application guidelines at the grant website; review the trust's funding history (link is available from the grant website); review the online application questions in advance; and review the list of required attachments. These will generally include: a list of board members, financial statements (audited, reviewed, or compiled by independent auditor); an organization summary; a list of other funding sources; an IRS Determination letter; and other required documents. All attachments must be uploaded in the online application as PDF, Word, or Excel files. The application deadline for the Marion Gardner Jackson Charitable Trust is 11:59 p.m., July 31. Applicants will be notified of grant decisions by January 15.
Requirements: As a condition for accepting grant funds, grantees must provide annual programmatic and financial reports detailing the use of the funds and documenting the progress of the capital campaign/capital project or documenting the impact achieved as a result of the funding. Receipt of annual funds from multi-year grants will be dependent on submission of an annual financial and project/programmatic grant report, due no later than December 15.
Restrictions: For program support grants, the yearly request may not be more than 50% of the program's budget. Organizations can submit one application per year and will not receive more than one award from the trust in any given year. Organizations receiving a multi-year award from the trust that continues into the next grant year are not eligible to apply for an additional grant until the end of the grant cycle. The trust does not support requests from individuals, organizations attempting to influence policy through direct lobbying, or any political campaigns.
Geographic Focus: Illinois
Date(s) Application is Due: Jul 31
Samples: John Wood Community College Foundation, Quincy, Illinois, $37,000 (2010); Quincy Society of Fine Arts, Quincy, Illinois, $25,000 (2010); Access Health Adams County, Quincy, Illinois, $25,000 (2010).
Contact: Debra Grand, Senior Vice President; (312) 828-4154; ilgrantmaking@bankofamerica.com
Internet: https://www.bankofamerica.com/philanthropic/fn_search.action
Sponsor: Marion Gardner Jackson Charitable Trust
231 South LaSalle Street, IL1-231-13-32
Chicago, IL 60604

BAML Marjorie Moore Charitable Foundation Grants 233

The Marjorie Moore Charitable Foundation was established in 1957 to support and promote quality educational, cultural, human-services, environmental, and health-care programming for underserved populations. Grants from the Moore Foundation made in support of operations or programming are one year in duration. Multi-year grants for long-term capital projects will be considered on a case-by-case basis. Applicants must apply online at the grant website. Applicants are strongly encouraged to do the following before applying: review the downloadable state application procedures for additional helpful information and clarifications; review the downloadable online-application guidelines at the grant website; review the foundation's funding history (link is available from the grant website); review the online application questions in advance; and review the list of required attachments. These will generally include: a list of board members, financial statements (audited, reviewed, or compiled by independent auditor); an organization summary; a list of other funding sources; an IRS Determination letter; and other required documents. All attachments must be uploaded in the online application as PDF, Word, or Excel files. The Marjorie Moore Charitable Foundation has biannual deadlines of June 1 and December 1. Applications must be submitted by 11:59 p.m. on the deadline dates. Applicants will be notified of grant decisions by letter within two to three months after each respective proposal deadline.
Requirements: Applicant organizations must have 501(c)3 tax-exempt status and serve the people of Kensington or Berlin, Connecticut. A breakdown of number/percentage of people served by specific towns is required on the online application. Preference is given to organizations that provide human services or health care programming.
Restrictions: The foundation does not support requests from individuals, organizations attempting to influence policy through direct lobbying, or any political campaigns.
Geographic Focus: Connecticut
Date(s) Application is Due: Jun 1; Dec 1
Contact: Kate Kerchaert, Senior Foundation Officer; (860) 657-7016; kate.kerchaert@baml.com
Internet: https://www.bankofamerica.com/philanthropic/fn_search.action
Sponsor: Marjorie Moore Charitable Foundation
200 Glastonbury Boulevard, Suite # 200, CT2-545-02-05
Glastonbury, CT 06033-4056

BAML Mary Reinhart Stackhouse Foundation Grants 234

The Mary Reinhart Stackhouse Foundation was established in 1999 to provide scholarships for golf caddies in New Jersey and to promote preservation of the natural environment in the state of New Jersey. In addition, annual gifts may be awarded to The Conservancy of Southern Florida. Grant requests for general operating support are strongly encouraged. Program support will also be considered. Small, program-related capital expenses may be included in general operating or program requests. The majority of grants from the Stackhouse Foundation are one year in duration; on occasion, multi-year support is awarded. Applicants must apply online at the grant website. Applicants are strongly encouraged to do the following before applying: review the downloadable state application procedures for additional helpful information and clarifications; review the downloadable online-application guidelines at the grant website; review the foundation's funding history (link is available from the grant website); review the online application questions in advance; and review the list of required attachments. These will generally include: a list of board members, financial statements (audited, reviewed, or compiled by independent auditor); an organization summary; a list of other funding sources; an IRS Determination letter; and other required documents. All attachments must be uploaded in the online application as PDF, Word, or Excel files. The application deadline for the Mary Reinhart Stackhouse Foundation is 11:59 p.m. on September 15. Applicants will be notified of grant decisions before December 31.
Requirements: Applicants must have 501(c)3 tax-exempt status.
Restrictions: In general, grant requests for endowment campaigns, capital projects, or scholarly research will not be considered. Grant requests from individuals, organizations attempting to influence policy through direct lobbying, or any political campaigns will not be considered.
Geographic Focus: New Jersey
Date(s) Application is Due: Sep 15
Samples: Greater Newark Conservancy, Newark, New Jersey, $20,000, Environmental Education and Advocacy Program (2010); New Jersey State Golf Association Caddie Scholarship Foundation, Kenilworth, New Jersey, to provide scholarships to high school seniors and college students who quality for the Caddie Scholarship Program (2010); Reeves-Reed Arboretum, Summit, New Jersey, $25,000, general operations (2010).
Contact: Ken Goody, Senior Vice President; (646) 855-0956; kenneth.l.goody@baml.com
Internet: https://www.bankofamerica.com/philanthropic/fn_search.action
Sponsor: Mary Reinhart Stackhouse Foundation
One Bryant Park, NY1-100-28-05
New York, NY 10036

BAML Perpetual Trust for Charitable Giving Grants 235

The Perpetual Trust for Charitable Giving was established in 1957 to support and promote quality educational, human-services, and health-care programming for underserved populations. Special consideration is given to medical aid and medical research organizations, as well as to institutions of higher learning. Grant requests for general operating support are strongly encouraged. Program support will also be considered. Small, program-related capital expenses may be included in general operating or program

requests. To better support the capacity of nonprofit organizations, multi-year funding requests are strongly encouraged. Applicants must apply online at the grant website. Applicants are strongly encouraged to do the following before applying: review the downloadable state application procedures for additional helpful information and clarifications; review the downloadable online-application guidelines at the grant website; review the trust's funding history (link is available from the grant website); review the online application questions in advance; and review the list of required attachments. These will generally include: a list of board members, financial statements (audited, reviewed, or compiled by independent auditor); an organization summary; a list of other funding sources; an IRS Determination letter; and other required documents. All attachments must be uploaded in the online application as PDF, Word, or Excel files. The application deadline for the Perpetual Trust is 11:59 p.m. on September 1. Applicants will be notified of grant decisions before November 30.
Restrictions: The trust does not support requests from individuals, organizations attempting to influence policy through direct lobbying, or any political campaigns.
Geographic Focus: Massachusetts
Date(s) Application is Due: Sep 1
Samples: Forsyth Institute's Forsyth Dental Infirmary for Children, Boston, Massachusetts, $60,000, ForsythKids Program (2010); Bridge Over Troubled Waters, Boston, Massachusetts, $30,000, general operating support (2010); Codman Academy Foundation, Dorchester, Massachusetts, $25,000, general operating support (2010).
Contact: Miki C. Akimoto, Vice President; (866) 778-6859; miki.akimoto@baml.com
Internet: https://www.bankofamerica.com/philanthropic/fn_search.action
Sponsor: Perpetual Trust for Charitable Giving
225 Franklin Street, 4th Floor, MA1-225-04-02
Boston, MA 02110

BAML Roy and Christine Sturgis Charitable Trust Grants **236**

The Roy and Christine Sturgis Charitable Trust was established in 1981 to support and promote quality educational, cultural, human-services, and health-care programming for all people. Roy Sturgis was one of ten children of an Arkansas farmer and homemaker. He dropped out of school after the tenth grade to join the Navy during World War I. Mr. Sturgis returned to his family home in southern Arkansas after the war and went to work in the local sawmills. In 1933, he married Texas native Christine Johns. They became very successful in the timber, lumber, and sawmill industries in Arkansas, owned other prosperous business enterprises, and had notable success managing their investments. Mr. and Mrs. Sturgis spent most of their lives in Arkansas and Dallas, Texas. They did not have children, but were particularly interested in educational opportunities for young people. In addition, Mr. and Mrs. Sturgis supported organizations working in the areas of health, social services, and the arts. The Sturgis Charitable Trust encourages requests for the following types of grants: capital, project-related, medical research, and endowment campaign. Funding for start-up programs and limited general-operating requests will also be considered. Approximately 65% of the trust's annual distributions are made within the state of Arkansas. The remaining 35% of grants are distributed within the state of Texas with strong preference given to organizations located in the Dallas area. The majority of grants from the Sturgis Charitable Trust are one year in duration; on occasion, multi-year support is awarded. Applicants must apply online at the grant website. Applicants are strongly encouraged to do the following before applying: review the downloadable state application procedures for additional helpful information and clarifications; review the downloadable online-application guidelines at the grant website; review the trust's funding history (link is available from the grant website); review the online application questions in advance; and review the list of required attachments. These will generally include: a list of board members, financial statements (audited, reviewed, or compiled by independent auditor); an organization summary; a list of other funding sources; an IRS Determination letter; and other required documents. All attachments must be uploaded in the online application as PDF, Word, or Excel files. The application deadline for the Roy and Christine Sturgis Charitable Trust is 11:59 p.m. on December 31. Applicants will be notified of grant decisions before July 31.
Requirements: 501(c)3 nonprofit organizations in Texas and Arkansas are eligible.
Restrictions: Former grantees must skip a year before submitting a subsequent application. The trust does not support requests from individuals, organizations attempting to influence policy through direct lobbying, or any political campaigns.
Geographic Focus: Arkansas, Texas
Date(s) Application is Due: Dec 31
Samples: University of Arkansas, Little Rock, Arkansas, $150,000, for Endowed Professorship at Nanotechnology and Educational Center (2010); Bishop Lynch High School, Dallas, Texas, $50,000, to construct new science labs (2010); Access Group, Little Rock, Arkansas, $25,000, ACCESS Evaluation and Resource Center (program support) (2010).
Contact: David Ross, Senior Vice President; (214) 209-1965; tx.philanthropic@baml.com
Internet: https://www.bankofamerica.com/philanthropic/fn_search.action
Sponsor: Roy and Christine Sturgis Charitable Trust
901 Main Street, 19th Floor, TX1-492-19-11
Dallas, TX 75202-3714

BAML Sophia Romero Trust Grants **237**

The Sophia Romero Trust was established in 1948 to support and promote quality human-services and health-care programming for underserved elders living in Bristol County, Massachusetts. Special consideration will be given to organizations that serve older women living in Bristol County, Massachusetts. Grant requests for general operating support or program support are strongly encouraged. The majority of grants from the Romero Trust are one year in duration. Applicants must apply online at the grant website. Applicants are strongly encouraged to do the following before applying: review the downloadable state application procedures for additional helpful information and clarifications; review the downloadable online-application guidelines at the grant website; review the trust's funding history (link is available from the grant website); review the online application questions in advance; and review the list of required attachments. These will generally include: a list of board members, financial statements (audited, reviewed, or compiled by independent auditor); an organization summary; a list of other funding sources; an IRS Determination letter; and other required documents. All attachments must be uploaded in the online application as PDF, Word, or Excel files. The application deadline for the Sophia Romero Trust is 11:59 p.m. on February 1. Applicants will be notified of grant decisions before April 30.
Requirements: Applicants must have 501(c)3 tax-exempt status and serve the residents of Bristol County, Massachusetts.
Restrictions: The fund does not support requests from individuals, organizations attempting to influence policy through direct lobbying, or any political campaigns.
Geographic Focus: Massachusetts
Date(s) Application is Due: Feb 1
Samples: Family Services Association of Greater Fall River, Fall River, Massachusetts, $20,000, continuing support (2011); Southeast Massachusetts Home Health Aides, $4,000, program development (2011); YWCA of Southeastern Massachusetts, New Bedford, Massachusetts, $4,000, Widowed Person Program (WPP) (2011).
Contact: Emma Greene, Director; (617) 434-0329; emma.m.greene@baml.com
Internet: https://www.bankofamerica.com/philanthropic/fn_search.action
Sponsor: Sophia Romero Trust
225 Franklin Street, 4th Floor, MA1-225-04-02
Boston, MA 02110

BAML Swindells Charitable Foundation **238**

The Swindells Charitable Foundation was established in 1933 to support and promote quality health and human-services programming for underserved children and adults. The Swindells Charitable Foundation also makes grants to public charitable hospitals. Preference is given to organizations that serve sick or economically disadvantaged children or older adults. Special consideration is given to organizations that provide for the "basic human needs" of individuals. Grants from the Swindells Charitable Foundation are one year in duration. Applicants must apply online at the grant website. Applicants are strongly encouraged to do the following before applying: review the downloadable state application procedures for additional helpful information and clarifications; review the downloadable online-application guidelines at the grant website; review the foundation's funding history (link is available from the grant website); review the online application questions in advance; and review the list of required attachments. These will generally include: a list of board members, financial statements (audited, reviewed, or compiled by independent auditor); an organization summary; a list of other funding sources; an IRS Determination letter; and other required documents.

All attachments must be uploaded in the online application as PDF, Word, or Excel files. The Swindells Charitable Foundation has biannual deadlines of February 1 and August 1. Applications are by 11:59 p.m. on the deadline dates. Applicants will be notified of grant decisions by letter within two to three months after each respective proposal deadline.
Requirements: Applicants must have 501(c)3 tax-exempt status.
Restrictions: Applicants will not be awarded a grant for more than three consecutive years. The trust does not support requests from individuals, organizations attempting to influence policy through direct lobbying, or any political campaigns. Capital requests will not be considered.
Geographic Focus: Connecticut
Date(s) Application is Due: Feb 1; Aug 1
Samples: Mercy Housing and Shelter Corporation, Hartford, Connecticut, $4,000, to cover portion of anticipated budgetary shortfall (2011); Plymouth Community Food Pantry, Terryville, Connecticut, $3,000, general operations (2011); Christian Fellowship Center, Bristol, Connecticut, $3,000, general program support (2011).
Contact: Kate Kerchaert, Senior Foundation Officer; (860) 657-7016; kate.kerchaert@baml.com
Internet: https://www.bankofamerica.com/philanthropic/fn_search.action
Sponsor: Swindells Charitable Foundation
200 Glastonbury Boulevard, Suite # 200, CT2-545-02-05
Glastonbury, CT 06033-4056

BAML Victor E. Speas Foundation Grants **239**

The Victor E. Speas Foundation was established in 1947 to provide medical care for the needy, to further medical research, and to support and promote quality educational, cultural, human-services, and health-care programming. In the area of arts, culture, and humanities, the foundation supports programming that: fosters the enjoyment and appreciation of the visual and performing arts; strengthens humanities and arts-related education programs; provides affordable access; enhances artistic elements in communities; and nurtures a new generation of artists. In the area of education, the foundation supports programming that: promotes effective teaching; improves the academic achievement of, or expands educational opportunities for, disadvantaged students; improves governance and management; strengthens nonprofit organizations, school leadership, and teaching; and bolsters strategic initiatives of area colleges and universities. In the area of health, the foundation supports programming that improves the delivery of health care to the indigent, uninsured, and other vulnerable populations and addresses health and health-care problems that intersect with social factors. In the area of human services, the foundation funds programming that: strengthens agencies that deliver critical human services and maintains the community's safety net and helps agencies respond to federal, state, and local public policy changes. In the area of community improvement, the foundation funds capacity-building and infrastructure-development projects including: assessments, planning, and implementation of technology for management and programmatic functions within an organization; technical assistance on wide-ranging topics, including grant writing, strategic planning, financial management services, business development, board and volunteer management, and marketing; and mergers, affiliations, or other restructuring efforts. Grant requests for general operating support and program support will be considered. Grants from the foundation are one year in duration. Application materials are available for download at the grant website. Applicants are strongly encouraged to review the state application guidelines for additional helpful information and clarifications before applying. Applicants are also encouraged to review the foundation's funding history (link is available from the grant website). There are no application deadlines for the Victor E. Speas Foundation. Proposals are reviewed on an ongoing basis.
Requirements: Applicants must have 501(c)3 tax-exempt status and serve the residents of Kansas City, Missouri. Applications must be mailed.
Restrictions: Grant requests for capital support will not be considered. The trust does not support requests from individuals, organizations attempting to influence policy through direct lobbying, or any political campaigns.
Geographic Focus: Missouri
Samples: Childrens Mercy Hospital Foundation, Kansas City, Missouri, $100,000, to fund research and clinical trials of reformulated adult drugs to benefit pediatric patients with rare and neglected blood and other cancers (2010); Open Options, Kansas City, Missouri, $25,000, United Cerebral Palsy of Greater Kansas City technology upgrade (2010); Metropolitan Community Colleges Foundation, Kansas City, Missouri, $50,000, for medical equipment for the Health Science Institute training facility (2010).
Contact: Spence Heddens, Market President; (816) 292-4301; Spence.heddens@baml.com
Internet: https://www.bankofamerica.com/philanthropic/fn_search.action
Sponsor: Victor E. Speas Foundation
1200 Main Street, 14th Floor, P.O. Box 219119
Kansas City, MO 64121-9119

BAML Vigneron Memorial Fund Grants **240**

The Vigneron Memorial Fund was established in 1959 to support charitable organizations that work to improve the lives of physically disabled children and adults. Preference is given to charitable organizations that serve the people of the city of Providence or the town of Narragansett, Rhode Island. Capital requests that fund handicapped assistive devices (wheelchairs, walkers, etc.) or adaptive equipment (lift installation, ramp installation, etc.) are strongly encouraged. Grant requests for general operating or program support will also be considered. The majority of grants from the Vigneron Memorial Fund are one year in duration. Applicants must apply online at the grant website. Applicants are strongly encouraged to do the following before applying: review the downloadable state application procedures for additional helpful information and clarifications; review the downloadable online-application guidelines at the grant website; review the foundation's funding history (link is available from the grant website); review the online application questions in advance; and review the list of required attachments. These will generally include: a list of board members, financial statements (audited, reviewed, or compiled by independent auditor); an organization summary; a list of other funding sources; an IRS Determination letter; and other required documents. All attachments must be uploaded in the online application as PDF, Word, or Excel files. The Vigneron Memorial Fund shares a mission and grantmaking focus with the John D. & Katherine A. Johnston Foundation. Both foundations have the same proposal deadline date of 11:59 p.m. on April 1. Applicants will be notified of grant decisions before May 31.
Requirements: Applicants must have 501(c)3 tax-exempt status.
Restrictions: The fund does not support requests from individuals, organizations attempting to influence policy through direct lobbying, or any political campaigns.
Geographic Focus: Rhode Island
Date(s) Application is Due: Apr 1
Samples: Homefront Health Care, Providence, Rhode Island, $10,000, general operations (2010); Nickerson Community Center, Providence, Rhode Island, $5,000, for disability access ramp for the main entrance (2010); WaterFire Providence, Providence, Rhode Island, WaterFire Access Program (a highly successful outreach program for children and adults with disabilities and/or mobility restrictions) (2010).
Contact: Emma Greene, Director; (617) 434-0329; emma.m.greene@baml.com
Internet: https://www.bankofamerica.com/philanthropic/fn_search.action
Sponsor: Vigneron Memorial Fund
225 Franklin Street, 4th Floor, MA1-225-04-02
Boston, MA 02110

BAML William J. Brace Charitable Trust **241**

The William J. Brace Charitable Trust was established in 1958 to support and promote quality educational, cultural, human-services, and health-care programming, with a preference for the following three areas: the education and health of children; the health and care of older adults; and hospitals in Kansas City, Missouri. Grant requests for general operating support and program support will be considered. Grants from the Trust are one year in duration. There are no application deadlines for the Brace Charitable Trust. Proposals are reviewed on an ongoing basis. Applicants may download the application and Missouri state guidelines at the grant website. Applicants are strongly encouraged to review the state guidelines for additional helpful information and clarifications on the three areas of interest.
Restrictions: The Brace Charitable Trust generally supports organizations that serve the residents of Kansas City, Missouri. Grant requests for capital support will not be considered.
Geographic Focus: Missouri
Samples: Childrens Mercy Hospital Foundation, Kansas City, Missouri, $105,000 (2010); Nonprofit Connect Network Learn Grow, Kansas City, Missouri, $5,000 (2010); Kansas City Repertory Theater, Kansas City, Missouri, $10,000 (2010).
Contact: Spence Heddens, Market President; (816) 292-4301; Spence.heddens@baml.com
Internet: https://www.bankofamerica.com/philanthropic/fn_search.action

Sponsor: William J. Brace Charitable Trust
1200 Main Street, 14th Floor, P.O. Box 219119
Kansas City, MO 64121-9119

BancorpSouth Foundation Grants 242
The BancorpSouth Foundation supports organizations involved with orchestras, secondary and higher education, legal aid, housing, youth development, and human services. Support is available in the form of general/operating grants in areas of operation, that include Arkansas, Mississippi and Tennessee. Applications for funding are accepted on a rolling basis and reviewed quarterly.
Requirements: Arkansas, Mississippi and Tennessee 501(c)3 non-profit organizations are eligible to apply. There is no application deadline nor is there an application form required when applying for funding. Applicants should include a detailed description of project and amount of funding requested in the proposal.
Restrictions: No grants to individuals.
Geographic Focus: Arkansas, Mississippi, Tennessee
Amount: 5,000 - 15,000 USD
Samples: Southern Arkansas University, Magnolia, AR, $15,000 (2008); Alpha House Home For Boys, Tupelo, MS, $5,000 (2008); Affordable Housing, Jackson, TN, $5,000 (2008).
Contact: Nash Allen, Grants Manager; (662) 680-2000
Sponsor: BancorpSouth Foundation
P.O. Box 789
Tupelo, MS 38802-0789

Banfi Vintners Foundation Grants 243
The foundation awards general operating grants to nonprofits in its areas of interest, including higher education, civic and public affairs, arts and humanities, wildlife protection, health (hospitals and disease research/prevention), religion, science, social services, and international. Grants are made nationwide, with preference given to requests from Massachusetts and the New York, NY, area.
Geographic Focus: Massachusetts, New York
Amount: 100 - 465,000 USD
Samples: Colgate U (Hamilton, NY)—for operating support, $75,000; Friends for Long Island's Heritage (Syosset, NY—for operating support, $25,000; Huntington Hospital Assoc (Huntington, NY)—for operating support, $25,000; Cornell U (Ithaca, NY)—for operating support, $465,000.
Contact: Philip Calderone, Executive Director; (516) 626-9200
Sponsor: Banfi Vintners Foundation
1111 Cedar Swamp Road
Glen Head, NY 11545

BankAtlantic Foundation Grants 244
The Foundation was created in 1994 as a 501(c)3 corporate foundation. Since then, the BA Foundation and BankAtlantic have awarded more than $10 million to charitable organizations throughout the state of Florida. The Foundation supports four key areas: community and economic development; human services; education; and the arts. The Foundation considers requests for specific projects, as well as for general operations. The majority of the grants made by the Foundation fall within the $1000 to $3000 range.
Requirements: Giving is limited to Florida. Funding consideration will be given to programs where BankAtlantic has a business presence. The Foundation will fund an organization one time per calendar year, up to three consecutive years. After three consecutive years of support, an organization may reapply after a one-year non-funding period.
Restrictions: No support is offered for hospitals, K-12 schools, national health-related organizations, political or lobbying organizations, religious, veteran, or fraternal organizations, school athletic teams, cheerleading squads, bands, or choirs. No grants are given to individuals, or for capital or building campaigns, courtesy or goodwill advertising to benefit publications, endowments, fund raising events, ticket purchases , travel, medical research, social functions, or sporting events.
Geographic Focus: Florida
Date(s) Application is Due: Mar 30; Oct 31
Amount: 1,000 - 3,000 USD
Contact: Marcia Barry-Smith; (954) 940-5058; (954) 940-5030
Internet: https://www.bankatlantic.com/bafoundation/
Sponsor: BankAtlantic Foundation
2100 West Cypress Creek Road
Fort Lauderdale, FL 33309-1823

Bank of America Charitable Foundation Anchor Institutions Grants 245
Bank of America's local leaders, working within their communities, look for opportunities to support community stakeholders; opportunities that will further economic and community development, that will do more than put bricks and mortar on your block. When it does find those opportunities, the Foundation invites anchor institutions to apply for a grant. Such institutions might include: arts and cultural institutions such as museums, zoos, and performance halls; colleges, universities, and community colleges that attract and educate the workforce; and hospitals that provide excellent health care.
Geographic Focus: All U.S. States
Samples: Apollo Theater, New York, New York; Children's Hospital, Boston, Massachusetts; Cook Children's Hospital, Fort Worth, Texas; New Jersey Performing Arts Center, Newark, New Jersey.
Contact: Anne Finucane, Foundation Chairperson/Chief Marketing Officer; (800) 218-9946 or (617) 434-9405; anne.m.finucane@bankofamerica.com
Internet: http://www.bankofamerica.com/foundation/index.cfm?template=fd_anchorinstitutions
Sponsor: Bank of America Charitable Foundation
100 North Tryon Street
Charlotte, NC 28255

Bank of America Charitable Foundation National Programs and Partners Grants 246
Part of the Foundation's philanthropic objective is to sustain community efforts and provide funding flexibility so nonprofits can distribute funds as they know will best serve their clients and build their organizations. Its national partners are an integral part of the neighborhoods they serve. These are organizations that complement what the Foundation is able to do in a local community and collectively impact hundreds of neighborhoods across the country. It's possible an organization needs funding for capacity building or operating support at the national level; it may be just as possible the funding needs to be directed to the local level to strengthen that office's reach. And when disaster strikes, the Foundation is prepared to respond nationally when need overwhelms local capabilities to respond.
Requirements: To be considered for a local grant, an organization must be: tax-exempt under section 501(c)3 of the Internal Revenue Code; must be based and serve communities in particular markets; and must be aligned with funding priorities for those markets. A map of markets is available online.
Restrictions: The following organizations are not eligible for funding: organizations that deny service to a potential client or beneficiary on the basis of race, religion, color, sex, sexual orientation, age, national origin, ancestry, citizenship, veteran, or disability status, individuals, including those seeking scholarships or fellowship assistance; political, labor, fraternal organizations, or civic clubs; religious organizations (for example, churches and synagogues). Some secular community service programs such as soup kitchens, shelters for the homeless, and job banks are eligible, even when sponsored by religious groups; individual pre-K-12 schools (public or private); sports, athletic events, or athletic programs; travel-related events, including student trips or tours; development or production of books, films, videos, or television programs; or memorial campaigns.
Geographic Focus: All U.S. States
Contact: Program Administrator; (800) 218-9946
Internet: http://www.bankofamerica.com/foundation/index.cfm?template=fd_nationalprograms
Sponsor: Bank of America Charitable Foundation
100 North Tryon Street
Charlotte, NC 28255

Bank of America Charitable Foundation Neighborhood Builders Grants 247
The Foundation awards $200,000 ($100,000 annually for 2 years) grants to two organizations from each of the 45 Bank of America markets with programs designed to create vibrant neighborhoods. The foundation provides general operating support and leadership development workshops. Recently, the program went international with a new market in London, United Kingdom. Applications for these awards are accepted beginning January 1 through June 30 each year.
Requirements: To be considered for the program, an applicant: qualifying nonprofit organizations must have a tax-exempt status by the Internal Revenue Service and are not classified as a private foundation; must be registered with the Charity Commission for England and Wales for the London, United Kingdom market; and must be based and serve communities in Neighborhood Excellence Initiative markets listed at the web site.

Restrictions: The following categories are ineligible for funding: individuals, including those seeking scholarships or fellowship assistance; political, labor, fraternal organizations, or civic clubs; religious organizations (for example, churches and synagogues); individual pre-K through 12 schools (public or private); Pre-Sixth Form/College (London, United Kingdom); sports, athletic events, or athletic programs; travel-related events, including student trips or tours; development or production of books, films, videos, or television programs; memorial campaigns; national health organizations (or their local affiliates) or research/disease advocacy groups; and colleges and universities.
Geographic Focus: All U.S. States
Date(s) Application is Due: Jun 30
Amount: 200,000 USD
Contact: Anne Finucane, Foundation Chairperson/Chief Marketing Officer; (800) 218-9946 or (617) 434-9405; anne.m.finucane@bankofamerica.com
Internet: http://www.bankofamerica.com/foundation/index.cfm?template=fd_neighborbuilders
Sponsor: Bank of America Charitable Foundation
100 North Tryon Street
Charlotte, NC 28255

Bank of America Charitable Gift Fund - General Fund Grants 248
The Bank of America Charitable Gift Fund - General Fund was established in 1955 to support and promote quality educational, human services, and health care programming for underserved populations. Grant requests for general operating support are strongly encouraged. Program support will also be considered. Small, program-related capital expenses may be included in general operating or program requests. The application deadline is September 1, and applicants will be notified of grant decisions before November 30.
Requirements: 501(c)3 organizations serving the residents of Massachusetts are eligible to apply.
Restrictions: The majority of grants from the Bank of America Charitable Gift Fund - General Fund are 1 year in duration. On occasion, multi-year support is awarded.
Geographic Focus: Massachusetts
Date(s) Application is Due: Sep 1
Contact: George Thorn, Vice President; (866) 778-6859; george.thorn@baml.com
Internet: https://www.bankofamerica.com/philanthropic/grantmaking.action
Sponsor: Bank of America Charitable Gift Fund
100 Federal Street, MA5-100-16-01
Boston, MA 02110

Bank of America Client Foundation Grants 249
The Foundation gives primarily to the arts, education, human services, natural science, youth and family organizations, and historic preservation. Fields of interest include: adult education; aging; AIDS; arts; children and youth services; community and economic development; crime and violence prevention; economically disadvantaged; education; the environment; family services; health care; historic preservation and historical societies; human services; marine science; media; mental health/crisis services; museums; performing arts; recreation; and urban/community development.
Requirements: Giving is limited to organizations operating in or providing services to residents of Sarasota County, Florida.
Restrictions: Generally the Foundation will not provide grants for: endowments, deficit financing, debt reduction, or ordinary operating expenses; conferences, seminars, workshops, travel, surveys, advertising, fund-raising costs or research; annual giving campaigns; individuals; projects that have already been completed; public or private schools; or child care facilities.
Geographic Focus: Florida
Date(s) Application is Due: Apr 15; Sep 15
Amount: 35,000 USD
Samples: Jewish Family and Children's Service of Sarasota-Manatee, Inc., $50,000 - to purchase conference room equipment and Brain Fitness Center technology and furnishings (2008); Pines of Sarasota Foundation, Inc., $45,000 - to renovate sections of The Garden - The Pines Alzheimer's/Dementia Facility (2008); Forty Carrots of Sarasota, Inc., $50,000 - Capital Campaign to purchase building and property and create a reserve to cover long-term maintenance (2008).
Contact: Renee Armbruster, CTFA Senior Vice President; (941) 952-2804; (941) 952-2768; renee.armbruster@ustrust.com
Sponsor: Bank of America Client Foundation
Bank of America Private Wealth Management, 1605 Main Street, Suite 800
Sarasota, FL 34236

Bank of Tokyo-Mitsubishi Community Grants 250
The foundation provides financial support to community-based organizations and programs that provide affordable housing, promote community economic development, and provide supportive community services targeted to low- and moderate-income people and neighborhoods. Established, well-managed organizations that are directly involved in serving low- and moderate-income individuals and neighborhoods, and administering programs that respond to community needs using a comprehensive, integrated approach, will be given priority. In general, the grants may be used for general operating purposes unless otherwise specified in the grant letter. The deadline for proposal submissions is generally the last business day of May. Applicants should send a letter including the following information: address of organization; detailed description of service provided to the local community by the organization; amount requested; names, addresses, and affiliations of managers, directors, trustees, and board members; copy of IRS exemption letter; audited financial statement for the previous two years and projected budget; list of grants and board giving for current and previous fiscal years; and references.
Requirements: New York, NY, nonprofits are eligible.
Restrictions: Grants are not awarded to support individuals; religious, sectarian, fraternal,veterans, or labor organizations; political or lobbying groups; organizations outside operating areas; fund-raising activities; or for deficit reduction.
Geographic Focus: New York
Date(s) Application is Due: May 28
Contact: Fiona Aitken, (212) 782-4548 or (212) 782-4000; (212) 782-6420; bgilroy@btmna.com or nahq@btmna.com
Sponsor: Bank of Tokyo-Mitsubishi Trust Company
1251 Avenue of the Americas, 15th Floor
New York, NY 10020-1104

Barbara Delano Foundation Grants 251
The foundation awards grants internationally in its fields of interest, including environmental conservation and wildlife preservation. Types of support include annual campaigns, building construction/renovation, equipment acquisition, challenge/matching grants, and general operating support. The board meets in the spring and fall.
Requirements: BDF only accepts proposals for programs outside the United States, primarily in developing countries. BDF only supports research directly related to the implementation of a conservation program.
Geographic Focus: All U.S. States
Date(s) Application is Due: Sep 1; Oct 15
Amount: 1,000 - 80,000 USD
Samples: Environmental Investigation Agency (Washington, DC)— for the Tigers in Crisis Campaign, $80,000; Environmental Investigation Agency (Washington, DC)—for Tigers in Crisis Campaign, $70,000.
Contact: Stephanie Carnow, Program Assistant; (415) 834-1758; (415) 834-1759; bdfoundation@usa.net
Internet: http://www.bdfoundation.org
Sponsor: Barbara Delano Foundation
450 Pacific Avenue, 2nd Floor
San Francisco, CA 94133-4640

Barker Foundation Grants 252
The foundation offers funding to New Hampshire non-profit organizations in the areas of: children/youth services; education; health organizations, association; hospitals (general); and human services. Giving primarily for health associations, social services and youth. Grants are awarded in the following types: Annual campaigns building/renovation; capital campaigns; continuing support; equipment; general/operating support and; program development.
Requirements: New Hampshire nonprofit organizations are eligible for funding. The Foundation accepts written requests only. No formal application form is required. Send a 1 page concept paper and request for guidelines to the Foundation with a SASE for response.
Restrictions: Grants are not made to individuals.
Geographic Focus: New Hampshire
Amount: 2,000 - 13,000 USD
Samples: Boys and Girls Club of Greater Nashua, Nashua, NH, $10,000; Senior Activity Center, Nashua, NH, $2,000; Nashua Soup Kitchen and Shelter, Nashua, NH, $13,000.
Contact: Allan Barker, Treasurer
Sponsor: Barker Foundation
P.O. Box 328
Nashua, NH 03061-0328

Barker Welfare Foundation Grants 253

The mission of the foundation is to make grants to qualified charitable organizations whose initiatives improve the quality of life, with an emphasis on strengthening youth and families and to reflect the philosophy of Catherine B. Hickox, the Founder. Consideration will be given to applications from institutions and agencies operating in the fields of health, welfare, education and literacy, cultural activities, and civic affairs, primarily serving the metropolitan area of New York, NY, and Michigan City, IN. The foundation board meets twice per year to consider requests.
Requirements: In advance of submitting a request, a brief letter or telephone call is suggested to determine if the organization seeking to apply for a grant falls within the current general policy of the Foundation. Before the Foundation sends out its application form, a brief 2-3 page letter describing the organization, the purpose and amount requested should be sent. A copy of the first page of the most recent 990 filed with the IRS and a current budget for the whole organization and a budget for program/project (if requesting program/ project support) including income and expense should be sent with the letter of inquiry. Grants are made to tax-exempt organizations which have received a ruling by the Internal Revenue Service that they are organizations described in Section 501(c)3 and classified in Section 509(a)(1),(2), or (3) of the Internal Revenue Code (publicly supported organizations and their affiliates).
Restrictions: Appeals for the following will be declined: organizations not located in nor directly serving the defined areas; national health; welfare; or education agencies; institutions or funds; scholarships; fellowships; loans; student aid; appeals from individuals; medical and scientific research; private elementary and secondary schools; colleges; universities; professional schools; trade organizations; films; program advertising; conferences; seminars; benefits and fund raising costs; start-up organizations; emergency funds; and deficit financing; lobbying-related or legislative activities; endowment funds; and intermediary organizations.
Geographic Focus: Indiana, New York
Date(s) Application is Due: Feb 1; Aug 1
Amount: 7,500 - 15,000 USD
Contact: Sarane Ross, President; (516) 759-5592; BarkerSMD@aol.com
Internet: http://www.barkerwelfare.org
Sponsor: Barker Welfare Foundation
P.O. Box 2
Glen Head, NY 11545

Barr Fund Grants 254

The fund awards grants to Illinois nonprofits in its areas of interest, including services for children and youth, orchestras, higher education, mental health/ crisis services, Jewish temples and organizations, and social services. Grants are awarded for general operating support. There are no application forms or deadlines. Submit a letter of request.
Requirements: Illinois nonprofits are eligible.
Restrictions: Individuals are not eligible.
Geographic Focus: Illinois
Amount: 100 - 75,000 USD
Samples: Rush University Medical Center, Chicago, IL, $10,000 (2008); New Israel Fund, Washington, DC, $1,000 (2008); Highland Park Community Foundation, Highland Park, IL, $1,000 (2008); The Barr Harris Center of the Institute For Psychoanalysis, Chicago, IL, $50,000 (2008).
Contact: Donald Lubin, President; (312) 782-4710; (312) 876-8000
Sponsor: Barr Fund
230 West Monroe Street, Suite 330
Chicago, IL 60606-4701

Batchelor Foundation Grants 255

The foundation supports food banks and organizations involved with arts and culture, education, the environment, animals and wildlife, health, human services, and economically disadvantaged people. Special emphasis is directed toward programs designed to engage in medical research and provide care for childhood diseases; and promote study, preservation, and public awareness of the natural environment. Funding is available in the form of: capital campaigns; continuing support; endowments; general/operating support; and program development grants. There are no application forms. Initial approach should be a letter that details the grant proposal.
Requirements: Florida area nonprofits are eligible.
Restrictions: Individuals are not eligible.
Geographic Focus: Florida
Amount: 1,000 - 1,000,000 USD
Samples: Community Partnership for Homeless, Miami, FL, $1,056,600—for general operating support and endowment (2008); Fairchild Tropical Botanic Garden, Coral Gables, FL, $540,000— For general operating support (2008); University of Miami, Miami, FL, $525,000— for general operating support (2008).
Contact: Anne Batchelor-Robjohns, Co-C.E.O; (305) 416-9066 or (305) 534-5004; jbatchelor@bellsouth.net
Sponsor: Batchelor Foundation
111 NE 1st Street, Suite 820
Miami, FL 33132

Batts Foundation Grants 256

Established in 1988, the Batts Foundation supports organizations involved with arts and culture, K-12 and higher education, disease, and human services. Types of support include: annual campaigns, building and renovation; capital campaigns; continuing support; operating support; endowments; matching grants; program development; and scholarship funding. Grants will be awarded primarily in the western Michigan area, particularly the communities of Huron, Zeeland, and Grand Rapids. There are no application forms or deadlines with which to adhere, and applicants should begin by submitting a one page letter summarizing the project.
Requirements: Michigan nonprofit organizations are eligible.
Restrictions: Individuals are ineligible.
Geographic Focus: Michigan
Amount: 250 - 25,000 USD
Contact: Robert Batts, Director; (616) 956-3053; jsand@battsgroup.com
Sponsor: Batts Foundation
3855 Sparks Drive SE, Suite 222
Grand Rapids, MI 49546-2427

Baughman Foundation Grants 257

The foundation awards grants to eligible nonprofit organizations in its areas of interest, including civic affairs, community development, higher education, and youth programs. Types of support include building construction/renovation, endowment funds, operating budgets, and special projects. Giving is primarily in southwest Kansas, the Oklahoma panhandle, and southeast Colorado. The board meets monthly; application deadlines are the first Wednesday of each month. Please contact the Foundation for guidelines.
Requirements: Grants are only available to charitable organizations as defined under IRS Code Section 501(c)3.
Geographic Focus: Colorado, Kansas, Oklahoma
Contact: Carol Feather-Francis, President; (620) 624-1371
Sponsor: Baughman Foundation
112 West 3rd Street, P.O. Box 1356
Liberal, KS 67905-1356

Bay and Paul Foundations, Inc Grants 258

General operating and project grants are awarded for support of children's services and precollege educational programs, with an emphasis on technology and enhancement of science, math, and writing curricula; preservation of cultural and natural history collections and collections care training in museums, zoos, libraries, and botanical gardens; advocacy and research programs for preserving biodiversity; and Native American cultural heritage preservation and economic development programs. There are no application forms. Proposals should be directed to the executive director and should include a brief description of the applicant organization and of the program for which funding is requested, including objectives and numbers served; a project budget or financials; other expected sources of support; qualifications of key personnel; and evidence of tax-exempt status. The foundation's directors meet three times a year, usually in January, May, and October, to consider grant proposals. Requests are not accepted via fax. Regular postal service delivery is the preferred method of proposal acceptance.
Requirements: Nonprofits in Connecticut, Massachusetts, Maine, New Hampshire, New Jersey, New York, Rhode Island, and Vermont are eligible.
Restrictions: Grants do not support requests for endowments, building campaigns, building construction or maintenance, sectarian religious programs, books or studies, individual scholarships or fellowships, loans, travel, film, television or video productions, programs consisting primarily of conferences, for annual fund appeals, or to other than publicly recognized charities. First time grants for K-12 arts-in-education programs and K-12 science and math programs are currently geographically restricted to the New York City metropolitan area.

Geographic Focus: Connecticut, Maine, Massachusetts, New Hampshire, New Jersey, New York, Rhode Island, Vermont
Samples: American Assoc for State and Local History (Nashville, TN)—to update the book Starting Right: A Guide to Museum Planning, $13,100.
Contact: Frederick Bay, Executive Director; (212) 663-1115; (212) 932-0316; info@bayandpaulfoundations.org
Internet: http://www.bayandpaulfoundations.org/areas.html
Sponsor: Bay and Paul Foundations
17 West 94th Street
New York, NY 10025

Bay and Paul Foundations Grants 259

The majority of grants are now directed to professional development with an emphasis on facilitative, distributive leadership and to the intentional interruption of inequitable policies, practices, and cultural norms. Many grants support a variety of efforts to empower students and teachers by promoting the practice of democracy in schools, encouraging student voice, advancing an ethic of environmental stewardship, and integrating academic course work with meaningful community service. In addition, math and science projects and projects that seek to strengthen the developmentally critical role of the arts are supported.
Requirements: Proposals should be addressed to the Executive Director and submitted by mail. Please prepare applications with a concern for the environment. Submit only one copy of the proposal and limit the amount of supporting materials. There is no required application form.
Restrictions: Grants are not made to individuals (except Biodiversity Leadership awards), building campaigns, sectarian religious programs, or to other than publicly recognized charities.
Geographic Focus: All U.S. States
Date(s) Application is Due: Mar 1; Sep 1; Dec 1
Amount: 3,000 - 10,000 USD
Contact: Frederick Bay, Executive Director; (212) 663-1115; (212) 932-0316; info@bayandpaulfoundations.org
Internet: http://www.bayandpaulfoundations.org/grants.html
Sponsor: Bay and Paul Foundations
17 West 94th Street
New York, NY 10025

Bayer Foundation Grants 260

The Bayer Foundation supports programs that enhance the quality of life, provide unique and enriching opportunities that connect diverse groups and ensure preparedness for tomorrow's leaders. The Foundation welcomes proposals from 501(c)3 organizations whose programming matches at least one of the following areas: Civic and Social Service Programs; Education and Workforce Development; Arts and Culture and Health and Human Services.
Requirements: 501(c)3 nonprofit organizations in Bayer operating communities are eligible. Submit proposals to regional offices in California, Connecticut, Georgia, Indiana, Kansas, Massachusetts, New Jersey, New York, North Carolina, Ohio, Pennsylvania, Texas and West Virginia.
Restrictions: The Foundation will not fund: For-profit organizations or those without Internal Revenue Service code 501(c)3 nonprofit, tax-exempt status; Organizations that discriminate on the basis of race, color, creed, gender, sexual orientation or national origin; General operating support for United Way affiliated agencies. Only support for special projects will be considered; Organizations or programs designed to influence legislation or elect candidates to public office; General endowment funds; Deficit reduction or operating reserves; Religious organizations; Charitable dinners, events or sponsorships; Community or event advertising; Individuals; Student trips or exchange programs; Athletic sponsorships or scholarships; Telephone solicitations; Organizations outside of the United States or its territories
Geographic Focus: California, Connecticut, Georgia, Indiana, Kansas, Massachusetts, New Jersey, New York, North Carolina, Ohio, Pennsylvania, Texas, West Virginia
Samples: Robert Morris College (Moon Township, PA)—for the Bayer Ctr for Nonprofit Management, which awards master's degrees in business administration with a focus on nonprofit management and that offers technical and consulting services, educational programs, and research and referral services to nonprofit organizations in Pennsylvania, $500,000.
Contact: Bayer Foundation; (800) 422-9374
Internet: http://www.bayerus.com/about/community/i_foundation.html
Sponsor: Bayer Foundation
100 Bayer Road, Building 4
Pittsburgh, PA 15205-9741

Bearemy's Kennel Pals Grants 261

The program provides direct support for animals in domestic pet programs including animal welfare organizations, pet rescue and rehabilitation organizations, and therapeutic and humane education pet programs. Grants will be a one-time contribution and generally range from $1,000 to $10,000, but the average grant tends to be $4,000. Programs that will be funded include: (1) Individual Project grants generally for one-time purchases or to fulfill a short-term need. Examples include equipment purchases or spay/neuter events, etc; (2) Organization Program grants - start-up or operational costs for ongoing programs. Examples include spay/neuter programs, humane education initiatives, and service dog training programs.
Requirements: While the geographic focus of the program is broad (United States and Canada), priority is given to organizations located near Build-A-Bear Workshop stores. United States applicants must be a tax-exempt organization under Section 501(c)3 of the IRS Code, and not a private foundation, within the meaning of Code Sections 509(a)(1) or 509(a)(2), or a state college or university within the meaning of Code Section 511(a)(2)(B) (a Public Charity). In addition, grant recipients must certify that they are not a supporting organization within the meaning of Code Section 509(a)(3). Canadian applicants must be a registered Canadian charity.
Restrictions: Grant types not funded: (1) Capital Campaigns; (2) Construction or new facility expenses; (3) Fundraising or Event Sponsorships; (4) Political Activities; (5) Religious organizations for religious purposes.
Geographic Focus: All U.S. States, Canada
Date(s) Application is Due: Mar 31; Jun 30; Sep 31; Dec 31
Amount: 1,000 - 10,000 USD
Samples: Animal Advocates of South Carolina (Barnwell, SC); Bunny Castle Rabbit Rescue (Bishop, CA); EquiFriends (Snohomish, WA); Hearing and Service Dogs of Minnesota (Minneapolis, MN); Pet Adoption Fund (Canoga Park, CA).
Contact: Maxine Clark, President; (314) 423-8000, ext. 5366; giving@buildabear.com
Internet: http://www.buildabear.com/aboutus/community/bearhugs.aspx
Sponsor: Build-A-Bear Workshop Bear Hugs Foundation
1954 Innerbelt Business Center Drive
Saint Louis, MO 63114

Beattie-McCay Sancuary Grants 262

The Foundation is focused on animal welfare, with funding going toward general operations and to individuals involved in helping animals. Giving is primarily in the Los Angeles metropolitan area of California. Though an application form is required, the Foundation requires an initial letter of inquiry. There are no deadlines.
Geographic Focus: California
Contact: Peggy McCay, President; (323) 650-8588
Sponsor: Beattie-McCay Sancuary
2714 Carmar Drive
Los Angeles, CA 90046-1009

Bedford Community Health Foundation Grants 263

The foundation awards grants to nonprofit health associations. Types of support include general operating support, equipment acquisition, and scholarships to individuals. Application forms are not required. Grants may be submitted throughout the year, however the Board of Trustees will only review grants at the May and November meetings. Applicants should call the executive director to discuss the proposal and to arrange a meeting.
Requirements: Nonprofits serving Bedford and Bedford County are eligible.
Restrictions: Individuals are not eligible.
Geographic Focus: Virginia
Date(s) Application is Due: Apr 1; Oct 1
Amount: 250 - 50,000 USD
Contact: Program Contact; (540) 586-5292; (540) 587-5819; bchf@bchf.org
Internet: http://www.bchf.org
Sponsor: Bedford Community Health Foundation
P.O. Box 1104
Bedford, VA 24523

Beerman Foundation Grants 264

The foundation awards general support grants to nonprofits in Ohio in its areas of interest, including Christian and Jewish religion, higher education, community services, Holocaust, Israel, Jewish education, Jewish welfare, museums, religious higher education, social issues, temples, and youth groups such as YMCA/YWCA. Applicants should submit a brief letter of inquiry

describing the program and organization. Specify charitable function and purpose of funds sought. There are no application deadlines.
Requirements: Nonprofit organizations in Ohio are eligible.
Geographic Focus: Ohio
Contact: Timothy D. Albro, Executive Vice President; (937) 222-1285, ext. 104; talbro@beermanrealty.com
Internet: http://www.beermanrealty.com/beerman_foundation.asp
Sponsor: Beerman Foundation
11 West Monument Building, 8th Floor
Dayton, OH 45402

Beim Foundation Grants **265**
The foundation awards grants to eligible nonprofit organizations in its areas of interest, including arts and culture, environmental conservation, education, and social services. Types of support include program grants, general operating grants, capital campaigns, building construction/renovation, land acquisition, equipment acquisition, and seed grants. High priority is given to the following types of projects: capital drives and equipment purchases; innovative start-up programs that require a moderate amount of grant money; intergenerational projects that involve community service; cooperative projects that involve several agencies or volunteers; on-going programs that have proven themselves unique and essential; matching funds drives. Low priority is given to the following types of projects: medical research, debt retirement, national fundraising programs, and requests from public schools and governmental agencies due to the lack of good financial data. Deadlines are February 3 for education, and human services; and July 3 for arts, arts small capital equipment, and environment. Guidelines are available online.
Requirements: 501(c)3 tax-exempt organizations located within Minnesota, as well as the city of Denver, CO; counties of Park and Gallatin in Montana; county of Santa Fe in New Mexico; and county of Cumberland in Maine are eligible.
Restrictions: The foundation does not fund individuals; private foundations; political organizations or campaigns; religious organizations, including schools, except for secular human service activities; memberships, subscriptions, tickets for benefits, conferences, fundraising events, or annual campaigns; organizations that have as a substantial part of their purpose the influencing of legislation; endowment; multi-year commitments; or international efforts.
Geographic Focus: Colorado, Maine, Minnesota, New Mexico
Date(s) Application is Due: Jan 17; Jul 18
Amount: 2,000 - 10,000 USD
Contact: Grants Administrator; (612) 605-8192; contact@beimfoundation.org
Internet: http://www.beimfoundation.org/guide.html
Sponsor: Beim Foundation
3109 W 50th Street, Suite 120
Minneapolis, MN 55410-2102

Beldon Fund Grants **266**
The fund focuses project and general support grants in two programs: human health and the environment, and key states. Human health and the environment—the fund seeks proposals that engage new constituencies in exposing the connection between toxic chemicals and human health and in promoting public policies that prevent or eliminate environmental risks to people's health. The program focuses grant making in three areas: new advocates, human exposure to toxic chemicals, and environmental justice. Key states—the fund believes that states hold the key to bringing about rapid, real change on environmental issues and policy in the United States. By strengthening public support for environmental protection in several of these key states, the fund hopes to transform the nation's approach to environmental protection. The fund is currently accepting proposals from Florida, Michigan, Minnesota, Wisconsin, and North Carolina for this program. Proposals do not need to be tied to any particular issue or set of issues, but targeted issues must be those that will build active public support for the environment. From time to time, the fund will add and remove states from this program. Types of support include special projects, seed money, general operating budgets, and technical assistance. One-year and multiyear grants are awarded. Due date applies to the letter of intent; full proposals are by invitation.By supporting effective, nonprofit advocacy organizations, the Beldon Fund seeks to build a national consensus to achieve and sustain a healthy planet. The Fund plans to invest its entire principal and earnings by 2009 to attain this goal.
Requirements: 501(c)3 tax-exempt organizations are eligible.
Restrictions: Grants do not support international efforts, academic or university efforts, school-based environmental education, land acquisition, wildlife or habitat preservation, film or video production, deficit reduction, endowments, capital campaigns, acquisitions of museums, service delivery, scholarshp, publications, or arts/culture.
Geographic Focus: Florida, Michigan, Minnesota, North Carolina, Wisconsin
Date(s) Application is Due: Feb 28; Jun 13
Amount: 5,000 - 100,000 USD
Samples: Ctr for Public Interest Research (Boston, MA)—for its Campaign Staff Training Institute Program to ameliorate the shortage of skilled activists, $75,000; Institute for Conservation Leadership (Takoma Park, MD)—for its outreach and hands-on support efforts, along with Environmental Support Ctr, $10,000; State Environmental Leadership Program (Madison, WI)—for general support, $175,000; Washington Environmental Alliance for Voter Education (Seattle, WA)—for general support, $50,000.
Contact: Holeri Faruolo, Grants Manager; (800) 591-9595 or (212) 616-5600; (212) 616-5656; info@beldon.org
Internet: http://www.beldon.org
Sponsor: Beldon Fund
99 Madison Avenue, 8th Floor
New York, NY 10016

Belk Foundation Grants **267**
The Foundation makes grants to a wide variety of community-based nonprofit organizations and institutions whose missions and actions support the advancement of Christian causes and the up-building of mankind. The Foundation supports local and regional organizations by: assisting secondary schools, colleges and universities and their programs; assisting religious institutions and organizations and their programs; supporting area arts and other cultural organizations and their programs; supporting community-based human services organizations and their programs; and aiding hospitals and health care organizations and their programs.
Requirements: 501(c)3 nonprofits in communities in the 14 states where Belk stores are located. Preference is given to organizations in North Carolina.
Restrictions: Grants are not awarded to: individuals, including students; public, government or quasi-governmental programs, agencies or organizations (excluding certain public secondary schools, colleges and universities); or international programs and/or organizations. Additionally, the Foundation does not provide door prizes, gift certificates, merchandise or other giveaways.
Geographic Focus: Alabama, Arkansas, Florida, Georgia, Kentucky, Louisiana, Maryland, Mississippi, North Carolina, South Carolina, Tennessee, Texas, Virginia, West Virginia
Date(s) Application is Due: Apr 15; Oct 15
Contact: Susan C. Blount, Foundation Administrator; (704) 426-8396; susan_blount@belk.com
Internet: http://www.belk.com/AST/Misc/Belk_Stores/About_Us/Belk_Community/Belk_Foundation.jsp
Sponsor: Belk Foundation
2801 W Tyvola Road
Charlotte, NC 28217-4500

Belo Foundation Grants **268**
The foundation supports primarily Dallas-Fort Worth area nonprofits. The company's giving focuses on two main areas: enhancing urban parks and open spaces, and journalism education that promotes an informed citizenry. Past grant winners include local groups that commissioned art works for downtown public places, schools, universities, and children's agencies. Belo provides funds for capital and endowment campaigns, scholarship funds, operating budgets, and building construction and renovation.
Requirements: The foundation supports charitable organizations focusing on its areas of interest in the cities where Belo has companies.
Geographic Focus: All U.S. States
Samples: YMCA of Metropolitan Dallas (Dallas, TX)—for capital support of its campaign to build eight new facilities and to expand and improve 15 existing branches, $75,000; Bacone College (Muskogee, OK)—for its capital campaign, $10,000.
Contact: Amy Meadows, Executive Director; (214) 977-6661; (214) 977-6620
Internet: http://www.belo.com/about/foundation.x2
Sponsor: Belo Foundation
P.O. Box 655237
Dallas, TX 75625-5237

Belvedere Fund Enivronmental Grants 269

The fund awards grants to grassroots state and regional environmental organizations, toxics organizations, and multi-issue organizations that make environmental advocacy a high priority. Areas of interest include organizational development and capacity building, including diversifying and expanding sources of funding; citizen participation; outreach to new constituencies; coalition building; and training and technical assistance. Types of support include general operating support and project development. A letter of inquiry may be submitted via email or postal mail. Application information is available online.

Restrictions: Requests are not accepted for academic or university grants; school, classroom, museum, or park-based environmental education; deficit reduction; land acquisition; capital campaigns; endowments; museum acquisition or collections; service delivery programs; research; film, video, or other visual media production; arts and culture; or scholarships.

Geographic Focus: All U.S. States

Amount: Up to 25,000 USD

Samples: Western Organization of Resource Councils Education Project (Billings, MT)—to support the Western Mining Activist Network, $25,000; Institute for Conservation Leadership (Takoma Park, MD)—to help grassroots environmental groups address the impact of September 11 terrorism and its aftermath on their work, $10,000; Northeast Action (Boston, MA)—to support the ePower Project, $80,000 over two years; Dakota Rural Action (Brookings, SD)—to organize citizens and promote public policy relating to the food industry in South Dakota, $90,000 over three years.

Contact: Catherine Lerza, Funds Advisor; (202) 293-0062; belvedere@tides.org

Sponsor: Belvedere Fund
2000 P Street NW, Suite 408
Washington, DC 20036

Bemis Company Foundation Grants 270

Funding is concentrated on those institutions, programs and organizations that encourage the development of educational, social welfare and health, cultural and civic institutions. Programs such as the Bemis Scholarship Program are designed to benefit employees. Additionally, funds are directed to organizations reflecting employees' volunteerism wherever possible, and employee matching programs such as FoodShare and the Educational and Nonprofit Gift Matching Plans are designed to enhance employees' personal donations.

Requirements: Grant proposals need not follow a specific format, but all proposals should cover the following points: name of organization and amount requested, brief description of the objectives for which the grant is sought, details regarding how the objectives are to be met, budget-including information about existing and other sources of income, and officers and Board members. Grant applications should also include a statement that the organization has tax-exempt status under Section 501(c)3 of the Internal Revenue Code and that contributions to it are tax deductible.

Restrictions: All initial inquiries should be made by mail, not by telephone or personal visit. Bemis does not make grants to individuals or organizations for religious or political purposes, either for lobbying efforts or campaigns. Bemis generally does not make grants for educational capital funds programs, endowment purposes, or for trips or tours. No grants will be made for more than three years.

Geographic Focus: All U.S. States

Samples: Regional Domestic Abuse Services (Neenah, WI)—$50,000; Science Museum of Minnesota (MN)—$260,000; YMCA of Metropolitan Minneapolis (MN)—$25,000.

Contact: Grant Administrator; BemisFoundation@bemis.com

Internet: http://www.bemis.com/citizenship

Sponsor: Bemis Company Foundation
222 South Ninth Street, Suite 440
Minneapolis, MN 55402-3373

Ben & Jerry's Foundation Grants 271

The foundation funds grassroots projects that typically are initiated and run by young people, that demonstrate long-term viability, and that empower those who traditionally have been disenfranchised in society. A variety of youth-led efforts will be funded, including ones that support minority or at-risk youths in leadership skills. Additional grantmaking areas include children and families and the environment. Each quarter, the foundation also funds a small number of material grants. The foundation accepts and reviews letters of intent throughout the year. Formal proposals will be invited, and the deadlines are listed. Small awards of under $1000 require only a letter. A letter of interest cover page is available on the website.

Requirements: Grants are distributed to organizations with IRS 501(c)3 status or who have a sponsoring agency with this status. Generally, the foundation funds projects with budgets less than $250,000. For all correspondence, use recycled paper, and print on both sides. Avoid plastic covers, sheet protectors, and glossy photos.

Restrictions: The foundation does not fund discretionary or emergency requests, colleges or universities, individuals or scholarship programs, research projects, capital campaigns, state agencies, religious programs, international or foreign-based programs, or social service programs.

Geographic Focus: All U.S. States

Amount: 1,001 - 15,000 USD

Samples: People Escaping Poverty Project (Moorhead, MN)—for general and program support, $10,000; Sunshine Project (Austin, TX)—for a national grassroots coalition that brings together arms-control, biotechnology, health, and social-justice organizations in order to monitor U.S. biodefense research, $10,000; Swell Cinema (San Francisco, CA)—to produce a collection of 10 short films designed to increase voter participation in the 2004 elections, $10,000; Tennesseans for Fair Taxation (Knoxville, TN)—to strengthen its Workshop Facilitator Network, which trains members and volunteers to advocate a revamped tax structure in Tennessee that would ensure adequate revenue for the benefit of all state residents, $10,000.

Contact: Program Contact; (802) 846-1500; (802) 846-1556; info@benjerry.com

Internet: http://www.benjerry.com/foundation/index.html

Sponsor: Ben and Jerry's Foundation
30 Community Drive
South Burlington, VT 05403-6828

Bender Foundation Grants 272

The foundation supports projects for higher education, health agencies, Jewish welfare funds and organizations, Christian youth organizations, and social welfare. Emphasis is support for programs to assist the elderly and aging, children and parenting, and environmental programs. Grants are awarded for challenge/matching grants, endowments, general operations, and scholarships.

Requirements: Grants are made to organizations and institutions in Maryland and Washington, DC. An applicant should initially send a brief letter of intent. Full proposals are by invitation.

Restrictions: Grants are not made to individuals.

Geographic Focus: District of Columbia, Maryland

Date(s) Application is Due: Nov 30

Amount: 100 - 100,000 USD

Samples: Jewish Community Center of Greater Washington (Rockville, MD)—for fitness center, $87,500; Discovery Creek Childrens Museum (Washington, DC)—general support, $50,000; Anti-Defamation League of Bnai Brith(Washington, DC)—for Concert Against Hate, $25,000.

Contact: Julie Bender Silver, President; (202) 828-9000; (202) 785-9347

Sponsor: Bender Foundation
1120 Connecticut Avenue NW, Suite 1200
Washington, DC 20036

Beneficia Foundation Grants 273

The foundation awards grants in support of the arts and environmental conservation, with an emphasis on tropical and marine ecosystems. The foundation favors programs that are innovative, catalytic, address unmet needs, strive for self-sustainability, and have limited alternative sources of funding. Project grants and general operating grants are awarded.

Requirements: Nonprofit tax-exempt organizations are eligible.

Restrictions: Individuals are not eligible.

Geographic Focus: All U.S. States

Date(s) Application is Due: Jan 31

Amount: 1,000 - 50,000 USD

Samples: Opera Co of Philadelphia (PA)—for general support, $45,000; Ctr for Marine Conservation (Washington, DC)—for general support, $30,000; The Nature Conservancy, New Jersey Field Office (Chester, NJ)—for the Johnson Swamp Preserve, $5000.

Contact: Feodor Pitcairn, Executive Director; (215) 887-6700

Sponsor: Beneficia Foundation
1 Pitcairn Place, Suite 3000
Jenkintown, PA 19046

Berks County Community Foundation Grants 274

The foundation supports a broad range of community projects in this Pennsylvania county, including the arts and culture, economic development, education, the environment, and health and human services. Types of support include general operating grants, capital campaigns, demonstration grants, seed grants, and program grants. Although applicants do not have to be located in Berks County, they must provide programs and services within the county.

Requirements: Tax exempt or public benefit organizations, individuals, associations and private or public agencies are eligible to apply. The grant must be used for charitable purposes only. Organizations are eligible to apply to more than one grant program in the same year.

Geographic Focus: Pennsylvania

Contact: Richard Mappin, Vice President; (610) 685-2223; (610) 685-2240; info@bccf.org

Internet: http://www.bccf.org/pages/grants.html

Sponsor: Berks County Community Foundation
501 Washington Street, Suite 801, P.O. Box 212
Reading, PA 19603-0212

Bernard F. Reynolds Charitable Trust Grants 275

The independent foundation, eastablished in New York in 1999, is interested in supporting human rights programs and agencies, both in the U.S. and internationally. The brainchild of Bernard F. Reynolds, chief executive officer of ASI Solutions, the charitable group hopes to battle hunger, homelessness, and displacement of the world's most vulnerable population. There are no specific applications required or deadlines with which to adhere. Applicants should contact the charitable trust via written proposal.

Geographic Focus: All U.S. States

Amount: Up to 140,000 USD

Samples: Save the Children, Westport, Connecticut, $2,000—general support; Cold Spring Harbor Labs, Cold Spring Harbor, New York, $5,200—for general support; Ramallah Center for Human Rights Studies, Palestine, Israel, $160,000—for general support.

Contact: Bernard F. Reynolds, (631) 367-9513

Sponsor: Bernard F. Reynolds Charitable Trust
6 Merry Meeting Lane
Lloyd Harbor, NY 11743-1609

Bernard Osher Foundation Grants 276

The purpose of the foundation is to improve the quality of life in San Francisco, Alameda and the State of Maine. Grantees over the years have included performing arts groups, literary programs, educational and environmental groups, and social service organizations. Growing emphasis now is on assisting arts and cultural organizations. The first step is to submit a letter or email providing a brief overview of the proposed project. There are no application deadlines.

Requirements: California 501(c)3 organizations are eligible to apply with preference given to those serving Alameda and San Francisco Counties.

Restrictions: Individuals are ineligible.

Geographic Focus: California, Maine

Samples: Texas Tech U (TX)—for its Lifelong Learning Community, which enables people over 50 to enroll in classes and participate in discussion groups, special events, and other activities, $100,000; U of New England (Biddeford, ME)—for scholarships for students from Biddeford, Old Orchard Beach, and Saco, ME, $1 million.

Contact: Jeanie Hirokane, Corporate Secretary; (415) 861-5587; (415) 677-5972; jhirokane@osherfoundation.org

Internet: http://www.osherfoundation.org/index.php?culture

Sponsor: Bernard Osher Foundation
One Ferry Building, Suite 255
San Francisco, CA 94111

Berrien Community Foundation Grants 277

The community foundation awards grants to nonprofits in Berrien County, Michigan, that address community needs. The Foundation is very interested in providing start-up funding for programs that address our focus areas of nurturing children, building community spirit/arts and culture and youth leadership and development. Higher priority is given to requests that demonstrate community-based collaborative solutions likely to stay in place after Foundation funding concludes. Low priority is given to requests for bricks and mortar, operational funds on a repetitive basis, annual fund drives, equipment, and ongoing programs where alternative funding is not planned to carry a program/project forward following a Foundation grant. Low priority is also given to advertising and capital campaigns and grants to cover deficits or other previously incurred obligations. Applicants must first call the Foundation's program director to discuss the proposed program/project.

Requirements: Grant applications will only be accepted from nonprofit 501(c)3 and grass roots organizations serving Berrien County residents.

Restrictions: Grants are not made for sectarian religious purposes, national fundraising efforts, political organizations or campaigns. Grants are not made to individuals, and form letters/emails are neither reviewed nor acknowledged.

Geographic Focus: Michigan

Date(s) Application is Due: Sep 1

Amount: Up to 10,000 USD

Contact: Anne McCausland, Program Director; (269) 983-3304, ext. 2; AnneMcCausland@BerrienCommunity.org

Internet: http://www.berriencommunity.org

Sponsor: Berrien Community Foundation
2900 South State Street, Suite 2 East
Saint Joseph, MI 49085

Besser Foundation Grants 278

The foundation limits its giving to nonprofits in the Alpena, MI area. Areas of interest include education, social services, civic affairs, arts and culture, religion, and international. Types of support include scholarship funds, matching funds, operating budgets, and continuing support. The board meets quarterly to consider requests.

Requirements: Only nonprofits in Michigan may apply.

Restrictions: Unless specifically requested by a Trustee, the Foundation will not consider grant requests from organizations outside of Alpena; nor for endowment funds, to defray meeting or conference expenses, or to pay for travel of individuals or groups. We will not relieve organizations or the public of their responsibilities, nor make grants to individuals for any purpose.

Geographic Focus: Michigan

Samples: Jesse Besser Museum, Alpena, MI, $220,00; Alpena Community College, Alpena, MI, $100,000; Child and Family Services of Northeast Michigan, Alpena, MI, $40,000.

Contact: J. Richard Wilson, President; (989) 354-4722; (517) 354-8099; besserfoundation@verizon.net

Sponsor: Besser Foundation
123 North Second Avenue, Suite 3
Alpena, MI 49707-2801

Bethesda Foundation Grants 279

The foundation awards grants to nonprofits in Hornell, NY, in its areas of interest, including education, hospitals, health care, substance abuse services, nutrition, AIDS research, and social services. Types of support include general operating support, equipment acquisition, program development, and scholarship funds. Application forms must be obtained from the office. The board meets in March, June, September, and December.

Requirements: Nonprofit organizations in Hornell, NY, are eligible.

Geographic Focus: New York

Amount: 1,000 - 24,000 USD

Contact: Grants Administrator; (513) 745-1616; (513) 745-1623; bethesdafoundation@trihealth.com

Internet: http://www.bethesdafoundation.com

Sponsor: Bethesda Foundation
10506 Montgomery Road, Suite 304
Cincinnati, OH 45242

Bildner Family Foundation Grants 280

The foundation awards grants to nonprofit organizations in its areas of interest, including arts and performing arts, health care and health organizations, Jewish and social service delivery. Types of support include continuing support, general operating support, and program support. The majority of grants are awarded in New Jersey and New York. There are no application forms or deadlines.

Restrictions: The foundation does not support private foundations or individuals.

Geographic Focus: New Jersey, New York

Amount: 2,000 - 300,000 USD

Samples: Dartmouth College, $6 million for residence hall construction; Rutgers, (New Brunswick, NJ)—for general support, $162,197; Bergen

Community College (Paramus, NJ)—to develop the Center for the Study of International Understanding, $225,000.
Contact: Allen Bildner, President
Sponsor: Bildner Family Foundation
293 Eisenhower Parkway, Suite 150
Livingston, NJ 07039

Bill and Melinda Gates Foundation Grants 281

The foundation awards grants in its areas of interest, including increasing access to innovations in technology, education, libraries, and global health. Education grants are intended to provide teachers with opportunities to learn together the best ways to use technology to enhance student learning. Global health grants are awarded to improve the health of women and children, particularly in developing countries, by expanding services to enable women to safely carry and deliver babies and to prevent cervical cancer. Grants to libraries bridge the digital divide between those who have access to computers and the Internet and those who lack such access.
Requirements: 501(c)3 tax-exempt organizations are eligible. Priority is given to requests in the Pacific Northwest, including Idaho, Oregon, and Washington.
Geographic Focus: All U.S. States
Samples: CARE (Atlanta, GA)—for relief efforts following tsunamis in South Asia and Africa, $750,000; Experience Music Project (Seattle, WA)—for general operating support, $250,000; CARE (Atlanta, GA)—to assist victims of flooding in eastern Nepal, $300,000; Korean Women's Assoc (Tacoma, WA)—for its capital campaign for a domestic-violence shelter, $200,000.
Contact: Program Contact; (206) 709-3140; info@gatesfoundation.org
Internet: http://www.gatesfoundation.org/ForGrantSeekers
Sponsor: Bill and Melinda Gates Foundation
P.O. Box 23350
Seattle, VA 98102

Blade Foundation Grants 282

The foundation awards general operating grants to cultural, educational, and social service organizations in Ohio. Scholarships also are awarded to children of employees of Toledo Blade with at least three years of employment. There are no application deadlines for grants.
Requirements: Ohio nonprofits and individuals are eligible.
Geographic Focus: Ohio
Contact: Dave Huey, (419) 724-6417
Sponsor: Blade Foundation
541 N Superior Street
Toledo, OH 43660

Blanche and Julian Robertson Family Foundation Grants 283

The Blanche and Julian Robertson Family Foundation is totally committed to the goal of improving the quality of life in Salisbury and Rowan County. The general direction of the Foundation's interest is: programs which address social problems and nurture positive social relationships; efforts aimed at enriching lives through exposure to the cultural arts; neighborhood revitalization programs, especially when such programs encourage development of transitional housing and enable first-time homeowners to purchase homes; programs that improve opportunities for youth at risk and families in crisis; efforts to improve broad-based educational, recreational, and athletic opportunities; efforts which address health and the environment. The Foundation is also interested in programs and projects that demonstrate the attributes of leverage (where a grant will attract matching gifts or other funding), as well as innovation, thoroughness, passion, and commitment. Contact the office for application and guidelines.
Requirements: North Carolina nonprofit organizations serving Salisbury and Rowan County.
Restrictions: Foundation does not make grants outside Salisbury and Rowan County.
Geographic Focus: North Carolina
Date(s) Application is Due: Mar 30
Samples: Rowan Regional Medical Ctr Foundation (Salisbury, NC)—for its capital campaign for a new emergency department, patient-care facility, and community-education center, $1 million.
Contact: David Setzer, Executive Director; (704) 637-0511; (704) 637-0177; bjrfoundation@aol.com
Sponsor: Blanche and Julian Robertson Family Foundation
141 East Council Street, P.O. Box 4242
Salisbury, NC 28145-4242

Blandin Foundation Grants 284

Foundation grantmaking activities are reviewed in two different geographic categories: grants for activities in Itasca County and the adjoining communities of Remer, Hill City, Blackduck and Northome and grants for rural areas and issues that extend beyond the local giving area. A minimum of 55 percent of the Foundation's grant making activities will be directed to the local giving area. Economic opportunity is the primary emphasis. Responsive grants are intended to address a range of social and cultural issues with priority on addressing the root causes of barriers faced by disadvantaged populations. Low priority is being placed on large capital grants, recreation, and community amenities. Initial inquiries by letter or phone are encouraged. Typically, grants will not exceed $250,000; however, in instances of exceptional impact, larger amounts will be considered.
Requirements: Grants will be made to organizations with a nonprofit 501(c)3 tax exempt status. Units of government may also apply for a grant, but only if the purpose of the grant request goes beyond the normal limits of expected government services and taxpayer responsibility.
Restrictions: Blandin Foundation does not make grants directly to individuals, except in the case of its Educational Awards Program. Funding does not support: grants outside the state of Minnesota; religious activities; medical research; publications, films or videos; travel grants for individuals or groups; camping and athletic programs; ordinary government services; grants to individuals; grants solely intended to influence legislation.
Geographic Focus: Minnesota
Date(s) Application is Due: Mar 15; Sep 15; Dec 15
Amount: Up to 250,000 USD
Contact: Wade Frauth, Grants Director; (877) 882-2257 or (218) 326-0523; (218) 327-1949; bfinfo@blandinfoundation.org
Internet: http://www.blandinfoundation.org/html/grants.cfm
Sponsor: Blandin Foundation
100 N Pokegama Avenue
Grand Rapids, MN 55744

Blowitz-Ridgeway Foundation Grants 285

The foundation supports nonprofit agencies that provide medical, psychiatric, and psychological care to economically disadvantaged children and adolescents. Program and capital grants are awarded, primarily in Illinois, in support of medical, psychiatric, psychological, and/or residential care; and research programs in medicine, psychology, social science, and education. The foundation supports operating budgets, and applicants may request commitments that extend beyond one year, but requests for annual funding will not be considered. Applications are accepted throughout the year and are reviewed in the order in which they are received. Guidelines and applications are available online.
Requirements: 501(c)3 nonprofit organizations that offer services to people who lack resources to provide for themselves may apply.
Restrictions: Grants will not be awarded to government agencies or to organizations that subsist mainly on third-party funding and have demonstrated no ability or expended little effort to attract private funding. Grants will not be made for religious or political purposes or for the production or writing of audio-visual materials.
Geographic Focus: Illinois
Amount: 5,000 - 30,000 USD
Samples: Elizabeth Ann Seton Program, $5,000 in general operating support of programs for pregnant and parenting mothers; The Enterprising Kitchen, $15,000 for programs improving self-sufficiency and employability of low-income women; Faith in Action of McHenry County, $7,000 to recruit volunteers; Gospel Rescue Mission, $10,000 for children's social and recreational activities; Guardian Angel Community Services, $5,000 for the Groundwork Domestic Violence Program.
Contact: Serena Moy, Administrator; (847) 330-1020; (847) 330-1028; serena@blowitzridgeway.org
Internet: http://www.blowitzridgeway.org/information/information1.html
Sponsor: Blowitz-Ridgeway Foundation
1701 E Woodfield Road, Suite 201
Schaumburg, IL 60173

Blue Mountain Community Foundation Grants 286

The Foundation administers charitable funds to benefit people of the Blue Mountain Area. Most of the money for discretionary grants is designated by donors for use by agencies serving Walla Walla County. The Foundation's grant making policies are generally directed toward the fields of social and community services, the arts and humanities, education and health. In

reviewing grant applications, careful consideration will be given to: potential impact of the program/project on the community and the number of people who will benefit; local volunteer involvement and support; commitment of the organization's Board of Directors; degree to which the applicant works with or complements the services of other community organizations; organization's fiscal responsibility and management skills; possibility of using the grant as seed money for matching funds from other sources; ability of the organization to obtain additional funding and to provide ongoing funding after the term of the grant.
Requirements: Nonprofit organizations serving the Walla Walla Valley, from Dayton to Milton-Freewater are encouraged to submit proposals.
Restrictions: Grants usually will not be made for the following: programs outside the Blue Mountain Area, operating expenses, annual fund drives, field trips, travel to or in support of conferences. No grants will be made for sectarian religious purposes nor to influence legislation or elections.
Geographic Focus: Oregon, Washington
Date(s) Application is Due: Jul 1
Amount: 125 - 4,000 USD
Samples: Blue Mountain Action Council, WA, $7,000 - Volunteer Adult Literacy Program (2008); Walla Walla Community College Foundation, WA, $1,500 - Parent Education Program Scholarships (2008); Carnegie Art Center, WA, $3,000 - general support (2008).
Contact: Lawson F. Knight, Executive Director; (509) 529-4371; (509) 529-5284; BMCF@bluemountainfoundation.org
Internet: http://www.bluemountainfoundation.org/grant-making-programs.php
Sponsor: Blue Mountain Community Foundation
8 South Second, Suite 168, P.O. Box 603
Walla Walla, WA 99362-0015

Blue River Foundation Grants 287

Grantmaking is a big part of what the Blue River Community Foundation does. This helps us to serve as an integrating force throughout Shelby County, helping our residents create a viable and vibrant community in which all people can thrive. Since our inception in 1988, BRCF's assets have grown from $500,000 to more than $20 million in over 180 funds, allowing us to award more than $5 million in grants to date. Our grantmaking process is driven and informed by rich community knowledge, relying on the contributions of staff, board members and a broad and diverse group of community volunteers. Each year, the Foundation awards grants to nonprofit organizations and charitable endeavors in several different ways - Unrestricted Grants: These grants come from a collection of funds, such as our large Community Fund and from several named Family Funds, which allow the Foundation to decide where the money is most needed in the community. Unrestricted grants are used to support long-term solutions for community issues, respond quickly to emergencies and to meet changing social, cultural, educational or environmental needs in our local communities. These funds can address a broad range of issues and keep the donor's gift from becoming outdated. Field of Interest Grants: These grants are made from funds where the donor designated one or more general areas of interest, such as education, youth, beautification, etc. Scholarship funds would be a good example of a field of interest fund. Donor Advised Grants: These grants are made based on recommendations of the donor advisor(s) to the fund. A family may sponsor one of these funds as a way of teaching their children the act of giving by allowing them participate in the selection process to award the grant. It can also be used for companies to meet their charitable goals. Designated Grants: These grants are made from funds where the donor has specified one or more nonprofit organizations to receive the annual payout from the growth of the fund. If the specified nonprofit ceases operations, the Foundation is legally authorized to select an alternate beneficiary to continue to fulfill the donor's charitable intent. Agency Endowment Grants: These grants are annual payouts from the growth of funds that nonprofits have set aside in an endowment to be administered by the BRCF. The nonprofit thereby can grow its assets and ensure operating dollars for years to come, while they focus on their mission of service to the community. The agency benefits because our Board of Directors provides strong investment oversight and staff provides administrative services for very low cost. Special Project Grants: These grants are made from nonpermanent funds that have been given for a specific project. They may be grant monies from another foundation that are to be administered by the Blue River Community Foundation on behalf of a nonprofit, such as the 4Community Project. Or they can be a collection of donations from the community for a special event, such as Shelby County Reads. This is a limited service the Foundation provides in special situations to help further a vital project or cause.
Requirements: Application and guidelines available on website application form.
Geographic Focus: Indiana
Date(s) Application is Due: Feb 1; Jun 1; Oct 1
Contact: Lynne Ensminger, Program Administrator; (317) 392-7955; (317) 392-4545; lensminger@blueriverfoundation.com
Internet: http://blueriverfoundation.com/main.asp?SectionID=6&TM=34779.5
Sponsor: Blue River Community Foundation
54 W Broadway Street, Suite 1, P.O. Box 808
Shelbyville, IN 46176

Blum-Kovler Foundation Grants 288

The foundation awards general operating grants to eligible Illinois nonprofit organizations in its areas of interest, including child welfare, civic affairs, cultural programs, health care, higher education, hospitals, medical research, and social services. Grants are awarded primarily in the Chicago metropolitan area. There are no application forms or deadlines. Submit a letter of request.
Requirements: Illinois nonprofit organizations are eligible.
Geographic Focus: Illinois
Amount: 2,500 - 50,000 USD
Contact: Hymen Bregar, Secretary; (312) 664-5050
Sponsor: Blum-Kovler Foundation
875 N Michigan Avenue, Suite 3400
Chicago, IL 60611

Blumenthal Foundation Grants 289

The foundation focuses the majority of its grants on programs and projects that have an impact on Charlotte, and the state of North Carolina. The foundation also believes that it is important to provide basic operational funding for non-profits, not just support for special programs or projects. The philanthropic efforts of the Foundation are focused in nine areas of grantmaking: arts, science and culture; civic and community; education; environment; foundation affiliates; health; Jewish institutions and philanthropies; religious and interfaith; social sciences.
Requirements: Nonprofit, tax-exempt charitable organizations and institutions that are exempt under Section 501(c)3 of the Internal Revenue code, or governmental agencies are eligible.
Restrictions: Grants are not made to individuals for any purpose.
Geographic Focus: North Carolina
Samples: Carolina Agency for Jewish Education (Charlotte, NC)—$35,000; Lubavitch of North Carolina (Charlotte, NC)—$12,000, Presbyterian Hospital Foundation (Charlotte, NC)—$10,000.
Contact: Philip Blumenthal, (704) 688-2305; (704) 688-2401; foundation@gunk.com
Internet: http://www.blumenthalfoundation.org/BFGrantListings.htm
Sponsor: Blumenthal Foundation
P.O. Box 34689
Charlotte, NC 28234-4689

Bodman Foundation Grants 290

The Foundation concentrates its programs in New York City, but also makes some grants in northern New Jersey. Funding is concentrated in six program areas: Arts and Culture, Education, Employment, Health, Public Policy, and Youth and Families. In both Health and Arts and Culture, the Foundation tends to focus its grants on leading institutions, generally where there is a longstanding relationship. In other areas, special consideration is given to competition, self-help, volunteerism, leadership and character development, parental involvement, consumer choice, economic empowerment, independent living, prevention and earlier intervention, independent research, faith-based programs, free markets, social entrepreneurship, advancing the state of the art, measuring participant outcomes and programs results, and strengthening traditional marriages and families.
Requirements: Nonprofit organizations based in New York City and northern New Jersey that are tax-exempt under Section 501(c)3 of the Internal Revenue Code and fall within the program areas of the Foundations are welcome to submit an inquiry or proposal letter. Initial contact should only include: an inquiry or proposal letter briefly summarizing the history of the project, need, research, objectives, time period, key staff, project budget, and evaluation plan emphasizing measurable outcomes and specific program results; latest annual report; current and complete audited financial statements; copy of IRS 501(c)3 tax-exemption letter.

Restrictions: The Foundations generally do not offer the following types of support, nor participate in the following program areas: nonprofit organizations outside of New York and New Jersey; annual appeals, dinner functions, and fundraising events; endowments and capital campaigns; loans and deficit financing; direct grants to individuals (such as scholarships and financial aid); individual day-care and after-school programs; housing; international; films and travel; projects for the elderly; small art, dance, music, and theater groups; independent or public K-12 schools (except charter schools); national health and mental health organizations; government agencies and nonprofit programs and services significantly funded or substantially reimbursed by government.
Geographic Focus: New Jersey, New York
Amount: 10,000 - 100,000 USD
Samples: Catholic Relief Services (Baltimore, MD)—for relief efforts for refugees and other victims of the fighting in Afghanistan, $20,000; STRIVE/East Harlem Employment Services (New York, NY)—for its Community Partnership, a citywide job training and placement effort by 15 nonprofit groups to assist workers displaced by the terrorist attacks and the economic recession, $75,000 (2001); Manhattan Institute for Policy Research (New York, NY)—for research, articles, panels, and other events on rebuilding New York, as part of a round of grants responding to the September 11 attacks and their aftermath, $100,000; New York Historical Society (NY)—for an exhibition and public program series in collaboration with the Skyscraper Museum on the conception, design, engineering, building, and destruction of the World Trade Center, $20,000.
Contact: Joseph S. Dolan, Executive Director; (212) 644-0322; (212) 759-6510; main@achelis-bodman-fnds.org
Internet: http://fdncenter.org/grantmaker/achelis-bodman
Sponsor: Bodman Foundation
767 Third Avenue, 4th Floor
New York, NY 10017-2023

Boeckmann Charitable Foundation Grants **291**

The foundation awards grants to nonprofits in support of education—colleges and universities, parochial secondary education, religious education, and campus crusades; community, family, and youth services; national and international ministries and missions; religious welfare; religious broadcasting; and temples. Grants support general operations. Applicants should submit a brief letter of inquiry describing the program and the organization. There are no application deadlines.
Requirements: Christian, Evangelical, and Presbyterian nonprofits in California are eligible.
Geographic Focus: California
Amount: Up to 17,000,000 USD
Samples: Church on Way (Van Nuys, CA)—operating support, $300,200; Hispanic Christian Communications Network (Los Angeles, CA)—operating support, $10,000; Valley Interfaith Council (Chatsworth, CA)—operating support, $2000.
Contact: Herbert Boeckmann II, Chief Executive Officer; (818) 787-3800
Sponsor: Boeckmann Charitable Foundation
15505 Roscoe Boulevard
North Hills, CA 91343

Boettcher Foundation Grants **292**

Grant support is given to promote the general well-being of humanity. Grants are awarded for arts and culture, community and social service, education and healthcare. Organizations seeking support from the Foundation should send a preliminary letter, describing the organization that wishes to submit a proposal and the project for which funding is being requested. The letter should be signed by the head of the applicant agency and should include a statement related to the priority of the project within the organization's overall plans. Letters of inquiry should be mailed or emailed.
Requirements: Capital grants are made in the form of challenges, conditional on an applicant agency's ability to raise the balance of the funds needed for a project. Although no absolute guidelines have been established, 50 to 75 percent of the goal should already be in hand before the grant request will be considered.
Restrictions: The Foundation does not accept proposals, or provide grants, for the following giving interests: operations; gymnasiums/athletic fields; housing; purchase of tables or tickets for dinner/events; individuals; large urban hospitals; out-of-state projects; media presentations; small business start-ups; open space/parks; conferences, seminars, workshops; organizations that primarily serve animals; debt reduction; pilot programs; endowments; religious groups or organizations for their religious purposes; scholarships; travel.
Geographic Focus: Colorado
Samples: Children's Hospital (Denver, CO)—for its fund-raising campaign to build a new hospital, $5 million; Colorado College (Colorado Springs, CO)—to renovate Palmer Hall, a classroom building, $400,000; Johnson and Wales U (Denver, CO)—for renovations and restoration at its Park Hill Campus, $100,000.
Contact: Grants Administrator; (800) 323-9640 or (303) 534-1937; grants@boettcherfoundation.org
Internet: http://www.boettcherfoundation.org/grants/index.html
Sponsor: Boettcher Foundation
600 Seventeenth Street, Suite 2210 South
Denver, CO 80202-5422

Bohemian Foundation Pharos Fund Grants **293**

The foundation awards grants to improve the quality of life in Fort Collins in its areas of interest, including youth, building the capacity of organizations working together, and citizen involvement. In the area of youth, the foundation makes grants that support youth at all social, economic, and developmental stages to achieve their greatest potential; support youth development in the areas of education and training; strengthen and align systems that affect learning and life-long opportunities; and support youth within the context of their families, communities, and the policy environment. In the area of building the capacity of organizations working together, the foundation makes grants that facilitate collaboration among community service entities to improve their effectiveness; strengthen the effectiveness of organizations working together to discover solutions to community concerns and issues; and support the development of relationships among organizations. In the area of citizen involvement, the foundation makes grants to support programs that demonstrate the need of greater public awareness; support programs that utilize existing research or information and make it more accessible to the public; and support programs, projects, or events that raise consciousness about community issues. Types of support include general operating grants, capital grants, equipment purchase, program support, and technical assistance. One request per grant cycle is permitted. Complete guidelines are available online.
Requirements: Grants are available to nonprofit, 501(c)3 organizations (other than private foundations) in Fort Collins, Colorado.
Restrictions: The program will not fund requests with the following criteria: multi-year requests; multi-program requests; fundraising events; tuition-based private schools; political campaigns or specific legislative issues; activities that have a specific religious purpose; non-501(c)3 organizations; private foundations, including private operating foundations; individual team requests; discriminatory programs; programs serving individuals; debt reduction.
Geographic Focus: Colorado
Date(s) Application is Due: Feb 1; Sep 15
Amount: Up to 30,000 USD
Samples: Colorado State U (CO)—for the University Center for the Arts, an academic facility for programs in music, theater, and dance, and to renovate an athletic stadium, $20.1 million.
Contact: Grants Administrator; (970) 482-4642; (970) 482-6139; info@bohemianfoundation.org
Internet: http://www.bohemianfoundation.org
Sponsor: Bohemian Foundation
103 West Mountain Avenue
Fort Collins, CO 80524

Boise Cascade Corporation Contributions Grants **294**

The corporate contributions program makes grants to charitable organizations and programs in communities where Boise Cascade operates. Areas of interest include education, environment, and culture. General operating grants, capital grants, and grants for programs/projects are awarded. Requests must be made in writing and sent to the location nearest the requesting organization.
Requirements: U.S. 501(c)3 nonprofit organizations in company-operating areas may apply.
Restrictions: The corporation will not support areas where the corporation has minimal or no operations; individuals, private foundations, or international organizations; trips, athletic teams, scholarships, or sports vehicle sponsorships; or religious, fraternal, social, labor, or veterans organizations.
Geographic Focus: All U.S. States
Contact: Corporate Contributions, Contribution Program Manager; (208) 384-6161; (208) 384-7189; bcweb@bc.com
Internet: http://www.bc.com/corporate/community.jsp

Sponsor: Boise Cascade Corporation
P.O. Box 50
Boise, ID 83728-0001

Bonfils-Stanton Foundation Grants 295

Colorado nonprofit organizations are eligible to apply, and funds must be used within the state for the benefit of Colorado citizens. The focus of the foundation is to advance excellence in the areas of arts and culture, community service, and science and medicine. Types of support include operating grants, capital campaigns, and capacity-building grants. Proposals will be reviewed at quarterly meetings. Guidelines and forms are available online.
Requirements: Colorado 501(c)3 organizations are eligible.
Restrictions: Areas generally not eligible for funding include loans, grants, or scholarships to individuals; events, media productions, seminars, conferences, or travel expenses related to meetings; activities or initiatives that have a religious purpose or objective; endowment funding, fellowships, endowed chairs; funding to retire operating debt; requests from organizations outside the State of Colorado or that are not for the benefit of Colorado citizens.
Geographic Focus: Colorado
Date(s) Application is Due: Jan 31; Apr 30; Jul 31; Oct 31
Samples: ArtReach (CO)—for a Web-based ticket reservation system; Capitol Hill Community Services (CO)—to fund meal sites for the homeless; Kids in Need of Dentistry (CO)—to develop a comprehensive technology plan.
Contact: Susan France, Vice President of Programs; (303) 825-3774; (303) 825-0802; susan@bonfils-stanton.org
Internet: http://www.bonfils-stantonfoundation.org
Sponsor: Bonfils-Stanton Foundation
1601 Arapahoe Street, Suite 500
Denver, CO 80202

Booth Ferris Foundation Grants 296

The foundation awards grants in the fields of education (K-12, private higher education, theological education, smaller colleges, secondary schools, and adult basic education) and civic and urban programs for social services, environmental conservation, and cultural activities. Types of support include project, capital, and capacity- building grants. Grants are awarded nationwide, with a focus on the metropolitan New York area. There are no application forms or deadline dates. Awards are decided on a quarterly basis.
Requirements: Organizations must be classified by the Internal Revenue Service as public charities and tax-exempt under section 501(c)3 of the Internal Revenue Code of 1986.
Restrictions: A minimum of three years must elapse between grant awards. No grants are made to individuals, private foundations or for loans. Grants are not made to organizations whose primary work is conducted outside of the U.S., to individuals, to federated campaigns, or to work with specific diseases or disabilities. Proposals from educational institutions for scholarships, fellowships and for unrestricted endowment are discouraged, as are proposals for individual research efforts at such institutions. Proposals from social services and cultural institutions from outside the metropolitan New York area will not be considered.
Geographic Focus: New York
Amount: 50,000 - 400,000 USD
Samples: Harlem RBI (New York, NY)—for organizational development, $150,000; Bowdoin College (Brunswick, ME)—to construct an academic building, $150,000.
Contact: Booth Ferris Foundation, c/o JPMorgan Private Bank (212) 464-2487; (212) 464-2487
Internet: http://fdncenter.org/grantmaker/boothferris
Sponsor: Booth Ferris Foundation
NY1-N040, 345 Park Avenue, 4th Floor
New York, NY 10154

Borkee-Hagley Foundation Grants 297

The foundation awards grants in a wide range of interests, including social services to children and families, religious organizations, and environmental programs. Delaware nonprofits receive preference. The board meets in December to consider requests.
Requirements: Delaware nonprofits are eligible to apply.
Restrictions: No support for specific churches or synagogues. Grants are not made to individuals.
Geographic Focus: Delaware
Date(s) Application is Due: Nov 1
Amount: 1,000 - 25,000 USD
Samples: Artistic Productions Inc (Hockessin, DE)—$1000; Delaware Hospice (Wilmington, DE)—$13,000; Better Life Outreach Ministries (Newport, DE)—$5000; Children and Families First (Wilmington, DE)—$13,000.
Contact: Henry H. Silliman Jr., President; (302) 652-8616
Sponsor: Borkee-Hagley Foundation
P.O. Box 4590
Wilmington, DE 19807-4590

Boston Foundation Grants 298

The Boston Foundation has a particular concern for low income and disenfranchised communities and residents and supports organizations and programs whose work helps advance the Foundation's high priorities in a variety of subject areas: Arts and Culture; Civic Engagement; Community Safety, Economic Development; Education/Out-of-School Time, Health and Human Services; Housing and Community Economic Development; the Nonprofit Sector, Urban Environment and Workforce Development. The Foundation generally makes the following types of grants: Project or program support for community-based efforts that improve the quality of life in the community, test new models, and promote collaborative and innovative ventures; advocacy and public policy research that is linked to specific action; support for planning to enable organizations and residents to assess community needs, respond to new challenges and opportunities, and provide for the inclusion of new populations; organizational support to develop and build the capacity of nonprofit organizations - support that helps organizations keep pace with the changing requirements and demands of their communities and broader environments; small grants awarded on a rolling basis for one-time organizational development needs through the Vision Fund. In addition, on a very limited basis, the Foundation will consider development grants and strategic alliances.
Requirements: Grants are made only to tax-exempt organizations in Massachusetts.
Restrictions: The committee does not consider more than one proposal from the same organization within a 12-month period. Discretionary grants are generally not made to the following applicants: city or state government agencies or departments; individuals; medical research; endowments; equipment; replacement of lost/expired government funding or gap funding to cover the full cost of providing services; scholarships and fellowships; video and film production; construction and renovation projects and capital campaigns; programs with religious content; travel; summer camps and lobbying. Activities that are generally lower priorities for the Foundation are conferences, lectures, one-time events, programs benefiting only a small number of participants or routine service delivery and/or operating expenses.
Geographic Focus: Massachusetts
Date(s) Application is Due: Jan 5; Jul 1
Samples: Raw Art Works in Lynn, MA, $75,000 - for arts-based youth development programs to young people in Lynn (2009); Boston Private Industry Council, Boston, MA, $200,000 - to administer the Accuplacer assessment to all program participants to determine the need for remedial writing support, and provide college transition coaching to 75 participating students headed to Bunker Hill and Roxbury Community College (2009)
Contact: Corey Davis, Grants Manager; (617) 338-1700; (617) 338-1604; info@tbf.org
Internet: http://www.tbf.org
Sponsor: Boston Foundation
75 Arlington Street, 10th Floor
Boston, MA 02116

Boston Foundation Initiative to Strengthen Arts and Cultural Service Organizations 299

The program supports Boston-area nonprofits with missions and programs that are substantially focused on serving and enhancing the capacity of individual artists and/or arts and cultural organizations. Organizations may submit proposals in either of two categories: externally focused activities that enhance or expand service delivery to artists and/or cultural organizations; or internally focused work or activities that build a service organization's own management and service capacity. Proposals that blend the two approaches are also welcomed. Evaluation criteria include management excellence, capacity to serve, and impact on and service to artists and/or small, community-based arts organizations within the greater Boston area. The listed application deadline is for letters of inquiry; full proposals are by invitation.
Requirements: 501(c)3 nonprofit agencies that provide services to artists and/or cultural nonprofits within the greater Boston service area are eligible.
Geographic Focus: Massachusetts

Date(s) Application is Due: Oct 14
Samples: American Composers Forum, Boston Area Chapter, (MA)—to implement a strategic plan, $7000; Cultural Access Consortium (MA)—to work with five theater companies to develop and implement access strategies, $20,000; StageSource (MA)—to enhance current and launch new professional development and job resource programs for theater artists, $15,000; The Art Connection (MA)—to frame works of art, facilitating donations from and placements to less affluent artists and nonprofit agencies, $10,000.
Contact: Ann McQueen, (617) 338-1700; mcg@tbf.org
Internet: http://www.tbf.org/current/current-L2.asp?id=3177
Sponsor: Boston Foundation
75 Arlington Street, 10th Floor
Boston, MA 02116

Boston Globe Foundation Grants **300**
The foundation concentrates on three focus areas: strengthen the reading, writing, and critical thinking of young people, while fostering their inherent love of learning; strengthen the roads that link people to culture; and strengthen the civic fabric of the city. The foundation also sponsors the Neighbor to Neighbor Initiative, which funds exceptional Dorchester focused nonprofits.
Requirements: Massachusetts nonprofit organizations in the greater Boston area are eligible.
Restrictions: The Foundation will only review one proposal per year from any organization.
Geographic Focus: Massachusetts
Amount: 5,000 - 15,000 USD
Contact: Leah P. Bailey, Director; (617) 929-2895; (617) 929-2041; foundation@globe.com
Internet: http://bostonglobe.com
Sponsor: Boston Globe Foundation
P.O. Box 55819
Boston, MA 02205-55819

Boston Women's Fund Grants **301**
The fund gives grants to support community-based projects in the greater Boston, MA, area run by and for women/girls organized for social and economic change. Also funded are direct service projects that have an organizing component. Types of support include challenge/matching grants, general operating grants, grants in aid, project grants, seed money grants, and technical assistance. Groups just getting started are encouraged to apply, particularly those including women/girls who are most vulnerable and have the least access to other resources—minority women, low-income women, girls, disabled women, lesbians, and older women. To apply, send a letter of intent to the foundation by September ninth. Letter of intent is available on the website.
Requirements: Applicant must be a Boston-area group with an organizational budget of less than $150,000 per year.
Geographic Focus: Massachusetts
Date(s) Application is Due: Oct 1
Amount: Up to 15,000 USD
Contact: Catherine Joseph, Program Director; (617) 725-0035, ext. 3002; (617) 725-0277; Catherine@bostonwomensfund.org
Internet: http://www.bostonwomensfund.org/grantinfo.html
Sponsor: Boston Women's Fund
14 Beacon Street, Suite 805
Boston, MA 02108

Brainerd Foundation Grants **302**
The foundation is dedicated to protecting the environmental quality of the Pacific Northwest, including Washington, Oregon, Idaho, Montana, Alaska, and British Columbia. Program grants are made in the following areas: endangered ecosystems—conservation biology, conservation assessment, and mining reform and roadless areas; and communications and capacity building—organizational development, and allied voices. Program grants are awarded to cover costs associated with activities such as public education and grassroots outreach, media strategies, litigation, scientific and economic studies, computer networking, and building organizational capacity. Opportunity Fund grants are awarded to organizations for support such as outreach, litigation, applied research, and other unexpected needs. Additional types of support include general operating support, continuing support, equipment acquisition, conferences and seminars, seed money, research, technical assistance, and employee matching gifts. Applications are available online.
Requirements: Nonprofit organizations in the Pacific Northwest are eligible.
Restrictions: The foundation does not favor proposals for school education programs, land acquisition, endowments, capital campaigns, projects sponsored by government agencies, basic research, fellowships, or books or videos that are not part of a broader strategy.
Geographic Focus: Alaska, Idaho, Montana, Oregon, Washington, Canada
Amount: 250 - 25,000 USD
Samples: Cook InletKeeper, $1,500 to protect Alaskan salmon streams and intact ecosystems from a one-billion ton coal strip mining project in the Beluga Coal fields; Georgia Strait Alliance, Nanaimo, BC, $8,500 for a summer outreach program to educate citizens in the lower mainland about untreated sewage; Institutes for Journalism & Natural Resources, Missoula, MT, $30,000 to increase organizational capacity and bolster fundraising and programmatic successes; Sierra Club of British Columbia Foundation $3,000 to launch an outreach campaign to raise public awareness and build leverage to enable a well-funded and legitimate recovery strategy for Mountain Caribou.
Contact: Ann Krumboltz, Executive Director; (206) 448-0676; (206) 448-7222; annk@brainerd.org
Internet: http://www.brainerd.org/grants/intro.php
Sponsor: Brainerd Foundation
1601 Second Avenue, Suite 610
Seattle, WA 98101-1541

Brett Family Foundation Grants **303**
The foundation awards grants in two focus areas: Boulder County nonprofits that provide direct services and support for underserved and frequently marginalized populations; and organizations throughout the state of Colorado advocating for social, economic, gender, and racial justice. The foundation accepts proposals in two general grant cycles: March and September. The March cycle will be devoted entirely to Social Justice grants (primarily community organizing and advocacy organizations), while the September cycle will be dedicated to Direct Services in Boulder County.
Requirements: 501(c)3 nonprofit organizations serving the communities of Boulder County are eligible.
Geographic Focus: Colorado
Date(s) Application is Due: Mar 1; Sep 1
Contact: Brian Hiatt, (303) 442-1200; (303) 442-1221; bhiatt@brettfoundation.org
Internet: http://www.brettfoundation.org
Sponsor: Brett Family Foundation
1123 Spruce Street
Boulder, CO 80302

Brico Fund Grants **304**
The mission of the fund is to effect systemic change—to change attitudes, policies and societal patterns. Grants are made to secure full participation in society for women and girls; restore and sustain the earth's natural systems; promote a just and equitable society; and nourish the creative spirit. Types of support include general operating, program, and rarely, capital and endowment grants. Applicants should complete the fund's preliminary application form and a two-page letter of intent, describing the organization's intended project or program.
Requirements: The fund supports organizations with projects and programs within the Greater Milwaukee community. Some funding is done statewide or nationally for programs of broader scope.
Restrictions: Grants do not support conferences and meetings, disease-specific programs, educational institutions, individuals, media projects, medical institutions, religions, or organizations with a focus on animals.
Geographic Focus: Wisconsin
Date(s) Application is Due: Jan 15; Jul 15
Amount: 1,000 - 500,000 USD
Samples: 1000 Friends (WI)—for the opening of a Milwaukee office to explore transportation and smart growth issues, $30,000; Fondy Market—to support building of the market, $50,000; Growing Power—for operating support, $115,000; Midtown Neighborhood Assoc—to support an urban tree house and education program, $35,000.
Contact: Melissa Nimke, Grants Administrator; (414) 272-2747; (414) 272-2036; mbn@bricofund.org or bricofund@bricofund.org
Internet: http://www.bricofund.org
Sponsor: Brico Fund
205 E Wisconsin Avenue, Suite 200
Milwaukee, WI 53202

Bright Family Foundation Grants 305

Established in 1986, the foundation primarily serves the Stanislaus County area of California. Areas of interest include: religion; education; medical services; medical school/education; internships; human services; children/youth services; arts & culture. The Board meets once a year in December to review proposals. Deadline date for applications is November 1.

Requirements: Stanislaus County, CA, IRS 501(c)3 tax-exempt organizations within a 20 mile radius of Modesto, CA, are eligible to apply.

Geographic Focus: California

Date(s) Application is Due: Nov 1

Amount: 5,000 - 50,000 USD

Samples: Beggs High School, Beggs, OK, $32,000—scholarship program (2008); UCSF School of Medicine, San Francisco, CA, $45,000 (2008); Modesto Symphony Orchestra, Modesto, CA, $20,000 (2008).

Contact: Calvin Bright, President; (209) 526-8242

Sponsor: Bright Family Foundation
1620 North Carpenter Road, Building B
Modesto, CA 95351-1155

Brinson Foundation Grants 306

The foundation supports education, public health, and scientific research programs that engage, inform, and inspire committed citizens to confront the challenges that face humanity. Grantmaking priorities are education—awareness and outreach, democracy and citizenship, economically disadvantaged, and libraries and literacy; public health—awareness and outreach, and economically disadvantaged; and scientific research—astrophysics, cosmology, geophysics, medical research (i.e., Alzheimer's disease, cancer, Lou Gehrig's Disease (ALS), and stroke). Types of support include general operating grants and project grants. The foundation does not accept unsolicited grant applications. Grantseekers are asked to review the foundation's mission, vision, beliefs, priorities (accessed from the Who We Are link), and guidelines. If a grantseeker believes the request would match one or more of the foundation's grantmaking priorities, they can make an inquiry by completing the online Grantseeker Information Form. The completed form should be emailed to the office. Further application is by invitation.

Requirements: The foundation will consider inviting grant applications from organizations: whose request matches one or more of the Foundation's grantmaking priorities; located in the United States of America that are exempt from tax under Section 501(c)3 of the Internal Revenue Code and are defined as charitable organizations as described in Section 509(a)1, 2 or 3 or 170(b)1A; located outside the United States of America provided they produce a written legal opinion stating that they are a charitable equivalency to a qualifying U.S. organization and/or a written affidavit containing sufficient information for the Foundation to make a reasonable judgment that the organization is charitable. The Foundation's education and public health grants are generally made to organizations that serve individuals and communities in the greater Chicago area. It also considers leading U.S.-based programs that reach broader populations across the U.S. and internationally or have the potential to have a meaningful impact on best practices at the national or international level. The Foundation's physical science research grants are made to leading organizations across the United States. In this priority area, the location of the program is less critical than the match with the Foundation's grantmaking priorities.

Restrictions: The Foundation will not consider grant inquiries from organizations that: discriminate on the basis of race, gender, religion, ethnicity or sexual orientation. The Foundation will not consider grant inquiries that request funding for: activities that attempt to influence public elections; voter registration; political activity; lobbying efforts; promotion of a specific religious faith; medical research involving human cloning. The Foundation discourages grant inquiries requesting funds for: capital improvements; endowments; fundraising events.

Geographic Focus: All U.S. States

Samples: Adler Planetarium and Astronomy Museum, Chicago, Illinois, $80,000 - for cosmology and astrophysics research (2010); Lincoln Park Zoo, Chicago, Illinois, $55,000 - for general support (2010); Institute for Humane Studies, Arlington, Virginia, $20,000 - summer seminars for college students (2010).

Contact: Cheryl A. Heads, Grants Manager; (312) 799-4500; (312) 799-4310; mail@brinsonfoundation.org

Internet: http://www.brinsonfoundation.org/grant_seekers/grantseekers.shtml

Sponsor: Brinson Foundation
737 N Michigan Avenue, Suite 1850
Chicago, IL 60611

Bristol-Myers Squibb Foundation Health Disparities Grants 307

One mission of the Foundation is to reduce health disparities by strengthening community-based health care worker capacity, integrating medical care and community-based supportive services, and mobilizing communities to fight disease. To this end, this Program attempts to address health disparities in four strategic disease areas representing major public health burdens and in four highly affected geographies: hepatitis in Asia, HIV/AIDS in Africa, serious mental illness in the U.S., and cancer in Europe. Additional areas of concern include: metabolic diseases, infectious diseases; rheumatoid arthritis; cardiovascular diseases; substance abuse; women's health issues; and overal health care giving.

Requirements: Nonprofit organizations in communities where Bristol-Myers Squibb maintains a facility should submit their requests for company contributions directly to that location. Contact persons are listed at the company website.

Restrictions: The foundation does not support individuals; conferences, special events, or videos; political, fraternal, social, or veterans organizations; religious or sectarian activities, unless they benefit the entire community; organizations funded through federated campaigns; endowments; or courtesy advertising.

Geographic Focus: Connecticut, Indiana, Massachusetts, New Jersey, New York

Contact: John Damonti, President; (212) 546-4000; (212) 546-9574

Internet: http://www.bms.com/foundation/reducing_health_disparities/Pages/default.aspx

Sponsor: Bristol-Myers Squibb Foundation
345 Park Avenue, Suite 4364
New York, NY 10154

British Columbia Arts Council Basic Assistance for Community Arts Councils 308

Grants support the operations of community arts councils throughout British Columbia. Awards may cover up to 50 percent of the overall operating budget of an arts council. Support levels are determined by the population served and the applicant community's distance from major urban centers. Applications are evaluated on the amount requested, the justification for expenditures, the level of the organization's activity, and its financial need. Arts councils should contact the office for guidelines and eligibility criteria.

Requirements: Applicants must be registered nonprofit societies in British Columbia.

Restrictions: Awards are not available for capital expenditures. Awards will not be made retroactively.

Geographic Focus: Canada

Date(s) Application is Due: Sep 30

Amount: Up to 25,000 CAD

Contact: Monique Lacerte-Roth, Community Arts, Training, and Scholarship Programs; (250) 356-5488; (250) 387-4099; bcartscouncil@gems2.gov.bc.ca or Monique.Lacerte-Roth@gov.bc.ca

Internet: http://www.bcartscouncil.ca/programs/program.php?active_page=790&p=1

Sponsor: British Columbia Arts Council
P.O. Box 9819, Station Provincial Government
Victoria, BC V8W 9W3 Canada

British Columbia Arts Council Community Arts Councils Local Government Matching Assistance 309

This program assists British Columbia arts councils that have received financial assistance from municipal or regional governments in the previous fiscal year.

Requirements: British Columbia community arts councils who have received financial assistance from municipal or regional governments in the previous fiscal year are eligible to apply.

Restrictions: In-kind contributions are not eligible for matching funds.

Geographic Focus: Canada

Date(s) Application is Due: Sep 30

Amount: Up to 3,500 CAD

Contact: Monique Lacerte-Roth, Community Arts, Training, and Scholarship Programs; (250) 356-5488; (250) 387-4099; bcartscouncil@gems2.gov.bc.ca or Monique.Lacerte-Roth@gov.bc.ca

Internet: http://www.bcartscouncil.ca/programs/program.php?active_page=790&p=1

Sponsor: British Columbia Arts Council
P.O. Box 9819, Station Provincial Government
Victoria, BC V8W 9W3 Canada

British Columbia Arts Council Community Arts Development Incentive 310

Grants will assist community arts councils to address the changing needs of their communities. Community arts councils can request additional project funds from this program at the time of their annual request for Basic Assistance. Examples of eligible proposals to the incentive include, but are not limited to, projects that will enhance the fiscal self-reliance of the arts council; projects that will enable new, productive relationships with key community players; projects that will animate under-served artistic disciplines or cultural traditions of the community; and projects that may require subsidy for more than one fiscal year. The award will not exceed 50 percent of eligible expenses.
Restrictions: The following kinds of proposals are ineligible for support: capital development, facility renovations or capital development planning costs; community celebrations, such as centennial celebrations, Canada Day, First Night or Millennium parties; primary research for new initiatives; initiatives that have previously been funded by the BC Arts Council or projects that are eligible for other BC Arts Council programs of assistance or affiliated programs, including projects that have or are eligible to receive assistance under the Artists and Communities, Community Presenters, Strategic Initiatives or the ARTS – Partners in Organizational Development programs.
Geographic Focus: Canada
Date(s) Application is Due: Apr 15; Oct 15
Amount: 500 USD
Contact: Richard Brownsey, Executive Director; (250) 356-1721; (250) 387-4099; Richard.Brownsey@gov.bc.ca
Internet: http://www.bcartscouncil.ca/programs/program.php?active_page=755
Sponsor: British Columbia Arts Council
P.O. Box 9819, Station Provincial Government
Victoria, BC V8W 9W3 Canada

British Columbia Arts Council Operating Assistance for Organizations 311

This program is intended to provide operating assistance to organizations whose primary objective is to serve the development of a specific artistic discipline or the arts and cultural communities in general on a province-wide basis. Applicants are judged on the merits of their entire operation from program content to administrative and financial management. Operating awards are made once each fiscal year for current or future operations. Eligibility in this category is reviewed on an annual basis. Organizations that have not previously received funding in this category are requested to establish their eligibility with the Cultural Services Branch (CSB) prior to filing an application. Areas eligible for assistance include performing arts, arts festivals, museums and galleries, arts training institutions, arts periodicals, and media information and deadlines. The March 15 deadline applies to theater, dance, music, and literary organizations; and the September 30 deadline applies to arts festivals, museums, galleries, and media arts organizations. Organizations that have not previously received funding for operating assistance are required to contact the office.
Requirements: An applicant must be registered as a nonprofit society in the province of British Columbia; have completed at least one full year of operation, be able to present a financial statement for that year, and have guarantees and firm program proposals for a second consecutive year of operation; show a high standard of professionalism in all areas of activity; employ full-time paid administration; be able to demonstrate a diversified revenue base; and have previously received at least one professional development project award from the CSB. Applicant organizations are required to provide detailed submissions regarding programs, administration, financing, long-range planning, leadership, and artistic program.
Restrictions: Awards in this category are not available for start-up costs, seed money, capital expenditures (construction, renovation, feasibility studies, or property or equipment purchase), or budget deficits.
Geographic Focus: Canada
Date(s) Application is Due: Mar 15; Sep 30
Amount: Up to 25,000 CAD
Contact: Richard Brownsey, Executive Director; (250) 356-1721; (250) 387-4099; bcartscouncil@gems2.gov.bc.ca or Richard.Brownsey@gov.bc.ca
Internet: http://www.bcartscouncil.ca/programs/program.php?active_page=13
Sponsor: British Columbia Arts Council
P.O. Box 9819, Station Provincial Government
Victoria, BC V8W 9W3 Canada

British Columbia Arts Council Operating Assistance for Public Museums and Visual Arts Organizations 312

Funds are available to professional, non-profit public museums that engage people in the recognition, understanding, and development of human and natural history and the visual arts, including the diverse cultures of first peoples and the world. Awards under this program are intended to support the public programming of established museums with stable curatorial and administrative leadership.
Requirements: Eligible applicants must: be registered as a non-profit society in the Province of British Columbia, or be a public museum operated by a municipality with a community-based board of management that sets policy for the museum's public programs and services; have received at least two Project Assistance awards from the British Columbia Arts Council in the previous three years and have completed at least two full years of operation; provide year-round public programming, and have done so during the immediately preceding two years; compensate artists by paying fees to professional artists at industry standard; employ competent curatorial and administrative leadership; provide an audited or independently prepared financial statement for the most recently completed fiscal year; demonstrate a diversified revenue base; if the applying organization has members, be able to demonstrate a range of membership that is representative of its constituency; and demonstrate financial need for assistance.
Restrictions: Awards under this program are not available for: start-up costs, seed money, capital expenditures (construction, renovation, or purchase of property or equipment), feasibility studies, budget deficits, or for-profit entities. Awards under this program are not available for archives-only organizations, single theme or specialty museums or industrial or heritage sites, organizations dedicated to a temporary exhibition or those which quality for operating assistance under other programs.
Geographic Focus: Canada
Contact: Sue Donaldson, Program Coordinator; (250) 356-1721; (250) 387-4099
Internet: http://www.bcartscouncil.ca/programs/program.php?active_page=759
Sponsor: British Columbia Arts Council
P.O. Box 9819, Station Provincial Government
Victoria, BC V8W 9W3 Canada

British Columbia Arts Council Regional Arts Councils Assistance 313

Awards support nonprofit regional arts councils to provide access to a range of artistic and cultural activities; develop and encourage leadership for the arts and culture at the community level; and encourage support for the arts and culture from local and regional governments. The three components to community arts council assistance are basic assistance, local government matching, and community arts development incentive. The priority for this assistance program is the support of activities that achieve a standard of excellence as determined in a peer review process. As a condition of funding, the support of the British Columbia Arts Council must be acknowledged in all promotional materials. Arts councils are advised to contact the program staff for information about program guidelines and eligibility criteria.
Requirements: To be eligible for assistance, a regional arts council must have a constitution and by-laws; elect officers at open meetings on a regular basis; be registered as a non-profit society in good standing with the British Columbia Corporate Registry; demonstrate significant financial assistance from its local government; present a diversified program of services for its community; have been in operation for a minimum of one year; and have demonstrated need of assistance.
Restrictions: Awards are not available for capital expenditures; awards for activity that has already taken place at the time of application (retroactive funding); or awards for more than 50 percent of the forecast budget of any applicant.
Geographic Focus: Canada
Date(s) Application is Due: Sep 30
Amount: Up to 3,500 USD
Contact: Richard Brownsey, Executive Director; (250) 356-1724; (250) 387-4099; Richard.Brownsey@gov.bc.ca
Internet: http://www.bcartscouncil.ca/programs/program.php?active_page=790&p=1
Sponsor: British Columbia Arts Council
P.O. Box 9819, Station Provincial Government
Victoria, BC V8W 9W3 Canada

British Columbia Arts Council Strategic Initiatives Program Grants 314

This program provides assistance to arts and cultural organizations of strategic and innovative initiatives that enhance long-term self-sufficiency and/or the organization's ability to respond to economic change. Specific projects may involve accessing a new market, undertaking an organizational review or planning process, or developing ancillary or new revenue sources. Projects must specifically focus on one or more of the following disciplines: visual, literary, media, dance, theater, music, or museums. As a condition of funding, the support of the British Columbia Arts Council must be acknowledged in all promotional materials. All applicants must contact the appropriate program coordinator prior to making application.

Requirements: Eligible organizations include nonprofit arts and cultural organizations whose principal activity is the production, distribution, or promotion of cultural products or services. Organizations must have previously received assistance under council programs. Organizations may receive assistance under the program for only one project in each year.

Restrictions: Capital projects or projects that primarily involve the creation of artistic or cultural products, and projects that begin before submission of an application are not eligible for funding.

Geographic Focus: Canada

Date(s) Application is Due: Sep 30

Contact: Program Coordinator; (250) 356-1718; (250) 387-4099; BCArtsCouncil@gems2.gov.bc.ca

Internet: http://www.bcartscouncil.ca/programs/program.php?active_page=766&p=1

Sponsor: British Columbia Arts Council
P.O. Box 9819, Station Provincial Government
Victoria, BC V8W 9W3 Canada

Broms Family Foundation Grants 315

The major purpose of the Foundation is its support of Jewish organizations and federated giving programs. The primary fields of interest include cancer, diabetes, education, girls clubs, and Jewish agencies and temples.

Requirements: An application form is required. Applicants should submit the following: listing of board of directors, trustees, officers and other key people and their affiliations; and a copy of current year's organizational budget and/or project budget.

Restrictions: Giving primarily in Minnesota and New York. No grants to individuals.

Geographic Focus: Minnesota, New York

Contact: Richard Broms, President; (952) 829-7850

Sponsor: Broms Family Foundation
6600 City West Parkway, Suite 100
Eden Prairie, MN 55344

Brookdale Foundation Relatives as Parents Grants 316

The foundation awards seed grants to community-based organizations to develop services for grandparents and other relatives acting as surrogate parents and to state agencies planning to offer such services. The program awards seed grants of $10,000 over a two-year period in two categories: local agencies and state public agencies. The RAPP Local Initiative is designed to establish community-based services to grandparents and other relatives who have assumed the responsibility of surrogate parenting. The RAPP Statewide Initiative asks grantees to initiate five new relative support groups, develop a statewide network of local organizations, and establish an inter-system task force of state agencies, so that collaborative efforts to meet the service needs of grandparent caregivers can be developed from the highest state levels. It is designed to encourage and promote the creation or expansion of services for grandparents and other relatives who have taken on the responsibility of surrogate parenting due to the absence of the parents. RAPP is designed to encourage and promote the creation or expansion of services for grandparents and other relatives who have taken on the responsibility of surrogate parenting when the biological parents are unable to do so.

Requirements: Applicants may apply for either the local or regional initiatives. Organizations applying must have a 501(c)3 or equivalent tax-exempt status. The applicant must show linkages to other community agencies (letters of support, etc.); must assign a senior staff member who will have overall administrative and supervisory responsibility for the Program, and should also designate a person to serve as RAPP Coordinator to manage the day-to-day operations. In addition to the General Guidelines, Local RAPP sponsors are subject to the following additional guidelines: (1) New Services/Programs to caregivers and their families may be proposed by agencies that are not currently part of the Brookdale Relatives As Parents Program. (2) Expanded Services may be proposed by agencies that are currently part of the Brookdale Relatives As Parents Program who wish to initiate additional services or replicate their programs in another area. (3) A Community Advisory Committee should be established to facilitate the program goals. (4) Grant recipients will be eligible to apply for renewed funding at the end of their two year grant period if they have demonstrated tangible results. In addition to the General Guidelines, Regional RAPP Sponsors are subject to the following additional guidelines: (1) Regional sponsors (for example: area agencies on aging, universities, cooperative extensions, local departments on aging, counties. Legal services, legal aid offices) will be responsible for serving a broad geographic area and support the development of a variety of local or regional group activities. (2) Sponsors must demonstrate that they have experience in developing and operating services for relative caregivers and their families. (3) A broad-based Regional Advisory Committee should be created to bring together representatives from various fields and communities to: facilitate program goals and serve as a focal point of information on programs and policies; stimulate the development of services to caregivers and their families across the region; and link local programs and interested agencies into a regional network to address the issues faced by relative caregivers and their families. Download the specific guidelines from the website.

Restrictions: Grants cannot be used for building funds, renovations, or capital improvements; to support existing services; or for indirect costs or overhead.

Geographic Focus: All U.S. States

Date(s) Application is Due: Dec 3

Amount: 10,000 USD

Contact: Melinda Perez-Porter, Program Director; (212) 308-7355, ext. 105; (212) 750-0132; mpp@brookdalefoundation.org

Internet: http://www.brookdalefoundation.org/RAPP/rapp.html

Sponsor: Brookdale Foundation
950 Third Avenue, 19th Floor
New York, NY 10022-3668

Brooklyn Benevolent Society Grants 317

The society awards general support grants to nonprofits of the Christian and Roman Catholic faiths, including the Salvation Army. Youth organizations such as YMCA/YWCA and child welfare groups, community service organizations, religion (divinity schools, parochial schools, missions, religious welfare) and religious organizations, and welfare groups. Grant making is focused in the New York, NY, area. Send a brief letter of inquiry describing the program and organization descriptions.

Requirements: Nonprofit organizations of the Christian and Roman Catholic faiths in New York are eligible.

Geographic Focus: New York

Samples: Fordham U (New York, NY)—for general support, $10,000; Our Lady of Perpetual Help High School (Brooklyn, NY)—for general support, $7500; Salvation Army Wayside Home and School for Girls (NY)—for general support, $6000.

Contact: Grants Administrator; (718) 624-0176

Sponsor: Brooklyn Benevolent Society
57 Willoughby Street
Brooklyn, NY 11201

Brooklyn Community Foundation Caring Neighbors Grants 318

The Caring Neighbors Fund assists vulnerable Brooklyn families and individuals with immediate need for a social safety net and seeks to provide access to health and mental health services. Its goals are to: offer paths out of poverty by supporting the work of emergency food providers and human services agencies; provide access to care for unaddressed physical or mental health needs in accessible community settings; ensure that homeless individuals and families can access safe temporary shelter and support services. The Foundation typically has two grant cycles annually, Letter of Inquiry are accepted then. Contact the Foundation directly for current grant cycles. Organizations invited to submit a complete proposal should expect a final decision from the Foundation within eight to twelve weeks of receipt.

Requirements: Organizations applying for a grant from the Brooklyn Community Foundation must be classified as tax-exempt under Section 501(c)3 of the Internal Revenue Code and as public charities under Section 509(a) of that Code. Fiscally sponsored organizations may also apply. Your organization need not be based in Brooklyn; however grants from the Brooklyn Community Foundation must directly benefit Brooklyn neighborhoods and/or Brooklyn residents. Applying for funding is a two part process: Ist step—begins with a Letter of Inquiry (LOI). This is the opportunity for an organization to provide the Foundation with an overview of the group and its proposed activities,

project or program; 2nd step—applicants who have been selected to proceed to the next stage will receive an email from the Foundation's staff indicating that the organization has been approved to submit a complete proposal which best describes in detail the activities, program or project. If selected, your organization will have 30 days to submit a complete a proposal online.
Restrictions: The Foundation does not: fund individuals; support for-profit organizations; purchase tickets for dinners, golf outings or similar fundraising events; make contributions to candidates for elective office or for partisan political purposes; provide funding for religious purposes.
Geographic Focus: New York
Samples: New York Asian Women's Center, $10,000 (2009); Street John's Bread & Life, $250,000 (2009); Brooklyn Bureau of Community Service, $25,000 (2009).
Contact: Diane John, (718) 722-5952 or (718) 722-2300; (718) 722-5757; info@BrooklynCommunityFoundation.org
Internet: http://www.brooklyncommunityfoundation.org/grants/caring-neighbors
Sponsor: Brooklyn Community Foundation
45 Main Street, Suite 409
Brooklyn, NY 11201

Brooklyn Community Foundation Community Arts for All Grants 319

The Arts for All Fund makes the arts a fun and essential component of life in Brooklyn, New York. Its goals are to: serve Brooklynites with diverse interests by supporting the outreach efforts of local arts and cultural organizations integrate the arts into schools and after-school programs; promote collaborations that employ the arts to address pressing community issues. Types of support available include: program, capacity building, capital, and operating support. The Foundation typically has two grant cycles annually, Letter of Inquiry are accepted then. Contact the Foundation directly for current grant cycles. Organizations invited to submit a complete proposal should expect a final decision from the Foundation within eight to twelve weeks of receipt.
Requirements: Organizations applying for a grant from the Brooklyn Community Foundation must be classified as tax-exempt under Section 501(c)3 of the Internal Revenue Code and as public charities under Section 509(a) of that Code. Fiscally sponsored organizations may also apply. Your organization need not be based in Brooklyn; however grants from the Brooklyn Community Foundation must directly benefit Brooklyn neighborhoods and/or Brooklyn residents. Applying for funding is a two part process: Ist step—begins with a Letter of Inquiry (LOI). This is the opportunity for an organization to provide the Foundation with an overview of the group and its proposed activities, project or program; 2nd step—applicants who have been selected to proceed to the next stage will receive an email from the Foundation's staff indicating that the organization has been approved to submit a complete proposal which best describes in detail the activities, program or project. If selected, your organization will have 30 days to submit a complete a proposal online.
Restrictions: The Foundation does not: fund individuals; support for-profit organizations; purchase tickets for dinners, golf outings or similar fundraising events; make contributions to candidates for elective office or for partisan political purposes; provide funding for religious purposes.
Geographic Focus: New York
Samples: Bedford Stuyvesant Restoration Corp., Brooklyn, NY, $25,000—education, arts & culture, project support (2008); Arts of Street Anna's, Brooklyn, NY, $10,000—arts & culture education, theater, project support (2008); Asian American Women Artist Alliance, Brooklyn, NY, $500—arts & culture education, arts/culture, project support (2008).
Contact: Diane John, (718) 722-5952 or (718) 722-2300; (718) 722-5757; info@BrooklynCommunityFoundation.org
Internet: http://www.brooklyncommunityfoundation.org/grants/arts-for-all
Sponsor: Brooklyn Community Foundation
45 Main Street, Suite 409
Brooklyn, NY 11201

Brooklyn Community Foundation Community Development Grants 320

The Community Development Fund supports efforts to provide affordable housing and neighborhood stability. It encourages thoughtful planning initiatives, quality urban design and sensitivity to the historic character of Brooklyn, New York neighborhoods. It also promotes family and individual economic health through support services and effective job training programs. The Fund's goals are to: strengthen and preserve access to affordable housing in Brooklyn neighborhoods; raise individual and family income by providing Brooklyn residents access to quality job training, career placement and financial support services; build the local economy by supporting neighborhood entrepreneurs and local efforts to improve our retail corridors. Types of support available include: program, capacity building, capital, and operating support. The Foundation typically has two grant cycles annually, Letter of Inquiry are accepted then. Contact the Foundation directly for current grant cycles. Organizations invited to submit a complete proposal should expect a final decision from the Foundation within eight to twelve weeks of receipt.
Requirements: Organizations applying for a grant from the Brooklyn Community Foundation must be classified as tax-exempt under Section 501(c)3 of the Internal Revenue Code and as public charities under Section 509(a) of that Code. Fiscally sponsored organizations may also apply. Your organization need not be based in Brooklyn; however grants from the Brooklyn Community Foundation must directly benefit Brooklyn neighborhoods and/or Brooklyn residents. Applying for funding is a two part process: Ist step—begins with a Letter of Inquiry (LOI). This is the opportunity for an organization to provide the Foundation with an overview of the group and its proposed activities, project or program; 2nd step—applicants who have been selected to proceed to the next stage will receive an email from the Foundation's staff indicating that the organization has been approved to submit a complete proposal which best describes in detail the activities, program or project. If selected, your organization will have 30 days to submit a complete a proposal online.
Restrictions: The Foundation does not: fund individuals; support for-profit organizations; purchase tickets for dinners, golf outings or similar fundraising events; make contributions to candidates for elective office or for partisan political purposes; provide funding for religious purposes.
Geographic Focus: New York
Samples: Bedford Stuyvesant Restoration Corp., Brooklyn, NY, $10,000—project support (2008); Brand New Day, Inc., Elizabeth, NJ, $20,000—neighborhood renewal, community development, general operating support grant (2008); Bridge Street Development, Corp., $600—neighborhood renewal, housing, sponsorship grant (2008).
Contact: Diane John, (718) 722-5952 or (718) 722-2300; (718) 722-5757; info@BrooklynCommunityFoundation.org
Internet: http://www.brooklyncommunityfoundation.org/grants/community-development
Sponsor: Brooklyn Community Foundation
45 Main Street, Suite 409
Brooklyn, NY 11201

Brooklyn Community Foundation Education and Youth Achievement Grants 321

The Education and Youth Achievement Fund promotes access to quality education and academic success for all children and adults in the Brooklyn area of New York. It also supports programs that help young people make smart life choices and nurture their social and emotional well-being. Its goals are to: combine tutoring, academic support networks, and enrichment activities to advance student achievement; encourage action-oriented, youth-led community projects that promote collaboration, leadership development, and critical thinking; build bridges between youth and trusted, responsible adult role models through effective mentoring programs. Types of support available include: program, capacity building, capital, and operating support. The Foundation typically has two grant cycles annually, Letter of Inquiry are accepted then. Contact the Foundation directly for current grant cycles. Organizations invited to submit a complete proposal should expect a final decision from the Foundation within eight to twelve weeks of receipt.
Requirements: Organizations applying for a grant from the Brooklyn Community Foundation must be classified as tax-exempt under Section 501(c)3 of the Internal Revenue Code and as public charities under Section 509(a) of that Code. Fiscally sponsored organizations may also apply. Your organization need not be based in Brooklyn; however grants from the Brooklyn Community Foundation must directly benefit Brooklyn neighborhoods and/or Brooklyn residents. Applying for funding is a two part process: Ist step—begins with a Letter of Inquiry (LOI). This is the opportunity for an organization to provide the Foundation with an overview of the group and its proposed activities, project or program; 2nd step—applicants who have been selected to proceed to the next stage will receive an email from the Foundation's staff indicating that the organization has been approved to submit a complete proposal which best describes in detail the activities, program or project. If selected, your organization will have 30 days to submit a complete a proposal online.
Restrictions: The Foundation does not: fund individuals; support for-profit organizations; purchase tickets for dinners, golf outings or similar fundraising events; make contributions to candidates for elective office or for partisan political purposes; provide funding for religious purposes.

Geographic Focus: New York
Samples: Shoot Hoops Not Guns Basketball, Association, Inc., Brooklyn, NY, $500—community quality of life, youth, program support grant (2008); United Community Centers, Inc., Brooklyn, NY, $30,000—neighborhood renewal, youth, project support grant (2008); Refuge Inc., Staten Island, NY, $450—quality of life, youth, project support grant (2008).
Contact: Diane John, (718) 722-5952 or (718) 722-2300; (718) 722-5757; info@BrooklynCommunityFoundation.org
Internet: http://www.brooklyncommunityfoundation.org/grants/education-youth
Sponsor: Brooklyn Community Foundation
45 Main Street, Suite 409
Brooklyn, NY 11201

Brooklyn Community Foundation Green Communities Grants 322
The Green Communities Fund fosters the development of green spaces, jobs, and neighborhoods. Its goals are to: encourage the protection and creation of open space, parks and community gardens; seek new ways to introduce and encourage environmental awareness in all neighborhoods through grassroots programming; train job seekers for green careers and connect them to employment opportunities. Types of support available include: program, capacity building, capital, and operating support. The Foundation typically has two grant cycles annually, Letter of Inquiry are accepted then. Contact the Foundation directly for current grant cycles. Organizations invited to submit a complete proposal should expect a final decision from the Foundation within eight to twelve weeks of receipt.
Requirements: Organizations applying for a grant from the Brooklyn Community Foundation must be classified as tax-exempt under Section 501(c)3 of the Internal Revenue Code and as public charities under Section 509(a) of that Code. Fiscally sponsored organizations may also apply. Your organization need not be based in Brooklyn; however grants from the Brooklyn Community Foundation must directly benefit Brooklyn neighborhoods and/or Brooklyn residents. Applying for funding is a two part process: Ist step—begins with a Letter of Inquiry (LOI). This is the opportunity for an organization to provide the Foundation with an overview of the group and its proposed activities, project or program; 2nd step—applicants who have been selected to proceed to the next stage will receive an email from the Foundation's staff indicating that the organization has been approved to submit a complete proposal which best describes in detail the activities, program or project. If selected, your organization will have 30 days to submit a complete a proposal online.
Restrictions: The Foundation does not: fund individuals; support for-profit organizations; purchase tickets for dinners, golf outings or similar fundraising events; make contributions to candidates for elective office or for partisan political purposes; provide funding for religious purposes.
Geographic Focus: New York
Contact: Diane John, (718) 722-5952 or (718) 722-2300; (718) 722-5757; info@BrooklynCommunityFoundation.org
Internet: http://www.brooklyncommunityfoundation.org/grants/green-communities
Sponsor: Brooklyn Community Foundation
45 Main Street, Suite 409
Brooklyn, NY 11201

Brown Foundation of Houston Grants 323
The foundation distributes funds for public charitable purposes, principally for support, encouragement and assistance to education, community service and the arts. The Foundation's current emphasis is in the field of public education at the primary and secondary levels with focus on supporting non-traditional and innovative approaches designed to improve public education primarily within the State of Texas. The visual and performing arts remain an area of interest. The Foundation also focuses on community service projects which serve the needs of children and families. The Foundation is interested in funding projects which fulfill one or more of the following criteria: addressing root causes of a concern rather than treating symptoms; serving as a catalyst to stimulate collaborative efforts by several sectors of the community; resulting in a long-lasting impact on the situation beyond the value of the grant itself; reflecting and encouraging sound financial planning and solid management practices in administration of the project. Proposals should be submitted a minimum of 4 months before funds are required.
Requirements: 501(c)3 tax-exempt organizations, public charities, and units of government are eligible.
Restrictions: Grants are not made to individuals. Only one application within a twelve month period will be considered. No proposal from an organization previously funded by the Foundation will be considered unless a full and timely report of expenditure of the previous grant has been submitted. The Foundation does not expect to support: grants to religious organizations for religious purposes; testimonial dinners, fundraising events or marketing events; grants intended directly or indirectly to support candidates for political office or to influence legislation; grants to other private foundations; grants to cover past operating deficits or debt retirements.
Geographic Focus: Texas
Samples: Saint Luke's Episcopal Hospital (Houston, TX)—to construct a patient-care center, $10,000; U of Arkansas (Fayetteville, AR)—to endow a chair in English literacy designed to increase the reading and writing competency of Arkansas high-school graduates through summer workshops and graduate-assistant tutoring, $1.5 million.
Contact: Nancy Pittman, Executive Director; (713) 523-6867; (713) 523-2917; bfi@brownfoundation.org
Internet: http://www.brownfoundation.org/Guidelines.asp
Sponsor: Brown Foundation of Houston
P.O. Box 130646
Houston, TX 77219-0646

Brunswick Foundation Grants 324
The Brunswick Foundation Grants awards direct donations to 501(c)3 organizations that enhance marine, fitness, bowling or billiards activities and related industry interests, or any other Brunswick business interest. The foundation also supports programs where Brunswick Corporation employees volunteer and efforts to provide a higher education for children of employees. Types of support include employee-related scholarships, employee-matching gifts, general operating budgets, building construction/renovation, capital campaigns, special projects, research, and continuing support. Requests for guidelines must be in writing, or applicants may submit a letter describing the purpose of the organization and the request.
Requirements: IRS 501(c)3 organizations in Alabama, Arizona, Connecticut, Florida, Georgia, Illinois, Indiana, Kentucky, Louisiana, Maryland, Michigan, Minnesota, Mississippi, Nebraska, North Carolina, Oklahoma, Oregon, South Carolina, Tennessee, Texas, Washington, and Wisconsin are eligible.
Restrictions: Grants are not made to religious organizations for religious purposes; for any form of political activity; to veterans groups, fraternal orders, or labor groups; for loans of any kind; or for trips, tours, dinners, tickets, or advertising.
Geographic Focus: Alabama, Arizona, Connecticut, Florida, Georgia, Illinois, Indiana, Kentucky, Louisiana, Maryland, Michigan, Minnesota, Mississippi, Nebraska, North Carolina, Oklahoma, Oregon, South Carolina, Tennessee, Texas, Washington, Wisconsin
Date(s) Application is Due: Mar 22
Amount: 500 - 2,000 USD
Samples: Grand Valley State U (Allendale, MI)—for the fresh water research program, $50,000; Texas Department of Parks and Wildlife (Austin, TX)—for capital support, $50,000.
Contact: Carol Stame, President; (847) 735-4467
Internet: http://www.brunswickcorp.com
Sponsor: Brunswick Foundation
1 N Field Court
Lake Forest, IL 60045

Build-A-Bear Workshop Foundation Grants 325
The foundation is committed to improving communities and impacting lives through meaningful philanthropic programs that help children and families, animals and the environment. Grants range between $1,000 and $10,000 with the average grant being $2,500. Application and guidelines are available online.
Requirements: Priority is given to 501(c)3 tax-exempt organizations.
Restrictions: The foundation does not awards grants to support: capital campaigns; fundraising sponsorships or events; political activities; religious organizations for religious purposes.
Geographic Focus: All U.S. States
Amount: 1,000 - 10,000 USD
Contact: Maxine Clark, President; (314) 423-8000, ext. 5366; giving@buildabear.com
Internet: http://www.buildabear.com/aboutus/community/babwfoundation.aspx
Sponsor: Build-A-Bear Workshop Bear Hugs Foundation
1954 Innerbelt Business Center Drive
Saint Louis, MO 63114

Bullitt Foundation Grants 326

The foundation functions to protect and restore the environment of the Pacific Northwest, including Washington, Oregon, Idaho, western Montana, coastal rainforests in Alaska, and British Columbia, Canada. Program priorities include aquatic ecosystems; terrestrial ecosystems; conservation and stewardship in agriculture; energy and climate change; growth management and transportation; toxic and radioactive substances; training, organizational development, and unique opportunities (including education and public outreach). Areas of interest include air pollution, climate change, endangered species, energy conservation, environmental education and justice, human health, transportation, and tribal communities. The foundation supports challenge/matching, general operating, project/program, seed money, demonstration, and development grants, as well as requests for conferences/seminars and technical assistance support. Grants will be awarded for one year with possible renewal.

Requirements: Nonprofit organizations in the Pacific Northwest, including Washington, Oregon, Idaho, western Montana, coastal rainforests in Alaska, and British Columbia, Canada are eligible.

Geographic Focus: Alaska, Idaho, Montana, Oregon, Washington, Canada

Date(s) Application is Due: May 1; Nov 1

Samples: North Seattle Community College Foundation (WA)—to support a model project for watershed educational activities, $10,000; Washington's National Park Fund (WA)—to support a program for youth from local school districts, $5000.

Contact: Program Officer; (206) 343-0807; (206) 343-0822; info@bullitt.org

Internet: http://www.bullitt.org

Sponsor: Bullitt Foundation
1212 Minor Avenue
Seattle, WA 98101-2825

Bunbury Company Grants 327

The company seeks to assist organizations primarily in Mercer County, but also in Burlington, Camden, Hunterdon, Mercer, Middlesex, Monmouth, Ocean, and Somerset with programs in the following areas: educational programs that provide opportunities for intellectual, societal or cultural growth to youth and families; environmental programs that help conserve threatened farmland, habitat or waterways and regional planning efforts that help advance these goals; community building and social service programs that empower the undeserved; cultural programs that promote local artistic initiatives. The Foundation is particularly interested in programs that are local and have the ability to positively impact the quality of life within their community. The Foundation provides basic needs support for: general operating support; building funds; challenge or matching funds; and funds for special programs.

Requirements: An applicant must have tax-exempt status under Section 501(c)3 of the Internal Revenue Service Code and be a publicly supported charity under Section 509. Nonprofit organizations additionally must be registered with the State of New Jersey as a charity unless they are schools that file their cirricula with the Department of Education and are exempted from the provisions of the New Jersey Charitable Registration and Investigation Act.

Restrictions: The Foundation will not provide support for the following: endowment campaigns; sporting activities, outings or events; fraternal or religious organizations, including schools with religious affiliation; individual fellowships or scholarships; summer camps or day care facilities, unless part of a comprehensive after care program; organizations with multiple chapters if outside Mercer County; specific cultural performances; publications or surveys.

Geographic Focus: New Jersey

Date(s) Application is Due: Mar 1; May 3; Aug 2; Nov 7

Amount: 15,000 USD

Contact: Grants Manager; (609) 333-8800; (609) 333-8900; BunburyCo@aol.com

Internet: http://www.bunburycompany.org/grant-guidelines.html

Sponsor: Bunbury Company
2 Railroad Place
Hopewell, NJ 08525

Burlington Northern Santa Fe Foundation Grants 328

The foundation is focused on the communities where the company operates and areas where its railways pass. The foundation supports education, including scholarships for Native Americans and scholarships for children of employees in conjunction with the National Merit Scholarships program; the arts, including museums, performing arts, and libraries; and civic and public affairs. Support goes to the Nature Conservancy and for local fire departments and law enforcement. Types of support include general operating support, continuing support, annual campaigns, capital campaigns, and program development. Health and human services funding concentrates on the United Way. Awards are made for a single year and for continuing support. The company also matches employee funds given to public and private colleges and universities, cultural organizations, and hospitals in the United States. Requests for applications should describe the purpose for the grant. Requests are reviewed every six weeks.

Requirements: Any 501(c)3 organization located in Schaumburg, IL, and communities where the corporation operates, including 28 states and two Canadian provinces, are eligible to apply.

Geographic Focus: All U.S. States

Samples: Texas Christian University, Fort Worth, TX, $600,000 - for Career Services Center and Neeley Schools Next Generation Leadership Program; Hastings Rural Fire District, Glenvil, NE, $20,000 - for replacement of rescue truck and grass firefighting rig; Foss Waterway Seaport, Tacoma, WA, $50,000 - for restoration and development of waterfront cultural center and maritime museum.

Contact: Deanna Dugas, Manager Corporate Contributions; (817) 867-6407; (817) 352-7924; Deanna.dugas@bnsf.com

Sponsor: Burlington Northern Santa Fe Foundation
2650 Lou Menk Drive, 2nd Floor, P.O. Box 961057
Fort Worth, TX 76131-2830

Burton D. Morgan Foundation Adult Entrepreneurship Grants 329

The Foundation is interested in supporting organizations that assist innovative entrepreneurs with launching their ventures and building sustainability. The Foundation believes that innovative entrepreneurship draws upon creativity, involves an element of risk, and creates value. Support is awarded to charitable organizations that provide the following kinds of entrepreneurship-related services: information, incubation, networking, continuing education, access to capital, risk management, and business planning. The Foundation is particularly interested in building entrepreneurial networks that foster a stronger entrepreneurial culture in Northeast Ohio.

Requirements: Grants are made to organizations recognized as tax-exempt under the Internal Revenue Service code section 501(c)3 which are not private foundations. The Foundation's geographic preferences complement its program and project focus by targeting: entrepreneurship-related programs in Summit County, Ohio, and surrounding counties, known collectively as the Northeast Ohio region; and Hudson, Ohio-based nonprofit organizations.

Restrictions: The Foundation does not usually make multi-year grants and does not ordinarily consider grants to annual fund drives, to units of government, or to organizations and institutions which are primarily tax supported, including state universities. The Foundation no longer makes grants to arts, mental health, and social service organizations and programs.

Geographic Focus: Ohio

Date(s) Application is Due: Mar 1; Jun 1; Oct 1

Contact: Deborah D. Hoover, President; (330) 665-1630 or (330) 655-1660; dhoover@bdmorganfdn.org

Internet: http://www.bdmorganfdn.org/Adult_entrepreneurship.php

Sponsor: Burton D. Morgan Foundation
22 Aurora Street
Hudson, OH 44236

Burton D. Morgan Foundation Collegiate Entrepreneurship Grants 330

The Burton D. Morgan Foundation supports entrepreneurship programs and activities on college and university campuses primarily in Northeast Ohio. Morgan believed that entrepreneurship should have a home on college campuses, but separate from schools of management. Accordingly, he encouraged the Foundation to establish campus entrepreneurship centers that combine a variety of disciplines and programs. The Foundation has since expanded its emphasis on cross-campus entrepreneurship programs at the collegiate level through its collaboration with the Ewing Marion Kauffman Foundation.

Requirements: Grants are made to organizations recognized as tax-exempt under the Internal Revenue Service code section 501(c)3 which are not private foundations. The Foundation's geographic preferences complement its program and project focus by targeting: entrepreneurship-related programs in Summit County, Ohio, and surrounding counties, known collectively as the Northeast Ohio region; and Hudson, Ohio-based nonprofit organizations.

Restrictions: The Foundation does not usually make multi-year grants and does not ordinarily consider grants to annual fund drives, to units of government, or to organizations and institutions which are primarily tax supported, including state universities. The Foundation no longer makes grants to arts, mental health, and social service organizations and programs.
Geographic Focus: Ohio
Date(s) Application is Due: Mar 1; Jun 1; Oct 1
Contact: Deborah D. Hoover, President; (330) 665-1630 or (330) 655-1660; dhoover@bdmorganfdn.org
Internet: http://www.bdmorganfdn.org/Collegiate_entrepreneurship.php
Sponsor: Burton D. Morgan Foundation
22 Aurora Street
Hudson, OH 44236

Burton D. Morgan Foundation Youth Entrepreneurship Grants 331
The Burton D. Morgan Foundation supports youth education programs for elementary, middle, and high school students with a focus on the free enterprise system, financial literacy and entrepreneurship. The Foundation values programs that inspire students to become financially independent and fiscally responsible and to envision a future that includes the highest educational attainment possible. To achieve these goals, teachers must receive the necessary training to incorporate entrepreneurial thinking and economic concepts into coursework and extracurricular activities. While not every student will become an entrepreneur, every student will benefit from learning about entrepreneurship and, thereby, be better equipped to chart their own futures. The Foundation also believes that Northeast Ohio youth entrepreneurship programs will benefit from networking and collaborating and that students will be best served by the creation of educational pathways from one educational level to another.
Requirements: Grants are made to organizations recognized as tax-exempt under the Internal Revenue Service code section 501(c)3 which are not private foundations. The Foundation's geographic preferences complement its program and project focus by targeting: entrepreneurship-related programs in Summit County, Ohio, and surrounding counties, known collectively as the Northeast Ohio region; and Hudson, Ohio-based nonprofit organizations.
Restrictions: The Foundation does not usually make multi-year grants and does not ordinarily consider grants to annual fund drives, to units of government, or to organizations and institutions which are primarily tax supported, including state universities. The Foundation no longer makes grants to arts, mental health, and social service organizations and programs.
Geographic Focus: Ohio
Date(s) Application is Due: Mar 1; Jun 1; Oct 1
Contact: Deborah D. Hoover, President; (330) 665-1630 or (330) 655-1660; dhoover@bdmorganfdn.org
Internet: http://www.bdmorganfdn.org/youth_entrepreneurship.php
Sponsor: Burton D. Morgan Foundation
22 Aurora Street
Hudson, OH 44236

Burton G. Bettingen Grants 332
The fields of activity of the corporation are education at all levels, mental health, crime and abuse victims and public protection programs, religion (Christian, Roman Catholic, and Salvation Army), environment, and welfare. Top funding priority is children and youth. The current focus is on child prostitutes, runaways, and abandoned children. Nonprofits servicing the economically disadvantaged also may apply. The corporation provides broad types of support, including operating, capital, research, challenge/matching grants, and endowments. A letter of inquiry stating the applicant's background, goals and objectives, and the specific need for funding is welcome. Unsolicited submissions are considered but receive low priority.
Requirements: IRS 501(c)3 organizations are eligible. Giving primarily, but not limited to, Southern California.
Restrictions: The corporation does not award grants to individuals; for general fund-raising events, dinners, or mass mailings; or to grantmaking organizations.
Geographic Focus: California
Amount: 5,000 - 200,000 USD
Samples: Childrens Hospital of Los Angeles (Los Angeles, CA)—for capital campaign, $700,000; Phoenix House (New York, NY)—for general support, $50,000; Children's Defense Fund (Washington, DC)—for general support, $750,000.
Contact: Patricia Brown, Executive Director; (323) 938-8478; (323) 938-8479; burtonbet@aol.com
Sponsor: Burton G. Bettingen Corporation
134 S Mansfield Avenue
Los Angeles, CA 90036-3019

Bush Foundation Arts & Humanities Grants: Short-Term Organizational Support 333
These grants are approved for one or more years and are intended to support particular activities for a finite period. Successful applicants typically propose activities that are part of a plan to achieve long-term organizational goals. Applicants should determine their own priorities when applying - the purposes of successful proposals are broad; however, the foundation typically approves only 10 to 15 requests each year.
Requirements: To be eligible for consideration, your organization must: Operate year-round programs based in Minnesota, North Dakota or South Dakota; Create or present performing, visual, humanities or media and/or literary arts; Have at least a three-year programming history in Minnesota or the Dakotas; Have had an average annual operating expense of more than $100,000 during the three most recently completed fiscal years; And, pay artists a reasonable salary or fee.
Restrictions: Funds are not available for sponsorship or presentation of one-time productions, events such as festivals or programs that operate only in the summer.
Geographic Focus: Minnesota, North Dakota, South Dakota, Wisconsin
Date(s) Application is Due: Mar 1; Jul 1; Nov 1
Contact: Program Officer; (651) 227-0891; info@bushfoundation.org
Internet: http://www.bushfoundation.org/grants/arts_humanities.asp#Short_Term_Support
Sponsor: Bush Foundation
332 Minnesota Street, Suite East 900
Street Paul, MN 55101-1315

Bush Foundation Ecological Health Grants 334
As part of the foundation's goal to improve the ecological health of their region, it seeks to help people and organizations develop ways to treat ecological health as an interdependent system, rather than as isolated problems to be solved. Through these efforts, the foundation hopes to help restore, preserve, and protect our resources in order to sustain the interdependent health of humans, animals, and ecosystems. This condition of interdependence is captured in the term 'ecological health.' Guidelines are available at the Bush Foundation website.
Requirements: The Foundation will make grants to benefit ecological health work in the three-state Bush region of Minnesota, North Dakota and South Dakota. Proposals that incorporate ecological health in other program areas (e.g., arts and culture) are encouraged. The preference is for initiatives that have a direct and practical bearing on humans and their communities. Specifically, the foundation will support work that: Promotes clean and renewable energy in order to improve ecological health; Protects and improves human health by reducing exposure to environmental toxins; Improves water quality by reducing pollutants in surface and ground water; Promotes decisions on land use that protect and preserve ecological health; Or, encourages farming and ranching practices that benefit the environment and the health of communities.
Restrictions: The Foundation does not make grants to environmental education programs, animal welfare organizations, humane societies, nature centers, outdoor recreation programs or day care centers. Single-issue environmental requests are unlikely to receive support.
Geographic Focus: Minnesota, North Dakota, South Dakota
Samples: Examples of desired results: A better informed public (community) that understands the link between human health and ecological health; Increased working relationships among environmental, health, and child development professionals; Improved quality of ground and surface water achieved through behavior change, policy change, and civic action.
Contact: Kelly Kleppe, Grants Manager; (651) 379-2222; kkleppe@bushfoundation.org
Internet: http://www.bushfoundation.org/grants/ecological_health.asp
Sponsor: Bush Foundation
332 Minnesota Street, Suite East 900
Street Paul, MN 55101-1315

Bush Foundation Health & Human Services Grants 335
The foundation responds to a broad range of human services proposals. Proposals are reviewed on a case-by-case basis; applicant organizations take the lead in identifying promising solutions to the challenges faced by people who use their programs. In recent years, most grant dollars given to human services

organizations have been for programs serving children, youth, and families. The foundation also considers program proposals that will improve the quality, accessibility, and efficiency of health care services in the region.
Requirements: The foundation is most interested in proposals that: (1) Promote opportunities for individuals and communities to become fully contributing members of society by supporting organizational projects that remove barriers to effective education, economic security and good health; (2) Improve the abilities of immigrant and refugee organizations, groups and individuals to obtain basic needs and rights, promote refugee and immigrant civic engagement and enhance their contribution to economic and cultural life; (3) The foundation will also consider proposals for comprehensive capital campaigns for building purchases, major building renovations and new construction to improve physical facilities. To be eligible for consideration, your organization must be a 501(c)3 nonprofit, tax-exempt organization, located in Minnesota, North Dakota or South Dakota, and able to demonstrate that you can take the lead in identifying promising solutions to challenges faced by people who use your programs. The two-step application process begins with a letter of inquiry. Guidelines for writing the letter of inquiry are on the information sheet which is available by contacting the sponsor or by download at the website.
Restrictions: The foundation does not make grants to: Individuals; Government agencies (except in special cases dictated by foundation priorities); Projects not benefiting the three-state region of Minnesota, North Dakota and South Dakota; Or, projects outside the United States. Download the Grant Restrictions file from the website for more details.
Geographic Focus: Minnesota, North Dakota, South Dakota
Date(s) Application is Due: Mar 1; Jul 1; Nov 1
Contact: Program Officer; (651) 227-0891; grants@bushfoundation.org
Internet: http://www.bushfoundation.org/grants/human_services.asp
Sponsor: Bush Foundation
332 Minnesota Street, Suite East 900
Street Paul, MN 55101-1315

Bush Foundation Regional Arts Development Program II Grants **336**
This program is an investment in the vitality, creative potential and long-term sustainability of mid-size arts and humanities organizations throughout Minnesota, North Dakota and South Dakota as a strategy towards the foundation's goal — to maintain a diverse, vibrant and sustainable environment for the arts and humanities. Grants through this program are long-term (10 years) and non-prescriptive in the use of grant funds.
Requirements: This program is open to organizations that meet all of the following criteria: Are based in Minnesota, North Dakota or South Dakota; Create, present or serve the performing, visual, media or literary arts or humanities; Have at least a five-year programming history; Have an annual operating budget larger than $250,000 but no greater than $5 million during the three most recently completed fiscal years; Pay artists a reasonable salary or fee; Produce, present or develop year-round arts programs for the public, rather than sponsor one-time events; Have filed a final report on all previous Foundation grants, with the exception of capital grants; Have 501(c)3 tax-exempt status. The two-step application process begins with a preliminary proposal. The Foundation will consider preliminary proposals one time per year.
Restrictions: This program is not open to organizations that exist as a government agency, local arts council, public education institution, library or public broadcasting entity, such as a nonprofit radio or television station.
Geographic Focus: Minnesota, North Dakota, South Dakota
Date(s) Application is Due: Mar 1; Jul 1
Amount: Up to 100,000 USD
Samples: Ballet Works, Inc. - Minneapolis, MN; Duluth Art Institute Association - Duluth, MN; Fargo-Moorhead Orchestral Association - Moorhead, MN; Graywolf Press - Street Paul, MN; North Dakota Museum of Art - Grand Forks, ND
Contact: Program Officer; (651) 227-0891; info@bushfoundation.org
Internet: http://www.bushfoundation.org/grants/arts_humanities.asp#RADP
Sponsor: Bush Foundation
332 Minnesota Street, Suite East 900
Street Paul, MN 55101-1315

Bushrod H. Campbell and Adah F. Hall Charity Fund Grants **337**
Grants are awarded to organizations in the Boston area devoted to basic needs for the elderly, projects relating to medicine and medical research, health care, hospitals, the blind and deaf, and certain discretionary projects. Grants are also awarded countrywide for projects addressing population control. Types of support include capital grants, general operating grants, program grants, and research grants.
Requirements: Tax-exempt organizations located within Boston and neighboring communities and U.S. tax-exempt organizations devoted to population control are eligible.
Restrictions: Grants are not awarded to individuals.
Geographic Focus: Massachusetts
Date(s) Application is Due: Jan 15; Apr 15; Aug 15; Oct 15
Amount: 3,000 - 7,500 USD
Contact: Brenda Taylor, c/o Palmer & Dodge; (617) 239-0556; (617) 227-4420
Sponsor: Bushrod H. Campbell and Adah F. Hall Charity Fund
111 Huntington Avenue at Prudential Center
Boston, MA 02199-7613

Butler Manufacturing Company Foundation Grants **338**
The foundation's purpose is to provide sustained financial assistance to worthy charitable, educational, and health and welfare programs in the United States and to enhance the quality of life in those communities where employees of Butler Manufacturing Company reside. The focus of the support includes youth programs, minority development, job training for the disadvantaged, neighborhoods, and support of nonresidential building programs using the company's products; scholarships for children of employees, and grants to colleges and universities serving locations where employees reside; and the community's principal arts organizations. Types of support include capital grants, general operating grants, employee matching gifts, program development grants, and scholarships to children of employees. Applications are considered quarterly.
Requirements: Applicants must be nonprofit institutions meeting the human needs of society in the greater Kansas City area and other communities where employees reside.
Geographic Focus: Missouri
Amount: 500 - 50,000 USD
Samples: Missouri Repertory Theatre (MO)—for project support, $5000; Kansas City Neighborhood Alliance (MO)—for operating support, $5000.
Contact: Foundation Administrator; (816) 968-3208; (816) 968-3211; blfay@butlermfg.org
Internet: http://www.butlermfg.org/faq/index.asp#Ans10
Sponsor: Butler Manufacturing Company Foundation
P.O. Box 419917
Kansas City, MO 64141-0917

Bydale Foundation Grants **339**
The foundation emphasizes international understanding, public policy research, environmental quality, cultural programs, the law and civil rights, social services, higher education, and economics. Funding includes support for: conference/seminars, continuing support, general operating support, matching/challenging support, program development, publication, research, and seed money. An application form is not required. Submit an initial approach in the form of a letter or proposal.
Requirements: U.S. 501(c)3 nonprofits are eligible.
Geographic Focus: All U.S. States
Date(s) Application is Due: Nov 1
Samples: Clean Water Fund (Washington, DC)—$5000; Greenhouse Crisis Foundation (Washington, DC)—$20,000; Greenpeace U.S. A (Washington, DC)—$2500.
Contact: Milton Solomon, Vice President; (914) 428-3232; (914) 428-1660
Sponsor: Bydale Foundation
11 Martine Avenue
White Plains, NY 10606

Byron W. and Alice L. Lockwood Foundation Grants **340**
The foundation awards grants to Washington nonprofit organizations in its areas of interest, including arts, biomedical research, higher education, hospitals and health care organizations, housing and homelessness, museums, religion and religious welfare programs, and social services. Types of support include capital improvements, continuing support, general operating grants, professorships, projects grants, and research grants. There are no application forms; submit a letter of request.
Requirements: Washington nonprofit organizations are eligible. Grants are awarded primarily in Washington's Seattle and Puget Sound areas.
Geographic Focus: All U.S. States
Date(s) Application is Due: Oct 31

Amount: 900 - 56,000 USD
Samples: Seattle's Union Gospel Mission (Seattle) for capital improvements at the men's shelter, $50,000; Youth Suicide Prevention Plan for Washington State,.
Contact: Lee Kraft, Executive Director; (206) 230-8489
Sponsor: Byron W. and Alice L. Lockwood Foundation
P.O. Box 4
Mercer, WA 98040

C.W. Titus Foundation Grants **341**
The foundation awards grants to eligible nonprofit organizations in Missouri and Oklahoma for programs in its areas of interest, including arts and culture, healthcare and health organizations, and social services. Types of support include building construction/renovation, general operating support, and materials/equipment acquisition. There are no application forms or deadlines.
Requirements: Missouri and Oklahoma nonprofit organizations are eligible.
Geographic Focus: Missouri, Oklahoma
Amount: 1,000 - 10,000 USD
Samples: Southwest Missouri State U Foundation (Springfield, MO)—to construct and equip a new master-control facility for the university's Ozarks Public Television station, $1 million.
Contact: Grants Administrator
Sponsor: C.W. Titus Foundation
950 Philtower Building, Suite 950
Tulsa, OK 74103-4123

Cabot Corporation Foundation Grants **342**
The objective of the company's corporate giving is to support community outreach objectives, with priority given to science and technology education; safety health and environment (SH&E); and community and civic improvement efforts in the communities where the company has major facilities or operations. Types of support include capital grants, challenge grants, employee matching gifts, fellowships, general support, professorships, project support, research, scholarships, and seed money. The board meets in January, April, July, and October to consider requests. Applications must be received at least 30 days before a board meeting.
Requirements: The foundation supports only nonprofit 501(c)3 tax-exempt organizations in Georgia, Illinois, Louisiana, Massachusetts, Pennsylvania, Texas, and West Virginia. Modest support is available for international organizations that qualify under U.S. tax regulations.
Restrictions: Contributions are not made to individuals; fraternal, political, athletic or veterans organizations; religious institutions (except for projects that are open to individuals without regard to religious preference); capital and endowment campaigns; sponsorships of local groups/individuals to participate in regional, national, or international competitions, conferences or events; advertising, dinner-table sponsorship, or fund-raising events.
Geographic Focus: Georgia, Illinois, Louisiana, Massachusetts, Pennsylvania, Texas, West Virginia
Amount: 1,000 - 25,000 USD
Samples: Gilbertsville Elementary School (PA)—to enhance science curriculum with LEGO products and training materials, $3700; Pact Malaysia (Malaysia)—to support literacy programs in Malaysia, $5000; Children's Hands-On Art Museum (MA)—equipment grant, $2500.
Contact: Karen Morrissey, Executive Director; (617) 345-0100; (617) 342-6312; Karen_Morrissey@cabot-corp.com
Internet: http://w1.cabot-corp.com/controller.jsp?N=21+3030
Sponsor: Cabot Corporation Foundation
Two Seaport Lane, Suite 1300
Boston, MA 02210

CACHH General Assistance Program Expansion Arts Support Grants **343**
Grants provide general operational support for Houston multicultural arts groups. The organization should be deeply rooted in and reflective of the culture of a minority, innercity, tribal, or disabled community; present a regular season of arts or cultural programs; and be primarily devoted to providing art to its community.
Requirements: Houston 501(c)3 nonprofit multicultural arts organizations are eligible. The organization must be governed by a board of directors that meets regularly and have been in operation at least one year before the deadline.
Geographic Focus: Texas
Date(s) Application is Due: Apr 1
Contact: Joseph Wilson, Director of Grants; (713) 527-9330, ext. 15; (713) 630-5210; joe@cachh.org or info@cachh.org
Internet: http://www.cachh.org/programsgrants.html
Sponsor: Cultural Arts Council of Houston/Harris County
3201 Allen Parkway, Suite 250
Houston, TX 77019-1800

CACHH General Assistance Program Organizational Support Grants **344**
Grants provide general operational support for Houston arts groups in operation for at least three years. The organization should present a regular season of arts or cultural programs and provide programs and events open to the appropriate public constituencies. All applications must be submitted on-line.
Requirements: Houston 501(c)3 nonprofit cultural arts or university arts organizations are eligible. The organization must be governed by a board of directors that meets regularly, and have been in operation at least three years before the deadline.
Geographic Focus: Texas
Date(s) Application is Due: Mar 26
Contact: Liz Alexander, Grants Management Officer; (713) 527-9330, ext. 14; (713) 630-5210; liz@cachh.org or grants@cachh.org
Internet: http://www.cachh.org/grants.html
Sponsor: Cultural Arts Council of Houston/Harris County
3201 Allen Parkway, Suite 250
Houston, TX 77019-1800

Caddock Foundation Grants **345**
The foundation supports nonprofit national and international Evangelical Christian religious organizations including churches and religious institutions, community groups, hospitals, international missions and ministries, religious centers and facilities, and youth organizations. Types of support include conferences/seminars, fellowships, and general operating support. Application must be made in writing and include a description of the organization and its objectives and the purpose of the grant. There are no application deadlines.
Restrictions: Grants are made to Evangelical Christian organizations. Grants are not made to individuals.
Geographic Focus: All U.S. States
Amount: 1,800 - 390,000 USD
Samples: Set Free Prison Ministries (Riverside CA)—for operating support, $152,000; Grace Evangelical Society (Roanoke, TX)—for operating support, $40,000.
Contact: Richard E. Caddock, Jr., Treasurer, (951) 683-5361
Sponsor: Caddock Foundation
1717 Chicago Avenue
Riverside, CA 92507

Caesar Puff Foundation Grants **346**
The Caesar Puff Foundation was established in Pennsylvania by a donation from Virginia A. Campana, and serves non-profit organizations in Ohio, Pennsylvania, and West Virginia. The Foundation's primary fields of interest include: animal welfare, Christian agencies and churches, food banks, higher education, public libraries, media/communications programs, and residential/custodial care units (including hospices). There are no specific application forms or deadlines, and applicants should contact the Foundation officer before sending a full application.
Restrictions: No grant support is offered to individuals.
Geographic Focus: Ohio, Pennsylvania, West Virginia
Date(s) Application is Due: Mar 14
Amount: 4,000 - 100,000 USD
Samples: Rostraver Public Library, Belle Vernon, Pennsylvania, $90,692 (2009); Family Hospice and Palliative Care, Pittsburgh, Pennsylvania, $4,000 (2009); Franciscan University of Steubenville, Steubenville, Steubenville, Ohio, $4,000 (2009).
Contact: Beverly Suchenek, (313) 222-6297
Sponsor: Caesar Puff Foundation
P.O. Box 75000, MC 3302
Detroit, MI 48275-3302

Caleb C. and Julia W. Dula Educational and Charitable Foundation Grants **347**
Grants are given in the areas of the arts and humanities (particularly museums and libraries), child welfare, the aged, community funds and appeals, health care, religion, and historical preservation. Most groups receiving foundation

grants have an established reputation in their particular field. There are no set requirements. Applicants should submit a letter that describes the organization, project, and amount requested.
Requirements: Grants are given to support projects of tax-exempt organizations.
Restrictions: Support is not available to individuals.
Geographic Focus: All U.S. States
Date(s) Application is Due: Apr 1; Oct 1
Amount: 5,000 - 50,000 USD
Contact: James F. Mauze, (314) 726-2800; (314) 863-3821; jfmauze@msn.com
Sponsor: Caleb C. and Julia W. Dula Educational and Charitable Foundation
112 S Hanley Road
Saint Louis, MO 63105

California Arts Council Creating Public Value Grants **348**
The California Arts Council's (CAC) Creating Public Value Program (CPV) is designed to promote a framework for thinking about the intrinsic and instrumental benefits of the arts; and to recognize that the resources artists, arts organizations, and others bring to a community play a key role in making a positive contribution to the individual and collective lives of all Californians. Through CPV, the CAC will partner with small California arts organizations in rural and underserved communities to support new or expanded projects to highlight the fact that the arts are of benefit to all Californians and are worthy of state and federal investment. CPV proposals must utilize the tools of the program identified as The Three Rs: relationships (building new or expanding existing partnerships); relevance (to audiences and community by expanding public participation); and, return on investment (through public awareness, promoting your organization's public value and social/economic impact to civic and political leaders, community supporters, audiences, and participants).
Requirements: CPV supports small arts organizations based in rural or underserved communities to implement new or expanded projects. The base of operations must be located within these communities. Applicants may apply under one of two categories: rural or underserved.
Restrictions: The Council does not fund: former grantee organizations not in compliance with CAC grant requirements (as stipulated in grant agreement); continuation of current work or previously funded CPV projects; non-arts organizations not involved in arts activities; for-profit organizations; other state agencies; programs not accessible to the public; projects with religious or sectarian purposes; organizations or activities that are part of the curricula base of schools, colleges, or universities; indirect costs of schools, colleges, or universities; trust or endowment funds; purchase of equipment, land, buildings, or construction (capital outlay or expenditures); out-of-state travel activities; hospitality or food costs; and expenses incurred before the starting or after the ending date of the grant.
Geographic Focus: California
Date(s) Application is Due: Feb 11
Amount: Up to 10,000 USD
Contact: Lucy Mochizuki, Contract and Procurement Administration; (916) 322-6337 or (916) 322-6555; (916) 322-6575; lmochizuki@cac.ca.gov
Internet: http://www.cac.ca.gov/programs/cpv201011.php
Sponsor: California Arts Council
1300 I Street, Suite 930
Sacramento, CA 95814

California Arts Council State-Local Partnerships **349**
The State-Local Partnership Program fosters cultural development on the local level through a partnership between the California Arts Council and the designated local arts agency of each county. The Partnership provides grant opportunities for general operating support and technical assistance for county-designated local arts agencies. This partnership includes funding, cooperative activities, information exchange, and leadership enabling individuals, organizations, and communities to create, present, and preserve the arts of all cultures to enrich the quality of life for all Californians. The grant application and eligibility list is available online at the California Arts Council website. May 3 is the annual deadline for submitting grant applications.
Requirements: Local arts agencies in California are eligible to apply. A local arts agency is a nonprofit organization, or agency of city or county government, officially designated to provide financial support, services, and/or other programs to a variety of arts organizations, individual artists, and the community as a whole. Matching funds, at a level of 1:1, are mandatory. The required match may be from any public or private source. In some instances, in-kind donated services for which a market value can be determined may be used for up to 50% of the required match. Applicants must: be a current grantee through the State-Local Partnership Program; be designated by resolution of their county board of supervisors to serve as the local partner; meet the legal eligibility requirements of all California Arts Council program grantees listed under Requirements; and provide a public office staffed by, at the minimum, a part-time director/professional administrator to be accessible during normal business hours.
Geographic Focus: California
Date(s) Application is Due: May 3
Contact: Lucy Mochizuki, Contract and Procurement Administrator; (916) 322-6337 or (916) 322-6555; (916) 322-6575; lmochizuki@cac.ca.gov
Internet: http://www.cac.ca.gov/programs/slp201011.php
Sponsor: California Arts Council
1300 I Street, Suite 930
Sacramento, CA 95814

California Arts Council Statewide Networks Grants **350**
The Statewide Networks Program (SN) is a California Arts Council (CAC) partnership with culturally specific, multicultural, and discipline-based statewide and regional arts networks and service organizations. Its goal is to promote the public value of the arts in communities by strengthening and expanding an organization's delivery of services to its constituents through communications, professional development opportunities, networking and arts advocacy. For this purpose, SN supports new approaches or expansions to an organization's work in the areas of organizational capacity and community building through advocacy, thus fostering an environment where all California cultures are represented. SN grants will be based on a ranking system and will range between $5,000 and $20,000.
Requirements: Statewide and regional culturally specific, multicultural, and discipline-based arts networks and service organizations are eligible to apply. Applicant organizations must have at least a two-year track record of developing its field and providing services to its constituent base (individual artists and/or arts organizations). All grant recipients must provide a dollar-for-dollar (1:1) match. The cash match may be from corporate or private contributions, local or federal government, or earned income. Other State funds cannot be used as a match. A combination of cash and in-kind contributions may be used to match CAC request.
Restrictions: SN requests cannot exceed an organization's total income based on its last completed budget. The Council does dot fund: previous grantee organizations that have not completed grant requirements (progress and final reports, final invoice, etc.); continuation of current work or previously funded SN projects; for-profit organizations; non-arts service organizations; indirect costs of schools, community colleges, colleges, or universities; trust or endowment funds; programs not accessible to the public; projects with religious or sectarian purposes; organizations or activities that are part of the curricula base of schools, colleges, or universities; purchase of equipment, land, buildings, or construction (capital outlay expenditures); out of state travel activities; hospitality or food costs; or expenses incurred before the starting or after the ending date of the contract.
Geographic Focus: California
Date(s) Application is Due: Mar 8
Amount: 5,000 - 20,000 USD
Contact: Lucero Arellano, SN Program Specialist; (916) 322-6338 or (916) 322-6555; (916) 322-6575; larellano@cac.ca.gov
Internet: http://www.cac.ca.gov/programs/sn200910.php
Sponsor: California Arts Council
1300 I Street, Suite 930
Sacramento, CA 95814

California Endowment Local Opportunities Fund Grants **351**
The fund will support a full spectrum of programs or activities to assist organizations in addressing the health needs of their local communities. The most common types of grants available include program grants—for specific projects or programs, including expansion of an existing project or program, pilot projects, or start-up of a new project or program; core operating support—day-to-day core operating costs for an existing program or for the general work of an organization; capacity building—to develop either the management or administrative capacity of an organization or to develop the organization's capacity to effectively implement a particular program; and planning—to develop a detailed plan and strategy for implementation of a project or program that will address a locally defined health need or health-related priority. Priority will be given to applications that address a locally

defined health need or health-related priority in an underserved community; are from a grassroots, nontraditional and/or emerging organization, or that address an issue or community that traditionally does not benefit from mainstream funding resources; and utilize the talents, cultures, and assets of the local community to address the health priorities of that community.
Requirements: California nonprofit organizations are eligible. Requests for core operating support will only be considered from organizations with annual operating budgets of less than $500,000 (as determined by financial statements and the annual operating budget submitted with the application).
Geographic Focus: All U.S. States
Date(s) Application is Due: Jan 10; May 15; Sep 15
Amount: Up to 50,000 USD
Samples: Horizons Foundation (San Francisco, CA)—for organizational development and regranting assistance needed to expand programs that address disparities in health and well-being among lesbian, gay, bisexual, and transgender residents of the San Francisco Bay area, $150,000; Asian Pacific Fund (San Francisco, CA)—to strengthen community institutions and expand programs and services needed to address disparities among Asian residents of the San Francisco Bay area, $150,000; Los Angeles Brotherhood Crusade (CA)—for organizational development and regranting assistance needed to expand programs that address disparities in health and well-being among minorities in South Central Los Angeles, $150,000.
Contact: Fund Coordinator; (800) 449-4149 or (818) 703-3311; (818) 703-4193
Internet: http://www.calendow.org/apply/frm_apply.htm
Sponsor: California Endowment
1000 N Alameda Street
Los Angeles, CA 90012

California Wellness Foundation Work and Health Program Grants 352
The foundation focuses its activities on specific priority areas where it has a significant, long-term commitment. Within each priority area, the foundation allocates the majority of its funds toward initiatives. Initiatives are targeted grantmaking programs with distinct objectives and are generally announced through requests for proposals. The foundation awards general grants and project grants. Under general grants, requests for core operating support for organizations that provide direct services to Californians for disease prevention or health promotion are of primary interest. Priority areas under general grants are diversity in the health professions, environmental health, healthy aging, mental health, teenage pregnancy prevention,, violence prevention, women's health, and work and health. Special projects grants are awarded to areas that fall outside the priority areas. Of particular interest are proposals to help California communities respond to cutbacks in federally funded programs. Activities commonly supported under special projects include strengthening traditional safety-net providers, educating consumers about changes in health care systems, advocating for underserved communities in health policy debates, and informing public decision making through policy analysis.
Requirements: Eligible applicants are California 501(c)3 nonprofit organizations, or organizations with a preapproved fiscal sponsor. An organization should first write a succinct letter of interest (one to two pages) that describes the organization, its leadership, the region and population(s) served, and the activities for which funding is needed, including the amount requested.
Geographic Focus: California
Amount: 5,000 - 200,000 USD
Samples: California Institute for Rural Studies (Davis, CA)—to articulate and distribute research findings on the health of farmworkers to policy makers, opinion leaders, the news media, and the public, $125,000 over three years; California State U, Stanislaus Foundation (Modesto, CA)—to provide holistic, prevention-based health-education services to Southeast Asian women and children living in Stanislaus County, $180,000 over three years; California State U, Auxiliary Services (CA)—to strengthen community organizations working to meet the health needs of residents of East Los Angeles and California's West San Gabriel Valley, $135,000 over three years; California Institute for Nursing and Healthcare (Berkeley, CA)—to develop and disseminate a plan for diversifying the nursing work force in California, $120,000 over three years.
Contact: Grants Administrator; (818) 702-1900; (818) 593-6614
Internet: http://www.tcwf.org/grants_program/index.htm
Sponsor: California Wellness Foundation
6320 Canoga Avenue, Suite 1700
Woodland Hills, CA 91367-7111

Callaway Foundation Grants 353
The Foundation awards grants for the benefit of projects and people in LaGrange and Troup County, Georgia. Areas of interest, include: arts and entertainment, elementary, higher, and secondary education; libraries; health and hospitals; community funds; care for the aged; community development; historic preservation; and church support. Types of support include annual campaigns, building construction/renovation, capital campaigns, continuing support, equipment acquisition, general operating support, land acquisition, and matching/challenge support. Preference is given to enduring construction projects and capital equipment. The Foundation Board meets four times per year in January, April, July, and October. Grant requests and applications are due the last day of the month preceding the meetings.
Requirements: IRS 501(c)3 nonprofit organizations in LaGrange and Troup County, Georgia are eligible to apply. Letters of request should briefly cover all aspects of the project, including complete financial planning and costs involved. Copies of budgets and current financial statements should also be included. An application form is available at the Foundation's website.
Restrictions: Grants are usually not made for loans, debt retirement, endowment or operating expenses. Requests from churches outside of Troup County, Georgia, are not considered.
Geographic Focus: Georgia
Date(s) Application is Due: Dec 31; Mar 31; Jun 30; Sep 30
Amount: 1,000 - 4,000,000 USD
Samples: Chattahoochee Valley Art Museum, LaGrange, GA, $59,000—for operating support (2008); Georgia Cities Foundation, Atlanta, GA, $367,772—for Downtown Revitalization Fund (2008); LaGrange College, LaGrange, GA, $4,000,000—for library building and renovation (2008).
Contact: H. Speer Burdette, President; (706) 884-7348; (706) 884-0201; hsburdette@callaway-foundation.org
Internet: http://www.callawayfoundation.org/grant_policies.php
Sponsor: Callaway Foundation
209 Broome Street, P.O. Box 790
La Grange, GA 30241

Callaway Golf Company Foundation Grants 354
The foundation strives to support initiatives in communities where Callaway Golf Company employees live and work. The geographic area of focus is primarily North San Diego County, California. The foundation offers support in the form of: matching funds, special projects, and general operating budgets. Areas of interest include but are not limited to: children and youth; biomedical research, with a special interest in the field of cancer; golf; education; boys & girls clubs of America; drug prevention; American Red Cross, housing, veterans; youth programs; food banks; social services; emergency programs; scholarship program for dependents of Callaway Golf employees; grants for training, competition and equipment needs. The foundation does not require the completion of a formal application document but requests a description of the organization and its history, the project at issue including goals and time lines, the qualifications of the leadership personnel involved in the project, and a detailed project budget. Grants are awarded semiannually. The Callaway Golf Company Foundation does not accept unsolicited requests for grants.
Requirements: IRS 501(c)3 nonprofit organizations in California are eligible.
Restrictions: The foundation will not fund applicants that illegally discriminate on the basis of gender, race, color, religion, national origin, ancestry, age, marital status, medical condition, or physical disability, either in the services they provide or in the hiring of staff; or promote political or particular religious doctrines.
Geographic Focus: California
Amount: 500 - 10,000 USD
Samples: Saint Judes Children's Research Hospital, $300 (2008); Utah Food Bank Services, $100 (2008); Purdue Foundation, $1,000 (2008).
Contact: Paul Thompson, Executive Director; (760) 930-8686; (760) 930-5021; cgcfoundation@callawaygolf.com
Internet: http://www.callawaygolf.com/Global/en-U.S. /Corporate/CallawayGolf Foundation.html
Sponsor: Callaway Golf Company Foundation
2180 Rutherford Road
Carlsbad, CA 92008-7328

Cambridge Community Foundation Grants 355
Cambridge Community Foundation is dedicated to improving the quality of life for the residents of Cambridge, Massachusetts. The CCF serves Cambridge through our support of nonprofit community organizations, by making direct financial grants, providing technical assistance, and forming

partnerships among organizations to coordinate services, address gaps, and highlight emerging issues. CCF primarily supports work in: early childhood services; youth service; senior services; community services; emergency outreach; arts; and the environment. See, the Foundations website http://www.cambridgecf.org/grant.html to download Proposal Summary Sheets, and additional guidelines.
Requirements: To be eligible to apply, the agency must be tax-exempt 501(c)3 under the IRS code), and the program must serve the people of Cambridge, Massachusetts.
Restrictions: Support is not provided to municipal, state, or federal agencies. Grants for individuals, scholarships, research studies, conferences, films, capital fund drives, or loans are not eligible.
Geographic Focus: Massachusetts
Date(s) Application is Due: Apr 1; Oct 1
Amount: 500 - 60,000 USD
Samples: Family First, Cambridge, MA — funding for the Family First parenting education and support programs for low-income and homeless families living in Cambridge (2008); Big Sister Association of Greater Boston, Boston, MA — funding to support Cambridge girls who participate in Big Sister's traditional one-to-one community-based mentoring program (2008); YNA Care Network, Inc./Hospice of Cambridge, Cambridge, MA — funding to support the patient care needs and running of the Chilton House, Cambridge's hospice, as well as bereavement support groups and counseling services to patient family members (2008).
Contact: Robert S. Hurlbut, Jr., Executive Director; (617) 576-9966; (617) 876-8187; RHurlbut@CambridgeCF.org or info@cambridgecf.org
Internet: http://www.cambridgecf.org
Sponsor: Cambridge Community Foundation
99 Bishop Richard Allen Drive
Cambridge, MA 02139

Camp-Younts Foundation Grants 356
The foundation supports social services, higher and secondary education, youth organizations, Protestant religion, and hospitals and other health organizations in Florida, Georgia, North Carolina, and Virginia. Applicants should submit a letter describing the program, a copy of the 501(c)3 tax-determination letter, listing of board members, and an audited budget for the previous year.
Requirements: Nonprofit organizations in Florida, Georgia, North Carolina, and Virginia may request grant support.
Geographic Focus: Florida, Georgia, North Carolina, Virginia
Date(s) Application is Due: Sep 1
Amount: 1,000 - 55,000 USD
Samples: Virginia Baptist General Board (Richmond, VA)—for operating support, $40,000; Saint Edwards School (Bon Air, VA)—for operating support, $25,000.
Contact: Bobby Worrell, Executive Director; (757) 562-3439
Sponsor: Camp-Younts Foundation
P.O. Box 4655
Atlanta, GA 30302

Campbell Hoffman Foundation Grants 357
The mission of the Campbell Hoffman Foundation is to promote and fund efforts to increase access to comprehensive health care for underserved and uninsured populations in the Northern Virginia region. Northern Virginia is defined as the counties of Arlington, Fairfax, Loudoun and Prince William and the cities of Alexandria, Falls Church, Fairfax, Manassas and Manassas Park. A letter of Inquiry should be submitted, as the initial approach, when approaching the Foundation for funding. Upon review, if the letter of inquiry meets with Foundations criteria, the applicant will be asked to submit a proposal; guidelines will be provided to them when the proposal is requested.
Requirements: Eligible organizations include nonprofit 501(c)3 organizations, government agencies and faith-based organizations. Eligible organizations must be both located in and serve the target populations of Northern Virginia.
Restrictions: The Foundation will not provide funding for capital campaigns, endowment campaigns, special events and/or conferences (including travel to and participation in same) , emergency funding, loans, capital projects (including but not limited to building, construction or renovation), land purchases, lawsuits, films, video or publications. The Foundation may choose to provide general operating support.
Geographic Focus: Virginia
Samples: Northern Virginia Family Service, $12,200—expand Dentral Resource Recruitment Program (2008); Arlington Free Clinic, $30,000—continue integration of mental health into primary care setting (2008); Loudoun Community Health Center, $45,000—initiate mental heatlh program; integrate w/ primary care; create community mental health provider coalition (2008).
Contact: Lyn S. Hainge, Executive Director; (703) 749-1794; (703) 442-0846; lhainge@campbellhoffman.org
Internet: http://www.campbellhoffman.org/applicants/default.aspx
Sponsor: Campbell Hoffman Foundation
1420 Spring Hill Road, Suite 600
McLean, VA 22102

Campbell Soup Foundation Grants 358
Since 1953, the Campbell Soup Foundation has provided financial support to local champions that inspire positive change in communities throughout the United States where Campbell Soup Company employees live and work. The Foundation places particular emphasis on Camden, New Jersey, birthplace of Campbell's flagship soup business and world headquarters. The Campbell Soup Foundation focuses its giving on four key areas: hunger relief-supporting food bank organizations in the communities of operation; wellness-addressing the health of consumers in the communities where they live; education-leveraging the Campbell brand portfolio to support educational programs; community revitalization-enhancing the quality of life in the communities that Campbell operates in. The Foundation only considers applications that meet the following criteria: the proposal must fit one of the key focus areas; the organization must display strong and effective leadership; the proposed plan must be clear and compelling, with measurable and sustainable commitments expressed in terms of real results; the proposed activity must be sufficiently visible to leverage additional support from other funding sources. There is no formal deadline. Proposals are accepted and reviewed on a rolling basis.
Requirements: The Foundation limits grants to nonprofit organizations which are tax-exempt under Section 501(c)3 of the Internal Revenue Code. Grants are made to institutions that serve: Camden, New Jersey; Davis, California; Sacramento, California; Stockton, California; Bloomfield, Connecticut; Norwalk, Connecticut; Lakeland, Florida; Downers Grove, Illinois; Marshall, Michigan; Maxton, North Carolina; Camden, New Jersey; South Plainfield, New Jersey; Napoleon, Ohio; Wauseon, Ohio; Willard, Ohio; Denver, Pennsylvania; Downingtown, Pennsylvania; Aiken, South Carolina; Paris, Texas; Richmond, Utah; Everett, Washington; Milwaukee, Wisconsin. Organizations do not need to be located in these communities in order to qualify for funding. However, the programs to be funded must serve these communities. Proposals must be submitted electronically via email to community_relations@campbellsoup.com. Proposals should be prepared in a concise, narrative form, without extensive documentation.
Restrictions: Grants are not made to the following: organizations that are based outside the United States and its territories; individuals; organizations that limit their services to members of one religious group or whose services propagate religious faith or creed; political organizations and those having the primary purpose of influencing legislation of/or promoting a particular ideological point of view; units of government; events and sponsorships; sports related events, activities and sponsorships. Organizations may not submit the same or similar proposals more than once in a Foundation fiscal year (July 1 - June 30). Proposals submitted via regular mail will not be reviewed.
Geographic Focus: Connecticut, Florida, Illinois, Michigan, New Jersey, North Carolina, Ohio, Pennsylvania, South Carolina, Texas, Utah, Washington, Wisconsin
Samples: Coriell Institute for Medical Research, $12,500 (2008); Scotland County Literacy Council, $15,000 (2008); Delaware County Christian School, $500 (2008).
Contact: Grant Administrator; (856) 342-6423 or (800) 257-8443; (856) 541-8185; community_relations@campbellsoup.com
Internet: http://www.campbellsoupcompany.com/community_center.asp
Sponsor: Campbell Soup Foundation
1 Campbell Place
Camden, NJ 08103-1701

Cape Branch Foundation Grants 359
The foundation awards grants to New Jersey nonprofit organizations in its areas of interest, including education and secondary education, natural resource conservation, and museums. Types of support include general operating support, building construction/renovation, land acquisition, scholarship

funds, and research grants. There are no application forms or deadlines. A letter should be submitted outlining purpose and amount of request.
Requirements: New Jersey nonprofit organization are eligible.
Geographic Focus: New Jersey
Amount: 1,000 - 329,268 USD
Samples: Edison Wetlands Assoc (Edison, NJ)—for the Raritan River project, $10,000.
Contact: Dorothy Frank, (609) 987-0300; (609) 452-1024
Sponsor: Cape Branch Foundation
P.O. Box 86
Oldwick, NJ 08858

Capezio/Ballet Makers Inc Grants and Awards 360

Grants are awarded to dance organizations to create a greater awareness and appreciation of dance as an art form and support efforts which preserve the legacy of the past, recognize the accomplishments of the present and encourage new or emerging talents, trends and practices. Types of support include awards, conferences and seminars, general operating grants, program grants, scholarships, and seed money grants. The Capezio Dance Award is also made by the trustees annually to an individual, company, or organization that brings respect, stature, and distinction to dance. Contact the program office for guidelines.
Requirements: Organizations must provide evidence of nonprofit status in their letters of application.
Restrictions: Awards are not made to individuals, companies, schools, or organizations for which dance is not a major priority.
Geographic Focus: All U.S. States
Date(s) Application is Due: Apr 1
Amount: 500 - 1,000 USD
Contact: Program Director; (973) 595-9000, ext. 203; (973) 595-0341
Internet: http://capeziodance.com/about/foundation/index.html
Sponsor: Capezio/Ballet Makers Dance
1 Campus Road
Totowa, NJ 07512

CarEth World Peace and Justice Grants 361

The foundation's mission is to promote peace with justice and encourage social, economic, and political equality. The foundation is currently interested in projects that involve youth. The main funding priorities are peace and justice worldwide and the promotion of democracy in the United States. Toward this end, grants are awarded for a wide range of proposals to U.S. democratic institutions working for peace and social justice. The foundation also supports proposals that address reversing the arms race and empowering people who have been excluded from full economic and political participation. Annual deadline dates may vary; contact the office for exact dates.
Restrictions: The foundation does not consider requests for conferences, fund-raising events, capital improvements, human rights organizations, relief aid, research, groups based outside the United States, schools, or film/video projects. Due to a high number of virus-infected proposals, the foundation is unable to accept any emailed proposals at this time. The foundation does not accept faxed proposals either, so please allow time for mailing your proposal to us so that we receive it by the deadline.
Geographic Focus: All U.S. States
Date(s) Application is Due: Jul 11
Samples: Grassroots Global Justice Jobs with Justice Education Fund (Washington, DC)—to support work related to the U.S. Social Forum, $10,000; Institute for Public Accuracy (San Francisco, CA)—to encourage press coverage of fairness and equity in the global economy and the need for for global governance, $7000; Institute for Southern Studies (Durham,NC)—to support the Sour Southern Studies for the Southern Peace Research and Education center, $12,000.
Contact: Amy Clough, Grants Manager; (413) 256-0349, ext. 12; (413) 256-3536; aclough@proteusfund.org
Internet: http://www.funder.org/grantmaking/careth
Sponsor: CarEth Foundation
264 N Pleasant Street, 2nd Floor
Amherst, MA 01002

Cargill Citizenship Fund-Corporate Giving Grants 362

Cargill's purpose is to be the global leader in nourishing people. Cargill measures their performance through engaged employees, satisfied customers, profitable growth and enriched communities. Corporate giving is one important way Cargill works to enrich the 1,000 communities where they conduct business. With 149,000 employees in 63 countries, Cargill people are working everyday to nourish the lives of those around us. The Cargill Citizenship Fund provides strategic grants to organizations serving communities where Cargill has a presence. The Fund provides direct grants for regional, national and global partnerships and provides matching grants for selected local projects supported by our businesses. Cargill seeks to build sustainable communities by focusing our human and financial resources in three areas: Nutrition and Health-support for programs and projects that address long-term solutions to hunger, increase access to health education and/or basic health care in developing and emerging countries, and improve youth nutrition and wellness; Education-support for innovative programs that improve academic achievement, develop logic and thinking skills, promote leadership development, and/or increase access to education for socio-economically disadvantaged children. Cargill also supports mutually beneficial partnerships with selected higher education institutions; Environment-support for projects that protect and improve accessibility to water resources; promote biodiversity conservation in agricultural areas; and educate children about conservation and/or proper sanitation. Application and additional guidelines are available at: http://www.cargill.com/wcm/groups/public/@ccom/documents/document/doc-giving-funding-app.pdf
Requirements: Applicants must have 501(c)3 status or the equivalent; and they must be located in communities where Cargill has a business presence. Only under special circumstances will Cargill consider general operating or capital support. Organizations requesting capital or operating support should contact the Cargill Citizenship Fund staff before applying.
Restrictions: Cargil will not fund: organizations without 501(c)3 status or the equivalent; organizations that do not serve communities where Cargill has a business presence; individuals or groups seeking support for research, planning, personal needs or travel; public service or political campaigns; lobbying, political or fraternal activities; benefit dinners or tickets to the same; fundraising campaigns, walk-a-thons, or promotions to eliminate or control; specific diseases; athletic scholarships; advertising or event sponsorships; religious groups for religious purposes; publications, audio-visual productions or special broadcasts; endowments; medical equipment.
Geographic Focus: All U.S. States
Amount: 500 - 100,000 USD
Contact: Stacey Smida, Grants Administrator; (952) 742-4311; stacey_smida@cargill.com
Internet: http://www.cargill.com/wcm/groups/public/@ccom/documents/document/doc-giving-funding-app.pdf
Sponsor: Cargill Corporation
P.O. Box 5650
Minneapolis, MN 55440-5650

Cargill Foundation Eliminating Barriers Grants 363

The Foundation seeks to fulfill its mission to prepare the next generation for success in school, work and life by investing in organizations and programs that demonstrate leadership and effectiveness in educating socio-economically disadvantaged children and eliminating barriers to their educational success. The Eliminating Barriers program specifically supports services that occur before or after the school day. Generally, paid program staff or volunteers provide these services.
Requirements: Only funds programs in Minneapolis and its northern and western suburbs.
Restrictions: The Foundation generally does not consider: programs outside the Minneapolis area; individuals; athletic scholarships; religious organizations for religious purposes; membership in civic organizations or trade associations; benefit fundraising events or tickets for the same; endowments or endowment campaigns; recognition or testimonial events; fundraising campaigns for specific diseases or medical research; public service or political campaigns or political lobbying activities; or participation in conferences or travel for groups or individuals.
Geographic Focus: Minnesota
Date(s) Application is Due: Apr 17
Contact: Stacey Smida, Grants Manager; (952) 742-4311; (952) 742-7224; stacey_smida@cargill.com
Internet: http://www.cargill.com/worldwide/usa/cargill-foundation/index.jsp
Sponsor: Cargill Foundation
P.O. Box 5650
Minneapolis, MN 55440-5650

Carl and Eloise Pohlad Family Foundation Grants 364

The mission of the foundation is to improve the lives of economically disadvantaged children and youth and participate in projects that positively impact the quality of life in the Minneapolis/St.Paul area. The foundation awards grants to Minnesota nonprofits in its areas of interest, including arts and culture, economic development, education, environment, health care, housing, and social services. Types of support include general operating support, continuing support, capital campaigns, building construction/ renovation, endowments, emergency funds, scholarship funds, and research.
Requirements: Minnesota nonprofits are eligible.
Restrictions: Individuals are not eligible. Capital request are considered only for physical plant improvements or significant technology investments. Capital requests for housing construction, endowment, program start-up or expansion or to establish operating reserves are not considered.
Geographic Focus: Minnesota
Amount: Up to 32,000,000 USD
Samples: Abbott Northwestern Hospital (Minneapolis, MN)—to construct a cardiology hospital, $3 million.
Contact: Josette Elstad, Grants Manager; (612) 661-3910; (612) 661-3715; info@pohladfamilygiving.org
Internet: http://www.pohladfamilyfoundation.org/pff/pff_default.aspx
Sponsor: Carl and Eloise Pohlad Family Foundation
60 South Sixth Street, Suite 3900
Minneapolis, MN 55402

Carl C. Icahn Foundation Grants 365

The foundation awards grants to New York and New Jersey nonprofits in the areas of education, arts and culture, health care, child welfare, and Jewish temples and organizations. Types of support include general operating support, annual campaigns, building construction/renovation, and matching funds. There are no application deadlines or forms.
Requirements: New York and New Jersey nonprofits are eligible to apply.
Restrictions: No grants are provided to individuals.
Geographic Focus: New Jersey, New York
Amount: 500 - 1,600,000 USD
Samples: Randall's Island Sports Foundation, New York, NY, $1,666,000—to support program/general purposes (2008); Wildlife Conservation Society, Pelham, NY, $10,000—to support program/general purposes (2008); The Ladies' Village Improvement Society, East Hampton, NY, $500—to support program/general purposes (2008).
Contact: Gail Golden-Icahn, Vice Presicent; (212) 702-4300; (212) 750-5815
Sponsor: Carl C. Icahn Foundation
767 5th Avenue, 47th Floor
New York, NY 10153-0023

Carl Gellert and Celia Berta Gellert Foundation Grants 366

The foundation funds religious, charitable, scientific, literary or educational purposes restricted in the nine counties of the greater San Francisco Bay Area (Alameda, Contra Costa, Marin, Napa, San Francisco, San Mateo, Santa Clara, Solano and Sonoma). No grants are made to individuals. Types of support include general operations, annual and capital campaigns, building construction/ renovation, equipment acquisition, debt reduction, program/ project development, medical research, publication, and scholarships.
Requirements: California 501(c)3 tax-exempt nonprofit organizations that are not private foundations are eligible.
Restrictions: Grants are not awarded to individuals.
Geographic Focus: California
Date(s) Application is Due: Aug 15
Amount: 1,000 - 10,000 USD
Samples: U of San Francisco, School of Business and Management (CA)—to renovate and add a new wing to the McLaren Center, home of the School of Business and Management, $500,000.
Contact: Jack Fitzpatrick, Executive Director; (415) 255-2829
Internet: http://home.earthlink.net/~cgcbg
Sponsor: Carl Gellert and Celia Berta Gellert Foundation
1169 Market Street, Suite 808
San Francisco, CA 94103

Carl J. Herzog Foundation Grants 367

The foundation awards grants, primarily in Connecticut, for research and general operating support in its areas of interest, including medical research, dermatology research, hospitals, and education. There are no application deadlines or forms.
Requirements: 501(c)3 tax-exempt organizations are eligible.
Geographic Focus: Connecticut
Amount: 1,000 - 200,000 USD
Samples: Meharry Medical College (Nashville, TN)—for scholarships for minority students, $250,000.
Contact: David Babson, (203) 629-2424
Sponsor: Carl J. Herzog Foundation
321 Railroad Avenue
Greenwich, CT 06836-0788

Carl M. Freeman Foundation FACES Grants 368

Founded in 2000 in Delaware, FACES stands for Freeman Assists Communities with Extra Support. The FACES program is designed to find and fund the smaller, overlooked projects in it's neighborhoods. The grants are limited to Montgomery County nonprofit organizations with operating budgets of $750,000 or less and Sussex County nonprofit organizations with operating budgets of $500,000 or less. Funding applications are available in five areas of interest: arts/culture; education/environment; health & human services; housing and; other-this may include anything you feel does not fit in the above categories, for example spaying cats/dogs.
Requirements: 501(c)3 tax-exempt organizations in Montgomery & Sussex County are eligible. Nonsectarian religious programs also are eligible.
Restrictions: Grants will not be distributed to: individuals; political associations or candidates; organizations that would disperse the funding to others; organizations that discriminate by race, creed, gender, sexual orientation, age, religion, disability or national origin.
Geographic Focus: Delaware, Maryland, West Virginia
Samples: Charles Town Health Right, Inc., Charles Town, WV—to help purchase needed medical and support supplies in order to meet daily medical needs (2008); Olney Community Band, Silver Spring, MD—to support the 2009 Concert Series and help present affordable concerts to diverse crowds (2008); Sussex Technical Adult Division, Georgetown, DE—to support the Even Start Family Literacy Program, which helps improve the literacy skills of low income and low literate families (2008).
Contact: Trish Schechtman, Relationship Manager; (302) 436-3555; trish@freemanfoundation.org
Internet: http://www.freemanfoundation.org/carl/CarlMFreemanFoundation/Grants/FACES/tabid/204/Default.aspx
Sponsor: Carl M. Freeman Foundation
36097 Sand Cove Road
Selbyville, DE 19975

Carl M. Freeman Foundation Grants 369

The Carl M. Freeman Foundation has historically emphasized it's support in the following communities: Montgomery County, Maryland; Sussex County, Delaware; and the Eastern Panhandle of West Virginia . Funding is available for a wide variety of community organizations, having supported everything from arts organizations and hunger centers to educational and health related organizations. To simplify the application process, funding applications are available in five areas of interest: arts/culture; education/ environment; health & human services; housing and; other-this may include anything you feel does not fit in the above categories, for example spaying cats/dogs. Additional guidelines and applications are available at: http://www.freemanfoundation.org/carl/CarlMFreemanFoundation/Grants/GrantGuidelines/ApplyForaGrant/tabid/185/Default.aspx
Requirements: 501(c)3 tax-exempt organizations in Maryland, Delaware and West Virginia are eligible. Nonsectarian religious programs also are eligible.
Restrictions: Grants will not be distributed to: individuals; political associations or candidates; organizations that would disperse the funding to others; organizations that discriminate by race, creed, gender, sexual orientation, age, religion, disability or national origin.
Geographic Focus: Delaware, Maryland, West Virginia
Amount: 5,000 - 30,000 USD
Contact: Trish Schechtman, Relationship Manager; (302) 436-3555; trish@freemanfoundation.org
Internet: http://www.freemanfoundation.org/carl/CarlMFreemanFoundation/Grants/GrantGuidelines/tabid/181/Default.aspx
Sponsor: Carl M. Freeman Foundation
36097 Sand Cove Road
Selbyville, DE 19975

Carl W. and Carrie Mae Joslyn Trust Grants 370

Grants support activities providing services to resident children, elderly, and the disabled in El Paso County, Colorado. Areas of interest include education, medical care, rehabilitation, children and youth services, and aging centers and services. Types of support include general operating support, annual campaigns, building construction and renovation, equipment acquisition, endowment funds, and program development. Application must be in writing and must specifically describe the use of the funds. Grants are not sustaining and new applications must be submitted semiannually for renewal.

Requirements: Nonprofit organizations located in, or serving the residents of, El Paso County, Colorado, are eligible.

Restrictions: Grants are not made to individuals or for research, scholarships, fellowships, loans, or matching gifts.

Geographic Focus: Colorado

Date(s) Application is Due: Apr 30; Oct 31

Amount: 500 - 15,000 USD

Samples: Pikes Peak Hospice, Colorado Springs, Colorado, $5,000 (2010); Silver Key Senior Services, Colorado Springs, Colorado, $5,000 (2010); Saint Marys High School, Colorado Springs, Colorado, $3,000 (2010).

Contact: Susan Bradt Laabs, Grants Administrator; (719) 227-6435 or (719) 227-6439; (719) 2276448

Sponsor: Carl W. and Carrie Mae Joslyn Charitable Trust
Trust Department, P.O. Box 1699
Colorado Springs, CO 80942

Carnahan-Jackson Foundation Grants 371

The foundation's areas of interest include higher and other education, libraries, hospitals, youth, the disabled, drug abuse programs, ecology, housing, community development, dance and other performing arts groups, and churches. Types of support include general operating support, continuing support, capital campaigns, building construction/renovation, equipment acquisition, programs/projects, seed grants, curriculum development, scholarship funds, and matching funds.

Requirements: IRS 501(c)3 organizations serving western New York, particularly Chautauqua County, are eligible.

Geographic Focus: New York

Amount: 2,500 - 125,000 USD

Contact: Stephen E. Sellstrom, (716) 483-1015

Sponsor: Carnahan-Jackson Foundation
13 East 4th Street, P.O. Box 3326
Jamestown, NY 14701-3326

Carnegie Corporation of New York Grants 372

The foundation provides research, study, and support for projects to improve government at all levels, to increase public understanding of social policy issues, to equalize opportunities for minorities and women, and to increase participation in political and civic life. Also supported are projects that promote electoral reform; education reform from early childhood through higher education; early childhood development; and urban school reform. The foundation will also fund research on the increasing availability and success of after-school and extended service programs for children and teenagers, particularly those in urban areas, that promote high academic achievement. Dissemination of best practices in teacher education will also be emphasized. There is no formal procedure for submitting a proposal. To apply under any of the corporation's grantmaking programs, applicants should submit a full proposal that describes the project's aims, duration, methods, amount of financial support required, and key personnel. The board meets four times a year, in October, February, April, and June.

Restrictions: Grants are not made for construction or maintenance of facilities or endowments. The Corporation does not generally make grants to individuals except through the Carnegie Scholars Program, that supports the work of select scholars and experts conducting research in the foundation's fields of interest.

Geographic Focus: All U.S. States

Amount: Up to 80,000,000 USD

Samples: American Academy of Arts and Sciences, Cambridge, Massachusetts, $500,000—toward an initiative on minimizing the risks of nuclear energy expansion (2009); George Washington University, Washington, DC, $349,900— toward research and writing on the effects of domestic foreign policy debates on U.S. global engagement (2009).

Contact: Sarina Cipriano, Grants Manager; (212) 371-3200; (212) 754-4073

Internet: http://www.carnegie.org/sub/program/grant.html

Sponsor: Carnegie Corporation of New York
437 Madison Avenue
New York, NY 10022

Carolyn Foundation Grants 373

Priorities for funding include community and environmental grantmaking. In the community focus area needs are addressed only in the communities of interest to the foundation: Minneapolis, Minnesota and, New Haven, Connecticut. There are two community focus areas for funding: economically disadvantaged children and youth; and community and cultural vitality. The foundation works to empower economically disadvantaged children and youth by supporting their families and others to inspire, nurture, educate and guide them to achieve long-term stability and well-being. In the environmental focus area, the Carolyn Foundation environmental committee is currently most interested in funding renewable energy programs. The Foundation will consider other environmental proposals if funds allow. All proposals submitted must: address root causes and create systemic and sustainable solutions and change; address global issues with local interventions that address local needs, as well as global needs; develop and implement solutions that can be replicated in other areas; collaborate effectively with others in the community: government, non-government, foundations and private parties. The Carolyn Foundation makes grants twice a year, in June and January. Applications must be submitted by January 15 for June grants, and July 15 for January grants. This is a postmark deadline. Grant applications will be reviewed by the Executive Director and a committee of foundation volunteers. Declinations will be sent at the time a decision is made to no longer consider a proposal, typically before the end of the review cycle. Successful applicants will be notified in June and January.

Requirements: IRS 501(c)3 nonprofit organizations in Minnesota and Connecticut may apply for the environmental grants. The Community grants program is limited to the cities of Minneapolis, Minnesota and New Haven, Connecticut. The foundation encourages use of Carolyn Foundation Application Form adapted from the Minnesota Common Grant Application Form. Applicants choosing not to use the common grant form must address the same information as required by the common grant. All proposals must use the Carolyn Foundation Cover Sheet, available at the Foundation's website. It is request that summary information and description of the project be no longer than six pages, printed on one side on 8 1/2 x 11-inch paper. Supporting documents, such as financial information, list of Officers, Directors, and Executive Staff, IRS determination letter may be in addition to the six pages. Do not send bound proposals, cassettes or VCR tapes.

Restrictions: Grants are not awarded to individuals, political organizations or candidates, veterans organizations, fraternal societies or orders, annual fund drives, umbrella organizations, or to deficits already incurred. The foundation does not generally make grants to religious organizations for religious purposes or to organizations in support of operations carried on in foreign countries.

Geographic Focus: Connecticut, Minnesota

Date(s) Application is Due: Jan 15; Jul 15

Amount: 5,000 - 50,000 USD

Samples: Clean Water Fund, Minneapolis, MN, $25,000—for development and use of safer alternatives for toxic substances (2009); Indian Child Welfare Law Center, Minneapolis, MN, $15,000—for Indian Children's Stability Program (2009); Hiawatha Leadership Academy, Minneapolis, MN, $20,000—for increasing salaries of the teaching staff (2009).

Contact: Becky Erdahl, Executive Director; (612) 596-3279 or (612) 596-3266; (612) 339-1951; berdahl@carolynfoundation.org

Internet: http://www.carolynfoundation.org/guidelines.html

Sponsor: Carolyn Foundation
706 2nd Avenue South, Suite 760
Minneapolis, MN 55402

Carpenter Foundation Grants 374

The foundation's primary areas of interest include the arts, education, public interest, and human services. The foundation is deeply concerned with the well-being of children and families and their relationship to their neighborhoods and communities. Also of concern is the health of the web of agencies and organizations which serve them. Grants are awarded for general operating support, program development, capital campaigns, equipment acquisition, scholarship funds, seed money, matching funds, and technical support. Deadlines are generally about six weeks before the quarterly board meetings, held in January, March, June, and September.

Requirements: Tax exempt agencies in the Jackson and Josephine Counties of Oregon may submit proposals.

Restrictions: Grants are not made to individuals. The foundation rarely makes grants for historical applications, hospital construction or equipment, group or individual trips, or activities for religious purposes.
Geographic Focus: Oregon
Amount: 250 - 25,000 USD
Samples: Community Health Center (Medford, OR)—fir a program to provide discounted medications to low-income/uninsured patients, $15,000; Science Works Hands-On Museum, (Ashland, OR)—in support of a life science hands-on exhibition for local schools and students, $6,000; Southern Oregon State College (Ashland, OR)—for faculty development opportunities which improve teaching, $25,000; Oregon Water Trust, (Portland, OR)—for a community outreach and education project to locally distribute the General Elections Voter's Guide, $12,000.
Contact: Polly Williams, Program Officer; (541) 772-5732; (541) 773-3970; carpfdn@internetcds.com
Internet: http://www.carpenter-foundation.org
Sponsor: Carpenter Foundation
711 E Main Street, Suite 10
Medford, OR 97504

Carrie E. and Lena V. Glenn Foundation Grants 375
Established in 1971, the Glenn Foundation provides annual grants in the following areas of interest: arts; children/youth, services; Christian agencies & churches; Elementary/secondary education; Environment; and Human services.
Requirements: Federally tax-exempt institutions and not-for-profit agencies that serve Gaston County, NC. agencies or out-of-county agencies whose projects have an impact on Gaston County citizens are eligible to apply.
Restrictions: Funding is not available for: planning grants; grants to individuals; scholarships; capital campaigns; umbrella campaigns; and multi-year grants.
Geographic Focus: North Carolina
Date(s) Application is Due: Mar 1
Amount: 3,000 - 25,000 USD
Samples: Community Foundation of Gaston County, Gastonia, NC., $25,000 - for purchase and installment of This Little Light of Mine, a painting by John Biggers, recreated as mosaic time mural; Gastonia Potters House, Lowell, NC., $10,000 - for operating expenses for residential drug rehabiliation program for women; Alliance for Children and Youth, Gastonia, NC., $8,885 - for Strengthening Families program for parents and their children
Contact: Barbara H. Voorhees, Executive Director; (704) 867-0296; (704) 867-4496; glennfnd@bellsouth.net
Sponsor: Carrie E. and Lena V. Glenn Foundation
1552 Union Road, Suite D
Gastonia, NC 28054

Carrie Estelle Doheny Foundation Grants 376
The foundation primarily funds local, not-for profit organizations endeavoring to advance education, medicine and religion, to improve the health and welfare of the sick, aged, incapacitated, and to aid the needy. Educational funding includes support of inner city Catholic schools, and scholarship funds for Catholic high schools and universities. Adult education programs and religious education are also supported. Medical funding is focused in two areas: research and care of the disadvantaged. Religious funding is directed to support the gospel values as expressed in the Roman Catholic faith. Health and welfare funding is directed to organizations who assist individuals to lead independent satisfying lives. Specific areas of interest include adoption and foster care service groups, programs for the disabled, health education programs, and senior programs. Aiding the needy funding includes inner city youth clubs, summer camps, and food banks. Applications are accepted anytime, an application form is required for submission and may be downloaded from the foundation web site. The board meets on the last Friday of each month, except for the month of September. Requests should be submitted approximately 6 weeks in advance to allow sufficient time for processing and for distribution to the Board members prior to the meeting. Allow 2 or 3 months for notification of the Board's decision. This is done in writing following the Board of Directors Meeting each month.
Requirements: The Foundation limits its grants to programs located within the fifty states and certified as 501(c)3 non-profit public charities by the Internal Revenue Service. The vast majority of funding is done in the Greater Los Angeles area.
Restrictions: Grant requests are not considered from individuals or from tax-supported entities. Areas also excluded from consideration include support for individuals, endowment funds, publishing books, television or radio programs, travel funds, advertisement, scholarships, or political purposes in any form.
Geographic Focus: All U.S. States
Amount: 5,000 - 150,000 USD
Samples: Boys & Girls Club of Venice, Venice, CA, $7,000—collaborative mentoring program support; YMCA of Greater Los Angeles, CA, $10,000—camperships for disadvantaged youth; South Central Lamp, Los Angeles, CA, general operating support.
Contact: Shirley Bernard, Senior Grants Administrator; (213) 488-1122; (213) 488-1544; doheny@dohenyfoundation.org
Internet: http://www.dohenyfoundation.org/grant/grant.htm
Sponsor: Carrie Estelle Doheny Foundation
707 Wilshire Boulevard, Suite 4960
Los Angeles, CA 90017

Carrier Corporation Contributions Grants 377
Carrier donates approximately $2 million around the world to registered nonprofit organizations. In the United States, Carrier funds only qualified 501(c)3 organizations that meet its eligibility criteria and operate in locations where the company has a significant employee base. Carrier believes in helping people in the communities where they live, work and do business. To better serve those communities and to better align its corporate contributions with mission and values, it focuses giving on the following these areas: environment and sustainability; civic & community; education; arts & culture; health & human services. All U.S. non-profits are required to complete an online grant application. Applications are accepted from March 1 through June 1 of each year, and are reviewed for funding to be paid the following year. Applicants will receive notification in the first quarter of the calendar year in which funding will occur.
Requirements: Carrier funds only qualified 501(c)3 organizations that meet eligibility criteria and operate in locations where it has a significant employee base.
Restrictions: Carrier will not fund: individuals; religious organizations; alumni groups, sororities or fraternities; booster clubs; political groups; any organization determined by Carrier to have a conflict of interest; any organization whose practices are inconsistent with the company's Code of Ethics
Geographic Focus: Alabama, Arizona, Connecticut, Georgia, Illinois, Indiana, Michigan, Nevada, New York, North Carolina, South Carolina, Tennessee, Texas
Date(s) Application is Due: Jun 1
Contact: Rajan Goel, Vice President; (860) 674-3420; (860) 622-0488
Internet: http://www.corp.carrier.com/vgn-ext-templating/v/index.jsp?vgnextoid=6afa80757d7e7010VgnVCM100000cb890b80RCRD
Sponsor: Carrier Corporation
One Carrier Place
Farmington, CT 06034-4015

Carylon Foundation Grants 378
The foundation awards general support grants to nonprofits of the Christian, interdenominational, Jewish, and Presbyterian faiths. Higher education institutions, health care organizations, international missions/ministries, medical centers, religious organizations, and temples receive support. Application may be made by submitting a brief letter describing the organization and program. There are no application deadlines.
Geographic Focus: All U.S. States
Amount: 50 - 50,000 USD
Samples: Rush-Presbyterian-Saint Lukes Medical Center (Chicago, IL)—for educational programs, $25,000; Holocaust Museum (Chicago, IL)—for operating support, $220,500; Weizmann Institute of Science (Palm Beach, FL)—for operating support, $10,000.
Contact: Marcie Mervis, Trustee; (312) 666-7700
Sponsor: Carylon Foundation
2500 W Arthington
Chicago, IL 60612-4108

Castle and Cooke California Corporate Giving Grants 379
Castle and Cooke Real Estate makes charitable contributions to nonprofit organizations on a case by case basis. Support is given primarily in Sierra Vista, Arizona, Bakersfield, California, and Keene's Pointe, Florida. The primary type of support is for general operating expenses. Application forms are required and are sent out annually in January. Initial approach is to contact

the headquarters directly to be added to application form mailing list. The deadline for applications is the end of March.
Requirements: 501(c)3 organizations serving the residents of Sierra Vista, Arizona, Bakersfield, California, and Keene's Pointe, Florida, are eligible to apply.
Geographic Focus: Arizona, California, Florida
Date(s) Application is Due: Mar 31
Contact: Renee Massey, Manager; (661) 664-6562; (661) 664-6500; rmassey@castlecooke.com
Sponsor: Castle and Cooke California
10000 Stockdale Highway, Suite 300, P.O. Box 11165
Bakersfield, CA 93389-1165

Castle Rock Foundation Grants 380
The foundation's grants are awarded to promote a better understanding of the free-enterprise system; preserve principles on which democracy was founded, ensure a limited role for government, and protect individual rights; encourage personal leadership; and uphold traditional American values. Types of support include general operating grants and special project grants.
Requirements: U.S. 501(c)3 organizations are eligible.
Restrictions: Grants requests from human service agencies, museums, organizations primarily supported by tax-derived funding, endowments, scientific or medical research, publications or media projects, churches, debt retirement, special events, or individuals will be denied.
Geographic Focus: All U.S. States
Date(s) Application is Due: Mar 15
Amount: 25,000 - 75,000 USD
Samples: College Fund/United Negro Fund, Fairfax, VA, $40,000 for scholarships; Congressional Medal of Honor Society, Mt. Pleasant, SC, $20,000 for general operating expense; Foundation for Research on economics and the Environment, $50,000 for general operating expense; Fund for American Studies, Washington, DC, $25,000 for general operating expense.
Contact: Sally W. Rippey, Executive Director; (303) 388-1683; (303) 388-1684; generalinfo@castlerockfdn.org
Internet: http://www.castlerockfoundation.org
Sponsor: Castle Rock Foundation
4100 E Mississippi Avenue, Suite 1850
Denver, CO 80246

Caterpillar Foundation Grants 381
The foundation awards grants internationally to nonprofits in company-operating locations in support of arts, community development, environment, higher education, and health and human services. Youth health is a priority of small grants given under the civic and community activities program. Types of support include general operating support, capital campaigns, program development, and employee matching gifts. There are no application deadlines or required forms.
Requirements: Go to the Caterpillar Foundation website (above) for details about what to include in a proposal.
Restrictions: Grants do not support fraternal organizations, religious organizations for religious purposes, political activities, individuals, United Way organizations, ticket purchase, or advertising for fund-raising benefits.
Geographic Focus: All U.S. States
Contact: Grants Administrator; (309) 675-4464
Internet: http://www.cat.com/cda/layout?m=39201&x=7
Sponsor: Caterpillar Foundation
100 NE Adams Street
Peoria, IL 61629-1480

Catherine Manley Gaylord Foundation Grants 382
The foundation awards grants to supplement the operating budgets of recognized public charities in the metropolitan Saint Louis, MO, area. Grants support general operations, materials and equipment, scholarships, symposiums and conferences, education and adult basic education, community development, and religious programs. Applications are accepted at any time.
Requirements: Saint Louis metropolitan area 501(c)3 nonprofit organizations may apply.
Geographic Focus: Missouri
Contact: Cindy Davis, Secretary; (314) 621-5757; (314) 621-5799
Sponsor: Catherine Manley Gaylord Foundation
1015 Locust Street, Suite 500
Saint Louis, MO 63101

Catholic Campaign for Human Development Economic Development Grants 383
The program focus of CCHD's Economic Development Program concentrates on Economic Development Institutions (EDIs). EDIs typically are community-based organizations and businesses. They create good jobs and just workplaces, and they develop assets for low-income people that are owned by families and communities. EDIs coincide with the CCHD mission by their commitment to the development of low income people. All EDIs have structures that promote low income leadership and ownership. CCHD funds may be used for general operating expenses, including staff salaries/training, procurement of technical assistance, board development costs and other overhead costs. For business development, CCHD funds may be used as part of a financing package for start-up or expansion, including start-up costs or working capital. For real estate development, CCHD funds may be used for pre-development or continuing operating expenses.
Requirements: In order to be considered for funding by CCHD, an applicant organization must demonstrate that it is committed to both goals. Priority will be given to eligible applicants that address one or more of the following four priorities: (1) To advance economic development models that enhance the scale of impact through replication or the transformation of an established model. (2) To encourage collaboration that generates cooperation and solidarity among diverse groups in the interest of a more integrated and mutually understanding society. (3) To link economic development with community organizing so that beneficiaries work together and with others on additional efforts to effect institutional change. (4) To facilitate the development of information systems in organizations that enhance planning, accountability and mutual learning by organizations and by CCHD. See the sponsor's website for specific criteria and guidelines. Eligibility Quizzes are accepted on a rolling basis between September 1st and November 1st. Organizations are strongly encouraged to submit their quiz prior to the November 1st deadline. This will allow your organization more time for completion of the online application.
Restrictions: Funds may not be used for capital expenditures (e.g. real estate, vehicles, equipment). Additionally, the following are also ineligible for funding: (a) Economic Development Institutions (EDIs) structured without opportunities for participatory control and ownership by low income people. (b) EDIs structured without opportunities to develop community-held assets (e.g. sole proprietorships, simple partnerships or fee-simple housing projects are not eligible). (c) EDIs owned or controlled by governmental agencies (federal, state or local), educational or ecclesiastical bodies. (d) EDIs the primary focus of which is direct service (e.g. job training, business consulting, financial literacy, savings programs, or homeownership education programs by themselves are not eligible). Such services may complement an eligible EDI, but they cannot be the EDI's primary focus. (e) Economic development programs that are not structured to stand on their own as sustainable institutions. (f) EDIs that intend to re-grant CCHD monies to other organizations.
Geographic Focus: All U.S. States
Date(s) Application is Due: Nov 1; Dec 1
Amount: Up to 50,000 USD
Samples: Inner City Revitalization Corporation - Alexandria, LA ($25,000); Deborah's Place - Chicago, IL ($50,000); Northern Communities Land Trust - Duluth, MN ($35,000); Northwest Missouri Enterprise Facilitation - Kansas City and Street Joseph, MO ($20,000); Green Worker Cooperatives - New York, NY ($35,000).
Contact: Ralph McCloud, Grants Administrator; (202) 541-3367 or (202) 541-3210; rmccloud@usccb.org
Internet: http://www.usccb.org/cchd/economicdevelopment.shtml
Sponsor: United States Conference of Catholic Bishops
3211 Fourth Street, NE
Washington, DC 20017-1194

CCA Assistance to Artist-Run Centres Grants 384
Canada Council for the Arts Assistance to Artist-Run Centres Grants provide funding to artist-run centres that provide visual artists and their audiences with an informed and professional forum for research, production, presentation, promotion and dissemination of new works in contemporary visual arts. The Grants also contribute to various services offered to visual artists, in addition to activities such as discussions, symposiums or publications on issues arising from visual arts practices. Awards begin at $20,000 with no upper limit.
Requirements: Applicants must: be incorporated, non-profit and Canadian; be directed by a board and the majority of the board members must be practicing visual artists; have a principle mandate to encourage research, production, presentation, promotion and dissemination of new works in contemporary visual arts; maintain a permanent, dedicated space that is accessible to the

public; have maintained an annual program of artistic activities, accessible to the public, for a minimum of three consecutive years; and pay professional artists' fees to artists participating in programming activities with fees which meet or exceed national standards. Visual arts include drawing, painting, sculpture, photography, printmaking, installation, performance art, architecture and craft.
Restrictions: Organizations including video, film, new media, audio and interdisciplinary works in its programming must apply to for the Council's Media Arts or Inter-Arts grants.
Geographic Focus: Canada
Date(s) Application is Due: Oct 15
Contact: Jim Logan, Program Officer; (800) 263-5588 or (613) 566-4414, ext. 5266; (613) 566-4332; jim.logan@canadacouncil.caFrancois Dion, Program Officer; (800) 263-5588 or (613) 566-4414, ext. 5268; (613) 566-4332; francios.dion@canadacouncil.ca
Internet: http://www.canadacouncil.ca/grants/visualarts/au127227986137031250.htm
Sponsor: Canada Council for the Arts
350 Albert Street, P.O. Box 1047
Ottawa, ON K1P 5V8 Canada

CCA Grants to Media Arts Organizations 385
The Canada Council for the Arts Grants to Media Arts offers funding to Canadian organizations that demonstrate a sustained commitment to research and development and the creation, presentation, dissemination, distribution or acquisition of independent Canadian media artworks. The purpose is to strengthen organizations throughout Canada to ensure the conditions necessary for the vitality and advancement of independent media arts in Canada. There are three Grant components: multi-year operating; initiatives; and emergency fund. The multi-year operating component is offered on a multi-year basis for three consecutive years to support organizations in carrying out their planned activities. It may include an amount for the acquisition of equipment. The initiatives component is for organizations receiving assistance from the multi-year operating component that wish to carry out a one-time initiative over a well-defined period that was not initially included in the three-year activity plan. The emergency fund component is intended solely for organizations that are already receiving assistance from the multi-year operating component. The award is to provide one-time non-recurring funding on an exceptional basis to organizations with an emergency. The maximum multi-year operating amount (including equipment) is $40,000 for the first year, $20,000 for the second year, and $20,000 for the third year. The maximum initiatives amount is $75,000. The maximum emergency amount is $5,000.
Requirements: All eligible organizations must: be incorporated as a non-profit organization or constituted as a non-profit cooperative under federal or provincial legislation for non-profit companies and have been active for at least two full years; have a board of directors, the majority of whose members are artists or professionals working in the field of Canadian independent media arts (or for festivals and cinematheques, an advisory committee made up of artists or professionals); support the practice of Canadian independent media arts; demonstrate a sustained commitment to research and development and the creation, presentation, dissemination, distribution or collection of Canadian independent media artworks; have an administrative structure and a management system suited to the nature of its activities; demonstrate sound financial management; pay artists' fees, distribution or dissemination rights to artists or pay fees to distributors for independent Canadian media artworks presented or acquired. Eligibility is contingent upon having received Council funding previously. See website for prior funding requirements. There are additional eligibility criteria for organizations relating to the activities performed which include: dissemination, distribution, production, national arts service, and cinematheque. See guidelines at website for requirements related to organizational activities. Aboriginal arts organizations and arts organizations of diverse cultural and regional communities of Canada are eligible.
Restrictions: Overdue final reports must be submitted and approved prior to applying. Organizations that have received a notice of exclusion from the Council are ineligible. Museums, public art galleries, libraries and educational institutions, crown corporations and municipal or governmental organizations are ineligible.
Geographic Focus: Canada
Date(s) Application is Due: Dec 1
Contact: Michele Stanley, Program Officer, Multi-Year and Emergency Fund Components; (800) 263-5588 or (613) 566-4414, ext. 5251; (613) 566-4409; michele.stanley@canadacouncil.caFelipe Diaz, Program Officer, Initiatives Component; (800) 263-5588 or (613) 566-4414, ext. 5252; felipe.diaz@canadacouncil.ca
Internet: http://www.canadacouncil.ca/mediaarts/
Sponsor: Canada Council for the Arts
350 Albert Street, P.O. Box 1047
Ottawa, ON K1P 5V8 Canada

CCA Opera/Music Theatre Annual Funding Grants 386
Canada Council for the Arts Opera/Music Theatre Annual Funding Grants contribute to the development and presentation of traditional and alternative repertoire (including Canadian repertoire), and to the creation, production and presentation of new, original Canadian opera and music theatre works. Funding is based on the program's assessment criteria and available funds.
Requirements: Eligible applicants must: be a professional, non-profit Canadian opera/music theatre company; have a board of directors; have completed at least three full years of professional activities; produce and stage at least two productions a year and give at least two performances of each production (small music theatre companies must produce and stage at least one major production a year along with relevant public activities such as workshops, public readings or training sessions for singers and/or performers in techniques appropriate to this repertoire); receive significant support from other levels of government, the public and the private sectors; and engage professional artistic and administrative personnel. First time applicants must: have received project grants in each of the last two competitions and meet the basic eligibility criteria. The peer assessment committee's decision to award an annual grant for the first time will be based on the organization's performance against the assessment criteria, the organization's ability to demonstrate that it fulfills a distinctive role within its community, and the availability of funds. Aboriginal arts organizations and arts organizations from diverse cultural and regional communities of Canada are eligible.
Restrictions: Opera/music theatre organizations cannot request operating support from more than one Council grant. Activities involving market-driven forms of music and/or music for which an established commercial support structure exists are not eligible.
Geographic Focus: Canada
Date(s) Application is Due: Dec 1
Contact: Daniel Swift, Program Officer; (800) 263-5588 or (613) 566-4414, ext. 5248; (613) 566-4409; daniel.swift@canadacouncil.ca
Internet: http://www.canadacouncil.ca/grants/music/lm127227298757031250.htm
Sponsor: Canada Council for the Arts
350 Albert Street, P.O. Box 1047
Ottawa, ON K1P 5V8 Canada

CCA Operating Grants to Professional Theater Organizations 387
Canada Council for the Arts Operating Grants to Professional Theatre Organizations provide multi-year and annual funding to non-profit, professional Canadian theatre organizations. Funding contributes to the general operating expenses. Funding is based on the assessment criteria and funds available.
Requirements: Eligible applicants must: be incorporated, non-profit Canadian theatre organizations; be directed by recognized theatre professionals; operate on a full-time basis and support ongoing activities; have received at least one Council production grant in the three preceding years or have produced five preceding seasons with an average of at least two productions per year; and if not previously funded by this Grant, have had at least one production from the last two years of sustained activity assessed by the Council. Aboriginal arts organizations and arts organizations of diverse cultural and regional communities of Canada are eligible.
Geographic Focus: Canada
Date(s) Application is Due: Mar 1
Contact: Robert Allen, Program Officer; (800) 263-5588 or (613) 566-4414, ext. 4485; (613) 566-4410; Nancy Guertin, Program Officer; (800) 263-5588 or (613) 566-4414, ext. 4485; (613) 566-4410; Kim Selody, Program Officer; (800) 263-5588 or (613) 566-4414, ext. 4485; (613) 566-4410; Bruce Sinclair, Program Officer; (800) 263-5588 or (613) 566-4414, ext. 4485; (613) 566-4410; Linda Nicholson, Assistant; (800) 263-5588 or (613) 566-4414, ext. 4485; (613) 566-4410; linda.nicholson@candacouncil.ca
Internet: http://www.canadacouncil.ca/grants/theatre/ho127227295916250000.htm
Sponsor: Canada Council for the Arts
350 Albert Street, P.O. Box 1047
Ottawa, ON K1P 5V8 Canada

CCA Professional Choir Program Annual Funding Grants 388

Canada Council for the Arts Professional Choir Program Annual Funding Grants assist professional Canadian choirs to develop and present choral repertoire. The program's particular emphasis is excellence in the presentation of Canadian music and encouragement to showcase Canadian artists. The goals of the Grants are: to contribute to the activities of professional Canadian choirs, from any cultural background, devoted to the development and presentation of choral music; to encourage innovative education and outreach programs that attract and serve new audiences for choral music, including young audiences; to stimulate the appreciation and enjoyment of choral music in Canada; and to encourage exemplary management and governance practices within the choral field. Funding is based on the assessment criteria and available funds.

Requirements: Eligible applicants must: be an incorporated, non-profit Canadian professional choir; have completed at least three seasons of professional activities; have a consistent core or membership of singers; have a season of activities (concerts) planned that includes a variety of self-produced programs showcasing Canadian choral music works; have a paid, professional Choral Conductor/Artistic Director; have a paid, professional administrative staff to support their artistic activities; have a board of directors; have experienced financial stability for at least the past two years and receive significant support from other levels of government, the public or the private sector; be adult choirs that have received project grants in each of the last two competitions and meet the basic eligibility criteria in order to apply for annual funding. Eligible choirs that received at least $20,000 at the last competition may be eligible for multi-year funding. All other choirs must apply for annual funding. Aboriginal arts organizations and arts organizations from diverse cultural and regional communities of Canada are eligible.

Restrictions: Choirs cannot request operating support from more than one Council grant.

Geographic Focus: Canada

Date(s) Application is Due: Jan 15

Contact: Andre Jutras, Program Officer; (800) 263-5588 or (613) 566-4414, ext. 5071; (613) 566-4409; andre.jutras@canadacouncil.ca

Internet: http://www.canadacouncil.ca/grants/music/dk127245411285312500.htm

Sponsor: Canada Council for the Arts
350 Albert Street, P.O. Box 1047
Ottawa, ON K1P 5V8 Canada

CCA Professional Orchestra Program Annual and Multi-Year Grants 389

Canada Council for the Arts Professional Orchestra Program Annual and Multi-Year Grants provide funding to professional Canadian orchestras for their activities. Grants contribute to the development and presentation of orchestra repertoire, with particular concern for excellence in the presentation of Canadian composition and of Canadian artists. Funding is awarded using a competitive process with award amounts based on the assessment criteria and available funds.

Requirements: Eligible organizations must: be a Canadian professional, non-profit orchestra; have a board of directors; have completed at least three year of professional activities; receive significant support from other levels of government, the public or the private sector; engage professional artistic and administrative personnel; and demonstrate a strong commitment to Canadian creation/repertoire as part of their ongoing annual programming. Applicant organizations eligible for first time annual funding must have received project grants in each of the last two competitions. If applicant organizations have received multi-year funding in the past or have received annual funding from each of the last two years, they must apply for multi-year funding, unless stipulated otherwise by the Music Section. Aboriginal arts organizations and arts organizations from diverse cultural and regional communities of Canada are eligible.

Restrictions: Applicants cannot request operating support from more than one Council grant.

Geographic Focus: Canada

Date(s) Application is Due: Feb 1

Contact: Daniel Swift, Program Officer; (800) 263-5588 or (613) 566-4414, ext. 5248; (613) 566-4409; daniel.swift@canadacouncil.ca

Internet: http://www.canadacouncil.ca/grants/music/be129038237771080058.htm

Sponsor: Canada Council for the Arts
350 Albert Street, P.O. Box 1047
Ottawa, ON K1P 5V8 Canada

CCFF Clinical Fellowships 390

Canadian Cystic Fibrosis Foundation (CCFF) Clinical Fellowships are intended for those physicians who have already obtained their residency training and who wish to pursue additional clinical training in Cystic Fibrosis (CF) care. The purpose is to train physicians to become CF specialists, so that they can provide ongoing clinical care to individuals with CF in Canada. This training would include developing competence to allow them to participate in clinical trials. This fellowship is not intended to train individuals from other countries who will not stay in Canada. Up to two highly-ranked competitive Clinical Fellowships will be offered by the Foundation each year. The value of a CCFF Clinical Fellowship is dependent upon academic qualifications, and/or research experience. Award levels are reviewed on an annual basis, and will correspond with prevailing Canadian rates. Additional guidelines are available at: http://www.cysticfibrosis.ca/en/treatment/TrainingAwards_ClinicalFellowships.php.

Requirements: Canadian citizens or permanent residents who have an M.D. degree, have recently completed their clinical training, are exam eligible, and have obtained medical licensure in Canada, are eligible to apply. Clinical Fellowships are tenable in Canada or abroad and it is intended that this experience will directly benefit the Canadian CF community.

Restrictions: Clinical Fellowships will not be awarded to individuals who have not completed residency training.

Geographic Focus: Canada

Date(s) Application is Due: Oct 1

Contact: Grants Administrator; (416) 485-9149; (416) 485-0960; info@cysticfibrosis.ca

Internet: http://www.cysticfibrosis.ca/en/treatment/TrainingAwards_ClinicalFellowships.php

Sponsor: Canadian Cystic Fibrosis Foundation
2221 Yonge Street, Suite 601
Toronto, ON M4S 2B4 Canada

CCFf Special Travel Grants For Fellows & Students 391

The Foundation encourages Canadian Cystic Fibrosis Foundation (CCFF) supported Fellows and Students to attend and participate in scientific meetings related to cystic fibrosis. In addition, allowances may be utilized to acquire new knowledge (i.e. visit another lab). Special Travel allowances may be awarded to CCFF-supported Fellows and Students, for each year of their award, upon written application and pending the availability of funds. No CCFF-supported Fellow or Student may receive more than one grant per year. Subject to the availability of funds and under certain circumstances, CCFF-supported Scholars, physicians who are not CF clinic directors but who specialize in the clinical care of adults with cystic fibrosis at Canadian CF clinics, and recipients of the Skelly and Lackey Summer Studentship awards, may also be eligible. Special Travel allowances are intended to cover travel costs not to exceed the lowest applicable advance booking airfare, and reasonable accommodation and meals, up to a $1,800. Additional guidelines are available at: http://www.cysticfibrosis.ca/en/research/TravelAllowancesStudents.php.

Requirements: Applications should be made in the form of a letter, and must be submitted prior to the proposed travel. The letter should indicate the conference or meeting for which the allowance is requested and must include a proposed travel and accommodation budget, along with the supervisor's signed endorsement. Proof of active participation (i.e. abstract acceptance, etc.) is also required.

Restrictions: An itemized breakdown of expenses incurred and the original receipts must be submitted to the Foundation upon return from the conference or meeting, and any unexpended funds returned to the Foundation.

Geographic Focus: Canada

Amount: Up to 1,800 USD

Contact: Grants Administrator; (416) 485-9149; (416) 485-0960; ResearchPrograms@cysticfibrosis.ca or info@cysticfibrosis.ca

Internet: http://www.cysticfibrosis.ca/en/research/TravelAllowancesStudents.php

Sponsor: Canadian Cystic Fibrosis Foundation
2221 Yonge Street, Suite 601
Toronto, ON M4S 2B4 Canada

CCFF Transplant Center Incentive Grants 392

The grants are intended to enhance the quality of care available to cystic fibrosis transplant candidates by providing eligible centers with supplementary funding for support of personnel directly involved in the provision of patient services; travel to the annual North American Cystic Fibrosis conference; and

administrative costs associated with providing data to the Canadian Cystic Fibrosis Lung Transplant Registry. Grants are renewable on an annual basis.
Requirements: Any Canadian lung transplant center which currently has one or more individuals with cystic fibrosis listed for transplant may apply for a Transplant Center Incentive grant. (
Restrictions: Under no circumstances will funding be provided to more than one transplant centers in the same city.
Geographic Focus: Canada
Date(s) Application is Due: Oct 1
Contact: Grants Administrator; (416) 485-9149; (416) 485-0960; info@cysticfibrosis.ca
Internet: http://www.cysticfibrosis.ca/en/treatment/TransplantCentreIncentiveGrants.php
Sponsor: Canadian Cystic Fibrosis Foundation
2221 Yonge Street, Suite 601
Toronto, ON M4S 2B4 Canada

CE and S Foundation Grants 393
The foundation is interested in supporting projects that improve people's lives. Focus areas for grant making include higher education; international cooperation; urban environmental improvement, and emergency disaster relief. Preference is given to those programs that have developed methods for measuring success. Before a grant proposal is submitted, the foundation requests that organizations first call the executive director to discuss the particulars of the project and the ways in which it fits the foundation guidelines.
Requirements: Nonprofit organizations are eligible to apply.
Restrictions: The foundation does not support individuals or for medical research.
Geographic Focus: All U.S. States
Amount: 500 - 100,000 USD
Samples: Bellarmine University, Louisville, a 6-year grant to fund a principled and innovative enhancement of teaching and learning, to benefit both students and faculty; Greater Louisville Project, supporting the largest city-county government consolidation in 40 years anticipating transitional needs of the new Metro government and its stewardship of the now 16th largest city in the nation; Metro Parks and Louisville Olmsted Parks Conservancy.
Contact: Bruce Maza, Executive Director; (502) 583-0546; (502) 583-7648; bruce@cesfoundation.com
Internet: http://www.cesfoundation.com/grantmaking.html
Sponsor: CE and S Foundation
1650 National City Tower
Louisville, KY 40202

Cemala Foundation Grants 394
The Cemala Foundation is a private family foundation established in 1986 by Martha A. and Ceasar Cone II to continue the family tradition of commitment to enhancing the quality of life of the community through grants to qualified charitable organizations. Areas of interest are: arts/culture; education; health; homelessness; human services; the state of North Carolina and; public interest. Application and additional guidelines are available at the Foundation's website.
Requirements: Grants are made only to non-profit charitable organizations which are tax exempt under Section 501(c)3 of the Internal Revenue Code or to public governmental units. Generally, grants are limited to projects which benefit the citizens of Guilford County, North Carolina. Occasionally, projects which benefit the state of North Carolina as a whole are considered.
Restrictions: The Foundation does not consider support for annual campaigns, endowments, sectarian religious activities, or requests under $1,000. Grants are not made to individuals. Grants from the Cemala Foundation are usually awarded for one year only. Only one grant application may be submitted in any twelve-month period. Organizations receiving grants are required to complete an evaluation report within twelve months after receipt of the funds.
Geographic Focus: North Carolina
Date(s) Application is Due: Mar 1; Sep 1
Amount: 3,000 - 200,000 USD
Samples: Eastern Music Festival for the MYEMF, $25,000—Community Outreach Project (2009); Bennett College, $25,000—for general operating support (2009); Women's Resource Center of Greensboro, $15,000—for the New Choices Program to provide pre-employment training and placement case management support to assist displaced homemakers (2009); Salvation Army in Greensboro, $75,000—for emergency financial assistance program (2009).
Contact: Susan S. Schwartz, Executive Director; (336) 274-3541; (336) 272-8153; cemala@cemala.org
Internet: http://www.cemala.org/grant/guidelines.php
Sponsor: Cemala Foundation
330 South Greene Street, Suite 101
Greensboro, NC 27401

Central Minnesota Community Foundation Grants 395
The community foundation administers charitable funds in the form of grants to nonprofit organizations for the benefit of residents of central Minnesota. The goal of the foundation is to identify and address social and cultural needs and to foster a sense of human interdependence dedicated to building self-capacity and fullness of life for all. The board of directors gives preference to applications that address themselves to developing capacity and self-help by attempting to address the causes of problems rather than dealing only with the symptoms; enhancing human dignity by providing support for those who participate actively in determining the course of their own lives; responding to new, innovative programs of organizations by addressing opportunities and dilemmas of emerging and changing needs; preserving the historic sense of voluntarism; fostering equal opportunity and enhancement of cultural heritage and diversity; supporting programs and projects that will enable charitable agencies to reduce costs and increase efficiency; and supporting community studies, programmatic research, or other types of projects intended to help citizens understand their problems and options, foster the refinement of public policy, and encourage coordination and cooperation. Applications are accepted four times each year; contact program staff for dates. Only one grant application per year will be considered from eligible applicants.
Requirements: The primary geographic focus of the foundation includes Benton, Sherburne, and Stearns Counties, but grants also are made to organizations located in rural central Minnesota counties. IRS 501(c)3 organizations are eligible, but applicants not meeting this requirement may apply through a fiscal agent.
Restrictions: The foundation will not fund individuals, endowments, medical research, capital campaigns to which the foundation can contribute no more than a tiny fraction of the total need, debt retirement or deficit financing, dollar-for-dollar replacement of government funding that has been reduced or eliminated, religious organizations for direct religious activities, political organizations or political campaigns, fraternal organizations, societies or orders, telephone solicitations, national fundraising efforts, or grants for travel.
Geographic Focus: Minnesota
Amount: Up to 31,000,000 USD
Contact: Susan Lorenz, Program Officer; (877) 253-4380 or (320) 253-4380; (320) 240-9215; slorenz@communitygiving.org
Internet: http://www.communitygiving.org/about_us_cm_6.php4
Sponsor: Central Minnesota Community Foundation
101 S 7th Avenue, Suite 100
Saint Cloud, MN 56301

Central New York Community Foundation Grants 396
The foundation is looking for innovative programs that address problems to be solved or opportunities to be seized in the Central New York area, specifically Onondaga and Madison Counties. Proposals are invited that suggest practical approaches to community problems; promote cooperation among agencies without duplicating services; generate community support, both professional and volunteer; demonstrate the organization's ability to secure realistic funding; strengthen an agency's effectiveness or stability; and address prevention as well as remediation. Types of support include capital grants, program development, seed money grants, and training grants. Prospective applicants are strongly encouraged to discuss the appropriateness of their grant request with staff before beginning the application process. Applications will not be accepted by fax.
Requirements: New York 501(c)3 tax-exempt organizations in Onondaga and Madison Counties are eligible.
Restrictions: The foundation generally does not make grants for annual operating budgets, except when it is seed or bridge money; endowments; sectarian purposes; loans or assistance to individuals; or medical research.
Geographic Focus: New York
Amount: 500 - 50,000 USD
Samples: Urban League of Onondaga County (Syracuse, NY)—for salary support of technicians at its computer centers in inner-city Syracuse, $15,000; Earlville Opera House (Carlville, NY)—to renovate a workshop and studio space for year-round use, $20,000; Syracuse Community Health Ctr (Syracuse, NY)—to construct an education and resource center for patients, $39,500; Interreligious Council of Central New York (Syracuse, NY)—for its Communitywide Dialog on Racism, Race Relations, and Racial Healing program, $20,000.

Contact: Kim Scott, Program Contact; (315) 422-9538; (315) 471-6031; kim@cnycf.org
Internet: http://www.cnycf.org/seekers/grants.cfm
Sponsor: Central New York Community Foundation
500 S Salina Street, Suite 428
Syracuse, NY 13202-3302

Chahara Foundation Grants 397

The foundation awards general operating grants to Boston-area nonprofit organizations run by and for lower-income women. Grants are focused on community-based and community-driven nonprofits that serve those with the least access to funding, particularly women of color, older women, girls, lesbians, bisexual and transgendered women, and women with disabilities.
Requirements: Nonprofit organizations run by and for lower-income women in the greater Boston, MA, area are eligible.
Geographic Focus: Massachusetts
Amount: Up to 20,000 USD
Samples: Association of Haitian Women in Boston (Boston, MA)— to human rights to have representation, to have health, education, and decent housing, $20,000; Homes for Families (Boston, MA)—to educate, organize and advocate for improved public policies to address the root causes of family homelessness with holistic and community-based solutions, $20,000.
Contact: Program Contact; (617) 247-1580; (617) 247-7177; carol@chahara.org
Internet: http://www.chahara.org
Sponsor: Chahara Foundation
4 Copley Place
Boston, MA 02116-6504

Chamberlain Foundation Grants 398

The foundation awards grants to Pueblo, CO, nonprofit organizations in its areas of interest, including arts and culture, education, religion, and science. Types of support include general operating support, equipment acquisition, and program development. Submit a brief proposal that includes the purpose of the request and its relevance to the foundation; amount requested; brief history of the organization and its achievements; names, titles, and qualifications of key personnel; name of agency that conducted the last annual audit; copy of the IRS tax-exemption letter; list of other sources of financial support during the past 12 months; and names and affiliations of board members, trustees, and officers of the organization by either of the two deadlines.
Requirements: 501(c)(30 Pueblo, CO, nonprofit organizations are eligible.
Restrictions: Grants do not support individuals; conferences; political activities; religious organizations whose services are limited to members; veteran, labor, fraternal, athletic, or social clubs; national health agencies concerned with specific diseases or health issues; operating expenses for United Way-supported organizations; publications, advertising campaigns, or travel expenses.
Geographic Focus: Colorado
Amount: 1,000 - 20,000 USD
Samples: YMCA of Pueblo, Pueblo, CO, $20,000 (2008); Bessemer Historical Society, Pueblo, CO, $8,000 (2008); Animal Welfare and Protection Society, Pueblo, CO, $20,000 (2008).
Contact: David Shaw, Foundation Chair; (719) 543-8596; (719) 543-8599
Sponsor: Chamberlain Foundation
501 North Main Street, Suite 222
Pueblo, CO 81003

Champ-A Champion Fur Kids Grants 399

Grants for children's health and wellness are awarded twice each year. The program provides direct support for children in the areas of health and wellness such as childhood disease research foundations, child safety organizations and organizations that serve children with special needs. The goal is to provide grants to help many programs that are working hard to make the world a healthier and happier place for kids. Programs funded include: (a) Individual Project grants (generally for one-time purchases or to fulfill a short-term need, such as the purchase of materials or equipment); or, (b) Organization Program grants (start-up or operational costs for ongoing programs. Examples include funds for research, health and wellness educational programs, or financial assistance for children and families in-need.)
Requirements: United States applicants must be a tax-exempt organization under Section 501(c)3 of the IRS Code, and 'not a private foundation,' within the meaning of Code Sections 509(a)(1) or 509(a)(2), or a state college or university within the meaning of Code Section 511(a)(2)(B) (a 'Public Charity'). In addition, grant recipients must certify that they are not a supporting organization within the meaning of Code Section 509(a)(3). Canadian applicants must be a registered Canadian charity.
Restrictions: Programs that will not be funded include: (1) Annual Appeals or Capital Campaigns; (2) Construction or New Facility expenses; (3) Fundraising or Event Sponsorships; (4) Political Activities; (5) Religious organizations for religious purposes.
Geographic Focus: All U.S. States, Canada
Date(s) Application is Due: Feb 28; Aug 30; Nov 30
Amount: 1,000 - 10,000 USD
Samples: Angels with Special Needs (Columbia, SC); Building A Generation (Redlands, CA); Hearts and Noses Hospital Clown Troupe (Needham, MA); Catholic Charities of the Diocese of Santa Rosa (Santa Rosa, CA); Hole in the Wall Gang Fund (New Haven, CT); Street Patrick Center (Street Louis, MO); The Children's Hospital Foundation (Omaha, NE); Youth in Need (Street Charles, MO)
Contact: Maxine Clark, President; (314) 423-8000, ext. 5366; giving@buildabear.com
Internet: http://www.buildabear.com/aboutus/community/bearhugs.aspx
Sponsor: Build-A-Bear Workshop Bear Hugs Foundation
1954 Innerbelt Business Center Drive
Saint Louis, MO 63114

Changemakers Grants 400

Changemakers makes grants to the following types of community-based philanthropic organizations: local, regional, national, and international public foundations; alternative community foundations; affinity groups/networking organizations; groups that administer donor-advised funds; donor organizing/service providers; federations/alternative workplace giving programs; groups that recruit and train grassroots development staff; groups that provide research, media, education, or advocacy on philanthropy; and fundraising and grantmaking collaboratives. Types of support include capacity building grants, collaborative initiatives, general support grants, and technical assistance.
Requirements: Community-based philanthropic organizations that are committed to the principles of community-based philanthropy, have a record of success or a potential for increased success, and demonstrate that they have a vision for the future are eligible.
Restrictions: Grants do not support service providers.
Geographic Focus: All U.S. States
Samples: Ctr for Third World Organizing (Oakland, CA)—to expand and update its fundraising and communications training program, $25,000; eGrants.org (San Francisco, CA)—for general support, $15,000; Pride Foundation (Seattle, WA)—to strengthen and link lesbian, gay, bisexual, and transgendered individuals and groups throughout Washington State, $20,000; Boston Women's Fund (Boston, MA)—to provide technical assistance programs to women and girls in the Boston area, $20,000.
Contact: Grants Administrator; (415) 561-2363; (415) 561-2366; grants@changemakers.org
Internet: http://www.changemakersfund.org/grantsprograms.htm
Sponsor: Changemakers
1550 Bryant Street, Suite 850
San Francisco, CA 94103

Charitable Leadership Foundation Housing Grants 401

CLF's housing efforts are focused on community-based solutions to the four specific problem areas outlined below: moderate- and middle-income homeownership support; innovative low-income rental models; sustaining volunteer-based homeownership programs, and; long term supported housing. Types of support include grants, loans, and technical assistance for projects, programs, and capacity building. Letters of inquiry and formal proposals are reviewed on an on-going basis. Applicants are required to discuss formal proposals with the staff prior to submission. Preference will be given to projects in upstate New York; however, projects will be considered in any geographic area of the United States.
Requirements: 501(c)3 charitable organizations are eligible.
Restrictions: The foundation does not normally fund organizations with substantial amounts of other resources, or arts or cultural organizations, unless the proposed project presents a compelling need or opportunity and substantially matches the funding criteria described above. Any grants to religious organizations will be restricted to nonsectarian purposes. Grants are not awarded to individuals.
Geographic Focus: All U.S. States
Amount: 20,000 USD

Contact: William Dessingue, Jr., Senior Program Officer; (518) 877-6701, ext. 305; (518) 877-6260; wdessingue@charitableleadership.org
Internet: http://www.charitableleadership.org/housing/housing.html
Sponsor: Charitable Leadership Foundation
747 Pierce Road
Clifton Park, NY 12065

Charity Incorporated Grants **402**
Grants are awarded to eligible Minnesota nonprofit organizations in support of Christian churches and organizations; elementary, secondary, and higher education; and social services for children/youth and families. Types of support include general operating grants, matching gifts, program development, and seed money grants. Submit a letter of proposal describing the organization and request, and include a copy of the IRS tax-exemption letter.
Requirements: Minnesota 501(c)3 tax-exempt organizations are eligible.
Restrictions: The foundation does not provide grants to individuals.
Geographic Focus: Minnesota
Amount: Up to 344,529 USD
Contact: Deanna Hulme, Grants Administrator; (320) 743-5466
Sponsor: Charity Incorporated
5786 118th Avenue
Clear Lake, MN 55319

Charles A. Frueauff Foundation Grants **403**
The foundation considers proposals 501(c)3 organizations that support private four-year colleges and universities, social service agencies, and health-related agencies and institutions. Types of support include building construction/renovation, capital campaigns, equipment acquisition, general operating support, matching/challenge grants, annual campaigns, and emergency funds. Consideration will be given to programs that support persons leaving welfare, preparing students for employment in non-profit agencies, tutoring at-risk youth, and revitalizing neighborhoods. Applicants are requested to send via postal service a one-page letter of inquiry and include the following information: very brief agency mission and purpose; agency location; brief purpose of request and amount requested; and email address if you wish to receive notification via email.
Requirements: Applicants must be private nonprofit corporations with 501(c)3 status.
Restrictions: The foundation funds nationwide except: Arizona, Alaska, California, Hawaii, Idaho, Iowa, Michigan, Minnesota, Montana, Nevada, New Mexico, North Dakota, Ohio, Oregon, Utah, Washington, Wisconsin, and Wyoming. K-12 schools are ineligible. Grants are not awarded to individuals, provide emergency funds, fund research, or for loans. Multi-year grants, international projects, state supported colleges or universities, primary and secondary schools, churches, or fund raising drives and special events are not supported.
Geographic Focus: Alabama, Arkansas, Colorado, Connecticut, Delaware, District of Columbia, Florida, Georgia, Illinois, Indiana, Kansas, Kentucky, Louisiana, Maine, Maryland, Massachusetts, Mississippi, Missouri, Nebraska, New Hampshire, New Jersey, New Mexico, New York, North Carolina, Oklahoma, Pennsylvania, Rhode Island, South Carolina, South Dakota, Tennessee, Texas, Vermont, Virginia, West Virginia
Date(s) Application is Due: Mar 15; Sep 15
Samples: Melmark Home (Berwyn, PA)—for classroom and office renovation, $50,000; Stetson U (Deland, FL)—to provide scholarships to students majoring in the natural sciences, $100,000.
Contact: Sue Frueauff, (501) 324-2233; (501) 324-2236
Internet: http://www.frueaufffoundation.com/application/default.asp
Sponsor: Charles A. Frueauff Foundation
200 South Commerce, Suite 100
Little Rock, AR 72201

Charles Delmar Foundation Grants **404**
Established in 1957, the Foundation supports organizations involved with inter-American studies, higher, secondary, elementary, and other education, underprivileged youth, the disadvantaged, the aged, the homeless and housing issues, general welfare organizations, and fine and performing arts. Giving primarily in the Washington, DC area in the U.S., and in Europe and South America. There are no specific deadlines with which to adhere. Contact the Foundation for further application information and guidelines.
Restrictions: No grants to individuals, or for building or endowment funds, or matching gifts; no loans.
Geographic Focus: District of Columbia, Maryland, Virginia, West Virginia, Albania, Andorra, Argentina, Armenia, Austria, Azerbaijan, Belarus, Belgium, Bolivia, Bosnia & Herzegovina, Brazil, Bulgaria, Chile, Colombia, Croatia, Cyprus, Czech Republic, Denmark, Ecuador, Estonia, Finland, France, Georgia, Germany, Greece, Guyana, Hungary, Iceland, Ireland, Italy, Kosovo, Latvia, Liechtenstein, Lithuania, Luxembourg, Macedonia, Malta, Moldova, Monaco, Montenegro, Norway, Paraguay, Peru, Poland, Portugal, Romania, Russia, San Marino, Serbia, Slovakia, Slovenia, Spain, Sweden, Switzerland, The Netherlands, Turkey, Ukraine, United Kingdom, Vatican City
Amount: 500 - 10,000 USD
Samples: James River Association, Mechanicsville, VA, $4,000 - for general support; Pan American Development Foundation, Washington, DC, $5,000 - for environmental operations; College of Wooster, Wooster, OH, $9,000 - for general support
Contact: Mareen D. Hughes, President; (703) 534-9109
Sponsor: Charles Delmar Foundation
5205 Leesburg Pike, Suite 209
Falls Church, VA 22041-3858

Charles G. Koch Charitable Foundation Grants **405**
The foundation provides funding for academic and public policy research directed at solving social problems through voluntary action and free enterprise. In the area of research, the foundation primarily funds organizations working with doctorate-level investigators in disciplines such as economics, history, philosophy, political science, and organizational behavior. Types of support include general operating, scholarship funds, conferences and seminars, research, special projects, and seed money. There are no application deadlines. Submit preproposal letters (three-page limit).
Geographic Focus: All U.S. States
Amount: 25,000 - 300,000 USD
Samples: George Mason U (Fairfax, VA)—to recruit faculty members, and for programs in experimental economics, $3 million.
Contact: Kelly Young, Vice President; (202) 393-2354; (202) 393-2355; email@cgkfoundation.org
Internet: http://www.cgkfoundation.org
Sponsor: Charles G. Koch Charitable Foundation
655 15th Street NW, Suite 445
Washington, DC 20005-2001

Charles H. Price II Family Foundation Grants **406**
The Charles H. Price II Family Foundation, established in Kansas City, Missouri, by a prominent American businessman and former Ambassador of the United States, offers support to educational programs and research primarily in Missouri and California (though funding is also occasionally provided outside of these two states). Grants are given for general operating support and scholarships. There are no specific applications or deadlines with which to adhere, and applicants should approach the Foundation in writing via a letter of application.
Geographic Focus: California, Missouri
Amount: 500 - 5,000 USD
Samples: Baker University, Baldwin, Kansas, $1,000 - scholarship fund (2009); Eisenhower Medical Center, Rancho Mirage, California, $5,000 - general operating support (2009); Nelson-Atkins Museum of Art, Kansas City, Missouri, $2,000 - general operating support (2009).
Contact: Charles H. Price II, Director; (816) 360-6174 or (816) 360-6176
Sponsor: Charles H. Price II Family Foundation
1 W. Armour Boulevard, Suite 300
Kansas City, MO 64111-2004

Charles M. and Mary D. Grant Foundation Grants **407**
The foundation awards grants primarily in the U.S. southeast in its areas of interest, including community and economic development, health and human services, education, and literacy. The foundation prefers to support projects, but may consider requests for operating support from organizations with budgets of less than $1 million. Grants are made in September. A minimum of three years must elapse between grant awards. Guidelines are available online.
Requirements: Southeast U.S. 501(c)3 tax-exempt organizations are eligible.
Restrictions: Individuals are ineligible, and loans are not awarded.
Geographic Focus: All U.S. States
Date(s) Application is Due: Apr 30
Amount: 10,000 - 50,000 USD

Samples: Free Clinic of Danville (VA)—for building renovations, $15,000; United Negro College Fund (New York, NY)—for the Faculty Advancement Program of the technology enhancement capital campaign, $30,000; Mountain Assoc for Community Economic Development (Berea, KY)—for general support, $35,000; Atlanta Legal Aid Society (GA)—for the Health Law Partnership, $25,000.
Contact: Jacqueline Elias, c/o JPMorgan Private Bank,
Internet: http://fdncenter.org/grantmaker/grant
Sponsor: Charles M. and Mary D. Grant Foundation
345 Park Avenue, 4th Floor
New York, NY 10154

Charles M. Bair Family Trust Grants 408

The trust awards general support grants to Montana nonprofits in its areas of interest, including museums, performing arts, arts and culture, higher education, youth, and social services. Application forms are required.
Requirements: Montana nonprofit organizations are eligible, with emphasis on Yellowstone, Meagher and Wheatland counties.
Restrictions: Funding is not provided for: churches, conventions, or associations of churches; individuals; conferences; symposiums; or for fundraising events.
Geographic Focus: Montana
Date(s) Application is Due: Jan 15; Aug 1
Amount: 2,000 - 300,000 USD
Contact: Grants Administrator, c/o U.S. Bank, Tax Department
Sponsor: Charles M. Bair Family Trust
P.O. Box 20678
Billings, MT 59115

Charles Stewart Mott Foundation Anti-Poverty Program 409

This program focuses on improving education, expanding economic opportunity, building organized communities, and special initiatives as pathways out of poverty. The overall goal is to help people vocalize and mobilize around local concerns, grow through participation in educational opportunities, and attain economic self-sufficiency by engaging more fully in the economy. Types of support include challenge/matching grants, conferences and seminars, demonstration grants, general operating grants, program grants, seed money grants, technical assistance, and training grants. The board meets in March, June, September, and December. Organizations should apply at least four months prior to the start date of the project for which they are seeking funds.
Requirements: Nonprofits and K-12 organizations are eligible to apply. A proposal may be submitted by a church-based or similar organization if the project falls clearly within program guidelines and is intended to serve as broad a segment of the population as the program of a comparable nonreligious organization.
Geographic Focus: All U.S. States
Amount: Up to 100,000,000 USD
Samples: Children's Aid Society (New York, NY)—to expand its Carrera program, a long-term, holistic approach to working with adolescents who are at high risk for teenage pregnancy, $873,782; Corp for a Skilled Workforce (Ann Arbor, MI)—to strengthen workforce development organizations in Michigan, $250,000; Pacific Institute for Community Organization (Oakland, CA)—for the Louisiana Interfaith Together project's work to engage residents of low-income communities in improving the educational outcomes of children in Louisiana, $220,000 over two years; Public/Private Ventures (Philadelphia, PA)—to assist and evaluate the Fathers at Work Initiative, which seeks to reduce poverty by increasing employment, earnings, and responsible fatherhood among young, low-income fathers, $787,047.
Contact: Office of Proposal Entry; (810) 238-5651; (810) 766-1753; info@mott.org
Internet: http://www.mott.org/programs/poverty.asp
Sponsor: Charles Stewart Mott Foundation
503 S Saginaw Street, Suite 1200
Flint, MI 48502-1851

Charles Stewart Mott Foundation Grants 410

The focus of the foundation's grant making is organized in four programs: civil society; environment; Flint, Michigan; and poverty. Flexibility to investigate new opportunities is maintained through an exploratory and special projects program. The civil society program promotes and supports civil society in the United States; Central/Eastern Europe and South Africa. The environment program supports efforts to achieve a healthy global environment capable of sustaining all forms of life. The Flint program seeks to strengthen the capacity of local institutions, including schools and school districts, in the foundation's home community of Flint, Michigan, to respond to economic and social needs. The poverty program addresses issues that contribute to improved life outcomes for children, youth, and families in low-income communities. Programs in low-income communities that connect schools and communities through systemic reform, improved teaching, leadership development, networking, technical assistance, and advocacy are also applicable. In all grant making, particular interest will be given to fresh approaches to solving community problems in the defined program areas; approaches that can generate long-term support from other sources and/or can be replicated in other communities; public policy development and research and development activities to further existing programs as well as to explore new fields of interest; and approaches and activities that lead to systemic change. Although proposals may be submitted at any time, applicants are strongly encouraged to submit during the first quarter of the year for which funding is requested. Grant expenditures are determined by September 1 of each year. The review process takes up to four months from the time the proposal is received. Therefore, proposals should be submitted at least four months prior to the start of the proposed grant period. Funding for unsolicited proposals is limited. It is recommended that letters of inquiry be submitted instead of a full proposal.
Requirements: Only 501(c)3 organizations are eligible, including schools and school districts.
Restrictions: Grants are not made to/for individuals; religious activities or programs that serve, or appear to serve, specific religious groups or denominations; or local projects outside the Flint area unless the projects are part of a national demonstration or foundation-planned network of grants that have clear and significant implications for replication in other communities.
Geographic Focus: All U.S. States
Samples: Regional Foundation for Local Development Zamah, Croatia, $82,000—Civil Society Grant for general purposes (2010); Clean Wisconsin, Wisconsin, $100,000—Environmental Grant (2010); Direct Action and Research Training Center, Florida, $300,000—Pathways Out of Poverty Grant for general purposes (2010).
Contact: Mary A. Gailbreath, Director; (810) 238-5651; (810) 766-1753; info@mott.org
Internet: http://www.mott.org/about/programs.aspx
Sponsor: Charles Stewart Mott Foundation
503 S Saginaw Street, Suite 1200
Flint, MI 48502-1851

Charles T. Beaird Foundation Grants 411

The foundation focuses its grantmaking on efforts to improve the Shreveport, LA, area. Grants are made to organizations that offer opportunity, freedom of action and choice, self-betterment and promote a climate for change to the people they serve. The foundation prefers to support those programs that are small, local, innovative, and perhaps even unpopular. The foundation awards general operating support, special program/project grants, capital expenditures, start-up costs, endowment funding, and technical assistance.
Requirements: Nonprofit organizations in, or projects that take place in, the Shreveport, LA, area are eligible. Requests from other areas, if they have the potential to be replicated in the Shreveport area, may be considered.
Geographic Focus: Louisiana
Date(s) Application is Due: Mar 1; Sep 1
Contact: Grants Administrator; (318) 221-8276; (318) 221-5993; BeairdP@aol.com or info@beairdfoundation.org
Internet: http://www.beairdfoundation.org
Sponsor: Charles T. Beaird Foundation
330 Marshall Street, Suite 1112
Shreveport, LA 71101

Chatlos Foundation Grants 412

The Chatlos Foundation supports nonprofit organizations in the U.S. A and around the globe. Support is provided to organizations currently exempt by the Internal Revenue Service of the United States. The Foundation's areas of interest are: Bible Colleges/Seminaries, Religious Causes, Medical Concerns, Liberal Arts Colleges and Social Concerns.
Requirements: Applicants must be U.S. tax-exempt, nonprofit organizations that provide services in the following areas: bible colleges, religious causes, medical concerns, liberal arts colleges, and social concerns. Proposals must include cover letter, specific request, tax-exemption letter, and budget. If proposal is to be considered at board level, additional information will be requested.

Restrictions: The foundation will not accept requests from individual church congregations, individuals, organizations in existence for less than two years as indicated by IRS tax-exempt letter of determination, for education below the college level, for medical research projects, or for support of the arts.
Geographic Focus: All U.S. States
Amount: 10,000 - 25,000 USD
Contact: C. J. Leff, Administrator; (407) 862-5077; cj@chatlos.org
Internet: http://www.chatlos.org/AppInfo.htm
Sponsor: Chatlos Foundation
P.O. Box 915048
Longwood, FL 32791-5048

Chautauqua Region Community Foundation Grants 413

Grants support projects serving communities in Chautauqua County in its areas of interest, including arts and culture, libraries, education, housing and shelters, children and youth, human services and general charitable giving, and government and public administration. Types of support include general operating support, continuing support, building construction/renovation, equipment acquisition, conferences and seminars, publication, seed grants, emergency funds, and undergraduate and graduate scholarships to individuals.
Requirements: Nonprofit organizations may apply for grants in support of projects serving communities in Chautauqua County, excluding the Fredonia/Dunkirk area, which is served by the Northern Chautauqua Community Foundation.
Geographic Focus: New York
Date(s) Application is Due: Jan 31; Mar 1; Nov 1
Samples: Salvation Army (NY)—to support the purchasing of infant formula and diapers, $500; James Prendergast Library Assoc (NY)—to support acquisition of books on and for small business, $2500; Research and Planning for Human Services (NY)—to support human services coordination activities, $4000.
Contact: June Diethrick, Grants Coordinator; (716) 661-3392; (716) 488-0387; jdiethrick@crcfonline.org
Internet: http://www.crcfonline.org/
Sponsor: Chautauqua Region Community Foundation
418 Spring Street
Jamestown, NY 14701

Chazen Foundation Grants 414

The foundation awards grants nationwide to eligible nonprofit organizations in its areas of interest, including arts; business education; higher education; hospitals; human services; Israel; Jewish agencies, temples, and federated giving programs; museums; and music performance. Types of support include building construction/renovation, capital campaigns, general operating support, grants and scholarships to individuals, professorships, and scholarship funds. Education grants are awarded to students of the Rockland County, NY, area. There are no application deadlines.
Geographic Focus: All U.S. States
Contact: Grants Administrator; (212) 750-6600
Internet: http://www.chazenscholar.com/project.php3
Sponsor: Chazen Foundation
767 5th Avenue, 26th Floor
New York, NY 10153-2696

CHC Foundation Grants 415

The foundation awards general operating grants to southeastern Idaho nonprofit organizations in its areas of interest, including children and youth, community development, natural resource conservation and protection, and social services. Applicants should submit a letter of inquiry; the foundation will invite full proposals.
Requirements: 501(c)3 southeastern Idaho nonprofit organizations may apply.
Geographic Focus: Idaho
Date(s) Application is Due: Mar 15; Sep 1
Amount: 750 - 150,000 USD
Samples: Tautphaus Park Zoo Animal Health Care Center—for building a hospital/quarantine facility for zoo animals, $250,000.
Contact: Ralph Isom, President; (208) 522-2368
Sponsor: CHC Foundation
P.O. Box 1644
Idaho Falls, ID 83403-1644

Chesapeake Bay Trust Environmental Education Grants 416

The Environmental Education Grants is designed to engage Maryland students and citizens in activities that raise public awareness and participation in the restoration and protection of the Chesapeake Bay and its rivers. The Trust seeks to increase environmental stewardship though hands-on education and public involvement in the Bay and its rivers by providing grants that build and expand K through 12 environmental education programs and increase student access to Meaningful Watershed Experiences. Requests up to $20,000 per project are available for funding. Application forms are available online and must be submitted by October 16. I
Requirements: The Trust welcomes requests from the following organizations: municipal and county agencies and school districts; public and independent higher educational institutions; 501(c)3 private nonprofit organizations; soil/water conservation districts & resource conservation and development councils. The strongest proposals will show committed partnerships that provide funding, technical assistance, or other in-kind services to support the successful implementation of the project.
Restrictions: The Trust does not fund the following: endowments, deficit financing, individuals, building campaigns, annual giving, research, fund raising or venture capital; mitigation or capital construction activities such as structural erosion control measures; political lobbying; reimbursement for a project that has been completed or materials that have been purchased; projects and programs located outside of Maryland; budget items that are considered secondary to the project's central objective. These items include, but are not limited to, food and refreshments, t-shirts and related materials, cash prizes, cameras and video equipment, and microscopes; funding is generally restricted to projects on public property, property owned by non-profit organizations, community-owned property, and property with conservation easements, unless otherwise specified in a grant program.
Geographic Focus: Maryland
Date(s) Application is Due: Oct 16
Amount: 20,000 USD
Contact: Jamie Baxter, Grant Manager; (410) 974-2941, ext. 105; (410) 269-0387; jbaxter@cbtrust.org
Internet: http://www.cbtrust.org/site/c.miJPKXPCJnH/b.5457277/k.75AD/Environmental_Education.htm
Sponsor: Chesapeake Bay Trust
60 West Street, Suite 405
Annapolis, MD 21401

Chesapeake Bay Trust Outreach and Community Engagement Grants 417

The Outreach and Community Awareness Grants, seeks to increase public awareness and public involvement in the restoration and protection of the Bay and its rivers. In light of the Trust's commitment to the advancement of diversity in its grant-making and environmental work, the Trust strongly encourages grant applications for projects that increase awareness and participation of communities of color in the restoration and protection of the watershed. Available funding will range between $5,000 - $20,000. All eligible projects should be a component of a clearly defined plan to engage communities, raise awareness and ultimately change citizen behaviors. The strongest proposals will show committed partnerships that provide funding, technical assistance, or other in-kind services to support the successful implementation of the project. Applications must be received via the new Online Grants System, available at the Chesapeake Bay Trust website.
Requirements: The Trust welcomes requests from the following Maryland organizations: 501(c)3 private nonprofit organizations; faith-based organizations; community associations; service, youth, and civic groups; municipal, county, regional, state, federal public agencies; soil/water conservation districts & resource conservation and development councils; forestry boards & tributary teams; public and independent higher educational institutions.
Restrictions: The Trust does not fund the following: endowments, deficit financing, individuals, building campaigns, annual giving, research, direct mail fund raising, or venture capital; mitigation or capital construction activities such as structural erosion control measures; political lobbying; reimbursement for a project that has been completed or materials that have been purchased; projects and programs located outside of Maryland; budget items that are considered secondary to the project's central objective. These items include, but are not limited to, cash prizes, cameras and video equipment, and microscopes. Funding is generally restricted to projects on public property, property owned by non-profit organizations, community-owned property, and property with conservation easements, unless otherwise specified in a grant

program. Projects should be completed within approximately one year upon receipt of the grant award.
Geographic Focus: Maryland
Amount: 5,000 - 20,000 USD
Contact: Jamie Baxter, Grant Manager; (410) 974-2941, ext. 105; (410) 269-0387; jbaxter@cbtrust.org
Internet: http://www.cbtrust.org/site/c.miJPKXPCJnH/b.5457559/k.48A4/Outreach_and_Community_Awareness.htm
Sponsor: Chesapeake Bay Trust
60 West Street, Suite 405
Annapolis, MD 21401

Chesapeake Corporation Foundation Grants 418
The foundation supports U.S. and international nonprofits in its areas of interest, including civic affairs, community development, cultural programs, higher education, and health. Types of support include endowments, capital grants, matching gifts, and scholarships. Grants are awarded for one year with the possibility of renewal.
Requirements: Nonprofits internationally are eligible.
Restrictions: Grants do not support athletic purposes or individuals, except for employee-related scholarships.
Geographic Focus: All U.S. States
Amount: 1,000 - 10,000 USD
Samples: David I. Clay II (Williamsburg, VA)—Chesapeake Employees' Children Scholarship, $3500 annually.
Contact: J.P. Causey Jr., (804) 697-1000; (804) 697-1199
Internet: http://www.cskcorp.com
Sponsor: Chesapeake Corporation Foundation
P.O. Box 2350
Richmond, VA 23218-2350

Chestnut Hill Charitable Foundation, Inc Grants 419
The foundation awards grants to nonprofit organizations in the greater Boston, MA, area in support of medical research, children and youth, and arts and education. Specifically, the foundation's interests include visual arts, museums, humanities, arts and culture, early childhood education and development, education at all levels, hospitals and medical research (cancer, heart and lungs, AIDS, and diabetes), social services, and general charitable giving. Types of support include general operating support, annual campaigns, capital campaigns, building construction/renovations, programs and projects, seed grants, curriculum development, research, and matching funds. There are no application forms, submit a letter of request.
Requirements: Nonprofit organizations in the greater Boston, MA, area may submit letters of request.
Restrictions: Grants are not awarded to support individuals or political or religious organizations.
Geographic Focus: Massachusetts
Amount: 1,000 - 15,000 USD
Samples: Leslie Berg, U of Massachusetts Medical Ctr (Worcester, MA)—for the Chestnut Hill Award for Excellence in Medical Research, administered by the Medical Foundation, in Boston, $15,000.
Contact: Kay Kilpatrick, Director Corporate Giving; (617) 630-2415
Sponsor: Chestnut Hill Charitable Foundation
27 Boylston Street
Chestnut Hill, MA 02167-1700

Chicago Board of Trade Foundation Grants 420
The foundation provides grant support to organizations in the metropolitan Chicago, IL, area in its areas of interest: arts and culture, including libraries and museums; education, including higher education, adult basic education and literacy training, and science and technology; health care, including mental health services, cancer research, and rehabilitation; child and youth development; minorities; the economically disadvantaged; wildlife; and media and communication. Grants are awarded for general operating support, continuing support, annual campaigns, capital campaigns, and endowments. An application form is not required; the initial approach should be by letter, or via the CBOT Foundation form on the website. The board meets during the first quarter annually to consider requests.
Requirements: Nonprofit organizations in a 75-mile radius of the metropolitan Chicago, IL, area may apply for grant support.
Restrictions: Support is not given to hospitals or foundations. Loans and program-related investments will also be denied.
Geographic Focus: Illinois
Date(s) Application is Due: Oct 1
Samples: Kent State U (Kent, OH)—to coordinate research symposia on derivative markets and instruments, $1.2 million.
Contact: Grants Administrator; (312) 435-3456; (312) 341-3306
Internet: http://www.cbot.com/cbot/pub/page/0,3181,948,00.html
Sponsor: Chicago Board of Trade Foundation
141 W Jackson Boulevard, Suite 600-A
Chicago, IL 60604

Chicago Community Trust Grants 421
The community trust supports charitable programs that provide mental, moral, intellectual and physical improvement, assistance, and relief for people in Cook County, IL. Grants are made in the areas of education—teaching and learning in public schools, with emphasis on improved literacy rates, professional development for teachers and administrators, and alternative educational models; arts and humanities—arts education, dance, and leadership transitions at arts groups; basic human needs—food, shelter, and related needs; community development—job training, criminal and juvenile justice, and strengthening nonprofits; and health—violence prevention, health and the environment, and healthful lifestyles. From time to time, guidelines are developed for specific programs or areas of grantmaking. In considering grants for either general operating support of a continuing program or for a specific time-limited program or project, the initial grant usually will be for one or two years. Consecutive funding, including the initial grant, rarely will extend beyond five years. The listed application deadlines are for letters of intent; full proposals are by invitation.
Requirements: Trust funds support 501(c)3 charitable organizations that serve residents of Cook, DuPage, Kane, Lake, McHenry, or Will Counties, IL. In general, grant requests from organizations that do not directly serve this geographic area will not be considered.
Restrictions: The trust generally will not make grants for scholarships, individuals, religious purposes, endowments, or operating support of government agencies.
Geographic Focus: Illinois
Date(s) Application is Due: Mar 15; Jul 15; Nov 15
Samples: ABJ Community Services, $25,000—Sunshine Food Pantry-basic human needs grant (2009); ACCION Chicago, $25,000—Microloan Program-community development grant (2010); Access Community Health Network, $50,000—to provide health care services to low income individuals-health grant (2009).
Contact: Sandy Phelps, Grant Manager, (312) 616-8000, ext. 112, (312) 616-7955; sandy@cct.org
Internet: http://www.cct.org/apply/funding-opportunities
Sponsor: Chicago Community Trust
111 E Wacker Drive, Suite 1400
Chicago, IL 60601

Chicago Sun Times Charity Trust Grants 422
The trust supports nonprofit organizations serving the Chicago metropolitan area by awarding grants to support projects in the areas of arts and culture and education/literacy. Grants will be awarded primarily as seed money for new ideas or approaches to problems affecting the quality of life in the community. Although applications for general operating support and capital projects are considered, the trust prefers to fund efforts that solve specific problems. Proposals are reviewed two times each year.
Requirements: IRS 501(c)3 organizations serving the Chicago, IL, metropolitan area are eligible.
Restrictions: The trust does not make grants to individuals, religious organizations for religious purposes, scholarships or fellowships, medical research or national health agency drives, or to political activities.
Geographic Focus: Illinois
Amount: Up to 5,000 USD
Contact: Patricia Dudek, Client and Community Services Supervisor; (312) 321-3000; (312) 321-2278; pdudek@hollingerintl.com
Sponsor: Chicago Sun Times Charity Trust
350 N Orleans Street
Chicago, IL 60654

Chicago Title and Trust Company Foundation Grants 423
The company foundation supports nonprofit organizations dedicated to improving the quality of life in Chicago. Grants are awarded to support higher education; city and neighborhood cultural organizations; and community

issues, such as job training, literacy, and economic development. Types of support include program development, general operating support, annual campaigns, building construction/renovation, and matching gifts.
Requirements: Nonprofit organizations serving Chicago, IL, may apply.
Geographic Focus: Illinois
Amount: 100 - 150,000 USD
Contact: Eileen Hughes, c/o Miami Corp, Treasurer; (312) 223-2911
Sponsor: Chicago Title and Trust Company Foundation
410 N Michigan Avenue
Chicago, IL 60611

Chicago Tribune's Corporate Contributions Grants **424**
The foundation's mission is to promote public knowledge and strengthen the Chicago metropolitan community by encouraging journalistic excellence, diversity and liberty; supporting diverse cultural institutions; and promoting civic efforts. Program areas for the foundation are civic, culture, and journalism. Grants in the civic program area support business, nonprofit or educational initiatives. These grants are considered by invitation only and are accepted throughout the year. The range is $2,500 to $25,000. Grants in the culture area support cultural organizations within the Chicago metropolitan area that provide educational programs in the arts for children from low-income communities or that foster diverse art. The range for these grants is $5,000 to $7,500. Proposals are due February 1. Grants in the journalism are support organizations on a national level that offer programs for professional journalists that lead to journalistic excellence, promote diversity in the newspaper industry and protect freedom of the press. Support is considered for journalism programs in the metropolitan Chicago area that promote diversity. Support is not provided to high school or college newspapers. The grant range is $5,000 to $20,000. Proposals are due June 1. Types of support include general operating grants, matching gifts, and program development grants. A brief summary proposal should be sent; if interested, the foundation will request a full proposal.
Requirements: Grants are made to Chicago-area tax-exempt organizations.
Restrictions: Grants are not made to individuals nor for fund-raising events.
Geographic Focus: Illinois
Date(s) Application is Due: Feb 1; Jun 1
Amount: 2,500 - 25,000 USD
Samples: Innovations for Learning (Evanston, IL)—for its reading programs for first graders supported by online tutors, $10,000; Chicago History Museum (Chicago, IL)—for curriculum development for Great Chicago Stories for schools, $5,000; Young Chicago Authors (Chicago, IL)—for in-school and after-school creative writing programs, $5,000; Association for Women Journalists-Chicago (Chicago, IL)—a survey about careers of women employed in the news media in the Chicago area; McCormick Tribune YMCA—Kids Need Heroes campaign, $1,000.
Contact: Community Relations Manager; (312) 222-4300; (312) 222-3751; ctcommunityrelations@tribune.com
Internet: http://www.chicagotribune.com/about/custom/community/chi-foundationspage-htmlstory,0,7165967.htmlstory
Sponsor: Chicago Tribune Foundation
435 N Michigan Avenue, 2nd Floor
Chicago, IL 60611-4041

Chiles Foundation Grants **425**
The foundation has a deep concern for and confidence in the future of Oregon and the Pacific Northwest. Although the foundation has made a steady commitment to the improvement of the quality of life for those who live and work in this area, it is not restricted in its grant making to the Pacific Northwest. The foundation has traditionally made grants to certain select institutions of higher education for business schools, scholarships, and athletics; supports basic research in certain select medical institutions; supports religion through divinity schools and religious education; and believes that the arts and cultural activities of a community are important and supports certain select, established institutions. Types of support include building construction/renovation, equipment acquisition, and scholarship funds. Annual deadline dates may vary; contact Foundation by a letter of Inquiry. The Foundation does not accept unsolicited proposals.
Requirements: The preferred initial method of contact is a phone call to the grants administration office to determine whether a prospective proposal is within guidelines; if so, an applicant will be invited to submit a one-page written preliminary proposal. An application form will be sent after approval of the preliminary proposal by the executive committee.
Restrictions: No support for projects involving litigation. Grants are not made to individuals, for deficit financing, mortgage retirement, or projects and conferences already completed.
Geographic Focus: California, Oregon, Germany
Amount: 1,000 - 270,000 USD
Samples: Boston Symphony Orchestra, Boston, MA, $100,000— general operating support (2008); Stanford University, Stanford, CA, $159,000—scholarship assistance (2008); Ludwig-Maximilians University, Munich, Germany, $180,000—support continuing clinical and experimental research (2008).
Contact: Earle M. Chiles, President; (503) 222-2143; (503) 228-7079; cf@uswest.net
Sponsor: Chiles Foundation
111 SW Fifth Avenue, Suite 4050
Portland, OR 97204-3643

Chingos Foundation Grants **426**
The foundation awards grants to Florida nonprofit organizations for protection of endangered wildlife and natural resource conservation. Grants support program development, general operations, land acquisition, and other purposes. There are no application deadlines or forms.
Requirements: Florida nonprofit organizations are eligible.
Restrictions: Grants do not support humane societies or spay/neuter clinics.
Geographic Focus: Florida
Amount: 5,000 - 20,000 USD
Samples: Zoological Society of Florida (FL)—$7000; Nature Conservancy (FL)—$5000.
Contact: William Manikas, (561) 737-7111
Sponsor: Chingos Foundation
639 E Ocean Avenue, Suite 307
Boynton Beach, FL 33435

Chinook Fund Grants **427**
The fund supports progressive social change, organizing, and activism efforts in Colorado. Emphasis is placed on groups with diverse membership and leadership that represent diverse populations. Priority is given to organizations that are based in minority, low-income, or other oppressed communities; operate in a democratic manner; empower communities; have difficulty obtaining funding from traditional sources; draw parallels between local problems and global issues; and work in cooperation with other organizations. The standard grant program awards grants to new and established groups working for social change. Types of support include general operating support, special projects, technical assistance, and emergency funds. Application forms are available on the website.
Requirements: Applicants do not have to be tax-exempt, but the activities for which funds are sought must fit within the IRS eligibility requirements for 501(c)3 organizations.
Restrictions: Groups with annual budgets over $350,000 are not eligible for grants. Groups whose purpose is to provide direct services are generally not funded. Individuals are ineligible for funding.
Geographic Focus: Colorado
Date(s) Application is Due: Feb 21; Aug 21
Amount: 500 - 7,000 USD
Samples: Jobs with Justice (Englewood, CO)—to create a series of educational forums and hearings on the growing unemployment rate in Colorado, develop programs to better serve displaced workers, and develop strategies to create jobs, $7000; Two Spirit Society of Denver (CO)—to confront and combat issues of homophobia, racism, and cultural oppression toward the Native American, non-Native, gay, lesbian, bisexual, and transgender communities, $3000; Domestic Violence Initiative for Women with Disabilities (CO)—to provide support and intervention for disabled women who are victims/survivors of domestic violence and abuse, $3000.
Contact: Eva Benavidez Clayton, Program Coordinator; (303) 455-6905; (303) 477-1617; ebenavidez@chinookfund.org
Internet: http://www.chinookfund.org
Sponsor: Chinook Fund
2418 W 32nd Avenue
Denver, CO 80218

Christensen Fund Regional Grants **428**
The fund (TCF) focuses its grantmaking on maintaining the biological and cultural diversity of the world by focusing on four geographic regions: the greater South West (Southwest United States and Northwest Mexico);

Central Asia and Turkey; the African Rift Valley (Ethiopia); and Northern Australia and Melanesia. Grants within these programs are generally directed to organizations based within those regions or, where appropriate, to internationally based organizations working in support of people and institutions on the ground. In general, grants are one year or less; currently grants up to two years are by invitation only.
Requirements: 501(c)3 nonprofit organizations and non-U.S. A institutions with nonprofit or equivalent status in their country of origin are eligible. Partnerships or associations with U.S. A-based nonprofit organizations are preferred.
Restrictions: The fund does not make grants directly to individuals but rather assists individuals through institutions qualified to receive nonprofit support with which such individuals are affiliated.
Geographic Focus: All U.S. States
Amount: Up to 200,000 USD
Contact: Administrator; (415) 644-1600; (415) 644-1601; info@christensenfund.org
Internet: http://www.christensenfund.org/index.html
Sponsor: Christensen Fund
260 Townsend Street
San Francisco, CA 94107

Christian A. Johnson Endeavor Foundation Grants 429

The foundation contributes primarily to educational projects in the eastern United States. More specifically, it concentrates its giving on private institutions of higher learning at the baccalaureate level and on educational outreach programs of visual and performing arts organizations. Types of support include general operating support, seed money grants, building construction/renovation funds, equipment acquisition, matching funds, endowments, professorships, and scholarship funds. Applicants should first submit a brief letter of inquiry describing the project, its purposes, and potential impact on the program or service of the applicant organization. If the project falls within the foundation's support areas, a formal, more detailed proposal will be requested. Proposals requested by the foundation should be submitted during the first six months of the foundation's fiscal year, specifically between October 1 and March 30.
Restrictions: The foundation does not award grants to individuals; neighborhood or community projects; city, county, state, or federal government-affiliated agencies; institutions controlled by religious institutions; or in the areas of health care and medical research.
Geographic Focus: All U.S. States
Amount: 10,000 - 250,000 USD
Samples: New England College (Henniker, NH)—to develop the college's curriculum, with an emphasis on its liberal arts courses, $250,000.
Contact: Julie Kidd, President; (212) 534-6620; (212) 410-5909
Sponsor: Christian A. Johnson Endeavor Foundation
1060 Park Avenue, Apt 1F
New York, NY 10128

CICF Indianapolis Foundation Community Endowment Grants 430

CICF's mission is to inspire, support, and practice philanthropy, leadership, and service in the community. Proposed programs should align with any of the Vision Priority Areas: Response to Basic Needs; Develop Productive Citizens; Build Strong Neighborhoods; Embrace Inclusiveness; Promote Community Amenities; Promote Philanthropy; or Promote Our Community.
Requirements: CICF welcomes grant applications from charitable organizations that are tax exempt under section 501(c)3 of the Internal Revenue Code, and from governmental agencies. New projects or organizations with pending 501(c)3 status may submit an application with the assistance of a fiscal sponsor. Grant inquiries and proposals will be prioritized using the following criteria: Organizations that serve primarily Marion County residents; Organizations with a demonstrable track record; Programs serving populations disadvantaged due to income, age, ethnicity, language, education, disability, transportation or other adverse conditions; Project/program ideas must be fully developed; Projects that strongly connect to existing community initiatives (e.g. the Blueprint to End Homelessness, Indianapolis Cultural Development Initiative, and Family Strengthening Coalition); The leverage of additional resources, both financial and non-financial. Application information is available online.
Restrictions: Priority will be given to organizations that serve Marion County residents. Capital projects only from organizations in which there is an existing relationship with the Foundation.
Geographic Focus: Indiana
Date(s) Application is Due: Mar 1; May 1; Sep 1; Nov 1
Amount: 1,000 - 100,000 USD
Contact: Joanna Nixon, Vice President for Grantmaking; (317) 634-2423, ext. 175; (317) 684-0943; joannan@cicf.org or program@cicf.org
Internet: http://www.cicf.org/newsarticle.cfm?articleid=98397&PTSidebarOptID=14412&returnTo=page26544.cfm&returntoname=The%20Indianapolis%20Foundation&SiteID=1824&pageid=26544&sidepageid=26544&thetitle=Apply%20for%20Funding%20from%20the%20Indianapolis%20Foundation&
Sponsor: Central Indiana Community Foundation
615 N Alabama Street, Suite 119
Indianapolis, IN 46204-1498

CICF Legacy Fund Noblesville Community Fund Grants 431

The City of Noblesville Community Fund was established to support the charitable intentions of the City of Noblesville. Further purposes of the fund include, but are not limited to, providing for the promotion of and public awareness of the human services, recreational programming, art, cultural, and humanities needs and issues of the City of Noblesville.
Requirements: Priority is given to programs and projects most likely to have a positive effect on the city's residents. In reviewing grant applications, the foundation gives careful consideration to: The potential impact of the grant and the number of Noblesville residents who will benefit; Programs and projects which promote inclusiveness and diversity; Programs and projects which are responsive to basic human needs; Program and projects which connect individuals and families to the community; The extent of commitment and capacity of the organization's directors, trustees, and volunteers to carry out the program or project; The degree to which the applicant works with or complements the services of other organizations in an attempt to eliminate duplication of services; The organization's fiscal responsibility and management qualifications; The possibility of using the grant to match funds from other sources; The ability of the organization to obtain the necessary additional funding to implement the project and provide or obtain ongoing funding after the grant has been expended. Organizations interested in applying must first submit an Application (available for download at website).
Restrictions: Limited to programs and services benefiting the residents of Noblesville, Indiana.
Geographic Focus: Indiana
Date(s) Application is Due: Mar 1; May 1; Sep 1; Nov 1
Amount: 1,000 - 5,000 USD
Contact: Liz Tate, Program Officer; (317) 843-2479, ext. 302; (317) 848-5463; lizt@cicf.org
Internet: http://www.cicf.org/newsarticle.cfm?articleid=99280&ptsidebaroptid=0&returnto=page26581.cfm&returntoname=What%20We%20Fund&siteid=1824&pageid=26545&sidepageid=26581&banner1img=banner%5F1%2EJPG&banner2img=banner%5F2%2EJPG&bannerbg=bannerbg%2Egif
Sponsor: Central Indiana Community Foundation
615 N Alabama Street, Suite 119
Indianapolis, IN 46204-1498

CIGNA Foundation Grants 432

CIGNA Foundation has identified four areas for grant consideration—health and human services, education, community and civic affairs, and culture and the arts. Health and education are of primary concern and receive priority. Under education, priority is placed on public secondary education, higher education for minorities, and adult basic education/literacy. The foundation also considers requests from U.S. cultural, educational, and public policy organizations that have international components. Requests are accepted and reviewed throughout the year. Consideration will be given to requests for general operating support, program development, annual campaigns, conferences and seminars, fellowships, scholarship funds and employee-related scholarships, and matching gifts and funds.
Requirements: Organizations with 501(c)3 tax-exempt status are eligible.
Restrictions: The foundation will not consider applications for grants to individuals, organizations operating to influence legislation or litigation, political organizations, or religious activities. In general, the foundation will not consider applications from organizations receiving substantial support through the United Way or other CIGNA-supported federated funding agencies; hospitals' capital improvements; or research, prevention, and treatment of specific diseases.
Geographic Focus: All U.S. States
Amount: 5,000 - 50,000 USD
Contact: Program Contact; communityrelations@cigna.com

Internet: http://www.cigna.com/general/about/community/grant_information.html
Sponsor: CIGNA Foundation
1601 Chestnut Street, TL06B
Philadelphia, PA 19192-1540

Cincinnati Bell Foundation Grants **433**

The foundation awards grants to Ohio organizations in support of elementary and secondary school programs that improve education for disadvantaged youths, such as mentoring or tutoring programs. Grants also support social services, colleges and universities, and local civic and cultural groups that make the arts accessible to everyone. Types of support include capital grants, challenge/matching grants, organizational development grants, general operating grants, and program development grants. There are no application deadlines; grant notification is made quarterly.
Requirements: 501(c)3 nonprofit organizations in the Cincinnati Bell service area are eligible. Giving primarily in northern KY, the greater Cincinnati, OH, area, and in other cities in which the company has a significant corporate presence.
Geographic Focus: Kentucky, Ohio
Samples: Cincinnati Zoo (Cincinnati, OH)—for general support, $100,000; College of Mount Saint Joseph (Cincinnati, OH)—to equip a media and video center in the college's new student center, $75,000.
Contact: Robert Horine, Public Affairs Director; (513) 397-7545
Internet: http://home.cincinnatibell.com/corporate/community
Sponsor: Cincinnati Bell Foundation
201 E Fourth Street, Room 102-560
Cincinnati, OH 45202

Cincinnati Milacron Foundation Grants **434**

The Cincinnati Milacron Foundation awards grants, gifts, and loans to eligible Michigan and Ohio nonprofit organizations in its areas of interest, including the arts, community development, higher education, youth programs, and religion. Types of support include annual campaigns, building/renovations, general operations, and seed money. Grants are awarded for one year and are renewable.
Requirements: Michigan and Ohio 501(c)3 nonprofit organizations are eligible.
Restrictions: Grants are not made to individuals.
Geographic Focus: Michigan, Ohio
Amount: 5,000 - 200,000 USD
Contact: George G. Price, (513) 487-5912; (513) 487-5586
Sponsor: Cincinnati Milacron Foundation
2090 Florence Avenue
Cincinnati, OH 45206-2484

Cinnabar Foundation Grants **435**

The foundation awards grants to nonprofits to promote environmental and wildlife conservation and protection. Types of support include general operating support, conferences and seminars, research, and scholarships to individuals. There are no application forms.
Requirements: Idaho, Montana, and Wyoming nonprofit organizations may apply.
Geographic Focus: Idaho, Montana, Wyoming
Date(s) Application is Due: Mar 15
Amount: 1,000 - 15,000 USD
Contact: James Posewitz, c/o Holmes and Turner, (406) 449-2795; (406) 449-9985; cinnabar@mt.net
Sponsor: Cinnabar Foundation
P.O. Box 5088
Helena, MT 59604

Citigroup Foundation Grants **436**

The foundation supports nonprofits worldwide in Citibank communities in the areas of financial education, educating the next generation, and building communities and entrepreneurs. Financial Education grants support efforts that help increase family stability, encourage better consumer habits, increase the individual's stake in his/her community, and deliver economic and financial education to young people. Educating the Next Generation grants support educational opportunities in low-income communities, early literacy development, technology-based curriculum resources, career and college preparation programs, teacher training and strategies that increase student achievement, student and curriculum development for graduate and undergraduate business programs, access for minorities and women within higher education and the workplace, and access to arts through curriculum and cultural institutions. Building Communities and Entrepreneurs grants reinforce community-led efforts to revitalize low-income neighborhoods through affordable housing, economic development, welfare-to-work initiatives, community infrastructure improvements, environmentally sustainable growth to local economies, community-based health and human services programs, and disaster relief efforts. Citigroup and the Citigroup Foundation prefer to solicit proposals from prospective grantees with demonstrated successes in the areas they fund. Unsolicited proposals will be accepted, but a favorable decision is less likely. Nonprofit organizations that are encouraged to submit proposals may do so at any time during a calendar year; the earlier, the better. There are no application deadlines.
Requirements: 501(c)3 nonprofit organizations in communities served by Citibank or a Citigroup company are eligible. The Citigroup Foundation receives all U.S. grant applications through an online submission system. For information on applying for a U.S. grant, contact your closest U.S. Contributions Coordinator. For information on applying for an international grant, contact the International Contributions Coordinator. Contacts are listed at the Foundation's website (given above).
Restrictions: The foundation does not to make grants to individuals for educational or other purposes; political causes or candidates; religious, veteran, or fraternal organizations, unless they are engaged in a significant project benefiting the entire community; fundraising events, telethons, marathons, races, or benefits; or courtesy advertising.
Geographic Focus: All U.S. States
Samples: Enterprise Community Partners (Columbia, MD)—for the Green Communities program a nationwide effort to build 8500 low-coast houses that conserve energy and natural resources and provide easy access to jobs, schools, and services, $1.5 million; Junior Achievement Worldwide (Colorado Springs, CO)—to expand its classroom-based program that teaches young people in more than 25 countries about finance, the principles of the banking industry, and the challenges of operating a bank, $2.7 million over three years; American National Red Cross (Washington, DC)—for relief efforts in the wake of the tsunamis in South Asia, and for the rebuilding of affected communities, $1 million, plus $2 million to be be distributed.
Contact: Pamela P. Flaherty, President; (212) 559-9163; (212) 793-5944; citigroupfoundation@citigroup.com
Internet: http://www.citigroup.com/citigroup/corporate/foundation/guide.htm
Sponsor: Citigroup Foundation
850 Third Avenue, 13th Floor
New York, NY 10022-6211

City of Oakland Cultural Arts Department Grants **437**

The arts program awards grants to Oakland-based individuals and nonprofit organizations. Organization Project Support grants support Oakland-based nonprofit organizations producing art activities in Oakland that culminate in a local public outcome for the benefit of the community. Individual Artist Project grants support Oakland resident individual artists producing art activities in Oakland that culminate in a local public outcome for the benefit of the community. Art in the Schools grants support quality, hands-on arts experiences in school settings to educate students about the process of creating and producing arts; support and enhance the classroom curriculum; and support arts residencies on the school site before, during, or after school hours. The January 6 application deadline is for organizations and individual artists; the January 13 deadline is for art in the schools. Guidelines are available online.
Requirements: Oakland-based individuals and nonprofit organizations are eligible.
Geographic Focus: All U.S. States
Date(s) Application is Due: Jan 6; Jan 13
Contact: Andrea Leal, (510) 238-6843; aleal@oaklandnet.com
Internet: http://oaklandculturalarts.org/main/programoverview.htm
Sponsor: City of Oakland Cultural Arts Department
1 Frank H Ogawa Plaza, 9th Floor
Oakland, CA 94612

Clarcor Foundation Grants **438**

Clarcor, through its foundation, seeks to improve the quality of life in the communities in which the company operates. Grants support nonprofits in the categories of health, human services, education, culture and art, and civic activities. Types of support include general operating support, annual campaigns, capital campaigns, and employee matching gifts. There are

no application deadlines. The board meets in February, May, August, and November.
Requirements: Tax-exempt organizations in company-operating areas in Rockford, IL; Louisville, KY; Kearney and Gothenburg, NE; Cincinnati, OH; Oklahoma, and Lancaster, PA; are eligible.
Restrictions: Grants are not made to support individuals, endowment funds, research, scholarships, fellowships, or loans.
Geographic Focus: Illinois, Kentucky, Nebraska, North Carolina, Ohio, Oklahoma, Pennsylvania
Amount: 500 - 50,250 USD
Samples: Boys & Girls Assoc of Rockford (IL)—to support the Crime Prevention program, $3000; New American Theater (Rockford, IL)—for educational outreach, $6000; Lancaster Theological Seminary (Lancaster, PA)—to fund creation of a computerized card catalog system, $2500; Boy Scouts of America (Kearney, NE)—to support the annual campaign, $1000.
Contact: Pete Nangel, (815) 962-8867; (815) 962-0417
Sponsor: Clarcor Foundation
840 Crescent Centre Drive, Suite 600
Franklin, TN 37067

Clarence E. Heller Charitable Foundation Grants **439**
The charitable foundation supports nonprofit organizations, with priority given to proposals from California, in its areas of interest, including environment and health—to prevent serious risk to human health from toxic substances and other environmental hazards by supporting programs in research, education, and policy development; management of resources—to protect and preserve the earth's limited resources by assisting programs that demonstrate how natural resources can be managed on a sustainable and an ecologically sound basis, and supporting initiatives for sustainable agriculture, and for promoting the long-term viability of communities and regions; music—to encourage the playing, enjoyment, and accessibility of symphonic and chamber music by providing scholarship and program assistance at selected community music organizations and schools, and by helping community-based ensembles of demonstrated quality implement artistic initiatives, diversify and increase audiences, and improve fund-raising capacity; and education—to focus on support for programs that improve the teaching skills of educators and artists in environmental and arts education. Types of support include continuing support, general operating expenses, publications, research, seed money, and special projects. The foundation's board meets typically in March, June, and October. Letters of inquiry are accepted at any time.
Requirements: 501(c)3 tax-exempt organizations are eligible.
Restrictions: Grants are not made to individuals.
Geographic Focus: California
Amount: 5,000 - 600,000 USD
Samples: Crossroads School, Santa Monica, CA, $50,000— to support the Elizabeth Mandell Music Institute (2008); Brentwood Agricultural Land Trust, Brentwood, CA, $50,000—for a program to save productive agricultural lands on the urban edge and market farm products from family-scale farms (2008); Graduate School of Education, UC Berkeley, Berkeley, CA, $10,000—for the Principal Leadership Institute Scholarship Endowment Fund (2008).
Contact: Bruce Hirsch, Executive Director; (415) 989-9839; (415) 989-1909; info@cehcf.org
Internet: http://cehcf.org/app_info.html
Sponsor: Clarence E. Heller Charitable Foundation
44 Montgomery Street, Suite 1970
San Francisco, CA 94104

Clarence T.C. Ching Foundation Grants **440**
The Clarence T. C. Ching Foundation provides funding opportunities to nonprofits primarily in Honolulu, Hawaii. The Foundation's areas of interest include education and health. Types of support available are: scholarship funds; general program support and; building/renovation. Grant applications are accepted year round with no application deadline date.
Requirements: Nonprofits in Honolulu, Hawaii are eligible for funding. When applying for a grant include the following in with your proposal: copy of IRS Determination Letter; detailed description of project and amount of funding requested; listing of additional sources and amount of support; five (5) copies of the proposal.
Restrictions: No grants to individuals.
Geographic Focus: Hawaii
Amount: 500 - 70,000 USD
Samples: Contemporary Museum, Honolulu, HI, $500—general program support; Street Francis Healthcare of Hawaii, Honolulu, HI, $70,000—general program support; Street Louis Scholarship Fund, Hawaii, Honolulu, HI, $70,000—general program support.
Contact: R. Stevens Gilley, Executive Director; (808) 521-0344
Sponsor: Clarence T.C. Ching Foundation
1001 Bishop Street, Suite 960
Honolulu, HI 96813

Clark-Winchcole Foundation Grants **441**
The foundation awards grants to nonprofit organizations in the District of Columbia, with an emphasis on higher education, hospitals and health care, cultural programs, youth, the disabled, and religion. Types of support include general operating support, scholarships, and building construction/renovation. Applicants should submit a letter of inquiry that includes a description of the project, amount requested, audited financial report, budget, and proof of tax-exempt status. Further information will be requested by the foundation if interested.
Requirements: Only nonprofit organizations in the District of Columbia are eligible to apply.
Restrictions: No support for individuals and private foundations.
Geographic Focus: District of Columbia
Amount: 5,000 - 225,000 USD
Samples: Capital Hospice, Falls Church, VA, $75,000—for Patient Care program (2008); Wesley Theological Seminary, Washington, DC, $125,000—for urban ministry program (2008); Wolf Trap Foundation for the Performing Arts, Vienna, VA, $225,000—for Institute for Early Learning, Opera at Wolf Trap, Fund for Artistic Initiative (2008).
Contact: Vincent Burke, President; (301) 654-3607
Sponsor: Clark-Winchcole Foundation
3 Bethesda Metro Center, Suite 550
Bethesda, MD 20814-5358

Clark Charitable Foundation Grants **442**
The foundation awards operating grants to nonprofit organizations in the District of Columbia and Maryland in its areas of interest, including arts, community funds, higher education, support also for health and hospitals, and social services.
Geographic Focus: District of Columbia, Maryland
Date(s) Application is Due: Mar 1; Sep 1
Amount: 5,000 - 50,000 USD
Contact: Courtney Clark Pastrick, Secretary; (301) 657 7166
Sponsor: Clark Charitable Foundation
7500 Old Georgetown Road, 15th Floor
Bethesda, MD 20814

Clark Charitable Trust Grants **443**
The trust awards grants to nonprofit organizations in its areas of interest, including basic human needs, environmental conservation and preservation, animal welfare, music, and higher education. Types of support include general operating support, annual campaigns, capital campaigns, building construction/renovation, equipment acquisition, endowment funds, scholarship funds, and matching funds. There are no application forms or deadlines. Submit a letter describing the project's purpose and an audited financial statement.
Requirements: Nonprofit organization are eligible.
Geographic Focus: All U.S. States
Amount: Up to 417,000 USD
Contact: Timothy Taylor, Trustee; (781) 259-8800
Sponsor: Clark Charitable Trust
P.O. Box 681
Lincoln, MA 01773

Clark Foundation Grants **444**
The foundation awards grants in New York, NY, and upstate New York for charitable and educational purposes and in support of health care, youth, cultural, environmental, and community organizations. Types of support include general operating support, continuing support, annual campaigns, capital campaigns, building construction/renovation, equipment acquisition, program development, seed money, and scholarships to Cooperstown County residents.
Requirements: Nonprofit organizations in upstate New York and New York, NY, are eligible.
Geographic Focus: New York

Date(s) Application is Due: Jan 1; Apr 1; Jul 15; Oct 1
Amount: 20,000 - 200,000 USD
Samples: Harlem RBI (New York, NY)—for general operating support, $100,000; Partnership with Children (New York, NY)—for general support, $150,000.
Contact: Charles Hamilton, Executive Director; (212) 977-6900
Sponsor: Clark Foundation
1 Rockefeller Plaza, 31st Floor
New York, NY 10020

Claude Worthington Benedum Foundation Grants 445
Grants are made in the areas of education, health and human services, community and economic development, environment, and the arts. Grants have been awarded to support education reform, teacher education, higher education, workforce development, rural health, professional developing in healthcare, human services, affordable housing, and economic development. Grants are awarded to organizations in West Virginia and southwestern Pennsylvania. Funds are provided for general operations for projects, sometimes including building and equipment, in West Virginia, and for projects in Pittsburgh that address regional problems and needs, that establish demonstration projects with strong potential for replication in West Virginia, or make outstanding contributions to the area. Additional types of support include matching funds, consulting services, technical assistance, capital campaigns, conferences and seminars, research, and seed grants. Organizations wishing to apply should request a copy of the annual report, which includes application guidelines. Applications may be submitted at any time; the board meets for review in March, June, September, and December.
Requirements: Southwestern Pennsylvania and West Virginia nonprofit organizations may apply.
Restrictions: Support is not given for national health and welfare campaigns, medical research, religious activities, fellowships, scholarships, annual campaigns, or travel.
Geographic Focus: Pennsylvania, West Virginia
Contact: Margaret M. Martin, Grants Administrator; (800) 223-5948 or (412) 246-3636; (412) 288-0366; mmartin@benedum.org
Internet: http://www.benedum.org/pages.cfm?id=10
Sponsor: Claude Worthington Benedum Foundation
1400 Benedum-Trees Building, 223 Fourth Avenue
Pittsburgh, PA 15222

Clayton Baker Trust Grants 446
The trust awards grants to Maryland nonprofit organizations for programs targeting the disadvantaged, with an emphasis on the needs of children. Grants are awarded nationally in the areas of environmental protection, population control, arms control, and nuclear disarmament. Types of support include general operating support, seed grants, and special projects.
Requirements: Nonprofit organizations in Maryland are eligible to apply.
Restrictions: Grants do not support the arts, research, higher educational institutions, individuals, building construction/renovation, or endowment funding.
Geographic Focus: Maryland
Date(s) Application is Due: Apr 5; Aug 5; Dec 5
Amount: 2,000 - 100,000 USD
Contact: John Powell, Jr., Executive Director; (410) 837-3555; (410) 837-7711
Sponsor: Clayton Baker Trust
2 East Read Street, Suite 100
Baltimore, MD 21202

Cleveland-Cliffs Foundation Grants 447
Contributions are made to nonprofit organizations to enhance the quality of life of Cleveland-Cliffs Inc employees and in recognition of a corporate responsibility toward educational, health, welfare, civic, and cultural matters within the communities where the company operates. The foundation was formed for the purpose of making contributions to groups organized and operated exclusively for religious, charitable, scientific, literary, or educational purposes and for the prevention of cruelty to children or animals. Types of support include general operating support, annual campaigns, capital campaigns, building/renovation, professorships, scholarship funds, research, and employee matching gifts. The foundation's major emphasis is on supporting education through a matching gift program and direct contributions to educational institutions. Requests for support must be in writing.
Requirements: Nonprofit organizations in the mining communities in which Cleveland-Cliffs Inc operates, including Alabama, Michigan, Minnesota, Ohio and, West Virginia are eligible.
Geographic Focus: Alabama, Michigan, Minnesota, Ohio, West Virginia
Amount: 250 - 50,000 USD
Samples: Bell Memorial Hospital, Ishpeming, MI, $400,000 (2008); University of Saint Thomas, Minneapolis, MN, $10,000 (2008); Michigan Tech Fund, Houghton, MI, $9,550 (2008).
Contact: Dana W. Byrne, Vice President; (216) 694-5700; (216) 694-4880; publicrelations@cleveland-cliffs.com
Internet: http://www.cliffsnaturalresources.com/Development/CommunityRelations/Pages/Cleveland-CliffsFoundation.aspx
Sponsor: Cleveland-Cliffs Foundation
1100 Superior Avenue, Suite 1500
Cleveland, OH 44114-2589

Clorox Company Foundation Grants 448
The Foundation makes grants primarily in its headquarters community of Oakland, California. Clorox manufacturing plants operate small giving programs in their local communities. These programs are administered independently and serve a three- to five-mile radius of the facility. The Foundation concentrates on two focus areas: education/youth development and culture/civic programs. The Foundation may shift funding priorities from year to year.
Requirements: Must be a 501(c)3 nonprofit organization located in Oakland, California.
Restrictions: In general, the Foundation does not fund the following: fund-raising events; athletic events or league sponsorships; field trips, tours and travel expenses; advertising or promotional sponsorships; benefit or raffle tickets; conferences, conventions, meetings; media productions; projects of a national scope; direct assistance to individuals or individual sponsorships; religious-based activities for the purpose of furthering religious doctrine; political parties, organizations, candidates or activities; exclusive membership organizations; association or membership dues; deficits or retroactive funding; capital projects; individual school projects.
Geographic Focus: California
Date(s) Application is Due: Jul 1; Oct 1; Jan 1; Apr 1
Contact: Victoria Jones, Community Relations Manager; (510) 836-3223; cloroxfndt@eastbaycf.org
Internet: http://www.thecloroxcompany.com/community/guidelines.html
Sponsor: Clorox Company Foundation
De Domenico Building, 200 Frank Ogawa Plaza
Oakland, CA 94612

Clowes Fund Grants 449
Funding is concentrated in the states of Indiana, Washington, Massachusetts, and parts of northern New England. Program interest areas and priorities vary among the different geographic areas: Washington—the arts and art education in the greater Seattle area; Indiana—social services and education in greater Indianapolis (Marion County and the seven surrounding counties), education focus is on primary and secondary schools with an emphasis on classroom instruction; Massachusetts (greater Boston area)—arts, education, and social services. In the area of social services (applicable in Indiana, Massachusetts, and northern New England) the current priority is for projects or programs that address the needs of immigrant and refugee populations, and/or workforce development. Types of support include capacity building, capital, challenge, matching operating, project/program, and seed grants. Requests for funding are limited to one request per organization per calendar year. Organizations that have no prior or recent (within the past five years) grant relationship with the fund must submit a Preliminary Proposal to be considered for funding. Guidelines and application are available online.
Requirements: Nonprofit organizations in northern New England and the metropolitan Indianapolis, IN; Boston, MA; and metropolitan Seattle, WA, areas are eligible.
Restrictions: The fund does not make grants to individuals or for publications, conferences, videos, or seminars. No grants are made to organizations in foreign countries. No grants are made for programs promoting specific religious doctrine. The fund will not accept unsolicited proposals from any organization for operating support. The fund will not accept unsolicited proposals of any sort from colleges and universities.
Geographic Focus: Connecticut, Indiana, Maine, Massachusetts, New Hampshire, Rhode Island, Vermont, Washington
Date(s) Application is Due: Nov 1; Jan 31

Amount: 10,000 - 50,000 USD
Samples: Alternatives for Community & Environment, Roxbury, Massachusetts, $15,000; Indiana Latino Institute, Indianapolis, Indiana, $10,000; Girls Incorporated of Indianapolis, Indiana, $100,000.
Contact: Elizabeth Casselman, Program Manager; (800) 943-7209 or (317) 833-0144; (317) 833-0145; staff@clowesfund.org
Internet: http://www.clowesfund.org/index.asp?p=3
Sponsor: Clowes Fund
320 N Meridian, Suite 316
Indianapolis, IN 46204

CMA Foundation Grants **450**
The foundation seeks to improve the quality of life for central Ohio residents through the promotion of wellness, prevention of disease, and delivery of services and research. The foundation will review funding requests for matching or challenge grants, multiyear commitments, and capital expenditures on a project-by-project basis. The foundation is the leading local source of funding for health care projects benefiting the local community. Application may be made online.
Requirements: Nonprofit organizations in central Ohio, including Franklin, Delaware, Fairfield, Licking, Madison, Pickaway, and Union Counties, are eligible.
Geographic Focus: Ohio
Samples: Children's Hunger Alliance (Columbus, OH)—to promote school-breakfast programs, $30,000; Educational Council Foundation (Columbus, OH)—to train middle- and high-school educators to provide information about positive health behaviors, $50,000 maximum; Franklin County Health Dept (Columbus, OH)—to expand its anti-tobacco activities, $30,000 maximum; Mount Carmel Health Systems Foundation (Columbus, OH)—to provide education, information, and self-care skills training to people who have experienced heart failure, $90,000.
Contact: Program Contact; (614) 240-7410; yourthoughts@goodhealthcolumbus.org
Internet: http://www.cmaf-ohio.org/cmaf/grants.html
Sponsor: Columbus Medical Association Foundation
431 E Broad Street
Columbus, OH 43215

CNA Foundation Grants **451**
The CNA Foundation concentrates its support primarily in programs designed to: meet the education needs of children, assist and support children, youth and adults in developing vocational skills. Support economically disadvantaged children and families. Requests for funding are accepted year-round. However, grants will be made only in accordance with the Foundation's budgetary guidelines. Proposals must be clear and brief. The Foundation will contact the organization if more information is needed.
Requirements: IRS 501(c)3 tax-exempt organizations are eligible.
Restrictions: Grants are not made to/for individuals; political causes, candidates, or organizations; veterans, labor, alumni, military, athletic clubs, or social clubs; sectarian organizations or denominational religious organizations; capital improvement or building projects; endowed chairs or professorships; United Way-affiliated agencies; or national groups whose local chapters have already received support.
Geographic Focus: All U.S. States
Amount: 10,000 - 250,000 USD
Samples: Chicago 2016 Exploratory Committee, Chicago, IL, $250,000; National Chamber Foundation, Washington, DC, $100,000; Starlight Starbright Childrens Foundation Midwest, Chicago, IL, $50,000.
Contact: Marlene Rotstein, Director; (312) 822-7065; marlene.rotstein@cna.com or cna_foundation@cna.com
Internet: http://www.cna.com/portal/site/cna/menuitem.7204aaf0316757e8715f09f6556631a0/?vgnextoid=b1e940fa11056010VgnVCM1000005566130aRCRD
Sponsor: CNA Foundation
333 South Wabash Avenue
Chicago, IL 60604

CNCS Foster Grandparent Projects Grants **452**
Dual purposes of the program are to provide part-time volunteer service opportunities for income-eligible persons age 60 and over and to give supportive person-to-person service in health, education, human services, and related settings to help address the physical, mental, and emotional needs of infants, children, or youth having special or exceptional needs. The grants may be used for low-income foster grandparent stipends, transportation, physical examinations, and meals; staff salaries and fringe benefits; staff travel; equipment; and space costs; etc. An amount equal to 90 percent of the federal share must be used for foster grandparent direct benefits. Assignment of foster grandparents to children and youth may occur in residential and nonresidential facilities including preschool establishments and to children living in their own homes. In addition, eligible agencies or organizations may, under a Memorandum of Agreement with the Corporation for National Service, receive technical assistance and materials to aid in establishing and operating a noncorporation-funded foster grandparent program project using local funds.
Requirements: Grants are made only to state and local government agencies and private nonprofit organizations.
Restrictions: Volunteers are not to supplant hiring or displace employed workers or impair existing contracts for service. No agency supervising volunteers shall request or receive compensation for services of the volunteers. Volunteers are not to be involved in and funds are not to be used for religious activities, labor or antilabor organization, lobbying, or partisan or nonpartisan political activities.
Geographic Focus: All U.S. States
Amount: 12,000 - 19,000,000 USD
Contact: Ruth Archie, Foster Grandparent Program, National Senior Service Corps; (202) 606-5000, ext. 289 or (800) 424-8867; rarchie@cns.gov
Internet: http://www.nationalservice.gov/about/search/search_results.asp?strSearchWords=foster%20grandparent
Sponsor: Corporation for National and Community Service
1201 New York Avenue NW
Washington, DC 20525

Coastal Bend Community Foundation Grants **453**
The community foundation awards grants to nonprofit organizations in the Aransas, Bee, Jim Wells, Kleberg, Nueces, Refugio and San Patricio counties of Texas. Grants are usually made to provide seed money for innovative and start-up programs that will generate additional future funding or revenues. Capital projects will also receive favorable consideration. The board of directors approves grant recipients in early November after considering recommendations presented by the Grants Committee. Areas of interest include alcohol and drug abuse, libraries and literacy, arts and culture, higher and other education, adult basic education, child welfare, hospitals, community development, animal welfare, human services, and general charitable giving. Grants are awarded for general operating support, program and project development, equipment, seed money, scholarship funds, and fellowships. Application forms are not required.
Requirements: Nonprofit organizations in Texas in Aransas, Bee, Jim Wells, Kleberg, Nueces, Refugio, and San Patricio counties, may submit grant proposals.
Geographic Focus: Texas
Date(s) Application is Due: Sep 1
Amount: 250 - 50,000 USD
Samples: Texas A&M U (Corpus Christi, TX)—for program support, $10,000;HIV/AIDS Housing Ctr (Corpus Christi, TX)—for operating support, $12,500.
Contact: Jim Moloney, Executive Vice President; (361) 882-9745; (361) 882-2865; jmoloney@cbcfoundation.org
Internet: http://www.cbcfoundation.org/grant.html
Sponsor: Coastal Bend Community Foundation
600 Building, Suite 1716
Corpus Christi, TX 78473

Coastal Community Foundation of South Carolina Grants **454**
The foundation awards grants to South Carolina nonprofit organizations in its areas of interest, including arts and culture, education, environment, health, religion, justice and equity, and social services. Types of support include general operating support, emergency funds, program development, publication, seed money, scholarship funds, and technical assistance. Deadlines vary per program; check website for exact dates.
Requirements: 501(c)3 South Carolina nonprofits located in the following coastal counties are eligible to apply: Beaufort, Berkeley, Charleston, Colleton, Dorchester, Georgetown, Hampton and Jasper.
Restrictions: Grants do not support individuals (except for designated scholarship funds), endowments, deficit financing, dinners, and rarely building funds.
Geographic Focus: South Carolina

Date(s) Application is Due: Jun 1
Amount: 500 - 10,000 USD
Samples: To each, a $15,000 annual grant for 3 years: Boys & Girls Clubs for Rural Units; Child Abuse Prevention Association; Citizens Opposed to Domestic Abuse; Colleton County Arts Council; Friends of Caroline Hospice; Hope Haven of the Lowcountry (formerly Hope Cottage); Literacy Volunteers of the Lowcountry; Lowcountry Food Bank; Second Helpings;.
Contact: George C. Stevens, President-CEO; (843) 723-3635; (843) 577-3671; gstevens@tcfgives.org or info@ccfgives.org
Internet: http://www.ccfgives.org
Sponsor: Coastal Community Foundation of South Carolina
90 Mary Street
Charleston, SC 29403

Cobb Family Foundation Grants **455**
The foundation awards grants to Florida nonprofits in its areas of interest, including community development, higher and secondary education, libraries, Protestant religion, recreation, and zoos. Grants are awarded primarily in Dade County.
Requirements: Nonprofit organizations in Florida are eligible to apply.
Geographic Focus: Florida
Amount: Up to 525,319 USD
Contact: Charles Cobb Jr., (305) 441-1700; (305) 445-5674
Sponsor: Cobb Family Foundation
355 Alhambra Circle, Suite 1500
Coral Gables, FL 33134

Coca-Cola Foundation Grants **456**
The foundation has established education as its philanthropic focus and set aside most of its funds to support educational initiatives that address pressing needs. To help prepare youth for life, the foundation gives in three areas: higher education—pipeline programs that connect various levels of education and help students stay in school, scholarships, and minority advancement; classroom teaching and learning—innovative K-12 projects, teacher development, and small projects that deal with classroom activities; and global education—projects that encourage international studies, global understanding, and student exchange. Grants are awarded to both public and private institutions at all levels of education: universities, colleges, and secondary and elementary schools. International educational institutions and health care organizations also receive consideration. Types of support include annual campaigns, donated equipment, employee matching gifts, operating budgets, special projects, capital campaigns, continuing support, fellowships, internships, endowment funds, matching funds, and scholarship funds. Proposals may be submitted at any time.
Requirements: The following are eligible to apply: IRS 501(c)3 non-profits; a foreign organization that has received a ruling from the IRS that it is a section 501(c)3 tax exempt organization; or a foreign organization that is the equivalent of a U.S. charity.
Restrictions: The foundation does not make grants to individuals, religious endeavors, political or fraternal organizations, or organizations without 501(c)3 status.
Geographic Focus: All U.S. States
Amount: 10,000 - 6,000,000 USD
Samples: Holyfield Foundation, Inc., Fairburn, GA, $75,000—contribution to the Giving Disadvantaged Youth a Fighting Chance scholarship program; United Way of Metropolitan Atlanta, Atlanta, GA, $15,000—support for Samaritan House, Impact Group and Atlanta Union Mission; Atlanta Children's Shelter, Inc., Atlanta, GA, $10,000—contribution to support shelter programs.
Contact: Helen Smith Price, Executive Director; (404) 676-2568; (404) 676-8804
Internet: http://www.thecoca-colacompany.com/citizenship/our_communities.html
Sponsor: Coca-Cola Foundation
P.O. Box 1734
Atlanta, GA 30301

Coeta and Donald Barker Foundation Grants **457**
The foundation awards grants to California and Oregon nonprofit organizations in its areas of interest, including arts, children and youth, community development, disabled, environmental conservation, family services, federated giving, health care and health organizations, heart and circulatory research, higher education, hospitals, mental health, and secondary school education. Types of support include building construction/renovation, equipment acquisition, general operating support, program development, and scholarship funds.
Requirements: California and Oregon nonprofit organizations are eligible.
Restrictions: Grants do not support sectarian religious purposes, federal and tax-dependent organizations, individuals, or endowment funds.
Geographic Focus: California, Oregon
Date(s) Application is Due: Mar 1; Aug 1
Amount: 100 - 20,450 USD
Samples: Santa Barbara Zoological Gardens (Santa Barbara, CA), $5000.
Contact: Nancy Harris, Executive Administrator; (760) 324-2656; (760) 321-8662
Sponsor: Coeta and Donald Barker Foundation
P.O. Box 936
Rancho Mirage, CA 92270

Colgate-Palmolive Company Grants **458**
Nonprofit organizations with IRS tax-exempt status located primarily in the U.S. tristate area of New York, New Jersey, and Connecticut and in locations of foreign subsidiaries may apply for support of programs that are directed toward youth, women, minorities, education, health and welfare, culture and arts, and civic and community activities. Priority will be given to programs that address the educational needs of youth and minorities. Types of support include program grants, scholarships, general support grants, multiyear support, and employee matching gifts. Proposals are accepted at any time and should include information on the organization, purpose of request, proof of tax-exempt status, and current operating budget.
Geographic Focus: All U.S. States
Samples: American Public Health Assoc (Washington, DC)—for program support, $1 million over five years; Boys and Girls Club of Milwaukee (Milwaukee, WI)—to implement a youth credit union run by and for members, $1000; Star Seekers 4-H Club (Bartlett, IL)—to form a sister club for residents of a learning center for disabled children, $1000.
Contact: Sally Phills, Contributions Administrator; (212) 310-2000; (212) 310-2873; sally_phipps@colpal.com
Internet: http://www.colgate.com/app/Colgate/U.S. /Corp/CommunityPrograms/HomePage.cvsp
Sponsor: Colgate-Palmolive Company
300 Park Avenue
New York, NY 10022

Colin Higgins Foundation Grants **459**
The foundation supports organizations that help people respond to a variety of life challenges, with a focus on responding to the AIDS pandemic by supporting innovative programs in the areas of education, service, and advocacy for people infected, affected, and at risk for HIV; and empowering lesbian, gay, bisexual, and transgender peoples by supporting community-based organizations that combat homophobia and foster leadership. The foundation is particularly interested in organizations that have a significant impact working in underserved, rural areas with traditionally underserved constituencies. The process of applying consists of two stages: submission of a letter of inquiry, and, if requested, a full proposal.
Requirements: The foundation only considers organizations with overall budgets under $2 million, or project budgets under $500,000.
Restrictions: Grants do not support projects that had previously fallen within its funding priorities, including any organizations or programs based in urban areas (population over 1 million); film and video projects; or organizations with overall budgets of over $2 million, or project budgets over $500,000. The one exception to the exclusion of programs in urban areas is those organizations and projects working with underserved communities (i.e., communities of color, low-income communities, transgender people, etc.). The foundation does not accept letters of inquiry from universities, schools, individuals, or corporations. It does not support political or legislative activities, endowments, or deficit budgets. Additionally, the foundation does not support capital campaigns, although it will consider requests for capital improvements, and does not award grants to organizations outside the United States.
Geographic Focus: All U.S. States
Date(s) Application is Due: Jul 1
Amount: 5,000 - 15,000 USD
Samples: Iowa Pride Network, Des Moines, IA, $10,000—general support (2008); Out Youth, Austin, TX, $15,000—Texas Gay-Straight Alliance Network (2008); Equality Florida, Street Petersburg, FL, $15,000—Youth Voices for Equality (2008).

Contact: Administrator; (212) 509-4975; (212) 509-1059; info@colinhiggins.org
Internet: http://www.colinhiggins.org/grantmaking/index.cfm
Sponsor: Colin Higgins Foundation
55 Exchange Place, Suite 402
New York, NY 10005

Collins C. Diboll Private Foundation Grants 460

The foundation awards grants to Louisiana nonprofit organizations in the areas of higher education, human services, and youth. Field of interest include: Catholic churches and agencies; education; higher education; human services; museums (art); and protestant agencies and churches. Types of support include building construction/renovation, capital campaigns, endowment funds, and general operating support. Applicants should submit a detailed description of the project and the amount of funding requested, along with a copy of an IRS determination letter.
Requirements: Louisiana nonprofit organizations are eligible.
Restrictions: Individuals are not eligible to apply.
Geographic Focus: Louisiana
Amount: 500 - 200,000 USD
Samples: Alton Ochsner Medical Foundation (New Orleans, LA)—for Golden Jubilee/Initiative Campaign, $100,000; New Orleans Museum of Art (New Orleans, LA)—$100,000; Junior Achievement of New Orleans (New Orleans, LA)—$35,000; Preservation Resource Ctr of New Orleans (New Orleans, LA)—for renovations, $11,000.
Contact: Donald W. Diboll, Chair; (504) 582-8103
Sponsor: Collins C. Diboll Private Foundation
201 Saint Charles Avenue, 50th Floor
New Orleans, LA 70170-5100

Collins Foundation Grants 461

Grants are awarded to organizations in Oregon with emphasis on higher education, youth and health agencies, social welfare, natural resource and wildlife conservation, religion, and arts and cultural programs. A special area of support includes building and medical equipment, and programs for those who are physically or mentally disabled. Challenge/matching grants, general operating support, scholarships, and internships also are awarded. Applications may be submitted at any time, additional guidelines are available at the Foundation's website.
Requirements: Grants are made to 501(c)3 nonprofit agencies domiciled in Oregon. The proposed project must directly benefit the citizens of Oregon.
Restrictions: Grants are not made to individuals or to organizations sponsoring requests intended to be used by or for the benefit of an individual. Grants normally are not made to elementary, secondary, or public higher education institutions; or to individual religious congregations. Grants normally are not made for development office personnel, annual fundraising activities, endowments, operational deficits, financial emergencies, or debt retirement.
Geographic Focus: Oregon
Samples: Portland Reading Foundation, Portland, OR, $9,000—support a literacy program in two inner-city elementary schools to advance students reading skills to grade level (2008); Children's Community Clinic, Portland, OR, $25,000—provide healthcare services for low-income children (2008); The Nature Conservancy, Portland, OR, $450,000 (3 year grant)—acquire and conserve six areas identified as the agency's highest priorities (2008).
Contact: Cynthia Knowles, Director of Programs; (503) 227-7171; (503) 295-3794; information@collinsfoundation.org
Internet: http://www.collinsfoundation.org/submission-guidelines
Sponsor: Collins Foundation
1618 South West First Avenue, Suite 505
Portland, OR 97201

Colonel Stanley R. McNeil Foundation Grants 462

Colonel Stanley R. McNeil and his wife Merna created the Colonel Stanley R. McNeil Foundation in 1993 to support and promote quality educational, human-services, and health-care programming for underserved populations. Special consideration is given to charitable organizations that serve the needs of children. During their lifetimes, the McNeils were actively involved in their local church and community. Colonel McNeil also served on a number of boards, including Lake Bluff Children's Home and Ravenswood Hospital. Although the McNeils had no children, they were strong supporters of children's causes. The foundation is particularly interested in funding programs or organizations that focus on children's causes, start-up initiatives within the human-services or arts and culture arenas, and healthcare. To better support the capacity of nonprofit organizations, multi-year funding requests are considered. Grant requests for naming opportunities that honor the donors are strongly encouraged. Applicants must apply online at the grant website. Applicants are strongly encouraged to do the following before applying: review the downloadable state application procedures for additional helpful information and clarifications; review the downloadable online-application guidelines at the grant website; review the foundation's funding history (link is available from the grant website); review the online application questions in advance; and review the list of required attachments. These will generally include: a list of board members, financial statements (audited, reviewed, or compiled by independent auditor); an organization summary; a list of other funding sources; an IRS Determination letter; and other required documents. All attachments must be uploaded in the online application as PDF, Word, or Excel files. The Colonel Stanley R. McNeil Foundation has biannual deadlines of February 1 and June 1. Applications must be submitted by 11:59 p.m. on the deadline dates. Applicants for the February deadline will be notified of grant decisions by June 30. Applicants for the June deadline will be notified by November 30.
Requirements: Illinois nonprofit organizations serving the Chicago metropolitan area are eligible.
Restrictions: Because requests for support usually exceed available resources, organizations can only apply to either the Lang Burk Fund or the Colonel Stanley McNeil Foundation in the same calendar year. Grant requests to both foundations during the same calendar year will no longer be accepted. The Foundation will consider requests for general operations only if the organization's operating budget is less than $1 million. In general, grant request for individuals, endowment campaigns or capital projects will not be considered.
Geographic Focus: Illinois
Date(s) Application is Due: Feb 1; Jun 1
Samples: Gads Hill Center, Chicago, Illinois, $35,000 (2010); Field Museum of Natural History, Chicago, Illinois, $50,000 (2010); Organic School Project, Chicago, Illinois, $35,000 (2010).
Contact: George Thorn, Vice President; (312) 828-4154; ilgrantmaking@bankofamerica.com
Internet: https://www.bankofamerica.com/philanthropic/fn_search.action
Sponsor: Colonel Stanley R. McNeil Foundation
231 South LaSalle Street, IL1-231-13-32
Chicago, IL 60604

Colorado Council on the Arts Grants for Artists and Organizations 463

The purpose of this grant is to support arts and cultural activities that directly address one or more of the Council's goals. Make the arts more accessible to all Coloradoans; expand access to quality arts education for young people; participate in local and regional economic development; preserve and promote cultural heritage; assist and encourage artists and art organizations; strengthen the financial stability of the arts industry; recognize diversity and inclusiveness; encourage artistic excellence and support freedom of artistic expression.
Requirements: Applicants must be Colorado artists, nonprofit organizations, educational institutions or government agencies that meet one of the following eligibility criteria: (1) an individual who has been a full-time resident of Colorado for at least three (3) consecutive years prior to application deadline; (2) an organization that has been providing public programs in Colorado for at least three (3) consecutive years by application deadline and is a Colorado-based nonprofit tax-exempt 501(c)3 organization by application deadline; (religious or sectarian organizations are excluded from eligibility by Article 9, Section 7 of the Colorado Constitution); or an agency of government in Colorado. Schools or school districts are not eligible unless they are collaborating with an arts organization or an artist on the proposal; (3) a partnership of two or more individually identified entities that undertake a shared project which requires combining capital and human resources. The lead applicant must meet one of the previously stated eligibility criteria. A key requirement of the program is that applicants must have a minimum dollar-for-dollar cash match. Proposed programs must align with one of four categories: Learning in the Arts for Children and Youth, Increasing Cultural Participation in Communities, Preserving and Promoting Our Cultural Heritage, or Professional Development Services.
Restrictions: Only online applications will be accepted. You must hit the submit button by 11:59 p.m. on the deadline date. Current recipients of the YouthReach Colorado Grant are not eligible. The recipient of public funds must provide assurances of compliance with all state and federal laws and regulations pertaining to fair labor standards, nondiscrimination, audit, drug free workplace, fair language, handicapped access and credit/acknowledgment.

Geographic Focus: Colorado
Date(s) Application is Due: Mar 15
Amount: 2,000 - 25,000 USD
Samples: City of Delta (Delta, CO)—for marketing of Council Tree Pow Wow and Cultural Festival through all media, $7000; Greeley Rodarte Dancers (Greeley, CO)—for dance instruction and performances to strengthen at-risk Hispanic youth and families by promoting cultural pride in Colorado's Latino and Indian heritages, $11,250.
Contact: Elaine Mariner, Executive Director; (303) 892-3870; elaine.mariner@state.co.us
Internet: http://www.coloarts.state.co.us/grants/apply/index.htm
Sponsor: Colorado Council on the Arts
1625 Broadway, Suite 2700
Denver, CO 80202

Colorado Interstate Gas Grants 464

Nonprofits in communities served by the company are eligible to apply for grants in the categories of education, including early child development, K-12, and higher education; civic; health and welfare; minorities; cultural programs; environmental programs, particularly those focusing on air quality; and youth groups that concentrate on improving areas where CIG employees live and work. The company also supports special event sponsorships, corporate memberships, joint projects with other organizations, and employee participation in volunteer activities.
Requirements: Colorado, Wyoming, Texas, Utah, and Kansas 501(c)3 tax-exempt organizations where the company has pipelines are eligible.
Geographic Focus: Colorado
Date(s) Application is Due: Aug 1
Amount: 200 - 20,000 USD
Contact: Richard Wheatley, Media Relations; (713) 420-6828
Internet: http://www.cigco.com
Sponsor: Colorado Interstate Gas Company
P.O. Box 1087
Colorado Springs, CO 80944

Colorado Renewables in Performance Contracting Grants 465

The purpose of the program is to reduce the cost of incorporating renewable energy into a performance contract to the extent that the system fits within an acceptable payback period for the entire project. Additionally, this incentive is designed to promote renewable technology after, or in conjunction with, energy efficiency upgrades. The funding for this grant will be allocated on a first come, first serve basis and is a 100% matching grant.
Requirements: Organizations that are in the process of executing a performance contract, or have completed one within the last 5 years may be eligible to receive up to $25,000 in matching grant funds from the Governor's Energy Office (GEO) to add renewable energy technology to its facility. The organization's energy service company or a professional solar installer must complete the application and submit it electronically. The application form can be downloaded at the program website.
Geographic Focus: Colorado
Amount: Up to 25,000 USD
Contact: Sean Mandel, Development Manager; (303) 866-2407; (303) 866-2930; Sean.mandel@state.co.us
Internet: http://www.colorado.gov/energy/resources/funding-opportunities.asp#RenewPC
Sponsor: Colorado Governor's Energy Office
1580 Logan Street, Suite 100
Denver, CO 80203

Columbia Foundation Grants 466

The foundation currently has three program areas: arts and culture, human rights, and sustainable communities and economies. Types of support include general operating support, program development, publication, seed money, and research. Multiyear grants are made on occasion. A complete application includes application, one-page proposal summary, proposal not to exceed five pages, budgets, funding sources, board of directors, certificate of tax-exempt status, and other descriptive materials. The board of directors generally meets twice a year to consider grant applications. Applicants should submit a one- to two-page inquiry letter with cover sheet. Proposals are invited from the foundation. The deadline is May 1 for arts and culture grants; August 1 for human rights grants; and December 1 for sustainable communities and economies grants. Annual deadlines may vary; contact program staff for exact dates.
Requirements: The foundation considers proposals only from organizations certified by the IRS as public charities. Priority will be given to applications from the San Francisco Bay, CA, area. International grants support the arts in London.
Restrictions: The foundation does not customarily provide support for operating budgets of established agencies, recurring expenses for direct services or ongoing administrative costs, individual fellowships or scholarships, or agencies wholly supported by federated campaigns or heavily subsidized by government funds.
Geographic Focus: California, United Kingdom
Date(s) Application is Due: May 1; Aug 1; Dec 1
Amount: 25,000 - 100,000 USD
Samples: Royal National Theatre (London, England)—for the world premiere of The Talking Cure, a new play about Sigmund Freud and Carl Jung by leading United Kingdom playwright Christopher Hampton, $50,000; Gender Public Advocacy Coalition (Washington, DC)—to support its work to end gender-based stereotypes, discrimination and violence at the national level, $25,000; Ctr for Food Safety (Washington, DC)—for the California Food and Agriculture Initiative, to establish and staff a California office to focus on legal issues, policy initiatives, and a statewide public-education campaign about the opportunities for California to make the transition to sustainable food systems, $40,000.
Contact: Susan Clark, Executive Director; (415) 561-6880; (415) 561-6883; info@columbia.org
Internet: http://www.columbia.org
Sponsor: Columbia Foundation
P.O. Box 29470
San Francisco, CA 94129

Columbus Foundation Central Benefits Health Care Foundation Grants 467

The Foundation was established in 1997 with a focus on preventative health care for indigent children and adults; the Trustees have taken a step further by focusing grantmaking for the preventative health care needs of children, prenatal through age six. Proposals for funding are accepted at anytime. Funding is limited to the central Ohio area, giving primarily in Columbus, Ohio.
Requirements: Central Ohio, tax-exempt organizations are eligible to apply.
Restrictions: Individuals are ineligible.
Geographic Focus: Ohio
Samples: Ohio Health Foundation, Columbus, OH, $350,000—health care grant (2008)
Contact: Tamera Durrence, Assistant Vice President and Director of Supporting Foundations; (614) 251-4000; (614) 251-4009; tdurrence@columbusfoundation.org
Internet: http://www.columbusfoundation.org/find/support/cenben_usa.aspx
Sponsor: Columbus Foundation
1234 E Broad Street
Columbus, OH 43205

Columbus Foundation Community Arts Fund Grants 468

The Community Arts Fund (CAF) helps provide central Ohioans with a rich diversity of art and cultural activities by providing operating support to small and medium-sized arts organizations. These organizations make contributions to the ethnic and artistic diversity of the arts and increase access to the arts at a community level. To qualify, organizations must have annual budgets of less than $350,000 and have been in existence for at least two years. A Letter of Intent (LOI) is required as the first step in the application process. The LOI will give an opportunity to provide an overview of the organization's mission and funding request. Timely feedback will be received about whether a request is competitive to move to full proposal submission. All LOIs and full proposals must be submitted using the online grantmaking process.
Requirements: Central Ohio, tax-exempt public charities under Section 501(c)3 of the Internal Revenue Service Code may submit grant requests.
Restrictions: Individuals are ineligible. Requests for religious purposes, budget deficits, endowments, conferences, scholarly research, or projects that are normally the responsibility of a public agency are generally not funded. Funding is not available for projects when funds are available elsewhere.
Samples:
Geographic Focus: Ohio
Date(s) Application is Due: Nov 5

Samples: Worthington Arts Council—$10,302 (2008); Columbus Music and Arts Academy—$5,980 (2008); Little Theatre Off Broadway, Inc.—$6,121 (2008).
Contact: Sandi Smith, Senior Community Research and Grants Management Officer; (614) 251-4000; (614) 251-4009; ssmith@columbusfoundation.org
Internet: http://www.columbusfoundation.org/gogrants/innovative_operations/arts_culture.aspx
Sponsor: Columbus Foundation
1234 E Broad Street
Columbus, OH 43205

Columbus Foundation Competitive Grants **469**
The foundation's competitive grants are made in the following fields: advancing philanthropy, arts and humanities, conservation, education, health, social services, and urban affairs. The Governing Committee approves distributions from unrestricted and field of interest funds through competitive grants. Competitive grants are the most common way nonprofit organizations request funding from the Foundation. Submit a Letter of Intent or a Full Proposal by accessing our online grant application system.
Requirements: Central Ohio, tax-exempt public charities under Section 501(c)3 of the Internal Revenue Service Code may submit grant requests.
Restrictions: Individuals are ineligible. Requests for religious purposes, budget deficits, endowments, conferences, scholarly research, or projects that are normally the responsibility of a public agency are generally not funded. Funding is not available for projects when funds are available elsewhere.
Geographic Focus: Ohio
Contact: Emily Savors, Director; (614) 251-4000; (614) 251-4009; esavors@columbusfoundation.org
Internet: http://www.columbusfoundation.org/gogrants/index.aspx
Sponsor: Columbus Foundation
1234 E Broad Street
Columbus, OH 43205

Columbus Foundation Major Arts Organizations Grants **470**
The Foundation accepts applications from regional Arts organizations with budgets at or above $350,000 per year. Criteria for awarding grants to major art organizations include the following: financial stability; attendance; inclusiveness; artistic quality; leadership; and overall administration. A Letter of Intent (LOI) is required as the first step in the application process. The LOI will give an opportunity to provide an overview of the organization's mission and funding request. Timely feedback will be received about whether a request is competitive to move to full proposal submission. All LOIs and full proposals must be submitted using the online grantmaking process. Organizations that have never received funding must contact Sandi Smith by email or at (614) 251-4000 prior to applying for arts funding. The deadline for arts proposals is the first Friday in November.
Requirements: Central Ohio, tax-exempt public charities under Section 501(c)3 of the Internal Revenue Service Code may submit grant requests.
Restrictions: Individuals are ineligible. Requests for religious purposes, budget deficits, endowments, conferences, scholarly research, or projects that are normally the responsibility of a public agency are generally not funded. Funding is not available for projects when funds are available elsewhere.
Geographic Focus: Ohio
Date(s) Application is Due: Nov 6
Contact: Sandi Smith, Senior Community Research and Grants Management Officer; (614) 251-4000; (614) 251-4009; ssmith@columbusfoundation.org
Internet: http://www.columbusfoundation.org/gogrants/innovative_operations/arts_culture.aspx
Sponsor: Columbus Foundation
1234 E Broad Street
Columbus, OH 43205

Columbus Foundation Traditional Grants **471**
The Traditional Grants creates quality opportunities and meets community need by focusing on three areas: Basic Needs funds programs and projects that provide food, shelter, and clothing. Priority will be given to programs and projects that meet current needs and simultaneously integrate services designed to support long-term stability; Disadvantaged Children funds programs and projects that meet the diverse needs of at-risk children. Priority will be given to programs and projects that are in the home, build relationships with the family, and create a support network around and for the families of disadvantaged children; Developmental Disabilities funds programs and projects that address the needs of children and adults with physical or cognitive disabilities that impair functions or behavior and that occurred before a person reaches the age of 22. (Blindness/visual impairments and deafness/hearing impairments are not considered within this category.) If you are implementing your project in a Columbus City School building, or collaborating with the district on a project, and asked to submit a full application, you must request a letter of endorsement from the Office of Development.
Requirements: Central Ohio, tax-exempt public charities under Section 501(c)3 of the Internal Revenue Service Code may submit grant requests .If you are implementing your project in a Columbus City School building, or collaborating with the district on a project, and asked to submit a full application, you must request a letter of endorsement from the Office of Development. Letter of Intent deadlines are twice a year on the first Friday in February and September. See Foundations website for further guidelines.
Restrictions: Operating support will only be considered when the applicant demonstrates continuous innovation that enhances services.
Geographic Focus: Ohio
Date(s) Application is Due: Feb 5; Sep 3
Contact: Emily Savors, Director; (614) 251-4000; (614) 251-4009; esavors@columbusfoundation.org
Internet: http://www.columbusfoundation.org/gogrants/targeted_needs/traditional_grants.aspx
Sponsor: Columbus Foundation
1234 E Broad Street
Columbus, OH 43205

Comer Foundation Grants **472**
The foundation awards grants to U.S. nonprofits in its areas of interest, including needle-exchange programs grounded in harm-reduction practice and programs providing direct services addressing health related to drug use; education—AIDS education, job training, and career guidance for low-income groups; health, with an emphasis on AIDS; social services—temporary shelters for homeless people and organizations offering diverse child, youth, and family services; and arts, culture, and humanities—to make programs of established organizations accessible to the public at large. Types of support include operating budgets, special projects, and staff development. There are no application deadlines.
Restrictions: Individuals are ineligible for grant support.
Geographic Focus: Illinois
Date(s) Application is Due: Mar 1; Jul 1; Nov 1
Amount: 5,000 - 30,000 USD
Contact: Stephanie Comer, (415) 256-9917; (415) 256-9918; scomer@comer-foundation.org
Internet: http://www.comer-foundation.com/home.html
Sponsor: Comer Foundation
P.O. Box 78154
San Francisco, CA 94107

Commission on Religion in Appalachia Grants **473**
The commission supports Christian and interdenominational nonprofits in U.S. Appalachian regions. Churches and ministries and nonprofits in the areas of parochial education, religious welfare, civil rights, health care, and social services (domestic violence, housing, women's affairs, and food distribution) are awarded grants. The commission strongly encourages applicants to obtain guidelines prior to submitting proposals.
Requirements: Nonprofits in the Appalachian regions of Mississippi, Alabama, Georgia, South Carolina, North Carolina, Tennessee, Kentucky, Virginia, West Virginia, Ohio, Pennsylvania, Maryland, and New York are eligible.
Geographic Focus: Mississippi
Date(s) Application is Due: Jan 31
Amount: 5,000 - 15,000 USD
Contact: Grant Administrator; (304) 720-2672; (304) 720-2673; corainappa@aol.com
Internet: http://www.geocities.com/appalcora/About.html
Sponsor: Commission on Religion in Appalachia
P.O. Box 11908
Charleston, WV 25339-1908

Community Foundation for Greater Buffalo Grants **474**
The Community Foundation for Greater Buffalo (CFGB) is a public charity holding more than 800 different charitable funds, large and small, established by individuals, families, nonprofit agencies and businesses to benefit Western New York. Since 1919, the foundation has served the needs of it's community and the wishes of it's donors through personalized service, financial stewardship,

local expertise, and community leadership. The Foundation focuse's on four main areas of interest: strengthen the region as a center for arts and culture; natural, historic, and architectural resources; reduce racial and ethnic disparities; increase economic self-sufficiency for low-income individuals and families. Special funding will also be available to support the following: AIDS research and its cure ($5,000); programs that serve the visual, speech or hearing impaired ($5,000). Preference will be given to requests that align with one or more of the four focus areas.
Requirements: Applicants must be 501(c)3 not-for-profit organizations located within the eight counties of Western New York: Allegany, Cattaraugus, Chautauqua, Erie, Genesee, Niagara, Orleans, and Wyoming.
Restrictions: The Foundation will not consider competitive funding for: endowments; religious purposes; schools not registered with the New York State Education Department; attendance at or sponsorship of fundraising events for organizations; annual events or festivals; any partisan political activity. Funds from the foundation cannot be used to support or oppose a candidate for political office. Projects and activities that have occurred. The Foundation will not, except in extraordinary cases, provide payment or reimbursement for expenses incurred prior to the funding decision being communicated to the applicant.
Geographic Focus: New York
Date(s) Application is Due: Mar 1
Amount: 1,000 - 25,000 USD
Samples: Carnegie Art Center, $4,500—to support the continued restoration of the landmark Carnegie Art Center building (2009); Grassroots Gardens, $25,000—to support new community gardens that provide beautification, food and employment (2009); Youth Character Development, $9,100—to aid refugee students in the transition to formal education and encourage college enrollment (2009).
Contact: Jean McKeown, Senior Program Officer; (716) 852-2857, ext. 204; (716) 852-2861; jeanm@cfgb.org
Internet: http://www.cfgb.org/page17000.cfm
Sponsor: Community Foundation for Greater Buffalo
712 Main Street
Buffalo, NY 14202

Community Foundation for Greater New Haven $5,000 and Under Grants 475

The Community Foundation for Greater New Haven (CFFGNH) is a philanthropic institution that was established in 1928. The foundation's mission is to create positive and sustainable change in Connecticut's Greater New Haven region by increasing the amount of and enhancing the impact of community philanthropy. Funding through the CFFGNH $5,000 and Under Grants process are available to any organization with an operating budget of $2 million or less.
Requirements: IRS 501(c)3 nonprofit organizations are eligible to apply in the greater New Haven area, which includes: Ansonia; Bethany; Branford; Cheshire; Derby; East Haven; Guilford; Hamden; Madison; Milford; New Haven; North Branford; North Haven; Orange; Oxford; Seymour; Shelton; Wallingford; West Haven and; Woodbridge.
Restrictions: No organization shall be eligible to receive a grant under this process more often than once in any period of two calendar years. Grants are not made to support religious activities, lobbying, or travel.
Geographic Focus: Connecticut
Amount: 5,000 USD
Samples: Christ Episcopal Church, $5,000—to support the Kathleen Samela Memorial Food Bank (2009); Connecticut Alliance to Benefit Law Enforcement, Inc., $2,100—to support training for Hamden Fire and EMS personnel (2009); Connecticut Pre-Engineering Program, $4,000—to provide operating support for science, technology, engineering and math (STEM) enrichment programming to students in High School in the Community, East Rock, Clinton Avenue, Micro-Society and Troupe schools (2009).
Contact: Denise Canning, Grants Manager; (203) 777-2386 or (203) 777-7076; (203) 787-6584; dcanning@cfgnh.org
Internet: http://www.cfgnh.org/GrantsScholarships/TypesofGrants/tabid/199/Default.aspx
Sponsor: Community Foundation for Greater New Haven
70 Audubon Street
New Haven, CT 06510

Community Foundation for Greater New Haven Responsive New Grants 476

The Community Foundation for Greater New Haven is a philanthropic institution that was established in 1928. The foundation's mission is to create positive and sustainable change in Connecticut's Greater New Haven region by increasing the amount of and enhancing the impact of community philanthropy. The Responsive New Grants is generally awarded to address an agency's general operating, programmatic, capital or technical assistance needs. This funding source is open to all requests for projects and organizational support.
Requirements: IRS 501(c)3 nonprofit organizations are eligible to apply in the greater New Haven area, which includes: Ansonia; Bethany; Branford; Cheshire; Derby; East Haven; Guilford; Hamden; Madison; Milford; New Haven; North Branford; North Haven; Orange; Oxford; Seymour; Shelton; Wallingford; West Haven and; Woodbridge.
Restrictions: Grants are not made to support religious activities, lobbying, or travel.
Geographic Focus: Connecticut
Date(s) Application is Due: Mar 5
Amount: 10,000 - 185,000 USD
Samples: Arts Council of Greater New Haven, New Haven, CT, $50,000—to provide general operating support (2009); Beth El Center Inc., Milford, CT, $25,000— general operating support for transitional shelter programs for homeless individuals and families and a soup kitchen/food pantry that feeds individuals and families from Greater New Haven and Lower Naugatuck Valley (2009); Area Congregations Together Inc., Shelton, CT, $150,000—to establish a development program (2009).
Contact: Denise Canning, Grants Manager; (203) 777-2386 or (203) 777-7076; (203) 787-6584; dcanning@cfgnh.org
Internet: http://www.cfgnh.org/GrantsScholarships/TypesofGrants/tabid/199/Default.aspx
Sponsor: Community Foundation for Greater New Haven
70 Audubon Street
New Haven, CT 06510

Community Foundation for Monterey County Grants 477

The community foundation supports nonprofits in Monterey, CA, in the areas of social services, education, environment, arts, health, historic preservation, and general charitable giving. Collaboratives are highly encouraged. The foundation awards grants through its General Endowment. Technical Assistance grants and Neighborhood Grants also are awarded. Types of support include seed money, emergency funds, general operating support, building funds, equipment acquisition, land acquisition, matching funds, projects, consulting services, and technical assistance. Information on how to apply for each type of grant can be accessed online.
Requirements: 501(c)3 tax-exempt organizations in Monterey, CA, may submit applications.
Restrictions: The foundation does not support individuals, religious activities, scholarships, fellowships, travel, research, salaries and other operating expenses of schools and public agencies, annual campaigns, or special events; create or add to endowment funds; or pay off debt.
Geographic Focus: California
Date(s) Application is Due: Jan 3; May 2; Aug 1
Amount: 5,000 - 40,000 USD
Contact: Jackie Wendland, Grants Administrator; (831) 375-9712, ext. 11; (831) 375-4731; jackie@cfmco.org
Internet: http://www.cfmco.org/grantsOverview.php
Sponsor: Community Foundation for Monterey County
2354 Garden Road
Monterey, CA 93940

Community Foundation for Southeastern Michigan Grants 478

The community foundation's grantmaking activity focuses on a seven-county region and supports a wide variety of activities benefiting arts and culture, education, health, human services, civic affairs, neighborhood and regional economic development, workforce development, and environment and land use. Usually grants provide start-up or short-term funding for innovative projects that meet new needs or demonstrate new solutions for old ones. Additional types of support include scholarship funds, technical assistance, and general operating support. Priority will be given to applications that develop or test new solutions to community challenges, increase the effectiveness or efficiency of nonprofit activities, enhance the quality of an organization's efforts and its stature, facilitate cooperation and collaboration among organizations, increase the diversity and competitiveness of the region's economy, and encourage civic

development and volunteerism. Grant proposals may be submitted at any time. The application must be in writing and include a cover letter outlining purpose, background, amount requested, and time limits of the proposed activity.
Requirements: 501(c)3 nonprofit organizations in the following seven Michigan counties are eligible to apply: Livingston, Macomb, Montclair, Monroe, Oakland, Washtenaw, Wayne.
Restrictions: Normally, grants will not be made for buildings or equipment, general operating support (except in the first few years of an organization's existence), endowments, sectarian religious programs, fund-raising campaigns, grants to individuals, conferences and annual meetings, or projects outside the seven-county region.
Geographic Focus: Michigan
Date(s) Application is Due: Mar 1; Jun 1; Sep 1; Dec 1
Amount: 10,000 - 75,000 USD
Samples: Michigan Opera Theatre (Detroit, MI)—to produce and perform two operas at elementary, middle, and high schools throughout Wayne County, MI, that deal with such topics as race, ethnicity, and tolerance, $10,750; Latin Americans for Social and Economic Development (Detroit, MI)—to renovate commercial space in two historic structures located on West Vernor in southwest Detroit, $50,000; Holy Cross Children's Services (Clinton, MI)—for a cultural-diversity project at its facilities in southeastern Michigan, $15,000; Oakland U, School of Education and Human Services (Rochester, MN)—to develop and implement a comprehensive recreation program at its new facility for children with autism and their families, $20,000.
Contact: Grant Administrator; (313) 961-6675; (313) 961-2886; cfsem@cfsem.org
Internet: http://www.cfsem.org/grants/index.html
Sponsor: Community Foundation for Southeastern Michigan
333 W Fort Street, Suite 2010
Detroit, MI 48226-3134

Community Foundation for Southern Arizona Grants 479

The foundation awards grants in southern Arizona for a broad array of charitable purposes in the areas of arts and humanities, education, the environment, health, social services. Types of support include challenge/matching grants, conferences and seminars, scholarships, equipment acquisition, fellowships, general support, multiyear support, project development, publications, research, seed funding, and technical assistance. Priority is given to proposals that promote collaboration and build on the strengths of individuals and communities. Deadlines are determined on a yearly basis.
Requirements: Nonprofit and grassroots organizations in southern Arizona communities are eligible. Southern Arizona communities include all of Cochise, Santa Cruz, and Pima Counties; and the areas of Yuma, Mariposa, Pinal, Graham, and Greenlee Counties that lie south of the Gila River.
Restrictions: Funds are generally not available for ongoing operating or capital campaigns, debt retirement, endowments, individuals, individual schools, sectarian activities, or underwriting of fund-raising events.
Geographic Focus: Arizona
Amount: 1,000 - 10,000 USD
Samples: Arizona's Children Association (AZ)—for KARE legal services, $7200; Tucson Clean and Beautiful (Tucson, AZ)—for Adopt-A-Park Program, $2000; Tucson Children's Museum, Inc (Tucson, AZ)—to cover admission costs for low-income children, $2250; Tucson Cinema Foundation Inc (Tucson, AZ)—funding for a ten-month program for high school students, $5600.
Contact: Barbara Brown, Executive Vice President; (520) 770-0800, ext. 107; (520) 770-1500; bbrown@CFSoAZ.org
Internet: http://www.cfsoaz.org/page17480.cfm
Sponsor: Community Foundation for Southern Arizona
2250 E Broadway Boulevard
Tucson, AZ 85719

Community Foundation for the Fox Valley Region Alcoholism and Drug Abuse Grants 480

The Community Foundation for the Fox Valley Region (CFFVR) was established as a public, nonprofit organization in 1986 to enhance the quality of life for all people of the region. Since it was founded, funds within the Foundation have awarded more than $125 million in grants to nonprofit organizations, primarily in Wisconsin's Fox Valley region. The purpose of the Alcoholism and Drug Abuse Grants program is to: supports new; existing programs and projects that address the prevention and/or treatment of alcohol; other drug abuse in the Fox Valley and surrounding area.
Requirements: Organizations serving residents of Outagamie, Calumet, Waupaca, Shawano and northern Winnebago counties are eligible to apply. The grant application form is available at the CFFVR website.
Geographic Focus: Wisconsin
Amount: 2,500 USD
Contact: Laurel Filapek, Community Engagement Officer; (920) 830-1290, ext. 28; (920) 830-1293; lfilapek@cffoxvalley.org
Internet: https://www.cffoxvalley.org/Page.aspx?pid=415
Sponsor: Community Foundation for the Fox Valley Region
4455 West Lawrence Street, P.O. Box 563
Appleton, WI 54912-0563

Community Foundation for the Fox Valley Region Appleton Education Foundation Grants 481

The Appleton Education Foundation (AEF) seeks to improve the well being of children, teachers and community by enhancing the quality of education within the Wisconsin, Appleton Area School District. AEF role is to fund initiatives that fall outside the school budget. Grants are available up to $500 for a single classroom or up to $1,500 for multiple classes, disciplines or schools. Grant application is available online. Grant deadline dates are April 10 and November 10.
Requirements: Any educator employed by the Wisconsin, Appleton Area School District or any community member in partnership with an educator is eligible to apply for a grant.
Restrictions: Generally, equipment alone does not qualify for a grant. Equipment required to complete a project or implement a program that meets the mission of the Foundation will be considered. Equipment upgrades are considered on an individual basis.
Geographic Focus: Wisconsin
Date(s) Application is Due: Apr 10; Nov 10
Amount: 500 - 1,500 USD
Contact: Julie Krause, Executive Director; (920) 832-1517; jkrause@cffoxvalley.org
Internet: https://www.cffoxvalley.org/Page.aspx?pid=415
Sponsor: Community Foundation for the Fox Valley Region
4455 West Lawrence Street, P.O. Box 563
Appleton, WI 54912-0563

Community Foundation for the Fox Valley Region Basic Needs Giving Partnership Grants 482

Supported by the U.S. Oil Open Fund for Basic Needs within the Community Foundation and the J.J. Keller Foundation, the partnership assists established charitable organizations with successful programs that address root causes of poverty. Available forms of support include: capacity building; general operating support; project support; project analysis & advocacy. A single organization may request up to $15,000 per year for three years, and collaborative proposals may request up to $100,000 per year for three years. Multiple years of support will be considered only if there is a compelling case for multi-year funding and the project clearly demonstrates how progression shall occur over time. Application deadlines are February 15 & September 1, applications should be submitted no later then 4:00 pm.
Requirements: Eligible applicants are well-established charitable organizations that are exempt from federal income taxes under the Internal Revenue Code and have been in operation for a minimum of three years. Wisconsin organizations must serve residents in Outagamie, Calumet, Waupaca, Shawano, or northern Winnebago counties.
Restrictions: Grants from the Basic Needs Giving Partnership will not support the following: technology projects; capital campaigns or building projects; organizational set-up costs; annual fund drives or endowments; lobbying for specific legislation; activities that occur before funding is awarded; organizations with past-due or incomplete grant reports.
Geographic Focus: Wisconsin
Date(s) Application is Due: Feb 15; Sep 1
Amount: 45,000 - 300,000 USD
Contact: Martha Hemwall, Community Engagement Officer; (920) 830-1290, ext. 26; mhemwall@cffoxvalley.org
Internet: https://www.cffoxvalley.org/Page.aspx?pid=400
Sponsor: Community Foundation for the Fox Valley Region
4455 West Lawrence Street, P.O. Box 563
Appleton, WI 54912-0563

Community Foundation for the Fox Valley Region Bridge Grants 483

The Community Foundation for the Fox Valley Region (CFFVR) Bridge Program, is a temporary grant program that's to be used as a financial bridge through the economic downturn. Bridge grants will provide general operating support to charitable organizations which, due to the current economic decline, are in need of temporary funding to help maintain programs necessary to their core mission, and demonstrated prior financial health and high potential for future stability. These charitable organizations must serve residents in the Community Foundation service area, which includes Calumet, Outagamie, Shawano, Waupaca and northern Winnebago counties of Wisconsin. Applicants may request up to $25,000 for general operating support. Multiple organizations seeking to collaborate or merge for reasons of efficiency may be eligible for additional funding. .

Requirements: Eligible applicants are established Wisconsin, 501(c)3 charitable organizations that can provide compelling evidence of an urgent or impending financial need caused by the economic downturn and are able to demonstrate prior financial health and high potential for future stability. Charitable organizations must serve residents in the Community Foundation service area, which includes Calumet, Outagamie, Shawano, Waupaca and northern Winnebago counties.

Restrictions: Not eligible: educational institutions, government programs or entities, religious organizations, churches and funding for endowments. Programs and offices within an organization and organizations with a fiscal sponsor are not eligible to apply.

Geographic Focus: Wisconsin

Amount: 25,000 USD

Contact: Marti Hemwall, Program Director; (920) 830-1290, ext. 26; mhemwall@cffoxvalley.org

Internet: https://www.cffoxvalley.org/Page.aspx?pid=654

Sponsor: Community Foundation for the Fox Valley Region
4455 West Lawrence Street, P.O. Box 563
Appleton, WI 54912-0563

Community Foundation for the Fox Valley Region Clintonville Area Foundation Grants 484

Clintonville Area Foundation (CAF) grants are awarded from unrestricted funds to support specific projects or new programs for which a moderate amount of grant money can make an impact on an area of need. Grants are made for a broad range of purposes to a wide variety of charitable organizations in the focus areas of health, education and community development. The Foundation is interesting in supporting: creative new activities or services—new programs, one-time projects, events, exhibits, studies or surveys; enhancement or strengthening of existing activities—projects to enhance, expand or strengthen the range, quantity and/or quality of an organization's programs and services; small capital investments—items that are directly related to program delivery or service to clients, such as a refrigerator for a food pantry or equipment to comply with ADA requirements. Qualifying Wisconsin nonprofits serving the residents of the Clintonville area are eligible for this funding. Grant applications are available online and are accepted annually from September 1 through Dececember 31.

Requirements: Wisconsin 501(c)3 nonprofit organizations that serve the residents of the Clintonville area are eligible to apply. Submit a grant application form by December 31, 4 p.m, preferably via email to clintonvillefoundation@gmail.com, or mail to CAF, P.O. Box 244, Clintonville, WI 54929. General questions about the grant process can also be directed to CAF Grants Committee Chair Jenny Goldschmidt at (715) 823-7125, ext. 2603 or, staff at the Community Foundation for the Fox Valley Region at (920) 830-1290.

Restrictions: The Clintonville Area Foundation will not generally fund the following: general operating expenses not related to the proposed project; annual fund drives or fundraising events; endowment funds; programs with a sectarian or religious purpose that promote a specific journey of faith; major capital projects such as the acquisition of land or buildings; medical research; travel for individuals or groups such as bands, sports teams or classes; activities that occur before funding is awarded; organizations with past-due or incomplete grant reports.

Geographic Focus: Wisconsin

Date(s) Application is Due: Dec 31

Contact: Jenny Goldschmidt, Chair; (715) 823-7125, ext. 2603; clintonvillefoundation@gmail.com

Internet: https://www.cffoxvalley.org/Page.aspx?pid=415

Sponsor: Community Foundation for the Fox Valley Region
4455 West Lawrence Street, P.O. Box 563
Appleton, WI 54912-0563

Community Foundation for the Fox Valley Region Doug & Carla Salmon Foundation Grants 485

The Doug & Carla Salmon Foundation provides need-based college scholarships to highly motivated students and financial support to local charitable organizations in the Fox Valley region of Wisconsin. Grants support capital campaigns and, the development of administrative endowments. There are no deadline dates for submitting your funding requests. Mail a letter of inquiry, to begin the application process to: Doug & Carla Salmon Foundation, 660 West Ridgeview Drive, Appleton, WI, 54911. Students interested in learning more about Salmon Foundation scholarships should request information through: UWO Foundation, *contact:* Lori Kroening at (920) 424-2228; Fox Valley Technical College Foundation, *contact:* Deb Woodworth at (920) 735-2478; UW-Fox Valley Student Services, *contact:* Brenda Rickert at (920) 832-2623.

Requirements: Wisconsin 501(c)3 tax-exempt organizations serving residents of Outagamie, Calumet, Waupaca, Shawano and northern Winnebago counties are eligible to apply.

Geographic Focus: Wisconsin

Contact: Sue Detienne, Executive Director; rdetienne@new.rr.com

Internet: https://www.cffoxvalley.org/Page.aspx?pid=403

Sponsor: Community Foundation for the Fox Valley Region
4455 West Lawrence Street, P.O. Box 563
Appleton, WI 54912-0563

Community Foundation for the Fox Valley Region Environmental Stewardship Grants 486

The Environmental Stewardship Fund was established by the Community Foundation in 2006 to support the Wisconsin, Fox Valley-area charitable organizations and projects that further the conservation of nature and enhance education about and enjoyment of the natural world. Grants awarded from the Environmental Stewardship Fund typically are for no more than $5,000. Funding priority is given to projects that: strengthen the connection between the people and the land; further environmental values; have a wide impact; are visible and inspiring; match groups with similar aspirations.

Requirements: Wisconsin 501(c)3 tax-exempt organizations serving residents of Outagamie, Calumet, Waupaca, Shawano and northern Winnebago counties are eligible to apply. The grant application form is available at the CFFVR website. The application deadlines are February 1 and August 1, applications must be received no later then 4:00 pm.

Restrictions: Projects that will not be funded: major capital expenses; ongoing operating expenses unrelated to the proposed project; annual fund drives or fund-raising events; recurring events; endowment funds; conference fees; lobbying; activities that occur before funding is awarded; organizations with past-due or incomplete grant reports.

Geographic Focus: Wisconsin

Date(s) Application is Due: Feb 1; Aug 1

Amount: 5,000 USD

Samples: Wisconsin League of Conservation Voters, $2,000—a Green Bay based organizer will educate members of Fox Valley environmental groups on such tools as working with the media and advocating with legislators to further a conservation agenda endorsed by more than 80 Wisconsin environmental and conservation groups (2009); Town of Greenville Pebbleidge Park, $2,250—shoreline planting will accompany a 2.5-acre prairie in this 13-acre park on Design Drive (2009); Appleton Area School District, $3,000—Author Paul Fleischman will present three days of classroom workshops on the diversity and nature themes in his book Seedfolks (2009).

Contact: David Horst, Communications Specialist; (920) 830-1290, ext. 24; dhorst@cffoxvalley.org

Internet: https://www.cffoxvalley.org/Page.aspx?pid=347

Sponsor: Community Foundation for the Fox Valley Region
4455 West Lawrence Street, P.O. Box 563
Appleton, WI 54912-0563

Community Foundation for the Fox Valley Region Frank C. Shattuck Community Grants 487

The Frank C. Shattuck Community Fund supports new or supplements existing services for youth and the elderly and benefits education, the arts and health care in Winnebago and Outagamie counties of Wisconsin. Funding is available for programs, capital expenses or operating expenses of qualifying charitable organizations. Grants to projects may be either one-time payments or multi-year commitments. Application forms are available online with deadline dates of March 1, and September 1.

Requirements: Wisconsin 501(c)3 organizations that serve residents in Outagamie or northern Winnebago counties are eligible to apply. To begin the application process, submit the following prior to the application deadline: grant application form; list of the organization's governing board members, including their professional or community affiliation; current year (board-approved) operating budget.
Restrictions: The Shattuck Fund will not typically support the following: grants for religious or political purposes; grants to support endowment funds of organizations; travel for individuals or groups such as bands, sports teams or classes; reimbursement for previously incurred expenses.
Geographic Focus: Wisconsin
Date(s) Application is Due: Mar 1; Sep 1
Contact: Shelly Leadley, Donor Relations Officer; (920) 830-1290, ext. 34; sleadley@cffoxvalley.org
Internet: https://www.cffoxvalley.org/Page.aspx?pid=339
Sponsor: Community Foundation for the Fox Valley Region
4455 West Lawrence Street, P.O. Box 563
Appleton, WI 54912-0563

Community Foundation for the Fox Valley Region Mielke Family Foundation Grants 488

Mielke Family Foundation grants, enhance the quality of life for residents of Appleton and, Shawano, Wisconsin. Priority areas of giving are: projects that primarily serve individuals residing within either the Appleton Area School District or the Shawano School District; special events, start-up expenses of projects expected to become self-sustaining, studies to determine future courses of action or needs, enrichment programs, or actions to meet similar objectives. Application forms are available online at the Community Foundation for the Fox Valley Region website. Application deadline dates are April15 & October 15.
Requirements: Applicants must: be a nonprofit 501(c)3 or qualifying tax-exempt organization; be able to demonstrate, to the satisfaction of the Foundation, that it has the capability to complete the proposed project.
Restrictions: The Mielke Family Foundation typically will not support: transportation costs for individuals or groups such as bands, sports teams or classes; general operating expenses not related to the proposed project; deficits incurred for past activities; programs or needs that do not serve residents in the Appleton Area School District or the Shawano Area School District. The Foundation typically prefers not to engage in long-term grant commitments.
Geographic Focus: Wisconsin
Date(s) Application is Due: Apr 15; Oct 15
Contact: Laurel Filapek, Community Engagement Officer; (920) 830-1290, ext. 28; (920) 830-1293; lfilapek@cffoxvalley.org
Internet: https://www.cffoxvalley.org/Page.aspx?pid=415
Sponsor: Community Foundation for the Fox Valley Region
4455 West Lawrence Street, P.O. Box 563
Appleton, WI 54912-0563

Community Foundation for the Fox Valley Region Myra M. & Robert L. Vandehey Foundation Grants 489

The Myra M. & Robert L. Vandehey Foundation's mission is support the charitable interests of the Myra and Robert Vandehey family. Areas of interest include: education; children and youth; health care and; family services. Contact Cathy Mutschler prior to submission of a formal request to see if the need aligns with current priorities. Unsolicited grant requests are not accepted from organizations who have not previously received funding support. Funding opportunities are limited to nonprofit organizations that serve residents in the Fox Cities or Keshena areas of Wisconsin. No application form is required, nor is there a deadline date to adhere to. The grant committee meets quarterly, all requests should be submitted 10 days prior to quarterly meeting.
Requirements: Wisconsin 501(c)3 nonprofit organizations that serve residents in the Fox Cities or Keshena are eligible for funding.
Restrictions: No grants to individuals.
Geographic Focus: Wisconsin
Amount: 5,000 - 30,000 USD
Samples: Fox Valley Technical College Foundation, Appleton, WI, $20,000—educational grant (2008); Boys & Girls Clubs of the Fox Valley, Appleton, WI, $25,000—youth development grant (2008).
Contact: Cathy Mutschler, VP Community Engagement; (920) 830-1290, ext. 29; cmutschler@cffoxvalley.org
Internet: https://www.cffoxvalley.org/Page.aspx?pid=415
Sponsor: Community Foundation for the Fox Valley Region
4455 West Lawrence Street, P.O. Box 563
Appleton, WI 54912-0563

Community Foundation for the Fox Valley Region (CFFVR) SAC Developmental Disabilities Grants 490

The Community Foundation for the Fox Valley Region Inc. was established as a public, nonprofit organization in 1986 to enhance the quality of life for all people of the region. Since it was founded, funds within the Foundation have awarded more than $125 million in grants to nonprofit organizations, primarily in Wisconsin's Fox Valley region. The service region includes Outagamie, Calumet, Waupaca, Shawano and northern Winnebago counties. The SAC Developmental Disabilities Fund supports projects or programs that address the recreational, social and educational needs of people with developmental disabilities and other handicapping conditions. Grants awarded range up to $5,000.
Requirements: Wisconsin 501(c)3 tax-exempt organizations serving residents of Outagamie, Calumet, Waupaca, Shawano and northern Winnebago counties are eligible to apply. The grant application form is available at the CFFVR website. The application deadline dates are January 2 and, June 1.
Geographic Focus: Wisconsin
Date(s) Application is Due: Jan 2; Jun 1
Amount: 5,000 USD
Contact: Laurel Filapek, Community Engagement Officer; (920) 830-1290, ext. 28; (920) 830-1293; lfilapek@cffoxvalley.org
Internet: https://www.cffoxvalley.org/Page.aspx?pid=415
Sponsor: Community Foundation for the Fox Valley Region
4455 West Lawrence Street, P.O. Box 563
Appleton, WI 54912-0563

Community Foundation for the Fox Valley Region Schmidt Family G4 Grants 491

The Schmidt Family G4 grants provide funding to improve the quality of life of those most in need in the Fox Valley, Wisconsin region, with a focus on at-risk youth and self-sufficiency for women. This goal will be accomplished by seeking to address immediate needs and to affect meaningful change in the following areas: at-risk youth—especially those with a physical or mental illness, those who have experienced abuse or those who have significant financial need; adult self-sufficiency—with a priority on issues that affect the stability and independence of women, as well as literacy, job skills training and transitional living for all. The G4 Committee prefers: not to be the sole funder for most projects it considers, unless the amount requested is small and/or a one-time request; to support specific projects or new programs for which a moderate amount of grant money can make a significant impact on an area of need and sustainability. A broad array of requests will be considered, including capital campaigns, existing programs or recurring events as long as they fall within the other listed giving guidelines. Grant awards will typically not exceed $15,000. To assist with the educational aspect of this fund, a formal application is required (available online). Prior to submitting an application, organizations are strongly encouraged to contact Cathy Mutschlerto, discuss the potential proposal and process. Complete and submit the application prior to the March 1, October 1 deadlines.
Requirements: IRS 501(c)3 nonprofit organizations, as well as government agencies are eligible to apply for funding. Organizations that are not public charities may apply through a fiscal sponsor. Organizations must serve Fox Valley residents, particularly in Outagamie, Calumet or northern Winnebago counties of Wisconsin.
Restrictions: The G4 Fund typically will not support the following: organizations that have received funding from the G4 Committee in the most recent 20 months; multi-year requests; programs with a sectarian or religious purpose that promote a specific journey of faith; travel for individuals or groups such as bands, sports teams or classes; reimbursement for previously incurred expenses; endowment funds; fund-raising events; requests from organizations with past-due or incomplete grant reports; a program or need previously declined unless the organization is invited back by the committee; programs or needs that do not serve Fox Valley residents, particularly Outagamie, Calumet or northern Winnebago counties.
Geographic Focus: Wisconsin
Date(s) Application is Due: Mar 1; Oct 1
Amount: 15,000 USD
Contact: Cathy Mutschler, VP Community Engagement; (920) 830-1290, ext. 29; cmutschler@cffoxvalley.org
Internet: https://www.cffoxvalley.org/Page.aspx?pid=340
Sponsor: Community Foundation for the Fox Valley Region
4455 West Lawrence Street, P.O. Box 563
Appleton, WI 54912-0563

Community Foundation for the Fox Valley Region Shawano Area Community Foundation Grants 492

Shawano Area Community Foundation works to preserve and improve the quality of life in Shawano, Wisconsin and, the surrounding area, including communities having economic, educational, cultural and recreational ties with the area. Grants are available up to $5,000. Grant application is available online, with an application deadline of September 1.
Requirements: Wisconsin 501(c)3 non-profits in or serving surrounding area of Shawano are eligible to apply.
Geographic Focus: Wisconsin
Date(s) Application is Due: Sep 30
Amount: 5,000 USD
Samples: City of Shawano/County Library, Shawano, WI, $3,000—reading machine for visually impaired (2009); Shawano Oral Health Fund, Shawano, WI, $1,500—program support for ssecond grade children in Shawano County (2009); Street John's Trinity Lutheran Church, Shawano, WI, $1,000—food purchase grant (2009).
Contact: Susan Hanson, Grants Manager; (715) 253-2580; shawanofoundation@granitewave.com
Internet: https://www.cffoxvalley.org/Page.aspx?pid=412
Sponsor: Community Foundation for the Fox Valley Region
4455 West Lawrence Street, P.O. Box 563
Appleton, WI 54912-0563

Community Foundation for the Fox Valley Region Wisconsin Branch of the King's Daughters & Sons Grants 493

The Wisconsin Branch of the International Order of King's Daughters and Sons, in alignment with the priorities of its national parent organization, will provide grants to Fox Valley charitable organizations who provide services related to autism and literacy. Grant requests may not exceed $5,000.
Requirements: Wisconsin 501(c)3 non-profit organizations in the Fox Valley region may apply. Organizations that are not public charities may apply through a fiscal sponsor. Application is available online. Submit one copy of the completed application form and attachments by 4pm on October 15.
Geographic Focus: Wisconsin
Date(s) Application is Due: Oct 15
Amount: 5,000 USD
Contact: Patti Habeck, Community Engagement Officer; (920) 830-1290, ext. 27; (920) 830-1293; phabeck@cffoxvalley.org
Internet: https://www.cffoxvalley.org/Page.aspx?pid=415
Sponsor: Community Foundation for the Fox Valley Region
4455 West Lawrence Street, P.O. Box 563
Appleton, WI 54912-0563

Community Foundation for the Fox Valley Region Women's Fund for the Fox Valley Region Grants 494

The Women's Fund provides grants for programs that inspire women and girls to flourish personally, economically and professionally. Grants have been distributed to programs supporting the following areas: arts & culture; physical and mental health; economic, self-sufficency; education; parenting & child care; violence prevention. The Women's Fund believes that no project is too small or too new to be considered. Innovative approaches and projects with limited access to other funding are encouraged. Collaborative efforts are welcome. Grant applicants should address one or more of these funding priorities as they relate to women and girls: promotes economic self-sufficiency; improves safely from violence; provides opportunities to develop life skills; promotes physical and/or mental health; enhances dignity and self-worth; promotes leadership development; provides opportunities for artistic development and/or exposure to the arts; provides gender-specific solutions to problems facing women and girls; creates an environment that encourages social change. To apply for funding, submit a letter of interest byÂ February 1. A completed grant application must be received by March 1. Application forms are available online.
Requirements: To be eligible for a grant, the project must be consistent with the Women's Fund mission; benefits women and girls in the Wisconsin, Fox Valley region; organization must be a tax-exempt, not-for-profit organization under the Internal Revenue Code, section 501(c)3.
Restrictions: The Women's Fund will not fund: individuals, endowments, government agencies (however educational institutions may qualify), projects with a religious focus, and political parties, candidates or partisan activities.
Geographic Focus: Wisconsin
Date(s) Application is Due: Feb 1; Mar 1
Contact: Becky Boulanger, Program Director; (920) 830-1290, ext. 17; bboulanger@cffoxvalley.org or grants@womensfundfvr.org
Internet: https://www.cffoxvalley.org/Page.aspx?pid=415
Sponsor: Community Foundation for the Fox Valley Region
4455 West Lawrence Street, P.O. Box 563
Appleton, WI 54912-0563

Community Foundation for the National Capital Region Competitive Grants 495

The Community Fund has a particular interest in supporting groups in the metropolitan Washington, DC, area working in the following issue areas: violence prevention; education; community building; cross-cultural or cultural partnership building; family literacy; and healthcare and dental services for underprivileged children, youth, and families. Types of support include general operating support, program development, technical assistance, and program evaluation. Approximately 20 to 30 grants per year will be awarded in two competitive cycles. Letters of inquiry (three-page maximum) must meet the listed application deadlines. Proposals will be invited.
Requirements: 501(c)3 nonprofits in the metropolitan Washington region, including the District of Columbia, northern Virginia, and suburban Maryland may submit letters of inquiry. Applicants must represent a neighborhood, citywide, or regional coalition effort, with one nonprofit organization serving as project sponsor.
Geographic Focus: District of Columbia, Maryland, Virginia
Samples: Nine nonprofit organizations (Washington, DC)—for awards through the Bridge Builders Fund, which supports projects that promote communication and understanding between the lesbian, gay, and bisexual populations and other city residents, $60,000 divided; George Washington U (Washington, DC)—for the Ctr for Excellence in Municipal Management, $150,000; Henry Ford Health System (Troy, MI)—to develop a set of standards for measuring the quality of health care provided to minority patients in managed-care plans, $179,464.
Contact: Alicia Reid, Program Officer; (202) 263-4774; (202) 955-8084; areid@cfncr.org
Internet: http://www.cfncr.org/page13847.cfm
Sponsor: Community Foundation for the National Capital Region
1201 15th Street NW, Suite 420
Washington, DC 20005

Community Foundation of Central Illinois Grants 496

The foundation funds programs in the fields of education, arts, human services, community service, or community development, and that advance one or more of the following objectives: address and help resolve important existing or emerging community issues; support new and creative projects and organizations offering the greatest opportunity for positive and significant change; promote cooperation and collaboration among organizations; identify, enhance, and develop leadership in the community through creative and innovative activities that empower individuals; and improve the quality or scope of charitable works in our community. Application guidelines are available online.
Requirements: Nonprofit organizations within a 50-mile radius of Peoria, IL, are eligible.
Restrictions: The foundation will not fund annual campaigns, individuals, or endowments, or make grants for sectarian religious purposes.
Geographic Focus: Illinois
Date(s) Application is Due: Apr 15; Sep 15
Amount: 2,500 - 3,000 USD
Contact: Kristan Creek, Program Officer; (309) 674-8730; (309) 674-8754; Kristan@communityfoundationci.org
Internet: http://www.communityfoundationci.org/grant_guidelines.asp
Sponsor: Community Foundation of Central Illinois
331 Fulton Street, Suite 310
Peoria, IL 61602

Community Foundation of Collier County Capacity Building Grants 497

The Community Foundation believes that all nonprofits can benefit from the best practices developed over time in excellent organizations. The Foundation wishes to help nonprofits become successful and sustainable, long term businesses. Capacity Building Grants are given to support best practices and sustainability for a variety of nonprofit organizational needs. The Foundation's focus is on substantial projects that: encourage and facilitate collaborations; improve communications between nonprofits with similar missions; engage in public-private partnerships; facilitate the development of strategic plans,

business plans, plans for marketing & communications, fund raising plans; encourage program evaluation that focuses on results for participants; fund updated technology systems; and other projects that improve the sustainability of the organization. This grant program includes a Letter of Intent, an interview and donor briefings. The Letter of Intent must be submitted by 5:00 on September 18th. The most common grant will be between $5,000-$8,000 per/applicant. The grant award from the Foundation will require a 50% match by the organization.
Requirements: 501(c)3 tax-exempt organizations serving Collier County and are not deemed as not a private foundation under Section 509(a) are eligible to apply.
Restrictions: The Foundation does not fund the following through this grant program: grants to individuals; endowments; private schools; political campaigns/lobby activities; scholarly research; annual campaigns; organizations which exclude individuals based on the Foundation statement of diversity; reimbursement of funds spent; projects that present a clear or perceived conflict of interest.
Geographic Focus: Florida
Date(s) Application is Due: Sep 18
Amount: 5,000 - 8,000 USD
Contact: Mary Barrett, Vice President; (239) 649-5000; (941) 649-5337; mbarrett@cfcollier.org
Internet: http://www.cfcollier.org/new_grant_program.php
Sponsor: Community Foundation of Collier County
2400 Tamiami Trail N, Suite 300
Naples, FL 34103

Community Foundation of Greater Birmingham Grants 498
The community foundation serving the greater Birmingham, AL, area awards grants in arts and culture, education, environment, health, and welfare. Types of support include capital campaigns, operating support, building/renovation, equipment, program development, publication, seed money, curriculum development, and matching funds. Grant requests are considered twice a year at distribution committee meetings. The foundation requires that grant requests be submitted in writing. There is no application form. Applicants are asked to submit a cover letter and a complete statement of the purpose of the grant, including the need for the project and population and number of people to be served, project budget, other funding sources, length of time for which foundation aid is needed, a method to evaluate the project's success, description of applicant organization including annual budget, copy of IRS determination letter, and names of the board of directors or trustees.
Requirements: IRS 501(c)3 organizations that provide services in the greater Birmingham metropolitan area (Jefferson, Shelby, Street Clair, Blount and Walker counties) are eligible.
Restrictions: Grants are not made to or for individuals, operating expenses of organizations, religious organizations for religious purposes, national fund-raising drives, conference or seminar expenses, tickets for benefits, political organizations or candidates for public office, organizations with IRS 501(h) status, budget deficits, replacement of government funding cuts, or scholarships or endowment funds.
Geographic Focus: Alabama
Date(s) Application is Due: Mar 15; Sep 15
Samples: Exchange Club Family Skills Center, $2,200—program support (2009); Catholic Family Services, $4,600— to expand outpatient psychiatric care for uninsured women and children in metro Birmingham (2009); Birmingham Civil Rights Institute, $20,000— toward operating costs as the institute continues to serve the general public, tourists and students, particularly in kindergarten through second grade (2009).
Contact: James McCrary, Senior Program Officer; (205) 327-3812 or (205) 327-3800; (205) 328-6576; jmccrary@foundationbirmingham.org or guidelines@foundationbirmingham.org
Internet: http://www.foundationbirmingham.org/page30508.cfm
Sponsor: Community Foundation of Greater Birmingham
2100 First Avenue N, Suite 700
Birmingham, AL 35203-4223

Community Foundation of Greater Flint Grants 499
The community foundation is interested in funding charitable organizations that are able to demonstrate they have planned their projects with respect to the community's needs in the areas of arts and humanities, community services, education, environment and conservation, ethics, health, human and social services, and philanthropy. The foundation's current objectives for the allocation of discretionary funds give top priority to programs that: advance the health and well-being of children; and/or improve the capacity of public education. Types of support include general operating support, program development, seed money, scholarship funds, and technical assistance. Applications are available on the website.
Requirements: IRS 501(c)3 organizations with programs of direct relevance to the residents of Genesee County, Michigan are eligible. Types of support include general operating support.
Restrictions: Grants will not be made to individuals. In general, requests for sectarian religious purposes, budget deficits, routine operating expenses of existing organizations, litigation, endowments, and other capital fund drives or projects are not funded.
Geographic Focus: Michigan
Samples: Greater Flint Health Coalition, $40,000—towards the Flint Healthcare Employment Opportunities (FHEO) program, which helps unemployed or low-income individuals in Genesee County to obtain employment opportunities or to advance in the healthcare industry (2009); Genesee Chamber Foundation,$30,000— towards the Summer Youth Initiative, a summer employment and leadership development program for Genesee County youth ages 14-18 (2009); United Way of Genesee County, $66,000- in support of the BEST Project (Building Excellence, Sustainability and Trust) BEST provides technical assistance and resources designed to build the capacity of area nonprofit organizations (2009).
Contact: Lynn Larkin, Senior Program Officer; (810) 767-8270; (810) 767-0496; llarkin@cfgf.org
Internet: http://www.cfgf.org/page32610.cfm
Sponsor: Community Foundation of Greater Flint
500 South Saginaw Street
Flint, MI 48502-1206

Community Foundation of Greater Greensboro Grants 500
The foundation supports community projects that strengthen the community, embrace the diversity of the community, demonstrate community support and in-kind investment, outline well-established proposed plans, and focus on collaborative efforts. Grants are awarded in the areas of community building, cultural and civic programs, arts, community development, health, environment, and social services. Types of support include general support, program development, seed grants, and emergency community funding. Annual deadline dates may vary; contact program staff for exact dates.
Requirements: Nonprofit organizations in Greensboro, NC, are eligible.
Restrictions: The Foundation does not award grants from the Community Grants for individuals, debt retirement, political organizations or campaigns, for-profit entities, capital campaigns, programming that promotes religious instruction or doctrine, or endowments.
Geographic Focus: North Carolina
Date(s) Application is Due: Feb 15; Jun 15; Oct 15
Amount: 10,000 USD
Samples: Eastern Music Festival (Greensboro, NC)—for the 2003 Piedmont Jazz Festival, $10,000; Guilford County Council of PTAs (Greensboro, NC)—to promote greater parental involvement in schools, $40,000; Piedmont Authority of Regional Transportation (Greensboro, NC)—to coordinate a regional medical-transportation program, $10,000 over two years; North Carolina Ctr for Nonprofits (Raleigh, NC)—for scholarships to enable local nonprofit groups to attend a statewide conference, $10,000.
Contact: Melissa Johnson, Program Officer; (336) 379-9100, ext. 124; (336) 378-0725; mjohnson@cfgg.org
Internet: http://www.cfgg.org/guidelines-new.htm
Sponsor: Community Foundation of Greater Greensboro
P.O. Box 20444
Greensboro, NC 27420

Community Foundation of Greenville Hollingsworth Funds Grants 501
The Hollingsworth Funds, Inc. has a competitive grant process that is administered by the Community Foundation. Consistent with the purposes established by its benefactor, John D. Hollingsworth, Jr., an astute textile executive and real estate investor. The Hollingsworth Funds will serve a broad range of charitable, educational, religious, literary and cultural purposes. The Hollingsworth Funds has adopted initial guidelines in order to assist its evaluation of charitable organizations for funding. The Hollingsworth Funds will make grants: to health and human service agencies dedicated to improving quality of life for residents of Greenville County and particularly for those which deliver services to the poor, homeless, and illiterate; to interdenominational faith-based programs that benefit a broad cross-section of the community; to a wide variety of arts and education related initiatives

including high quality preschool and after school programs; for grants for capital projects that provide a public benefit on a nondiscriminatory basis; to increase the organizational capacity of a non-profit organization; to public/private partnerships. The Hollingsworth Funds will give priority to new and innovative projects that are outside of the scope of an organization's ongoing operating budget. To submit a request for funding, a charitable organization must deliver or mail two (2) complete application packets to the Community Foundation of Greenville by 4:00 pm on September 3. All applicants will be notified of their status by December 31.
Requirements: A 501(c)3 charitable organization can submit one grant application per year for an amount not to exceed $50,000 to fund innovative projects for the benefit of charitable uses within Greenville County, South Carolina, or for the benefit of residents of Greenville County.
Restrictions: The Hollingsworth Funds will not make grants: to sponsor special fundraising events, celebration functions, dinners or annual meetings; for areas that are traditionally the primary responsibility of local, state or federal governments; for core operating expenses of public, private or parochial schools; that primarily benefit the religious activities of a church, synagogue, mosque or other house of worship; to pay off existing debts; scholarship awards or grants to individuals.
Geographic Focus: South Carolina
Date(s) Application is Due: Sep 3
Amount: Up to 50,000 USD
Contact: Debbie Cooper, Director of Donor Services; (864) 233-5925 or (864) 331-8414; (864) 242-9292; dcooper@cfgg.com or Cfgg@cfgg.com
Internet: http://www.cfgreenville.org/page18741.cfm
Sponsor: Community Foundation of Greenville
27 Cleveland Street, Suite 101
Greenville, SC 29601

Community Foundation of Herkimer and Oneida Counties Grants 502
The community foundation serves Oneida and Herkimer Counties, NY, and awards grants for programs that have direct relevance to needs in these areas. Preference is given to requests for support of particular programs or projects that are expected to benefit the community and to requests for capital expenditures and seed money. Additional types of support include general operating support, endowment funds, fellowships, scholarship funds, consulting services, demonstration grants, matching funds, and technical assistance. Applications from organizations not previously known to the foundation are given the same consideration as requests from those it knows well. The foundation may cut off acceptance of applications at any time if it is deemed that its current grant agenda is full. A grant request should be initiated by an application in writing on the organization's letterhead, if it has one, signed by the chairperson or president of its governing board.
Requirements: The community foundation supports only nonprofit organizations in Oneida and Herkimer Counties in New York.
Restrictions: Grants will not normally be made for endowments, ongoing operations, annual budgets or deficit financing, religious purposes, or financial assistance or scholarships to individuals.
Geographic Focus: New York
Contact: Margaret O'Shea, Director of Programs; (315) 735-8212, ext. 229; (315) 735-9363; moshea@foundationhoc.org
Internet: http://www.foundationhoc.org
Sponsor: Community Foundation of Herkimer and Oneida Counties
1222 State Street
Utica, NY 13502

Community Foundation of Louisville Grants 503
The mission of the community foundation is to enrich the quality of life for all citizens in the Louisville area by being a leader in attracting, mobilizing, and focusing philanthropic resources to meet community needs for generations to come. The foundation's focus is the four areas of community, arts and humanities, historic preservation, and the Lee Look Fund for Spinal Injury. Community grants supportsprojects designed to help prevent poverty by better preparing children and youth to achieve economic self-sufficiency through educational, leadership, mentoring, recreational, cultural, and other activities. Arts and humanities grants supports visual arts, crafts, theater, and the Louisville Free Public Library. The historic preservation fund supports the preservation of prehistoric and historic resources in Louisville and Jefferson County. The Lee Look Fund for Spinal Injury supports public charities that help people with spinal injuries or that develop new therapies and cures for disabilities resulting from spinal injuries. Scholarships in a wide array of areas are also available. The foundation does not accept unsolicited grant proposals for any grant programs. All potential applicants should review a grant program's guidelines for more detailed information.
Requirements: Only Kentucky non-profit organizations are eligible to apply. For the community grants, programs must serve populations in Algonquin, California, Chickasaw, Limerick, Old Louisville, Park DuValle, Park Hill, Parkland, Phoenix Hill, Portland, Russell, Shawnee, Shelby Park, Smoketown, or South Louisville neighborhoods.
Geographic Focus: Kentucky
Amount: 100 - 150,000 USD
Samples: West Louisville Boys Choir (Louisville, KY)—for operating support, $25,000; Big Brothers and Big Sisters of Kentuckiana (Louisville, KS)—to enable police officers to provide weekly educational, mentorship, and safety programs at Coleridge-Taylor Elementary School and King Elementary School, $10,000; Health Promotion Schools of Excellence (Louisville, KY)—to promote healthy behavior for K-12 students at 10 schools, $25,000 matching grant.
Contact: Alexandra Spoelker, Director of Grants; (502) 585-4649, ext. 1005; (502) 587-7484; alexs@cflouisville.org
Internet: http://www.cflouisville.org/page13464.cfm
Sponsor: Community Foundation of Louisville
325 W Main Street, Suite 1110, Waterfront Plaza
Louisville, KY 40202

Community Foundation of Muncie and Delaware County Grants 504
The Community Foundation of Muncie and Delaware County Grants provide funding in the following areas of interest: arts and culture, human services, economic development, education, and community betterment. The Foundation focus on: new and innovative projects and programs for which there is a demonstrable need or community benefit; capital needs of community institutions and organizations; emerging needs of Muncie and Delaware County; establishment of community priorities; monitoring of community services to avoid duplication and ineffective programs; acting as a catalyst for action and community participation. Applications are encouraged for types of projects that address one or more of the following: yield substantial benefits to the community for the resources invested; promote cooperation among agencies without duplicating services; enhance or improve institutional or organizational self-sufficiency; provide "seed money" for innovative community programs; encourage matching gifts or additional funding from other donors; and reach a broad segment of the community with needed services which are presently not provided. The Board of Directors review applications on a quarterly basis in the months of February, May, August, and November.
Requirements: First-time applicants must contact the Foundation to discuss their proposal prior to submission. Organizations are required to submit 18 copies of the application packet, but must submit different items depending on the type of funding requested. See website for submission details.
Restrictions: Requests of $25,000 or more are preferred during the first cycle of each year. The Foundation does not make grants to individuals or grants for religious purposes, budget deficits, for travel, fundraising events, endowments or projects normally the responsibility of a government agency.
Geographic Focus: Indiana
Amount: Up to USD
Samples: Animal Rescue Fund, to defray the cost of a van to transport animals to the vet and pick up strays in danger, $15,000 (2011); United Way of Delaware County, support to the Technology Wrap-Around Project, a pilot project to create access to computers and the Internet to ensure that those using these services can improve their lives in education, income, and health, $40,000 (2011); Gateway Health Clinic, to increase clinic hours to reduce the waiting list of patients, $25,000 (2011).
Contact: Suzanne Kadinger, Program Officer; (765) 747-7181; (765) 289-7770; skadinger@cfmdin.org or info@cfmdin.org
Internet: http://www.cfmdin.org/main/grant-seekers/
Sponsor: Community Foundation of Muncie and Delaware County
201 East Jackson Street
Muncie, IN 47305

Community Foundation of South Alabama Grants 505
The Community Foundation of South Alabama is the platform for building community in Baldwin, Clarke, Conecuh, Choctaw, Escambia, Mobile, Monroe and Washington counties. The Foundation provides grant support to South Alabama nonprofit organizations in four major program areas: community and civic affairs, education, arts and recreation, and social services (health and human services). Priority consideration is given to projects that clearly provide innovative responses to community needs, are collaborative

in nature when appropriate, and potentially affect broad segments of the community. Types of support include general operating support, capital campaigns, endowment funds, program development, and scholarship funds. The board of directors meets annually to consider grant requests. Application forms may be obtained from the office.
Requirements: Nonprofit organizations that have a 501(c)3, government entities and religious organizations that are located in Mobile, Baldwin, Clarke, Conecuh, Washington, Choctaw, Escambia and Monroe counties are eligible.
Restrictions: Grants generally are not provided for or to individuals, recurring requests for the same purpose for which foundation grant funds have already been awarded, research that is noncommunity-related or that does not have short-range results, films, conferences and workshops, lobbying activities, and tickets to fund-raising events.
Geographic Focus: Alabama
Amount: 2,500 - 28,000 USD
Contact: Janine Phillips, Director and Program Officer; (334) 438-5591; (334) 438-5592; info@communityendowment.com or program@communityendowment.com
Internet: http://communityendowment.com/grants/grants.htm
Sponsor: Community Foundation of South Alabama
212 Street Joseph Street, P.O. Box 990
Mobile, AL 36601-0990

Community Foundation of South Puget Sound Grants 506

The foundation awards grants to a variety of charitable, cultural, education, health, and welfare organizations. Grants from the unrestricted funds are considered for general operational or program support. Typical grants range from $1,000 to $7,500. Emergency grants may be considered on a case-by-case basis. Application and guidelines for grants and scholarships are available online.
Requirements: The foundation awards grants to Washington tax-exempt organizations primarily for use in Thurston, Mason, and Lewis Counties, except on instructions of the donor at the time of the gift or bequest.
Restrictions: Grants do not support religious organizations for religious purposes; individuals; annual campaigns of organizations (direct mail or special events); political or lobbying activities; organizations that discriminate based on race, creed, or ethnic group; capital campaigns for bricks and mortar or endowment funds; or for multiple year commitments.
Geographic Focus: Washington
Date(s) Application is Due: Apr 3; Oct 2
Amount: 1,000 - 7,500 USD
Samples: Rochester Organization of Families, $7,000—to help maintain ROOF's Kid's Place academic enrichment program for 50 low -income, at-risk children in the first through fifth grades (2008); Harmony Hill, $4,500—to purchase a computer server to maintain its extensive database of clients and donors; which in turn supports their mission to improve the quality of life for those affected by cancer (2008); Thurston Mason Project Access, $4,000—to make donated medical services available to uninsured, low-income Thurston County residents with acute, urgent conditions (2008).
Contact: Norma Schuiteman, Executive Director; (360) 705-3340; (360) 705-2656; legacy@thecommunityfoundation.com
Internet: http://www.thecommunityfoundation.com/grants.php
Sponsor: Community Foundation of South Puget
111 Market Street NE, Suite 375
Olympia, WA 98501

Community Foundation of Street Joseph County ArtsEverywhere Grants 507

The ArtsEverywhere Fund seeks to raise artistic quality, strengthen volunteer and staff leadership, enhance the capacity of arts organizations and the arts community, foster and support local talent, and inspire community pride. Grants will be competitively awarded in the following categories: capacity building (matching grants of up to $5,000); program or project support (matching grants of up to $5,000); and major venture funding (matching grants of up to $50,000, potentially renewable for up to three years, for a maximum commitment of $150,000). Applicants may apply for any or all types of funding.
Requirements: Street Joseph County nonprofit or public agencies with a demonstrated, substantial (though not necessarily exclusive) commitment to the arts as part of its overall mission and appropriate participation in the ArtsEverywhere initiative are eligible to apply for grant funding. Detailed guidelines and application information for each grant category are available at the website.
Restrictions: Grants are not made to fund: operational phases of established programs; endowment campaigns; religious organizations for religious purposes; individuals directly; development or public relations activities (e.g. literature, videos, etc.); retirement of debts; camperships; annual appeals or membership contributions; travel for bands, sports teams, classes, etc; computers (unless presented as a necessary component of larger program or objective); and post-event or after-the-fact situations.
Geographic Focus: Indiana
Date(s) Application is Due: May 1; Nov 1
Amount: Up to 50,000 USD
Contact: Angela Butiste, Senior Program Officer; (574) 232-0041; (574) 233-1906; angela@cfsjc.org
Internet: http://www.cfsjc.org/initiatives/artseverywhere/artseverywhere_grants.html
Sponsor: Community Foundation of Street Joseph County
205 W Jefferson Boulevard, P.O. Box 837
South Bend, IN 46624

Community Foundation of Street Joseph County Indiana Arts Commission (IAC) Regional Partnership 508

The Community Foundation of Street Joseph County is one of 12 regional partners with the Indiana Arts Commission (IAC), dedicated to advancing arts and culture throughout Indiana. Indiana Arts Commission grants awarded through the Regional Arts Partnership are available to qualifying nonprofit organizations through a competitive application process. Nonprofit, tax-exempt organizations or public entities with eligible arts programming and addresses in the following counties are eligible to apply for funding from the Region 2 Partner, the Community Foundation of Street Joseph County: Elkhart, Fulton, Kosciusko, Marshall, Street Joseph, and Starke. Three separate grant categories are funded, based on the need and size of the organization. The Arts Project Support Grant funds arts and non-arts organizations to support a distinct aspect of the organization's arts activities, such as a one-time event, single production or exhibition, educational seminar, or training sessions. The Arts Organization Support I Grant funds one year of annual operating support for the ongoing artistic and administrative functions of eligible arts organizations. These organizations must have arts as primary mission, with an annual income of less than $250,000. The Arts Organization Support II Grant funds two years of operating support for the ongoing artistic and administrative functions of an organization of an operating budget of over $250,000. Detailed information about each category is posted on the website.
Restrictions: Each grant has specific guidelines for approval.
Geographic Focus: Indiana
Contact: Indiana Arts Commission Grants Contact; (574) 232-0041; (574) 233-1906
Internet: http://www.cfsjc.org/grants/iac/iac_grants.html
Sponsor: Community Foundation of Street Joseph County
205 W Jefferson Boulevard, P.O. Box 837
South Bend, IN 46624

Community Foundation of Street Joseph County Special Project Challenge Grants 509

The Special Project Challenge Grants assist public and other 501(c)3 agencies in their efforts to serve community needs. For every $1 raised by the chosen agency, the Community Foundation will match $1. The foundation encourages projects in the following areas: community development and urban affairs; health and human services; parks, recreation, and environment; and youth and education.
Requirements: In additional to the online application, all applicants must submit the following materials online: up to a two page proposal narrative; a detailed project budget; current board roster with officers identified; fiscal year income statement; proof of nonprofit status. Application materials must be submitted via email to grants@cfsjc.org in word processing format (narrative or budget) or Microsoft Excel (budget). Hard copy applications are no longer accepted.
Restrictions: Grants are not made to fund: operational phases of established programs; endowment campaigns; religious organizations for religious purposes; individuals directly; development or public relations activities (e.g. literature, videos, etc.); retirement of debts; camperships; annual appeals or membership contributions; travel for bands, sports teams, classes, etc; j) computers (unless presented as a necessary component of larger program or objective); and post-event or after-the-fact situations.
Geographic Focus: Indiana

Date(s) Application is Due: Mar 1; Oct 1
Samples:
Contact: Angela Butiste, Senior Program Officer; (574) 232-0041; (574) 233-1906; angela@cfsjc.org
Internet: http://www.cfsjc.org/grants/sproj/special_project_grants.html
Sponsor: Community Foundation of Street Joseph County
205 W Jefferson Boulevard, P.O. Box 837
South Bend, IN 46624

Community Foundation of Switzerland County Grants 510

The Community Foundation of Switzerland County is a nonprofit organization created by and for the people of the Switzerland County area with one goal, making our community a better place to live, now and for future generations. Organizations applying for a grant may request up to $1,000. In addition, the Community Foundation will give priority to grant applications that focus on the basic needs of the community. While the term basic needs can be interpreted differently, in general, the Community Foundation uses the term to describe food, housing, shelter, health care, clothing, personal care, transportation services and other essential needs that people in our community may not have due to the weakened economy. While grant applications addressing basic needs of the community will be given priority, the Community Foundation still welcomes applications for other programs and projects that benefit Switzerland County. To make grant dollars available on a timely basis, there are no deadlines. Grant letters will be reviewed and decided upon monthly. Any request in by the 1st of each month will be notified of a decision by the end of that month.
Requirements: Any organization with a 501(c)3 or any organization that provides a program with charitable intent and has a fiscal agent is eligible to apply. To apply for a grant, an organization must write a one page letter explaining: who will be doing the requested program/project; what will be done (program, purchase, training, etc); when it will be done; where it will be done; and how much it will cost (short budget). If the cost is more than being requested from the Community Foundation, indicate where the rest of the money will come from. There will be no match required for these grants, so a program or project can be totally funded by a request or it may be part of a larger project.
Geographic Focus: Indiana
Amount: 1,000 USD
Contact: Pam Acton, Grants DIrector; (812) 427-9160; (812) 427-4033; pacton@cfsci.org
Internet: http://www.cfsci.org/
Sponsor: Community Foundation of Switzerland County
303 Ferry Street, P.O. Box 46
Vevay, IN 47043

Community Foundation of the Eastern Shore Technical Mini Grants 511

Twice each year, the Community Foundation of the Eastern Shore awards Technical Mini Grants through its Nonprofit Support Program to a wide range of organizations, whose programs benefit health and human services, education, arts and culture, community affairs, environmental conservation, and historic preservation. The purpose of the program is to provide grants of up to $1000 to nonprofit agencies for the purchase of equipment, attendance at training or other such resources necessary to enhance staff's capability. Grants are given to individual organizations.
Requirements: To be eligible, an organization must be a designated 501(c)3 nonprofit under the Internal Revenue Code and provide evidence of that designation. The organization must be located in Maryland, providing services for residents of the lower three counties of the Eastern Shore: Worcester, Wicomico, and Somerset.
Restrictions: The Community Foundation's Technical Mini Grants does not make grants for: building campaigns; operational deficits; operational support; debt retirement; sectarian religious programs; endowment funds; fundraising campaigns; program development. Governmental organizations/agencies and religious organizations are not eligible to apply.
Geographic Focus: Maryland
Date(s) Application is Due: Jan 20; Jul 20
Amount: 100 - 1,000 USD
Contact: Erica N. Joseph, Program Officer; (410) 742-9911; (410) 742-6638; joseph@cfes.org
Internet: http://www.cfes.org/non_profit_support.php
Sponsor: Community Foundation of the Eastern Shore
1324 Belmont Avenue, Suite 401
Salisbury, MD 21804

Community Foundation of the Verdugos Educational Endowment Fund Grants 512

The Educational Endowment Fund provides financial support to innovative as well as traditional educational programs and projects in public and private schools and community organizations in the Crescenta Valley, California region. The goal is to enrich educational opportunities by supporting building, equipment, instruction, guidance, coaching, practical application, classroom activities, in-service, training and/or practice programs. Grants will support: equipment purchase, replacement & modernization; improvement to facilities including athletic facilities; printed materials; fundraising events or capital campaigns; classroom materials; public/private schools and colleges; child day care/development centers; libraries; hospitals; community enrichment projects; salaries. All qualified organizations are invited to submit grant applications once a year for grants that will be awarded at the Crescenta Valley Chamber of Commerce Installation Luncheon in early January. Average grant sizes are from $500 to $3,000. The grant application is available at the Community Foundation of the Verdugos website. The application must be submitted by October 9th.
Requirements: 501(c)3 IRS nonprofit public charities in the Crescenta Valley region of California (includes La Crescenta, Montrose, Tujunga and La Canada) and, organizations located outside the Crescenta Valley but delivering educational programs in the Crescenta Valley are eligible to apply. Please indicate the number of Crescenta Valley residents who will be served by your program. An organization may apply for no more than two grants during a grant cycle. Note, the president, school principal or leader must indicate awareness of multiple requests and each application must be for different types of support.
Restrictions: Grants will not support: uniforms or clothing; travel expenses; fiscal agents; individuals and individual scholarships; endowment funds; feasibility studies or consulting fees; advertising; research; political lobbying, voter registration or political campaigns; insurance or maintenance contracts; faith-based projects.
Geographic Focus: California
Date(s) Application is Due: Oct 9
Amount: 500 - 3,000 USD
Samples: Crescenta Valley Arts Council, $500 (2009); Verdugo Hills Hospital Foundation, $1,000 (2009); YMCA of the Foothills & Rosemont School, $750 (2009).
Contact: Edna Karinski, Executive Director; (818) 241-8040; (818) 241-8045; info@communityfoundationoftheverdugos.org
Internet: http://www.glendalecommunityfoundation.org/grants_endowment.php
Sponsor: Community Foundation of the Verdugos
330 Arden Avenue, Suite 130
Glendale, CA 91203

Community Foundation of the Verdugos Grants 513

The Community Foundation of the Verdugos welcomes grant requests from public agencies and nonprofit organizations that serve the Verdugo region including Burbank, Glendale, La Canada Flintridge, La Crescenta, Montrose, and Verdugo City of California. Grant recipients must have appropriate fiscal and program accountability. Average grant amounts range from $2,500 to $10,000. Grants are provided in the following areas of interest: arts and culture; civic; health and human services (examples include projects and services for the disabled/handicapped, general community health, or homeless services); education programs; senior services; student aid (scholarships); youth services; environment and; community. Grant application and, application guidelines are available at the Foundation's website. Grants are made three times a year. Deadline for grant applications are February 1, June 1, and September 1. Scholarship deadline is March 5. Only one proposal from an organization is permitted per grant cycle. Approval or denial of your request will be provided to you in writing.
Requirements: The Foundation funds nonprofit organizations that: have IRS nonprofit status; predominantly serve the Verdugo region of California (Glendale, La Canada Flintridge, La Crescenta, Montrose, Verdugo City) and adjacent areas; capital equipment that helps to increase your organization's long-term sustainability or services to increase impact in the Verdugo region; programs (including related overhead, supplies and administrative expenses) responsive to changing community needs and which increase impact in the Verdugo region. Requests that provide significance and impact for the Verdugo region in the areas of arts and culture, children/youth, education and literacy, health and human services, civic activities, senior services, and environmental/animal related programs.

Restrictions: The Foundation does not make grants or loans to individuals unless they are students receiving scholarships. The Foundation also does not provide funds for religious or political purposes, for budget deficits, or projects that are usually the responsibility of a public agency.
Geographic Focus: California
Date(s) Application is Due: Feb 1; Mar 5; Jun 1; Sep 1
Amount: 25,000 - 10,000 USD
Samples: San Gabriel Valley Habitat for Humanity, $10,000—toward handicapped lifts (2009); Salvation Army Glendale Corporation, $10,000—ZONE after school program for low-income and at-risk children (2009); College View School, $10,000—toward a new playground structure (2009).
Contact: Edna Karinski, Executive Director; (818) 241-8040; (818) 241-8045; info@communityfoundationoftheverdugos.org
Internet: http://www.glendalecommunityfoundation.org/grants.php
Sponsor: Community Foundation of the Verdugos
330 Arden Avenue, Suite 130
Glendale, CA 91203

Community Foundation Serving Boulder County Grants 514
The foundation awards grants to eligible Colorado nonprofit organizations in its areas of interest, including arts, civic involvement, education, the environment, and health and human services. Types of support include capital campaigns, endowments, general operating support, and program support. The foundation also offers a variety of programs to build capacity and the organizational structure of nonprofits. Deadlines vary depending on program, check website or contact staff for exact dates.
Requirements: Colorado 501(c)3 nonprofit organizations serving the Boulder area are eligible.
Geographic Focus: Colorado
Samples: Colorado Music Festival (CO)—$2000; Imagination Makers Theatre Co (CO)—$2500; Old Firehouse Art Ctr (CO)—$1000; Turning the Wheel Productions (CO)—$1000.
Contact: Carly Hare, (303) 442-0436, ext. 111; (303) 442-1221; Carly@commfound.org
Internet: http://www.commfound.org/grants/index.html
Sponsor: Community Foundation Serving Boulder County
1123 Spruce Street
Boulder, CO 80302

Community Foundation Silicon Valley Advancing the Arts Initiative 515
The initiative is designed to strengthen and connect local arts organizations to one another and with the community. The primary focus of the grants program is to advance the work of individual organizations and the sector by providing one-year general support grants and technical support to small and mid-sized arts organizations with budgets between $50,000 and $2 million. The foundation will select 15 to 20 participants that represent diverse geographies, budget sizes, and disciplines. Grantees may apply for a technical assistance grant, and will meet at least twice during the year to attend workshops and network with one another. Complete guidelines are available online.
Requirements: California 501(c)3 nonprofit organizations located in Santa Clara County or Southern San Mateo County and that provide arts activities in Santa Clara County and/or Southern San Mateo County are eligible.
Restrictions: For-profit organizations; elementary schools, high schools, and colleges; and government entities are not eligible. Grants may not be applied toward support for political or religious purposes, debt retirement, or costs already incurred. Applicant organization may not be a current grantee of both The David and Lucile Packard Foundation and the James Irvine Foundation.
Geographic Focus: California
Date(s) Application is Due: Jan 9
Amount: 5,000 - 15,000 USD
Contact: Melissa Downey, (408) 278-2255; (408) 278-0280; mdowney@cfsv.org
Internet: http://www.cfsv.org/grants_advancingarts.html
Sponsor: Community Foundation Silicon Valley
60 S Market Street, Suite 1000
San Jose, CA 95113

Community Foundation Silicon Valley Grants 516
The foundation supports California nonprofits in its areas of interest, including arts and cultural participation, education and lifelong learning, self-reliant individuals and family, and neighborhood and civic projects. The foundation also supports the Youth in Philanthropy program and early literacy grants. Preference is given to proposals that focus on the prevention of problems rather than the cure, equip people to become self-sufficient, encourage programs that take a comprehensive approach to addressing interrelated problems, promote cooperation and collaboration among agencies, encourage leveraging and matching grant opportunities, and provide seed funding for innovative projects. Additional types of support include program development, technical assistance, consulting services, and general operating grants. Grants generally are made for one year of support; long-term commitments are contingent upon annual review of progress and available funds. Guidelines and application are available online.
Requirements: Nonprofit organizations benefiting Santa Clara County and southern San Mateo County, CA, are eligible.
Restrictions: In general, the foundation does not consider fundraising events, capital equipment and endowment campaigns, on-going operating expenses, existing debts/obligations, for-profit schools, or individuals.
Geographic Focus: California
Amount: Up to 25,000 USD
Samples: Child Advocates of Santa Clara and San Mateo Counties (San Jose, CA)—to recruit and train new child-advocacy volunteers, $225,000 over three years; Project H.E.L.P (High Expectations Learning Program) (Sunnyvale, CA)—to expand this early-intervention program that provides high-quality supplemental academic instruction to poorly performing students at public elementary schools in Santa Clara County, CA, $225,0000 over three years.
Contact: Jeff Sunshine, Director of Programs; (408) 278-2200; (408) 278-0280; jsunshine@cfsv.org or info@cfsv.org
Internet: http://www.cfsv.org/grants_focusareas.html
Sponsor: Community Foundation Silicon Valley
60 S Market Street, Suite 1000
San Jose, CA 95113

Community Memorial Foundation Grants 517
The foundation encourages public/private endeavors in Illinois by nurturing the formation of creative initiatives and innovative funding strategies. Collaborative efforts may include participation with nonprofit organizations, governments, schools, and the business sector. In general, the foundation gives preference to organizations that reach underserved segments of the population. A broad range of funding includes service delivery programs for vulnerable populations, start-up funds, building construction/renovation, project support, general operating support, and educational programs. Generally, the foundation does not consider more than one proposal from any one institution and favors funding noncapital programs.
Requirements: 501(c)3 organizations located in the Illinois communities of Argo, Bridgeview, Broadview, Brookfield, Burr Ridge, Clarendon Hills, Countryside, Darien, Downers Grove, Hickory Hills, Hinsdale, Hodgkins, Indian Head Park, Justice, La Grange, La Grange Park, Lyons, McCook, North Riverside, Oak Brook, Riverside, Stickney, Summit, Westchester, Western Springs, Westmont, Willow Springs, and Willowbrooks may apply.
Restrictions: Grants are not awarded to individuals, sectarian or religious organizations, or for purposes to influence legislation or other political activities.
Geographic Focus: Illinois
Date(s) Application is Due: Mar 31; Sep 30
Amount: Up to 250,000 USD
Samples: All Saints Episcopal Church & First Congregational Church (Western Springs, IL)—to establish a program to match volunteers with service opportunities, with a particular focus on older adults, $19,750. Parent & Community Network (Western Springs, IL) —to sponsor a conference and workshops on relevant issues to parents of children in School District 204 and feeder schools, $5,000. Boy Scouts of America-Des Plaines Valley Council (La Grange, IL)—for general operating support, $10,000 challenge grant.
Contact: Deborah Kustra, Grants Manager; (630) 654-4729; (630) 654-3402; info@cmfdn.org
Internet: http://www.cmfdn.org/guidelines.html
Sponsor: Community Memorial Foundation
15 Spinning Wheel Road, Suite 326
Hinsdale, IL 60521

COMPAS Grants 518
COMPAS helps support the creation of art in communities across Minnesota through its granting programs through support of arts organizations' work in schools and communities. Grant programs include 3M Award for Innovation in the Arts—honors creative approaches to arts education and outreach;

American Express Audience Development Fund—helps Minnesota arts organizations outside of the seven-county metropolitan area reach new audiences; Community Art Program—through the McKnight Foundation, provides grants for neighborhood arts projects; General Fund—provides resources for established arts organizations striving to reach new audiences; Medtronic Arts Access Program—promotes cross-cultural understanding and offers increased accessibility to the arts; and School Arts Fund—supports partnerships between schools and community arts organizations. Application and guidelines are available online.
Requirements: Any group, organization, or individual is eligible to apply. All proposed activities must occur within the cities of Saint Paul and/or Minneapolis.
Restrictions: Grants do not support capital improvements, mortgage payments, property purchase, or building construction; deficit financing; administrative costs unrelated to the CAP sponsored project; fundraising events; or projects that result in lobbying for particular legislation, promoting of a particular religious belief, are discriminatory, or in any way violate federal, state or local laws.
Geographic Focus: Minnesota
Amount: Up to 15,000 USD
Contact: John Mentzos, (651) 292-3287; (651) 292-3258; john@compas.org
Internet: http://www.compas.org/pages/grants.html
Sponsor: COMPAS
304 Landmark Center, 75 W Fifth Street
Saint Paul, MN 55102-1414

Compass Bank Foundation Grants 519
The Foundation, established in 1981, supports organizations involved with arts and culture, higher and law education, health, heart disease, multiple sclerosis, medical research, youth development, human services, and philanthropy. Giving is primarily centered in the states of Alabama, Arizona, Colorado, Florida, New Mexico, and Texas. There are no specific deadlines with which to adhere. Contact the Foundation for further application information and guidelines.
Restrictions: No support is provided for religious organizations, and there are no grants to individuals (except for employee-related scholarships).
Geographic Focus: Alabama, Arizona, Colorado, Florida, New Mexico, Texas
Samples: University of Alabama, Tuscaloosa, AL, $375,000; United Way, Mile High, Denver, CO, $29,167; Alabama Symphonic Association, Birmingham, AL, $55,000; John P. McGovern Museum of Health and Medical Science, Houston, TX, $20,000
Contact: Jerry W. Powell, Treasurer; (205) 297-3960
Sponsor: Compass Bank Foundation
P.O. Box 10566, MC AL/BI/CH/ACT
Birmingham, AL 35296-0002

Comprehensive Health Education Foundation Grants 520
The foundation awards grants to support programs that address health inequities. The initial grantmaking effort will focus on Clark, Pierce, and Spokane Counties in Washington State. One-year grants of up to $20,000 each will be awarded to culturally appropriate, community-led collaborations to test their best idea on how to make it easier for people who suffer from health inequities to move more and eat healthier. Health inequities are defined as differences in the incidence, prevalence, mortality, and burden of diseases that exist for specific populations in the United States. Low-income individuals and people of color within the United States generally have higher rates of poor health and injury than those who are in higher-income groups and are Caucasian.
Requirements: 501(c)3 tax-exempt organizations located in Clark, Pierce, and Spokane Counties in Washington State and units of government that are nondiscriminatory in policy and practice regarding disabilities, age, sex, sexual orientation, race, ethnic origin, or creed are eligible.
Restrictions: Support will not be provided for building or land acquisitions; equipment or furniture purchases; endowment funds; emergency funds; grants to individuals; fellowships/scholarships; research; debt retirement; fundraising activities; general fund drives; indirect overhead; or CHEF programs or products.
Geographic Focus: Washington
Amount: 500 - 20,000 USD
Contact: Kari L. Lewis, Grant Coordinator; (800) 323-2433, ext. 1899; (206) 824-3072; KariL@chef.org
Internet: http://www.chef.org/about/grants.php
Sponsor: Comprehensive Health Education Foundation
159 S Jackson Street, Suite 510
Seattle, WA 98104

Compton Foundation Grants 521
The foundation was founded to address community, national, and international concerns in the fields of peace and world order, population, and the environment. Other concerns of the foundation include equal educational opportunity, community welfare and social justice, and culture and the arts. The foundation makes three kinds of grants. Project grants generally are made to national organizations for projects that fall within the primary areas of peace and world order, population, and the environment. These grants may be for regional (Pacific Coastal states), national, or international activities and are usually for projects of limited duration. Project grants are considered by the board two times a year. Discretionary grants are made at the discretion, and usually at the initiation, of individual board members. Most grants in this area are made for community welfare and social justice, and culture and the arts. Renewal grants provide general support to organizations whose activities have been funded by the foundation for many years and whose work continues to be considered particularly effective by the board. Many of the foundation's grants in the area of equal educational opportunity, and some grants in peace and world order and population, are renewal grants.
Requirements: The foundation makes grants only to tax-exempt organizations and institutions.
Restrictions: Grants will not be made to individuals.
Geographic Focus: All U.S. States
Date(s) Application is Due: Mar 7; Sep 7
Amount: 5,000 - 50,000 USD
Samples: Colorado Environmental Coalition—for Colorado Instream Flow Project, $20,000; Klamath Forest Alliance—for Klamath Riverkeeper and Karuk Tribe Klamath Dams Campaign, $30,000; San Francisco Education Fund—for Peer Resources Program, $10,000.
Contact: Edith T. Eddy, Executive Director; (650) 508-1181; (650) 508-1191; info@comptonfoundation.org
Internet: http://www.comptonfoundation.org/application_procedures.html
Sponsor: Compton Foundation
255 Shoreline Drive, Suite 540
Redwood City, CA 94065

ConAgra Foods Foundation Community Impact Grants 522
The Community Impact Grants (CIG) program will award grants between $10,000 and $100,000 to impactful, grassroots organizations that leverage innovation and creativity to address childhood hunger and nutrition needs in communities where ConAgra Foods' employees live and work or states where 20% or more of children are food insecure. Organizations that demonstrate a strong alignment with the Foundation's giving strategies (i.e., direct service, capacity building, and advocacy) and core funding priorities have the greatest chance of receiving a grant. The CIG program is a two-step, competitive process that first requires the submission of an Letter of Inquiry (LOI) and then the subsequent completion of a full application if invited to apply for a grant. For more detailed program information and guidelines see: http://www.nourishkidstoday.org/downloads/pdf/CIGGuidelines.pdf.
Requirements: The preference of ConAgra Foods Foundation is to award Community Impact Grants to organizations located in states with a child food insecurity rate of 20% or more according to Feeding America's Child Hunger Study as well as those communities where ConAgra Foods has a significant employee presence.
Restrictions: ConAgra Foods Foundation does not fund: professional or amateur sports organizations and teams, or athletic events and programs; political organizations; terrorist organizations or those not compliant with the U.S. A Patriot Act; fundraising events; emergency funding; loans, debt reduction or operating deficits; individuals; endowments; capital campaigns (unless solicited at the founder's discretion); memorial campaigns; elementary and secondary education.
Geographic Focus: Arizona, Arkansas, California, Colorado, District of Columbia, Florida, Georgia, Idaho, Illinois, Indiana, Iowa, Louisiana, Massachusetts, Michigan, Minnesota, Mississippi, Missouri, New Mexico, North Carolina, Ohio, Oregon, Pennsylvania, South Carolina, Tennessee, Texas, Washington, Wisconsin
Date(s) Application is Due: Jan 29
Amount: 10,000 - 100,000 USD
Contact: Program Contact; foundation@conagrafoods.com
Internet: http://www.nourishkidstoday.org/about-us/application-guidelines.jsp
Sponsor: ConAgra Foods Foundation
One ConAgra Drive, CC-304
Omaha, NE 68102-5001

ConAgra Foods Foundation Nourish Our Community Grants 523

The Foundation awards Nourish Our Community Grants to non-profit organizations based on recommendations from employees. While any organization that is working to address community needs is eligible for funding, preference will be given to those that seek to provide children and their families with access to food and nutrition education. Organizations must be located in the communities where ConAgra Foods employees live and work in order to be considered for a Nourish Our Community grant. Nourish Our Community grants typically range from $5,000 to $25,000, with an average grant of $10,000. The grant requests are reviewed by a committee representative of a cross-section of employees within the company. Organizations can receive funding for up to three consecutive years and then must postpone applying for support for one grant making cycle. Applications for Nourish Our Community grant requests are reviewed annually. The application process for the current fiscal year is June 1-May 31. Additional guidelines are available at: http://www.nourishkidstoday.org/about-us/application-guidelines.jsp

Requirements: Non-profit organizations based in AR, AZ, CA, CO, DC, FL, GA, IA, ID, IL, IN, LA, MA, MI, MN, MO, MS, NC, NE, NM, OH, OR, PA, SC, TN, TX, WA, and WI are eligible to apply for this grant.

Restrictions: ConAgra Foods Foundation does not fund: professional or amateur sports organizations and teams, or athletic events and programs; political organizations; terrorist organizations or those not compliant with the U.S. A Patriot Act; fundraising events; emergency funding; loans, debt reduction or operating deficits; individuals; endowments; capital campaigns (unless solicited at the founder's discretion); memorial campaigns; elementary and secondary education.

Geographic Focus: Arizona, Arkansas, California, Colorado, Connecticut, District of Columbia, Florida, Georgia, Idaho, Illinois, Indiana, Iowa, Louisiana, Maine, Massachusetts, Michigan, Minnesota, Mississippi, Missouri, New Hampshire, New Mexico, North Carolina, Ohio, Oregon, Pennsylvania, Rhode Island, South Carolina, Tennessee, Texas, Vermont, Washington, Wisconsin

Date(s) Application is Due: May 31

Amount: 5,000 - 25,000 USD

Contact: Program Contact; foundation@conagrafoods.com

Internet: http://www.nourishkidstoday.org/about-us/application-guidelines.jsp

Sponsor: ConAgra Foods Foundation
One ConAgra Drive, CC-304
Omaha, NE 68102-5001

Connecticut Commission on Culture & Tourism Organizational Support Grants 524

The Organizational Support Program (OSP) offers funding designed to advance the mission of arts organizations and support a broad range of arts programs in Connecticut. Connecticut arts organizations (registered as 501(c)3 non-profits) are eligible to apply for General Operating Support (GOS) to assist with administrative and/or artistic expenses. Non-arts organizations (including colleges and universities) as well as arts organizations may apply for Project Support funding for a specific activity, such as an exhibition or music series, or for an ongoing arts program.

Requirements: Organizations must be incorporated in Connecticut for at least two years and have a minimum two-year history of public programming to be eligible. Projects eligible for funding must also have a two-year history. Applicants are required to match funds received from the Commission with cash income from other sources. GOS applicants must have a minimum operating income of $25,000. Projects must have a minimum budget of $10,000.

Restrictions: Ineligible Entities: Past CCT grantees with overdue final reports; Elementary and secondary schools; colleges and universities; Park and recreation departments or other units of local government; Local Arts Agencies; For-profit organizations; Religious institutions and organizations; Organizations acting as fiscal agents for individual artists or other groups. Ineligible Activities: Brick and mortar activities, equipment expenditures, facility construction, or capital improvements; Hospitality expenses, such as food and beverages; Interest expenses paid on loans or payments to eliminate or reduce existing deficits; Scholarships; Projects that are primarily fundraisers, such as social events or entrepreneurial activities; Arts programs/activities that are essentially recreational or avocational.

Geographic Focus: Connecticut

Date(s) Application is Due: Feb 6

Contact: Kathleen DeMeo, Program Manager; (860) 256-2735; kathleen.demeo@ct.gov

Internet: http://www.cultureandtourism.org

Sponsor: Connecticut Commission on Culture and Tourism
1 Constitution Plaza, 2nd Floor
Hartford, CT 06103

Connelly Foundation Grants 525

To achieve its mission to foster learning and improve the quality of life, Connelly Foundation provides grants toward costs associated with programs, direct services, general operations and capital projects to non-profit organizations and institutions working in the following fields: education; health and human services; arts and culture and civic enterprise. The Foundation supports non-profits with strong leadership, sound ideas, future viability, and attainable and well defined goals. It directs its philanthropy toward 501(c)3 organizations and institutions based in and serving Philadelphia and the counties of Bucks, Chester, Delaware, Montgomery and the City of Camden. The Foundation values the proposal process. Given its preference to review a comprehensive package as a primer for discussion, letters of inquiry or requests for pre-proposal discussions are not deemed necessary. Written proposals from nonprofit organizations are accepted and reviewed by the Connelly Foundation throughout the year, there are no deadlines.

Requirements: 501(c)3 organizations and institutions based in and serving in Philadelphia and its surrounding counties of Bucks, Chester, Delaware, and Montgomery in Pennsylvania and in the City of Camden, New Jersey are eligible to apply. There are determined parameters to the Foundation's financial support. It provides non-profit organizations only one grant within a twelve month period. As a general practice, it does not fund advocacy, annual appeals, charter schools, conferences, environmental projects, feasability or planning studies, general solicitations, historic preservation projects, national organizations, organizations focused on a single disease, public schools or research.

Restrictions: The foundation does not award grants to individuals, or political or national organizations; Nor does it respond to annual appeals or general letters of solicitation.

Geographic Focus: Pennsylvania

Contact: Emily C. Riley, Executive Vice President; (610) 834-3222; (610) 834-0866; info@connellyfdn.org

Sponsor: Connelly Foundation
1 Tower Bridge, Suite 1450
West Conshohocken, PA 19428

ConocoPhillips Foundation Grants 526

The foundation makes charitable grants (primarily in the communities where it has operations) in support of education, medical programs, human services, civic, cultural, youth, and other services. Contributions will be considered for organizations such as: federated organizations; educational institutions, both public and private, primarily at the college level; youth organizations; hospital and medical facilities and programs such as hospital buildings and equipment, improvement campaigns and other medical facilities; cultural organizations; civic services; and human service organizations. Applicants may download the application form from the website. There are no application deadlines.

Requirements: 501(c)3 tax-exempt organizations and, where appropriate 170(c) organizations, and international nonprofit organizations are eligible. Proof of the exemption must be submitted with grant applications.

Restrictions: Grants do not support religious organizations for religious purposes; war veterans and fraternal service organizations; endowment funds; national health organizations and programs; grants or loans to individuals; fund-raising events; corporate memberships or contributions to chambers of commerce, taxpayer associations and other bodies whose activities are expected to directly benefit the company; or political organizations, campaigns and candidates.

Geographic Focus: Alaska, California, Illinois, Louisiana, Montana, New Jersey, Oklahoma, Pennsylvania, Texas, Washington

Date(s) Application is Due: Aug 1

Amount: Up to 46,000,000 USD

Samples: Christian Community Service (Houston, TX)—$25,000; Jewish Day School of Metropolitan Seattle (Seattle, WA)—$25,000; YMCA of Greater Seattle (Seattle, WA)—$15,000.

Contact: Community Relations Manager

Internet: http://www.conocophillips.com/about/Contribution+Guidelines/index.htm

Sponsor: ConocoPhillips Foundation Grants
600 N Dairy Ashford
Houston, TX 77079

ConocoPhillips Grants 527

ConocoPhillips maintains a philanthropic contributions budget for nonprofit, charitable programs closely tied to its corporate goals and focused primarily in locations of strong business interests. Submit an executive summary outlining the purpose of the program or project, how it will be accomplished, expected results, a budget (noting administrative expenses such as: salaries and fees, program expenses and total income), other sources of financial support and a copy of the IRS tax determination letter that confirms 501(c)3 status. The grant must be used in the United States. Requests for grants in non-U.S. locations should be made directly to the ConocoPhillips international office doing business in that part of the world. Education and youth, civic and arts, employee volunteerism, safety and social services, and the environment are focus areas.

Requirements: Applications are accepted from areas where ConocoPhillips has a strong business presence, e.g., Texas and Oklahoma. All contributions are to be used within the United States.

Restrictions: ConocoPhillips does not award funds to individuals, sectarian or religious organization, promotional sponsorship and advertising (marketing related) or an endowment.

Geographic Focus: Alaska, California, Illinois, Louisiana, Montana, New Jersey, Oklahoma, Pennsylvania, Texas

Samples: Houston Baptist U (Houston, TX)—for the Cultural Arts Ctr capital campaign, $50,000; U of Texas (Austin, TX)—for scholarships, fellowships, and special programs in business, engineering, law, and the natural sciences, $1 million.

Contact: Program Contact; (281) 293-2685

Internet: http://www.conocophillips.com/about/Contribution+Guidelines/index.htm

Sponsor: ConocoPhillips Corporation
600 N Dairy Ashford, MA 3144
Houston, TX 77079

Constellation Energy Corporate EcoStar Grants 528

Environmental stewardship is one of Constellation Energy's core foundational values. Because of this commitment to use natural resources responsibly, prevent pollution, improve energy efficiency and enhance it's stewardship efforts, EcoStar Grants are now being offered to local communities where Constellation Energy does business. See, Constellation Energy's website for: listing of funding locations; on-line application; additional guidelines. Project should fit at least one of five environmental focus areas: Pollution Prevention; Education; Energy Efficiency; Conservation; Community Activism.

Requirements: Organization must be a 501(c)3 nonprofit with a Board of Directors.

Restrictions: Grant funds limited to maximum of 20% administration and office expenses (i.e., salaries, phone and postage)

Geographic Focus: All U.S. States

Date(s) Application is Due: Mar 16

Amount: 5,000 USD

Contact: Larry McDonnell, Director; (401) 470-7433; media@constellation.com

Internet: http://www.constellation.com/portal/site/constellation/menuitem.999b6fed85785a2399084010016176a0

Sponsor: Constellation Energy Corporate
100 Constellation Way, Suite 1000C
Baltimore, MD 21202

Constellation Energy Corporate Grants 529

Constellation Energy provides its philanthropic resources to non-profit organizations that make an impact in these key focus areas: energy Initiatives; environment; education; economic development. Applications are accepted at various times throughout the year. Grant, Sponsorship, Banner Hanging, and In-Kind requests under $10,000 are reviewed on a rolling basis. The Corporate Contributions Committee meets bi-annually, in May and October, to review significant financial grant requests of $10,000 or more. Grant requests should be submitted by April 1 and September 1 respectively. Additional guidelines and the online applications are available at the companies website.

Requirements: The company makes charitable donations to 501(c)3 tax-exempt, nonprofit organizations.

Restrictions: Constellation Energy does not make grants to: individuals; churches or religious causes; individual schools; athletic teams or events; programs located outside Constellation Energy communities.

Geographic Focus: All U.S. States

Date(s) Application is Due: Apr 1; Sep 1

Contact: Larry McDonnell, Director; (401) 470-7433; media@constellation.com

Internet: http://www.constellation.com/portal/site/constellation/menuitem.94939662e40191875fb60610025166a0/

Sponsor: Constellation Energy Corporate
100 Constellation Way, Suite 1000C
Baltimore, MD 21202

Consumers Energy Foundation 530

Since its creation in 1990, the Consumers Energy Foundation has touched countless lives and communities through it's grant programs, corporate giving and employee volunteers. The Foundation accepts grant applications from nonprofit organizations for innovative projects and activities creating measurable impact in five areas: Social Welfare, Michigan Growth and Environmental Enhancement, Education, Community and Civic, and Culture/Arts. The Foundation's areas of support include, operating budgets and capital funds.

Requirements: The Consumers Energy Foundation provides financial support primarily to Michigan organizations classified by the Internal Revenue Service as tax-exempt under section 501(c)3 of the Internal Revenue Code.

Restrictions: The following are ineligible for funding: individuals; individual scholarships; individual sponsorship related to fund-raising; organizations that do not qualify as charitable organizations as defined by the Internal Revenue Service; organizations that practice discrimination on the basis of sex, age, height, weight, marital status, race, religion, sexual orientation, creed, color, national origin, ancestry, disability, handicap, or veteran status; organizations whose operating activities are already supported by the United Way (except when the request is approved by the appropriate community United Way organization); political organizations and political campaigns; religious organizations when the contribution will be used for denominational or sectarian purposes; labor or veterans organizations; fraternal orders; social clubs; sports tournaments; talent or beauty contests; loans for small business; debt reduction campaigns.

Geographic Focus: Michigan

Amount: 500 - 10,000 USD

Samples: Saginaw Basin Land Conservancy, $6,000—for educational outreach efforts supporting wetlands preservation and land conservation within the Saginaw Bay Watershed (2009); American Red Cross Mid-Michigan Chapter, $10,000—for a disaster response vehicle (2009); Kalamazoo Department of Public Safety, $15,000—for development of a Kalamazoo Regional Police and Fire Training Center (2009).

Contact: Carolyn Bloodworth, Secretary/Treasurer; (517) 788-0432; (517) 788-2281; foundation@consumersenergy.com

Internet: http://www.consumersenergy.com/welcome.htm

Sponsor: Consumers Energy
1 Energy Place, Room EP8-210
Jackson, MI 49201-2276

Conwood Charitable Trust Grants 531

The Conwood Charitable Trust was established to make a positive impact upon the communities where Conwood employees live and work by financially supporting organizations with a demonstrated ability to assist individuals in need. The elderly, underprivileged, youth, educational institutions and the arts are supported through the Conwood Charitable Trust. Funds from the Trust are donated primarily in the company's hometown of Memphis and in the surrounding Mid-South area. Additionally, contributions are made to organizations in other areas of Tennessee (Tennessee Independent Colleges and Universities Association) and in North Carolina (Independent College Fund of North Carolina).

Requirements: Eligible applicants include any 501(c)3 organization that supports the people of Tennessee.

Geographic Focus: Tennessee

Amount: 2,500 - 30,000 USD

Samples: Rhodes College, Memphis, Tennessee, $28,000; Neighborhood Christian Centers, Memphis, Tennessee, $15,000; Madonna Learning Center, Germantown, Tennessee, $5,000.

Contact: Ed Roberson, Vice-President; (901) 761-2050; (901) 767-1302

Internet: http://www.reynoldsamerican.com/Responsibility/Community8.aspx

Sponsor: Conwood Charitable Trust
813 Ridge Lake Boulevard
Memphis, TN 38119

Cooke Foundation Grants 532

Grants are awarded primarily for culture and the arts, social services, education, programs for youth and the elderly, humanities, health, and the environment. Organizations receiving grants must be located in Hawaii or serve the people of Hawaii. Preference will be given to requests from Ohau. Types of support include general operating support, capital campaigns, building and renovations, program development, seed money, and matching funds.
Requirements: Grant making is limited to the state of Hawaii.
Restrictions: Grants are not made to individuals, churches, or religious organizations, or for endowment funds, scholarships, or fellowships.
Geographic Focus: Hawaii
Date(s) Application is Due: Mar 2; Sep 1
Amount: 5,000 - 25,000 USD
Samples: Maui Community Arts and Cultural Ctr (HI)—to support the capital campaign to complete construction, $10,000; Honolulu Dance Theatre (HI)—for a ballet performance, $2,500; Kauai Historical Society (HI)—to support the lecture series, $2,500; Honolulu Academy of Arts (HI)—annual grant, $100,000.
Contact: Carrie Shoda-Sutherland, Senior Program Officer; (808) 566-5524 or (888) 731-3863, ext. 524; (808) 521-6286; csutherland@hcf-hawaii.org
Internet: http://www.cookefdn.org/
Sponsor: Cooke Foundation, Limited
1164 Bishop Street, Suite 800
Honolulu, HI 96813

Cooper-Levy Trust Grants 533

The trust provides financial support for the United Way and other nonprofit agencies providing food, shelter, basic services, and medical care to low-income families and children in Washington state. Types of support include general operating support and project support. The majority of grants will be made in the Puget Sound area. Application guidelines are available online.
Requirements: Washington 501(c)3 nonprofit organizations in Washington's King, Pierce, Spokane, Snohomish, and Yakima Counties are eligible.
Restrictions: Funds are not awarded for capital campaigns; computer or office equipment; book, video, or website production; event sponsorship; scholarships; medical research; or to individuals. Grants are not directed toward projects serving older adults or indigent adults without dependent children.
Geographic Focus: Washington
Date(s) Application is Due: May 15; Oct 15
Amount: 5,000 - 10,000 USD
Contact: Therese Ogle, Grants Consultant, c/o The Private Bank, Union Bank of California; (206) 781-3472; (206) 784-5987; oglefounds@aol.com
Internet: http://fdncenter.org/grantmaker/cooperlevy
Sponsor: Cooper-Levy Trust
P.O. Box 3123
Seattle, WA 98114

Cooper Foundation Grants 534

The objectives of the foundation are to fund innovative ideas that promise substantial impact in Nebraska and that encourage others to make similar or larger grants for the same purpose. All grants are made in Nebraska, with the majority in Lincoln and Lancaster County. The foundation's highest priorities are education, including projects to improve teaching and learning and parent education at pre-school and K-12 levels as well as educational solutions to human service issues; human services; the arts, especially in the area of non-traditional areas of curriculum to increase accessibility by under-served audiences; the humanities; and the environment. Types of support include seed money, technical assistance, matching funds, and programs and projects. Requests for general operating funds and capital campaigns for physical facilities receive less priority.
Requirements: Nebraska 501(c)3 organizations are eligible.
Restrictions: Grants will not be made to support individuals, endowments, private foundations, businesses, proposals devoted to health issues, or proposals of a religious nature.
Geographic Focus: Nebraska
Date(s) Application is Due: Jan 15; Apr 1; Aug 1; Oct 1
Amount: Up to 10,000 USD
Samples: Lincoln Literacy Council (NE)—to support the Refugee Women's Group, $10,000; Nebraska Statewide Arboretum—to support an exhibition in eight venues across Nebraska, $5,000; Foundation for Lincoln Public Schools (NE)—for program support, to enhance reading, math and science programs, expand opportunities for low income students and families and provide additional resources to schools and teachers, $50,000.
Contact: Grants Administrator; (402) 476-7571; (402) 476-2356; info@cooperfoundation.org
Internet: http://www.cooperfoundation.org
Sponsor: Cooper Foundation
870 Wells Fargo Center, 1248 O Street
Lincoln, NE 68508

Cooper Industries Foundation Grants 535

Cooper and the Cooper Industries Foundation annually donate more then $3 Million to nonprofit organizations serving the communities where their employees live and work. The Cooper Industries Foundation accepts and reviews grant requests throughout the year. There is no deadline; however, budgets are compiled annually each fall for the following year. Applicants must submit a brief letter explaining the purpose of the request with: concise description of organization and its mission; purpose and amount of request; budget information and other funding sources; evidence of 501(c)3 tax-exempt status; current listing of board members.
Requirements: Only 501(c)3 tax-exempt-status organizations are eligible. Programs must: benefit a community where Cooper is a significant employer; be endorsed by local Cooper management when applicable; not duplicate the efforts of the four Cooper-created programs; fulfill an important community need. Program objectives must coincide with that of the company.
Restrictions: The following types of organizations are generally ineligible for funding: United Way-funded organizations; national and state organizations; religious organizations; veterans organizations; political candidates, labor and lobbying organizations; hospitals; primary and secondary schools; scholarship organizations (except National Merit).
Geographic Focus: Alabama, Georgia, Illinois, Missouri, New York, North Carolina, South Carolina, Texas, Wisconsin, United Kingdom
Contact: Victoria B. Guennewig, VP Public Affairs; (713) 209-8800; (713) 209-8982; info@cooperindustries.com
Internet: http://www.cooperindustries.com/common/aboutCooper/corporateGiving.cfm?CFID=160327&CFTOKEN=61243618
Sponsor: Cooper Industries Foundation
P.O. Box 4446
Houston, TX 77210

Cord Foundation Grants 536

The foundation makes grants to a variety of groups in three broad areas: education, social services, and the arts. Grant recipients have included higher education institutions, research groups, youth organizations, community service agencies, religious organizations, and performing and visual arts centers. Types of support include general operating support, building construction/renovation, equipment acquisition, emergency funds, program development, scholarship funds, research, and matching funds. Grants are awarded nationwide, with preference given to requests from northern Nevada. Application forms are not required.
Requirements: Nonprofit organizations are eligible but giving is primarily in the northern NV area.
Restrictions: The foundation does not support general fund-raising events, memorial campaigns, deficit fundings, conferences, dinners, or mass mailings.
Geographic Focus: Nevada
Amount: 10,000 - 250,000 USD
Samples: Saint Marys Hospital Foundation, Reno, NV, $200,000—for hospice program; Reno, City of, Reno, NV, $500,000—for purchase of YMCA property; Food Bank of Northern Nevada, Sparks, NV, $200,000—for new distribution center.
Contact: William Bradley, Trustee; (775) 323-0373
Sponsor: Cord Foundation
418 Flint Street
Reno, NV 89501-2008

Corina Higginson Trust Grants 537

The Corina Higginson Trust makes grants to organizations based in or benefiting the greater Washington Metropolitan area. The Trust's goals are: to increase opportunities for individuals for the purpose of improvement and development of their capabilities; to provide relief of the poor, distressed, and underprivileged; to promote social welfare by organizations designed to accomplish any of the above purposes or to lessen neighborhood tensions; to enhance opportunities for education about the arts and about the environment; and to eliminate prejudice and discrimination; or to defend civil rights secured by law.

Requirements: 501(c)3 District of Columbia, Maryland, and Virginia nonprofit organizations are eligible.
Restrictions: Grants do not support individuals, fixed assets, religious organizations, medical or health-related programs, endowment funds to individual schools, or scholarship funds.
Geographic Focus: District of Columbia, Maryland, Virginia
Date(s) Application is Due: Mar 1; Sep 1
Amount: 5,000 - 10,000 USD
Contact: Wilton C. Corkern, Jr. , (301) 283-2113; (301) 283-2049
Internet: http://www.corinahigginsontrust.org/instructionsforloi.html
Sponsor: Corina Higginson Trust
3400 Bryan Point Road
Accokeek, MD 20607

Cornerstone Foundation of Northeastern Wisconsin Grants **538**
The community foundation supports nonprofit organizations primarily in Brown County, Wisconsin. The foundations area of interest are: education, cultural programs, social service and, youth agencies. With an additional interest in supporting healthcare facilities. The foundation offers the following types of support: annual campaigns; building/renovation; capital campaigns; continuing support; debt reduction; emergency funds; endowments; equipment; general/operating support; matching/challenge support; program; development. Contact the foundation by telephone for guidelines before submitting a proposal, no application form is required.
Requirements: Nonprofit organizations in Green Bay and northeastern Wisconsin may submit applications for grant support. The primary focus is Brown County.
Restrictions: No grants are available to: individuals, religious, or political organizations.
Geographic Focus: Wisconsin
Date(s) Application is Due: Jan 15; Sep 15
Amount: 10,000 - 400,000 USD
Samples: Green Bay Symphony Orchestra, Green Bay, WI, $10,000—for youth orchestra program; Boys and Girls Club of Green Bay, Green Bay, WI, $400,000—for capital campaign; Salvation Army of Green Bay, Green Bay, WI, $24,900—for transitional housing program; N.E.W. Community Clinic, Green Bay, WI, $50,000—for medical expense program.
Contact: Sheri Prosser, Executive Director; (920) 490-8290; (920) 490-8620; cornerstone@cfnew.org
Sponsor: Cornerstone Foundation of Northeastern Wisconsin
111 North Washington Street, Suite 450
Green Bay, WI 54301-4208

Corning Incorporated Foundation Educational Grants **539**
The grants improve education by supporting selected K-12 school districts, community colleges and four-year institutions of higher learning primarily in communities where the sponsor company has operations. Areas of involvement have included community service programs for students, curriculum enrichment, student scholarships, facility improvement, and instructional technology projects for the classroom.
Requirements: Support goes to institutions that are tax-exempt under Section 501(c)3 of the Internal Revenue Code and which are public charities as defined in Section 509(a) of the Code. All requests to the foundation for support must be made in writing. Grant seekers are advised to submit a two- to three-page letter of inquiry, signed by the senior administrative officer of the organization.
Restrictions: Grants do not support individuals; political parties, campaigns, or causes; labor or veterans' organizations; religious or fraternal groups; volunteer emergency squads; athletic activities; courtesy advertising; or fundraising events.
Geographic Focus: All U.S. States
Amount: 1,000 - 25,000 USD
Samples: Wilson College (Chambersburg, PA)—for the Learning Resources Ctr, $5000; Corning City School District (Painted Post, NY)—to support computerization and curriculum enrichment, $33,000; Junior Achievement of Elmira (Corning, NY)—for general program support, $3000.
Contact: Karen Martin, Associate Director; (607) 974-8722; (607) 974-4756; martinkc@corning.com
Internet: http://www.corning.com/inside_corning/foundation.asp
Sponsor: Corning Foundation
1 Riverfront Plaza, MP-BH-07
Corning, NY 14831

Coughlin-Saunders Foundation Grants **540**
The foundation awards grants to nonprofit organizations in its areas of interest, including arts and arts education, higher education, religion, social services, and youth organizations. Types of support include general operating support, capital campaigns, building construction/renovation, equipment acquisition, emergency funds, program development, professorships, and scholarship funds. Proposals are preferred in January or February. Grants are made primarily for projects which benefit Alexandria, Louisiana, and the surrounding area. New Orleans and the surrounding area will be considered.
Requirements: 501(c)3 tax-exempt organizations in central Louisiana may apply.
Restrictions: Grants are not made to individuals or for fund raisers. Endowments will not be funded.
Geographic Focus: Louisiana
Amount: 100 - 40,000 USD
Contact: Ed Crump Jr., Grants Administrator; (318) 561-4070; (318) 487-7339; csfoundation@kricket.net
Sponsor: Coughlin-Saunders Foundation
2010 Gus Kaplan Drive
Alexandria, LA 71301

Covenant Mountain Ministries Grants **541**
The program, established in 1995, is a non-profit foundation dedicated to spreading the gospel through the establishment of churches and assisting in the creation of new ministries. Grants are given primarily to West Virginia organizations (Christian agencies, churches, and family service offices) that give aid to abused spouses and children. Funding comes in the form of general operations support. Though there are no deadlines, an application form can be secured by contacting the Ministries directly.
Geographic Focus: West Virginia
Amount: 500 - 1,500 USD
Samples: Sam's Place, Princeton, West Virginia, $1,500—to assist abused spouses and children.
Contact: Marilyn L. Perkins, (304) 487-1680; Marilyn@Marilynperkins.com
Sponsor: Covenant Mountain Ministries
573 Pigeon Roost Trail
Princeton, WV 24740-4246

Cowles Charitable Trust Grants **542**
The foundation awards grants, primarily in New York, Florida, and on the East Coast, for the arts and culture, including museums and the performing arts; environment; education, including early childhood education, secondary and higher education, medical school education, adult basic education and literacy, and adult continuing education; hospitals and AIDS programs, including research; social services, including family planning, human services, and federated giving; and community funds, including leadership development, civil rights, and race relations. Types of support include general operating support, capital campaigns, annual campaigns, equipment acquisition, endowment funds, continuing support, seed money, building construction/renovation, matching funds, professorships, and program development. Application forms are required; initial approach should be by letter. The board meets in January, April, July, and October.
Requirements: Nonprofit organizations may apply for grant support. Grants are awarded primarily along the Eastern Seaboard.
Geographic Focus: Florida, New York
Date(s) Application is Due: Mar 1; Jun 1; Sep 1; Dec 1
Amount: 1,000 - 40,000 USD
Samples: Church of the Holy Comforter, Burlington, NC, $53,200; Miami Art Museum of Dade County, Miami, FL, $30,000; Allen-Stevenson School, New York, NY, $27,500.
Contact: Mary Croft, Treasurer; (732) 936-9826
Sponsor: Cowles Charitable Trust
P.O. Box 219
Rumson, NJ 07760

Crail-Johnson Foundation Grants **543**
The Crail-Johnson Foundation (CJF) has defined itself as a children's charity, and the vast majority of grant-making is directed toward programs benefiting children, youth and families in the greater Los Angeles area. Proposals, which are not relevant to the foundation's mission and funding priorities, will not be considered. CJF provides grants for program initiatives and enhancements, general operating support and capital projects as well as selected endowments. CJF provides technical assistance to selected community-based initiatives

benefiting children and families. The majority of Crail-Johnson Foundation funding supports organizations located in the greater Los Angeles area and projects that directly benefit Los Angeles area residents. National organizations providing services in Los Angeles are also considered. Occasionally, grants are made to programs and projects that are regional or national in scope, where potential benefits to children and families in Los Angeles can be clearly demonstrated. Initial contact with the Crail-Johnson Foundation should be in the form of a letter of inquiry, letters are accepted October through December each year for the following year's grant cycle and are generally considered in the order in which they are received. Organizations selected to submit proposals will be asked to complete a Grant Application Form provided by the Foundation.
Requirements: The foundation provides financial support primarily through grants to public non-profit organizations that are exempt under Section 501(c)3of the Internal Revenue code and are not a private foundation under Section 509(a).
Restrictions: Support is not granted for programs and projects benefiting religious purposes, university level education, research, events recognizing individuals or organizations, political causes or programs attempting to influence legislation. No grants are made directly to individuals.
Geographic Focus: California
Amount: 5,000 - 50,000 USD
Samples: Heart of Los Angeles Youth, Los Angeles, CA, $25,000—Smart Start Elementary Education Program (2009); Mentor LA, Los Angeles, CA, $25,000—staffing and special program enrichment (2009); Strive Foundation, Houston, TX, $20,000—expansion of academic and arts Program (2009).
Contact: Pat Christopher, Program Officer; (310) 519-7413; (310) 519-7221; pat-christopher@crail-johnson.org
Internet: http://www.crail-johnson.org/grants-application.htm
Sponsor: Crail-Johnson Foundation
222 W Sixth Street, Suite 1010
San Pedro, CA 90731

Cralle Foundation Grants 544
The foundation awards grants to Kentucky nonprofits, with an emphasis on Louisville, in the areas of education, children and youth, community development, and human services. Types of support include: building/renovation; capital campaigns; continuing support; endowments; equipment; general/operating support; matching/challenge support; program development; scholarship funds; and seed money.
Requirements: Nonprofit organizations in Kentucky are eligible.
Restrictions: No grants to individuals.
Geographic Focus: Kentucky
Date(s) Application is Due: Mar 1; Sep 1
Amount: 5,000 - 50,000 USD
Samples: Summit Academy of Greater Louisville, Middletown, KY, $35,000 - for challenge grant (20009); Americana Community Center, Louisville, KY, $20,000 - for youth programming (2009); Maryhurst School, Louisville, KY, $25,000 - for Neuville Program (2009)
Contact: James Crain Jr., Executive Director; (502) 581-1148; (502) 581-1937; jcrain37@bellsouth.net
Sponsor: Cralle Foundation
614 West Main Sreet, Suite 2500
Louisville, KY 40202

Cranston Foundation Grants 545
The foundation directs most of its grants to the geographic areas where Cranston Print Works Company has operations and a large number of employees, including Rhode Island, Massachusetts, Louisiana, and New York. Targeted priority areas are education, health and welfare, culture and the arts, and civic and community programs. Types of support include general operating support, employee matching gifts, and employee-related scholarships. All requests should be made in writing and should contain details and funding requirements pertaining to the project. The February deadline is for scholarships; the August deadline is for grants.
Requirements: IRS 501(c)3 organizations serving Rhode Island, Massachusetts, Louisiana, and New York are eligible.
Geographic Focus: Massachusetts, New York, Rhode Island
Date(s) Application is Due: Feb 15; Aug 31
Amount: 200 - 5,000 USD
Contact: Trustee; (401) 943-4800
Sponsor: Cranston Foundation
1381 Cranston Street
Cranston, RI 02920

Crescent Porter Hale Foundation Grants 546
The foundation places emphasis on organizations engaged in Catholic endeavors, with preference given to organizations in the San Francisco Bay area counties of Alameda, Contra Costa, Marin, San Francisco, and San Mateo. Areas of concern considered desirable for funding include organizations devoted to Catholic elementary and high school, education in the fields of art and music, agencies serving disadvantaged and at-risk youth, families and elderly. Applications for capital funds, scholarship funds, requests for special projects, as well as for general operating program support will be considered. The foundation will consider other worthwhile programs that can be demonstrated as serving broad community purposes, leading toward the improvement of the quality of life. Agencies serving disadvantaged youth, the disabled, or the elderly are of particular interest. Organizations wishing to apply should address a brief letter of intent to the foundation indicating the nature of the program and/or the specific project for which funding is sought. The board meets in April, September, and December to consider requests.
Requirements: To be eligible for consideration, organizations must meet the following criteria: be a corporate non-profit organization; qualify for tax exemption by the State in which said organization or institution is incorporated; be a organization to which contributions are deductable by donors for income tax purposes, generally of the type described in Section 501(c)3 of the Internal Revenue Code of 1954 and the corresponding Sections of the 1939 Code and prior Revenue Acts; be classified as a non-private foundation pursuant to the 1969 Tax Reform Acts; have and annual financial audit in accordance with approved accounting practices.
Restrictions: Individuals are ineligible. Healthcare-related, research, or postgraduate education programs are ineligible.
Geographic Focus: California
Amount: 5,000 - 250,000 USD
Samples: The BASIC Fund, San Francisco, San Francisco, CA, $240,000—to support scholarships for elementary school children in Bay Area schools (2009); Stagebridge, Oakland, CA, $15,000—to support its Healthy Aging theatre program (2009); Summer Search, San Francisco, CA, $25,000—in support of its leadership development programs for low-income high school students (2009).
Contact: Ulla Davis, Executive Director; (415) 388-2333; (415) 381-4799
Internet: http://www.crescentporterhale.org/policy/policy.htm
Sponsor: Crescent Porter Hale Foundation
655 Redwood Highway, Suite 301
Mill Valley, CA 94941

Crestlea Foundation Grants 547
The foundation supports Delaware nonprofits in its areas of interest, including secondary education, higher education, natural resource conservation, health care, housing development, community development, social services, and public affairs. Types of support include annual campaigns, general operating support, capital campaigns, building construction/renovation, and equipment acquisition. There are no application forms.
Requirements: Delaware nonprofits are eligible.
Geographic Focus: Delaware
Date(s) Application is Due: Nov 1
Amount: 5,000 - 50,000 USD
Samples: Philadelphia Museum of Art (Philadelphia, PA)—for operating support, $82,500; Archmere Academy (Claymont, DE)—for capital campaign, $20,000.
Contact: Stephen Martinenza, Secretary-Treasurer; (302) 654-2477
Sponsor: Crestlea Foundation
100 W 10th Street, Suite 1109
Wilmington, DE 19801

CRH Foundation Grants 548
The foundation awards general operating grants to U.S. nonprofit organizations in its areas of interest, including health and human services. Religious organizations also are eligible. Preference is given to requests from New Jersey and New York. Applications are accepted each year between May 1 and October 31. Inquiries must be in writing.
Requirements: U.S. 501(c)3 nonprofit organizations may apply.
Geographic Focus: All U.S. States
Date(s) Application is Due: Oct 31
Amount: Up to 74,000 USD
Samples: United Jewish Community (River Edge, NJ)—$4000; New York Times Neediest Cases (New York, NY)—$1000; American Cancer Society (Atlanta, GA)—$1000.

Contact: Grants Administrator; (201) 568-9300; (201) 568-6374
Sponsor: CRH Foundation
175 N Woodland Street
Englewood, NJ 07631

Cricket Foundation Grants **549**

The foundation awards grants to New England nonprofit organizations in its areas of interest, including the arts, museums, and environmental conservation and protection. Types of support include program development, matching funds, seed grants, publication, general operating support, and building construction/renovation. Telephone inquiries are welcome.
Requirements: 501(c)3 New England nonprofit organizations may apply.
Restrictions: Grants do not support endowment funds, fellowships, scholarships, or loans.
Geographic Focus: Connecticut, Maine, Massachusetts, New Hampshire, Rhode Island, Vermont
Date(s) Application is Due: Apr 30; Oct 31
Amount: 3,000 - 10,000 USD
Samples: New England Forestry Foundation (Groton, MA)—to purchase the largest forestland easement in U.S. history, which will protect 762,192 acres in Maine from development, $10,000.
Contact: George Butterworth, Counsel; (617) 570-1130; (617) 523-1231; gbutterworth@goodwinprocter.com
Sponsor: Cricket Foundation
Exchange Place, Suite 2200
Boston, MA 02109-2881

Crossroads Fund Seed Grants **550**

The fund supports organizations working on issues of social and economic justice in the Chicago metropolitan area. This grants program supports new, emerging, and small community based organizations that are actively engaged in social change work. Types of support include general operating grants, start-up costs, and project development. The maximum grant in this program is $10,000.
Requirements: Community organizations rooted in the Chicago metropolitan area, including northwestern Indiana, with annual expenses under $300,000 in the last completed fiscal year are eligible. Additionally, organizations must meet the Fund's general funding criteria: Working for Social Change—organizing community members to examine and challenge the underlying causes of their problems and conditions; Cross-Issue Organizing—working with an understanding of the connectedness among the various people and issues that make up the whole community; Grassroots Leadership—involving the people who are directly affected at all levels of the organization in planning, organizing and leading, and working to continue building leadership within the grassroots community; Solid Plan—having a clear purpose to the project with well-planned goals, objectives, activities and a tool to measure outcomes and impact; a timeline and budget that reflects the proposed objectives and activities; a realistic fundraising plan.
Restrictions: The fund does not support organizations that are involved in electoral campaigns; contribute substantially to support lobbying at the federal, state, or local levels; or support private, in contrast to public, interest.
Geographic Focus: Illinois, Indiana
Amount: Up to 10,000 USD
Samples: (2008) Center for Immigrant Resources and Community Arts ($5,000): youth-focused organization that uses theater and art to organize various immigrant communities across social, economic and political issues; First Defense Legal Aid ($4,000): provides legal advice and aid in Chicago Police Department stations to low-income individuals who cannot afford attorneys; Blocks Together ($7,500) grassroots, multi-issue social justice organization on the West Side of Chicago addressing affordable housing, public education & restorative justice; Next Steps ($3,000) organizes mentally disabled and often homeless individuals for greater voice in the systems that affect them, particularly major boards, institutions and decision-making bodies addressing homelessness and mental health; Waukegan Leadership Council ($3,000): protects the welfare of immigrant and Latino residents in a city that is predominately Latino from current immigration policies of indiscriminate arrest, detainment and deportation through voter registration, education and building collaborations with non-immigrant communities of color; Young Women's Empowerment Project ($9,000): run by and for women and girls with life experiences in the sex trade and street economies who use social justice, transformative justice and harm-reduction strategies to address issues affecting them. These grants included support for a research project documenting violence against their constituency.
Contact: Jane Kimondo, Program Director; (773) 227-7676; (773) 227-7790; jane@crossroadsfund.org
Internet: http://www.crossroadsfund.org/seedfund.html
Sponsor: Crossroads Fund
3411 W Diversey Avenue, #20
Chicago, IL 60647

Crossroads Technical Assistance Program Grants **551**

Grants support Chicago area organizations working on social and economic justice issues. The program supports the specific technical assistance needs of smaller organizations, focusing on projects that reach beyond a group's regular, ongoing work to build the organization's internal capacity. Types of support include funding for technology; training; conferences; or hiring a consultant or facilitator for evaluation, planning, or a retreat. Priority is given to organizations that have been funded by the foundation in the last 2 years.
Requirements: Community-based organizations in the Chicago metropolitan area, including northwestern Indiana, that have annual expenses under $150,000, and that have been in operation for at least three years are eligible.
Restrictions: The fund does not support organizations that are involved in electoral campaigns; contribute substantially to support lobbying at the federal, state, or local levels; or support private, in contrast to public, interest.
Geographic Focus: Illinois, Indiana
Date(s) Application is Due: Mar 1; Sep 1
Amount: Up to 3,000 USD
Contact: Inhe Choi, Program Director; (773) 227-7676; (773) 227-7790; inhe@crossroadsfund.org or info@crossroadsfund.org
Internet: http://www.crossroadsfund.org/techassist.html
Sponsor: Crossroads Fund
3411 W Diversey Avenue, #20
Chicago, IL 60647

Crowell Trust Grants **552**

The Trustees of the Trust continue to follow the directives for grantmaking which Henry Parsons Crowell established in his original indenture. Crowell identified candidates for grants from among agencies whose purpose is: Evangelism and discipleship; international cross-cultural missions; U.S. focused missions; Christian higher education; and Christian leadership development. Types of support include matching funds, operating budgets, building funds, equipment, and scholarship funds. There are no application deadlines.
Restrictions: As a general rule grants are not made to individuals, local churches, pre-kindergarten through high school education, endowment funds, land acquisition, or building construction.
Geographic Focus: All U.S. States
Amount: 10,000 - 100,000 USD
Contact: Executive Director; (719) 272-8300; (719) 272-8305; grantadmin@crowelltrust.org or info@crowelltrust.org
Internet: http://www.crowelltrust.org/page.php?id=8
Sponsor: Crowell Trust
1880 Office Club Pointe, Suite 2200
Colorado Springs, CO 80920

Cullen Foundation Grants **553**

The foundation awards grants to eligible Texas nonprofit organizations in its areas of interest, including arts and culture, education, health, and public service programs. There are no application deadlines or forms. Proposals should detail the purpose and scope of the grant; the amount requested; other sources of anticipated funding; a list of trustees, directors, and staff; financial statements and tax returns of the last two years; and anticipated project budgets. Preference is given to requests from Houston.
Requirements: Texas 501(c)3 or 170(c) nonprofit organizations are eligible.
Restrictions: The board prefers not to consider galas, testimonials, and various other types of fundraising events; organizations that in turn make grants to others; activities whose sole purpose is the promotion or support of a specific religion, denomination, or church; purchase of uniforms, equipment, or trips for school-related organizations or amateur sports teams; applications from an organization more frequently than once every 12 months, whether the previous application was approved or denied; applications from an organization that has received a multi-year grant from the foundation, until all payments of that grant have been made; or oral presentations from potential applicants.
Geographic Focus: Texas
Amount: Up to 100,000,000 USD

Samples: Reasoning Mind (Houston, TX)—Bringing the internet-based 5th grade math curriculum to Houston students, $50,000; Child Advocates, Inc. (TX)—Operating support, $20,000; The Heritage Society (Houston, TX)—for the relocation and restoration of the 1868 Pilot House, $25,000; Camp for All Foundation (Houston, TX)—Improvements to the camp's drainage system and main thoroughfare, $72,950
Contact: Sue Alexander, Grant Administrator; (713) 651-8837; salexander@cullenfdn.org
Internet: http://www.cullenfdn.org
Sponsor: Cullen Foundation
601 Jefferson, 40th Floor
Houston, TX 77002

Cummins Foundation Grants 554
The Foundation's areas of interest include: children and youth; education; elementary and secondary schools; civil rights; women; minorities; leadership development; increasing minority economic participation. Inquiries and proposals may be submitted in writing at any time during the year. A preliminary proposal should include a brief description of the problem being addressed, specifically what the program hopes to achieve, operating plan and cost, description of key leadership and how one will be able to tell whether or not the program worked. Upon receipt of the proposal, the Foundation staff will respond regarding the possibility of funding.
Requirements: The Foundation makes virtually all its local grants in communities where Cummins and its subsidiaries have manufacturing plants or affiliate businesses. These communities are: Columbus and Seymour, Indiana and their environs; Charleston, South Carolina; Jamestown, New York; Findlay, Ohio; Cookeville, Nashville and Memphis, Tennessee; Lake Mills, Iowa; Rocky Mount, North Carolina; El Paso, Texas; Fridley, Minnesota; Stoughton, Wisconsin. International grants are also reviewed by the Foundation Board. Proposals from the non-Indiana plant communities should be submitted first to the local plant manager or business leader.
Restrictions: The Foundation does not support political causes or candidates, or sectarian religious activities. No grants are made to individuals.
Geographic Focus: Indiana, Iowa, Minnesota, New York, North Carolina, Ohio, South Carolina, Tennessee, Texas, Wisconsin, Brazil, Japan, Mexico
Amount: 2,500 - 100,000 USD
Contact: Gayle Dudley Nay, (812) 377-3114; (812) 377-7897; Cummins.Foundation@cummins.com
Internet: http://www.cummins.com/cmi/content.jsp?siteId=1&langId=1033&menuId=82&overviewId=5&menuIndex=0
Sponsor: Cummins Foundation
500 Jackson Street
Columbus, IN 47201

D. W. McMillan Foundation Grants 555
The D. W. McMillan Foundation, established in 1956, supports organizations involved with youth services, health care, health organizations, homelessness, hospitals, human services, mental health/crisis services, residential/custodial care, hospices, people with disabilities, and the economically disadvantaged population. Giving is primarily centered in the states of Alabama, and Florida. There are no specific deadlines with which to adhere. Contact the Foundation for further application information and guidelines.
Geographic Focus: Alabama, Florida
Samples: Manna Food Bank, Pensacola, FL, $20,000; Baptist Health Care Foundation, Pensacola, FL, $76,000; Boy Scouts of America, Pensacola, FL, $20,000
Contact: Ed Leigh McMillan II, Treasurer; (251) 867-4881
Sponsor: D. W. McMillan Foundation
329 Belleville Avenue
Brewton, AL 36426-2039

Dade Community Foundation Community AIDS Partnership Grants 556
The Community AIDS Partnership, is a special funding initiative established in 1990 through the National AIDS Fund and local funders to increase the availability of private funds to address gaps in the local HIV/AIDS service system, particularly in the area of prevention. The Community AIDS Partnership represents one of the major sources of private philanthropic funds for HIV prevention in Miami-Dade County. As the result of a public/private partnership with Miami-Dade County, the Foundation also awards $350,000 in county funds, which represents a significant increase in the local public sector's commitment to funding HIV prevention. Through the Community AIDS Partnership, the Foundation supports quality programs that respond to the local population risk profile and that incorporate strategies with the greatest potential to effectively address the priority populations, communities and service needs related to HIV prevention in Miami-Dade County. Grant Size: $30,000 Single Organization, $60,000 for Collaborations.
Requirements: Eligible applicants include nonprofit tax-exempt organizations, as defined by the Internal Revenue Code, which are serving the residents of Miami-Dade County. Preference will be given to or- ganizations based in Miami-Dade County or if located outside the county, are working in partnership with an organization based in Miami-Dade.
Geographic Focus: Florida
Amount: 30,000 - 60,000 USD
Samples: Camillus House, $30,000 - to support a comprehensive HIV/AIDS program that targets homeless members of racial/ethnic minority communities who are either HIV positive or are at very high risk for HIV infection due to injection drug use and/or heterosexual contact; MUJER, $30,000 - to continue the Nosotras Viviremos project which seeks to increase awareness about HIV/AIDS in migrant farmworker communities in South Miami-Dade County
Contact: Gianne Ewing-Chow, Senior Program Officer; (305) 371-2711; (305) 371-5342; gianne.ewingchow@dadecommunityfoundation.org
Internet: http://www.dadecommunityfoundation.org/Site/wc/wc145.jsp
Sponsor: Dade Community Foundation
200 S Biscayne Boulevard, Suite 505
Miami, FL 33131-5330

Dade Community Foundation Grants 557
The funding for this program is made available through the Foundation's unrestricted and field of interest funds. This program is designed to honor both the donors interests and address significant community issues such as: education; health; human services; arts and culture; environment; economic development; at-risk youth; abused and neglected children; living with HIV/AIDS; homelessness; social justice; care of animals; heart disease and more.
Requirements: Eligible applicants include nonprofit tax-exempt organizations, as defined by the Internal Revenue Code, which are serving the residents of Miami-Dade County. Preference will be given to organizations based in Miami-Dade County or if located outside the county, are working in partnership with an organization based in Miami-Dade.
Restrictions: The Foundation does not provide grants to individuals, for memberships, fundraising events or memorials. Grants to government agencies are made on a very restricted basis.
Geographic Focus: Florida
Date(s) Application is Due: Nov 15
Amount: 7,500 USD
Samples: Alliance for Musical Arts Productions, $7,500 - to provide after school and summer camp services to youth from low-income households living in Opa-locka; Chai Lifeline, $6,500 - to support Smile S'more, a unique program designed to bring fun and love to children who are being treated for cancer and other life-threatening illnesses on pediatric specialty units of hospitals; Earth Learning, $10,000 - to create an EarthFest network that will form an umbrella to unite Earth Day celebrations across South Florida under one banner.
Contact: Charisse Grant, Vice President for Programs; (305) 371-2711; (305) 371-5342; charisse.grant@dadecommunityfoundation.org
Internet: http://www.dadecommunityfoundation.org/Site/programs/overview.jsp
Sponsor: Dade Community Foundation
200 S Biscayne Boulevard, Suite 505
Miami, FL 33131-5330

DaimlerChrysler Corporation Fund Grants 558
The fund contributes to organizations grouped under the general categories of education, health and human services, civic and community, religion, and culture and the arts. Within these categories, grants are made available for public welfare or for charitable, scientific, educational, environmental, safety, building, and affirmative action purposes. Higher education grants largely support science and engineering education and business management. A major interest of the corporation is the establishment of national certification standards for elementary and secondary teachers. Another area of concern is the encouragement of early reading skills, and a pilot project has been funded for research in this area. The fund earmarks funds for its future workforce initiatives, which support business and engineering departments, community-based job-skill training, and entry-level work preparation. Types of support include matching gifts, program grants, scholarships, annual campaigns, building construction/renovation,

general support, and employee matching gifts. In considering requests, the fund evaluates each applicant organization on its own merits; considered are the programs in which it is engaged, constituencies served, operation procedures, services offered, quality of management, its accountability, finances, and fund-raising practices. Applications are accepted at any time.
Requirements: Eligible for support are nonprofit, tax-exempt educational, health, civic, and cultural organizations primarily in locations where the greatest number of employees of Chrysler and its U.S. -based subsidiaries live and work (Alabama, Delaware, Illinois, Indiana, Michigan, Missouri, New York, Ohio, and Wisconsin). Some support is targeted for national organizations as well.
Restrictions: Grants are not awarded to support endowments, conferences, trips, direct health care delivery, multiyear pledges, capital campaigns, fund-raising activities related to sponsorships, advertising, or debt retirement.
Geographic Focus: All U.S. States
Samples: Charles H. Wright Museum of African American History (Detroit, MI)—$1 million to complete an exhibit area; Second Harvest Food Bank of Central Florida, $25,000 and food via convoy of Dodge Rams, and $50,000 to help residents affected by recent tornadoes.
Contact: Brian Glowiak, Vice President; (248) 512-2502; (248) 512-2503; mek@dcx.com
Internet: http://www.fund.daimlerchrysler.com
Sponsor: DaimlerChrysler Corporation Fund
1000 Chrysler Drive
Auburn Hills, MI 48326-2766

Dale and Edna Walsh Foundation Grants **559**
The foundation joins hands with effective charitable organizations to meet human need and promote the common good worldwide. Grants support ministries, religious activities, health, relief efforts, education, community services, and arts organizations. Guidelines are available online.
Requirements: Tax-exempt, nonprofit charities are eligible.
Restrictions: The foundation does not contribute toward normal church operation; culturally liberal activist causes or organizations that primarily seek to influence legislation or government spending; or political parties or associated political organizations.
Geographic Focus: All U.S. States
Contact: Grants Administrator; (847) 230-0056; (847) 901-9193; Info@dewfoundation.org
Internet: http://dewfoundation.org
Sponsor: Dale and Edna Walsh Foundation
6461 Valley Wood Drive
Reno, NV 89523

Dallas Women's Foundation Grants **560**
The Foundation promotes women's philanthropy and raises money to support community programs that help women and girls realize their full potential. Priority will be given to funding programs that include elements of the following: effect long-term, positive changes to help women succeed in reaching their full potential; expanded choices and opportunities for women and girls; evaluation tools that include measurement for effectiveness with clean definition of program success; and programs specifically designed to take into consideration the gender-specific needs and differences of women and girls. The Foundation also encourages projects developed in consultation and collaboration with other agencies, and which promote coordination, cooperation and sharing among organizations. Effective use of volunteers, as well as Board diversity and involvement, are equally encouraged.
Requirements: To be eligible to receive a grant from the Foundation, applicants must meet all of the following criteria: be in receipt of a current 501(c)3 tax-exempt designation from the Internal Revenue Service (dated within the last 10 years); at least 50% of the population served must be residents of Dallas, Denton, or Collin County, with priority given to organizations serving residents of Dallas County; 75% of the clients benefiting from the grant funding must be women and/or girls.
Geographic Focus: Texas
Samples: Avance (Dallas, TX)—for equipment and operating support of this organization that promotes academic achievement among Hispanics in Dallas, $10,000; U of North Texas, Division of Equity and Diversity (Dallas, TX)—for a seminar on critical issues affecting lesbians, $15,000; Interfaith Housing Coalition (Dallas, TX)—to provide transitional housing, training, and support services to Dallas-area homeless families, $20,000; English Language Ministry (Dallas, TX)—to provide free child care and English-language instruction to non-English speaking adults, particularly women, $17,500.
Contact: Pat Alexander, (214) 965-9977; (214) 526-3633; palexander@dallaswomensfoundation.org
Internet: http://www.dallaswomensfoundation.org/grants/highlights.html
Sponsor: Dallas Women's Foundation
4300 MacArthur Avenue, Suite 255
Dallas, TX 75209

Dana Corporation Foundation Grants **561**
The foundation gives to communities throughout the country. Social services and education are top priorities. Most education grants are awarded to colleges and universities through a matching gifts program. Other grants go to civic affairs, environmental, youth, and health organizations with the smallest percentage awarded in the areas of culture and arts. Types of support include annual campaigns, building construction/renovation, continuing support, equipment acquisition, land acquisition, operating budgets, seed grants, and capital campaigns.
Requirements: 501(c)3 organizations in communities where Dana Corporation facilities are located are eligible.
Restrictions: The foundation does not make grants to individuals or to organizations that practice discrimination, religious groups for denominational purposes, political activities, or United Way-supported organizations for operating expenses. The foundation does not purchase tickets to charitable or fund-raising events or support goodwill advertising.
Geographic Focus: All U.S. States
Amount: 1,000 - 20,000 USD
Samples: Big Brothers/Big Sisters of Iredell County (Statesville, NC)—$10,000; Toledo Museum of Art (Toledo, OH)—$50,000.
Contact: Ed McNeal, (419) 535-4500
Internet: http://www.dana.com
Sponsor: Dana Corporation Foundation
P.O. Box 1000
Toledo, OH 43697

Danellie Foundation Grants **562**
The foundation's primary areas of interest include services for the financially disadvantaged, including housing and social services. The types of support offered are: building/renovation; capital campaigns; continuing support; general/operating support; program development; scholarship funds and; sponsorships. Contact foundation for application guidelines. New York/New Jersey Area Common Application Form and New York/New Jersey Common Report Form accepted. Application form required.
Requirements: Nonprofit organizations in Southern New Jersey, (including Mercer and portions of Monmouth counties), the Greater Philadelphia, Pennsylvania area and, the Balimore, Maryland region are eligible to apply. The foundation also has an international interest in Guatemala and Haiti.
Restrictions: No support for political organizations or professional sports, libraries or museums. No grants to individuals, or for endowments or radio and television.
Geographic Focus: Maryland, New Jersey
Amount: 4,000 - 180,000 USD
Samples: University of Medicine and Dentistry, Stratford, NJ, $71,000 - for Latino health clinic; Doctors of the World U.S. A, New York, NY, $65,000 - for medical needs in Third World countries; Aid for Friends, Philadelphia, PA, $20,000 - for needy, disabled, and the elderly homebound.
Contact: Nancy Dinsmore, (856) 810-8320; danelliefoundation@verizon.net
Sponsor: Danellie Foundation
P.O. Box 376
Marlton, NJ 08053

Dan Murphy Foundation Grants **563**
The foundation awards grants to eligible nonprofit organizations in its areas of interest: support of activities and charities of Roman Catholic Church Archdiocese of Los Angeles, including education, health care, and social service programs. Types of support include building construction/renovation, capital support, continuing support, general operating support, matching grants, and program development. The majority of grants are awarded to Los Angeles, CA, nonprofits. There are no application forms or deadlines.
Geographic Focus: California
Amount: 10,000 - 100,000 USD
Samples: Council of Major Superiors of Women Religious (Washington, DC)—for general operating support, $150,000; Notre Dame High School

of Sherman Oaks (CA)—for a matching grant for the capital campaign, $350,000; Thomas Aquinas College (Santa Paula, CA)—for the scholarship endowment fund, $545,511.
Contact: Daniel J. Donohue, President; (213) 623-3120
Sponsor: Dan Murphy Foundation
P.O. Box 711267
Los Angeles, CA 90071

Dave Coy Foundation Grants 564
The foundation awards grants to Texas nonprofits in the areas of children and youth, social services for the economically disadvantaged, and religion (religious organizations, religious education, and religious welfare). Types of support include general operating support, capital campaigns, building construction/renovation, equipment acquisition, and emergency funds. Application forms are required.
Requirements: Nonprofits in Bexar County, TX, are eligible.
Restrictions: Grants are not made to individuals.
Geographic Focus: Texas
Date(s) Application is Due: Jun 1
Amount: 10,000 - 250,000 USD
Samples: Baptist Childrens Home Ministries (San Antonio, TX)—for South Texas Campus Project, $250,000; Carver Academy (San Antonio, TX)—for capital campaign, $75,000; Salvation Army (San Antonio, TX)—for operating support for a program for male substance abusers, $125,000; Jewish Community Center of San Antonio (San Antonio, TX)—for senior transportation, $40,000; San Antonio Metropolitan Ministry (San Antonio, TX)—to upgrade housing beds and mattresses, $35,000; Amarillo Senior Citizens Assoc (Amarillo, TX)—for operating support, $15,000.
Contact: Gregg Muenster, (210) 270-5371
Sponsor: Dave Coy Foundation
P.O. Box 121
San Antonio, TX 78291-0121

David and Barbara B. Hirschhorn Foundation Grants 565
Seeking to improve the lives of families and children and cultivate a level playing field, the David and Barbara B. Hirschhorn Foundation supports Jewish and secular initiatives that expand educational opportunity, address human service needs, and promote intergroup tolerance and understanding. Support is primarily given within the state of Maryland, providing grants of annual campaigns, capital campaigns, endowments, general/operating support. Letters of inquiry and proposals are accepted on a rolling basis. Your application will be acknowledged by postcard within two weeks.
Requirements: 501(c)3 non-profit organizations are eligible to apply. To begin the application process submit a letter of inquiry to the Foundation, no longer then 3 pages long. The initial application should include the following: information about the programs(s) for which funding is requested; need, purpose, activities, and evaluation plan of the proposed program(s); program budget (including sources of anticipated income as well as expenditure) and timeline; dollar amount of funding requested. Information about your organization: history, mission, and key accomplishments; information on Board members and key staff; current institutional operating budget (including major sources of revenue as well as expenditures); copy of IRS tax status determination letter or information about your fiscal agent. The Foundation will also accept initial applications that conform to the Association of Baltimore Area Grantmakers [ABAG] Common Grant Application.
Restrictions: No support available for: scholarships to individuals; unsolicited proposals for academic, scientific, or medical research; direct mail, annual giving, membership campaigns, fundraising and commemorative events.
Geographic Focus: All U.S. States
Amount: 2,500 - 350,000 USD
Samples: American Committee for Shaare Zedek Medical Center in Jerusalem, Baltimore, MD, $20,000 (2008); AMIT Women, Inc. New York, NY, $10,000 (2008); Institute for Christian and Jewish Studies, Inc., Baltimore, MD, $100,000 (2008)
Contact: Betsy Ringel, Executive Director; (410) 347-7103; (410) 347-7210; info@blaufund.org
Internet: http://www.blaufund.org/foundations/davidandbarbara_f.html
Sponsor: David and Barbara B. Hirschhorn Foundation
10 E Baltimore Street, Suite 1111
Baltimore, MD 21202

David Bohnett Foundation Grants 566
The foundation's mission is to improve society through social activism. Focus areas include the promotion of the positive portrayal of lesbians and gay men in the media; voter registration activities; animal language research, animal companions, and eliminating rare animal trade; environmental conservation; the reduction and elimination of the manufacture and sale of handguns in the United States; community-based social services that benefit gays and lesbians; and the development of mass transit and non-fossil fuel transportation. Types of support include general operating support, program specific grants, seed money, and multiyear grants. Applicants should email a letter of inquiry to the program officer.
Requirements: Nonprofit organizations are eligible.
Restrictions: Grants do not support individuals, videos or other film productions, or organizations outside the United States.
Geographic Focus: All U.S. States
Date(s) Application is Due: Jan 27; Jul 28
Amount: 5,000 - 50,000 USD
Samples: Disability Rights Education and Defense Fund (Berkeley, CA)—for a project to ensure that voting booths in California are accessible to disabled people, $25,000; Proteus Fund (Amherst, MA)—for the Civil Marriage Collaborative, a group of organizations working to achieve civil marital rights and oppose efforts that limit or deny those rights to lesbian, gay, bisexual, and transgender people, $100,000; Service Members Legal Defense Network (Washington, DC)—for operating support and for legal fees to support active-duty service members who are gay or lesbian, $35,000; Bill Foundation (Beverly Hills, CA)—to find permanent, safe homes for abandoned and unwanted dogs as companion animals, $10,000.
Contact: Michael Fleming, Executive Director; (310) 277-4611; (310) 203-8111; mfpfleming@yahoo.com
Internet: http://www.bohnettfoundation.org/grants/grantapplication.htm
Sponsor: David Bohnett Foundation
2049 Century Park E, Suite 2151
Los Angeles, CA 90067-3123

David Geffen Foundation Grants 567
The foundation supports nonprofits in Los Angeles, California, and New York, New York, with some giving in Israel as well. The Foundation offers support in its five principal funding areas: AIDS/HIV, civil liberties, the arts, issues of concern to the Jewish community, and health care. Support is provided for general operations and special projects. There are no application deadlines. Applicants are asked to submit a letter of request.
Requirements: 501(c)3 tax-exempt organizations in Los Angeles, CA, and New York, NY, may submit a proposal letter (without folder or binder) including description of the project, objectives, constituents served, evaluation criteria; background on the organization including key staff, volunteers, and board; copy of IRS letter confirming tax-exempt status; financial information including line-item budget for the project; and copy of non-discrimination policy from the organization's hiring guidelines.
Restrictions: The Foundation does not fund individuals, or organizations based outside of the United States. The foundation generally does not support documentaries or other types of audio-publication of books or magazines.
Geographic Focus: California, New York, Israel
Samples: Natural Resources Defense Council, New York, NY, $50,000; Childrens Diabetes Foundation at Denver, Denver, CO, $25,000; Morehouse College, Atlanta, GA, $50,000.
Contact: J. Dallas Dishman, Program Director; (310) 581-5955; (310) 581-5949; ddishman@geffenco.com
Sponsor: David Geffen Foundation
12011 San Vicente Boulevard, Suite 606
Los Angeles, CA 90049-4926

David Robinson Foundation Grants 568
Founded by David Robinson, a former National Basketball Association center who played his entire career for the San Antonio Spurs. The foundation awards grants to Texas nonprofit organizations in its areas of interest, including agriculture, family services, single parents, social services, and spirituality. The majority of grants will be awarded in the San Antonio area.
Requirements: Texas nonprofit organizations are eligible. Contributes only to pre-selected organizations.
Geographic Focus: Texas
Amount: 200 - 500,000 USD

Samples: Oak Hills Church of Christ, San Antonio, TX, $150,000; Mile High Ministries, Denver, CO, $25,000; San Antonio Food Bank, San Antonio, TX, $10,000.
Contact: Grants Administrator; (210) 696-8061; (210) 696-7754; drfoundation@express-news.net
Sponsor: David Robinson Foundation
24165 IH-10 West, Suite 217-628
San Antonio, TX 78257

Dayton Power and Light Foundation Grants **569**
The foundation contributes general operating grants to nonprofit organizations in the greater Dayton, OH, area in support of education and charitable activities and programs. Education grants are made to support adult basic education/literacy-skills development and engineering school education. Direct donations are made to civic, cultural, and health and welfare organizations that do not participate in community funds, such as United Way or community chests, but serve a real need. There is no official application form. Requests should be made in writing and must include a description of the history, structure, purpose, and program of the organization and a summary of the support needed and how it will be used. Contributions are planned a year in advance and based on a calendar-year budget. The distribution committee normally meets quarterly.
Requirements: 501(c)3 organizations in the greater Dayton, OH, area are eligible.
Restrictions: The foundation prefers not to support capital campaigns; college fund-raising associations; conduit organizations; endowment or development funds; fraternal, labor, or veterans organizations; hospital operating budgets; individual members of federated campaigns; individuals; national organizations outside the DP&L service territory; religious organizations; sports leagues; or telephone or mass-mail solicitations. Grants are rarely made to tax-supported institutions.
Geographic Focus: Ohio
Amount: 1,000 - 20,000 USD
Samples: Dayton Art Institute (OH)—to support the capital campaign, $25,000; United Way of the Greater Dayton Area (OH)—to support the annual campaign, $200,000.
Contact: Ginny Strausburg, Executive Director; (937) 259-7925; (937) 259-7923
Internet: http://www.waytogo.com/cc/cc.phtml
Sponsor: Dayton Power and Light Company Foundation
1065 Woodman Drive
Dayton, OH 45432

Daywood Foundation Grants **570**
The Foundation distributes available funds primarily to community service organizations focusing on the arts, and health and human services. Grants are available in the following types: annual campaigns; building/renovation; capital campaigns; continuing support; debt reduction; emergency funds; equipment; general/operating support; matching/challenge support; seed money.
Requirements: Nonprofit 501(c)3 organizations situated in, and benefiting Charleston, Lewisburg, Barbour, Greenbrier and Kanawha counties Of West Virginia are eligible to apply. There is no standardized grant application form. Send proposal to: William W. Booker, 1500 Chase Tower, Charleston, WV 25301.
Restrictions: Grants do not support endowment funds, research, individuals, or individual scholarships or fellowships.
Geographic Focus: West Virginia
Date(s) Application is Due: Sep 15
Samples: Clay Center for the Arts and Sciences of West Virginia, Charleston, WV, $150,000—for endowment; University of Charleston, Charleston, WV, $125,000— for pharmacy school; West Virginia Symphony Orchestra, Charleston, WV, $100,000- for endowment.
Contact: William W. Booker, Treasurer; (304) 343-4841
Sponsor: Daywood Foundation
707 Virginia Street E, Suite 1600
Charleston, WV 25301

Deaconess Community Foundation Grants **571**
The foundation awards grants to eligible Ohio nonprofit organizations in its areas of interest, including health, education, welfare, community, and social service activities. Proposals that are of greatest interest to the Foundation are those that have the strongest fit to the mission statement and that have some or all of the following characteristics: projects that have specific measurable outcomes and a tangible ability to evaluate results and measure success; projects that are supported by other funding sources; and projects that have identified potential for ongoing support beyond the life of the grant. Application information is available online.
Requirements: Only qualified non-profit organizations located in Cuyahoga County which are classified by the Internal Revenue Code as tax-exempt 501(c)3 organizations are eligible for funding consideration.
Restrictions: Grant requests for the following will not be considered: individuals, governmental agencies or any other organization that is not a tax exempt 501(c)3 organization; internal operations and capital campaigns of churches; research projects; or endowments. Grant funds may not be used to carry on propaganda or otherwise attempt to influence legislation, participate in, or intervene in, any political campaign on behalf of or in opposition to any candidate for public office, or to conduct, directly or indirectly, any voter registration drive (within the meaning of Section 4945(d)(2) of the Internal Revenue Code).
Geographic Focus: Ohio
Date(s) Application is Due: Jan 15; May 15; Sep 15
Samples: Junior Achievement, $10,000—Workforce Readiness & Entrepreneurship programs (2008); Magnolia Clubhouse, $35,000—part-time senior development consultant, $2,000 —general operating support (2008); The Intergenerational School, $28,000—establishment of a development department (2008).
Contact: Deborah Vesy, Executive Director; (216) 741-4077; (216) 741-6042; dvesy@deacomfdn.org
Internet: http://www.deacomfdn.org/guidelines.html
Sponsor: Deaconess Community Foundation
7575 Northcliff Avenue, Suite 203
Brooklyn, OH 44144

Deaconess Foundation Grants **572**
The foundation supports work in two main areas: Capacity Building and Public Policy. Capacity Building means providing resources to child-serving organizations that will enable them to improve measurably their internal operational systems so as to increase their services and enhance their chances of long-term survivability. In other words, capacity building is about giving organizations more horsepower to fulfill their missions. Public Policy means providing support to key public policy organizations which serve as the voice of children and families in the places of power and policy making both in the Street Louis Region and the State of Missouri. Without supporting good public policy, children are likely to fall further and further behind in the community's priorities. Currently, Deaconess Foundation supports public policy and advocacy organizations such as Citizens for Missouri's Children. On occasion, at the discretion of Board and Staff, Deaconess Foundation also supports specific child-related advocacy initiatives.
Requirements: Nonprofit groups and organizations in the metropolitan Saint Louis area are eligible for funding. Organizations should send a one- to two-page letter of intent that should include name of organization, mission, and history; purpose for which the organization is seeking funding; issues that will be addressed; anticipated outcomes; other participating organizations; amount of funding requested; time frame; and contact person's name, address, and phone and fax numbers.
Geographic Focus: Illinois, Missouri
Amount: Up to 100,000,000 USD
Contact: Rev. Jerry Paul, President; (314) 436-8001; (314) 436-5352; jerryp@deaconess.org or info@deaconess.org
Internet: http://www.deaconess.org/grantmaking.phtml
Sponsor: Deaconess Foundation
211 N Broadway, Suite 1260
Saint Louis, MO 63102

DeKalb County Community Foundation Grants **573**
The DeKalb County Community Foundation Grants support programs for DeKalb County, Indiana citizens that address today's needs and prepare for tomorrow's challenges. Grant guidelines are intentionally broad in order to meet the community's ever-changing charitable needs. Grants are awarded for charitable programs and projects in the following areas of interest: art and culture; community development; education; environment; health and human services; and youth development. Grants are also available for the general operating expenses of organizations that address local charitable needs. Applicants are encouraged to contact the Foundation before submitting a proposal to be certain it follows the grant guidelines. They are also encouraged

to attend a free one hour workshop to help them understand the Foundation's grant process and learn basic proposal writing tips. The Foundation gives priority to grant proposals for programs/projects that: will be completed within one year of receiving a grant; strengthen the grant seeking organization; directly relate to the grant seeker's mission; project a high degree of community impact; benefit many local people; and are proactive rather than reactive.
Requirements: After reviewing the grant guidelines, applicants will fill out the online proposal form. Applicants should include their contact information, financial information, a brief summary of the request, their organization's mission statement, and a detailed explanation of the benefits they'll receive from the grant. They should also include their operating expenses, total budget, and their source of funds. Applicants will then email the proposal form to the Foundation contact person or mail a printed copy to the Foundation address.
Restrictions: Grants are less likely to be awarded for: repeat funding for a program/project that has received a Foundation grant within the last two years; or a funding debt. The Foundation grants to religious organizations for charitable purposes but does not award grants for religious purposes.
Geographic Focus: Indiana
Date(s) Application is Due: Jul 1
Amount: 500 - 7,000 USD
Samples: American Red Cross of Northeast Indiana, disaster services for DeKalb County; $2,500 (2010): Street Martin's Healthcare, operating expenses for medical clinic; $7,000 (2010): DeKalb County Council on Aging, exercise equipment; $2,500 (2010); Community Care Food Pantry, food pantry/garage infrastructure construction and new commercial freezer/refrigerator equipment; $3,000 (2010).
Contact: Rosie Shinkel, Program Manager; (260) 925-0311; rshinkel@dekalbfoundation.org
Internet: http://www.dekalbfoundation.org/g_grantmaking.php
Sponsor: DeKalb County Community Foundation
650 West North Street
Auburn, IN 46706

Delaware Division of the Arts General Operating Support Grants **574**

Grants are provided to Delaware arts organizations in support of their annual operating expenses. All general operating support grants are funded on a matching basis. Matching funds must be cash and may not come from the NEA. Other federal grant sources may be used as match in accordance with authorizing legislation. Awards are calculated as a percentage of the actual operating expenses of the most recent fiscal year as reported on the IRS 990 form. No one organization is awarded more than 10% of the Division's General Operating Support grant award budget.
Requirements: To be eligible for General Operating Support, applicants must: Have the promotion, presentation, production, and/or teaching of the arts as their primary purpose as outlined in their charter, incorporation papers, bylaws, and IRS nonprofit determination letter; Have a stable, functioning board of directors that meets at least quarterly; Be based and chartered in Delaware as a nonprofit organization; exempt from federal income tax under Section 501(c)3 or 501(c)(4) or 509(a) of the Internal Revenue Code; and eligible to receive donations allowable as charitable contributions under Section 170(c) of the Internal Revenue Code of 1954.
Restrictions: DDOA will not accept applications through fiscal agents. No individual may compile or submit an application on behalf of an organization if that individual is a member or relative of a member of the Delaware State Arts Council (DSAC) or DDOA staff.
Geographic Focus: Delaware
Date(s) Application is Due: Mar 1
Contact: Delaware Division of the Arts, Kent and Sussex Coordinator; (302) 739-5304
Internet: http://www.artsdel.org/grants/artsorggrants.shtml
Sponsor: Delaware Division of the Arts
820 N French Street, Carvel State Office Building
Wilmington, DE 19801

Delaware Division of the Arts Opportunity Grants—Arts Organizations **575**

Arts organizations may apply for funding for staff and/or board members to attend conferences, workshops, or mentoring sessions that will enable the organization to further develop administrative and/or artistic skills. Arts organizations with unique and unanticipated opportunities to present the literary, performing, visual, media, or folk arts in ways that will reach new audiences may apply for funding. Arts organizations may apply for funding to enable them to take advantage of unique opportunities to present their programs at events of regional, national, or international significance outside Delaware. Applicants may request up to 80 percent of the cost of the project with requests not to exceed $750. New arts organizations, including those who have not yet received their IRS nonprofit status, may apply for funding to support their early programming and organizational development efforts. Arts organizations may apply for funding to help make their programs more accessible to people with disabilities. Note: Organizations will be eligible to receive only one grant award in this category per calendar year. Annual deadline dates may vary; contact the council for exact dates.
Requirements: To be eligible to apply applicants must: Have the promotion, presentation, production, and/or teaching of the arts as their primary purpose as outlined in their charter, incorporation papers, bylaws, and IRS nonprofit determination letter; Have a stable, functioning board of directors that meets at least quarterly; Be based and chartered in Delaware as a nonprofit organization; exempt from federal income tax under Section 501(c)3 or 501(c)(4) or 509(a) of the Internal Revenue Code; and eligible to receive donations allowable as charitable contributions under Section 170(c) of the Internal Revenue Code of 1954.
Restrictions: No individual may compile or submit an application on behalf of an organization if that individual is a member or relative of a member of the Delaware State Arts Council (DSAC) or DDOA staff.
Geographic Focus: Delaware
Date(s) Application is Due: Feb 1; Apr 1; Jun 1; Aug 1; Oct 1; Dec 1
Amount: Up to 750 USD
Contact: Kent and Sussex Grants Administrator; (302) 739-5304
Internet: http://www.artsdel.org/grants/artistgrants.shtml
Sponsor: Delaware Division of the Arts
820 N French Street, Carvel State Office Building
Wilmington, DE 19801

Delaware Division of the Arts Project Support Grants **576**

Project Support funding is available for arts projects that accomplish one or more of the following: Provide experiences of artistic merit and integrity for the public; Reach audiences and participants with limited access to the art or to a particular art form; Provide opportunities for conservation, documentation, and appreciation of the artistic traditions of diverse cultures and communities; Involve collaborations with artists, arts organizations, community and civic groups, government entities, or social service agencies; Provide new or non-traditional venues for arts programs; Offer opportunities for the creation of new works of art; Provide lifelong learning opportunities in the arts beyond the school setting; Provide opportunities for artistic expression of a community's unique history, culture, or circumstances; Contribute to a community's enhanced quality of life or economic revitalization. All Project Support grants are funded on a matching basis. Applicants may request grants of up to 75 percent of the direct expenses for the actual artistic portion of their project. For arts projects that are part of a festival that is a fundraiser, grant requests may not exceed 50 percent of the cash expenses for contracted vendors and services.
Requirements: To be eligible for Project Support as a community-based organization, you must: Be a Delaware-based nonprofit organization whose primary purpose is not the arts. This includes libraries, civic groups, community/senior centers, festivals, parts/recreation programs, and university/college non-credit programs intended to serve the community. Public, private, and parochial schools are eligible only if the proposed arts project is taking place after school hours and is open and promoted to the public; Have a stable, functioning board of directors that meets at least quarterly; Be based and chartered in Delaware as a nonprofit organization; exempt from federal income tax under Section 501(c)3 or 501(c)(4) or 509(a) of the Internal Revenue Code; and eligible to receive donations allowable as charitable contributions under Section 170(c) of the Internal Revenue Code of 1954. Organizations that have not received Delaware incorporation or IRS nonprofit designation are not eligible to apply for Project Support; Be an established unit of municipal, county, or state government within Delaware.
Restrictions: Expenses not eligible for Project Support are: Activities for which academic credit is given; Activities outside Delaware; Awards or cash prizes; Bad debt; Building, renovating, or remodeling of facilities; Capital expenditures and non-consumables valued over $3,000; Circus and athletic activities; Contingency funds; Expenses incurred outside the grant period; Investments of any type; Meals/refreshments; Private entertainment; Projects restricted to exclusive participation or enjoyment; Projects which have sectarian or religious purposes; Scholarships or research by individuals.
Geographic Focus: Delaware
Date(s) Application is Due: Mar 1

Amount: 2,500 USD
Contact: Kent and Sussex Grants Administrator; (302) 739-5304
Internet: http://www.artsdel.org/grants/cbogrants.shtml
Sponsor: Delaware Division of the Arts
820 N French Street, Carvel State Office Building
Wilmington, DE 19801

Delaware Division of the Arts Public Impact Grant **577**

The Division of the Arts has established Public Impact grants to: Acknowledge and encourage exemplary community impact initiatives by Delaware arts organizations; to offer competitive, merit-based funding to supplement formula-based General Operating Support grants for arts organizations; to invest DDOA funds to advance the goals of the National Endowment for the Arts' Challenge America program.
Requirements: To be eligible for Public Impact grants, applicants must apply for and receive a General Operating Support grant, meeting all of the eligibility requirements for that grant category.
Geographic Focus: Delaware
Date(s) Application is Due: Mar 1
Contact: Paul Weagraff, Director; (302) 577-8278; Paul.Weagraff@state.de.us
Internet: http://www.artsdel.org/grants/artsorggrants.shtml
Sponsor: Delaware Division of the Arts
820 N French Street, Carvel State Office Building
Wilmington, DE 19801

Delaware Division of the Arts Stabilization Grants **578**

Funding is provided for needed maintenance, repairs, or renovations of existing facilities owned and operated by the non-profit arts organization and for repair, upgrade or replacement of capital equipment owned and operated by the non-profit arts organization. No match is required. However, organizations that can provide some level of cash match may receive a more favorable review by the panel.
Requirements: To be eligible for Arts Stabilization, applicants must: Have the promotion, presentation, production, and/or teaching of the arts as their primary purpose as outlined in their charter, incorporation papers, bylaws, and IRS nonprofit determination letter; Have a stable, functioning board of directors that meets at least quarterly; and be based and chartered in Delaware as a nonprofit organization; exempt from federal income tax under Section 501(c)3 or 501(c)(4) or 509(a) of the Internal Revenue Code; and eligible to receive donations allowable as charitable contributions under Section 170(c) of the Internal Revenue Code of 1954.
Restrictions: DDOA will not accept applications through fiscal agents. No individual may compile or submit an application on behalf of an organization if that individual is a member or relative of a member of the Delaware State Arts Council (DSAC) or DDOA staff. Arts organizations that are members of the Arts Consortium of Delaware, Inc. (ArtCo) are not eligible to apply for Arts Stabilization Grants through the Delaware Division of the Arts. Ineligible organizations include: The Christina Cultural Arts Center, Delaware Art Museum, Delaware Symphony Orchestra, Delaware Theatre Company, Grand Opera House, OperaDelaware, Rehoboth Art League, and the Wilmington Music School.
Geographic Focus: Delaware
Date(s) Application is Due: Mar 1
Contact: Paul Weagraff, Director; (302) 577-8278; Paul.Weagraff@state.de.us
Internet: http://www.artsdel.org/grants/artsorggrants.shtml
Sponsor: Delaware Division of the Arts
820 N French Street, Carvel State Office Building
Wilmington, DE 19801

Delaware Division of the Arts Technical Assistance Grant **579**

Technical Assistance grants assist Delaware arts organizations in building organizational capacity to present and produce the arts. The three established goals for Technical Assistance grants are: To support efforts to build administrative capacity; support professional development initiatives for board members and staff and support marketing and audience development initiatives. Technical Assistance grants are funded on a matching basis. Arts organizations may request up to 75 percent of the cost of a Technical Assistance project. Requests may not exceed $7,500.
Requirements: To be eligible for Technical Assistance, applicants must: Have the promotion, presentation, production, and/or teaching of the arts as their primary purpose as outlined in their charter, incorporation papers, bylaws, and IRS nonprofit determination letter; Have a stable, functioning board of directors that meets at least quarterly; Be based and chartered in Delaware as a nonprofit organization; exempt from federal income tax under Section 501(c)3 or 501(c)(4) or 509(a) of the Internal Revenue Code; and eligible to receive donations allowable as charitable contributions under Section 170(c) of the Internal Revenue Code of 1954.
Restrictions: DDOA will not accept applications through fiscal agents. No individual may compile or submit an application on behalf of an organization if that individual is a member or relative of a member of the Delaware State Arts Council (DSAC) or DDOA staff.
Geographic Focus: Delaware
Date(s) Application is Due: Mar 1
Contact: Paul Weagraff, Director; (302) 577-8278; Paul.Weagraff@state.de.us
Internet: http://www.artsdel.org/grants/artsorggrants.shtml
Sponsor: Delaware Division of the Arts
820 N French Street, Carvel State Office Building
Wilmington, DE 19801

Dennis and Phyllis Washington Foundation Grants **580**

The foundation supports a broad spectrum of worthy causes benefiting people of all ages primarily serving the State of Montana and surrounding states where the Washington Companies are located. Priorities for funding are direct service, youth oriented programs and the advancement of educational opportunities through scholarships to units of higher education in Montana. The Foundation also focuses on the needs of economical and socially disadvantaged people, troubled or at-risk youth and individuals with special needs.
Requirements: Eligible applicants must be a charitable, nonprofit entity with tax exempt status under Section 501(c)3. Organizations applying for support must be categorized in one of the four giving areas of education, health and human services, community service and arts and culture. The Foundation places particular emphasis on those organizations and programs that provide a direct service to economically and socially disadvantaged youth and their families, at-risk or troubled youth, and individuals with special needs. Preference is given to applicants who are able to demonstrate that a majority, if not all, of Foundation funds will be used for direct services. The Foundation prefers giving to organizations with no or low administrative costs. Organizations may apply for funding only in the year in which funds will be used. The Foundation prefers that organizations show evidence of substantial financial support from their community, constituency groups or other funding sources prior to applying.
Restrictions: Applications will not be considered for the following organizations or purposes: organizations that, in policy or practice, unfairly discriminate against race, ethnic origin, sex, creed, or religion; to fund loans, debt retirement or operational deficits; to fund on-going, general operations; to individuals, unless under an approved educational scholarship program; to sectarian or religious organizations for religious purposes where the principal activity is for the benefit of their own members or adherents; to veterans or fraternal organizations, unless their programs are available to members of the community as a whole; for travel expenses or trips; to general endowment funds, private or public foundations and most capital campaigns; for operation expenses of tax-supported groups; for sponsorships including auctions, dinners, tickets, advertising, or annual fundraising events; for political action or legislative advocacy groups or influencing legislation or elections; for operational costs or curriculum development at educational institutions; the purchase of motor vehicles or other forms of transportation; to organizations acting on behalf of, but without the authority of, qualified tax exempt organizations.
Geographic Focus: Montana
Samples: Horatio Alger Assoc (Alexandria, VA)—to provide college scholarships for students from Montana who plan to attend the U of Montana, $1 million over four years.
Contact: Mike Halligan, Executive Director; (406) 523-1325
Internet: http://www.dpwfoundation.org/home.htm
Sponsor: Dennis and Phyllis Washington Foundation
P.O. Box 16630
Missoula, MT 59808-6630

Denver Foundation Technical Assistance Grants **581**

All nonprofit organizations need help from time to time in order to function more effectively and efficiently. This is especially true of new or emerging nonprofit organizations or those with smaller budgets. The Denver Foundation has set aside funds specifically to provide grants for nonprofit organizations to get this kind of help, usually called technical assistance. Technical Assistance

(TA) can be many things, and what is most important is that TA helps the staff and/or board of the organization learn something new and increase its capacity to lead, manage and direct the organization. Examples of Technical Assistance include: obtaining training on a specific topic, such as marketing, volunteer management, financial management or fund raising; hiring a facilitator for a board retreat; or working with a consultant to develop a fund raising plan or a strategic plan for the organization.
Requirements: To qualify for a grant an organization must be a 501(c)3 tax-exempt nonprofit organization, serve residents in seven specific Denver counties, and provide a service that falls under one of the four funding areas.
Restrictions: The Foundation will not consider requests to fund the following: requests from organizations that have received funding from the program for the three previous consecutive calendar years; organizations with fund balance deficits in their most recently completed fiscal year; organizations that discriminate on the basis of race, color, religion, gender, age, national origin; disability, marital status, sexual orientation, or military status; debt retirement; endowments or other reserve funds; membership or affiliation campaigns, dinners, or special events; conferences and symposia and related travel; grants that further political doctrine; grants that further religious doctrine; grants to individuals; scholarships or sponsorships; individual medical procedures; medical, scientific, or academic research; grants to parochial or religious schools; grants to governmental agencies, except public schools; requests from individual public schools that have not coordinated the request with their central school district administration; requests from foundations/organizations that raise money for individual public schools; creation or installation of art objects; development, production, or distribution of books, newspapers, or video productions; grants for re-granting programs; requests for capital campaigns that have not met 75% of their goal; activities, projects, or programs that will have been completed before funding becomes available; and multi-year funding requests.
Geographic Focus: Colorado
Date(s) Application is Due: Feb 2; Jun 1; Oct 1
Contact: Jeff Hirota, Vice President; (303) 300-1790, ext. 129; (303) 300-6547; jhirota@denverfoundation.org
Internet: http://www.denverfoundation.org/page16399.cfm
Sponsor: Denver Foundation
55 Madison, 8th Floor
Denver, CO 80206

DeRoy Testamentary Foundation Grants 582

Established in 1979, the Foundation gives primarily in the state of Michigan. Giving primarily for youth development and services, education, human services, health care, and the arts. The Foundation offers support in the form of: scholarship funds; annual campaigns; building/renovation; continuing support; general/operating support; program development grants. There are no application deadlines. The board meets monthly.
Requirements: Michigan nonprofit organizations are eligible.
Restrictions: Grants are not made to individuals.
Geographic Focus: Michigan
Amount: 10,000 - 300,000 USD
Samples: National Bone Marrow Transplant Link, Southfield, MI, $10,000; Oakland Family Services, Pontiac, MI, $65,000; Interlochen Center for the Arts, Interlochen, MI, $300,000.
Contact: Julie Rodecker Holly, Vice President; (248) 827-0920; (248) 827-0922; deroyfdtn@aol.com
Sponsor: DeRoy Testamentary Foundation
26999 Central Park Boulevard, Suite 160N
Southfield, MI 48076

DHHS ARRA Strengthening Communities Fund - State, Local, and Tribal Government Capacity Building Grants 583

The purpose of this grant program is to build the capacity of government offices (or their authorized designee) that provide outreach to faith-based and community-based organizations and to assist nonprofit organizations in addressing the broad economic recovery issues present in their communities, including helping low-income individuals secure and retain employment, earn higher wages, obtain better-quality jobs, and gain greater access to State and Federal benefits and tax credits. The Administration for Children and Families (ACF) will award funds to State, city, county, and Indian/Native American Tribal government offices (e.g., offices responsible for outreach to faith-based and community organizations or those interested in initiating such an effort), or their designees, to build their own capacity to partner with community-based and faith-based non-profits and to provide training and technical assistance to help nonprofit faith-based and community organizations better serve those in need and to increase nonprofit organizations' involvement in the economic recovery. Grantees will use program funds to provide free capacity building services to nonprofit organizations, such as a beneficiary benefits clearinghouse, outreach and education, facilitation of partnerships between and among nonprofits and other government agencies, and training and technical assistance to improve awareness of and access to ARRA efforts/benefits and to improve organizational capacity to be active participants in ARRA efforts/benefits. Grantees will also use program funds to build their own capacity to provide these services to nonprofits. The average projected award amount is $250,000 per project period.
Requirements: An applicant must be a State, city, county, or Indian/Native American Tribal government office or a designated private nonprofit organization authorized by such an office. All applicants, whether a government office or a private nonprofit organization, must be authorized by the State, city, county, or Indian/Native American Tribal government to apply for a SCF State, Local, and Tribal Government Capacity Building program grant through a statute, resolution, or executive order. Applicants must include a copy of the authorizing document in the application. If the document is not signed or approved prior to the application due date, a letter from the executive officer of the governing body may be submitted, with an approved statute, resolution, or executive order to be submitted by the start of the grant. This authorizing document must specify the role of the Authorized Entity as well as detail the support, access, and authority to be provided by the State, city, county, and Indian/Native American Tribal government with regard to the activities to be conducted under the grant. A State, city, county, or Indian/Native American Tribal government may designate only one authorized entity to apply for this program. All applicants must have a D&B Data Universal Numbering System (D-U-N-S) number.
Restrictions: Applications with requests that exceed the ceiling on the amount of individual awards will be deemed non-responsive and will not be considered for funding. These grants cannot be used to provide direct client services. Under the SCF State, Local, and Tribal Government Capacity Building program, organizations shall not use direct Federal grants or contracts to support inherently religious activities, such as religious instruction, worship, or proselytization. Therefore, any organization receiving funds must take steps to separate, in time or location, their inherently religious activities from the grant-funded activities. Some of the ways organizations may accomplish this include, but are not limited to, promoting only the Federally funded program in materials or websites created with any portion of the Federal funds. Further, participation in such inherently religious activity by individuals receiving services must be voluntary. Any criteria for selecting nonprofit organizations to receive training and technical assistance must be neutral to whether the nonprofits are religious or secular groups.
Geographic Focus: All U.S. States
Date(s) Application is Due: Jul 7
Contact: Thom Campbell, Office of Community Services Operations Center; (800) 281-9519; ocs@lcgnet.com
Internet: http://www.acf.hhs.gov/grants/open/HHS-2009-ACF-OCS-SN-0092.html
Sponsor: U.S. Department of Health and Human Services
370 L'Enfant Promenade SW
Washington, DC 20447

DHHS Community Services Block Grant Training and Technical Assistance Program: Capacity-Building for Ongoing CSBG Programs and Strategic Planning and Coordination Supported by the ARR Act of 2009 584

This program is intended to support Statewide capacity development projects for technical assistance in the Community Services Block Grant program. In addition, it supports Statewide strategic planning efforts related to the American Recovery and Reinvestment Act of 2009. The Recovery Act projects supported through this announcement are a part of the Federal government's overall support for training and technical assistance activities. As specified in the CSBG Act, training and technical assistance activities may support improved financial management practices, program performance measurement, information and reporting systems, coordination between fragmented State and local programs, and ensure responsiveness to locally identified community needs. The focus of strategic planning efforts supported through this grant will be on informing communities of available services supported under the Recovery Act, documenting community results, and preparing communities to sustain the impact of Recovery Act funds after additional Federal support received through the Recovery Act ends.

Requirements: Eligible applicants include Non-profits with 501(c)3 IRS status (other than institutions of higher education); Non-profits without 501(c)3 IRS status (other than institutions of higher education); or statewide or local organizations or associations, with demonstrated expertise in providing training to individuals and organizations on methods of effectively addressing the needs of low-income families and communities. Faith-based and community organizations are eligible to apply under this announcement. Organizations that applied for and received funding under funding opportunity HHS-2008-ACF-OCS-ET-0041 are eligible for funding under this announcement. However, applicants that received funding under HHS-2008-ACF-OCS-ET-0041 must describe new proposed capacity-building projects proposed in Part 1 of the grant project (Capacity-Building for Ongoing CSBG Programs) that do not duplicate those supported under the previous application. Applicants for funding under this announcement must be recognized by the State CSBG Lead Agency as a technical assistance provider for eligible entities within the State and must include a letter of endorsement from the State CSBG Lead Agency. All applicants must have a D&B Data Universal Numbering System (D-U-N-S) number. A D-U-N-S number is required whether an applicant is submitting a paper application or using the government-wide electronic portal, Grants.gov.
Restrictions: Applications with requests that exceed the ceiling on the amount of individual awards will be deemed ineligible. Applications that do not include a letter of endorsement from the State CSBG Lead Agency will not be considered for funding. Foreign entities are not eligible under this announcement.
Geographic Focus: All U.S. States
Date(s) Application is Due: Jun 12
Amount: 105,000 USD
Contact: Seth Hassett, Office of Community Services Operations Center; (800) 281-9519; OCS@lcgnet.com
Internet: http://www.acf.hhs.gov/grants/open/HHS-2009-ACF-OCS-EQ-0037.html
Sponsor: U.S. Department of Health and Human Services
370 L'Enfant Promenade SW
Washington, DC 20447

DHHS Health Centers Grants for Migratory and Seasonal Farmworkers **585**
The grants support the development and operation of migrant health centers and projects that provide primary health care services, supplemental health services, and environmental health services that are accessible to migrant and seasonal agricultural farm workers and their families as they move and work. Funds may be used for the planning, development, and operation of clearly defined migrant health centers and programs; for the acquisition and modernization of existing buildings; and for training related to the management of programs assisted through grants and contracts.
Requirements: Any public or nonprofit private entity may apply. Preference will be given to applications submitted by community-based organizations that are representative of the populations to be served.
Restrictions: For-profit organizations are ineligible.
Geographic Focus: All U.S. States
Amount: 50,000 - 2,500,000 USD
Contact: Grants Management Officer, Bureau of Primary Health Care; (301) 594-4235
Internet: http://www.bphc.hrsa.gov
Sponsor: U.S. Department of Health and Human Services
4350 East-West Highway
Bethesda, MD 20814

DHHS Individual Development Accounts for Refugees Project Grants **586**
The Office of Refugee Resettlement invites qualified entities to submit competing grant applications for new projects that will establish, support, and manage Individual Development Accounts (IDAs) for eligible low-income refugee individuals and families. This program represents an anti-poverty strategy built on asset accumulation for low-income refugee individuals and families with the goal of promoting refugee economic independence. In particular, the objectives of this program are to: increase the ability of low-income refugees to save; promote their participation in the financial institutions of this country; assist refugees in advancing their education; increase home ownership; and assist refugees in gaining access to capital. These new projects will accomplish these objectives by establishing programs that combine the provision of matched savings accounts with financial training and counseling.
Requirements: Eligible applicants include states and private, nonprofit organizations.
Geographic Focus: All U.S. States
Amount: 5,000 - 19,000,000 USD
Contact: Office of Refugee Resettlement; (202) 401-9246; (202) 401-5487
Internet: http://www.acf.hhs.gov/programs/orr/programs/individual.htm
Sponsor: U.S. Department of Health and Human Services
370 L'Enfant Promenade SW
Washington, DC 20447

DHHS Oral Health Promotion Research Across the Lifespan **587**
The National Institute of Dental and Craniofacial Research has invited proposals for improving the oral health of people of all ages. The research team must include someone with extensive experience in health promotion, behavioral and/or social science research. The health promotion intervention proposed for funding must be based on a previously conducted assessment of the epidemiology, social, behavioral and/or environmental factors related to the disease or condition under study. Research could focus on maternal and child health, adolescent and young adult health, or health of adults with complex diseases. For example, an applicant might propose to study approaches to involving families, social networks, communities, or neighborhoods in behaviors that promote and improve oral health; improving patient-provider communication related to oral preventive measures; or effective ways to train oral health professional students to communicate with diverse patient populations.
Requirements: Any person with the skills, knowledge, and resources necessary to carry out the proposed research as the project director/principal investigator (PD/PI) is invited to work with his/her organization to develop an application for support. Applications must be submitted electronically through Grants.gov (http://www.grants.gov) using the SF424 research and related forms and the SF424 application guide.
Geographic Focus: All U.S. States
Date(s) Application is Due: Mar 5; Jul 5; Nov 5
Contact: Maria Teresa Canto, (301) 594-5497; (301) 480-8322; maria.canto@nih.gov
Internet: http://grants.nih.gov/grants/guide/pa-files/PA-07-225.html
Sponsor: National Institute of Dental and Craniofacial Research
45 Center Drive, Natcher Building
Bethesda, MD 20892

DHL Charitable Shipment Support **588**
The corporation provides free shipment of materials supporting charitable programs. Applicants must submit a complete web questionnaire.
Requirements: Application by internet only.
Restrictions: Religious organizations are ineligible for religious sectarian activities, and political organizations are not eligible for political purposes.
Geographic Focus: All U.S. States
Contact: Technical Support; (800) 527-7298
Internet: http://www.dhl-usa.com
Sponsor: DHL International, Ltd.
1220 South Pine Island Road, Suite 600
Plantation, FL 33324

DHS ARRA Fire Station Construction Grants (SCG) **589**
The Department of Homeland Security's Assistance to Firefighters Fire Station Construction Grants (SCG) will provide financial assistance directly to fire departments on a competitive basis to build new or modify existing fire stations in order for departments to enhance their response capability and protect the community they serve from fire and fire-related hazards.
Requirements: Non-Federal Fire Departments and state and local governments that fund/operate fire departments are eligible to apply. SCG seeks to support organizations lacking the tools and resources necessary to effectively protect the health and safety of the public and their emergency response personnel with respect to fire and all other hazards.
Geographic Focus: All U.S. States
Date(s) Application is Due: Jul 10
Contact: Help Desk; (866) 274-0960; firegrants@dhs.gov
Internet: http://www.firegrantsupport.com/afscg/
Sponsor: U.S. Department of Homeland Security
500 C Street SW
Washington, DC 20472

DHS ARRA Port Security Grants (PSGP) **590**

The purpose of the FY 2009 ARRA PSGP is to create a sustainable, risk-based effort to protect critical port infrastructure from terrorism, particularly attacks using explosives and non-conventional threats that could cause major disruption to commerce. Funds will support increased port-wide risk management; enhanced domain awareness; and further capabilities to prevent, detect, respond to and recover from attacks involving improvised explosive devices (IEDs) and other non-conventional weapons. It is expected that about 200 awards will be granted from the estimated total program funding of $150,000,000.

Requirements: All entities covered by an Area Maritime Security Plans (AMSP) may submit an application for consideration of funding. A facility that is not expressly identified in an AMSP will be considered covered under an AMSP if the facility in question has had a risk analysis completed by the U.S. CG utilizing the MSRAM tool. Congress has specifically directed DHS to apply these funds to the highest risk ports. In support of this, the ARRA PSGP includes a total of 147 specifically identified critical ports, representing approximately 95% of the foreign waterborne commerce of the United States. Applicants must provide a Dun and Bradstreet Data Universal Numbering System (DUNS) number with their application.

Geographic Focus: All U.S. States

Date(s) Application is Due: Jun 29

Contact: Program Director; (866) 927-5646; ASK-GMD@dhs.gov

Internet: http://www.fema.gov/government/grant/arra/index.shtm#2

Sponsor: U.S. Department of Homeland Security

500 C Street SW

Washington, DC 20472

DHS ARRA Transit Security Grants (TSGP) **591**

The ARRA is an economic stimulus package that was designed to jumpstart the U.S. economy, create or save millions of jobs, and put a down payment on addressing long-neglected challenges nationally. Funds received under this Act are intended to support these goals, and unprecedented levels of transparency, oversight, and accountability are required of the expenditure of Act dollars. ARRA TSGP specifically will focus on the use of visible, unpredictable deterrence through the funding of Operational Packages for canine teams, mobile explosives detection screening teams, and Anti-Terrorism Teams both due to their effectiveness in reducing risk to transit systems and their potential for job creation. In addition, funding will be provided for capital projects including Multi-User High-Density Key Infrastructure Protection, Single-User High-Density Key Infrastructure Protection, Key Operating Asset Protection, and Other Mitigation Activities. These funds are intended to preserve and create jobs across the nation through projects that can be implemented quickly. Based on those considerations, the following project types are eligible: Priority 1a Operational Packages - Hiring of transit law enforcement officers to enhance visible, unpredictable deterrence efforts in transit (e.g., K-9 teams, mobile screening teams, and Anti-Terrorism teams); Priority 1b Support and Equipment for Operational Packages - Related support and equipment costs for new officers/capability; Priority 2 Shovel Ready Capital Projects for Asset Hardening - Capital Projects including Multi-User High-Density Key Infrastructure Protection, Single- User High-Density Key Infrastructure Protection, Key Operating Asset Protection, and Other Mitigation Activities that can certifiably begin within 90 days of release of funds and will be completed within 24 months from the release of funds date. Failure to meet the 90 day requirement may result in a loss of ARRA TSGP funding for the specific project; Priority 3 Other Security Projects - Capital Projects including Multi-User High-Density Key Infrastructure Protection, Single-User High-Density Key Infrastructure Protection, Key Operating Asset Protection, and Other Mitigation Activities.

Requirements: With the exception of ferry systems, those eligible under the FY 2009 TSGP, as well as Amtrak are eligible for FY 2009 ARRA TSGP funds. Transit agencies eligible for FY 2009 TSGP funding were identified using a comprehensive, empirically-grounded risk analysis model. The risk methodology for the TSGP is consistent across modes and is linked to the risk methodology used to determine eligibility for the core DHS State and local grant programs. TSGP basic eligibility is derived from the Urban Areas Security Initiative (UASI). Eligibility for Operational Packages (Priority 1) is determined based on the number of authorized sworn positions for transit agency police departments and law enforcement agencies with dedicated transit bureaus. Eligible transit agencies and request thresholds were determined by the following transit police force or law enforcement provider characteristics: Transit police forces or law enforcement provider must have at least 100 authorized sworn positions dedicated to transit security; Funding requests are limited to no more than five percent (5%) of the force's current authorized sworn positions and the associated support equipment requests are based on number of officers requested. Law enforcement agencies with dedicated transit bureaus are eligible through the transit agency they provide security for; the transit agency itself is the grantee, and as such must apply on behalf of the law enforcement agency. To qualify for a Priority 2 Project, Shovel Ready Capital Projects for Asset Hardening, applicants must certify that the project can begin within 90 days of the release of funds. Applicants must also certify that the project will be completed within 24 months of the release of funds date.

Restrictions: Security service providers with unsworn law enforcement officers or guards are not eligible.

Geographic Focus: All U.S. States

Date(s) Application is Due: Jun 15

Contact: Program Director; (866) 927-5646; ASK-GMD@dhs.gov

Internet: http://www.fema.gov/government/grant/arra/index.shtm#1

Sponsor: U.S. Department of Homeland Security

500 C Street SW

Washington, DC 20472

DHS FY 2009 Transit Security Grants (TSGP) **592**

The Transit Security Grants (TSGP) is one of six grant programs that constitute the Department of Homeland Security (DHS) Fiscal Year (FY) 2009 transportation infrastructure security activities. These grant programs are part of a comprehensive set of measures authorized by Congress and implemented by the Administration to help strengthen the nation's critical infrastructure against risks associated with potential terrorist attacks. The TSGP is an important component of the Department's effort to enhance the security of the Nation's critical infrastructure. The program provides funds to owners and operators of transit systems (which include intra-city bus, commuter bus, and all forms of passenger rail) to protect critical surface transportation infrastructure and the traveling public from acts of terrorism, major disasters, and other emergencies.

Requirements: Transit agencies eligible for FY 2009 TSGP funding were identified using a comprehensive, empirically-grounded risk analysis model. The risk methodology for the TSGP is consistent across modes and is linked to the risk methodology used to determine eligibility for the core DHS State and local grant programs. TSGP basic eligibility is derived from the Urban Areas Security Initiative (UASI). Certain ferry systems are eligible to participate in the FY 2009 TSGP, and receive funds under the Tier I cooperative agreement process. However, any ferry system electing to participate and receive funds under the FY 2009 TSGP cannot participate in the FY 2009 Port Security Grants (PSGP), and will not be considered for funding under the FY 2009 PSGP. Likewise, any ferry system that participates in PSGP cannot be considered for funding under TSGP.

Restrictions: Eligibility does not guarantee grant funding.

Geographic Focus: All U.S. States

Date(s) Application is Due: Jun 29

Contact: Program Director; (866) 927-5646; ASK-GMD@dhs.gov

Internet: http://www.fema.gov/government/grant/tsgp/index.shtm

Sponsor: U.S. Department of Homeland Security

500 C Street SW

Washington, DC 20472

Dick and Marsha Sands Family Ministry **593**

Established in Maryland, the Dick and Marsha Sands Family Ministry has a primary interest in supporting human and social service programs, helping the needy, and the distribution of religious materials. There are no specific application materials or deadlines with which to adhere, and applicants should forward the completed proposal. Amounts range up to $1,000.

Geographic Focus: Florida, Maryland

Samples: Gospel Crusade Ministerial Fellowship, Bradenton, Florida, $380 - general operating support (2010).

Contact: Dick Sands, President; (410) 726-7224

Sponsor: Dick and Marsha Sands Family Ministry

12 Worcester Street, P.O. Box 351

Ocean City, MD 21843

District of Columbia Commission on the Arts City Arts Grants **594**

The program encourages the growth of quality and diverse arts activities throughout the city, supports local artists, and makes arts experiences accessible to District residents. City Arts projects provide art exposure to the broader community or to persons traditionally underserved or separate from the mainstream due to geographic location, economic constraints, or disability.

Eligible projects include, but are not limited to: festivals, concerts, visual arts exhibitions, literary readings, and salary support to enhance the cultural diversity of staff. Contact the program officer for deadline dates.
Requirements: Grants and awards are made to individuals and nonprofit 501(c)3 organizations based in the District of Columbia.
Geographic Focus: District of Columbia
Contact: Lionell Thomas, Assistant Director; (202) 724-5613; (202) 727-4135; lionell.thomas@dc.gov or dcart@dc.gov
Internet: http://dcarts.dc.gov
Sponsor: District of Columbia Commission on the Arts and Humanities
410 Eighth Street NW, 5th Floor
Washington, DC 20004

DJ and T Foundation Grants **595**
The foundation supports low cost or free spay/neuter clinics in the United States. Preference will be given to grassroots-level, underfunded clinics that provide free or low-cost dog and cat spaying and neutering services. There are no application deadlines. Grant applications may be downloaded from the foundation's website.
Requirements: IRS 501(c)3 nonprofits operating a stationary and/or mobile clinic and nonprofits in the process of creating such a clinic are eligible.
Restrictions: The foundation does not underwrite voucher programs or other fees. Grants are not made to individuals.
Geographic Focus: All U.S. States
Amount: 15 - 26,597 USD
Samples: Colorado Humane Society (Boulder, CO)—for operating support; Adopt-A-Pet (Columbus, OH)—for operating support; Pasco Animal Welfare Society (FL)—for operating support.
Contact: William Prappas, (310) 278-1160; WillPrappas@msn.com
Internet: http://www.djtfoundation.org
Sponsor: DJ and T Foundation
9201 Wilshire Boulevard, Suite 204
Beverly Hills, CA 90210

Donald and Sylvia Robinson Family Foundation Grants **596**
The foundation awards grants to U.S. nonprofit organizations in its areas of interest, including animal and wildlife protection, arms control, arts (general, performing arts, and visual arts), environmental conservation and protection, eye diseases and eye research, family planning and human reproductive health, food distribution, international affairs, Israel, Jewish social services, and social service delivery programs. Types of support include annual campaigns, building construction/renovation, capital campaigns, and general operating support. There are no application deadlines or forms.
Requirements: National nonprofit organizations are eligible to apply.
Restrictions: Individuals are ineligible.
Geographic Focus: Pennsylvania
Amount: 500 - 5,000 USD
Samples: Phipps Conservatory and Botanical Gardens, Pittsburgh, PA, $5,000; Jewish Residential Services, Pittsburgh, PA, $5,000; Jewish Family and Childrens Service of Pittsburgh, Pittsburgh, PA, $500.
Contact: Donald Robinson, Treasurer; (412) 661-1200; (412) 661-4645
Sponsor: Donald and Sylvia Robinson Family Foundation
6507 Wilkins Avenue
Pittsburgh, PA 15217

Donald P. and Byrd M. Kelly Foundation Grants **597**
The foundation awards grants to eligible nonprofit organizations in its areas of interest, including adult, elementary, preschool, higher, and secondary education; educational organizations; educational research; and minorities. Types of support include continuing support, endowment funds, general operating grants, and scholarship funds. Contact the office for application materials.
Requirements: Nonprofit organizations are eligible. Illinois nonprofits, with an emphasis on Chicago, receive preference.
Geographic Focus: Illinois
Samples: Big Shoulders Fund (Chicago, IL)—for general operating support, $25,000; Foundation Fighting Blindness (Hunt Valley, MD)—for general operating support, $76,191; Robert Crown Ctr for Health Education (Hinsdale, IL)—for general operating support, $12,500; Museum of Science and Industry (Chicago, IL)—for general operating support, $30,000.
Contact: Marcia Stone, Grants Coordinator; (630) 575-2344
Sponsor: Donald P. and Byrd M. Kelly Foundation
701 Harger Road
Oak Brook, IL 60523

Donald W. Reynolds Foundation Charitable Food Distribution Grants **598**
In 2002, the Foundation's trustees launched an initiative to improve the charitable food distribution systems in Arkansas, Nevada and Oklahoma, working closely with the food banks in those states. The Charitable Food Distribution Initiative builds on the success of the Foundation's previous capital support of the Regional Food Bank of Oklahoma in Oklahoma City. Application to the Charitable Food Distribution Initiative is by invitation only. Unsolicited requests will not be accepted.
Geographic Focus: Arkansas, Nevada, Oklahoma
Amount: 800,000 - 1,000,000 USD
Contact: Craig Willis, Program Director; (702) 804-6000; (702) 804-6099; craig.willis@dwrf.org
Internet: http://www.dwreynolds.org/Programs/Regional/Food.htm
Sponsor: Donald W. Reynolds Foundation
1701 Village Center Circle
Las Vegas, NV 89134-6303

Donald W. Reynolds Foundation Special Projects Grants **599**
Special Projects of the Foundation are awarded at the discretion of the board and encompass areas outside of the established programs of the Foundation. While these grants might result in the construction of a facility, provide for the acquisition of equipment or fund a specific program, they are unique and considered for funding based upon their individual merits. Often, Special Projects present a unique opportunity to advance patriotism, entrepreneurship, or another special lifetime interest held by Mr. Reynolds. Proposal invitations are usually generated directly by our Trustees. There is no application and no designated staff contact. Unsolicited proposals are rarely approved. Brief proposals may be sent to the Foundation, addressed to the attention of Special Projects.
Geographic Focus: All U.S. States
Contact: Courtney Latta Knoblock, Program Director; (702) 804-6000; (702) 804-6099; capitalquestions@dwrf.org or GeneralQuestions@dwrf.org
Internet: http://www.dwreynolds.org/Programs/Special/Special.htm
Sponsor: Donald W. Reynolds Foundation
1701 Village Center Circle
Las Vegas, NV 89134-6303

Dora Roberts Foundation Grants **600**
The foundation awards general operating grants to eligible Texas organizations in its areas of interest, Arts, Social Services, Health and Education. Most grants are awarded in Big Spring, TX. There are no application forms. Trustees meet annually in the Fall to review all requests received prior to the deadline.
Requirements: The Foundation can distribute grants only to qualified charitable organizations in the State of Texas. Persons who represent an organization which they believe might qualify for our support are welcome to submit an application in letter form containing: a brief narrative history of the organization's purpose and work; a specific description of the program or project for which support is asked; a statement of the amount of funds requested; proof of tax exempt status; a list of Trustees or Directors and principal staff; and budgetary information pertaining to the requested grant.
Restrictions: The Foundation does not give or lend money to individuals.
Geographic Focus: Rhode Island
Date(s) Application is Due: Sep 30
Contact: Konnie Darrow, c/o JP Morgan Chase Bank, N.A., (817) 884-4772
Sponsor: Dora Roberts Foundation
P.O. Box 2050
Fort Worth, TX 76113

Do Right Foundation Grants **601**
The foundation's grant-making interests include the reduction of violent crime, efforts to combat joblessness, increasing productivity of the U.S. legal system, helping people with the basic transition from welfare to work, parenting education, and the improvement of integrity and efficiencies of government. Funding targets small, controlled pilot programs. The foundation has a formal grant application that is available on its website or by contacting the foundation. Preliminary inquiry letters are not accepted. Preliminary inquiries are mandatory.
Requirements: Nonprofit 501(c)3 organizations in the United States are eligible.
Restrictions: Support is not granted to individuals, schools, or police departments.
Geographic Focus: All U.S. States
Amount: Up to 190,000 USD

Samples: Broken Connections (East Cleveland, OH)—for a parenting program for women with substance abuse and criminal backgrounds, $7000; Sweetwater Educational Ctr (Sweetwater, FL)—for a tutoring program for at-risk youth, $8000.
Contact: James McCrink, President; (619) 233-5634; dorightfdn@aol.com
Internet: http://www.doright.org
Sponsor: Do Right Foundation
991-C Lomas Santa Fe, #413
Solana Beach, CA 92075

Doris and Victor Day Foundation Grants **602**
The foundation supports local community organizations providing food, shelter, clothing, medical care, and education in Illinois/Iowa Quad Cities region. Preference will be given to preventive programs and projects that foster pride in the local community. Types of support include general operating support, building/renovation, equipment, emergency funds, seed grants, and scholarship funds.
Requirements: Illinois/Iowa Quad Cities region nonprofit organizations may apply.
Restrictions: The Foundation is committed to programs that are non-sectarian, and therefore, will not contribute toward programs and capital projects for religious purposes, except for modest contributions to the churches in which the Days held membership. However, clearly non-sectarian, community serving programs of religious organizations will be considered for funding.
Geographic Focus: Illinois, Iowa
Date(s) Application is Due: May 1
Samples: Transitions Mental Health Rehabilitation, $4,000—Client Home Renovation (2009); Rock Island Economic Growth Corporation, $50,000—Neighborhood Stabilization Program (2009); Martin Luther King Center, $175,000 — expansion and renovation (2009).
Contact: Program Contact; (309) 788-2300; info@dayfoundation.org
Internet: http://www.dayfoundation.org/guide.htm
Sponsor: Doris and Victor Day Foundation Grants
1800 3rd Avenue, Suite 302
Rock Island, IL 61201-8019

Dorothy Hooper Beattie Foundation Grants **603**
The Foundation primarily supports higher education, health care, and religious programs in and around the Greenville, South Carolina, region. Its program interests include: camps; cancer treatment; Catholicism; children and youth programs; higher education; health services; literacy; and the environment. Grants range from $620 to $6,500, and there are no specific deadlines or application forms. Initial approach should be by letter, with telephone contacts discouraged. Mail applications to: Bank of America, 7 North Laurens Street, Greenville, SC 29601.
Geographic Focus: South Carolina
Amount: 620 - 6,500 USD
Samples: The Bernardine Fund Street Francis, Greenville, SC, $620; Upstate Forever, Greenville, SC, $1,345; Greenville Free Medical Clinic, Greenville, SC, $4,000; United Ministries, Greenville, SC, $6,500.
Contact: Mary W. Green, Bank of America Contact; (864) 271-5789
Sponsor: Dorothy Hooper Beattie Foundation
101 South Tryon Street
Charlotte, NC 28255

Dorrance Family Foundation Grants **604**
The Dorrance Family Foundation was founded by Bennett Dorrance, co-owner of the Campbell Soup Company. The Foundation gives primarily in the state of Arizona, offering support in the areas of education and natural resource conservation.
Requirements: No formal application form is required, non-profits operating in Arizona are eligible to apply for these grants. Applicants should submit a proposal consisting of a detailed description of project and amount of funding requested.
Restrictions: No funding available to individuals.
Geographic Focus: Arizona
Samples: Arizona Community Foundation, Phoenix, AZ, $1,980,412; scholarship program,(2008). Nature Conservancy, Phoenix, AZ, $1,778,000; precious lands and water preservation (2008).
Contact: Carolyn O'Malley, Executive Director; (480) 367-7000
Sponsor: Dorrance Family Foundation
7600 East Doubletree Ranch Road, Suite 300
Scottsdale, AZ 85258

Douty Foundation Grants **605**
The Foundation, established in 1968, supports projects in the fields of elementary and other education, youth, and community welfare, with special emphasis on services to disadvantaged people. Grants are sometimes made to small organizations for general operations. Preference is given to organizations that operate in Philadelphia and Montgomery counties, Pennsylvania.
Requirements: Organizations with annual budgets greater than $2 million are discouraged from applying for grants.
Restrictions: Grants for capital expenditures or endowments are not a priority for the Foundation, nor are grants for agency promotion, such as marketing, development, publication of annual reports or sponsorship of fund-raising events. Grants are not made for religious or political purposes.
Geographic Focus: Pennsylvania
Date(s) Application is Due: Feb 15; Mar 15; May 15; Oct 15
Amount: Up to 5,000 USD
Samples: ArtReach, Philadelphia, PA, $3,000—Museum and Arts Education Program (2008); Brandywine Graphic Workshop, Philadelphia, PA, $2,500—after-school programs for Philadelphia high school students (2008); Cunningham Community Center, Philadelphia, PA, $2,500—summer camp (2008).
Contact: Judith L. Bardes, Manager; (610) 828-8145; (610) 834-8175; judy1@aol.com
Internet: http://www.grants-info.org/douty/index.htm
Sponsor: Douty Foundation
P.O. Box 540
Plymouth Meeting, PA 19462-0540

Dover Foundation Grants **606**
The primary purpose of the foundation is to serve the interests of Cleveland County and other areas of North Carolina. Foundation grants seek to strengthen the spiritual, mental, and moral fiber of the community; give priority to those initiatives and programs that will elevate the life and educational opportunities of deserving recipients; and discover ways to encourage others to come together to address needs for the common welfare of the community. Types of support include general operating support, annual campaigns, capital campaigns, building/renovation, emergency funds, scholarship funds, and research. A formal grant request must be submitted by letter. The board of directors meets four times a year to consider grant awards—January, April, July, and October.
Requirements: Applicants must reside in North Carolina.
Restrictions: The foundation ordinarily does not make grants to organizations whose principal activities are outside the United States; political activities or entities; individuals or their projects; advertising; newsletters, magazines, or books; or trips or tours.
Geographic Focus: North Carolina
Amount: 500 - 25,000 USD
Samples: Gardner-Webb U, School of Business (Boiling Springs, NC)—to endow a faculty position at the School of Business, $500,000; Heineman Medical Research Center of Charlotte (Charlotte, NC)—for support, $50,000.
Contact: Hoyt Bailey, President; (704) 487-8888; (704) 482-6818; doverfnd@shelby.net
Sponsor: Dover Foundation
P.O. Box 208
Shelby, NC 28151

DPA Promoting Policy Change Advocacy Grants **607**
The program seeks to broaden public and political support for drug policy reform and will fund strategic and innovative approaches to increase such support. Proposals should be designed to: educate the public and policymakers about the negative consequences of current local, state or national drug policies; promote better awareness and understanding of alternatives to current drug policies; and broaden awareness and understanding of the extent to which punitive prohibitionist policies are responsible for most drug-related problems around the country.
Requirements: 501(c)3 tax-exempt organizations and organizations with 501(c)3 fiscal sponsors are eligible. All grantmaking will be directed to organizations working within the United States, and possibly Canada, with particular emphasis on state-based activity.
Geographic Focus: All U.S. States
Date(s) Application is Due: Jun 15
Amount: 50,000 USD

Contact: Asha Bandele, (212) 613-8020; (212) 613-8021; abandele@drugpolicy.org or grants@drugpolicy.org
Internet: http://www.drugpolicy.org/about/jobsfunding/grants/index.cfm
Sponsor: Drug Policy Alliance
70 West 36th Street, 16th Floor
New York, NY 10018

Drive Bob and Jean Smith Foundation Grants **608**
The foundation awards grants to Texas nonprofit organizations in its areas of interest, including arts and culture, higher education, medical education, medical research, and health care. Types of support include annual campaigns, building construction/renovation, capital campaigns, general operating support, matching/challenge grants, and scholarship funds. There are no application deadlines; the board meets quarterly.
Requirements: Texas nonprofit organizations are eligible. Preference is given to Dallas-based organizations.
Restrictions: Individuals are ineligible.
Geographic Focus: Texas
Amount: 100 - 500,000 USD
Samples: Southwestern Medical Foundation (Dallas, TX)—to conduct neuromuscular research at the U of Texas Southwestern Medical Ctr at Dallas, $1 million.
Contact: Sally Smith, Grants Administrator; (214) 521-3461
Sponsor: Drive Bob and Jean Smith Foundation
3811 Turtle Creek Center, #2150 LB 53
Dallas, TX 75219

Dreitzer Foundation Grants **609**
The foundation awards general operating grants to nonprofit organizations in its areas of interest, including health, homeless, social services, and youth programs. Grants are awarded nationally, with preference given to New York nonprofits. Applications are available by mail or fax. Phone calls are strongly discouraged.
Requirements: 501(c)3 tax-exempt organizations in New York are eligible.
Geographic Focus: New York
Date(s) Application is Due: Jul 1
Amount: 5,000 - 65,000 USD
Samples: Partnership for the Homeless (New York, NY)—grant recipient, $50,000; Ethical Culture Society of Queens (Bayside, NY)—grant recipient, $25,000.
Contact: Alan Seget c/o Davidson, Dawson and Clark LLP, (212) 557-7700; (212) 286-8513
Sponsor: Dreitzer Foundation
60 E 42nd Street, 38th Floor
New York, NY 10165

Dresher Foundation Grants **610**
The foundation awards grants to eligible Maryland nonprofit organizations in its areas of interest, including capital campaigns, endowments, new or ongoing programs, operating support and scholarships. Summer camp and after-school program letters of inquiry are accepted for review only for the January and March deadlines. Letters of inquiry are accepted; full proposals are by request.
Requirements: Fund requests are generally limited to the Maryland jurisdictions of Baltimore City and Baltimore and Harford Counties. The Foundation will only make grants to organizations that are exempt from federal tax under section 501(c)3 of the IRS Code and that are not classified as private foundations under section 509(a) of the Code.
Restrictions: Support is not provided for: agencies that redistribute grant funds to nonprofits; annual giving; charter schools; public elementary or high schools; galas, special events, or golf tournaments; literacy programs; national or local chapters for specific diseases; one-time only events, seminars, or workshops; or political activities. The Foundation will not consider inquiries or proposals from any organization more than once every twelve months.
Geographic Focus: Maryland
Date(s) Application is Due: Jan 12; Mar 9; May 4; Aug 10; Oct 5
Samples: Johns Hopkins U (Baltimore, MD)—to establish a professorship in cardiac surgery in the department of medicine, $2 million.
Contact: Robin Platts, Executive Director; (410) 933-0384; robin@dresherfoundation.org
Internet: http://www.dresherfoundation.org
Sponsor: Dresher Foundation
4940 Campbell Boulevard, Suite 110
Baltimore, MD 21236

Dreyer's Foundation Large Grants **611**
This grant focuses on young people from preschool to grade 12, primarily in Oakland and the East Bay. Grants will be awarded to K-12 public education and programs that help students to succeed in core academic subjects and graduate to post secondary education and/or vocational training. Priority will be given to programs, either in-school or after school, which are provided in sequential, consistent basis to students throughout the year. Organizations may request support for capital items, program expenses, operating expenses, start-up costs, materials, and/or supplies. Priority will be given to those programs/projects that support low and middle income youth and minority youth.
Requirements: Grants are awarded to nonprofit youth-serving organizations and K-12 public education organizations.
Restrictions: The Foundation does not fund basic health, clothing or shelter needs. An organization may submit only one proposal annually.
Geographic Focus: All U.S. States
Date(s) Application is Due: Jan 15
Amount: 3,000 USD
Contact: Large Grants Coordinator; (510) 450-4586
Internet: http://www.dreyersinc.com/dreyersfoundation/large_grants.asp
Sponsor: Dreyer's Foundation
5929 College Avenue
Oakland, CA 94618

Duchossois Family Foundation Grants **612**
The foundation focuses its efforts in the Chicago metropolitan area and gives primary consideration to nonprofit organizations that contribute to the community in the area of health. The foundation supports organizations involved with mental health/crisis services, cancer, HIV/AIDS, cancer research, AIDS research and, human services. A one-page summary-request letter should include a description of the organization and its specific needs and purposes, the amount requested, and a list of members of the board of directors and their business/professional affiliations.
Requirements: 501(c)3 tax-exempt public charities serving the Chicago metropolitan area are eligible.
Geographic Focus: Illinois
Samples: American Cancer Society, Chicago, IL, $50,000 (2008); Metropolitan Family Services, Chicago, IL, $125,000 (2008); Barrington Area Council on Aging, Barrington, IL, $2,500 (2008).
Contact: Iris Krieg, Executive Director; (312) 641-5765; iriskrieg1@aol.com
Sponsor: Duchossois Family Foundation (Chicago)
203 N Wabash Avenue, Suite 1800
Chicago, IL 60601

Duke Endowment Education Grants **613**
The Education Division of the Duke Endowment awards grants to four specific institutions of higher education named in the trust indenture. Funds are provided annually both for general operating support and for special projects and programs. Application forms for individual grants are not required. Faculty and administrators at Duke University should contact the Office of the Provost, while faculty and administrators at the other eligible institutions should contact the Office of the President.
Requirements: The endowment awards education grants to four institutions: Davidson College, Duke University, Furman University, and Johnson C. Smith University.
Restrictions: The Endowment does not accept grant proposals from individual academic units or faculty members.
Geographic Focus: North Carolina, South Carolina
Samples: Five organizations in North and South Carolina (NC, SC)—for programs that promote collaboration among child-welfare groups, $467,680 divided; Thirty-two organizations in North and South Carolina (NC, SC)—for programs designed to strengthen and improve hospital care, $9.62 million divided; Johnson C. Smith U (Charlotte, NC)—to endow professorships in English and biology, for scholarships, and to support the university's role in a local literacy program, $2.875 million; Ninety-seven churches in rural North Carolina (NC)—for maintenance and operating support, and for child-care, community, and leadership-development programs, $3.806 million.
Contact: Susan L. McConnell, Program Officer; (704) 376-0291; (704) 376-9336; smcconnell@tde.org
Internet: http://www.dukeendowment.org/program-areas/higher-education
Sponsor: Duke Endowment
100 N Tryon Street, Suite 3500
Charlotte, NC 28202-4012

Duke Endowment Rural Churches Grants 614

The majority of grants awarded through this program go to individual rural United Methodist churches, defined as those churches in communities of fewer than 1,500 people. While North Carolina is becoming increasingly an urban state, almost 1,300 rural United Methodist churches meet eligibility requirements for Endowment grants. While the foundation makes many for capital projects such as sanctuaries and fellowship halls, recent years have seen the Endowment award an increasing number of grants for programs that help rural churches conduct ministries that meet the changing needs of modern communities. Grants are also made to the North Carolina and Western North Carolina Annual Conferences of the United Methodist Church, and to the districts of those conferences, for programs or projects addressing needs and concerns of groups of churches. The Endowment also awards grants to Duke University Divinity School, with special focus on programs that train and support pastors in rural churches.
Requirements: Nonprofit United Methodist in North Carolina and South Carolina in communities of less than 1,500 people.
Geographic Focus: North Carolina, South Carolina
Samples: Wesley Community Development, Iredell County, North Carolina; Sandy Plains United Methodist Church, Pembroke, North Carolina
Contact: W. Joseph Mann, Director, Rural Church Division; (704) 376-0291; (704) 376-9336; jmann@tde.org
Internet: http://www.dukeendowment.org/program-areas/rural-church
Sponsor: Duke Endowment
100 N Tryon Street, Suite 3500
Charlotte, NC 28202-4012

Duke Energy Foundation Grants 615

The Duke Energy Foundation gives primarily in areas of company operations in Indiana, Kentucky, North Carolina, Ohio and South Carolina. At the core of The Duke Energy Foundation is its commitment to the community, with a focus in three areas: Environment and Energy Efficiency; Economic Development; and Community Vitality.
Requirements: Organizations with a 501(c)3 verification from the IRS or are a part of a governmental entity are eligible. All organizations applying for a grant must have: completed the Online Grant Application; a clear reason for making the contribution that relates to the areas of focus; regular reports on the measurable results of the project.
Restrictions: Foundation funds are not provided for: organizations that discriminate by race, creed, gender, age or national origin; political activities and organizations; grants to individual agencies of the United Way or the Charlotte Arts and Science Council, capital campaigns and endowments, except in extremely rare and specialized situations that relate directly to our areas of expertise in business; individuals; athletics, including individual sports teams and all-star teams; underwriting of films, video and television productions; reducing the cost of utility service; sectarian or religious activities; conferences, trips or tours; fraternal, veteran or labor groups serving only their members; advertising; membership fees or association fees, either personal or corporate; dinners or tables at fund-raisers are rarely considered; family foundations.
Geographic Focus: Indiana, Kentucky, North Carolina, Ohio, South Carolina
Amount: 1,000 - 1,250,000 USD
Samples: Arts and Science Council of Charlotte-Mecklenburg, Charlotte, NC., $1,250,000 - for capital support; United Way of Cleveland County, Shelby, NC., $12,610 - for operating support; Greater Cincinnati Arts and Education Center, Cincinnati, OH., $550,000 - for capital support
Contact: Deanita McCall, Vice President; (704) 382-7200; (704) 382-7600
Internet: http://www.duke-energy.com/community/foundation.asp
Sponsor: Duke Energy
P.O. Box 35469
Charlotte, NC 28254

Duluth-Superior Area Community Foundation Grants 616

The foundation supports a wide variety of activities in five interest areas: Arts, Community and Economic Development, Education, Environment, and Human Services. Consideration is given to regional needs, the availability of other funding sources, and level of foundation resources. The foundation concentrates its funding support towards new projects and organizational start-up for a limited time; however, some field of interest and donor advised funds consider requests for ongoing project or organizational support, and capital and equipment support.
Requirements: Eligible organizations include: those classified as charitable organizations under Section 501(c)3 of the Internal Revenue Code; or classified as an organization under Section 170(c)(1) of the Internal Revenue Code; located in or that provide services to residents within the seven counties of northeast Minnesota (Aitkin, Carlton, Cook, Itasca, Koochiching, Lake, and Street Louis) and/or the two counties in northwest Wisconsin (Bayfield, Douglas). Some funds have a specific geographic focus area.
Restrictions: The foundation does not make grants to/for: individuals (aside from scholarships initiated or managed by the Community Foundation), fundraising activities, requests from re-granting organizations for its own grant making activities, tickets for benefits, telephone solicitations, endowments, religious organizations for religious activities, medical research, debt retirement, political organizations or campaigns, organizations with significant activity considered influencing of legislation.
Geographic Focus: Minnesota, Wisconsin
Date(s) Application is Due: Feb 1; Apr 1; Aug 1; Oct 1
Amount: 1,000 - 10,000 USD
Samples: Hibbing Kinship Mentoring Program, Hibbing, Minnesota, $3,000 (2009); ISD 381 Lake Superior Public Schools, Two Harbors, Minnesota, $4,864—for Community Education Preschool scholarships, kindergarten transition activities and Weekly Readers for Preschool children (2009); Minnesota Ballet, Duluth, Minnesota, $5,000—for operating support (2009).
Contact: Katie Gellatly, (218) 726-0232; KGellatly@dsacommunityfoundation.com
Internet: http://www.dsacommunityfoundation.com/grants
Sponsor: Duluth-Superior Area Community Foundation
324 West Superior Street, Suite 212
Duluth, MN 55802

Dunspaugh-Dalton Foundation Grants 617

The foundation awards grants to eligible nonprofit organizations in the areas of higher, secondary, and elementary education; social services; youth; health associations and hospitals; cultural programs; and civic affairs. Types of support include capital campaigns, continuing support, endowment funds, matching funds, operating support, professorships, and special projects. The board meets monthly to consider requests.
Requirements: U.S. nonprofit organizations are eligible. The foundation primarily supports programs in California, Florida, and North Carolina.
Restrictions: Individuals are not eligible.
Geographic Focus: California, Florida, North Carolina
Amount: 5,000 - 50,000 USD
Samples: Barry U—for program support, $1.5 million over five years; Bertha Abess Children's Ctr (Miami, FL)—for operating support, $3000.
Contact: William Lane Jr, (305) 668-4192; (305) 668-4247
Sponsor: Dunspaugh-Dalton Foundation
1533 Sunset Drive, Suite 150
Coral Gables, FL 33143-5700

Dwight Stuart Youth Foundation Capacity-Building Initiative Grants 618

The Dwight Stuart Youth Foundation was endowed by Dwight L. Stuart (1924 - 1998). As a philanthropist, Mr. Stuart was honored for his work and generosity on behalf of underserved and disadvantaged children and youth. The foundation looks for projects and programs that provide direct services to underserved children and youth within Los Angeles County. The foundation's Capacity-Building Initiative builds on its regular grantmaking, which already has provided support for capacity building to a number of grantees. The Initiative's objective is to increase the foundation's commitment to strengthening youth-serving nonprofits in Los Angeles County, helping them achieve their missions by offering grant support for such purposes as staff training, creation of new staff positions such as development director, board training, facilities development and technology purchases. In addition, the Capacity-Building Initiative includes a Cornerstone Grants, which is by invitation only - you cannot apply for a Cornerstone grant and only current or past DSYF grantees are eligible to be invited. The purpose of these special grants is to provide up to three years of operating support (support for specific capacity-building activities also can be included) to a select group of youth-serving nonprofits in Southern California, based upon their demonstrated excellence and growth potential. Those invited to apply will be contacted by the Foundation.
Requirements: Nonprofit organizations with 501(c)3 status and in the Los Angeles County area are eligible to apply. The application process starts with a letter of inquiry. Letters of inquiry are accepted year round and are reviewed in the order they are received. If it is determined from your letter of inquiry that your request is consistent with the foundation's funding priorities and

interests, you may be asked to participate in a conference call with foundation staff to further refine your request and clarify questions. During the conference call, if it is decided that your organization's objectives and activities match the foundation's criteria, you will be asked to submit a full proposal and application materials will be mailed to you at that time. Unsolicited full proposals are not accepted. Youth-serving nonprofits can apply for grant funds to support capacity-building activities of their own choosing; these requests will be considered independent of any program requests, and you may ask for both program and capacity building support at the same time. If you are seeking capacity-building support, use the Quick Assessment Tool in the Resources section (see website) to help define your needs, and include brief responses to its five questions in your Letter of Inquiry. The maximum grant amount that can be requested for capacity building is $25,000. Submit your capacity building request separately from any program requests.
Restrictions: Funding is not available for individuals; private foundations; annual giving campaigns; buildings or capital campaigns; unrestricted endowments or deficit reduction; political parties, candidates, campaigns, or lobbying activities; fundraising activities, benefit sponsorship, advertisements, or tables; medical or health programs (this includes hospitals, clinics, and mental or physical trauma recovery programs). The foundation also does not fund programs for children and youth who are diagnosed as emotionally and/or developmentally disabled, or chronically and terminally ill; organizations which, in their constitution or practice, discriminate against a person or group on the basis of age, political affiliation, race, national origin, ethnicity, gender, disability, sexual orientation, or religious belief; programs outside Los Angeles County; institutions outside the United States of America.
Geographic Focus: California
Amount: Up to 25,000 USD
Contact: Wendy Chang, Program Director; (310) 777-5050; (310) 777-5060
Internet: http://www.dsyf.org/grantmaking_capacitybuilding.asp
Sponsor: Dwight Stuart Youth Foundation
9595 Wilshire Boulevard, Suite 212
Beverly Hills, CA 90212

Dwight Stuart Youth Foundation Grants **619**
The Dwight Stuart Youth Foundation was endowed by Dwight L. Stuart (1924 - 1998). As a philanthropist, Mr. Stuart was honored for his work and generosity on behalf of underserved and disadvantaged children and youth. The foundation looks for projects and programs that provide direct services to underserved children and youth within Los Angeles County. The four funding areas that are of interest are education enrichment, mentoring, leadership and school readiness.
Requirements: Nonprofit organizations with 501(c)3 status and in the Los Angeles County area are eligible to apply. The application process starts with a letter of inquiry. Letters of inquiry are accepted year round and are reviewed in the order they are received. If it is determined from your letter of inquiry that your request is consistent with the foundation's funding priorities and interests, you may be asked to participate in a conference call with foundation staff to further refine your request and clarify questions. During the conference call, if it is decided that your organization's objectives and activities match the foundation's criteria, you will be asked to submit a full proposal and application materials will be mailed to you at that time. Unsolicited full proposals are not accepted.
Restrictions: Funding is not available for individuals; private foundations; annual giving campaigns; buildings or capital campaigns; unrestricted endowments or deficit reduction; political parties, candidates, campaigns, or lobbying activities; fundraising activities, benefit sponsorship, advertisements, or tables; medical or health programs (this includes hospitals, clinics, and mental or physical trauma recovery programs). The foundation also does not fund programs for children and youth who are diagnosed as emotionally and/or developmentally disabled, or chronically and terminally ill; organizations which, in their constitution or practice, discriminate against a person or group on the basis of age, political affiliation, race, national origin, ethnicity, gender, disability, sexual orientation, or religious belief; programs outside Los Angeles County; institutions outside the United States of America.
Geographic Focus: California
Samples: (2009) Actor's Gang - Student Education Initiative; California Conference for Equality & Justice - Talking in Class; City Scholars Foundation - AfterSchool Leadership Academy; Free Arts for Abused Children - General Operating Support; Los Angeles Gay & Lesbian Center - GED Preparation Program; Red Hen Press - Writing in Schools; Southeast Asian Community Alliance - Youth Leadership Project; Uncommon Good - Clinic to College
Contact: Wendy Chang, Program Director; (310) 777-5050; (310) 777-5060
Internet: http://www.dsyf.org/grantmaking_areas.asp
Sponsor: Dwight Stuart Youth Foundation
9595 Wilshire Boulevard, Suite 212
Beverly Hills, CA 90212

Dyson Foundation Mid-Hudson Valley General Operating Support Grants **620**
General operating support grants are sometimes referred to as core support or unrestricted grants. Many organizations use general operating support grants to cover day-to-day activities or ongoing expenses such as administrative salaries, utilities, office supplies, technology maintenance, etc. Other organizations use this type of funding to cover project costs, capital, technology purchases, and professional development. The use of these funds is totally at the discretion of the organization's board and/or executive staff, although the Foundation expects all organizational expenditures to be part of a board-approved annual budget. The first step in applying for a general operating support grant is to submit a letter of inquiry.
Restrictions: The Foundation places no restrictions on the use of these funds, unlike project or management technical assistance grants that are restricted by the Foundation to a particular project or activity. Colleges and universities, hospitals, faith-based institutions, and organizations with annual budgets in excess of $15 million dollars are not eligible to apply for general operating support grants.
Geographic Focus: New York
Amount: 1,000 - 1,000,000 USD
Contact: Diana M. Gurieva, Executive Vice President; (845) 677-0644; (845) 677-0650; dgurieva@dyson.org or info@dyson.org
Internet: http://www.dysonfoundation.org/programareas/programareas_show.htm?doc_id=328141
Sponsor: Dyson Foundation
25 Halcyon Road
Millbrook, NY 12545-9611

Eastern Bank Charitable Foundation Grants **621**
The goal of the foundation is to contribute to the health and vitality of northeastern Massachusetts communities served by Eastern Bank. The program provides financial support to nonprofit medical, cultural, educational, community service, or voluntary relief organizations operating within communities served by the bank. Types of support include capital grants, demonstration grants, development grants, endowments, general operating grants, and program grants. Requests for major gifts ($10,000-$25,000) must be submitted in the Associated Grantmakers of Massachusetts Application Form plus Eastern Bank donation request summary. Listed application deadlines are for major grants; there are no deadlines for community grants (less than $10,000). Guidelines are available online.
Requirements: Nonprofit organizations operating in northeastern Massachusetts communities served by Eastern Bank are eligible for funding.
Restrictions: Recipients of major gifts generally will be considered ineligible to reapply for a major gift for a period of three years.
Geographic Focus: Massachusetts
Date(s) Application is Due: May 1; Nov 1
Amount: 100 - 25,000 USD
Samples: Special Children's Outing Committee (MA)—charitable support, $1000; Northeastern U (MA)—pledge payment, $2000; Visiting Nurse Assoc Foundation (MA)—program support, $1000.
Contact: Laura Kurzrok, Foundation Coordinator; (781) 598-7888; (978) 740-6329; Lkurzrok@easternbk.com
Internet: http://www.easternbank.com/a_charitable_foundation.html
Sponsor: Eastern Bank Charitable Foundation
1 Eastern Place, 195 Market Street
Lynn, MA 01901

Eastman Kodak American Greenways Awards **622**
The program is a partnership project of Kodak, The Conservation Fund, and the National Geographic Society that provides small grants to stimulate the planning and design of greenways in communities throughout America. Grants may be used for activities such as mapping, ecological assessments, surveying, conferences, and design activities; developing brochures, interpretative displays, audiovisual productions, or public opinion surveys; hiring consultants, incorporating land trusts; and building foot bridges, bike paths, or other creative projects. In general, grants can be used for all appropriate expenses needed to complete a greenway project, including planning, technical assistance, legal, and other costs. The program also

honors groups and individuals whose ingenuity and creativity foster creation of greenways. Applications are available online.
Requirements: Local, regional, and statewide nonprofit organizations are eligible. Public agencies also may apply, but community organizations will receive preference.
Geographic Focus: All U.S. States
Date(s) Application is Due: Jul 15
Amount: Up to 2,500 USD
Contact: Grants Administrator; (703) 525-6300; (703) 525-4610; kodakawards@conservationfund.org
Internet: http://www.conservationfund.org/awards_and_grants
Sponsor: Conservation Fund
1655 N Fort Myer Drive, Suite 1300
Arlington, VA 22209-2156

Eaton Charitable Fund Grants **623**

The Fund is dedicated to supporting programs that improve the quality of life in communities where the company operates. The Fund gives primary consideration to requests for programs located in an Eaton community, recommended by an Eaton manager and where employees demonstrate leadership involvement. Programs selected for funding will have clearly defined objectives, measurable end results, and provide a positive return on the Funds investment. The Fund's primary interests are in support of community improvement, education, and arts and cultural programs. Program, project and capital grants are awarded. Capital grants are made for special purposes that meet specific community needs within the company's funding focus. On occasion, operating grants are awarded. Proposals should be sent to the manager of the Eaton facility located in an Eaton community.
Requirements: Applicant organizations must be 501(c)3 tax exempt charities and be located in communities where the company has operations.
Restrictions: Eaton does not make contributions to: annual operating budgets of United Way agencies or hospitals; medical research; endowment funds; debt retirement; religious organizations unless they are engaged in a significant program benefiting the entire community; fraternal or labor organizations; individuals or individual endeavors; fund raising benefits, sponsorships or other events.
Geographic Focus: Arkansas, Colorado, Florida, Georgia, Kansas, Kentucky, Louisiana, Maine, Maryland, Michigan, Minnesota, New Jersey, New York, North Carolina, Ohio, Pennsylvania, South Carolina, Texas, Wisconsin
Samples: 81,640 Eaton Multicultural Scholars Program, Cleveland, OH; $15,000 Habitat for Humanity, Sumter, SC; $7,500 United Performing Arts Fund, Milwaukee, WI; and $5,000 YMCA of North Oakland County, Rochester Hills, MI.
Contact: Grants Administrator; (216) 523-4944; (216) 479-7013
Internet: http://www.eaton.com/EatonCom/OurCompany/AboutUs/CorporateResponsibility/SocialCommitment/CorporateGiving/index.htm
Sponsor: Eaton Charitable Fund
1111 Superior Avenue
Cleveland, OH 44114-2584

eBay Foundation Community Grants **624**

The mission of the Foundation is to make investments that improve the economic and social well-being of local communities. The Foundation works to fulfill its mission by collaborating with non-profit organizations and funding innovative programs primarily in microenterprise development. The Foundation also provides support to community organizations in areas where employees are located.
Requirements: 501(c)3 nonprofit organizations in communities where eBay has a major employment base, which includes San Jose, CA, and Salt Lake City, UT, are eligible.
Geographic Focus: California, Utah
Amount: 1,000 - 15,000 USD
Samples: Friends of Farm Drive (San Jose, CA)—for operating support of this organization, which is dedicated to improving the quality of life for residents of a neighborhood rampant with drug dealing and gang activity; U Research Expedition Program (U of California)—for scholarships to send California elementary and high school teachers on UREP trips, where they learn by working with university scientists and local residents in countries around the world, to increase awareness of current events and to foster understanding of different cultures among both students and teachers.
Contact: Grants Administrator; ebayfdn@cfsv.org
Internet: http://pages.ebay.com/community/aboutebay/foundation/grantapp.html
Sponsor: eBay Foundation
60 South Market Street, Suite 1000
San Jose, CA 95113

EcoLab Foundation Youth and Educaton Grants **625**

The funds major focus is on youth and preparing children to grow up as contributing members of society. Programs of interest are those designed for learning readiness, and for mentoring troubled youth and students eager to learn about career opportunities in the business world.
Requirements: 501(c)3 nonprofit in Beloit, WI; City of Industry, CA; Elk Grove Village, IL; Garland, TX; Grand Forks, ND; Greensboro, NC; Hebron, OH; Huntington, IN; Joliet, IL; Martinsburg, WV; McDonough, GA; San Jose, CA; and Saint Paul, MN, are eligible.
Restrictions: Contributions will not be made to or in support of: individuals; sectarian/denominational religious organizations, except where funds are to be used in the direct interest of the whole community; loans or investments; political/lobbying organizations; industry, trade or professional association memberships; disease-specific organizations; sports/athletic programs and facilities; and fundraising events/sponsorships.
Geographic Focus: California, Georgia, Illinois, Indiana, Minnesota, North Carolina, North Dakota, Ohio, Texas, West Virginia, Wisconsin
Date(s) Application is Due: Sep 21
Contact: Grants Administrator; (651) 293-2658; ecolabfoundation@ecolab.com
Internet: http://www.ecolab.com/companyprofile/foundation/default.asp
Sponsor: EcoLab
370 Wabasha Street North
Street Paul, MN 55102

Ecosystem Protection Grants **626**

The foundation supports small, local environmental groups working to protect key threatened wild rivers in the Western United States and larger campaigns for ecosystems that contain significant wild rivers (i.e., the Arctic Refuge, southern Utah, Oregon, and California). Grants also support regional and national organizations that disseminate information and training on national policy issues that directly impact the work of local groups and projects that provide training and information in communication skills and strategies. Types of support include general operating support, technical assistance, capacity building, advocacy, and special projects. Previous grant recipients are eligible for opportunity grants.
Requirements: 501(c)3 nonprofit organizations in British Columbia or the Western United States, including Alaska, Arizona, California, Colorado, Idaho, Montana, Nevada, New Mexico, Oregon, Utah, Washington, and Wyoming, are eligible. Organizations must have annual operating budgets under $740,000, collaborate with other groups, be innovative, and produce measurable results.
Restrictions: Grants do not support watershed restoration, land acquisition, endowments, research, or legal work.
Geographic Focus: Alaska, Arizona, California, Colorado, Idaho, Montana, Nevada, New Mexico, Oregon, Utah, Washington, Wyoming, Canada
Contact: Grants Administrator; (415) 977-0772; (415) 369-9180; grants@kenneyfdn.org
Internet: http://www.kenneyfdn.org/grants.html
Sponsor: William C. Kenney Watershed Protection Foundation
P.O. Box 267
San Francisco, CA 94104

Edler G. Hawkins African American Culture Preservation Grants **627**

Each year the foundation provides funding to nonprofit African American arts organizations in, but not limited to, the New York City metropolitan area. The foundation awards general operating and program support to organizations working in the following artistic disciplines: visual arts; dance; music; and theater. The foundation encourages organizations to submit proposals detailing programs for young people that focus on African American culture in classrooms and other arts education settings. Application and guidelines are available online.
Geographic Focus: New York
Date(s) Application is Due: May 7
Contact: Grants Administrator; (212) 937-2020; eghf@eghf.org
Internet: http://www.eghf.org/grants04.htm
Sponsor: Edler G. Hawkins Foundation
Grand Central Station, P.O. Box 217
New York, NY 10163-0217

Edna Wardlaw Charitable Trust Grants 628

The trust awards general operating grants nationwide to nonprofit organizations in its areas of interest, including children and youth services, community funds, cultural programs, environmental and natural resources conservation, health and hospitals, homelessness, international peace, and reproductive health.

Geographic Focus: All U.S. States
Amount: Up to 12,000,000 USD
Samples: National Coalition for the Homeless (Washington, DC)—for general operating support, $6000; Ctr for Democratic Renewal and Education (Atlanta, GA)—for general operating support, $40,000; Ecology Action of the Mid-Peninsula (Willits, CA)—for general operating support, $25,000; Peace House (Ashland, OR)—for general operating support, $5000.
Contact: Mark Drake, SunTrust Bank Contact; (404) 827-6921
Sponsor: Edna Wardlaw Charitable Trust
P.O. Box 4655, MC 217
Atlanta, GA 30302-4655

Edward and Helen Bartlett Foundation Grants 629

Established by a single donor, Edward E, Bartlett, in Oklahoma in 1961, the Foundation primarily offers grant support for: education, particularly public schools; community programs and services; health care; children and youth; and social services. There are no specific application forms or deadlines with which to adhere, and applicants should begin by forwarding a letter of application to the contact listed. In the recent past, grant amounts have ranged between $5,000 to $150,000.

Requirements: Preference id given to non-profit 501(c)3 organizations located in, or serving the residents of, Oklahoma.
Restrictions: No grants are to individuals directly.
Geographic Focus: Oklahoma
Amount: 5,000 - 150,000 USD
Samples: Clarehouse, Tulsa, Oklahoma, $150,000 (2008); Creek County Literacy Program, Sapulpa, Oklahoma, $30,000 (2008); Retired Senior Volunteer Program of Tulsa, Tulsa, Oklahoma, $20,000 (2008).
Contact: Bruce A. Currie, (918) 586-5273
Sponsor: Edward and Helen Bartlett Foundation
P.O. Box 3038
Milwaukee, WI 53201-3038

Edward S. Moore Foundation Grants 630

The foundation awards grants to nonprofits in Connecticut and New York in its areas of interest, including youth, hospitals, education, cultural programs, museums, and Christian religion. Types of support include operating budgets, continuing support, annual campaigns, seed money, emergency funds, building funds, equipment, land acquisition, endowment funds, matching funds, internships, scholarship funds, special projects, and research. There are no application deadlines. The board meets in January, April, July, and October to consider proposals.

Requirements: Nonprofits in Connecticut and New York may submit proposals.
Restrictions: Grants are not awarded to individuals or for deficit financing, publications, or conferences.
Geographic Focus: Connecticut, New York
Amount: 10,000 - 50,000 USD
Samples: Children's Aid Society (New York, NY)—$50,000; Metropolitan Opera (New York, NY)—$35,000; Stamford Hospital Foundation (Stamford, CT)—$430,000.
Contact: John W. Cross III, President; (203) 629-4591
Sponsor: Edward S. Moore Foundation
30 Lismore Lane
Greenwich, CT 06831

Edwards Memorial Trust Grants 631

The trust awards grants to eligible Minnesota nonprofit organizations in support of health care for people without health insurance or who are underinsured, preventive health care for children, and programs for the disabled. Areas of support include health care and hospitals, mental health crisis services, social services, children and youth, and the disabled. Types of support include building construction/renovation, equipment acquisition, general operating grants, and program development. A copy of the tax determination letter and most recent audited financial statements must accompany applications.

Requirements: Minnesota 501(c)3 tax-exempt organizations in the greater Saint Paul area are eligible.
Geographic Focus: Minnesota
Date(s) Application is Due: May 1; Nov 1
Amount: 2,000 - 50,000 USD
Contact: Cheryl Nelson, c/o U.S. Bank; (651) 466-8441; (651) 244-4267
Sponsor: Edwards Memorial Trust
P.O. Box 64713
Saint Paul, MN 55164-0713

Edward W. and Stella C. Van Houten Memorial Fund Grants 632

Stella C. Van Houten resided in Bergen County, New Jersey. This foundation, providing funding for health and human services, education, education of medical professionals, and the care of children, was established in 1978 in memory of her husband and herself. The Van Houten's had a particular fondness for the Valley Hospital of Ridgewood, New Jersey and for the Rollins College in Florida. The Foundation continues to honor their preferences with grants to these two organizations in addition to grants to other organizations. The Foundation's mission is to: supports agencies, institutions and services in Passaic and Bergen Counties, New Jersey, having to do with the care or cure of sick or disabled persons or for the care of orphaned children or aged persons; educates students in the medical profession; support for educational purposes; support for the care of children. A target of 10% of the grants each year is for medical scholarships.

Requirements: Passaic and Bergen Counties, New Jersey non-profits are eligible to apply. The application form & guidelines are available online at the Wachovia website. The applications must be submitted by January 31 for a March meeting & August 1 for an October meeting.
Geographic Focus: New Jersey
Date(s) Application is Due: Jan 31; Aug 1
Amount: 6,000 - 100,000 USD
Samples: Therapeutic Learning Center, Ramsey, NJ, $6,000—speech therapy; William Paterson University Foundation, $20,000—scholarships for undergraduate, minority, and/or graduate nursing students; Christian Health Care Center Foundation, $100,000—to build a Great Room at Heritage Manor East.
Contact: Trustee, c/o Wachovia Bank; grantinquiries2@wachovia.com
Internet: https://www.wachovia.com/foundation/v/index.jsp?vgnextoid=00c78689fb0aa110VgnVCM1000004b0d1872RCRD&vgnextfmt=default
Sponsor: Edward W. and Suitella C. Van Houten Memorial Fund
190 River Road, NJ3132
Summit, NJ 07901

Edwin S. Webster Foundation Grants 633

The policy of the foundation is to support charitable organizations that are well known to the trustees, with emphasis on special projects and capital programs, or operating income for hospitals, medical research, education, youth agencies, cultural activities, and programs addressing the needs of minorities. Types of support include operating budgets, continuing support, annual campaigns, building funds, equipment, land acquisition, endowment funds, matching funds, scholarship funds, professorships, internships, fellowships, special projects, and research.

Requirements: The Foundation confines its grants primarily to the New England area. Grantees must provide evidence of their tax-exempt status. The AGM common proposal format, available on the Internet at http://agmconnect.org is suitable for submission of proposals but not required. There are no set deadlines, but for consideration at the spring meeting, proposals should arrive by May 1 and by November 1 for consideration at the fall meeting. Proposals received after the trustees meet will be held for consideration at the next meeting.
Restrictions: Grants are not made to organizations outside the United States or to individuals.
Geographic Focus: Massachusetts
Date(s) Application is Due: May 1; Nov 1
Amount: 15,000 - 50,000 USD
Samples: Massachusetts Institute of Technology, Office of Minority Education, Cambridge, MA, $40,000 - Mentor Advocate Partnership (2008); Eastern Virginia Medical School, Norfolk, VA, $25,000 - general operations and interdisciplinary research (2008); Museum of Science, Boston, MA, $50,000 - capital support for the Hayden Planetarium (2008).
Contact: Michelle Jenney, Administrator; (617) 391-3087; (617) 426-7080; mjenney@gmafoundations.com
Sponsor: Edwin S. Webster Foundation
GMA Foundations, 77 Summer Street, 8th Floor
Boston, MA 02110-1006

Edwin W. and Catherine M. Davis Foundation Grants 634

The foundation awards grants to U.S. nonprofit organizations in its areas of interest, including arts, elderly, environment, higher education, housing, mental health, religion, social services,and youth. Types of support include annual campaigns, endowment funds, fellowships, operating grants, research grants, and scholarship funds. There are no application deadlines. The board meets in May or June; submit a proposal that is three pages or less in length.
Requirements: U.S. nonprofit organizations are eligible.
Geographic Focus: Washington
Amount: 1,000 - 10,000 USD
Samples: Fulfillment Fund, Los Angeles, CA, $150,000; Childrens Health Council, Palo Alto, CA, $21,000; Trust for Public Land, Seattle, WA, $88,000.
Contact: Gayle Roth, Grants Administrator; (651) 215-4408; (651) 228-0776
Sponsor: Edwin W. and Catherine M. Davis Foundation
30 East 7th Street, Suite 2000
Saint Paul, MN 55101-1394

Edwin W. Pauley Foundation Grants 635

The foundation awards grants to California nonprofit organizations in its areas of interest, including children and youth development and higher education. Types of support include annual campaigns, building construction/renovation, continuing support, general operating support, and professorships. There are no application deadlines or forms.
Requirements: California nonprofit organizations are eligible.
Restrictions: Grants are not made to individuals.
Geographic Focus: California
Amount: 10,000 - 50,000 USD
Samples: Pomona College (Claremont, CA)—to endow a professorship in environmental analysis, $1.5 million.
Contact: Stephen Pauley, President; (323) 954-3131
Sponsor: Edwin W. Pauley Foundation
5670 Wilshire Boulevard, Suite 1450
Los Angeles, CA 90036

Effie and Wofford Cain Foundation Grants 636

The foundation gives primarily for higher and secondary education, medical research, and public service organizations. Grants also are awarded to religious organizations (Baptist, Christian, Episcopal, Presbyterian, Salvation Army, and United Methodist), and for aid for the handicapped. Additional fields of interest include elementary and secondary education, early childhood development and education, medical school education, nursing school education, hospitals and general health care and health organizations, religious federated giving programs, government and public administration, African Americans, Latinos, the disabled, the aging, and economically disadvantaged and homeless. Types of support include general operating support, continuing support, annual campaigns, capital campaigns, building/renovations, equipment acquisition, endowment funds, program development, seed money, curriculum development, fellowships, internships, scholarship funds, research, and matching funds. Organizations may reapply for funding every other fiscal year.
Requirements: The foundation only makes grants to 501(c)3 tax-exempt organizations in Texas.
Restrictions: Individuals are ineligible.
Geographic Focus: Texas
Amount: 1,000 - 100,000 USD
Samples: U of Texas at Austin (TX)—to acquire works of art for its collection, $500,000; Texas College (Tyler, TX)—for its concert choir, $100,000 over four years.
Contact: Lynn Fowler, Executive Director; (512) 346-7490; (512) 346-7491
Sponsor: Effie and Wofford Cain Foundation
4131 Spicewood Springs Road, Suite A-1
Austin, TX 78759

Eisner Foundation Grants 637

The Eisner Foundation exists to provide access and opportunity for disadvantaged children and the aging of Los Angeles County. The Eisner Foundation has been funding innovative and effective non-profit organizations that improve and enrich the lives of underserved children in Southern California since 1996. In 2008, the Foundation recognized that many of the same attributes that the children unfortunately possess physical and emotional vulnerability, extreme poverty, lack of advocacy on their behalf, minimal access to the arts, and general powerlessness also applied to many members of our rapidly aging population in the community. The Foundation elected to broaden the funding focus to include those at both ends of the spectrum of life, the young and the old. The Foundation's now dedicated to bringing about lasting changes in the lives of disadvantaged and vulnerable people starting and ending their lives in Los Angeles County.
Requirements: California nonprofit organizations serving Los Angeles and Orange Counties are eligible to apply. Applicants can apply at any time, but should know that these proposals will be reviewed and approved at the June or December board meetings. Applying to the Foundation is a two step process. The first step is to submit a Letter of Inquiry (see Eisner Foundation website for guidelines). If Letter of Inquiry meets the Foundation's criteria, a full application will be sent to the applicant for completion and submission, completing the second step.
Restrictions: Proposals for endowments are rarely excepted.
Geographic Focus: California
Amount: 5,000 - 100,000 USD
Samples: LA Scores, Los Angeles, CA, $100,000—to provide project support for an after-school program that combines creative writing, soccer, and community service (2008); California Institute of the Arts, Los Angeles, CA, $1,250,000—to support the Community Arts Partnership program which provides new media arts education programs to local youth (2008); Friendship Circle, Los Angeles, CA, $25,000—to provide support for an organization that addresses the challenges of families with special-needs children in the South Bay (2008); Eisner Pediatric & Family Medical Center, Los Angeles, CA, $1,000,000—to support the endowment campaign for a pediatric and family medical center serving low-income, uninsured and under-insured families (2008); Aquarium of the Pacific, Los Angeles, CA, $100,000—to provide support for a project that increases science learning access to Title I school communities in the South Bay (2008); Street Barnabas Senior Center, Los Angeles, CA, $75,000—to support a program that provides education on sustained nutrition, adult day care, and other health promotion services for 3,000 seniors in the greater downtown Los Angeles area (2008).
Contact: Trent Stamp, Executive Director; (310) 228-6808; trent.stamp@eisnerfoundation.org
Internet: http://www.eisnerfoundation.org/what_we_do/
Sponsor: Eisner Foundation
233 South Beverly Drive
Beverly Hills, CA 90212

Eli Lilly & Company Foundation Grants 638

Discretionary grants are awarded in two categories: nonprofit groups aligned with company interests, and grants in Indianapolis and several other communities with significant employee populations. Company-aligned giving focuses on public policy research, health and human services aligned with major therapeutic interests, and academic relations. Community-aligned giving focuses on culture, K-12 education and youth development, locally aligned healthcare organizations, fencerow neighborhood groups, and diversity. The foundation supports organizations within these categories that have a well-defined sense of purpose, a demonstrated commitment to maximizing available resources, and a reputation for meeting objectives and delivery quality programs and services.
Restrictions: Grants do not support individuals; endowments; debt reduction; religious or sectarian programs for religious purposes; bands or fraternal, labor, athletic, or veterans organizations; political contributions; beauty or talent contests; fundraising activities related to individual sponsorship; conferences or media productions; nonaccredited education groups; or memorials.
Geographic Focus: All U.S. States
Date(s) Application is Due: Jun 30; Dec 31
Samples: American National Red Cross (Washington, DC)—for relief efforts in South Asia and Africa, $1 million; Oklahoma Medical Research Foundation Foundation (Oklahoma City, OK)—to endow two professorships in biomedical research, $6 million.
Contact: Thomas King, President; (317) 276-3177; (317) 277-2025
Internet: http://www.lilly.com
Sponsor: Eli Lilly and Company Foundation
734 N LaSalle Street, #1167
Indianapolis, IN 46285

Elisabeth Severance Prentiss Foundation Grants 639

The foundation awards the majority of its support in the field of health and medicine. Scientific and medical research, hospitals, health projects, medical education, and care and support of the elderly are funded. Types of support

include building programs, equipment needs, research, operating budgets, continuing support, seed grants, endowment funds, and projects/programs. Decision makers favor specific projects over general operating support. The maximum term of a commitment is five years, with preference for proposals for three years or less. Special consideration will be given to requests from applicants in the Cuyahoga County area. The board meets in June and December.
Requirements: Grants are awarded to promote and improve medical services in the greater Cleveland, OH, area.
Restrictions: Grants are not awarded to individuals for scholarships, fellowships, or grants in aid; or to organizations for fund-raising campaigns, surveys, assessments, studies, or planning activities.
Geographic Focus: Ohio
Date(s) Application is Due: May 15; Nov 15
Amount: 10,000 - 100,000 USD
Samples: University Hospitals of Cleveland (OH)—to create an inpatient psychiatric unit for children and adolescents at Rainbow Babies and Children's Hospital, $5 million.
Contact: Michael Galland, National City Bank Contact; (216) 222-2736
Sponsor: Elisabeth Severance Prentiss Foundation
P.O. Box 94651
Cleveland, OH 44104

Elizabeth & Avola W. Callaway Foundation Grants **640**
The Elizabeth & Avola W. Callaway Foundation supports non-profit organizations primarily in the state of Georgia. General/operating support is available in the areas of : education; human services; Protestant agencies and; churches.
Requirements: Georgia 501(c)3 non-profits are eligible to apply, begin the application process by submitting a letter of inquiry to the Foundation. Letters of inquiry are accepted year round and should contain a detailed description of project and amount of funding requested.
Restrictions: No grants to individuals.
Geographic Focus: Georgia
Amount: 100 - 5,000 USD
Samples: Athens, Academy, Athens, GA, $1,200—education grant (2008); First Methodist Church, Washinton, GA, $4,300—religious/education grant (2008); Wills Memorial Hospital Foundation, Washington, GA, $1,750—public welfare grant (2008).
Contact: Michael Benson, Grants Director; (706) 274-3392
Sponsor: Elizabeth and Avola W. Callaway Foundation
869 Callaway Road
Rayle, GA 30660-1421

Elizabeth M. Irby Foundation Grants **641**
The foundation awards grants to Mississippi nonprofits in its areas of interest, including arts and culture, elementary education, secondary education, higher education, social services, and Christian churches and religious organizations. Types of support include general operating support, continuing support, annual campaigns, capital campaigns, building construction/renovation, endowment funds, emergency funds, program development, research, scholarship funds, and matching funds. There are no application forms or deadlines.
Requirements: Mississippi nonprofit organizations may apply.
Restrictions: Individuals are ineligible.
Geographic Focus: Mississippi
Amount: 250 - 500,000 USD
Contact: Stuart Irby, President; (601) 989-1811
Sponsor: Elizabeth M. Irby Foundation
P.O. Box 1819
Jackson, MS 39215

Ellen Abbott Gilman Trust Grants **642**
The Trust, established in Massachusetts, has designated a number of fields of interest, including: aging centers and services; multipurpose art centers; children and youth services; education; human and community services; and museums. Support is restricted to the State of Massachusetts, and most often comes in the form of general operations. There are no application form or deadlines with which to adhere, and applicants should inquire directly to the Trust for more information.
Requirements: Applicants must be 501(c)3 organizations supporting the residents of Massachusetts.
Geographic Focus: Massachusetts
Amount: 2,000 - 3,000 USD
Samples: Northampton Council on Aging, Northampton, Massachusetts—in support of its Elder Vision program, $3,000; Freedom House, Boston, Massachusetts, $3,000—for general operating support.
Contact: Walter G. Van Dorn, Trustee c/o Kirkpatrick & Lockhart Nicholson Graham; (617) 261-3100; (617) 261-3175; walter.vandorn@klgates.com
Sponsor: Ellen Abbott Gilman Trust
1 Lincoln Street
Boston, MA 02111-2901

Ellie Fund Grants **643**
The foundation awards grants to organizations located in Cuyahoga County, OH, whose activities benefit the county's residents. Applications outside of the area must be preapproved by a trustee. Preference is given to services for children within these priorities: crisis intervention, literacy, mental health, physical health, safety, and shelter. The trustees favor requests to support program development, as well as operating needs (especially for start-up, emergency, or bridge funding). Types of nonprofit organizations that receive support include start-up organizations; grassroots and community-based organizations; smaller organizations that do not receive wide public support; religious organizations, but only for secular programs that provide social services to the general community; and established organizations, but only for innovative programs. Organizations that have received a foundation grant for four consecutive years must go on a one-year hiatus before they can reapply for a grant.
Requirements: Grants are awarded only to tax-exempt, nonprofit organizations, and never to individuals.
Restrictions: Requests for annual appeals, fundraisers, symposia, and seminars will not be considered.
Geographic Focus: Ohio
Date(s) Application is Due: Aug 15
Amount: 1,000 - 7,500 USD
Contact: Foundation Management Services; (216) 621-2901; ellie@fmscleveland.com
Internet: http://www.fmscleveland.com/ellie/guidelines.cfm
Sponsor: Ellie Fund
1422 Euclid Avenue, Suite 627
Cleveland, OH 44115-1952

Elliot Foundation Inc Grants **644**
The Elliot Foundation Inc. formerly known as Elliot Foundation for Medical Research and Education, Inc. is a independent foundation, operating primarily in the state of Indiana. The foundation offers funding in the form of general/operating support. The fields of interest include: Christian agencies & churches; crime/violence prevention; environment; natural resources; child abuses; education.
Requirements: Contact Foundation for more information.
Geographic Focus: Indiana
Contact: Richard E. Bond, Secretary; (575) 293-1165
Sponsor: Elliot Foundation
2210 East Jackson Boulevard
Elkhart, IN 46516-1165

Elmer L. and Eleanor J. Andersen Foundation Grants **645**
The foundation exists to enhance the quality of the civic, cultural, educational, environmental, and social aspects of life in Minnesota, primarily in the metropolitan area of Saint Paul and Minneapolis. Types of support include general operating support, continuing support, annual campaigns, capital campaigns, building construction/renovation, endowment funds, program development, deficit reduction, publication, seed money, curriculum development, research, technical assistance, and matching funds. The board meets four times annually.
Requirements: Minnesota nonprofit organizations are eligible.
Geographic Focus: Minnesota
Date(s) Application is Due: Feb 1; May 1; Aug 1; Nov 1
Amount: 500 - 75,000 USD
Contact: Mari Oyanagi Eggum, Foundation Administrator; (651) 642-0127; (651) 645-4684; eandefdn@mtn.org
Sponsor: Elmer L. and Eleanor J. Andersen Foundation
2424 Territorial Road
Saint Paul, MN 55114

El Paso Community Foundation Grants 646

The Foundation is a facilitator linking the generosity of the region's donors to local non-profit organizations to meet the charitable needs of the El Paso area. In this capacity, the Foundation helps to provide funding for programs and initiatives of these organizations for the broader good of the El Paso Community. Major areas of interest are: arts and humanities; education; public benefit; health and disabilities; environment;animals and; human services. Types of support offered include: equipment acquisition; general/operating support; management development/capacity building; matching/challenge support; program development; scholarship funds; seed money; technical assistance. Priority is given to: more effective ways of doing things; projects where a moderate amount of grant money can have an impact; and projects that show collaboration with other organizations. Application deadlines are February 1 and August 1.

Requirements: Grant requests will be considered only from agencies located within or offering services to the citizens of our community, which includes far west Texas, southern New Mexico and northern Chihuahua, Mexico. Applicants must be exempt from income taxes under Section 501(c)3 of the Internal Revenue Service Code. Application form is available on the El Paso Community Foundation website.

Restrictions: Funding is not available for/to: individuals; capital campaigns; fundraising events or projects; religious organizations for religious purposes; annual appeals and membership contributions; organizations that are political or partisan in purpose; travel for individuals or groups; organizations outside the El Paso geographic area; endowment funds; past operating deficits.

Geographic Focus: Texas

Date(s) Application is Due: Feb 1; Aug 1

Amount: 3,000 - 10,000 USD

Samples: American Cancer Society, 42,000—provide local patients transportation to and from treatments (2009); Angelo Catholic School, $11,000— teachers' salary (2009); Animal Rescue League of El Paso, Inc., $8,000—animal rescue, rehabilitation and placement (2009).

Contact: Bonita Johnson, Grants Manager; (915) 533-4020; (915) 532-0716; info@epcf.org

Internet: http://www.epcf.org/grant_guidelines

Sponsor: El Paso Community Foundation
P.O. Box 272
El Paso, TX 79943

El Pomar Foundation Awards and Grants 647

The Foundation is one of the largest and oldest private foundations in the Rocky Mountain West and contributes annually through direct grants and Community Stewardship Programs to support Colorado nonprofit organizations. The Foundation's primary focus is in health, human services, education, arts and humanities, and civic and community initiatives.

Requirements: The foundation makes grants to 501(c)3 nonprofit Colorado organizations and for activities that take place within the state.

Restrictions: The Foundation does not accept grant applications for: other foundations or nonprofits that distribute money to recipients of its own selection; endowments; individuals; organizations that practice discrimination of any kind; organizations that do not have fiscal responsibility for the proposed project; organizations that do not have an active 501(c)3 nonprofit IRS determination letter; camps, camp programs, or other seasonal activities; religious organizations for support of religious programs; cover deficits or debt elimination; cover travel, conferences, conventions, group meetings, or seminars; influence legislation or support candidates for political office; produce videos or other media projects; fund research projects or studies; primary or secondary schools (K-12).

Geographic Focus: Colorado

Amount: 500 - 500,000 USD

Samples: Four Miles Historical Park (Denver, CO)—to construct a visitors center on the history of Denver, $50,000; Saint Paul Catholic Church (Colorado Springs, CO)—to construct a community center, $333,333; Pikes Peak Hospice and Palliative Care (Colorado Springs, CO)—for a new system for managing patient information, $75,000; Colorado Assoc of Nonprofit Organizations (Denver, CO)—for general operating support for statewide nonprofit programs, $20,000.

Contact: Executive Office; (719) 633-7733 or (800) 554-7711; (719) 577-5702; grants@elpomar.org

Internet: http://www.elpomar.org/grant2.html

Sponsor: El Pomar Foundation
10 Lake Circle
Colorado Springs, CO 80906

Elsie H. Wilcox Foundation Grants 648

The Foundation provides partial support to programs and projects of tax-exempt, public charities in Hawaii to improve the quality of life in the state, particularly the island of Kauai. Areas of interest to the Foundation, include: education, health organizations, people with disabilities; human services, performing arts, theater, religion, YM/YMCAs & YM/YWHAs. Types of support include building/renovation; equipment; general/operating support. Grants average from $5,000 - $15,000.

Requirements: 501(c)3 nonprofit organizations in Hawaii are eligible to apply. The Foundation places a special emphasis on the island of Kauai. Contact Paula Boyce to acquire the cover sheet/application forms and any additional guidelines required to begin the application process. Proposals must be submitted by October 1st.

Restrictions: No grants to individuals, or for endowments.

Geographic Focus: Hawaii

Date(s) Application is Due: Oct 1

Amount: 5,000 - 15,000 USD

Samples: Girl Scouts of Hawaii, Honolulu, HI, $5,000—scholarships for Kauai girls in grades K-5 (2008); Bishop Museum, Honolulu, HI, $5,000—educational program support (2008); American Cancer Society, Hawaii Pacific Division, Hawaii, Honolulu, HI, $5,000—quality of life services for cancer patients on Kauai (2008).

Contact: Paula Boyce, c/o Bank of Hawaii; (808) 538-4944; (808) 538-4647; pboyce@boh.com

Internet: http://www.hawaiicommunityfoundation.org/index.php?id=290

Sponsor: Elsie H. Wilcox Foundation
Bank of Hawai'i, Foundation Administration Department 758
Honolulu, HI 96802-3170

Elsie Lee Garthwaite Memorial Foundation Grants 649

Established in 1943, the Foundation supports organizations primarily in Philadelphia, Chester, Montgomery and Delaware counties of Pennsylvania. Giving to organizations that: provide for the physical and emotional well-being of children and young people; seek to enable young people, particularly the needy, to reach their fullest potential through education, empowerment, and exposure to the arts; are smaller organizations, with budgets under $1 million per year.

Requirements: Non-profits are eligible in the Philadelphia, Chester, Montgomery and Delaware counties, PA. Contact the Foundation at least 30 days prior to deadlines with a Letter of Intent. An application form can be obtained from the Foundation after reviewing the Letter of Intent, unsolicited applications will not be excepted. Contact the Foundation for further guidelines.

Restrictions: No grants to individuals, public, private, or parochial schools, colleges and universities.

Geographic Focus: Pennsylvania

Date(s) Application is Due: Mar 31; Aug 31

Amount: 3,000 - 16,000 USD

Samples: United States Fund for UNICEF, New York, NY, $15,000 - for Pakistan earthquake victim relief; Citizen Schools, Boston, MA, $10,000 - for program support; Center for Grieving Children, Teens and Families, Philadelphia, PA, $3,000 - for general operating support

Contact: Thomas Kaneda, Secretary; (610) 527-8101; (610) 527-7808

Sponsor: Elsie Lee Garthwaite Memorial Foundation
1234 Lancaster Avenue, P.O. Box 709
Rosemont, PA 19010-0709

Emerson Charitable Trust Grants 650

Established in 1944 in Missouri as the Emerson Electric Manufacturing Company Charitable Trust, the Foundation supports: arts and culture—fine arts and cultural institutions to enrich the diversity, creativity, and liveliness of the community; education—programs designed to promote educational systems at all levels; health and human services—programs designed to help individuals and families in times of need, including sickness, old age, family crisis, and natural disasters; civic affairs—programs designed to protect citizenry; further economic health of the community; and build and maintain assets such as parks and zoos; and youth—programs designed to give young people the opportunity to recognize their potential, confidence, and skills to achieve their dreams. The foundation awards college scholarships to children and step-children of employees of Emerson Electric. No specific application form is required, and initial approach should be the complete proposal,

Geographic Focus: All U.S. States

Amount: 5,000 - 300,000 USD

Samples: Alvin J. Siteman Ctr, Washington U School of Medicine and Barnes-Jewish Hospital (Saint Louis, MO)—for a new cancer-research facility and for cancer research, $6 million challenge grant.
Contact: Jo Ann Harmon, Senior Vice President; (314) 553-3722; (314) 553-1605
Internet: http://www.emerson.com/en-us/about_emerson/company_overview/pages/our_approach_to_corporate_philanthropy.aspx
Sponsor: Emerson Charitable Trust
8000 W Florissant Avenue, P.O. Box 4100
Saint Louis, MO 63136

Emily Hall Tremaine Foundation Grants 651

The foundation seeks to fund innovative projects that advance solutions to basic problems within society. Emphasis is placed on U.S. elementary and secondary education. The foundation also supports programs in the arts, environmental conservation, and learning disabilities. There are no application forms or deadlines. Unsolicited proposals rarely develop into a grant; submit informative letters of inquiry that highlight the organization's mission, goals, history, strategies, and programmatic scope.
Requirements: Education-related nonprofits may apply for grant support.
Geographic Focus: All U.S. States
Amount: 1,000 - 50,000 USD
Samples: Columbia U (New York, NY)—to teach two semesters of a course designed for Master of Fine Arts students to equip them with critical skills to manage their careers as a visual artist, $44,000; Side Street Projects (Los Angeles, CA)—t support the enhancement and implementation of a program to assist visual artists in Los Angeles with obtaining skills that will help them in their lives as artists, $45,000; Volunteer Lawyers for the Arts of Massachusetts (Boston, MA)—to support the development and implementation of a program to assist visual artists in Boston to obtain critical life and career management skills, $90,000.
Contact: Stewart Hudson, President; (203) 639-5544; (203) 639-5545; chevalier@tremainefoundation.org
Internet: http://www.tremainefoundation.org
Sponsor: Emily Hall Tremaine Foundation
290 Pratt Street
Meriden, CT 06450

Emma B. Howe Memorial Foundation Grants 652

The Emma B. Howe Memorial Foundation makes grants through the Minneapolis Foundation. The focus of all grants is to improve: the health and well-being of children, youth and families; opportunities for educational achievement; access to quality affordable housing; and economic vitality throughout the region. Information on the application process is available online.
Requirements: Eligible organizations include 501(c)3 nonprofits, public institutions; and emerging groups organized for nonprofit purposes.
Restrictions: Funds are not available for: individuals; organizations/activities outside of Minnesota; conference registration fees; memberships; direct religious activities; political organizations or candidates; direct fundraising efforts; telephone solicitations; courtesy advertising; financial deficits.
Geographic Focus: Minnesota
Samples: Kids in Distressed Situations (KIDS)—(New York, NY)—to provide donated products to low-income children and families in the Minneapolis area through Bridging Inc, $75,000 over three years.
Contact: Grants Manager; (612) 672-3836; grants@mplsfoundation.org
Internet: http://www.mplsfoundation.org/partners/emma.htm
Sponsor: Emma B. Howe Memorial Foundation
80 S Eighth Street
Minneapolis, MN 55402

Enterprise Rent-A-Car Foundation Grants 653

The Foundation's mission is to give back to and to strengthen the thousands of communities where employees and customers work and live. The Foundation supports four key focus areas: local causes by joining employees and providing a fifty percent match of contributions to United Way through the community; provides financial resources to worthwhile nonprofit initiatives that are actively supported by employees and customers; provides more sizable special grants to nonprofit groups or causes of significant strategic or social importance; and supports relief projects or causes the company deems important as they arise, such as natural disasters. A brief written proposal is requested. The Foundation Board meets three times each year.
Requirements: The Foundation provides grants only to qualified tax exempt 501(c)3 organizations in the United States.
Restrictions: Neither the Foundation nor the company donates vehicles or rentals. The Foundation considers the support of schools, churches, and sports teams a personal responsibility, and therefore discourages requests for Foundation support of these types of organizations.
Geographic Focus: All U.S. States
Date(s) Application is Due: Jan 19; Apr 6; Sep 7
Amount: 2,500 - 5,000 USD
Samples: Harris-Stowe State College—for the business-administration program, $1 million; Washington U (Saint Louis, MO)—to endow undergraduate scholarships and financial assistance for minority and other student's, as part of the university's campaign, $25 million.
Contact: Jo Ann Kindle, President; (314) 512-2754
Internet: http://206.196.101.205/what_we_believe/our_foundation.html
Sponsor: Enterprise Rent-A-Car Foundation
600 Corporate Park Drive
Saint Louis, MO 63105

Essex County Community Foundation Discretionary Fund Grant 654

The grant awards funds across the broad areas of nonprofit activity, including arts and culture, education, environment, health, social and community services and youth services. The fund will assist nonprofits with projects which strengthen the capacity of the organization to perform its work. Application information is available online.
Requirements: Eligible organizations must be Massachusetts 501(c)3 agencies that serve Essex County citizens with operating budgets of less than $500,000.
Restrictions: Funds are not available for: individuals; costs associated with programs or services provided to citizens outside of Essex County; sectarian or religious purposes; political purposes; debt or deficit reduction; capital campaigns for buildings, land acquisition or endowment; or to support academic research.
Geographic Focus: Massachusetts
Date(s) Application is Due: Jan 15
Amount: 1,000 - 5,000 USD
Contact: Julie Bishop, Vice President of Grants and Nonprofit Services; (978) 777-8876; (978) 777-9454; j.bishop@eccf.org or info@eccf.org
Internet: http://eccf.org/discretionaryfund42.html
Sponsor: Essex County Community Foundation
175 Andover Street, Suite 101
Danvers, MA 01923

Ethel and Raymond F. Rice Foundation Grants 655

The foundation awards grants to eligible Kansas nonprofit organizations in its areas of interest, including arts and culture; elementary, secondary, and higher education; environmental programs; elderly and youth; and social services. Types of support include capital campaigns, equipment, general support, land acquisition, scholarship funds, and federated giving funds. An application form is required.
Requirements: 501(c)3 nonprofit organizations and colleges and universities, school districts, and schools in Kansas are eligible. The foundation focuses on the areas of Lawrence and Douglas counties.
Geographic Focus: Kansas
Amount: 1,000 - 150,000 USD
Contact: James Paddock, President; (785) 841-9961
Sponsor: Ethel and Raymond F. Rice Foundation
1617 Street Andrews Drive, 200A
Lawrence, KS 66047

Ethel Sergeant Clark Smith Foundation Grants 656

The activities of the Ethel Sergeant Clark Smith (ESCS) Memorial Fund focuses on grants to organizations located in Southeastern Pennsylvania, with primary emphasis on those serving community needs in Delaware County. Grants will be made for capital projects, operating expenses and special programs in amounts that are meaningful to the success of the individual endeavors of the organizations. However, operating expense grants are typically awarded for charities without capital requirement and under circumstances where continuing funding is not expected. Grants will be made in areas of medical, educational, cultural, arts, health and welfare, and such other areas as the trustee shall identify and determine from time to time, to be responsive to changes in community needs. Application forms are available online and must be submitted by March 1 or September 1 annually.

Requirements: Southeastern Pennsylvania 501(c)3 non-profit organizations with primary emphasis on those serving community needs in Delaware County, Pennsylvania are eligible to apply. Complete applications should include the following: one original copy of the Proposal which includes the purpose and general activities of the organization should be included as well as a description of the proposed project and its justification, a budget and timetable for the project are also required; one copy of audited financial statements for the last fiscal year (or if not audited, Internal Revenue Service form 990) plus an operating budget for the current period and budgets for future period if appropriate; copy of the Internal Revenue Service tax determination letter which shows the organization is tax-exempt under Section 501(c)3 and that it is not a private foundation under section 509 (a) of the Internal Revenue Code. Any organization that is awarded a grant will be required to sign a Grant Agreement Form prior to the distribution of funds. Approximately one year after a grant has been awarded, a Progress Report should be completed by the organization. This information must be submitted prior to the consideration of any new proposals.
Restrictions: Grants will not be considered for the following: deficit financing; construction or renovations to real estate not owned by the charitable entity; salaries; professional fund raiser fees; multi-year grants over three years; to any organization more than once in a given year; to any organization more than three years in succession; any organization receiving a grant over a three year period or in three successive years will not be eligible for a future grant until two years transpire after the three year period.
Geographic Focus: Pennsylvania
Date(s) Application is Due: Mar 1; Sep 1
Contact: Wachovia Bank, N.A., Trustee; grantinquiries4@wachovia.com
Internet: https://www.wachovia.com/foundation/v/index.jsp?vgnextoid=3b38 52199c0aa110VgnVCM1000004b0d1872RCRD&vgnextfmt=default
Sponsor: Ethel Sergeant Clark Smith Foundation
620 Brandywine Parkway, Mail Code PA 5042
West Chester, PA 19380

Ethyl Corporation Grants 657
The corporation supports nonprofit organizations internationally in company operating locations. Education grants are awarded to public and private institutions at the secondary, undergraduate, and graduate levels. The program matches employee grants of $25-$2500 and also supports but does not administer a scholarship fund. Economic education grants for all age groups are awarded. Health and welfare grants support programs in the areas of health care, social services, recreation, and physical fitness. Requests also are considered for culture/arts and civic affairs, including federated giving. Types of support include general operating support, building funds, community advertising, employee-matching gifts, endowment support, professorships, and scholarships. Applicants should submit proposals, including a statement of purpose of the organization, a brief description of the organization and list of current board members, proof of tax-exempt status, and a brief statement on why Ethyl should contribute to the organization.
Requirements: Organizations in company-operating locations worldwide are eligible, including the United States, Australia, Belgium, Brazil, Canada, England, France, Germany, Japan, Russia, Saudi Arabia, and Singapore.
Restrictions: Grants are not awarded to religious organizations for religious purposes, individuals for personal gain, or fraternal groups.
Geographic Focus: All U.S. States
Date(s) Application is Due: Sep 1
Amount: 25 - 2,500 USD
Contact: Human Resources and External Affairs; (804) 788-5720; (804) 788-5636; contributions@ethyl.com
Internet: http://www.ethyl.com/About+Ethyl/Our+History.htm
Sponsor: Ethyl Corporation
P.O. Box 2189
Richmond, VA 23218

Eugene and Agnes E. Meyer Foundation Grants 658
The Foundation awards grants to nonprofit organizations that serve the people and communities in the Washington, D.C. region. Grants are awarded in ten program areas: arts; heritage, and culture; children, youth and families; civic engagement; education; employment and skills training; health and mental health; homelessness and hunger; housing and community development; immigrant communities; and law and justice. Candidates are required to first submit a letter of inquiry. Instructions for completion of LOI are available online.
Requirements: Eligible applicants must be a nonprofit organization with tax-exempt status and be located within and primarily serve the Washington, D.C. region which is defined as: the District of Columbia; the Maryland counties of Montgomery, Prince George's, Calvert, Charles, and Street Mary's; and the Virginia counties of Arlington, Fairfax, Loudoun, Prince William, and Stafford and cities of Alexandria, Falls Church, Manassas, and Manassas Park in Virginia.
Restrictions: The Foundation generally will not consider requests to fund: individuals, either through scholarships or other forms of financial assistance; scientific or medical research; sectarian purposes (programs that promote religious doctrine); special events or conferences; endowments.
Geographic Focus: District of Columbia, Maryland, Virginia
Date(s) Application is Due: Feb 9; Jun 8; Oct 1
Samples: Theatre Downtown, Washington Stage Guild (Washington, DC)—for general operating support, $20,000; Empower Program (Washington, DC)—to support local youth-services programs, $20,000; Community Family Life Services (Washington, DC)—to revamp and document its financial accounting and reporting systems, $10,000; Independent Sector (Washington, DC)—for its conference program, $10,000.
Contact: Julie Rogers, President; (202) 483-8294; (202) 328-6850; jrogers@meyerfdn.org
Internet: http://www.meyerfoundation.org
Sponsor: Eugene and Agnes E. Meyer Foundation
1400 16th Street, NW Suite 360
Washington, DC 20036

Eugene B. Casey Foundation Grants 659
The foundation awards grants to nonprofit organizations in the District of Columbia and Maryland. Nonprofit organizations of the Christian and Roman Catholic faiths also are eligible. Organizations receiving grants include colleges and universities, community service organizations, government agencies, medical centers, parochial schools, and religious groups. Types of support include capital grants and general support grants. There are no application forms or deadlines. Applicants should submit written proposals that include an annual report, the purpose for which the funds are requested, and the amount requested compared with the total sought.
Requirements: Nonprofits in Maryland or the District of Columbia are eligible to apply.
Geographic Focus: District of Columbia, Maryland
Amount: 10,000 - 100,000 USD
Samples: Redlands Christian Migrant Association, Immokalee, FL, $10,000—for general operating support (2008); Cystic Fibrosis Foundation, Bethesda, MD, $20,000—for general operating support (2008); United States Department of State, Washington, DC, $50,000—for general operating support (2008).
Contact: Betty Brown Casey, Treasurer; (301) 948-4595
Sponsor: Eugene B. Casey Foundation
800 South Frederick Avenue, Suite 100
Gaithersburg, MD 20877-1701

Eugene M. Lang Foundation Grants 660
The foundation awards grants in New York and Pennsylvania in its areas of interest, including education (early childhood education and higher education), medical and health programs, arts, health organizations, medical research, minorities, and performing arts. Types of support include annual campaigns, conferences and seminars, continuing support, fellowships, general operating support, internship funds, professorships, program development, scholarship funds, and seed money. The foundation favors social services such as those helping homeless or single mothers. Locally based groups wanting support must involve a Lang family member. There are no application deadlines; initial approach should be by letter.
Requirements: Organizations in New York and Pennsylvania are eligible to apply.
Restrictions: Grants are not made to individuals, or for building funds, equipment and materials, capital or endowment funds, deficit financing, publications, or matching gifts.
Geographic Focus: New York, Pennsylvania
Amount: 500 - 50,000 USD
Samples: New York-Presbyterian Hospital (New York, NY)—for a six-year health-sciences education program for selected inner-city youths, designed to boost their academic success and facilitate their entry into health careers, $1.25 million.
Contact: Program Contact; (212) 949-4100

Sponsor: Eugene M. Lang Foundation
535 5th Avenue, Suite 906
New York, NY 10017

Eugene McDermott Foundation Grants **661**

The foundation awards grants to Texas nonprofit organizations in its areas of interest, including children and youth, community development, education (early childhood through higher education), health care/organizations, international human rights, medical research, minorities, and social service delivery programs. Types of support include annual campaigns, building construction/renovation, capital campaigns, equipment/land acquisition, general operating grants, matching/challenge grants, professorships, programs/project support, research grants, scholarship funds, and seed grants. There are no application deadlines or forms. The board meets quarterly to consider requests.
Requirements: Texas nonprofit organizations are eligible.
Geographic Focus: Texas
Amount: 1,000 - 25,000 USD
Samples: Nasher Sculpture Center (Dallas, TX)—for endowment, $500,000; U of Texas Southwestern Medical Center (Dallas, TX)—to refurbish Medical School, $400,000; U of Texas Southwestern Medical Ctr (Dallas, TX)—to establish a chair in cardiothoracic anesthesiology, $1 million.
Contact: Grants Administrator; (214) 521-2924
Sponsor: Eugene McDermott Foundation
3808 Euclid Avenue
Dallas, TX 75205

Eulalie Bloedel Schneider Foundation Grants **662**

The Foundation's mission is to support secular grassroots programs that enhance individual and family self-sufficiency and economic stability. Areas of interest are skill-building and training programs that empower at-risk youth, women and families to develop skills that would bring them towards economic self-sufficiency. The Foundation supports programs that provide job-related educational and skill building opportunities, and those seeking to build character and develop self-reliance and accountability. Artistic and cultural skill-building programs for youth and families that enhance educational and future career opportunities are also of interest.
Requirements: Washington 501(c)3 groups in the Puget Sound area are eligible.
Restrictions: The Foundation will not support: groups outside the Puget Sound area; national organizations, even those with projects in the Pacific Northwest; human services or low-income services projects or organizations that are not specifically providing skill-building or training opportunities; programs with a religious or proselytizing approach or mission; educational and outreach programs of large artistic or cultural institutions; museum exhibits or related outreach programs for schools or communities; traditional academic-oriented literacy, tutoring, and mentorship programs; individual requests for research or scholarships; childcare centers, schools, or classroom projects; book, video, film, or home-page productions, unless the expenses occur within the context of a project that fits the foundation's major areas of interest; computer, software, or office equipment purchases unless clearly a component of a project that fits foundation areas of interest; and capital campaigns for building construction or renovations.
Geographic Focus: All U.S. States
Date(s) Application is Due: Feb 1; Aug 1
Amount: 1,000 - 3,500 USD
Samples: Creative Theatre Experience Olympia, WA)—to provide hands-on training for teen interns about behind-the-scenes work necessary to put on a show, $1500; Washington CASH (Seattle, WA)—general operations for this microcredit organization, $2500; Seattle Youth Garden Works (WA)—general operations for a market-gardening job-skills training program for homeless and low-income youth, $2500.
Contact: Therese Ogle, Grants Consultant; (206) 781-3472; (206) 784-5987; oglefounds@aol.com
Internet: http://fdncenter.org/grantmaker/schneider
Sponsor: Eulalie Bloedel Schneider Foundation
6723 Sycamore Avenue NW
Seattle, WA 98117

Evelyn Haas and Walter Haas Jr. Fund Grants **663**

The Foundation's vision is to help those who live and work at society's margins gain opportunities to participate, succeed and contribute. Guided by the values of fairness, equality and opportunity, the Foundation aims to help revitalize low-income neighborhoods and to improve the lives of the children and families who live there. The Foundation promotes equal rights and dignity for gays, lesbians, immigrants, and people of color. Applicants should submit a two to three page letter of inquiry. Information regarding the LOI process is available online.
Requirements: IRS 501(c)3 organizations in California not classified as private foundations under section 509(a) are eligible. Matching funds are required.
Restrictions: The fund generally does not make grants for capital campaigns, major equipment, basic research, conferences, publications, films or videos, deficit or emergency funding, scholarships, direct mail campaigns, fundraising events, annual appeals, or endowment contributions. Exceptions may be made for requests that form part of a larger effort in which the fund is engaged or for requests from organizations with which the fund has a long-term funding relationship. No exceptions will be made for aid to individuals
Geographic Focus: California
Samples: Community Youth Ctr (CA)—to pilot an after-school youth leadership program for Asian/Pacific Islander youth living in Visitacion Valley and Bayview/Hunter???s Point, $35,000; New Leaf Services for Our Community (CA)—for HIV and substance abuse prevention among gay and bisexual men, $65,000; Tides Ctr (San Francisco, CA)—to expand its services that assist individuals and nonprofit organizations working in such areas as economic development, the environment, and social justice, $100,000; San Francisco Symphony (CA)—for its Keeping Score campaign, a multimedia effort to develop new audiences for classical music, $10 million challenge grant.
Contact: Clayton Juan, Grants Administrator; (415) 856-1400; (415) 856-1500; haasjr.org
Internet: http://www.haasjr.org
Sponsor: Evelyn Haas and Walter Haas Jr. Fund
One Market, Landmark, Suite 400
San Francisco, CA 94105

Evert B. and Ruth Finley Person Foundation Grants **664**

The foundation supports nonprofits in Northern California, primarily Sonoma County, in the areas of music, musical arts, health associations, higher education, journalism, engineering, religion, and science education. Types of support include operating budgets, matching funds, and scholarship funds. There are no application deadlines.
Requirements: 501(c)3 nonprofit organizations in northern California may apply.
Geographic Focus: California
Amount: 5,000 - 500,000 USD
Contact: Evert Person, Trustee; (707) 545-3136; (707) 575-5778
Sponsor: Evert B. and Ruth Finley Person Foundation
1400 N Dutton Avenue, Suite 12
Santa Rosa, CA 95401-4644

Every Voice in Action Foundation Grants **665**

The Foundation is a private foundation based in Tucson, Arizona that makes grants to non-profit organizations to encourage and support youth voice in the Tuscon community. It defines youth voice as young people having an authentic voice in their lives and in the life of the community. This means the community recognizing youth as important resources, and encouraging them to express their unique perspectives and ideas. In addition to grant making, the Foundation operates and supports programs to teach youth about philanthropy and engage them in making grants that benefit other youth and the community.
Requirements: Tucson and Pima County, Arizona, serving nonprofit organizations are eligible.
Restrictions: Programs with a primary focus on academics, athletics, health, recreation, or other topics are not eligible if mentor relationships are a secondary focus or byproduct of the program.
Geographic Focus: Arizona
Amount: Up to 20,000 USD
Contact: Judith Anderson, President; (520) 615-2100; (520) 615-2112; judith@everyvoicefoundation.org
Internet: http://www.everyvoicefoundation.org/funding_areas.php
Sponsor: Every Voice in Action Foundation
2851 N Country Club Road
Tucson, AZ 85716

Ewing Marion Kauffman Foundation Grants and Initiatives **666**

The vision of the Foundation is to foster a society of economically independent individuals who are engaged citizens, contributing to the improvement of

their communities. The Foundation focuses its grant making and operations on two areas: advancing entrepreneurship and improving the education of children and youth. In entrepreneurship, the Foundation works nationwide to catalyze an entrepreneurial society in which job creation, innovation, and the economy flourish. In education, the Foundation works to improve the academic achievement of disadvantaged children and works with partners to support programs that directly impact a child's academic achievement, with a concentrated focus on math, science, and technology skills. The Foundation does not use a grant application form or formal application process. There are no proposal deadlines or established funding limits. Information regarding submission of a letter of inquiry is available online.
Requirements: The foundation only funds programs within the United States. The majority of education grants go to organizations within the Kansas City metropolitan area. The foundation's entrepreneurship efforts fund programs and activities nationally and within the Kansas City area.
Restrictions: The Foundation does not fund: requests from individuals, political, social, or fraternal organizations; endowments, special events, arts, or international programs; provide loans, start-up expenses or seed capital funding for private businesses or scholarships requested by individuals; proposals submitted via audiotape or videotape; institutions that discriminate on the basis of race, creed, gender, national origin, age, disability or sexual orientation in policy or in practice; programs in furtherance of sectarian religious activities, impermissible lobbying, legislative or political activities; programs targeted for people with a specific physical, medical or psychological condition; or medical research or profit-making enterprises.
Geographic Focus: All U.S. States
Samples: Center for a New American Security, Washington, DC, $25,000—support the Center for a New American Security's effort to make a meaningful contribution to our nation's debate over economic growth (2009); Duke University, Pratt School of Engineering, Durham, NC, $40,000—support research on the contributions of immigrants to the U.S. economy and the role immigrant and native entrepreneurial and social networks play in fostering entrepreneurship and successful businesses (2009).
Contact: Grants Administrator; (816) 932-1000; (816) 932-1100; info@emkf.org
Internet: http://www.kauffman.org/grants.cfm
Sponsor: Ewing Marion Kauffman Foundation
4801 Rockhill Road
Kansas City, MO 64110-2046

ExxonMobil Education Foundation Grants **667**
The program addresses the use of mathematics specialists in grades K-3, the status of mathematics instruction at the college level, and the analysis of policy issues in mathematics education. Types of support include general operating grants, matching gifts, scholarship funds, and program grants. The foundation also funds the Elementary and Secondary School Improvement program, which is intended to help the educational community gain a better understanding of the changing demographics of the school-age population and the implications for changes in the schools; to help educators learn how to restructure schools to make them instructionally more effective with more students, particularly with educationally at-risk and minority students; and to improve teacher education to help teachers take better advantage of changing school structures. The foundation also sponsors a program addressing the reform of undergraduate science, technology, engineering, and mathematics education.
Requirements: The foundation makes grants only to tax-exempt organizations. A two-page letter of inquiry is required.
Restrictions: The foundation rarely contributes to endowments or make grants for construction or remodeling of facilities. Funds are not provided for equipment acquisition. Scholarships and grants to individuals are not awarded.
Geographic Focus: All U.S. States
Samples: American Mathematical Assoc of Two-Year Colleges (Memphis, TN) and Mathematical Assoc of America (Washington, DC)—for professional-development activities for mathematics instructors at two-year colleges, $475,000 jointly over three years; U of Texas at Austin, Ctr for American History (TX)—to catalog and preserve a collection of ExxonMobil's historical archives, $300,000; Society of Women Engineers (Chicago, IL)—to develop curricula to prepare girls in elementary and high school for careers in scientific fields, $600,000; Texas State History Museum Foundation (Austin, TX)—to produce a large-screen film about Texas, and to create accompanying education materials for use by schools and the museum, $1.5 million and $63,000 respectively Tom Joyner Foundation (Dallas, TX)—for scholarships for students at engineering, mathematics, and science 11 historically black colleges and universities, $200,000.
Contact: Program Contact; (972) 444-1106; (972) 444-1405; contributions@exxonmobil.com
Internet: http://www.exxonmobileurope.com/corporate/Citizenship/Corp_Cit_EducationInter.asp
Sponsor: ExxonMobil Education Foundation
5959 Las Colinas Boulevard
Irving, TX 75039-2298

F.B. Heron Foundation Grants **668**
The foundation focuses on core wealth-creation strategies for low-income families and communities. Grantmaking is considered for programs that promote home ownerships, enterprise development, access to capital, quality and affordable child care, and comprehensive community development. There are no application deadlines or forms. Submit a two- to three-page letter of inquiry.
Requirements: U.S. 501(c)3 nonprofits may apply.
Geographic Focus: All U.S. States
Amount: 25,000 - 125,000 USD
Samples: Rosalie Manor, Inc. (Milwaukee, WI)—to support a First Time Parents program to promote health child development, $75,000; Wheelock College (Boston, MA)—for the Ctr for Career Development in Early Child Care, $50,000; Beyond Shelter (Los Angeles, CA)—for general support, $50,000.
Contact: Mary Jo Mullan, Program Officer, c/o Rockefeller and Company Inc; (212) 404-1800; (212) 404-1805
Internet: http://www.fbheron.org
Sponsor: F.B. Heron Foundation
100 Broadway, 17th Floor
New York, NY 10005

F.J. O'Neill Charitable Corporation Grants **669**
The corporation awards general operating grants to eligible Ohio nonprofit organizations in its areas of interest, including higher and secondary education, medical research, and Roman Catholic organizations and churches. There are no application deadlines or forms.
Requirements: Ohio nonprofit organizations serving the Cleveland area are eligible.
Geographic Focus: Ohio
Amount: 25,000 - 100,000 USD
Contact: Grants Administrator; (216) 464-2121
Sponsor: F.J. O'Neill Charitable Corporation
3550 Lander Road
Cleveland, OH 44124

FAF Community Arts Fund Operating Support Program Grants **670**
Operating support grants are available to provide unrestricted financial assistance to arts organizations that operate or sponsor cultural programs in the greater Cincinnati area. In addition to generally assisting the operation of these groups, grants may be used to develop the professionalism of the organization; encourage the growth and/or stabilization of an organization; improve technical, fund-raising, marketing, accounting, or management skills; identify ways to increase audience participation, especially those audiences not served by other organizations in the community and stimulate collaboration within the greater Cincinnati arts community. Maximum operating support requests may not exceed 10 percent of an organization's operating expenses for the last fiscal year. Applications are available on the website.
Requirements: Organizations must have 501(c)3 tax-exempt status; three or more years of incorporated operation; an active board of volunteers that advises the organization in areas such as audience development, publicity, community relations, fund-raising, and finance; proof of fiscal accountability and management; policies and programming that demonstrate attendance by, as well as accessibility to, a broad public audience; and demonstrated focus on the greater Cincinnati area.
Restrictions: Individuals and units or support groups of state agencies, community centers, government, college or university departments, school systems, ar churches and synagogues are not eligible for operating support.
Geographic Focus: Ohio
Date(s) Application is Due: Jul 12
Amount: Up to 16,000 USD
Contact: Grants Administrator; (613) 871-2787, ext. 28; (513) 871-2706; faf@artsincincinnati.org
Internet: http://www.artserv.org/grant.html

Sponsor: Fine Arts Fund
2649 Erie Avenue
Cincinnati, OH 45208-2087

Fairfield County Community Foundation Grants **671**
As a community foundation, FCCF makes discretionary grants to nonprofits in the broad program areas of economic opportunity (including affordable housing, neighborhood development, and workforce development); children, youth and families; health and human services; the environment; arts and culture; and nonprofit organizational effectiveness. The Foundation is particularly interested in proposals focused on: economic opportunity; education and youth development; advancing school readiness in Fairfield County; organizational effectiveness; and regionalism. Applicants must first submit a letter of inquiry. Application information is available online.
Requirements: Nonprofit organizations in Fairfield County, CT, are eligible.
Restrictions: Funds are not used to provide support for religious or political purposes, deficit financing, annual appeals, fundraising events, open space purchases, for-profit, parochial, charter or private schools, or nonprofit endowments. Grants are not given to individuals.
Geographic Focus: Connecticut
Samples: Cardinal Shehan Center, Bridgeport, CT, $20,000—to support the Made for Talent Program that offers youth arts education throughout the year (2008); ACORN Housing Corporation, Bridgeport, CT, $30,000—to support ACORN's foreclosure counseling program in Bridgeport that prevents mortgage foreclosures as well as assists homeowners impacted by the subprime loan crisis (2008); Danbury Youth Services, Danbury, CT, $20,000—to support the Target After School Program that offers after-school education to children who live in Danbury public housing (2008).
Contact: Karen Brown, Vice President of Programs; (203) 750-3200; (203) 750-3232; kbrown@fccfoundation.org
Internet: http://www.fccfoundation.org/cm/grantseekers/what_we_fund.html
Sponsor: Fairfield County Community Foundation
383 Main Avenue
Norwalk, CT 06851-1543

Fales Foundation Trust Grants **672**
The foundation provides financial support to social service agencies addressing issues of homelessness and hunger; and to artistic and cultural organizations in the city of Seattle, with strong emphasis in this category directed toward community-based arts programs related to issues of homelessness and hunger, providing arts opportunities for underserved constituencies. Types of support include general operating grants and special project grants. Preference is given to organizations receiving past support from the Fales Foundation. Application materials should be mailed to Cynthia Crawford, Trustee, Union Bank of California, The Private Bank, at the address listed. Guidelines are available online.
Requirements: Seattle 501(c)3 nonprofit organizations are eligible. Additional requirements for applicants include: successful program capability, sound fiscal policies, and responsible management; and in existence for five years or more.
Restrictions: The foundation will not support groups located outside the city of Seattle, even if the program serves a Seattle clientele or constituency; capital campaigns or expenditures; loans or investments; fundraising events; projects of a political or religious nature; individual requests for research or scholarships; computer, software, or office equipment purchases; projects of an individual artist, even if under the sponsorship of a 501(c)3 organization; video or film productions; or book publications.
Geographic Focus: All U.S. States
Date(s) Application is Due: Apr 1; Oct 1
Amount: 1,000 - 5,000 USD
Samples: Pike Market Senior Ctr (Seattle, WA)—to support the meal program and food bank $5000; Archdiocesan Housing Authority (Seattle, WA)—for general operations for five housing/shelter programs, $15,000; Ladies Musical Club (Seattle, WA)—artist fees for school programs $2000; Seattle Opera (WA)—for the Experience Opera program, $5000.
Contact: Therese Ogle, Grants Consultant; (206) 781-3472; (206) 784-5987; oglefounds@aol.com
Internet: http://fdncenter.org/grantmaker/fales
Sponsor: Fales Foundation Trust
P.O. Box 3123
Seattle, WA 98114

Fallon OrNda Community Health Fund Grants **673**
The purpose of the health fund is to advance projects that increase access to health care or health promotion services that improve the health status of vulnerable populations. Of particular interest are projects that result in: the support or creation of primary care outreach services to vulnerable populations; the development of continuing managed care services rather than episodic or uncoordinated care; and the removal of barriers that prevent people from receiving services such as lack of transportation, cultural competency of providers, language differences, or others. Grants may be for operational expenditures such as personnel costs, or for construction, renovation, equipment purchase or other physical improvements. Past grants have ranged from $6,500 to $30,000.
Requirements: Funding will not be provided for long-term underwriting of operational costs for any one program.
Geographic Focus: Massachusetts
Date(s) Application is Due: Feb 15
Amount: 6,500 - 30,000 USD
Contact: Lois Smith, Senior Program Officer; (508) 755-0980, ext. 107; lsmith@greaterworcester.org
Internet: http://www.greaterworcester.org/grants/Fallon.htm
Sponsor: Greater Worcester Community Foundation
370 Main Street, Suite 650
Worcester, MA 01608-1738

Fan Fox and Leslie R. Samuels Foundation Grants **674**
The foundation's areas of funding are the performing arts and healthcare. Healthcare funding supports patient-based and social service activities that directly help the elderly of New York City. The foundation supports performing arts organizations in the City of New York, principally, but not exclusively, in the borough of Manhattan. The foundation's primary mission is to support major performing arts institutions of national or international eminence. In addition to providing direct support, the foundation also assists presenting entities that have the requisite expertise, knowledge, and artistic judgment to present groups or individuals, new works, varied repertoire, and arts-in-education projects that will be contributions to the aesthetic and intellectual life of New York. Application guidelines are available on the website or upon request.
Requirements: The foundation funds organizations in the New York City area only. Only 501(c)3 tax-exempt organizations are invited to apply.
Restrictions: The foundation does not give grants to individuals or for scholarships, and does not support research, film, or video, nor does it fund education or social services. The foundation no longer actively solicits applications for support of arts-in-education programs at the primary and secondary level.
Geographic Focus: New York
Date(s) Application is Due: Mar 1; Jun 1; Dec 1
Amount: 25,000 - 250,000 USD
Samples: Hebrew Home for the Aged at Riverdale (New York, NY)—for a comprehensive center dedicated to preventing and treating elder abuse, including a shelter for abused senior citizens, $200,000 over two years; Jamaica Hospital Medical Ctr (New York, NY)—to establish an interdisciplinary family-medicine program for predominantly poor, minority, and elderly patients who do not have access to palliative-care services, $150,000; Metropolitan Jewish Health System (New York, NY)—to establish a palliative-medicine program based on home visits, $201,000 over two years; Calvary Hospital (New York, NY)—for a program to increase access to comprehensive hospice and palliative care for nursing-home residents, $250,000.
Contact: Joseph Mitchell, President; (212) 239-3030; (212) 239-3039; info@samuels.org
Internet: http://www.samuels.org
Sponsor: Fan Fox and Leslie R. Samuels Foundation
350 Fifth Avenue, Suite 4301
New York, NY 10118

Fannie E. Rippel Foundation Grants **675**
The foundation aids, assists, funds, equips, and provides maintenance for corporations, institutions, associations, organizations, or societies maintained for the relief and care of aged women; provides funds for the building, equipping, and maintenance of hospitals; and provides funds for corporations, institutions, and other organizations existing for treatment of and/or research on heart disease or cancer. The foundation gives emphasis to the equipment and programmatic needs of major teaching medical centers and local rural hospitals, particularly where opportunities exist for leveraging the expertise or capabilities of the medical centers/rural hospitals. Programs should reach

underserved rural and urban groups, advocate preventive care, present strategies to change behaviors of the people served, and promote humanistic medicine and mind-body-spirit connections in the healing process. Preference also is given to proposed projects where the benefits can be leveraged through challenge grants.
Requirements: Organizations, associations, institutions, and hospitals in the Northeast are eligible.
Restrictions: Grants are not awarded to individuals.
Geographic Focus: Connecticut, Maine, Massachusetts, New Hampshire, Rhode Island, Vermont
Amount: 50,000 - 300,000 USD
Contact: Grants Administrator; (973) 540-0101; (973) 540-0404; pmacbain@rippelfoundation.org
Internet: http://fdncenter.org/grantmaker/rippel
Sponsor: Fannie E. Rippel Foundation
14 Maple Avenue, Suite 200
Morristown, NJ 07960

FAR Fund Grants **676**
The FAR Fund Project is a New Orleans-based program exploring Hurricane Katrina's effects on New Orleans therapists and therapeutic practice. It was designed by and for clinicians. The project's mission is two fold: to offer support and concrete help to local clinicians, and to develop a model for better understanding how shared trauma affects therapists and therapy. Through this project, the FAR Fund wishes to unite and revitalize clinician communities following large-scale disasters wherever they occur, starting in New Orleans.
Requirements: The FAR Fund Project is open to New Orleans psychotherapists of all disciplines and theoretical orientations. Their mission is two-fold: to offer support and concrete help to local mental health clinicians, and to develop a psychodynamic model to better understand how shared trauma affects therapists and therapy.
Geographic Focus: Louisiana
Contact: Shirlee Taylor, Director; (212) 982-8400; (212) 982-8477; FARFund@mac.com
Sponsor: Far Fund
928 Broadway, Suite 902
New York, NY 10010

Faye McBeath Foundation Grants **677**
The Faye McBeath Foundation is a private, independent foundation providing grants to tax-exempt nonprofit 501(c)3 organizations in the metropolitan Milwaukee, Wisconsin area, including Milwaukee, Waukesha, Ozaukee and Washington counties. The major areas of interest are: children; aging and elders; health; health education; civic and governmental affairs. The Foundation's Trustees are primarily interested in promising or established programs, operated by well-managed organizations. Benchmarks that will be applied to projects and organizations in all five interest areas are the following: strength of proposal - Foundation guidelines match; quality and creativity in project design, implementation and evaluation; quality of the applicant nonprofit's leadership and organizational capacity; potential to stretch or leverage McBeath funds; specific interests of Trustees and/or staff. The majority of grants support specific programs. On occasion, operating and capacity-building grants are awarded. Capital grants are limited to projects with community-wide impact that reflect the program interests of the Foundation. Any invited requests for operating or capacity-building support must include an organization's results-oriented annual plan, covering both programs and management. The trustees meet four times each year to consider grant proposals. Written notification of the Trustees' decision regarding a grant proposal will be sent within ten days of the meeting. Organizations awarded grants will receive written notification of grant conditions, payment dates and reporting requirements
Requirements: 501(c)3 nonprofit organizations in the metropolitan Milwaukee area are eligible. To begin the application process, submittal of a letter of intent, 1-2 pages long that includes: a brief description of the applicant organization, the program to be funded, the corresponding match between the Foundation's guidelines and the request, the amount requested and the estimated total project budget. Include the name and address of the organization, and the name, phone number and email address of a contact person. There are no deadlines for letters of intent. Upon receipt of a letter of intent, Foundation staff will formally acknowledge by email or letter. If the request is clearly outside the current program or geographical focus of the Foundation, a decline letter will be sent informing you of this determination. If you are formally invited by McBeath staff to submit a full proposal, you will be asked to use the Wisconsin Common Grant Application Form. The Foundation requires that a volunteer serving on the Board sign the application.
Restrictions: The Foundation does not award grants for annual fund drives, scholarships, support of individuals, sponsorship of fundraising events, or emergency funds. The Foundation does not consider or acknowledge general solicitation letters. Basic health sciences research is not funded by the Foundation. Single disease or condition organizations are typically not funded by the Foundation. An exception may be made for a creative project involving one or more of the following: service to multiple populations, collaboration and/or creation of a replicable model. There are no published deadlines for letters of intent or grant proposals. Proposal deadlines are established based upon discussion with Foundation staff. Organizations serving the disabled will be considered only if the project targets children or older adults. Any discussion of the availability of funding in a subsequent year should be initiated by the grantee and discussed with staff at least 60 days in advance of a project anniversary.
Geographic Focus: Wisconsin
Amount: 1,000 - 50,000 USD
Samples: Aurora Sinai Medical Center, Milwaukee, WI, 45,000—for improvement of access to Health Care Services (2009); Greater Milwaukee Foundation, Milwaukee, WI, $25,000—for the Camps For Kids Forever Fund (2009); NAMI Waukesha, Waukesha, WI, $10,000—for Housing Support and Advocacy Program (2009).
Contact: Scott Gelzer, Executive Director; (414) 272-2626; (414) 272-6235; info@fayemcbeath.org
Internet: http://www.fayemcbeath.org/ProgramPriorities/index.html
Sponsor: Faye McBeath Foundation
101 West Pleasant Street, Suite 210
Milwaukee, WI 53212

Feldman Foundation Grants **678**
Giving is concentrated in the areas of community development, social welfare, and Jewish causes. Types of support include annual campaigns, building construction/renovation, general operating support, program development, research, and scholarship funds. Initial contact should be by proposal letter. Foundation trustees meet in the spring and fall to review proposals under serious consideration. Applications are accepted at any time.
Requirements: Organizations based in New York and Texas are eligible to apply.
Restrictions: Grants will not be awarded to individuals.
Geographic Focus: New York, Texas
Amount: 10,000 - 50,000 USD
Contact: Robert Feldman, Trustee; (214) 689-4337
Sponsor: Feldman Foundation
P.O. Box 1046
Dallas, TX 75221

FEMA Assistance to Firefighters Grants (AFG) **679**
The program provides financial assistance directly to fire departments and nonaffiliated EMS organizations to enhance their abilities with respect to fire and fire-related hazards. The primary goal is to help fire departments and nonaffiliated EMS organizations meet their firefighting and emergency response needs. AFG seeks to support organizations that lack the tools and resources necessary to more effectively protect the health and safety of the public and their emergency response personnel with respect to fire and all other hazards. The project period for any award under AFG will be twelve months from the date of the award.
Requirements: The application will be accessible from the AFG website (www.firegrantsupport.com), the U.S. Fire Administration's (U.S. FA) website (www.usfa.fema.gov), and grants.gov website (www.grants.gov). Paper applications will be accepted, but are discouraged due to the inherent delays associated with processing them. Fire departments or nonaffiliated EMS organizations operating in any of the 50 States plus the District of Columbia, the Commonwealth of the Northern Mariana Islands, the Virgin Islands, Guam, American Samoa, and Puerto Rico are eligible for funding. A fire department is defined as an agency or organization that has a formally recognized arrangement with a State, territory, local, or tribal authority (city, county, parish, fire district, township, town, or other governing body) to provide fire suppression to a population within a fixed geographical area on a first-due basis. A nonaffiliated EMS organization is defined as a public or private nonprofit emergency medical services organization that provides direct emergency medical services, including medical transport, to a specific

geographic area on a first-due basis but is not affiliated with a hospital and does not serve a geographic area where emergency medical services are adequately provided by a fire department. Fire departments may submit applications for either or both of the following program areas: Firefighter Operations and Safety; Firefighter Vehicle Acquisition. EMS applicants may apply for assistance under either the Operations and Safety program area or the Vehicle Acquisition program area, or both using separate applications. Any eligible applicant, whether a fire department or a nonaffiliated EMS organization, may act as a host applicant and apply for large-scale or regional projects on behalf of itself and any number of organizations in neighboring jurisdictions. The only activities available for application under a regional project are training and equipment acquisition that positively affect interoperability.
Restrictions: Fire departments that are Federal, or contracted by the Federal Government, and are solely responsible under a formally recognized agreement for suppression of fires on Federal installations or land are ineligible for funding. Fire stations that are not independent entities, but are part of, controlled by, or under the day-to-day operational direction of a larger fire department or agency are not eligible for funding. Fire departments that are for-profit departments (i.e., do not have specific nonprofit status or are not municipally based) are not eligible for funding. Auxiliaries, fire service organizations or associations, and State/local agencies such as a forest service, fire marshals, hospitals, and training offices are not eligible for funding. Dive teams and search and rescue teams, or any similar organizations that do not provide medical transport, are not eligible for assistance as nonaffiliated EMS organizations.
Geographic Focus: All U.S. States
Date(s) Application is Due: May 4
Samples: Falmouth Fire Department ($169,833) - Falmouth, KY; Asotin Fire Department ($234,000) - Asotin, WA; Baldwin Volunteer Fire Department ($101,650) - Baldwin, LA; Brush Valley Twp. Vol. Fire Co. Relief Association ($39,900) - Homer City, PA
Contact: Help Desk; (866) 274-0960; firegrants@dhs.gov
Internet: http://www.firegrantsupport.com/afg/
Sponsor: U.S. Department of Homeland Security
245 Murray Lane - Building 410, SW
Washington, DC 20528-7000

FHL Foundation Grants 680

The foundation supports efforts of eligible New Mexico nonprofit organizations to eliminate systems that support abuse and oppression of people and animals. Areas of interest include education to increase public understanding; discovery to uncover systems that allow abuse to happen; and service to provide care for victims of abuse. There are three levels of support: Level One for organizations new to the theory of attachment, or to provide ongoing support to organizations actively applying attachment theory (whether at the program or project level); Level Two for organizations that are actively applying attachment theory to their programs but not necessarily their projects; and Level Three for organizations that are applying attachment theory to both their programs and their projects. Different levels of funding have different deadline dates.
Requirements: New Mexico nonprofit organizations are eligible.
Restrictions: Grants are not made to individuals.
Geographic Focus: New Mexico
Date(s) Application is Due: Feb 28; May 31; Aug 31; Nov 30
Amount: 1,000 - 20,000 USD
Contact: Grants Administrator; (505) 247-2400; (505) 247-2300; fhlfound@thuntek.net
Internet: http://www.fhlfoundation.com
Sponsor: FHL Foundation
P.O. Box 27650
Albuquerque, NM 87125

Field Foundation of Illinois Grants 681

The Foundation awards grants only to institutions and agencies operating in the fields of urban and community affairs, culture, education, community welfare, health, and environment, primarily serving the people of Chicago with extremely limited grant making in the metropolitan area. Preference will be given to funding innovative approaches for addressing program areas.
Requirements: Applicants must reside in Illinois. Grant applications are not provided; however, a formal proposal is required. The Foundation does not accept grant requests via email or fax.
Restrictions: No grants will be made to support: endowments; individuals; medical research or national health agency appeals; propaganda organizations or committees whose efforts are aimed at influencing legislation; printed materials, video or computer equipment; fund-raising events or advertising; appeals for religious purposes; other granting agencies or foundations for ultimate distribution to agencies or programs of its own choosing; custodian afterschool programs or tutoring; most disease specific programs, research or activities; or operating support of established neighborhood health centers or clinics, day care centers for children, or small cultural groups. Requests for computer equipment will not be considered.
Geographic Focus: Illinois
Date(s) Application is Due: Jan 15; May 15; Sep 15
Amount: 50,000 USD
Samples: Catholic Charities of the Archdiocese of Chicago (IL)—to support expansion of the Emergency Assistance Services program, $15,000; Jobs for Youth/Chicago (IL)—to support the Workforce Advancement Initiative, $10,000; Palliative Care Center and Hospice of the North Shore (IL)—to support the capital campaign for a new community facility, $25,000; Puerto Rican Alliance (IL)—to support the Community Arts Program, $10,000.
Contact: Joann Ross, (312) 831-0910; (312) 831-0961; jross@fieldfoundation.org
Internet: http://www.fieldfoundation.org
Sponsor: Field Foundation of Illinois
200 S Wacker Drive, Suite 3860
Chicago, IL 60606

Fieldstone Foundation Grants 682

The Foundation was created to provide grants, leadership and development and service to nonprofit organizations working to support individuals in the communities where the company does business. The Foundation gives emphasis to programs that serve children and families and allocates its resources in four general areas: Humanitarian, Community and Education, Cultural Arts and Christian Ministries. Faxed and emailed proposals will not be accepted. Application information is available online.
Requirements: Funding is limited to non-profit organizations serving the communities where the company is currently operating: Orange, Riverside, and San Diego counties in Southern California and Salt Lake City in Utah.
Restrictions: Support will not be provided for individuals; political parties, candidates and partisan political organizations; veteran, labor, fraternal or athletic organizations except for specific projects that benefit the broad community; advertising; or individual churches. The Foundation does not make multi-year commitments or fund capital campaigns.
Geographic Focus: California, Utah
Date(s) Application is Due: Jun 30
Samples: Discovery Science Museum (Santa Ana, CA)—for operating support, $10,000; San Diego Museum of Art (San Diego, CA)—for a biennial exhibition of student art, $20,000 over two years.
Contact: Janine Mason, Executive Director; janinem@fieldstone-homes.com
Internet: http://www.fieldstone-homes.com/foundation
Sponsor: Fieldstone Foundation
14 Corporate Plaza Drive
Newport Beach, CA 92660

FirstEnergy Foundation Community Grants 683

The Foundation believes it takes commitment to help make communities strong, resilient, and responsive to the needs of citizens. It also takes vision, cooperation, and financial support. The Foundation considers grants in the following areas that: ensure the safety and overall health of the community; support employee involvement and investment; promote economic development; and advance professional development and education. Interested applicants should submit a one or two page proposal letter. Guidelines are available online.
Requirements: 501(c)3 organizations within the FirstEnergy Corp. operating companies' service areas - Ohio Edison, The Illuminating Company, Toledo Edison, Penn Power, Met-Ed, Penelac, and Jersey Central Power and Light are eligible to apply.
Restrictions: Funding is not considered for: direct grants to individuals, political or legislative activities; organizations that receive sizable public tax funding; fraternal, religious, labor, athletic, social or veterans organizations - unless the contribution is earmarked for an eligible program or campaign open to all beneficiaries, including those not affiliated with the host organization; national or international organizations; organizations supported by federated campaigns, such as United Way; research; equipment purchases; loans or second party giving, such as endowments, debt retirement, or foundations; or public or private schools.
Geographic Focus: New Jersey, Ohio, Pennsylvania

Samples: United Way Services (Cleveland, OH)—for operating support, $493,000; Musical Arts Assoc (Cleveland, OH)—for operating support, $43,394; Cleveland Initiative for Education (Cleveland, OH)—for operating support, $40,000.
Contact: Mary Beth Carroll, President; (330) 761-4246
Internet: http://www.firstenergycorp.com/community
Sponsor: FirstEnergy Foundation
76 South Main Street
Akron, OH 44308

Fisa Foundation Grants **684**

The foundation's mission is to build a culture of respect and improve the quality of life for three populations in southwestern Pennsylvania: women, girls, and people with disabilities. Emphasis is given to addressing gaps and unmet needs in the community. The foundation will consider support for new and ongoing programs and projects, operating needs, capacity building, equipment, and capital expenditures. Applicants are encouraged to submit a letter of inquiry outlining the needs to be addressed, a brief description of the proposed project or program, and the amount of the request. Letters of inquiry are reviewed on a monthly basis; full proposals are by invitation. Application and guidelines are available online.
Requirements: 501(c)3 and 509(a) nonprofit organizations in the 10-county southwestern Pennsylvania area, including Allegheny, Armstrong, Beaver, Butler, Fayette, Greene, Indiana, Lawrence, Washington and Westmoreland Counties, are eligible.
Restrictions: The foundation does not make grants in support of individuals; political campaigns or lobbying; religious organizations for religious purposes; travel, study and scholarships; services for people with disabilities that result from the aging process; renovations to improve physical accessibility of buildings; programs with the primary mission of serving individuals with mental illness; clinical research; or parenting programs, unless they specifically relate to parents with disabilities.
Geographic Focus: Pennsylvania
Amount: 5,000 - 75,000 USD
Samples: City Theatre (Pittsburgh, PA)—for disability-awareness training for employees and for the development of audio-description services for visually impaired audience members, $10,000; Women and Girls Foundation of Southwest Pennsylvania (Pittsburgh, PA)—to train high-school girls to be grantmakers, $19,000 over three years; Hosanna House (Pittsburgh, PA)—to provide permanent housing and coordinated support services for families with disabled members, $15,000; Gwen's Girls (Pittsburgh, PA)—for a long-term residential facility for teenage mothers who are in the foster-care or juvenile-justice systems and their babies, $40,000.
Contact: Mary Delaney, (412) 456-5550; (412) 456-5551; info@fisafoundation.org
Internet: http://www.fisafoundation.org/grtmk.ivnu
Sponsor: Fisa Foundation
1001 Liberty Avenue, Suite 650
Pittsburgh, PA 15222

Fisher Foundation Grants **685**

The foundation awards grants to Connecticut nonprofits that benefit education, health and human services, housing, community needs, and arts and culture. The majority of grants are single year awards. Before submitting an application, a letter of inquiry or conversation with staff to discuss the specific purpose for which the funds are being requested is strongly recommended. Application information and guidelines are available online. Do not submit applications by fax or email.
Requirements: Nonprofits located in, and/or serving the residents of the Greater Hartford area, including: Andover, Avon, Bloomfield, Bolton, Canton, East Hartford, East Granby, East Windsor, Ellington, Enfield, Farmington, Glastonbury, Granby, Hartford, Hebron, Manchester, Marlborough, Newington, Rocky Hill, Simsbury, Somers, South Windsor, Suffield, Tolland, Vernon, West Hartford, Wethersfield, Windsor, and Windsor Locks are eligible.
Restrictions: Foundation policy does not allow funding for: organizations which are not tax-exempt under IRS Code section 501(c)3; organizations which have the IRS private foundation designation; individuals; performances, conferences, retreats, one-time events, trips; annual campaigns.
Geographic Focus: Connecticut
Date(s) Application is Due: Jan 15; Apr 15; Sep 15
Contact: Beverly Boyle, Executive Director; (860) 570-0221; (860) 570-0225; bboyle@fisherfdn.org
Internet: http://www.fisherfdn.org/application/instructions.htm
Sponsor: Fisher Foundation
36 Brookside Boulevard
West Hartford, CT 06107

FleetBoston Financial Foundation Grants **686**

Grants are made in company-operating areas with a focus on community-based local nonprofit organizations providing services and opportunities for children, families, and individuals in low/moderate-income areas. Priority areas include economic opportunity (community development programs; microenterprise, entrepreneurial, and small business development; job creation and employment training; affordable housing initiatives and homebuyer seminars; and selected programs that serve low- and moderate-income individuals; youth development (programs that promote healthy development, adult mentoring support, job readiness and skill building, and leadership skills through community service; public education (literacy programs, business and finance education, transition from school to career, and long-term education reform efforts); and arts and culture (major exhibits, community and grassroots performances, educational outreach to low- and moderate-income youth, and projects that promote increased access to the arts). Grants are awarded for operational support and facilities improvement. Applications are reviewed in June, September, December, and March. Grant applications are available online, and inquiries should be made to the appropriate regional contact.
Requirements: Charitable support focuses on nonprofits in states where Fleet Bank operates, including Connecticut, Maine, Massachusetts, New Hampshire, New Jersey, New York, eastern Pennsylvania, and Rhode Island.
Restrictions: The foundation does not support individuals; religious, fraternal, political, or veterans organizations; national organizations, including state and local chapters; organizations that are not open to the general public; annual funds of hospitals, colleges, universities, grade schools, or high schools; trips, tours, or conferences; scientific or medical research; or deficit spending or debt liquidation.
Geographic Focus: Connecticut, Maine, Massachusetts, New Hampshire, New Jersey, New York, Pennsylvania, Rhode Island
Amount: Up to 100,000,000 USD
Samples: Shakespeare Theatre of New Jersey (Madison, NJ)—for performances of the musical, A Child's Christmas in Wales, for students, $10,000; Literacy Partners (New York, NY)—for a financial-education program, $50,000; 88 organizations in the Northeast—for services for disadvantaged people, GLBT (gay, lesbian, bisexual, and transgender) people with disabilities, women, and low-income parents, $260,000 distributed.
Contact: Gail Snowden, President; (617) 434-2804; (617) 434-6072
Internet: http://www.bankofamerica.com/foundation/index.cfm?template=fd_funding
Sponsor: FleetBoston Financial Foundation
100 Federal Street, MADE 10018A
Boston, MA 02110

Fleishhacker Foundation Education Grants **687**

The Foundation funds precollegiate education, K-12, with an emphasis on the K-8 level. The Foundation's general interest is in programs and projects which: take place at the school site, preferably during the school day; are innovative; involve coordination of programs and services which support the educational process; connect in-school learning to the student's home, community, and cultural life; are cost effective; and show potential for longevity. Application information is available online.
Requirements: Nonprofits in the San Francisco Bay area are eligible.
Restrictions: The foundation does not support: deficit financing; annual funds; endowment campaigns; capital campaigns over $10 million; youth who have dropped out of school; adult education; fundraising events; and travel.
Geographic Focus: California
Date(s) Application is Due: Jan 15; Jul 15
Amount: 5,000 - 10,000 USD
Samples: Fine Arts Museums of San Francisco (San Francisco, CA)—for permanent installation of ancient Mexican Teotihuacan murals at M.H. de Young Museum, $40,000; KQED-TV (San Francisco, CA)—to support the arts programming endowment of the capital campaign, $10,000; Asian American Dance Collective (San Francisco, CA)—for production costs of West Coast Sweep, to commemorate the 50th anniversary of Japanese American internment during World War II, $2500.
Contact: Christine Elbel, Executive Director; (415) 561-5350; info@fleishhackerfoundation.org

Internet: http://www.fleishhackerfoundation.org/education.html
Sponsor: Fleishhacker Foundation
P.O. Box 29918
San Francisco, CA 94129-0918

Fleishhacker Foundation Small Grants in the Arts **688**
The particular emphasis of the Program is to support the development and presentation of the work of living Bay Area artists. New work is the first priority, however retrospectives and classical repertory of non-living artists will be considered. Grants may be awarded for: artists' fees for creative time; production costs for performances or film/video projects; exhibition/installation costs for visual, media, or interdisciplinary arts projects; activities that contribute to overall artistic development; and efforts to strengthen an organization's artistic impact within the community.
Requirements: Applicants must be: arts and cultural organizations incorporated as not-for-profit [501(c)3]; organizations residing and offering programming in the greater San Francisco Bay Area; able to demonstrate a consistent artistic presence in the Bay Area for at least 3 years; and of budget size between $100,000 and $750,000.
Restrictions: Not eligible for funding are: programs/projects whose fundamental purpose or benefit falls within the social services, health, youth, or community development fields; individuals (unless conducting a project under the sponsorship of an eligible nonprofit organization; organizations based outside the greater San Francisco Bay Area; or deficit financing, endowment campaigns, major capital campaign requests (campaigns over $10 million).
Geographic Focus: California
Date(s) Application is Due: Jan 15; Jul 15
Amount: 1,000 - 10,000 USD
Contact: Christine Elbel, Executive Director; (415) 561-5350; info@fleishhackerfoundation.org
Internet: http://www.fleishhackerfoundation.org/small.html
Sponsor: Fleishhacker Foundation
P.O. Box 29918
San Francisco, CA 94129-0918

Fleishhacker Foundation Special Arts Grants **689**
Periodically grants which exceed the scope of the Small Grants are made to groups with budgets greater than $750,000. The project must clearly demonstrate potential for broad and long-term impact on the local community and the art form involved. This might involve: facility access or use, community-wide program initiatives, or exceptional artistic projects. Grants normally do not exceed $25,000.
Requirements: Applicants must be: arts and cultural organizations incorporated as not-for-profit [501(c)3]; organizations residing and offering programming in the greater San Francisco Bay Area; and able to demonstrate a consistent artistic presence in the Bay Area for at least 3 years.
Restrictions: Not eligible are capital campaigns over $1 million and endowment campaigns.
Geographic Focus: California
Date(s) Application is Due: Jan 15; Jul 15
Amount: Up to 25,000 USD
Contact: Christine Elbel, Executive Director; (415) 561-5350; info@fleishhackerfoundation.org
Internet: http://www.fleishhackerfoundation.org/special.html
Sponsor: Fleishhacker Foundation
P.O. Box 29918
San Francisco, CA 94129-0918

Flinn Foundation Grantss **690**
The foundation's grantmaking programs, limited to Arizona, include enhancing community-based solutions to local health care needs, especially those for children and youth; strengthening medical education and biomedical research programs in Arizona; strengthening Arizona's universities through an undergraduate scholarship program for outstanding Arizona high school students; and enhancing the visibility and long-term artistic mission of Arizona's principal visual and performing arts organizations. Types of support include program development, seed money, scholarship funds, and research grants.
Requirements: Arizona-based institutions or organizations whose programs are operated for the benefit of Arizona institutions and individuals are eligible to apply. Applications are accepted at any time. There is no application form, but a preliminary letter of inquiry or phone call is requested to determine the appropriateness of a full submission.
Restrictions: The foundation rarely provides grants to individuals, building projects (capital campaigns), purchase of equipment, endowment projects, annual fund-raising campaigns, ongoing operating expenses, or deficit needs. Requests to support conferences and workshops, publications, or the production of films and video are considered only when these activities are an integral component of a larger foundation initiative.
Geographic Focus: Arizona
Amount: 2,500 - 150,000 USD
Samples: Northern Arizona U (Flagstaff, AZ)—to expand teacher-preparation programs in the biological sciences, $517,100 over three years; Homeward Bound (Phoenix, AZ)—to coordinate access to health care services for disadvantaged children, $10,000; Ballet Arizona (Phoenix, AZ)—for 15 months of support, $200,000.
Contact: JoAnn Fazio, Grants Coordinator; (602) 744-6800; (602) 744-6815; info@flinn.org
Internet: http://www.flinn.org/about/grants.cms
Sponsor: Flinn Foundation
1802 N Central Avenue
Phoenix, AZ 85004-1506

Florida BRAIVE Fund of The Community Foundation in Jacksonville **691**
The Florida BrAIve Fund of The Community Foundation in Jacksonville was created to provide assistance to North Florida military personnel and families affected by deployment to Afghanistan or Iraq. Grants will be made to non-profit agencies in North Florida to support services that assist military personnel and their families before, during, and after deployment. Specific priority target populations include: military personnel returning from deployment to Afghanistan or Iraq and their families; military personnel with physical or mental health needs as a result of deployment to Afghanistan or Iraq; families of military personnel currently deployed or preparing for imminent (within 120 days) deployment to Afghanistan or Iraq; families of those killed in action during deployment to Afghanistan or Iraq; and individual augmentees or others deployed without a typical support structure. Grant applications for The Florida BrAIve Fund of The Community Foundation in Jacksonville will be considered on a rolling basis as they are received. You may submit an application at any time. Once the Foundation have received your application and all supplemental materials, you may expect to receive a decision from The Community Foundation in Jacksonville within 60 days. See the Foundations website for a application form and additional guidelines.
Requirements: Nonprofit 501(c)3organization providing services to meet the unmet needs of North Florida military personnel and families affected by deployments to Iraq and Afghanistan as part of Operation Enduring Freedom or Operation Iraqi Freedom, may be eligible to apply for a grant.
Geographic Focus: Florida
Contact: Cheryl Riddick, Vice President of Grantmaking Services; (904) 356-4483; info@jaxcf.org
Internet: http://www.jaxcf.org/NetCommunity/Page.aspx?pid=430
Sponsor: Community Foundation in Jacksonville
121 W Forsyth Street, Suite 900
Jacksonville, FL 32202

Florida Division of Cultural Affairs Cultural Endowment Grants **692**
The purpose of this program is to create an endowment matching funds program that will provide operating resources to participating cultural organizations. The Cultural Endowment Program is comprised of two components: Cultural Sponsoring Organization (CSO) designation, and receipt of a $240,000 State Matching Share (SMS). Although both parts require the submission of application material, each contains eligibility criteria that are unique to the components. An organization may be designated as a CSO without submitting an application for an SMS. However, CSO designation is an eligibility criterion for the receipt of a SMS.
Requirements: Applicant must be a not-for-profit, tax exempt Florida corporation according to these definitions: Incorporated or authorized as a not-for-profit corporation, in good standing, pursuant to Chapter 617, Florida Statutes; designated as a tax exempt organization as defined in Section 501(c)3 or (4) of the Internal Revenue Code of 1954; designated as in compliance with S.170 of the Internal Revenue Code of 1954. Eligible organizations must be able to provide a description and documentation of a program that qualifies it as a sponsoring organization within a cultural discipline. The description and documentation shall include printed performance or printed exhibition material such as brochures, programs, or catalogues. When an organization raises $360,000 in eligible contributions, the State of Florida will match the local contributions with a State Matching Share (SMS) in the amount of $240,000.

The State Matching Share, when combined with the local match, creates an endowment fund for the organization. The funds in the endowment fund are invested by the Cultural Sponsoring Organization (CSO), and the interest that is generated on the investment(s) is used for general operating support.
Restrictions: The income that is generated from the investment of the SMS and the local match shall be expended only for operating cost while engaged in programs directly related to cultural activities. The income from the investments may not be used for: expenses associated with lobbying or attempting to influence federal, state, or local legislation, the judiciary branch, or any state agency; debt reduction; private entertainment, food, beverages, plaques, awards, or scholarships; projects which are restricted to private or exclusive participation which shall include restricting access to programs on the basis of gender, race, creed, national origin, disability, age, or habitat; regranting; building, renovation, or remodeling of facilities; contingencies, fines and penalties, interest and other financial cost; contributions or donations; neither the corpus nor the income of the trust may be pledged as security for any debt or purchase.
Geographic Focus: Florida
Date(s) Application is Due: Jun 1
Amount: 240,000 USD
Contact: Donald R. Blancett, (850) 245-6483; dblancet@dos.state.fl.us
Internet: http://www.florida-arts.org/grants/endowment/
Sponsor: Florida Arts Council, Division of Cultural Affairs
R.A. Gray Building, 500 South Bronough Street, 3rd Floor
Tallahassee, FL 32399-0250

Florida Division of Cultural Affairs Cultural Support Grants 693
The goal of the Cultural Support Grants is to provide state recognition through competitive grants for significant public programs that preserve, strengthen, and foster excellence and diversity in art or culture for Florida's residents and visitors. The Division of Cultural Affairs, through the Cultural Support Grants, encourages a commitment to outreach and educational services to underserved areas and populations, and increased access for persons with disabilities. Funded by the Florida Legislature, this program is dedicated to fund not-for-profit cultural organizations, recurring cultural programs, museums, and arts programs of non-arts organizations. Discipline categories available in dance, discipline service, folk arts, interdisciplinary, literature, media arts, multidisciplinary, art museums, science museums, youth and children's museums, music, sponsor/presenter, community theatre, professional theatre, and visual arts are designed to support grant proposals, which make possible programs that promote excellence in the discipline and make such excellence accessible for general community-wide audiences. Two types of funding are offered through this program: Specific Project (SP) and General Program Support (GPS). Organizations can receive funding for either Specific Projects or General Program Support through this program, but not both. Annual deadline dates may vary; contact program staff for exact dates.
Requirements: Nonprofit organizations in Florida are eligible. The amount requested must be matched dollar-for-dollar, cash and in-kind. Matching funds may be anticipated at the time of application, but must be obligated by the grant period ending date. At least 50% of the matching funds must be cash. Applications must be submitted in OASIS (http://www.florida-arts.org/oasis/) by midnight Eastern Time of the deadline date. This means applications submitted from a location in Central Time must be submitted by 11pm local time. There are no waivers or exceptions to a deadline. All applicants must have an email address to utilize OASIS. Support material packages must be postmarked by midnight of the deadline. Packages postmarked by the U.S. Postal Service no later than midnight of the deadline date shall be deemed to have been submitted in a timely fashion.
Geographic Focus: Florida
Amount: Up to 25,000 USD
Samples: Young at Art of Broward (Broward, FL)—for general support, $39,862; Miami Children's Museum (Miami, FL)—for operating support, $45,617.
Contact: Sarah Thomas Stage, Administrator; (850) 245-6459; sthomas@dos.state.fl.us
Internet: http://www.florida-arts.org/grants/csg/index.htm
Sponsor: Florida Arts Council, Division of Cultural Affairs
R.A. Gray Building, 500 South Bronough Street, 3rd Floor
Tallahassee, FL 32399-0250

Florida Division of Cultural Affairs Organizations Grants—Community Theater 694
The community theater program is designed to support producing Florida community theaters and local community service organizations for the creation of projects that promote excellence in community theater performance, and to make programs available for community-wide audiences. Included in this category are American musical theater and related genre programs, excluding opera. The program also supports nonarts organizations that undertake projects consistent with the community theater discipline. A guidelines booklet with application forms should be obtained from the Bureau of Grant Services prior to submitting a formal application. General program support is for up to 10 percent of the last completed fiscal year's revenue, not to exceed $50,000; specific project grants to arts organizations is for up to 20 percent of the last completed fiscal year's revenue, not to exceed $25,000; and specific project grants to nonarts organizations is for up to 10 percent of the last completed fiscal year's revenue, not to exceed $25,000. Annual deadline dates may vary; contact program staff for exact dates.
Requirements: An organization must qualify as a political subdivision of a municipal, county, or state government in Florida; or be a nonprofit, tax-exempt Florida corporation. A dollar-for-dollar match is required, with 25 percent in kind allowed.
Restrictions: Organizations applying for general program support may not apply for a specific project grant. Arts organizations that have been incorporated for less than one year are not eligible for general program support.
Geographic Focus: Florida
Samples: Fort Lauderdale Children's Theater (Fort Lauderdale, FL)—for classes, plays, and outreach, $14,734; South Florida Theater of the Deaf (FL)—for performances and workshops, $4454.
Contact: Sarah Thomas Stage, Administrator; (850) 245-6459; sthomas@dos.state.fl.us
Internet: http://www.florida-arts.org/grants/csg/index.htm
Sponsor: Florida Arts Council, Division of Cultural Affairs
R.A. Gray Building, 500 South Bronough Street, 3rd Floor
Tallahassee, FL 32399-0250

Florida Division of Cultural Affairs Organizations Grants—Dance 695
The dance category is designed to assist Florida dance companies and dance service organizations to develop their artistic and administrative skills. This category encourages the creation of projects that promote excellence in dance performance and strive to bring such excellence to communitywide audiences. General program support is for up to 10 percent of the last completed fiscal year's revenue, not to exceed $50,000; specific project grants to arts organizations is for up to 20 percent of the last completed fiscal year's revenue, not to exceed $25,000; and specific project grants to nonarts organizations is for up to 10 percent of the last completed fiscal year's revenue, not to exceed $25,000. Obtain specific guidelines and application forms from the Bureau of Grant Services. Annual deadline dates may vary; contact program staff for exact dates.
Requirements: Florida dance-producing organizations or local service organizations and arts organizations established primarily for the purpose of dance programming and seeking funding for its annual operations are eligible to apply for general support. Nonarts organizations, such as political subdivisions, and public and private educational institutions for which dance is not a primary mission may apply for specific project support. A dollar-for-dollar match is required.
Restrictions: Organizations applying for general program support may not also apply for a specific project grant. Arts organizations that have been incorporated for less than one year are not eligible for general program support.
Geographic Focus: Florida
Samples: Florida Dance Association (FL)—for general operating support, $15,878; Dance Alive (FL)—for season support, $7868; Black Door Dance Ensemble (FL)—for the Metropolis Dance Theater, $1000.
Contact: Sarah Thomas Stage, Administrator; (850) 245-6459; sthomas@dos.state.fl.us
Internet: http://www.florida-arts.org/grants/csg/index.htm
Sponsor: Florida Arts Council, Division of Cultural Affairs
R.A. Gray Building, 500 South Bronough Street, 3rd Floor
Tallahassee, FL 32399-0250

Florida Division of Cultural Affairs Organizations Grants—Folk Arts 696
The folk arts category is designed to help organizations preserve and present traditional arts by assisting these groups to present performances, exhibitions, or festivals featuring traditional artists and their work. Folk artistic practices

have emerged from occupational, ethnic, religious, generational, or regional communities that have endured through several generations and that express a sense of a community's aesthetics. These art forms are usually learned informally through a relative or the community and are maintained without formal instruction. The folk arts program encourages Florida's communities to honor their folk traditions, both native and immigrant, long-standing and evolving, by preserving and encouraging public awareness of and appreciation for them. General program support is for up to 10 percent of the last completed fiscal year's revenue, not to exceed $50,000; specific project grants to arts organizations is for up to 20 percent of the last completed fiscal year's revenue, not to exceed $25,000; and specific project grants to nonarts organizations is for up to 10 percent of the last completed fiscal year's revenue, not to exceed $25,000.
Requirements: Arts organizations in Florida whose primary mission is to produce or to encourage public awareness of and appreciation for traditional arts and crafts in keeping with the purpose of the discipline and are seeking funding for their annual operations are eligible to apply for general program support. Organizations eligible to apply for specific project support include political subdivisions, public and private educational institutions, and other organizations for which folk arts programming is not a primary mission, as well as arts organizations seeking support for a particular project, program, or series. A dollar-for-dollar match is required, with 25 percent in kind allowed.
Restrictions: Organizations applying for general program support may not also apply for a specific project grant. Grants are generally not funded for research for scholarly purposes only, historical presentations or re-creations, exhibits limited to historical objects, highly choreographed or orchestrated interpretations of traditional folk or ethnic dance or music, contemporary studio crafts or reproductions, or competitive events. Arts organizations that have been incorporated for less than one year are not eligible for general program support.
Geographic Focus: Florida
Samples: Sosyete Koukouy, Miami (FL)—for the project The Death of Jozafa, $7348; Florida A&M U, Division of Sponsored Research (FL)—for the project Folk Arts as Cultural History, $6685.
Contact: Sarah Thomas Stage, Administrator; (850) 245-6459; sthomas@dos.state.fl.us
Internet: http://www.florida-arts.org/grants/csg/index.htm
Sponsor: Florida Arts Council, Division of Cultural Affairs
R.A. Gray Building, 500 South Bronough Street, 3rd Floor
Tallahassee, FL 32399-0250

Florida Division of Cultural Affairs Organizations Grants—Literature 697

The literature discipline program supports projects by small presses, noncommercial publishing houses, professional literary groups, and other organizations involved in literary arts. Florida arts organizations established primarily for the purpose of literary arts may apply for funding. Organizations must provide documentation of publishing history or professional status; a proposed publication schedule, where applicable; previous conference programs or samples of published material; support letters that demonstrate a strong commitment from contributors; and other support materials that best reflect the strengths of the organization. General program support is for up to 10 percent of the last completed fiscal year's revenue, not to exceed $50,000; specific project grants to arts organizations is for up to 20 percent of the last completed fiscal year's revenue, not to exceed $25,000; and specific project grants to nonarts organizations is for up to 10 percent of the last completed fiscal year's revenue, not to exceed $25,000. Annual deadline dates may vary; contact program staff for exact dates.
Requirements: An organization must qualify as a political subdivision of a municipal, county, or state government in Florida; or be a nonprofit, tax-exempt Florida corporation. A dollar-for-dollar match is required, and 25 percent in-kind is allowed.
Restrictions: Organizations applying for general program support may not apply for a specific project grant. Arts organizations that have been incorporated for less than one year are not eligible for general program support.
Geographic Focus: Florida
Samples: Florida International U Creative Writing Program (FL)—for Writers on the Bay, $4145; U of South Florida, Division of Sponsored Research (FL)—for the Florida Suncoast Writers' Conference, $2083.
Contact: Sarah Thomas Stage, Administrator; (850) 245-6459; sthomas@dos.state.fl.us
Internet: http://www.florida-arts.org/grants/csg/index.htm
Sponsor: Florida Arts Council, Division of Cultural Affairs
R.A. Gray Building, 500 South Bronough Street, 3rd Floor
Tallahassee, FL 32399-0250

Florida Division of Cultural Affairs Organizations Grants—Media Arts 698

The media arts program provides support to producing Florida media arts organizations and local media arts service organizations for the creation of projects that promote excellence in film, video, radio, and television, in which the media is the art form. This program also helps sponsor film and videotape festivals and exhibitions, conferences, and seminars that provide access to the media arts for the general community. The media arts category also supports nonarts organizations that undertake similar activities. General program support is for up to 10 percent of the last completed fiscal year's revenue, not to exceed $50,000; specific project grants to arts organizations is for up to 20 percent of the last completed fiscal year's revenue, not to exceed $25,000; and specific project grants to nonarts organizations is for up to 10 percent of the last completed fiscal year's revenue, not to exceed $25,000. Annual deadline dates may vary; contact program staff for exact dates.
Requirements: An organization must qualify as a political subdivision of a municipal, county, or state government in Florida; or be a nonprofit, tax-exempt Florida corporation. A dollar-for-dollar match is required, with 25 percent in kind allowed.
Restrictions: Organizations applying for general program support may not apply for a specific project grant. Arts organizations that have been incorporated for less than one year are not eligible for general program support.
Geographic Focus: Florida
Samples: Alliance for Media Arts (FL)—general program support, $15,432; Film Society of Miami (FL)—to support the 14th Miami Film Festival, $16,014; Louis Wolfson II Media History Ctr (FL)—to support archival screenings, seminars, exhibitions, and workshops, $9772.
Contact: Sarah Thomas Stage, Administrator; (850) 245-6459; sthomas@dos.state.fl.us
Internet: http://www.florida-arts.org/grants/csg/index.htm
Sponsor: Florida Arts Council, Division of Cultural Affairs
R.A. Gray Building, 500 South Bronough Street, 3rd Floor
Tallahassee, FL 32399-0250

Florida Division of Cultural Affairs Organizations Multidisciplinary Grants 699

The multidisciplinary program is intended to support Florida organizations and programs that produce events that incorporate two or more separate artistic disciplines. This category includes, but is not limited to, the support of festivals and other creative projects involving two or more separate artistic disciplines. General program support is for up to 10 percent of the last completed fiscal year's revenue, not to exceed $50,000; specific project grants to arts organizations is for up to 20 percent of the last completed fiscal year's revenue, not to exceed $25,000; and specific project grants to nonarts organizations is for up to 10 percent of the last completed fiscal year's revenue, not to exceed $25,000. Annual deadlines may vary; contact program staff for exact dates.
Requirements: An organization must qualify as a political subdivision of a municipal, county, or state government in Florida; or be a nonprofit, tax-exempt Florida corporation. A dollar-for-dollar match is required, with 25 percent in kind allowed.
Restrictions: Organizations applying for general program support may not apply for a specific project grant. Arts organizations that have been incorporated for less than one year are not eligible for general program support.
Geographic Focus: Florida
Samples: Artsfusion (FL)—for the project Ogun: Iron, Conflict and Creativity, $1169; Coral Gables International Festival of Craft Arts (FL)—for general program support, $5760.
Contact: Sarah Thomas Stage, Administrator; (850) 245-6459; sthomas@dos.state.fl.us
Internet: http://www.florida-arts.org/grants/csg/index.htm
Sponsor: Florida Arts Council, Division of Cultural Affairs
R.A. Gray Building, 500 South Bronough Street, 3rd Floor
Tallahassee, FL 32399-0250

Florida Division of Cultural Affairs Organizations Grants—Music 700

The music program is designed to assist Florida music organizations and music service groups to develop their artistic and administrative skills. This program encourages the creation of projects that promote excellence in music performance and strive to bring such excellence to communitywide audiences. This category includes, but is not limited to, such organizations as symphonies, community or youth orchestras, opera companies, community operas, musical theater, chamber or jazz ensembles, choral groups, and community bands. Each

category carries its own eligibility criteria in addition to general requirements. A guidelines booklet with application forms must be obtained from the Bureau of Grant Services prior to submitting an application. General program support is for up to 10 percent of the last completed fiscal year's revenue, not to exceed $50,000; specific project grants to arts organizations is for up to 20 percent of the last completed fiscal year's revenue, not to exceed $25,000; and specific project grants to nonarts organizations is for up to 10 percent of the last completed fiscal year's revenue, not to exceed $25,000. Annual deadline dates may vary; contact program staff for exact dates.
Requirements: An organization must qualify as a political subdivision of a municipal, county, or state government in Florida; or be a nonprofit, tax-exempt Florida corporation. A dollar-for-dollar match is required, with 25 percent in kind allowed.
Restrictions: Organizations applying for general program support may not apply for a specific project grant. Arts organizations that have been incorporated for less than one year are not eligible for general program support.
Geographic Focus: Florida
Samples: Gainesville Chamber Orchestra (Gainesville, FL)—to support the Celebration and Family Series, $3594; Gold Coast Opera (FL)—for season support, $10,717.
Contact: Sarah Thomas Stage, Arts Administrator; (850) 245-6459; sthomas@dos.state.fl.us
Internet: http://www.florida-arts.org/grants/csg/index.htm
Sponsor: Florida Arts Council, Division of Cultural Affairs
R.A. Gray Building, 500 South Bronough Street, 3rd Floor
Tallahassee, FL 32399-0250

Florida Division of Cultural Affairs Organizations Grants—Professional Theater 701

The professional theater category is designed to support producing, professional Florida theaters and local professional theater service organizations for the creation of projects that promote excellence in professional theater performance, and to make programs accessible for communitywide audiences. Organizations applying to this category must compensate their artistic staff and actors on a regular and continuing basis. American musical theater and related genre programs (excluding opera) may be included in this category. This category also supports nonarts organizations that undertake activities described here. Annual deadline dates may vary; contact program staff for exact dates.
Requirements: An organization must qualify as a political subdivision of a municipal, county, or state government in Florida; or be a nonprofit, tax-exempt Florida corporation. A dollar-for-dollar match is required, with 25 percent in kind allowed.
Restrictions: Organizations applying for general program support may not apply for a specific project grant. Arts organizations that have been incorporated for less than one year are not eligible for general program support.
Geographic Focus: Florida
Samples: Florida Professional Theaters Association (FL)—for general program support, $8956.
Contact: Sarah Thomas Stage, Arts Administrator; (850) 245-6459; sthomas@dos.state.fl.us
Internet: http://www.florida-arts.org/grants/csg/index.htm
Sponsor: Florida Arts Council, Division of Cultural Affairs
R.A. Gray Building, 500 South Bronough Street, 3rd Floor
Tallahassee, FL 32399-0250

Florida Division of Cultural Affairs Organizations Grants—Sponsor Presenter 702

This program provides general program assistance in the development of local Florida organizations solely dedicated to presenting, as opposed to producing, the performing arts; and support for other projects involving the sponsorship or presentation of high-quality performing arts groups and individual artists. Any organization for which sponsor-presenter activity is the primary mission that is seeking funding for its annual operations may apply for general program support or specific project support. A guidelines booklet with application forms must be obtained from the Bureau of Grant Services prior to submitting an application. General program support is for up to 10 percent of the last completed fiscal year's revenue, not to exceed $50,000; specific project grants to arts organizations is for up to 20 percent of the last completed fiscal year's revenue, not to exceed $25,000; and specific project grants to nonarts organizations is for up to 10 percent of the last completed fiscal year's revenue, not to exceed $25,000.
Requirements: An organization must qualify as a political subdivision of a municipal, county, or state government in Florida; or be a nonprofit, tax-exempt Florida corporation. A dollar-for-dollar match is required, with 25 percent in kind allowed.
Restrictions: Organizations applying for general program support may not apply for a specific project grant. Arts organizations that have been incorporated for less than one year are not eligible for general program support.
Geographic Focus: Florida
Amount: 1,000 - 500,000 USD
Samples: Community Concert Assoc (FL)—for season program support, $15,387; Miami Light Project (Miami, FL)—for season presenting activities, $16,982.
Contact: Sarah Thomas Stage, Arts Administrator; (850) 245-6459; sthomas@dos.state.fl.us
Internet: http://www.florida-arts.org/grants/csg/index.htm
Sponsor: Florida Arts Council, Division of Cultural Affairs
R.A. Gray Building, 500 South Bronough Street, 3rd Floor
Tallahassee, FL 32399-0250

Florida Division of Cultural Affairs Organizations Grants—Visual Arts 703

The visual arts program is designed to foster professional development among Florida visual arts institutions and service organizations and to promote public appreciation for the state's visual arts resources. Projects may include publications, exhibits, lectures, artist workshops, and technical assistance programs for visual artists. Programs employing or involving outstanding Florida artists will be given priority consideration, as will programs originating in Florida and designed to travel to qualified institutions either in-state or out-of-state. Publication of exhibition catalogs or other program documentation designed to contribute to scholarship is encouraged. An applicant organization is expected to originate a significant portion of the programs for which general support is requested. A guidelines booklet with application forms must be obtained from the Bureau of Grant Services prior to submitting a formal application. General program support is for up to 10 percent of the last completed fiscal year's revenue, not to exceed $50,000; specific project grants to arts organizations is for up to 20 percent of the last completed fiscal year's revenue, not to exceed $25,000; and specific project grants to nonarts organizations is for up to 10 percent of the last completed fiscal year's revenue, not to exceed $25,000. Annual deadline dates may vary; contact program staff for exact dates.
Requirements: An organization must qualify as a political subdivision of a municipal, county, or state government in Florida; or be a nonprofit, tax-exempt Florida corporation. Accreditation by the American Association of Museums, though not required, is encouraged for museum applicants. A dollar-for-dollar match is required, and 25 percent in kind is allowed.
Restrictions: Organizations applying for general program support may not apply for a specific project grant. Arts organizations that have been incorporated for less than one year are not eligible for general program support.
Geographic Focus: Florida
Samples: Miami-Dade Community College, Wolfson Galleries (FL)—for exhibition support, $12,607; Pensacola Museum of Art (Pensacola, FL)—for season support, $14,622.
Contact: Sarah Thomas Stage, Administrator; (850) 245-6459; sthomas@dos.state.fl.us
Internet: http://www.florida-arts.org/grants/csg/index.htm
Sponsor: Florida Arts Council, Division of Cultural Affairs
R.A. Gray Building, 500 South Bronough Street, 3rd Floor
Tallahassee, FL 32399-0250

Florida Division of Cultural Affairs State Service Organization Grants 704

The State Service Organization Grants's purpose is to support the efforts of state service organizations through stabilized funding and to encourage collaborative work between the Division and these organizations to achieve state goals and objectives. For purposes of the state service organization program, statewide is defined as reaching at least 50% of the state's population, or 34 or more Florida counties. Funding is available for state service organizations on a matching basis for general program support of their ongoing activities and programs.
Requirements: Organizations may apply to the program once every 3 years. All State Service Organizations may apply for general program support only. State Service Organizations that receive general program support under this program are ineligible to receive support under the Cultural Support Grants but are eligible for additional funding through any of the Division's other grant programs. To be eligible to apply, an applicant organization must: Be a

public entity governed by a county, municipality, school district, community college, college, university, or agency of state government; Be a not-for-profit, tax-exempt Florida corporation.
Restrictions: The following are nonallowable project costs for grant or matching funds: Expenses incurred or obligated prior to, or after, the grant period; Lobbying or attempting to influence federal, state, or local legislation; Building, renovation, or remodeling of facilities, capital expenditures (includes acquisitions, building projects, renovations, etc.), collections acquisitions (whether inanimate or live); Bad debts, contingencies, fines and penalties, interest, and other financial costs; and private entertainment, food, beverages, plaques, awards, or scholarships; Projects restricted to private or exclusive participation, which includes restricting access to programs on the basis of sex, race, color, national origin, religion, handicap, age, or marital status; Regranting; Contributions and donations.
Geographic Focus: Florida
Contact: Morgan Barr Lewis, Division of Cultural Affairs; (850) 245-6477 or (850) 245-6356; (850) 245-6497; mhbarr@dos.state.fl.us
Internet: http://www.florida-arts.org/grants/sso/index.htm
Sponsor: Florida Department of State, Division of Cultural Affairs, R.A. Gray Building, 3rd Floor, 500 South Bronough Street
Tallahassee, FL 32399-0250

Florida Division of Cultural Affairs Underserved Arts Communities Assistance Grants **705**

The Underserved Arts Communities Assistance Program (UACAP) fosters the development of underserved arts organizations by providing access to grants for salary assistance, organizational development, and consultancy. Salary assistance grants are also available to consulting organizations that specifically target underserved organizations and provide evidence of service to such organizations in their particular plan. The UACAP program is only open to ARTS organizations, which meet basic eligibility criteria and the underserved definition. Non-arts organizations may not apply to any of the UACAP categories.
Requirements: To be eligible to apply, an applicant organization must: be a public entity governed by a county, municipality, school district, community college, college, university, or a state government agency; or be a not-for-profit, tax exempt Florida corporation as a result of being incorporated or authorized as a not-for-profit corporation, in good standing, pursuant to Chapter 617, Florida Statutes. Match requirements are dollar-for-dollar.
Restrictions: Application to this program must be made through OASIS (http://www.florida-arts.org/oasis/) Grants are for administrative purposes only, not for artistic programs.
Geographic Focus: Florida
Date(s) Application is Due: Apr 12
Contact: Gaylen Phillips, Program and Development Manager; (850) 245-6482; gphillips@dos.state.fl.us
Internet: http://www.florida-arts.org/grants/uacap/index.htm
Sponsor: Florida Arts Council, Division of Cultural Affairs
R.A. Gray Building, 500 South Bronough Street, 3rd Floor
Tallahassee, FL 32399-0250

Fluor Foundation Grants **706**

The Fluor Corporation achieves its contribution objectives through the Fluor Foundation and corporate giving. The Foundation's areas of interest are: education; human services; cultural outreach; and public/civic affairs. The Foundation considers requests for operating, program, capital or endowment support. Priority is given to funding organizations with employee volunteer participation. Application information is available online.
Requirements: Fluor's giving programs focus on community organizations in those locations around the world where the company has a presence. See website for local contact information: http://www.fluor.com/sustainability/community/fluor_giving/Pages/applying_for_fluor_foundation_grants.aspx
Restrictions: Funding is not available for: film production/publishing activities; individuals; sports organizations/programs; veterans, fraternal, labor or religious organizations; or lobbying/political organizations or campaigns.
Geographic Focus: Alaska, California, Louisiana, New Jersey, New York, North Carolina, Pennsylvania, South Carolina, Tennessee, Texas, Virginia, Washington, Albania, Andorra, Armenia, Australia, Austria, Azerbaijan, Belarus, Belgium, Bosnia & Herzegovina, Bulgaria, Canada, Caribbean, China, Croatia, Cyprus, Czech Republic, Denmark, Estonia, Finland, France, Georgia, Germany, Greece, Hungary, Iceland, Ireland, Italy, Japan, Kosovo, Latvia, Liechtenstein, Lithuania, Luxembourg, Macedonia, Malta, Mexico, Moldova, Monaco, Montenegro, New Zealand, Norway, Peru, Philippines, Poland, Poland, Portugal, Romania, Russia, Russia, San Marino, Serbia, Slovakia, Slovenia, Spain, Sweden, Switzerland, The Netherlands, Turkey, Ukraine, United Kingdom, Vatican City, Venezuela
Contact: Suzanne Esber, Executive Director of Community Relations; (949) 349-7847; (949) 349-7694; suzanne.esber@fluor.com
Internet: http://www.fluor.com/sustainability/community/fluor_giving/Pages/applying_for_fluor_foundation_grants.aspx
Sponsor: Fluor Foundation
3 Polaris Way
Aliso Viejo, CA 92698

FMC Foundation Grants **707**

The foundation supports education, community improvement, urban affairs, health and human services, and public issues/economic education. Higher education is supported through scholarships and employee matching gifts. Education support tends to be in business, engineering, chemistry, and some minority education programs. Eligible applicants need to contact the FMC in their geograhic area. Each individual FMC location determines how their contributions will be given.
Requirements: Grants are awarded to 501(c)3 organizations in FMC-plant communities. U.S. -based organizations with an international focus are also eligible.
Restrictions: Grants are not made to individuals.
Geographic Focus: Arizona, California, Delaware, Florida, Illinois, Louisiana, Maine, Maryland, Missouri, New Jersey, New York, North Carolina, Pennsylvania, Tennessee, Texas, West Virginia, Wyoming, Canada
Contact: Program Contact; (215) 299-6000; (215) 299-6140
Internet: http://www.fmc.com
Sponsor: FMC Foundation
1735 Market Street
Philadelphia, PA 19103

Foellinger Foundation Grants **708**

The foundation awards grants primarily in Fort Wayne and Allen County, IN, to improve the quality of life in the areas of early child development, youth development, strengthening family services, strengthening organizations, and community concerns. Special emphasis is given to projects/programs that help children and their families, particularly those with the greatest economic need and least opportunity. By doing so, the Foundation hopes to help children and their families move from dependence to independence. In addition to programs and projects, the foundation also awards grants for general operating, capital, seed money, renovation projects, conferences and seminars, consulting services, equipment, challenge/matching, and planning purposes.
Requirements: Indiana organizations are eligible to apply.
Restrictions: The foundation does not fund scholarships, travel assistance, conference fees, religious groups, public or private elementary or secondary schools, sponsorships, special events, advertising, or endowments.
Geographic Focus: Indiana
Date(s) Application is Due: Feb 1; May 1; Nov 1
Amount: 10,000 - 100,000 USD
Samples: Public Broadcasting of Northeast Indiana (IN)—for general operating support; Arthur J. Blaising Social Services (IN)—for its after-school program and its 10-week summer day camp, $75,585; Turnstone (IN)—for a transportation program that serves elderly and disabled people, $187,500 over 18 months; Taylor U—for the Allen County Postsecondary Education Consortium, $219,690 over two years.
Contact: Cheryl Taylor; (219) 422-2900; (219) 422-9436; info@foellinger.org
Internet: http://www.foellinger.org
Sponsor: Foellinger Foundation
520 E Berry Street
Fort Wayne, IN 46802

Ford Family Foundation Grants **709**

The foundation supports nonprofit organizations in Oregon and California in its areas of interest, including rural education (K-12), rural human services (family and youths), and rural civic and community enhancement. Types of support include general operating support, building construction/renovation, challenge grants, equipment acquisition, program development, and scholarship funds. Preapplication letters are accepted at anytime. Information about the preapplication process is available online.

Requirements: Nonprofit organizations in Oregon, with emphasis given to requests from Douglas and Coos Counties, and small and midsize communities in rural Oregon and in Siskiyou County, CA, are eligible.
Restrictions: The Foundation generally will not consider funding requests for: endowments or reserve funds; general fund drives, such as United Way; indirect or overhead expenses; debt retirement or operating deficits; sponsorship of fundraising events; on-going operating expenses, such as salaries and general administration; on-going operating expenses for places of worship or conducting religious services by churches or other religious organizations; propagandizing or influencing elections or legislation; purchase of art; exhibits and construction of history museums; general funding projects of governmental units; environmental preservation activities that have the intent or effect of depriving property owners of the use of their property or reducing the gainful employment of legal residents of the United States.
Geographic Focus: California, Oregon
Samples: Doernbecher Children's Hospital (Portland, OR)—to expand the Children's Cancer Center, $2 million challenge grant.
Contact: Norman Smith, President; (541) 957-5574; (541) 957-5720
Internet: http://www.tfff.org/cms/Default.aspx?tabid=57
Sponsor: Ford Family Foundation
1600 NW Stewart Parkway
Roseburg, OR 97470

Forest Foundation Grants 710

The foundation awards grants to eligible Washington nonprofit organizations in its areas of interest, including the arts, community development, environment, and social services delivery. Types of support include building construction/renovation, capital campaigns, general operating support and matching/challenge grants. While the foundation does not support religious groups for religious purposes, programs that are not restricted to religious affiliation are considered. The board meets six times annually. Submit two copies of a letter of inquiry; full proposals are by invitation.
Requirements: Washington nonprofit organizations in Pierce County are eligible. Capital requests outside of Pierce County will be considered.
Restrictions: Grants do not support individuals, endowment funds, debt retirement, annual appeals, research, fellowships, films, publications, or scholarships.
Geographic Focus: Washington
Amount: 1,000 - 50,000 USD
Samples: Seattle Ctr Foundation (WA)—for its capital campaign for the Marion Oliver McCaw Hall performing arts center, $250,000.
Contact: Frank Underwood, Executive Director; (253) 627-1634
Sponsor: Forest Foundation
820 A Street, Suite 345
Tacoma, WA 98402

Forest Lawn Foundation Grants 711

The foundation awards grants in Los Angeles and Orange Counties, CA, to organizations serving youth and the disabled and to hospitals, welfare, and social service agencies. Types of support include continuing support, emergency funds, general purposes, matching funds, operating budgets, and special projects. Contact office for program availability.
Requirements: Nonprofit organizations in Los Angeles County and Orange County may apply.
Restrictions: Grants do not support federated appeals, political purposes, or projects/programs normally funded by the government.
Geographic Focus: California
Amount: 1,000 - 200,000 USD
Samples: Weingart Center Association (Los Angeles, CA)—for general operating support, $100,000.
Contact: Program Contact
Sponsor: Forest Lawn Foundation
1712 S Glendale Avenue
Glendale, CA 91205

Forever Young Foundation Grants 712

The Foundation serves children facing significant physical, emotional, and financial challenges. Grants are considered for organizations seeking to provide academic, athletic, and therapeutic opportunities currently unavailable to these children. The foundation has determined the best way to accomplish its mission is through the development and support of charitable organizations with a proven track record in delivering these services.
Requirements: In reviewing grant requests, FYF requires: requests to be from the Northern California, Utah, and Arizona region; the organization have a non-profit 501(c)3 tax-exempt charity status; goals fall under the mission of the Forever Young Foundation; organizations that do not discriminate by race, religion, color, creed, sex, or national origin; adequate financial resources for performance, the necessary experience, organizational, and technical qualifications, or a firm commitment, arrangement, or ability to obtain such, and; adequate financial management system and audit procedures that provide efficient and effective accountability and control of all property, funds, and other assets.
Geographic Focus: Arizona, California, Utah
Contact: Sterling Tanner, President & Executive Director; (800) 994-3837; sterling@foreveryoung.org
Internet: http://www.foreveryoung.org/donations.html?charityid=fore&homeurl=http://www.foreveryoung.org/foundation/
Sponsor: Steve Young Foundation
1424 S Stapley Drive
Mesa, AZ 85204

Foster Foundation Grants 713

The Foundation funds effective, nonprofit organizations that can provide tangible benefits and ongoing support to improve the quality of life for individuals, families and communities within the Pacific Northwest. The Foundation's primary field of interests are: basic human welfare issues, education, medical research, treatment and care and cultural activities. The Foundation places special emphasis on meeting the needs of the underserved and disadvantaged segments of the population, especially children, women and seniors.
Requirements: Eligible applicants must: be a nonprofit located in or serving the populations of the Pacific Northwest; address as their mission or project intent one of the Foundation's priority issues for funding; not have any delinquent final reports due to the Foundation from previous grant cycles.
Restrictions: The Foundation will not consider requests for: direct grants, scholarships or loans for the benefit of specific individuals; projects of organizations whose policies or practices discriminate on the basis of race, ethnic origin, sex, creed or sexual orientation; contributions or program support for sectarian or religious organizations whose activities benefit only their members; or loans.
Geographic Focus: Alaska, Idaho, Montana, Oregon, Washington
Contact: Jill Goodsell, Executive Director; (206) 726-1815; (206) 903-0628; info@thefosterfoundation.org
Internet: http://thefosterfoundation.org/Grants_Guide.asp
Sponsor: Foster Foundation
601 Union Street, Suite 3707
Seattle, WA 98101

Foundation Northwest Grants 714

Grants are awarded to organizations in the Inland Northwest—eastern Washington and northern Idaho—for charitable and educational purposes in the fields of music and drama; education; civic categories which include culture, education, civic and community development; and human services. The foundation has five distinct grant programs and types of support include matching funds, special projects, seed money, and occasional operating support and capital funding. Deadlines vary according to area and contributing sponsorship; contact program support for exact dates.
Requirements: Grant applications are accepted for projects that will enrich the quality of life in the communities of eastern Washington and northern Idaho. Eligible Washington counties include Adams, Asotin, Columbia, Ferry, Garfield, Lincoln, Pend Oreille, Spokane, Steven, and Whitman. Eligible Idaho counties include Benewah, Bonner, Boundary, Clearwater, Idaho, Kootenai, Latah, Lewis, Nez Perce, and Shoshone.
Restrictions: Grants do not support endowments, debt retirement, lobbying, sectarian religious purposes, individuals, travel, sports teams and classes, projects that taxpayers or commercial interests normally support, fundraising campaigns, publications or films (unless an integral part of a foundation-supported program), or nondonor-supported research.
Geographic Focus: Idaho, Washington
Amount: 2,500 - 7,500 USD
Contact: Program Contact; (509) 624-2606; (509) 624-2608; admin@foundationnw.org
Internet: http://www.foundationnw.org
Sponsor: Foundation Northwest
221 Wall Street N, Suite 624
Spokane, WA 99201-0826

Foundations of East Chicago Grants 715

Foundations of East Chicago, Indiana is funded by the Resorts East Chicago Casino and Hotel. Foundations supports churches, schools, and nonprofit organizations that know the community best and put money where it does the most good.

Requirements: Must be a registered 501(c)3 organization & located in East Chicago, Indiana. If you are not located in East Chicago, you may still qualify if you comply with at least one of the following *requirements:* the program that you are applying for operates in East Chicago; the funding that you are applying for will go toward assisting East Chicagoans participate in the programs you provide.

Restrictions: All applications MU.S. T be submitted via Foundations of East Chicago website. The Foundations will not accept any applications in person.

Geographic Focus: Indiana

Date(s) Application is Due: Feb 27; Feb 27

Amount: Up to 15,000 USD

Samples: City Of East Chicago, Indiana, $12,550, Picnic in the Park for Children Project;2008; Healthy East Chicago, Indiana, $6,100, Women Family Health Initiative Program;2008

Contact: Russell G. Taylor, Executive Director; (219) 392-4225; (219) 392-4245; grantinfo@foundationsofeastchicago.org

Internet: http://foundationsofeastchicago.org/shaping-the-future-many-ways/make-a-donation-request

Sponsor: Foundations of East Chicago
905 W Chicago Avenue
East Chicago, IN 46312

Fourjay Foundation Grants 716

The Foundation supports only those organizations whose chief purpose is to improve health and/or promote education, within Philadelphia, Montgomery, and Bucks counties in southeastern Pennsylvania. The Fourjay Foundation requires no specific application form. It will consider proposals that address a well-defined need, offer a concrete plan of action, and request a specific amount, from organizations whose staff has the ingenuity, commitment, and motivation to carry out the proposal's objectives. Requests may be for operating support, project specific funds, or capital funds.

Requirements: Organizations serving Philadelphia, Montgomery, and Bucks Counties in southeastern Pennsylvania are eligible.

Restrictions: Funding is not available for: charities operating outside Montgomery, Bucks, or Philadelphia counties; individuals; elementary or secondary educational institutions; museums, musical groups, theaters, or cultural organizations; religious organizations in support of their sacramental or theological functions; political groups or related think tanks; athletic organizations or alumni associations; libraries; public radio or television; United Way or the YMCA; civic organizations; organizations that have applied or been funded within the last 12 month period.

Geographic Focus: Pennsylvania

Date(s) Application is Due: Mar 1; Jun 1; Sep 1; Dec 1

Amount: 1,000 - 10,000 USD

Contact: Ann T. Bucci, Grant Coordinator; (215) 830-1437; (215) 830-0157; abucci@fourjay.org

Internet: http://www.fourjay.org/grantGuidelines.asp

Sponsor: Fourjay Foundation
2300 Computer Avenue, Building G, Suite 1
Willow Grove, PA 19090-1753

Frances and Benjamin Benenson Foundation Grants 717

The foundation awards grants to nonprofit organizations in support of community services, international ministries and missions, Jewish education, Jewish welfare, and religious welfare. Types of support include general operating support and scholarships. There are no application deadlines. Applications must be made in writing, stating the purpose of the grant and the amount requested.

Requirements: Nonprofits of the Jewish and Roman Catholic faiths are eligible.

Restrictions: Grants are not made to individuals.

Geographic Focus: All U.S. States

Samples: School of American Ballet, New York, New York, $7,500; Feminist Majority Foundation, Arlington, Virginia, $10,000.

Contact: Bruce W. Benenson, Vice President; (212) 867-0990; (212) 983-1952; bbenenson@benensoncapital.com

Sponsor: Frances and Benjamin Benenson Foundation
708 Third Avenue, 28th Floor
New York, NY 10017

Francis A. and Jacquelyn H. Harrington Foundation Grants 718

The foundation supports requests from health, educational, and cultural organizations that are providing solutions to, or prevention of, problems within the immediate Worcester, MA, community area and that are receiving additional support from other funding sources. Types of support include capital campaigns, equipment acquisition, general operating support, and program development. A proposal should be in letter form and should include the goals and objectives of the request together with a plan for accomplishing the same. The trustees meet twice each year, once in late summer to review requests received to date and again in December to review requests and confirm grants. The foundation does not make human service grants. Instead, all human service requests should be sent to the Greater Worcester Community Foundation, where the foundation has established the Francis A. and Jacquelyn H. Harrington Fund.

Requirements: The foundation provides grants to 501(c)3 tax-exempt organizations that are based in the Worcester, MA, area.

Geographic Focus: Massachusetts

Date(s) Application is Due: Jun 1

Samples: Quinsigamond Community College (Worcester, MA)—to create a one-stop enrollment center in the college's administration building, $1 million.

Contact: Sumner Tilton Jr., Trustee; (508) 798-8621

Sponsor: Francis A. and Jacquelyn H. Harrington Foundation
370 Main Street, 12th Floor
Worcester, MA 01608

Francis Families Foundation Grants 719

In carrying out its mission, the foundation awards grants to educational and art and cultural institutions in the greater Kansas City metropolitan area. Areas of interest under education include child and youth development and higher education. Under arts and culture, priority consideration is given to programs that benefit major arts institutions, provide stability, enhance programming, or assist the artistic or fiscal growth of such organizations; and educational arts programming that has children as its focus. Support may be ongoing or a one-time contribution and may include capital campaigns, pledges, general operations, fellowships, or special projects. Interested persons should call or write to determine whether their organization/project falls within foundation guidelines. Eligibility varies between programs; contact program staff for eligibility.

Requirements: The applying entity must be tax-exempt under the IRS code and geographically located within the greater Kansas City area (60 mile radius).

Restrictions: The foundation does not make grants to individuals.

Geographic Focus: Missouri

Date(s) Application is Due: Jul 28

Samples: Child and youth development programs and organizations (Kansas City, KS)—$1.3 million total; Art and cultural programs and organizations (Kansas City, KS)—$265,428 total.

Contact: Lyn Knox, Program Officer; (816) 531-0077; webmaster@francisfoundation.org

Internet: http://www.francisfoundation.org/application.htm

Sponsor: Francis Families Foundation
800 W 47th Street, Suite 717
Kansas City, MO 64112

Frank and Lydia Bergen Foundation Grants 720

The mission and goals of the Frank and Lydia Bergen Foundation are: to arrange for musical entertainments, concerts and recitals of a character appropriate for the education and instruction of the public in the musical arts. Paramount consideration is given to traditional classical music programs; to aid worthy students of music in securing a complete and adequate musical education; to aid organizations in their efforts to present fine music to the public, provided that such organizations are operated exclusively for educational purposes. Support is offered in the form of: scholarships; program development; capital campaigns; financial aid; community outreach programs; community programs; artist-in-residency programs and; general operating support. Applications are due April 10, for the June meeting & August 15, for the October meeting. Grant applications forms are available online. Applicants will receive notice acknowledging receipt of the grant request, and subsequently be notified of the grant declination or approval.

Requirements: Qualifying tax-exempt 501(c)3 organizations are eligible to apply. There is no geographic restriction but applying organizations must be operating exclusively for educational purposes. Proposals should be submitted in the following format: completed Common Grant Application Form; an original

Proposal Statement; an audited financial report and a current year operating budget;a copy of your official IRS Letter with your tax determination; a listing of your Board of Directors. Proposal Statements (second item in the above Format) should answer these questions: what are the objectives and expected outcomes of this program/project/request; what strategies will be used to accomplish your objective; what is the timeline for completion; if this is part of an on-going program, how long has it been in operation; what criteria will you use to measure success; if the request is not fully funded, what other sources can you engage; an Itemized budget should be included; please describe any collaborative ventures. Prior to the distribution of funds, all approved grantees must sign and return a Grant Agreement Form, stating that the funds will be used for the purpose intended. Progress reports and Completion reports must also be filed as required for your specific grant. All current grantees must be in good standing with required documentation prior to submitting new proposals to any foundation.
Restrictions: Grants are not made for political purposes, nor to organizations which discriminate on the basis of race, ethnic origin, sexual or religious preference, age or gender.
Geographic Focus: All U.S. States
Date(s) Application is Due: Apr 10; Aug 15
Amount: 3,000 - 60,000 USD
Samples: New Jersey Symphony Orchestra, $60,000—Greater Newark Youth/ Chamber Orchestras, program support; Newark School of the Arts, $20,000—financial aid and scholarship assistance for music students; Harmonium, A Classical Choral Society, Inc., $8,000—orchestra funding and artists' fees.
Contact: Gale Y. Sykes, Grant Administrator; (908) 598-3576; grantinquiries2@wachovia.com
Internet: https://www.wachovia.com/foundation/v/index.jsp?vgnextoid=990852199c0aa110VgnVCM1000004b0d1872RCRD&vgnextfmt=default
Sponsor: Frank and Lydia Bergen Foundation
190 River Road, NJ3132
Summit, NJ 07901

Frank E. and Seba B. Payne Foundation Grants **721**

The foundation awards grants in the Chicago, IL, area and in Pennsylvania in its areas of interest, including AIDS prevention, children and youth, cultural activities, education, and hospitals. Types of support include building construction/renovation, equipment acquisition, and general operating support.
Requirements: Nonprofit organizations in the greater Chicago, IL, metropolitan area and in Pennsylvania are eligible.
Restrictions: Grants are not made to individuals.
Geographic Focus: Illinois, Pennsylvania
Contact: M. Catherine Ryan, c/o Bank of America, (312) 828-1785
Sponsor: Frank E. Payne and Seba B. Payne Foundation
231 S LaSalle Street
Chicago, IL 60697

Frank G. and Freida K. Brotz Family Foundation Grants **722**

The Foundation supports Wisconsin nonprofits of the Christian, Lutheran, and Roman Catholic faiths, including Salvation Army. Types of support include capital support and general support. Organizations eligible to receive support include colleges and universities, community service groups, hospitals, ministries, parochial schools and religious education organizations, religious welfare organizations, and youth organizations. There are no application forms or deadlines. Applicants should submit a brief letter of inquiry that contains a description of the organization, its purpose, purpose of grant, and proof of tax-exempt status.
Requirements: Grants are awarded to publicly supported, Section 170(c) IRS qualified organizations, primarily in the State of Wisconsin.
Restrictions: No grants are awarded to individuals or organizations that require expenditure responsibility under Treasury Regulations.
Geographic Focus: Wisconsin
Contact: Stuart W. Brotz, Grants Committee Contact; (920) 458-2121; (920) 458-1923
Sponsor: Frank G. and Freida K. Brotz Family Foundation
3518 Lakeshore Road, P.O. Box 551
Sheboygan, WI 53082-0551

Frank S. Flowers Foundation Grants **723**

The Frank S. Flowers Foundation primarily serves the Gloucester County, New Jersey area. The Foundation's area of interest include: Education—supporting public high schools of Gloucester County, New Jersey, to provide scholarships for college or graduate study, vocational or technical training; Youth—supporting chapters or councils or branches of Y.M.C.A. and Boys Scouts of America located in Gloucester and/or Salem Counties, grants are also considered for organizations having branches or offices in Gloucester County, New Jersey which treat and educate children with special needs; Health-Related—support to non-profit Gloucester County hospitals; Religious organizations—support to churches in the boroughs of Paulsboro and Wenonah, New Jersey. The Foundation also has a specific interest in The Shriner's Hospital for Crippled Children in Philadelphia, Pennsylvania and the Masonic Home Charity Foundation of New Jersey. Grants range from $1,000 - $8,000. Application deadline date is February 15th, application available online. Requestors will receive a letter acknowledging the receipt of their request.
Requirements: Qualifying tax-exempt 501(c)3 organizations are eligible for grants if they meet the purpose of the foundation. Proposals should be submitted in the following format: completed Common Grant Application Form; an original Proposal Statement*; an audited financial report and a current year operating budget; a copy of your official IRS Letter with your tax determination; a listing of your Board of Directors. *Proposal Statement should answer these questions: what are the objectives and expected outcomes of this program/project/request; what strategies will be used to accomplish your objective; what is the timeline for completion; if this is part of an on-going program, how long has it been in operation; what criteria will you use to determine your success; if the request is not fully funded, what other sources can you engage. A Proposal budget should be included if this is for a specific program within your annual budget. Please describe any collaborative ventures.
Restrictions: Grants are not made for political purpose, nor to organizations which discriminate on the basis of race, ethnic origin, sexual or religious preference, age or gender.
Geographic Focus: New Jersey, Pennsylvania
Date(s) Application is Due: Feb 15
Amount: 1,000 - 8,000 USD
Samples: Holy Trinity Episcopal Church, Parking Lot Rehabilitation—$8,000; Deptford Township High School, $3,000—scholarships; Ronald McDonald House of Southern New Jersey, $5,000—general operations support.
Contact: Gale Y. Sykes, Trustee c/o Wells Fargo Bank; (908) 598-3576; grantinquiries2@wachovia.com
Internet: https://www.wachovia.com/foundation/v/index.jsp?vgnextoid=68d78689fb0aa110VgnVCM1000004b0d1872RCRD&vgnextfmt=default
Sponsor: Frank S. Flowers Foundation
190 River Road
Summit, NJ 07901

Frank Stanley Beveridge Foundation Grants **724**

The foundation welcomes proposals in the areas of: animal care; arts, culture and humanities; civil rights, social action, advocacy; education; employment/jobs; environmental quality, protection and beautification; food, nutrition and agriculture; health; housing; human services; medical research; mental health; philanthropy; safety; recreation; religion; science; social services; and youth development. The board meets in October and April to consider requests. Multiyear grants are rare. Contact the foundation via the website only. No phone or written inquiries will be accepted.
Requirements: Applicants must be 501(c)3 nonprofit organizations or foundations in Massachusetts's Hampden and Hampshire Counties.
Restrictions: The Foundation prefers not to support: awards or prizes; commissioning of new artistic work; conferences/seminars; curriculum development; debt reduction; employee matching gifts; employee-related scholarships; endowment funds; exhibitions; faculty/staff development; fellowship funds; fellowships to individuals; film/video/radio production; foundation administered programs; general operating support; grants to individuals; income development; internship funds; management development; performance/production costs; professorships; program-related investment/loans; publications; scholarships to individuals; student aid; technical assistance.
Geographic Focus: Massachusetts
Date(s) Application is Due: Feb 1; Aug 1
Amount: 50,000 USD
Contact: Philip Caswell, President; (800) 229-9667; (561) 748-0644; administrator@beveridge.org or caswell@beveridge.org
Internet: http://www.beveridge.org/
Sponsor: Frank Stanley Beveridge Foundation
1340 U.S. Highway 1, Suite 102
Jupiter, FL 33469

Fraser-Parker Foundation Grants 725

The foundation awards general operating grants in its areas of interest, including Christian religion organizations, education and higher education, and hospitals. There are no application forms.

Geographic Focus: Georgia
Date(s) Application is Due: Apr 15; Oct 15
Amount: 5,000 - 50,000 USD
Contact: John Stephenson, Executive Director; (404) 658-9066
Sponsor: Fraser-Parker Foundation
50 Hurt Plaza, Suite 850
Atlanta, GA 30303

Fred C. and Katherine B. Andersen Foundation Grants 726

Fred C. and Katherine B. Andersen Foundation, formerly known as the Andersen Foundation gives on a national basis for higher education. The foundation provides funds locally in Minnesota and western Wisconsin for all areas of interest, which include: arts; health care; higher education; hospitals; and youth development. Funding is available in the forms of: capital campaigns; general/operating support and; program development.

Requirements: 501(c)3 tax-exempt organizations are eligible. Giving is on a national basis although preference is given to requests from Minnesota.
Restrictions: The foundation does not make grants to institutions that receive federal funding.
Geographic Focus: All U.S. States
Date(s) Application is Due: Mar 18; Jul 22; Oct 21
Amount: 5,000 - 12,000,000 USD
Samples: Nichols College, Dudley Hall, Dudley, MA, $250,000—unrestricted, general grant (2008); Bayport Public Library Foundation, Bayport, MN, $36,000—program support grant (2008).
Contact: Mary Gillstrom, Director; (651) 264-5150
Sponsor: Fred C. and Katherine B. Andersen Foundation
P.O. Box 8000
Bayport, MN 55003-0080

Fred C. and Mary R. Koch Foundation Grants 727

The foundation mainly supports organizations in its geographic area of interest. Particular interest is given to education (programs that promote the application of economic and scientific principles to problem-solving); environmental stewardship (projects that apply innovative solutions to solve local environmental problems); and human services (projects that promote self-sufficiency, individual responsibility, tolerance, and respect for others) The foundation prefers to support specific projects with clearly defined parameters and measurable results rather than fund-raising events, endowments, capital campaigns, or general operating support.

Requirements: The foundation supports nonprofit, tax-exempt organizations and institutions in communities that have Koch employees and facilities: Kansas, Minnesota, Texas, Oklahoma, Louisiana, and Alberta, Canada.
Restrictions: Grants are not made to individuals.
Geographic Focus: All U.S. States, Canada
Samples: Exploration Place (Wichita, KS)—for interactive, family-oriented educational programs for visitors to this science center, children's museum, and park, $500,000.
Contact: Susan Addington, Community Affairs Manager; (316) 828-2646; philanthropy@kochind.com
Internet: http://www.kochind.com/community/default.asp
Sponsor: Fred C. and Mary R. Koch Foundation
4111 E 37th Street N
Wichita, KS 67220

Freddie Mac Foundation Grants 728

The Foundation focus is on children whose families have limited resources and who are vulnerable to poor outcomes. The Foundation emphasizes the integration of services that focus on family strengthening and youth development in order to maximize the benefit to children and their families. Grants will be made for direct service projects, general operating support, capacity building, public awareness, planning and capital projects. The following funding priorities will be considered: the early years; elementary school years; junior high and high school years; children and families in crisis; and public awareness education. Proposals must be submitted online.

Requirements: Eligible organizations must be tax exempt under IRS code 501(c)3 and defined as a public charity. The Foundation's grantmaking program services the following metropolitan Washington, DC areas: District of Columbia; Virginia - the counties of Arlington, Fairfax, Loudoun and Prince William and the cities of Alexandria, Falls Church, Manassas Park, and Leesburg; Maryland - the counties of Charles, Frederick, Howard, Montgomery, and Prince George's.
Restrictions: The Foundation will not fund organizations that discriminate in the provision of services or in employment practices based on race, color, religion, ethnicity, sex, age, national origin, disability, sexual orientation, marital status, and any other characteristics protected by applicable law. Unless approved by the board, the Foundation does not fund: individuals; training in/promotion of religious doctrine; incurring a debt liability; endowment campaigns.
Geographic Focus: District of Columbia, Maryland, Virginia
Date(s) Application is Due: Sep 9
Amount: 5,000 - 50,000 USD
Samples: Distributed among nonprofit organizations to aid support-relief efforts following Hurricane Katrina, $10 million; CrossChildren's Law Ctr (Washington, DC)—to support the caregivers of children in the Washington, DC, foster-care system who are seeking adoption and guardianship, $90,000; Ctr for Multicultural Human Services (Falls Church, VA)—to acquire five transitional-housing units that will provide 16 homeless families in northern Virginia, many of whom are recent immigrants, with safe housing and intensive support services, $550,000; American National Red Cross (Washington, DC)—to assist tsunami-relief efforts, $150,000.
Contact: Ralph F. Boyd, President and CEO; (703) 918-8888; freddie_mac_foundation@freddiemac.com
Internet: http://www.freddiemacfoundation.org
Sponsor: Freddie Mac Foundation
8250 Jones Branch Drive, MS A40
McLean, VA 22102-3110

Frederick S. Upton Foundation Grants 729

The foundation awards grants, primarily in southwestern Michigan. Areas of interest include arts, child welfare, education, youth programs, and religion. Types of support include annual campaigns building construction/renovation, capital campaigns, general operating support, and special projects. The application deadline is in mid-March, and there are no specific application forms.

Geographic Focus: Michigan
Date(s) Application is Due: Mar 15; Jun 15; Oct 15
Contact: Stephen E. Upton, President; (312) 732-4260; (269) 982-0323; fsuptonfdn@opexonline.com or uptonfoundation@comcast.net
Sponsor: Frederick S. Upton Foundation
100 Ridgeway Street
Street Joseph, MI 49085

Fred Meyer Foundation Grants 730

The Foundation is dedicated to enriching the quality of life in the communities where stores operate and where customers and associates live and work. The Foundation focuses grants on organizations that work toward youth development or hunger reduction. Grant recipients must be invited to apply by a Fred Meyer associate.

Requirements: Grants will be awarded to nonprofits in communities served by Fred Meyer Stores.
Restrictions: The Foundation does not accept unsolicited letters of inquiry.
Geographic Focus: Alaska, Idaho, Oregon, Washington
Samples: Perseverance Theater (Juneau, AK)—for a series of arts and cultural presentations for school-age children, $10,500; Community Transitional School (Portland, OR)—to purchase a school bus for this private alternative school serving homeless preschool through eighth-grade students in the Portland area, $25,000; Share Our Strength's Portland Operation Frontline (Portland, OR)—for a six-week class in which volunteer chefs teach basic cooking, food budgeting, and nutritional skills to low-income teenage parents, $15,000.
Contact: Community Affairs Manager; (503) 232-8844; foundation@fredmeyer.com
Internet: http://www.thekrogerco.com/corpnews/corpnewsinfo_charitablegiving_fredmeyer.htm
Sponsor: Fred Meyer Foundation
3800 SE 22nd Avenue
Portland, OR 97202

Freeman Foundation Grants 731

The foundation's major objectives include strengthening the bonds between the United States and the Far East; preservation and protection of the forests, lands,

and natural resources of the United States and land conservation and farmland preservation in Vermont; and development of a vibrant, international, free enterprise system. Giving primarily in VT for conservation and environment grants; Asian studies grants are awarded nationally. Grants are awarded four times annually.
Restrictions: Grants are not made to individuals.
Geographic Focus: All U.S. States
Samples: Johns Hopkins U (MD)—for the Freeman Southeast Asia Fellowships at the Paul H. Nitze School of Advanced International Studies, $1 million; Institute of International Education (New York, NY)—to rebuild schools devastated by the December tsunamis and provide educational resources to students in Indonesia and Thailand, $1.75 million.
Contact: George S. Tsandikos, (212) 649-5853; gtsandikos@rockco.com
Sponsor: Freeman Foundation
30 Rockefeller Plaza
New York, NY 10012

Fremont Area Community Foundation Amazing X Grants 732
The Amazing X Charitable Trust, a supporting organizaton of the Fremont Area Community Foundation (FACF), was established in the late 1970s by members of the Gerber family to benefit people with disabilites and address general charitable needs in Newaygo County, Michigan. Grant requests are accepted for: projects or programs that serve people with disabilities; projects or programs that address general charitable needs. Preferred programs are innovative, collaborative, and have a significant impact on the residents of Newaygo County. Grants range from $1,000 - $60,000 range. Grant applications are due each year by July 15.
Requirements: Michigan 501(c)3 organizations located in or supporting Newaygo County are eligible for funding. When submitting your proposal, include your organizations: mission, history, description of current programs, activities, and accomplishments; purpose of the grant (describe in detail and include supporting evidence); grant proposal budget form/narrative (form available at the Foundation's website). The following list of attachments must also be included: a copy of the current IRS 501(c)3 determination letter; roster of current governing board, including addresses and affiliations; finances: organization's current annual operating budget, including all expenses and revenues, audited financial statement (most recently completed), IRS Form 990 (most recently filed), annual report, if available; resumes and job descriptions of the key project personnel; organizational chart; letters of support (up to five).
Restrictions: The foundation typically does not fund requests for projects that have previously been denied, grants to individuals, programs that advocate specific religions, or services which are government or school obligations.
Geographic Focus: Michigan
Date(s) Application is Due: Jul 15
Amount: 1,000 - 60,000 USD
Samples: Newaygo County Commission on Aging, $32,000—Alzheimer Congregate Respite program (2008); Grant Area District Library, $6,500—circulating materials for people with disabilities (2008); Pioneer Resources, $2,500—Pioneer Trails Day Camp for Newaygo County youth (2008).
Contact: Jeff Jahr, Senior Program Officer; (231) 924-5350; (231) 924-5391; jjahr@tfacf.org
Internet: http://www.tfaf.org/grants/amazingx.html
Sponsor: Fremont Area Community Foundation
P.O. Box B
Fremont, MI 49412

Fremont Area Community Foundation Elderly Needs Grants 733
The Foundation is focusing its grantmaking resources primarily on expanding opportunities that enhance the well being of residents from the Newaygo County, Michigan area. The purpose of the Elderly Needs Fund is to make grants to support health and enrich aging for the elderly of Newaygo County. The strategies of the Elderly Needs Fund include: promote the physical health of the elderly; promote the mental/emotional well being of the elderly and their caregivers; promote the social enrichment and prevent the social isolation of the elderly; promote the provision of basic human services for the elderly. Application deadlines are February 15 and October 15 each year.
Requirements: Michigan 501(c)3 organizations located in or supporting Newaygo County are eligible for funding. When submitting your proposal, include your organizations: mission, history, description of current programs, activities, and accomplishments; purpose of the grant (describe in detail and include supporting evidence); grant proposal budget form/narrative (form available at the Foundation's website). The following list of attachments must also be included: a copy of the current IRS 501(c)3 determination letter; roster of current governing board, including addresses and affiliations; finances: organization's current annual operating budget, including all expenses and revenues, audited financial statement (most recently completed), IRS Form 990 (most recently filed), annual report, if available; resumes and job descriptions of the key project personnel; organizational chart; letters of support (up to five).
Geographic Focus: Michigan
Date(s) Application is Due: Feb 15; Oct 15
Amount: 1,000 - 200,000 USD
Samples: Newaygo County MSU Extension, $10,830—Senior Project Fresh food vouchers for use at area farmer's markets (2008); Newaygo County Commission on Aging, $281,000—senior programs (2008); Baldwin Family Health Care, $6,200—Adult Screening and Prevention Program (ASAP) (2008).
Contact: Jeff Jahr, Senior Program Officer; (231) 924-5350; (231) 924-5391; jjahr@tfacf.org
Internet: http://www.tfaf.org/grants/elderlyneeds.html
Sponsor: Fremont Area Community Foundation
P.O. Box B
Fremont, MI 49412

Fremont Area Community Foundation Grants 734
The Foundation is focusing its grantmaking resources primarily on expanding opportunities that enhance the well being of children, youth and families in Newaygo County. The Foundation's areas of interest include: arts and culture, community development, education, the environment, and human services. Type of support offered include: building/renovation; capital campaigns; conferences/seminars; consulting services; continuing support; curriculum development; emergency funds; employee matching gifts; endowments; equipment; general/operating support; management development/capacity building; matching/challenge support; program-related investments/loans; program development; program evaluation; scholarship funds; scholarships-to individuals; seed money; technical assistance. Grant applications have a deadline date of February 15, May 15 and, September 15. Scholarship applications are due on March 15th.
Requirements: Michigan 501(c)3 organizations located in or supporting Newaygo County are eligible for funding. When submitting your proposal, include your organizations: mission, history, description of current programs, activities, and accomplishments; purpose of the grant (describe in detail and include supporting evidence); grant proposal budget form/narrative (form available at the Foundation's website). The following list of attachments must also be included: a copy of the current IRS 501(c)3 determination letter; roster of current governing board, including addresses and affiliations; finances: organization's current annual operating budget, including all expenses and revenues, audited financial statement (most recently completed), IRS Form 990 (most recently filed), annual report, if available; resumes and job descriptions of the key project personnel; organizational chart; letters of support (up to five).
Restrictions: The foundation typically does not fund requests for projects that have previously been denied, grants to individuals, programs that advocate specific religions, or services which are government or school obligations.
Geographic Focus: Michigan
Date(s) Application is Due: Feb 15; Mar 15; May 15; Sep 15
Samples: Grant Public Schools, Grant, MI, $13,750—for fitness equipment for student and community use (2008); Newaygo County Regional Educational Service Agency, Fremont, MI, $305,000—for Newaygo County Parents as Teachers Plus program (2008); Newaygo County Community Services, Fremont, MI, $566,130—for general operating and program support (2008).
Contact: Jeff Jahr, Senior Program Officer; (231) 924-5350; (231) 924-5391; jjahr@tfacf.org
Internet: http://www.tfaf.org/grants.html
Sponsor: Fremont Area Community Foundation
P.O. Box B
Fremont, MI 49412

Fremont Area Community Foundation Ice Mountain Environmental Stewardship Fund (IMESF) Grants 735
In 2002, through the generosity of Great Spring Waters of America, Inc., the Ice Mountain Environmental Stewardship Fund (IMESF) was established at the Fremont Area Community Foundation (FACF). The FACF serves the community of Newaygo County, Michigan. Grants from the IMESF will be

made for the following purpose: to support the waters and water-dependent natural resources of the Muskegon River Watershed by supporting conservation, enhancement, and restoration projects that will result in improvements to the physical, chemical, and biological integrity of the watershed. Proposals will be accepted for projects located in any county within the Muskegon River Watershed. Up to $50,000 is available annually for projects, typical grants are in the $5,000 to $20,000 range. Application deadline date is August 1st.
Requirements: Michigan 501(c)3 organizations located in any county within the Muskegon River Watershed are eligible to apply. When submitting your proposal, include your organizations: mission, history, description of current programs, activities, and accomplishments; purpose of the grant (describe in detail and include supporting evidence); grant proposal budget form/narrative (form available at the Foundation's website). The following list of attachments must also be included: a copy of the current IRS 501(c)3 determination letter; roster of current governing board, including addresses and affiliations; finances: organization's current annual operating budget, including all expenses and revenues, audited financial statement (most recently completed), IRS Form 990 (most recently filed), annual report, if available; resumes and job descriptions of the key project personnel; organizational chart; letters of support (up to five).
Restrictions: Projects or programs that are primarily educational or recreational in nature or designed to increase or improve river access will NOT be considered.
Geographic Focus: Michigan
Date(s) Application is Due: Aug 1
Amount: 5,000 - 50,000 USD
Contact: Jeff Jahr, Senior Program Officer; (231) 924-5350; (231) 924-5391; jjahr@tfacf.org
Internet: http://www.tfaf.org/grants/icemountain.html
Sponsor: Fremont Area Community Foundation
P.O. Box B
Fremont, MI 49412

Fremont Area Community Foundation Summer Youth Grants 736

The Summer Youth Initiative is a special grantmaking program of the Fremont Area Community Foundation which awards grants of up to $8,000 to provide summer programs for Michigan youth residing in Newaygo County. Priority will be given to Summer Youth Initiative programs that: involve a minimum of ten youth; last for a minimum of one week; provide education and recreation; be open and accessible to all interested youth; enhance participants' self-esteem; challenge participants' creativity; involve participants in some physical exercise and teach healthy lifestyle. Grant application and proper materials are due by February 15 each year.
Requirements: Organizations applying for a Summer Youth Initiative grant must: be designated as a 501(c)3 non-profit organization or utilize a 501(c)3 organization as a fiscal sponsor; conduct programs to benefit Newaygo County residents; be experienced youth program providers; have oversight of the program by personnel with appropriate credentials; have appropriate youth/staff ratio; provide a positive and safe environment; provide nutritious snack/meal if time warrants; not discriminate on the basis of race, sex, or religious preference; include a plan for evaluation with clearly stated goals and objectives; partner with colleagues and collaborate with other organizations when possible to avoid duplication of services and overlapping of projects. When submitting your proposal, include your organizations: mission, history, description of current programs, activities, and accomplishments; purpose of the grant (describe in detail and include supporting evidence); grant proposal budget form/narrative (form available at the Foundation's website). The following list of attachments must also be included: a copy of the current IRS 501(c)3 determination letter; roster of current governing board, including addresses and affiliations; finances: organization's current annual operating budget, including all expenses and revenues, audited financial statement (most recently completed), IRS Form 990 (most recently filed), annual report, if available; resumes and job descriptions of the key project personnel; organizational chart; letters of support (up to five).
Restrictions: Fremont Area Community Foundation will not fund: t-shirts; vacation bible schools; camps whose purpose is primarily athletics; traditional or mandated summer school.
Geographic Focus: Michigan
Date(s) Application is Due: Feb 15
Amount: 8,000 USD
Contact: Jeff Jahr, Senior Program Officer; (231) 924-5350; (231) 924-5391; jjahr@tfacf.org
Internet: http://www.tfaf.org/grants/summeryouth.html
Sponsor: Fremont Area Community Foundation
P.O. Box B
Fremont, MI 49412

Friedman Family Foundation Grants 737

The purpose of the family foundation is to fund programs that attempt to end the cycle of poverty. To this end, programs are sought that provide tools, support, and opportunity to people in need to overcome the root causes of their poverty, and in which the people to be helped are part of the design and decision making of the organization or project. Priority is given to organizations in the nine counties of the San Francisco Bay area of California. Occasionally projects are considered beyond this region if they offer lessons or benefits for the Bay area. Application deadlines vary; call for dates and application forms.
Requirements: California 501(c)3 nonprofit organizations or public entities with a board or advisory group that is reflective of the population or community being served are eligible.
Restrictions: The foundation generally does not fund films, videos, conferences, seminars, capital, scholarships, individuals, research, or special or fund-raising events.
Geographic Focus: California
Amount: 1,000 - 15,000 USD
Samples: Shefa Fund (Wyndmoor, PA)—to leverage investments from Jewish institutions and individuals for use by community development financial institutions, $100,000; Juma Ventures (San Francisco, CA)—for general support, $10,000.
Contact: Lisa Kawahara, Grants Administrator; (650) 342-8750; (650) 342-8750
Internet: http://www.friedmanfamilyfoundation.org
Sponsor: Friedman Family Foundation
204 E 2nd Avenue, PMB 719
San Mateo, CA 94401

Frist Foundation Grants 738

The foundation supports a variety of organizations in the fields of health, human services, civic affairs, education, and the arts. Grants support building the capacity of nonprofit organizations by strengthening their management structure and systems. Types of support include capital, management, operating, project, and technology grants. Deadline listed is for technology grants.
Requirements: 501(c)3 nonprofits in Davidson County, TN, area may apply.
Restrictions: The foundation does not support: individuals or their projects, private foundations, political activities, or advertising or sponsorships. The foundation does not ordinarily support: projects, programs, or organizations that serve a limited audience or a relatively small number of people; organizations during their first three years of operation; disease-specific organizations seeking support for national projects and programs; biomedical or clinical research; hospitals; organizations whose principal impact is outside of Middle Tennessee; endowments; social events or similar fund-raising activities; or religious organizations for religious purposes.
Geographic Focus: Tennessee
Date(s) Application is Due: Apr 1
Amount: 500 - 10,000 USD
Samples: Domestic Violence Intervention Ctr (TN)—to translate domestic violence educational materials into Spanish, $3000; Mockingbird Theatre (TN)—for general support, $5000; Metropolitan Nashville Public Schools (TN)—to establish a pilot reading program at Haywood Elementary School, $65,000; Faith Family Medical Clinic of Nashville (TN)—to help establish a medical clinic for low-income working people, $105,000.
Contact: Peter Bird, (615) 292-3868; (615) 292-5843; askfrist@fristfoundation.org
Internet: http://www.fristfoundation.org/grants/general.asp
Sponsor: Frist Foundation
3100 W End Avenue, Suite 1200
Nashville, TN 37203

Frost Foundation Grants 739

The foundation awards grants in the areas of human service needs, environmental programs, and education programs in New Mexico and Louisiana. Preference will be given to programs that have potential for wider service or educational exposure than an individual community. The foundation encourages collaborations, mergers, and the formation of alliances among agencies within the community to reduce duplication of effort and to promote

a maximum effective use of funds. Applicants are urged to call the foundation for guidelines before sending a proposal. Application information is available online.
Requirements: 501(c)3 nonprofits in Louisiana and New Mexico are eligible.
Geographic Focus: Louisiana, New Mexico
Date(s) Application is Due: Jun 1; Dec 1
Samples: Santa Fe Children's Museum, Santa Fe, New Mexico, $200,000 (2008); Share Your Care Adult Day Services, Albuquerque, New Mexico, $4,500 (2008); Lafayette Community Health Care Clinic, Lafayette, Louisiana, $15,000 (2008).
Contact: Mary Amelia Whited-Howell, President; (505) 986-0208; info@frostfound.org
Internet: http://www.frostfound.org
Sponsor: Frost Foundation
511 Armijo, Suite A
Santa Fe, NM 87501

Fuller E. Callaway Foundation Grants **740**

The foundation awards grants to nonprofit organizations and individuals in LaGrange and Troup County, GA. Grants are awarded in the areas of religion, higher and other education, social services, youth, and health. Types of support include general operating budgets, annual campaigns, building funds, equipment, matching funds, and student aid. Letters of application from organizations are accepted and have deadlines at the end of December, March, June, and September. Application forms are required for the scholarship program. Scholarship deadlines are February 15 and June 30 for law school scholarships. The board meets in January, April, July, and October to consider scholarship requests.
Requirements: Nonprofit organizations and individuals in LaGrange and Troup County, GA, are eligible for support.
Geographic Focus: Georgia
Amount: 500 - 25,000 USD
Contact: H. Speer Burdette, President; (706) 884-7348; (706) 884-0201; hsburdette@callaway-foundation.org
Sponsor: Fuller E. Callaway Foundation
P.O. Box 790
LaGrange, GA 30241

Fuller Foundation Grants **741**

The Fuller Foundation is a family foundation, inspired by its forward-thinking founder, Alvan T. Fuller. It's purpose is to support non-profit agencies which improve the quality of life for people, animals and the environment. The Foundation also funds the Fuller Foundation of New Hampshire which supports horticultural and educational programs for the public at Fuller Gardens. The geographic focus area is predominately the Boston area and the immediate seacoast area of New Hampshire. Through these grants the foundation strives to effect change, make an impact on the community, and inspire good deeds. Application information is available online. Faxed or emailed grant requests will not be accepted.
Requirements: Nonprofits in the Boston, MA, area and the immediate seacoast region of New Hampshire are eligible.
Restrictions: Funding is not available for: capital projects (unless in the opinion of the Trustees, the Foundation gift will have significant impact); individuals; or multi-year grants. Incomplete grants are not considered.
Geographic Focus: Massachusetts, New Hampshire
Date(s) Application is Due: Jan 15; Jun 15
Amount: 3,500 - 7,500 USD
Samples: Nature Connection, Concord, MA, $3,000—for education and outreach programs (2008); Dolphin Research Center, Grassy Key, FL, $10,000—for Dolphin Child Pathway programs (2008); Womens Crisis Center of Greater Newburyport, Newburyport, MA, $5,000—for Children Overcoming Violence Program (2008).
Contact: John Bottomley, Executive Director; (603) 964-6998; (603) 964-8901; atfuller@aol.com
Internet: http://www.fullerfoundation.org/FullerFoundation/HomePage.cfm?page=appprocedures
Sponsor: Fuller Foundation
P.O. Box 479
Rye Beach, NH 03871

Fund for New Jersey Grants **742**

Grants support nonprofit organizations in New Jersey or organizations that benefit the state, with particular attention given to projects seeking to affect public policy. Although a few grants are provided for local activities, direct services, and general operating support, such proposals are considered usually at the fund's invitation. Grant applicants are asked to submit a single-page proposal cover sheet containing the following information: organization and contact person, summary of request, amount requested, and problem or need addressed by proposed activity. All proposals must be accompanied by a copy of the IRS tax-exemption letter, names and affiliations of the board of directors, and a budget. The board normally meets in March, June, September, and December to consider proposals.
Requirements: 501(c)3 tax-exempt organizations are eligible. Proposals are not accepted via email.
Restrictions: The fund does not accept proposals for support of individuals nor for capital projects such as acquisition, renovation, or equipment. The fund is unable to support day care centers, drug treatment programs, arts programs, health care delivery, or scholarships.
Geographic Focus: New Jersey
Amount: Up to 33,000,000 USD
Samples: CityWorks (Trenton, NJ)—for its efforts to develop commercial real-estate projects in selected urban neighborhoods, $100,000; New Jersey Community Capital (Trenton, NJ)—for a campaign intended to attract investments for community- and economic-development projects in low-income communities, $85,000; Pinelands Preservation Alliance (Southampton, NJ)—for advocacy efforts designed to help protect New Jersey's Pinelands region, $30,000; New Jersey Immigration Policy Network (Newark, NJ)—to support a coalition of civil-rights, community, immigrant, and labor groups that promote fair policies for recent immigrants, $100,000.
Contact: Mark Murphy, Executive Director; (732) 220-8656; (732) 220-8654; info@fundfornj.org
Internet: http://www.fundfornj.org/app_guide.html
Sponsor: Fund for New Jersey
94 Church Street, Suite 303
New Brunswick, NJ 08901

Fund for Santa Barbara Grants **743**

The fund gives preference to projects working to address the root causes of social, economic, and environmental problems. Types of support include seed grants to new grassroots projects, general support, or project grants to small organizations, and grants to larger, more established organizations only for specific targeted purposes. Affirmative action considerations are among the criteria used in all funding decisions.
Requirements: Applications are invited from organizations that are working against discrimination based on race, sex/gender, age, religion, economic status, sexual orientation, physical/mental ability, ethnicity, language, or immigration status; struggling for the rights of workers; promoting self-determination in low-income and disenfranchised communities; promoting international peace and organizing locally for a just foreign policy; working on improving the environment, especially organizing a constituency usually without access or input to environmental concerns; and operating in a democratic manner, responsive to and directed by the constituency being served.
Restrictions: Grants do not support projects involved in electoral campaigns on behalf of candidates or parties; private (vs. public) interests; direct labor organizing; projects located outside of Santa Barbara County; projects providing direct services without a social change component; or direct support to individuals, capital ventures, or building improvements.
Geographic Focus: California
Date(s) Application is Due: Mar 12; Sep 9
Amount: Up to 10,000 USD
Samples: Committee for Social Justice (CA)—to pay for a Spanish-speaking coordinator to extend their reach, and run workshops and clinics, $3750; Men Against Rape (CA)—for office supplies, training materials, conference attendance, poster printing, and school outreach expenses, $4000; Clergy United for Equality of Homosexuals (CA)—for seminars and workshops on biblical oppression and its relief, including models for change for pastors and churches, $3750.
Contact: Fund Administrator; (805) 962-9164; (805) 965-0217; email@fundforsantabarbara.org
Internet: http://www.fundforsantabarbara.org/apply/apply.htm
Sponsor: Fund for Santa Barbara
924 Anacapa Street, Suite 4H
Santa Barbara, CA 93101-2192

Fund for the City of New York Grants 744

The fund is dedicated to improving the quality of life in the city by supporting efforts to increase the efficiency and effectiveness of government agencies and the nonprofit organizations that are instrumental in promoting a healthy civic environment. The fund's programs concentrate on children and youth and community development and the urban environment. The grants provide project or general support for nonprofit organizations, including a number of watchdog and advocacy organizations, and project support for special initiatives of government agencies. Short-term consultancy grants also are awarded to enable organizations to hire the right person at the right time to help projects through difficult periods. Between 40 and 50 grants are made each year. The fund's board of directors meets three times a year. Proposals must be received by April 15 to be considered for the spring cycle and August 15 to be considered for the fall cycle.
Requirements: Individuals, academic studies, scholarships, endowments and capital campaigns are not eligible.
Restrictions: The fund cannot make grants to individuals, to support endowment and capital campaigns, nor to support academic studies.
Geographic Focus: New York
Date(s) Application is Due: Apr 15; Aug 15; Dec 15
Contact: Safiya McCrea, Project Assistant; (212) 925-6675; smcrea@fcny.org
Internet: http://www.fcny.org/portal.php/support/grants
Sponsor: Fund for the City of New York
121 Avenue of the Americas, 6th Floor
New York, NY 10013

G. Harold and Leila Y. Mathers Charitable Foundation Grants 745

The foundation awards grants to support research in the basic life sciences. Requests for general operating support also will be considered. There are no application forms or deadlines. The board meets two or three times each year.
Requirements: U.S. research organizations are eligible.
Geographic Focus: All U.S. States
Amount: 10,000 - 200,000 USD
Samples: Fox Chase Cancer Ctr (Philadelphia, PA)—for genetic research, $660,000 over three years.
Contact: James Handelman, Executive Director; (914) 242-0465; bcheikin@mathersfoundation.org
Internet: http://www.mathersfoundation.org
Sponsor: G. Harold and Leila Y. Mathers Charitable Foundation
118 N Bedford Road, Suite 203
Mount Kisco, NY 10549-2555

G.N. Wilcox Trust Grants 746

The trust provides partial support to programs and projects of tax-exempt, public charities in Hawaii to improve the quality of life in the state, particularly the island of Kauai. Grants of one year's duration are awarded in categories of interest to the trust, including education, literacy programs and adult basic education, health, Protestant religion, delinquency and crime prevention, social services, youth services, and culture and the performing arts. Types of support include general operating grants, capital grants, equipment acquisition, seed grants, scholarship funds, and challenge/matching grants. Deadlines dates for general grants are: January 1; April 1; July 1; October 1. The deadline date for scholarships is February 15th.
Requirements: Giving is limited to Hawaii, with emphasis on the island of Kauai. To begin application process, contact Paula Boyce for additional guidelines.
Restrictions: Grants are not awarded to support government agencies (or organizations substantially supported by government funds), individuals, or for endowment funds, research, deficit financing, or student aid in scholarships or loans.
Geographic Focus: Hawaii
Date(s) Application is Due: Jan 1; Feb 15; Apr 1; Jul 1; Oct 1
Samples: Save our Seas—to support scholarships for youth to participate in the Second Annual Clean Oceans Conference, $2,954; Church of the Crossroads—to support the capital campaigns for renovations, $10,000; Hawaii Public Radio—to support the membership challenge grant, $3,000.
Contact: Paula Boyce, c/o Bank of Hawaii; (808) 538-4944; (808) 538-4647; pboyce@boh.com or emoniz@boh.com
Sponsor: G.N. Wilcox Trust
Bank of Hawai'i, Foundation Administration Department 758
Honolulu, HI 96802-3170

Gallo Foundation Grants 747

The foundation primarily supports nonprofits in Modesto, CA, in its areas of interest, including higher and other education, disabled, community funds, social services, and religion. Types of support include employee matching gifts and general operating budgets. There are no application deadlines or forms.
Requirements: Northern California nonprofits may submit grant requests.
Geographic Focus: California
Amount: 250 - 891,500 USD
Contact: Ronald Emerzian, (209) 341-3141
Sponsor: Gallo Foundation
P.O. Box 1130
Modesto, CA 95353

Gamble Foundation Grants 748

Founded in 1968, The Gamble Foundation is primarily interested in supporting organizations that serve disadvantaged children and youth in San Francisco, Marin and Napa counties. Within the field of youth development, the Foundation focuses on literacy, educational and personal enrichment programs designed to open doors of opportunity for at-risk youth in order to help them succeed in school and become productive, self-sufficient members of society. The Foundation is particularly interested in agricultural/environmental education, financial & computer literacy, vocational training and programs that prevent substance abuse and teen violence. To a lesser degree, the Foundation supports environmental organizations that focus on land preservation and sustainability, animal welfare and management, and pollution control. The foundation is interested in promoting green concepts that increase awareness of science based solutions that help reduce consumption of finite resources. The Foundation prefers to fund specific projects rather than annual appeals. Grants range from $5,000 to $20,000.
Requirements: Northern California 501(c)3 nonprofit organizations, with an emphasis on San Francisco, Marin, and Napa Counties, are eligible to apply. The Board meets in the spring each year and makes grants in late summer. The Foundation will accept proposals for the April meeting from January 25 - February 10. The Foundation encourages submission of proposals and attachments by email. For those submitting by email, the proposal and required attachments should be emailed in PDF format only. Send your proposals to Fiona Barrett at fbarrett@pfs-llc.net. If you do not receive an email within 24 hours confirming that your proposal has been received, please contact Fiona at (415) 561-6540, ext. 221. The Foundation will also accept a proposal submitted by mail as long as it is postmarked on or before February 10th. Proposals must include the following in the order listed: cover letter, on organization letterhead with address and phone number, including a brief summary of the request and a list of attachments (not more than one page); proposal narrative (not to exceed 5 pages); concise description of the organization (not more than two pages) including: relevant history, mission, geography and populations served, overview of programs; description of the project (not more than three pages) including: need, purpose, goals, timeline, project budget, including secured and projected sources of funding; financial statement, including actual revenue and expenses for the organization's most recently completed fiscal year; organizational budget for the present year, detailing proposed expenditures and projected sources of funding (not more than two pages); list of major public and private funders, identifying both secured and planned for funds; list of the Board of Directors, with affiliations; copy of the agency's IRS 501(c)3 tax-exempt determination letter. When submitting proposal, clasp the proposal materials with a single binder clip; do not use staples. Do not send audio-visual materials, binders, folders, or pamphlets unless requested. Receipt of proposals will be acknowledged with a written response within a reasonable period of time. Should additional information be required, applicants will be contacted.
Restrictions: In general, the Foundation does not support medical research, individuals, endowments, or capital improvements.
Geographic Focus: California
Date(s) Application is Due: Feb 10
Amount: 5,000 - 20,000 USD
Samples: WildCare: Terwilliger Nature Education and Wildlife Rehabilitation, San Rafael, CA, $20,000—for No Child Left Indoors program, providing outdoor education for Marin and San Francisco youth (2009); Canal Alliance, San Rafael, CA, $25,000—for Youth Education and Development program, providing academic, leadership, and personal development for low-income San Rafael youth (2009); Bay Area Discovery Museum, Sausalito, CA, $25,000—for Connections program (2009).
Contact: Eric Sloan, Grants Manager; (415) 561-6540, ext. 205; (415) 561-6477; esloan@pfs-llc.net

Internet: http://www.pfs-llc.net/gamble/gamble.html
Sponsor: Gamble Foundation
1660 Bush Street, Suite 300
San Francisco, CA 94109

Gardiner Howland Shaw Foundation Grants **749**
The Foundation is committed to awarding grants that can make a real difference in the way the justice system operates. The following are funding priorities: research, analysis, and journalism, that examine important criminal and juvenile justice issues and offer ways to improve the administrations of justice in Massachusetts; initiatives that demonstrate innovative approaches to the reintegration of adult and juvenile offenders leaving correctional and detention facilities; programs that demonstrate effective inter-agency and community collaboration models for crime prevention; initiatives that address the legal, social and rehabilitative needs of juvenile and adult offenders through advocacy, public education and training. Potential applicants are encouraged to telephone the office to discuss ideas prior to submitting a proposal.
Requirements: Nonprofit Massachusetts organizations are eligible.
Restrictions: The foundation does not support capital requests, the arts, endowments, grants to individuals, or scholarships.
Geographic Focus: Massachusetts
Date(s) Application is Due: Feb 1
Amount: 15,000 - 25,000 USD
Contact: Thomas Coury, Executive Director; (781) 455-8303; (781) 433-0980; admin@shawfoundation.org
Internet: http://www.shawfoundation.org/guidelines.php
Sponsor: Gardiner Howland Shaw Foundation
355 Boylston Street
Boston, MA 02116

Gates Family Foundation Community Development & Revitalization Grants **750**
The mission of the Foundation is to invest in Colorado-based projects and organizations primarily through capital grants which have meaningful impact and enhance the quality of life for those who live, work and visit the state. Funding goals in the area of Community Development and Revitalization include: investing in organizations that have the potential to reinforce and enhance the economic vitality of a community; supporting organizations that further the broad education of the population in the maintenance of the free enterprise system; supports educational programs that effectively teach the principles of entrepreneurship and business ethics; and supporting projects that involve partnerships between public and private sector organizations that seek to improve the economic and cultural health of communities.
Requirements: The Foundation: generally makes grants only to organizations in the state of Colorado; expects strong support for the project from the community; will grant funds only to properly documented tax-exempt organizations; and generally confines its grants to campaigns for capital improvement or projects.
Restrictions: The Foundation does not: provide loans, grants, or scholarships to individuals, or loans to organizations; make grants for projects that have been completed prior to the next trustees' meeting; make grants for conferences, meetings, or studies that are not initiated by the trustees; consider more than one proposal from an organization in a calendar year; make grants to other foundations or organizations engaged in grant making; grant funds for general operating support or to retire operating debt; make grants for the purchase of vehicles or office equipment; make grants directly to individual public schools or public school districts; make grants for the construction of medical facilities or for medical research; schedule interviews with the Foundation trustees unless the trustees initiate the meeting. The Foundation will not purchase tickets for fundraising dinners, parties, benefits, balls, or other social fundraising events.
Geographic Focus: Colorado
Date(s) Application is Due: Jan 15; Apr 1; Jul 15; Oct 1
Contact: Karen White Mather, Program Officer; (303) 722-1881; (303) 316-3038; info@gatesfamilyfoundation.org
Internet: http://www.gatesfamilyfoundation.org/www/gates.php?section=grant_applications&p=funding_priorities&fp=community
Sponsor: Gates Family Foundation
3575 Cherry Creek North Drive, Suite 100
Denver, CO 80209-3600

GATX Corporation Grants **751**
Local community investment programs support organizations and projects that improve the quality of life in GATX communities across the U.S. . Each year, GATX contributes to nonprofit organizations committed to the issues surrounding culture, education, the environment, families, healthcare and social services. GATX has active community investment committees in Buffalo, Chicago, and San Francisco, which serve their respective regions as well as several other locations. Types of support include challenge grants, employee matching gifts, general operating support, project grants, and seed grants. Applications are accepted year-round. Funding decisions are made by the contributions committee, which meets quarterly in February, May, August, and November. Proposals received after these dates will be held for a subsequent meeting.
Requirements: Eligible to apply are nonprofit 501(c)3 tax-exempt organizations located in company-operating areas and that serve the economically disadvantaged.
Restrictions: Grants are not awarded to individuals, political organizations, religious organizations, private foundations, capital campaigns, endowment funds, health research, national organizations, or for fund-raisers.
Geographic Focus: Illinois
Amount: 7,000 - 80,000 USD
Samples: Suzuki-Orff School for Young Musicians (Chicago, IL)—for the Clap, Sing, and Read program, which uses music to promote reading skills among at-risk children, $15,000; Chicago Anti-Hunger Federation (Chicago, IL)—for the Oliver's Kitchen Employment Training Program, which provides culinary training to formerly homeless and low-income individuals, $20,000; National Lekotek Ctr (Evanston, IL)—to provide learning and recreational services for disabled children in Chicago's West Humboldt Park neighborhood, as well as supportive services for their parents, $19,534.
Contact: Allison Dean, Community Affairs Specialist; (312) 621-4274; (312) 621-8062; community@gatx.com
Internet: http://www.gatx.com/common/about/community/about.asp
Sponsor: GATX Corporation
500 W Monroe
Chicago, IL 60661

Gaylord and Dorothy Donnelley Foundation Grants **752**
The foundation accepts unsolicited proposals for projects under the environment/conservation and arts/culture areas of interest. Applicants must be located in the Chicago Region or the Lowcountry of South Carolina. Types of support include general operating support, program development grants, building construction/renovation, and capital campaigns. Proposals are accepted on an ongoing basis for review at board meetings in March, June and November. Applications are due three months prior to board meetings. Obtain required application forms from the office.
Requirements: IRS 501(c)3 organizations serving the Chicago region or the South Carolina low country are eligible. The Chicago region includes 13 counties in three states: Illinois—Lake, McHenry, Kane, Cook, DuPage, Kendall, Grundy, and Will; Wisconsin—Kenosha, and Walworth; and Indiana—Lake, Porter, and LaPorte. Lowcountry of South Carolina counties include Beaufort, Colleton, Charleston, Berkeley, Georgetown, Dorchester, Jasper, Horry, and Hampton.
Restrictions: The foundation usually will not support requests for individuals; endowments or capital campaigns; fund-raising events; publications, films, or videos; eradication of deficits or loans; conferences; or religious purposes.
Geographic Focus: Illinois, Indiana, South Carolina, Wisconsin
Date(s) Application is Due: Dec 2
Amount: Up to 85,000,000 USD
Samples: Hubbard Street Dance Chicago (IL)—for its audience development project, $40,000; Land Trust Alliance (Chicago, IL)—for the Northeastern Illinois Project, to increase the quality and pace of land conservation in the United States, $23,000.
Contact: Grants Manager; (312) 977-2700; (312) 977-1686; gddf@gddf.org
Internet: http://www.gddf.org/grant/process.asp
Sponsor: Gaylord and Dorothy Donnelley Foundation
35 E Wacker Drive, Suite 2600
Chicago, IL 60601-2102

Gebbie Foundation Grants **753**
The Foundation's mission is to support appropriate charitable and humanitarian programs to improve the quality of life, primarily in Chautauqua County, New York by focusing on: children, youth and education; arts; human services; and community development. The foundation's strategic focus is to rejuvenate

downtown Jamestown, New York, through economic development. Types of funding include: annual campaigns; building/renovation; capital campaigns; continuing support; endowments; equipment; general/operating support; matching/challenge support; program-related investments/loans; scholarship funds and; seed money.
Requirements: Organizations requesting funding must be approved as (or sponsored by) a 501(c)3 organization. The Board meets quarterly and proposals are accepted throughout the year. Before preparing a complete proposal, applicants are urged to submit a letter of inquiry addressed to the Executive Director. The letter should contain a descriptive title for the project, the project's intent, objectives, outcome measures, short and long term funding needs, and other relevant factual information. After reviewing the letter of inquiry, a detailed proposal may be requested. It should not be assumed that such a request is an indication of funding. The full proposal should include a detailed narrative, budgets, a board list, an IRS determination letter, other funding sources and financial documentation. In addition, the proposal should describe expected future funding sources and should indicate whether and to what extent additional funding by the Foundation will be necessary for the proposed project to be successful. The Foundation will respond to all inquiries from eligible organizations.
Restrictions: Grants are not made to individuals or sectarian or religious organizations. Because the Foundation makes annual contributions to the United Way of Southern Chautauqua County, applications for assistance from United Way-funded agencies will not be considered unless there is a strong link to the strategic focus.
Geographic Focus: New York
Amount: 1,000 - 1,000,000 USD
Samples: Jamestown Audobon Society, Jamestown, NY, $20,000—attractors grant (2008); City of Jamestown, Jamestown, NY, $188,599—economic development grant (2008); Rodger Tory Peterson Institute, Jamestown, NY, $37,500—attractors grant/loan relief (2008).
Contact: John C. Merino, Executive Director; (716) 487-1062; (716) 484-6401; jmerino@gebbie.org or info@gebbie.org
Internet: http://www.gebbie.org
Sponsor: Gebbie Foundation
111 West Second Street, Suite 1100
Jamestown, NY 14701

Genentech Corporate Charitable Contributions Grants **754**
The Foundation's primary focus areas are health science education, patient education/advocacy, and community. The Foundation supports nonprofits through its contributions in two primary ways: project-specific or general support funding to organizations whose mission aligns with the Foundation's focus areas; and sponsorships of selected events that fall into the Foundation's focus areas. Interested applicant's are encouraged to submit applications online.
Requirements: Nonprofit organizations recognized by the IRS as tax exempt, public charities, located in the United States are eligible to apply. Eligible grantees may include public elementary and secondary schools, as well as public colleges and universities and public hospitals.
Restrictions: The Foundation does not provide funding to organizations that discriminate on the basis of age, political affiliation, race, national origin, ethnicity, gender, disability, sexual orientation or religious beliefs. Funding is not provided for: advertising journals or booklets; alumni drives; capital campaigns/building funds; continuing medical education; infrastructural requests (e.g. salaries, equipment); memorial funds; memberships; organizations based outside of the United States; political or sectarian organizations; professional sports events or athletes; religious organizations; scholarships; yearbooks.
Geographic Focus: California
Samples: To be distributed among 19 organizations (CA)—for science programs for students in the San Francisco Bay area, $1 million.
Contact: Program Manager; (650) 467-9494; give@gene.com
Internet: http://www.gene.com/gene/about/community/overview.jsp
Sponsor: Genentech
1 DNA Way
South San Francisco, CA 94080-4990

General Dynamics Corporation Grants **755**
Corporate contributions funding goes to education, civic and public affairs, health and welfare, and arts and culture. Types of support include capital campaigns, general support, and operating funds. Grants are made nationally and communities where the company has operations. There is no formal application process. Interested applicants may submit a letter of application.
Geographic Focus: All U.S. States
Contact: Arlene Nestle, (703) 876-3305; (703) 876-3600
Internet: http://www.generaldynamics.com
Sponsor: General Dynamics Corporation
2941 Fairview Park Drive, Suite 100
Falls Church, VA 22042-4513

General Mills Foundation Grants **756**
The Foundation was created to focus its philanthropic resources on community needs. Strategic objectives are to: demonstrably improve the quality of life in communities with GM facilities and employees; initiate innovative solutions and approaches to improve youth nutrition and fitness; and to support GM employees and retirees giving to United Way, education, and arts and culture organizations through gift matching. Funding priorities include: social services; youth nutrition and fitness; education; and arts and culture. Priority is given to organizations meeting the following criteria: their mission is closely related to the Foundation's priorities; programs or activities are based in communities with GM operations and employees; programs or activities involve GM employees and retirees; and services create sustainable community improvement. Applications are accepted at any time.
Requirements: U.S. and Canadian charitable 501(c)3 and 509(a) nonprofits in communities where General Mills operates (California, Georgia, Illinois, Indiana, Iowa, Maryland, Massachusetts, Missouri, Minnesota, Missouri, Montana, New Jersey, New York, Ohio, Oklahoma, Pennsylvania, Tennessee and Wisconsin) are eligible.
Restrictions: The Foundation does not support: organizations without 501(c)3 and 509(a) status; organizations that do not comply with the Foundation's non-discrimination policy; individuals; social, labor, veterans, alumni or fraternal organizations serving a limited constituency; travel by groups; recreational, sporting events or athletic associations; religious organizations for religious purposes; basic research; organizations seeking underwriting for advertising; political causes, candidates or legislative lobbying efforts; conferences, seminars and workshops; campaigns to eliminate or control specific diseases; publications, films or television programs; underwriting for program sponsorship.
Geographic Focus: Arizona, Arkansas, California, Georgia, Illinois, Indiana, Iowa, Maryland, Massachusetts, Michigan, Minnesota, Missouri, Montana, New Jersey, New Mexico, New York, Ohio, Oklahoma, Pennsylvania, Tennessee, Wisconsin
Contact: Christina L. Shea, President; (763) 764-2211; (763) 764-4114
Internet: http://www.generalmills.com/corporate/commitment/foundation.aspx
Sponsor: General Mills Foundation
1 General Mills Boulevard, P.O. Box 1113
Minneapolis, MN 55440

General Motors Foundation Grants Support Program **757**
With a strong commitment to diversity in all areas, the targeted areas of focus for the Foundation are: education; health and human services; civic and community; public policy; arts and culture; and environment and energy. Primary consideration is given to requests that meet the following criteria: exhibit a clear purpose and defined need in one of the foundation's areas of focus; recognize innovative approaches in addressing the defined need; demonstrate an efficient organization and detail the organization's ability to follow through on the proposal; and, explain clearly the benefits to the foundation and the plant city communities. Paper applications are no longer accepted. Completion of an online eligibility quiz is the first step in the application process.
Requirements: Nonprofit, tax-exempt organizations and institutions are eligible to apply. Applications must be made online.
Restrictions: The Foundation not not support organizations that discriminate on the basis of race, religion, creed, gender, age, veteran status, physical challenge or national origin. Contributions are generally not provided for: individuals; religious organizations; political parties or candidates; U.S. hospitals and health care institutions (general operating support); capital campaigns; endowment funds; conferences, workshops or seminars not directly related to GM's business interests.
Geographic Focus: All U.S. States
Samples: American National Red Cross (Washington, DC)—for relief efforts in South Asia and Africa, $1 million; Pierre Chambon, College de France (Paris, France) and Ronald Evans, Salk Institute for Biological Studies (La

Jolla, CA)—to honor their contributions to the diagnosis, prevention, and treatment of cancer, $250,000 jointly.
Contact: Grant Coordinator; (313) 556-5000
Internet: http://www.gm.com/company/gmability/community/guidelines/index.html
Sponsor: General Motors Foundation
300 Renaissance Center, P.O. Box 300
Detroit, MI 48265-3000

Genesis Foundation Grants 758

The Foundation funds projects and program in the areas of health and formal education, benefiting children 0 to 18 years old, as well as training programs in these two areas. Capital, operating, program and general grants are funded. Approximately eighty percent of grant-making is devoted to Colombian entities, with the remainder devoted to projects in the U.S. , specifically in Southern Florida, Washington, DC and the New York Metropolitan area.
Requirements: Preliminary criteria to apply for a grant include: must be located in Colombia, Southern Florida, Washington, DC or the New York Metropolitan Area; must be incorporated as a non-profit, charitable institution in the appropriate jurisdiction; must have been in operation for a minimum of two (2) full years; must include at least three (3) people in decision-making process at all times; must benefit a minimum of 50 people per year; in Colombia, must have raised at a minimum the equivalent of U.S. $10,000 in the previous two years; in the U.S. must have raised a minimum of $20,000 in the previous two years; must have an independent financial auditor; must be able to provide audited financial statements for the previous three years; must be able to provide a budget for the organization and the project for which the grant is sought; must not be a political organization; and must not have a religious purpose.
Restrictions: Individuals and political or religious causes are ineligible.
Geographic Focus: District of Columbia, Florida, New York, Colombia
Date(s) Application is Due: Mar 15; Sep 15
Amount: 10,000 - 100,000 USD
Samples: Asociacion Social Popular (Bello, Colombia)—to purchase an educational facility, $35,000; Fundacion Estructurar (Bucaramanga, Colombia)—to provide education to working children, with an emphasis on training in design and graphic arts, $15,000; Fundacion Neumologica Colombiana (Bogota, Colombia)—to create an asthma center for children, $240,000; Nutrir (Bogota, Colombia)—to construct an additional facility that will provide nutritional and social services to underserved children, $40,000.
Contact: Grants Administrator; (212) 763-3703; (917) 591-7858; genesis@genesid-foundation.org
Internet: http://www.genesis-foundation.org
Sponsor: Genesis Foundation
140 East 45th Street, 2 Grant Central Tower 18th Floor, Suite A
New York, NY 10017

George and Ruth Bradford Foundation Grants 759

The foundation awards grants to local nonprofit organizations in the San Francisco Bay Area and Mendocino, California region. Areas of interest include: children and youth; families; education/higher education; environmental/wildlife conservation; housing and; social services. Types of support include general operating support and scholarship funds.
Requirements: California nonprofit organizations in the San Francisco peninsula and Mendocino, California region are eligible to apply. There is no deadline date to adhere to. The Board meets monthly, letters of inquiry may be submitted throughout the year for review.
Restrictions: No grants to individuals.
Geographic Focus: California
Samples: Frank R. Howard Foundation, Willits, CA, $10,000-hospital building fund (2009); Ukiah Valley Cultural & Recreation Center. Ukiah, CA, $5,000—youth recreation grant (2009); MC Aids Volunteer Network, Ukiah, CA, $1,000—health services grant (2009).
Contact: Myrna Oglesby, Director; (707) 462-0141; (707) 462-0160
Sponsor: George and Ruth Bradford Foundation
P.O. Box 720
Ukiah, CA 95482-0720

George A Ohl Jr. Foundation Grants 760

The purpose of the George A Ohl Jr. Foundation is to improve the well-being of the citizens of the State of New Jersey through science, health, recreation, education and increased good citizenship. Grants are made to organizations engaged in such work whether through research, publications, health, school or college activities. The Foundation's mission is the relief of the poor; the improvement of living conditions; the care of the sick, the young, the aged, the homeless, the incompetent and the helpless. The foundation will target: 35% of its grants to Community Redevelopment; 35% to Health and Human Services organizations; 15% for Arts and culture; 15% for Educational requests. Application deadlines are: January 22 for a March meeting and, June 15 for an August meeting. Application forms are available online. Applicants will receive notice acknowledging receipt of the grant request, and subsequently be notified of the grant declination or approval.
Requirements: New Jersey 501(c)3 nonprofit organizations are eligible to apply. Proposals should be submitted in the following format: completed Common Grant Application Form; an original Proposal Statement; an audited financial report and a current year operating budget; a copy of your official IRS Letter with your tax determination; a listing of your Board of Directors. Proposal Statements (second item in the above Format) should answer these questions: what are the objectives and expected outcomes of this program/project/request; what strategies will be used to accomplish your objective; what is the timeline for completion; if this is part of an on-going program, how long has it been in operation; what criteria will you use to measure success; if the request is not fully funded, what other sources can you engage; an Itemized budget should be included; please describe any collaborative ventures. Prior to the distribution of funds, all approved grantees must sign and return a Grant Agreement Form, stating that the funds will be used for the purpose intended. Progress reports and Completion reports must also be filed as required for your specific grant. All current grantees must be in good standing with required documentation prior to submitting new proposals to any foundation.
Restrictions: Grants are not made for political purposes, nor to organizations which discriminate on the basis of race, ethnic origin, sexual or religious preference, age or gender
Geographic Focus: New Jersey
Date(s) Application is Due: Jan 22; Jun 15
Amount: 3,000 - 35,000 USD
Samples: Mountainside Hospital Foundation, $35,000—Modernization of Internal Medicine Residents' Learning Center; Bloomfield College, $10,000—Improving Academic Success Through Technological Support Project; Medical Missions for Children, $5,000—Giggles Theater Programming Support (12 performances).
Contact: Wachovia Bank, N.A., Trustee; grantinquiries2@wachovia.com
Internet: https://www.wachovia.com/foundation/v/index.jsp?vgnextoid=e0f78689fb0aa110VgnVCM1000004b0d1872RCRD&vgnextfmt=default
Sponsor: George A Ohl Jr. Foundation
190 River Road, NJ3132
Summit, NJ 07901

George B. Page Foundation Grants 761

The foundation awards grants to Santa Barbara, CA, nonprofit organizations in support of programs for children and youth and the needy. Types of support include capital campaigns, building construction/renovation, material acquisition, and program development.
Requirements: Santa Barbara 501(c)3 tax-exempt organizations are eligible.
Geographic Focus: California
Date(s) Application is Due: Oct 1
Amount: 2,000 - 50,000 USD
Contact: Sara Kaufman, Trustee
Sponsor: George B. Page Foundation
P.O. Box 1299
Santa Barbara, CA 93102-1299

George B. Storer Foundation Grants 762

The foundation awards grants, primarily in Florida, in its areas of interest, including higher education, social services—particularly for the blind, youth organizations, conservation, hospitals, and cultural programs. Types of support include building construction/renovation, capital campaigns, general operating support, matching/challenge grants, and research grants. There are no application forms. Applications should be submitted between October 15 and the listed deadline.
Geographic Focus: All U.S. States
Date(s) Application is Due: Nov 15
Contact: Grants Administrator, c/o Thomas McDonald
Sponsor: George B. Storer Foundation
P.O. Box 1040
Tavernier, FL 33070

George F. Baker Trust Grants **763**

Grants are awarded nationwide, with preference given to nonprofits in the eastern United States, primarily for K-12, higher, and secondary education; hospitals; social services; civic affairs; environmental conservation; religion; and international affairs. Types of support include general operating support and matching funds. There are no application forms or deadlines. The board meets in June and November to consider requests.
Restrictions: Grants are not made to individuals.
Geographic Focus: All U.S. States
Amount: 10,000 - 100,000 USD
Samples: West Granville Christian Academy (West Granville, MA)—for operating support, $25,000; Saint Paul's Community Development Corp (Patterson, NJ)—for operations and program support, $20,000.
Contact: Rocio Suarez, Executive Director; (212) 755-1890; (212) 319-6316; rocio@bakernye.com
Sponsor: George F. Baker Trust
477 Madison Avenue, Suite 1650
New York, NY 10022

George Foundation Grants **764**

The George Foundation strive to support organizations and programs that assist in developing strong, stable families across Fort Bend County region of Texas. The Foundation's areas of interest include: family stability; scholarships; foundation initiated programs, current programs include, Youth in Philanthropy (YIP), Leadership Excellence for Non-Profits, Integrated Mental Health Care, and Transportation. The Foundation prefers to fund the following types of grants to support Fort Bend organizations in their delivery of services to the community (listed in order of priority): program/project support; foundation initiated; general operating; capital. Proposal deadlines for making grant applications to the Foundation are January 15, April 15, July 15 and October 15 of each year. All proposals for capital support will be grouped together for review. The deadline for capital proposals will be October 15 of each year.
Requirements: Non-profit organizations in Fort Bend County, Texas may submit grant proposals.
Restrictions: The Foundation does not fund: grants to organizations that do not have a current 501(c)3 determination letter; churches or other organized religious bodies; grants to another organization that distributes money to recipients of its own selection, i.e., a regranting organization; regional, national or international programs; grants for research or studies; grants for travel, conferences, conventions, group meetings, or seminars; the purchase of event tickets, tables, ads or sponsorships; support to fairs and festivals; religious or private schools; request for funds to develop films, videos, books or other media projects; direct mail campaigns; loans of any kind; grants to individuals; grants to fraternal organizations; political interests of any kind; and institutions that discriminate on the basis of race, creed, gender, national origin, age, disability or sexual orientation in policy or in practice.
Geographic Focus: Texas
Date(s) Application is Due: Jan 15; Apr 15; Jul 15; Oct 15
Amount: 1,000 - 4,000,000 USD
Samples: Wharton County Junior College, $110,000—to provide scholarships for Fort Bend County residents; YMCA of the Greater Houston Area, $250,000—to assist in acquiring facility to offer outdoor education/recreation experiences to Fort Bend families and children; OakBend Medical Center, $4,000,000—four year grant to provide indigent healthcare to Fort Bend County residents.
Contact: Dee Koch, Grant Officer; (281) 342-6109; (281) 341-7635; dkoch@thegeorgefoundation.org
Internet: http://www.thegeorgefoundation.org
Sponsor: George Foundation
310 Morton Street, PMB Suite C
Richmond, TX 77469

George Frederick Jewett Foundation Grants **765**

The foundation is concerned primarily with people and values. The grants program focuses on the future and on stimulating and supporting activities and projects of established, voluntary, nonprofit organizations that are of importance to human welfare. Grants are made in the fields of arts and humanities, conservation and preservation, education, health care and medical services, population, religion, and social welfare. The foundation may support research on and studies of important problems of public concern solely for the purpose of aiding in the gathering and presenting of facts that may assist the public to better understand such problems and to arrive at realistic and effective solutions to them. From time to time, support may be given to the scholarship, fellowship, and research programs of established institutions when sufficient evidence is available to establish clearly that the applicant organization is awarding such grants in accordance with the regulations established by the IRS. Grants are awarded to support activities in progress, research into potential projects, building and equipment, general operations, program development, seed funding, research, technical assistance, and matching funds. Inquiries for clarification of the foundation's policy and program emphasis are encouraged.
Requirements: Preference is given to public charities or nonprivate foundations. The foundation confines its grants largely to requests from eastern Washington and the San Francisco Bay area.
Restrictions: Grants do not support advertising; advocacy, athletic, international, religious, political, or veterans organizations; or individuals.
Geographic Focus: California, Washington
Amount: 5,000 - 50,000 USD
Samples: American U of Beirut (New York, NY)—general support, $15,000; Committee to Restore the Opera House (San Francisco, CA)—for a three-year commitment for restoration of the San Francisco War Memorial Opera House, $120,000.
Contact: Ann Gralnek, (415) 421-1351; (415) 421-0721; ADGjewettf@aol.com or tfbjewettf@aol.com
Sponsor: George Frederick Jewett Foundation
235 Montgomery Street, Suite 612
San Francisco, CA 94104

George Gund Foundation Grants **766**

The Foundation's long-standing interests include: arts; economic development; community revitalization; education; environment; and human services. The Foundation considers global climate change an urgent issue that cuts across all of the Foundation's programs. The Foundation takes seriously it's own responsibility and wants to hear from grant applicants what they are doing or considering to reduce or to eliminate their organizational impact on climate change. The Foundation also supports special projects grants, which currently include: Retinal Degenerative Diseases research grants, making an annual commitment for research on the causes, nature and prevention of inherited retinal degenerative diseases and; philanthropic services grants, offering support to organizations that strengthen the infrastructure of the nonprofit and philanthropic communities. The George Gund Foundation also supports capital requests but only for projects that are clearly aligned with their program priorities and that meet Green Building Council LEED (Leadership in Energy and Environmental Design) certification. The Foundation's green building policy covers both planning and construction grants. In addition, the Foundation supports opportunities that cross program boundaries and that integrate elements of the Foundation's interests. Although the Foundation's focus is centered in the Greater Cleveland, Ohio region, a portion of their grantmaking will continue to support state and national policy making that bolsters their work. Proposals should be mailed directly to the George Gund Foundation. All proposals are screened and evaluated by the staff before presentation at Trustee Meetings. Receipt of proposals will be acknowledged by mail.
Requirements: 501(c)3 nonprofit organizations are eligible to apply for funding, with a special interest in Greater Cleveland, Ohio region. Proposals are accepted three times: March 15, July 15 and November 15. Proposals are due the next business day if a deadline falls on a weekend. The grant application form is available on the George Gund Foundation website. All proposals must include a climate change statement, the Foundation's website includes resources to assist grantees with this task. Applicants also must include a completed Grant Application Cover Sheet, which is signed by the organization's board chair and executive director. Proposals should also include: organizational background; history; mission; types of programs offered; constituencies served; project description; justification of need; specific goals and objectives; activities planned to meet goals and objectives; project time line; qualifications of key personnel; methods of evaluation; project budget; anticipated expenses, including details about how Foundation funds would be used; anticipated income, including information about other sources approached for funding; organizational budget; previous and current year budget and proposed budget for project year(s) showing both income and expenses; the organization's most recent audited financial statement, do not include IRS 990 forms; supporting documents; list of current trustees; letters of support; readily available printed material about organization such as annual reports and brochures; IRS letter confirming Internal Revenue Code 501(c)3 status and classification as a public charity or information confirming status as a government unit or agency. The Foundation also will accept the Ohio Common Grant Form, available at www.

ohiograntmakers.org, if organizations are using it to apply to multiple funders. Faxed or electronic proposals are not accepted.
Restrictions: Do not submit proposals in notebooks, binders or plastic folders and print proposals on both sides of each sheet of paper. The Foundation normally does not consider grants for endowments. Capital requests must meet the Foundation's program goals and also adhere to green building standards of environmental sustainability. Details on these requirements are available from the Foundation. Grants are not made for debt reduction or to fund benefit events. The Foundation does not make grants to individuals, nor does it administer programs it supports. Grants are limited to organizations located in the United States.
Geographic Focus: All U.S. States
Date(s) Application is Due: Mar 15; Jul 15; Nov 15
Samples: Progressive Arts Alliance Incorporated, Cleveland, OH, $20,000—database capacity building project (2010); Cleveland Restoration Society, Incorporated, Cleveland, OH, $20,000—preservation programs (2010); Center for Community Solutions, Cleveland, OH, $360,000—two year grant for policy and fiscal analysis and GroundWork early childhood campaign (2010).
Contact: David Abbott, Executive Director; (216) 241-3114; (216) 241-6560; info@gundfdn.org
Internet: http://www.gundfdn.org/what.asp
Sponsor: George Gund Foundation
1845 Guildhall Building, 45 Prospect Avenue, West
Cleveland, OH 44115

George K. Baum Foundation Grants 767

The foundation supports nonprofits in the greater Kansas City, MO, area in its areas of interest, including arts and cultural programs, education, health care, Jewish federated giving, and general charitable giving. There are no application deadlines or forms.
Requirements: Nonprofits in the metropolitan Kansas City, MO, area are eligible.
Geographic Focus: Missouri
Amount: Up to 392,000 USD
Samples: Jewish Federation of Greater Kansas City (MO)—general support, $20,000; University of Missouri, Conservatory of Music—general support, $7500.
Contact: Jonathan Baum, Trustee; (816) 474-1100 or (800) 821-7195; (816) 283-5171
Sponsor: George K. Baum Foundation
120 W 12th Street, Suite 800
Kansas City, MO 64105

George P. Davenport Trust Fund Grants 768

The trust fund awards grants to Maine nonprofits in its areas of interest, including education and higher education, health care, community development, and religion. Types of support include general operating support, building construction/renovation, seed grants, scholarships to individuals, matching grants, and emergency funds. There are no application deadlines. The board meets two times each year.
Requirements: Nonprofit organizations serving Bath, ME, are eligible.
Restrictions: Grants are not awarded for continuing support, annual campaigns, deficit financing, equipment, programs, research, demonstration projects, or publications.
Geographic Focus: Maine
Amount: 500 - 25,000 USD
Samples: Salvation Army (Bath, ME)—for program support, $17,000; U of Maine (Orono, ME)—for scholarships, $10,750.
Contact: Barry Sturgeon, Treasurer; (207) 443-3431
Sponsor: George P. Davenport Trust Fund
65 Front Street
Bath, ME 04530

George R. Wallace Foundation Grants 769

The foundation's fields of interest are culture, education, and the environment. Giving is primarily in the Fitchburg/Leominster, Massachusetts, area. Priority will be given to support education, particularly programs benefiting low income students. Grants will be awarded to support building/renovation, capital campaigns, endowment, general operating, multi-year pledges, special projects, and equipment. Initial contact should be by telephone or email inquiry. There is no set form of application, but letters should contain a concise statement of the purpose for which the grant is sought. All applicants should include the current year's operating budget; the most recent audited financial statements; a list of board members; and a copy of the IRS determination letter.
Requirements: Organizations in Massachusetts are eligible to apply.
Restrictions: Grants will not be awarded to individuals or for scholarships, fellowships, or loans.
Geographic Focus: Massachusetts
Amount: 10,000 USD
Samples: Philharmonic Ctr for the Arts (Naples, FL)—for general operating support, $105,000; Walnut Hill School (Natick, MA)—for program support, $53,000.
Contact: Lucia Thompson, (617) 570-1355; lthompson@goodwinprocter.com
Sponsor: George R. Wallace Foundation
Goodwin Procter LLP, Exchange Place
Boston, MA 02109-2881

George S. and Dolores Dore Eccles Foundation Grants 770

The foundation awards grants to eligible Utah organizations in its areas of interest, including arts, children and youth, economics, higher education, hospitals, medical research, performing arts, visual arts, and social services. Types of support include building construction/renovation, capital campaigns, equipment acquisition, general operating grants, matching/challenge grants, professorships, program development, research grants, and scholarship funds. A request for application is available online.
Requirements: Giving primarily in Utah.
Restrictions: Funding requests will not be considered from the following types of organizations: those that have not received a tax exemption letter establishing 501(c)3 status from the Internal Revenue Service, unless they are a unit of government, in which case such a letter is not required; other private foundations; those of a political nature that attempt to influence legislation and/or candidacy of persons for elected public office; conduit organizations, unified funds, or those that use funds to make grants to support other organizations; those that do not have fiscal responsibility for the proposed project. Funds will also not be considered for: contingencies, deficits, or debt reduction; general endowment funds; direct aid to individuals; conferences, seminars, or medical research; requests which do not fall within the Foundation's specified areas of interest.
Geographic Focus: Utah
Samples: Westminster College of Salt Lake City (UT)—for undergraduate scholarships, $1.2 million over three years.
Contact: Director; (801) 246-5340; (801) 350-3510; gseg@gseccles.org
Internet: http://www.gsecclesfoundation.org
Sponsor: George S. and Dolores Dore Eccles Foundation
79 South Main Street, 12th Floor
Salt Lake City, UT 84111

Georgia-Pacific Foundation Grants 771

The Foundation primarily invests it's resources in four key areas that are essential to creating and sustaining strong communities: education; environment; community enrichment; and entrepreneurship. Funding is available in communities, in which Georgia-Pacific operates. The following is a list of states are eligible to apply for funding: Alabama; Arkansas; California; Florida; Georgia; Illinois; Indiana; Iowa; Kentucky; Louisiana; Massachusetts; Michigan; Mississippi; New Jersey; New York; North Carolina; Ohio; Oklahoma; Oregon; Pennsylvania; South Carolina; Tennessee; Texas; Virginia; Washington; West Virginia and; Wisconsin. There is no specific dollar amount for a request for grants, scholarships or in-kind support. The dollar amount varies based on the budget requested, program value and Georgia-Pacific funds available. Types of support available are: annual campaigns; building/renovation; capital campaigns; conferences/seminars; continuing support; employee-related scholarships; employee volunteer services; equipment; general/operating support; in-kind gifts; program development; scholarship funds; sponsorships; scholarships for individuals.
Requirements: Nonprofit organizations in Georgia-Pacific communities are eligible to apply for funding. To find out whether your program qualifies for consideration for a Georgia-Pacific Foundation grant, sponsorship, in-kind donation or other assistance, complete the Eligibility Survey available online. Once you have successfully completed Eligibility Survey, the How to Apply section will be presented and will guide you through the process to submit your request to the Georgia-Pacific Foundation. The Georgia-Pacific Foundation will accept proposals for grants and in-kind donations from Jan 1 - Oct 31. It is recommended that you submit your proposal early in the grant cycle. (only one copy of the proposal is required).

Restrictions: No support for discriminatory organizations, political candidates, churches or religious denominations, religious or theological schools, social, labor, veterans', alumni, or fraternal organizations not of direct benefit to the entire community, athletic associations, national organizations with local chapters already receiving support, medical or nursing schools, or pass-through organizations. No grants to individuals (except for scholarships), or for emergency needs for general operating support, political causes, legislative lobbying, or advocacy efforts, goodwill advertising, sporting events, general operating support for United Way member agencies, tickets or tables for testimonials or similar benefit events, named academic chairs, social sciences or health science programs, fundraising events, or trips or tours.
Geographic Focus: Alabama, Arkansas, California, Florida, Georgia, Illinois, Indiana, Iowa, Kentucky, Louisiana, Massachusetts, Michigan, Mississippi, New Jersey, New York, North Carolina, Ohio, Oklahoma, Oregon, Pennsylvania, South Carolina, Tennessee, Texas, Virginia, Washington, West Virginia, Wisconsin
Date(s) Application is Due: Oct 31
Samples: Church of the Sacred Heart, $1,000—program support (2008); United Way of Camden County, $10,000—foundation support (2008); Chattahoochee Nature Center, $25,000—contribution support (2008).
Contact: James Hannan, CEO and President; (404) 652-4182; (404) 749-2754
Internet: http://www.gp.com/gpfoundation/index.html
Sponsor: Georgia-Pacific Foundation
133 Peachtree Street, North East, 39th Floor
Atlanta, GA 30303

Georgia Council for the Arts Organizational Grants **772**
The council is dedicated to supporting the arts in Georgia by providing grant funding and services for non-profit arts and cultural organizations throughout the state in an effort to make quality arts programming available to all Georgians. Organizational grants include general operating support and project support. Organizations can be funded only once per fiscal year for general operating support. Project support allows organizations that do not apply for general operating support to be funded for specific arts-related projects. Deadlines vary depending on programs, check website, or contact program staff for specific dates.
Requirements: Georgia nonprofits are eligible.
Geographic Focus: Georgia
Samples: Cobb County (GA)—for the Georgia Ballet, $2500; Muscogee County (GA)—for The Columbus Museum, $68,616.
Contact: Karen Lawton, Program Manager; (404) 685-2796; (404) 685-2788; klawton@gaarts.org
Internet: http://www.web-dept.com/gca/resources_forms.asp#
Sponsor: Georgia Council for the Arts
260 14th Street NW, Suite 401
Atlanta, GA 30318-5360

Geraldine R. Dodge Foundation Arts Grants **773**
The Dodge Foundation invite proposals for general operating or project-specific support from organizations that: enhance the cultural richness of the community in which they reside and contribute to New Jersey's creative economy. Priority will be given to those that: pursue and demonstrate the highest standards of artistic excellence; provide opportunities for meaningful connections between people and art within their communities, and partner with others to expand the inclusiveness and the impact of the arts; contribute to the diverse human narrative by creating new work and/or re-imagining the classics; provide creative opportunities and living wages for New Jersey artists; use the arts to revitalize public places and natural spaces and/or help citizens engage in and advocate for the environmental well-being of their communities. Application guidelines are available online.
Requirements: All applicants must either have 501(c)3 status under the Internal Revenue Code, or be a public entity.
Restrictions: Funding is not provided for: higher education; health; religion; capital programs; equipment purchases; indirect costs; endowment funds; and deficit reduction. The Foundation does not make direct awards to individuals or support lobbying efforts.
Geographic Focus: New Jersey
Samples: New Jersey Repertory Company, Long Branch, NJ, $75,000—for general operating support of core programs and new initiatives; Cape May Stage, Cape May, NJ, $25,000—for general operating support; Peters Valley Craftsmen, Layton, NJ, $75,000—for general operating support of artistic and educational activities including scholarships to New Jersey artists to participate in a residency program.
Contact: Laura Aden Packer, Program Director, Arts; (973) 540-8442; (973) 540-1211; info@grdodge.org
Internet: http://www.grdodge.org/arts/index.htm
Sponsor: Geraldine R. Dodge Foundation
14 Maple Avenue, P.O. Box 1239
Morristown, NJ 07962-1239

Geraldine R. Dodge Foundation Environment Grants **774**
The Program focuses on organizations and leaders working in New Jersey to improve livability as it relates to current patterns of land consumption and development. The Foundation seeks proposals that strengthen and uphold: nonprofit groups whose primary work is preserving major ecosystems and open space; nonprofit groups who work on livable communities; and the community of advocates and innovators who work to accelerate the achievement of ecosystem, open space and livable community goals. New applicants should submit a one-page letter of inquiry to determine if a project falls within our guidelines. Letters of inquiry may be submitted throughout the year, but must be received at least two weeks prior to the corresponding proposal submission deadline.
Requirements: All applicants must either have 501(c)3 status under the Internal Revenue Code, or be a public entity.
Restrictions: The Foundation does not make capital grants, nor does it fund individuals. Dodge does not generally make grants to institutions of higher learning, except for their outreach efforts which complement and enhance the Foundation's other efforts.
Geographic Focus: New Jersey
Date(s) Application is Due: May 1
Samples: American Farmland Trust, Washington, DC, $30,000—for support of programs to facilitate township adoption of model farm ordinances, disseminate new local and state policy recommendations, and help Burlington County tell the story of its local agriculture innovations (2008); New Jersey Conservation Foundation, Far Hills, NJ, $170,000—for general operating support that will enable NJCF to maintain its leadership role in preserving New Jersey's most critical ecosystems through land acquisition and stewardship, public policy, and strategic partnerships (2008); The Land Conservancy of New Jersey, Boonton, NJ, $60,000—to support the Partners for Greener Communities program (2008).
Contact: Michelle Knapik, Program Director; (973) 540-8442; (973) 540-1211; info@grdodge.org
Internet: http://www.grdodge.org/environment/index.htm
Sponsor: Geraldine R. Dodge Foundation
14 Maple Avenue, P.O. Box 1239
Morristown, NJ 07962-1239

Gertrude and William C. Wardlaw Fund Grants **775**
The fund awards general operating grants to Georgia nonprofit organizations in its areas of interest, including cultural activities, community development, education and higher education, and health and hospitals.
Requirements: Georgia nonprofit organizations are eligible.
Geographic Focus: Georgia
Date(s) Application is Due: Feb 15
Amount: Up to 675,546 USD
Contact: Mark Drake, Secretary
Sponsor: Gertrude and William C. Wardlaw Fund
P.O. Box 4655, MC 217
Atlanta, GA 30302

Gibson Foundation Grants **776**
The Foundation is committed to making the world a better place for children by creating, developing and supporting programs and other non-profit organizations in their efforts to advance education, music and the arts, the environment and health & welfare causes. The Foundation actively seeks out programs that will be a direct mission-fit and further its goals.
Requirements: Applicants must be 501(c)3 organizations.
Restrictions: The Foundation does not support religious or political affiliations, and does not award individual scholarships.
Geographic Focus: All U.S. States
Contact: Nina Miller, Executive Director; (615) 871-4500, ext. 2114; (615) 884-9597; nina.miller@gibson.com
Internet: http://www.gibson.com/en-us/Lifestyle/GibsonFoundation/
Sponsor: Gibson Foundation
309 Plus Park Boulevard
Nashville, TN 37217

Gilroy and Lillian P. Roberts Charitable Foundation Grants 777

The foundation awards grants to eligible nonprofit organizations in its areas of interest, including arts and fine arts, health care and health organizations, higher education, Jewish temples and organizations, and social services. Types of support include annual campaigns, capital campaigns, continuing support, fellowships, general operating grants, professorships, program development, and scholarships. Most grants are awarded in Montgomery and Delaware Counties, PA. There are no application deadlines or forms.
Restrictions: Individuals are not eligible.
Geographic Focus: Pennsylvania
Amount: Up to 408,750 USD
Samples: Temple University (Philadelphia, PA)—for Merves Professorship in Accounting, $155,000.
Contact: Stanley Merves, Treasurer; (610) 668-1998
Sponsor: Gilroy and Lillian P. Roberts Charitable Foundation
101 W Elm Street, Suite 500
Conshohocken, PA 19428

Ginger and Barry Ackerley Foundation Grants 778

The Ginger & Barry Ackerley Foundation makes grants to public and private organizations that sponsor programs enhancing the education of young learners under the age of five, in the greater Puget Sound region. The Foundation focuses on organizations involved in skills support, literacy development, mentoring relationships and programs that connect school and home in order to produce specific and measurable results in early learning. Grants are usually made for capital drives, endowments and specific program objectives, not operating budgets. Grants are generally to be expended within one year, without expectation of further support. Priority will be given to requests that show specific plans for funding beyond the present.
Requirements: Washington State 501(c)3 tax-exempt organizations, with an active board of directors, with policy-making authority are eligible to apply. The board should demonstrate competence in the sound financial management of the organization. Organizations seeking grant support must receive an invitation from the Ackerley Foundation prior to submitting an application. To initiate the process, organizations that fit within the Foundation's mission and guidelines should submit a letter of inquiry describing the organization, the program the request is for, and the amount of funding sought. The process continues as follows: the Foundation arranges visits and meetings to learn more about the organization; suitable organizations are invited to apply for funding (Grant Request Summary form available online at the Foundation's website); all organizations must fulfill the written application requirements. The Foundation evaluates funding requests twice annually, typically in March and October. Application deadlines will be established according to funding needs and program timing.
Restrictions: Funding is not available for: organizations that discriminate on the basis of race, color, creed, sex, marital status, or handicap; individuals, except scholarship recipients chosen by educational institutions; political candidates, organizations, or committees; religious organizations whose mission, policies or practices declare a purely denominational intent; debt retirement or operating deficits, loans, or investments; team sponsorships, individual athletic endeavors, or travel expenses; annual fund drives; administrative salaries.
Geographic Focus: Washington
Amount: 100 - 500,000 USD
Samples: Kidsquest Children's Museum, Bellevue, WA, $5,000—general support (2008); First Place School, Seattle, WA, $100,000—general support (2008); Kirlin Charitable Foundation, Bellevue, WA. $25,000—general support (2008).
Contact: Twyla McFarlane, (206) 624-2888; (206) 623-7853; info@ackerleyfoundation.com
Internet: http://www.ackerleyfoundation.org/apply/guidelines.html
Sponsor: Ginger and Barry Ackerley Foundation
4105 East Madison Street, Suite 210
Seattle, WA 98112

Ginn Foundation Grants 779

The foundation's mission is to address educational and community-based health care needs through supporting effective programs and services that bring about long-term solutions for individuals and the community, principally in Cuyahoga County, OH. The Foundation will consider not only grants to academic institutions, but also to organizations that meet non-academic educational needs, such as, programs that address issues of disease avoidance, child and family counseling, after-school training, arts, housing, and employment. Preference in all of these areas will be given to organizations and programs that serve low-income recipients. Faxed applications will not be considered. Application information is available online.
Requirements: Nonprofit organizations in Cuyahoga County, OH, may apply. Consideration will also be given to trustee-sponsored grants to similar types of organizations in the Chicago, Washington, DC, and Minneapolis-Street Paul metropolitan areas.
Restrictions: The foundation will not fund requests for support of advocacy activities. Nor will it make grants to endowment, capital, or annual fund campaigns. The foundation will not fund special events or attendance at conferences or symposia.
Geographic Focus: District of Columbia, Illinois, Minnesota, Ohio
Date(s) Application is Due: Mar 15; Sep 15
Amount: 5,000 - 30,000 USD
Samples: Bellflower Center for the Prevention of Abuse, Cleveland, OH, $10,000—general operating support for support services directly addressing healthy child development through the prevention & treatment of child abuse (2008); Cleveland Playhouse, Cleveland, OH, $15,000—collaboration with Cleveland School of the Arts (2008); Cleveland Hearing & Speech, Cleveland, OH, $15,000—Speech-Language Pathology Program (2008).
Contact: Walter Pope Ginn, Trustee; info@ginnfoundation.org
Internet: http://www.ginnfoundation.org/index.html
Sponsor: Ginn Foundation
13938 A Cedar Road, P.O. Box 239
Cleveland Heights, OH 44118

Girl's Best Friend Foundation Grants 780

The foundation supports and promotes programs by and for girls and young women in Illinois (ages eight through 21). The foundation is dedicated to effecting change at the grassroots level by funding community-based organizations statewide. Types of grants made include general operating support, project specific support, planning or start-up support, technical assistance, and collaborative action research (research that lays the groundwork for policy changes conducted by a partnership between two nonprofits or a nonprofit contracting with a researcher or academic institution). When multiyear funding is requested, the foundation will consider making two-year grants if the requesting organization has received at least two previous grants from GBF, is seeking two years of funding for the same purpose, and has clearly demonstrated the need for a two-year grant. Applications are due the first Monday in August.
Requirements: Letters of intent will be accepted from 501(c)3 nonprofits for projects that serve or have a direct impact on girls living in the Chicago metropolitan area including Cook, DuPage, Kane, Lake, McHenry, and Will counties.
Restrictions: Organizations with budgets that exceed $650,000 may apply only for technical assistance and/or collaborative action research grants. The foundation generally does not fund individuals, capital campaigns, debt reduction, scholarships, or government or religious organizations.
Geographic Focus: Illinois
Amount: 5,000 - 20,000 USD
Samples: Chicago Health Connections (IL)—for school-based support services for pregnant teenagers and teenage parents, $11,000; Chicago Women in Trades (IL)—to develop the leadership and advocacy skills of young women enrolled in vocational classes, $16,500; Family Matters (Chicago, IL)—for a program that focuses on community building, entrepreneurial skills, and academics, $16,500; Girls in the Game (Chicago, IL)—for sports and leadership programs for girls, $49,400.
Contact: Robin Dixon, Senior Program Officer; (312) 266-2842; (312) 266-2972; robin@girlsbestfriend.org or contact@girlsbestfriend.org
Internet: http://www.girlsbestfriend.org/apply/index.html
Sponsor: Girl's Best Friend Foundation
900 N Franklin, Suite 210
Chicago, IL 60610

Gladys Marinelli Coccia Awards 781

The awards were launched in 2009 to recognize two young female social entrepreneurs, ages 14 to 17, whose initiatives serve the common good. The awards are created in memory of Gladys Coccia, who began her entrepreneurial career when she was a young girl in West Virginia and later became a very successful businesswoman in Washington, DC. The award include $2,000 for the social enterprise; travel and registration to YSA's Youth Service Institute; service as a spokesperson for YSA's initiatives; invitation to serve on the executive board of Girls Helping Girls; and, access to YSA's resources to support and expand social enterprise.

Requirements: Girls who meet the following criteria are eligible for the award: between the ages of 14 and 17 on December 31; located in the United States; have her own social enterprise; be supported by contributions of at least $1,000 (cash and/or in-kind); and, have a business plan, including an itemized budget. Special consideration will be given to nominees located in West Virginia and Metro Washington DC. Nominations from across the country are welcome; special consideration will be given to nominees from West Virginia and metropolitan Washington, DC. Self-nominations are accepted. The deadline to begin an online nomination is June 15. After this date, nominations cannot be initiated. The deadline to complete a nomination is June 30. To access the eligibility quiz and the nomination form, visit www.ysa.org/awards or email coccia@ysa.org.
Restrictions: Materials must be in electronic format and uploaded as part of the nomination. Materials sent by mail/email will not be considered.
Geographic Focus: All U.S. States
Date(s) Application is Due: Jun 15; Jun 30
Amount: 2,000 USD
Contact: Nandini Assar, Manager; (202) 296-2992, ext. 123; nassar@ysa.org
Internet: http://ysa.org/MyYSA/YSAContent/YSANews/tabid/219/articleType/ArticleView/articleId/147/TheGladysMarinelliCocciaAwards.aspx
Sponsor: Youth Service America
1101 15th Street NW, Suite 200
Washington, DC 20005

Glaser Progress Foundation Grants **782**

The foundation awards grants to U.S. nonprofit organizations in its areas of interest, including progress definition and measurement—efforts to improve understanding and measurement of human progress; animal advocacy—address issues such as wildlife cruelty, farm animals, vivisection, primate rights and protection, and use of technology for animal advocacy; and independent media—to support efforts to strengthen democracy by making independent voices heard. There are no application deadlines or forms. Application form is available online.
Requirements: U.S. 501(c)3 tax-exempt organizations are eligible.
Restrictions: Grants are not awarded to influence legislation or support candidates for political office.
Geographic Focus: All U.S. States
Amount: 1,000 - 25,000 USD
Samples: Yale U (New Haven, CT)—for the G-ECON Project, to explore the relationship between economics and geography, $100,000; Doris Day Animal Foundation (Washington, DC)—for general support of the Chimpanzee Collaboratory, $14,000; Independent Media Institute (San Francisco, CA)—to support AlterNet's online magazine and digest, $20,000; Columbia University (New York, NY)—to support the Access Project for the Global Fund to Fight AIDS, Tuberculosis, and Malaria, $450,000.
Contact: Melessa Rogers, (206) 728-1050; (206) 728-1123; melessa@glaserprogress.org or grants@glaserprogress.org
Internet: http://www.glaserprogress.org
Sponsor: Glaser Progress Foundation
P.O. Box 91123
Seattle, WA 98111

Global Fund for Children Grants **783**

The Global Fund for Children's (GFC) mission is to advance the dignity of children and youth around the world through small grants to innovative community-based organizations working with some of the world's most vulnerable children and youth. The Fund selects its grantee partners based on their potential to grow in effectiveness and to become valuable resources or models for others. Selection criteria include exceptional leadership, sound management, strong community participation, innovative and effective programs, and direct engagement with the most vulnerable children. Fund focus is on four specific issues: learning, enterprise, safety, and healthy minds and bodies. Organizations may submit a letter of inquiry at any time. If a letter of inquiry falls within GFC's priorities, GFC will follow up with the organization to solicit a full proposal.
Requirements: Nonprofit organization worldwide are eligible.
Geographic Focus: All U.S. States
Amount: 5,000 - 20,000 USD
Samples: Anandan, Kolkata, India, $8,000—education grant (2009); Benishyaka Association, Kigali, Rwanda, $15,000—academic scholarships (2009); Children in the Wilderness, Lilongwe, Malawi, $15,000—education grant (2009).
Contact: Andrew Barnes, Grants Manager; (202) 331-9003; (202) 331-9004; info@globalfundforchildren.org
Internet: http://www.globalfundforchildren.org/applyforagrant/index.html
Sponsor: Global Fund for Children
1101 Fourteenth Street, North West, Suite 420
Washington, DC 20005

Global Fund for Women Grants **784**

The fund provides flexible, timely financial assistance to women's groups around the world. Grantees address a wide variety of issues critical to women, such as women's political participation and leadership, poverty and economic opportunity, women's rights in religious traditions, reproductive health and choice, lesbian rights, violence against women, and access to communications technology and to the media. Types of support include conferences and seminars, equipment acquisition, general operating support, program development, publication, seed money grants, and technical assistance. The fund supports work on emerging issues as groups identify their importance to women. Groups may apply by sending a letter providing information about the group, its work, its financial resources and needs, and the specific grant request. Letters of inquiry may be handwritten or typed, and may be sent via post, fax, or email. Applicants should check the online contact guide for various countries around the world.
Requirements: The board prefers to fund organizations that demonstrate a clear commitment to women's causes, are governed by women, have long-term plans to strengthen the work of their group, and are unlikely to receive support from other funding sources.
Restrictions: The fund does not make grants to individuals; groups based and working primarily or solely in the United States; groups whose main or only purpose is to generate income for individuals or welfare-oriented projects; groups headed and managed by men, and without women in important management functions; groups in the global north proposing partnerships with the global south; or groups that do not have any female human rights focus.
Geographic Focus: All U.S. States
Amount: 500 - 20,000 USD
Samples: Central African Region (Yaounde, Cameroon)—to train and provide income-generating activities for indigenous African women, $10,000; Assoc of Samaritan Women (Antananarivo, Madagascar)—to provide vocational training and education and counseling on HIV and sexually transmitted infections to workers in the sex industry, $20,000; Mano River Women's Peace Network (Freetown, Sierra Leone)—to establish a secretariat that will coordinate regional efforts to monitor and document gender-based violence, strengthen reconstruction strategies, and include women in peace-building processes, $40,000.
Contact: Erika Guevara Rosas, American Program Officer; (415) 202-7640; (415) 202-8604; proposals@globalfundforwomen.org
Internet: http://www.globalfundforwomen.org/cms/grant-criteria/
Sponsor: Global Fund for Women
1375 Sutter Street, Suite 400
San Francisco, CA 94109

Golden LEAF Foundation Grants **785**

The mission of the foundation is to support organizations that promote the social welfare of North Carolina's citizens and to receive and distribute funds to lessen the economic impact of changes in the state's tobacco economy. The Foundation looks for projects with the following characteristics: serving unmet needs in communities; supporting new technology, crops, and applications to increase the areas advantage in agriculture; job creation and retention in rural tobacco-dependent counties; creation, expansion and improvement of business activity in rural tobacco-dependent counties; training/workforce preparedness initiatives; and public infrastructure improvement projects. Applicants seeking funding are encouraged to contact the Foundation for more information regarding the grants application process and funding priorities.
Requirements: Government and 501(c)3 tax-exempt organizations in North Carolina are eligible to apply.
Restrictions: Grants will not be awarded to: endowments; capital campaigns; construction projects - except as noted; infrastructure - except as noted; debt relief; revolving loan funds; purchase of land; after-school or day care programs; general employability training programs; general use community centers/facilities.
Geographic Focus: North Carolina
Date(s) Application is Due: Aug 1

Samples: North Carolina Agricultural Foundation (Raleigh, NC)—to help middle school students develop entrepreneurial and financial literacy skills, $65,762; Johnston Community College (NC)—for a training program to help farmers move into other agricultural enterprises, $100,000; North Carolina A&T State U (NC)—to help former tobacco farmers move into other agricultural enterprises, $100,000; North Carolina Central U (NC)—to train displaced tobacco workers and other unemployed people for careers in hospitality and tourism, $175,000.
Contact: Grants Administrator; (888) 684-8404 or (252) 442-7474; (252) 442-7404; info@goldenleaf.org
Internet: http://www.goldenleaf.org
Sponsor: Golden LEAF (Long-term Economic Advancement Foundation) Foundation
107 SE Main Street, Suite 500
Rocky Mount, NC 27801

Goodrich Corporation Foundation Grants **786**

The Foundation makes charitable grants in four categories: education; arts and culture; civic and community; and health and human services. Preference shall be given to requests for projects or programs in areas having a significant number of employees, employees serving on boards of charitable organizations or other noticeable corporate presence. The Foundation staff accepts and reviews grant requests quarterly. To request funding, applicants will need to complete the application form which is available online. Telephone and email requests or inquiries are not accepted.
Requirements: 501(c)3 tax-exempt organizations are eligible.
Restrictions: The foundation generally will not support: multiyear grants in excess of five years; individuals, private foundations, endowments, churches or religious programs, fraternal/social/ labor/veterans organizations; groups with unusually high fundraising or administrative expenses; political parties, candidates, or lobbying activities; travel funds for tours, exhibitions, or trips by individuals or special interest groups; organizations that discriminate because of race, color, religion, national origin, or areas covered by applicable federal, state, or local laws; local athletic/sports programs or equipment, courtesy advertising benefits, raffle tickets and other fundraising events; organizations that receive sizable portions of their support through municipal, county, state, or federal dollars; individual United Way agencies that already benefit from Goodrich contributions to the United Way; or international organizations.
Geographic Focus: All U.S. States
Date(s) Application is Due: Feb 1; Aug 1
Contact: Foundation Contact, Foundation Contact; (704) 423-7011
Internet: http://www.goodrich.com/CDA/GeneralContent/0,1136,59,00.html
Sponsor: Goodrich Foundation
Four Coliseum Center, 2730 West Tyvola Road
Charlotte, NC 28217-4578

Good Works Foundation Grants **787**

The Foundation was established to support good works wherever they are found and encourage innovative programs which involve collaboration in education, the arts, and the environment. In particular, the Foundation focuses on initiatives and programs that impact children, especially the culture and environment in which they learn and grow. The Foundation generally meets quarterly to evaluate requests for funding programs. Guidelines and application information is available online.
Requirements: 501(c)3 tax-exempt organizations in the Santa Monica and West Los Angeles area are eligible.
Restrictions: No fax or email proposals are accepted. You may not apply for fellowships, capital expenditures, construction, or endowment.
Geographic Focus: California
Contact: Laura Donnelley-Morton, (310) 828-1288; (310) 829-6090; info@goodworks.org
Internet: http://www.goodworks.org/pages/guidelines
Sponsor: Good Works Foundation
2101 Wilshire Boulevard, Suite 225
Santa Monica, CA 90403

Google Grants Beta **788**

The Google Grants program supports organizations sharing their philosophy of community service to help the world in areas such as science and technology, education, global public health, the environment, youth advocacy, and the arts. Google Grants has awarded AdWords advertising to non-profit groups whose missions range from animal welfare to literacy, from supporting homeless children to promoting HIV education. Recipients use their award of free AdWords advertising on Google.com to raise awareness and increase traffic. Application available online only.
Requirements: In the United States - Organizations must have current 501(c)3 status, as assigned by the Internal Revenue Service to be considered for a Google Grant. Outside the U.S - currently accepting applications from eligible charitable organizations based in Australia, Brazil, Canada, Denmark, France, Germany, India, Ireland, Italy, Japan, the Netherlands, Spain, Sweden, Switzerland and the United Kingdom.
Restrictions: Organizations already participating in the Google AdSense program are not eligible for Google Grants consideration. In addition, organizations that are either religious or political in nature are not eligible, including those groups focused primarily on lobbying for political or policy change.
Geographic Focus: All U.S. States
Samples: Three award recipients have achieved these results: - Room to Read, which educates children in Vietnam, Nepal, India and Cambodia, attracted a sponsor who clicked on its AdWords ad. He has donated funds to support the education of 25 girls for the next 10 years. - The U.S. Fund for UNICEF's e-commerce site, Shop UNICEF, has experienced a 43 percent increase in sales over the previous year. - CoachArt, supporting children with life-threatening illnesses through art and athletics programs, has seen a 60 to 70 percent increase in volunteers.
Contact: Google Grants Team Contact; googlegrants@google.com
Internet: http://www.google.com/grants/
Sponsor: Google
1600 Amphitheatre Parkway
Mountain View, CA 94043

Gottlieb Daimler and Karl Benz Foundation Grants **789**

Grants are awarded to individuals for doctoral research, to German nationals wishing to conduct research abroad, and to foreign young scientists carrying out research at German institutions. In addition, several grants support the scientific cooperation with the Kaliningrad State University (open for applications), with young economists from East Europe, with Peking University, with Vietnam, and with South Africa. Types of support include awards, general operating support, basic research, dissertation research support, fellowships, international exchange programs and grants, seed grants, and conferences and workshops.
Geographic Focus: All U.S. States
Date(s) Application is Due: Mar 1; Oct 1
Contact: Drive Jorg Klein, Managing Director; 49 6203 1092 0; 49 6203 1092-5; klein@daimler-benz-stiftung.de
Internet: http://www.daimler-benz-stiftung.de/home/fellowship/en/start.html
Sponsor: Gottlieb Daimler and Karl Benz Foundation
Dr Larl-Benz-Platz 2
Ladenburg, 68526 Germany

Grace and Franklin Bernsen Foundation Grants **790**

The Grace and Franklin Bernsen Foundation provide grants primarily within the metropolitan Tulsa, Oklahoma area. Areas of interest supported are: religious; charitable; scientific; literary and; educational purposes. Grant applications for programs and projects that will provide a defined benefit such as capital projects, building programs, specific program needs or ongoing operations from time to time are all considered. Grant applications from elementary or secondary education institutions will be considered if they involve programs for at-risk, handicapped or learning-disabled children; or if they are innovative and apply to all schools in the system.
Requirements: Applicant should submit a narrative summary no more than three pages in length. This letter should be addressed to the Trustees of the Foundation, see website for detailed description of narrative requirements. IRS 501(c)3 non-profit organizations in the metropolitan Tulsa, Oklahoma area are eligible to apply. Application may be made at any time for support of activities consistent with the Foundation's guidelines. The Foundation's Board meets monthly to review grant applications. Applications received on or before the 12th day of the month (unless the 12th falls on a Saturday, Sunday, or a holiday, in which event applications are due on the preceding business day) preceding a next regularly scheduled Board meeting are normally considered at such meeting.
Restrictions: Grant applications for individuals are not considered. The Foundation discourages applications for general support or reduction of debt,

or for continuing or additional support for the same programs. The Foundation will only review one grant request per agency during our fiscal year
Geographic Focus: Oklahoma
Amount: 2,000 - 1,000,000 USD
Samples: Parent Child Center of Tulsa, Tulsa, OK, $10,000—program funds (2009); Street John Medical Center Foundation, Tulsa, OK, $106,000—funds for programs and capital improvements (2009); Tulsa Air & Space Museum, Tulsa, OK, $10,000—provide funds for capital improvements (2009).
Contact: Margaret Skyles, Administrator; (918) 584-4711; (918) 584-4713; mskyles@bernsen.org or info@bernsen.org
Internet: http://www.bernsen.org/grant.html
Sponsor: Grace and Franklin Bernsen Foundation
15 West Sixth Street, Suite 1308
Tulsa, OK 74119-5407

Greater Columbus Arts Council Operating Grants 791
GCAC grants fund the operation of arts organizations that demonstrate high-quality artistic programming, stable artistic and administrative staffing, healthy financial structures, and significant impact on the city's economy and tourism. Operating support grants allow the organization to develop and maintain managerial and artistic capacity through methods the organization deems most valuable. Operating support grants are unrestricted as to use.
Requirements: Applicant organizations must have had 501(c)3 status for at least three consecutive years prior to the date of application, demonstrate that the organization's primary focus and actual operation are artistic in nature, provide cultural programming of the highest caliber, employ professional management staff, demonstrate a wide-ranging impact on the city of Columbus, operate with a community-based board of trustees, operate with a clearly articulated artistic plan, and demonstrate fiscal accountability.
Geographic Focus: Ohio
Date(s) Application is Due: Feb 1
Contact: Program Officer, Community Funding; (614) 224-2606; (614) 224-7461; grants@gcac.org
Internet: http://www.gcac.org/org/guidelines_operating_support.php
Sponsor: Greater Columbus Arts Council
100 E Broad Street, Suite 2250
Columbus, OH 43215

Greater Tacoma Community Foundation Fund for Women and Girls Grant 792
The mission of the fund is to promote the power of generosity among women and fund opportunities for women and girls in Pierce County. Distributions from the Fund shall provide assistance to programs that promote intellectual, physical, emotional, social, economic, and cultural growth of women and girls of all ages. Grants will be considered for general operations, equipment, and project support. Application information is available online.
Requirements: Grants will be made to organizations, located primarily in, and serving women and girls of, the greater Tacoma-Pierce County area.
Restrictions: Grants will not be made for annual campaigns, fund raising events, travel expenses, political or lobbying activities, religious organizations for sacramental/theological purposes, endowments, or publications except those that grow out of research and experiments underwritten by the Foundation. Grants will not be awarded for deficit reduction. Grant requests from agencies that are discriminatory to race, sex, age, national origin, religion, physical or mental handicap, veteran status or sexual orientation will not be considered.
Geographic Focus: Washington
Date(s) Application is Due: May 15; Jun 15
Amount: 1,700 USD
Contact: Sherrana Kempton, (253) 383-5622; (253) 272-8099; sherrana@gtcf.org
Internet: http://www.tacomafoundation.org/newsarticle.cfm?articleid=67374&ptsidebaroptid=0&returnto=page19700.cfm&returntoname=Fund%20for%20Women%20and%20Girls&siteid=1735&pageid=19538&sidepageid=19700&banner1img=banner%5F1%2EJPG&banner2img=banner%5F2%2EJPG&bannerb
Sponsor: Greater Tacoma Community Foundation
950 Pacific Avenue, Suite 1220, P.O. Box 1995
Tacoma, WA 98402

Greater Tacoma Community Foundation Grants 793
The Foundation invests in the community through grants to vital nonprofit agencies in Pierce County. While grants are made across all fields, principal funding areas include: arts and culture; civics; education; the environment; health; and human services. The Foundation also makes capital, equipment, project and operating support grants. Application information is available online.
Requirements: Eligible applicants must meet the following criteria: attest to non-discrimination on the basis of race, sex, age, national origin, religion, physical or mental handicap, veteran status or sexual orientation; provide a service primarily for residents of Pierce County; qualify as tax-exempt under section 501(c)3 of the IRS Code; and apply no more than once a year for any one governing or umbrella organization.
Restrictions: Grants will not be made for: fundraising events or fundraising feasibility projects; individuals; religious organizations for sacramental/theological purposes; production of books, videos, films, or other publications; annual campaign appeals; travel; political or lobbying activities; endowments; debt reduction; events or programs that occur prior to the board of directors decision/notification dates.
Geographic Focus: Washington
Samples: Kids in Distressed Situations (New York, NY)—to provide donated products to low-income children and families in Tacoma and Pierce County, WA, through the Emergency Food Network, $25,000.
Contact: Rose Lincoln Hamilton, President & CEO; (253) 383-5622; (253) 272-8099; rlincoln@gtcf.org
Internet: http://www.tacomafoundation.org
Sponsor: Greater Tacoma Community Foundation
950 Pacific Avenue, Suite 1220, P.O. Box 1995
Tacoma, WA 98402

Greater Worcester Community Foundation Jeppson Memorial Fund for Brookfield Grants 794
The Fund provides money to civic and community projects that help improve the lives of residents and enrich the cultural environment. The Fund provides support for: cultural or artistic performances; public seminars; festivals or exhibitions; services that help frail or vulnerable citizens, or that contribute to public health and safety; opportunities for educational enrichment; youth involvement in recreation, sports and the arts; and projects that foster community awareness and connections among different groups. Application information is available online.
Requirements: Any nonprofit or civic organization that serves the residents of Brookfield may apply.
Restrictions: Grant funds may not be used for expenses already incurred by the applicant. Fund awards are not intended to replace municipal funds.
Geographic Focus: Massachusetts
Date(s) Application is Due: Jul 15
Contact: Pamela B. Kane, (508) 755-0980; pkane@greaterworcester.org
Internet: http://www.greaterworcester.org/grants/Jeppson.htm
Sponsor: Greater Worcester Community Foundation
370 Main Street, Suite 650
Worcester, MA 01608-1738

Greenburg-May Foundation Grants 795
Grants are almost entirely awarded for medical research, primarily in the fields of cancer, heart, and neurological research. In addition, some support is given to hospitals, Jewish welfare funds, temple support, and the aging. Types of support include general operating support, continuing support, annual campaigns, endowment funds, emergency funds, program development, internships, scholarship funds, research, and consulting services. Organizations in Florida and New York City receive the largest part of the funds. Applications may be submitted at any time.
Requirements: Nonprofit organizations in southern Florida and New York are eligible.
Restrictions: Grants are not given to individuals or for endowment funds, special projects, publications, or conferences, and generally not for scholarships and fellowships.
Geographic Focus: Florida, New York
Amount: Up to 295,282 USD
Samples: Miami Jewish Home and Hospital for the Aged (Miami, FL)—$75,200; Greater Miami Opera (Miami, FL)—$4,220.
Contact: Isabel May, President; (305) 864-8639
Sponsor: Greenburg-May Foundation
P.O. Box 54-5816
Miami Beach, FL 33154

GreenPoint Foundation Grants **796**

The foundation awards grants in operating communities to organizations dedicated to increasing the availability of affordable housing and that meet basic health and human service needs. Submit grant requests on organization letterhead, which is signed by an officer, and include specific details, including budget, about the project or event; the organization's mission statement; details regarding the organization's services to low- to moderate-income individuals and/or its activities to revitalize/stabilize low- to moderate-income areas (include statistics if possible); and the IRS determination letter with the organization's federal (not state) tax ID number.
Requirements: 501(c)3 nonprofits that serve the needs of the communities in which GreenPoint Bank does business are eligible.
Restrictions: Grants do not support capital campaigns, endowments, scholarship funds, special events, other short-term projects, religious organizations, or membership organizations.
Geographic Focus: New York
Amount: Up to 28,000,000 USD
Samples: Families of employees of Keefe, Bruyette and Woodf (New York, NY)—for families of employees killed in the September 11 attacks on the World Trade Center, $250,000; American Red Cross, Disaster Relief Fund (Washington, DC)—to provide disaster-relief services to victims of the September 11 terrorist attacks, $25,000.
Contact: Gwen Perry, Foundation Manager; (212) 834-1215; (212) 834-1406; gperry@GreenPoint.com
Internet: http://www.greenpoint.com/index.cfm?spPathname=static/com-grants5less.htm
Sponsor: GreenPoint Foundation
90 Park Avenue, 4th Floor
New York, NY 10016

Grotto Foundation Project Grants **797**

The foundation is interested in local programs in Minnesota that improve education and promote economic, physical, and social well-being, particularly programs focusing on children and youth, ethnic groups, immigrants and refugees, gays and lesbians, and the economically disadvantaged. Grants support new, innovative projects with special consideration given to programs that show potential to continue after the grant period. General operating grants also are awarded. Application procedures are available on the website.
Requirements: Minnesota 501(c)3 nonprofits may submit grant applications.
Restrictions: Policy precludes grants being awarded for capital fund projects, travel, publication of books or manuscripts, undergraduate research projects, or grants to individuals.
Geographic Focus: Minnesota
Date(s) Application is Due: Jan 15; Mar 15; Jul 15; Nov 15
Amount: Up to 10,000 USD
Samples: W. Harry Davis Leadership Institute (Minneapolis, MN)—for the African American Youth Leadership Training Initiative, $4500; Girl Scout Council of Saint Croix Valley (MN)—for a volleyball program for Asian American girls, $3000; Mankato State U (MN)—for a dental health program for Native Americans, $2467.
Contact: Sarah Marquardt, Grants Manager; (763) 277-3434; (763) 277-3444; info@grottofoundation.org
Internet: http://www.grottofoundation.org
Sponsor: Grotto Foundation
5323 Lakeland Avenue N, Suite 100
Minneapolis, MN 55429-3115

Grundy Foundation Grants **798**

The foundation awards capital grants to eligible Pennsylvania nonprofit organizations in its areas of interest, including children and youth, culture, health care and hospitals, elderly, disabled, and historic preservation. Projects are generally funded for one year and often on a one-time basis. Potential applicants should submit a letter that describes the organization, project or activity, and funds requested. Applications are accepted at any time.
Requirements: Pennsylvania 501(c)3 organizations in Bucks County are eligible.
Restrictions: Grants are not made to support operating expenses, political or religious organizations, or individuals.
Geographic Focus: Pennsylvania
Amount: 1,000 - 75,000 USD
Samples: Bristol Riverside Theater (Bristol, PA)—for the performance season; Behanna (Southampton, PA)—for renovations to Swigart House.
Contact: Roland Johnson, Executive Director; (215) 788-5460; (215) 788-0915; grundyf@voicenet.com
Sponsor: Grundy Foundation
680 Radcliffe Street, P.O. Box 701
Bristol, PA 19007

Gulf Coast Foundation of Community Capacity Building Grants **799**

The Capacity Building Grants program offers Grant Writer Assistance funding, which helps local nonprofits that are unable to compete for grant opportunities because of complex, lengthy grant applications. Funds may be used to hire an experienced grant writer with the capabilities to attract dollars from regional or national funders and private or government programs. Requests for grant writing assistance will be judged on the following criteria: amount is significant enough to warrant the use of grant funds to hire a grant writer; the source of the grant is non-local; the expertise of the selected grant writer is appropriate; the agency has a reasonable chance of receiving the grant; the cost to hire a grant writer would have been prohibitive to the agency if these funds were not available; and all fund requests will require a minimum 50 percent cash match by the agency.
Requirements: The Foundation will make grants to qualified organizations classified as 501(c)3 tax-exempt public charities by the Internal Revenue Service in the counties of Brevard, Charlotte, Citrus, Collier, DeSoto, Glades, Hardee, Hendry, Hernando, Highlands, Hillsborough, Indian River, Lake, Lee, Manatee, Okeechobee, Orange, Osceola, Pasco, Pinellas, Polk, Sarasota, Seminole, Sumter, and Street Lucie.
Geographic Focus: Florida
Contact: Kirstin Fulkerson, Philanthropic Advisor; (941) 486-4600; (941) 486-4699; info@gulfcoastcf.org
Internet: http://www.gulfcoastcf.org/resources.php
Sponsor: Gulf Coast Foundation of Community
601 Tamiami Trail South
Venice, FL 34285

Gulf Coast Foundation of Community Operating Grants **800**

Through grants and strategic community initiatives, Gulf Coast invests in the work of effective nonprofit organizations that improve quality of life in our region. The Foundation will award operating grants over $10,000, with grant funds to be expended within one year of approval. Currently, the Foundation has four grant cycles for operating grants, which fund the core operating needs of nonprofits and help make them stronger. This includes staff and training, database and accounting systems, marketing and fundraising operations. Organizations that want to diversify income streams and generate new revenue sources may apply for an operating – earned revenue grant. Examples of successful proposals in this category include using existing facilities to generate rental income or marketing and selling a packaged program/service to other organizations. Groups that want to reduce operating costs may apply for an operating – efficiency grant. Examples of successful proposals in this category include consolidating services with other nonprofits, implementing new or improved technologies such as databases or financial systems, or "greening" offices.
Requirements: The Foundation will make grants to qualified organizations classified as 501(c)3 tax-exempt public charities by the Internal Revenue Service in the counties of Brevard, Charlotte, Citrus, Collier, DeSoto, Glades, Hardee, Hendry, Hernando, Highlands, Hillsborough, Indian River, Lake, Lee, Manatee, Okeechobee, Orange, Osceola, Pasco, Pinellas, Polk, Sarasota, Seminole, Sumter, and Street Lucie. All operating – earned revenue grant applications must provide realistic revenue estimates that result in a return on investment that exceeds the grant amount. Operating – efficiency grant applications must provide a cost?benefit analysis showing how proposed funding approaches will produce cost savings.
Geographic Focus: Florida
Samples: Special Operations Warrior Foundation, $500,000 - immediate financial assistance for special operations personnel, who have been severely wounded, to have his/her family travel and be bedside (2009); Charlotte Behavioral Health Care, $200,000 - addressing mental health, substance abuse, and related psychosocial needs of veterans and their families (2009).
Contact: Kirstin Fulkerson, Philanthropic Advisor; (941) 486-4600; (941) 486-4699; info@gulfcoastcf.org
Internet: http://www.gulfcoastcf.org/resources.php
Sponsor: Gulf Coast Foundation of Community
601 Tamiami Trail South
Venice, FL 34285

Guy's and Street Thomas' Charity Grants 801

The Charity's grants program supports both small (under 20,000 British pounds) and large (between 20,000 and 1 million British pounds) projects under three themes: staff benefits and development; clinical and service innovation; and buildings and the environment. Applications for grants under 20,000 British pounds are considered by the Small Grants Committee, and grants over 20,000 British pounds are assessed by the New Services and Innovations Committee. The small grants deadline dates are: August, 14; September, 25; October 16. Deadline dates for the large grants are: December, 1; March, 6; June, 5; September, 4; November, 20.
Requirements: The Charity only considers applications from anyone working in one of the four NHS Trusts in Lambeth or Southwark, although there are some restrictions for mental health staff.
Geographic Focus: United Kingdom
Date(s) Application is Due: Aug 14; Sep 25; Oct 16; Dec 1; Mar 6; Jun 5; Sep 4; Nov 20
Amount: 20,000 - 1,000,000 GBP
Samples: Julie Brown, Midwifery Practice Leader for Parent Education, 5,000 pounds; Drive Danielle Harari, Consultant Physician in Elderly Medicine, 20,000 pounds; Improving dermatology training for primary care professionals, NHS Foundation Trust, 254,000 pounds.
Contact: Anne Rigby, Grants Manager; 020 7188 1227; anne.rigby@gsttcharity.org.uk
Internet: http://www.gsttcharity.org.uk/grants/index.html
Sponsor: Guy's and Street Thomas' Charity
Freepost Lon 15724
London, SE1 9YA England

GVF Elgin Grant Works 802

The foundation awards a limited number of general operating grants per year to Elgin-based nonprofit organizations. Organizations may apply for renewed support for two additional years. After the third year of funding, a full calendar year must elapse before an organization may apply for another general operating grant. Application deadlines are the first Friday in February, June, and October. Application and guidelines are available online.
Requirements: Eligible organizations are 501(c)3; based in Elgin, IL, providing services to Elgin residents; and have a dedicated Elgin budget; have an annual operating budget between $50,000 and $4 million; are well managed and fiscally sound; have a balanced budget or an operating deficit of less than 10 percent; have at least one paid staff person; have been in business and operating as a 501(c)3 nonprofit for at least three years; are willing to abide by the grant agreement; and are willing to submit a final report.
Restrictions: Grants are not available to support endowments, organizations not based in Elgin, fundraising events, debt or deficit reduction, grantmaking organizations, federated funds, scholarships, political campaigns, religious purposes, or individuals.
Geographic Focus: Illinois
Date(s) Application is Due: Feb 3; Jun 3; Oct 7
Amount: Up to 10,000 USD
Samples: Elgin Children's Chorus (IL)—general operating support, $10,000; The Literacy Connection (Elgin, IL)—general operating support, $10,000; Little Angels Parents ARC (Elgin, IL)—general operating support, $10,000; Sybaquay Girl Scout Council (Elgin, IL)—general operating support, $10,000.
Contact: Grants Administrator; (847) 289-8575; (847) 289-8576; info@grandvictoriafdn.org
Internet: http://www.grandvictoriafdn.org
Sponsor: Grand Victoria Foundation
60 S Grove Avenue
Elgin, IL 60120

H&R Block Foundation Grants 803

The foundation supports the arts and culture, community development, education, and health and human services. Grants for operational support; special projects; and capital improvements for construction, renovation, and equipment will be considered. The foundation usually makes one-year grants but may consider requests for up to five years for special project funding. Guidelines and application are available online.
Requirements: 501(c)3 tax-exempt organizations are eligible. Major emphasis is placed on support of activities in the Kansas City metropolitan area.
Restrictions: Except in most unusual circumstances, the foundation does not make grants to individuals or businesses; publications; projects for which the foundation must exercise expenditure responsibility; single-disease agencies; travel or conferences; historic preservation; or telethons, dinners, advertising, or other fundraising events.
Geographic Focus: Kansas, Missouri
Date(s) Application is Due: Jan 28; Apr 29; Jul 29; Oct 14
Amount: 500 USD
Contact: Grants Administrator; (816) 932-8324; (816) 753-1585; foundation@hrblock.com
Internet: http://www.hrblockfoundation.org/grants/index.html
Sponsor: HandR Block Foundation
4400 Main Street
Kansas City, MO 64111

H.A. and Mary K. Chapman Charitable Trust Grants 804

The H.A. and Mary K. Chapman Charitable Trust and The Mary K. Chapman Foundations are private foundations, each formed as a perpetual entity in trust, that maintain endowments to fund charitable grants to public charities. The trustees and staff that administer the foundations also provide public stewardship through service to charitable organizations and causes. Though not limited geographically, most grants and public service are within Oklahoma. Grants to human services and civic and community programs and projects are primarily focused in the area of Tulsa. There are two steps in the process of applying for a grant. The first is a Letter of Inquiry from the applicant. This letter is used to determine if the applicant will be invited to take the second step of submitting a formal Grant Proposal.
Requirements: IRS 501(c)3 non-profits are eligible to apply.
Restrictions: Grant requests for the following purposes are not favored: endowments, except as a limited part of a capital project reserved for maintenance of the facility being constructed; deficit financing and debt retirement; projects or programs for which the Chapman Trusts would be the sole source of financial support; travel, conferences, conventions, group meetings, or seminars; camp programs and other seasonal activities; religious programs of religious organizations; project or program planning; start-up ventures are not excluded, but organizations with a proven strategy and results are preferred; purposes normally funded by taxation or governmental agencies; requests made less than nine months from the declination of a previous request by an applicant, or within nine months of the last payment made on a grant made to an applicant; requests for more than one project.
Geographic Focus: All U.S. States
Samples: Thackerville Community Foundation, Tuksa, OK, $52,500—purchase of brush truck & equipment (2008); Tulsa Symphony Orchestra, Tulsa, OK, $10,000—operating funds (2008); Holland Hall School, Tulsa, OK, $1,250,000—primary school renovation (2008).
Contact: Andrea Doyle, Program Officer; (918) 496-7882; (918) 496-7887; andie@chapmantrusts.com
Internet: http://www.chapmantrusts.org/grants_programs.html
Sponsor: H.A. and Mary K. Chapman Charitable Trust
6100 South Yale, Suite 1816
Tulsa, OK 74136

H.J. Heinz Company Foundation Grants 805

The Foundation is committed to promoting the health and nutritional needs of children and families. Priority is given to programs in communities where Heinz operates with a special focus given to southwestern Pennsylvania. The Foundation proactively donates funds to develop and strengthen organizations that are dedicated to nutrition and nutritional education, youth services and education, diversity, healthy children and families, and quality of life. Application information is available online.
Requirements: Only organizations that have 501(c)3 tax status under the U.S. Internal Revenue Code are eligible for support domestically. International organizations are encouraged to submit a letter of inquiry prior to preparing a full proposal to determine eligibility. International organizations will need to provide a 501(c)3 determination letter from the United States Internal Revenue Service or sufficient documentation to demonstrate that the non-U.S. grantee is the equivalent of a U.S. public charity. Documentation should be provided in English. The Foundation will also accept proposals in the Common Grant Application Format. All proposals must be submitted in writing. Electronic submissions are not accepted at this time.
Restrictions: The Foundation will not provide grants to individuals nor make multi-year pledges except for major capital or grant campaigns. Generally, the Foundation does not make loans and does not provide grants for individuals, equipment, conferences, travel, general scholarships, religious programs, political campaigns, and unsolicited research projects.
Geographic Focus: All U.S. States

Samples: King Edwards Memorial Hospital, Subiacio, Perth, Australia, $28,000—Micronutrient long-term development study (2008); The Children's Medical & Research Foundation, Dublin, Ireland, $25,000—new adolescent Hematology/Oncology unit (2008); Pittsburgh Public Theater, Pittsburgh, PA, $30,000—program support (2008).
Contact: Tammy B. Aupperle, Program Director; (412) 456-5773; (412) 442-3227; heinz.foundation@hjheinz.com
Internet: http://www.heinz.com/sustainability.aspx/social/heinz-foundation.aspx
Sponsor: H.J. Heinz Company Foundation
P.O. Box 57
Pittsburgh, PA 15230-0057

H. Leslie Hoffman and Elaine S. Hoffman Foundation Grants 806
The foundation awards general operating grants to California non-profits, primarily focusing on education. Additional funding is also available in the following areas of interest: arts; social services; hospitals; health organizations; children/youth services, including children's hospitals and, social services. There are no application forms or deadlines.
Requirements: California IRS 501(c)3 non-profits are eligible to apply. The majority of grants are funded in the Los Angeles area with a special emphasis on Pasadena.
Restrictions: Individuals are ineligible.
Geographic Focus: California
Amount: 1,000 - 200,000 USD
Samples: All Saints Church, Pasadena, CA, $10,000—general funding (2008); Hillsides Home For Children, Pasadena, CA, $5,000—general funding (2008); Descanso Gardens, Lacanada, CA, $1,000—annual benefit (2008).
Contact: J. Kristoffer Popovich, Treasurer; (626) 793-0043
Sponsor: H. Leslie Hoffman and Elaine S. Hoffman Foundation
225 S Lake Avenue, Suite 1150
Pasadena, CA 91101-3005

Haddad Foundation Grants 807
The Haddad Foundation, established in West Virginia in 2003, offers grant support primarily in Boone and Kanawha counties of West Virginia. Its identified fields of interest include: children and youth services; higher education; and human services. Funding comes in the form of general operations support. There are no specific application forms or deadlines with which to adhere, and initial approach should be with a letter of application. Amounts range up to $10,000.
Requirements: Applicants must be a 501(c)3 organization that serves the residents of either Boone or Kanawha counties, West Virginia.
Geographic Focus: West Virginia
Amount: Up to 10,000 USD
Samples: Smile Train, New York, New York, $10,000 - general operating support (2009); University of South Florida, Tampa, Florida, $6,400 - general operating support (2009).
Contact: Susan L. Haddad, Director; (304) 925-5418
Sponsor: Haddad Foundation
707 Virginia Street East, Suite 900
Charleston, WV 25301-2716

Hagedorn Fund Grants 808
William Hagedorn directed that the remainder of his estate be dedicated to this fund, in memory of his late wife, Tillie Hagedorn, that would support religious or charitable organizations in the New York City region. Funding interests include: health (including cancer, HIV/AIDS, blindness), gardens, social services, youth, education, senior services and housing and community development. All applications to the Hagedorn Fund must be submitted online, additional information is available at the Hagedorn Fund website.
Requirements: New York nonprofit organizations are eligible to apply.
Restrictions: No grants are made to individuals or private foundations or for matching gifts or loans.
Geographic Focus: New York
Date(s) Application is Due: Sep 1
Amount: 5,000 - 45,000 USD
Samples: Cornell University, New York, NY, $10,000 (2009); Brooklyn Botanic Garden Corporation, Brooklyn, NY, $20,000 (2009); Riverdale Presbyterian Church, Bronx, NY, $20,000 (2009).
Contact: Erin K. Hogan, Fund Manager; (212) 464-2476; (212) 464-2305; erin.k.hogan@jpmorgan.com
Internet: http://fdncenter.org/grantmaker/hagedorn
Sponsor: Hagedorn Fund
270 Park Avenue, 16th Floor
New York, NY 10017

Halliburton Foundation Grants 809
The foundation supports education at all levels and charitable organizations in the following ways: matching U.S. - based employee donations on a two-for-one basis up to $20,000 annually per employee for accredited junior colleges, colleges, and universities; matching U.S. -based employee donations to accredited elementary and secondary schools on a two-for-one basis up to $500 annually per employee; making direct donations to U.S. -based elementary and secondary schools and colleges and universities; and recognizing and supporting active U.S. -based employee volunteerism with direct donations through the Halliburton Volunteer Incentive Program. The corporate giving program makes donations to tax-exempt nonprofit organizations dedicated to education, health/welfare, civic issues, and arts and culture. The board meets quarterly. There are no application deadlines or forms.
Geographic Focus: Arizona, Texas
Amount: 250 - 20,000 USD
Contact: Margaret Carriere, (713) 676-3717; fhoufoundation@halliburton.com
Internet: http://www.halliburton.com/about/community.jsp
Sponsor: Halliburton Foundation
4100 Clinton Drive, Building 1, 7th Floor
Houston, TX 77020

Hallmark Corporate Foundation Grants 810
The mission of the Foundation is to help create communities where: all children have the chance to grow up as healthy, productive and caring persons; vibrant arts and cultural experiences enrich the lives of all citizens; there is a strong infrastructure of basic institutions and services, especially for persons in need; and all citizens feel a responsibility to serve their community. Proposals are accepted and reviewed throughout the year. There are no deadlines. The application process can be completed online using the Hallmark General Grant Application, which is available on the Hallmark website.
Requirements: IRS Non-profit 501(c)3 organizations are eligible to apply in the following areas: Kansas City metropolitan area; Center, Texas; Columbus, Georgia; Enfield, Connecticut; Lawrence, Kansas; Leavenworth, Kansas; Liberty, Missouri; Metamora, Illinois and; Topeka, Kansas.
Restrictions: Funding is not available for: individuals for any purpose, including travel, starting a business or paying back loans; religious organizations unless they can demonstrate that services are provided to the community at large and separated from religious purposes; fraternal, international and veterans organizations; sports teams and athletic organizations; individual youth clubs, troops, groups or school classrooms; social clubs; disease-specific organizations whose local chapters primarily raise funds for national research; past operating deficits; endowment or foundation funds; conferences; scholarly or health-related research; scholarship funds.
Geographic Focus: Connecticut, Georgia, Illinois, Kansas, Missouri, Texas
Contact: Community Development Manager; (816) 545-6906; contributions@hallmark.com.
Internet: http://corporate.hallmark.com/Community/Community-Involvement-Program-Guidelines
Sponsor: Hallmark Corporate Foundation
Mail Drop 323, P.O. Box 419580
Kansas City, MO 64141-6580

Hamilton Family Foundation Grants 811
The Foundation provides financial support primarily in the area of education, grades K-12 with a particular emphasis on literacy projects in underserved Philadelphia area schools. The Foundation considers applications for high school enrichment projects, as well as academically based after-school, arts and culture, and summer programs. Colleges and universities are not generally considered. The grant application is available online.
Requirements: Nonprofit organizations in Pennsylvania's Chester, Camden, Montgomery, and Delaware Counties are eligible.
Restrictions: Grant requests for individuals, bricks and mortar projects, endowments, and other foundations are not processed.
Geographic Focus: Pennsylvania
Date(s) Application is Due: Nov 1; Feb 1; May 1; Aug 1
Amount: 3,000 - 15,000 USD
Samples: Academy of Natural Sciences (Philadelphia, PA)—to upgrade technology in its auditorium, $250,000.

Contact: Nancy Wingo, (610) 975-0517; (610) 293-0967; nwingo@HamiltonFamilyFoundation.org
Internet: http://www.hamiltonfamilyfoundation.org/guidelines.html
Sponsor: Hamilton Family Foundation
200 Eagle Road, Suite 316
Wayne, PA 19087

Handsel Foundation Grants **812**
The Handsel Foundation provides grants to organizations working to end companion animal cruelty, neglect, and overpopulation. It is most interested in supporting organizations with effective plans to reduce animal suffering through targeted spay/neuter programs to address companion animal overpopulation. These projects will be given special consideration, particularly for larger grants. The foundation occasionally provides grants for adoption and/or education programs relating to companion animals. However, these grants are rare and typically small relative to our spay/neuter grants.
Requirements: Prospective grant recipients must meet the following criteria: only 501(c)3 nonprofit organizations will be considered, as defined by the IRS; organization must have been in operation for at least one year; total expenses of less than $1 million for latest fiscal year; and must be seeking funds for programs in Oregon, Washington, or California.
Geographic Focus: All U.S. States
Date(s) Application is Due: Mar 31; Jun 30; Sep 30; Dec 31
Amount: 3,000 - 25,000 USD
Contact: Grants Coordinator; (206) 905-9887; inquiries@handselfdn.org
Internet: http://www.handselfdn.org/howtoapply.htm
Sponsor: Handsel Foundation
P.O. Box 6476
Olympia, WA 98507-6476

Hannaford Charitable Foundation Grants **813**
The foundation awards grants to nonprofit organizations in its areas of interest, including arts and culture, education, environment, children and youth, community development, neighborhoods, and United Way organizations. Types of support include general operating support, capital campaigns, scholarship funds, and exchange programs. There are no application forms or deadlines.
Requirements: Nonprofit organizations are eligible, with preference given to requests in Maine and New Hampshire.
Geographic Focus: Maine, Massachusetts, New Hampshire, New York, Vermont
Amount: 1,000 - 10,000 USD
Contact: Grants Administrator, c/o Scholarship America; (507) 931-1682
Internet: http://www.hannaford.com/Contents/Our_Company/Community/index.shtml
Sponsor: Hannaford Charitable Foundation
P.O. Box 1000
Portland, ME 04104

Harden Foundation Grants **814**
The goals of the foundation are to improve the well-being of youth, strengthen families, prevent inappropriate institutionalization of individuals, improve the quality of life through the arts, encourage humane treatment of animals, and improve coordination of social and community services in Monterey County, with emphasis on the Salinas Valley, areas. The foundation supports one-time capital projects, special initiatives, and general operating support.
Requirements: 501(C)3 organizations who provide services or programs in Monterey County, California are eligible to submit grant proposals.
Restrictions: The foundation does not fund sectarian religious programs, educational projects (except agriculture-related requests), endowments, annual events, conferences, or fund-raising events.
Geographic Focus: California
Date(s) Application is Due: Mar 1; Sep 1
Amount: Up to 100,000 USD
Samples: Boys and Girls Clubs of Monterey County (Seaside, CA)—for youth center at Salinas Sports Complex, $400,000. Kinship Center (Monterey, CA)—for capital campaign for new building in Salinas, $100,000.
Contact: Joseph Grainger, Executive Director; (831) 442-3004; (831) 443-1429; jgrainger@hardenfoundation.org
Internet: http://www.hardenfoundation.org
Sponsor: Harden Foundation
P.O. Box 779
Salinas, CA 93902

Harder Foundation Grants **815**
The foundation focuses grant making on environmental efforts. The foundation's four main interest areas are large forest ecosystem protection, grizzly bear habitat preservation in the 48 contiguous states, wild salmon recovery in the Pacific Northwest, and protection of the Everglades. Funded projects usually offer long-term protection of specific public lands and waterways and may concentrate on a particular environmental problem. The foundation gives priority to advocacy projects of statewide or regional significance aiming to protect undeveloped habitat areas facing immediate threats. Types of support include operating budgets, continuing support, annual campaigns, seed grants, land acquisition, endowment funds, and matching funds.
Requirements: Nonprofit environmental groups or projects in Alaska, Colorado, Florida, Idaho, Montana, Nevada, Oregon, Utah, Washington, and Wyoming are eligible.
Restrictions: Local projects with limited scope, environmental education programs, and public policy development are not funded.
Geographic Focus: Alaska, Colorado, Florida, Idaho, Montana, Nevada, Oregon, Utah, Washington, Wisconsin
Amount: 10,000 - 50,000 USD
Samples: Greater Yellowstone Coalition—to support a project for grizzly bear protection, $12,000; Save Our Wild Salmon Coalition—for general support, $14,500.
Contact: Mary Martin, Office Manager; (253) 593-2121; (253) 593-2122; grants@theharderfoundation.org
Sponsor: Harder Foundation
401 Broadway Avenue, Suite 303
Tacoma, WA 98402

Harold and Arlene Schnitzer CARE Foundation Grants **816**
The Foundation's principal purpose is to assist with Jewish, cultural, youth, education, medical, social service, and community activities. Foundation focus is on proposals for projects that enhance the quality of life in Oregon and Southwest Washington. The Foundation funds grant requests for operating expenses, special projects, matching grants, multiple-year grants and capital campaigns as well as for purchase of specific items. There is no formal application form. Interested applicants may contact the Foundation for guidelines.
Requirements: Nonprofit organizations in Oregon and Washington are eligible. Organizations located in Portland are given first funding priority. Approximately 90% of grant funds stay in the Portland metropolitan area.
Restrictions: The Foundation does not provide funds for individuals, non tax-exempt organizations, other private foundations or political groups.
Geographic Focus: Oregon, Washington
Date(s) Application is Due: Feb 28; May 31; Aug 31; Nov 30
Amount: 1,000 - 5,000,000 USD
Samples: Mittleman Jewish Community Center, Portland, OR, $400,000—for operating support; Oregon Health and Science University Foundation, Portland, OR, $5,500,000— for Diabetes Center; Give Them Wings, Hood River, OR, $25,000—for Wyeth Work Camp renovation.
Contact: Barbara Hall, Vice President; (503) 973-0286; (503) 450-0810
Sponsor: Harold and Arlene Schnitzer Foundation
P.O. Box 2708
Portland, OR 97208-2708

Harold Simmons Foundation Grants **817**
The foundation awards grants to Texas nonprofit organizations, with emphasis on social services, religion, health, the arts, and youth. Grants also support community programs and projects, child development, and adult basic education/literacy programs. The foundation also supports international development and relief efforts in Third World countries. Grants are awarded for general operating support, annual campaigns, capital campaigns, building construction/renovation, continuing support, seed money, and program development. Application forms are not required, and there are no deadline dates.
Requirements: Dallas, TX, nonprofits are eligible.
Restrictions: Grants are not awarded to support individuals or for endowment funds or loans.
Geographic Focus: Texas
Samples: Children's Medical Ctr Dallas (TX)—to establish a hospital within the medical center devoted to the needs of child cardiac patients, $5 million; U of Texas Southwestern Medical Ctr (Dallas)—to enhance the Simmons Comprehensive Cancer Center, including supporting the work of its newly recruited director, $15.4 million.
Contact: Lisa Simmons Epstein, President; (972) 233-2134

Sponsor: Harold Simmons Foundation
5430 LBJ Freeway, Suite 1700
Dallas, TX 75240-2697

Harold Whitworth Pierce Charitable Trust Grants **818**

The trust awards grants to Boston-area nonprofit organizations in its areas of interest, including green and public spaces—projects that support community gardens, parks, and other natural areas, and projects that enhance space for recreation; capital projects—projects that reduce the operating costs for an institution and projects that improve and/or restore the physical heritage of Boston; and research—environmental research and/or for making the results of such research available for public policy. Occasionally other areas are supported. Types of support include program development, seed money, capital projects, and operating grants on occasion. The first step in the application process is a phone call to determine whether the project is eligible. The listed application deadlines are for concept letters (two-page maximum). Full proposals are by invitation.
Requirements: 501(c)3 tax-exempt organizations in the Boston area are eligible.
Restrictions: Grants do not support scholarships, individuals, fund-raising events or training, films, videos, travel, or advocacy.
Geographic Focus: Massachusetts
Date(s) Application is Due: Mar 1; Sep 15
Amount: 1,000 - 100,000 USD
Contact: Elizabeth Nichols, (617) 523-8368; (617) 523-8949; piercetrust@nichols-pratt.com
Sponsor: Harold Whitworth Pierce Charitable Trust
50 Congress Street, Suite 832
Boston, MA 02109

Harris and Eliza Kempner Fund Grants **819**

The foundation provides grants primarily in the Galveston, TX, area to qualifying organizations in the broad areas of the arts, historic preservation, community development, education, health, and human services. The foundation gives preference to requests for seed money, operating funds, small capital needs, and special projects partnering with other funding sources. Application information is available online.
Requirements: Grants are made primarily to Texas qualifying organizations in the greater Galveston area.
Restrictions: Funding is not available for: fund-raising benefits; direct mail solicitations; grants to individuals; and grants to non-U.S. A based organizations.
Geographic Focus: Texas
Date(s) Application is Due: Mar 15; Oct 15
Samples: Galveston Art League, Galveston, TX, $5,000—matching grant to purchase gallery space (2008); Avenue L Missionary Baptist Church, Galveston, TX, $20,000—renovation and restoration repairs to Fellowship Hall (2008); Galveston Island Swim Team, Galveston, TX, $$4,600—program expansion to include all Galveston Island youth (2008).
Contact: Harrette N. Howard, Grants Administrator; (409) 762-1603; (409) 762-5435; information@kempnerfund.org
Internet: http://www.kempnerfund.org/app/programs.html
Sponsor: Harris and Eliza Kempner Fund
2201 Market Street, Suite 601
Galveston, TX 77550-1529

Harris Bank Foundation Grants **820**

Grants are made to a broad range of cultural, educational, community, and civic organizations in Chicago, IL, including organizations that help ethnic and/or minority groups. Education grants are made to private four-year institutions to help defray operating expenses, limited to colleges and universities within Cook County that provide comprehensive accredited programs. Education-related grants considered are unrestricted for operating expenses of recognized, nonprofit Chicago educational institutions other than schools, such as museums, public television, career development programs, and so forth. Culture and fine arts grants are given to organizations that foster an appreciation of the arts such as opera companies, art institutes, and symphony orchestras. Health care grants are available to local health organizations that increase minority community access to primary health care. The bank will fund programming for handicapped, drug rehabilitative, and other health care services on a selective basis. For civic affairs grants, the foundation considers organizations whose work and service enhance the business and community spirit of greater Chicago. Harris Bank also supports the revitalization of Chicago's neighborhoods throughout the city, makes grants for initial expenses of new organizations or new projects of established organizations that provide social services, especially to minority groups, and also provides funding for capital expenses of metropolitan organizations whose objectives are to respond to charitable, educational, scientific, medical, or cultural needs. Grants are approved at bimonthly meetings, usually on a yearly basis; however, the committee may approve multiple-year grants.
Requirements: Grants are given only to tax-exempt organizations located in the Chicago metropolitan area. A proposal should include a statement of the proposed project; project budget and potential funding sources; background information about the organization; evidence of tax-exempt status; and current, audited financial statements.
Restrictions: Grants are not made for or to political activities, individuals, individual sectarian or religious organizations, fraternal organizations, nor for testimonial drives, advertisements in souvenir or program books, or raffle tickets.
Geographic Focus: Illinois
Amount: 5,000 - 20,000 USD
Samples: Art Institute of Chicago (IL)—for general operating support, $14,000; YMCA of Metropolitan Chicago (IL)—for Duncan YMCA renovation and expansion, $10,000; Habitat for Humanity Uptown Chicago (IL)—for general operating support, $10,000.
Contact: Mary Houpt, Secretary Treasurer; (312) 461-5834; (312) 293-4702
Sponsor: Harris Bank Foundation
111 W Monroe Street, P.O. Box 755
Chicago, IL 60690

Harry A. and Margaret D. Towsley Foundation Grants **821**

The foundation awards grants to Michigan organizations in its areas of interest, including environment, medical and preschool education, social services, continuing education, and research in the health sciences. Types of support include annual campaigns, building construction and renovation, capital campaigns, continuing support, employee matching gifts, endowments, general operating support, matching/challenge support, professorships, program development, research, and seed grants. There are no application forms; submit a letter of inquiry between January and the listed application deadline.
Restrictions: Grants are not awarded to individuals or for travel, scholarships, fellowships, conferences, books, publications, films, tapes, audio-visual or communication media, or loans.
Geographic Focus: Michigan
Date(s) Application is Due: Mar 31
Samples: U of Michigan at Ann Arbor, School of Music ((MI)—to construct a theater and performing-arts center, $1.5 million; Nature Conservancy, Michigan Chapter (Lansing, MI)—for the Northern Great Lakes Forest Project, which will protect 271,000 acres across eight counties in Michigan's Upper Peninsula and link more than 2.5 million acres of protected federal, state, and natural areas, $2 million.
Contact: Lynn White, President; (989) 837-1100; (989) 837-3240
Sponsor: Harry A. and Margaret D. Towsley Foundation
140 Ashman Street, P.O. Box 349
Midland, MI 48640

Harry and Grace Steele Foundation Grants **822**

The foundation's giving emphasizes higher and secondary education including scholarship funds, the fine arts, population control, hospitals and clinics, religion, and youth agencies. Types of support include building funds, endowment funds, scholarship funds, matching funds, continuing support, general purposes, special projects, and equipment grants. Grants are made primarily to California organizations. Application guidelines may be requested; there is no deadline date.
Requirements: IRS 501(c)3 tax-exempt organizations in Orange County, CA, are eligible.
Restrictions: Grants are not made to individuals.
Geographic Focus: California
Amount: 100,000 - 250,000 USD
Samples: Borrego Community Health Society (Borrego Springs, CA)—for general support, $1 million,; Traveler's Aid Society (Garden Grove, CA)—for an additional case worker, $50,000; Canine Companions for Independence (Rancho Santa Fe, CA)—for training of working dogs, $12,000; Chapman U—for renovation of the biotechnology laboratory, $200,000.
Contact: Audrey Burnand, (949) 631-0418
Sponsor: Harry and Grace Suiteele Foundation
441 Old Newport Boulevard, Suite 301
Newport Beach, CA 92663

Harry and Helen Sands Charitable Trust Grants 823

Established in Milwaukee, Wisconsin, in 2007, the Harry and Helen Sands Charitable Trust offers its support primarily in West Virginia. Its primary field of interest is to assist in the funding of Christian churches and agencies through general operations money. Applicants should adhere to the Foundation guidelines by first requesting a formal application and submitting the completed request by the annual November 1 deadline.

Requirements: Applicants must be 501(c)3 or Christian organizations either located in, or serving the residents of, Wheeling, West Virginia.

Geographic Focus: West Virginia

Date(s) Application is Due: Nov 1

Amount: Up to 5,000 USD

Samples: Soup Kitchen of Greater Wheeling, Wheeling, West Virginia, $4,000 (2009); Wheeling Health Right, Wheeling, West Virginia, $4,000 (2009); Kings Daughters Child Care Centers, Wheeling, West Virginia, $2,500 (2009).

Contact: Debbie Broemsen, Trust Administrator; (866) 300-6222; (800) 883-7695; debbie.x.broemsen@jpmorgan.com

Sponsor: Harry and Helen Sands Charitable Trust
P.O. Box 3038
Milwaukee, WI 53201-3038

Harry and Jeanette Weinberg Foundation Grants 824

The foundation awards grants to support organizations in the areas of aging/gerontology, disabled, disadvantaged (economically), food distribution, and social services. Types of support include building construction/renovation, capital campaigns, challenge/matching grants, endowments, general operating support, and material acquisition. Submit a letter of inquiry at any time.

Restrictions: Grants are not awarded to institutions of higher education or museums.

Geographic Focus: All U.S. States

Amount: 10,000 - 1,000,000 USD

Samples: Punahou School (Honolulu, HI)—to construct Case Middle School, $3 million; Metropolitan Career Ctr (Philadelphia, PA)—for general operating support of its work with low-income and unemployed people, $330,000 over three years; Strive (New York, NY)—to strengthen and expand its job training and placement network, and for endowment, $5 million challenge grant.

Contact: Grants Administrator; (410) 654-8500

Internet: http://www.hjweinbergfoundation.org

Sponsor: Harry and Jeanette Weinberg Foundation
7 Park Center Court
Owings Mills, MD 21117

Harry Bramhall Gilbert Charitable Trust Grants 825

The Harry Bramhall Gilbert Charitable Trust supports tax-exempt organizations that contribute to the health, education, and cultural life of the Tidewater, Virginia region. The Trust currently and substantially funds nonprofits based in the cities of Norfolk, Chesapeake, and Virginia Beach, Virginia. To apply, submit a letter to the Trust (no application form is required) containing the following information: copy of IRS Determination Letter; copy of most recent annual report/audited financial statement/990; listing of board of directors, trustees, officers and other key people and their affiliations; detailed description of project and amount of funding requested. Include two copies.

Requirements: Virginia nonprofit organizations based in the cities of Norfolk, Chesapeake, and Virginia Beach are eligible.

Restrictions: No support for religious or political organizations. No grants to individuals.

Geographic Focus: Virginia

Date(s) Application is Due: Sep 30

Amount: 2,500 - 100,000 USD

Samples: Chesapeake Public Library Foundation, Chesapeake, VA, $5,000—for additions to collections of books, magazines, newspapers, computers, and software at Central Library (2008); University of Virginia, Charlottesville, VA, $100,000—for merit scholarships for undergraduate students in their fourth-year at UVA meeting certain criteria, who have graduated from Public High School of City of Chesapeake, VA (2008); Virginia Symphony, Norfolk, VA, $25,000—for general support and the Virginia Symphony Endowment Fund (2008).

Contact: Stuart D. Glasser, Treasurer; (757) 204-4858; sdglasser@cox.net

Internet: http://fdncenter.org/grantmaker/gilbert

Sponsor: Harry Bramhall Gilbert Charitable Trust
316 Scone Castle Loop
Chesapeake, VA 23322

Harry C. Trexler Trust Grants 826

The trust supports charitable organizations located in the city of Allentown or in Lehigh County, Pennsylvania. The trust provides that one-fourth of the income shall be added to the corpus, one-fourth paid to the city of Allentown for park purposes, and the remainder distributed to such charitable organizations and objects as shall be of the most benefit to humanity, but limited to Allentown and Lehigh County, Pennsylvania, particularly for hospitals, churches, institutions for the care of the crippled and orphans, youth agencies, social services, cultural programs, and support of ministerial students at two named Pennsylvania institutions. Types of support include: building construction/renovation, capital campaigns, continuing support, land acquisition, equipment acquisition, program development, general operating support, and matching/challenge grants.

Requirements: Potential grantees are nonprofit organizations located in Allentown or Lehigh County, PA, and rendering exclusive or substantial services to the people residing therein.

Restrictions: Grants are not made to individuals or for endowment funds, research, scholarships, or fellowships.

Geographic Focus: Pennsylvania

Date(s) Application is Due: Dec 1

Amount: 1,000 - 100,000 USD

Samples: Allentown Art Museum, Allentown, PA, $200,000—to construct a new wing (2009); Lehigh Valley Public Telecommunications Corporation, Allentown, PA, $15,000—underwrite a reading program in the Allentown School District (2009); Sacred Heart Hospital , Allentown, PA, $80,000—underwrite the operating expenses of the Parish Nurse Program in center-city Allentown (2009).

Contact: Janet Roth, Executive Director; (610) 434-9645; (610) 437-5721

Internet: http://www.TrexlerTrust.org/

Sponsor: Harry C. Trexler Trust
33 South 7th Street, Suite 205
Allentown, PA 18101

Harry W. Bass, Jr. Foundation Grants 827

The Dallas-based Harry W. Bass, Jr. Foundation seeks to enrich the lives of the citizens of Texas by providing support to qualified organizations in the areas of education, health, human services, civic & community, science, research, arts and culture. Grant applications for specific programs or projects, capital projects or, less often, general operations are considered. Endowment gifts are rare. The Harry W. Bass, Jr. Foundation also considers program-related investments as part of its grant-making activities. The foundation strives to be responsive to the needs of all eligible organizations and considers requests of any amount. There is no formal application form. Grant requests are accepted at any time throughout the year. Each organization is limited to one application within a twelve-month period. Requests are usually processed within three to four months. Electronic grant applications should be submitted to dcalhoun@hbrf.org (no file attachments, please). For more information, contact the Harry W. Bass, Jr. Foundation.

Requirements: Texas 501(c)3 tax-exempt organizations are eligible.

Restrictions: In general, grants are not made for purposes of: church or seminary construction; annual fundraising events or general sustentation drives; professional conferences and symposia; out-of-state performances or competition expenses; to other private foundations. Unsolicited grant requests are restricted to organizations based in the Greater Dallas area. In the event a grant is approved, the recipient organization will be unable to submit another grant request for two years due to the foundation policy of not providing subsequent year grants.

Geographic Focus: Texas

Samples: Southwestern Medical Foundation, $3,000,000—Heart, Lung & Vascular Center of Excellence at UT Southwestern University Hospital - Street Paul (2008); Child Protective Services Community Partners, $10,000—Rainbow Room; Health & Human Services Grant (2008); Wilkinson Center, $20,000—CLIMB After-School and Summer Program (2008).

Contact: F. David Calhoun, Executive Director; (214) 599-0300; (214) 599-0405; dcalhoun@hbrf.org

Internet: http://www.harrybassfoundation.org/about.asp

Sponsor: Harry Bass Foundation
4809 Cole Avenue, Suite 252
Dallas, TX 75205

Hartford Aging and Health Program Awards 828

The foundation's two principal programs are Health Care Cost and Quality and Aging and Health. The Health Care Cost and Quality program supports

the community health management initiative, health care quality measures, and reducing inappropriate health care services. The Aging and Health program supports strengthening physicians' knowledge of geriatrics, reducing medication problems of the elderly, and demonstrating integrated financing and service delivery for comprehensive geriatric services. Types of support include operating budgets, continuing support, projects/programs, research, publications, and conferences and seminars. The foundation also welcomes inquiries regarding projects that may not fit these specific interests but would further its broad goal of improving health care in America. Types of support include general operations, continuing support, projects/programs, research, publications, and conferences and seminars. Applications are accepted at any time and are reviewed four times each year when the board meets.
Requirements: U.S. health, education, and social service organizations may apply.
Restrictions: Requests will be denied for general research or for projects lasting more than three years.
Geographic Focus: All U.S. States
Samples: New York Academy of Medicine (NY)—to help start rotational field-training components, with a focus on working with older adults, in programs that offer master's degrees in social work, $5.1 million over four years; U of California (San Diego, CA) and U of Pittsburgh (PA)—to create new centers of excellence in geriatric medicine in order to increase the number of physician faculty members in the field of geriatrics, $450,000 each over three years; American Federation for Aging Research (New York, NY)—for the Medical Student Summer Research Training in Aging Program, $1.9 million over five years.
Contact: Corinne Rieder; (212) 832-7788; (212) 593-4913; mail@jhartfound.com
Internet: http://www.jhartfound.org
Sponsor: John A. Hartford Foundation
55 E 59th Street, 16th Floor
New York, NY 10022-1178

Hartford Foundation Regular Grants 829

The Foundation awards grants for a broad range of purposes to a wide variety of nonprofit organizations in social services, health, education, early childhood and youth services, arts and culture, housing and neighborhood development, and other charitable fields. These grants: enhance or strengthen existing activities; provide start-up for organizations and new programs; provide support for capital improvements. Interested applicants are encouraged to phone a program contact to discuss their project before beginning the application process.
Requirements: Nonprofit organizations in the following Connecticut towns are eligible to apply for funding: Andover, Avon, Bloomfield, Bolton, Canton, East Granby, East Hartford, East Windsor, Ellington, Enfield, Farmington, Glastonbury, Granby, Hartford, Hebron, Manchester, Marlborough, Newington, Rocky Hill, Simsbury, Somers, South Windsor, Suffield, West Hartford, Wethersfield, Windsor, Windsor Locks, Tolland, and Vernon. Proposals for statewide programs may be considered when there is a substantial benefit to residents of these communities.
Restrictions: The Foundation does not make grants from its unrestricted funds for: sectarian or religious activities; grants directly to individuals; grants to private foundations; endowments or memorials; direct or grass-roots lobbying efforts; conferences; research; or informational activities on topics that are primarily national or international in perspective. In addition, the Foundation generally does not make grants for: federal, state, or municipal agencies or departments supported by taxation; sponsorship of or support for one-time events; liquidation of obligations incurred at a previous date; or sustaining support for recurring operating expenses.
Geographic Focus: Connecticut
Amount: Up to 500,000 USD
Samples: Town of Farmington, Farmington, CT, $19,749 - for construction of a tower and zip line at the youth center and for the Farmington High School's McDonough School Math and Literacy Tutoring Program; The ARC of the Farmington Valley, Inc., Canton, CT, $375,000 - for remodeling, code compliance, and upgrades to the Alleluia property.
Contact: Cheryl L. Gerrish, Grants Manager; (860) 548-1888; (860) 524-8346; gerrish@hfpg.org or hfpg@hfpg.org
Internet: http://www.hfpg.org/GrantmakingPrograms/Overview/tabid/163/Default.aspx
Sponsor: Hartford Foundation
10 Columbus Boulevard, 8th Floor
Hartford, CT 06106

Hartford Foundation Transitional Operating Support Grants 830

The Foundation offers transitional operating support grants to enable well-run nonprofits that have experienced unexpected income shortfalls to continue important community programs. Support is designed for programs that: address critical needs, especially those involving disadvantaged or vulnerable populations; have been operated competently and demonstrate evidence of positive effects on the lives of the population served; and would be particularly difficult or expensive to reestablish if they ceased operations. Interested applicants should call the Foundation and speak with a program officer.
Requirements: Nonprofit organizations in the following Connecticut towns are eligible to apply for funding: Andover, Avon, Bloomfield, Bolton, Canton, East Granby, East Hartford, East Windsor, Ellington, Enfield, Farmington, Glastonbury, Granby, Hartford, Hebron, Manchester, Marlborough, Newington, Rocky Hill, Simsbury, Somers, South Windsor, Suffield, West Hartford, Wethersfield, Windsor, Windsor Locks, Tolland, and Vernon. Proposals for statewide programs may be considered when there is a substantial benefit to residents of these communities.
Restrictions: The Foundation does not make grants from its unrestricted funds for: sectarian or religious activities; grants directly to individuals; grants to private foundations; endowments or memorials; direct or grass-roots lobbying efforts; conferences; research; or informational activities on topics that are primarily national or international in perspective. In addition, the Foundation generally does not make grants for: federal, state, or municipal agencies or departments supported by taxation; sponsorship of or support for one-time events; liquidation of obligations incurred at a previous date; or sustaining support for recurring operating expenses.
Geographic Focus: Connecticut
Amount: Up to 200,000 USD
Contact: Cheryl L. Gerrish, Grants Manager; (860) 548-1888; (860) 524-8346; gerrish@hfpg.org or hfpg@hfpg.org
Internet: http://www.hfpg.org/GrantmakingPrograms/AboutOurGrantmaking/TypesofGrants/tabid/168/Default.aspx#transitionaloperating
Sponsor: Hartford Foundation
10 Columbus Boulevard, 8th Floor
Hartford, CT 06106

Harvest Foundation Grants 831

Formed by the sale of Memorial Health Systems, the foundation is managing an endowment to invest in programs and initiatives that will address local challenges in the areas of health, education, and welfare in Martinsville/Henry County. The foundation is committed to honoring the legacy of Memorial Hospital by emphasizing prevention, safety and access to health care; by facilitating opportunities for local citizens to help their community reach its potential, and by improving the learning environment for citizenship, academic, and vocational preparedness. Application and guidelines are available online.
Requirements: To be eligible for consideration, an organization must: be located within, or have its program focused within Martinsville and/or Henry County; have a letter from the IRS stating its 501c3 status; and propose a project within one of the Foundation's three interest areas of health, education or welfare.
Restrictions: The foundation does not fund organizations that discriminate based upon race, creed, gender, or sexual orientation; scholarships, fellowships, or grants to individuals; sectarian religious activities, political lobbying, or legislative activities; profit-making businesses; emergency needs or extremely time sensitive requests; or direct replacement of discontinued government support.
Geographic Focus: Virginia
Samples: Dan River Basin Association, $8,000— to enhance the Uptown Spur Trail (2009); Boy Scouts of America, Blue Ridge Mountains Council, $45,300—to launch the Scoutreach Program aimed at recruiting underserved boys in Martinsville/Henry County to join the Boy Scouts (2009); MARC Workshop, Inc., $241,900—funding paid over 3 years to start-up a mobile employment program for disabled adults, creating competitive, minimum wage jobs for special education students graduating out of the public school system (2009).
Contact: Allyson Rothrock, Executive Director; (276) 632-3329; (276) 632-1878; arothrock@theharvestfoundation.org
Internet: http://www.theharvestfoundation.org/page.cfm/topic/strategic-map
Sponsor: Harvest Foundation
1 Ellsworth Street, P.O. Box 5183
Martinsville, VA 24115

Hattie M. Strong Foundation Grants 832

The Foundation awards grants in support of projects designed to provide educational opportunities and services to youth and adults in the Greater Washington Area, with a concentration on programs in Washington, D.C. The Foundation considers innovative and effective programs that strengthen academic education (enrichment and remedial), promote literacy, and provide vocational skills training. Organizations interested in submitting a proposal for consideration by the Board should first contact the Foundation for written materials explaining the Foundation's proposal procedure and requirements.

Requirements: Nonprofit organizations serving the Washington, DC, metropolitan area may apply.

Restrictions: Funding is not available for building or endowment funds, requests for equipment, research, conferences, special events or benefits, projects designed to educate the general public, or programs of national or international scope. The Foundation does not make grants to individuals nor does it give scholarships.

Geographic Focus: District of Columbia

Date(s) Application is Due: Jan 15; Apr 15; Jul 15; Oct 15

Samples: Campagna Ctr (Alexandria, VA)—to support the Reading Specialist Program for first- to third-grade students at Mount Vernon Elementary School, $6000; Carlos Rosario Adult and Career Ctr (Washington, DC)—for general support to expand this adult education program, $6500.

Contact: Director; (202) 331-1619; (202) 466-2894; hmsf@hmstrongfoundation.org

Internet: http://www.hmstrongfoundation.org

Sponsor: Hattie M. Strong Foundation
1620 I Street NW, Suite 700
Washington, DC 20006-4005

Hawaii Community Foundation Geographic-Specific Fund Grants 833

With its Geographic-Specific program, the Foundation supports grant making in Ewa Beach, Kamuela, Kauai, Lanai, Maui, and West Hawaii via eleven distinct funds. Generally, these funds hope to improve the lives of residents living within these distinct geographic regions of Hawaii. Funding levels and deadlines vary throughout the course of year by fund, and applicants should visit the website for specific details.

Requirements: Nonprofit, tax-exempt 501(c)3 organizations, public schools, or units of government are eligible to apply. The Richard Smart Fund program supports projects that benefit the Waimea community.

Geographic Focus: Hawaii

Contact: Georgianna deCosta, Philanthropic Services Assistant; (808) 537-6333 or (888) 731-3863; gdecosta@hcf-hawaii.org

Internet: http://hawaiicommunityfoundation.org/index.php?id=71&categoryID=22

Sponsor: Hawai'i Community Foundation
1164 Bishop Street, Suite 800
Honolulu, HI 96813

Hawaii Community Foundation Health Education and Research Grants 834

The program provides support from three distinct funds: Tobacco Prevention & Control Trust Fund; the Leahi Fund Research Fund; and the Medical Research Program. Funding will be provided for medical education and research in the fields of: cancer; heart disease; lung disease and research. Priority is given to projects that: demonstrate a foreseeable benefit to the people of Hawaii; support new investigators in Hawaii; and support collaborative efforts. Proposal submission information is available online.

Requirements: To be eligible for consideration an organization must be a 501(c)3 organization or a unit of government. The Principal Investigator must be based in Hawaii and conducting the research in Hawaii.

Geographic Focus: Hawaii

Date(s) Application is Due: Feb 27; Jul 17; Aug 14; Sep 10

Amount: 25,000 - 50,000 USD

Contact: Christel Wuerfel, Philanthropic Services Assistant; (808) 537-6333 or (888) 731-3863; cwuerfel@hcf-hawaii.org

Internet: http://www.hawaiicommunityfoundation.org/index.php?id=71&categoryID=23

Sponsor: Hawai'i Community Foundation
1164 Bishop Street, Suite 800
Honolulu, HI 96813

Hawaii Community Foundation Human Services Grants 835

The purpose of the Foundation's Human Services program is to support children and youth, and family strengthening. Six distinct funds have been established to support various facets of the program, including: the Hawaii Children's Trust Fund (awareness & prevention); the Oscar and Rosetta Fish Fund for Speech Therapy; the Persons In Need (PIN) Program; the Reverend Takie Okumura Family Fund for Children and Youth; the Theodore A. Vierra Fund and Kitaro Watanabe Fund; and the Victoria S. and Bradley L. Geist Foundation Supporting Enhancements for Foster Children. Deadlines and funding levels of each program vary, and applicants should contact the Foundation for further details.

Requirements: Nonprofit, tax-exempt 501(c)3 organizations, public schools, or units of government are eligible to apply.

Geographic Focus: Hawaii

Amount: 3,000 - 10,000 USD

Contact: Jennifer Murphy, Program Officer; (808) 537-6333 or (888) 731-3863; csutherland@hcf-hawaii.org

Internet: http://hawaiicommunityfoundation.org/index.php?id=71&categoryID=24

Sponsor: Hawai'i Community Foundation
1164 Bishop Street, Suite 800
Honolulu, HI 96813

Haymarket People's Fund Sustaining Grants 836

The fund is an activist-controlled foundation committed to radical social change. Haymarket funds groups that organize or provide resources for organizing around a wide spectrum of issues, and who reflect in their action as well as their vision the principles Haymarket upholds. Groups must engage in grassroots organizing or provide resources for grassroots organizing efforts. Grant sizes are between $2000 and $10,000, and they average around $5,000.

Requirements: Both incorporated organizations (with or without established 501(c)3 status) and unincorporated organizations may apply. Applicants must conduct work within New England (Connecticut, Maine, Massachusetts, New Hampshire, Rhode Island, and Vermont).

Restrictions: Grants do not support social services if they do not demonstrate some organizing strategies to challenge the systems that lead to oppression; alternative business (food co-ops and alternative schools, for example); organizations with access to traditional or mainstream funding sources, including those with significant government and/or corporate funding and those with relatively large budgets; government agencies; individuals, or individual projects, such as graduate research or fellowships; or other grantmaking foundations. Groups with budgets over $350,000 will not be funded.

Geographic Focus: Connecticut, Maine, Massachusetts, New Hampshire, Rhode Island, Vermont

Date(s) Application is Due: Dec 3

Amount: 2,000 - 10,000 USD

Contact: Anne Richmond, Grantmaking Organizer; (617) 522-7676; (617) 522-9580; anne@haymarket.org

Internet: http://www.haymarket.org/grants.html

Sponsor: Haymarket People's Fund
42 Seaverns Avenue
Boston, MA 02130

Haymarket Urgent Response Grant 837

Grants of up to $1,000/year to help grassroots, social change organizations respond quickly to unforeseen crises or opportunities that critically affect an organization and its constituency. This includes unexpected events, political crises or organizing opportunities. Applications are accepted on a rolling basis, as long as funding is available.

Requirements: To receive an application, you must first call and speak with a Haymarket staff person about your request.

Restrictions: Grants are not to be used for ongoing program work (including expenses the organization should have anticipated), for financial crises or a shortfall in projected funding, or because the group missed a funding deadline. Additionally, the foundation does not fund: 1) Groups primarily providing direct services that focus on meeting people's basic needs or that focus primarily on individual empowerment or self-help. Social service organizations can apply for a project-specific organizing grant if it fits Haymarket's criteria. 2) Publications, reports, workshops, classes, conferences, media events, arts or theater productions unless they are part of an ongoing community organizing effort or are accountable to social change movements. 3) Groups based outside of New England (unless they have a strong base in New England which holds them accountable) or work focused outside of New England. 4) Legal or

research expenses unless they are part of an overall organizing strategy. 5) Capital campaigns or endowment drives. 6) Individuals or individual projects (such as graduate research, fellowships or scholarships). 7) Projects sponsored by a government agency. 8) Organizations with budgets over $350,000. 9) Small businesses, alternative businesses or business associations. 10) Other foundations. 11) Electoral work that promotes specific candidates.
Geographic Focus: Connecticut, Maine, Massachusetts, New Hampshire, Rhode Island, Vermont
Amount: Up to 1,000 USD
Contact: Anne Richmond, Grantmaking Organizer; (617) 522-7676; (617) 522-9580; anne@haymarket.org
Internet: http://www.haymarket.org/uresponse.htm
Sponsor: Haymarket People's Fund
42 Seaverns Avenue
Boston, MA 02130

HCA Foundation Grants **838**

The Foundation is committed to the care and improvement of human life. Grants are made in the areas of health and well being, childhood and youth development, and the arts. Preference will be given to requests from organizations where an HCA employee volunteers or serves on the board. New applicants are asked to send a one-or two-page letter of inquiry to the Foundation, describing the proposed project, its goals and objectives and the approximate level of funding required. Foundation staff will review each request and will notify the organization as to whether the project coincides with funding priorities.
Requirements: 501(c)3 nonprofit organizations are eligible. Because the foundation focuses its giving in Middle Tennessee, all requests outside of the Nashville area should be submitted to the closest HCA facility location or division office. Organizations must have a full updated GivingMatters.com profile to be considered for funding. For more information please go to www.givingmatters.com.
Restrictions: Funding is not available for: individuals or their projects; private foundations; political activities; advertising or sponsorships of events; social events or similar fund-raising activities. The Foundation does not ordinarily support: organizations in their first three years of operation and organizations involved in research, sports, environmental, wildlife, civic and international affairs. The Foundation does not accept proposals from individual churches or schools, but will support broad faith-based initiatives consistent with it's mission and guidelines.
Geographic Focus: Tennessee
Date(s) Application is Due: Dec 12; Mar 12; Jun 11; Sep 10
Amount: 20,000 - 100,000 USD
Samples: Campus for Human Development Public Charity, Nashville, TN, $100,000—capital funding (2008); Second Harvest Food Bank Middle Tennessee, Nashville, TN, $35,000—general operating (2008); Mental Health Association of Middle, Tennessee, Nashville, TN, $20,000—program funding (2008).
Contact: Lois Abrams, Grants Manager; (615) 344-2390; (615) 344-5722; lois.abrams@hcahealthcare.com
Internet: http://www.hcacaring.org/CustomPage.asp?guidCustomContentID=BBB7D8F2-B906-4302-A164-07643DB2582E
Sponsor: HCA Foundation
1 Park Plaza, Building 1, 4th Floor East
Nashville, TN 37203

Head Start Replacement Grantee: Colorado **839**

The Administration for Children and Families solicits applications from local public or private non-profit organizations, including faith-based organizations or local for-profit organizations, that wish to compete for funds that are available to provide Head Start services to children and families residing in the City of Alamosa, Colorado. The intent of this announcement is to provide for the continuation of services as previously provided by the former grantee, Alamosa Head Start, Inc. Funds in the amount of $987,663 annually will be available to provide Head Start program services to eligible children and their families. The former grantee was funded for a total enrollment of 161 children and families. Interested applicants should call the ACYF Operations Center at (866) 796-1591 to receive pre-application materials and additional information.
Requirements: Eligibility is limited to local public or private non-profit organizations, including faith-based organizations or local for-profit organizations, that can provide Head Start services to children and families residing in the City of Alamosa, Colorado.
Restrictions: Grantees are required to meet a non-Federal share of the project costs, in accordance with section 640(b) of the Head Start Act. Grantees must provide at least 20 percent of the total approved cost of the project.
Geographic Focus: Colorado
Date(s) Application is Due: Mar 28
Amount: 987,663 USD
Contact: Karen McKinney, Coordinator; (866) 796-1591; OHS@dixongroup.com
Internet: http://www.acf.hhs.gov/grants/open/HHS-2007-ACF-OHS-CH-0801.html
Sponsor: Administration for Children and Families
ACYF Operations Center, 118 Q Street NE
Washington, DC 20002

Head Start Replacement Grantee: Florida **840**

The Administration for Children and Families solicits applications from local public or private non-profit organizations, including faith-based organizations or local for-profit organizations, that wish to compete for funds that are available to provide Head Start services to children and families residing in Polk County, Florida. The intent of this announcement is to provide for the continuation of services as previously provided by the former grantee, the Polk County Opportunity Council, Inc. Funds in the amount of $6,896,580 annually will be available to provide Head Start program services to eligible children and their families. The former grantee was funded for a total enrollment of 942 children and families. Interested applicants should call the ACYF Operations Center at (866) 796-1591 to receive pre-application materials and additional information.
Requirements: Applicants should propose a design or designs that best address the needs of the proposed service area. Applicants have flexibility in determining the appropriate number of children to be served by the various program options (center-based, home-based, or combination) and program designs (hours per day, days per week, weeks per year). Preference will be given to applicants who can demonstrate efficient management of several or all of the service areas.
Restrictions: Grantees are required to meet a non-Federal share of the project costs, in accordance with section 640(b) of the Head Start Act. Grantees must provide at least 20 percent of the total approved cost of the project.
Geographic Focus: Florida
Date(s) Application is Due: Apr 13
Amount: 69,000,000 USD
Contact: Karen McKinney, Program Coordinator; (866) 796-1591; OHS@dixongroup.com
Internet: http://www.acf.hhs.gov/grants/open/HHS-2007-ACF-OHS-CH-0402.html
Sponsor: Administration for Children and Families
ACYF Operations Center, 118 Q Street NE
Washington, DC 20002

Head Start Replacement Grantee: West Virginia **841**

The Administration for Children and Families solicits applications from local public or private non-profit organizations, including faith-based organizations or local for-profit organizations, that wish to compete for funds that are available to provide Head Start services to children and families residing in Calhoun, Doddridge, Pleasants, Tyler, Wirt and/or Wood Counties, West Virginia. The intent of this announcement is to provide for the continuation of services as previously provided by the former grantee, Family Development, Inc. Applicants may apply to operate a Head Start program for one or more of the listed areas. Interested applicants should call the ACYF Operations Center at (866) 796-1591 to receive pre-application materials and additional information.
Requirements: Applicants should propose a design or designs that best address the needs of the proposed service area. Applicants have flexibility in determining the appropriate number of children to be served by the various program options (center-based, home-based, or combination) and program designs (hours per day, days per week, weeks per year). Preference will be given to applicants who can demonstrate efficient management of several or all of the service areas.
Restrictions: Grantees are required to meet a non-Federal share of the project costs, in accordance with section 640(b) of the Head Start Act. Grantees must provide at least 20 percent of the total approved cost of the project.
Geographic Focus: West Virginia
Date(s) Application is Due: Apr 23
Amount: Up to 23,000,000 USD

Contact: Karen McKinney, Program Coordinator; (866) 796-1591; OHS@dixongroup.com
Internet: http://www.acf.hhs.gov/grants/open/HHS-2007-ACF-OHS-CH-0303.html
Sponsor: Administration for Children and Families
ACYF Operations Center, 118 Q Street NE
Washington, DC 20002

Healthcare Georgia Foundation Grants **842**
The foundation's mission is to advance the health of all Georgians and to expand access to affordable, quality healthcare for underserved individuals and communities. Grantmaking priority areas include addressing health disparities, strengthening nonprofit health organizations, and expanding access to primary healthcare. The foundation will award grants that support: policy development and advocacy, research and evaluation, technical assistance/capacity building, organizational improvement, leadership development and recognition, direct service delivery, professional development and training, and public education and awareness. The grant application process begins with the submission of a two-page letter of inquiry that describes the funding request specifying who, what, where, when, for whom, and for what cost. Full proposals are by invitation.
Requirements: Georgia organizations, including community-based/health service, education, government, public policy, and other nonprofits, are eligible.
Geographic Focus: Georgia
Samples: Lowndes County Partnership for Health (Atlanta, GA)—to expand the Well Workplace health promotion program, to implement a strategic plan, and to help a church-based program become a self-sustaining, community-based nonprofit group, $145,000; National Council of La Raza-Atlantic Program Office (GA)—for the Georgia Latino/Hispanic Health Agenda and Leadership Project, $235,000; Planned Parenthood of Georgia (Atlanta, GA)—to strengthen its ability to provide health services to low-income women and to enhance the self-sustainability of its programs in Augusta, $50,000; Meridian Educational Resource Group (Atlanta, GA)—to establish a fitness, health-promotion, and weight-loss program for children served by the Whitefoord and Coan School Health Clinics, $150,000.
Contact: Grants Administrator; (404) 653-0990; (404) 577-8386; info@healthcaregeorgia.org
Internet: http://www.healthcaregeorgia.org
Sponsor: Healthcare Georgia Foundation
50 Hurt Plaza, Suite 550
Atlanta, GA 30303

Health Foundation of Greater Indianapolis Grants **843**
The foundation promotes health care for children, youth, and families in Marion County, IN, and seven contiguous Indiana counties. Programs of interest include school-based health, adolescent health, and HIV/AIDS Grants also are awarded to support the development of health careers and to promote cooperative effort between health professionals. Types of support include general operations, building/renovations, equipment, program/project development, conferences and seminars, seed money, technical assistance, and matching funds. Prior to submitting a proposal, contact Stephen L. Everett, Vice President of Programs, to determine if your program and proposal matches The Health Foundation of Greater Indianapolis' funding priorities and application guidelines.
Requirements: Grants are awarded to neighborhood-based service centers in Indiana's Marion County and the seven contiguous counties of Boone, Hamilton, Hancock, Hendricks, Johnson, Morgan and Shelby. Applicants must be a 501(c)3 group, organization or agency that provides health-related programs or services.
Restrictions: Grants will not be provided for: individuals; sectarian religious organizations; research projects; purchase of advertising or tickets to events; production and design of educational materials already available; endowments; short or long term loans or payment of financial obligations.
Geographic Focus: Indiana
Amount: 10,000 - 100,000 USD
Samples: Indiana AIDS Fund (Indianapolis, IN)—for a fundraising event for HIV/AIDS organizations, $25,000; Indianapolis Medical Society Foundation (IN)—for a project designed to improve access to health care for low-income, uninsured Indianapolis residents, $40,000; Little Red Door Cancer Agency (Indianapolis, IN)—to provide baskets filled with personal-care items to people with cancer, $15,000; Damien Ctr (Indianapolis, IN)—to implement its HIV Care Network, $50,000.
Contact: Stephen Everett, Program Officer; (317) 630-1805; (317) 630-1806; severett@thfgi.org
Internet: http://www.thfgi.org
Sponsor: Health Foundation of Greater Indianapolis
429 East Vermont Street, Suite 300
Indianapolis, IN 46202

Health Foundation of Southern Florida Responsive Grants **844**
The foundation awards Responsive Grants through two grant cycles per year. With exceptions, the foundation focuses on providing one to three year grants that do not exceed $300,000 annually. The majority of grants are funded in the $50,000 to $150,000 range over one or two years. Funding is provided in four categories: Project Planning; Health Services; Organizational Capacity Building and Health System/Health Policy Development.
Requirements: Though the foundation welcomes proposal applications anytime, the applications are reviewed on a semi-annual basis. Applicant organizations must be tax-exempt nonprofit under section 501(c)3 of the Internal Revenue Code or a local or state governmental agency. The project must serve exclusively the residents of Broward, Miami-Dade and/or Monroe counties. Initially, a preliminary proposal is required (see the sponsor's website for specific details). If approved, the sponsor will then invite a full proposal. Download the sponsor's grant guide from the website.
Restrictions: The foundation does not fund: Biomedical research or other research that will not impact local residents within the immediate future (1-3 years) or that does not have a direct application to implementing a community-driven health intervention; Capital campaigns of over $1 million (versus grants toward specific health-related equipment or the 'build out' of a specific health-focused space); Secondary and tertiary services (versus preventive and primary medical, oral and behavioral health care services); Health promotion and/or health care with a high per capita cost (this figure will vary depending upon the type of intervention, but over $1,000 per person/year cost may be a rule of thumb); Service expansion or new projects without viable sustainability (unable to reach sustainability without the foundation's resources within a four-year period).
Geographic Focus: Florida
Date(s) Application is Due: Mar 13; Apr 24
Amount: Up to 300,000 USD
Contact: Eliane Morales, (305) 374-7200; (305) 374-7003; emorales@hfsf.org
Internet: http://www.hfsf.org/ORIGHTML/responsive.html
Sponsor: Health Foundation of South Florida
2 South Biscayne Boulevard
Miami, FL 33131

Hearst Foundation and William Randolph Hearst Foundation Grants **845**
The Hearst Foundations support well-established nonprofit organizations that address important issues within our major areas of interests: education, health, culture, social services that primarily serve large demographic and/or geographic constituencies. Within these areas, the Foundations generally provide endowment, program, and capital grant support. Private nonprofits with significant support from the philanthropic community are favored over those financed through government sources. Proposals may be submitted throughout the year; board meetings on grant decisions are held in March, June, September, and December. Only fully documented appeals will be considered. As a general policy, meetings are arranged between foundation staff and applicant only if serious consideration of the appeal is anticipated. Programs headquartered east of the Mississippi River should mail appeals to the Hearst Foundations at the New York address. Those west of the Mississippi River should mail requests to Hearst Foundations, 90 New Montgomery Street, Suite 1212, San Francisco, CA 94105; phone: (415) 543-0400; fax: (415) 348-0887.
Requirements: Grants are made only to 501(c)3 tax-exempt organizations that are not private foundations.
Restrictions: Funding is not available for: individuals; loans and program-related investments; multi-year grants; start-up or seed funding; equipment of any kind, including computers and transportation; publishing projects; radio, film, television or other media-related projects; conferences, workshops or seminars; public policy research; special events, tickets, tables or advertising for fundraising events.
Geographic Focus: All U.S. States
Samples: The Archer School for Girls, Los Angeles, CA, $50,000—scholarship support (2009); YMCA of Greater New York, New York, NY, $80,000—Y Scholars Program to prepare middle and high school students for college

(2009); Cerebral Palsy International Research Foundation, Washington, DC, \$200,000—to support one investigator-initiated research project and two career development awards (2009); The Village of Arts and Humanities Inc., Philadelphia, PA, \$50,000—general support (2009)
Contact: Mason Granger, Director; (212) 586-5404; (212) 586-1917
Internet: http://www.hearstfdn.org/fp_home.html
Sponsor: Hearst Foundation
300 West 57th Street, 26th Floor
New York, NY 10019-3741

Heckscher Foundation for Children Grants **846**
The Heckscher Foundation for Children was founded in 1921 to promote the welfare of children, primarily in New York City. Funding organizations serving youth in the fields of education, family services, job training, health, arts and recreation. The Foundation's giving takes the form of program support, capacity-building, capital projects and general operating support. The Foundation does not participate in annual appeals, endowments, fundraising events or political efforts. The Heckscher Foundation provides support in the following categories: Education & Academic Support; Arts; Social Services; Health; Recreation and; Workforce Development. The Foundation accepts applications online only. To begin the application process. fill out the application template provided online. Do not submit additional information or materials unless asked to do so. All inquiring organizations will be notified of the outcome of the Foundation's review, and any further necessary materials will be requested at that time.
Requirements: 501(c)3 nonprofit organizations are eligible.
Restrictions: Funding is not available for annual appeals, endowments, fundraising events or political efforts.
Geographic Focus: New York
Amount: 25,000 - 500,000 USD
Samples: University of Pennsylvania, Philadelphia, PA, \$150,000—for LEAD Program; Miami Art Museum of Dade County, Miami, FL, \$500,000—for outreach and education programs; Saint Vincents Services, Brooklyn, NY, \$50,000—for capacity building.
Contact: Virginia Sloane, President; (212) 744-0190; (212) 744-2761
Internet: http://fdncenter.org/grantmaker/heckscher
Sponsor: Heckscher Foundation for Children
123 East 70th Street
New York, NY 10021

Heinz Endowments Grants **847**
The endowments support efforts to make southwestern Pennsylvania a premier place to live and work, a center of learning and educational excellence, and a home to diversity and inclusion. Committed to helping its region thrive as a whole community—economically, ecologically, educationally and culturally—the foundation works within Pennsylvania and elsewhere in the nation to develop solutions to challenges that are national and even international in scope. Fields of emphasis include arts and culture; children, youth and families; economic opportunity; education; the environment; and innovation economy. The two-step application process begins with submitting an online letter of inquiry (LoI) available at the Heinz website. The second step is a formal application process for those requests that are determined to meet the endowments' basic funding criteria. Information for submission of an LOI is available online.
Requirements: Grants are limited to 501(c)3 nonprofit organizations and 509(a) public charities in Pennsylvania and generally to the southwestern Pennsylvania region.
Restrictions: Individuals and for-profit organizations are not eligible.
Geographic Focus: Pennsylvania
Date(s) Application is Due: Feb 1; Aug 1
Samples: Greater Pittsburgh Arts Council, \$300,000—operating support (2009); Mount Ararat Community Activity Center, \$50,000—support for the Urban Male Mentoring Project (2009); 10,000 Friends of Pennsylvania, \$300,000—operating support for state-level policy work on transportation, land use, and municipal governance (2009).
Contact: Program Contact; (412) 281-5777; (412) 281-5788
Internet: http://www.heinz.org/programs.aspx
Sponsor: Heinz Endowments
30 Dominion Tower, 625 Liberty Avenue
Pittsburgh, PA 15222-3115

Helen and Merrill Bank Foundation Grants **848**
The foundation awards general operating grants to nonprofit organizations nationwide, including religious organizations (Christian, Jewish, and Salvation Army), hospitals, museums, organizations serving the disabled, parochial schools, temples, and organizations addressing issues affecting women. The foundation requests applications be made in writing. Include a description of the organization and activities for which funds are sought. There are no application deadlines.
Requirements: Nonprofit organizations in Florida and Maryland are eligible.
Geographic Focus: Florida, Maryland
Amount: Up to 548,025 USD
Samples: Raymond F. Kravis Ctr for the Performing Arts (West Palm Beach, FL)—for operating support, \$79,150; Temple Israel (Boston, MA)—for operating support, \$45,000.
Contact: Herbert Bank, (410) 363-6767
Sponsor: Helen and Merrill Bank Foundation
8 Roland Mews
Baltimore, MD 21210

Helena Rubinstein Foundation Grants **849**
The Foundation supports programs in education, community services, arts/arts in education, and health with emphasis on projects which benefit women and children. Grants are primarily targeted to organizations in New York City. Although general operating grants are made, the Foundation prefers to support specific programs. Grant proposals are accepted throughout the year. There is no formal application form; however, the New York Common Application Form may be used. Organizations seeking funds are asked not to make telephone inquiries, but to submit a brief letter outlining the project.
Requirements: U.S. nonprofit organizations are eligible.
Restrictions: Support is not offered to individuals, or for film or video projects. Grants are rarely made to endowment funds and capital campaigns. The foundation does not make loans and cannot provide emergency funds. Funding of new proposals is limited by ongoing commitments and fiscal constraints.
Geographic Focus: New York
Samples: New York City Outward Bound Ctr (NY)—for programs to help high school students develop self-esteem, self-reliance, social responsibility, and improved academic performance, \$10,000; Goodwill Industries of Greater New York (NY)—to support the capital campaign, \$10,000; Winston Preparatory School (NY)—salary support for a vocational guidance counselor, \$5000.
Contact: Diane Moss, President; (212) 750-7310
Internet: http://www.helenarubinsteinfdn.org/guide.html
Sponsor: Helena Rubinstein Foundation
477 Madison Avenue, 7th Floor
New York, NY 10022-5802

Helen Bader Foundation Grants **850**
The foundation supports innovative pilot projects and programs that are research based, have strong evaluation components, and involve community collaboration. The foundation's primary focus areas are Alzheimer's disease and dementia, early childhood development in Israel, education, economic development, and Jewish life and learning. Modest grants are awarded to support neighborhood renewal and youth development in Milwaukee's Sankofa area. Grants will be awarded primarily in the Delaware River Valley and in particular Milwaukee, WI, with the exception of the Alzheimer's disease and dementia program, which accepts applications from organizations nationwide. International grants are made for projects conducted in Israel. The foundation often funds multiple-year projects but rarely for a period of more than three years. Preliminary proposals must be received by the listed application deadline dates. If the foundation is interested in exploring the grant request further, a member of the program staff will contact the applicant to arrange a meeting or site visit. Applications are available on the website.
Requirements: Grants are awarded for projects consistent with one or more of the Helen Bader Foundation's program areas. Grants are given only to U.S. organizations which are tax exempt under Section 501(c)3 of the Internal Revenue Code or to government entities. Grants will only be approved for foreign entities which meet specific charitable status requirements.
Restrictions: The Foundation does not provide direct support for individuals, such as individual scholarships.
Geographic Focus: Wisconsin
Date(s) Application is Due: Feb 24; Mar 24
Amount: 10,000 - 100,000 USD

Samples: Donors Forum of Wisconsin, Inc., Milwaukee, WI, $45,000—this grant dupports the Donors Forum of Wisconsin's organization of the Milwaukee Area Workforce Funding Alliance, which includes private and public funders that seek to maximize outcomes for low-income families (2009); Aging & Disability Resource Center of Portage County, Stevens Point, WI, $7,000—this grant supports the Aging and Disability Resource Center of Portage County's instituting the Project Lifesaver Program, providing equipment and training to quickly located persons with dementia (2009); Mental Health America of Wisconsin, Inc., Milwaukee, WI, $10,000—this Grant supports the Grantee's emergency assistance to families living with mental illness (2009).
Contact: Tamara Hogans, Grants Manager; (414) 224-6464; (414) 224-1441; tammy@@hbf.org
Internet: http://www.hbf.org/apply.htm
Sponsor: Helen Bader Foundation
233 North Water Street, 4th Floor
Milwaukee, WI 53202

Helen Brach Foundation Grants **851**

The foundation operates to prevent cruelty to animals or to children; for religious, charitable, scientific, literary, and education purposes; and for public safety testing through support of Midwest 501(c)3 tax-exempt organizations carrying out programs and activities in these areas. Brach provides grants nationally and has wide-ranging interests. For example, it supports homeless and women's emergency shelters, teen pregnancy prevention programs, parenting education, summer school for disadvantaged children, job training for welfare mothers, orphanages, and scholarships for economically disadvantaged students. Types of support include annual campaigns, building construction/renovation, equipment, general operating support, publications, research, and special projects. The foundation ordinarily does not make multiyear grants or commitments. Applicants are required to complete in full a brief application form, which may be obtained from the office. The board of directors gives final consideration to all applications received in a given year at the board's meeting, which is usually held in March.
Requirements: Although 501(c)3 nonprofits from across the nation are eligible, giving is primarily made in California, Massachusetts, Ohio, Pennsylvania, and South Carolina.
Restrictions: Grants are not made to individuals or to organizations outside the United States. Typically grants are not made in excess of 10 percent of a group's operating budget, which automatically excludes start-up grants.
Geographic Focus: All U.S. States
Date(s) Application is Due: Dec 31
Amount: 10,000 - 25,000 USD
Samples: Zoological Society of Florida (Miami, FL)—to purchase dinosaur and bird artifacts to be used in an educational program called Are Birds Really Dinosaurs?, $20,000.
Contact: John P. Hagnell, Associate Director; (312) 372-4417; (312) 372-0290
Sponsor: Helen V. Brach Foundation
55 W Wacker Drive, Suite 701
Chicago, IL 60601-1609

Helen K. and Arthur E. Johnson Foundation Grants **852**

The foundation makes grants to a wide variety of nonprofit organizations in an attempt to solve community problems and enrich the quality of life in Colorado in the following areas: education, youth, health, community and social services, civic and cultural, and senior citizens. Requests are welcomed throughout the year. However, to be considered at the next board meeting, complete written proposals must be received by the listed application deadline dates. Proposal submission information is available online.
Requirements: IRS 501(c)3 tax-exempt organizations serving Colorado residents may apply.
Restrictions: Funding is not available for: loans or fund endowments; individuals; conferences; scholarships to individuals; multiple year grants; fundraising dinners or special events. The Foundation does not support organizations whose primary purpose is to influence (directly or indirectly) the legislative or judicial process in any manner or for any cause. In addition, the Foundation will not consider grant requests that pass through the nominal grant recipient to another organization.
Geographic Focus: Colorado
Date(s) Application is Due: Jan 1; Apr 1; Jul 1; Oct 1
Samples: Little Sisters of the Poor, Denver, CO, $250,000—for heating and air conditioning system; Educare Colorado, Denver, CO, $100,000—for program support.
Contact: John H. Alexander, President; (800) 232-9931 or (303) 861-4127; (303) 861-0607; info@johnsonfoundation.org
Internet: http://www.johnsonfoundation.org
Sponsor: Helen K. and Arthur E. Johnson Foundation
1700 Broadway, Suite 1100
Denver, CO 80290-1718

Helen S. Boylan Foundation Grants **853**

The Helen S Boylan Foundation is a private family foundation established in 1982 to continue the family tradition of commitment to enhancing the quality of life of the community through grants to qualified charitable organizations. In carrying out its mission, the Foundation considers a wide range of proposals within the following areas: arts, education, health, human services, environment, and public interest. Generally, grants are limited to projects that benefit the citizens of Jasper County, Missouri, Smith County, Texas and, Kansas City, Metropolitan area. Occasionally, projects that benefit the state of Missouri as a whole may be considered as well. The Foundation prefers to support proposals for new initiatives, special projects, expansion of current programs, capital improvements or building renovations. Grants from the Foundation are usually awarded for one year only. For projects in those areas in which the Foundation has a special interest, requests for multi-year funding and general operating support may be considered. The Board of Directors meet four times a year to consider grant requests. Applications must be received by March 31, June 30, September 30 or December 31 to be acted upon at the following meeting.
Requirements: IRS 501(c)3 nonprofit organizations operating in the Carthage, Kansas City Metro and Lindale Texas area are eligible to apply for funding. Application form is available online at the Foundation's website.
Restrictions: No support for political organizations or religious activities. No grants to individuals, or for annual campaigns or endowments.
Geographic Focus: Missouri, Texas
Date(s) Application is Due: Mar 31; Jun 30; Sep 30; Dec 31
Amount: 500 - 50,000 USD
Samples: Lindale Independant Schools, Lindale, TX, $52,000—supplies, systems, books, programs (2009); Heartland Hoops, Kansas City, MO, $10,000—uniforms & fees (2009); Art Central, Carthage, MO, $7,500—children's art camp (2009).
Contact: James R. Spradling, President; (417) 358-4033; (417) 358-5937; spradlinglaw@hotmail.com
Internet: http://www.boylanfoundation.org/
Sponsor: Helen S. Boylan Foundation
320 Grant Street, P.O. Box 731
Carthage, MO 64836

Helen Steiner Rice Foundation Grants **854**

The Foundation awards grants to worthy charitable programs that assist the needy and the elderly. Essential objectives for grant consideration are: basic necessities and human needs for the poor and elderly; preference for meeting the immediate needs of the poor; and innovative approaches. Organizations in the Greater Cincinnati area should use the contact information for Cincinnati. Organizations in Lorain County should *contact:* Linda Weaver, Community Foundation Center of Lorain County, (440) 277-0142, Ext. 23. Application forms and instructions are available online.
Requirements: Nonprofit organizations in the greater Cincinnati area and Lorain, OH, may submit grant applications.
Restrictions: Funding is not available for building or endowment programs, direct gifts to individuals, or capital fund drives.
Geographic Focus: Ohio
Date(s) Application is Due: Jul 1
Contact: James D. Huizenga, Director; (513) 241-2880; (513) 768-6122; huizengai@greatercincinnatifdn.org or hrice@cincymuseum.org
Internet: http://www.helensteinerrice.com/grants.html
Sponsor: Helen Suiteiner Rice Foundation
200 West Fourth Street
Cincinnati, OH 45202-2602

Henrietta Tower Wurts Memorial Foundation Grants **855**

The Foundation supports organizations which are engaged in helping or caring for people in need, or alleviating the conditions under which they live,

primarily for the elderly, women, family and child welfare services. Giving is limited to Philadelphia, Pennsylvania.
Requirements: Non-profits in Philadelphia, Pennsylvania are eligible. The initial approach should be a letter requesting an application form from the Foundation.
Restrictions: No grants to individuals, or for endowment funds, scholarships, fellowships, or matching gifts; no loans. Organizations or programs serving disadvantaged youth and the elderly in Philadelphia, Pennsylvania must have an annual budget of less than 3 million.
Geographic Focus: Pennsylvania
Date(s) Application is Due: Feb 1; May 1; Sep 1
Amount: 1,000 - 7,000 USD
Samples: Empowerment Group, Philadelphia, PA, $7,000; Juvenile Law Center, Philadelphia, PA, $5,000; Supportive Older Womens Network, Philadelphia, PA, $4,000
Contact: Andrew Swinney, President; (215) 563-6417
Sponsor: Henrietta Tower Wurts Memorial Foundation
1234 Market Street, Suite 1800
Philadelphia, PA 19107-3704

Henry and Ruth Blaustein Rosenberg Foundation Grants 856
The Henry and Ruth Blaustein Rosenberg Foundation provides support primarily in the Baltimore, Maryland region. Areas of interest are: arts and culture; youth development; health; and adult self-sufficiency. The goal of the arts and culture program is to enable cultural institutions in the Baltimore metropolitan area to reach underserved youth and to diversify audiences. Youth Development funding is provided to promote recreation, learning, and leadership development through after-school programs; prevent teen pregnancy; and advocate for policies and practices that improve outcomes for youth. Health funding is available to improve the prevention and treatment of breast cancer, diabetes, multiple sclerosis, and kidney disease. Adult Self-Sufficiency funding is provided to promote adult literacy; provide job training; improve parenting skills, especially for parents of children under age three; and eliminate domestic violence. The foundation meets three or four times a year to consider proposals. Letters of intent and proposals are accepted on a rolling basis. Applications that conform to the Association of Baltimore Area Grantmakers (ABAG) Common Grant Application are accepted and this form is available at the Henry and Ruth Blaustein Rosenberg Foundation website.
Requirements: 501(c)3 tax-exempt charitable organizations located in and/or primarily serving the metropolitan Baltimore area are eligible to apply. The initial application should include the following: information about the program(s) for which funding is requested; need, purpose, activities, and evaluation plan of the proposed program(s); program budget (including sources of anticipated income as well as expenditures) and timeline; dollar amount of funding requested; history, mission, and key accomplishments of your organization; information on Board members and key staff; current institutional operating budget (including major sources of revenue as well as expenditures); copy of your IRS tax status determination letter or information about your fiscal agent.
Restrictions: The foundation does not: make grants or scholarships to individuals; accept unsolicited proposals for academic, scientific, or medical research; support direct mail, annual giving, membership campaigns, fundraising and commemorative events. The foundations rarely make capital grants unless there is a prior relationship with the applicant organization.
Geographic Focus: Maryland
Amount: 1,000 - 40,000 USD
Samples: Heifetz International Music Institute, Ellicott City, MD, $30,000—support for a six-week summer program for aspiring young musicians (2009); Open Society Institute, Baltimore, MD, $15,000—sponsorship support for the Community Fellows Program (2009); Street Agnes Hospital Foundation, Baltimore, MD, $45,000—support for the Beacon of Hope capital campaign (2009).
Contact: Michael J. Hirschhorn, President; (410) 347-7201; (410) 347-7210; info@blaufund.org
Internet: http://www.blaufund.org/foundations/henryandruth_f.html
Sponsor: Henry and Ruth Blaustein Rosenberg Foundation
10 E Baltimore Street, Suite 1111
Baltimore, MD 21202

Henry J. Kaiser Family Foundation Grants 857
The foundation concentrates giving in the following areas: U.S. government's role in health, health of low-income and minority groups with major emphasis on HIV/AIDS policy, reproductive health policy, and health system innovation and reform in California. The foundation also operates a major program to improve health and health care and promote social justice in South Africa. Grants are awarded for one to three years and support a range of activities, including policy analysis, applied research to define and measure public health problems, demonstration and pilot projects, and communications activities that help sharpen health care debates and improve quality of health information. Prospective applicants should submit a preliminary letter (two to three pages in length) that briefly describes the proposed project, along with an estimate of the total budget and the amount requested from the foundation. There are no deadlines and no application forms. Inquiries for projects in South Africa may be addressed to Drive Michael Sinclair, Senior Vice President, The Henry J. Kaiser Family Foundation, 1450 G Street NW, Suite 250, Washington, DC 20005, (202) 347-5270, fax: (202) 347-5274.
Requirements: Grants in response to unsolicited proposals are made only to governmental agencies and to private organizations with IRS 501(c)3 tax-exempt status.
Restrictions: The foundation does not award grants to individuals. Support is not given to ongoing general operating expenses, indirect costs, capital campaigns, annual appeals or other fundraising events, construction, purchase or renovation of facilities, or equipment purchases.
Geographic Focus: All U.S. States
Amount: 1,000 - 500,000 USD
Samples: Alliance for Justice (Washington, DC)—for general operating support, $600,000 over three years; U of Florida, Tropical Conservation and Development Program (Gainesville, FL)—for a community-based conservation and training program for organizations working in protected areas of Colombia and Ecuador, $240,000 over three years; U of California at Los Angeles (CA)—for the Network on Youth Mental Health Care, $5 million over four years; Ctr for Defense Information (Washington, DC)—for policy research and advocacy on nuclear-weapons systems and their vulnerabilities, $650,000 over three years.
Contact: Renee Wells, Grants Manager; (415) 854-9400; (415) 854-4800; rwells@kff.org
Internet: http://www.kff.org
Sponsor: Henry J. Kaiser Family Foundation
2400 Sand Hill Road
Menlo Park, CA 94025

Henry P. Kendall Foundation Grants 858
The foundation focuses almost entirely on the environment and securing its physical, biological, and aesthetic wealth for future generations. Geographic priorities for grants are New England and the Maritime Provinces of Eastern Canada and the Pacific Northwest, including Western Canada and Alaska. Current program themes include Gulf of Maine ecosystem, Northeastern landscape, Northeast climate change initiative, North country institution capacity-building, Yellowstone to Yukon conservation, watershed innovations in North America, public lands management, and special project initiatives. The foundation provides funding for general operating needs and for specific programs and initiatives. Activities funded include advocacy, public education, policy research and analysis, on-the-ground resource management experiments, and institutional development. Grants are normally made for one or two years. Unsolicited proposals and inquiries will not be reviewed.
Restrictions: Grants do not support endowments or capital fund campaigns, land acquisition, television and film projects, fellowships, basic scientific research, building construction or maintenance, equipment, debt reduction, or conferences unrelated to current foundation institutional grants. Nor does the foundation normally fund waste clean-ups, toxics or air/water pollution prevention or pollution monitoring initiatives, individual land trusts, or species-specific preservation efforts.
Geographic Focus: Alaska, Canada
Date(s) Application is Due: Feb 1; May 1; Oct 1
Amount: 20,000 - 50,000 USD
Samples: Alaska Conservation Foundation (Anchorage, AK)—to create a strategic transition fund dedicated to strengthening and expanding efforts to build a popular majority for conservation values—terrestrial and marine—throughout Alaska over the next two decades, $100,000; Earth Day Network (Seattle, WA)—to support preparatory organizing efforts in New England for Earth Day 2000, $35,000; Montana Wilderness Assoc (Helena, MT)—for general support to advance the protection of public wildlands and naturally functioning ecosystems in the Montana portion of the Yellowstone to Yukon landscape, $40,000.
Contact: Jennifer Patrick, Associate Program Officer; (617) 951-2525; (617) 443-1977

Internet: http://www.kendall.org/grants/types.html
Sponsor: Henry P. Kendall Foundation
176 Federal Street
Boston, MA 02110

Henry W. Bull Foundation Grants **859**

Established in 1960 in California, the foundation was established by Maud Bull in memory of her husband, Henry W. Bull. The foundation grants awards on a nationwide basis, giving primarily in the areas of: arts/performing arts; education; health and; human services. Types of support include annual campaigns, building construction/renovation, capital campaigns; program development, equipment acquisition, matching/challenge grants; general operating support, continuing support, and research. There is no formal grant application form. Submit a simple, concise statement of needs and objectives with pertinent supportive data, c/o Janice Gibbons, Santa Barbara Bank & Trust, P.O. Box 2340, Santa Barbara, CA, 93120-2340.
Requirements: 501(c)()3 nonprofits are eligible.
Restrictions: No grants to individuals or private foundations.
Geographic Focus: All U.S. States
Date(s) Application is Due: Apr 1; Sep 1
Amount: 500 - 20,000 USD
Samples: Shiloh Christian Childrens Ranch, Shelbina, MO, $2,000—general support; FamiliesFirst, Davis, CA, $3,000—to help expand child abuse prevention program; Dunn School, Los Olivos, CA, $10,000—purchase of new biology countertops, data collection equipment and laptop computers for Science Department.
Contact: Janice Gibson, Vice-President, Santa Barbara Bank & Trust; (805) 899-8405; (805) 884-1404
Sponsor: Henry W. Bull Foundation
P.O. Box 2340
Santa Barbara, CA 93120-2340

Herbert and Gertrude Latkin Charitable Foundation Grants **860**

The foundation awards grants to eligible California nonprofit organizations to assist and promote the welfare and health of the elderly. Areas of interest include human services, aging centers and services, and family services. Additional focus areas include animal cruelty, child abuse, emergency medical services, and scholarships to college students. Types of support include general operating support, emergency funds, and equipment acquisition.
Requirements: California nonprofit organizations serving Santa Barbara County are eligible.
Geographic Focus: California
Date(s) Application is Due: Apr 1; Oct 1
Amount: 1,000 - 16,000 USD
Contact: Janice Gibbons, (805) 564-6211
Sponsor: Herbert and Gertrude Latkin Charitable Foundation
P.O. Box 2340
Santa Barbara, CA 93120-2340

Herbert H. and Grace A. Dow Foundation Grants **861**

The Foundation has charter goals to improve the educational, religious, economic and cultural lives of Michigan's people. Priority is given to organizations that: have clearly stated objectives, strong and purposeful management and are publicly accountable; have needs which are in areas not normally funded by governmental or public financing; are not hesitant to explore, initiate, volunteer, or execute original ideas or concepts; are willing to collaborate with other persons or organizations to give synergy to a common objective or goal; have purposes which tend to advance private enterprise and the preservation of a free, open and self-resourceful society. Application information is available online.
Requirements: Only organizations in Michigan are eligible to apply.
Restrictions: The Foundation does not make grants directly to individuals. It cannot legally support: organizations to which contributions are not tax deductible, according to Internal Revenue Service regulations; organizations that practice discrimination by race, sex, creed, age or national origin; political organizations or organizations whose purposes are to influence legislation.
Geographic Focus: Michigan
Samples: Grand Valley State U, Dorothy A. Johnson Ctr for Philanthropy and Nonprofit Leadership (Grand Rapids, MI)—for the Growing the Greater Good Endowment Campaign, with a focus on identifying and disseminating best practices of nonprofit organizations, $1 million; Nature Conservancy, Michigan Chapter (Lansing, MI)—for the Northern Great Lakes Forest Project, which will protect 271,000 acres across eight counties in Michigan's Upper Peninsula and link more than 2.5 million acres of protected federal, state, and natural ares. $4.5 million.
Contact: Margaret Ann Riecker, President; (989) 631-3699; (989) 631-0675; info@hhdowfoundation.org
Internet: http://www.hhdowfdn.org
Sponsor: Herbert H. and Grace A. Dow Foundation
1018 West Main Street
Midland, MI 48640-4292

Herman Abbott Family Foundation Grants **862**

The Foundation, established in 1996 in New York, supports the arts, performing arts, and Jewish agencies and temples. Grant funding most often comes in the form of general operating support. There are no applications or deadlines with which to adhere, and applicant should approach the foundation initially in writing.
Geographic Focus: All U.S. States
Contact: David Y. Bailey, Treasurer; (203) 481-1120; (203) 488-3027
Sponsor: Herman Abbott Family Foundation
1224 Main Street, Lockworks Square
Branford, CT 06405-3778

Herman Goldman Foundation Grants **863**

The foundation's broad purpose is to enhance the quality of life in the areas of health, education, social justice, and the arts. Applications submitted by organizations sponsoring projects that will benefit those in need will be considered. With few exceptions, grant making is confined to the New York metropolitan area. A written proposal should include the specific funds requested, a thorough description of existing or intended activities and their expected impact, additional sources of funding on hand as well as those anticipated, and the prospects for the project's continuance and the support envisioned at the expiration of the requested grant. Where possible, a budget should be submitted. The board meets monthly. Grants are considered in April, July, and November. Proposals are due the middle of the month preceding the board meeting.
Requirements: Applicant organizations must submit a copy of the IRS determination letter.
Restrictions: Grants to individuals will not be considered.
Geographic Focus: New York
Amount: 5,000 - 25,000 USD
Samples: Boca Raton Community Hospital (Boca Raton, FL)—to support construction of an urgent care center, $20,000; New York U School of Medicine—to support Medical Ctr scholarships, $20,000; American Civil Liberties Union Foundation—to continue support of the Children's Rights Project, $10,000; Dramatic Risks—to support the development of exemplary projects in the performing arts, theatrical writing, and the arts in education, $5000.
Contact: Richard Baron, Executive Director; (212) 797-9090
Sponsor: Herman Goldman Foundation
61 Broadway, 18th Floor
New York, NY 10006

HFSF Grants **864**

The foundation conducts two separate grant programs: responsive grants and strategic initiative grants. With exceptions, the foundation will focus on developing one- to two-year grants. The following responsive grant categories have been established: project planning—to support the planning of projects requiring outside expertise, significant amounts of inter-agency collaboration, or other aspects needing additional resources to develop; health system/health policy development—to support a variety of activities specifically designed to improve public policies, infrastructure, and/or inter-agency procedures leading to increased system effectiveness, efficiency, sustainability, and overall capacity; organizational capacity building/core operating support—to organizations with a clear plan for increasing their agencies' effectiveness, efficiency, and sustainability; and health services—to support a range of preventive and primary health care services. The listed deadlines are for preliminary proposals; full proposals are by invitation. Application and guidelines are available online.
Requirements: 501(c)3 tax-exempt organizations serving southern Florida are eligible.
Geographic Focus: Florida
Date(s) Application is Due: Mar 31; Oct 22
Amount: 50,000 - 300,000 USD

Samples: Broward House (Fort Lauderdale, FL)—to support operational efficiency and improve its technology, $86,380; Community Committee for Developmental Handicaps (Miami, FL)—to develop a plan designed to strengthen its board development, marketing, staffing, and technology, $23,925; Human Services Coalition (Miami, FL)—to increase organizational capacity by improving communications and increasing membership, revenue, and donations, $20,000; Florida International U, Ctr on Aging (FL)—for efforts to improve the health of older adults who are at high risk for poor health due to obesity and physical inactivity, $263,394.
Contact: Peter Wood, Chief Program Officer; (305) 374-2282; (305) 374-7003; pwood@hfsf.org
Internet: http://www.hfsf.org
Sponsor: Health Foundation of South Florida
601 Brickell Key Drive, Suite 901
Miami, FL 33131

HHK Employment Grants **865**
The majority of the foundation's grants are directed toward increasing employment opportunities for people with physical disabilities. Grants are awarded to organizations that work toward improving the employment and career advancement of people with physical disabilities living in New Jersey. Areas of interest include programs that focus on transition to work for youth and adults; transportation to and from work; workplace accommodations—overcoming barriers to employment, such as access to assistive technology, providing accessible facilities and services, employee education on disabilities; equipment and training programs focusing on workplace preparation and vocational training; supported employment programs; mentoring; school-based enterprises; work-based learning; alternative work solution, such as telecommuting; and employment strategies to support disability recruitment, hiring practices, placement, and retention. Types of support include project/program funds and general operating funds. Grants are awarded for one year. Preference is given to organizations seeking matching funds and that collaborate with other organizations or entities. Guidelines are available online.
Requirements: 501(c)3 tax-exempt organizations are eligible.
Restrictions: The foundation does not support grants to individuals; grants to underwrite fundraising events, such as benefits, dinners, or theater events, ticket purchases, or advertising; endowment campaigns; scholarship funds; deficit reduction or loans; or international causes.
Geographic Focus: New Jersey
Amount: 20,000 - 50,000 USD
Samples: Brain Injury Assoc of New Jersey (Edison, NJ)—for training, technical assistance, and resources for people with brain injuries, $49,980; Cheshire Home (Florham Park, NJ)—for salary support of a teacher for GED and job preparation and computer-skills training, $12,000; Employment Horizon (Cedar Knolls, NJ)—for salary support of a driver to transport people with disabilities to work centers in their community, $10,000.
Contact: Elaine Katz, Director of Development; (973) 324-8367; (973) 324-8373; ekatz@hhkfdn.org
Internet: http://www.hhkfdn.org
Sponsor: Henry H. Kessler Foundation
300 Executive Drive, Suite 150
West Orange, NJ 07052

High Meadow Foundation Grants **866**
The foundation grants funds in support of the performing arts, especially theater and music, and other cultural organizations. Organizations supported are usually located in Berkshire County, MA. Types of support include continuing support, annual campaigns, capital campaigns, building construction/renovation, equipment acquisition, emergency funds, program development, employee-related scholarships, and matching funds. Applications are accepted at any time. Forms are not necessary; a letter outlining the proposed project should include budget and administrative information.
Requirements: Western Massachusetts 501(c)3 tax-exempt organizations in Berkshire County are eligible.
Geographic Focus: Massachusetts
Samples: Massachusetts Museum of Contemporary Art, North Adams, MA, $100,000; Berkshire Theater Festival, Stockbridge, MA, $60,000; Lenox Library Association, Lenox, MA, $10,000
Contact: Jane Fitzpatrick, Treasurer; (413) 298-5565 or (413) 243-1474; (413) 298-4058
Sponsor: High Meadow Foundation
30 Main Street
Stockbridge, MA 01262

Hillman Foundation Grants **867**
The foundation provides grants to nonprofit organizations in the city of Pittsburgh and the southwestern Pennsylvania region for programs and projects designed to improve the quality of life in the area. The foundation's areas of interest include community affairs, social services, culture and the arts, education at all levels, and youth services including medical and health. Grants range widely in size and are allocated for large and small capital projects, endowment, new and expanding programs, and on a limited basis, operating support. Applications should include an annual budget of the organization, project information, and evidence of tax-exempt status. Application information is available online.
Requirements: The Foundation considers requests only from organizations classified as tax-exempt under Section 501(c)3 of the U.S. Internal Revenue Code and designated as public charities under Section 509(a).
Restrictions: Grants are not made to individuals, organizations located outside of the United States, for travel expenses for groups, or in support of events, sponsorships and meetings such as conferences, institutes and seminars.
Geographic Focus: Pennsylvania
Samples: Strong Women, Strong Girls, INc., $10,000—towards program for at-risk and low-income girls (2009); Greater Pittsburgh Community Food Bank, $65,000—toward food pantry and outreach program (2009).
Contact: David K. Roger, President; (412) 338-3466; (412) 338-3463; foundation@hillmanfo.com
Internet: http://www.hillmanfdn.org/grantprograms.html
Sponsor: Hillman Foundation
330 Grant Street, Suite 2000
Pittsburgh, PA 15219

Hilton Hotels Corporate Giving Program Grants **868**
Hilton makes charitable contributions to nonprofit organizations involved with K-12 education, youth development, public policy, homelessness, and civic affairs. Support is given primarily in areas of company operations, with emphasis on California, including Los Angeles and San Francisco, and Tennessee, including Memphis; giving also to national organizations. Contact Ellen Gonda for additional information at: corporate_communications@hilton.com.
Requirements: 501(c)3 tax-exempt organizations are eligible.
Restrictions: No support for sport teams, religious organizations not of direct benefit to the entire community, government-supported organizations (over 20 percent of budget), hospitals, private schools, pre-schools, or day care facilities, film and video production, or promotional materials. No grants to individuals (except for employee related scholarships), or for fellowships, sports activities, debt reduction, capital campaigns or endowments, film or video projects, or promotional merchandise.
Geographic Focus: California, Tennessee
Contact: Ellen Gonda, Senior Vice President; (310) 278-4321; (310) 205-7678; corporate_communications@hilton.com
Internet: http://www.hiltonworldwide.com
Sponsor: Hilton Hotels Corporation
9336 Civic Center Drive
Beverly Hills, CA 90210-3604

Hirtzel Memorial Foundation Grants **869**
The foundation awards grants to eligible organizations in New York and Pennsylvania in its areas of interest, including medical research and health care; community and neighborhood improvement; higher education; and social and human services. Types of support include building construction and renovation, capital campaigns, scholarships, equipment acquisition, general operating support, research, and scholarships. There are no application deadlines; contact the office for appropriate forms.
Requirements: New York nonprofit organizations in Ripley, Chautauqua County, and Pennsylvania nonprofit organizations in North East, Erie County, are eligible.
Geographic Focus: New York, Pennsylvania
Amount: 750 - 250,000 USD
Samples: Mercyhurst College (Erie, PA)—to establish the Institute on Aging and Geriatric Health, $1 million.
Contact: Laurie Moritz, Grants Administrator, c/o Mellon Financial Corporation; (412) 234-0023
Sponsor: Orris C. Hirtzel and Beatrice Dewey Hirtzel Memorial Foundation
P.O. Box 185
Pittsburgh, PA 15230

Historic Landmarks Legal Defense Grants 870

While the foundation regards legal action as a last resort, it is recognized that it is sometimes required to save endangered structures and support preservation processes. The defense grants cover 80% of the total cost of legal counsel up to $2,000.

Requirements: Nonprofit preservation organizations may request grants of up to $2,000 for legal fees to defend or compel conformance with a local preservation ordinance, enforce protective covenants, or seek an injunction to prevent the demolition of a historic building.

Restrictions: Limited to Indiana only.

Geographic Focus: Indiana

Amount: Up to 2,000 USD

Contact: Carla Jones, Receptionist, State Headquarters; (317) 639-4534; (317) 639-6734; info@historiclandmarks.org

Internet: http://www.historiclandmarks.org/help/grants.html

Sponsor: Historic Landmarks Foundation of Indiana
340 W Michigan Street
Indianapolis, IN 46202

HNHfoundation Grants 871

The foundation awards general operating and program support to New Hampshire healthcare organizations. Preference will be given to programs providing services to children and youth. There are no application deadlines; obtain application forms and procedures from the office.

Requirements: New Hampshire nonprofit organizations are eligible.

Geographic Focus: New Hampshire

Amount: 250 - 250,000 USD

Samples: Home Health and Hospice Care (Nashua, NH)—to support an outreach program for uninsured children, $10,000; North Country Health Consortium (NH)—for health insurance for small businesses, $35,361; Community Health Access Network (Newmarket, NH)—to support chronic-disease education programs, $34,433.

Contact: Sandi Van Scoyoc, President; (603) 229-3260; (603) 229-3259; info@hnhfoundation.org

Internet: http://www.hnhfoundation.org

Sponsor: HNHfoundation
14 Dixon Avenue
Concord, NH 03301

Hoglund Foundation Grants 872

The foundation supports nonprofits working in the areas of education, health science and services, social services, and children's health and development. Grants are made primarily in Dallas, and Houston, Texas, with a limited number of grants awarded outside of this area. Types of support include project support, capital support, and general operating support. Application guidelines are available on the foundation's website.

Requirements: To be eligible for consideration, an organization must provide proof that they have received a determination letter from the Internal Revenue Service indicating that it is a tax exempt organization as described in Section 501(c)3 of the Internal Revenue Code of 1986 and is treated as other than a private foundation as within the meaning of Section 509(a) of the Code. An organization may also qualify under Section 170(c)(1) if the grant requested is to be used exclusively for public purposes as described in the Code.

Restrictions: Grants are not made to individuals.

Geographic Focus: Texas

Date(s) Application is Due: Mar 15; Jul 15; Nov 15

Amount: 1,000 - 200,000 USD

Samples: University of Virginia Fund, Charlottesville, VA, $33,000-Global Scholarship Fund (2008); Vickery Meadow Learning Center, Dallas, TX, $10,000—Family Literacy program (2008); Victims Outreach, Dallas, TX, $5,000—program services for victims of crime & violence (2008); Reasoning Mind, Inc., Houston, TX, $250,000—program expansion and general operating support (2008).

Contact: Kelly Compton, Executive Director; (214) 987-3605; (214) 363-6507; info@hoglundfoundation.org

Internet: http://www.hoglundfoundation.org/grants.html

Sponsor: Hoglund Foundation
5910 North Central Expressway, Suite 255
Dallas, TX 75206

Homeland Foundation Grants 873

The foundation awards grants to nonprofit organizations in its areas of interest, including the environment and natural resource conservation—primarily the U.S. West Coast (including Baja, CA, and Hawaii)and the Caribbean and Western Pacific; and women's issues—physical, mental, and financial health—in California's Los Angeles and Orange Counties. Types of support include general operating grants, program grants, continuing support, and multiyear grants. The board meets quarterly; contact the office for guidelines prior to submitting proposals.

Requirements: 501(c)3 nonprofit organizations are eligible.

Restrictions: Grants are not awarded to support political campaigns, individuals, scholarships, fellowships, or film or video projects.

Geographic Focus: California, Hawaii

Date(s) Application is Due: Mar 1; Jun 1; Sep 1; Dec 1

Amount: 1,000 - 328,000 USD

Contact: Glenda Menges, Grants Administrator; (949) 494-0365; (949) 494-8395

Sponsor: Homeland Foundation
412 N Pacific Coast Highway, PMB 359
Laguna Beach, CA 92651

Homer A. Scott and Mildred S. Scott Foundation Grants 874

The foundation awards grants to Wyoming nonprofit organizations in its areas of interest, including children and youth, higher education, and social services. Types of support include employee matching gifts and matching funds. Preference is given to requests that intervene in and prevent the problems of young people, build public awareness of youth issues, promote coordination and communication among programs serving young people, develop leadership skills, build self-esteem, and can become sustainable. Application deadlines vary; contact program staff for exact dates. Application forms must be obtained from the office. The board meets quarterly to consider requests.

Requirements: Sheridan, WY, nonprofit organizations are eligible.

Restrictions: No grants to individuals.

Geographic Focus: Montana, Wyoming

Contact: Lynn Mavrakis, Executive Director; (307) 672-1448; (307) 672-1443; lynn.mavrakis@fib.com

Sponsor: Homer A. Scott and Mildred S. Scott Foundation
P.O. Box 2007
Sheridan, WY 82801-2007

Honeywell Foundation Grants 875

The foundation awards grants to nonprofits in communities where company plants are located. Areas of interest include education, community funds, health, aging, human services, youth agencies, cultural programs, and international exchange programs. Types of support include general operating support, continuing support, annual campaigns, building/renovation, equipment acquisition, employee matching gifts, and fellowship and scholarship aid to colleges and universities that are major sources of future employees.

Requirements: Nonprofit organizations in company-operating areas are eligible. Areas include Arizona, Florida, Illinois, Minnesota, and New Mexico.

Restrictions: Grants do not support individuals, church-related programs, special interest groups (such as labor or veterans) unless activity benefits entire community, political organizations, or for international organizations.

Geographic Focus: Arizona, Florida, Illinois, Minnesota, New Mexico

Amount: 1,000 - 25,000 USD

Contact: Andre Lewis, Vice President and Executive Director; (973) 455-5876; (612) 951-0433

Internet: http://www.honeywell.com/about/foundation.html

Sponsor: Honeywell Foundation
101 Columbia Road
Morristown, NJ 07962

Honor the Earth Grants 876

The mission of Honor the Earth is to provide funding and public support for Native environmental initiatives. Grantmaking focuses on three program areas: environmental justice—defense and protection of homelands and traditional ways of life; building sustainable communities—innovative initiatives that foster Indigenous thinking and use of traditional language addressing sustainable community development, providing tools for addressing conflict resolution, and learning principles of de-colonization; and nuclear waste/safe clean energy—addressing fossil fuel, mega-hydro, nuclear power, nuclear waste issues, and promoting alternative, clean renewable energy initiatives. Grants support Native communities and groups working to protect the earth; organizations working with Native youth and young adults to develop leadership skills; and projects designed to encourage youth to protect and restore Native communities. There are no application deadlines.

Requirements: Native American individuals or organizations may apply. Priority is given to Native grassroots, community-based organizations and groups with a lack of access to federal and/or tribal funding resources.
Geographic Focus: All U.S. States
Amount: 1,000 - 5,000 USD
Samples: Eyak Rainforest Preservation Fund (Cordova, AK)—for operating support, $5000.
Contact: Executive Director; (800) 327-8407 or (612) 879-7529; (612) 278-7162; honorearth@earthlink.net
Internet: http://honorearth.org/grants.html
Sponsor: Honor the Earth
2104 Stevens Avenue S
Minneapolis, MN 55404

Horace A. Kimball and S. Ella Kimball Foundation Grants **877**

The Kimball Foundation makes grants almost exclusively to Rhode Island operatives (charities) or those benefitting Rhode Island residents and causes. Although, the Foundation considers gifts to all areas in the state, greater emphasis is placed on South County. Areas of interest for the Foundation are: human services, the environment, and health care.
Requirements: The Foundation will consider any organization which has proper 501(c)3 and 509(a) I.R.S. tax classification status. Application form and guidelines available on foundation website. Application form required. Applicants should submit the following: copy of IRS Determination Letter; brief history of organization and description of its mission; copy of most recent annual report/audited financial statement/990.
Restrictions: No support for religious organizations. No grants to individuals, or for feasibility studies, capital projects or multi-year commitments.
Geographic Focus: Rhode Island
Date(s) Application is Due: Jul 15
Amount: 1,000 - 50,000 USD
Contact: Thomas F. Black III, President; (401) 364-3565
Internet: http://www.hkimballfoundation.org/index2.htm
Sponsor: Horace A. Kimball and S. Ella Kimball Foundation
130 Woodville Road
Hope Valley, RI 02832

Horizon Foundation for New Jersey Grants **878**

The Foundation's purpose is to promote health, well-being, and quality of life in New Jersey communities. Foundation goals are to improve health by promoting quality health care programs and access and to enhance arts and cultural opportunities. Application information is available online. Only electronic grant applications will be accepted. Application are accepted between January 1 and September 31.
Requirements: 501(c)3 tax-exempt organizations in New Jersey communities located in and served by Horizon Blue Cross Blue Shield of New Jersey are eligible.
Restrictions: Funding is not available for: capital campaigns; endowments; hospitals or hospital foundations; individuals; political causes; political candidates; political organizations; political campaigns.
Geographic Focus: New Jersey
Amount: 10,000 - 50,000 USD
Samples: ChoiceOne Pregnancy & Sexual Health Resource Centers, Lawrenceville, NJ, $25,000—to support the Sexually Transmitted Diseases Education and Prevention component of its Straight Talk Program (2008); Family Guidance Center, Hamilton, NJ, $15.000—to support its Behavioral Health Services-Depression Recovery Program (2008); American Repertory Ballet, New Brunswick, HJ, $7,500—to support the Dance Power Program (2008).
Contact: Michele Berry, Grants Coordinator; Foundation_Info@horizonblue.com
Internet: http://www.horizon-bcbsnj.com/foundation/about/funding.html?WT.svl=leftnav
Sponsor: Horizon Foundation for New Jersey
Three Penn Plaza East, PP-15V
Newark, NJ 07105-2200

Horizons Community Issues Grants **879**

Grants support program activities or projects serving lesbian, gay, bisexual, and transgender (LGBT) people of all ages in designated California counties focusing on the following issue areas: arts and culture; advocacy, awareness, and civil rights; children, youth, and families; and community and social services. Application information is available online.
Requirements: To be eligible, an organization must: be a nonprofit, 501(c)3 organization, or provide documentation that the organization is sponsored under a fiscal agent umbrella that has 501(c)3 status. Organizations or programs must request support for one or more of the following counties: Alameda; Contra; Costa; Marin; Napa; San Francisco; San Mateo; Santa Clara; Solano; Sonoma.
Restrictions: The following are not eligible for support: costs incurred prior to the date of the grant award; government agencies; capital support, including construction and renovation; fundraising or event sponsorship; individuals; Non-LGBT organizations with budget over $1 million.
Geographic Focus: California
Amount: 10,000 - 20,000 USD
Contact: Jewelle Gomez, Program Officer; (415) 398-2333, ext. 116; jgomez@horizonsfoundation.org
Internet: http://www.horizonsfoundation.org/page/organizations/ci
Sponsor: Horizons Foundation
870 Market Street, Suite 728
San Francisco, CA 94102

Hormel Family Foundation Business Plan Award **880**

The purpose of this competition is to stimulate entrepreneurship and economic development in McCook, Nebraska. Competition is different from many other business plan competitions in the sense that the prize is not a simple cash award, but an actual investment by which the Hormel Family Foundation becomes a shareholder in the winning business. In addition to the $25,000 investment, the winner will receive business, legal and advertising services valued at $10,000. The Foundation views this competition not only as an investment in an individual or team, but primarily in the community of McCook.
Requirements: The proposed business must be located in or near McCook, Nebraska. Business owners located outside McCook city limits must be willing to relocate their business to McCook, or within a proximity acceptable to the Foundation. The business plan must be an original idea, and must be written by the applicant(s). Any copyright or intellectual property infringement will result in immediate disqualification and possible legal action. While the operations of the business must be based in the McCook area, and any tax dollars earned by the business must benefit McCook, sales of proposed products or services are not limited to McCook. This is important to note, especially in the case of internet-based businesses and businesses that might distribute products throughout the United States.
Restrictions: Applicants must be: local business owners interested in expanding or improving their existing business; any individual or team with a brand new business idea, willing to launch their business in McCook; or business owners elsewhere who are willing to relocate their business to McCook.
Geographic Focus: Nebraska
Amount: 35,000 USD
Contact: Susan Harris-Broomfield, Project Manager; (308) 340-0856; susan@hormelfamilyfoundation.com
Internet: http://www.hormelfamilyfoundation.com/businessplancompetition.html
Sponsor: Hormel Family Foundation
1 Prairie Hills Road
McCook, NE 69001

Household International Corporate Giving Program Grants **881**

Grants made in support of Household's corporate social responsibility fall into three main focus areas: education, housing, and community enrichment. Special attention is given to requests from nonprofits that address issues related to financial and credit education, economic development, housing, youth development, and education, particularly for low-income and minority populations. Types of support include annual campaigns, capital campaigns, challenge/matching grants, employee-related scholarships, scholarship funds, equipment, fellowships, general operating support, continuing support, research grants, and technical assistance. Grants are made at three levels: companywide grants, local-facility grants, and the Help for Communities program administered through local branch offices. Each level has its own deadline. Obtain guidelines, which contain a list of contacts for the company's U.S. and foreign subsidiaries.
Requirements: Nonprofit organizations in corporate operating areas are eligible.
Restrictions: The corporation generally does not support the following: nonprofit organizations that do not have 501(c)3 tax deductible status; fraternal, veteran, labor, athletic, or religious organizations serving a limited

constituency; for-profit student aid or scholarship programs, aside from those already established by Household or its business groups; political, lobbying, or voter registration programs, or those supporting the candidacy of a particular individual; funds to support travel for groups or individuals; organizations that might in any way pose a conflict with corporate values, products, customers, or employees; unsolicited requests from secondary, elementary, and post-secondary schools; single disease research initiatives outside of corporate sponsored programs; unsolicited proposals from colleges and universities; advertising; or individuals.
Geographic Focus: All U.S. States
Date(s) Application is Due: Dec 15
Amount: Up to 8,000,000 USD
Samples: Beacon Light Community Housing Development Organization (Hampton, VA)—for money-management classes for low- and middle-income people, $109,000; Catholic Charities Community Development Corp (Saint Petersburg, FL)—to provide homeownership and financial education to low- and moderate-income adults, and for a program to teach youths about budgeting and investing, $215,000; Vecinos Unidos (Dallas, TX)—for educational courses for low- and middle-income Latinos buying homes, $60,950; FAIM Economic Development Corp (Dallas, TX)—for a money-management and credit-education program for members of African-American churches and other Dallas residents, $114,000 over two years.
Contact: Contributions Administrator; (847) 564-6010; (847) 564-7094; communityrelations@household.com
Internet: http://www.hsbcusa.com/corporateresponsibility/contributions_grants
Sponsor: Household International Corporate Giving Program
2700 Sanders Road
Prospect Heights, IL 60070

Howard County Community Foundation Grants **882**
The foundation awards grants to Maryland nonprofit organizations in its areas of interest, including human services, arts and culture, and education and community affairs. The board meets monthly. Project grants are reviewed in March, and operating grants are reviewed in November. Contingency grants are available year-round. Contact the office for application forms and deadlines.
Requirements: Howard County, MD, nonprofit organizations are eligible.
Restrictions: Grants do not support individuals, sectarian religious purposes, or medical research.
Geographic Focus: Maryland
Contact: Program Contact; (410) 730-7840; (410) 997-6021; info@columbiafoundation.org
Internet: http://www.columbiafoundation.org/nonprofits/index.html
Sponsor: Columbia Foundation/Howard County Community Foundation
10227 Wincopin Circle, Suite G-15
Columbia, MD 21044

Howard Gilman Foundation Grants **883**
The foundation is dedicated to the preservation of natural and cultural resources, with a focus on environmental, especially animal, conservation; the preservation and advancement of artistic and cultural endeavors; and medical research, especially in the fields of HIV/AIDS, cardiology, and sports medicine. The arts and culture component of the program is focused primarily in the New York metropolitan area. Types of support include general operating grants, program grants, research grants, and seed money grants. Staff prefer to respond to a brief letter of inquiry outlining the project's aim and general budgetary requirements before asking potential grantees to prepare full proposals.
Requirements: 501(c)3 nonprofit organizations are eligible.
Restrictions: Religious and political agencies are ineligible.
Geographic Focus: New York
Amount: 1,000 - 100,000 USD
Samples: Brooklyn Academy of Music (Brooklyn, NY)—for endowment and operating support, $5 million.
Contact: Harry Brown, Program Associate; (212) 307-1073; (212) 262-4108; hbrown@gilman.com
Sponsor: Howard Gilman Foundation
111 W 50th Street, 40th Floor
New York, NY 10020

Howard H. Callaway Foundation Grants **884**
The Howard H. Callaway Foundation offers support in the form of general operation grants primarily in the state of Georgia. The Foundations areas of interest include: athletics/sports, baseball; federated giving programs; higher education; human services and; public affairs. Applications are accepted year round, submit a letter of inquiry to the Foundation to begin the application process.
Requirements: Georgia 501(c)3 non-profit organizations are eligible for funding. There is neither a deadline date to adhere to nor, is there a specific application form to submit. Begin the application process by submitting a letter of inquiry to the Foundation containing: copy of IRS Determination Letter; descriptive literature about organization; detailed description of project and amount of funding requested.
Restrictions: No grants to individuals.
Geographic Focus: Georgia
Amount: 5,000 - 25,000 USD
Samples: Columbus Baseball Foundation, Columbus, GA, $5,000—general operational grant (2008); National Infantry Museum, Fort Benning, GA, $25,000—general operational grant (2008); Free Congress Foundation, ALexandria, VA, $5,000—general operational grant (2008).
Contact: Howard H. Callaway, President; (706) 663-5075
Sponsor: Howard H. Callaway Foundation
P.O. Box 1326
Pine Mountain, GA 31822-1326

HRK Foundation Grants **885**
The foundation focuses its resources on single-year funding for special projects in the areas of health care, AIDS, and children and youth services. Within the Twin Cities metro area, the Saint Croix Valley, and Ashland and Bayfield Counties of Wisconsin, the board will consider programming related to the issue of AIDS and programming that addresses children's health issues. Within the Saint Croix Valley and Ashland and Bayfield Counties in Wisconsin, the board will consider local community-specific projects. Types of support include general operating support, seed funding, community development, matching/challenge grants, equipment acquisition, and annual campaigns. Requests are considered two times each year.
Requirements: The foundation makes grants only to qualified IRS 501(c)3 organizations that specifically benefit people in the area surrounding Bayport and Saint Paul, MN, and western Wisconsin.
Restrictions: The foundation does not make loans or provide grants to individuals.
Geographic Focus: Minnesota, Wisconsin
Date(s) Application is Due: Mar 15; Sep 15
Amount: 1,000 - 25,000 USD
Samples: American Red Cross, Saint Croix Valley Chapter (Stillwater, MN)—for general operating support, $3000; A Chance to Grow (Minneapolis, MN)—to support the EEG neurofeedback program, $1000; Minnesota DARE (Saint Paul, MN)—for workbooks for the drug education and prevention program, $1000.
Contact: Kathleen Fluegel, Foundation Director; (866) 342-5475 or (612) 293-9001; (612) 298-0551; info@HRKFoundation.org
Internet: http://www.hrkfoundation.org/grants/index.htm
Sponsor: HRK Foundation
345 Street Peter Street, Suite 1200
Saint Paul, MN 55102-1639

Huber Foundation Grants **886**
The Foundation focuses its grants program on three specific aspects of reproductive rights: keeping abortion safe, legal, and preferably increasingly rare; contraceptive choice and availability; and relevant education. The Foundation's major interest lies in funding organizations that will impact these issues on a national level. There is no formal application procedure. A letter describing the project, a budget for the project, and proof of tax-exempt status is required. Though the Foundation board meets four times annually, there are no fixed deadline dates.
Requirements: U.S. nonprofits, including advocacy groups, hospitals, legal defense groups, family planning agencies, educational organizations, universities, and women's groups may submit grant applications.
Restrictions: The foundation does not encourage proposals for projects that are local or regional in scope. It will not consider grants to individuals, foreign organizations, capital campaigns, scholarships, endowment funds, research, international projects, or film productions.
Geographic Focus: All U.S. States

Amount: 10,000 - 100,000 USD
Samples: Planned Parenthood Federation of America (New York, NY)—for general support and Responsible Choices Campaign, $700,000; Feminist Majority Foundation (Arlington, VA)—for the National Clinic Access Project, $100,000; Planned Parenthood of Northern New England (Williston, VT)—for general support, $90,000.
Contact: Lorraine Barnhart, Executive Director; (732) 933-7700
Sponsor: Huber Foundation
P.O. Box 277
Rumson, NJ 07760-0277

Hudson Webber Foundation Grants **887**
The purpose of the Foundation is to improve the vitality and quality of life of the metropolitan Detroit community. The Foundation concentrates its giving primarily within the City of Detroit and has a particular interest in the revitalization of the urban core because this area is a focus for community activity and pride and is of critical importance to the vitality of the entire metropolitan community. The Foundation presently concentrates its efforts and resources in support of projects within five program missions: Detroit Physical Revitalization; Economic Development; The Arts; Safe Community; and the Detroit Medical Center. A brief letter signed by a senior officer of the requesting organization is the preferred form of application. Information for completing the letter of request are available online.
Requirements: The foundation concentrates its giving within Detroit.
Geographic Focus: Michigan
Samples: Habitat for Humanity - Metro Detroit, Inc., Detroit, MI, $150,000—Partnership to Build Capacity; Detroit Renaissance Foundation, Inc., Detroit, MI, $100,000—Business Attraction Program; Detroit Science Center, Inc., Detroit, MI, $10,000—General program support; Michigan Community Service Commission, Detroit, MI, $75,000—Winning Futures Program-Mentor Michigan; Harper Hospital, Detroit, MI, $200,000—Renal Transplant Unit.
Contact: Katy Locker, Program Director; (313) 963-7777; (313) 963-2818; HWF@hudson-webber.org
Internet: http://www.hudson-webber.org/HowToApply_Instructions.html
Sponsor: Hudson Webber Foundation
333 West Fort Street, Suite 1310
Detroit, MI 48226-3134

HUD Supportive Housing Program Grants **888**
The program is designed to promote the development of supportive housing and supportive services, including innovative approaches to assist homeless persons in the transition from homelessness and to enable them to live as independently as possible. Funds may be used to provide transitional housing, permanent housing, supportive housing, supportive services for homeless individuals not provided in conjunction with supportive housing, or facilities in which supportive services are provided. Seven types of assistance may be provided, including: acquisition of structures for use as supportive housing or in providing supportive services; rehabilitation of structures for use as supportive housing or in providing supportive services; new construction of buildings for use as supportive housing under limited circumstances; leasing of structures for use as supportive housing or in providing supportive services; operating costs of supportive housing; costs of providing supportive services to homeless persons; and administrative costs not to exceed five percent of the SHP grant. Funding of up to 75 percent of the annual operating costs is allowed for the first two years. Funding of up to 80 percent for supportive services cost and, the program provides grants for leasing costs for up to three years.
Requirements: States, local governments, other governmental entities; Native American tribes; private nonprofit organizations; and public, nonprofit community mental health associations are eligible to apply.
Geographic Focus: All U.S. States
Amount: 200,000 - 400,000 USD
Contact: Mark Johnston, Program Director; (202) 708-4300; Mark.Johnston@hud.gov
Internet: http://www.hud.gov/offices/cpd/homeless/programs/shp/index.cfm
Sponsor: U.S. Department of Housing and Urban Development
451 Seventh Street SW
Washington, DC 20410

Huffy Foundation Grants **889**
The foundation awards grants in company-operating areas in support of the arts, including museums, theaters, and cultural programs; education and higher education; hospitals, health associations, and substance abuse programs; human services, including women, youth, and child welfare; federated giving; and government/public administration. Types of support include general operating support, continuing support, annual campaigns, capital funds, program development, seed grants, scholarship funds, consulting services, and matching gifts. All requests must be in writing. Applications are accepted at any time and are considered four times each year, generally in February, May, August, and November. Grant applications for a local community should be submitted to the president of the local corporation. Requests for the Dayton community and for Ohio or national programs should be submitted to the office listed.
Requirements: Nonprofit organizations in company locations may apply. Requests should include a description of the organization and its history and purpose, a description of the people it serves, summary of total budget and funding for the past and present years, and names of Huffy employees who serve on the organization's governing board.
Restrictions: Grants are not made to individuals, in support of political activities or of religious organizations for religious purposes, or non tax-exempt organizations. Grants are seldom made for medical research; to organizations receiving support from United Way; to endowments; or for operating funds for organizations located outside the corporation communities.
Geographic Focus: California, Ohio, Pennsylvania, Wisconsin
Amount: 100 - 2,500 USD
Contact: Pam Booher, Secretary; (937) 866-6251
Sponsor: Huffy Foundation
225 Byers Road
Miamisburg, OH 45342

Hugh J. Andersen Foundation Grants **890**
The mission of the Hugh J. Andersen Foundation is to give back to our community through focused efforts that foster inclusivity, promote equality, and lead to increased human independence, self sufficiency and dignity. To fulfill this mission, the Foundation acts as a grantmaker, innovator, and convener. The Foundation's primary geographic area of focus is the Street Croix Valley: Washington County in Minnesota and Pierce, Polk and Street Croix Counties in Wisconsin. Secondarily, there is an interest in Street Paul, Minnesota. From time to time the Foundation may consider programs in other parts of the Metro Area and Greater Minnesota. Please contact the Program Director prior to submitting a proposal to determine if the program might be of interest to the Foundation. The Board generally considers requests in June, September, December and February. Faxed or emailed applications will not be considered.
Requirements: The Hugh J. Andersen Foundation awards grants only to qualified charitable organizations that are designated as tax exempt under Internal Revenue Service Code 501(c)3 and are not classified as private foundations.
Restrictions: The Hugh J. Andersen Foundation: does not make loans, and does not provide grants or scholarships to individuals; does not provide grants for lobbying activities, fundraising dinners and events, or travel; will generally not consider the following types of organizations and programs for funding: agencies/divisions/councils/programs that have counterparts in Street Paul or the Street Croix Valley; arts organizations exclusively focused on music, dance or visual arts; athletic teams; business/economics education; child care centers; civic action groups; debt or after the fact situations; immigration/refugee issues and programs; independent media productions; political/voter education; private or alternative schools; religious institutions. In addition, the Foundation: will generally not fund the entire project budget, but prefers to be part of an effort supported by a number of sources; considers major endowment and capital requests for funding to be a low priority; does not provide funding through fiscal agents; considers letters of inquiry. Letters of inquiry are reviewed at the Foundation's next board meeting. If the board determines that the request falls within its guidelines and interests, a full proposal will be requested from the applicant for review at the following board meeting.
Geographic Focus: Minnesota, Wisconsin
Date(s) Application is Due: Mar 15; Jun 15; Aug 15; Nov 15
Contact: Brad Kruse, Program Director; (651) 275-4489 or (888) 439-9508; (651) 439-9480; hjafdn@srinc.biz
Internet: https://www.srinc.biz/hja/documents/HJAGuidelines09-10.pdf
Sponsor: Hugh J. Andersen Foundation
White Pine Building, 342 Fifth Avenue North
Bayport, MN 55003

Huie-Dellmon Trust Grants 891

The trust awards grants to Louisiana nonprofits in its areas of interest, including hospitals, higher and secondary education, libraries, and Protestant churches and organizations. Types of support include general operating support, capital campaigns, building construction/renovation, equipment acquisition, program development, scholarship funds, research, and matching funds. There are no application forms or deadlines.
Requirements: Central Louisiana nonprofit organizations are eligible.
Geographic Focus: Louisiana
Amount: 1,000 - 100,000 USD
Samples: Christus Cabrini Foundation, Alexandria, LA, $100,000 (2008); Calvary Baptist Church, Alexandria, LA, $12,500 (2008); Rapides Parish Library, Alexandria, LA, $30,000 (2008).
Contact: Richard Crowell Jr., Trustee; (318) 748-8141
Sponsor: Huie-Dellmon Trust
P.O. Box 330
Alexandria, LA 71309-0330

Huisking Foundation Grants 892

The foundation awards grants in its areas of interest, including Catholic higher and secondary education, church support and social services, hospitals, and religion associations. Types of support include general operating support, building construction/renovation, research grants, endowment funds, scholarship funds, special projects, and continuing support. The board meets in April and November; letters of intent are due in February and August.
Geographic Focus: All U.S. States
Amount: 200 - 60,000 USD
Contact: Frank Huisking, Treasurer; (203) 426-8618
Sponsor: Huisking Foundation
291 Peddlers Road
Guilford, CT 06437

Hulman & Company Foundation Grants 893

The Hulman & Company Foundation was established in 1998 in the state of Indiana. The Foundation giving primarily in Indianapolis and the Terre Haute area. The Foundation supports community foundations and organizations involved with engineering education, animal welfare, and youth services.
Requirements: Contact the Foundations office with a proposal for initial approach, no application form required.
Restrictions: NO grants available to individuals.
Geographic Focus: Indiana
Amount: 5,000 - 95,000 USD
Contact: Jeffrey G. Belskus, Treasurer; (812) 232-9446
Sponsor: Hulman and Company Foundation
P.O. Box 150
Terre Haute, IN 47808-0150

Humanitas Foundation Grants 894

The Foundation considers proposals from Catholic organizations in the U.S. in the areas of church renewal, education and relief work. Areas of interest are: projects that promote the spirituality of the laity, high quality religious and lay leadership, vital parish life, Hispanic ministry, pastoral research, quality religious education, and direct service to the needy within disadvantaged populations. Proposal information is available online.
Requirements: Proposals for funding are accepted from Roman Catholic organizations, dioceses, groups of parishes, social agencies, religious orders, associations and other groups in the U.S. that are listed in The Official Catholic Director. Roman Catholic organizations with individual, federal tax-exempt status may also apply.
Restrictions: The Foundation does not fund capital campaigns, endowments, debt repayment, building construction, major renovations, scholarships, community organizing, or political lobbying efforts, nor does it fund already completed projects. It does not provide general support for well established programs. The Foundation does not accept proposals from individual parishes, schools, colleges, universities, seminaries or retreat houses for projects serving the ongoing functions of a particular institution. It does not make grants to support individuals. The Foundation does not accept applications from organizations outside of the U.S., or from U.S.-based organizations seeking funds for international projects.
Geographic Focus: All U.S. States
Date(s) Application is Due: Feb 1; Jul 1
Amount: 15,000 - 25,000 USD
Samples: Woodstock Theological Ctr (Washington, DC)—for the Preaching the Just Word program, $25,000; Catholic Charities U.S. A (Alexandria, VA)—for the emergency assistance fund, $40,000; Kidane-Mehret Geez Rite Catholic Church (Washington, DC)—for pastoral work among Ethiopian and Eritrean communities, $30,000.
Contact: Program Contact; (212) 704-2300; (212) 704-2301; humanitas@humanitasfoundation.org
Internet: http://www.humanitasfoundation.org/infograntseekers.html
Sponsor: Humanitas Foundation
1114 Avenue of the Americas, 28th Floor
New York, NY 10036

Human Source Foundation Grants 895

The Human Source Foundation is the charitable, non for profit arm of PALMEA. The Foundation is organized to support charitable and educational initiatives that improve the human condition, by providing assistance and financial support for programs involved with botany, higher education, and human services, with grants coming in the form of general operating funds. Giving is restricted to the State of Texas, primarily in Denton and Fort Worth counties. There are no specific deadlines or application forms with which to adhere, and applicants should begin by forwarding a letter of request.
Requirements: 501(c)3 tax-exempt organizations serving Texas, primarily Denton and Fort Worth counties, are eligible to apply.
Geographic Focus: Texas
Contact: Mary G. Palko, (817) 926-2799; (817) 926-5202; mary@ftw.com or mpalko@compuserve.com
Sponsor: Human Source Foundation
2409 Winton Terrace West, P.O. Box 100423
Fort Worth, TX 76185-0423

Humboldt Area Foundation Technical Assistance Program Grants 896

TAP is a small award program which provides nonprofits with one-on-one technical assistance in a variety of forms: consultants, training workshops, self-pace manuals, software, or any other form identified by applicants. TAP awards typically range from $500 to $2,000. Funds must be used to improve the organization, its leadership or operations, as a whole; not on programs or projects of the agency. Areas of assistance may include: strategic planning, financial management, operational assessments, board development, program assessments, personnel issues, collaborations, and fundraising. TAP applications and information are confidential and will not affect other potential Humboldt Area Foundation grant funding. TAP grant applications are accepted on the first of each month and grants that are awarded are paid directly to a consultant to cover the costs of their consulting services.
Restrictions: TAP will not pay for grant writing, programmatic development or for duties that are typically handled by staff (e.g. data entry). Organizations less than a year old and government entities are not eligible for TAP funds.
Geographic Focus: California
Date(s) Application is Due: Jan 1; Feb 1; Mar 1; Apr 1; May 1; Jun 1; Jul 1; Aug 1; Sep 1; Oct 1; Nov 1; Dec 1
Amount: 500 - 2,000 USD
Contact: Peter Pennekamp, Executive Director; (707) 442-2993, ext. 304; (707) 442-3811; peterp@hafoundation.org
Internet: http://www.hafoundation.org/index.php?option=content&task=view&id=74
Sponsor: Humboldt Area Foundation
373 Indianola Road
Bayside, CA 95524

Hyams Foundation Grants 897

The Foundation's mission is to increase economic and social justice and power within low-income communities in Boston and Chelsea, Massachusetts. The Foundation's focus is on four community priorities or outcomes: increased civic engagement, with a special focus on immigrant communities; more affordable housing, especially for very low-income families; increased family economic self-sufficiency; and expanded opportunities for low-income, older teens. Application information is available online.
Requirements: Massachusetts 501(c)3 charitable organizations are eligible. The foundation will give priority to programs that have a substantial impact on low-income neighborhoods/populations in Boston, and Chelsea.
Geographic Focus: Massachusetts
Date(s) Application is Due: Mar 1; Sep 1; Dec 1
Amount: 20,000 - 50,000 USD

Samples: Center for the Development of Teen Empowerment Programs, Boston, MA, $30,000—Youth Organizing Initiative (2009); East Boston Ecumenical Community Council, Boston, MA, $15,000—Immigrant Leadership Fund/Technical assistance (2009); Hyde Square Task Force, Inc., Boston, MA, $30,000—Affordable Housing/Operating expenses (2009).
Contact: Susan Perry, (617) 426-5600, ext. 307; (617) 426-5696; sperry@hyamsfoundation.org
Internet: http://www.hyamsfoundation.org
Sponsor: Hyams Foundation
50 Federal Street, 9th Floor
Boston, MA 02110

I.A. O'Shaughnessy Foundation Grants 898

The Foundation is concerned that too many schools lack sufficient resources; that students in high-poverty areas have lower achievement scores, higher drop-out rates, and lower rates of college graduation; that low-income families lack the resources to choose better schools; and that the gap between the rich and the poor is increasing. The Foundation has set its current funding interest to help address these critical matters of public concern. The Foundation is currently interested in making grants to support high quality education that prepares students in disadvantaged communities for educational and life success. Priority is given to organizations that provide support networks; remove impediments to student success; are broadly supported by the community, and have a record of demonstrated success. Additional guidelines and application forms are available at the foundation's website.
Requirements: Eligible applicant must be: nonprofit organizations; mission-consistent; fiscally sound; demonstrate a need; and capable and accountable.
Restrictions: The Foundation will not fund: grants that are not consistent with Foundation values; national or umbrella organizations that raise funds through broad-based solicitations to the general public; organizations that become overly dependent on the Foundation for on-going operational support; capital campaign gifts exceeding 20% of the campaign goal; political campaigns, events, or organizations whose purpose is to promote political candidates; lobbying; individuals.
Geographic Focus: Illinois, Kansas, Minnesota, Texas
Samples: Chicago Communities in Schools, $15,000; Church of Street Michael Stillwater, $200,000; Museum of New Mexico Foundation, $88,000.
Contact: Eileen A. O'Shaughnessy, Secretary; (952) 698-0959; (952) 698-0958; info@iaoshaughnessyfdn.org
Internet: http://www.iaoshaughnessyfdn.org/guidelines.htm
Sponsor: I.A. O'Shaughnessy Foundation
2001 Killebrew Drive, Suite 120
Bloomington, MN 55425

Ian Hague Perl 6 Development Grants 899

In May 2008 The Perl Foundation (TPF) received an unprecedented gift from Ian Hague, a finance executive in New York. The amount of the gift was $200,000 and was given to TPF to support Perl 6 development. Roughly half of the donation would be used to develop TPF's own capabilities to further search for Perl 6 support, and the balance would be used to directly and indirectly support developers working on Perl 6. The nominal maximum monthly payment is $5,000 for full-time work on the grant. This amount is not changed based on changes to the schedule of the grant once the grant is in process. Payments for varying levels of part-time work will be pro-rated against this nominal amount.
Requirements: Grants will be made to projects which obviously and concretely advance the completion of a Perl 6 implementation. Other Perl 6 projects, while potentially very worthwhile, are not the focus of Hague grants. The main goal is the release of a Perl 6 implementation, so critical path elements have preference. In order to demonstrate the criticality of your grant, supporting documentation of a complete project milestone list for your implementation will be very useful. Obviously, grants that support well-documented and well planned implementations have preference.
Restrictions: Residents and nationals of countries that are prohibited by U.S. law from engaging in commerce, are ineligible to participate.
Geographic Focus: All U.S. States
Amount: Up to 15,000 USD
Contact: Richard Dice, President; rdice@perlfoundation.org
Internet: http://www.perlfoundation.org/ian_hague_perl_6_development_grants
Sponsor: Perl Foundation
6832 Mulderstraat
Grand Ledge, MI 48837

IBM Community Development Grants 900

IBM's philanthropic resources are allocated to specific projects and programs that fit within our targeted areas of interest. IBM realizes the power and importance of education. Wherever IBM does business around the globe, the Corporation forms connections to communities and supports a range of civic and nonprofit activities that help those in need through its Community Development grants. In all of its efforts, the Corporation demonstrates how technology can enrich and expand access to services and assistance. Nonprofit organizations wishing to submit unsolicited proposals to IBM should make an initial inquiry in the form of a two-page letter. In the event that the proposal is of interest to IBM, additional information will be requested. The letter should include the following information: a brief statement fully describing the mission of the organization, the amount of money requested, and the purpose of the contribution; a description of the problem you wish to address, the solution you propose, and how IBM technology, and IBM volunteers, if appropriate, will be incorporated; proposed project budget with all other anticipated sources of income; plans to measure and evaluate program results; and the name, address and telephone number of the project contact person.
Requirements: IBM only considers requests submitted by organizations which have a tax-exempt classification under Sections 170(c) or 501(c)3 of the U.S. Internal Revenue Code. Priority is assigned to requests involving IBM technology or the volunteer efforts of its employees. In making a grant decision, they also consider what other types of IBM support (Matching Grants, Fund for Community Service, United Way) an organization may already be receiving. Videotapes and other supplemental materials are strongly discouraged at the initial stage of application.
Restrictions: IBM does not make equipment donations or grants from corporate philanthropic funds to: individuals, political, labor, religious, or fraternal organizations or sports groups; fund raising events such as raffles, telethons, walk-a-thons or auctions; capital campaigns, construction and renovation projects; chairs, endowments or scholarships sponsored by academic or nonprofit institutions; special events such as conferences, symposia or sports competitions; or, organizations that advocate, support, or practice activities inconsistent with IBM's non-discrimination policies, whether based on race, color, religion, gender, gender identity or expression, sexual orientation, national origin, disability, age or status as a protected veteran.
Geographic Focus: All U.S. States
Contact: Ann Cramer, Director; (404) 238-6660; (404) 238-6138; acramer@us.ibm.com or alfredat@us.ibm.com
Internet: http://www.ibm.com/ibm/ibmgives/grant/index.shtml
Sponsor: IBM Corporation
4111 Northside Parkway NW
Atlanta, GA 30327-3098

Icahn Family Foundation Grants 901

Established in 1996, the Foundation awards grants in primarily for education, higher education, and medical schools. Areas of interest include arts, children and youth services, and education. Of particular interest are elementary and secondary education, as well as education reform. There are no application forms or deadlines with which to adhere, and organizations interested in appealing for funding should submit a copy of their IRS Determination Letter, a detailed description of the project, and the amount of funding requested.
Geographic Focus: New Jersey, New York
Amount: Up to 500,000 USD
Samples: Princeton University (Princeton, NJ)—for Carl C. Icahn Laboratory for Genomics, $3,650,000; Mount Sinai School of Medicine of New York University (New York, NY)—for medical research, $1,010,000.
Contact: Gail Golder-Icahn, Vice-President; (212) 702-4300; (212) 750-5815
Sponsor: Icahn Family Foundation
767 Fifth Avenue, 47th Floor
New York, NY 10153

Idaho Power Company Corporate Contributions 902

The company awards grants in company operating territories in its areas of interest, including arts and culture, civic and community, education, and health and human services. Types of support include building construction/renovation, capital campaigns, continuing support, equipment, general operating support, matching gifts, scholarships, and sponsorships. The corporate contribution request form is available online. There are no application deadlines.
Requirements: Nonprofit organizations in southern Idaho and eastern Oregon are eligible.

Restrictions: Grants do not support: individuals; loans or investments; churches or religious organizations for purposes of religious advocacy; tickets for contests, raffles, or other prize-oriented activities; organizations that discriminate for any reason, including race, color, religion, creed, age, sex, or national origin; individual school programs or projects with limited participation; fraternal or labor organizations; unrestricted operating funds; special occasion good-will advertising.
Geographic Focus: Idaho, Oregon
Contact: Contribution Program Manager; (208) 388-2200
Internet: http://www.idahopower.com/aboutus/community/corporateContributions.htm
Sponsor: Idaho Power Company
P.O. Box 70
Boise, ID 83707

Iddings Foundation 903
Grants are given to Ohio nonprofits for operating budget support, capital improvements, upper-class collegiate scholarships to designated institutions, expansion of programs, and equipment in the areas of physical and mental health; education; culture and the environment; community welfare; and human services. Types of support include challenge/matching grants, equipment acquisition, demonstration grants, development grants, seed grants, annual campaigns, conferences and seminars, publication, and scholarship funds. and project grants. Proposals are reviewed quarterly; the distribution committee meets the month following the application deadline date.
Requirements: Applicants must be Ohio-based, tax-exempt organizations whose purpose is to improve the community environment and lives of the citizens, and whose primary focus is on the greater Dayton area.
Restrictions: Grants are not made to individuals or to organizations outside Ohio. Additionally, there will be no endowment support.
Geographic Focus: Ohio
Date(s) Application is Due: Mar 1; Jun 1; Sep 1; Nov 1
Amount: 500 - 50,000 USD
Samples: AIDS Foundation of Miami Valley (OH)—for staff support over two years, $19,125;Miami Valley Literacy Council (OH)—for salary support of a curriculum director, $5000.
Contact: Maribeth Graham, Administrator; (937) 224-1773; (937) 224-1871
Sponsor: Iddings Benevolent Trust
Ketting Tower, Suite 1620
Dayton, OH 45423

IDEM Section 319(h) Nonpoint Source Program Grants 904
This program funds projects that will work on a watershed level to reduce nonpoint source pollution in Indiana's lakes, rivers, and streams. Nonpoint source pollution does not come from a pipe. It results when water (rain or snowmelt) moves across land, such as city streets, agricultural fields and residential backyards, and picks up dirt, fertilizers, pesticides, animal wastes, road salt, motor oil and other pollutants. Nonpoint source pollution is also caused by wind, which like rain, can pick up soil particles and deposit them in lakes and streams. These pollutants have harmful effects on drinking water supplies, recreation, fisheries and wildlife. Nonpoint source pollution is the leading cause of water quality problems in Indiana and is responsible for many of the impairments identified on the 303(d) List of Impaired Waterbodies. Funding for selected projects will be provided by Clean Water Act Section 319 grant funds and match is provided by grant recipients and partners.
Requirements: To be considered for funding, the project sponsor (the entity responsible for the project and its overall success), must be one of the following: 1) Municipality; 2) County Government; 3) State Government; 4) Federal Government; 5) College/University; 6) Nonprofit 501(c)3. The program provides funding and technical assistance to groups that work on the watershed level with citizens to develop locally-based solutions to nonpoint source pollution. Specific ways to address nonpoint source water pollution include education/outreach on watershed management, information gathering activities such as conducting watershed inventories and water quality assessments for the purpose of developing comprehensive watershed management plans and implementing those plans, including implementation of best management practices that directly reduce sources of nonpoint source pollution. IDEM provides sixty percent (60%) of an approved project's total cost with Section 319 funds. A grant recipient must provide the remaining forty percent (40%) of the total project cost as match. Match may be in-kind services or cash. Match cannot come from any federal funding sources. Guidelines and application forms are available for download at the website. Do not use forms from previous years - they will not be accepted by IDEM.
Restrictions: The following is a list of activities that cannot be funded with Section 319 funds and cannot be counted as matching funds for a Section 319 grant: Permit fees; Food for meetings or other events; Purchase of agricultural equipment, or other large pieces of equipment (equipment modifications and leasing are allowable); Purchase of land or land easements (these activities can be counted as matching funds in some cases); Any project which is directed at water quantity rather than water quality, such as dredging, drainage, or flood control; Any practices, equipment, or supplies used to fulfill the requirements of any federal permit (NPDES permit, Section 401 Water Quality Certification, permits from the U.S. Army Corps of Engineers, as examples) or to comply with IDEM's Confined Feeding Operation rule or permit requirements, or to meet enforcement requirements; Wetland mitigation sites; Incentive payments or yield losses; Nonpoint source best management practices not sanctioned by IDEM or not sanctioned by a partner agency of IDEM; Practices not installed in accordance with standards and specifications developed by NRCS, IDNR or other recognized standards; Office furniture; Sales tax. Additionally, the following will not be funded by this grant program: Septic system pump outs, repairs, rehabilitations, or demonstrations of alternative septic systems; Projects whose sole purpose is data collection, research, demonstration of best management practices, or education/outreach. However, these activities may be incorporated as elements into a proposal that meets one of the three priorities.
Geographic Focus: Indiana
Date(s) Application is Due: Sep 1
Contact: Laura Bieberich, Team Leader; (317) 233-1863
Internet: http://www.in.gov/idem/resources/grants_loans/319h/index.html
Sponsor: Indiana Department of Environmental Management
Indiana Government Center North, 100 N Senate Avenue, MC-64-00, IGCS W041
Indianapolis, IN 46204

IEDC Industrial Development Grant Fund (IDGF) 905
The IEDC provides financial support for infrastructure improvements in conjunction with projects creating jobs and generating capital investment in Indiana. This grant provides money to local governments for off-site infrastructure projects associated with an expansion of an existing Indiana company or the location of a new facility in Indiana. State funding through the IDGF program must be matched by a combination of local government and company financial support. The grant may be awarded to communities or other eligible applicants who have a commitment letter from representatives of the affected industry/industries indicating their plans to locate or expand a facility. Applicants will be reviewed based on the number and quality of jobs being created, the community's economic need, a local match of funding and capital investment being made by the company. Typically this grant does not exceed 50% of the total project costs.
Requirements: Eligible applicants include the following entities: City; Town; County; Special taxing district; An economic development commission; Nonprofit corporation; Corporation established under I.C. 23-17 for the purpose of distributing water for domestic and industrial use; Regional water, sewage, or solid waste district; Conservancy district that includes in its purpose the distribution of domestic water or the collection and treatment of waste. Projects which may qualify include: (1) Construction of airports, airport facilities, and tourist attractions; (2) Construction, extension, or completion of: (a) Sanitary sewer lines, storm sewers, and other related drainage facilities; (b) Waterlines; (c) Roads and storms; (d) Sidewalks; (e) Rail spurs and sidings; and (f) Information and high technology infrastructure; (3) Leasing, purchase, construction, repair, and rehabilitation of property, both real and personal; and (4) Preparation of surveys, plans, and specifications for the construction of publicly owned and operated facilities, utilities, and services.
Restrictions: Funds are limited to existing Indiana companies or the location of a new facility in Indiana.
Geographic Focus: Indiana
Contact: Charlie Sparks, Director, Central Region; (317) 233-5122; (317) 232-4146; csparks@iedc.in.gov
Internet: http://www.in.gov/iedc/incentives/idgf.html
Sponsor: Indiana Economic Development Corporation
1 North Capitol Avenue, Suite 700
Indianapolis, IN 46204

IEDC International Trade Show Assistance Program 906
The program provides financial assistance for small Indiana businesses to participate in international trade shows. TSAP is designed to promote Indiana exports by encouraging companies to explore overseas markets. The maximum

amount of funding is $5,000, or 100% of exhibit space rental fees, whichever is less. The State Fiscal Year runs from July 1 through June 30.
Requirements: Small businesses eligible for this program are to be defined as a manufacturing concern with worldwide employment of 500 employees or less within the preceding 12 months (this includes parent companies, subsidiaries, divisions of, etc.). Firms must be prequalified with the IEDC in order to receive reimbursement. To receive this assistance, firms must: promote their company's products at an applicable trade show, exposition or fair; have an official company representative attend the show; have less than 500 employees worldwide; manufacture at least 51% of their product in Indiana; provide market research for applicable market. NOTE: Full stay at the show is required. Those companies not exhibiting ALL days of the show are disqualified from receiving funding from TSAP. See the website for detailed guidelines and application instruction.
Restrictions: Funding for trade shows is limited to one (1) show per company per fiscal year. Also, companies may not receive funding to attend the same show every year and may not exhibit by catalog only.
Geographic Focus: Indiana
Amount: Up to 5,000 USD
Contact: Steve Akard, Director, Office of International Development; (317) 234-2083; (317) 232-4146; sakard@iedc.in.gov
Internet: http://www.in.gov/iedc/incentives/tradeShow.html
Sponsor: Indiana Economic Development Corporation
1 North Capitol Avenue, Suite 700
Indianapolis, IN 46204

IEDC Skills Enhancement Fund (SEF) **907**
The fund is a tool to encourage companies to invest in their existing workforce and train new employees. SEF provides reimbursement for eligible training expenses over a two year term. Companies may reapply for additional SEF Funds after their initial two year term. The maximum amount awarded through the SEF program typically does not exceed 50% of a company's training budget.
Requirements: Companies may claim reimbursement for training expenses that result in improved basic or transferable skills. Company specific and quality assurance training expenses are also eligible.
Restrictions: IEDC typically does not provide reimbursement for training that is required by law. Those businesses that receive SEF training assistance must commit to continue their operations at the location where the SEF training assistance is provided for at least five years after the date that the training grant is completed.
Geographic Focus: Indiana
Contact: Karen Northrop, Business Development Specialist; (317) 232-0160; (317) 232-4146; knorthrop@iedc.in.gov
Internet: http://www.in.gov/iedc/incentives/sef.html
Sponsor: Indiana Economic Development Corporation
1 North Capitol Avenue, Suite 700
Indianapolis, IN 46204

Illinois Arts Council Local Arts Agencies Program Grants **908**
Local Arts Agencies Program Grants are designed to provide project and/or operational support to Illinois local arts agencies (defined as a community-based organization or an agency of city or county government that supports the growth and development of all of the arts in the identified area of service). Available funding ranges from $500 to $30,000, depending upon the applicant organization's overall past operating budget.
Requirements: Nonprofit organizations applying for funding must be chartered in the state of Illinois.
Geographic Focus: Illinois
Date(s) Application is Due: Mar 15
Amount: 500 - 30,000 USD
Contact: Rose Parisi, Director of Programs; (312) 814-4991; rose.parisi@illinois.gov
Internet: http://www.state.il.us/agency/iac/Guidelines/guidelines.htm
Sponsor: Illinois Arts Council
100 W Randolph Street, Suite 10-500
Chicago, IL 60601-3298

Illinois Arts Council Multidisciplinary Program Grants **909**
These grants are designed to support organizations offering programming that involves or fuses two or more distinct artistic disciplines. Programs should be distinct, not supplemental in nature, and must integrally involve each of the participating art forms rather than be in service to a single art form. Grants are available for ongoing programming, new projects, staff, production costs, marketing, and audience development. Available funding ranges from $500 to $30,000, depending upon the applicant organization's overall past operating budget.
Requirements: Nonprofit organizations applying for funding must be chartered in the state of Illinois.
Geographic Focus: Illinois
Date(s) Application is Due: Mar 15
Amount: 500 - 30,000 USD
Contact: Rose Parisi, Director of Programs; (312) 814-4991; rose.parisi@illinois.gov
Internet: http://www.state.il.us/agency/iac/Guidelines/guidelines.htm
Sponsor: Illinois Arts Council
100 W Randolph Street, Suite 10-500
Chicago, IL 60601-3298

Illinois Arts Council Music Program Grants **910**
Music Program Grants are designed to support professional, regional, and community companies including opera, vocal ensembles, orchestras, chamber music, jazz ensembles, contemporary and early music groups, and concert and wind bands. Available funding ranges from $500 to $30,000, depending upon the applicant organization's overall past operating budget.
Requirements: Nonprofit organizations applying for funding must be chartered in the state of Illinois.
Geographic Focus: Illinois
Date(s) Application is Due: Mar 15
Amount: 500 - 30,000 USD
Contact: Rose Parisi, Director of Programs; (312) 814-4991; rose.parisi@illinois.gov
Internet: http://www.state.il.us/agency/iac/Guidelines/guidelines.htm
Sponsor: Illinois Arts Council
100 W Randolph Street, Suite 10-500
Chicago, IL 60601-3298

Illinois Arts Council Theater Program Grants **911**
Theatre Program grants are designed to support professional, regional, and community companies, including experimental, street, and children's theater. This includes experimental, musical theatre, street performance, and theatre for young audiences. Available funding ranges from $500 to $30,000, depending upon the applicant organization's overall past operating budget.
Requirements: Nonprofit organizations applying for funding must be chartered in the state of Illinois.
Geographic Focus: Illinois
Date(s) Application is Due: Mar 15
Amount: 500 - 30,000 USD
Contact: Rose Parisi, Director of Programs; (312) 814-4991; rose.parisi@illinois.gov
Internet: http://www.state.il.us/agency/iac/Guidelines/guidelines.htm
Sponsor: Illinois Arts Council
100 W Randolph Street, Suite 10-500
Chicago, IL 60601-3298

Illinois Tool Works Foundation Grants **912**
The corporate foundation awards grants in areas of company operations, with emphasis on Chicago, Ilinoise. Grants support organizations that focus on: education, the arts, health and human services, social welfare, housing, environmental and youth issues. The Foundation contributes financial support to not-for-profit organizations through two major giving programs: a direct-giving program and a three-for-one matching gift program for employees.
Requirements: Not-for-profit organizations are eligible to apply.
Geographic Focus: All U.S. States
Amount: 5,000 - 1,000,000 USD
Samples: United Way of Metropolitan Chicago, Chicago, IL, $1,110,732 (2008); Scholarship America, Saint Peter, MN, $478,350 (2008); Scott & White Memorial Hospital / Scott Sherwood & Brindley Foundation, Temple, TX, $60,000 (2008).
Contact: Mary Ann Mallahan, Secretary; (847) 724-7500; (847) 657-4261; mmallahan@itw.com
Internet: http://www.itwinc.com/itw/corporate_citizenship/itw_foundation
Sponsor: Illinois Tool Works Foundation
3600 West Lake Avenue
Glenview, IL 60026

IMLS Grants to State Library Administrative Agencies **913**

The through the program, the Institute of Museum and Library Services provides funds to State Library Administrative Agencies (SLAAs) using a population-based formula. State libraries may use the appropriation to support statewide initiatives and services. They also may distribute the funds through subgrant competitions or cooperative agreements to public, academic, research, school, and special libraries in their state.

Requirements: State library administrative agencies located in one of the 50 states of the United States, the District of Columbia, the Commonwealth of Puerto Rico, Guam, American Samoa, the U.S. Virgin Islands, the Commonwealth of the Northern Mariana Islands, the Republic of the Marshall Islands, the Federated States of Micronesia, and the Republic of Palau are eligible to submit five-year plans.

Geographic Focus: All U.S. States

Date(s) Application is Due: Apr 1

Amount: 1 - 2,000,000 USD

Contact: Laurie C. Brooks, Associate Deputy Director; (202) 653-4650; stateprograms@imls.gov

Internet: http://www.imls.gov/programs/programs.shtm

Sponsor: Institute of Museum and Library Services
1800 M Street NW, 9th Floor
Washington, DC 20036-5802

Inasmuch Foundation Grants **914**

The foundation was established for charitable, scientific, and educational projects primarily in Oklahoma; however, select projects in Colorado Springs, CO, also are supported. The foundation consistently provides funding and support to educational, health and human service, cultural, artistic, historical, and environmental concerns. This funding is not available to individuals, but is available to formal organizations seeking capital and support for existing programs that meet the emerging needs of the community. In order to initiate a proposal, submit a one-page letter of inquiry by the listed application deadlines. Application information is available online.

Restrictions: The foundation generally does not fund endowments or scholarships.

Geographic Focus: Colorado, Oklahoma

Date(s) Application is Due: Feb 15; Aug 15

Samples: Colorado College (Colorado Springs, CO)—to construct a facility for arts education and performances, $4 million.

Contact: Program Contact; (405) 604-5292

Internet: http://www.inasmuchfoundation.org/application.html

Sponsor: Inasmuch Foundation
210 Park Avenue, Suite 3150
Oklahoma City, OK 73102

Independence Community Foundation Education, Culture & Arts Grant **915**

The Foundation recognizes that cultural and educational institutions create positive change in communities. The Foundation provides program and project support to institutions that seek to bolster economic and social development, and act as stabilizing forces in their communities. Interested applicants should submit a letter of inquiry. Application information is available online.

Requirements: Program or project grants are made on a competitive basis to nonprofit organizations located within New York City, Nassau, Suffolk and Westchester counties in New York, and Essex, Bergen, Union, Hudson, Middlesex, Ocean, and Monmouth counties in New Jersey.

Restrictions: Funding is not available to support individual artists.

Geographic Focus: New Jersey, New York

Date(s) Application is Due: Mar 30; Sep 30

Contact: Program Contact; (718) 722-2300; (718) 722-5757; inquiries@icfny.org

Internet: http://www.icfny.org/education_arts.html

Sponsor: Independence Community Foundation
182 Atlantic Avenue
Brooklyn, NY 11201

Independence Foundation Grants **916**

The foundation awards grants to Philadelphia nonprofit organizations in its areas of interest, including community-based nurse managed health care, health promotion, family planning, and comprehensive health care services where issues of quality, access, and cost are considered; arts and culture; legal aid; and assistance to the disadvantaged. Types of support include development grants, endowments, general operating grants, professorships, program development grants, seed money grants, and scholarships. A brief letter outlining a proposed project is a prerequisite to a formal application.

Requirements: 501(c)3 tax-exempt organizations serving Philadelphia and the surrounding counties including Bucks, Chester, Delaware, and Montgomery are eligible.

Restrictions: Grants will not be made to individuals or for building and development funds or to support travel, research, or publications.

Geographic Focus: Pennsylvania

Amount: 1,000 - 100,000 USD

Contact: Grants Administrator; (215) 985-4009; (215) 985-3989

Internet: http://www.independencefoundation.org

Sponsor: Independence Foundation
200 S Broad Street, Suite 1101
Philadelphia, PA 19102

Indiana 21st Century Research and Technology Fund Awards **917**

The Indiana 21st Century Research and Technology Fund of the Indiana Economic Development Corporation (IEDC) is open to proposals from all public and private entities for technology-based commercialization activities encompassing science/technology creation, innovation, and transfer intended to have commercial impacts. The fund intends to increase the numbers, and rates of development, of new and expanding technology-based companies by funding promising opportunities that, in some cases, the financial markets might find too risky. The Fund makes awards in two broad categories: Science and Technology Commercialization and Centers of Excellence. In addition, the Fund provides cost-share on behalf of Federal proposals submitted by Indiana-based entities. Generally awards are made in multiples of $50,000 up to $2,000,000. Support for awards in excess of $2,000,000 will be rare.

Requirements: The IEDC defines a technology-based company as one that is involved in transferring advanced technology into products, developing technologies with the near-term intention of creating products, or using new or advanced technologies in its design, development, and/or manufacturing of products. The Fund emphasizes the creation of academic-sector - commercial-sector partnerships. In making awards, the Fund expects significant leverage from the partners involved in the projects. Important: before applying, contact Fund staff (email preferred) to discuss your interest in submitting a proposal and to discuss your technology and commercialization goals. While not a review criterion, the fund encourages the inclusion of interns from any academic institution, or participating commercial sector partner, in order to increase project-related involvement of students at all levels.

Restrictions: Only direct costs will be supported. Institutions will not be provided indirect (overhead) cost support. Entities with previous Fund awards that are not current with regard to financial or technical reporting requirements will be disqualified from making new submissions to the Fund. Resubmissions of previously declined proposals will be considered only if substantive changes have been made to the proposal. Fund staff will determine whether to review resubmissions.

Geographic Focus: Indiana

Amount: 500,000 - 2,000,000 USD

Samples: 2K Corporation: $400,000 - Commercialization of a Neutron Based Explosives Detection Device (Car Bomb Detection). Arxan Technologies, Inc.: $1,944,096 - Protecting Critical IP in the 21st Century: Advancing Anti-Tamper Technologies. BioVitesse Inc.: $1,300,000 - Rapid Detection and Identification of Live Bacteria. CIS LLC: $1,075,000 - Commercialization of Satellite Radio for Cell Phone Applications.

Contact: Carla Phelps, Financial Manager; (317) 233- 4336; cphelps@21fund.org

Internet: http://www.21fund.org/

Sponsor: Indiana Economic Development Corporation
1 North Capitol Avenue, Suite 900
Indianapolis, IN 46204

Indiana Arts Commission Capacity Building Grants **918**

The program is a stabilization process that provides IAC support, over a 24-month period, for organizational assessment, long range planning, and plan implementation utilizing a standardized assessment tool. It is designed to allow arts providers to comprehensively examine their 'reason for being,' mission, markets, programs, services, and governance and management structures and general operations with the aim of increased organizational effectiveness. The program is not designed to address single issue needs such as developing marketing or fund raising plans, program planning or evaluation, or feasibility studies. Grant amount is 75 percent of project costs or $20,000 over a 24-month period. Grantees must provide at least a 25 percent match. The match may be

a combination of cash and in-kind (the value of necessary donated goods and services). However, at least one-half of the matches must be cash. Letters of Intent are due by February 16, with final applications due by April 20.
Requirements: Organizations must meet five basic requirements to apply: 1) Must have arts programming and/or services as its primary mission. 2) Must be a private, nonprofit, tax-exempt organization, incorporated in the state of Indiana. 3) Must have received recognition of tax-exempt status from the Internal Revenue Service. 4) Must be Indiana-based and have an Indiana address. Nonprofit corporations that are based in another state must be registered in Indiana as a Foreign Corporation, have an Indiana address, and provide arts activities in Indiana to be eligible. 5) Must be in good standing with the IAC and in compliance with all IAC requirements. Consider participation if your Indiana-based arts services organization fits into one of the following categories: (a) The organization is healthy and interested in re-evaluating the organization's mission, exploring assumptions about the organization's service and audience, and balancing the need to ensure artistic quality and fostering participation; (b) The organization has recurring problems (i.e. deficit, turnover, poor audience participation) that may relate to overall organizational issues not specific situations, or; (c) The organization has completed some type of overall organizational assessment in the last 5 years. The IAC requires any organization interested in applying to this grant program to submit a Notice of Intent to Apply form. This form can be found at http://www.in.gov/arts/grants/program.html
Restrictions: A complete list of restrictions can be found in the guidelines, instructions, and application packet available at the website.
Geographic Focus: Indiana
Date(s) Application is Due: Feb 16; Apr 20
Amount: Up to 20,000 USD
Contact: Kristina Davis, Program Coordinator; (317) 232-1279; (317) 232-5595; kdavis-smith@iac.in.gov
Internet: http://www.in.gov/arts/2550.htm
Sponsor: Indiana Arts Commission
150 W Market Street, Suite 618
Indianapolis, IN 46204

Indiana Arts Commission Statewide Arts Service Organization Grants 919
This program strengthens the capacity of arts providers and arts providing organizations by providing financial support to organizations that offer quality training and technical assistance services on a statewide or multi-regional basis, with special attention to arts providers in underserved communities. Technical assistance includes workshops, publications and other organizational training. Funding is limited to project support for a distinct aspect of the organization's arts-related technical assistance activities. Organizations may request up to 50 percent of project expenses for two years or $20,000. Applicants must provide a local match. Letters of Intent should be received by March 9, with applications due by April 9.
Requirements: An underserved community is one in which individuals lack access to arts programs due to: geography, economic conditions, ethnic background, disability or age. Organizations must be Indiana-based and have an Indiana address or registered in Indiana as a Foreign Corporation and provide arts activities in Indiana. Indiana public or private, nonprofit, tax-exempt agency or part of an Indiana public agency with a separate organizational structure. In addition to the general eligibility requirements, an organization applying in this category will have: 1) mission to provide arts-related technical assistance; 2) membership or constituency; 3) two-year history of planning and delivering arts-related technical assistance; 4) process for determining the training needs of consumers and an evaluation of the effectiveness; 5) process for planning and evaluation with input from the community; 6) a governing body that is representative of the service area; 7) operated for one year according to a strategic plan adopted by the governing body; 8) statewide presence.
Restrictions: All applicants must provide a local match. In general, applicants must match IAC funds on a dollar-for-dollar basis. In some cases, the match may be a combination of cash and the value of necessary donated goods and services up to 50 percent of the required match amount.
Geographic Focus: Indiana
Date(s) Application is Due: Mar 9; Apr 9
Amount: 1,000 - 20,000 USD
Contact: Kristina Davis, Program Coordinator; (317) 232-1279; (317) 232-5595; kdavis-smith@iac.in.gov
Internet: http://www.in.gov/arts/2556.htm
Sponsor: Indiana Arts Commission
150 W Market Street, Suite 618
Indianapolis, IN 46204

Indianapolis Preservation Grants 920
Grants are available for professional architectural and engineering feasibility studies and other preservation consulting services, as well as organizational development and fundraising projects. The foundation makes the preservation grants on a four-to-one matching basis, with four dollars from us matching each local cash dollar. Grants will fund 80% of the total project cost up to $2,000.
Requirements: Nonprofit community preservation organizations and historic neighborhood foundations in Marion County are eligible to apply.
Restrictions: The grants may not be used for physical restoration work.
Geographic Focus: Indiana
Amount: Up to 2,000 USD
Contact: Chad Lethig, Indianapolis Preservation Coordinator, Central Regional Office; (317) 639-4534; (317) 639-6720; flip@historiclandmarks.org
Internet: http://www.historiclandmarks.org/help/grants.html
Sponsor: Historic Landmarks Foundation of Indiana
340 W Michigan Street
Indianapolis, IN 46202

Indiana Preservation Grants 921
Grants are available for professional architectural and engineering feasibility studies and other preservation consulting services, as well as organizational development and fundraising projects. The foundation makes the preservation Grants on a four-to-one matching basis, with four dollars from us matching each local cash dollar. Grants will fund 80% of the total project cost up to $2,500.
Requirements: Nonprofit organizations in Indiana are eligible to apply. Contact the Historic Landmarks regional office that serves your community (see website for list of regional offices or contact the state headquarters office) for guidelines and forms.
Restrictions: The grants may not be used for physical restoration work.
Geographic Focus: Indiana
Amount: Up to 2,500 USD
Samples: Clinton, IN (Vermillion County) $3,040 grant for a feasibility study led to a $700,000 restoration of the town's 1905 passenger depot.
Contact: Carla Jones, Receptionist, State Headquarters; (317) 639-4534; (317) 639-6734; info@historiclandmarks.org
Internet: http://www.historiclandmarks.org/help/grants.html
Sponsor: Historic Landmarks Foundation of Indiana
340 W Michigan Street
Indianapolis, IN 46202

Indiana Recycling Grants 922
Indiana Recycling Grants are designed to help start or expand source reduction, recycling, and recycling education programs in Indiana. Funds are available for the costs associated with establishing curbside recycling, drop off recycling, recycling processing, and yard waste collection and management. These grants are intended to create sustainable projects with no state funding for ongoing program costs.
Requirements: A matching contribution of 50% of the total project cost is required. Solid waste management districts, counties, municipalities, townships, schools, and nonprofit organizations with 501(c) status are eligible. Detailed guidelines, application and forms are available at the website.
Restrictions: Limited to Indiana only.
Geographic Focus: Indiana
Date(s) Application is Due: May 25; Sep 28
Contact: Kristin Brier, Program Officer; (800) 988-7901; kbrier@idem.in.gov
Internet: http://www.in.gov/recycle/funding/irg.html
Sponsor: Indiana Department of Environmental Management
100 North Senate Avenue, MC 64-01
Indianapolis, IN 46204-2251

Initiative Foundation Grants 923
The Foundation exists to improve the quality of life in central Minnesota. The Foundation's highest priorities are: to strengthen children, youth and families; promote economic stability; preserve space, place and natural resources; build capacity of nonprofit organizations; embrace diversity and reduce prejudice; and increase utilization of technology. Application information is available online.
Requirements: Grants are awarded to organizations or programs that deliver specific services on a regular basis to residents of the following Minnesota counties: Benton, Cass, Chisago, Crow Wing, Isanti, Kanabec, Mille Lacs, Morrison, Pine, Sherburne, Stearns, Todd, Wadena, and Wright.

Restrictions: Funding is not available for: any programs or projects that do not directly benefit residents in the Initiative Foundation's 14-county service area; replacement of government or other funding; endowments, local fund drives, grants to individuals and businesses; religious activities; capital expenses (e.g. buildings, equipment, signs, vehicles, etc.); development or purchase of school curriculum; expenses incurred prior to receipt of grant award; lobbying or campaigning for a candidate, issue or referendum vote; school athletic programs. Arts, health related and media production project applications are discouraged, unless they are a part of a strategic plan developed through an Initiative Foundation Partnership program. Multiple applications from a single organization at the same time are discouraged.
Geographic Focus: Minnesota
Amount: 2,000 - 15,000 USD
Contact: Grants Director; (877) 632-9255; (320) 632-9258; grants@ifound.org
Internet: http://www.ifound.org/grants_index.php
Sponsor: Initiative Foundation
405 First Street SE
Little Falls, MN 56345

Inland Foundation Inc Grants **924**

Nonprofit organizations located in communities where Inland Container has facilities and employees are invited to apply for grants in the areas of community services, education, art and culture, and health. Types of support include employee-related scholarships, annual campaigns, continuing support, general operating budgets, and special projects. Proposals should consist of a brief letter that includes a description of the sponsoring organization and project; statement of the importance of the project and why it meets the foundation's guidelines; geographical area served by the project; total funds needed and the amount requested from the foundation; other sources of income and funding; and proof of the organization's tax-exempt status. Grant proposals are accepted throughout the year.
Requirements: Grants are awarded to nonprofits in plant locations, including Fort Smith, AR; Buena Park, El Centro, Los Angeles, Neward, Santa Fe Springs, and Tracy, CA; Denver, CO; Orlando, FL; Rome, GA; Chicago, IL; Crawfordsville, Evansville, Indianapolis, and Newport, IN; Garden City and Kansas City, KS; Louisville and Maysville, KY; Minden, LA; Minneapolis, MN; Hattiesburg, MS; Saint Louis, MO; Edison and Spotswood, NJ; Middletown, OH; Biglerville, and Hazleton, PA; Vega Alta, Puerto Rico; Lexington and Rock Hill, SC; Elizabethton and New Johnsonville, TN; Dallas, Edinburg, and Orange, TX; and Petersburg, VA.
Restrictions: The foundation does not make grants to individuals, religious organizations for sectarian purposes, or individual professors or departments within universities.
Geographic Focus: All U.S. States
Amount: 1,000 - 30,000 USD
Contact: Evonne Nerren, Secretary/Treasurer; (936) 829-1721
Internet: http://www.templeinland.com
Sponsor: Inland Foundation
303 S Temple Drive
Diboll, TX 75941

Intergrys Corporation Grants **925**

Integrys supports the giving initiatives of Wisconsin Public Service Foundation in Michigan, Minnesota and Wisconsin. Other significant giving by Integrys occurs through programs operated by Peoples Gas and North Shore Gas in Illinois, including the city of Chicago and its 54 suburban communities in northeastern Illinois. Areas if interest include: arts and culture; education (all levels); human services and health; community and neighborhood development; and the environment. Employee volunteers allow staff to give back to the neighborhoods they cherish. Matching funds energize charitable involvement. Categories of giving include health and welfare, civic and community, higher education, and cultural. Most corporate contributions are in the form of unrestricted grants. Types of support include capital grants, endowments, general operating grants, matching gifts, and program grants. Before eligibility is determined, consideration will be given to the background of the organization, the organization's legal status, how the program will benefit the community, whether the organization receives broad community support, the quality of the organization's leadership, and the organization's financial status.
Requirements: Organizations in Illinois, Michigan, Minnesota, and Wisconsin are eligible.
Restrictions: Contributions will not be made to individuals; organizations that discriminate by race, color, creed, or national origin; political organizations or campaigns; organizations whose prime purpose is to influence legislation; religious organizations for religious purposes; agencies owned and operated by local, state, or federal governments; or for trips or tours, or special-occasion or goodwill advertising.
Geographic Focus: Illinois, Michigan, Minnesota, Wisconsin
Amount: Up to 5,000 USD
Contact: Community Contributions Officer; (312) 240-7516 or (800) 699-1269; (312) 240-4389
Internet: http://www.integrysgroup.com/corporate/corporate_giving.aspx
Sponsor: Intergrys Corporation
130 E Randolph Drive, 18th Floor
Chicago, IL 60601

Iowa Arts Council Operational Support Grants for Major and Mid-Size Arts Organizations **926**

A limited number of grants are awarded annually for operational support to major and midsize arts organizations providing cultural and managerial excellence on a continuing basis to the citizens of Iowa. Organizations receiving Operational Support grants are required to demonstrate the ability to cash match the award. Application forms will be mailed to organizations on request or on receipt of the required letter of intent. Applicants who are currently in the operating support grant cycle must submit an Interim Application for the second year of funding on or before May 1. Contact program staff for current funding schedule.
Requirements: Organizations must be located and incorporated in Iowa, federally tax-exempt, and must have had an annual cash operating budget of between $50,000 and $250,000 (for midsize) for at least three years before filing an application. Applicant organizations must be unattached to an educational institution, must operate year-round, and must have at least one professional staff member.
Restrictions: Organizations requesting operational support are not eligible to apply for project grants.
Geographic Focus: Iowa
Date(s) Application is Due: May 1
Amount: 3,000 - 22,000 USD
Contact: Bruce Williams, Program Contact; (515) 281-4406; bruce.williams@iowa.g or bruce.williams@dca.state.ia.us
Internet: http://www.iowaartscouncil.org/funding/overview.shtml
Sponsor: Iowa Arts Council
600 E Locust, Capitol Complex
Des Moines, IA 50319-0290

IREX Kosovo Civil Society Project (KCSP) Grants **927**

The Program is aimed at assisting Kosovo's Nongovernmental Organization (NGO) community in becoming a truly indigenous, viable sector that plays an important role in representing and serving Kosovo's diverse citizenry and shaping public policy. IREX works with individual NGOs and coalitions to strengthen their capacity to advocate for public policy issues while progressing toward forming an inclusive, transparent, and credible Kosovo network of NGOs. In partnership with the Advocacy Training and Resource Center (ATRC), the Program provides grants to support issue-specific campaigns, coalition-building and training on effective advocacy, coalition-building techniques, and public relations through the media.
Geographic Focus: All U.S. States
Samples: Building Partnerships for Economic Development—this project promotes partnerships among local government, the NGO sector and the business community in order to attract more foreign investment in the Gjakove region, $100,000; Municipal Court as a Place of Justice—the project provides space for Kosovar nongovernmental organizations to participate with policymakers in the creation of future laws related to the status of women in Kosovo, $100,000.
Contact: Program Officer; (202) 628-8188; (202) 628-8189; kcsp@irex.org
Internet: http://www.irex.org/programs/kcsp/index.asp
Sponsor: International Research and Exchanges Board
2121 K Street NW, Suite 700
Washington, DC 20037

IREX Russia Civil Society Support Program (CSSP) Grants **928**

The Program is aimed at strengthening the nongovernmental organization (NGO) sector in Russia, particularly in the Russian Far East. CSSP promotes an environment where the government actively reaches out to involve NGOs in policy development and, in turn, NGOs demonstrate the skills and capacity to advocate their positions in a constructive manner. Small grants support NGO coalitions and alliances for advocacy projects benefiting their constituents.

To date, regional and inter-regional coalitions have been initiated to advocate for housing rights, welfare of disabled children, education reform, and environmental protection in twenty regions of the Russian Federation.
Geographic Focus: All U.S. States, Russia
Contact: Program Officer; (202) 628-8188; (202) 628-8189; csd@irex.org
Internet: http://www.irex.org/programs/cssp/index.asp
Sponsor: International Research and Exchanges Board
2121 K Street NW, Suite 700
Washington, DC 20037

IREX Small Grant Fund for Civil Society Projects in Africa and Asia 929
IREX will provide a select number of grants of up to U.S. $10,000 to local private, nongovernmental institutions in Africa and Asia. Proposed project must focus on strengthening civic engagement in one of the following ways: institutional development of civil society organizations, to include support for training and technical assistance. Preference given to organizations and/or initiatives focused on advocacy, transparency and accountability, anti-corruption and/or citizen participation; women's empowerment initiatives that promote the full participation of women in all levels of economic, political and /or social life (special use of technology is encouraged); and vocational training or educational programs addressing child labor or trafficking, child soldiers, HIV/AIDS, learning disabilities or special needs. In lieu of a formal application or proposal, IREX requests that interested organizations submit a brief letter of inquiry, of no more than two pages, to help determine whether the proposed project would address IREX's present interests. Inquiry letters will be reviewed on a rolling basis and if they meet current interests, the grant seeker will be asked to submit a formal proposal. Inquiry letters can be sent by mail, fax or email.
Requirements: Applicants must be a private nongovernmental organization based solely in Africa or Asia.
Restrictions: The Program will not fund: grants to individuals; grants for university study, graduate study or research; or grants to attend conferences, trainings or workshops.
Geographic Focus: All Countries
Amount: Up to 10,000 USD
Contact: Program Officers; (202) 628-8188; (202) 628-8189; sgfcsd@irex.org
Internet: http://www.irex.org/programs/sgf/index.asp
Sponsor: International Research and Exchanges Board
2121 K Street NW, Suite 700
Washington, DC 20037

IREX Small Grant Fund for Media Projects in Africa and Asia 930
IREX will provide a select number of grants of up to U.S. $10,000 to local private, nongovernmental institutions in Africa and Asia. Proposed project must focus on promoting professionalism and independence in media in one of the following ways: journalism training, to include basic reporting skills, environmental reporting, business and economics reporting, investigative reporting, and other specialized reporting skills; media advocacy, to include education on the value of professional media, development of media legislation, community outreach, and training in issues related to free media; and institutional development of media and media-related institutions, to include support for equipment and operational costs. In lieu of a formal application or proposal, IREX requests that interested organizations submit a brief letter of inquiry, of no more than two pages, to help determine whether the proposed project would address IREX's present interests. Inquiry letters will be reviewed on a rolling basis and if they meet current interests, the grant seeker will be asked to submit a formal proposal. Inquiry letters can be sent by mail, fax or email.
Requirements: Applicants must be a private nongovernmental organization based solely in Africa or Asia.
Restrictions: The Program will not fund: grants to individuals; grants for university study, graduate study or research; or grants to attend conferences, trainings or workshops.
Geographic Focus: All Countries
Amount: Up to 10,000 USD
Contact: Program Officers; (202) 628-8188; (202) 628-8189; sgfmdd@irex.org
Internet: http://www.irex.org/programs/sgf/index.asp
Sponsor: International Research and Exchanges Board
2121 K Street NW, Suite 700
Washington, DC 20037

Irving and Harriet Sands Foundation Grants 931
The Irving and Harriet Sands Foundation (formerly known as the Sands Family Foundation) was established in 1991 by Irving Sands. Giving is limited primarily in Florida, Boston, Massachusetts, Akron, Ohio, and Seattle, Washington. Specific fields of interest include Jewish agencies and synagogues. There are no specific deadlines or application forms with which to adhere, and applicants should begin by forwarding a narrative request by mail.
Geographic Focus: Florida, Massachusetts, Ohio, Washington
Amount: Up to 1,000 USD
Samples: Atlantic Street Center, Seattle, Washington, $1,000 (2009); Food Lifeline, Shoreline, Washington, $1,000 (2009); Dale Turner Family YMCA, Shoreline, Washington, $1,000 (2009).
Contact: Richard Sands, President; (617) 283-0027; richsands1@rich-sands.com
Sponsor: Irving and Harriet Sands Foundation
37 Beverly Road
Arlington, MA 02474

Irving S. Gilmore Foundation Grants 932
The Irving S. Gilmore Foundation endeavors to develop and to enrich the Greater Kalamazoo community of Michigan and, its residents by supporting the work of nonprofit organizations. The Foundation's funding priorities are: health and well-being; arts; human services; education; community development; culture and humanities. Organizations that are first time Foundation applicants or have not received Foundation funding since 2007 must contact the Foundation at least four weeks prior to an applicable submission deadline.
Requirements: The Foundation supports Kalamazoo County projects, programs, and purposes carried out by charitable institutions, primarily public charities and governmental entities.
Restrictions: Grants are not made to individuals.
Geographic Focus: Michigan
Date(s) Application is Due: Jan 4; Mar 1; May 3; Jul 1; Sep 1; Nov 1
Samples: Michigan Festival of Sacred Music—Operational Support (2008); Hospice Care of Southwest Michigan—Capital Campaign (2008); Volunteer Services of Greater Kalamazoo— BoardConnect Program (2008).
Contact: Janice C. Elliott, Vice President of Administrations; (269) 342-6411; (269) 342-6465
Internet: http://www.isgilmorefoundation.org/communityinvolvement.htm
Sponsor: Irving S. Gilmore Foundation
136 East Michigan Avenue, Suite 900
Kalamazoo, MI 49007-3912

Irvin Stern Foundation Grants 933
The Foundation awards grants to nonprofits primarily in the following areas: human services; civic affairs; and Jewish welfare. Other grant requests should be in the Foundation's other areas of interest which include: aiding the underserved, poor, and disadvantaged; improving the quality of life in urban communities; and enhancing Jewish community, education and spirituality. Interested applicants may submit an online letter of inquiry or applications may be mailed to the Foundation office.
Requirements: The Foundation makes grants to tax-exempt organizations.
Restrictions: The Foundation does not contribute to endowments, capital campaigns, capital construction projects, and academic or medical research programs of any kind.
Geographic Focus: All U.S. States
Samples: Book Worm Angels, Chicago, IL—general operating funds; Hand in Hand/Center for Jewish-Arab Education in Israel, Portland OR—Hand in Hand Expansion Project. Project will expand capacity of Hand in Hand's bilingual, multicultural schools for Jewish and Arab students in Israel; Metropolitan College of New York, New York, NY—to support the Office of Career Services.
Contact: Christine Flood, Grants Administrator; christine@irvinstern.org
Internet: http://www.irvinstern.org/guidelines.html
Sponsor: Irvin Suitern Foundation
25 West Hubbard Street, 4th Floor
Chicago, IL 60610

Island Foundation Grants 934
Grants are awarded in the New England states for the support of arts and culture, civic and public affairs, community development, elementary and secondary education, environmental advocacy as it relates to alternatives in wastewater technology, and social services. Types of support include general

operating budgets, matching funds, special projects, and research. Interested persons should request a copy of the foundation's annual report and guidelines before submitting their request.
Requirements: Nonprofit organizations in Maine, Massachusetts, and Rhode Island are eligible for grant support.
Restrictions: Grants do not support individuals, international organizations, religious organizations, special events, benefit dinners, or political campaigns.
Geographic Focus: Maine, Massachusetts, Rhode Island
Amount: Up to 17,000,000 USD
Samples: Woods Hole Oceanographic Institution (Woods Hole, MA)—to support research on solar aquatic systems, $231,000; Coalition for Buzzards Bay (Buzzards Bay, MA)—for the protection of Buzzards Bay, $45,000.
Contact: Julie Early, Executive Director; (508) 748-2809; (508) 748-0991; islandfdn@earthlink.net
Sponsor: Island Foundation
589 Mill Street
Marion, MA 02738

Ittleson Foundation AIDS Grants **935**

In regards to AIDS, the foundation is particularly interested in new model, pilot, and demonstration efforts: addressing the needs of underserved at-risk populations and especially those programs recognizing the overlap between such programs; responding to the challenges facing community-based AIDS service organizations and those organizations addressing systemic change; providing meaningful school-based sex education; making treatment information accessible, available and easily understandable to those in need of it; or, addressing the psycho-social needs of those infected and affected by AIDS, especially adolescents.
Requirements: Tax-exempt organizations may apply.
Restrictions: The foundation generally does not provide funds for capital building projects, endowments, grants to individuals, scholarships or internships (except as part of a program), direct service programs (especially outside New York City), projects that are local in focus and unlikely to be replicated, continuing or general support, projects and organizations that are international in scope or purpose, or biomedical research.
Geographic Focus: All U.S. States
Date(s) Application is Due: Sep 1
Samples: AIDS Alliance for Children Youth and Family, Washington, DC, $5,000—to transform the National Consumer Leadership Corps Training Program into one that can be replicated by local AIDS organizations around the nation (2008); Cesar E. Chavez Institute, New York, NY, $40,000—one-time grant to develop new family interventions and a new family-related model of care to reduce risk for HIV and mental health problems in lesbian, gay, bisexual and transgender (LGBT) youth (2008).
Contact: Anthony C. Wood, Executive Director; (212) 794-2008; (212) 794-0351
Internet: http://www.ittlesonfoundation.org/aids.html
Sponsor: Ittleson Foundation
15 E 67th Street, 5th Floor
New York, NY 10021

Ittleson Foundation Environment Grants **936**

The foundation supports innovative pilot, model and demonstration projects that will help move individuals, communities, and organizations from environmental awareness to environmental activism by changing attitudes and behaviors. This program seeks to encourage and nurture environmental action through: supporting the present generation of environmental activists, whether professionals or volunteers through education, training and other activities; educating and engaging the next generation of environmentalists with a special interest in supporting the training of those who are teaching that generation; strengthening the infrastructure of the environmental movement with a particular focus on efforts at the grassroots and statewide levels; activating new constituencies, particularly those focused on environmental equity issues.
Requirements: Tax-exempt organizations may apply.
Restrictions: The foundation generally does not provide funds for capital building projects, endowments, grants to individuals, scholarships or internships (except as part of a program), direct service programs (especially outside New York City), projects that are local in focus and unlikely to be replicated, continuing or general support, projects and organizations that are international in scope or purpose, or biomedical research.
Geographic Focus: All U.S. States
Date(s) Application is Due: Sep 1
Samples: Antioch University New England, Keene, NH, $45,000—to advance the emerging field of Conservation Psychology; Cornell University Cooperative Extension, New York, NY, $40,000—one-time grant for the Participatory Development of an Urban Forestry Community Engagement Model involving the public in the planning planting and stewardship of urban forestry efforts (2008).
Contact: Anthony C. Wood, Executive Director; (212) 794-2008; (212) 794-0351
Internet: http://www.ittlesonfoundation.org/enviro.html
Sponsor: Ittleson Foundation
15 E 67th Street, 5th Floor
New York, NY 10021

Ittleson Foundation Mental Health Grants **937**

For this program, the foundation is interested in innovative, pilot, model and demonstration projects that are: fighting the stigma associated with mental illness and working to change the public's negative perception of people who have mental illness; utilizing new knowledge and current technological advances to improve programs and services for people who have mental illness; bringing the full benefits of this new knowledge and technology to those who presently do not have access to them; or, advancing preventative mental health efforts, especially those targeted to youth and adolescents, with a special focus on strategies that involve parents, teachers, and others in close contact with these populations.
Requirements: Tax-exempt organizations may apply.
Restrictions: The foundation generally does not provide funds for capital building projects, endowments, grants to individuals, scholarships or internships (except as part of a program), direct service programs (especially outside New York City), projects that are local in focus and unlikely to be replicated, continuing or general support, projects and organizations that are international in scope or purpose, or biomedical research.
Geographic Focus: All U.S. States
Date(s) Application is Due: Sep 1
Samples: Active Minds, Inc., Washington, DC, $10,000—to dramatically expand the network of chapters on college campuses (2008); Partnership with Children, New York, NY, $50,000—one-time grant to develop the Center for Capacity Building to enable the dissemination of the successful counseling and prevention care program for inner-city boys and girls, Open Heart-Open Mind to over 100 schools by 2012 (2008); Horticultural Society of New York, New York, NY, $30,000—to launch their new Nonprofit Partnership for Horticultural Therapy to formalize and expand their ability to help a wide range of organizations working with the mentally and physically ill, formerly homeless, HIV+, victims of substance abuse, the elderly, at-risk juveniles and those re-entering society from incarceration, use horticultural therapy programs to address the needs of these marginalized populations (2008).
Contact: Anthony C. Wood, Executive Director; (212) 794-2008; (212) 794-0351
Internet: http://www.ittlesonfoundation.org/mental.html
Sponsor: Ittleson Foundation
15 E 67th Street, 5th Floor
New York, NY 10021

J.B. Reynolds Foundation Grants **938**

The foundation makes grants in the local Kansas City, MO, area, up to a 150-mile radius of the city. Grants are awarded for building and equipment, community development, medical research, social welfare, and the arts and humanities. Some support is given to colleges and universities. Additional types of support include general operating support, continuing support, annual campaigns, endowment funds, publications, and research. The board meets in April and December of each year to consider letters of requests, and only invited proposals are reviewed. All grants are awarded in December.
Requirements: 501(c)3 organizations in the Kansas City, MO, area may submit applications.
Geographic Focus: Missouri
Amount: 5,000 - 50,000 USD
Contact: Richard L. Finn, Secretary-Treasurer; (816) 753-7000; (816) 753-1354
Sponsor: J.B. Reynolds Foundation
P.O. Box 219139
Kansas City, MO 64141-6139

J. F. Maddox Foundation Grants 939

The mission of the Foundation is to significantly improve the quality of life in southeastern New Mexico. The Foundation is most interested in supporting initiatives that strive to obtain well-planned project outcomes. The Foundation has redirected its focus toward economic and community development initiatives in an effort to provide opportunities for long-term economic vitality within Lea County. Application information is available online.

Requirements: Nonprofit organizations and governmental agencies seeking grants for the explicit benefit of Lea County, New Mexico are eligible.

Restrictions: Grants are not made to individuals, for the express benefit of an individual, or to other private foundations.

Geographic Focus: New Mexico

Amount: 5,000 - 700,000 USD

Samples: New Mexico Junior College, Hobbs, NM, $2,500—to provide funding to bus Lea County, New Mexico elementary children to the Western Heritage Museum to tour the museum and participate in hands-on activities related to the Handmade Books of New Mexico exhibit (2009); City of Hobbs, Hobbs, NM, $25,000—to purchase outdoor movie theatre equipment for the annual outdoor summer movie series event held in Del Norte Park (2009); City of Hobbs, Senior Center, Hobbs, NM, $5,000—a matching grant to help replace computers in the Senior Center computer lab (2009).

Contact: Jennifer Townsend, Grants Manager; (575) 393-6338, ext. 23; (575) 397-7266; jtownsend@jfmaddox.org

Internet: http://www.jfmaddox.org/areas_of_emphasis.asp

Sponsor: J. F. Maddox Foundation
P.O. Box 2588
Hobbs, NM 88241-2588

J. Homer Butler Foundation Grants 940

The foundation awards grants to Roman Catholic nonprofits nationwide and internationally, with a focus on New York. Recipient organizations include child welfare organizations, churches, community service organizations, health care organizations and hospitals, international ministries and relief organizations, missions, parochial schools and religious education organizations, seminaries, and women affairs organizations. Types of support include emergency funds, general support grant, multiyear grants, project development grants, special project grants, and scholarships. Application must be made in writing.

Geographic Focus: All U.S. States

Date(s) Application is Due: Jun 30; Dec 31

Amount: 1,000 - 3,000 USD

Samples: Xavier Jesuit Community (New York, NY)—for general support, $5000; Gospel Outreach (Hillsboro, MO)—for leprosy programs in India, $2000.

Contact: Grant Administrator; (212) 242-7340; (718) 442-5088

Sponsor: J. Homer Butler Foundation
30 W 16th Street
New York, NY 10011

J.M. McDonald Foundation Grants 941

Grants are awarded to nonprofit organizations for educational purposes; for the aged, orphans, and children who are sick, infirm, blind, or crippled; for youth and child care in an effort to combat juvenile delinquency; and to aid underprivileged, mentally or physically handicapped children. Grants are also given for building funds, equipment, and general purposes to educational institutions and hospitals. Application guidelines will be sent upon written request.

Requirements: New York organizations classified as IRS 509(a) tax-exempt are eligible to apply.

Restrictions: Grants are not made to individuals, or for seminars, workshops, endowment funds, fellowships, travel, exhibits, or conferences.

Geographic Focus: New York

Date(s) Application is Due: Apr 15; Sep 15

Amount: 5,000 - 100,000 USD

Samples: Nazareth College (Rochester, NY)—for its capital campaign, which includes the purchase of new property, construction, and the renovation of existing buildings, $30,000.

Contact: Donald McJunkin, President; (303) 674-9300; (303) 674-9216

Sponsor: J.M. McDonald Foundation
P.O. Box 3219
Evergreen, CO 80437

J.W. and Ida M. Jameson Foundation Grants 942

The foundation supports higher and theological education, hospitals, medical research, cultural programs, and Protestant and Catholic religion. Types of support include research and general operating budgets. Applicants should submit a proposal.

Requirements: California nonprofits may submit applications for grant support.

Geographic Focus: California

Date(s) Application is Due: Feb 1

Amount: 5,000 - 50,000 USD

Contact: Les Hugn, President; (626) 355-6973

Sponsor: J.W. and Ida M. Jameson Foundation
P.O. Box 397
Sierra Madre, CA 91025

J.W. Kieckhefer Foundation Grants 943

The foundation awards grants to support medical research; hospice; health; family planning; disabled; social services; higher, medical, and other education; youth; child welfare; conservation; community funds; public policy; and cultural programs. The grants are awarded for operating budgets, continuing support, annual campaigns, emergency funds, building funds, equipment, land acquisition, endowment funds, matching funds, research, publications, conferences and seminars, and special projects. Applications should be submitted between May and November. The board meets in November and December to consider requests.

Restrictions: Grants are not awarded to individuals or for seed money, deficit financing, scholarships, or demonstration projects.

Geographic Focus: All U.S. States

Amount: 350 - 100,000 USD

Contact: John Kieckhefer, Trustees; (928) 445-4010

Sponsor: J.W. Kieckhefer Foundation
116 E Gurley Street, P.O. Box 1151
Prescott, AZ 86302

J. Walton Bissell Foundation Grants 944

The foundation's yearly giving programs are available primarily in the Connecticut River Valley and focus on higher and secondary education, hospitals, youth agencies, care of the aged, aid to the blind, and encouragement of the arts. Brief letters describing projects to be funded, history and current status of requesting organization, and amount desired will be reviewed as received. Organizations interested in applying should apply at least three months before funding is needed. Requests should be submitted three months before funding is needed.

Requirements: Grants are awarded to 501(c)3 charitable organizations in Connecticut, Massachusetts, New Hampshire, and Vermont that are not private foundations.

Restrictions: Grants are not awarded to support campaigns or endowment funding, nor are they awarded to individuals.

Geographic Focus: Connecticut, Massachusetts, New Hampshire, Vermont

Amount: 1,500 - 20,000 USD

Contact: J.D. Anthony Jr., President; (860) 275-0136; (860) 275-0343

Sponsor: J. Walton Bissell Foundation
P.O. Box 370067
Hartford, CT 06137

J. Willard and Alice S. Marriott Foundation Grants 945

The Foundation awards grants to nonprofit organizations in its areas of interest: scholarship programs; inner city work and; youth programs, with special interest in employment opportunities for young people with disabilities. Interested applicants should prepare a written request which should include a project narrative and attachments. The Board of Trustees meets two times per year, usually in the Spring and Fall.

Requirements: Nonprofit organizations in Maryland, Virginia and the District of Columbia are eligible to apply.

Restrictions: Individuals are ineligible.

Geographic Focus: District of Columbia, Maryland, Virginia

Contact: Anne Gunsteens, Executive Director; (301) 380-2246; (301) 380-8957; kimberly.howes@marriott.com

Sponsor: J. Willard and Alice S. Marriott Foundation
P.O. Box 150
Washington, DC 20058

Jackson Foundation Grants 946

The Jackson Foundation was established October 1960 pursuant to the last will of Maria C. Jackson. Its purpose is to respond to the requests deemed appropriate to promote the welfare of the public of the City of Portland or the State of Oregon, or both. The Foundation considers projects located outside the Portland metropolitan area only if the project is of statewide appeal, rather than of local concern.

Requirements: Grants are awarded to nonprofit 501(c)3 tax-exempt agencies located within the state of Oregon.

Restrictions: Funding is not available for individuals or private businesses. Grants are generally not made to a K-12 school. Do not contact the Foundation by phone to check the status of an application.

Geographic Focus: Oregon

Date(s) Application is Due: Mar 31; Jun 30; Sep 30; Dec 31

Amount: 1,000 - 25,000 USD

Samples: Emanuel Medical Center Foundation (Portland, OR)—for general support, $10,000; Portland Community College Foundation (OR)—for program support, $5000.

Contact: Robert H. Depew, c/o U.S. Bank, (503) 275-4414

Internet: http://www.thejacksonfoundation.com

Sponsor: Jackson Foundation
P.O. Box 3168
Portland, OR 97208

Jacob and Charlotte Lehrman Foundation Grants 947

The foundation makes grants to establish scholarships and fellowships at institutions of learning and to foster research in medicine and science. Grants are also given for Jewish welfare funds, care of the aged and sick, the establishment of trade schools, the fostering of religious observance, recreation, and aid to refugees. Additional types of support include general operating grants and matching funds. The Foundation Board generally makes grants once a year, typically in October. The deadline for RFPs as well as proposals submitted from current grant recipients is April 1.

Requirements: Grants are made primarily to organizations in the greater metropolitan Washington, DC, area.

Restrictions: Grants are not made to individuals.

Geographic Focus: District of Columbia

Date(s) Application is Due: Apr 1

Amount: 1,000 - 10,000 USD

Contact: Robert Lehrman, Vice President; (202) 338-8400; (202) 338-8405; info@lehrmanfoundation.org

Internet: http://www.lehrmanfoundation.org

Sponsor: Jacob and Charlotte Lehrman Foundation
1027 33rd Street NW, 2nd Floor
Washington, DC 20007

Jacob and Hilda Blaustein Foundation Grants 948

The Foundation promotes social justice and human rights through its five program areas: Jewish life; strengthening Israeli democracy; health and mental health; educational opportunity; and human rights. Support is provided to organizations in the United States and abroad, with a preference to the Baltimore, Maryland area. The Foundation supports organizations that promote systemic change; involve constituents in planning and decision-making; encourage volunteer and professional development; and engage in ongoing program evaluation. Additional guidelines and application information is available online.

Requirements: Nonprofit organizations are eligible to apply.

Restrictions: Support is unavailable for the following: individuals; scholarships to individuals; unsolicited proposals for academic, scientific, or medical research; direct mail; annual giving; membership campaigns; fundraising; commemorative events.

Geographic Focus: Maryland

Samples: The Foundation for Jewish Campus Life, Washington, DC, $150,000—support offered over a two year period, for Tzedek Hillel, a program that promotes social justice activities among Jewish college students across the country, and support for the Tzedek Leadership Mission to Israel; Fund for Educational Excellence, Baltimore, MD, $250,000—support for over five years, for the implementation of a reform plan for Baltimore's neighborhood high schools (2008); Mental Disability Rights International, Washington, DC, $70,000—support paid over two years, to promote the human rights of people with mental disabilities worldwide (2008).

Contact: Betsy Ringel, Executive Director; (410) 347-7103; (410) 347-7210; info@blaufund.org

Internet: http://www.blaufund.org/foundations/jacobandhilda_f.html

Sponsor: Jacob and Hilda Blaustein Foundation
10 E Baltimore Street, Suite 1111
Baltimore, MD 21202

Jacobs Family Foundation Village Neighborhoods Grants 949

The Foundation primarily serves the four neighborhoods immediately surrounding The Village at Market Creek: Chollas View, Emerald Hills, Lincoln Park, and Valencia Park; proposals are considered from throughout the Fourth City Council District of southeastern San Diego. The Neighborhood Grants funds programs or strategies that: strengthen and expand health, environmental, education and family resources; foster opportunities for ownership and building assets through economic and business development; create vibrant places and spaces which express and enhance the cultures and environment of the community; and/or strengthen the ability of the community to get things done and include the voice of residents in decision-making, advocacy, and planning. The Village Neighborhoods Fund makes grants to resident groups and neighborhood organizations that serve or support The Village at Market Creek. Funding is also available for a limited number of grants that support projects outside the neighborhoods that demonstrate innovative community and economic development strategies and a commitment to share what works, what doesn't, and why. Applications are excepted year round, however unsolicited applications are not. Call the Foundation to discuss your project. If the project meets the Foundations criteria, you may be asked to send a brief letter of interest and/or complete a full Village Neighborhoods Fund application.

Requirements: 501(c)3 non-profits may apply that: work with the Jacobs Center to develop The Village at Market Creek in southeastern San Diego; provide programs or services that benefit the neighborhoods surrounding The Village at Market Creek; or provides neighborhood strengthening strategies or models that can inform and advance The Village at Market Creek work.

Geographic Focus: California

Amount: 10,000 - 75,000 USD

Contact: Program Contact; (619) 527-6161 or (800) 550-6856; (619) 527-6162; communications@jacobscenter.org

Internet: http://www.jacobsfamilyfoundation.org/how.htm

Sponsor: Jacobs Family Foundation
Joe & Vi Jacobs Center, 404 Euclid Avenue
San Diego, CA 92114

James & Abigail Campbell Family Foundation Grants 950

The James & Abigail Campbell Family Foundation embraces the values and beliefs of James and Abigail Campbell by investing in Hawwaii's people and the communities that nuture them. The Foundation supports projects in the following areas: Youth—programs that address the challenges of young people; Education—support for public schools, early childhood education and environmental stewardship; Hawaiian—support for programs that promote values and the health and welfare of Hawaiians. Priority is given to programs located in or serving communities in the following areas of West Oahu: Ewa/Ewa Beach, Kapolei, Makakilo and the Wai'anae Coast. The following types of requests are eligible for consideration: support for special projects that are not part of an organization's ongoing operations; program support when unforeseen circumstances have affected the financial base of an organization; financial assistance to purchase items such as office equipment and to fund minor repairs and renovations. Grants range from $5,000 - $50,000. Your grant application must be postmarked by February 1 for the April/May meeting, August 1 for the October/November meeting.

Requirements: The Foundation will only consider requests from organizations which qualify as non-profit, tax-exempt public charities under Section 501(c)3 and 170(b) of the Internal Revenue Code. To apply for a grant, summarize the following information in a two - three page proposal letter: the nature and purpose of your organization; the objectives of your program, include the grant amount requested and the proposed use of funds; a brief outline on how you plan to accomplish your objectives; a statement of a community problem, need or opportunity that this project will address; the duration for which Foundation funds are needed; other sources of funding currently being sought and future funding sources; methods used to measure the program's effectiveness. In addition to the proposal letter, submit a copy of the following: Internal Revenue Service notification of tax-exempt status; most recent annual financial statement; list of the current Board of Directors; the project's proposed budget; one (1) copy of your complete grant proposal package.

Restrictions: The Foundation will not consider funding for: individuals, endowments, sectarian or religious programs, loans, political activities or

highly technical research projects. Only one request per organization will ordinarily be considered in a calendar year. Funds are usually not committed for more than one year at a time.
Geographic Focus: Hawaii
Date(s) Application is Due: Feb 1; Aug 1
Amount: 5,000 - 50,000 USD
Samples: Kapolei High School, $20,000—scholarships grant (2008); Kahikolu Ohana Hale O Wai'anae, $50,000—Hawaiian culture grant (2008); KAMP Hawai'i, $5,000—youth grant (2008); International Dyslexia Association, $10,000—educational grant (2008).
Contact: D. Keola, Grant Manager; (808) 674-3167; (808) 674-3349; keolal@jamescampbell.com
Internet: http://www.campbellfamilyfoundation.org/grant_procedures.cfm
Sponsor: James and Abigail Campbell Family Foundation
1001 Kamokila Boulevard
Kapolei, HI 96707

James A. and Faith Knight Foundation Grants 951
Primarily serving Jackson and Washtenaw counties, Michigan, the Foundation is dedicated to improving communities by providing grant support to qualified nonprofit organizations including, but not limited to, those that address the needs of women and girls, animals and the natural world, and internal capacity. In general, the foundation supports organizations that believe in good nonprofit practices including sound financial management, developed governance practices, and clarity of mission. Attention to gender, diversity, and outcomes are important. Giving is primarily for human services, including a neighborhood center, women's organizations, and family services; support also for nonprofit management, the United Way, housing, the arts, education, and environmental conservation. Fields of interest include: adult education and literacy; basic skills; GED; arts; environment and natural resources; family services; housing development; human services; nonprofit management; and women's services. There are two annual deadlines, and initial approach should be by letter.
Requirements: Giving is limited to Michigan, with emphasis on Jackson and Washenaw counties.
Restrictions: No support is offered for religious or political organizations. No grants to individuals, or for conferences or special events, or for annual campaigns.
Geographic Focus: Michigan
Date(s) Application is Due: Jan 28; Sep 16
Samples: Center for the Childbearing Year, Ann Arbor, Michigan, $23,000—to increase capacity of the Doulas Care program, with targeted emphasis to improve maternal/infant health outcomes and develop a health career pathway for women; Dahlem Conservancy, Jackson, Michigan, $18,000—to purchase a van to initiate outreach programs.
Contact: Margaret A. Talburtt, Executive Director; (734) 769-5653; (734) 769-8383; peg@KnightFoundationMi.org or info@knightfoundationmi.org
Internet: http://www.knightfoundationmi.org/guidelines.htm
Sponsor: James A. and Faith Knight Foundation
180 Little Lake Drive, Suite 6B
Ann Arbor, MI 48103-6219

James and Elsie Nolan Charitable Trust Grants 952
The trust awards grants, primarily in southeastern Alaska, in its areas of interest, including museums, hospitals, and public administration. General operating and project grants are awarded. There are no application deadlines. The board meets in early October.
Requirements: Alaska nonprofit organizations are eligible.
Restrictions: Individuals are ineligible.
Geographic Focus: Alaska
Amount: Up to 22,000,000 USD
Samples: Catholic Community Services of Juneau (AK)—for wheelchair-accessible vehicles, $17,000; Junior Achievement in Anchorage (AK)—for computer equipment; Wrangell Medical Ctr (AK)—for mammogram machine and endoscopes, $105,000; Irene Ingle Public Library (Wrangell, AK)—for library book purchases and a learning project, $4164.
Contact: Gwendolyn Feltis, c/o Wells Fargo Bank Alaska, N.A., N.A
Sponsor: James and Elsie Nolan Charitable Trust
P.O. Box 927
Wrangell, AK 99929

James F. and Marion L. Miller Foundation Teaching Awards 953
A major problem facing public high schools is the large number of teachers who drop out of the profession during their first five years of teaching. This award was established to encourage more teachers to stay in the profession and improve their skills. The Miller Foundation is offering up to 50 awards a year to provide public high school teachers with opportunities for growth and development, with the goal of strengthening their commitment to, interest in, and effectiveness in a long-term classroom teaching career. The ultimate goal is helping teachers pursue activities that will stimulate and nurture student achievement. The awards will range from $1,000 to $5,000, depending upon the nature of the individual projects. See website for additional guidelines and application: http://www.millerfound.org/teaching-awards/guidelines/.
Requirements: Any public high school principal in Oregon may nominate a teacher who has less than five years in the profession and who develops a promising plan of activities designed to benefit the teacher's performance and professional satisfaction.
Restrictions: Within three months after his or her project is completed, a teacher and the recipient school's principal will report on the use of the funds and the benefits gained from the supported activities.
Geographic Focus: Oregon
Date(s) Application is Due: Jan 19
Amount: 1,000 - 5,000 USD
Samples: Condon High School, Teacher: Michelle Densmore, $5,000—to purchase three Vernier LabQuest portable units with manuals and to upgrade science technology and learning tools (2009); Madras High School, Teacher: Nate Tyler, $4,800—to purchase a touch tank with 30 organisms to teach Marine Biology (2009); South Medford High, Teacher: Daniel Woodward, $5,000—to become proficient in project-based learning with technology and multi-media instruction. Project includes computer lab (2009).
Contact: Suzanna S. McKirdie, Grants Manager; (503) 546-3191; info@millerfnd.org
Internet: http://www.millerfound.org/teaching-awards/guidelines/
Sponsor: James F. and Marion L. Miller Foundation
520 SW Yamhill Street, Suite 520
Portland, OR 97205

James Ford Bell Foundation Grants 954
The Foundation supports organizations primarily in Minnesota. Emphasis is on cultural programs, support is also available for wildlife preservation and conservation, youth agencies, the environment, education, health and human services. A high priority is given to projects with historical connections to the Bell Family. The Trustees meet in the Spring and Fall. Contact the Foundation prior to sending in a proposal. Unsolicited requests for funds are not accepted.
Requirements: Nonprofit organizations in Minnesota are eligible to apply.
Restrictions: No grants are made directly to individuals, nor for scholarships, fellowships, or political campaigns. No funding is available to units of local government. The Foundation does not respond to requests for memberships, annual appeals, or special events and fundraisers.
Geographic Focus: Minnesota
Samples: University of Minnesota Foundation, Minneapolis, MN, $3,000,000 - for general operating support; Minneapolis College of Art and Design, Minneapolis, MN, $1,020,000 - for general operating support; Minnesota Environmental Partnership, Saint Paul, MN, $58,000 - for general operating support.
Contact: Ellen George, Chief of Operations; (612) 377-8400; (612) 377-8407; ellen@fpadvisors.com
Internet: http://www.fpadvisors.com/jamesfordbell/jamesfordbell.htm
Sponsor: James Ford Bell Foundation
1818 Oliver Avenue South
Minneapolis, MN 55405-2208

James Irvine Foundation Creative Connections Grants 955
The Creative Connections Fund supports creativity and the expansion of diverse, relevant cultural offerings in local communities across California and primarily outside San Francisco, San Mateo and Santa Clara counties. The Fund targets small and midsize arts organizations and offers project grants of up to $50,000, over a maximum of 24 months, through an open, competitive review process. The Creative Connections Fund aims to support small and midsize arts organizations with a diversity of projects and ideas. The Foundation's rationale is two-fold. First, small organizations play an important role in the arts ecosystem. They have close ties to the communities they serve, present aesthetics that have particular relevance to their audiences, and

involve local artists. In this way, community-based arts organizations support grassroots creativity and add to the cultural offerings of the neighborhoods and cities they serve, which, in turn, adds to the cultural vibrancy of the state. Second, because we frequently partner with organizations that have annual budgets greater than $2 million, the Creative Connections Fund is an important complement to our invitational portfolio and a way to reach arts organizations of all artistic disciplines and aesthetics, located in all geographic locations in California. See Foundations website for additional guidelines.
Requirements: To be considered for a grant organizations and requests must meet all the following *requirements:* 501(c)3 status or an established relationship with an approved fiscal sponsor; California focus; no more than 50 percent of revenue from government sources; annual revenue of at least $100,000; grant request of no more than $50,000 or 10% of organizations annual budget; no active grant or outstanding reports due to the Foundation.
Restrictions: Irvine does not make direct grants to individual artists.
Geographic Focus: California
Amount: 50,000 USD
Samples: San Diego Asian Film Foundation, San Diego, CA, $50,000—for Connect, a community-based media arts training program in two diverse San Diego communities that is designed to increase communication and interaction among immigrants and underserved ethnic groups (2009); Venice Arts In Neighborhoods, Venice, CA, $50,000—for broadening participation of youths by developing and implementing an expanded Art Mentoring Program for instruction in filmmaking, photography and media arts (2009); Laxart, Los Angeles, CA, $50,000—to support the creation and exhibition of new works by five culturally diverse California artists (2009); A Window Between Worlds, Venice, CA, $50,000—for the Pearls of Wisdom/End the Violence Project to bring artists and domestic violence programs together to create an original mixed media art piece that will be exhibited in 2011 (2009).
Contact: Fund Coordinator; (800) 374-6851; artsfund@irvine.org
Internet: http://www.irvine.org/grantmaking/our-programs/arts-program/fundingguidelines/creativeconnectionsfund
Sponsor: James Irvine Foundation
575 Market Street, Suite 3400
San Francisco, CA 94105

James L. and Mary Jane Bowman Charitable Trust Grants **956**
Established in 1997 in Virginia through a donation by James L. Bowman, the James L. and Mary Jane Bowman Charitable Trust Supports both education and libraries within Virginia. The Trust's primary fields of interest include: Christian agencies and churches, higher education, human services, public libraries, and recreation. There are no specific application forms or deadlines with which to adhere, and applicants should forward a letter of application that includes a needs statement, population to be served, and the project budget.
Requirements: 501(c)3 nonprofit organizations Serving residents of Virginia are eligible.
Restrictions: The foundation does not award grants to individuals in the form of scholarships or other direct support; orpolitical causes or candidates.
Geographic Focus: Virginia
Date(s) Application is Due: Apr 1
Amount: 1,000 - 15,000 USD
Samples: Lord Fairfax Community College, Middletown, Virginia, $19,151 - general operations support (2009); Blue Ridge Hospice, Winchester, Virginia, $10,000 - to provide hospice care for local chronically ill patients (2009); Museum of the Shenandoah Valley, Winchester, Virginia, $6,500 - to preserve regional art, history, and culture (2009).
Contact: Beverley B. Shoemaker, Trustee; (540) 869-1800; (540) 869-4225
Sponsor: James L. and Mary Jane Bowman Charitable Trust
P.O. Box 480
Stephens City, VA 22655-0480

James L. Stamps Foundation Grants **957**
The foundation awards grants to nonprofits primarily in southern California to support Protestant religion schools, churches, seminaries, and organizations. Types of support include operating budgets, continuing support, emergency funds, matching funds, special projects, and scholarship funds for Christian colleges only. There are no application deadline dates or forms. Applicants should submit a letter of request. The board meets bimonthly beginning in February.
Requirements: Southern California nonprofit organizations may apply.
Geographic Focus: California
Amount: 1,000 - 50,000 USD
Samples: Azusa Pacific U (CA)—for furniture and shelving for its new theology library, $100,000.
Contact: Delores Boutault, Manager; (714) 568-9740
Sponsor: James L. Stamps Foundation
2000 E 4th Street, Suite 230
Santa Ana, CA 92705-3814

James R. Dougherty Jr. Foundation Grants **958**
The James R. Dougherty, Jr. Foundation, established in 1950, gives to organizations primarily in Texas. Areas of interest include: family services, domestic violence, human services and women. Support is offered in the form of: annual campaigns, building/renovation, capital campaigns, continuing support, curriculum development, endowments, equipment, general/operating support, income development, management development/capacity building, matching/challenge support, program development, program evaluation, research, scholarship funds, seed money and, technical assistance grants. The board meets twice a year, in the Spring and Fall. No application form is required, contact the Foundation, before submitting a proposal.
Requirements: Nonprofit organizations in Texas are eligible to apply.
Geographic Focus: Texas
Date(s) Application is Due: Mar 1; Sep 1
Contact: Daren Wilder, Grants Administrator; (512) 358-3560
Sponsor: James R. Dougherty Jr. Foundation
P.O. Box 640
Beeville, TX 78104-0640

James R. Thorpe Foundation Grants **959**
The Foundation is interested in supporting organizations, programs or projects which address the needs of the Elderly and Youth. The Thorpe Foundation is most likely to make general operating or program support grants. In the area of Youth, the Foundation supports organizations and programs that: engage youth in the arts; encourage character development; support academic and social development; provide safety and support to youth. In the area of the Elderly, the Foundation fosters the vital aging of seniors through support of services which help them to live independently. The Foundation will give special consideration to services which address the needs of economically disadvantaged seniors, immigrant seniors and the frail elderly. The Foundation supports organizations and programs that: provide transportation services; assist seniors in remaining in their own homes; educate seniors about housing options; provide social and recreational opportunities for seniors. Additional guidelines are available at: http://www.jamesrthorpefoundation.org/2010procedures.html.
Requirements: The Thorpe Foundation supports 501(c)3 non-profit organizations located in and serving the Minneapolis and the western Minneapolis metro suburbs of the Twin Cities.
Restrictions: The Foundation does not: make multi-year grants or fund individuals; make grants in the east metro area, greater Minnesota, or outside the State of Minnesota; make grants through fiscal agents; support endowment drives, conferences, seminars, tours, or fundraising events; support organizations with operating budgets over $2 million; support organizations with no paid staff.
Geographic Focus: Minnesota
Date(s) Application is Due: Mar 1; Sep 1
Contact: Kerrie Blevins, Foundation Manager; (612) 822-3412; kerrieblevins@jamesrthorpefoundation.org
Internet: http://www.jamesrthorpefoundation.org/2010guidelines.html
Sponsor: James R. Thorpe Foundation
318 West 48th Street
Minneapolis, MN 55419

Jane's Trust Grants **960**
The Jane's Trust has particular interest in organizations and projects which primarily benefit underserved populations and disadvantaged communities. Jane's Trust will support grants for general operating purposes, as well, as it's Fields of Interest, which are: arts and culture, education, the environment, health and welfare. The Trust will make grants in the states of Florida, with a preference for southwest and central Florida; Massachusetts, with a preference for greater Boston and eastern Massachusetts; and in the northern New England states of Maine, New Hampshire and Vermont. Preference will be given to organizations located in those states for projects which will primarily provide benefits within those states. The application process begins by submitting of a concept paper. Guidelines are available at the Trusts website.

Requirements: 501(c)3 tax-exempt organizations in Florida, Maine, Massachusetts, New Hampshire, and Vermont are eligible.
Restrictions: Jane's Trust will not support: loans to charitable organizations; attempts to influence legislation; requests from individuals. Please note: Jane's Trust will normally not support public entities, such as municipalities, municipal departments, or public schools directly, but will entertain applications from tax-exempt fiscal agents or partners for collaborative projects with municipalities or schools. This does not apply to public colleges and universities.
Geographic Focus: Florida, Maine, Massachusetts, New Hampshire, Vermont
Date(s) Application is Due: Jan 25; Jul 15
Amount: 50,000 - 1,000,000 USD
Samples: Good Shepherd Food-Bank, Auburn, ME, $30,000—for operating support, payable over one year for agency matching funds project to provide for local food pantries and agencies across Maine (2008); Boca Grande Health Clinic Foundation, Inc., Boca Grande, FL, $150,000—capital support in the amount of $100,000 for the renovation of the Boca Grande Health Clinic Annex, $50,000 in endowment support, for the Boca Grande Health Clinic (2008); The Conservation Fund, Arlington, VA, $100,000—capital support for protection of the Three Sisters Springs in Crystal River, Florida, a wintering manatee habitat (2008); Kimball Union Academy, Meriden, NH, $150,000—capital support, payable over two years for construction and renovation of school campus (2008); Vermont Symphony Orchestra, Burlington, VT, $100,000—endowment support for Symphony Kids education programs (2008).
Contact: Susan Fish, Grants Administrator; (617) 227-7940, ext. 775; (617) 227-0781; sfish@hembar.com
Internet: http://www.hembar.com/selectsrv/janes/index.html
Sponsor: Hemenway and Barnes LLP
60 State Street
Boston, MA 02109-1899

Jaquelin Hume Foundation Grants **961**

Major grants of the foundation support activities or organizations having a national impact and fall into two primary areas: education of young people to be better citizens, to have sound values, and to appreciate the value of the free-enterprise; and incentive-based economy and improvement of the structure and function of government and the reduction of the influence of the federal government in citizens' lives. Grants will be made for general operations, project development, and research but not for equipment or buildings. Special projects are generally preferred. Preference will be given to requests from the San Francisco Bay area or that are national in scope. One request per organization per year will be considered.
Requirements: U.S. 501(c)3 nonprofit organizations may apply.
Restrictions: The foundation generally will not consider institutions or organizations primarily supported by tax-derived funding. The foundation will not consider organizations that discriminate on the basis of race, creed, or sex.
Geographic Focus: All U.S. States
Date(s) Application is Due: Mar 15; Sep 15
Amount: 25,000 - 100,000 USD
Contact: Gisele Huff, Executive Director; (415) 705-5115
Sponsor: Jaquelin Hume Foundation
600 Montgomery Street, Suite 2800
San Francisco, CA 94111

Jean and Louis Dreyfus Foundation Grants **962**

The Jean and Louis Dreyfus Foundation was established in 1979 from the estate of Louis Dreyfus, a music publisher, and that of his wife, Jean. The mission of the Foundation is to enhance the quality of life of New Yorkers, particularly the aging and disadvantaged. The Foundation disburses grants mainly within the five boroughs of New York City, and supports programs in the arts, health and social services (including youth agencies, women, and the elderly), and education (including literacy). Support is given for program development and matching funds. Application forms are not required. The board meets each year in the spring and in the fall. Initial inquiries should consist of a one or two page letter describing the organization and outlining the project in question. The January 15th and July 15th deadlines are for Letters of Intent.
Requirements: New York City nonprofits are eligible.
Restrictions: Grants are never made to individuals.
Geographic Focus: New York
Date(s) Application is Due: Jan 15; Jul 15
Contact: Jessica Keuskamp, Program Director; (212) 599-1931; (212) 599-2956; jldreyfusfdtn@hotmail.com
Internet: http://foundationcenter.org/grantmaker/dreyfus/guide.html
Sponsor: Jean and Louis Dreyfus Foundation
420 Lexington Avenue, Suite 626
New York, NY 10170

Jean and Price Daniel Foundation Grants **963**

The Jean and Daniel Price Foundation, established in Texas in 1985, has the primary purpose of supporting historical preservation programs. The Foundation's current fields of interest include: historical societies, libraries, archives, protestant agencies and churches, and public health initiatives. Types of support include building and renovation, general operating support, land acquisition, and program development. There are no specific application forms or deadlines with which to adhere, and potential applicants should contact the office initially by letter. Past grants have ranged from $5,000 to $100,000.
Requirements: Applicants should be 501(c)3 organizations located in, or serving the residents of, Texas.
Geographic Focus: Texas
Amount: 5,000 - 100,000 USD
Samples: Coppell Historical Society, Coppell, Texas, $50,000 - historical preservation projects (2009); Texas Governor's Mansion Restoration Project, Austin, Texas, $100,000 - restoration and preservation (2009); Wallisville Heritage Park, Wallisville, Texas, $10,000 - general operating expenses (2009).
Contact: Jean Daniel Murph, President; (936) 336-7355
Sponsor: Jean and Price Daniel Foundation
P.O. Box 789
Liberty, TX 77575-0789

JELD-WEN Foundation Grants **964**

The Foundation seeks to improve the quality of life in company-operating areas and awards grants in the areas of capital campaigns, education, youth activities, community development, health and medical, and arts and humanities. Types of support include building construction/renovation, equipment, general operating support, land acquisition, matching/challenge support, program development, scholarship funds, and seed money. Prescreening and application information are available online.
Requirements: Nonprofits in the Foundation's area of operations.
Geographic Focus: All U.S. States
Amount: 1,000 - 1,000,000 USD
Samples: Knox Community Hospital, Mt. Vernon, OH, $500,000—grant to help build an outpatient cancer treatment center (2008); Crater Lake Science and Learning Center, Crater Lake, OR, $500,000—to help build the Science and Learning Center at Crater lake National Park (2008); Yakima Valley Museum, Yakima, WA, $250,000—to upgrade and improve the museum facility (2008).
Contact: JELD-WEN Foundation Headquarters; (503) 478-4478; (503) 478-4474
Internet: http://www.jeld-wenfoundation.org/
Sponsor: Jeld-Wen Foundation
200 SW Market Street, Suite 550
Portland, OR 97201

Jenkins Foundation: Improving the Health of Greater Richmond Grants **965**

The foundation is committed to expanding access to community-based services through programs and organizations that have the potential to make a significant impact on the quality of health, especially for the youth in its local area.
Requirements: The current areas of focus are: Expanding access to health care services for the uninsured and underserved; Substance abuse prevention services that promote healthy lifestyles and increase availability of services; Violence prevention services that promote safe and healthy environments for children and their families and work toward the elimination of violence in the local communities; In addition, the foundation is committed to the long-term viability of the organizations it supports, and will consider capacity building grants that strengthen an agency's ability to better serve its clients. The foundation will also consider a limited number of proposals outside the above stated focus areas.
Restrictions: Proposals will be accepted from charitable organizations, which serve the residents of the City of Richmond and the counties of Chesterfield, Hanover, Henrico, Goochland, and Powhatan.

Geographic Focus: Virginia
Date(s) Application is Due: May 5; Nov 5
Amount: Up to 50,000 USD
Contact: Elaine Summerfield, Program Officer; (804) 330-7400; (804) 330-5992; esummerfield@tcfrichmond.org
Internet: http://www.tcfrichmond.org/Page2954.cfm#Jenkins
Sponsor: Community Foundation Serving Richmond and Central Virginia
7501 Boulders View Drive, Suite 110
Richmond, VA 23225

Jerome Foundation Grants 966

The Foundation supports programs in dance, literature, media arts, music, theater, performance art, the visual arts, multidisciplinary work and arts criticism. The Foundation seeks to support artists who exhibit significant potential yet are not recognized as established creators by fellow artists and other arts professionals. Examples of recognition include exhibitions, reviews, commissions, performances, grant awards, residencies, fellowships, publications and productions. Applications are available online.
Requirements: Artists and nonprofit, tax-exempt organizations in Minnesota and New York are eligible.
Geographic Focus: Minnesota, New York
Samples: Aperture Foundation (New York, NY)—to publish the work of emerging photographers, $30,000 over two years; SASE, the Write Place (Minneapolis, MN)—for fellowships and mentoring for emerging writers, $49,500; Art in General (New York, NY)—for commissions, exhibitions, residencies, and artists' services, $38,000 over two years; Zeitgeist (Saint Paul, MN)—for a program for musicians and composers, $27,000 over two years.
Contact: Program Contact; (800) 995-3766 or (651) 224-9431; (651) 224-3439; info@jeromefdn.org
Internet: http://www.jeromefdn.org
Sponsor: Jerome Foundation
400 Sibley Street, Suite 125
Saint Paul, MN 55101-1928

Jessie Ball Dupont Fund Grants 967

The fund is a national foundation having a special, though not exclusive, interest in issues affecting the South. Grants awarded include competitive grants—program grants, institutional development, and capacity building; and feasibility grants—smaller grants that enable institutions to carefully explore and develop new concepts and programs. Areas of interest include six focus areas: strengthening the independent sector; organizing and nurturing philanthropy; building assets of people, families, and communities; building the capacity of eligible organizations; stimulating community problem solving; and helping people hold their communities accountable. The fund supports four initiatives: the religion initiative, the nonprofit initiative, the small liberal arts colleges initiative, and the independent schools initiative. Types of support include general operating support, building construction/renovation, equipment acquisition, program development, seed money grants, publication, consulting services, professorships, curriculum development, matching funds, and technical assistance. Grants are awarded generally for one year. The trustees meet in January, March, May, July, September, and November to consider requests.
Requirements: Applying organizations must have received a contribution from Mrs. DuPont between the five-year period of January 1, 1960, and December 31, 1964.
Amount: 2,000 - 5,000 USD
Samples: Jacksonville Symphony Assoc (FL)—to implement a strategic marketing program, $50,000; Historical Society of Delaware (Wilmington, DE)—to hire a consultant to lead a community-based strategic-planning process, $52,690; Episcopal Diocese of Southern Ohio (Cincinnati, OH)—to support a partnership with Scioto Christian Ministries to conduct a needs-assessment in Ohio's Scioto County, $28,000; U of Richmond (VA)—to support the creation of an Internet-based resource center that will serve community organizations in the Northern Neck region of Virginia, $219,975.
Contact: Geana Potter, Grants Manager; (904) 353-0890 or (800) 252-3452; (904) 353-3870; contactus@dupontfund.org
Internet: http://www.dupontfund.org
Sponsor: Jessie Ball Dupont Fund
One Independent Drive, Suite 1400
Jacksonville, FL 32202-0511

Jessie Smith Noyes Foundation Grants 968

The foundation is committed to preventing damage to the natural systems upon which all life depends and to strengthening individuals and institutions committed to protecting natural systems and ensuring a sustainable society. The foundation makes grants primarily in the interrelated areas of environment and reproductive rights. The program components include toxics, sustainable agriculture (both with emphasis on southern and Rocky Mountain states), and U.S. reproductive rights. In addition, a few grants are made in four areas of special concern: sustainable communities, U.S. environmental justice, strengthening the U.S. nonprofit sector, and environmental issues in the metropolitan New York region. Letters of inquiry are received at any time; proposals will be requested from the foundation after review.
Requirements: 501(c)3 tax-exempt organizations are eligible.
Restrictions: Normally, the foundation will not consider requests for direct service, endowments, loans or scholarships to individuals, capital construction funds, conferences, media events, production of media and TV programming, or general fund-raising drives. General research projects are not funded per se.
Geographic Focus: All U.S. States
Samples: Northwest Women's Law Ctr (Seattle, WA)—for its contributions to the field of reproductive-health care and rights in Alaska, Idaho, Montana, Oregon, and Washington State, $100,000.
Contact: Millie Buchanan, Program Officer; (212) 684-6577; (212) 689-6549; noyes@noyes.org
Internet: http://www.noyes.org
Sponsor: Jessie Smith Noyes Foundation
6 E 39th Street, 12th Floor
New York, NY 10016-0112

Jewish Fund Grants 969

The fund awards grants to sustain, enrich, and address the overall health care needs of both the Jewish community and general community in the metropolitan Detroit area. Funding priorities include programs that address priorities and program initiatives of the DMC/Sinai Hospital; the health care needs of vulnerable/at- risk populations in the general community; and efforts to further positive relationships between the Jewish community and the Detroit community. The fund gives priority to requests for start-up or short-term operating support; new programs within a defined period that address a critical need; and geographical priority to the metropolitan Detroit area of Wayne, Oakland, and Macomb counties. Preference will be given to proposals that can be funded and replicated by others; have a specific plan for continuation funding beyond the grant period; include a financial or in-kind contribution from the organization; involve collaboration with others; and have a well-defined outcome-based evaluation plan. The fund generally will not support a project for more than three years. The first step in the application process is to submit a letter of intent in March or September. Obtain an application packet containing complete guidelines from the office.
Requirements: Michigan 501(c)3 nonprofit organizations that serve the Jewish and/or Detroit communities are eligible.
Geographic Focus: Michigan
Samples: Detroit Institute for Children (Detroit, MI)—to subsidize services for disadvantaged children with special needs, $100,000; Jewish Community Council (Bloomfield Hills, MI) and Kids Kicking Cancer (Detroit, MI)—to develop a program that uses the martial arts to empower Detroit Public School students to overcome adversity, $300,000 jointly over three years; City Connect (Detroit, MI)—for efforts to increase financial support from the federal government and foundations for the City of Detroit and nonprofit groups in the Detroit area, $20,000; Arthritis Foundation of Michigan (Southfield, MI)—to develop a comprehensive arthritis education and management program for Jews in the Detroit area, $50,000.
Contact: Jodee Fishman Raines, Director; (248) 203-1487; (248) 645-7879; raines@jfmd.org
Sponsor: Jewish Fund
6735 Telegraph Road
Bloomfield, MI 48303-2030

Joe W. and Dorothy Dorsett Brown Foundation Grants 970

The foundation awards grants to nonprofit organizations in Louisiana and the Gulf Coast of Mississippi. Areas of interest include medical research; housing for the homeless; support for organizations who care for the sick, hungry or helpless; religious and educational institutions; and organizations and groups concerned with improving the local community. Types of support include operating budgets, research, and student aid. The foundation also supports

Service Learning, a learn-by-doing approach to the curriculum. Students receive practical, hands-on experience in the subject matter studied by meeting identified community needs through active participation. The listed deadline date is for Service Learning grants.
Requirements: Louisiana and Mississippi nonprofit organizations, with a focus on South Louisiana, the New Orleans area, and the Mississippi Gulf Coast, are eligible. Service Learning grant applications are available yearly to sixth through 12th grades in the following parishes: Orleans, Jefferson, Plaquemines, Saint Bernard, Saint Charles, Tangipahoa, Saint James, Saint John, Saint Tammany, and Washington.
Geographic Focus: Louisiana, Mississippi
Date(s) Application is Due: Sep 30
Amount: 5,000 - 25,000 USD
Contact: Beth Buscher, (504) 834-3433; BethBuscher@thebrownfoundation.org
Internet: http://www.thebrownfoundation.org
Sponsor: Joe W. and Dorothy Dorsett Brown Foundation
320 Hammond Highway, Suite 500
Metairie, LA 70005

John and Margaret Post Foundation Grants **971**
The John and Margaret Post Foundation provides support to charitable organizations, which benefit the quality of life for families and society in general and primarily in Northwest New Jersey. The Foundations mission: first consideration for grants is given to organizations based in Northwest New Jersey, or the New Jersey chapters of national organizations; proposals are occasionally considered from groups outside of the state. Priority for funding will be given in the following order: capital needs, specific programs and general operating expenses for smaller organizations who do not have endowments that provide operating support or that can be considered grass roots. Application deadlines are April 1st for a June meeting & October 1st for a December meeting. Grants average $20,000.
Requirements: 501(c)3 organizations based in Northwest New Jersey, or the New Jersey chapters of national organizations are eligible to apply for funding. Contact the Foundation via email for Application Form and Instructions.
Geographic Focus: New Jersey
Date(s) Application is Due: Apr 1; Oct 1
Amount: 20,000 USD
Contact: Gale Y. Sykes, Grant Administrator; (908) 598-3576; grantinquiries2@wachovia.com
Internet: https://www.wachovia.com/foundation/v/index.jsp?vgnextoid=af878689fb0aa110VgnVCM1000004b0d1872RCRD&vgnextfmt=default
Sponsor: John and Margaret Post Foundation
190 River Road, NJ3132
Summit, NJ 07901

John D. and Catherine T. MacArthur Foundation Media Grants **972**
The goal of the foundation's media grantmaking is to improve the diversity of viewpoints and high-quality documentary content available in radio and television and to use media, especially television and radio production, to further the goals of the other foundation programs. The primary focus of funding is independent documentary film. The foundation usually supports films and programming that address subject matter close to MacArthur's grantmaking strategies; but also it occasionally supports projects on other subjects of overall relevance to the foundation's mission. The foundation also supports outreach efforts, especially related to films it has supported in the production stage and organizations serving filmmakers. Grants may be used for strategic planning, general operating support, publications, and to convene members of the field. Funding for public radio is intended to maintain and strengthen its program—production infrastructure. The program supports the production and distribution infrastructure of public radio through grants to selected national networks including National Public Radio and Public Radio International.
Requirements: Eligible applicants are media centers, which the foundation defines as organizations that provide community-based and independent producers with access to training and resources needed to produce, exhibit, and distribute film and video; and media organizations, which work at the national level to support independent producers, provide services to the field or support the exhibition of independent media. The foundation is particularly interested in projects that collaborate with nonprofit organizations, public institutions, and disadvantaged communities.
Restrictions: The foundation does not support film festivals, children's programming, or public affairs series. Funds are not provided for individual radio series or individual stations.
Geographic Focus: All U.S. States
Date(s) Application is Due: Sep 30
Amount: Up to 55,000,000 USD
Samples: Lichtenstein Creative Media (Cambridge, MA)—to produce a documentary film examining the intersection of the education, foster-care, juvenile- justice, and mental-health systems, $300,000; West Wind Productions (San Francisco, CA)—to produce a film about the multinational efforts to bring former Chilean dictator Augusto Pinochet and his associates to trial, $300,000; WGBH Educational Foundation (Boston, MA)—for the Frontline/World documentary series, $500,000 over two years; WNET (New York, NY)—for Wide Angle, a television series that features documentary films on international issues, $550,000 over two years.
Contact: Office of Grants Management; (312) 726-8000; (312) 920-6258; 4answers@macfdn.org
Internet: http://www.macfound.org/programs
Sponsor: John D. and Catherine T. MacArthur Foundation
140 S Dearborn Street, Suite 1100
Chicago, IL 60603

John Deere Foundation Grants **973**
The foundation invests in programs in education, health/human services, community improvement, arts and culture. Types of support include annual campaigns, building construction/renovation, continuing support, fellowships, general operating support, scholarship funds, and seed money grants. Foundation interest also includes support for Third World development through U.S. -based nonprofits with international building funds, research grants, general operating purposes, and continuing support. There are no application deadlines.
Requirements: Nonprofit organizations in communities with major John Deere operating units, and employee presence are eligible. Eligible U.S. locations are: Augusta, GA; Quad City Region, IL; Des Moines, IA, Dubuque, IA, Iowa Quad Cities, IA, Ottumwa, IA, Waterloo, IA, Coffeyville, KS, Lenexa, KS, Thibodaux, LA, Springfield, MO, Cary, NC, Fuquay-Varina, NC, Fargo, ND, Greeneville, TN, Madison, WI, Horicon, WI. Exceptions include: accredited colleges and universities; organizations focused on international development initiatives related to John Deere Solutions for World Hunger initiative. Because John Deere dealerships are owned and operated independently, their communities are not included in this geographic scope. Also eligible to apply are organizations and institutions of national or international scope that reflect the foundation's concerns.
Restrictions: Funds are not available for the following organizations or purposes: individual initiatives, including scholarships; sports teams, racing teams, athletic endeavors or scholarships designated for athletes; faith-based organizations for sectarian purposes; political candidates, campaigns or organizations; private clubs, fraternities or sororities; other foundations for purposes of building endowment; tax-supported entities.
Geographic Focus: Georgia, Illinois, Iowa, Kansas, Louisiana, Missouri, North Carolina, Tennessee, Wisconsin, Belarus, Brazil, Canada, Estonia, Latvia, Lithuania, Moldova, Ukraine
Contact: Amy Nimmer, Director; (309) 765-8000
Internet: http://www.deere.com/en_U.S. /globalcitizenship/socialinvestment/index.html
Sponsor: John Deere Foundation
1 John Deere Place
Moline, IL 61265-8098

John Edward Fowler Memorial Foundation Grants **974**
The foundation makes grants to qualified charitable organizations providing grassroots programs for people in need in the Washington, DC, metropolitan area. Preference is given to programs that address the issues of homelessness, hunger, at-risk children and youth (pre-school through high school), adult literacy, free medical care (prenatal to seniors), seniors aging in place, job training and placement. Types of support include general operating support, building construction/renovation, equipment acquisition, program development, and matching funds. The foundation is interested in supporting smaller, well-managed nonprofit organizations that have innovative ideas about how to help people help themselves. Contact the office for application forms. There are no application deadlines.
Requirements: Organizations in Washington, DC, and its close Maryland and Virginia suburbs are eligible.

Restrictions: Grants are not made outside the metropolitan Washington, DC, area, or to/for national health organizations; government agencies; medical research; public school districts; individuals; or arts (except for intensive arts-in-education programs that directly benefit at-risk children and youth).
Geographic Focus: District of Columbia, Maryland, Virginia
Amount: 5,000 - 20,000 USD
Samples: Carpenter's Shelter, Alexandria, VA, $20,000 - housing with intensive supportive services for homeless adults and children (2008); Bucknell University, Lewisburg, PA , $10,000 - general support (2008); All Souls' Episcopal Church, Mechanicsville VA, $15,000 - Orphans Program of the Maseno Mission in Kenya (2008).
Contact: Suzanne Martin, Grant Consultant; (301) 654-2700
Internet: http://fdncenter.org/grantmaker/fowler/about.html
Sponsor: John Edward Fowler Memorial Foundation
4340 East-West Highway, Suite 206
Bethesda, MD 20814

John Gogian Family Foundation Grants **975**
The foundation supports California nonprofit organizations that provide services and solutions for: developmentally disabled adults and children—life skills and vocational training, residential group home, employment, day services, therapeutic services, homelessness, and institutionalized or incarcerated youth; abused or neglected youth— domestic violence, residential group homes, therapeutic/social/educational services, emancipation, homelessness, and institutionalized or incarcerated youth; and Armenian causes in the United States. Types of support include core programming—new, expanding, or sustaining; and capital purchases and improvements. After receiving two consecutive grants, an organization is eligible to apply for a capacity grant—to build infrastructure, including technical, management and leadership capabilities. The foundation occasionally awards an impact grant for projects of special merit, opportunity, or potential impact (maximum award is $50,000). An organization may apply for and receive a grant annually, for up to three consecutive years. Thereafter, it must refrain from applying for at least one year. The foundation does not make multiple year pledges. Application and guidelines are available online.
Requirements: Organizations must provide a copy of their 501(c)3 tax-exempt status verification letter with IRS indication that they are not a private foundation; provide services to adults and/or children within Los Angeles County; be nonsectarian; and not discriminate in hiring staff or providing services on the basis of race, religion, ethnicity, national origin, sex, or disability.
Restrictions: The foundation does not fund individuals, research, debt reduction, endowments, loans, fundraising events, sectarian programs, or political campaigns/projects designed to influence legislation.
Geographic Focus: California
Date(s) Application is Due: Jan 12; Jun 28
Amount: 5,000 - 15,000 USD
Contact: Lindsey Stammerjohn, (310) 325-0954; jgff@gogianfoundation.org
Internet: http://www.gogianfoundation.org/grant/index.html
Sponsor: John Gogian Family Foundation
3305 Fujita Street
Torrance, CA 90505

John H. and Wilhelmina D. Harland Charitable Foundation Grants **976**
The foundation, offers support for: youth services, community services, cultural programs, education, and health. The focus is local rather than regional or national, and priority is given to institutions in metropolitan Atlanta, Georgia. Grants support: building/renovation; capital campaigns; equipment; general/operating support; matching/challenge support; and scholarship funds. The Foundation prefers a telephone call as opposed to a letter of inquiry for the initial approach.
Requirements: Grant support is available to nonprofit organizations in Georgia, with emphasis on the metropolitan Atlanta area.
Restrictions: Grants are not awarded to individuals.
Geographic Focus: Georgia
Date(s) Application is Due: Mar 1; Sep 1
Amount: 4,000 - 250,000 USD
Samples: Childrens Healthcare of Atlanta, Atlanta, GA, $151,068; Atlanta Botanical Garden, Atlanta, GA, $100,000; Georgia Shakespeare Festival, Atlanta, GA, $35,000.
Contact: Jane Hardesty, Executive Director; (404) 264-9912
Sponsor: John H. and Wilhelmina D. Harland Charitable Foundation
2 Piedmont Court, Suite 106
Atlanta, GA 30305-1567

John I. Smith Charities Grants **977**
The foundation supports nonprofit organizations, primarily in South Carolina. With its areas of interest, including: the visual and performing arts, higher education, medical education, theological education, literacy education and basic skills, Christian agencies and churches, child welfare, and programs for the disabled. Grants support general operations, capital campaigns, endowment funds, scholarship funds, and emergency funds. Application forms are not required. The board meets on a quarterly basis. Mail applications to: P.O. Box 1687, Greer, SC 29652
Requirements: Nonprofit organizations in South Carolina are eligible to apply.
Geographic Focus: South Carolina
Amount: 2,500 - 200,000 USD
Samples: Furman University, Greenville, SC, $100,000; Alliance for Quality Education, Greenville, SC, $27,000; Columbia Theological Seminary, Decatur, GA, $200,000.
Contact: Jefferson Smith, President; (864) 879-2455
Sponsor: John I. Smith Charities
P.O. Box 40200, FL9-100-10-19
Jacksonville, FL 32203-0200

John J. Leidy Foundation Grants **978**
The John J. Leidy Foundation was established in 1957. The foundation gives primarily in the metropolitan Baltimore, Maryland, area. Funding is available to people with disabilities, education, health, social services, and Jewish organizations in the form of, scholarship funds, building/renovation, equipment, general/operating support, and program development grants.
Requirements: Maryland non-profits are eligible to apply.
Restrictions: No grants to individuals.
Geographic Focus: Maryland
Samples: Maryland Food Bank, Baltimore, MD, $20,000; Baltimore Symphony Orchestra, Baltimore, MD, $5,000; Baltimore Hebrew Congregation, Baltimore, MD, $50,000.
Contact: Robert L. Pierson, President; (410) 821-3006; Leidyfd@attglobal.net
Sponsor: John J. Leidy Foundation
305 W Chesapeake Avenue, Suite 308
Towson, MD 21204-4440

John Jewett and Helen Chandler Garland Foundation Grants **979**
Established in 1959, the John Jewett & Helen Chandler Garland Foundation gives primarily in California, with emphasis on southern California. The foundations area of interest include: the arts, education, health care, children and social services. There are no application deadlines.
Requirements: California nonprofit organizations are eligible.
Restrictions: No telephone inquiries excepted, submit a letter of inquiry as your initial approach.
Geographic Focus: California
Amount: 2,500 - 610,000 USD
Samples: Huntington Library, Friends of the, San Marino, CA, $800,000 - for general support and educational programs at Botanical Center; Marlborough School, Los Angeles, CA, $25,000 - for general support and minority scholarships; Boys and Girls Clubs of Pasadena, Pasadena, CA, $110,000 - for general support and to make swimming pool accessible year-round.
Contact: Lisa M. Hausler, Manager
Sponsor: John Jewett and Helen Chandler Garland Foundation
P.O. Box 550
Pasadena, CA 91102-0550

John M. Ross Foundation Grants **980**
The John M. Ross Foundation provides funding to nonprofit organizations operating in the state of Hawaii. Funding priorities include youth services, scholarship funds and federated giving programs, offering support in the form of general/operating grants & scholarships. Grant proposals are due February 1st. Applicants are notified in writing of the Committee's action on their requests. Grants range from $250 - $10,000.
Requirements: Nonprofit organizations operating in the state of Hawaii are eligible. To begin the application process, contact the Foundation's administrative office for a Funding Cover Sheet (FCS) and application form. The (FCS) must accompany each grant proposal. The proposal should be no more then 3 pages in length. Include the following information and documentation with your proposal: 1 copy of IRS determination letter, charter, and bylaw, and annual report and financial statements; how project

will be sustained once grantmaker support is completed; qualifications of key personnel; statement of problem project will address; population served; copy of IRS Determination Letter; copy of most recent annual report/audited financial statement/990; how project's results will be evaluated or measured; listing of board of directors, trustees, officers and other key people and their affiliations; detailed description of project and amount of funding requested; organization's charter and by-laws; copy of current year's organizational budget and/or project budget; listing of additional sources and amount of support; 4 copies of proposal. Mail proposal to: John M. Ross Foundation c/o Bank of Hawaii, Corporate Trustee Foundation Administration #758 P. O. Box 3170 Honolulu, Hawaii 96802-3170.
Restrictions: No grants are made for endowments or capital campaigns. The recipient of a grant will be required to submit a narrative report on what has been accomplished as a result of the grant, and a fiscal accounting of the grant expenditures.
Geographic Focus: Hawaii
Date(s) Application is Due: Feb 1
Amount: 250 - 10,000 USD
Samples: YWCA of Hawaii Island, Hilo, HI, $5,000—operational & program Support for Hamakua youth (2009); Aloha Performing Arts Company, Kealakekua, HI, $6,893—Aloha Teen Theatre production of "A Christmas Story" (2009); University of Hawaii Foundation, Honolulu, HI, $10,000—scholarship (2009).
Contact: Paula Boyce, Grants Administrator; (808) 694-4945; paula.boyce@boh.com
Sponsor: John M. Ross Foundation
P.O. Box 3170
Honolulu, HI 96802-3170

John P. McGovern Foundation Grants 981
The John P. McGovern Foundation, established in 1961, supports the charitable interests of the donor to support the activities of established nonprofit organizations, which are of importance to human welfare with special focus on children and family health education and promotion, treatment and disease prevention. The Foundation gives primarily in Texas with an emphasis on the Houston area, but also provides funding in the Southwest region as well. The types of support offered are: building/renovation; conferences/seminars; continuing support; curriculum development; emergency funds; endowments; general/operating support; matching/challenge support; professorships; publication; research; and scholarship funds.
Requirements: Non-profits in Texas are eligible to apply.
Geographic Focus: Texas
Date(s) Application is Due: Aug 31
Amount: 10,000 - 100,000 USD
Samples: University of Texas Health Science Center, Houston, TX. $1,500,000 - for John P. McGovern, MD, Center for Health, Humanities, and Human Spirit/Certificate Program Endowment Fund; Community Family Centers, Houston, TX. $200,000- for John P. McGovern Community Sports and Recreation Building; Salvation Army of Houston, Houston, TX. $150,000 - for general operating fund.
Contact: Kathrine G. McGovern, President; (713) 661-4808; (713) 661-3031
Sponsor: John P. McGovern Foundation
2211 Norfolk Street, Suite 900
Houston, TX 77098-4044

John R. Oishei Foundation Grants 982
The foundation's primary mission is to support medical research and care and education, as well as cultural and social needs existing in the Buffalo Niagara region. The foundation favors creative programs that attempt to advance from the status quo, are strategically sound, and are strongly focused on excellence. Programs that provide opportunities for foundation support to be leveraged into greater support from other sources will be especially favored. The foundation generally does not fund operating expenses, though occasional exceptions may be made for organizations that address basic human needs. Requests for capital funds will not be considered unless they are an integral part of an otherwise eligible proposal. Contact the foundation to discuss eligibility before submitting an application. Grant applications are accepted throughout the year.
Requirements: It is the general policy of the foundation to confine its support to activities located in the Buffalo, NY, metropolitan region.
Restrictions: Grants do not support endowments; capital requests (buildings or equipment); deficit funding or loans; individual scholarships or fellowships (except within specific foundation programs); travel, conferences, seminars, or workshops; fundraising events; or 509(a) private foundations.
Geographic Focus: New York
Amount: 100,000 - 200,000 USD
Contact: Blythe T. Merrill, Senior Program Officer; (716) 856-9490, ext. 3; (716) 856-9493; btmerrill@oisheifdt.org
Internet: http://www.oisheifdt.org/Home/Fund/WhatWeFundOverview
Sponsor: John R. Oishei Foundation
1 HSBC Center, Suite 3650
Buffalo, NY 14203-2805

John Reynolds and Eleanor B. Allen Charitable Foundation Grants 983
The Foundation, established in Florida in 2004, is a 501(c)3 dedicated to supporting performing arts programs, particularly instrumental music, as well as other charitable organizations operating in and around Wauchula, Florida. The brainchild of W. Reynolds Allen, founding partner of a Labor and Employment Law firm, the Foundation is interested in offering its support throughout southern Florida. There are no specific application formats or deadlines, and applicants should contact the Foundation for further instructions.
Requirements: Applicants should be located in Florida.
Geographic Focus: Florida
Amount: 600 USD
Samples: Wednesday Musicale, Wauchula, Florida, $600—in support of general operations for a musical club; Southeastern Guide Dogs, Wauchula, Florida, $150—general fund support.
Contact: W. Reynolds Reynolds, (813) 251-1210; (813) 253-2006; rallen@anblaw.com
Sponsor: John Reynolds and Eleanor B. Allen Charitable Foundation
324 S Hyde Park Avenue, #225
Tampa, FL 33606-4127

John S. and James L. Knight Foundation Communities Grants 984
The program aims to improve the quality of life in 26 U.S. communities where the Knight brothers owned newspapers. Grants support six priority areas: education—to gain economic self-sufficiency, remain active learners, be good parents, and effective citizens in a democracy; well-being of children and families; housing and community development—to provide affordable, decent housing in safe, drug-free neighborhoods and to provide services for the homeless as well as affordable opportunities for home ownership; economic development—to help all adults gain access to jobs; civic engagement/positive human relations—to encourage residents to be good citizens, form ties to local institutions, and strengthen relationships with one another; and vitality of cultural life—to provide access to a wide variety of arts and cultural pursuits for all and to nourish creativity in children, youth, and adults. The foundation will work with local advisory committees to craft customized strategies for each Knight community, based on the priority areas, and to identify appropriate nonprofit partners. The foundation encourages interested organizations to send a one- to two-page letter of inquiry before submitting a proposal.
Requirements: Nonprofit organizations and institutions are eligible. The proposed project must serve at least one of the following target areas: Long Beach or San Jose, CA; Boulder, CO; Boca Raton, Bradenton, Miami, or Tallahassee, FL; Columbus, Macon, or Milledgeville, GA; Fort Wayne or Gary, IN; Wichita, KS; Lexington, KY; Detroit, MI; Duluth or Saint Paul, MN; Biloxi, MS; Charlotte, NC; Akron, OH; Philadelphia or State College, PA; Columbia or Myrtle Beach, SC; and Aberdeen, SD. Applicant organizations may be located outside of the project target area.
Geographic Focus: California, Colorado, Florida, Georgia, Indiana, Kansas, Kentucky, Minnesota, Mississippi, North Carolina, Ohio, Pennsylvania, South Carolina, South Dakota
Contact: Anne Corriston, Program Director; (305) 908-2600 or (305) 908-2673; (305) 908-2698; publications@knightfdn.org
Internet: http://www.knightfoundation.org/programs/communities/
Sponsor: John S. and James L. Knight Foundation
200 S Biscayne Boulevard, Suite 3300
Miami, FL 33131-2349

Johns Manville Fund Grants 985
The Johns Manville Fund, Inc. gives primarily in areas of company operations in Denver, Colorado, Etowah, Tennessee, and in Canada. The Fund offers support in the areas of: the arts; education; health care; human services; youth services and the American Red Cross. The grants are offered in the form of employee-related scholarships, employee volunteer services, general/operating

support, and program development. Contact the Johns Manville Fund, Inc. for a Informational brochure, including application guidelines.
Requirements: Non-profits operating in Denver, Colorado, Etowah, Tennessee, and in Canada are eligible.
Restrictions: No support for religious organizations not of direct benefit to the entire community, hospitals, or non-special needs private educational organizations. No grants for special events.
Geographic Focus: Colorado, Tennessee, Canada
Amount: 1,000 - 27,000 USD
Contact: Community Relations Manager; (303) 978-3863; (303) 978-2108
Internet: http://www.jm.com/corporate/careers/1241.htm
Sponsor: Johns Manville Fund
717 17th Street
Denver, CO 80202-3330

Johnson & Johnson Corporate Contributions Grants **986**
Johnson & Johnson and its many operating companies support community-based programs that improve health and well-being. The Company works with community-based partners that have the greatest insight into the needs of local populations and the strategies that stand the greatest chances of success. Giving focuses on: saving and improving the lives of women and children; building on the skills of people who serve community health needs, primarily through education; and preventing diseases and reducing stigma and disability in underserved communities where we have a high potential for impact.
Requirements: Grants are awarded to nonprofit and tax-exempt local, national, and international organizations and institutions.
Restrictions: Grants are not awarded to individuals, for deficit funding, capital or endowment funds, demonstration projects, or publications.
Geographic Focus: All U.S. States
Contact: Shaun Mickus, (732) 524-2086; smickus@corus.jnj.com
Internet: http://www.jnj.com/connect/caring/corporate-giving/
Sponsor: Johnson and Johnson
1 Johnson & Johnson Plaza
New Brunswick, NJ 08933-0001

Johnson Controls Foundation Arts and Culture Grants **987**
The Johnson Controls Foundation provides financial gifts to select U.S.-based organizations located in the communities in which the company has a presence. In the area of arts and culture, the Foundation supports organizations in the areas of visual, performing and literary arts, public radio and television, libraries, museums, and related cultural activities.
Requirements: In evaluating requests for funds, the Advisory Board has developed policies and guidelines for giving in Culture and the Arts. Contributions will be given to visual, performing, and literary arts, public radio and television, libraries, museums, and other related cultural activities. Priority will be extended to those serving communities in which Johnson Controls employees live and work, and to those in which these employees are involved with their time and/or funds.
Restrictions: In general, no grants will be made to any political campaign or organization; any municipal, state, federal agency, or department, or to any organization established to influence legislation; any private individual for support of personal needs; any sectarian institutions or programs whose services are limited to members of any one religious group or whose funds are used primarily for the propagation of a religion; for testimonial dinners, fund raising events, tickets to benefits, shows, or advertising; to provide monies for travel or tours, seminars and conferences or for publication of books and magazines or media productions; for specific medical or scientific research projects; foreign-based institutions nor to institutions or organizations for use outside of the United States; fraternal orders or veteran groups; private foundations or to endowment funds. The foundation does not donate equipment, products or labor.
Geographic Focus: All U.S. States
Amount: 500 - 40,000 USD
Contact: Charles A. Harvey, President; (414) 524-1200 or (414) 524-2296
Internet: http://www.johnsoncontrols.com/publish/us/en/about/our_community_focus/johnson_controls_foundation.html
Sponsor: Johnson Controls Foundation
5757 North Green Bay Avenue, P.O. Box 591
Milwaukee, WI 53201

Johnson Controls Foundation Civic Activities Grants **988**
The Johnson Controls Foundation provides financial gifts to select U.S.-based organizations located in the communities in which the company has a presence. In the area of civic activities, the Foundation provides assistance to programs in the areas of justice and law, community and neighborhood improvements, the environment, civic activities and equal opportunity, citizenship and safety.
Requirements: In evaluating requests for funds, the Advisory Board has developed policies and guidelines for giving in civic activities. Contributions will be given to programs in the areas of justice and law, community and neighborhood improvements, the environment, civil rights and equal opportunity, citizenship and safety. Requests to finance office equipment and computer systems do not have a high priority.
Restrictions: In general, no grants will be made to any political campaign or organization; any municipal, state, federal agency, or department, or to any organization established to influence legislation; any private individual for support of personal needs; any sectarian institutions or programs whose services are limited to members of any one religious group or whose funds are used primarily for the propagation of a religion; for testimonial dinners, fund raising events, tickets to benefits, shows, or advertising; to provide monies for travel or tours, seminars and conferences or for publication of books and magazines or media productions; for specific medical or scientific research projects; foreign-based institutions nor to institutions or organizations for use outside of the United States; fraternal orders or veteran groups; private foundations or to endowment funds. The foundation does not donate equipment, products or labor.
Geographic Focus: All U.S. States
Date(s) Application is Due: Aug 30
Contact: Charles A. Harvey, President; (414) 524-1200 or (414) 524-2296
Internet: http://www.johnsoncontrols.com/publish/us/en/about/our_community_focus/johnson_controls_foundation.html
Sponsor: Johnson Controls Foundation
5757 North Green Bay Avenue, P.O. Box 591
Milwaukee, WI 53201

Johnson Controls Foundation Health and Social Services Grants **989**
The Johnson Controls Foundation provides financial gifts to select U.S.-based organizations located in the communities in which the company has a presence. Operating support for organizations in the health and social services category largely occurs in communities where Johnson Controls has a local presence and is often directed through contributions to United Way.
Requirements: In evaluating requests for funds, the Advisory Board has developed policies and guidelines for giving in health and social services. Contributions will be given financial assistance to federated drives, hospitals, youth agencies and other health and human service agencies. Ordinarily, operating support of health and social service agencies is reserved for Johnson Controls communities.
Restrictions: In general, no grants will be made to any political campaign or organization; any municipal, state, federal agency, or department, or to any organization established to influence legislation; any private individual for support of personal needs; any sectarian institutions or programs whose services are limited to members of any one religious group or whose funds are used primarily for the propagation of a religion; for testimonial dinners, fund raising events, tickets to benefits, shows, or advertising; to provide monies for travel or tours, seminars and conferences or for publication of books and magazines or media productions; for specific medical or scientific research projects; foreign-based institutions nor to institutions or organizations for use outside of the United States; fraternal orders or veteran groups; private foundations or to endowment funds. The foundation does not donate equipment, products or labor.
Geographic Focus: All U.S. States
Date(s) Application is Due: Apr 30
Amount: 1,000 - 150,000 USD
Contact: Charles A. Harvey, President; (414) 524-1200 or (414) 524-2296
Internet: http://www.johnsoncontrols.com/publish/us/en/about/our_community_focus/johnson_controls_foundation.html
Sponsor: Johnson Controls Foundation
5757 North Green Bay Avenue, P.O. Box 591
Milwaukee, WI 53201

Johnson Foundation Wingspread Conference Support Grants **990**
The foundation sponsors conferences in the public interest. Meeting facilities include Wingspread and an adjacent building, The House. Conferences are intensive, one- to four-day meetings of small groups convened in partnership with nonprofit organizations, public agencies, universities, and other foundations. Strategic interests of the foundation are: education; sustainable development and

environment; democracy and community; and family. The foundation also seeks to advance the arts, help those with disabilities, and enhance the future of Racine and southeastern Wisconsin. The foundation's usual contribution to a conference sponsored by one or more other organizations consists of the provision of the full conference facilities of Wingspread, planning and logistical support by the staff, meals and other amenities for the period of the meeting, and local transportation between the conference center, airport, and the nearby hotel where conferees are lodged.
Requirements: To be invited to submit a full proposal, applicants first must submit a brief concept letter, consisting of: a clear statement of purpose; a draft agenda; the identification of key participants; and an estimated budget and schedule. The letter should describe how the conference will: enhance collaboration and community; include diverse opinions and perspectives; identify solutions; and result in action.
Restrictions: Proposals are limited to 501(c)3 organizations, educational institutions, or agencies of government. The foundation does not make grants, sponsor retreats, fundraisers, meetings of single organizations, or for-profit events. The facilities are not available for rent.
Geographic Focus: All U.S. States
Contact: Carole Johnson, Program Officer, Education; (262) 639-3211; (262) 681-3327; cjohnson@johnsonfdn.org
Internet: http://www.johnsonfdn.org/guidelines.html
Sponsor: Johnson Foundation
33 E Four Mile Road
Racine, WI 53402

Joseph Alexander Foundation Grants 991
Established in 1960 in New York, the Foundation supports primarily the New York, New York region. Offering support for: higher education, health organizations and medical research, particularly optic nerve research, social services, and Jewish organizations.
Requirements: Nonprofit organizations are eligible to apply.
Restrictions: Grants are not made to individuals.
Geographic Focus: New York
Amount: 1,000 - 100,000 USD
Samples: Bar-Ilan University in Israel, New York, NY, $50,000; Center for Jewish History, New York, NY, $15,000; Autism Speaks, New York, NY, $25,000.
Contact: Robert Weintraub, President; (212) 355-3688
Sponsor: Joseph Alexander Foundation
110 East 59th Street
New York, NY 10022-1304

Joseph Drown Foundation Grants 992
The foundation makes contributions in the areas of education; community, health and social services; and arts and humanities. It supports programs dealing with such issues as the high school drop-out rate, teen pregnancy, lack of sufficient health care, substance abuse, and violence. Types of support include general operating support, program development, seed money, scholarship funds, and matching funds. Most grant making is limited to programs or organizations in California. Requests are considered each year at March, June, September, and December meetings. The foundation makes grants for both operating support and program support but does not make multiyear commitments. No special application form is required. Proposal should include a letter with information about the organization and the project, a copy of 501(c)3 determination letter, a budget for the organization and the project, the most recent audited financial statements, a copy of the most recent IRS Form 990, and a list of the current board of directors. Any additional materials, such as an annual report, may be attached. Questions should be directed to the program director; proposals should be sent to the foundation president.
Requirements: California 501(c)3 organizations may apply.
Restrictions: The foundation does not provide funds to individuals, endowments, capital campaigns, or annual funds. The foundation does not underwrite annual meetings, conferences, or special events, nor does it fund religious programs or purchase tickets to fund-raising events.
Geographic Focus: California
Date(s) Application is Due: Jan 15; Apr 15; Jul 15; Oct 15
Amount: 10,000 - 100,000 USD
Samples: The Henry Mancini Institute, Los Angeles, CA, $15,000 - for support of the Community Outreach Initiative; The Museum of Tolerance, Los Angeles, CA, $50,000 - for Tolerance Youth Education programs; Friends of the Semel Institute for Neuroscience, Los Angeles, CA, $40,000 - for a postdoctoral fellowship; Los Angeles Leadership Academy, Los Angeles, CA, $30,000 - for a literacy coordinator and development director in initial year of operation.
Contact: Alyssa Eichelberger, Program Administrator; (310) 277-4488, ext. 100; (310) 277-4573; alyssa@jdrown.org
Internet: http://www.jdrown.org
Sponsor: Joseph Drown Foundation
1999 Avenue of the Stars, Suite 1930
Los Angeles, CA 90067

Joseph H. and Florence A. Roblee Foundation Grants 993
The foundation awards grants to enable organizations to promote change by addressing significant social issues in order to improve the quality of life and help fulfill the potential of individuals. The foundation arises out of a Christian framework, and values ecumenical endeavors. The foundation particularly supports programs which work to break down cultural, racial, and ethnic barriers. Organizations and churches are encouraged to collaborate in achieving positive change through advocacy, prevention, and systemic improvements.
Requirements: Giving limited to nonprofit organizations in the greater bi-state Street Louis region, and Miami/Dade, FL. Contact Foundation for additional guidelines.
Restrictions: Support is not given to individuals or for annual campaigns, research, or loans.
Geographic Focus: Florida, Illinois, Missouri
Date(s) Application is Due: Jan 15; Jun 15
Amount: 1,000 - 30,000 USD
Samples: Planned Parenthood of the Saint Louis Region, Saint Louis, MO, $20,000 - for comprehensive sex education programs for area teens; Christian Activity Center, East Saint Louis, IL, $15,000 - for Bridging the Gap after-school homework room program; Switchboard of Miami, Miami, FL, $30,000 - for Kevin Kline Suicide Awareness Initiative
Contact: Peggy Thomas c/o Bank of America, N.A., Bank of America; (314) 466-1304; kathydc@robleefoundation.org.
Sponsor: Joseph H. and Florence A. Roblee Foundation
P.O. Box 14737, MO2-100-07-19
Saint Louis, MO 63178-4737

Josephine S. Gumbiner Foundation Grants 994
The charitable foundation functions for the benefit of women and children in the Long Beach area. The funder supports a wide array of programs, such as the arts; day care; education health care intervention, prevention, and direct services; housing; and recreation. Organizations are not be eligible for funding more than once in any 12-month period. As a general rule, the foundation will not grant funding to any organization for more than three consecutive years. The two-step application process begins with requesting a letter of intent questionnaire, which should be requested through email. Full applications are by invitation. There are no application deadlines. The board meets three or four times each year.
Requirements: Southern California nonprofit organizations are eligible.
Restrictions: Grants do not support political campaigns, lobbying efforts, programs that supplant tradition schooling, pass-through organizations, or groups with endowments greater than $5 million.
Geographic Focus: California
Amount: 5,000 - 50,000 USD
Samples: Children's Dental, CA, $20,000 - I.V. Sedation for L.B. Children Program (2009); Children Today, Long Beach, CA, $15,000 - LCSW Support (2009); Helpline Youth Counseling, Norwalk, CA, $15,000 - L.B. Gang Prevention Program (2009).
Contact: Administrator; (562) 437-2882; (562) 437-4212; julie@jsgf.org
Internet: http://www.jsgf.org/
Sponsor: Josephine S. Gumbiner Foundation
333 West Broadway, Suite 302
Long Beach, CA 90802

Joshua M. Freeman Foundation Grants 995
The Joshua M. Freeman Foundation was established in 2007 to honor Josh Freeman, the former Chair of the Carl M. Freeman Foundation, after his untimely death in December of 2006. The Joshua M. Freeman Foundation is a nonprofit organization that conceptualizes, constructs, and operates buildings that promote community gathering primarily for the support and enjoyment of the arts, the environment, and athletic achievement.
Geographic Focus: Delaware, Maryland, West Virginia

Contact: Trish Schechtman, Relationship Manager; (302) 436-3555; trish@freemanfoundation.org
Internet: http://www.freemanfoundation.org/josh/
Sponsor: Joshua M. Freeman Foundation
36097 Sand Cove Road
Selbyville, DE 19975

Jostens Foundation Community Grants **996**
Jostens provides support to organizations that enhance the lives of youth and promote educational opportunities that significantly and positively impact children from birth through college. The foundation meets quarterly to review all Community Grant requests.
Requirements: Nonprofit organizations with 501(c)3 status are eligible. The foundation gives priority to organizations where Jostens facilities and employees are located and gives priority to nonprofit organizations that involve Jostens employees.
Restrictions: In general, grants are not made to support educational institutions or for scholarships, political organizations, churches or religious groups, fund-raising events, or endowment funds.
Geographic Focus: All U.S. States
Date(s) Application is Due: Mar 9; Jun 8; Sep 7; Dec 7
Amount: 500 - 10,000 USD
Contact: Mary Klimek, (952) 830-3235; (952) 897-4116; foundation@jostens.com
Internet: http://www.jostens.com/company/community/index.asp
Sponsor: Jostens Foundation
5601 American Boulevard W
Minneapolis, MN 55437

Journal Gazette Foundation Grants **997**
The foundation awards grants to northeastern Indiana nonprofit organizations in its areas of interest, including community funds, education, higher education, health organizations and hospitals, social services, Christian agencies and churches, and youth. Types of support include general operations and capital campaigns. There are no application deadlines; the board meets quarterly.
Requirements: Indiana nonprofit organizations are eligible. Preference is given to requests from northeastern Indiana.
Restrictions: Grants are not made to individuals.
Geographic Focus: Indiana
Amount: 25 - 112,000 USD
Samples: Lincoln Museum (Fort Wayne, Indiana)—for operating support, $6000.
Contact: Jerry Fox, (260) 424-5257
Sponsor: Journal Gazette Foundation
701 S Clinton
Fort Wayne, IN 46802-1883

Joyce Foundation Grants **998**
The foundation's program areas are education, employment, environment, gun violence, money and politics, and culture. Grantmaking is focused on initiatives that promise to have an impact on the Great Lakes region, specifically the states of Illinois, Indiana, Michigan, Minnesota, Ohio, and Wisconsin. A limited number of environment grants are made to organizations in Canada. Education grantmaking focuses on Chicago, Cleveland, and Milwaukee. Culture grants are primarily focused on the Chicago metropolitan area. The foundation is committed to improving public policy through its grant program. Public policy grants provide general operating support or fund educational advocacy such as nonpartisan research, technical assistance, or examinations of broad social issues. Grant applicants are encouraged to describe the nature of advocacy activities in their grant applications and reports, so the foundation can ensure that it is in compliance with federal tax laws. Guidelines are available online.
Requirements: Applications should be made only by organizations in the Great Lakes region that can demonstrate their tax-exempt status and that can supply complete financial information and permit the results of a grant to be audited.
Restrictions: The foundation generally does not support capital projects, endowment campaigns, religious activities, direct services, or scholarships.
Geographic Focus: Illinois, Indiana, Iowa, Michigan, Minnesota, Ohio, Wisconsin, Canada
Date(s) Application is Due: Apr 15; Aug 16; Dec 12
Amount: 20,000 - 100,000 USD
Samples: Environmental Defense (New York, NY)—to implement federal farm-conservation programs in Midwestern states in an effort to protect Great Lakes water resources, $500,000 over two years; Chicago Metropolis 2020 (Chicago, IL)—for efforts to revise the Illinois criminal code, $150,000 over two years; U of Michigan at Ann Arbor, Great Lakes Radio Consortium (MI)—to cover water-related stories in the region, $200,000 over two years; National-Louis U, Ctr for Early Childhood Leadership (IL)—to educate policy makers and others about the importance of highly qualified directors of early-childhood programs in achieving universal preschool, $200,000 over two years.
Contact: Veronica Salter, Grants Manager; (312) 782-2464; (312) 782-4160; info@joycefdn.org
Internet: http://www.joycefdn.org/seekingagrant/seekingmain-fs.html
Sponsor: Joyce Foundation
70 W Madison Street, Suite 2750
Chicago, IL 60602

Joy Family Foundation Grants **999**
The foundation awards grants to nonprofit organizations and individuals in the city of Buffalo, NY, and the counties of Erie and Niagara, NY, to improve the quality of life. Grants are awarded in support of human and family services, education and literacy, AIDS research, substance abuse, alcoholism, the aging, the economically disadvantaged, hospitals, women and children, and Roman Catholic churches and organizations. Grants will be awarded for programs and projects, general operating support, capital campaigns, building/renovation, technical assistance, and consulting services. The board meets quarterly.
Requirements: New York nonprofit organizations are eligible.
Geographic Focus: New York
Amount: 100 - 100,000 USD
Samples: Burchfield-Penny Art Center (Buffalo, NY)—for capital campaign, $25,000; Christ the King Seminary (East Aurora, NY)—grant recipient, $10,000; Computers for Children (Buffalo, NY)—for computer refurbishment, $10,000.
Contact: Marsha Sullivan, Executive Director; (716) 633-6600; (716) 633-0600; info@joyfamilyfoundation.org
Internet: http://www.joyfamilyfoundation.org
Sponsor: Joy Family Foundation
5436 Main Street, Suite 1
Williamsville, NY 14221

JP Morgan Chase Arts and Culture Grants **1000**
The foundation supports programs in the New York tri-state region, across the nation, and around the world that strengthen communities where JP Morgan Chase employees live and work. In its Arts and Culture grantmaking, the Foundation looks for opportunities to integrate the arts into children's educational opportunities and position arts organizations and artists as key drivers of local economic renewal. The Foundation supports: arts programs in schools and after school; building the capacity of community-based arts institutions; initiatives that stimulate the creation and growth of local cultural economies; broadening of access to artistic excellence and diversity by partnering with major arts and culture groups.
Requirements: Only charitable, not-for-profit organizations are eligible to apply. Refer to the website in order to identify the region in which your program will be administered.
Restrictions: The following types of organizations, activities or purposes are not funded: programs outside the geographic markets we serve; individuals; fraternal organizations; athletic teams or social groups; public agencies; private schools; public schools (K-12), unless in partnership with a qualified not-for-profit organization; parent-teacher associations; scholarships or tuition assistance; higher education, unless program is specifically within guidelines; fundraising events (e.g. golf outings, school events); advertising, including ads in event, performance or athletic programs; volunteer-operated organizations; funds to pay down operating deficits; programs designed to promote religious or political doctrines; endowments or capital campaigns (exceptions are made by invitation only); organizations that discriminate on the basis of race, sex, sexual orientation, age or religion; health or medical-related organizations, unless program fits within stated giving guidelines.
Geographic Focus: Arizona, California, Colorado, Connecticut, Delaware, Florida, Illinois, Indiana, Kentucky, Louisiana, Michigan, New Jersey, New York, Ohio, Oklahoma, Texas, Utah, West Virginia, Wisconsin
Contact: Kimberly B. Davis, President; (212) 270-6000
Internet: http://www.jpmorganchase.com/corporate/Corporate-Responsibility/corporate-philanthropy.htm

Sponsor: JP Morgan Chase & Company
270 Park Avenue
New York, NY 10017

JP Morgan Chase Community Development Grants 1001

Working with best-in-class community-based partners, the JP Morgan Chase goal is to help stabilize families living in high-poverty neighborhoods and to make that stability echo through a neighborhood in a manner that improves educational and job opportunities, reduces crime and dramatically raises the community's quality of life. The program supports both resident-focused programs and community-focused programs. Resident-focused programs that address workforce development, asset building, and financial literacy, will support: continuing education courses; adult literacy outreach; job training; money management basics; credit repair; EITC workshops; home ownership and home buyer workshops; and foreclosure prevention programs. Community-focused programming addresses economic development and affordable housing issues.
Requirements: Only charitable, not-for-profit organizations are eligible to apply. Refer to the website in order to identify the region in which your program will be administered.
Restrictions: The following types of organizations, activities or purposes are not funded: programs outside the geographic markets we serve; individuals; fraternal organizations; athletic teams or social groups; public agencies; private schools; public schools (K-12), unless in partnership with a qualified not-for-profit organization; parent-teacher associations; scholarships or tuition assistance; higher education, unless program is specifically within guidelines; fundraising events (e.g. golf outings, school events); advertising, including ads in event, performance or athletic programs; volunteer-operated organizations; funds to pay down operating deficits; programs designed to promote religious or political doctrines; endowments or capital campaigns (exceptions are made by invitation only); organizations that discriminate on the basis of race, sex, sexual orientation, age or religion; health or medical-related organizations, unless program fits within stated giving guidelines.
Geographic Focus: Arizona, California, Colorado, Connecticut, Delaware, Florida, Illinois, Indiana, Kentucky, Louisiana, Michigan, New Jersey, New York, Ohio, Oklahoma, Texas, Utah, West Virginia, Wisconsin
Contact: Kimberly B. Davis, President; (212) 270-6000
Internet: http://servicelearning.org/resources/funding_sources/index.php?popup_id=898
Sponsor: JP Morgan Chase & Company
270 Park Avenue
New York, NY 10017

JP Morgan Chase Foundation/Asian American Arts Alliance Grants 1002

Grants awarded for general program/project support. Arts groups with budgets up to $300,000 and who are members of the alliance are eligible to apply.
Geographic Focus: All U.S. States
Date(s) Application is Due: Apr 15
Amount: 1,000 - 3,000 USD
Contact: Executive Director; (212) 941-9208; (212) 941-7978; lcho@aaartsalliance.org
Internet: http://www.aaartsalliance.org/HTML/programsGrants.html
Sponsor: Asian American Arts Alliance
74 Varick Street, Suite 302
New York, NY 10013-1914

JPMorganChase Regrant Program for Small Ensembles 1003

This joint grant initiative of Meet The Composer and JPMorganChase is dedicated to general operating support for professional music organizations and music presenters with annual budgets of $300,000 or less. The goal of this program is to encourage the work of small New York City based music organizations and music presenters (Bronx, Brooklyn, Manhattan, Queens and Staten Island). The purpose of general operating support is to provide unrestricted support for ongoing institutional operating activities of organizations whose central mission is the creation, production, and performance of musical programming. Guidelines and application instructions are available online.
Requirements: 501(c)3 tax-exempt organizations in the five boroughs of New York City, with organized music programs for at least three years, and an annual budget of less than $300,000 are eligible. Eligible organizations must have an existing organizational structure and an on-going artistic product.
Geographic Focus: All U.S. States
Date(s) Application is Due: Mar 4
Amount: Up to 5,000 USD
Contact: Grants Administrator; (212) 645-6949, ext. 101; mtrevino@meetthecomposer.org
Internet: http://www.meetthecomposer.org/programs/fundforsmall.html
Sponsor: Meet the Composer
75 Ninth Avenue, Floor 3R, Suite C
New York, NY 10011

JP Morgan Community Life Grants 1004

JP Morgan Chase believes that thriving communities need quality of life through arts and culture, arts and civic programming that celebrates diversity, programs that help build arts and cultural capacity and sustainability and environmental awareness. Funding is available for: supporting organizations that focus upon capacity building, advocacy, technical assistance, and financial support to the broad arts and cultural community; arts exhibitions and performance that enhance the quality of life in the community, with emphasis on programming that addresses cultural enrichment and issues related to diversity; programs that promote ecologically sound practices and environmental conservation; organizations that focus on emerging or underrepresented artists to foster the creation of new work; projects for groups with budgets under $500,000 in the NY Tri-State Region.
Requirements: Only charitable, not-for-profit organizations are eligible to apply. Please refer to the grant contacts information online to identify the region in which your program will be administered.
Restrictions: The following types of organizations, activities or purposes are not funded: programs outside the geographic markets JP Morgan serves; individuals; fraternal organizations; athletic teams or social groups; public agencies; private schools; public schools (K-12), unless in partnership with a qualified not-for-profit organization; parent-teacher associations; scholarships or tuition assistance; higher education, unless program is specifically within guidelines; fundraising events (e.g. golf outings, school events); advertising, including ads in event, performance or athletic programs; volunteer-operated organizations; funds to pay down operating deficits; programs designed to promote religious or political doctrines; endowments or capital campaigns (exceptions are made by invitation only); organizations that discriminate on the basis of race, sex, sexual orientation, age or religion; health or medical-related organizations, unless program fits within state giving guidelines.
Geographic Focus: Arizona, California, Colorado, Connecticut, Delaware, Florida, Illinois, Indiana, Kentucky, Louisiana, Michigan, New Jersey, New York, Ohio, Oklahoma, Texas, Utah, West Virginia, Wisconsin
Contact: Community Relations Officer; (212) 270-6000
Internet: http://servicelearning.org/resources/funding_sources/index.php?popup_id=898
Sponsor: J.P. Morgan Chase
201 N Central Avenue
Phoenix, AZ 85004

JSPS Postdoctoral Fellowship for Foreign Researchers 1005

To facilitate cooperative research between young foreign researchers and hosting Japanese researchers, fellowships are awarded to enable postdoctoral researchers to undertake research at Japanese universities and institutions. The program also supports short-term fellowships of 15 days to 11 months. The fellowship includes round-trip airfare, a monthly stipend of @Y270,000, and an additional settling-in allowance. In addition, JSPS may provide a special research grant up to @Y1.5 million, depending on need of applicants.
Requirements: Fellowships are available to citizens of countries that have diplomatic relations with Japan. Candidates must hold the doctorate degree when the fellowship goes into effect; the degree must have been received within six years prior to April of the fiscal year in which the fellowship commences. The candidate must have arranged in advance a research plan with his/her Japanese host researcher, who must be employed at a Japanese university/research institution.
Geographic Focus: All U.S. States
Amount: 5,000 - 13,000 USD
Contact: Program Administrator, Foreign Fellowship Division; 81-3-3263-1721; 81-3-3263-1854
Internet: http://www.jsps.go.jp/english/e-fellow/postdoctoral.html#short
Sponsor: Japan Society for the Promotion of Science
Nihon Gakujutsu Shinko-kai, 5-3-1, Kojimachi, Chiyoda-ku
Tokyo, 102-8471 Japan

K. M. Hunter Charitable Foundation Social Welfare Grants 1006

The Foundation provides a number of major grants to social and health services programs in Ontario. In addition, a series of smaller grants are given to organizations, including housing shelters and hospices for the sick. The Foundation requests that applicants make all contacts through its web site. There are no specific applications or deadlines, and the Board meets two or three times annually to make its funding decisions.

Requirements: Grants are made to registered charitable organizations based in Ontario, with the exception of grants that support AIDS in Africa.

Geographic Focus: All U.S. States, Canada

Contact: Sarah Hunter, Vice President

Internet: http://www.kmhunterfoundation.ca/

Sponsor:

Kalamazoo Foundation Grants 1007

The foundation awards unrestricted grants in four priority areas: individuals and families, economic development, education and learning, and community engagement and youth development. Types of support include general operating support, capital campaigns, building construction/renovation, equipment acquisition, emergency funds, program development, seed grants, scholarship funds, technical assistance, employee matching gifts, and matching funds. The period for grant support is normally one year. Guidelines and application are available online.

Requirements: Kalamazoo, MI, organizations recognized (or in the process of applying for recognition) under IRS code 501(c)3 are encouraged to contact foundation staff before submitting a request to determine eligibility.

Restrictions: Generally, the foundation does not provide funding for debt retirement, endowments, individuals, travel for individuals or groups, religious organizations for religious purposes, meetings, conferences, publications, films, or television and radio programming.

Geographic Focus: Michigan

Samples: Interfaith Strategy for Advocacy and Action in the Community (Kalamazoo, MI)—for a voter-registration and community-engagement project, $40,000; Catholic Family Services (Kalamazoo, MI)—for the Kalamazoo Caring Network's Read Me a Story program, which promotes reading skills and literacy among teenage parents and their children, $25,297; Michiana Addictions and Prevention Services (Kalamazoo, MI)—to support the merger of this substance-abuse-treatment center with the Guidance Clinic in Kalamazoo, $100,000; Kalamazoo College (MI)—for a postgraduate fellowship position at the Mary Jane Underwood Stryker Institute for Service Learning, $45,000.

Contact: Program Contact; (269) 381-4416; (269) 381-3146; info@kalfound.org

Internet: http://www.kalfound.org/page8490.cfm

Sponsor: Kalamazoo Foundation
151 S Rose Street
Kalamazoo, MI 49007

Kaman Corporate Giving Program Grants 1008

The corporate giving program focuses on the needs of the handicapped and disabled, but funding is provided to cover a broad range of human needs. Grants are made for capital building, renovation campaigns, and selected operating programs. The majority of grants are awarded to nonprofits in the Hartford, CT, area. Requests are accepted throughout the year. Requests for funding should include the organization's latest financial report; a description of (and budget for) the project to be funded; information concerning the status of funding toward the goal; a listing of the organization's board of directors and key staff; and the name, address, and phone number of the person to be contacted for further information. Other material the organization feels would be helpful is welcomed.

Requirements: Nonprofits in the greater Hartford region of Connecticut are eligible.

Restrictions: Grants do not support endowment funds, recipients of state grants, agencies receiving funds from the United Way/Combined Health Appeal, or galas and events.

Geographic Focus: Connecticut

Amount: 25,000 - 500 USD

Contact: Russell Jones, Vice President; (860) 243-6308; (860) 243-6365; info.kaman-corp@kaman.com

Internet: http://www.kaman.com

Sponsor: Kaman Corporation
1332 Blue Hills Avenue
Bloomfield, CT 06002

Kansas Arts Commission Operational Support for Arts and Cultural Organizations 1009

Through operational support grants, the Commission offers financial assistance to nonprofit arts and cultural organizations with at least a three-year history of incorporation or operation as an independent entity. The award is based upon a percentage of the organization's projected expense budget and the amount of funds available for distribution in this program category. Arts organizations may apply for support of general operating, program, and administrative expenses; and on attached application components, arts organizations may apply for support of arts in education activities, and for support of Kansas touring program events. The purpose of the operational support grants is to strengthen the administrative and programming capability of arts organizations; enable arts organizations to provide high-quality, accessible arts activities, programs, and services to their constituencies; support arts organizations in planning and development of long-term goals; and augment, not supplant, local support for arts organizations.

Requirements: Single or multidisciplinary arts and cultural organizations based in Kansas are eligible to apply. Organizations must have as their primary missions planning, development, support or presentation of arts and cultural programs and services, as evidenced by their mission statement, total fiscal operations, and total activities.

Geographic Focus: Kansas

Date(s) Application is Due: Mar 4

Amount: 2,000 USD

Contact: Raena Sommers, Grants Administrator; (785) 296-4089; (785) 296-4989; raena@arts.state.ks.us

Internet: http://arts.ks.gov/grants/os/index.shtml

Sponsor: Kansas Arts Commission
700 SW Jackson, Jayhawk Tower, Suite 1004
Topeka, KS 66603-3774

Kansas Health Foundation Grants 1010

The foundation provides grants to Kansas organizations that share its mission to improve the quality of health in the state. Through solicited requests for proposals, the foundation proactively works as a partner with others in the state on programs that address the greatest health needs and achieve the most positive results. Grants are made in five primary categories, including primary care education, rural health, health promotion and disease prevention, public health, and health policy and research. At times, the foundation may respond to unsolicited proposals that are consistent with current programs. Types of support include fellowships, general operating budgets, special projects, and technical assistance. The foundation also awards recognition grants to honor Kansas grassroots organizations doing innovative work to improve the health of the people of the state.

Requirements: Kansas 501(c)3 nonprofit organizations are eligible.

Restrictions: The foundation does not support clinical or medical research; contributions to capital campaigns; organizations that practice discrimination by race, color, creed, sex, age or national origin; operating deficits or retirement of debt; endowment programs; construction projects or real estate acquisitions; political projects of any kind; and vehicles, such as vans or buses, or emergency medical services equipment.

Geographic Focus: Kansas

Date(s) Application is Due: Mar 15; Sep 15

Samples: Kansas Health Foundation Leadership Ctr (Wichita, KS)—to establish this center, which will help develop leaders who can spearhead efforts to improve the health of all Kansans, $30 million; Wichita State U, Elliott School of Communication (KS)—to endow a professorship in strategic communication, $2 million.

Contact: Grants Manager; (800) 373-7681 or (316) 262-7676; (316) 262-2044; info@khf.org

Internet: http://www.kansashealth.org/grants/recognition_grants.jsp

Sponsor: Kansas Health Foundation
309 E Douglas
Wichita, KS 67202-3405

Karma Foundation Grants 1011

The foundation awards grants on an international basis to support the following broad interest areas: arts and culture, education and literacy, health and human services, and development and enrichment of Jewish life. Types of support include operating expenses, special projects, capital grants, seed grants, equipment and materials. and disaster relief. The foundation also provides technical assistance and assists in proposal development. There are no application deadlines.

Requirements: National and international nonprofit organizations are eligible.
Restrictions: Grants do not support travel expenses for bands or sports teams, political or lobbying activities, advertising for fundraising events, litigation, charter schools, or loans.
Geographic Focus: California, New Jersey, Wisconsin
Amount: 500 - 25,000 USD
Samples: Wheaton Village—to purchase a computerized collection management system and to train personnel at the Museum of AmericanGlass, $15,900; Children's Hospital of Los Angeles (CA)—for medical equipment for the emergency transport team, $18,081; First Concern (Somerset, NJ)—to refurbish the kitchen and laundry room, $25,000; National Jewish Medical and Research Ctr—for asthma research, $10,000.
Contact: Dina Karmazin Elkins, Executive Director; (609) 924-5939; (609) 924-2714; info@karmafoundation.org
Internet: http://www.karmafoundation.org
Sponsor: Karma Foundation
140 Arreton Road
Princeton, NJ 08540

Kate B. Reynolds Charitable Trust Health Care Grants 1012

The Trust responds to health care and wellness needs and invests in solutions that improve the quality of health for financially needy residents throughout North Carolina. The Health Care Division seeks impact through two program areas: providing treatment and supporting prevention. The trust requires advanced consultation by phone or in writing. Application materials are available online, but applications are not accepted electronically.
Requirements: Nonprofit 501(c)3 organizations in North Carolina are eligible.
Restrictions: Grants are not awarded to individuals.
Geographic Focus: North Carolina
Date(s) Application is Due: Mar 15; Sep 15
Amount: 20,000 - 200,000 USD
Contact: John H. Frank, Director; (336) 397-5502 or (866) 551-0690; (336) 723-7765; john@kbr.org
Internet: http://www.kbr.org/health-care-division-fund.cfm
Sponsor: Kate B. Reynolds Charitable Trust
128 Reynolda Village
Winston-Salem, NC 27106-5123

Kate B. Reynolds Charitable Trust Poor and Needy Grants 1013

Through the Poor and Needy Division, the trust responds to basic life needs and invests in solutions that improve the quality of life for financially needy residents of Forsyth County. The Poor and Needy division seeks impact through two program areas by providing operating funds: Providing Basic Needs and Increasing Self Reliance. The Grant Application Process is a two-step process involving consultation with a staff Program Officer, followed by formal submission of a grant application. The consultation can be scheduled by calling our Winston-Salem offices.
Requirements: Nonprofit 501(c)3 organizations in Forsyth County, North Carolina, are eligible.
Restrictions: Grants are not awarded to individuals.
Geographic Focus: North Carolina
Date(s) Application is Due: Jan 15; Jul 15
Contact: Joyce T. Adger, Program Director; (336) 397-5503 or (336) 723-1456; (336) 723-7765; joyce@kbr.org
Internet: http://www.kbr.org/poor-and-needy-division-fund.cfm
Sponsor: Kate B. Reynolds Charitable Trust
128 Reynolda Village
Winston-Salem, NC 27106-5123

Katherine Mabis McKenna Foundation Grants 1014

The foundation awards grants to eligible Philadelphia nonprofit organizations in its areas of interest, including education, arts and culture, philanthropy, human services, environment, and community development. Types of support include annual campaigns, building construction/renovation, capital campaigns, equipment acquisition, general operating grants, program development, and seed grants. There are no application forms. The foundation prefers to receive proposals between January and July.
Requirements: Philadelphia nonprofit organizations are eligible. Preference is given to requests from Westmoreland County.
Geographic Focus: Pennsylvania
Date(s) Application is Due: Oct 1
Amount: 2,500 - 50,000 USD
Samples: Seton Hill U (Greensburg, PA)—to construct a recreational facility that will include fitness rooms, a gymnasium, and a running trace, $2 million.
Contact: Linda McKenna Boxx, (724) 537-6900
Sponsor: Katherine Mabis McKenna Foundation
P.O. Box 186
Latrobe, PA 15650

Kathryne Beynon Foundation Grants 1015

Founded in California in 1967, the Kathryne Beynon Foundation provides support primarily for: hospitals (with a special interest in Asthma); youth agencies; child welfare; Roman Catholic church; higher education, Types of support include: general operating support; building construction/renovation; endowment funds; and scholarship funds. The Board meets quarterly to review grant requests. Applicants should contact the office in writing, outlining their proposal. Application is by invitation only, and there is no deadline date when submitting grant proposals. Contact the Foundation directly for additional guidelines before submitting a full proposal.
Requirements: 501(c)3 southern California tax-exempt organizations are eligible. Preference is given to requests from Pasadena. There are no: deadline dates; formal application form required to submit proposal.
Restrictions: No support to individuals.
Geographic Focus: California
Amount: 500 - 50,000 USD
Samples: Artists of America, San Pedro, CA, $17,800—Laurel Elementary School, Prep art classes (2009); Assistance League of Southern California, Hollywood, CA, $4,000—children's club/ day nursery (2009); Scripps College, Claremont, CA, $20,000—science scholarship program (2009).
Contact: Robert D. Bannon, Trustee; (626) 584-8800
Sponsor: Kathryne Beynon Foundation
1111 South Arroyo Parkway, Suite 470
Pasadena, CA 91105-3239

Keith Campbell Foundation for the Environment Grants 1016

The foundation awards grants to Maryland nonprofit organizations serving children in the areas of culture and social services delivery. Types of support include building construction/renovation, equipment acquisition, program development, and general operating grants. Grants are awarded for one year. Submit a brief (two-page maximum) proposal describing the request and organization.
Requirements: Maryland 501(c)3 tax exempt organizations are eligible. The majority of grants are awarded in the Baltimore area.
Restrictions: Grants are not made to individuals.
Geographic Focus: Maryland
Amount: 150 - 500,000 USD
Contact: Keith Campbell, President; (410) 825-0545, ext. 103
Sponsor: Keith Campbell Foundation for the Environment
210 W Pennsylvania Avenue, Suite 770
Towson, MD 21204

Kellwood Foundation Grants 1017

The foundation makes grants to 501(c)3 charitable scientific, educational, and literary organizations for programs that provide basic human needs and improve the quality of life. Primary focus areas include cultural and performing arts; education; health services; and social welfare, civic, and community programs. Types of support include general operating support, annual campaigns, capital campaigns, program development, and employee matching gifts. The board meets in March, June, September, and December to consider requests. Requests should be submitted on organization letterhead and contain the name, address, and phone number of the contact person; statement of the problem to be addressed; identification of geographic area and number of people served; statement of the purpose for which funds are requested; specific dollar request; explanation of how the program differs from others providing similar services in the same geographic area; annual organizational budget; identification of sources of annual operating funds; identification of board of directors and key staff members; and copy of IRS 501(c)3 determination letter.
Requirements: Giving is primarily made to the greater Street Louis, MO, area.
Geographic Focus: Missouri
Amount: 25 - 70,000 USD

Samples: Central Institute for the Deaf (Saint Louis, MO)—for endowment, $10,000; Girl Scouts of the U.S. A (Saint Louis, MO)—for program support, $3000; American Red Cross (Saint Louis, MO)—for operating support, $10,000.
Contact: Terri Grandcolas, (314) 576-3431; (314) 576-3439
Sponsor: Kellwood Foundation
600 Kellwood Parkway
Chesterfield, MO 63017

Kelsey Trust Grants **1018**
The trust awards grants within its geographical territory to support organizations in its primary areas of interest, including child development education, adult basic education and literacy, vocational education, health care and health organizations, the environment and conservation, and services for children and families. Grants are awarded for general operating support, program development, seed money, scholarship funds, matching funds, and emergency funds.
Requirements: Nonprofit organizations in the Lake Champlain Valley drainage basin; eastern Adirondacks, in New York; and western Vermont, north of Rutland, may submit applications for grant support.
Restrictions: The trust does not typically make grants for most capital projects, debt reduction, normal operating budgets, to individuals, for sectarian religious purposes, for endowments, or where the trust may become a predominant source of support.
Geographic Focus: New York, Vermont
Date(s) Application is Due: Feb 1; Sep 1
Amount: 2,500 - 10,000 USD
Samples: Planned Parenthood of Northern Adirondack (Plattsburgh, NY)—for program support, $10,000; Fletcher Allen Health Care (Burlington, VT)—for program support, $3000; Bristol Family Center (Bristol, VT)—for program support, $1000.
Contact: Paula Johnson, Grants Manager, c/o Vermont Community Foundation; (802) 388-3355
Internet: http://www.vermontcf.org/guidelines-forms/kelsey-trust.html
Sponsor: Kelsey Trust
P.O. Box 30
Middlebury, VT 05753

Kelvin and Eleanor Smith Foundation Grants **1019**
The foundation awards grants to Ohio nonprofits in its areas of interest, including nonsectarian education, the performing and visual arts, health care, and environmental conservation and protection. Types of support include general operating support, continuing support, annual campaigns, capital campaigns, building construction/renovation, and equipment acquisition. There are no required application forms or deadlines.
Requirements: Nonprofit organizations in the greater Cleveland, OH, area are eligible.
Restrictions: Grants are not made in support of individuals or for endowment funds, scholarships, fellowships, matching gifts, or loans.
Geographic Focus: Ohio
Amount: 3,000 - 150,000 USD
Samples: Case Western Reserve University, Kelvin Smith Library (Cleveland, OH)—for capital campaign, $200,000; Cleveland Museum of Art (Cleveland, OH)—for annual fund, $125,000.
Contact: Carol Zett, Grants Manager; (216) 591-9111; (216) 591-9557
Sponsor: Kelvin and Eleanor Smith Foundation
30195 Chagrin Boulevard, Suite 275
Cleveland, OH 44124

Kenneth King Foundation Grants **1020**
The foundation awards grants to Colorado nonprofit organizations in its areas of interest, including agriculture, arts and culture, civic and public affairs, community development, disabled, disadvantaged (economically), education (elementary, secondary, and higher), environment, healthcare, international (Hungary, Russia), religion, social services, technology, and women's issues. Types of support include general operating support, matching/challenge grants, program development, research grants, and scholarship funds. Guidelines are available online.
Requirements: Colorado 501(c)3 nonprofit organizations are eligible. Organizations that received more than $1500 in the previous year should contact the office by phone or email before submitting a proposal.
Restrictions: Capital requests will not be considered.
Geographic Focus: Colorado
Date(s) Application is Due: Mar 1
Amount: 300 - 200,000 USD
Contact: Janice Fritsch, Program Contact; (303) 832-3200; (303) 832-4176; jfritsch@kennethkingfoundation.org
Internet: http://www.kennethkingfoundation.org
Sponsor: Kenneth King Foundation
900 Pennsylvania Street
Denver, CO 80203-3163

Kenneth T. and Eileen L. Norris Foundation Grants **1021**
The foundation supports Los Angeles County nonprofits in the areas of medicine—to improve access to health care, increase knowledge through research, and provide facilities for those activities to take place; youth—to provide constructive activities, positive role models, and opportunities for disadvantaged, disabled, and misguided children; community—to support law enforcement agencies, good citizenship, and environmental conservation; arts and culture—to support museums, symphony orchestras, and dance and theater companies; and education and science—to focus on private education, especially secondary and college levels. Types of support include general operating support, continuing support, building construction/renovation, equipment acquisition, endowment funds, program development, professorships, scholarship funds, research, and matching funds. Education/science projects are due between May 1 and June 30; youth requests are due between February 15 and March 31; community and cultural (the arts) requests are due between December 1 and January 31; and medicine proposals are due between May 1 and June 30.
Requirements: Grants are awarded to organizations in southern California.
Geographic Focus: California
Date(s) Application is Due: Jan 31; Mar 31; Jun 30
Amount: 5,000 - 25,000 USD
Samples: Los Angeles Regional Foodbank (Los Angeles, CA)—for general operating support, $10,000.
Contact: Ronald Barnes, Executive Director; (562) 435-8444; (562) 436-0584; grants@ktn.org
Internet: http://www.norrisfoundation.org/grant_funding.html
Sponsor: Kenneth T. and Eileen L. Norris Foundation
11 Golden Shore, Suite 450
Long Beach, CA 90802

Kenny's Kids Grants **1022**
The foundation awards grants to U.S. nonprofits in company-operating locations with a focus on programs that improve life for children and young adults. The primary target of grants is giving support to organizations which seek to give youth greater opportunities outside of the classroom to learn and grow, to teach them skills that will enable them to thrive in a technology-oriented society, and to offer them the guidance and attention necessary to develop such skills. Also consideration for youth-oriented organizations and other organizations that promote the welfare of youth, such as those that offer hope and encouragement to the sick and terminally ill, protect those who have suffered from abuse, and offer after-school programs for the underprivileged. There are no application deadlines. Allow eight to 12 weeks for proposal review.
Requirements: Nonprofits in company operating areas of Illinois are eligible.
Restrictions: No support for private foundations, schools (public or private), or corporations. Grants are not made to individuals, or for political campaigns, film, video, or audio productions.
Geographic Focus: Illinois
Amount: Up to 573,902 USD
Contact: Nicholas Pontikes, President
Sponsor: Kenny's Kids
1212 W Lill Street
Chicago, IL 60614

Kentucky Arts Council Community Arts Development Grants **1023**
The program is designed to nurture existing, and support the formation of new arts organizations in Kentucky communities and neighborhoods and to assist these organizations in establishing and maintaining viable, ongoing community-based arts programs and activities. The program provides operating, technical assistance, and program support over a three-year period. Application materials are available on the website.
Requirements: The program will provide technical assistance to new or emerging arts organizations in Kentucky to gradually increase organizational development and maturity over a three-year period. Organizations need not be

incorporated as a nonprofit, tax-exempt entity in their first year, but must have applied for this status by year two and secured such status by year three. Other eligible organizations include those which provide some arts programming (not year-round); organizations with budgets of $50,000 or more; and local arts agencies and discipline-based arts organizations (such as community theaters, visual art leagues, dance companies, etc.) with budgets under $50,000. Cash matches are required at every level of funding; amounts vary.
Restrictions: Funds cannot be used for deficits, capital expenditures, or major purchases of equipment.
Geographic Focus: Kentucky
Date(s) Application is Due: Jan 15
Amount: Up to 3,500 USD
Contact: Daniel Strauss, Arts Program Branch Manager; (888) 833-2787, ext. 4804 or (502) 564-3757; (502) 564-2839; kyarts@ky.gov
Internet: http://www.state.ky.us/agencies/arts/guide/prog7/ca_gdl.html
Sponsor: Kentucky Arts Council
500 Mero Street, 21st Floor, Capital Plaza Tower
Frankfort, KY 40601-1987

Kentucky Arts Council Organizational Support—Arts Development Grants 1024

Arts Development grants provide operating support primarily to Kentucky small and medium-sized nonprofit arts and cultural organizations to ensure that ongoing arts programs and activities are available to Kentucky citizens. Arts development grants focus on arts and cultural organizations which exist within a restricted fundraising environment. Arts Development funds will provide partial support of the operating costs of ongoing arts programming, as well as projected new initiatives. Grants may be used for personnel (artistic, administrative, technical/production), outside artistic or other professional fees and services, space rental, travel and marketing costs, subgranting and other operating costs. Grants generally range from 2 percent to 10 percent of an organization's prior year operating costs for arts programs (exclusive of capital expenditures, such as renovation or acquisition of facilities, or costs of auxiliary services, such as gift shops or food services). Annual deadline dates may vary; contact program staff for exact dates.
Requirements: Kentucky nonprofit arts organizations committed to providing arts programs and services to the public are eligible to apply. First-time organizations applying to the program must contact the program manager listed prior to making application. All applicants with operating expenses greater than or equal to $150,000 during their most recently completed fiscal year must submit an audit for that period.
Restrictions: Not eligible are internal programs of academic institutions and state or other agencies supported primarily with state or federal funds. Applicants to the Challenge or Community Arts programs are not eligible.
Geographic Focus: Kentucky
Date(s) Application is Due: Jan 1; Feb 1
Amount: Up to 140,000 USD
Contact: Dan Strauss, Branch Program Manager; (888) 833-2787, ext. 474; (502) 564-2839; dan.strauss@mail.state.ky.us
Internet: http://www.kyarts.org/guide/prog2/gos1_gdl.html
Sponsor: Kentucky Arts Council
500 Mero Street, 21st Floor, Capital Plaza Tower
Frankfort, KY 40601-1987

Kentucky Arts Council Organizational Support—Challenge Grants 1025

The intent of the challenge grant program is to stimulate broad-based ongoing support for Kentucky's arts organizations by matching net contributions from private and other nonstate, nonfederal sources. The program is designed to reward efforts in developing contributed income. The total eligible income for the organizations most recent accounting period may be matched by a grant of up to 33 1/3 percent, subject to the total state appropriation to the council for the challenge grants program. Funds may be used for general operating expenses. Application materials are available on the website. An intent to apply form is due by January 1; full proposal is due February 1. Annual deadline dates may vary; contact program staff for exact dates.
Requirements: Kentucky nonprofit arts organizations committed to providing arts programs and services to the public are eligible to apply. First-time organizations applying to the program must contact the program manager listed prior to making application. All applicants with operating expenses greater than or equal to $150,000 during their most recently completed fiscal year must submit an audit for that period.
Restrictions: Not eligible are internal programs of academic institutions and state or other agencies supported primarily with state or federal funds. Applicants to the Arts Development or Community Arts programs are not eligible.
Geographic Focus: Kentucky
Date(s) Application is Due: Jan 1; Feb 1
Contact: Dan Strauss, Branch Program Manager; (888) 833-2787, ext. 4804; (502) 564-2839; dan.strauss@mail.state.ky.us
Internet: http://www.state.ky.us/agencies/arts/guide/prog2/cg_gdl.html
Sponsor: Kentucky Arts Council
500 Mero Street, 21st Floor, Capital Plaza Tower
Frankfort, KY 40601-1987

Kentucky Arts Council Organizational Technical Assistance Grants 1026

The organizational technical assistance matching grant program provides funding assistance to organizations wishing to improve the effectiveness of their management and programs. Funds will generally go to an organization to hire knowledgeable consultants to address artistic or management problems or to strengthen organizational oversight, management, and programs. Funds may be used to send staff to appropriate training workshops and seminars or to bring a consultant into the organization for a specific assessment, planning, or training activity. Requests will be accepted throughout the year. Applications should be received at least six weeks before funds are needed and are subject to the availability of KAC funds. Application materials are available on the website.
Requirements: Kentucky arts organizations that are current Kentucky Arts Council grantees or applicants may apply. Applicants must match the KAC grant dollar-for-dollar in cash.
Restrictions: In-kind contributions are not eligible as matching funds.
Geographic Focus: Kentucky
Amount: Up to 1,000 USD
Contact: Daniel Strauss, Arts Program Branch Manager; (502) 564-8110, ext. 474; (502) 564-2839; kyarts@ky.gov
Internet: http://artscouncil.ky.gov/gtprogs.htm
Sponsor: Kentucky Arts Council
500 Mero Street, 21st Floor, Capital Plaza Tower
Frankfort, KY 40601-1987

KFC Allied Health Research Grants 1027

The foundation supports research into the incidence and cure of kidney and urinary tract disease, patient services, and public education. Preference will be given to allied health personnel undertaking research related to the kidney and urinary tract and to a new research project not supported by any other agency. Applications from investigators in related specialty areas also are considered. Types of support include capital grants, fellowships, general operating grants, program development grants, scholarships, and travel assistance. One- and two-year renewable grants are awarded.
Requirements: Application is open to individuals affiliated with Canadian universities for research conducted within Canada.
Restrictions: Grants will not be awarded for equipment only.
Geographic Focus: Canada
Date(s) Application is Due: Oct 15
Amount: Up to 50,000 CAD
Contact: National Research Programs Manager; (514) 369-4806, ext. 223 or (800) 361-7494, ext. 223; research@kidney.ca
Internet: http://www.kidney.ca/english/research/allied-funding-03.htm
Sponsor: Kidney Foundation of Canada
300-5165 Sherbrooke Street W
Montreal, QC H4A 1T6 Canada

KFC Biomedical Research Grants 1028

The program fosters and encourages research about the kidney and urinary tract and the understanding of kidney diseases. Types of support include general operating grants, research grants, materials and supplies, and travel assistance. One- and two-year renewable grants are offered.
Requirements: Canadian citizens or landed immigrants may apply. Research must be conducted in Canada by individuals holding staff appointments at Canadian universities or academic institutions.
Restrictions: Requests for equipment only are denied.
Geographic Focus: Canada
Date(s) Application is Due: Oct 15
Amount: Up to 50,000 CAD
Contact: National Research Programs Manager; (514) 369-4806, ext. 225 or (800) 361-7494, ext. 225; (514) 369-2472; research@kidney.ca
Internet: http://www.kidney.ca/english/research/biomed-funding-03.htm

Sponsor: Kidney Foundation of Canada
300-5165 Sherbrooke Street W
Montreal, QC H4A 1T6 Canada

Kimberly-Clark Foundation Grants **1029**

The foundation supports nonprofits within 50 miles of a Kimberly-Clark manufacturing plant or facility in a wide range of areas, including social welfare, medicine, and health; education; and civic and cultural activities. In the social welfare and health category, grants have supported groups such as boys' and girls' clubs, the Salvation Army, and visiting nurse associations. Educational funding includes NAACP and higher education institutions. The category of civic and cultural activities includes support for public broadcasting, museums, performing arts, and environmental groups. Types of support include annual campaigns, building construction funds, continuing support, equipment acquisition, operating budgets, seed grants, scholarship funds, and capital campaigns. Requests for the company's application form must be in writing.
Requirements: Nonprofit organizations in Kimberly-Clark locations are eligible.
Geographic Focus: All U.S. States
Amount: 1,000 - 75,000 USD
Samples: Marquette U (Milwaukee, WI)—for the Raynor Library's Information Commons and the Thompson Center for Excellence in Education, $1.1 million over five years; U.S. Fund for Unicef (New York, NY)—to provide education, health, legal, and mental-health services to African children orphaned because of AIDS, $2.6 million over four years; UNICEF—to provide services to the more than 13 million children worldwide orphaned as a result of AIDS, including health and nutritional services, community care, group homes, access to education, grief counseling, and legal advice on how to keep siblings together, $2.6 million.
Contact: Carolyn Mentesana, Vice President; (972) 281-1200; (972) 281-1490
Internet: http://www.kimberly-clark.com/aboutus/kc_foundation.asp
Sponsor: Kimberly-Clark Foundation
P.O. Box 619100
Dallas, TX 75261-9100

Kind World Foundation Grants **1030**

The foundation's purpose is to encourage and support charitable programs and activities that enhance the quality of life and best serve the public good. Funding priorities are environmental concerns, animal welfare, human services, education, and the arts. Types of support include general operating support, continuing support, annual campaigns, capital campaigns, building construction/renovation, equipment acquisition, endowment funds, seed grants, research, consulting services, and matching funds. Although the foundation supports regional and national programs, major grants are usually limited to the greater Siouxland area, including northwest Iowa, southeast South Dakota, and northeast Nebraska. Challenge grants and matching gift proposals receive special consideration. Proposals may be submitted at any time and are reviewed by the board of directors on a revolving basis. The board meets in January, April, July, October, and as needed. It is suggested that applicants contact the office prior to submitting a formal application.
Geographic Focus: California, Iowa
Amount: 500 - 250,000 USD
Samples: Morningside College (Sioux City, IA)—for marketing and financial aid programs, $125,000.
Contact: Arlene Curry, Executive Director; (605) 232-9139; (605) 232-3098; acurry@kindworld.org
Sponsor: Kind World Foundation
P.O. Box 980
Dakota Dunes, SD 57049

Kinsman Foundation Grants **1031**

The foundation awards grants to eligible nonprofit organizations in its areas of interest, including historic preservation, animal/wildlife welfare, and health care policy. Types of support include annual campaigns, building construction/renovation, capital campaigns, challenge/matching grants, conferences and seminars, consulting services, continuing support, curriculum development, endowments, equipment acquisition, general operating support, internships, program development, publication, research, seed grants, and technical assistance. Contact the office for application forms and guidelines.
Requirements: Oregon and southern Washington nonprofit organizations are eligible.
Geographic Focus: Oregon, Washington
Date(s) Application is Due: Aug 1
Samples: Kam Wah Chung and Company Museum (John Day, OR)—for restorations at this museum, a former trading post built in 1875, that documents the lives and culture of Chinese immigrants in eastern Oregon, $110,000.
Contact: Grants Administrator; (503) 654-1668; (503) 654-1759; grants@kinsmanfoundation.org
Sponsor: Kinsman Foundation
3727 SE Spaulding Avenue
Milwaukie, OR 97267-3938

Kiplinger Foundation Grants **1032**

The foundation awards grants to educational, health, welfare, civic, and cultural organizations, primarily in the Washington, DC, area. Building grants are also awarded to organizations in these areas of endeavor. The foundation also provides matching grants on a two-to-one basis to secondary schools and college-level institutions on behalf of Kiplinger Washington Editors employees and retirees of up to $5000 per year per employee or retiree. Areas of particular interest to the foundation include the arts and programs that provide better conditions for troubled and deprived youth. Grants also support annual campaigns, capital campaigns, continuing support, endowment funds, and special projects. Application should be a brief letter of proposal outlining the project for which funds are sought and objectives that the project should accomplish. Most grants are made for a period of one year.
Requirements: Organizations with IRS 501(c)3 status in the greater Washington, DC area are eligible.
Restrictions: The foundation does offer money for seed grants nor does it support scholarships.
Geographic Focus: District of Columbia
Amount: Up to 15,000,000 USD
Contact: Andrea Wilkes, Secretary; (202) 887-6559; foundation@kiplinger.com
Sponsor: Kiplinger Foundation
1729 H Street NW
Washington, DC 20006

Kirkpatrick Foundation Grants **1033**

Primary fields of interest are arts and culture, education, natural and built environments, and animal research and conservation. The board meets in March, June, September, and December. Contact the office for application forms.
Requirements: Grants are provided for nonprofit organizations qualified as public charities under Section 501(c)3 of the Internal Revenue Code. Public and private educational institutions and faith based educational programs are also available for funding. Priority is given to organizations serving Oklahoma, and particular emphasis is placed on programs and services directly benefiting citizens of the Oklahoma City metropolitan area.
Restrictions: Grants are not awarded to individuals or in support of hospitals.
Geographic Focus: Oklahoma
Date(s) Application is Due: Jan 15; Jul 15
Amount: 1,000 - 75,000 USD
Samples: Oklahoma City Art Museum (Oklahoma City, OK)—for general operating support, $20,000; Oklahoma Philharmonic Society (Oklahoma City, OK)—for general operating support, $20,000.
Contact: Susan McCalmont, Secretary; (405) 608-0934; (405) 608-0942
Internet: http://www.kirkpatrickfoundation.com/application.asp
Sponsor: Kirkpatrick Foundation
1001 W Wilshire Boulevard, Suite 201
Oklahoma City, OK 73116

Kitsap Community Foundation Grants **1034**

The foundation strives to address basic human needs in the Kitsap community. The foundation is primarily interested in funding programs in its focus areas that build on existing strengths of an organization; focus areas include arts and culture, civic and community improvement, education, social services, health, recreation, environment, and youth. Grants will be considered for general operational support and for capital needs of qualified institutions or organizations. Decisions are based on a number of factors including, but not limited to the number of people served, the potential for funding from other sources, whether the grant falls within the funding priority areas, the originality of the project, whether any other services of its kind exist, and the demonstrated need of the organization. Application guidelines and procedures are available online.

Requirements: Washington 501(c)3 nonprofit organizations in Kitsap County and its neighboring communities are eligible.
Restrictions: Generally, the foundation does not make grants to annual campaign appeals; endowments; individuals; political or lobbying activities; religious organizations for sacramental or theological purposes; publications except those that grow out of research and experiments underwritten by the foundation; or deficit reduction.
Geographic Focus: Washington
Date(s) Application is Due: Feb 15
Amount: Up to 2,000 USD
Contact: Executive Director; (360) 698-3622; kcf@kitsapfoundation.org
Internet: http://www.kitsapfoundation.org/grantgd.html
Sponsor: Kitsap Community Foundation
P.O. Box 3670
Silverdale, WA 98383

Klingenstein Fellowship Awards in the Neurosciences 1035
The purpose of these awards is to support, in the early stages of their careers, young investigators engaged in basic or clinical research that may lead to a better understanding of epilepsy. The fund recognizes that to accomplish this goal it is necessary to encourage a variety of new approaches. Several areas within the neurosciences are of particular interest to the fund: Cellular and molecular neuroscience—Studies of the mechanisms of neuronal excitability and development, and of the genetic basis of seizure disorders. Neural systems—Studies of the integrative function of the nervous system. Clinical research—Studies designed to improve the prevention, diagnosis, treatment and our understanding of the causes of epilepsy. Application may be made at any time.
Requirements: Applicants must hold the PhD and/or MD degrees, and have completed all research training, including post-doctoral training. U.S. citizenship is not a requirement, but it is expected that candidates will be permanent residents of the U.S. and that their research will be carried out in U.S. institutions.
Restrictions: The fund does not contribute to endowments and rarely contributes to buildings or other kinds of capital projects.
Geographic Focus: All U.S. States
Date(s) Application is Due: Dec 10
Samples: Teachers College Columbia U (New York, NY)—for program support, $578,595; American Jewish Committee (New York, NY)—for work on issues of separation of church and state, $40,000; Foundation for Biomedical Research (Washington, DC)—for animal biomedical research, $25,000.
Contact: Kathleen Pomerantz, Vice President; (212) 492-6181; kathleen.pomerantz@klingenstein.com
Internet: http://www.klingfund.org
Sponsor: Esther A. and Joseph Klingenstein Fund
787 7th Avenue, 6th Floor
New York, NY 10019

Klingenstein Third Generation Foundation Grants in Depression 1036
The foundation strives to improve the lives of families afflicted by clinical depression, including childhood and adolescent depression, and Attention Deficit/Hyperactive Disorder (ADHD). Grants are awarded in the areas of intervention and referral, prevention, public education/training, and infrastructure. The foundation will consider making capital grants, operating grants, challenge grants, seed grants, and grants given over more than a one-year period. The foundation also sponsors fellowships for postdoctoral research in depression. Funding proposals will be accepted from any geographic area, but the board expects to fund primarily in the New York, Chicago, and District of Columbia metropolitan areas. There is no formal application procedure or form. Applicants should submit a brief letter that succinctly describes the project and the amount sought and explains why the project is significant. The foundation will request a more detailed proposal.
Requirements: U.S. tax-exempt organizations are eligible.
Restrictions: Grants do not support direct services, unless they include a research or program evaluation component, or unless they represent the application of research findings to a clinical setting.
Geographic Focus: All U.S. States
Amount: 5,000 - 35,000 USD
Samples: American Academy of Child and Adolescent Psychiatry (Washington, DC)—for general support, $15,000; Columbia U, Carmel Hill Ctr for Early Diagnosis and Treatment (New York, NY)—to create brochures on mental-health disorders written in different languages and at a low reading level, $15,000; State U of New York (Buffalo, NY)—fellowship support for James Waxmonsky, for research on child and adolescent depression, $30,000 over two years.
Contact: Sally Klingenstein Martell, Executive Director; (212) 492-6179; (212) 492-7007; sally@ktgf.org
Internet: http://www.ktgf.org/depress.html
Sponsor: Klingenstein Third Generation Foundation
787 Seventh Avenue, 6th Floor
New York, NY 10019-6016

Knight Foundation Grants - Georgia 1037
The Foundation, established in 1992, serves a variety of programs and organizations in Savannah, Georgia. Its primary fields of interest include: children and youth services; human services; and Protestant churches and agencies. The primary type of support provided is by way of general operations funding. Applicants should submit: a detailed description of project and amount of funding requested; and the name, address and phone number of organization. The annual deadline is December 1st.
Restrictions: No funding is provided to individuals, and giving is primarily limited to 501(c)3 non-profits operating in Savannah, Georgia.
Geographic Focus: Florida, Georgia
Date(s) Application is Due: Dec 1
Amount: Up to 10,000 USD
Samples: White Bluff Methodist Church, Savannah, GA, $6,900—for general operations (2008); Westfield School, Perry, GA, $2,000—for educational programs (2008).
Contact: Stuart G. Knight, President; (912) 925-8092
Sponsor: Knight Foundation
28 Sherborne Road
Savannah, GA 31419-3261

Koessler Family Foundation Grants 1038
The family foundation awards grants to western New York nonprofits, with emphasis on Buffalo, NY. Areas of interest include higher education, hospitals, and hospices. Types of support include general operating support, building construction/renovation, capital campaigns, and matching grants. Submit a letter of request.
Requirements: Western New York nonprofits are eligible.
Geographic Focus: New York
Date(s) Application is Due: Nov 30
Amount: Up to 342,000 USD
Samples: Canisius College (Buffalo, NY)—for its capital campaign, $1 million matching grant; Childrens Hospital of Buffalo (Buffalo, NY)—for general support, $60,000; Kenmore Mercy Foundation (Kenmore, NY)—to construct a new patient tower, $24,000.
Contact: Stephen Juhasz, Grant Manager
Sponsor: Kenneth L. and Katherine G. Koessler Family Foundation
124 Brantwood Road
Snyder, NY 14226

Kongsgaard-Goldman Foundation Grants 1039
The foundation provides support to a wide range of nonprofit organizations in the Pacific Northwest in the areas of human rights, civic development, environmental protection and conservation, and the arts and humanities. Grants are awarded for both general operating support and special projects. Small technical assistance grants are also made throughout the year to assist organizations with training and skill development, expert consultation, leadership development, and networking. Preapplications must be submitted. Deadlines for preapplications are March 16 and September 16; proposals are due April 30 and October 31. There are no application forms.
Requirements: Organizations classified as 501(c)3 or 149(1)f (Canada) may apply. Grants are limited to organizations in the Pacific Northwest (Washington, Oregon, Idaho, Alaska, Montana) and British Columbia, Canada.
Restrictions: Grants are not awarded to support direct services, clinical and health services, medical research grants to individuals, wildlife rehabilitation programs, land acquisition, or funding of individual scholarships or fellowships.
Geographic Focus: Alaska, Idaho, Montana, Oregon, Washington, Canada
Date(s) Application is Due: Mar 16; Apr 30; Sep 16; Oct 31
Amount: Up to 1,500 USD
Samples: Chamber Music In Napa Valley (Napa, CA)—for general support, $5000; Pacific Crest Biodiversity Project (Seattle, WA)—to support the NW Old Growth Campaign and the Wildlands Restoration Program, $8000; Jewish Family Service (Seattle, WA)—to promote the growth and

development of Jews of all ages in greater King County to lead productive and meaningful lives, $20,000.
Contact: Aana Agee, Administrator; (206) 448-1874; (206) 448-1973; kgf@kongsgaard-goldman.org
Internet: http://www.kongsgaard-goldman.org/program.html
Sponsor: Kongsgaard-Goldman Foundation
1932 First Avenue, Suite 602
Seattle, WA 98101

Koret Foundation Grants **1040**
The foundation supports projects in the San Francisco Bay Area (Alameda, Contra Costa, Marin, San Francisco, San Mateo, and Santa Clara Counties) related to the arts and culture, community development, higher education, Jewish life and culture, primary and secondary education, and youth development. It also supports projects in Israel related to economic development, higher education, and security. Review of an application takes from three to six months; applicants are encouraged to submit applications well in advance of the need for funding.
Requirements: Applicant must first submit a one- to three-page preliminary letter briefly outlining the project or need for which support is being requested; the population(s) and geographic area(s) to be served; the proposed starting date and duration of grant-supported activities; an outline of the budget including all funding sources; highlights of organization's experience in the program or service area; list of board of directors; and IRS tax-exempt letter verifying applicant's 501(c)3 status.
Restrictions: Grants will not be made for direct support, scholarships, or loans to individuals; for general fund drives, annual appeals, or endowments; for emergency funding, debt retirement, or deficits; for indirect or overhead costs; to fiscal agents soliciting funds for projects or programs not conducted by the applicant; to organizations in support of propaganda or activities to influence legislation; to projects of sectarian/fraternal/religious/veteran/military organizations whose principal benefit is for their own members or adherents; or to grantees who have not fulfilled terms and conditions of a previous award.
Geographic Focus: All U.S. States, Israel
Amount: Up to 100,000,000 USD
Samples: Taube-Koret Campus for Jewish Life (Palo Alto, CA)—to construct a multipurpose, intergenerational Jewish community center and a residential complex for active senior citizens, $7.5 million; Ctr for Governmental Studies (Los Angeles, CA)—to increase civic participation in government through campaign-finance, governance, and media reforms, $200,000; City Arts and Lectures (San Francisco, CA)—for the Seriously Funny program, $15,000.
Contact: Director of Grants; (415) 882-7740; (415) 882-7775; info@KoretFoundation.org
Internet: http://www.koretfoundation.org/apply/application.shtml
Sponsor: Koret Foundation
33 New Montgomery Street, Suite 1090
San Francisco, CA 94105-4526

Kroger Company Foundation Grants **1041**
Kroger and the company's three foundations provide financial support to local schools, hunger relief agencies, youth sports teams, and nonprofit organizations in communities where the company operates stores or manufacturing facilities. Kroger focuses its charitable giving in five key areas: being a good neighbor; hunger relief; education; advancement of women and minorities; and women's health. Types of support include capital grants, general operating grants, scholarships, and seed money grants. Eligible organizations may submit proposals through the operating divisions of the company. Proposals must include an IRS tax-exempt determination letter, a statement of goals and objectives, and a list of the board of trustees.
Requirements: Nonprofit organizations in Kroger communities may submit grant proposals. National and regional organizations that provide services to areas of company operations also may be considered.
Restrictions: Support is not given to individuals or for religious purposes, endowment campaigns (unless the endowment is an important part of a broader campaign that meets the foundation's objectives), medical research, conferences, dinners, or sporting events.
Geographic Focus: All U.S. States
Amount: 250 - 50,000 USD
Contact: Foundation Administrator; (513) 762-4449, ext. 3; (513) 762-1295
Internet: http://www.kroger.com/corpnewsinfo_charitablegiving.htm
Sponsor: Kroger Company Foundation
1014 Vine Street
Cincinnati, OH 45202-1100

L. W. Pierce Family Foundation Grants **1042**
Established in 1997, The Foundation supports organizations involved with health, social, and educational services in the areas of alcohol and drug abuse, hospice care and children's welfare. Giving is limited to the Vero Beach, FL and Philadelphia, PA areas.
Requirements: Non-profits in the Vero Beach, FL and Philadelphia, PA areas are eligible.
Restrictions: No grants to individuals.
Geographic Focus: Florida, Pennsylvania
Date(s) Application is Due: Mar 1
Amount: 1,000 - 50,000 USD
Samples: Homeless Family Center, Vero Beach, FL, $50,000; Senior Resource Association, Vero Beach, FL, $20,000; Thomas Jefferson University, Philadelphia, PA, $20,000
Contact: Constance Buckley, President; (610) 862-2105; (610) 862-2120
Sponsor: L. W. Pierce Family Foundation
8 Tower Bridge, Suite 1060, 161 Washington Street
Conshohocken, PA 19428-2060

La-Z-Boy Foundation Grants **1043**
The foundation makes grants to nonprofit organizations in communities where it maintains plants and within a 15-mile radius of its corporate headquarters in Monroe, MI. Grants are awarded to public charities, civic organizations, and hospitals and health organizations. Support is given for general operating costs, building construction/renovation, education programs, and preservation/restoration. Potential applicants are asked to write to the office and describe the purpose of their project, time span, estimated costs, and benefits. Requests are reviewed at quarterly staff meetings held in March, June, September, and December.
Requirements: 501(c)3 nonprofit charities are eligible. Grants are awarded primarily in communities of company operations, including Siloam Springs, AR; Redlands, CA; Monroe, MI; Neosho, MO; Newton and Leland, MS; Lincolnton, NC; Florence, SC; Dayton, TN; and Tremonton, UT.
Geographic Focus: Arkansas, California, Michigan, Mississippi, Missouri, North Carolina, South Carolina, Tennessee, Utah
Date(s) Application is Due: Mar 1; Jun 1; Sep 1; Dec 1
Amount: 250 - 50,000 USD
Contact: Donald Blohm, Administrator; (734) 242-1444; (734) 457-2005
Internet: http://www.la-z-boy.com
Sponsor: La-Z-Boy Foundation
1284 N Telegraph Road
Monroe, MI 48162

Laclede Gas Charitable Trust Grants **1044**
The trust recognizes the civic responsibility of the company to the area it serves and the fact that the welfare of this area is essential to the customers, employees, and stockholders of the company. To this end, grants are awarded in the company's current areas of interest, including youth and human services, education and educational institutions, United Way, arts and culture, and civic and community projects. Types of support include capital grants, general operating grants, matching gifts, program development, and special projects. Requests for support for capital projects are presently considered by a committee of the company's board of directors. Proposals should be in writing and should include purpose of request, recent financials, list of members of board of directors, copy of IRS tax-exempt status letter, and past experience of fund raising. Meetings of the trustees of the trust are usually held in March, June, September, and December, at which time applications are reviewed.
Requirements: Contributions are limited to those organizations located in the company's service area. Contact program staff for locations.
Restrictions: The trust generally does not fund individuals or family support; advertising; political, labor, fraternal, or religious organizations or civic clubs; individual K-8 schools or school-affiliated clubs or events (public or private); sports, athletic events, or athletic programs; travel related events, including student trips or tours; development or production of books, films, videos, or television programs; or endowment or memorial campaigns.
Geographic Focus: All U.S. States
Amount: Up to 622,000 USD
Contact: Mary Kullman, Secretary; (314) 421-1979; mkullman@lacledegas.com
Internet: http://www.lacledegas.com/about/cs_charitable.htm
Sponsor: Laclede Gas Charitable Trust
720 Olive Street, Room 1517
Saint Louis, MO 63101

LaGrange Independent Foundation for Endowments (L.I.F.E.) **1045**
LaGrange Independent Foundation for Endowments, or L.I.F.E., is a philanthropic group of young people in LaGrange County. Representatives from four county schools are selected when they enter grade 8 and serve throughout their high school career as the advisory committee for the donor advised non-permanent fund held by the foundation. Grant applications submitted to the LCCF office are evaluated by the L.I.F.E Youth Pod in order to select recommended recipients.
Requirements: Nonprofit organizations including schools in LaGrange county are eligible to apply. Grants are awarded during the school year. The application is available at the foundation's website.
Geographic Focus: Indiana
Samples: LaGrange Communities Youth Centers, after school programming for youth (2011): Lakeland High School, Protective suits for use in Sheriff's Dept. Rape Agression Defense (RAD) training for women (2011): Prairie Heights Leo Club: Boomerang Backpack program for young people in elementary schools (2011).
Contact: Laura Lemings, Executive Director; (260) 463-4363; (260) 463-4856; llemings@lccf.net
Internet: http://www.lccf.net/life.html
Sponsor: LaGrange County Community Foundation
109 E Central Avenue, Suite 3
LaGrange, IN 46761

Land O'Lakes Foundation Mid-Atlantic Grants **1046**
The grassroots program serves Land O'Lakes dairy communities in the states of Maryland, New Jersey, New York, Pennsylvania, and Virginia, and works to improve quality of life by supporting valuable projects and charitable endeavors in the region. The foundation awards grants to projects that best address the following areas: hunger relief, youth and education, rural leadership, civic improvements, soil and water preservation, and arts and culture. Application procedures are available online.
Requirements: 501(c)3 community organizations serving Land O'Lakes dairy communities in Maryland, New Jersey, New York, Pennsylvania, and Virginia are eligible.
Restrictions: Grants will not be awarded for the following purposes: scholarship funds, gifts or fund raisers for individuals, or non-public church use.
Geographic Focus: Maryland, New Jersey, New York, Pennsylvania, Virginia
Amount: 500 - 5,000 USD
Contact: Bonnie Bassett, Executive Director; (651) 481-2222; (651) 481-2000; Bbbass@landolakes.com or MLAtkins Sakry@landolakes.com
Internet: http://www.foundation.landolakes.com/mida_desc.asp
Sponsor: Land O'Lakes Foundation
P.O. Box 64150
Saint Paul, MN 55164-0150

Lannan Foundation Indigenous Communities Program Grants **1047**
The program is designed to help Native Americans renew institutions and traditions. Funding priority is given to rural indigenous projects that are consistent with traditional values in the areas of education, Native cultures, the revival and preservation of languages, legal rights, and environmental protection. The foundation will consider multiyear requests for funding of project costs, operating costs, technical assistance, and collaborative activities that build organizational strength and community capacity. There are no application forms or deadlines; submit a letter of inquiry.
Geographic Focus: All U.S. States
Amount: 5,000 - 50,000 USD
Samples: Fort Yuma-Quechan Indian Tribe (Yuma, AZ)— for initiative to stop gold mine, $200,000; Pueblo of Zuni (Zuni, NM)—for legal support to stop coal mine and protect sacred lake, $200,000; Lost Children School (Browning, MT)—for a program where students in grades 5-8 are immersed in the Blackfoot language.
Contact: Grants Administrator; (505) 986-8160; (505) 986-8195; info@lannan.org
Internet: http://ee.lannan.org/lf/about/grant-guidelines
Sponsor: Lannan Foundation
313 Read Street
Santa Fe, NM 87501-2628

Laura B. Vogler Foundation Grants **1048**
The foundation supports innovative programs and projects in New York City and Long Island in the areas of education, health care, and social services. The foundation is particularly interested in organizations that serve and support children, the elderly, and the disadvantaged. Types of support include general operating support, program development, research grants, and seed money grants. Grants provide one-time, nonrenewable support.
Requirements: Nonprofit organizations in New York City and Long Island, NY, may submit proposals.
Restrictions: Grants are not awarded to support building or endowment funds, annual fund-raising campaigns, or matching gifts.
Geographic Focus: New York
Date(s) Application is Due: Mar 1; Jul 1; Nov 1
Amount: 1,000 - 5,000 USD
Contact: Lawrence D'Amato, President; (718) 423-3000; (718) 631-4808
Internet: http://fdncenter.org/grantmaker/vogler
Sponsor: Laura B. Vogler Foundation
P.O. Box 610508
Bayside, NY 11361-0508

Laurel Foundation Grants **1049**
The foundation awards grants in western Pennsylvania to nonprofit organizations operating in the fields of vocational education, the environment and conservation, cultural programs (including museums and the performing arts), health care and health organizations, population planning, and family planning. Grants are awarded to support general operations, capital campaigns, building construction/renovation, program development, conferences and seminars, publication, seed money, and curriculum development. Interested organizations should review the foundation's annual report before applying. Applicants may submit a brief letter of inquiry to the vice president or a formal proposal. Proposals may follow the format of the Common Grant Application of the Grantmakers of Western Pennsylvania. The narrative should be limited to 300 words. Application forms are not required. The board meets in June and December to consider requests.
Requirements: Nonprofit organizations in western Pennsylvania may submit applications.
Restrictions: Grants are not made to individuals.
Geographic Focus: Pennsylvania
Date(s) Application is Due: Apr 1; Oct 1
Amount: 1,000 - 100,000 USD
Samples: Frick Art and Historical Center (Pittsburgh, PA)—for general operating support, $25,000; Pennsylvania Assoc for the Blind (Pittsburgh, PA)—for facility improvements and program expansion, $10,000.
Contact: Donna Panazzi, Executive Director; (412) 765-2400; (412) 765-2407
Sponsor: Laurel Foundation
2 Gateway Center, Suite 1800
Pittsburgh, PA 15222

Lavelle Fund for the Blind Grants **1050**
The fund is dedicated to supporting programs that promote the spiritual, moral, intellectual, and physical development of blind and low-vision people of all ages, together with programs that help people avoid vision loss. Priority is given to agencies that concentrate on serving the New York City metropolitan area. The fund gives preference to program creation, expansion, or improvement. (General operating support is rarely provided.) Capital support is generally awarded only in connection with specific program support needs. Application guidelines are available online.
Requirements: 501(c)3 tax-exempt organizations are eligible.
Restrictions: The fund does not make grants to: individuals; medical research programs; conferences or media events (unless they are an integral part of a broader program of direct service); efforts to influence legislation or elections; or organizations seeking support for deficit reduction or emergency funding.
Geographic Focus: All U.S. States
Samples: Cancer Care (New York, NY)—to create a financial-assistance and support program for people with ocular cancers, $122,750 over 18 months; Catholic Near East Welfare Assoc (New York, NY)—for projects at five Palestinian schools for the blind or at vision-rehabilitation groups in the Jerusalem area and the West Bank and Gaza, $209,316 over three years; International Trachoma Initiative (New York, NY)—for a program that will provide sight-saving surgeries in Mali and Niger, two countries with extremely high rates of trachoma, $300,000 Over two years; Recording for the Blind and Dyslexic (Princeton, NJ)—to create 300 digitally recorded textbooks on mathematics, science, and technology, $320,000 over two years.
Contact: Andrew Fisher, Executive Director; (212) 668-9801; (212) 668-9803; afisher@lavellefund.org

Internet: http://fdncenter.org/grantmaker/lavellefund
Sponsor: Lavelle Fund for the Blind
80 Maiden Lane, Suite 1207
New York, NY 10038

Lawrence J. and Anne Rubenstein Charitable Foundation Grants 1051
The Foundation, established in 1963, supports organizations involved with early childhood services, and higher education, support also for programs for school preparedness. Giving primarily in Boston, MA and Philadelphia, PA. Contact the Foundation for further application information and guidelines.
Requirements: Nonprofits operating in the Boston, MA and Philadelphia, PA area are eligible.
Restrictions: No grants to individuals.
Geographic Focus: Massachusetts, Pennsylvania
Date(s) Application is Due: Apr 1; Oct 1
Samples: Dorchester Community Council, Dorchester, MA, $34,000 - for Pre-K literacy; Hebrew SeniorLife, Boston, MA, $20,000 - for senior fitness program; Camp Sunshine at Sebago Lake, Casco, ME, $15,000 - for general support
Contact: Susan W. Hunnewell, Foundation Contact c/o Ridgeway Advisors; (617) 279-8052; (617) 279-8059; shunnewelle@ridgewayadvisors.com
Sponsor: Lawrence J. and Anne Rubenstein Charitable Foundation
10 Post Office Square
Boston, MA 02109-4615

Lee and Ramona Bass Foundation Grants 1052
The foundation makes grants in Texas in the following categories: schools, colleges, and universities, with emphasis on faculty development and liberal arts programs; community programs and projects, particularly related to the arts and the environment, such as museums, zoos, and educational/research institutions; and national and regional conservation programs. Types of support include general operating support, building construction/renovation, endowment funds, and curriculum development. Preliminary inquiries are requested, in the form of a letter briefly describing the project or program, prior to the filing of formal applications. Proposals are by invitation. Guidelines are available online.
Requirements: Eligible organizations must have 501(c)3 status. Grant requests must be limited to programs and projects within the state of Texas.
Restrictions: No grants can be made to individuals.
Geographic Focus: Texas
Amount: 10,000 - 350,000 USD
Samples: All Saints' Episcopal School of Fort Worth (TX)—for its capital campaign, $1 million.
Contact: Valleau Wilkie Jr., Executive Director; (817) 336-0494; (817) 332-2176; cjohns@sidrichardson.org
Sponsor: Lee and Ramona Bass Foundation
309 Main Street
Fort Worth, TX 76102

Leicester Savings Bank Fund 1053
The Fund supports projects that improve the quality of life and build a stronger community in Leicester, Massachusetts. To receive funding, applicants must state how they will use the grant to do the following: make a positive difference for the Leicester community's vulnerable citizens; improve Leicester community life through community development, education, recreation, the arts, or human services; and attract other resources or secure matching funds from public or private sources. Grants are available for capital expenditures (to acquire or renovate property or equipment) or for operating expenses of specific programs or projects undertaken by associations or organizations.
Requirements: Any non-municipal association or nonprofit organization that serves residents of Leicester is invited to apply.
Restrictions: Grants will generally not be awarded to individuals or to municipal agencies.
Geographic Focus: Massachusetts
Date(s) Application is Due: Apr 15
Contact: Pamela B. Kane, (508) 755-0980; pkane@greaterworcester.org
Internet: http://www.greaterworcester.org/grants/LSB.htm
Sponsor: Greater Worcester Community Foundation
370 Main Street, Suite 650
Worcester, MA 01608-1738

Leland Fikes Foundation Grants 1054
Grants are awarded for medical research, mental health programs, social welfare, education, reproductive health care, and arts and culture. Building programs and equipment acquisition are supported in these areas. Support is rarely given to programs located outside of the Dallas area. Additional types of support include general operating support, continuing support, annual campaigns, capital campaigns, endowment funds, emergency funds, program development, professorships, seed money grants, scholarship funds, research, and matching funds. Contact the foundation for guidelines.
Requirements: Giving is primarily to Texas organizations.
Restrictions: Grants are not awarded to individuals.
Geographic Focus: Texas
Amount: 5,000 - 75,000 USD
Samples: Saint Marks School of Texas (Dallas, TX)—for capital campaign, $200,000; Texas Partnership for End-of-Life Care (Austin, TX)—for general support, $175,000; Planned Parenthood (TX)—for operating support.
Contact: Nancy Solana, (214) 754-0144
Sponsor: Leland Fikes Foundation
3050 Lincoln Plaza, 500 N Akard Street
Dallas, TX 75201

Leo Burnett Company Charitable Foundation Grants 1055
The charitable foundation supports at-risk youth projects and literacy programs in Chicago. The foundation currently is not making discretionary grants other than to local, major cultural institutions. Past support has been given in the areas of environmental affairs, wildlife protection, international affairs, and international relief efforts. Types of support include employee matching gifts, operating support, and project support. There are no application deadlines. Proposals are reviewed throughout the year.
Requirements: Illinois nonprofit organizations are eligible.
Geographic Focus: Illinois
Contact: Chris Kimball, (312) 220-5959; (312) 220-3299; belief@leoburnett.com
Internet: http://www.leoburnett.com
Sponsor: Leo Burnett Company Charitable Foundation
35 Wacker Drive
Chicago, IL 60601

Leo Goodwin Foundation Grants 1056
The foundation awards general operating grants, primarily in Florida, in the areas of cancer research, child welfare, education, hospitals, mental health, and youth. There are no application forms.
Requirements: Nonprofit organizations are eligible.
Restrictions: Individuals are not eligible.
Geographic Focus: Florida
Date(s) Application is Due: Oct 31
Amount: 1,000 - 80,000 USD
Contact: Helen Furia, Treasurer; (954) 491-2000
Sponsor: Leo Goodwin Foundation
800 Corporate Drive, Suite 510
Fort Lauderdale, FL 33334-3621

Leo Niessen Jr., Charitable Trust Grants 1057
Leo Niessen lived in Abington Township, Montgomery County, Pennsylvania. In 1993, his Foundation was funded from a testamentary bequest. He was a charitable man, who also made substantial philanthropic gifts to Holy Redeemer Hospital during his lifetime. He had a special affinity for Red Cloud Indian School of Pine Ridge, South Dakota. To this day, the Co-trustees of his Foundation continue to support this school, as well as the Hospital and The Society for the Propagation of the Faith. All grants are made in the memory of Leo Niessen and his family. The Foundation also supports organizations: that provide health services for all ages; which educate the needy and educable at all academic levels, without regard to age; working for and on behalf of youth and the elderly, and which provide assistance to the homeless and economically disadvantaged; which provide spiritual and emotional guidance. Application Deadlines are, January 31 and July 31. Application forms are available online. Applicants will receive notice acknowledging receipt of the grant request, and subsequently be notified of the grant declination or approval.
Requirements: Pennsylvania 501(c)3 nonprofit organizations are eligible to apply. Proposals should be submitted in the following format: completed Common Grant Application Form; an original Proposal Statement; an audited financial report and a current year operating budget; a copy of your official IRS Letter with your tax determination; a listing of your Board of Directors.

Proposal Statements (second item in the above Format) should answer these questions: what are the objectives and expected outcomes of this program/project/request; what strategies will be used to accomplish your objective; what is the timeline for completion; if this is part of an on-going program, how long has it been in operation; what criteria will you use to measure success; if the request is not fully funded, what other sources can you engage; an Itemized budget should be included; please describe any collaborative ventures. Prior to the distribution of funds, all approved grantees must sign and return a Grant Agreement Form, stating that the funds will be used for the purpose intended. Progress reports and Completion reports must also be filed as required for your specific grant. All current grantees must be in good standing with required documentation prior to submitting new proposals to any foundation.
Restrictions: Grants are not made for political purposes, nor to organizations which discriminate on the basis of race, ethnic origin, sexual or religious preference, age or gender. The Niessen Foundation normally does not consider grants for endowment.
Geographic Focus: Pennsylvania
Date(s) Application is Due: Jan 31; Jul 31
Amount: 10,000 - 60,000 USD
Contact: Wachovia Bank, N.A., Trustee; grantinquiries3@wachovia.com
Internet: https://www.wachovia.com/foundation/v/index.jsp?vgnextoid=345852199c0aa110VgnVCM1000004b0d1872RCRD&vgnextfmt=default
Sponsor: Leo Niessen Jr., Charitable Trust
Wachovia Bank, N A. PA 1279, 1234 East Broad Street
Philadelphia, PA 19109-1199

Leon Lowenstein Foundation Grants **1058**
The foundation awards grants to eligible organizations in its areas of interest, including education, medical research, and disaster relief. Types of support include research grants, general operating support, program development, and seed funding. There are no application deadlines or forms. The board meets twice each year to consider requests.
Requirements: Nonprofit organizations are eligible. Preference will be given to requests from the New York City metropolitan area.
Geographic Focus: All U.S. States
Samples: U of Pennsylvania (Philadelphia, PA)—to create a loan-forgiveness fund for MBA graduates of the Wharton School who pursue careers at public and nonprofit institutions, $2.5 million.
Contact: Executive Director; (212) 319-0670; (212) 688-0134
Sponsor: Leon Lowenstein Foundation
126 E 56th Street
New York, NY 10022

Levi Strauss Foundation Grantss **1059**
The Levi Strauss Foundation Community Partnership program awards contributions to nonprofit community agencies in the following areas: reducing poverty; youth and women; economic development (job creation and community-based economic development); job training, placement, and access; leadership development aimed at strengthening the economic development capacity of community organizations; international education, health care, and peace; and microenterprise. The program also supports AIDS and disease prevention (assistance to people with AIDS and their caregivers); risk reduction education for those with high-risk behaviors; and services to populations severely affected by AIDS. Contributions are also made in the field of social justice (programs that seek to remove racial and other discriminatory barriers, ease tension between groups, promote diversity in community leadership, and prevent violent acts of racial and cultural prejudice). Types of support include matching funds, continuing support, seed money, equipment, exchange programs, employee-related scholarships, employee matching gifts, technical assistance, special projects, and operating budgets. Contact the foundation for more information and application guidelines.
Requirements: Giving is on a national basis with emphasis on areas of company operations. Agencies receiving funding must be accredited charitable organizations or public entities and have boards or advisory groups that reflect the population or communities being served.
Restrictions: The company does not fund projects by individuals or for political, sectarian, or religious purposes; tickets for dinners or other special events; requests for sponsorships; or courtesy advertising. Research and conferences are generally not considered for funding unless they are an integral part of a larger effort that the company is supporting. The foundation does not accept unsolicited proposals.
Geographic Focus: All U.S. States
Samples: American Institute for Public Service (Wilmington, DE)—for support for 2003 Jefferson Awards, $20,000; The Asia Foundation (San Francisco, CA)— for the Labor Projects Workshop, $27,000; Citizens' Scholarship Foundation of America (Saint Peter, MN)—for the Families of Freedom Scholarship Fund, to provide undergraduate scholarships for the spouses and children of people injured or killed as a result of the September 11 terrorist attacks, $500,000.
Contact: Theresa Fay-Bustillos, Executive Director; (415) 501-3577; (415) 501-6575; lsf@levi.com
Internet: http://www.levistrauss.com/responsibility/foundation/guidelines.htm
Sponsor: Levi Strauss Foundation
1155 Battery Street, P.O. Box 7215
San Francisco, CA 94111

Lewis Preston Fund for Girls Education Grants **1060**
The fund supports women's groups that advance the human rights of women and girls. Grants support women's groups based outside the United States by providing small, flexible, and timely grants for operating and project expenses. Grantees address issues that include but are not limited to building peace and ending gender-based violence; advancing health and sexual and reproductive rights; expanding civic and political participation; ensuring economic and environmental justice; increasing access to education; and fostering social change philanthropy. In addition urgent requests for support to organize or participate in local, regional, or international meetings and conferences will be considered outside of the normal grant cycle. These types of requests must come from organizations, not individuals, and must be received at least eight weeks before the event. Funds for these types of grants are limited. Guidelines are available online.
Requirements: The applicant group must be based in a country outside the United States; demonstrate a strong commitment to women's equality and human rights that is clearly reflected in its activities; be a group of women working together; and be governed, directed, and led by women.
Restrictions: Grants do not support individuals; scholarships; academic research; groups based and working primarily or only in the United States; international organizations proposing projects with local partners; groups without a strong women's rights focus; groups headed and managed by men, or without women in the majority of leadership positions; groups whose sole purpose is to generate income or to provide charity to individuals; or political parties or election campaigns.
Geographic Focus: All U.S. States
Amount: 500 - 20,000 USD
Contact: Executive Assistant; (415) 202-7640; (415) 202-8604; proposals@globalfundforwomen.org
Internet: http://www.globalfundforwomen.org/1work/programs/preston.html
Sponsor: Global Fund for Women
1375 Sutter Street, Suite 400
San Francisco, CA 94109

Liberty Hill Foundation Seed Fund Grants **1061**
The hallmark of Liberty Hill's grant making is its Seed Fund, providing one-year grants of $10,000 to $20,000 to organizations tackling social, racial and economic justice issues that are often too new or too controversial to attract funding from more traditional sources. The Seed Fund is often the catalyst that turns someone's vision for a better future into a solid plan of action capable of changing lives as well as communities.
Requirements: Los Angeles County, California, grassroots, proactive, community organizations that are committed to diversity, with a record of leadership development through a democratic process, are eligible.
Restrictions: The foundation does not fund social service providers that do not have a strong community organizing component, projects directed at constituencies outside Los Angeles County, individual efforts, film projects, groups that received foundation funding in the previous funding cycle, direct union organizing, nor businesses or profit-making ventures. Liberty Hill generally does not fund travel expenses, equipment purchases, or research.
Geographic Focus: California
Date(s) Application is Due: Aug 15
Amount: 10,000 - 20,000 USD
Samples: A New Way of Life Re-Entry Program, Los Angeles, California, $20,000—support for the Empowering Communities for Change project; Coalition Against Militarism in Our School, Los Angeles, California, $10,000—funding for the CAMS Adopt-A-School Project.

Contact: James Williams, (310) 453-3611, ext. 114; (310) 453-7806; jwilliams@libertyhill.org or info@libertyhill.org
Internet: http://libertyhill.org/donor/seed.html
Sponsor: Liberty Hill Foundation
2121 Cloverfield Boulevard, Suite 113
Santa Monica, CA 90404

Libra Foundation Grants **1062**
The foundation awards operating grants to nonprofits in Maine in its areas of interest, including art, culture, and humanities; education; health; human services; environment; justice; public/society benefit; and religion. Application are due quarterly.
Requirements: Maine 501(c)3 nonprofits and nonprofits serving the state may apply.
Restrictions: Individuals are ineligible. Grants do not provide funding to supplement annual campaigns or for regular operating needs, multiyear projects, scholarships, or travel.
Geographic Focus: Maine
Date(s) Application is Due: Feb 15; May 15; Aug 15; Nov 15
Amount: Up to 25,000 USD
Samples: Maine Lighthouse Museum (ME)—to construct a home for the Maine Lighthouse Museum and its collection, $10,000; Colby College (Waterville, ME)—program support for Colby Cares About Kids, $20,000; Shalom House (Portland, ME)—for construction of a mixed-use development to provide affordable housing, $25,000; YWCA Bangor-Brewer (Bangor, ME)—to support the core programs and services that make the YWCA so important to the community, $10,000.
Contact: Elizabeth Flaherty, (207) 879-6280; (207) 879-6281
Internet: http://www.librafoundation.org
Sponsor: Libra Foundation
P.O. Box 17516
Portland, ME 04112-8516

Lifebridge Foundation Grants **1063**
U.S. nonprofit organizations receive foundation support for a wide range of environmental, educational, and arts projects that create bridges of understanding among diverse populations. Past grants have funded studies in parapsychology, land purchase for a shamanic learning center, and research on the survival of the personality after death. The foundation makes grants for projects, general operating support, seed money, and challenge/matching purposes. Funding generally extends for a maximum of three years.
Requirements: Nonprofit organizations, individuals sponsored by nonprofit organizations, and individuals working independently on specific projects are eligible for funding. The foundation generally preselects its grantees, but also accepts introductory letters. A letter should be no more than three pages and should describe how the organization or project specifically reflects foundation's purposes and aims. Do not include any other supporting materials. Individuals seeking support for a specific project should include a resume or brief biography only.
Restrictions: No introductory letters sent via email will be accepted.
Geographic Focus: All U.S. States
Amount: 2,000 - 10,000 USD
Contact: Robert Silverstein, Communications Manager; (212) 757-9711; (212) 757-0246; LifebridgeNYC@aol.com
Internet: http://www.lifebridge.org/policy.htm
Sponsor: Lifebridge Foundation
P.O. Box 793, Times Square Station
New York, NY 10108

Lightner Sams Foundation of Wyoming Grants **1064**
The foundation awards grants primarily to Texas nonprofit organizations in its areas of interest, including arts and culture, education, women, and social services. Types of support include general operating support, continuing support, annual campaigns, capital campaigns, building construction/renovation, equipment acquisition, and matching funds. There are no application deadlines or forms. The board meets quarterly to consider requests.
Requirements: Giving is limited to the Dallas, TX metroplex area.
Restrictions: Grants are not made to individuals.
Geographic Focus: Texas
Date(s) Application is Due: Feb 1; Jun 1; Oct 1
Amount: 300 - 42,000 USD
Samples: Goodwill Industries of Dallas (Dallas, TX)—for capital campaign, $12,500; American Foundation for the Blind (Dallas, TX)—for operating support, $1000.
Contact: Larry Lightner, (972) 458-8811; (972) 458-8812; foundation@lightnersams.org
Sponsor: Lightner Sams Foundation of Wyoming
5400 LBJ Freeway, Suite 515
Dallas, TX 75240

Lillian S. Wells Foundation Grants **1065**
The Lillian S. Wells Foundation established in 1976, primarily supports the Fort Lauderdale, Florida, and Chicago, Illinois regions with funding interests that include: medical research, with emphasis on brain cancer research, women's health, substance abuse, and at-risk youth. Additional funding for education and the arts. Contact the Foundation for an application form, the Board meets quarterly in January, April, July, and October.
Requirements: Nonprofit organizations in Chicago, Illinois and Fort Lauderdale, Florida area are eligible to apply.
Geographic Focus: Florida, Illinois
Date(s) Application is Due: Mar 15; Jun 15; Sep 15; Dec 15
Amount: 1,000 - 1,900,000 USD
Contact: Patricia Mulvaney, Executive Director; patricia.mulvaney@thewellsfamily.net
Sponsor: Lillian S. Wells Foundation
600 Sagamore Road
Fort Lauderdale, FL 33301-2215

Lilly Endowment Educational Leadership Grants **1066**
The program supports projects that foster educational reform in Indiana by improving the quality of the state's instructors; design creative and unconventional professional development experiences for school leaders' long- and short-term growth; and encourage administrators to expand their skills, explore new ideas, and sharpen their vision as advocates for Indiana's youth. Projects must fall between July 1 of the current year and June 30 of the next. Projects that seek to deepen a community's expertise about the key issues of leadership in schools will receive priority consideration.
Requirements: Only Indiana organizations are eligible to apply.
Geographic Focus: Indiana
Samples: Vincennes U Foundation (IN)—for the Tech Works Partnership Fund for Faculty and Program Excellence, $1.5 million; Indiana Institute of Technology (Fort Wayne, IN)—for a faculty-development fund, $1 million.
Contact: Sue Ellen Walker, Communications Associate; (317) 924-5471; (317) 926-4431
Internet: http://www.lillyendowment.org
Sponsor: Lilly Endowment
2801 N Meridian Street, P.O. Box 88068
Indianapolis, IN 46208-0068

Lilly Endowment Giving Indiana Funds for Tomorrow Grants **1067**
The goal of this program is to expand the concept of community foundations to Indiana counties and to increase the endowments of existing community foundations in the state.
Requirements: Applications will be accepted from viable community foundations in Indiana counties. Only one application will be accepted per county. Multicounty foundations may submit one application for each county served.
Restrictions: Only Indiana organizations are eligible to apply. The Endowment generally does not support loans or cash grants to private individuals; requests to discharge pre-existing debts of individuals or organizations; health-care projects; mass media projects; libraries; or organizations outside of Indianapolis.
Geographic Focus: Indiana
Samples: Community foundations throughout Indiana (IN)—for unrestricted use, operating funds, or both, through the GIFT Initiative, $189 million; Indiana Grantmakers Alliance Foundation (Indianapolis, IN)—to provide technical assistance to the GIFT Initiative, $504,364; Community Ctrs of Indianapolis (IN)—for transitional support, $1 million; Lawrence County Community Foundation (Bedford, IN)—for program support, $130,000.
Contact: W.R. 'Ace' Yakey Jr., (317) 916-7342
Internet: http://www.lillyendowment.org/communitydevelopment.html
Sponsor: Lilly Endowment
2801 N Meridian Street, P.O. Box 88068
Indianapolis, IN 46208-0068

Lilly Endowment Grants **1068**

Areas for which funds are granted include religion—denominational studies, congregational studies, urban ministry, etc; leadership education—training for trustees of educational institutions, including community leadership and other community-based nonprofit organizations; education—higher education, faculty and institutional development, minority doctoral education at Big Ten and UNCF-affiliated schools, dropout prevention, etc; youth—community guidance programs, support for African American males; and community development—improved low-income housing, the United Way, statewide expansion in support of community foundations, arts and culture, etc. Religion, public policy, and select research and pilot programs are national in scope. Community development and education grants are mainly restricted to Indiana and UNCF colleges and universities. Applications are accepted at any time.

Requirements: Applicant should send a letter describing credentials of organization, project proposed, and amount of funding requested.

Restrictions: The endowment does not consider applications for health care and biological science projects, mass media initiatives, endowments or endowed chairs, libraries, building campaigns, K-12 schools, or general operations.

Geographic Focus: All U.S. States

Amount: Up to 100,000,000 USD

Samples: Heartland Film Festival (Indianapolis, IN)—to expand its programs, strengthen its finances, and develop additional opportunities for filmmakers to showcase their work, $3.7 million; U of Indianapolis (IN)—for efforts to recruit and retain outstanding faculty members and students, $1 million; Indiana U at Bloomington (IN)—for life-sciences research, primarily for studies of genetic coding and the internal workings of cells, $53 million.

Contact: Sue Ellen Walker, Communications Associate; (317) 924-5471; (317) 926-4431

Internet: http://www.lillyendowment.org

Sponsor: Lilly Endowment
2801 N Meridian Street, P.O. Box 88068
Indianapolis, IN 46208-0068

Lilly Endowment Indiana Camp Ministries Enhancement Grants **1069**

The program awards grants to support general operations and capital improvements at Christian church-related youth camps. Grants are intended to enhance a camp's ability to provide young people with religious education and spiritual and leadership development. Send applications to P.O. Box 88068, Indianapolis, IN 46208.

Requirements: Christian denominations, congregations, and other religious organizations that own and operate camps in Indiana are eligible. The camps should serve more than one congregation.

Geographic Focus: Indiana

Amount: 100,000,000 USD

Samples: Independent Colleges of Indiana (Indianapolis, Indiana)—for Lilly Endowment Community Scholarship Program, $28 million; University of Evansville (Evansville, Indiana)—for capital support to develop Institute of Global Enterprise, effort to integrate liberal arts with business and professional programs through development of experiential education initiatives, $15 million.

Contact: Sue Ellen Walker, (317) 924-5471; (317) 926-4431

Internet: http://www.lillyendowment.org

Sponsor: Lilly Endowment
2801 N Meridian Street, P.O. Box 88068
Indianapolis, IN 46208-0068

Lilly Endowment National Clergy Renewal Grants **1070**

The program seeks to strengthen Christian congregations by providing an opportunity for pastors to step away briefly from the persistent obligations of daily parish life and to engage in a period of renewal and reflection. Renewal periods are not vacations, but times for intentional exploration and reflection, religious rejuvenation, and regaining enthusiasm and creativity for ministry. High-quality proposals should include a strong sense of purpose; a sense of balance; evidence that the congregation understands and affirms the value of a renewal program for its leader; and benefits for both the pastor and the congregation. It is anticipated that approximately 125 grants will be awarded directly to congregations for the support of a renewal program for their pastor. Up to $15,000 of the grant may be used for congregational expenses associated with the renewal program.

Requirements: A Christian congregation whose ordained pastor has a master of divinity degree is eligible.

Restrictions: The program for Indiana congregation continues, so Indiana pastors are ineligible for the national program.

Geographic Focus: All U.S. States

Date(s) Application is Due: May 15

Amount: Up to 45,000 USD

Contact: National Clergy Renewal Program Office; (317) 916-7302; (317) 926-4431; clergyrenewal@yahoo.com

Internet: http://www.clergyrenewal.org

Sponsor: Lilly Endowment
2801 N Meridian Street, P.O. Box 88068
Indianapolis, IN 46208-0068

Lincoln Community Foundation Grants **1071**

The foundation offers program, capital, and quick response grants. Program grants are available to fund the creation of new programs or the enhancement of existing programs within nonprofit organizations. These grants are given in support of programs that focus on the areas of basic needs, children and youth, older adults, human diversity, family issues, environmental enhancement and cultural arts. Capital grants are available to help nonprofit organizations fund the construction of a new facility or facility addition, the renovation or purchase of an existing facility, and/or the purchase of equipment (including furnishings and computer equipment). Quick response grants are available to nonprofit organizations to provide quick solutions to unexpected needs or special opportunities. These grants give nonprofits the opportunity to meet requests that could not typically be responded to due to the traditional application process and timeline or lack of funding sources. Deadlines listed are for program grants.

Requirements: IRS 501(c)3 organizations serving the Lincoln, NE, area are eligible.

Restrictions: Grants are not awarded to individuals, and requests are generally not considered for religious purposes, political purposes, endowments, programs outside the Lincoln/Lancaster County area, routine operating expenses, large capital expenditures, budget deficits, and projects with future annual commitments.

Geographic Focus: Nebraska

Date(s) Application is Due: Jun 1; Dec 1

Amount: 50 - 50,000 USD

Samples: 7th Street Loft Consortium (Lincoln, NE)—to develop a capital campaign, $11,500; Good Neighbor Community Ctr (Lincoln, NE)—for salary support of a part-time coordinator responsible for resource development and volunteer management, $14,000; Lincoln Literacy Council (Lincoln, NE)—for a program that promotes greater parental involvement in their children's education and activities, $14,736.

Contact: Debra Shoemaker, Program Director; (402) 474-2345; (402) 476-8532; debs@lcf.org or lcf@lcf.org

Internet: http://www.lcf.org

Sponsor: Lincoln Community Foundation
215 Centennial Mall S, Suite 200
Lincoln, NE 68508

Lippard-Clawiter Foundation Grants **1072**

The foundation awards grants in Chouteau County in its areas of interest, including children and youth services, community development, and recreation. Types of support include general operating support and equipment acquisition.

Requirements: Chouteau County, MT, nonprofits are eligible.

Restrictions: Individuals are ineligible.

Geographic Focus: Montana

Amount: Up to 275,000 USD

Samples: Chouteau County Fair Board (Fort Benton, MT)—for renovation of fair ground buildings and for chairs, $25,000; Chouteau County Free Library Foundation (Fort Benton, MT)—for installation of elevator, $15,000.

Contact: Rodney Thorne, Secretary-Treasurer; (406) 727-0888

Sponsor: Lippard-Clawiter Foundation
P.O. Box 1605
Great Falls, MT 59403

Little River Foundation Grants **1073**

The foundation supports nonprofit organizations in the Mid-Atlantic states, primarily New Jersey, New York, and Pennsylvania. Grants are awarded for hospitals, AIDS research, substance abuse services, higher education, secondary education, early childhood education, adult basic education, building funds, literacy programs, animal welfare, legal education, international studies

in Africa, environmental conservation, legal services, religious organizations, and community funds. Grants are awarded for general operating support, annual campaigns, endowment funds, conferences and seminars, research, and building construction/renovations. Application forms are not required. The board meets each year in the fall.
Requirements: Only residents of Maryland, New Jersey, New York, Pennsylvania, and Virginia may apply.
Geographic Focus: California, New York, Virginia
Amount: 100 - 175,000 USD
Samples: Grace Episcopal Church (The Plains, VA)—for facilities improvement, $25,000; Piedmont Environmental Council (Warrenton, VA)—for the building program, $87,000; Johns Hopkins U (Baltimore, MD)—for brain tumor research, $25,000; Princeton U (Princeton, NJ)—for annual support, $25,000.
Contact: Dale Hogoboom, Assistant Treasurer
Sponsor: Little River Foundation
101 Park Avenue, Suite 3500
New York, NY 10178-0061

Livingston Memorial Foundation Grants **1074**
The foundation awards grants to promote medical and health-related services of benefit to the underserved and uninsured people of Ventura County, CA. General operating grants support well-established programs that continue to have positive results. Special projects grants support organizations that can demonstrate the need for assistance in funding a special project or with the cost of medical equipment that promises significant positive results. Organizations should submit a brief letter of inquiry that includes a concise statement of the need for the funds, the amount requested, pertinent factual information, and state the desired type of grant. Include a copy of the tax-exemption letter.
Requirements: California nonprofit organizations serving Ventura County are eligible.
Restrictions: Grants are not awarded to individuals or for projects normally financed from government sources, conferences, seminars, workshops, exhibits, travel, or publication.
Geographic Focus: California
Amount: 2,500 - 156,000 USD
Contact: Laura McAvoy, (805) 495-7489; Lmcavoy@jdplaw.com
Sponsor: Livingston Memorial Foundation
2815 Townsgate Road, Suite 200
Westlake Village, CA 91361

Liz Claiborne Foundation Grants **1075**
Liz Claiborne Inc.'s founders established the Liz Claiborne Foundation to serve as the company's center for charitable activities. The Liz Claiborne Foundation is a separate nonprofit legal entity, which supports organizations in the U.S. communities where Liz Claiborne Inc.'s primary offices are located. These include the five boroughs of New York City; Hudson County, New Jersey; and Los Angeles County, California. In addition, a small portion of the grants may be directed to national organizations addressing critical issues for women, specifically women's economic independence. The mission of the Liz Claiborne Foundation is as follows: Established in 1981, the Liz Claiborne Foundation supports nonprofit organizations working with women to achieve economic independence by supporting multi-dimensional programs that offer essential job readiness training and increase access to tools that help women, including those affected by domestic violence, transition from poverty into successful independent living.
Requirements: Non-profits in the five boroughs of New York City; Hudson County, New Jersey; and Los Angeles County, California are eligible to apply for funding.
Restrictions: Religious organizations and individuals are ineligible for grants.
Geographic Focus: California, New Jersey, New York
Contact: Melanie Lyons, Vice President; (212) 626-5704; (212) 626-5304
Internet: http://www.lizclaiborneinc.com/foundation/default.asp
Sponsor: Liz Claiborne Foundation
1440 Broadway
New York, NY 10018

Lloyd A. Fry Foundation Grants **1076**
The foundation supports organizations with the strength and commitment to address persistent problems of urban Chicago resulting from poverty, violence, ignorance, and despair. The foundation is specifically interested in programs that improve conditions for low-income, underserved communities. Grants are made in four major fields: education, community services, health, and arts and culture. Generally, priority is given to proposals for the initiation of new programs or the strategic expansion or enhancement of existing programming. Programs that build the capacity of the individuals served also are encouraged. Former and current grantee organizations may submit proposals for projects that strengthen an organization's capacity, including requests for strategic planning, program evaluation, board and staff development, fundraising, and the application of technology. An organization that has received three years of funding for either general operating support or a specific program will generally be asked to take a year off in seeking support during the following year. Guidelines are available online. We are also interested in funding advocacy activities that focus on ensuring that low-income communities and individuals in Chicago are being treated fairly and are getting the services they deserve
Requirements: Grants are made only to tax-exempt organizations and are rarely made to organizations outside the Chicago metropolitan area.
Restrictions: The foundation does not fund government entities, political or religious activities, fundraising events, or medical research.
Geographic Focus: Illinois
Date(s) Application is Due: Mar 1; Jun 1; Sep 1; Dec 1
Samples: Changing Worlds (Chicago, IL)—for the Literacy and Cultural Connections Program and the Summer Institute for Teachers, $10,000; Hamdard Ctr for Health and Human Services (Addison, IL)—for the Employment Training Program serving Chicago residents, $20,000; Planned Parenthood of the Chicago Area (IL)—for the Community Partnership with Chicago Public Schools, $20,000; Chicago Children's Choir (IL)—for the in-school and neighborhood choir programs, $20,000.
Contact: Unmi Song, Executive Director; (312) 580-0310; (312) 580-0980; usong@fryfoundation.org
Internet: http://www.fryfoundation.org/guidelines.html
Sponsor: Lloyd A. Fry Foundation
120 S La Salle Street, Suite 1950
Chicago, IL 60603

Lloyd G. Balfour Foundation Attleboro-Specific Charities Grants **1077**
The Lloyd G. Balfour Foundation was established in 1973. The Foundation's 3 primary focus areas reflect Mr. Balfour's strong affinity for the employees of the Balfour Company; his commitment to the city of Attleboro, Massachusetts; and his lifelong interest in education. The Foundation supports organizations that specifically serve the people of Attleboro, with special consideration given to organizations that provide educational, human services, and health care programming for underserved populations. The application deadline for Attleboro-specific charities is February 1.
Requirements: 501(c)3 organizations serving the residents of Attleboro, Massachusetts, Maine, New Hampshire, Rhode Island, and Vermont are eligible to apply.
Geographic Focus: Massachusetts
Date(s) Application is Due: Feb 1
Amount: 75,000 - 200,000 USD
Contact: Miki C. Akimoto, Vice President; (866) 778-6859; miki.akimoto@baml.co
Internet: https://www.bankofamerica.com/philanthropic/fn_search.action
Sponsor: Lloyd G. Balfour Foundation
225 Franklin Street, 4th Floor, MA1-225-04-02
Boston, MA 02110

Loews Foundation Grants **1078**
The foundation supports Jewish causes and organizations in Israel. Types of support include matching gifts, general support grants, and scholarships.
Requirements: Organizations in Israel are eligible to apply.
Geographic Focus: All U.S. States
Amount: 1,000 - 50,000 USD
Contact: Candace Leeds, (212) 521-2650; (212) 521-2634
Sponsor: Loews Foundation
655 Madison Avenue
New York, NY 10021

Lois and Richard England Family Foundation Grants **1079**
The foundation is committed to improving the lives of those in need in the Washington metropolitan area. Grants focus on local human services—comprehensive services that enable low-income families or individuals to become self-sufficient, to live independently, or provide employment and training; education—preschool, elementary, and secondary education; and enrichment programs, particularly for children in underserved communities; and arts and culture—directed at local institutions, especially organizations

with community outreach. Access to arts education for disadvantaged children is a key interest. The foundation also supports targeted programs to enhance Jewish life and causes locally, nationally and internationally. There is no formal application procedure; the foundation requests a brief proposal.
Requirements: The foundation supports programs in the Washington, DC, metropolitan area, and for targeted programs to enhance Jewish life and causes locally, nationally, and internationally.
Geographic Focus: All U.S. States
Amount: 500 - 15,000 USD
Samples: Washington AIDS Partnership (Washington, DC)—to support AIDS prevention, education, and treatment, $10,000; New Israel Fund (Washington, DC)—to make small grants to nonprofit organizations in Israel, $15,000; Washington Ballet (Washington, DC)—for its educational programs, $10,000; Latin American Youth Ctr (Washington, DC)—for general operating support, $102,750.
Contact: Program Director; (202) 244-4636; (202) 244-9566; engfmfnd@mail.clark.net
Internet: http://fdncenter.org/grantmaker/england/guide.html
Sponsor: Lois and Richard England Family Foundation
P.O. Box 11582
Washington, DC 20008

Lotus 88 Foundation for Women and Children Grants **1080**
The foundation's mission is to promote the empowerment of women and children through supporting their economic, emotional, and spiritual development. The foundation's focus area is American Indian Country. Grants are awarded in Indian Country for two strategic purposes: revitalizing the council tipis as spiritual, cultural, and service centers; and providing the basic needs through community building. Community building grants are intended to promote and support community building in Indian Country to improve basic living conditions and to encourage a more positive future. Tipi project grants are made to help tribal women living on reservation or off reservation in building community. Grants support cultural and social services, tribal gatherings, educational programs, healing and purification ceremonies, and retreats. Each proposal should identify the specific needs and uses for the tipi and should identify a nonprofit program partner working in the tribal area who will work with the foundation on the project. Contact the Foundation directly for application and additional guideline information.
Requirements: Projects in American Indian communities are eligible.
Geographic Focus: All U.S. States
Contact: Patricia Stout, President; (510) 841-4123; (510) 841-4093; benita@lotus88.org
Internet: http://lotus88.net/
Sponsor: Lotus 88 Foundation for Women and Children
127 University Avenue, P.O. Box 10728
Berkeley, CA 94710

Louie M. and Betty M. Phillips Foundation Grants **1081**
The foundation supports a variety of organizations, primarily in Nashville, TN, in the fields of health, human services, civic affairs, education, and the arts. Types of support include annual operating grants for selected organizations contributing significantly to the Nashville area; one-year project and program grants for specific projects or equipment; and capital support (five-years maximum) for major capital projects of organizations with strong records of community service. Highest priority is given to nonprofits that were supported by Mr. and Mrs. Phillips.
Requirements: Nonprofit organizations are eligible. With rare exceptions, grants are limited to organizations in the greater Nashville, TN, area.
Restrictions: The foundation does not support individuals or their projects, private foundations, political activities, advertising, or sponsorships. In general, the foundation does not support projects, programs, or organizations that serve a limited audience or a relatively small number of people; disease-specific organizations; biomedical or clinical research; organizations whose principal impact is outside the Nashville area; or tax-supported institutions.
Geographic Focus: Tennessee
Date(s) Application is Due: Jun 1; Oct 31
Amount: 1,000 - 20,000 USD
Contact: Louie Buntin, (615) 385-5949; (615) 385-2507; louie@phillipsfoundation.org
Internet: http://www.phillipsfoundation.org
Sponsor: Louie M. and Betty M. Phillips Foundation
3334 Powell Avenue, P.O. Box 40788
Nashville, TN 37204

Louis Calder Foundation Grants **1082**
The Louis Calder Foundation seeks to promote the educational and scholastic development of children and youth by improving academic content at charter and parochial schools and at community based organizations. The Foundation's grant making will focus on opportunities for schools and community based organizations in communities within the Northeast Corridor with populations no greater than 500,000 to undertake such efforts during the regular school hours as well as the out-of-school or extended-day hours. New and existing charter schools, parochial schools and community based organizations are invited to submit a letter of inquiry with a summary of their plans to improve or initiate programs and projects designed to deliver classical education in areas of literacy, history, ethics, mathematics and the sciences. The Foundation has no formal application form and requests that organizations use the Philanthropy New York Common Application Form (available at the Foundation's website).
Requirements: New and existing charter schools, parochial schools and community based organizations are invited to submit a letter of inquiry with a summary of their plans to improve or initiate programs and projects designed to deliver classical education in areas of literacy, history, ethics, mathematics and the sciences. There is no application deadline when applying for funding.
Restrictions: The Foundation does not provide long term continuing program support and requests for renewed support are considered on the basis of reports received, site visits and Foundation priorities.
Geographic Focus: All U.S. States
Amount: 5,000 - 600,000 USD
Samples: Achievement First, Inc., New Haven, Connecticut, $300,000 - program expansion (2010); Friends of Catholic Urban Schools, Street Paul, Minnesota, $229,000 - curriculum development in three consortium schools (2010); Core Knowledge Foundation, Charlottesville, Virginia, $600,000 - Core Knowledge Language Arts K-2 curriculum (2010).
Contact: Holly Nuechterlein, Grants Director; (203) 966-8925; (203) 966-5785; proposals@calderfdn.org
Internet: http://www.louiscalderfdn.org/gguide.html
Sponsor: Louis Calder Foundation
175 Elm Street
New Canaan, CT 06840

Louisiana State Arts Council General Operating Support Program **1083**
The program provides support for organizations whose programming has major impact on their communities and on the state's cultural environment. There are two funding levels. Level One provides support for organizations whose annual budget is $500,000 or more and who have paid, professional staff responsible for the administrative and artistic functions of the organization. Level Two provides support for organizations whose budget is at least $250,000 but less than $500,000. Organizations intending to use grant money for the hiring of a director or supplementing a director's salary should contact the division staff for special technical assistance before making application. First-time applicants should also contact the staff for special technical assistance before applying.
Requirements: Louisiana nonprofit 501(c)3 organizations are eligible. Applicants for both Level One and Level Two funding must have been incorporated as an arts producing and programming organization for at least three years prior to the application deadline; have an independent governing board empowered to formulate policies and execute programs; have significant educational outreach for children and adults; provide a full season of 26 weeks or more of public programming to include production or exhibitions, educational activities, outreach programs, and free public performances; have produced at least one free community performance during the preceding year; and provided with the application a complete copy of an independent financial audit for the organization's prior year if such audit has not been previously submitted. In addition, Level One applicants must provide a copy of the organization's long-range plan with application. Level Two applicants must provide a three-year, long-range plan with their application addressing the following areas: artistic program, educational outreach, fund raising and development, personnel/staff development, financial development, and marketing. Grants must be matched by cash reflected in the operating budget approved by the organization's governing board.
Restrictions: Grants will not be made to fund exhibitions or productions by children or students in grades K-12 or performances or exhibitions primarily for student audiences. In addition, the program does not support projects that pay children or students in grades K-12 or in undergraduate degree programs. Applicants for these grants are not eligible to apply for funding under the project assistance program.

Geographic Focus: Louisiana
Date(s) Application is Due: Mar 1
Contact: Program Officer, Major Art Institutions; (225) 342-8180; (225) 342-8173; arts@crt.state.la.us
Internet: http://www.crt.state.la.us/arts/04_06Guidedwnld.htm
Sponsor: Louisiana State Arts Council and Division of the Arts
P.O. Box 44247
Baton Rouge, LA 70804-4247

Louisiana State Arts Council Local Arts Agency Level One Grants 1084
A local arts agency (LAA) is a government agency or nonprofit community organization, officially designated by municipal or parish governments to provide financing, services, or other programs for arts organizations and individual artists within a city, parish, or region of adjacent parishes. The Level One program is designed for established local arts agencies that provide diverse programs and services in their communities or region. There should be a significant relationship between local government and the LAA. Grant applications and plans submitted must indicate the impact of LAA activities on the economy of the community or region. This program is designed for mature organizations with a record of successful service and administrative competence. General support funds may be used at the discretion of the agency for a variety of purposes such as arts programs, salaries, artist fees, supplies, or operating expenses. Applicants may request general support grants of up to 25 percent of the agency's actual cash operating revenues for the prior fiscal year (excluding grants from the division).
Requirements: Louisiana 501(c)3 nonprofit organizations may apply. In addition, Level One applicants must be officially designated by the municipal or parish governing body with jurisdiction over the service area to act on its behalf as the local arts agency; have at least one full-time, paid professional staff member; have a governing board with the responsibility and the legal power to set agency policy; have had annual operating revenues of $100,000 or more for the preceding fiscal year; provide, with the application, a complete copy of an independent financial audit for the organization's prior year (if such audit has not previously been submitted); and provide a copy of the current community cultural plan.
Geographic Focus: Louisiana
Date(s) Application is Due: Mar 1
Amount: Up to 250,000 USD
Contact: Program Officer; (225) 342-8180; (225) 342-8173; arts@crt.state.la.us
Internet: http://www.crt.state.la.us/arts/04_06Guidedwnld.htm
Sponsor: Louisiana State Arts Council and Division of the Arts
P.O. Box 44247
Baton Rouge, LA 70804-4247

Louisiana State Arts Council Local Arts Agency Level Two Grants 1085
A local arts agency (LAA) is a government agency or nonprofit community organization, officially designated by municipal or parish governments to provide financing, services, or other programs for arts organizations and individual artists within a city, parish, or region of adjacent parishes. The Level Two program is designed to support smaller local arts agencies in early stages of development and communities committed to establishing an LAA. Grants may be used for planning, operations, special projects, or organizational and professional staff development. An application for a maximum grant must indicate cash resources of at least $25,000. Grants must be matched dollar for dollar in either cash or a combination of cash and in-kind contributions.
Requirements: Louisiana 501(c)3 nonprofit organizations may apply. In addition, Level Two applicants must be officially designated by the municipal or parish governing body with jurisdiction over the service area to act on its behalf as the local arts agency; have a governing board with the responsibility and the legal power to set agency policy; have had annual operating revenues of not more than $100,000 for the preceding fiscal year; and provide a copy of current community cultural plans.
Geographic Focus: Louisiana
Date(s) Application is Due: Mar 1
Amount: 10,000 USD
Contact: Program Officer; (225) 342-8180; (225) 342-8173; arts@crt.state.la.us
Internet: http://www.crt.state.la.us/arts/04_06Guidedwnld.htm
Sponsor: Louisiana State Arts Council and Division of the Arts
P.O. Box 44247
Baton Rouge, LA 70804-4247

Louis R. Lurie Foundation Grants 1086
The foundation awards one-year renewable grants to nonprofits in the metropolitan Chicago area and in the San Francisco Bay area to support local arts, community services, education, and health care programs. Types of support include program development, seed money, equipment, and general operating support. Applications are accepted by invitation only.
Requirements: Nonprofits serving the metropolitan Chicago area and the San Francisco Bay area are eligible for grant support.
Geographic Focus: California, Illinois
Amount: 5,000 - 60,000 USD
Samples: Chicago Children's Museum (IL)—for museum relocation, $25,000; Chicago Metro History Education Ctr (IL)—for general operating support, $1000.
Contact: Nancy Terry, Administrator; (415) 392-2470
Internet: http://fdncenter.org/grantmaker/lurie
Sponsor: Louis R. Lurie Foundation
555 California Street, Suite 5100
San Francisco, CA 94104

Lowe Foundation Grants 1087
The foundation awards grants to organizations in Texas, primarily for programs that support the critical needs of women and children. The arts and higher education also receive support. Grants are awarded to support capital campaigns, building construction/renovation, and general operations. The board meets in April of each year. The December 1 deadline listed is for pre-proposals, with full proposals by request due on December 31.
Requirements: 501(c)3 organizations in Texas may apply for grant support.
Geographic Focus: Texas
Date(s) Application is Due: Dec 1; Dec 31
Amount: 5,000 - 225,000 USD
Samples: U of Texas Southwestern Medical Ctr at Dallas (Dallas, TX)—to endow a professorship in pediatric critical care, $100,000.
Contact: Clayton Maebius, Trustee; (512) 322-0041; (512) 322-0061; info@thelowefoundation.org
Internet: http://www.thelowefoundation.org/guidelines.htm
Sponsor: Lowe Foundation
1005 Congress Avenue, Suite 895
Austin, TX 78701

Lowell Berry Foundation Grants 1088
Mr. Lowell W. Berry established The Lowell Berry Foundation in 1950 with the primary purpose of assisting in strengthening Christian ministry at the local church level. Mr. Berry's secondary purpose was that of assisting social service programs in the areas in California where he lived and operated his business. Guidelines are available at the Foundation's website.
Requirements: 501(c)3 tax-exempt organizations may apply, The Foundation provides funding primarily in Contra Costa and Alameda counties of California.
Restrictions: No grants to individuals, or for building or capital funds, equipment, seed money, or land acquisition.
Geographic Focus: California
Amount: 5,000 - 200,000 USD
Samples: Fuller Theological Seminary, Pasadena, CA, $115,000—Fellowship Program & Lowell Berry Institute (2008); Hawaiian Islands Ministries, Honolulu, HI, $60,000—Bay Area Conference (2008); Faith Network of the East Bay, Oakland, CA, $25,000—Urban School Adoption Program (2008).
Contact: Katherine Sanders, Office Manager; (925) 284-4427; (925) 284-4332; info@lowellberryfoundation.org
Internet: http://www.lowellberryfoundation.org/process.html
Sponsor: Lowell Berry Foundation
3685 Mount Diablo Boulevard, Suite 269
Lafayette, CA 94549-3776

Lubbock Area Foundation Grants 1089
The Lubbock Area Foundation is a nonprofit community foundation that manages a pool of charitable endowment funds, the income from which is used to benefit the South Plains community through grants to nonprofit organizations, educational programs and scholarships. Funding priorities are: art and culture; social services; civic and community; education; social services; health and human services. Grants may be made for start-up funding, general operating support, program support and demonstration programs. Typical grant awards range from $500 - $2,500 with $5,000 as the maximum

from the unrestricted funds. Grant application and additional guidelines are available on the Foundation's website.
Requirements: The Foundation restricts its support to organizations in Lubbock and the surrounding South Plains area which are 501(c)3 or the government equivalent.
Restrictions: The Foundation does not make grants to individuals, for political purposes, to retire indebtedness or for payment of interest or taxes.
Geographic Focus: Texas
Date(s) Application is Due: Jan 1; Mar 1; May 1; Jul 1; Sep 1; Nov 1
Amount: 500 - 5,000 USD
Samples: Louise Hopkins Underwood Center for the Arts Clay Studio, Lubbock, TX, $8,500—Firehouse Theatre and Marketing Staff Salaries (2009); The Haven Animal Care Shelter, Lubbock, TX—$8,000— funding for veterinary care for animals (2009); Lubbock Children's Health Clinic, Lubbock, TX, $3,600—Pharmacy Assistance Program (2009).
Contact: Kathleen Stocco, Executive Director; (806) 762-8061; (806) 762-8551
Internet: http://www.lubbockareafoundation.org/grant.shtml
Sponsor: Lubbock Area Foundation
1655 Main Street, Suite 202
Lubbock, TX 79401

Lubrizol Corporation Community Grants **1090**
The Lubrizol Corporation has a long-standing commitment to the local communities in which it operates. The Corporation believes that enhancing the quality of life and building and maintaining positive relationships is the right thing to do. It all began with its founders' corporate philosophy, whose legacy is a culture of active community support. Today, the Corporation continues their model by providing dollars and people to support a wide variety of educational, cultural and charitable organizations. One of the ways that Lubrizol and its employees provide support to its local communities is through various charitable outreach efforts. Employees volunteer their time to offer assistance to local organizations, making use of their individual skills. An annual event in Northeast Ohio that exemplifies this type of charitable outreach is the Building Bonds event. Applicants should contact the Corporate Community Involvement office for further guidelines.
Requirements: IRS 501(c)3 organizations in or serving the following regions may apply: Wickliffe, Ohio; Cleveland, Ohio; Brussels, Belgium; and Hong Kong.
Geographic Focus: Ohio, Belgium, Hong Kong
Contact: Karen Lerchbacher, Administrator; (440) 347-1797; (440) 347-1858; karen.lerchbacher@lubrizol.com
Internet: http://www.lubrizol.com/CorporateResponsibility/Community.html
Sponsor: Lubrizol Corporation
29400 Lakeland Boulevard
Wickliffe, OH 44092-2298

Lubrizol Foundation Grants **1091**
The Lubrizol Foundation makes grants in support of education, health care, human services, civic, cultural, youth and environmental activities of a tax-exempt, charitable nature. Scholarships, fellowships, and awards are generally made in the fields of chemistry and chemical and mechanical engineering at colleges and universities. Types of support include the following: annual campaigns; building/renovation; capital campaigns; continuing support; employee matching gifts; employee volunteer services; equipment; fellowships; general/operating support; scholarship funds. Priority is given to the greater Cleveland, Ohio and Houston, Texas areas. The Lubrizol Foundation typically reviews and decides upon requests quarterly. There are no deadlines by which you need to submit your proposal. Proposals may be submitted via postal mail or email, but not by fax. Applicants will receive written notification of the decision on their proposal.
Requirements: Written applications of established Ohio and Texas nonprofit charitable organizations will be considered on a case by case basis. Grant proposals should include the following: a cover letter that summarizes the purpose of the request, signed by the executive officer of the organization or development office; a narrative of specific information related to the subject of the request; current audited financial statements and a specific project budget, if applicable; documentation of the organization's Federal tax-exempt status, e.g., a copy of the 501(c)3 determination letter. Additional descriptive literature (e.g., an annual report, brochures, etc.) that accurately characterizes the overall activities of the organization is appreciated. Upon review, further information may be requested including an interview and site visit.
Restrictions: Grants are not made for religious or political purposes, to individuals nor, generally, to endowments.
Geographic Focus: Ohio, Texas
Amount: 2,000 - 250,000 USD
Samples: Big Brothers Big Sisters of Greater Cleveland, Cleveland, OH, $2,500 - for operating support (2008); American Red Cross, Houston, Texas, $25,000 - for Hurricane Ike Disaster Relief Fund (2008); Hospice of the Western Reserve, Cleveland, OH, $250,000 - toward construction of new faculty (2008).
Contact: Karen Lerchbacher, Administrator; (440) 347-1797; (440) 347-1858; karen.lerchbacher@lubrizol.com
Internet: http://www.lubrizol.com/CorporateResponsibility/Lubrizol-Foundation.html
Sponsor: Lubrizol Foundation
29400 Lakeland Boulevard, 053A
Wickliffe, OH 44092-2298

Lucile Horton Howe and Mitchell B. Howe Foundation Grants **1092**
The foundation supports youth organizations, social services, medical research, hospitals, religion, child welfare, drug abuse, education, and family services. Types of support include continuing support, general operating funds, and research. Requests from qualified organizations must be received prior to the second Tuesday of March for the grant year. There is only one consideration meeting a year.
Requirements: Only nonprofit organizations in the Prox-Pasadena area and the San Gabriel Valley of California are eligible. A brief letter and a copy of the organizations 501(c)3 form are the requirements for application.
Restrictions: No restricted grants will be funded by the foundation.
Geographic Focus: California
Date(s) Application is Due: Feb 28
Amount: 1,000 - 300,000 USD
Samples: Huntington Medical Research Institutes, Pasadena, CA., $60,000; Childrens Hospital Los Angeles, Los Angeles, CA., $12,000; Upward Bound Group Home, Pioneer, CA., $10,000
Contact: Mitchell B. Howe, President; (626) 792-2771; lhmbhowefoun@earthlink.net
Sponsor: Lucile Horton Howe and Mitchell B. Howe Foundation
180 South Lake Avenue
Pasadena, CA 91101-4932

Lucile Packard Foundation for Children's Health Grants **1093**
The foundation supports activities that have potential to promote, protect, and sustain the health of children in California's San Mateo and Santa Clara Counties. There are two areas of interest: protect children from injury (birth to age five), with an emphasis on preventing neglect, child abuse, and other forms of intentional injury; and promote emotional, mental, and behavioral health in preteens (ages nine to 13), with a focus to build on assets, foster resiliency, and promote the healthy development of this age group, thereby reducing the likelihood of high-risk behaviors. Types of support include (but are not limited to): capital expenses including equipment purchase, renovation, and construction; data development and dissemination; direct delivery of service; educational programs and public awareness activities; evaluation; operating expenses related to ongoing programs, services, or activities; technical assistance; and training and staff development. Letters of inquiry must received by the listed deadline date; full proposals are by invitation.
Requirements: Nonprofit organizations and public agencies providing healthcare services to children in California's San Mateo and Santa Clara Counties are eligible.
Restrictions: Grants do not support annual fund appeals; basic biomedical research; for-profit organizations; fundraising sponsorships; individuals; political activities, lobbying, or support of candidates for political office; private foundations 509(a); or religious organizations for religious purposes.
Geographic Focus: California
Date(s) Application is Due: Dec 1
Amount: 75,000 - 194,400 USD
Samples: Community Solutions for Children, Families, and Individuals (Morgan Hill, CA)—for programs for young children who are at high risk of abuse and neglect, and for programs designed to bolster the well-being of adolescents, $149,000 over two years.
Contact: Grants Administrator; (650) 736-0676; grants@lpfch.org
Internet: http://www.lpfch.org/grantmaking
Sponsor: Lucile Packard Foundation for Children's Health
770 Welch Road, Suite 350
Palo Alto, CA 94304

Lucille Lortel Foundation New York City Theater Grants 1094

The foundation awards general operating grants to small and mid-size nonprofit theater companies in New York City. The grants are paid in two annual installments. Annual deadline dates may vary; contact program staff for exact dates.
Requirements: An applicant theater must have been in operation as a professional, nonprofit, producing organization in New York, NY, for at least three years; have a current annual operating budget of $200,000 to $2.5 million; and have at least one paid professional manager or director.
Geographic Focus: New York
Date(s) Application is Due: Oct 25
Amount: 2,500 - 25,000 USD
Samples: 49 small and mid-size nonprofit theaters in New York City that were affected by the attacks on the World Trade Center (NY)—for operating support, $1 million total.
Contact: Shawn Willett, (212) 924-2817, ext. 208; (212) 989-0036; grants@lortel.org
Internet: http://www.lortel.org
Sponsor: Lucille Lortel Foundation
322 Eighth Avenue, 21st Floor
New York, NY 10001

Lucy Gooding Charitable Foundation Trust 1095

The trust awards grants to eligible Florida nonprofit organizations in its areas of interest, including child welfare, disabled children, disadvantaged people, homelessness, and hospices. Types of support include building construction/renovation, capital campaigns, equipment and land acquisition, general operating support, seed grants, and United Way. Contact the office for required application form.
Requirements: Florida 501(c)3 nonprofit organizations serving the Jacksonville area are eligible.
Geographic Focus: Florida
Date(s) Application is Due: Sep 30
Amount: 2,500 - 25,000,000 USD
Samples: Wolfson Children's Hospital (Jacksonville, FL)—to establish a pediatric neurosurgery center, $5 million; Community Foundation in Jacksonville (FL)—to endow a fund to support organizations that serve children or provide relief services, with an emphasis on Florida's Clay and Duval Counties, $25 million.
Contact: Bonnie Smith; (904) 786-4796; (904) 786-4796; bhsmith@bellsouth.net
Sponsor: Lucy Gooding Charitable Foundation Trust
P.O. Box 37349
Jacksonville, FL 32236-7349

Lumina Foundation for Education Grants 1096

The foundation focuses on three theme areas: addressing the multiple barriers that impede access to postsecondary education among traditionally underserved groups; supporting efforts that help these students attain sound educational objectives; and understanding and addressing the challenges faced by adult learners, particularly those who face barriers, such as low income or academic underpreparation. The following types of strategic activities are supported: research that casts new light on issues affecting postsecondary education access and success; programs that present innovative and practical approaches in overcoming challenges to access and attainment; leadership-development efforts to share the expertise of higher education executives and scholars working on issues of access and attainment; communication initiatives that bring about positive change by sharing the lessons of access and degree attainment with educational leaders, policy-makers, the news media, and the public; public policy initiatives that help policy-makers reach informed decisions on issues of postsecondary education access and attainment; and evaluation efforts that look closely at the work grantees and others have done to answer the questions: What have we learned? What works? What's next? The first step in seeking a grant is to write a preliminary letter of inquiry that is no more than three pages long. The letter should describe the organization, its mission, the project, and the amount requested. The foundation responds in writing to all preliminary inquiries. If the inquiry fits with funding priorities, the foundation will request additional information about the project, and will provide a grant-application packet. Guidelines are available online.
Requirements: IRS 501(c)3 or 509(a)(1, 2, or 3) tax-exempt organizations and public school organizations are eligible.
Restrictions: The foundation will not award grants that support corporate sponsorships and fundraising events; fund partisan political or lobbying efforts; or provide direct support for individuals, including scholarships or institutional scholarship funds.
Geographic Focus: All U.S. States
Amount: 75,000 - 200,000 USD
Samples: Excelencia in Education (Washington, DC)—for a study on the effects of institutional leadership on practices that improved Latino students' success at institutions that primarily serve Hispanics, $230,000; Ohio Assoc of Student Financial Aid Administrators (Delaware, OH)—for events put on by the College Goal Sunday program in Ohio, which helps students find ways to pay for college, $25,000; U of Michigan (Ann Arbor, MI)—to develop a model for dealing with local issues that affect access to and success in higher education, $769,200; Women in Government (Washington, DC)—to establish the Legislative Research Center and inform policy makers about access to higher education for women and minorities, $114,055.
Contact: Grants Manager; (800) 834-5756 or (317) 951-5300; (317) 951-5063
Internet: http://www.luminafoundation.org/grants/apply.html
Sponsor: Lumina Foundation for Education
30 S Meridian Street, Suite 700
Indianapolis, IN 46204

Lutheran Foundation Grants 1097

The foundation awards Regular, Partnership, and Emergency Grants. Regular grants are available to any congregation or nonprofit organization in northeast Indiana. Regular grants are awarded four times a year. The foundation will consider funding of one-time grants, single-year grants, and multi-year grants that do not exceed three years. Partnership grants are available to each of the foundation's member congregations. They are designed to assist congregations with their outreach ministries and also to enrich the internal life of their own membership. Emergency grants are designed to address unforeseen circumstances that disrupt the ongoing ministry or service provided by churches and organizations. The foundation also encourages, promotes, and supports Lutheran and Christian educational opportunities. Guidelines and application are available online.
Requirements: The foundation awards grants to ministries located in 10 counties in northeast Indiana, including Adams, Allen, DeKalb, Huntington, LaGrange, Noble, Steuben, Wabash, Wells, and Whitley counties.
Restrictions: Proposals for projects that have been completed, deficit financing, fundraising, and promotional items are not considered. In addition, the foundation does not fund individuals, endowments, other funds, or the general operating expenses of congregations or medical procedures that are destructive of life.
Geographic Focus: Indiana
Amount: Up to 10,000 USD
Samples: Allen County Non-Public School Assoc (Fort Wayne, IN)—to fund school nurse program expenses for parochial and independent schools $57,565 three-year grant; Bethlehem Evangelical Lutheran Church and School (Fort Wayne, IN)—for renovations to cafeteria, basement classrooms, and Fellowship Hall for handicap accessibility $9870 matching grant; Camp Lutherhave (Albion, IN)—to purchase multi-passenger van, $22,000; Cancer Services of Allen County (Fort Wayne, IN)—for operational support, $75,000 three-year grant.
Contact: Terri Kortokrax, (800) 677-2451 or (260) 458-2112, ext. 302; (260) 458-3069; tkortokrax@thelutheranfoundation.org
Internet: http://www.thelutheranfoundation.org/grants.htm
Sponsor: Lutheran Foundation
3024 Fairfield Avenue, Suite 200
Fort Wayne, IN 46807-1697

Luther I. Replogle Foundation Grants 1098

The foundation focuses its giving on the following areas: programs addressing the needs of youth and children living in, or at risk of, long-term poverty (especially children of inner-city residents and migrant workers); programs to improve educational opportunities for inner- city children, including enrichment programs in the arts and sciences, alternative schools, after-school tutoring and mentoring, and scholarship programs; programs for affordable and supportive housing that reach groups of people frequently left out of traditional shelter programs, including single mothers and families with children, the elderly, ex-offenders, and youth; projects, lectures, and fellowships in classical archaeology; projects and institutions working for the conservation of maps and globes, and dissemination and education in the area of geography; and a modest budget for support of the arts. Types of support include direct service efforts; advocacy at the local, state, and/or federal levels;

general operating support, new projects, and capital campaigns (limited). The board meets twice a year to make funding decisions, once in the autumn and once in the spring. Guidelines and application are available online.
Requirements: 501(c)3 nonprofits in Chicago, IL; Minneapolis, MN; Palm Beach County, FL; and Washington, DC, are eligible. Preference is given to organizations with small or modest operating budgets
Geographic Focus: District of Columbia, Florida, Illinois, Minnesota
Date(s) Application is Due: Mar 15; Sep 15
Amount: 500 - 45,000 USD
Samples: Bright Beginnings (Washington, DC)—day care for homeless children, $5000; The Enterprising Kitchen, (Chicago, IL)—for jobs training for women, $5000; First Presbyterian Church of Chicago (IL)—social service programming, $25,000; Oriental Institute, U of Chicago (Chicago, IL)—to support a conservation internship, $10,000.
Contact: Gwenn Gebhard, Executive Director; (202) 296-3686; (202) 296-3948; info@lirf.org
Internet: http://www.lirf.org
Sponsor: Luther I. Replogle Foundation
1111 19th Street NW, Suite 900
Washington, DC 20036

Lynde and Harry Bradley Foundation Grants **1099**
The foundation aims to encourage projects that focus on cultivating a renewed, healthier, and more vigorous sense of citizenship among the American people and among peoples of other nations. Projects likely to be supported will generally treat free people as self-governing, personally responsible citizens, not as victims or clients; aim to restore the intellectual and cultural legitimacy of common sense, the wisdom of experience, everyday morality, and personal character; seek to reinvigorate and re-empower the traditional, local institutions—families, schools, churches, and neighborhoods—that provide training in and room for the exercise of genuine citizenship, that pass on everyday morality to the next generation, and that cultivate personal character; and encourage decentralization of power and accountability away from centralized, bureaucratic, national institutions back to states, localities, and revitalized mediating structures. Eligible projects may address any arena of public life—economics, politics, culture, or civil society; the problem of citizenship at home or abroad; Milwaukee and Wisconsin community and state projects that aim to improve the life of the community through increasing cultural and educational opportunities, grassroots economic development, and social and health services; the resuscitation of citizenship in the economic, political, cultural, or social realms; policy research and writing about approaches encouraging that resuscitation; academic research and writing that explore the intellectual roots of citizenship; and popular writing and media projects that illustrate for a broader public audience the themes of citizenship. The foundation supports programs that research the needs of gifted children and techniques of providing education for students with superior skills and/or intelligence; research programs investigating how learning occurs in gifted children; and demonstration programs of instruction.
Requirements: Tax-exempt and nonprofit organizations should prepare a letter of inquiry presenting a concise description of the project, its objectives and significance, and the qualifications of the organizations and individuals involved. If the project appears to fall within the foundation's mandate, a brochure with detailed proposal requirements will be sent to the applicant.
Restrictions: The foundation favors projects that are normally not financed by public funds and will consider requests from religious organizations that are not denominational in character. Grants without significant importance to the foundation's areas of interest will only under special conditions be considered for endowment or deficit financing proposals. Grants will not be made to individuals, for overhead costs, or for fund-raising counsel.
Geographic Focus: All U.S. States
Date(s) Application is Due: Feb 1; May 1; Aug 1; Nov 1
Amount: 25,000 - 250,000 USD
Samples: Black Alliance for Educational Options, Washington, D.C., $250,000; Texas A&M University, College Station, Texas, $50,000; Evergreen Freedom Foundation, Olympia, Washington, $50,000.
Contact: Daniel Schmidt, Vice President; (414) 291-9915; (414) 291-9991
Internet: http://www.bradleyfdn.org/app.html
Sponsor: Lynde and Harry Bradley Foundation
1241 N Franklin Place
Milwaukee, WI 53202-2901

Lyndhurst Foundation Grants **1100**
The foundation concentrates its funding on a variety of strategic partnerships that serve to strengthen and enhance the design, animation, ecology, and livability of metropolitan Chattanooga and advance the protection and restoration of the region's forests, watersheds, and natural systems. Contact the Foundation before submitting any requests.
Requirements: Any Chattanooga-based nonprofit organization is eligible to apply.
Geographic Focus: All U.S. States
Date(s) Application is Due: Jan 11; Apr 1; Jul 5; Sep 30
Amount: 1,000 - 1,200,000 USD
Samples: Allied Arts of Greater Chattanooga, Chattanooga, TN, $100,000—to galvanize broad participation in and widespread support for the arts in Chattanooga and Hamilton County (2009); American Trails, Redding, CA, $10,000—for support of the 2010 National Trails Symposium and assistance for local planning and marketing activities in advance of the event (2009); Chattanooga Community Kitchen, Chattanooga, TN, $50,000—general support for food, shelter, and other basic services as provided by the Chattanooga Community Kitchen (2009).
Contact: Benic M. Clark III, President; (423) 756-0767; (423) 756-0770; bclark@lyndhurstfoundation.org
Sponsor: Lyndhurst Foundation
517 E Fifth Street
Chattanooga, TN 37403-1826

M.B. and Edna Zale Foundation Grants **1101**
The M.B. & Edna Zale Foundation honors the tradition of its founders through grants that stimulate change. To accomplish this mission, the Foundation acts as a catalyst for collaboration and makes grants in communities where the Directors live or have an interest. Grants are made primarily in the communities of Dallas (Dallas County) and Houston (Harris County), Texas; Boca Raton, Florida; Portland, Oregon; and New York, including Long Island. The Foundation has an interest in four areas of funding: community services; health; education; Jewish heritage.
Requirements: 501(c)3 nonprofits organizations in the communities of Dallas (Dallas County) and Houston (Harris County), Texas; Boca Raton, Florida; Portland, Oregon; and New York, including Long Island are eligible. Contact the Foundation for further application information and guidelines.
Restrictions: The Foundation does not ordinarily provide: major support for the arts; grants to individuals; scholarships and fellowships to individuals (except through colleges and universities).
Geographic Focus: Florida, New York, Oregon, Texas
Amount: 2,000 - 100,000 USD
Contact: Leonard Krasnow, President; (214) 855-0627; (972) 726-7252; mail@zalefoundation.org
Sponsor: M.B. and Edna Zale Foundation
6360 LBJ Highway, Suite 205
Dallas, TX 75240

M. Bastian Family Foundation Grants **1102**
The foundation supports nonprofit organizations in its areas of interest, including music, the arts, higher education, health care and health organizations, religion (Christian and Latter-day Saints), social services, and wildlife conservation. Types of support include general operating support and scholarship funds. Contact the office for application forms. There are no application deadlines.
Requirements: Funding focus is primarily in Utah.
Restrictions: Grants are not made to individuals.
Geographic Focus: All U.S. States
Amount: 2,000 - 200,000 USD
Samples: Brigham Young U (Provo, UT)—for scholarship endowment, $200,000; Pediatric AIDS Foundation (Los Angeles, CA)—for general support, $20,000; American Diabetes Assoc (Alexandra, VA)—for research, $100,000.
Contact: McKay Matthews, Program Contact; (801) 225-2455
Sponsor: M. Bastian Family Foundation
51 W Center Street, Suite 305
Orem, UT 84057

M.D. Anderson Foundation Grants **1103**
The foundation supports Texas nonprofit organizations, including religious organizations, higher education institutions, parochial education institutions, hospitals, and religious welfare organizations. Types of support include capital

grants, general support, program support, scholarships, and research grants. Applicants should send a brief letter describing the proposed project, along with an original and four copies of the proposal. If applying for a matching grant, indicate other sources of funding. There are no application deadlines. The board meets on the third Tuesday of each month. Applications should be received a month prior to the the meeting to be considered.
Requirements: Texas nonprofit organizations are eligible.
Geographic Focus: Texas
Amount: 25,000 - 100,000 USD
Samples: U of Texas (Austin, TX)—for the law school, $800,000; U of Saint Thomas (Houston, TX)—to construct a humanities and education building, $250,000.
Contact: Toloria Allen, Secretary-Treasurer; (713) 216-4513
Sponsor: M.D. Anderson Foundation
P.O. Box 2558
Houston, TX 77252-8037

M.E. Raker Foundation Grants **1104**
The foundation was established in 1984, serving the Allen County, Indiana area. Areas of interest include: children/youth, services; education; environment; natural resources; health care; historic preservation/historical societies; human services people with disabilities. Support is offered in the following areas: building/renovation; general/operating support; matching/challenge support; Program development. No support for the arts or to individuals.
Requirements: Indiana nonprofit organizations are eligible. Emphasis is given to requests from Fort Wayne. Send a letter requesting an application to the foundation office. Application form required for grant proposals.
Geographic Focus: Indiana
Amount: 5,000 - 40,000 USD
Contact: Jennifer Pickard, Grants Coordinator; (260) 436-2182
Sponsor: M.E. Raker Foundation
6207 Constitution Drive
Fort Wayne, IN 46804-1517

Mabel Y. Hughes Charitable Trust Grants **1105**
The trust awards grants to Denver-area nonprofit organizations in its areas of interest, including community funds, cultural programs, education, health, hospitals, museums, social services, and youth. Types of support include operating support, continuing support, annual campaigns, seed money, emergency funds, building funds, equipment acquisition, endowment funds, research grants, and special projects.
Requirements: Colorado nonprofit organizations are eligible.
Restrictions: Grants do not support conferences, individuals, or ticket purchases for benefits.
Geographic Focus: Colorado
Amount: 5,000 - 60,000 USD
Contact: Judy Dowling, c/o Wells Fargo Bank, (720) 947-6725
Sponsor: Mabel Y. Hughes Charitable Trust
1740 Broadway, MC 7300 #483
Denver, CO 80274

Maddie's Fund Grant **1106**
The foundation supports projects that work with veterinarians, animal rescue groups, and other organizations that find homes for every adoptable cat and dog in a given community within five years. Proposals should include a description of the geographic area to be served, contact and financial information for all participating groups, demographic information on human and stray-pet populations, and a timeline for eliminating the deaths of all adoptable animals. Preference is given to proposals from consortia of groups within the same geographic area. Grants may be used to seed start-up programs, initiate services, provide outreach, purchase equipment, fund staff positions, and underwrite marketing campaigns. Organizations must be able to demonstrate on a quarterly basis how the investment of the grant dollars will immediately and directly save additional animal lives. An application form and guidelines are available on the website.
Requirements: Eligible to apply are California 501(c)3 nonprofit animal welfare organizations that have a no-kill policy in place or a plan to establish one within two or three years and a timeline for eliminating the deaths of all adoptable animals in their area.
Geographic Focus: California
Samples: Mayor's Alliance for NYC's Animals (New York, NY) and the Veterinary Medical Assoc of New York City (NY)—to create programs designed to end the killing of healthy and treatable homeless animals in New York City, $15.5 million maximum jointly over seven years.
Contact: Grants Administrator; (510) 337-8989; (510) 337-8988; info@maddies.org
Internet: http://www.maddies.org/grant/index.html
Sponsor: Maddie's Fund
2223 Santa Clara Avenue, Suite B
Alameda, CA 94501-4416

Madison Community Foundation Grants **1107**
The foundation is a tax-exempt community trust that establishes permanent funds, invests those funds for long-term growth, and distributes the earnings to enhance the lives of Dane County citizens. The foundation awards grants to Wisconsin nonprofits in its areas of interest, including health and social services, youth development and social activities, cultural outreach, education, economic and community development, environment, and the elderly. The foundation offers capital grants that support the construction, purchase and renovation of facilities, land acquisition, and occasionally the purchase of vehicles or equipment; and program grants that support new programs or expansion of existing programs that have a track record of success. The foundation requires grantseekers to submit a letter of inquiry; this can be done electronically on MCF's website. Deadlines listed are for letters of inquiry.
Requirements: Nonprofit organizations serving Dane County, WI, are eligible.
Restrictions: Grants are not awarded to individuals or for religious purposes, annual campaigns, endowments, deficit financing, political activities, or equipment.
Geographic Focus: Wisconsin
Date(s) Application is Due: Jan 15; Jul 15
Amount: 20,000 USD
Samples: Briarpatch (Madison, WI)—to support a program that assists parents with the specific challenges of raising adolescents, $15,000; American Players Theatre (Madison, WI)—for construction of on-site restrooms, $10,000; Hospicecare (Madison, WI)—for a new computer system, $10,000; YWCA (Madison, WI)—for facility renovations, $30,000.
Contact: Tom Linfield, Vice President of Grantmaking; (608) 232-1763; (608) 232-1772; tlinfield@madisoncommunityfoundation.org
Internet: http://www.madisoncommunityfoundation.org
Sponsor: Madison Community Foundation
2 Science Court, P.O. Box 5010
Madison, WI 53705

Madison County Community Foundation - Immediate Need Grants **1108**
The Madison County Community Foundation - Immediate Need Grants are available to non-profit agencies who have a proven track record with the Foundation, with an urgent operational need for funding, rather than a program or project.
Requirements: Organizations contact the Program Director and complete a two page application. The application is sent to the grants committee who provide an answer generally within 72 hours.
Geographic Focus: Indiana
Amount: Up to 2,000 USD
Contact: Tammy Bowman, Program Director; (765) 644-0002; (765) 644-3392; tbowman@madisoncf.org
Internet: http://www.madisonccf.org/index.php?submenu=Grants&src=gendocs&ref=Grants&category=Non_Profits
Sponsor: Madison County Community Foundation
33 West 10th Street, Suite 600
Anderson, IN 46015-1056

Maine Community Foundation Grants **1109**
The foundation awards a wide variety of grants. The community building program focuses on proposals that build on community assets and resources and support/promote sustainable, healthy community networks. The goal of the organizational capacity building grant program is to strengthen the impact of Maine-based nonprofit organizations by improving their organizational capacity. The foundation considers requests for equipment purchases or operating expenses, especially if the group is in the start-up stage. The foundation has several fields of interest and donor-advised funds that make grants within specific interest areas. Several funds make grants to individuals for professional development and special projects (i.e., gay, lesbian, and transgender community, environmental conservation, and arts); there also is a scholarship program. Recent grants have support affordable housing, the

arts, economic and community development, education, environment, health, social capital, and youth. Grant sizes, deadlines, and priorities vary for each fund. The board meets quarterly to consider requests. Application deadlines and guidelines are available online.
Requirements: Maine 501(c)3 nonprofit organizations are eligible.
Restrictions: Support is not given to religious organizations for religious purposes; individuals, except scholarship funds; or for endowment funds, equipment, or annual campaigns for regular operations. Grants rarely are made to support capital campaigns.
Geographic Focus: Maine
Amount: 5,000 - 20,000 USD
Samples: College of the Atlantic (Bar Harbor, ME)—for the Cummings Scholarship Fund, to support students from the western mountain area of Maine to attend the college, $10,000.
Contact: Bethany Murray, Competitive Grants Associate; (877) 700-6800; (207) 667-0447; bmurray@mainecf.org or info@mainecf.org
Internet: http://www.mainecf.org/html/grants/available/index.html
Sponsor: Maine Community Foundation
245 E Main Street
Ellsworth, ME 04605

Maine Community Foundation Theater Grants **1110**
The foundation awards grants to professional and community theaters in Maine for the production and presentation of live theater. Types of support include capacity-building, operating, and capital grants. Application and guidelines are available online.
Requirements: Applicants must be nonprofit, 501(c)3 federal tax-exempt organizations, or have a fiscal sponsor that is a 501(c)3 organization, public school, public agency, or Indian tribal government.
Geographic Focus: Maine
Date(s) Application is Due: Sep 15
Amount: Up to 20,000 USD
Contact: Pam Cleghorn, (207) 761-2440; pcleghorn@mainecf.org
Internet: http://www.mainecf.org/html/grants/available/metheater.html
Sponsor: Maine Community Foundation
245 E Main Street
Ellsworth, ME 04605

Maine Women's Fund Grants **1111**
The fund's grantmaking program focuses on changing the landscape to improve the lives of women and girls, especially those who are low-income or otherwise marginalized. Grantmaking priorities include the following areas targeting women and/or girls: economic empowerment, health, prevention of violence, self-determination. Initiatives that promote systemic change through the empowerment, advancement, and full participation of women and girls in society are encouraged. Grant types include start-up expenses, new or special projects, programs, and general operating support.
Requirements: Maine 501(c) nonprofit organizations, groups that submit applications through a fiscal agent, and groups of women and nascent grassroots organizations that have come together for a specific project that is charitable in purpose are eligible.
Restrictions: Grants do not fund individuals; capital campaigns; endowments; campaigns to elect candidates to public office; programs that promote religious activities; programs or projects outside the state of Maine; or programs or projects that discriminate on the basis of race, color, creed, religion, sex, national origin, age, handicap, marital status, sexual orientation, or any veteran's status. Lower priority requests include requests to fund conferences or other one-time events or activities that do not result in ongoing organizing or public policy changes.
Geographic Focus: Maine
Amount: 5,000 - 7,500 USD
Contact: Shaye Robbins, Program Coordinator; (207) 774-5513; (207) 774-5533; shaye@mainewomensfund.org or thewomen@mainwomensfund.org
Internet: http://www.mainewomensfund.org/about.html
Sponsor: Maine Women's Fund
565 Congress Street, Suite 306, P.O. Box 5135
Portland, ME 04101

Manitoba Arts Council Literary Arts Publishers Operating Grants **1112**
Operating grants support the annual activities of professional Manitoba book publishers, periodicals publishers, and arts service organizations who publish in eligible genres. The periodicals publishers grants deadline is April 15; the book publishers grants deadline is December 1. The Arts Service Organizations grants deadline is May 15.
Requirements: Companies that maintain professional industry standards and practices, have published at least four eligible titles in the past two years, and are committed to a continuing and sustained book publishing program may apply. Eligible titles for the book publishers grants must account for 75 percent of the total title production.
Geographic Focus: Canada
Date(s) Application is Due: Apr 15; May 15; Dec 1
Contact:
Internet: http://www.artscouncil.mb.ca/english/liter_grantorg.html#operating
Sponsor: Manitoba Arts Council
525-93 Lombard Avenue
Winnipeg, MB R3B 3B1 Canada

Manitoba Arts Council Operating Grants for Visual Arts Organizations **1113**
The Operating Grants is available to provide ongoing, partial support to professional, not-for-profit visual arts organizations. An organization that receives support is expected to present and interpret works of art to the general public, participate in the development of Manitoba artists and maintain sound management and financial controls. Guidelines for this program are available through Marian Butler, the Program Consultant.
Requirements: Manitoba visual arts organizations are eligible.
Geographic Focus: Canada
Date(s) Application is Due: Apr 1
Amount: 2,000 - 20,000 USD
Contact: Marian Butler, Program Consultant; (204) 945-0399; mbutler@artscouncil.mb.ca
Internet: http://www.artscouncil.mb.ca/english/vis_grantorg.html
Sponsor: Manitoba Arts Council
525-93 Lombard Avenue
Winnipeg, MB R3B 3B1 Canada

Marcia and Otto Koehler Foundation Grants **1114**
Grants are made to support arts and culture, medical, education, and social organizations in San Antonio, Texas. Proposals must demonstrate leadership in effecting positive change; encourage collaborative effort; serve large and diverse sectors of the population; and demonstrate vision, effectiveness, and good fiscal management. Types of support include general operating support, building construction/renovation, and research. Grants are made for one time only. Applicants must send a letter of request for application by March 1 to receive an application.
Requirements: Grants are awarded only to organizations in Bexar County, Texas.
Restrictions: Grants will not be made to individuals or to support other foundations or endowments; salaries; operating deficits; political organizations; or churches, synagogues, or parishes.
Geographic Focus: Texas
Date(s) Application is Due: Jun 1
Amount: 2,500 - 50,000 USD
Samples: Centro Alameda (San Antonio, TX)—to restore a marquee, canopy, and facade, $30,000; McNay Art Museum (San Antonio, TX)—to sponsor an art exhibit, $50,000.
Contact: Thomas K. Killion, Senior Vice President, Bank of America; (210) 270-5422; (210) 270-5520; thomas.k.killion@ustrust.com
Sponsor: Marcia and Otto Koehler Foundation
P.O. Box 121
San Antonio, TX 78291-0121

Mardag Foundation Grants **1115**
The foundation is committed to making grants to qualified nonprofit organizations in Minnesota that help enhance and improve the quality of life. The foundation's focus is on children, the elderly, and other at-risk populations; education (including elementary education, adult basic education, and literacy programs); and the arts. Grants normally support capital, program, or expansion projects of a time-limited nature; start-up costs for promising new programs that demonstrate sound management and clear goals relevant to community needs; established agencies seeking to expand their services or experiencing temporary financial difficulty; grants payable over a number of years; and matching funds and challenge grants. The foundation expects an indication of the general process that will be used to monitor or evaluate the impact or effect of the grant. A potential applicant is encouraged to submit

a brief summary of the project prior to preparation of a full proposal to see if the project fits the guidelines and interests of the foundation. The foundation's grantmaking meetings are in April, August, and November. Generally, full proposals must be received approximately three and one-half months prior to a meeting date.
Requirements: Minnesota 501(c)3 tax-exempt organizations are eligible. The geographic focus of the grantmaking is the East Metro area of Ramsey, Washington, and Dakota counties, as well as greater Minnesota.
Restrictions: Normally the foundation will not fund grants for the West Metro area; individuals; annual grants; events, development offices or officers, medical research, conservation, and scholarship programs; or sectarian religious programs.
Geographic Focus: Minnesota
Date(s) Application is Due: May 1; Aug 1; Dec 31
Amount: 10,000 - 30,000 USD
Samples: The Evergreen House (MN)—for the Capacity Building Project, $20,000; Northwoods Interfaith Volunteer Caregivers Program (MN)—for the Senior Care Outreach and Coordination Project, $25,000; The Good Shepherd Foundation, Inc (MN)—for the Faith in Action Program, $25,000; Northwoods Coalition for Battered Women, Inc (MN)—for the Capital Campaign for New Construction, $75,000.
Contact: Program Contact; (612) 224-5463; (651) 224-8123; inbox@mardag.org
Internet: http://www.mardag.org
Sponsor: Mardag Foundation
55 Fifth Street E, Suite 600
Saint Paul, MN 55101

Margaret Abell Powell Fund Grants **1116**
The Margaret Abell Powell Fund of the William S. Abell Foundation makes grants to support traditional classical theater and classical ballet in the Washington, DC, metropolitan area including the counties of Montgomery, Prince George's, Charles, Calvert, Street Mary's and Arlington; and the city of Alexandria. Support will be given to local organizations producing English language, mainstream theater and classical ballet. Emphasis will be given to organizations which support specific performances, the staging or choreography of pieces, and the training of young artists. Applications for this program will be accepted for: the underwriting of specific performances; the training of actors, actresses, performers and dancers; and the staging and choreography of specific pieces. Proposals are reviewed only in June and December. Deadlines are April 15 and October 15.
Requirements: Nonprofit organizations in the District of Columbia and the nearby Maryland counties of Montgomery, Prince George's, Charles, Calvert, and Street Mary's, as well as the city of Arlington, Virginia, are eligible.
Geographic Focus: District of Columbia, Maryland, Virginia
Date(s) Application is Due: Apr 15; Oct 15
Amount: 5,000 - 65,000 USD
Samples: BlackRock Center for the Arts, Germantown, Maryland, $25,000 - to support young ballet students in their ballet program, "On Your Toes", which provides scholarships and free performance tickets for students (2011); Levine School of Music, Washington, DC, $25,000 - to produce Once Upon a Mattress and for 15 scholarships for low-income students (2011).
Contact: Carol Doolan, Executive Director; (301) 652-2224; (301) 652-9173; cdoolan@williamsabellfoundation.orgHeather Brooks, Program Assistant; (301) 652-2224; (301) 652-9173; info@williamsabellfoundation.org
Internet: http://www.williamsabellfoundation.org/margaret_abell_powell_fund
Sponsor: William S. Abell Foundation
8401 Connecticut Avenue, Suite 1204
Chevy Chase, MD 20815-5821

Margaret T. Morris Foundation Grants **1117**
The foundation awards grants, primarily in Arizona, in its areas of interest, including arts and culture, children and youth, higher education. family, environment and animal welfare, social services, mental health, medical research, marine sciences, music, and hospice. Types of support include general operating costs, building construction/renovation, scholarship funds, deficit financing, endowments, land acquisition, and program development. Proposals are accepted between May and November, and the board meets in August and December.
Restrictions: No support for religious organizations. Grants are not made to individuals.
Geographic Focus: Arizona
Amount: 350 - 100,000 USD
Contact: Eugene Polk, Trustee
Sponsor: Margaret T. Morris Foundation
P.O. Box 592
Prescott, AZ 86302

Margoes Foundation Grants **1118**
The foundation awards grants to California nonprofits in its areas of interest, including cardiac research, rehabilitation of mentally ill patients, and scholarships for minority students and for Asian and African nationals studying in the United States. Types of funding include general operating support, continuing support, program development, fellowships, scholarship funds, research, and matching funds. There are no application forms. Applicants should call or submit a preliminary letter prior to submitting a full proposal.
Requirements: California nonprofits are eligible, with preference given to the San Francisco Bay area.
Restrictions: Grants are not awarded to agencies supported by federated campaigns or to individuals.
Geographic Focus: California
Date(s) Application is Due: Apr 1; Oct 1
Amount: 10,000 - 20,000 USD
Samples: Community Music Center (San Francisco, CA)—for financial aid, $10,000; U of the Pacific (Stockton, CA)—to increase minority enrollment in the predentistry undergraduate programs, $20,000 over two years; Fred Finch Youth Ctr (Oakland, CA)—for salary support of a part-time counselor for a transitional independent living program for older adolescents and young adults with severe emotional problems, $15,000.
Contact: John Blum, Principal Manager; (415) 981-2966; (415) 981-5218; margoesfdn@aol.com
Sponsor: Margoes Foundation
57 Post Street, Suite 510
San Francisco, CA 94104

Marie C. and Joseph C. Wilson Foundation Grants **1119**
The mission of the foundation is to improve the quality of life through initiating and supporting projects that measurably demonstrate a means of creating a sense of belonging within the family and the community. Grants are awarded, primarily in the Rochester, NY, area, for programs that strengthen families and reduce alienation and isolation of the elderly and programs that support youth and the environment. The foundation supports early childhood and adult education including literacy training, health care, and human services. Types of support include general operating support, continuing support, conferences and seminars, seed money grants, and scholarship funds. Applicants should submit a one-page letter of request; full proposals will be requested. Annual deadline dates may vary; contact program staff for exact dates.
Requirements: 501(c)3 nonprofit organizations serving the Rochester, NY, area are eligible.
Restrictions: Grants will not be made to individuals, partisan political organizations, or to support lobbying efforts. Requests for capital projects also will not be considered.
Geographic Focus: New York
Date(s) Application is Due: Jul 11
Amount: 1,000 - 25,000 USD
Samples: Andrew Ctr (Rochester, NY)—to provide services to physically and emotionally disabled children, $10,000; Greater Rochester Enterprise (NY)—to support economic development in the Rochester region, $25,000; Sojourner House (Rochester, NY)—for a transitional-housing program for women and children, $10,000; Westside Health Services (Rochester, NY)—to purchase dental equipment, $11,000.
Contact: Ruth Fleischmann-Colgan, Executive Director; (585) 461-4699 or (585) 461-4696; (585) 473-5206; mcjcwilsonfdn@frontiernet.net
Internet: http://www.mcjcwilsonfoundation.org/funding.cfm
Sponsor: Marie C. and Joseph C. Wilson Foundation
160 Allens Creek Road
Rochester, NY 14618-3309

Marilyn Augur Family Foundation Grants **1120**
The foundation gives priority to organizations serving basic human needs primarily in the geographical area of Dallas, TX. Basic needs include food, shelter, clothing, health, and education aimed at transforming lives of those living in poverty or in prison. Christian organizations that minister to the needy are of particular interest. The foundation gives emphasis to children's

programs. The foundation prefers to support organizations and projects directly rather than supporting fundraising events.
Requirements: Texas nonprofit organizations are eligible.
Restrictions: Generally, the foundation does not give in the area of arts and culture.
Geographic Focus: Texas
Amount: 1,000 - 3,000 USD
Contact: Nancy Roberts, (214) 522-5586; (214) 526-0253; maf@waymark.net
Internet: http://fdncenter.org/grantmaker/augur/app.html
Sponsor: Marilyn Augur Family Foundation
4209 McKinney Avenue, Suite 202A
Dallas, TX 75205

Marion I. and Henry J. Knott Foundation Grants **1121**
Grants are awarded to organizations located in areas served by the Archdiocese of Baltimore for projects in private and nonsectarian private school elementary and secondary education, cultural arts and humanities, human and social services, Roman Catholicism, and health. Programs and projects that will be funded include endowment funds, capital and building campaigns, operating expenses, matching funds, equipment, seed money, and new or ongoing program support. All grant requests must be discussed with the foundation's executive director at least one month before submission. Requests should be submitted by a one-page letter; full proposals are by invitation. Deadlines listed are for letters of inquiry.
Requirements: Funding is limited to 501(c)3 organizations serving Baltimore City and the following counties in Maryland: Allegheny, Anne Arundel, Baltimore, Carroll, Frederick, Garrett, Harford, Howard, and Washington.
Restrictions: The following will not be funded: organizations that have not been in operation for at least one year, scholarships, public education/public sector agencies, pro-choice activities, individuals, annual giving, political activities, one-time only events/seminars/workshops, legal services, environment, medical research, day care centers, endowment funds for arts/humanities, national/local chapters for specific diseases, agencies that redistribute grant funds to other nonprofits, or government agencies that form 501(c)3 nonprofits to fund public sector projects.
Geographic Focus: Maryland
Date(s) Application is Due: Jun 1; Dec 1
Amount: 20,000 - 35,000 USD
Samples: Sisters Academy of Baltimore (MD)—for salary support of sixth-grade teachers at this tuition-free middle school for girls, $40,000; Family Crisis Ctr of Baltimore County (MD)—for operating support, $35,000, Maryland Institute College of Art (Baltimore, MD)—for its Community Arts Corps program, which works with young people living in poverty, $20,000; Saint Cecilia Roman Catholic Church (Baltimore, MD)—for capital support, $30,000.
Contact: Program Contact; (410) 235-7068; (410) 889-2577; knott@knottfoundation.org
Internet: http://knottfoundation.org
Sponsor: Marion I. and Henry J. Knott Foundation
3904 Hickory Avenue
Baltimore, MD 21211-1834

Mark and Catherine Winkler Foundation Grants **1122**
The foundation awards grants in its areas of interest, including children and youth, community development, education/higher education, environmental conservation/programs, health care/surgery, human services, and social sciences. Types of support include annual campaigns, building construction/renovation, capital campaigns and endowments, challenge/matching grants, conferences and seminars, equipment acquisition, fellowships, general operating support, professorships, program development, research, and seed grants. There are no application deadlines. The board meets in November to consider requests.
Requirements: Nonprofit organizations are eligible.
Geographic Focus: All U.S. States
Amount: 700 - 1,000,000 USD
Samples: Centre College of Kentucky (Danville, KY)—for program support, $500,000; Colorado College (Colorado Springs, CO)—to create a professorship and to add a new junior faculty position in the psychology department, $1.5 million.
Contact: Lynne Ball, Assistant Treasurer; (703) 998-0400
Sponsor: Mark and Catherine Winkler Foundation
4900 Seminary Road, Suite 900
Alexandria, VA 22311

MARPAT Foundation Grants **1123**
The foundation supports nonprofit organizations based in or benefiting the greater Washington metropolitan area. Grants are awarded to support organizations that promote the visual and performing arts; encourage family planning; conserve natural resources or advance knowledge of the natural world; promote international understanding; preserve historic resources or advance knowledge of American history and culture, or; expand opportunities in the District of Columbia's Wards 7 and 8 for low-income youth and adults. Grant support includes general operating support, building funds, equipment, programs/projects, and publications. Stage One summary sheets are due by the listed application deadline; full proposals are by invitation.
Requirements: Organizations determined to be tax-exempt under section 501(c)3 of the U.S. Internal Revenue Code of 1986 and which are not private foundations are eligible. Grants will only be made to organizations based in or benefiting the greater Washington metropolitan area.
Restrictions: The foundation does not make grants for medical research, to endowment funds, to individuals, or to organizations based outside the United States.
Geographic Focus: District of Columbia, Maryland, Virginia
Date(s) Application is Due: May 22
Amount: 5,000 - 50,000 USD
Samples: 2008: GALA (Grupo de Artistas Latino Americanos) - $35,000 to support artistic, education and community engagement programming; Textile Museum - $20,000 for general operating support; International Student House - $20,000 to update electrical service to the building; Earthwatch - $15,000 to support DC middle/high school teacher volunteers in ?????eld research; Catholics for a Free Choice - $15,000 to support 'Condoms4Life' and 'Prevention Not Prohibition' initiatives; Jewish Historical Society of Greater Washington $5,000 to support an exhibition about Jewish life in Washington, DC and Alexandria during the Civil War
Contact: Joan Koven, Secretary/Treasurer; jkoven@marpatfoundation.org
Internet: http://fdncenter.org/grantmaker/marpat
Sponsor: MARPAT Foundation
P.O. Box 1769
Silver Spring, MD 20915-1769

Mars Foundation Grants **1124**
The foundation awards grants to eligible nonprofit organizations primarily within the Washington, DC, metropolitan area, including Virginia, Maryland, and the District of Columbia. Areas of support include arts and culture, animal/wildlife, civic and community, education, environment, health and human services, and historic preservation. Types of support include capital grants, challenge grants, general operating grants, and project grants. Grants are awarded once a year. Requests must be submitted on the foundation's application form.
Requirements: U.S. 501(c)3 nonprofit organizations are eligible.
Geographic Focus: All U.S. States
Date(s) Application is Due: Oct 15
Amount: 1,000 - 100,000 USD
Contact: Grants Administrator; (703) 821-4900; (703) 448-9678
Internet: http://www.mars.com
Sponsor: Mars Foundation
6885 Elm Street
McLean, VA 22101

Marsh Corporate Giving Grants **1125**
The corporate giving program targets nonprofit organizations in corporate communities. Support goes to food banks—financial support and in-kind product donations, and nutrition programs that provide free hot meals for underprivileged children; education and youth programs—operating grants or project support to human service agencies that provide services to people, particularly children, in need in Marsh communities, and projects that directly benefit children, promote the education of children, or encourage the positive development of children; community development—support for operations or projects to community and civic organizations that focus on civic involvement, citizen participation, or positive improvements that benefit the community; arts—cultural and arts organizations that serve broad audiences with programming of the highest quality, and one-time capital grants for arts and cultural facilities; and hometown or neighborhood activities—grass-roots organizations that focus their efforts on improving their immediate community through activities that benefit families in their hometowns or neighborhoods. Guidelines are available online.

Restrictions: Marsh is unable to provide support to for-profit organizations (employee recognition programs, company events, etc.) and third-party organizations.
Geographic Focus: All U.S. States
Contact: Community Relations Manager; (317) 594-2100
Internet: http://www.marsh.net/ce_cg.html
Sponsor: Marsh Supermarkets
9800 Crosspoint Boulevard
Indianapolis, IN 46256

Mary Black Foundation Grants **1126**
The foundation makes grants to nonprofit organizations in the Spartanburg County, South Carolina, region in its areas of interest, including early childhood development, and active living. Grants support projects in preventive health care, community health and wellness, and education. The community health fund is a small grantmaking resource that allows the foundation to respond to grant applications outside of the active living and early childhood development priority areas, but still within the foundation's mission of improving health and wellness in Spartanburg County. Guidelines and applications are available on the foundation's website.
Requirements: Nonprofit organizations in Spartanburg County, SC are eligible.
Restrictions: The foundation does not accept applications from individuals or general fundraising solicitations.
Geographic Focus: South Carolina
Date(s) Application is Due: Mar 15; Jun 15; Sep 15; Dec 15
Samples: Health Resource Ctr (Spartanburg, SC)—to publish and distribute Parent Talk, a newsletter on child rearing, $15,000; Senior Ctrs of Spartanburg County (SC)—for a home-repair program for elderly people, $28,000; Healthy Spartanburg (SC)—for general operating support, $25,000; Stop the Violence Collaboration of Spartanburg (SC)—to hold a series of violence-prevention institutes for seventh and eighth graders, $25,000.
Contact: Program Contact; (864) 573-9500; (864) 573-5805; info@maryblackfoundation.org
Internet: http://www.maryblackfoundation.org/application.html
Sponsor: Mary Black Foundation
945 E Main Street
Spartanburg, SC 29302

Mary D. and Walter F. Frear Eleemosynary Trust Grants **1127**
Grants are awarded to Hawaii nonprofit organizations in the areas of child welfare and youth, education, social services, music, and the arts. Types of support include building construction/renovation, capital campaigns, conferences and seminars, equipment acquisition, general operating support, matching/challenge grants, program development, and seed grants.
Requirements: Grant applications are accepted from qualified tax-exempt charitable organizations in Hawaii.
Restrictions: Grants are not made to individuals, nor for endowments, reserve purposes, deficit financing, or travel.
Geographic Focus: Hawaii
Date(s) Application is Due: Jan 1; Jul 1; Oct 1
Amount: 5,000 - 25,000 USD
Samples: Daughters of Hawaii (HI)—to support capital projects at Queen Emma Summer Palace, $3000; Manoa Valley Theatre (HI)—to support the community outreach program, $2250; Hospice Hawaii (HI)—for bereavement support groups, $4000; Alzheimer's Assoc (HI)—toward start-up costs of the respite care center, $5000.
Contact: Paula Boyce, Grants Administrator, c/o Bank of Hawaii; (808) 538-4944; (808) 538-4006; pboyce@boh.com
Sponsor: Mary D. and Walter F. Frear Eleemosynary Trust
P.O. Box 3170
Honolulu, HI 96802-3170

Mary E. Bivins Foundation Grants **1128**
The foundation supports U.S. organizations and distributes funding for religious education, religious welfare, and scholarships. Types of support include building construction/renovation, capital campaigns, conferences and seminars, research, scholarship funds and scholarships to individuals, and seed grants. Applicants should submit a brief letter of inquiry, including program description and organization background, religious preference, and future plans.
Requirements: Christian nonprofits in Texas are eligible.
Geographic Focus: Texas
Amount: 5,000 - 50,000 USD
Samples: Ozark Christian College (Joplin, MO)—for scholarships, $23,805; Abilene Christian U (Abilene, TX)—for scholarships, $3300.
Contact: Linda Pitner, Program Coordinator; (806) 379-9400; (806) 379-9404; linda@bivinsfoundation.org
Internet: http://www.bivinsfoundations.org/grants.php
Sponsor: Mary E. Bivins Foundation
P.O. Box 1727
Amarillo, TX 79105

Mary Flagler Cary Charitable Trust Grants **1129**
Grants are awarded for general operating support and for program support. The trust considers grant proposals in three areas: for music in New York City (with an emphasis on the performance of contemporary music; and support of music education programs, primarily at community schools of the arts); for the conservation of natural resources (the protection of coastal wetlands, with an emphasis on the Virginia Barrier Islands and South Carolina Coastal Focus Areas, through the support of efforts to provide for the long-term protection of natural resources as a part of regional ecosystems); and for urban environmental programs in New York City (focused on support for community initiatives and to help develop local leadership to work on the environmental problems within low-income neighborhoods of the city). The balance of the trust's grant budget is devoted primarily to support the Mary Flagler Cary Arboretum and its scientific program, the Institute of Ecosystem Studies, in Millbrook, NY. Multiple-year grants may be awarded when appropriate. Initial contact should be by letter outlining the project for which funds are requested; the amount needed; and information on the structure, activities, budget, and staff of the requesting organization. Proposals are accepted at any time.
Requirements: Grants are made to tax-exempt organizations whose programs fall within the trust's interests.
Restrictions: Grants are not made to individuals or for scholarships, fellowships, capital funds, annual campaigns, seed grants, emergency funds, deficit financing, or endowment funds.
Geographic Focus: New York
Amount: 5,000 - 50,000 USD
Samples: American Symphony Orchestra (New York, NY)—for general support of its concert season at Avery Fisher Hall, $45,000; Uprose (Brooklyn, NY)—support for the Sunset Park Environmental Justice Community Organizing initiative, $20,000; National Audubon Society (New York, NY)—general support of the society's Florida Everglades program, $40,000.
Contact: Grants Administrator; (212) 953-7700; (212) 953-7720; info@carytrust.org
Internet: http://www.carytrust.org
Sponsor: Mary Flagler Cary Charitable Trust
122 E 42nd Street, Room 3505
New York, NY 10168

Mary Kay Foundation Domestic Violence Shelter Grants **1130**
Every October, The Mary Kay Foundation observes National Domestic Violence Awareness Month by awarding grants to deserving women's domestic violence shelters across the United States. During the past year, the Foundation awarded $20,000 grants to more than 150 women's domestic violence shelters across the nation for a total of $3 million. Each year, the Foundation awards a grant to at least one domestic violence shelter in every state. Any remaining funds are distributed based on state population. Grant applications are reviewed by the Domestic Violence Shelter Grant Committee, which makes recommendations to the TMKF Board of Directors. After reviewing these recommendations, the Foundation's Board of Directors selects the final grant recipients. Domestic violence shelter grant applications are available from this website or from The Mary Kay Foundation from January to June 30 each year. We announce grant recipients in the fall to coincide with National Domestic Violence Awareness Month in October.
Geographic Focus: All U.S. States
Amount: 20,000 USD
Samples: Abused Women's Aid in Crisis, Inc., Anchorage, Alaska, $20,000 (2010); Domestic Violence Services of Greater New Haven (DVS), New Haven, Connecticut, $20,000 (2010); Crisis Intervention Service Shelter, Mason City, Iowa, $20,000 (2010).
Contact: Lana Rowe, (972) 687-4822 or (877) 652-2737; Lana.Rowe@mkcorp.comJennifer Cook, (972) 687-5889 or (972) 687-4822; Jennifer.cook@mkcorp.com or MKCares@marykayfoundation.org

Internet: http://www.marykayfoundation.org/Pages/ShelterGrantProgram.aspx
Sponsor: Mary Kay Foundation
P.O. Box 799044
Dallas, TX 75379-9044

Mary Owen Borden Foundation Grants **1131**
The foundation supports programs that address the needs of economically disadvantaged youth and their families. This includes needs such as health, family planning, education, counseling, childcare, substance abuse, and delinquency. Other areas of interest for the foundation include affordable housing, conservation, environment, and the arts.
Requirements: New Jersey nonprofits in Monmouth and Mercer Counties are eligible.
Geographic Focus: New Jersey
Date(s) Application is Due: Mar 15; Sep 15
Amount: Up to 25,000 USD
Samples: Young Scholars' Institute (Trenton, NJ)—to support after-school, Saturday, and summer programs for more than 200 students (K-12), $18,500; Union Industrial Home (Trenton, NJ)—to provide residential care for young unwed mothers and their children, and support a program for young fathers, $14,000; Peace Action Education Fund (Princeton, NJ)—to provide conflict resolution training to Trenton youth, $12,500.
Contact: Quinn McKean, Executive Director; (732) 741-4645; (732) 741-2542; qmckean@aol.com
Internet: http://fdncenter.org/grantmaker/borden/guide.html
Sponsor: Mary Owen Borden Foundation
4 Blackpoint Horseshoe
Rumson, NJ 07760

Mary Reynolds Babcock Foundation Grants **1132**
The Foundation invites proposals from local, statewide and regional nonprofits in the Southeastern United States that have track records of helping low-wealth people build assets and transform economic conditions in their communities. The foundation supports people to build just and caring communities that nurture people, spur enterprise, bridge differences, and foster fairness. Its mission is to help people and places to move out of poverty and achieve greater social and economic justice. The foundation carries out this commitment through three funding areas: enterprise and asset development, community problem solving, and grassroots leadership development. Organizations may use grant funds in a variety of ways, including but not limited to: general operating support; project support; glue support for bringing together networks of grassroots and partner organizations; organizational development support; and efforts to bring 18- to 30-year-olds into leadership roles in the organization.
Requirements: Applicants must be located in the southeastern U.S., with emphasis on eastern Alabama, Arkansas, Georgia, Louisiana, Mississippi, North Carolina, South Carolina, Tennessee, north and central Florida, and the Appalachian regions of Kentucky and West Virginia.
Restrictions: No grants to individuals, capital improvements, direct services (such as food or medical assistance), or for satellite operations of organizations outside the southeast.
Geographic Focus: Alabama, Arkansas, Florida, Georgia, Kentucky, Louisiana, Mississippi, North Carolina, South Carolina, Tennessee, West Virginia
Date(s) Application is Due: Feb 1; Jul 1
Amount: 1,500 - 6,000,000 USD
Contact: Gayle Williams, Executive Director; (336) 748-9222; (336) 777-0095; info@mrbf.org
Internet: http://www.mrbf.org/whatWeDo.aspx
Sponsor: Peek-A-Boo

Mary Reynolds Babcock Foundation Grants **1133**
Throughout our region, people who live in low-wealth communities and individuals from the public, private and nonprofit sectors are forming creative partnerships to advance economic and social justice. The Foundation invites proposals from local, statewide and regional nonprofits in the Southeastern U.S. that have track records of helping low-wealth people build assets and transform economic conditions in their communities. It supports grassroots groups and networks in low-wealth communities that are poised to expand their scale of impact. The Foundation also supports statewide or regional organizations and networks that are achieving large-scale impact. It is interested in both new approaches and proven strategies that link together grassroots and larger organizations. Organizations may use grant funds in a variety of ways, including but not limited to: general operating support; project support; glue support for bringing together networks of grassroots and partner organizations; organizational development support; and efforts to bring 18- to 30-year-olds into leadership roles in the organization.
Requirements: The Babcock Foundation invites proposals from local, statewide and regional nonprofits in the Southeastern United States that have track records of helping low-wealth people build assets and transform economic conditions in their communities. Applicants must be located in the southeastern U.S., with emphasis on eastern Alabama, Arkansas, Georgia, Louisiana, Mississippi, North Carolina, South Carolina, Tennessee, north and central Florida, and the Appalachian regions of Kentucky and West Virginia.
Restrictions: No grants to individuals, capital improvements, direct services (such as food or medical assistance), or for satellite operations of organizations outside the southeast.
Geographic Focus: Alabama, Arkansas, Georgia, Kentucky, Louisiana, Mississippi, North Carolina, South Carolina, Tennessee, Virginia, West Virginia
Date(s) Application is Due: Feb 1; Jul 1
Amount: 1,500 - 6,000,000 USD
Samples: Alabama Appleseed Center for Law & Justice, Montgomery, Alabama, $100,000 - grant supports general operations (2010); Hope Community Credit Union, Jackson, Mississippi, $250,000 - general operations (2011); Mountain Association for Community Economic Development, Berea, Kentucky, $600,000 - general support for MACED's sustainable development efforts in Central Appalachia (2011).
Contact: Gayle Williams , Executive Director; (336) 748-9222; (336) 777-0095; info@mrbf.org
Internet: http://www.mrbf.org/applyForGrant.aspx
Sponsor: Mary Reynolds Babcock Foundation
2920 Reynolda Road
Winston-Salem, NC 27106-3016

MassMutual Foundation for Hartford Grants **1134**
Programs are supported in the areas of education, housing, and health. Grants in education support collaborative relationships between the Connecticut Mutual/Hartford Public High School and Connecticut Mutual/Quirk Middle School Alliances; an employee matching gifts contribution program; and scholarship funding earmarked for Hartford Public High School graduates granted directly to the institutions of higher education and training. In the area of health, the foundation gives special consideration to proposals concerned with increasing the efficiency and effectiveness of health care in such areas as health education and disease prevention, alternative modes of health care delivery, and programs for cost containment. In the area of housing, the foundation will give special consideration to contributions relating to the city of Hartford and the Asylum Hill neighborhood in particular. Types of support include general operating support, continuing support, capital campaigns, program development, seed grants, internships, scholarship funds, matching funds, employee matching gifts, and technical assistance.
Requirements: Grants are limited to Connecticut tax-exempt organizations.
Restrictions: No support for sectarian groups; political, fraternal, labor, or veterans' organizations; or federated drives outside the local area. No grants to individuals (including direct scholarships), or for endowment funds, deficit financing, emergency funds, publications, land acquisition, fellowships, capital fund drives outside the local area, or goodwill advertising.
Geographic Focus: Connecticut
Amount: 500 - 300,000 USD
Samples: Connecticut Assoc for Human Services (CT)—for operating support, $5000; Connecticut Housing Investment Fund (CT)—for operating support, $4000; Hartford College for Women (CT)—for financial aid for Hartford Public High School graduates, $3000.
Contact: Ronald Copes, Executive Director; (860) 987-2085
Sponsor: MassMutual Foundation for Hartford
140 Garden Street, H356
Hartford, CT 06154

Mathile Family Foundation Grants **1135**
The foundation awards grants to eligible Ohio nonprofit organizations in its areas of interest, including children, education, meeting basic human needs, and free enterprise education. Grants support food services, children and youth services, and human services for the homeless. Types of support include general operating support, capital campaigns, building construction/renovation, program development, and matching/challenge funds.
Requirements: Ohio nonprofit organizations are eligible. Giving primarily is limited to the Dayton area.

Restrictions: Grants are not made to individuals or for endowment funds.
Geographic Focus: Ohio
Date(s) Application is Due: Feb 1; May 1; Aug 1; Nov 1
Amount: 1,000 - 250,000 USD
Contact: Angela Hayes, Program Contact; (937) 264-4607; (937) 264-4805; angela.hayes@cymi.com
Sponsor: Mathile Family Foundation
6450 Sand Lake Road, Suite 100
Dayton, OH 45414

Matilda R. Wilson Fund Grants **1136**
The fund awards grants, primarily in southeast Michigan, in support of the arts, youth agencies, higher education, hospitals, and social services. Types of support include building construction/renovation, endowments, equipment acquisition, general operating support, matching/challenge grants, program development, research, and scholarship funds. There are no application forms; initial approach should be a letter of request. The board considers requests at quarterly board meetings, in January, June, September, and December.
Requirements: Michigan tax-exempt organizations are eligible.
Restrictions: Grants are not made to individuals.
Geographic Focus: Michigan
Amount: 10,000 - 100,000 USD
Samples: Oakland U (MI)—to repair and restore Meadow Brook Hall, the former home of the university's founder, Matilda Dodge Wilson, $7 million.
Contact: David Larsen, Grants Administrator; (313) 259-7777; (313) 393-7579; roosterveen@bodmanllp.com
Sponsor: Matilda R. Wilson Fund
100 Renaissance Center, 34th Floor
Detroit, MI 48243

Mattel International Grants **1137**
The corporation and its foundation award grants to charitable organizations that directly serve children in need. Funding priorities include international organizations or programs that creatively address a defined need directly impacting children in need, and international organizations or programs that align with Mattel's philanthropic priorities, including health—supporting the physical and mental health and well-being of children, and increasing access to health care services for children in need; education—increasing access to education, promoting literacy to children in need, and resources that promote after-school educational achievement; and girls empowerment—promoting self-esteem of girls and increasing access to education, health, and community resources for girls. Types of support include program-specific grants—funding for new programs or expansion of existing programs; and core operating support—support of organizations to sustain their programs. Applications must be submitted online. Applications will not be accepted by fax or mail. Submit questions via email.
Requirements: Organizations must serve children in non-U.S. communities; and must not discriminate against a person or a group on the basis of age, political affiliation, race, national origin, ethnicity, gender, disability, sexual orientation, or religious belief. Pilot projects and new organizations may be considered as long as all eligibility criteria are met; however, preference will be given to organizations that have at least two years of experience. Preference is given to organizations that have an annual operating budget of less than $1 million and are not affiliated with a national organization.
Restrictions: The program does not not fund capital funding for physical property purchase, renovation, or developments; individuals; political parties, candidates, or partisan political organizations; labor organizations, fraternal organizations, athletic clubs, or social clubs; sectarian or denominational religious organizations, except for programs that are available to anyone, broadly promoted, and free from religious orientation; schools and school districts; fundraising events (e.g., dinners, tournaments); advertising or marketing sponsorships; or research overhead and/or indirect costs (including fiscal sponsor fees) that exceed 15 percent of the direct project costs.
Geographic Focus: All U.S. States
Amount: 5,000 - 25,000 USD
Contact: Grants Administrator; (310) 252-2000; (310) 252-2180; foundation@mattel.com
Internet: http://corporate.mattel.com/about-us/philanthropy/internationalgrants.aspx
Sponsor: Mattel Children's Foundation
333 Continental Boulevard, M1-1418
El Segundo, CA 90245-5012

Maurice Amado Foundation Grants **1138**
The foundation awards grants to nonprofit organizations in the Los Angeles and New York City metropolitan areas primarily for activities that emphasize the Sephardic Jewish heritage, with special interest in educational and cultural projects. Types of support include general operating support, challenge grants, conferences and seminars, continuing support, endowment funds, program development, publication, curriculum development, fellowships, seed money grants, and research. Letters of request and proposals are accepted and reviewed throughout the year. The board meets in the fall and the spring, at which time funding decisions are made. Organizations interested in applying are asked to submit a letter of inquiry.
Requirements: 501(c)3 organizations in New York and California are eligible. Individuals applying for grants must be affiliated with a tax-exempt organization.
Restrictions: Grants are not made directly to individuals.
Geographic Focus: All U.S. States
Date(s) Application is Due: Feb 15; Aug 15
Amount: 500 - 200,000 USD
Samples: 92nd Street Y (NY)—for operating support, $15,000; American Jewish Historical Society (NY)—for operating support, $10,000.
Contact: Pam Kaizer, Executive Director; (818) 980-9190; (818) 980-9190; pkaizer@mauriceamadofdn.org
Internet: http://www.mauriceamadofdn.org
Sponsor: Maurice Amado Foundation
3940 Laurel Canyon Boulevard, #809
Studio City, CA 91604

Max A. Adler Charitable Foundation Grants **1139**
The foundation awards grants to eligible New York nonprofit organizations serving the greater Rochester area in its areas of interest, including arts, children and youth services, Jewish services, health care, higher education, and social services. Types of support include building construction/renovation, capital campaigns, general operating support, and program development. There are no application forms or deadlines.
Requirements: New York 501(c)3 nonprofit organizations serving the greater Rochester area are eligible.
Geographic Focus: New York
Amount: 1,000 - 25,000 USD
Samples: Nazareth College (Rochester, NY)—for its capital campaign to expand the size of its campus, $50,000.
Contact: David Gray, President; (585) 232-7290; (585) 232-7260
Sponsor: Max A. Adler Charitable Foundation
1010 Times Square Building
Rochester, NY 14614

Max and Anna Levinson Foundation Grants **1140**
Grants are awarded in three categories: the environment—including primarily preservation of ecosystems and biological diversity, environmental justice, alternative energy, alternative agriculture, and toxics; social—including primarily local economic development and responses to globalization, empowerment of youth, and direct aid and social service; Jewish/Israel—including Jewish culture and spirituality, building Jewish community in the diaspora, Jewish history and education, and social and environmental issues in Israel. Types of support include conferences and seminars, equipment acquisition, general operating support, grants to individuals, program development, publication, and seed money grants. Grants are awarded once a year.
Restrictions: Grants generally are not awarded to organizations with annual budgets in excess of $500,000. Grants do not support building programs, capital or endowment funds, expansion of existing services, fellowships or scholarships, matching gifts, programs serving local communities, or travel.
Geographic Focus: All U.S. States
Date(s) Application is Due: Apr 1
Amount: 10,000 - 20,000 USD
Contact: Program Contact; (505) 995-8802; (505) 995-8982; info@levinsonfoundation.org
Internet: http://www.levinsonfoundation.org
Sponsor: Max and Anna Levinson Foundation
P.O. Box 6309
Santa Fe, NM 87502-6309

May and Stanley Smith Trust Grants 1141

The trust awards grants to nonprofit organizations in its areas of interest, including children and youth, people with disabilities, the economically disadvantaged, education, the elderly, social services, and the visually impaired. Types of support include general operating grants and scholarship funds. Grants are awarded primarily in North America, with emphasis on the San Francisco Bay area, and Canada. Applications are accepted from January 1 through the listed deadline date; grants are considered beginning in April.
Restrictions: Grants are not made to individuals.
Geographic Focus: All U.S. States
Date(s) Application is Due: Sep 30
Amount: 500 - 6,000 USD
Contact: Dale Matheny, (415) 391-0292
Sponsor: May and Stanley Smith Trust
720 Market Street, Suite 250
San Francisco, CA 94102

Mayer and Morris Kaplan Family Foundation Grants 1142

Grants are available to nonprofit organizations serving inner-city Chicago residents in seven program areas: education, self-help, basic human needs, museums, cultural arts, civic affairs, and Jewish affairs. The foundation considers providing seed money, challenge grants, support for general operations, and special project funding. Agencies awarded multiyear grants are required to submit annual progress reports, including a current audit, board list, and statement of accomplishments prior to the release of precommitted support. The first step that must be followed by all applicants is submission of a two-page summary request letter and budget. If requested by the board, a full proposal will be invited.
Requirements: Illinois nonprofit organizations are eligible.
Restrictions: Grants are generally not given to sectarian institutions; purchase of tickets to testimonial events or goodwill advertising; medical, scientific, or academic research; individuals, films, or funding of meetings; capital and endowment campaigns, building and equipment acquisition, or fund-raising drives; health care institutions; national health, welfare, education, or cultural organizations; or an institution more than once during the fiscal year.
Geographic Focus: Illinois
Date(s) Application is Due: Jan 15; May 15; Sep 15
Amount: 5,000 - 120,000 USD
Contact: Jason Heeney, Executive Director; (847) 926-8350; Jheeney@kapfam.com
Sponsor: Mayer and Morris Kaplan Family Foundation
1780 Green Bay Road, Suite 205
Highland Park, IL 60035

MAZON Grants: A Jewish Response to Hunger 1143

MAZON's domestic grant program makes awards for general support or special projects in four categories. Advocacy Education/Research grants, ranging from $5000-$20,000, support programs to change public policy or opinion or the operation and administration of federal food assistance programs. Emergency/Direct Food Assistance grants, ranging from $5000-$7000, support food pantries, soup kitchens, and programs providing meals to special-needs populations. Food Bank grants, ranging from $5000-$15,000, are awarded to warehouses that collect and distribute food to nonprofit feeding programs; applicants must demonstrate that they participate in antihunger advocacy and education efforts. Multiservice Organization grants, ranging from $5000-$15,000, support organizations that provide food and a broad array of services to hungry and low-income people. Deadlines listed are for letters of inquiry.
Requirements: U.S. nonprofit organizations that meet program criteria may apply.
Restrictions: MAZON does not make grants to groups that proselytize or place any religious requirements on service; have national name recognition; are principally focused on homelessness; charge individuals for food; or are government entities, professional associations, job training programs, or grantmaking organizations. Capital grants for building projects are not eligible for support. Prepared and perishable food programs are not eligible unless they are in their first two years of operation. MAZON does not fund holiday meal programs.
Geographic Focus: All U.S. States
Date(s) Application is Due: May 15; Nov 15
Samples: 28 nonprofit organizations nationwide—for their work to relieve hunger in the United States, $110,500 divided.
Contact: Grants Administrator; (310) 442-0020; (310) 442-0030; mazonmail@mazon.org
Internet: http://www.mazon.org/What_We_Fund/Funding_Guidelines/
Sponsor: MAZON: A Jewish Response to Hunger
1990 S Bundy Drive, Suite 260
Los Angeles, CA 90025-5232

McCarthy Family Foundation Grants 1144

The McCarthy Family Foundation is a small private foundation established in 1988. Organized as a California public benefit nonprofit corporation, it operates from San Diego, California. The foundation's current program interest areas have been funded throughout its almost two decades history. These funding areas are: K-12 science education; HIV/AIDS research, education and direct services; assistance to homeless persons; and child abuse prevention and services for victims and families. The board will occasionally fund a special project outside these categorical areas and/or for regional, national or international charitable purposes. A small portion of the grantmaking budget is provided for director matching grants to encourage and amplify personal philanthropy by the foundation's board of directors. Proposals will be considered in the above general areas or for special project areas established by the Board. Proposals will only be accepted for programs within San Diego County. Multiple year proposals may be considered but it is not the foundation's intention to provide annual support. It is not normally the foundation's desire to be the sole source of funds for a project. Most grants are expected to be small, $5,000-$15,000, reflecting the foundation's limited budget although there are no fixed minimum or maximum amounts. Grant proposals received by March 15 will be considered for decision/funding in June. Grant proposals received by September 15 will be considered for decision/funding in December.
Requirements: Proposals will only be accepted for programs within San Diego County, California. All applicants should first submit a letter of inquiry, which can be submitted directly from the Foundation's web site. The letter (1-2 pages) must contain a brief statement describing the applicant and the need for funds with enough information for the foundation to determine whether or not the application falls within its program areas. Proposals submitted without an initial letter of inquiry will not be reviewed by the foundation. Applicants should briefly and clearly provide a statement of their needs and the specific request to the foundation, taking into account other possible sources of funding. Letters of inquiry will be acknowledged upon their receipt, but because the foundation operates without a professional staff, a more detailed response may be delayed. Applicants who receive a favorable response to their initial inquiry will be invited to submit a grant application. The foundation accepts the Common Grant Application of San Diego Grantmakers, which can be downloaded from the Foundation's web site. Five copies of the application (proposal) should be submitted. Only one copy of required attachments need be submitted. The application should be signed by the organization's board chair or the executive director (or equivalent individuals).
Restrictions: The foundation does not consider grants for individuals, scholarship funds, or sectarian religious activities. Normally the foundation does not consider requests for general fundraising drives. It does not make grants intended directly or indirectly to support political candidates or to influence legislation.
Geographic Focus: California
Date(s) Application is Due: Mar 15; Sep 15
Amount: 500 - 250,000 USD
Samples: United Way of San Diego County, $10,000—general operating support (2009); UCLA AIDS Institute, $50,000—stem cell research for HIV prevention (2009); Elementary Institute of Science, $10,000—-science and technology youth education (2009).
Contact: Rachel McCarthy Bender, President; (858) 485-0129; mail@mccarthyfamilyfdn.org
Internet: http://www.mccarthyfamilyfdn.org/guide.html
Sponsor: McCarthy Family Foundation
P.O. Box 27389
San Diego, CA 92198-1389

McColl Foundation Grants 1145

Established in 1996, the Foundation awards funding in its areas of interest, including: the arts; community and economic development; early childhood education; elementary and secondary education; federated giving programs; health organizations; higher education; and performing arts. Types of support include: annual campaigns, building and renovation, curriculum development, general operations, and scholarship funds. Giving is primarily focused in

North Carolina, with an initial approach requesting a Letter of Inquiry. The Board meets twice annually.
Geographic Focus: North Carolina
Amount: 500 - 25,000 USD
Contact: Jane McColl Lockwood, President; (704) 376-6978
Sponsor: McColl Foundation
P.O. Box 6144
Charlotte, NC 28207-0001

McCune Charitable Foundation Grants **1146**
The Marshall L. and Perrine D. McCune Charitable Foundation is dedicated to enriching the health, education, environment, and cultural and spiritual life of New Mexicans. The Foundation engages in proactive grantmaking that seeks to foster positive social change. Specifically, the Foundation funds projects that benefit New Mexico in the areas of arts, economic development, education, environment, health, and social services.
Requirements: Grants can be awarded to qualified 501(c)3 nonprofit organizations, federally recognized Indian tribes, public schools, and governmental agencies. Applications are available online via the Foundation's website.
Restrictions: Grants are not awarded to individuals or to support endowments.
Geographic Focus: New Mexico
Date(s) Application is Due: Sep 30
Amount: Up to 150,000 USD
Samples: New Mexico Community Capital, Albuquerque, New Mexico, $150,000- for general operating support (2008); Institute of American Indian Arts, Santa Fe, New Mexico, $10,000- for general operating support; Story Dancer Project, Santa Fe, New Mexico, $10,000- For intercultural and bilingual program of Connected-Learning (2008)
Contact: Norty Kalishman, M.D., Program Director; (505) 983-8300; (505) 983-7887; mccune@nmmccune.org
Internet: http://www.nmmccune.org
Sponsor: McCune Charitable Foundation
345 E Alameda Street
Santa Fe, NM 87501

MCF Human Needs Grants **1147**
The foundation was established to engage in, conduct, and promote charitable, religious, educational, artistic, and philanthropic activities primarily in Marin County, CA. The mission of the foundation is to help improve the human condition and to enhance the quality of life of the community. Toward this end, the foundation awards grants in seven areas: human needs, education and training, community development, religion, environment, the arts, and community programs. Types of support include continuing support, emergency funds, equipment, land acquisition, loans, matching funds, operating budgets, program-related investments, renovation projects, seed money, special projects, and technical assistance. Applicants should call or write for a copy of the guidelines as well as contact a program officer to determine if a proposed project or program is consistent with foundation goals.
Requirements: The applicant must be a public or nonprofit organization. The proposed project must be conducted either in Marin County or benefit the residents of Marin County. Projects with regional or multicounty benefits may be funded only in proportion to the extent that they benefit the Marin County community.
Restrictions: Ineligible activities include for-profit purposes, basic research, the start-up of new nonprofit organizations that duplicate existing programs or services or undertake services that can be more effectively provided by other organizations, and grants to individuals.
Geographic Focus: California
Samples: Bay Area Community Resources (San Rafael, CA)—to offer programs at a youth center, $1 million approximately over two years; MCF Property Holdings (Novato, CA)—to establish a youth center in San Rafael, CA, that will be operated by Bay Area Community Resources, $3.6 million in cash and loans.
Contact: Christy Vorhis, Grants Manager; (415) 464-2532; (415) 464-2555; cvorhis@marincf.org
Internet: http://www.marincf.org
Sponsor: Marin Community Foundation
5 Hamilton Landing, Suite 200
Novato, CA 94949

McGregor Foundation Grants **1148**
The program favors grants that address the following priority areas for elders in need: recruitment, education, training, and retention of health care professionals in geriatrics; access to care for underserved populations; promotion of health and wellness; and total quality of life for seniors. The board of directors particularly encourages requests for programs that increase the pool of workers trained in geriatrics, expand access to care for elders in need, or demonstrate effective new methods and approaches. In some instances, the foundation will consider requests for emergency operating support. The foundation will also consider requests for capital projects, with certain restrictions.
Requirements: Tax-exempt nonprofit organizations located within Cuyahoga County, OH, with preference given to communities traditionally served by The A.M. McGregor Home, are eligible. Currently no unsolicited grant applications from organizations outside Cuyahoga County will be accepted.
Restrictions: The foundation discourages capital requests from long-term residential care facilities or requests for debt reduction, annual funds, research, symposia, or endowments. No grants are awarded to individuals.
Geographic Focus: Ohio
Date(s) Application is Due: Mar 1; Sep 1
Samples: Access to the Arts (Cleveland, OH)—for art performances for elderly people in hospitals, nursing homes, and retirement communities, $15,270; Case Western Reserve U (Cleveland, OH)—to support the Gerontological Scholars Program of its Mandel School of Applied Social Sciences during the 2005-06 academic year, $20,000; Ohio Presbyterian Retirement Services (Cleveland, OH)—to implement a program on preventing and managing diabetes, $21,120; Recovery Resources (Cleveland, OH)—to collaborate with Fairhill Center to provide training for staff members caring for elderly people with a history of substance abuse and mental illness, $60,111.
Contact: Susan Althans, Executive Director; (216) 696-7273; (216) 621-8198; salthans@fmscleveland.com
Internet: http://mcgregorfoundation.org/guidelines.html
Sponsor: McGregor Foundation
1422 Euclid Avenue, Suite 627
Cleveland, OH 44115-1952

McGregor Fund Grants **1149**
The fund makes grants to organizations in the following areas: human services—emphasis on activities in southeastern Michigan addressing emergency needs in housing, food, clothing, and other direct aid; education—early child education and development, colleges and universities in the Detroit metropolitan area, liberal arts colleges and universities in Michigan and Ohio; arts and culture in southeastern Michigan; health care—improving access to primary care for underserved populations in Detroit; and public benefit—civic and community organizations that improve the quality of life in southeastern Michigan. Types of support include project support, operating support, special projects, and capital support. Grant decisions are made by the board of trustees four times annually, in February, May, September, and November. Grant requests may be submitted at any time, but requests may take up to three months for staff review. Application guidelines are available online.
Requirements: Organizations in the metropolitan Detroit, MI area, are eligible. Requests will be considered from organizations located elsewhere for programs or projects that significantly benefit the metropolitan Detroit area (city of Detroit and Wayne, Oakland, and Macomb Counties).
Restrictions: The fund discourages proposals for student scholarships, travel, seminars, conferences, workshops, film or video projects, as well as disease-specific organizations and their local affiliates.
Geographic Focus: Michigan
Amount: 25,000 - 50,000 USD
Samples: Detroit Institute of Arts (MI)—for its capital campaign to complete a building project, increase its endowment, and support operations, $2 million,
Contact: C. David Campbell, President; (313) 963-3495; (313) 963-3512; info@mcgregfund.org
Internet: http://www.mcgregorfund.org/guideline.html
Sponsor: McGregor Fund
333 W Fort Street, Suite 2090
Detroit, MI 48226

McKenzie River Gathering Foundation Grants **1150**
Grants are awarded to organizations located in Oregon that address peace, social justice, and environmental issues, such as anti-bigotry, domestic violence, homelessness, community-labor coalitions, HIV/AIDS, reproductive

rights, ancient forest and watershed protection, and anti-militarism. Types of support include general operating grants, matching grants, program grants, seed money grants, technical assistance, training grants, and travel grants. Interested groups should call the Eugene office which, after prescreening for adherence to MRG's basic criteria, will place prospective groups on a list to receive an application form.
Requirements: Applicant organizations must be located in Oregon, organizing for progressive social change, committed to developing diversity, and have limited access to other funding.
Restrictions: Grants are not awarded to/for social service agencies, schools, health centers, scholarships, cooperatives, individuals, or organizations based outside of Oregon, even if they have an Oregon project.
Geographic Focus: Oregon
Date(s) Application is Due: Feb 25; Sep 2
Amount: 3,000 - 5,000 USD
Samples: Central Oregon Environmental Ctr (Bend, OR)—for general support, $3000; Latino Coalition (Eugene, OR)—for general support, $3000.
Contact: Anita Rodgers, Program Director; (800) 489-6743 or (503) 234-2338; anita@mrgfoundation.org
Internet: http://www.mrgfoundation.org/html/apply
Sponsor: McKenzie River Gathering Foundation
2705 E Burnside, Suite 210
Portland, OR 97214

McKesson Foundation Grants **1151**

The foundation seeks to enhance the health and quality of life in communities where McKesson HBOC operates and its employees live. Emphasis is focused on youth, especially health services for underserved populations, educational enrichment, the environment, recreation, and youth development activities. The foundation also funds emergency services for children and families, and a variety of social, educational and cultural programs. For culture and the arts, support is given primarily to organizations that reach out to youth and other populations that do not have easy access to such programs. Grants are made for specific projects and programs, and general operating support will be considered in some circumstances. Grants are awarded for one to three years. The Foundation does not accept uninvited applications. Initial approach should be to contact the Foundation directly.
Requirements: 501(c)3 tax-exempt organizations are eligible.
Restrictions: Grants are not made to endowment campaigns, individuals or individual scholarships, religious organizations for religious purposes, political causes or campaigns, advertising in charitable publications, research studies or health organizations concentrating on one disease.
Geographic Focus: All U.S. States
Amount: 5,000 - 25,000 USD
Samples: LA Theater Work (CA)—for a project that creates hands-on performing arts and literary workshops aimed at finding a positive outlet for the aggression of 3000 at-risk and incarcerated youths, $7500; Massachusetts Coalition for School-Based Health Ctrs (MA)—to hire a coordinator and to continue providing school-based health care, $125,000 over three years.
Contact: Marcia Argyris, Foundation President; (415) 983-8673 or (415) 983-8300; (415) 983-7590; marcia.argyris@mckesson.com or community.relations@mckesson.com
Internet: http://www.mckesson.com/en_us/McKesson.com/About%2BUs/Corporate%2BCitizenship/McKesson%2BFoundation.html
Sponsor: McKesson Foundation
1 Post Street, 32nd Floor
San Francisco, CA 94104-5203

McKnight Foundation Mississippi River Environment Grants **1152**

The McKnight Foundation assists nonprofit organizations and public agencies to improve the quality of life for all people, particularly those in need. The goal of the Foundation's Mississippi River Environment Grants is to use their resources to restore the water quality and resilience of the Mississippi River. Three strategies are to: restore and protect floodplains and wetlands in the ten-state Mississippi River corridor; reduce agricultural pollution in four states along the northern half of the river (Minnesota, Wisconsin, Iowa, and Illinois), focusing on farmland and operations with high levels of nitrogen and phosphorus runoff; and achieve cross-boundary and interagency coordination that improves the river's water quality and resilience. Funding is provided for planning, operating, and projects.
Requirements: Applicants must be classified by the Internal Revenue Service as tax-exempt, nonprofit organizations. Applicants are encouraged to call the Foundation to discuss ideas with a Program Officer and to learn more about the Foundation's strategies. If the organization's work fits the Foundation's funding strategies, an initial application may be made on-line, with an email respond from the Foundation within 45 days either to decline funding or to provide instructions to submit a full proposal online.
Restrictions: The following are ineligible: advocacy efforts related to biofuels production; efforts broadly addressing endocrine disruptors; conventional water supply, waste water treatment, storm water conveyance, or flood control facilities; basic research in academic disciplines; scholarships or other types of assistance for individuals; conferences, including attendance or travel, except when related to existing McKnight support; endowments, except in rare cases; activities that have a specific religious purpose; or lobbying prohibited by the Internal Revenue Code.
Geographic Focus: Illinois, Iowa, Minnesota, Wisconsin
Date(s) Application is Due: Nov 1; Feb 1; May 1; Aug 1
Contact: Ron Kroese, Program Director; (612) 333-4220; rkroese@mcknight.org
Internet: http://www.mcknight.org/environment/river.aspx
Sponsor: McKnight Foundation
710 S Second Street, Suite 400
Minneapolis, MN 55401

McMurry Foundation Grants **1153**

The foundation was established to have a significant and beneficial impact on the communities within Wyoming with special emphasis in Natrona County. Areas of interest include education, religion, children and advocacy for children, health and human services, the arts and humanities, and a favorable business environment. The foundation invests in innovative ventures as well as established community programs that have the potential to make a lasting difference. Funds provide seed money to start new programs; general funds to expand or improve services offered by established agencies; and organizational support, such as strategic planning, increasing management capacity, and board development. Priority will be given to promote strengthening the capacity of nonprofit organizations to do their work, leveraging the dollars of the McMurry Foundation, collaboration and efficient use of nonprofit resources, and addressing the causes or prevention of community problems. Application process and guidelines are available online.
Requirements: Wyoming 501(c)3 nonprofit organizations and organizations who have applied and anticipate receiving such status are eligible.
Restrictions: Grants designated to influence legislation or elect public officials are rejected.
Geographic Focus: All U.S. States
Date(s) Application is Due: Jan 15; Apr 15; Jul 15; Oct 15
Samples: U of Wyoming (Laramie, WY)—to help renovate the College of Education facility, $250,000.
Contact: Trudi McMurry, Director; (307) 234-4631; trudie@mcmurry.net
Internet: https://online.foundationsource.com/public/home/mcmurryfoundation
Sponsor: McMurry Foundation
P.O. Box 2016
Casper, WY 82602-2016

Mead Johnson Nutritionals Charitable Giving Grants **1154**

Mead Johnson Nutritionals considers requests for charitable giving from a broad range of charitable organizations. Requests for charitable giving must be made in connection with a general fund raising effort by the charitable entity, rather than a request directed only to Mead Johnson Nutritionals. In addition, the request for a contribution must come from the organization itself and not from an individual physician, pharmacist, or health care professional who is not an employee of the charity. Applicants should allow at least three months for the processing of a funding request. Grant applications submitted less than three months prior to an event may be rejected due to insufficient time to process the application. Organizations outside the U.S. that wish to request a charitable gift should refer to Mead Johnson contact information within their country or call the charitable giving department at (812) 429-7800.
Requirements: Charitable giving is permitted if the recipient is a tax-exempt organization under Section 501(c)3 of the Internal Revenue Code.
Restrictions: As with grants, charitable giving may not be tied, in any way, to past, present, or future prescribing, purchasing, or recommending (including formulary recommendations) of any product.
Geographic Focus: All U.S. States
Contact: Grants Administrator; (812) 429-7831; (812) 647-8674; meadjohnson.grants1@bms.com

Internet: http://www.mjn.com/app/iwp/MJN/Content2.do?dm=mj&id=/MJN_Home2/mjnBtnSocialResponsibility2/mjnBtnCharitableGivingApplication&iwpst=B2C&ls=0&csred=1&r=3435833953
Sponsor: Mead Johnson Nutritionals
2400 West Lloyd Expressway
Evansville, IN 47721-0001

Mead Witter Foundation Grants **1155**

Incorporated in Wisconsin in 1951, the Foundation awards grants to nonprofits in company operating locations, primarily in central and northern Wisconsin. Local community programs are funded, focusing on education, including scholarships in higher education and direct contributions to colleges and universities. Grants also are made to support the arts, health care, human services, youth organizations, environmental programs, and Christian and Roman Catholic organizations for nonreligious purposes. Types of support include general operating support, continuing support, annual campaigns, capital campaigns, building construction and renovation, equipment acquisition, endowment funds, professorships, seed grants, scholarship funds, and employee-matching gifts. The board meets twice annually to consider requests. Full proposal is by invitation only.
Requirements: Wisconsin 501(c)3 organizations may apply.
Restrictions: The foundation does not support religious, athletic, or fraternal groups, except when these groups provide needed special services to the community at large; direct grants or scholarships to individuals; community foundations; or flow-through organizations that redispense funds to other charitable causes.
Geographic Focus: Wisconsin
Amount: 25,000 - 18,000,000 USD
Samples: Carroll University, Waukesha, Wisconsin, $1,030,000; Medical College of Wisconsin, Milwaukee, $512,000; Beloit College, Beloit, $300,000.
Contact: Cynthia Henke, President; (715) 424-3004; (715) 424-1314
Sponsor: Mead Witter Foundation
P.O. Box 39
Wisconsin Rapids, WI 54495-0039

Medina Foundation Grants **1156**

The foundation makes grants to a wide range of nonprofits in the Puget Sound area. Grants support several causes: human services—emergency food and housing; education—private entities, grades preschool through 12, and programs in the areas of leadership and management, vocational and alternative schools, and tutoring and mentoring; persons with disabilities—work training and employment opportunities, self-sufficiency; alcohol and drug abuse—education, and treatment. Grants are awarded to fund direct service delivery programs, operating expenses, capital expenses, equipment, emergency funds, seed money grant, and technical assistance. Applications and guidelines are available on the website.
Requirements: Organizations operating within the greater Puget Sound region or to projects significantly affecting its residents are eligible. The greater Puget Sound region is defined as the following counties: Clallum, Grays Harbor, Island, Jefferson, King, Kitsap, Mason, Pacific, Pierce, San Juan, Skagit, Snohomish, Thurston, and Whatcom.
Restrictions: Requests will not be accepted from public schools or cultural programs.
Geographic Focus: Washington
Samples: Washington Families Fund (Seattle, WA)—for efforts in Washington State to create a reliable, long-term source of financing for support services for homeless children and their families, $100,000.
Contact: Jennifer Teunon, Program Officer; (206) 652-8783; info@medinafoundation
Internet: http://www.medinafoundation.org/index.php?p=Grants&s=3
Sponsor: Medina Foundation
801 2nd Avenue, Suite 1300
Seattle, WA 98104

Medtronic Foundation Full Life Patient Partnership Program—Heart Rescue Grants **1157**

The program funds organizations and government agencies that provide community-based education, training, and awareness programs related to sudden cardiac death and the use of automatic external defibrillators.
Requirements: National and local nonprofit organizations and government agencies that provide education, training, and awareness programs related to sudden cardiac death, early defibrillation, and early intervention are eligible.
Restrictions: The foundation does not support individuals, including scholarships for individuals; religious groups for religious purposes; fund-raising events or activities, social events or goodwill advertising; reimbursable health treatment or scientific research; general support of educational institutions; long-term counseling or personal development; lobbying, political, or fraternal activities; or programs that receive support from United Way of the Minneapolis area.
Geographic Focus: All U.S. States
Date(s) Application is Due: Oct 15
Amount: 5,000 - 50,000 USD
Contact: Penny Hunt, Executive Director; (763) 505-2646; (763) 505-2648
Internet: http://www.medtronic.com/foundation/about_news.html
Sponsor: Medtronic Foundation
710 Medtronic Parkway NE, MS LC110
Minneapolis, MN 55432-5604

Mellon Financial Corporation Foundation Grants **1158**

Mellon Bank supports economic development that strengthens communities and initiatives that focus on the needs of low- and moderate-income residents. Current focus is on efforts to attract and develop business and jobs, affordable housing and home ownership, literacy improvement, and technical assistance or capacity building for nonprofit organizations. Types of support include capital grants, program/project grants, matching gifts, technical assistance, and general operating grants. The fund makes grants primarily in its headquarters city of Pittsburgh, as well as in Boston and Philadelphia. Contributions to organizations in other Mellon locations, including outside the United States, are made through corporate donation programs customized to address the needs of specific communities. There are no application deadlines.
Requirements: IRS 501(c)3 charitable organizations in Mellon locations are eligible.
Restrictions: Support is not available for loans or assistance to individuals; ecclesiastical programs of churches or other sectarian organizations; political parties, campaigns, or candidates; or fraternal fraternal organizations. Grants do not support scholarships and fellowships; travel grants, conferences, specialized health campaigns; or endowment funds.
Geographic Focus: All U.S. States
Amount: 5,000 - 20,000 USD
Contact: Program Contact; (412) 234-2732
Internet: http://www.mellon.com/communityaffairs/charitablegiving.html
Sponsor: Mellon Financial Corporation Foundation
One Mellon Center, Suite 1830
Pittsburgh, PA 15258

Memorial Foundation Grants **1159**

The foundation awards grants each year to support nonprofit organizations that provide services in Middle Tennessee. Special emphasis is given to organizations that focus on health and rehabilitation; youth and children; senior citizens; education; human and social services; and substance abuse. Types of support include capital projects; general operating support; and start-up projects for new initiatives that address important, unmet community needs and that demonstrate a potential for ongoing operational support from other sources. The directors prefer that an applicant organization be able to demonstrate a broad base of financial support for a proposed grant from its own community and constituency prior to asking for support from the foundation. Multiyear grants are rarely awarded. There are no application deadlines. Guidelines are available online.
Requirements: 501(c)3 tax-exempt organizations that serve the Middle Tennessee area are eligible.
Restrictions: The foundation does not make grants to individuals; for newsletters, magazines, or books; to churches and religious organizations for projects that primarily benefit their own members (exception: church-based programs funded by multiple sources with broad community support); for tickets to charitable events or dinners for disease-specific organizations seeking support for national research projects and programs; to sponsor special events, productions, telethons, performances, or similar fundraising and advertising activities; for legislative lobbying or other political purposes; or to retire accumulated debt.
Geographic Focus: Tennessee
Contact: Grants Administrator; (615) 822-9499; (615) 822-7797
Internet: http://www.memfoundation.org
Sponsor: Memorial Foundation
100 Bluegrass Commons Boulevard, Suite 320
Hendersonville, TN 37075

Merck Company Foundation Grants 1160

The foundation advances the company's philanthropic outreach in helping to meet important needs of local and international communities that are consistent with Merck's overall mission to enhance the health and well-being of people around the world. Such needs include improving health care, fostering biomedical and science education; and supporting the arts, social services, and civic, environmental and other charitable organizations.

Requirements: Operating support of health and social service agencies is reserved for Merck communities and generally directed through annual contributions to United Way.

Restrictions: Grants are not made to political, labor, fraternal, or veterans organizations; sectarian groups; or to individuals. Except within foundation programs, grants are not given for elementary/secondary education, scholarships, fellowships, research, publications, conferences/seminars/symposia, and travel.

Geographic Focus: All U.S. States

Samples: Alliance of Community Health Plans (Washington, DC)—to help healthcare groups that use culturally and linguistically appropriate health services demonstrate that those services are financially sound options, $235,000; American National Red Cross (Washington, DC), UNICEF (NY), and several local relief organizations—for relief efforts in South Asia and Africa, $3 million divided; Task Force for Child Survival and Development (Atlanta, GA)—to expand programs to treat people in Africa who are suffering from onchocerciasis, more commonly known as river blindness, as part of the Mectizan Donation Program, $1 million over five years.

Contact: Drive Shuang Ruy Huang, (908) 423-1000; (908) 423-1987

Internet: http://www.merck.com/about/cr/policies_performance/social/philanthropy.html

Sponsor: Merck Company Foundation
P.O. Box 100 (WSIAF-35)
Whitehouse Station, NJ 08889-0100

Merck Family Fund Grants 1161

The goals of the fund are to restore and protect the natural environment and ensure a healthy planet for generations to come; and to strengthen the social fabric and the physical landscape of the urban community. In the environmental area, the foundation has two areas of priority to help achieve a healthy planet: protection of vital ecosystems in the eastern United States; and supporting the shift toward environmentally sustainable economic systems, incentives, and behaviors. In the area of strengthening the urban community, the fund's two areas of focus are to create green and open space, and support youth as agents of social change. These grants are limited to grassroots programs in New York, NY; Providence, RI; and Boston, MA. New requests for support should be made by a letter of inquiry rather than a full proposal. The letter should not exceed three pages and should concisely describe the project, its purpose, and its likely impact. The letter should also briefly describe the organization and its goals and specify the amount of funds requested. Letters of inquiry are acknowledged as soon as possible. Applicants will be contacted if a full proposal is warranted. Funding decisions are made twice each year. The fund prefers documents printed on nonchlorine bleached, 100 percent recycled paper.

Requirements: U.S. tax-exempt organizations are eligible.

Restrictions: The foundation does not generally support academic research or books. It does not fund endowments, debt reduction, annual fund-raising campaigns, capital construction, the purchase of equipment, the acquisition of land, film or video projects, or political candidates.

Geographic Focus: All U.S. States

Date(s) Application is Due: Mar 1; Aug 1

Amount: 10,000 - 35,000 USD

Samples: Hubbard Brook Research Foundation (Hanover, NH)—to support Science Links, a science-based information resource focused on mercury and carbon pollution, $25,000; SouthWings (Asheville, NC)—general support to use flights to bring awareness to conservation issues, $20,000; Sistas on the Rise (Bronx, NY)—to support the organizing campaigns of this collective run by teen mothers in the South Bronx, $20,000; Green Press Initiative (Ann Arbor, MI)—to support green paper practices in the book publishing industry. Fiscal Agent: Social and Environmental Entrepreneurs, $10,000. .

Contact: Jenny Russell, Executive Director; (617) 696-3580; (617) 696-7262; merck@merckff.org

Internet: http://www.merckff.org/grantguidelines.html

Sponsor: Merck Family Fund
303 Adams Street
Milton, MA 02186

Meriden Foundation Grants 1162

The foundation awards grants to eligible Connecticut nonprofit organizations in its areas of interest, including arts, children and youth, civic affairs, Christian organizations and churches, health organizations and hospitals, higher education, public libraries, and social services. Types of support include annual campaigns, general operating support, scholarships, and social services delivery. There are no application deadlines. A formal application is required, and the initial approach should be a letter, on organizational letterhead, describing the project and requesting an application.

Requirements: Connecticut nonprofit organizations in the Meriden-Wallingford area are eligible.

Geographic Focus: Connecticut

Amount: 175 - 10,000 USD

Samples: Best Friends Animal Sanctuary, Kanab, Utah, $3,500 - general operations (2009); Church of the Holy Angels, Meriden, Connecticut, $3,296 - general operations (2009); Franciscan Home Care and Hospice, Meriden, Connecticut, $5,000 - to purchase laptop computers (2009).

Contact: Jeffrey F. Otis, Director; (203) 782-4531; (203) 782-4530

Sponsor: Meriden Foundation
123 Bank Street
Waterbury, CT 06702-2205

Merrill Lynch Philanthropic Program Grants 1163

The foundation supports a variety of charitable causes throughout the world, with a focus on education. Through 2005, the foundation has adopted children and youth as its global cause. Programs should meet the educational needs and interests of uderserved children and youth. Programs should support an ethnically diverse population of children and youth; provide direct services from early childhood to postsecondary education, and incorporate one or more of the following elements: academic support, global exchange, community service, internships, cultural enrichment, life skills, digital divide, mentoring, entrepreneurship, scholarships, personal finance, technology skills, GED programs linked with four-year colleges, and workforce preparation. The foundation gives priority to specific programs and projects, rather than general operating support. Preference will be given to requests from the five boroughs of New York City and national organizations that reflect that focus. Requests outside of New York City should be submitted to managers of local branches or offices.

Requirements: Tax-exempt 501(c)3 organizations are eligible.

Restrictions: Grants will not be made to private foundations; individuals; fundraising activities related to individual sponsorships (e.g., walk-a-thons, marathons); seed money for new organizations; political causes, candidates, and campaigns as well as organizations designed specifically for lobbying; religious, fraternal, social, or other membership organizations providing services mainly to their own constituencies; athletic events and sports tournaments (Special Olympics is eligible); and fundraising events (dinners, luncheons).

Geographic Focus: All U.S. States

Samples: Sesame Workshop (New York, NY)—for the WorldwideKids program, which will use multimedia tools and resources to educate three- to six-year olds about diverse people and cultures, $5 million; United Nations Assoc of the United States of America (Washington, DC)—to expand to 14 countries the Global Classrooms program, which supports Model United Nations activities in schools, and to develop a curriculum on global development, finance, and trade, $7.5 million.

Contact: Westina Matthews, Vice President, Philanthropic Programs; (212) 236-4319; (212) 236-8007; SDimaggio@exchange.ml.com

Internet: http://philanthropy.ml.com

Sponsor: Merrill Lynch and Company Foundation
2 World Financial Center, 5th Floor
New York, NY 10281-6100

Mertz Gilmore Foundation Grants 1164

The foundation makes general operating, project, challenge, and capacity-building grants, often over a multi-year period. The foundation makes grants in dance in New York City and New York City human and built environment. A brief letter outlining the organization's purpose and programs is the first step of application. If the foundation is interested, it will send an application form and request a full proposal.

Restrictions: The foundation does not make grants for political purposes such as lobbying or propaganda. In addition, proposals are not accepted for individuals; endowments, annual fund appeals, or fundraising events; conferences, workshops; sectarian religious concerns; scholarships, fellowships, research, loans, or travel; film or media projects; or publications.

Geographic Focus: All U.S. States
Amount: 20,000 - 75,000 USD
Contact: Program Officer; (212) 475-1137; (212) 777-5226; info@mertzgilmore.org
Internet: http://www.mertzgilmore.org
Sponsor: Mertz Gilmore Foundation
218 E 18th Street
New York, NY 10003-3694

Mervin Bovaird Foundation Grants **1165**

The foundation awards grants, with a focus on Tulsa, OK, to nonprofit organizations such as churches, homeless shelters, medical centers, nursing homes, parochial schools, religious welfare organizations, the Salvation Army, and youth organizations. Areas of interest include arts, community development, education, environment, health care and health organizations, and social services. Types of support include general operating support, matching, project, and research grants. The foundation also funds a scholarship program for Tulsa County High School graduating seniors and graduates of Tulsa Community College at the University of Tulsa (not for graduate or professional study). Applicants should submit a brief letter of inquiry, including program and organization descriptions.
Requirements: Nonprofits of the Christian, Methodist, Roman Catholic, and United Methodist faiths in Tulsa, OK, are eligible.
Geographic Focus: Oklahoma
Amount: 1,000 - 250,000 USD
Samples: Salvation Army (Tulsa, OK)—for facilities and program expansion, $50,000; John 3:16 Mission (Tulsa, OK)—for the family/youth center, $25,000.
Contact: R. Casey Cooper, President and Trustee, c/o Boesche, McDermott, and Eskridge; (918) 592-3300
Sponsor: Mervin Bovaird Foundation
401 S Boston Avenue, Suite 3300
Tulsa, OK 74103-4070

Metro Health Foundation Grants **1166**

The foundation awards grants in southeastern Michigan in its areas of interest, including children and youth, disabled, elderly, health associations, homeless, and women. Types of support include challenge grants, equipment acquisition, general operating support, project development, scholarship funds, seed grants, and federated giving. Obtain application materials from the office; the board meets in April and October.
Requirements: Nonprofit organizations in the metropolitan tri-county Detroit, MI, area are eligible to apply.
Restrictions: Grants do not support advertising, advocacy organizations, athletic groups, individuals, international organizations, political organizations, special events, benefit dinners, or state or local government agencies.
Geographic Focus: Michigan
Date(s) Application is Due: Feb 1; Aug 1
Amount: 1,000 - 25,000 USD
Contact: Theresa Sondys, Program Contact; (313) 965-4220; (313) 965-3626; metrohealthfdn@aol.com
Sponsor: Metro Health Foundation
333 W Fort Street, Suite 1370
Detroit, MI 48226-3134

Meyer Memorial Trust Emergency Grants **1167**

Emergency Grants provide expedited consideration of true emergencies. MMT's emergency fund is intended for sudden, unanticipated and unavoidable challenges that, if not addressed immediately, could threaten an organization's stability and/or ability to achieve its mission. Examples of Emergency Grants might include assistance for recovery from fire, flood, and other acts of nature. It is not intended to address failure of an organization to comply with legal requirements or problems that can be attributed to organizational neglect or failure to plan for likely contingencies, such as the breakdown of aging equipment.
Requirements: Grants are awarded to 501(c)3 nonprofit organizations in Oregon and Clark County, Washington.
Restrictions: Meyer does not fund general administrative overhead or indirect rate allocations.
Geographic Focus: Oregon, Washington
Contact: Barbara Gibbs, Grants Director; (503) 228-5512; barbara@mmt.org
Internet: http://www.mmt.org/grants_programs/
Sponsor: Meyer Memorial Trust
425 NW 10th Avenue, Suite 400
Portland, OR 97209

Meyer Memorial Trust Grassroots Grants **1168**

Grassroots Grants enable smaller organizations, often without development departments, to compete for MMT grants. While organizations with budgets up to $2 million may apply for Grassroots Grants, historically, 70% of small grants have gone to organizations with budgets of $250,000 or less. Grants of $1,000 to $25,000 are awarded for projects with budgets of up to $150,000. Grassroots Grants fund programs, outreach, equipment, facility expansions or repairs, strategic planning, website development, and more. Decisions on Grassroots Grants are made by trustees at the program meetings in February, June and October.
Requirements: Grants are awarded to 501(c)3 nonprofit organizations in Oregon and Clark County, Washington.
Restrictions: Meyer does not fund general administrative overhead or indirect rate allocations.
Geographic Focus: Oregon, Washington
Date(s) Application is Due: Mar 15; Jul 15; Oct 15
Amount: 1,000 - 25,000 USD
Samples: Assistance League of Klamath Basin, Klamath Falls, Oregon, $14,547—for safety improvements to its resale and consignment shop (2008); Central Oregon Environmental Center, Bend, Oregon, $24,750—to support a merger with reSource to strengthen environmental work in the region (2008).
Contact: Barbara Gibbs, Grants Director; (503) 228-5512; barbara@mmt.org
Internet: http://www.mmt.org/grants_programs/
Sponsor: Meyer Memorial Trust
425 NW 10th Avenue, Suite 400
Portland, OR 97209

Meyer Memorial Trust Operating Funds Grants **1169**

MMT has launched an Operating Funds grant program to help small- and mid-sized organizations that have been hit particularly hard by the current economic crisis. The purpose of this initiative is organizational stability. Organizations for which a cash infusion is not critical to stability, but wish to request funds to maintain or expand current programming, should continue to apply for support through MMT's Responsive and Grassroots Grant programs, as usual. Applications will be accepted beginning September 1. Application deadline is October 1. Awards announcement is anticipated in December. Applications will be accepted through MMT's Responsive Grant inquiry process.
Requirements: Any 501(c)3 nonprofit organizations the operates in Oregon and Clark County, Washington is eligible to apply.
Restrictions: Meyers does not support the following: direct grants, scholarships, or loans to individuals; endowments; general fund drives, annual appeals, special events, or sponsorships; elimination of operating deficits; projects of sectarian or religious organizations that principally benefit their own members or adherents; direct replacement funding for activities previously supported by federal, state, or local public sources; acquisition of land for conservation purposes (except through Program Related Investments); hospital capital construction projects (except through Program Related Investments); animal welfare organizations (both domestic and wild animals); projects that primarily benefit students of a single K-12 school, unless the school is an independent alternative school primarily serving low-income and/or special needs populations; MMT funds cannot be earmarked for purposes of influencing legislation, and the grantee cannot expend any part of the grant in a way that violates its tax-exempt status.
Geographic Focus: Oregon, Washington
Date(s) Application is Due: Oct 1
Amount: Up to 50,000 USD
Contact: Barbara Gibbs, Grants Director; (503) 228-5512; barbara@mmt.org
Internet: http://www.mmt.org/grants_programs/
Sponsor: Meyer Memorial Trust
425 NW 10th Avenue, Suite 400
Portland, OR 97209

Meyer Memorial Trust Responsive Grants **1170**

Responsive Grants are awarded in the areas of social services, health, affordable housing, community development, conservation and environment, public affairs and social benefit, arts and culture, and education. They generally

range from $30,000 to $500,000; grant periods are from one to three years in length. General purpose grants are given for a wide variety of projects in many fields of activity including program expansions, capacity building, capital projects, and start-ups. Final decisions on Responsive Grants proposals are made by trustees at program meetings every month except January, April and August. Final decisions on proposals for capital projects requesting more than $200,000 are made in May and November. Applicants should time their Initial Inquiry submission at least six months before they hope to have a final decision from MMT.
Requirements: General purpose and small grants are awarded to 501(c)3 nonprofit organizations in Oregon and Clark County, Washington.
Restrictions: Meyer does not fund general administrative overhead or indirect rate allocations.
Geographic Focus: Oregon, Washington
Amount: 30,000 - 500,000 USD
Samples: Confederated Tribes of Warm Springs, Warm Springs, Oregon, $150,000—to help construct a building to co-locate the newspaper office and KWSO radio station (2008); Oregon Ballet Theatre, Portland, Oregon, $200,000—for two years of operating support (2008); South Lane Mental Health Services Cottage Grove, Oregon, $150,000—to purchase and renovate a building as a mental health clinic (2008).
Contact: Barbara Gibbs, Grants Director; (503) 228-5512; barbara@mmt.org
Internet: http://www.mmt.org/grants_programs/
Sponsor: Meyer Memorial Trust
425 NW 10th Avenue, Suite 400
Portland, OR 97209

MGN Family Foundation Grants **1171**
The MGN Family Foundation makes grants to qualified 501(c)3 organizations specializing in the following areas: education; health care and medical research; children in need; armed service personnel. Areas of particular interest include: colleges, universities and private schools, examples would be: to fund a chair to provide lecturers in literature, philosophy or the arts, and provide scholarships; hospitals and clinics that specialize in excellent patient care and continuing medical research such as Memorial Sloan-Kettering Cancer Center and the Mayo and Cleveland Clinics are other examples, also under consideration would be hospice organizations that provide palliative care to the dying; organizations that support children in need whether due to emotional, physical abuse, neglect or disadvantaged circumstances. Support can be for basic necessities such as food, shelter, education, medical as well as, spiritual and emotional counseling; in light of recent events, this Foundation would like to offer assistance to our servicemen/ servicewomen and their families through those charities which give support to their unique needs. The examples provided above reflect the true mission and goals of the MGN Foundation. There should be no exclusions due to race or creed, provided all applicants have a strong moral base and core values in the areas of education, health care, welfare of children and service personnel and their families. The Foundation Board meets semi-annually in May and November. Applications are due by April 1st and October 1st. Application form is available online.
Requirements: Qualified 501(c)3 organizations specializing in the following areas: education; health care and medical research; children in need; armed service personnel. To apply, submit seven (7) sets of the following items: Grant application form completed, dated, and signed by the Chief Executive Officer or Chairman of the Board of the organization; list of Board of Directors; Financial Statement (audited if available), for the most recent complete fiscal year; copy of IRS 501(c)3 Determination Letter. If you wish, you may submit your proposal in a narrative format of not more than two pages in addition to the completed application form. Optional materials may be submitted but are not required (such as brochures discussing or depicting the activities of the organization).
Restrictions: Do not staple materials or place them in a bound notebook.
Geographic Focus: All U.S. States
Date(s) Application is Due: Apr 1; Oct 1
Amount: 1,000 - 10,000 USD
Samples: Agnes Scott College, $3,000—scholarship (2008); Vermont National Guard Charitable Foundation, Inc., $3,000—wounded veteran program (2008); Center for Molecular Medicine and Immunology/Garden State, $5,000—foster research for new technologies in the diagnosis, detection and treatment of cancer (2008).
Contact: Pamela Nothstein, Grants Manager; (843) 937-4614; grantinquiries7@wachovia.com
Internet: https://www.wachovia.com/foundation/v/index.jsp?vgnextoid=61078689fb0aa110VgnVCM1000004b0d1872RCRD&vgnextfmt=default
Sponsor: MGN Family Foundation
16 Broad Street (SC1000)
Charleston, SC 29401

MHRC Operating Grants **1172**
Grants in aid of research are designed to defray the normal direct costs of research including, among others, personnel costs, supplies and expendable materials, experimental animals, equipment costing less than $C5000, computer costs, and publication costs. Up to five percent of the operating grant may be used for travel related to the investigator's research program. Grants are normally awarded for one year. The council gives priority to new investigators and new projects. The starting date for successful grants is July 1.
Requirements: Normally only investigators holding academic appointments or equivalent in the province of Manitoba are eligible to apply. Investigators who do not hold academic appointments should consult with the council to establish their eligibility before applying.
Restrictions: Individuals holding continuing operating grants from the council are not eligible to apply for other operating grants that would become effective during the tenure of their present grants. Expenditures for student and postdoctoral salaries will not be considered on operating grants.
Geographic Focus: Canada
Amount: Up to 100,000 CAD
Contact: Program Contact; (204) 775-1096; (204) 786-5401; mhrc@cc.umanitoba.ca
Internet: http://www.umanitoba.ca/academic_support/MHRC/PROGRAMS.HTM#contents
Sponsor: Manitoba Health Research Council
770 Bannatyne Avenue
Winnipeg, MB R3E 0W3 Canada

Michael and Susan Dell Foundation Grants **1173**
The mission of the foundation is to encourage and inspire children to reach their greatest potential. The foundation proactively seeks out opportunities to support or develop programs that address five essential areas: children's health—access to affordable health care and insurance; education—improve study and college readiness skills, enable tutoring by licensed teachers, and guide parents and students through the college application process and financial aid process (including the grants and scholarships process); safety—foster care, residential treatment for neglected or abused children, law enforcement, agency child abduction programs, and sexual or domestic violence abuse counseling; youth development—affordable and enriching after school programs to protect and educate children; and early childhood care—increase the quality and reliability of child care. The foundation does not accept unsolicited proposals. Preliminary grant requests may be submitted via the foundation's online form; full application is by invitation. The foundation also sponsors the Dell Scholars Program, which strives to make the dream of a college education possible for a number of underserved youth, especially lower-income students who have experienced obstacles and hardships. Candidates for this particular scholarship are evaluated based on their individual determination to succeed and their demonstrated ability to overcome obstacles and challenges, not on academic record alone.
Requirements: Texas nonprofit organizations are eligible.
Geographic Focus: Texas
Samples: National Governors Assoc (Washington, DC)—for efforts to create and implement ways to improve high school-graduation and college-preparedness rates in 13 states, $4 million; College Board (New York, NY)—to expand its College Board Schools Initiative in New York City to 16 schools, as part of an effort to raise the achievement, graduation, and college-readiness rates of students attending New York City high schools, $3.6 million; Blanton Museum of Art (Austin, TX)—for its capital campaign, $250,000; For disaster relief in South Asia and Africa—$3 million distributed among relief organizations.
Contact: Janet Mountain, Executive Director
Internet: http://www.msdf.org
Sponsor: Michael and Susan Dell Foundation
P.O. Box 163867
Austin, TX 78716-3867

Michael Reese Health Trust Grants **1174**
The trust awards grants in the metropolitan Chicago area to nonprofits for community-based health services provided to vulnerable groups, including

children and youth, people with mental and physical disabilities, the elderly, immigrants and refugees, uninsured, medically indigent, and other underserved populations. Grants provide general and project support of innovative approaches to delivering health services to the target populations, efforts to improve community health through health promotion and disease prevention, and education to improve healthcare providers' ability to treat the underserved. Some research is funded, but emphasis is on direct service delivery. To apply, submit an inquiry letter. Deadlines listed are for letters of inquiry.
Requirements: Nonprofit organizations operating in the metropolitan Chicago area are eligible.
Restrictions: Grants do not support capital needs (i.e., building construction/renovation, vehicles, and equipment), endowments, fund-raising events, individuals, scholarships or debt reduction.
Geographic Focus: Illinois
Date(s) Application is Due: Jun 15; Dec 15
Contact: Dorothy Gardner, President; (312) 726-1008; (312) 726-2797; programs@healthtrust.net
Internet: http://www.healthtrust.net/index.php?option=com_content&task=view&id=13&Itemid=42
Sponsor: Michael Reese Health Trust
20 N Wacker Drive, Suite 760
Chicago, IL 60606

Michigan Arts Organization Development Program Grants **1175**
The program provides funding to small to midsized professional, arts-producing organizations to achieve increased levels of financial support and administrative stability, and to expand delivery of services. The two categories of grants provided are Strategic Planning and Administrative Development. Annual deadline dates may vary; contact program staff for exact dates.
Requirements: Professional arts-producing organizations in Michigan that meet the following criteria may apply development program: have produced or presented in each of the three fiscal years prior to the date of application; have an operating budget under $250,000 at the time of application; have administrative and artistic staff sufficient to satisfy program requirements; and have either an audit or review of financial statements prepared by an independent certified public accountant. Organizations that have successfully completed multiyear business/strategic plans through this program or completed a planning process within the past two years may apply for implementation grants.
Restrictions: No part of the net earnings may benefit a private individual.
Geographic Focus: Michigan
Date(s) Application is Due: May 1
Amount: 25,000 - 10,000 USD
Contact: Program Coordinator; (517) 241-4011; (517) 241-3979; artsinfo@michigan.gov
Internet: http://www.michigan.gov/hal/0,1607,7-160-18833_18834_18842—-,00.html
Sponsor: Michigan Council for Arts and Cultural Affairs
300 N. Washington Square
Lansing, MI 48913

Michigan Local Art Agencies and Service Grants **1176**
This program is intended to support those projects that are often unique to local arts agencies, regional, or statewide service providers in their efforts to promote, coordinate, fund, and/or improve the climate for the arts and cultural activities in their communities. Such activities include calendars of events, coordinated booking, regranting, cultural planning, workshops and conferences, board development, technical services, coordinated management, facility operations, etc. Annual deadline dates may vary; contact program staff for exact dates.
Requirements: Eligible to apply are local Michigan arts agencies and regional or statewide service organizations, which are defined as public or private nonprofit councils, commissions, societies, or organizations that, by their charters and operating policies, are publicly accountable to provide financial and/or service support for the arts in the communities that they serve. Applicants must provide a cash match of at least 50 percent of the grant amount requested. The remainder of the match requirement may be in any combination of cash and/or in-kind contributions.
Restrictions: No part of the net earnings may benefit a private individual. Funding may not exceed one-third of a project's total cost. State funds may not be used as a match. The same matching funds may not be utilized in more than one project application.
Geographic Focus: Michigan
Date(s) Application is Due: May 1
Amount: Up to 40,000 USD
Contact: Program Contact; (517) 241-4011; (517) 241-3979
Internet: http://www.michigan.gov/hal/0,1607,7-160-18833_18834_18840—-,00.html
Sponsor: Michigan Council for Arts and Cultural Affairs
300 N. Washington Square
Lansing, MI 48913

Microsoft Community Affairs Puget Sound Grants **1177**
Microsoft provides direct grants and matching support to a broad range of nonprofit organizations that address community needs in the Puget Sound region. Organizations with missions and work that align with funding areas - human services, arts and culture, civic affairs, work-force development, and K-12 math education - can apply. Human services focus is on assisting people in need to move toward self sufficiency. Arts and culture funding supports visual, literary, and performing arts, as well as cultural organizations such as science and history museums. Civic affairs funding supports organizations and projects that promote civic engagement, voter registration, and public policy education. Workforce development funding provides technology that will transform education, foster local innovation, and enable jobs. Education funding helps to improve middle school student academic performance and participation in math. Types of support include employee matching grants to health and human service organizations, general operating support, and capital grants. Applications for donations of software to Washington State nonprofits are considered on an ongoing basis. Grant proposals from community organizations are accepted throughout the year; proposals are requested by the listed application deadline to coincide with meeting schedules.
Requirements: The corporation contributes cash and software to 501(c)3 nonprofits in the Puget Sound, WA, area.
Restrictions: Ineligible organizations and projects include: individuals; private enterprises (for profit); private educational institutions; hospitals or medical clinics (though hospitals or medical clinics designated as Community Health Center Programs by the U.S. Department of Health are eligible to apply); private foundations; political, religious, or fraternal organizations; amateur or professional sports groups, teams, or events; conferences or symposia; or endowments.
Geographic Focus: Washington
Date(s) Application is Due: Oct 31
Samples: Elderhealth Northwest (Seattle, WA)—to construct low-cost housing units for elderly people, $50,000; Urban Enterprise Ctr (Seattle, WA)—to foster effective dialogues on race and to expand job creation and economic development in the Central and Rainier Valley neighborhoods of Seattle, $25,000; Washington Early Learning Foundation (Seattle, WA)—for a statewide public-awareness campaign on early childhood development, $15,000; Boys and Girls Clubs of King County (Seattle, WA)—for its capital campaign, $175,000.
Contact: Bruce Brooks, Director of Community Affairs; (425) 936-8185; (425) 936-7329; upinfo@microsoft.com or giving@microsoft.com
Internet: http://www.microsoft.com/About/CorporateCitizenship/Citizenship/giving/programs/grants.mspx
Sponsor: Microsoft Corporation
One Microsoft Way
Redmond, WA 98052-6399

Mid-Iowa Health Foundation Grants **1178**
The foundation is interested in supporting community-based health services in its geographic area of focus, comprising Iowa's Polk County and contiguous counties. A strong commitment exists toward programs involving children, elderly, disabled, and indigent populations, such as disadvantaged youth, isolated elderly, young mothers and their children, people with substance abuse, and chronically or terminally ill people. Types of support include general operating grants, capital campaigns, building construction/renovation, and matching funds. Request application forms by phone or mail.
Requirements: Organizations with nonprofit, tax-exempt status under IRS codes in Polk, IA, and contiguous counties are eligible.
Restrictions: The foundation does not provide grants for direct aid to individuals, religious programs, political organizations or projects, or dinners or tickets.
Geographic Focus: Iowa
Date(s) Application is Due: Apr 1; Oct 1
Amount: 15,000 - 40,000 USD

Samples: Drake University (Des Moines, IA)—for capital support of the Knapp Recreation and Sports Arena, $10,000.
Contact: Program Contact; (641) 277-6411; (515) 271-7579; info@midiowahealth.org
Internet: http://www.midiowahealth.org/grants.html
Sponsor: Mid-Iowa Health Foundation
550 39th Street, Suite 305
Des Moines, IA 50312

Midsouth Foundation Grants 1179

Two types of funding are available through this initiative– matching funds and operating funds. Matching funds are available for IDA Program Operators to match the savings of IDA program participants who are Entergy customers. Operating funds are available to organizations for the purpose of managing IDA programs. Annual deadline dates may vary; contact program staff for exact dates.
Requirements: Nonprofits in Arkansas, Louisiana, and Mississippi are eligible.
Geographic Focus: Arkansas, Louisiana, Mississippi
Amount: 500 - 25,000 USD
Samples: All Our Children (West Memphis, AR)—to aid low-income residents in community resource development, $10,000; Christian Children's Fund (Jackson, MS)—to strengthen a statewide child care advocacy organization, $60,000; East Arkansas Private Industry Council (West Memphis, AR)—to provide personal development training for parents, $10,000.
Contact: Program Officer; (601) 355-8167; (601) 355-6499
Internet: http://www.fndmidsouth.org/grants_opportunities.htm
Sponsor: Midsouth Foundation
1230 Raymond Road, Box 700
Jackson, MS 39204

Miles of Hope Breast Cancer Foundation Grants 1180

The Fund provides programs and support services for women and families in the Hudson Valley, New York, affected by breast cancer. All funds raised for the Foundation are used in the Hudson Valley. The Miles of Hope Breast Cancer Foundation is currently offering grants for projects in the areas of breast health and breast cancer education, outreach, screening, treatment and support projects.
Requirements: Services must be provided in the eight counties served by the Miles of Hope Breast Cancer Foundation, which include: Columbia, Dutchess, Greene, Orange, Putnam, Rockland, Westchester and Ulster.
Restrictions: Project must be specific to breast health and/or breast cancer. Applicants must be a U.S. nonprofit (federally tax-exempt) organization. Nonprofit organizations, known educational institutions (i.e. college or university), government agencies, and Indian tribes are eligible. Equipment costs, if applicable, may not exceed 30% of direct costs and should be used exclusively on this project. Salaries, if requested, are for personnel related to this project only and not the general work of the employee. Funds will not be awarded to capital campaigns
Geographic Focus: New York
Contact: Program Administrator; (845) 527-6884 or (845) 264-2005; info@milesofhopebcf.org
Internet: http://www.milesofhopebcf.org/funds.html#grants
Sponsor: Miles of Hope Breast Cancer Foundation
P.O. Box 405
La Grangeville, NY 12540

Milken Family Foundation Grants 1181

The purpose of the family foundation is to discover and advance inventive ways to build human resources and help people lead productive and satisfying lives, primarily in Los Angeles, CA. This mission is pursued in three areas: education, medical research and health care, and community welfare. Under education, the foundation seeks to recognize and reward outstanding educators, expand their professional leadership and policy influence, and encourage talented young people to become educators; stimulate creativity and productivity among educators; and foster the involvement of the family and the community in schools. The foundation supports basic and applied medical research, especially in the areas of cancer and epilepsy, and supports programs designed to improve and protect the health of people of all ages. Under community welfare, the foundation helps build vibrant communities and responds to basic human needs. Preventive programs with long-range goals receive the closest consideration. Types of support include general operations, research, conferences and seminars, scholarship funds, and building and renovation projects. Applicant should submit a brief written statement that includes a description of the project, goals, procedure, and personnel; brief background of the organization; and letter of exemption from the IRS. Approximately 80 percent of all funding is directed toward foundation initiatives. Requests are considered throughout the year.
Requirements: Grants are made to 501(c)3 tax-exempt organizations. Grant recipients must have the financial potential to sustain the program for which funding is sought following the period of foundation support.
Restrictions: Grants are not made directly to individuals.
Geographic Focus: California
Samples: Teacher Advancement Program Foundation (Santa Monica, CA)—for the work of this new organization, which uses a research-based strategy designed to attract, develop, and retain high-quality teachers, $5 million; To be distributed among 100 educators nationwide—for the Milken Educator Awards, which honor outstanding elementary and secondary teachers, principals, and other education professionals, $2.5 million.
Contact: Drive Julius Lesner, Executive Vice President; (310) 570-4800; (310) 570-4801; admin@mff.org
Internet: http://www.mff.org/about/about.taf?page=funding
Sponsor: Milken Family Foundation
1250 Fourth Street, 6th Floor
Santa Monica, CA 90401-1353

Miller Brewing Corporate Contributions Program Grants 1182

The corporate contributions program funds programs of nonprofit organizations in corporate operating communities. Applicants should call the local Miller community affairs manager to discuss an idea before submitting a proposal. The corporation also supports the Thurgood Marshall Scholarship Fund, which provides four-year merit scholarships to students attending the 44 historically black public colleges and universities, and two-year scholarships to law schools at Texas Southern, North Carolina Central, Southern, and Howard Universities; and ?Adelante! U.S. Education Leadership Fund, which awards scholarships to Hispanic-American students.
Requirements: Nonprofits must be near Miller operating locations, in Irwindale, California; Albany, Georgia; Trenton, Ohio; Eden, North Carolina; Fort Worth, Texas; and Milwaukee, Wisconsin.
Geographic Focus: California
Amount: 1,000 - 15,000 USD
Samples: Advocates of Ozaukee (West Bend, WI)—for a round-the-clock crisis line and other services for victims of domestic violence, $15,000; Goodwill Industries of Southeastern Wisconsin (Milwaukee, WI)—to purchase a vehicle for a program that provides elderly people with assistance with errands and shopping, $10,000; America's Second Harvest-Milwaukee (WI)—for a nutrition program for elderly people, $15,000; COA Youth and Family Ctrs (Milwaukee, WI)—for GED programs and job-readiness training and placement services, $15,000.
Contact: Grants Administrator; (414) 931-3110; (414) 931-6352
Internet: http://www.millerbrewing.com/inthecommunity/default.asp
Sponsor: Miller Brewing Corporation
3939 W Highland Boulevard
Milwaukee, WI 53201-0482

Millipore Foundation Grants 1183

The foundation supports nonprofit organizations in company operating communities in five main areas: education and research, social services, culture, health care, and public policy. Types of support include general operating support, employee matching gifts, and employee-related scholarships. Applications are accepted throughout the year.
Requirements: 501(c)3 tax-exempt organizations are eligible.
Geographic Focus: All U.S. States
Amount: 2,500 - 5,000 USD
Contact: Charleen Johnson, Executive Director; (978) 715-1268; (978) 715-1385; Charleen_Johnson@millipore.com
Internet: http://www.millipore.com/corporate/milliporefoundation.nsf/foundationhome
Sponsor: Millipore Foundation
290 Concord Road
Billerica, MA 01821-7037

Millstone Foundation Grants 1184

The foundation awards grants to eligible Missouri nonprofit organizations in its areas of interest, including education and higher education, Jewish services, and Israel. Types of support include annual campaings, continuing support,

deficit financing, emergency funds, general operating support, and research grants. There are no application forms or deadlines.
Requirements: Missouri tax-exempt organizations are eligible. Preference is given to requests from Saint Louis.
Geographic Focus: Missouri
Amount: Up to 100,000,000 USD
Contact: Colleen Millstone, Director; (314) 961-8500
Sponsor: Millstone Foundation
7701 Forsyth Boulevard, Suite 925
Saint Louis, MO 63105-1842

Minneapolis Foundation Community Grants **1185**
The foundation awards grants throughout Minnesota. Eligible activities include policy and systems change work in the following areas: affordable housing; economic opportunity; educational achievement; and the health and well-being of children, youth, and families. The foundation also focuses on systems and policy work that addresses the intersection of issues, such as housing and health. Types of support include program/project support, operating support, capital support (limited to the seven-county metro area); and some multiyear grants. Proposals are accepted throughout the year. Guidelines are available online.
Requirements: 501(c)3 nonprofit organizations located in the seven-county metropolitan area of Minneapolis and Saint Paul may apply.
Restrictions: The foundation does not fund individuals, organizations/activities outside of Minnesota, conference registration fees, memberships, direct religious activities, political organizations or candidates, direct fundraising activities, telephone solicitations, courtesy advertising, or financial deficits.
Geographic Focus: Minnesota
Date(s) Application is Due: Mar 15; Sep 15
Contact: Paul Verrette, Senior Grants Administrator; (612) 672-3836; pverrette@mplsfoundation.org
Internet: http://www.mplsfoundation.org/grants/guidelines.htm
Sponsor: Minneapolis Foundation
800 IDS Center, 80 South Eighth Street
Minneapolis, MN 55402

Minnesota State Arts Board Institutional Support Grants **1186**
Unrestricted operational support grants are awarded to arts organizations that produce or exhibit works of art and/or provide a broad range of programs and services to artists. Goals of this grants program are to support those outstanding Minnesota arts resources that provide cultural leadership within a region, the state, or the nation; to sustain existing creative activities and encourage new forms of artistic expression through the support of the state's cultural resources; to enable Minnesotans to have greater access to the arts through the support of the state's cultural resources; and to provide exposure to the work of Minnesota artists through the support of the state's cultural resources. Applicant organizations must demonstrate high standards of excellence in the areas of artistic leadership, management and financial responsibility, and outreach. Organizations can use the funds to pursue artistic goals and management objectives or to maintain ongoing programs, services, and facilities. Grants are awarded in three categories based on operating expenses.
Requirements: Nonprofit, tax-exempt arts-producing or arts service organizations that have been in existence for at least two years, are incorporated in Minnesota, have attained annual operating expenses of at least $132,000, and have at least one paid professional staff member are eligible to apply.
Restrictions: Institutions of primary, secondary, and higher education; public broadcasting organizations; libraries; and civic organizations such as chambers of commerce and community service agencies are not eligible to apply.
Geographic Focus: Minnesota
Date(s) Application is Due: Feb 1
Contact: Pam Todora, Program Secretary; (651) 215-1618 or (800) 866-2787; (651) 215-1602; pam.todora@arts.state.mn.us or msab@arts.state.mn.us
Internet: http://www.arts.state.mn.us/grants/institutional_support.htm
Sponsor: Minnesota State Arts Board
400 Sibley Street, Suite 200
Saint Paul, MN 55101-1928

Miranda Lux Foundation Grants **1187**
The foundation supports promising proposals for preschool education through community college programs in San Francisco, CA. Areas of interest include vocational education and training, adult basic education, literacy and reading programs, employment services, and children and youth services. Grants are awarded in support of general operating costs, continuing support, equipment, program/project development, seed money, fellowships, internships, scholarship funds, and matching funds. There are no application forms or deadlines. Proposals should be submitted five weeks prior to board meetings, in January, March, June, and September.
Requirements: Grants are awarded in San Francisco, CA.
Restrictions: Support will not be given to individuals or for annual campaigns, emergency funds, deficit financing, building or endowment funds, land acquisition, renovations, research, publications, or loans.
Geographic Focus: California
Amount: 1,500 - 34,000 USD
Samples: Bay Area Discovery Museum (San Francisco, CA)—for the My Story by the Bay Initiative, $10,000; Arriba Juntos Ctr (San Francisco, CA)—to support the Youth at Work program, $25,000; Youth Assistance Assoc (San Francisco, CA)— for the Auto Technician program, $17,500; YMCA, Embarcadero Branch (San Francisco, CA)—to support an employment readiness training program, $10,000.
Contact: Kenneth Blum, Executive Director; (415) 981-2966; (415) 981-5218; admin@mirandalux.org
Internet: http://www.mirandalux.org
Sponsor: Miranda Lux Foundation
57 Post Street, Suite 510
San Francisco, CA 94104-5020

Miriam and Peter Haas Fund Grants **1188**
The fund, which limits grant making to the San Francisco Bay area of California, supports nonprofit organizations in the areas of education, early childhood education and development (ages two to five), family services, arts, humanities, health, social services, public affairs, and the environment. Types of support include operating budgets, capital campaigns, equipment acquisition, continuing support, deficit financing funds, building challenge/ matching grants, equipment acquisition, special projects, and technical assistance. There are no application deadlines.
Requirements: Nonprofit organizations in the San Francisco Bay area of California may submit grant requests.
Restrictions: Individuals are not eligible.
Geographic Focus: California
Amount: 5,000 - 50,000 USD
Samples: Child Development Policy Institute Education Fund (CA)—for general operating support, $25,000; Ctr for the Arts, Yerba Buena Gardens (CA)—to support educational and marketing efforts, $100,000; Performing Arts Workshop (CA)—to train a core group of artists to teach creative movements in San Francisco preschools, $10,000.
Contact: David Thesell, Grants Manager; (415) 296-9249; (415) 296-8842; dThesell@mphf.org
Sponsor: Miriam and Peter Haas Fund
201 Filbert Street, 5th Floor
San Francisco, CA 94133

Mississippi Arts Commission Arts-Based Community Development Grants **1189**
The arts-based community development program responds to the commission's goal to support the development of Mississippi communities through the arts by working to stimulate increased participation in the arts and access to the arts by the entire community; advance community support for arts programs and local understanding of the benefits of the arts to community life; and increase the capacity of Mississippi communities and organizations to use the arts to effect positive community change. The program offers mini-grants, project grants, and operating grants. These grants must be matched dollar for dollar in cash. In addition, as a publicly funded agency, the commission works to ensure that the public at large has access to artistic resources of the state. Services include training seminars and information services, staff consultations, facilitation of board workshops and planning discussions that strengthen the capacities of community arts organizations, and access to national, regional, and statewide information and potential partnerships. Mini-grants and operating grants are paid in two installments: 50 percent as soon as possible following receipt and approval of a properly signed contract, and 50 percent as soon as possible following receipt and approval of the final report. Project grants are also paid in two installments: 75 percent after the contract is signed, and 25 percent after the final report is received. Grantee must submit a final report, which must be postmarked no later than 60 days after the completion of the project or by the deadline date, whichever comes first. Contact program staff for deadlines.

Requirements: Applicants must reside in Mississippi.
Geographic Focus: Mississippi
Amount: 50 - 25,000 USD
Contact: Beth Batton, Arts-Based Community Development Program Director; (601) 359-6546; bbatton@arts.state.ms
Internet: http://www.arts.state.ms.us/grants_abcd.html
Sponsor: Mississippi Arts Commission
501 North West Street, Suite 1101A
Jackson, MS 39201

Mississippi Arts Commission Arts in Education Grants **1190**
The goal of the arts in education program is to strengthen education in and through the arts with a focus on promoting sequential, comprehensive arts education in grades K-12 for all students throughout the state. The program offers minigrants, project grants, large-scale project grants, and operating grants, all requiring a dollar-to-dollar match. Mini-grants have quarterly deadlines and are paid in two installments: 50 percent of the grant award as soon as possible following receipt and approval of a properly signed contract, and 50 percent as soon as possible following receipt and approval of the final report. Grantees must submit a final report, which must be postmarked no later than 60 days after the completion of the project or by the deadline date, whichever comes first.
Requirements: Applicants must reside in Mississippi.
Geographic Focus: Mississippi
Amount: 50 - 25,000 USD
Contact: Wendy Shenefelt, Arts in Education Program Director; (601) 359-6037; wshenefelt@arts.state.ms.us
Internet: http://www.arts.state.ms.us/grants_education.html
Sponsor: Mississippi Arts Commission
501 North West Street, Suite 1101A
Jackson, MS 39201

Missouri Arts Council Community Arts Grants **1191**
The council assists community arts councils and other local arts coordinating agencies that sponsor programs in more than one art form to provide high-quality arts programs and services to nonmetropolitan areas of the state. To help local arts agencies upgrade their management and sponsorship capabilities, financial assistance is available for projects assistance up to a maximum of 50 percent of the costs of providing programs in the visual arts, music, dance, theater, media, architecture, folk art, arts education, literature, and technical assistance; and salary support for the cost of arts agency administration (funding for part- or full-time salary support is not limited to a specific dollar amount). Assistance is also available to help cover the expenses of an official arts council office. Contact the council for annual deadline dates.
Requirements: Applicants must be nonmetropolitan community arts councils and other local arts coordinating agencies in Missouri, must be nonprofit and tax-exempt, and must be governed by citizen boards. Organizations can request arts agency administration support only in conjunction with project support; funds are not available for arts agency administration only.
Geographic Focus: Missouri
Amount: 2,000 USD
Contact: Julie Hale, (314) 340-6845 or (866) 407-4752; (314) 340-7215; julie.hale@ded.mo.gov
Internet: http://www.missouriartscouncil.org/html/funding.shtml
Sponsor: Missouri Arts Council
815 Olive Street, Suite 16
Saint Louis, MO 63101-1503

Missouri Housing Trust Fund Grants **1192**
Grants provide funding to help meet the housing needs of very low-income families and individuals. It provides funding for a variety of eligible activities, including rental housing production, housing and related services for the homeless, and other activities. Grants are awarded for two years. Typically, a Notice of Funding Availability (NOFA) is published during the month of August. The deadline for proposal submission is typically in late October, and recommendations are made to the Commission in January or February. Application forms are available on the website.
Requirements: Any Missouri developers or nonprofit organizations involved in housing, community service, or community or economic development may apply. Applicants must demonstrate prior, successful housing experience and have the financial capacity to successfully complete and operate the housing and/or service proposed. Provider of services must have qualified and trained staff, and a successful recording of providing the proposed services.
Geographic Focus: Missouri
Samples: The Kitchen Inc (Springfield, MO)—for general operating support, $100,000; Economic Security of the Southwest Area (Joplin, MO)—for general operating support, $96,690; The Haven of Grace (Saint Louis, MO)—for general operating support, $25,000.
Contact: Valori Sanders, (816) 759-7226; vsanders@mhdc.com
Internet: http://www.mhdc.com/housing_trust_fund/index.htm
Sponsor: Missouri Housing Trust Fund
3435 Broadway
Kansas City, MO 64111-2415

Mitsubishi Electric America Foundation Grants **1193**
The foundation follows a long tradition of philanthropy by the Mitsubishi Electric America companies. It seeks to contribute to the greater good of society by assisting young Americans with disabilities, through education, technology, and other means, to lead fuller and more productive lives. Requests from all areas of the United States will be considered, though priority will be given to communities where MEA companies are located. A major program emphasis is to advance the independence, productivity, and community inclusion of young people with disabilities. Funding is available for projects and general organizational support. The foundation awards matching grants locally. Concept papers are accepted throughout the year. Invited proposals are due by the listed application deadline. Application and guidelines are available online.
Requirements: Grants are made only to 501(c)3 tax-exempt nonprofit organizations.
Restrictions: The foundation does not support individuals; intermediary organizations; ethnic, fraternal, labor, or political organizations; religious organizations for religious purposes; endowments; the purchase of tickets for fundraising; or advertising, mass mailing, or conference expenses.
Geographic Focus: All U.S. States
Date(s) Application is Due: Jul 1
Samples: American Assoc of People with Disabilities (Washington, DC)—for a Congressional internship program that provides internships to college students with disabilities, $222,000 over three years; Easter Seals (Chicago, IL)—for partnerships between six Easter Seals affiliates and local recreation groups that will serve as models for including disabled children and youths in recreational activities, $150,000; Wilderness Inquiry (Minneapolis, MN)—to support inclusive outdoor educational and recreational activities for youths with and without disabilities, in partnership with Girls Scouts and Boy Scouts groups in the Minneapolis-Saint Paul region, and to duplicate those partnerships nationwide, $165,000.
Contact: Program Officer; (703) 276-8240; (703) 276-8260
Internet: http://www.meaf.org/apply/priorities.html
Sponsor: Mitsubishi Electric America Foundation
1560 Wilson Boulevard, Suite 1150
Arlington, VA 22209

Molly Bee Fund Grants **1194**
The fund awards grants to support nonprofits in its areas of interest, including arts and cultural programs, education, and hospitals. Types of support include general operating support, capital campaigns, building construction/renovation, equipment acquisition, endowment funds, and program-related investments. Giving is primarily in Palm Beach and West Palm Beach, FL, and Cleveland, OH. There are no application forms or deadlines.
Restrictions: Grants are not made to individuals.
Geographic Focus: All U.S. States
Amount: 5,000 - 100,000 USD
Contact: Thomas Allen, (440) 331-8220
Sponsor: Molly Bee Fund
20325 Center Ridge Road, Suite 629
Rocky River, OH 44116

Monfort Family Foundation Grants **1195**
The foundation awards general operating grants to Colorado nonprofit organizations in its areas of interest, including education, health and medical research, arts and culture, agriculture, and general charitable giving. Application forms must be obtained.
Requirements: Colorado nonprofits, primarily in Weld County, are eligible.
Restrictions: Grants are not made to individuals.
Geographic Focus: Colorado
Date(s) Application is Due: May 1; Oct 1
Amount: 5,000 - 100,000 USD

Samples: U of Northern Colorado, College of Business Administration (Greeley, CO)—to bring nationally prominent business leaders to campus to teach; to create a technology center; and to establish an entrepreneurship institute, a lecture series, and an instruction-improvement fund, $10.5 million.
Contact: Dave Evans, Program Contact; (970) 454-1357
Sponsor: Monfort Family Foundation
Box 337300
Greeley, CO 80633

Montana Arts Council Cultural and Aesthetic Project Grants 1196

Applications must be for cultural and aesthetic projects in Montana, including, but not limited to, the visual, performing, literary, and media arts; history; archaeology; folklore; archives; collections; research; historic preservation; and the construction or renovation of cultural facilities. Applications are encouraged for projects serving rural communities, racial and ethnic groups, the disabled, institutionalized populations, youth and the aging, and projects addressing the role of women in Montana's cultural life. Grant categories include special project ($4500 or less), operational support, capital expenditure, and challenge grants for endowment development. Generally, each dollar in special projects grants is to be matched in cash or in-kind goods and services. Capital expenditures require three dollars or in-kind goods and services for each dollar granted. Annual deadline dates may vary; contact program staff for exact dates.
Requirements: Any person, association, or representative of a governing unit in Montana including, but not limited to, state, regional, county, city, town, or Indian tribal governments may submit an application. Examples of eligible applicants are county art or historical museums, public libraries, public educational institutions or school districts, state agencies, city arts commissions or parks and recreation departments, and tribal cultural or education committees.
Geographic Focus: Montana
Date(s) Application is Due: Aug 1
Contact: Program Contact; (406) 444-6430; (406) 444-6548; mac@mt.gov
Internet: http://www.art.state.mt.us/orgs/orgs_ca.asp
Sponsor: Montana Arts Council
316 N Park Avenue, Room 252, P.O. Box 202201
Helena, MT 59620-2201

Montana Arts Council Organizational Excellence Grants 1197

Grants are awarded every two years to outstanding Montana arts organizations for biennial funding. Eligible to apply are nonprofit organizations that have had 501(c)3 status for at least five years and have at least a half-time paid director. Grant funds may support artistically related expenses, and statewide arts service organizations may apply to support any operational expense. The applicant must match each dollar in grant funds with one dollar in cash. Annual deadline dates may vary; contact program staff for exact dates.
Requirements: Nonprofit organizations and units of government in Montana are eligible to apply.
Restrictions: Grant funds may not be used to fund permanent capital expenditures; purchase equipment, art, or artifacts; establish or develop a cash reserve; establish or add to a permanent endowment; or reduce a deficit.
Geographic Focus: Montana
Amount: 1,000 - 8,000 USD
Contact: Program Contact; (406) 444-6430; (406) 444-6548; khan@state.mt.us
Internet: http://www.art.state.mt.us/orgs/orgs_excellence.asp
Sponsor: Montana Arts Council
316 N Park Avenue, Room 252, P.O. Box 202201
Helena, MT 59620-2201

Montana Community Foundation Grants 1198

Unrestricted grants are made by the community foundation in five areas of interest: arts and culture, basic human needs, economic development, education, and natural resources and conservation. To be considered, the program/project must enhance community vitality and/or endowed philanthropy; be for charitable purposes; serve the people of Montana; and not discriminate on the basis of race, religion, sex, age, or national origin in hiring or business practices. In reviewing proposals, consideration will be given to programs or projects that address new and emerging needs or incorporate new approaches to meeting recognized needs; get more citizens involved in meeting community needs; encourage cooperation and eliminate duplication; focus on prevention as well as treatment; provide models for replication; and help nonprofit organizations more effectively manage themselves and their finances.
Requirements: The applicant program or project to be funded must be for charitable purposes, serve the people of Montana, and not discriminate on the basis of race, religion, sex, age, or national origin when employing staff or providing services.
Restrictions: The foundation will not make grants for religious purposes or lobbying. The foundation will place a lower priority on requests for endowment funds, capital campaigns, annual campaigns, debt retirement, or requests for funding from public agencies for mandated services.
Geographic Focus: Montana
Samples: Child Care Connections (Bozeman, MT)—for a year-long match of 50 college-age volunteers and senior citizens, including training, follow-up, and monitoring, $2000; Helena Symphony Society (Helena, MT)—to continue the youth symphony program and increase youth participation in Lewis and Clark County, $2500; Community After School Activities (Billings, MT)—to purchase equipment and resource library materials for a new after-school care program, $1000.
Contact: Program Officer; (406) 443-8313; (406) 442-0482; dianesands@mtcf.org
Internet: http://www.mtcf.org
Sponsor: Montana Community Foundation
101 N Last Chance Gulch, Suite 211
Helena, MT 59601

Montana Power Foundation Grants 1199

The foundation focuses its grant making in Montana on education, health and human services, civic and community, culture and the arts, and resource conservation. Education support is awarded primarily through gifts to university system foundations, scholarship programs, and employee matching gifts. Grants also are made to local colleges and special primary and secondary education programs in the fields of math, science, and youth leadership. Health and human services funding supports the United Way, youth homes, and community health and safety. Support is awarded for civic improvements, special community events, and youth and senior citizen organizations. Art grants support local museums, libraries, cultural centers, and the performing arts. The foundation also awards funding for resource conservation, namely habitat preservation and fish and wildlife protection. Application guidelines and forms are available on the website.
Requirements: Montana nonprofits in the service area of the power company and its subsidiaries may submit grant requests.
Restrictions: Health and human services funding does not support national health organizations, medical equipment purchases, or research.
Geographic Focus: Montana
Amount: Up to 314,000 USD
Samples: Butte Family YMCA (Butte, MT)—operating support, $27,500; Montana Race for the Cure (Helena, MT)—program support, $2000.
Contact: Kathy Vogelsang, (406) 497-2602; (406) 497-2451
Sponsor: Montana Power Foundation
130 N Main Street
Butte, MT 59701-9394

Montgomery County Community Foundation Grants 1200

The Montgomery County Community Foundation Grants help fund non-profit organizations and agencies in Montgomery County, Indiana. Significant grants have been awarded to organizations such as the Crawfordsville District Public Library, Boys and Girls Club, and the Family Crisis Shelter. Organizations should contact the Foundation for a grant proposal application and other documentation required.
Requirements: A strong proposal will have several or all of the following characteristics: an estimate of who and how many will benefit; show long term potential; address a community problem of some significance for which funding is not covered by the regular budget; present an innovative and practical approach to solve a community problem or project; identify possible future funding, if needed; give evidence of the stability and qualifications of the organization applying; show cooperation within the organization and avoid duplication effort.
Restrictions: The Foundation will usually not fund any of the following: grants to individuals; programs which are religious or sectarian in nature, except when the program is open to the entire community; operating expenses such as salaries and utilities; parades, festivals and sporting events; endowment funds; any propaganda, political or otherwise, attempting to influence legislation or

intervene in any political affairs or campaigns; an organization's past debts or existing obligations; or post-event or after-the-fact situations.
Geographic Focus: Indiana
Date(s) Application is Due: May 10
Amount: Up to 50,000 USD
Samples: Crawfordsville Main Street Program, $48,000 to ensure ongoing growth and fiscal sustainability of Athens of Indiana Arts Studio and Gallery (2011); Animal Welfare League, $17,000 to purchase a pre-owned pickup truck to be used for animal control (2011); Educational Foundation, $20,000 for teacher grants of up to $1,000 each for innovative and imaginative projects that go beyond the normal curriculum (2011); Lew Wallace Preservation Society, $9,500 to produce a Historic Structures Report considered vital for the preservation of significant structures (2011); Boys and Girls Club, $17,000 for operational costs of the After School Program (2011).
Contact: Cheryl Keim, Grant Coordinator; (765) 362-1267; (765) 361-0562; cheryl@mccf-in.org
Internet: http://www.mccf-in.org/Granthomenewpage.html
Sponsor: Montgomery County Community Foundation
119 East Main Street
Crawfordsville, IN 47933

MONY Foundation Grants **1201**
The foundation awards grants in its areas of interest, including after-school community service and volunteer programs for youth, New York, NY; meeting the essential after-school needs of children and teens at risk, Syracuse, NY; and meeting the essential needs of minority children nationwide (with local MONY sales office). Types of support include employee matching gifts, employee-related scholarships, general operating support, in-kind gifts, matching/challenge support, and program development. Contact headquarters or local office by mail to obtain guidelines.
Restrictions: Grants do not support private foundations; fully participating members of the United Way; religious, fraternal, athletic, social, or veterans' organizations; individuals; capital fund drives; endowments; or deficit financing.
Geographic Focus: All U.S. States
Amount: 1,500 - 10,000 USD
Samples: To be distributed among 19 nonprofit organizations—for awards through the Field Grants, which provides fund-raising and financial assistance to groups that offer services to minority children, $95,000.
Contact: Grants Administrator; (212) 708-2468; (212) 708-2001; lynn_stekas@mony.com
Internet: http://www.mony.com
Sponsor: MONY Foundation
1740 Broadway, Mail Drop 10-36
New York, NY 10019

Morgan Stanley Foundation Grants **1202**
The foundation awards grants to nonprofit organizations in its areas of interest, including education, civic and community development, culture and the arts, and health and welfare. In the area of education, programs are supported that work to strengthen the teaching profession, address adult literacy, and retrain seniors and the disadvantaged. Economic development organizations with innovative programs designed to enhance and broaden the economic stability of communities receive consideration. In the area of health and welfare, applied research, educational programs, and other innovative programs in preventive health care, particularly those targeted to youth and seniors, receive support. Under arts and culture, performing arts and cultural programs in major metropolitan serving areas with outreach potential receive consideration. Types of support include capital campaigns, general operating support, continuing support, employee matching gifts, and in-kind gifts. The foundation prefers to fund project-specific proposals rather than requests for grants to underwrite operating or capital budgets.
Requirements: New York 501(c)3 organizations in company-operating areas are eligible.
Restrictions: Grants do not support United Way member agencies, individuals, endowment or building funds, capital campaigns, deficit financing, equipment acquisition, scholarships, fellowships, special projects, journal advertisements, research, publications, conferences, fund-raising dinners, or benefit events.
Geographic Focus: New York
Amount: 500 - 25,000 USD
Samples: New York Presbyterian Hospital (New York, NY)—for the capital campaign for the Children's Hospital, $2 million.
Contact: Director of Community Affairs; (212) 259-1235 or (212) 761-4000; (212) 259-1253; whatadifference@msdw.com
Internet: http://www.morganstanley.com/about/inside/community.html?page=about
Sponsor: Morgan Stanley Foundation
1601 Broadway, 12th Floor
New York, NY 10019

Moriah Fund Grants **1203**
The fund awards grants to nonprofit organizations in its areas of interest, including women's rights, human rights and democracy; community development and education in Israel and Guatemala; and disadvantaged in the United States, with emphasis on housing and family planning. Priority will be given to funding requests for the disadvantaged in Washington, DC. Types of support include continuing support, matching funds, operating budgets, seed money, technical assistance, and program development. Submit a two-page letter of application. The board meets in May and November to consider requests.
Restrictions: Grants do not support political campaigns, private foundations, arts organizations, medical research, or individuals.
Geographic Focus: All U.S. States
Date(s) Application is Due: Mar 1; Aug 1
Amount: 20,000 - 50,000 USD
Samples: Ctr for Community Change (Washington, DC)—for general support, including work on welfare reform and public housing, $70,000; Washington Regional Assoc of Grantmakers (Washington, DC)—for Community Development Support Collaborative, to revitalize and stabilize low-income, distressed neighborhoods in the District of Columbia, $60,000; Shefa Fund, Tzedek Economic Development Campaign, (Philadelphia, PA)—for matching grant for Local Tzedek Challenge Fund, which facilitates increased investment by Jewish communal organizations in institutions that finance efforts to revitalize low-income communities, $55,000.
Contact: Program Contact; (202) 783-8488; (202) 783-8499; info@moriahfund.org
Internet: http://www.moriahfund.org/grants/index.htm
Sponsor: Moriah Fund
1634 I Street NW, Suite 1000
Washington, DC 20006

Morris Stulsaft Foundation Grants **1204**
The foundation awards grants to California nonprofits for programs that focus on the needs of homeless children and youth; services for children living in subsidized housing; the needs of children and youth in foster care, especially as they prepare for emancipation; early intervention development programs for children with disabilities; child care for low-income families; and training for child care providers and staff. Types of support include operating budgets, building construction/renovations matching funds, research, special projects, and seed money. There are no application deadlines. Applicant should request an application form. At the full proposal stage, review turn around time is six months.
Requirements: Nonprofits in California counties, including Alameda, Contra Costa, Marin, San Francisco, Santa Clara, and San Mateo, are eligible.
Restrictions: Grants do not support individuals, deficit funding, emergency funding, endowments, fundraising, or special events/benefit dinners.
Geographic Focus: California
Amount: 5,000 - 15,000 USD
Samples: Dance Palace (CA)—toward dance scholarships for low-income Latino children, $2500; Fort Milky Adventures Rope Course (CA)—to purchase and upgrade equipment for the Ropes Course, $5000; National Junior Tennis League of San Francisco (CA)—to expand summer after-school program for low-income minority children and youth, $7500.
Contact: Program Contact; (415) 986-7117; (415) 986-2521; Stulsaft@aol.com
Internet: http://www.stulsaft.org/approvedgrants.html
Sponsor: Morris Stulsaft Foundation
100 Bush Street, Suite 825
San Francisco, CA 94104-3911

Morton-Kelly Charitable Trust Grants **1205**
The trust awards grants to Maine nonprofits in its areas of interest, including historic preservation, arts and culture, education and vocational education, and environment. Types of support include general operating support, continuing support, annual campaigns, capital campaigns, building construction/renovation, endowment funds, equipment acquisition, fellowships, capital

campaigns, program development, seed grants, scholarship funds, and research. There are no application forms; submit a letter of request.
Requirements: Maine nonprofit organizations are eligible.
Geographic Focus: All U.S. States
Amount: Up to 209,000 USD
Contact: Program Contact; (207) 775-7271; (207) 775-7935
Sponsor: Morton-Kelly Charitable Trust
10 Free Street, Box 4510
Portland, ME 04112

Moses Cone-Wesley Long Community Health Foundation Grants 1206
The foundation awards grants to eligible North Carolina organizations and programs in its areas of interest, including access to necessary health services, with particular emphasis on eliminating the barriers often encountered by persons in need; or wellness, with particular attention to physical activity, nutrition/obesity, substance abuse (including tobacco use prevention/cessation), responsible sexual behavior (especially the prevention of HIV/AIDS, STDs, and adolescent pregnancy), mental health, and injury prevention. Grants are awarded through the community health improvement fund ($50,000 maximum), direct foundation grants ($50,000 minimum), and special funding initiatives. In addition, the foundation funds organizational development and technical assistance projects that help communities build the capacity to help themselves improve the health of those in their communities. Funding priorities will be reviewed annually, and change is expected to occur periodically every three to five years. Applications and guidelines are available online.
Requirements: North Carolina nonprofit organizations, government agencies, schools, academic and research institutions, and collaborative consortia serving Greensboro, Winston-Salem, and High Point are eligible.
Geographic Focus: North Carolina
Samples: Nonprofit groups in the metropolitan Greensboro, NC, area (NC)—to support activities related to healthcare access, health promotion, injury prevention, mental health, physical activity and nutrition, responsible sexual behavior, and substance abuse treatment and prevention, $2 million; Twenty-four nonprofit groups and government agencies (Greensboro, NC)—to support activities related to health-care access, health promotion, injury prevention, mental health, physical activity and nutrition, responsible sexual behavior, and substance-abuse treatment and prevention, $3.194 million.
Contact: Program Director; (336) 832-9555; (336) 832-9559; antonia.reaves@mosescone.com
Internet: http://www.mcwlhealthfoundation.org
Sponsor: Moses Cone-Wesley Long Community Health Foundation
721 Green Valley Road, Suite 102, P.O. Box 4426
Greensboro, NC 27404-4426

Motorola Foundation Grants 1207
Motorola concentrates its giving in the following areas: engineering, technical, science or mathematics programs in K-12 schools or in universities and colleges; programs reaching traditionally under-represented groups in the areas of math, science, engineering and business; programs providing technical assistance, research and statistical information on the state of science and engineering education, or; progams that support the protection and preservation of the environment.
Requirements: All grants are made to 501(c)3 tax-exempt organizations.
Restrictions: Grants may not be made to individuals (scholarships, travel, business loans), religious groups, fraternity or sorority programs, political campaigns, private foundations, benefit events or ads, single disease causes, national health organizations or their local chapters, trade schools, product donations, media projects, capital fund drives, sports sponsorships, or endowment funds.
Geographic Focus: Arizona, California, Florida, Georgia, Illinois, Massachusetts, New Jersey, Pennsylvania, Texas
Amount: 10,000 - 100,000 USD
Samples: National Ctr for Disability Services, National Business and Disability Council (Albertson, NY)—to develop a publication designed to help employers who hire people with disabilities, $22,540.
Contact: Matthew Blakely, (847) 576-7895; (847) 576-9440; giving@motorola.com
Internet: http://www.motorola.com/content.jsp?globalObjectId=8152
Sponsor: Motorola Foundation
1303 E Algonquin Road
Schaumburg, IL 60196

Motorola Foundation Innovation Generation Collaborative Grants 1208
The Innovation Generation Collaborative Grants Support medium to large-scale STEM education collaborations between two or more non-profit organizations, schools and/or school districts, with joint requests ranging from $150,000 to $500,000. Programming must have nationwide and/or online reach or take place near communities where Motorola has an employee presence: Tempe, Arizona; San Diego, California; Miami, Florida; Chicago, Illinois; Lowell, Massachusetts; New York City and Long Island, New York; Philadelphia, Pennsylvania; or Fort Worth, Texas. Program must demonstrate measurable outcomes & impact on at least 250 primary participants. Grants may be for up to two years of project work starting after June of this year. Grant applications are accepted at the Motorola Foundation website, with a deadline date of April 1st.
Requirements: Any U.S. non-profit organization, school or school district may apply. Programming must have nationwide and/or online reach or take place near communities where Motorola has an employee presence: Tempe, Arizona; San Diego, California; Miami, Florida; Chicago, Illinois; Lowell, Massachusetts; New York City and Long Island, New York; Philadelphia, Pennsylvania; or Fort Worth, Texas. All requests must be partnerships between two or more non-profit organizations or schools. Only prior Motorola Foundation Innovation Generation grant recipients may apply. Organizations will be expected to interact and share program attributes with other grantees through conferences and online forums. Applications must be accompanied by letters of support from each member of the partnership. Funding priority will be placed on partnerships that: focus on a key STEM interest area such as teacher training, girls programming, out-of-school programming or online programs; engage students and teachers in innovative, hands-on activities; teach not only STEM, but also innovative thinking and creative problem-solving skills; focus on girls and underrepresented minorities; engage Motorola employees as volunteers.
Restrictions: Only prior Motorola Foundation Innovation Generation grant recipients may apply.
Geographic Focus: All U.S. States
Amount: 150,000 - 500,000 USD
Samples: Society of Women Engineers, Chicago, IL,—encourages girls in grades K-12 to capture the spirit of innovation and open their eyes and minds to a rewarding profession through a host of events, resources and in-person outreach programs (Out-of-School Programming) (2009); Texas Alliance for Minorities in Engineering (TAME), Austin, TX, TAME Statewide Math and Science Competition engages hundreds of female and underrepresented middle school and high school students from across Texas through individual competition and a Team Design Challenge, encouraging teamwork, leadership, academic achievement and an interest in science and math-related careers. (Out-of—School Programming) (2009).
Contact: Matthew Blakely, (847) 576-7895; (847) 576-9440; giving@motorola.com
Internet: http://www.motorola.com/staticfiles/Business/Corporate/U.S.-EN/corporate-responsibility/society/community-investment-education-more-about-innovation-generation-grants.html?globalObjectId=8153
Sponsor: Motorola Foundation
1303 E Algonquin Road
Schaumburg, IL 60196

Motorola Foundation Innovation Generation Grants 1209
The Motorola Foundation's Innovation Generation program equips students with the skills essential to both their lives today and their future success. By making the complex concepts behind math and science real and relevant, students look at their world differently through strengthened problem-solving skills. The Innovation Generation Grants support targeted, innovative STEM education programs for U.S. pre-school through 12th grade students and teachers, with grants ranging from $25,000 to $50,000. Program must: impact at least 100 primary participants, teacher training programs are exempt; demonstrate measurable change in STEM awareness or education. At least 25 percent of total grant dollars will support new programming that has been operating for less than two years and is not simply an expansion of an existing program. At least 15 percent of total grant dollars will support environment-focused programming.
Requirements: Any U.S. non-profit organization, school or school district may apply. Programming must have nationwide and/or online reach or take place near communities where Motorola has an employee presence: Tempe, Arizona; San Diego, California; Miami, Florida; Chicago, Illinois; Lowell, Massachusetts; New York City and Long Island, New York; Philadelphia, Pennsylvania; or Ft. Worth, Texas

Geographic Focus: All U.S. States
Date(s) Application is Due: Mar 1
Amount: 25,000 - 50,000 USD
Samples: Discovery Science Center, Santa Ana, CA.—Future Scientists and Engineers of America develops and instills the thrill and excitement of science, technology, engineering and math through the use of real-world hands-on projects and curricula for 2,000 students grades 4-12 across the nation (2009); National Society of Black Engineers, Alexandria, VA— Summer Engineering Experience for Kids (SEEK) Academy engages hundreds of students across the country in grades 3-8 in team-based, interactive engineering projects designed to increase their aptitude in math and science and their interest in pursuing careers in STEM fields (2009).
Contact: Matthew Blakely, (847) 576-7895; (847) 576-9440; giving@motorola.com
Internet: http://www.motorola.com/staticfiles/Business/Corporate/U.S.-EN/corporate-responsibility/society/community-investment-education-more-about-innovation-generation-grants.html?globalObjectId=8153
Sponsor: Motorola Foundation
1303 E Algonquin Road
Schaumburg, IL 60196

MRBF Small Grants for Grassroots Organizations **1210**
The foundation supports organizations in the Southeast and is committed to reaching small, grassroots organizations that have few other sources of philanthropic support in the region. Areas of grantmaking include grassroots leadership development, community problem solving, enterprise and asset development, and organizational development. The foundation makes grants to small organizations that need a combination of general operating and organizational development support to further their work. Eligible organizations must hold values consistent with building just and caring communities, including justice, equity, fairness, democracy/representative power, and inclusiveness. Participating organizations receive two grants of 18 months each, with the second grant being contingent upon accomplishing outcomes the organization and the Foundation agree upon for the first grant. Application guidelines are available online.
Requirements: Southeastern organizations must be rooted in their local community, have a governing board that represents and is accountable to their constituency, have a track record of effectiveness in addressing racism or poverty in low-income communities, and have an annual operating budget of $350,000 or less (most funded organizations have budgets between $75,000-$150,000) to be eligible.
Geographic Focus: Alabama, Arkansas, Florida, Georgia, Kentucky, Louisiana, Mississippi, North Carolina, South Carolina, Tennessee, Virginia, West Virginia
Date(s) Application is Due: Mar 1; Aug 1
Amount: Up to 45,000 USD
Contact: Cynthia Stivender, (336) 748-9222; (336) 777-0095; info@mrbbf.org
Internet: http://www.mrbf.org/fund/gld.aspx
Sponsor: Peek-A-Boo

Ms. Foundation for Women Grants **1211**
The foundation funds in the areas of economic security; health and safety; and girls, young women and leadership. It also supports organizing and public policy advocacy work that cuts across these issue areas. Guidelines are available on the website.
Requirements: Applicants must be tax-exempt groups and organizations. Applications, in five pages or less, should describe the organization or group; project for which funds are requested and why the organization is particularly suited to carry it out; community affected; general budget and project budget with specific amount being requested; other funding sources, presently and in the past; references; and a copy of IRS letter of determination of tax exemption. The foundation does not accept or reply to unsolicited requests that are not sent in response to an RFP.
Restrictions: Grants do not support cultural or media projects, publications, individuals, scholarships, university-based research, state agencies, religious institutions, or international programs.
Geographic Focus: All U.S. States
Contact: Program Contact; (212) 742-2300; (212) 742-1653; info@ms.foundation.org
Internet: http://www.ms.foundation.org/wmspage.cfm?parm1=5
Sponsor: Ms. Foundation for Women
120 Wall Street, 33rd Floor
New York, NY 10005

Ms. Foundation for Women Reproductive Rights Coalition and Organizing Grants **1212**
Grants support individual organizations and coalitions implementing grassroots organizing strategies or other collective approaches to improve access to reproductive health services including abortion, contraception, prenatal care, well-baby care, and comprehensive sexuality education. Proposals will be reviewed with regard to the following criteria: specific goals of the organization for the grant period; use of grassroots organizing strategies to involve activists; use of coalition strategies to increase membership; organizational commitment to diversity; use of multiple tactics; partnering with new allies outside the reproductive rights community to support a reproductive health agenda; range of reproductive health issues addressed, involvement of young women; organization's access to other funding sources; influence of religious right organizations in the city or state; and the current political climate of the state legislature, governor, and judiciary regarding reproductive rights. Priority is given to local and state coalitions and organizations. One-year general support and project support grants are awarded. Application and guidelines are available online.
Requirements: Priority will be given to state coalitions and membership organizations mounting proactive strategies and that address reproductive rights in the context of women's health, consumer rights, patient rights, racial justice, economic justice, or other contexts that broaden beyond a single issue. Regional, national, or academically oriented organizations must have strong connections to grassroots groups, and/or their work must be informed by local organizing efforts.
Restrictions: The foundation does not support individuals, national organizations, state or regional intermediaries, research institutes or think tanks, or capital and endowment campaigns.
Geographic Focus: All U.S. States
Amount: 15,000 - 30,000 USD
Contact: Grants Administrator; (212) 742-2300; (212) 742-1563; info@ms.foundation.org
Internet: http://www.ms.foundation.org/wmspage.cfm?parm1=16
Sponsor: Ms. Foundation for Women
120 Wall Street, 33rd Floor
New York, NY 10005

Ms. Foundation Public Voices, Public Policy Grants **1213**
The foundation is actively seeking organizations that are led by women of color and that are engaged in public policy advocacy and action. Because the goals of this initiative are not issue specific but rather about broad issues of access and participation of women of color in the public policy process, grantee organizations can be engaged in either multi- or single-issue work. Types of support include general support grants, technical assistance, training, and peer-to-peer opportunities. Start-up organizations that have no track record or experience in advocating for policy change for their communities will be given priority. Preference will be given to applicants with a budget under $1 million, although organizations that fall outside of this range are encouraged to apply. The listed application is for letters of intent; full proposals are by invitation. Guidelines and application are available online.
Requirements: 501(c)3 nonprofit organizations in the United States or Puerto Rico that are implementing local, state, tribal, national, or collective approaches around organizing, research, advocacy, or communications for public policy change are eligible.
Geographic Focus: All U.S. States
Date(s) Application is Due: Nov 12
Amount: 35,000 - 75,000 USD
Contact: Grants Administrator; (212) 742-2300; (212) 742-1653; info@ms.foundation.org
Internet: http://ms.foundation.org/wmspage.cfm?parm1=5
Sponsor: Ms. Foundation for Women
120 Wall Street, 33rd Floor
New York, NY 10005

Ms. Foundation Women and AIDS Fund Grants **1214**
The Women and AIDS Fund supports and builds the capacity of community-based, peer-focused organizations led by women with HIV/AIDS. Proposals will be considered for efforts that seek to enhance organizational capacity around: advocacy programs that provide leadership training and skills building for HIV-positive women to increase their participation at the planning and decision-making level; advocacy programs that increase the understanding around the unique issues facing HIV-infected women to the general public and seek ways to enlist HIV-positive women to take action in seeking redress; and

expanding HIV-positive women's access to currently available resources, such as clinical trials, new medications, and funding, that have often overlooked or underutilized women. Three-year general operating and project specific grants are awarded. Annual deadline dates may vary; contact program staff for exact dates.
Requirements: Grants are awarded to nonprofit groups working in the United States and Puerto Rico. The leadership of the specific project must be substantially made up of women with HIV/AIDS. Priority will be given to independent, women-focused organizations and programs.
Restrictions: Start-up projects in organizations that have no track record in women and AIDS will not be considered. The fund does not support videos, stand-alone conferences, individuals, scholarships, fundraising events, university-based research, or government agencies.
Geographic Focus: All U.S. States
Amount: 10,000 USD
Contact: Grants Administrator; (212) 742-2300; (212) 742-1653; info@ms.foundation.org
Internet: http://www.ms.foundation.org/wmspage.cfm?parm1=5
Sponsor: Ms. Foundation for Women
120 Wall Street, 33rd Floor
New York, NY 10005

Musgrave Foundation Grants **1215**
The foundation awards grants to eligible Missouri tax-exempt organizations in its areas of interest, including civic and public affairs, community development, elementary education, secondary education, higher education, and social services. Types of support include annual campaigns, building construction/renovation, capital campaigns, continuing support, equipment acquisition, general operating support, matching grants, and scholarship funds.
Requirements: 501(c)3 tax-exempt organizations and colleges, universities, and schools in Missouri may apply.
Restrictions: Grants are not made to individuals.
Geographic Focus: Missouri
Date(s) Application is Due: May 31
Amount: 500 - 61,000 USD
Contact: Jerry Redfern, Program Contact; (417) 841-4698 or (417) 882-9090; (417) 882-2529; jredfern@musgravefoundation.org
Internet: http://www.musgravefoundation.org
Sponsor: Musgrave Foundation
P.O. Box 10327
Springfield, MO 65804

Myers Family Foundation Grants **1216**
The foundation awards grants to nonprofit organizations in its areas of interest, including arts and culture, education, hospitals, family services, and churches. Types of support include capital grants, general operating grants, programs grants, and seed money grants. There are no application deadlines.
Requirements: 501(c)3 nonprofit organizations are eligible. Giving is primarily made in California.
Geographic Focus: All U.S. States
Amount: 25 - 150,000 USD
Contact: William Myers, Trustee; (805) 963-2690
Sponsor: Myers Family Foundation
1114 State Street, Suite 232
Santa Barbara, CA 93101-9650

Naomi and Nehemiah Cohen Foundation Grants **1217**
The foundation awards grants primarily for Jewish organizations, especially welfare funds, community services, and educational institutions. Grants also are awarded to Christian nonprofits and to organizations for peace activities. Types of support include annual campaigns, building construction/renovation, capital campaigns, equipment acquisition, general operating support, project support, publications, seed money, and technical assistance. Nonprofits in the District of Columbia receive preference. There are no formal grant procedures or application deadlines. Initial approach should be a letter of inquiry.
Restrictions: Grants are not made to individuals.
Geographic Focus: All U.S. States, Israel
Amount: 1,000 - 50,000 USD
Samples: Jewish Federation of Greater Washington (Rockville, MD)—for the United Jewish Endowment Fund's annual campaign, $4 million; Shefa Fund (Wyndmoor, PA)—to leverage investments from Jewish institutions and individuals for use by community development financial institutions, $360,000; United Jewish Appeal Federation (Rockville, MD)—operating support, $200,000.
Contact: Alison McWilliams, Director; (202) 234-5454; (202) 234-8797; NNCF@erols.com
Sponsor: Naomi and Nehemiah Cohen Foundation
P.O. Box 73708
Washington, DC 20056

Narragansett Number One Foundation Grants **1218**
The foundation awards most of its grants to nonprofit organizations in Buxton, ME, and the surrounding areas. Grants are made to public charities including schools, fire departments, police departments, libraries, parks, recreational facilities, churches, religious groups, shelters for children, the homeless and abused persons, museums, and shelters for animals. Types of support include start-up expenses, new or special projects, projects, and general operating support. Guidelines and application are available online. Annual deadline dates may vary; contact program staff for exact dates.
Requirements: Maine 501(c)3 tax-exempt organizations are eligible.
Restrictions: Grants do not support individuals, campaigns to elect candidates to public office, lobbying or propaganda campaigns, or programs or projects that discriminate.
Geographic Focus: Maine
Date(s) Application is Due: Mar 1
Amount: 750 - 29,000 USD
Contact: Grants Administrator
Internet: http://www.nnof.org
Sponsor: Narragansett Number One Foundation
P.O. Box 779
Bar Mills, ME 04004

Natalie W. Furniss Charitable Trust Grants **1219**
The Mission of the Furniss Foundation is to promote the humane treatment of animals by providing funding to societies for the prevention of cruelty to animals.
Requirements: Qualifying tax-exempt 501(c)3 organizations operating in the state of New Jersey are eligible to apply. Applications are accepted Ocotber 1 - December 1. Complete the Common Grant Application form available at the Wachovi website to apply for funding.
Restrictions: Grants are not made for political purposes, nor to organizations which discriminate on the basis of race, ethnic origin, sexual or religious preference, age or gender.
Geographic Focus: New Jersey
Date(s) Application is Due: Dec 1
Samples: Oasis Animal Sanctuary, Inc., $4,200—animal sterilization program; Woodford Cedar Run Wildlife Refuge, Inc., $4,5000—winter operating support for wildlife rehab; Society for the Prtevention of Cruelty to Animals, $5,000—humane education in Cumberland Co. School system; Greyhound Friends of New Jersey, Inc., $5,000—broken leg program.
Contact: Wachovia Bank, N.A., Trustee; grantinquiries6@wachovia.com
Internet: https://www.wachovia.com/foundation/v/index.jsp?vgnextoid=61078689fb0aa110VgnVCM1000004b0d1872RCRD&vgnextfmt=default
Sponsor: Natalie W. Furniss Foundation
100 North Main Street
Winston Salem, NC 27150

Nathan Cummings Foundation Grants **1220**
The foundation's core programs are in arts and culture; the environment; health; Jewish life; children and youth; and interprogram, which includes two special initiatives—democratic values and contemplative practice. Several basic themes run through all of these programs, including concern for the poor, disadvantaged, and underserved; respect for diversity; promotion of understanding across cultures; and empowerment of communities in need. Types of support include general operating support, continuing support, program development, conferences and seminars, seed money, and program evaluation. The foundation seeks to work with partners in the public, private, and nonprofit sectors. The board meets in the spring and fall of each year to consider requests. Initial contact should be through a letter of intent.
Restrictions: The foundation does not contribute to endowments, debt reduction, capital campaigns, capital construction, equipment purchases, or museum collections acquisitions. Individuals are not eligible.
Geographic Focus: All U.S. States
Amount: 20,000 - 150,000 USD

Samples: Cultural Initiatives-Silicon Valley (San Jose, CA)—for research leading to a community arts program, $50,000; Better Government Assoc (Chicago, IL)—for campaign finance-reform efforts, $32,000; Hebrew Union College-JIR (New York, NY)—for a flexible master's-degree program for lay Jewish leaders, $67,700.
Contact: Program Contact; (212) 787-7300; (212) 787-7377; info@nathancummings.org
Internet: http://www.nathancummings.org/programs/index.html
Sponsor: Nathan Cummings Foundation
475 10th Avenue, 14th Floor
New York, NY 10018

Nathaniel and Elizabeth P. Stevens Foundation Grants **1221**

The foundation awards grants to eligible Massachusetts nonprofit organizations to improve the quality of life in the greater area comprising Lawrence and Merrimack Valley. Areas of interest include arts and culture, community services, education, religion, and youth programs. Types of support include building construction/renovation, capital campaigns, conferences and seminars, continuing support, consulting services, endowments, equipment acquisition, general operating support, land acquisition, matching funds, special projects, and technical assistance. Include a copy of the IRS 501(c)3 tax-exemption letter with application.
Requirements: Massachusetts 501(c)3 tax-exempt organizations serving the greater Lawrence and Merrimack Valley are eligible.
Restrictions: Grants do not support national organizations, state or federal agencies, individuals, annual campaigns, deficit financing, exchange programs, internships, professorships, scholarships, or fellowships.
Geographic Focus: Massachusetts
Amount: 2,000 - 8,000 USD
Contact: Josh Miner, Executive Director; (978) 688-7211; (978) 686-1620; grantprocess@stevensfoundation.com
Sponsor: Nathaniel and Elizabeth P. Suitevens Foundation
P.O. Box 111
North Andover, MA 01845

National Center for Outreach Challenge Grants **1222**

The purpose of these grants is threefold: to help stations promote outreach impact and visibility in the community, to strengthen the core infrastructure of station outreach departments, and to leverage local matching funds. NCO funds may be applied toward one of five designated purposes: promoting internal/external visibility and impact; community assessment; diversifying outreach audiences; beginning an outreach program; and evaluation. Applicants will have 12 months to implement their projects and meet a 2:1 NCO/Station cash fundraising challenge. To promote outreach/development collaboration, up to 50 percent of matching funds may be used toward general operating expenses. NCO funds must be used only for the project.
Requirements: Public broadcasting stations are eligible.
Geographic Focus: All U.S. States
Date(s) Application is Due: Jun 16
Amount: 5,000 - 8,000 USD
Contact: Tom Linfield; (866) 234-2016 or (608) 265-6052; linfield@wpt.org
Internet: http://www.nationaloutreach.org/Grants/Challenge/Index.html
Sponsor: National Center for Outreach
975 Observatory Drive
Madison, WI 53706

National Starch and Chemical Foundation Grants **1223**

The foundation supports nonprofits in company-operating locations in the areas of higher education, children's services, and hospitals. Types of support include general operating support, continuing support, employee-related scholarships, and employee matching gifts. There are no application guidelines. Applicants are asked to submit a written proposal.
Requirements: Nonprofits in company operating areas such as Georgia, Illinois, Indiana, Missouri, North Carolina, New Jersey, Pennsylvania, South Carolina, and Tennessee may apply.
Geographic Focus: Georgia, Illinois, Indiana, Missouri, New Jersey, North Carolina, Pennsylvania, South Carolina, Tennessee
Amount: 500 - 10,000 USD
Contact: Carmen Ortiz, (908) 685-5201; carmen.ortiz@nstarch.com
Internet: http://news.nationalstarch.com/NewsStory.asp?newsItemId=214
Sponsor: National Starch and Chemical Foundation
10 Finderne Avenue
Bridgewater, NJ 08807

Nationwide Foundation Grants **1224**

Grants are given to tax-exempt organizations located in central Ohio or recommended for funding by a state office or subsidiary/affiliate, In order of emphasis, grants support: health and human services, higher education, culture and arts, and civic and community. Funds are provided for arts programs, including fine arts, dance, music, museum, and theater programs; business and economics; children and youth; health programs, mental health, and programs dealing with alcoholism and drug abuse; assistance for and care of the aged; educational programs for minorities, persons with disabilities, and the disadvantaged; social service and social welfare programs; and urban affairs. Types of support include operating budgets, continuing support, annual campaigns, seed grants, projects and programs, employee matching gifts, and capital campaigns. Preference is given to organizations located in central Ohio.
Requirements: Seventy percent of grants are awarded to nonprofit organizations in the greater Columbus, OH, area, with the rest going to organizations in which Nationwide has a large number of employees and agents.
Restrictions: Individuals, organizations that support political candidates or political philosophies, public elementary and secondary schools, lobbying groups, and fraternal or veterans organizations are not eligible for these grants. Research is not funded.
Geographic Focus: Ohio
Date(s) Application is Due: Sep 1
Amount: 5,000 - 50,000 USD
Samples: To be divided among more than 1000 organizations nationwide—to benefit these nonprofit groups, which include more than 700 United Way chapters, $14 million.
Contact: Grants Administrator; (614) 249-4310 or (614) 249-0039; (614) 249-3147
Internet: http://www.nationwide.com/aboutus/community/fndatn.htm
Sponsor: Nationwide Foundation
1 Nationwide Plaza, MD 1-22-05
Columbus, OH 43215-2220

NCI Technologies and Software to Support Integrative Cancer Biology Research (SBIR) Grants **1225**

This Funding Opportunity Announcement (FOA), issued by the National Cancer Institute (NCI), invites Small Business Innovation Research (SBIR) grant applications from small business concerns (SBCs) that propose the development of commercial software tools, computational/mathematical methods, and technologies that will enable integrative cancer biology research. Integrative cancer biology focuses on understanding cancer as a complex biological system by utilizing both computational and experimental biology to integrate heterogeneous data sources and ultimately to generate predictive computational models of cancer processes. Phase I applications may request up to 2 years of support with total costs of up to $300,000 for the duration of the award (not to exceed $200,000 total costs in any one year). Budgetary requests of Phase II applications will conform to standard SBIR guidelines (up to $750,000 total costs for up to two years).
Requirements: Only United States small business concerns (SBCs) are eligible to submit SBIR applications.
Geographic Focus: All U.S. States
Date(s) Application is Due: Apr 5; Aug 5; Dec 5
Amount: 200,000 - 750,000 USD
Contact: Greg Evans, (301) 594-8807; (301) 480-4082; evansgl@mail.nih.gov
Internet: http://grants.nih.gov/grants/guide/pa-files/PA-09-188.html
Sponsor: National Cancer Institute
31 Center Drive, Building 31, Room 10A19, MSC 2580
Bethesda, MD 20892-2580

Nebraska Arts Council Basic Support Grants **1226**

Grants offer general operating support for arts organizations in Nebraska, allowing them to improve and extend the arts services they annually provide to their communities. Grants are awarded to community and volunteer organizations (BSG-C) or discipline-based organizations (BSG-D). Organizations that have been receiving BSG funds may request up to 25 percent more than their most recent BSG award. Organizations that are applying in the BSG category for the first time may request up to $2500. Community and volunteer organizations that do not currently receive funding but are interested in applying must contact NAC staff. Annual deadline dates may vary; contact the council for exact dates.

Requirements: Nebraska nonprofit, tax-exempt organizations that dedicate 51 percent or more of their budget to producing or sponsoring arts events or to providing arts services are eligible. In addition, if applying organizations are not currently participating in a community challenge grant program, they must have done so three years prior to application in this category.
Geographic Focus: Nebraska
Date(s) Application is Due: Mar 1
Contact: Elaine Buescher, Grants Manager; (800) 341-4067 or (402) 595-2122; (402) 595-2334; ebuescher@nebraskaartscouncil.org
Internet: http://www.nebraskaartscouncil.org/index_html?page=content/GRANTS/Categories/CatGrants.htm
Sponsor: Nebraska Arts Council
3838 Davenport Street
Omaha, NE 68131-2329

Needmor Fund Grants **1227**
The fund awards grants to grassroots, community-based organizations for a range of activities in the areas of justice, political liberty, human services (food, shelter, health care, and safety), and education that enables low- and moderate-income individuals to contribute to society and the opportunity to secure productive work with just wages and benefits. Needmor gives to groups that help people take control of their lives and change the conditions that adversely affect them. Preference will be given to groups that have a highly committed membership, develop leadership from within, can determine solutions to major problems facing their communities, and formulate effective strategic plans. Types of support include general operating budgets, seed money, and technical assistance. Grantees are encouraged to develop alternative means of long-term fundraising to promote self-sufficiency. The January dedline is for applicants located in Alabama, Arizona, southern California, Louisian, Mississippi, Nnew Mexico, and southern Texas (including San Antonio). The June deadline is for applicants in all other states.
Requirements: Nonprofit community-based organizations may apply for support.
Restrictions: Grants do not support individuals, capital funds, scholarships, fellowships, deficit financing, replacement of lost government funding, land acquisition, purchase of buildings or equipment, publications, media, films, TV or radio productions, computer projects, or university research. Nonprofits with access to traditional funding sources generally are denied support.
Geographic Focus: Arizona, California, Colorado, New Mexico, Wyoming
Date(s) Application is Due: Jan 10; Jun 30
Amount: 15,000 - 30,000 USD
Samples: Congregations United for Community Action (Saint Petersburg, FL)—for operating support, $20,000; Congregations Allied for Community Improvement (Saint Louis, MO)—for operating support, $9333; Farmworkers Self-Help Inc (Dade City, FL)—for operating support, $20,000; Greater Columbus Community Shares (Columbus, OH)—for operating support, $20,000.
Contact: Mary Sobecki, Grants Manager; (419) 255-5560; (419) 255-5561; needmors@sbcglobal.net
Internet: http://fdncenter.org/grantmaker/needmor
Sponsor: Needmor Fund
42 S Saint Clair Street
Toledo, OH 43602

NEFA National Dance Project Grants **1228**
These grants provide funding for the creation of new dance work that will tour nationally. Funds support a project's development through the time of its premiere, covering costs related to producing the work. Every season, 15 to 20 production grants are awarded. Each awardee also receives a touring grant, to support a tour of the new work.
Requirements: Production grants are awarded to dance projects based on nominations received from presenters, artists, artist managers, and agents.
Restrictions: Artists receiving production grants in any given season are not eligible to apply for production grant support in the following season.
Geographic Focus: Connecticut, Maine, Massachusetts, New Hampshire, Rhode Island, Vermont
Date(s) Application is Due: Apr 1
Amount: 15,000 - 35,000 USD
Samples: Nineteen contemporary-dance companies—for production grants that support the development of new dance projects, $560,000 divided.
Contact: Program Contact; (617) 951-0010; (617) 951-0016; dance@nefa.org
Internet: http://www.nefa.org/grantprog/ndp/ndp_prod_grant_app.html
Sponsor: New England Foundation for the Arts
145 Tremont Street, 7th Floor
Boston, MA 02111

Nevada Arts Council Partners Development Grants **1229**
Development grants are designed to assist Nevada's rural and urban arts groups in strengthening their abilities to stabilize existing operations, and to broaden public access to the arts and arts resources in communities that previously have been underserved in the area. Funds may be requested to develop and/or present first-time programs, expand existing programming, or solve organizational or community issues. Applicants may also apply for planning projects, consultant fees for technical assistance, and/or operating support. Annual deadline dates may vary; contact the program office for exact dates.
Requirements: 501(c)3 Nevada arts/cultural organizations applying for the first time to the grants program must apply in this category, no matter the age of the organization or its budget size.
Geographic Focus: Nevada
Date(s) Application is Due: Mar 15
Amount: 1,001 - 4,000 USD
Contact: Stacey Spain, Grants Coordinator; (775) 687-7102; (775) 687-6688; slspain@clan.lib.nv.us
Internet: http://dmla.clan.lib.nv.us/docs/ARTS/grants/grantgdlnsFY06.htm
Sponsor: Nevada Arts Council
716 N Carson Street, Suite A
Carson City, NV 89701

Nevada Arts Council Partners in Excellence Grants **1230**
Partners in Excellence grants provide organizational (programmatic and operational) support for nonprofit arts organizations that have completed at least two years of funding in the Development Grant category.
Requirements: Tier 1 grants are available to Nevada organizations with budgets smaller than $30,000 and with three years of effective programming, a cumulative operating cash budget of at least $35,000 for the past two-year fiscal period, and an operating cash budget of $25,000 in the last fiscal year. Tier 2 grants are available to Nevada organizations with budgets larger than $30,000 and smaller than $100,000; three years of effective programming, including at least one year with professional staff; an operating cash budget of $30,000 in the last fiscal year; and a multiyear plan.
Geographic Focus: Nevada
Date(s) Application is Due: Mar 31
Amount: 1,001 - 8,000 USD
Contact: Stacey Spain, Grants Coordinator; (775) 687-7102; (775) 687-6688; slspain@clan.lib.nv.us
Internet: http://dmla.clan.lib.nv.us/docs/ARTS/grants/grantgdlnsFY06.htm
Sponsor: Nevada Arts Council
716 N Carson Street, Suite A
Carson City, NV 89701

Nevada Arts Council Project Grants **1231**
Project Grants are designed to support activities/projects of non-arts organizations and public institutions that are: integral to the applicant's overall mission and goals; and achieved through community partnerships. Partnerships, including those that involve sectors outside of the arts, are key to the success of activities funded by Project Grants and must be reflected in every application. Eligible activities may include, but are not limited to, performances, ethnic festivals, film series, and visual arts exhibitions. Requests to fund ongoing programming are allowable. Applicants need to supply budget information that reflects the cost of the proposed project only, not a total organization budget.
Requirements: Nevada 501(c)3 nonprofit organizations are eligible.
Geographic Focus: Nevada
Date(s) Application is Due: Mar 15
Amount: 1,000 - 6,500 USD
Contact: Stacey Spain, Grants Coordinator; (775) 687-7102; (775) 687-6688; slspain@clan.lib.nv.us
Internet: http://dmla.clan.lib.nv.us/docs/ARTS/grants/grantgdlnsFY06.htm
Sponsor: Nevada Arts Council
716 N Carson Street, Suite A
Carson City, NV 89701

Nevada Community Foundation Grants **1232**
The foundation assists in funding organizations and programs that benefit the growing needs of the community. Currently, NCF offers two grant programs:

the capacity building grant program and the Edwin F. Wiegand Grants. See website for program details.
Requirements: Las Vegas, NV, nonprofits are eligible.
Geographic Focus: Nevada
Contact: Grants Administrator; (702) 892-2326; (702) 892-8580
Internet: http://www.nevadacf.org
Sponsor: Nevada Community Foundation
300 S Fourth Street, Suite 1009
Las Vegas, NV 89101

New-Land Foundation Grants **1233**
The foundation supports U.S. nonprofit organizations for programs that emphasize the areas of civil rights, justice, peace, and arms control. The foundation also focuses on the environment, population control, and leadership development in these areas. Types of support include general operating expenses, annual campaigns, seed grants, research, continuing support, internships, matching funds, and programs/projects. The foundation board generally meets in the fall and spring of each year to consider grant requests. Application form and guidelines should be requested in writing.
Restrictions: Individuals are ineligible.
Geographic Focus: All U.S. States
Date(s) Application is Due: Feb 1; Aug 1
Amount: 5,000 - 25,000 USD
Samples: Ms. Foundation for Women (New York, NY)—$60,000; Institute for Policy Studies (Washington, DC)—$40,000; Land and Water Fund of the Rockies (Boulder, CO)—$25,000.
Contact: Program Contact; (212) 479-6162
Sponsor: New-Land Foundation
1114 Avenue of the Americas, 46th Floor
New York, NY 10036-7798

New Covenant Farms Grants **1234**
The Program, established in Idaho in 2000 by the L.M. Davenport Warehouse, provides funding and goods for children and families in both Texas and Mexico. Types of support include: cash; housing; clothing; food; education; and other necessities. There are no specific deadlines, though written applications are required. Applicants should include: name and location; exemption status; what food products and distribution needs are required; and budget.
Geographic Focus: Texas, Mexico
Samples: Rick Caywood Ministries, Crawford, TX, $3,500—food distribution to the poor (2008); Rio Bravo W-4stries, Mission, TX,—home to 65 children in Reynosa Tam, Mexico (2008), Instituto De Magdiel, Matamoros Tam, Mexico—training students for Christian Ministry (2008).
Contact: Lewis M. Davenport III, CEO; (208) 934-5600 or (208) 934-5609
Sponsor: New Covenant Farms
1737 East 1800 South
Gooding, ID 83330-5095

New Earth Foundation Grants **1235**
The New Earth Foundation (NEF) supports nonprofit organizations in the following areas: education, social services, the arts, communication, and the preservation of sacred spaces, among other areas. NEF prefers to fund smaller and newer organizations. Typical grantee organizations are less than 15 years old with annual operating budgets of less than $350,000, including programs and administration. If you are a 501(c)3 organization, or are working under the umbrella of a 501(c)3 organization, you may apply for a grant of between $5,000 and $7,500. If you are working under an umbrella, a clear relationship between that organization and your project must be demonstrated. You must include a letter that shows that the board of directors (not just the staff or chair) agrees that the umbrella organization may act as your funding agent. The letter should address your project's relationship to the organization and be signed by the president/chair.
Requirements: 501(c)3 nonprofit organizations are eligible to apply. To begin the application process submit (electronically) a Letter of Inquiry to the foundation, providing basic information about your organization and about your program/project. After reviewing the Letter of Inquiry, you maybe invited to submit a complete application.
Restrictions: NEF does not fund organizations that: offer mainstream social services or are local organizations that are affiliated with a national organization such as Boys & Girls Clubs, Big Brothers/Big Sisters, Habitat for Humanity, the Cancer Society and other such organizations; are good candidates for governmental funding; are involved in community housing and renovation; have standard forms of after-school programs, outdoor summer camps/expeditions, or gardening programs; are land and building preservation programs; are capital improvement/building projects; are involved in land purchases.
Geographic Focus: All U.S. States
Amount: 5,000 - 7,500 USD
Contact: David Belskis, President; newearthfoundation@foundationsource.com
Internet: http://www.newearthfoundation.org/application.html
Sponsor: New Earth Foundation
Foundation Source, 55 Walls Drive
Fairfield, CT 06824

New England Biolabs Foundation Grants **1236**
The foundation has special program interests in marine conservation, estuary protection, sustainable economic development, sustainable organic agriculture, education in women's health issues (developing countries only), and environmental education for teachers or elementary age students. Additional funding supports local education and art programs. Education and community projects are limited to Boston and the North Shore. International grants are made to small developing countries, with priority given to environmental protection and education projects. Grants provide general operating support. Applicants should make preliminary inquiry by letter, phone, or email. Proposals are accepted online, and the foundation will also accept the NNG common grant application.
Requirements: The foundation makes grants to grassroots organizations, emerging support groups, and other charitable organizations, generally nonprofits with revenue under $3 million. International projects located in Cambodia, Cameroon, the Caribbean (not Haiti, Cuba, the U.S. Virgin Islands, or the Dominican Republic), Central America (not Mexico, Costa Rica, Panama or Belize), Guatemala (funding environmental education projects for students and/or teachers), Ghana (environmental projects only), Tanzania, Madagascar, Papua New Guinea, South America (not Argentina, Brazil, Fr. Guiana, Suriname, Uruguay, Columbia, or Venezuela), Viet Nam, and Zimbabwe will be considered. Under certain provisions, individuals also may be eligible.
Restrictions: Grants are not awarded to support religious activities, specific animal protection, services for the elderly or the disabled, projects normally funded by major agencies, or art projects outside the immediate community. Grants do not support capital endowment or building funds, fellowships, movies or videos, scholarships, or conferences.
Geographic Focus: All Countries
Date(s) Application is Due: Mar 1; Sep 1
Amount: 500 - 20,000 USD
Samples: Artcorps (Boston, MA)—to support inner city teens art design in Boston, $20,000; A Woman's Voice—to prevent female circumcision in young girls in Kenya, $5000; Lesson One (Peabody, MA)—for violence prevention programs in elementary schools in Peabody, MA, $7500; Idea Wild (Fort Collins, CO)—to continue a biodiversity and conservation program in Latin America, $5000.
Contact: Martine Kellett, Executive Director; (978) 927-2404; (508) 921-1350; kellett@nebf.org
Internet: http://www.nebf.org/application.html
Sponsor: New England Biolabs Foundation
8 Enon Street #2B
Beverly, MA 01915

New England Grassroots Environment Fund Grants **1237**
The purpose of the fund is to increase engagement and participation in grassroots environmental initiatives and to build and connect healthy, sustainable communities in New England. Applicants must be working at the grassroots level and must demonstrate a major element of volunteer involvement in their programs. A broad range of activities will be funded, including community needs, computer networking, capacity building, advocacy campaigns, institutional support, conferences, meeting travel, and enhancing partnerships in the region. Types of support include but are not limited to general operating support, equipment acquisition, program development, conferences and seminars, and scholarship funds. The fund has three funding cycles each year. Applications are accepted at any time.
Requirements: 501(c)3 nonprofit, grassroots organizations in Maine, Massachusetts, New Hampshire, Rhode Island, and Vermont are eligible. Grassroots groups are defined as being largely volunteer driven, having no more than two paid full-time staff members, and an annual budget (including

projects) of less than $100,000. Proposals may be considered from larger community-based groups for projects at the grassroots level.
Restrictions: Grants do not support lobbying or partisan political purposes.
Geographic Focus: Connecticut, Maine, Massachusetts, New Hampshire, Rhode Island, Vermont
Date(s) Application is Due: Jan 15; May 1; Sep 15
Amount: 500 - 2,500 USD
Samples: Maine Wolf Coalition (South China, ME)—to purchase a computer, other office equipment, and furniture, $2250; Toxics Action Ctr (Boston, MA)—to finance scholarships to allow local activists to attend an annual training conference, $175; New Hampshire Council of Churches (Concord, NH)—to hire an intern to set up a network of faith-based environmental groups and congregations, $2500; Saugatucket River Heritage Corridor (Wakefield, RI)—for general operating support, $2500.
Contact: Cheryl King Fischer, Executive Director; (802) 223-4622; (802) 229-1734; fischer@grassrootsfund.org
Internet: http://www.grassrootsfund.org/guide_1.html
Sponsor: New England Grassroots Environment Fund
P.O. Box 1057
Montpelier, VT 05601

Newfoundland and Labrador Arts Council Project Grants **1238**
Project grants support production, operating, travel, and study costs (but not capital costs, i.e., costs associated with the purchase of equipment such as typewriters or tape recorders; however, such items may be leased) relating to a specific project to be undertaken by an artist, arts group, or organization. Of the money available for projects, up to 12 percent is designated as seed funding. Less established artists, groups, and organizations may be considered in this separate category as determined by the council. Similarly, a portion, up to 8 percent, is earmarked for study. September 15 is the deadline for projects beginning after November 1, and March 1 is the deadline for projects beginning after May 1. Applications are available on the website and from the council.
Requirements: Individual applicants must be 18 years of age or hold postsecondary standing at the time of application; must ordinarily be either Canadian citizens or landed immigrants; must have been residents in Newfoundland or Labrador for a minimum of 12 consecutive months at the time of application; and applicants working outside the province at the time of application are eligible if it can be shown that their permanent place of residence is Newfoundland or Labrador. Groups, organizations, and companies must have been based in Newfoundland or Labrador for a minimum of 12 months at the time of application; and a majority of the executive committee must individually meet the individual residency requirements.
Restrictions: Students in degree- or diploma-granting courses of study for which Canada Student Aid is available are not eligible for assistance from the council. email submissions are not acceptable.
Geographic Focus: Canada
Date(s) Application is Due: Mar 1; Sep 15
Amount: 500 - 2,000 CAD
Contact: Program Contact; (709) 726-2212; (709) 726-0619; nlacmail@newcomm.net or kmurphy@nfld.net
Internet: http://www.nlac.nf.ca/grants/project.shtml
Sponsor: Newfoundland and Labrador Arts Council
Newman Building, 1 Springdale Street, P.O. Box 98
St Johns, NL A1C 5H5 Canada

Newfoundland and Labrador Arts Council Sustaining Grants **1239**
Grants are available to professional arts organizations to provide assistance toward administrative costs with a guaranteed minimum grant for a three-year period. Two types of sustaining funding are available: Professional Performing Arts Organization (PPAO), which provides funding for performing arts groups that produce work themselves. Applications under this category are due April 15, with payout on June 1. Visual, Literary, and Provincial Arts Organization (VLPAO) funding is for groups whose chief function is administrative. The deadline for VLPAO applications is September 30, with payout on January 2.
Requirements: Groups, organizations, and companies must have been based in Newfoundland or Labrador for a minimum of 12 consecutive months at the time of application; and a majority of the executive committee must individually meet the residency requirement outlined above.
Geographic Focus: Canada
Date(s) Application is Due: Apr 15; Sep 30
Contact: Katrina Rice, Program Officer; (709) 726-2212; (709) 726-0619; krice@nfld.net
Internet: http://www.nlac.nf.ca/grants/sustain.shtml
Sponsor: Newfoundland and Labrador Arts Council
Newman Building, 1 Springdale Street, P.O. Box 98
St Johns, NL A1C 5H5 Canada

Newman's Own Inc Grants **1240**
The corporate giving program awards general support grants to a broad array of charitable and educational causes, including children and youth, health, education, elderly, environment, the arts, handicapped, literacy, substance abuse education, programs for the needy (i.e., housing and food). More than 600 grants are made annually. Funding levels vary each year based on after-tax profits. Actor and company president, Paul L. Newman, reviews each proposal and selects the groups and organizations to receive contributions. He is interested in organizations outside of the charity mainstream that help those who often cannot help themselves. Social service agencies in Australia and Canada also receive support. Early submission of proposals is encouraged. Faxed or emailed proposals are not accepted.
Requirements: IRS 501(c)3 nonprofits are eligible for grant support.
Restrictions: Paul Newman and the Newman's Own Foundation do not support individual donations and scholarships.
Geographic Focus: All U.S. States
Amount: 2,000 - 15,000 USD
Contact: Paul L. Newman, c/o Newman's Own,
Internet: http://www.newmansownfoundation.org/giving/
Sponsor: Newman's Own
246 Post Road E
Westport, CT 06880-3615

Newman W. Benson Foundation Grants **1241**
Established in New York in 1990, the Foundation supports both human service programs and religious agencies. Generally, funding comes in the form of operating costs, with giving centered around Bradford and Towanda County, Pennsylvania. A selection of grants are also provided to organizations outside of Pennsylvania. There are no specific application forms or deadlines with which to adhere, and applicants should send a letter of request detailing the program or project, and include both a budget narrative and 501(c)3 letter.
Geographic Focus: All U.S. States
Amount: Up to 12,000 USD
Samples: First United Methodist Church, Towanda, Pennsylvania, $10,200; Wysox Presbyterian Church, Wysox Township, Pennsylvania, $675.
Contact: Newman W. Benson, President; (570) 265-3498
Sponsor: Newman W. Benson Foundation
P.O. Box 430, Lake Wesauking
Towanda, PA 18848-0430

New Prospect Foundation Grants **1242**
The foundation awards grants nationally and internationally (Central America and Israel) to support activities directed toward human rights. Nonprofits also are eligible for support of housing improvement, employment, health, welfare, and the economic viability of urban and inner-city neighborhoods. Additional areas of interest are pro-choice activities, health care policy and advocacy, human and civil rights, and public school reform. Types of support include general operating support, continuing support, program development, and seed money. Priority is given to requests from the Chicago metropolitan area. Applications are due six weeks before board meetings in March, June, October, and December.
Requirements: Priority is given to requests from the Chicago metropolitan area.
Restrictions: Grants do not fund the arts, higher education, individuals, capital or endowment requests, basic research, scholarships, fellowships, or loans.
Geographic Focus: Illinois
Amount: 1,500 - 7,500 USD
Samples: Shefa Fund (Wyndmoor, PA)—to leverage investments from Jewish institutions and individuals for use by community-development financial institutions, $180,000.
Contact: Paul Lehman, Director; (847) 328-2288
Sponsor: New Prospect Foundation
1603 Orrington Avenue, Suite 1880
Evanston, IL 60201

New World Foundation Grants 1243

The foundation supports grassroots organizations that foster citizen engagement and local empowerment in the areas of public education, equal rights and opportunities, public health, community initiatives, and the avoidance of war. Types of support include general operating grants, seed money grants, and technical assistance. To increase the impact small groups can make, the foundation works on providing opportunities for grassroots groups to come together to share experience, expertise, and constituencies. The foundation also aims to connect grassroots organizations with the wider philanthropic sector. Application consists of a brief letter outlining the project needing funding, amount needed, and specifics of the requesting organization. The foundation will advise if more detailed information is needed. Grants are usually awarded for one year and sometimes are renewable. Applications are accepted at any time.
Geographic Focus: All U.S. States
Amount: 5,000 - 25,000 USD
Contact: Grants Administrator; (212) 249-1023; (212) 472-0508; info@newwf.org
Internet: http://www.newwf.org/grant_programs/main.html
Sponsor: New World Foundation
666 W End Avenue
New York, NY 10025

New York Foundation Grants 1244

The foundation supports groups in New York City that are working on problems of urgent concern to residents of disadvantaged communities and neighborhoods. The foundation does not limit grants to specified issue areas, although half of the grants are reserved for projects involving youth or the elderly. Also supported are programs of public education and advocacy whose effect is to increase the participation of these target populations in the public debate on issues of pressing social concern. The foundation prefers to back advocacy or organizing projects, rather than the provision of services. Types of support include start-up grants to new, untested programs often involving a high element of risk, established nonprofits for new community projects that may need ongoing support in the future, general support to groups that offer relatively new programs, and technical assistance. Grants are made for one year, renewable for a total of three years. Proposals to coordinate and improve communication among programs working on similar issues are encouraged.
Requirements: A letter outlining proposed project, budget needs, and amount of grant to be requested should precede a formal application. Applicants must reside in New York.
Restrictions: The foundation never makes grants to individuals or to capital campaigns. It does not consider support of research studies, films, conferences, or publications; or requests outside New York City except from organizations working on statewide issues of concern to youth, the elderly, or the poor.
Geographic Focus: New York
Date(s) Application is Due: Mar 1; Jul 1; Nov 1
Amount: 40,000 - 60,000 USD
Samples: New York Statewide Senior Action Council(Albany, NY)—for general support of this statewide, membership-based advocacy organization, $45,000; Afghan Communicator (New York, NY)—to create an information center, assess community needs, and educate the public about Afghanistan, Islam, and the Afghan community, $40,000. New York AIDS Coalition (New York, NY)—to retain a community organizer to engage grassroots HIV/AIDS leaders in the Coalition's efforts $45,000; Picture the Homeless (New York, NY)— for an organization led by homeless people to end the criminalization of homelessness and build a movement that demands housing as a human right, $45,000.
Contact: Maria Mottola, Executive Director; (212) 594-8009
Internet: http://www.nyf.org/Guidelines.asp
Sponsor: New York Foundation
350 Fifth Avenue, Room 2901
New York, NY 10118

New York Life Foundation Grants 1245

The foundation awards grants to nonprofit organizations in its areas of interest. Periodically, the foundation selects an area of special priority. The current focus, Nurturing the Children, directs the majority of the foundation's resources toward organizations, programs, and services aimed at helping young people. This initiative specifically focuses on safe places to learn and grow; educational enhancement; and mentoring. The foundation has initiated a new grant award program for nonprofit organizations based in New York City. Youth In Action recognizes innovative Nurturing the Children programs that engage youth in planning, coordinating and/or helping to provide services.
Requirements: Nonprofit 501(c)3 organizations may submit grant requests. The foundation funds projects in New York City, where New York Life's Home Office is located. The foundation also considers multi-site projects implemented by national organizations. These projects must serve two or more of the following locations: Atlanta; Cleveland; Clinton/Hunterdon County, New Jersey; Dallas; Kansas City; Minneapolis; New York City; Parsippany/Morris County, New Jersey; Tampa; and Westchester County, New York.
Restrictions: The foundation does not support sectarian or religious organizations or activities; fraternal, social, professional, athletic, or veterans groups; seminars or conferences; preschool, primary, or secondary education; endowments; memorials; basic or applied research; capital campaigns; or fund-raising activities.
Geographic Focus: All U.S. States
Date(s) Application is Due: Dec 1
Samples: Coalition for the Homeless (New York, NY)—for its after-school programs at five New York City shelters and its summer camp programs for children living in homeless shelters, $140,000; Harlem Education Activities Fund (New York, NY)—to expand the Summer Quest Program, a six-week summer academic program for middle-school students, $290,750 over three years; New York Historical Society (New York, NY)—for a new educational program that will serve at-risk elementary- and middle-school students in New York, $160,000; Foundation for the National Archives (Washington, DC)—to produce a film and companion book for children as part of the National Archives Experience, an interactive learning program for students and families, and to expand exhibition spaces at the National Archives building, $1.2 million over three years.
Contact: Program Contact; (212) 576-7341; (212) 576-6220; NYLFoundation@newyorklife.com
Internet: http://www.newyorklife.com/foundation/index.html
Sponsor: New York Life Foundation
51 Madison Avenue, Room 1600
New York, NY 10010-1655

New York Times Company Foundation Grants 1246

The major areas in which the foundation entertains applications for grants are education, journalism, cultural affairs, community services, and environmental concerns, with the greatest portion going to cultural affairs. Types of support include general operating purposes, scholarship funds, building construction funds, employee matching gifts, seed grants, and programs/projects. Under education, direct grants are given to colleges as well as college associations; scholarship programs are also supported, especially for minorities, as are a number of general programs. Freedom of the press and of all channels of communications is a matter of highest priority to the foundation. The cultural affairs program makes grants to museums, libraries, the performing arts, and for general requests to improve arts-related activities. Foundation support of the disadvantaged is divided among urban, national, and international community services. Grants in the area of environmental concerns are made largely in the New York City area. All grants will be made in localities where there is a New York Times affiliate, or to organizations of national stature in wildlife protection and conservation. Applications may be submitted at any time. The board meets during the first and third quarters to award monies based on the president's recommendations. Giving is primarily in the New York, NY, metropolitan area and in localities served by business units of the company.
Requirements: A brief letter describing the purpose for which funds are requested, including details of other potential sources of support, is sufficient for an application. Proof of tax-exempt status is also required.
Restrictions: Grants are not made to individuals, to sectarian religious institutions and causes, or for drug, alcohol, or health-related purposes.
Geographic Focus: All U.S. States
Amount: 1,000 - 25,000 USD
Samples: Kids Voting (Boston, MA)—for programs on voting and civic participation, $5000; Goddard Riverside Community Ctr (New York, NY)—to provide college-related guidance to students in overburdened high schools, $10,000; Lower East Side Tenement Museum (NY)—for general operating support, $15,000; Committee to Protect Journalists (NY)—for programs that support journalists who are harassed or imprisoned abroad, $25,000.
Contact: Program Contact; (212) 556-1091; (212) 556-4450
Internet: http://www.nytco.com/company/foundation/index.html
Sponsor: New York Times Company Foundation
229 W 43rd Street, 2nd Floor
New York, NY 10036

New York Women's Foundation Grants 1247

The foundation's goal is to support women helping low-income girls and women in New York City to achieve sustained economic self-sufficiency and self-reliance. The foundation's specific program areas of interest include community organizing and advocacy, economic security, girls' positive development, violence against women and girls, and women's health and reproductive rights. For the current year, only organizations whose constituencies consist of or who serve a majority of women and/or girls are eligible to apply for general operating support. As part of its grantmaking, the foundation is committed to supporting the efforts of organizations to develop their administrative and programmatic infrastructure. Capacity-building initiatives may be included as part of an organization's proposal for general or program support. The foundation also encourages the collaboration of organizations to increase the efficiency and effectiveness of service delivery and advocacy efforts and welcomes proposals for collaborative activities within its five program areas. Guidelines are available online.

Requirements: Organization/program criteria include: are within the five boroughs of New York City; work in the following issue areas: community organizing and advocacy, economic security, girls' positive development, violence against women and girls, and women's health and reproductive rights; are community-based, led by women (board and staff), and include recognized leaders of their community; are designed specifically for low-income women and girls, particularly women of color, immigrants, lesbians, the elderly, or other underserved populations; strive toward the philosophy of women helping women, an active, consensus-driven form of management; encourage the involvement of program participants in the decision-making; have limited access to ongoing traditional funding sources, i.e., government, foundations, and individual donors; and have been in existence for at least six months.

Restrictions: The foundation does not provide funds to individuals; start a new project (seed money); capital fund projects; endowments; fundraising events; feasibility studies; real estate purchases; public or private schools; colleges or universities; campaigns to elect candidates to public office; programs to promote religious activities; statewide, national, or international organizations; programs that are primarily artistic or cultural; programs located outside the five boroughs of New York City; or programs that do not comply with federal, state, or local equal employment statutes.

Geographic Focus: New York

Date(s) Application is Due: Oct 14

Amount: 10,000 - 40,000 USD

Samples: Mercy Center (NY)—to provide job training and social services to low-income women who lives in the Mott Haven section of the South Bronx, $35,000; Picture the Homeless (NY)—to support organizing efforts of homeless women to advocate for better shelter services for themselves and their families, $30,000; Women for Afghan Women (NY)—to establish a leadership development and service-delivery program for the isolated Afghani women and girls living in Flushing, Queens, $25,000; Youth Ministries for Peace and Justice(NY)—to expand programming at the Center for Community Wellness to support the development of young women and girls by meeting their educational and physical developmental needs and strengthening their critical thinking skills by becoming aware of local political and social issues, $35,000.

Contact: Grants Administrator; (212) 414-4342; (212) 414-5708; info@nwf.org

Internet: http://www.nywf.org/grant.html

Sponsor: New York Women's Foundation
34 W 22nd Street
New York, NY 10010

NFF Collaboration Support Grants 1248

The intent of the Collaborative Support Program is to promote innovation and advancement in the field of community-based natural resource collaboration, and to support collaborative processes whose work benefits America's National Forests and Grasslands. Grants range up to $5,000 for Capacity grants, and up to $10,000 for Innovation grants. Technical assistance provided includes peer learning, mentoring and coaching opportunities. Examples of grant activities might include: collaborative work on an emerging topic (for example, newly recognized invasive species or private land transfer to public ownership); structured information sharing; new approaches to collaborative stewardship; and multiparty monitoring.

Requirements: Community-based collaborative groups working on stewardship issues on National Forests and Grasslands across the country are eligible to apply.

Geographic Focus: All U.S. States

Date(s) Application is Due: Feb 15; Apr 29

Amount: Up to 10,000 USD

Contact: Adam Liljeblad, Director, Conservation Awards; (406) 542-2805; (406) 542-2810; aliljeblad@nationalforests.org

Internet: http://nationalforests.org/conserve/grantprograms

Sponsor: National Forest Foundation
Fort Missoula Road, Building 27, Suite 3
Missoula, MT 59804

NFF Community Assistance Grants 1249

The NFF established the Community Assistance Program (CAP) in 2002 to promote the creation of locally based organizations or groups seeking to resolve natural resource issues through a collaborative, dialogue based process. The program proves support in the form of start-up funds for newly forming (or significantly reorganizing) groups or nonprofit organizations that intend to proactively and inclusively engage local stakeholders in forest management and conservation issues on and around the National Forests and Grasslands. CAP awards provide collaborative groups with start-up grants of $5,000 to $15,000, as well as basic tools and guidance, to enable them to resolve differences and play a more active role in the sustainable management of nearby National Forests, Grasslands and surrounding communities. Organizations applying for funding through CAP will be considered based on need, and will not be required to match the NFF funds. CAP funds can be used for a wide range of tools, including: technical assistance, training, consultants, community outreach, obtaining 501(c)3 status, group facilitation, basic startup and operating costs, materials and equipment, program development, nonprofit management kill building, and communications.

Requirements: In order to qualify for a grant through the CAP, the applicant must be: newly forming or significantly reorganizing collaborative community-based nonprofits or unincorporated groups; engaged in a collaborative process; based in the community in which the collaboration is taking place and be legitimate stakeholders in the collaborative process; working to develop solutions for sustainable management or restoration on and around National Forests and Grasslands that lead to on-the-ground work; specific issues should be related to community-based forest stewardship, recreation, watershed restoration, and/or wildlife habitat; incorporated as a 501(c)3 or utilize a fiscal sponsor organization with that designation; and seeking to build local ecological, social and economic sustainability.

Restrictions: Established organizations, fire safe councils, federal agencies, and state or local governmental entities are not eligible to apply.

Geographic Focus: All U.S. States

Date(s) Application is Due: Jan 15; Jul 7

Amount: 5,000 - 15,000 USD

Contact: Adam Liljeblad, Director, Conservation Awards; (406) 542-2805; (406) 542-2810; aliljeblad@nationalforests.org

Internet: http://nationalforests.org/conserve/grantprograms

Sponsor: National Forest Foundation
Fort Missoula Road, Building 27, Suite 3
Missoula, MT 59804

NFF Mid-Capacity Assistance Grants 1250

The primary purpose of the Mid-Capacity Assistance Grants is to assist mid-capacity collaborative organizations whose work benefits America's National Forests and Grasslands in building their organizational capacity. Examples of technical assistance and support include: peer learning, mentoring and coaching opportunities; and development of monitoring/outcome plans in coordination with the Western Collaboration Assistance Network (WestCAN). Grant supported activities may include: strategic planning, support for on-going collaborative process needs, training, and board development.

Requirements: Mid-capacity collaborative, community-based groups working on stewardship issues on National Forests and Grasslands are eligible to apply. Applicants may apply for up to $70,000 for a two-year period.

Geographic Focus: All U.S. States

Date(s) Application is Due: Feb 15; Apr 29

Amount: Up to 70,000 USD

Contact: Adam Liljeblad, Director, Conservation Awards; (406) 542-2805; (406) 542-2810; aliljeblad@nationalforests.org

Internet: http://nationalforests.org/conserve/grantprograms/capacitybuilding/ccls

Sponsor: National Forest Foundation
Fort Missoula Road, Building 27, Suite 3
Missoula, MT 59804

NFF Ski Conservation Grants **1251**

Through its Ski Conservation Fund, the National Forest Foundation (NFF) has teamed up with ski areas, lodges and resorts located on National Forest lands to raise money for the care of their local National Forest. Funds are raised through voluntary contributions from guests at participating ski areas and lodges throughout the country and are matched with NFF federal funds. These dollars are invested in on-the-ground conservation projects, completed by local nonprofit organizations, on or around the National Forest from which they originate. The projects advance the NFF's on-the-ground, action-oriented approach to wildlife habitat improvement, watershed restoration, community-based forestry programs and forest recreation improvements. Grants can range from $5,000 to $100,000, but typically average $35,000.

Requirements: Nonprofit organizations accomplishing conservation work on a participating National Forest can apply.

Geographic Focus: All U.S. States

Amount: 5,000 - 100,000 USD

Contact: Adam Liljeblad, Director, Conservation Awards; (406) 542-2805; (406) 542-2810; aliljeblad@nationalforests.org

Internet: http://nationalforests.org/conserve/grantprograms/ontheground/scf

Sponsor: National Forest Foundation
Fort Missoula Road, Building 27, Suite 3
Missoula, MT 59804

NHSCA Cultural Facilities Grants: Barrier Free Access for All **1252**

Cultural Facilities grants will support renovations, maintenance, and purchase of major equipment that supports creating a universal or inclusive environment for the arts where programs, services, and activities are accessible to everyone, including people with and without disabilities. Requests may be made for $1,000 to $8,000. Government agencies, municipalities and towns, county agencies, state agencies, or federal agencies that own a historic cultural facility; or nonprofit organizations that manage publicly owned historic cultural facilities, are encouraged to apply for a Cultural Conservation Grant.

Requirements: At a minimum, grants must be matched on a one-to-one basis. In-kind contributions may comprise one half of the required match and will also be considered by the reviewers as evidence of support and commitment by the community and/or partner organization. Organizations with 501(c)3 tax-exempt status from the IRS and not-for-profit incorporation in the State of New Hampshire may apply, provided that they: own or have a minimum three-year lease on the facility, or demonstrable ability to acquire by deed, or a minimum three-year lease on the proposed facility when it is built or rehabilitated for cultural use; operate or will establish a cultural facility in New Hampshire; have one year of experience in arts programming for the general public prior to the date of application, or have plans for at least one year of arts programming at the facility it plans to operate; must demonstrate that the facility is striving to be in full compliance with the Americans with Disabilities Act (ADA) requirements; have submitted all required reports on past State Arts Council grants; and are in good standing with the N.H. Secretary of State's Office and the N.H. Attorney General's Office.

Restrictions: State Arts Council funds may not be matched by other State Arts Council or National Endowment for the Arts funds.

Geographic Focus: New Hampshire

Date(s) Application is Due: Mar 31

Amount: 1,000 - 8,000 USD

Contact: Cassandra Erickson Mason, Grants Coordinator; (603) 271-7926 or (603) 271-2789; (603) 271-3584; cassandra.mason@dcr.nh.gov

Internet: http://www.nh.gov/nharts/grants/culturalfacilities.htm

Sponsor: New Hampshire State Council on the Arts
19 Pillsbury Street, 1st Floor
Concord, NH 03301

NHSCA Operating Grants **1253**

Operating grants are an investment in the cultural infrastructure and creative economy of New Hampshire. The creative economy is made up of artists, not for profit organizations and creative businesses that positively impact quality of life in communities, generate jobs and produce revenue for municipalities, cities and the state. These competitive and matching grants are awarded in two-year cycles to not-for-profit arts and cultural organizations that demonstrate excellence in planning, administration and programming. Grantees are expected to provide high quality arts experiences, activities and services for New Hampshire citizens and ensure that the arts are accessible to all. They are also expected to maintain close and productive relationships with other community organizations and businesses, ensuring that the arts are integral to community infrastructure.

Requirements: Not-for-profit organizations with incorporation in New Hampshire and a 501(c)3 tax-exempt status from the Internal Revenue Service, whose primary mission is to produce, present or serve the arts. In addition, applicant organizations must: have been in continuous operation as a 501(c)3 non-profit arts organization for at least five years prior to application for an Operating Grant; have an independent board of directors that meets at least quarterly; have a paid, full-time arts administrator; have a long-range plan in place that covers the two-year grant period; be fully in compliance with the Americans with Disabilities Act requirements; have submitted all required reports on past State Arts Council grants; and be in good standing with the State Arts Council and NH Attorney General's Office.

Restrictions: Requests are for unrestricted operational funds and may be made for up to $15,000 per year. The request for the first year of the grant period may not exceed 10% of income in the organization's last fiscal year prior to application. Applicants also must be able to leverage other support and project a cash match, excluding federal and state funds, of at least $10 for each $1 requested from the State Arts Council. Applicant organizations must be physically located in New Hampshire, not just incorporated in the state. In general, a college, university, library, or school is not eligible for Operating Grants unless its primary mission is the arts and the majority of its arts activities are open to the general public. Grant awards may not be used for previously incurred debts or deficits. Operating Grant awards may not be used for endowments or capital projects, and recipients are ineligible to receive additional General Project Grants, except for the Traditional Arts Project strand, during the Operating Grant period.

Geographic Focus: New Hampshire

Date(s) Application is Due: Mar 11

Amount: Up to 15,000 USD

Contact: Cassandra Erickson Mason, Chief Grants Officer; (603) 271-7926 or (603) 271-2789; (603) 271-3584; cassandra.mason@dcr.nh.gov

Internet: http://www.nh.gov/nharts/grants/organizations/operating.htm

Sponsor: New Hampshire State Council on the Arts
19 Pillsbury Street, 1st Floor
Concord, NH 03301

Nicholas H. Noyes Jr. Memorial Foundation Grants **1254**

The foundation awards grants to eligible Indiana nonprofit organizations in its areas of interest, including arts and culture, education from early childhood through higher education, disadvantaged, museums, social services, health, hospitals, family services, performing arts, and youth. Types of support include general operating support, endowment funds, and scholarship funds.

Requirements: Proposals are welcomed, and encouraged, to be submitted at any time after January 1st for the first funding cycle or after June 1st for the final funding cycle. Submit the following with your proposal: thirteen copies of the complete grant application (available at the foundations website or office) including attachments (i.e. applicable budget(s) as required). You may recreate the application form for ease in completing, but please limit your response to the space provided and use a minimum font of 12. It is also require that you use both sides of the paper i.e. side one is page 1 with page 2 on the flip-side etc; one copy of your organization's 501(c)3 tax determination letter from the IRS; one copy of your organization's most recent audited financial statement for all organizations requesting $25,000 or more.

Restrictions: Organizations may apply only one time in any calendar year. The Foundation does not make grants to individuals. The principle geographic region served by the Noyes Foundation is the greater Indianapolis area. If you intend to request a grant in excess of $50,000, please contact the Foundation's Program Officer before submitting your grant request.

Geographic Focus: Indiana

Date(s) Application is Due: Feb 1; Aug 29

Amount: Up to 150,000 USD

Contact: Kelly Mills, Executive Administrator; (317) 844-8009; (317) 844-8099; kmills@noyesfoundation.org

Internet: http://www.noyesfoundation.org

Sponsor: Nicholas H. Noyes Jr. Memorial Foundation
1950 E Greyhound Pass, #18
Carmel, IN 46033-7730

Nicor Corporate Contributions **1255**

Nicor Gas' philanthropy mission is to apply its charitable funds, company expertise and employee volunteer efforts to help fulfill the educational, health, cultural and community needs of the people who reside in our service territory. Its strategic focus is to help educators and those who support the educational

system by providing enrichment opportunities that will assist students in achieving their educational goals.
Requirements: Charitable contributions will be made only to eligible organizations that have a current determination letter exempting them from federal tax under Section 501(c)3 of the Internal Revenue Code. Eligible not-for-profit organizations requesting support from Nicor Gas must prepare and submit the required application form (available for downloading at the website) and all required attachments. Requests may be made for the following types of contributions: (a) General Operating - Only one operating gift will be made to an organization during a year. If an organization receives United Way funding, it will not be eligible for a general operating gift, but may be considered for funding an event if Nicor employees are involved. (b) Events - Requests for support of events in the communities Nicor serves and where Nicor Gas employees are involved will be given consideration. (c) Capital Campaigns - Support may be granted for building and remodeling programs of not-for-profit organizations that best advance Nicor Gas' priorities and add value to the communities where Nicor serves. Capital grants are not multi-year commitments. (d) In-Kind Support - Requests for surplus furniture, equipment or services will be reviewed upon receipt. The response will be based on contribution priorities and availability of the requested gift.
Restrictions: Grants will not be made to: organizations without IRS 501(c)3 designation or equivalent; individuals or foundations; social, athletic, recreational or union groups; endowment or debt reduction drives; churches or religious groups in support of their sacramental or theological functions; organizations with discriminatory practices; political parties, groups or candidates; organizations soliciting advertising space in newspapers or programs; specific schools or foundations supporting specific secondary or primary schools.
Geographic Focus: Illinois
Contact: Julian Brown, Corporate Contributions Manager; (630) 388-2763; jbrown@nicor.com
Internet: http://www.nicor.com/en_us/nicor_inc/nicor_in_the_community/grants_and_donations.htm
Sponsor: Nicor
P.O. Box 3014
Naperville, IL 60566-3014

Nina Mason Pulliam Charitable Trust Grants **1256**
The Nina Mason Pulliam Charitable Trust provides grants that focus on the areas of service Nina Pulliam supported during her lifetime: helping people in need; protecting animals and nature; enriching community life. The Trust awards grants for program projects and capital needs, and provides application opportunities three times during the calendar year. The Trust prefers to disperse funds as a one-year grant, but will consider projects of up to three years.
Requirements: Primary consideration is given to 501(c)3 charitable organizations that serve metropolitan Indianapolis and Phoenix. Secondary consideration is given to the states of Indiana and Arizona. National organizations whose programs benefit these priority areas and/or benefit society as a whole are occasionally considered.
Restrictions: Grants are not awarded for international purposes or academic research, Grants are not awarded to individuals, sectarian organizations for religious purposes, or to non-operating private foundations except in extraordinary circumstances.
Geographic Focus: Arizona, Indiana
Date(s) Application is Due: Jan 4; May 4; Sep 4
Samples: Chrysalis Academy of Life and Learning, $75,000 for a residential program to develop self-sufficiency among young men ages 18-24; Indiana Legal Services, to continue a project that helps individuals avoid losing their homes in inner-city Indianapolis neighborhoods because of abusive lending practices, $35,000; Camptown, Inc., to send 100 underprivileged youths on wilderness trips, $28,000; Street Francis Healthcare Foun dation, Inc., $35,000 to hire an additional social worker to serve residents in the Garfield Park area.
Contact: David Hillman, (317) 231-6075; (317) 231-9208
Internet: http://www.ninapulliamtrust.org
Sponsor: Nina Mason Pulliam Charitable Trust
135 N Pennsylvania Street, Suite 1200
Indianapolis, IN 46204

Nissan Foundation Grants **1257**
The foundation funds projects that support the following initiatives: Building Community Through Valuing Cultural Diversity—celebrating and embracing diverse cultural heritages as a means to promote respect for others, generate alternative ways of thinking, strengthen self-awareness, and enrich communities, also promote learning about diverse cultural traditions as an integral aspect of education; and Creating Career Opportunities for Young Adults in the Automotive Industry Age 15-24—seeking to inspire young adults to develop the skills and expertise necessary to meet the needs of future Nissan customers. The listed application deadline is for letters of inquiry. Guidelines are available online.
Requirements: 501(c)3 nonprofit organizations that serve communities surrounding Nissan's affiliate locations are eligible. These include southern California, middle Tennessee, south central Mississippi, Dallas/Fort Worth, and metropolitan Detroit.
Restrictions: The foundation does not support disease advocacy, research, religious or political activities, events, sponsorships, or capital campaigns.
Geographic Focus: California, Michigan, Mississippi, Tennessee, Texas
Date(s) Application is Due: Nov 23
Amount: 5,000 - 50,000 USD
Contact: Grants Administrator; (310) 771-3330; (310) 516-7967
Internet: http://www.nissandriven.com/insideNissan/CorporateOutreach/0,9396,,00.html#AS1341
Sponsor: Nissan North America
P.O. Box 191, Mail Stop N-3-A
Gardena, CA 90248-0191

NJSCA General Operating Support Grants **1258**
General Operating Support (GOS) is awarded to New Jersey based, nonprofit, arts-missioned organizations to help underwrite the expense of their total operation including the expenses of producing and presenting arts events. Receipt of a GOS grant usually carries the commitment of the Council to fund the program over a three-year period, although the funding level will be determined annually. Review and consideration of GOS requests occur only every three years. Applicants must file a Notice of Intent online as well as apply online. Deadline dates may vary; contact the program office for exact dates. Deadlines must be met by eFiling by midnight on the deadline date. The deadline for signed originals and support materials is within two business days of the eDeadline and can be met with either a postmark or actual delivery of the materials to NJSCA offices at 225 West State Street, 4th Floor in Trenton by 5:00 p.m on the deadline date. New Jersey State Council on the Arts is a Division in the New Jersey Department of State and Partner Agency with the National Endowment for the Arts.
Requirements: Applicants must be incorporated in the State of New Jersey as a 501(c)3 organization or be a unit of government; be registered with the New Jersey Charities Registration Bureau; have a clearly articulated mission relating to the arts; have been in existence and actively providing public programs or services for at least the past two years at time of application; have a board of directors empowered to formulate policies and be responsible for the governance and administration of the organization, its programs and finances; demonstrate regional or statewide public impact through the organization's programs or project (regional is defined as serving audiences across a two or more county region of New Jersey). Matching funds are required and must be cash, not in-kind. For each dollar received from the Council, the grantee must show three additional dollars raised and spent, based on operating income. Applicants must apply online and should be advised that the prerequisite pre-registraton process requires up to 72 hours for completion by the system administrator before they can access the system.
Restrictions: Applicants may apply either to the Council or to their County Arts Agency, not both, in a given year. Prospective NJSCA applicants that have been receiving support through their County Arts Agency up to now should attend a scheduled NJSCA grant workshop, work closely with Council staff and their County Arts Agency in filing their Notice of Intent to Apply, and may also want to schedule a meeting early in the process with Council staff. Because the funding periods for the County Arts Agency grants and the State Council grants overlap by six months, applicants should discuss their situation in advance of the Notice of Intent to Apply with the State Council to determine eligibility. K-12 schools and school districts are not eligible to apply, but may be a partner or collaborator on a project with an eligible applicant.
Geographic Focus: New Jersey
Date(s) Application is Due: Feb 23
Samples: American Repertory Ballet Comp (Middlesex)—for dance general operating support, $250,000; Haddonfield Symphony Society (Camden)—for music general operating support, $177,915; Paper Mill Playhouse—for theater general operating support, $1.05 million.

Contact: Steve Runk, Executive Director; (609) 292-6130; (609) 989-1440; steve.runk@sos.state.nj.us
Internet: http://www.njartscouncil.org/grant.cfm
Sponsor: New Jersey State Council on the Arts
225 West State Street, P.O. Box 306
Trenton, NJ 08625-0306

NNEDVF/Altria Doors of Hope Grants **1259**

The goal of this initiative is to strengthen the safety net available to survivors of domestic violence through the provision of grant awards that support organizational excellence, innovation, and leadership in the provision of shelter and legal advocacy services. Direct service grants are awarded to domestic violence service providers for shelter services and advocacy/legal services. There is a two stage application process; stage one consists of registration online, which includes key questions that will be used to determine which applicants will be invited to apply for stage two. For the current funding year, grantmaking will be by invitation only. Applicants will be contacted if they are eligible to apply. Additional assistance and information is provided at www.nnedv.org.
Requirements: Eligible organizations must have a primary mission which includes the provision of direct services to survivors of domestic violence; provide shelter and/or legal advocacy services to survivors of domestic violence; be a U.S. based non-profit, non-governmental, tax-exempt organization; have been in operation for a minimum of three years with an organization budget greater than or equal to $250,000; and have nondiscrimination policies that include ethnicity, race, religious creed, national origin, disability, sexual orientation, marital status, age, and gender.
Restrictions: Applications will only be accepted through the online RFP.
Geographic Focus: All U.S. States
Amount: 10,000 - 50,000 USD
Samples: Hmong American Friendship Association (Milwaukee, WI)—to provide group facilitators, education groups in the workplace, and domestic violence training for Hmong elders, $24,000; Susquehanna Valley Women in Transition (Lewisburg, PA)—to implement and teach a curriculum of safe living and violence prevention to group home residents with mental disabilities, $19,000.
Contact: Grants Administrator; (202) 543-5566; (202) 543-5626; altriadoorsofhope@nnedv.org
Internet: http://www.altria.com/responsibility/4_9_1_1_2_1_domviolprograms.asp
Sponsor: National Network to End Domestic Violence Fund
660 Pennsylvania Avenue SE, Suite 303
Washington, DC 20003

Nokomis Foundation Grants **1260**

The foundation seeks to make a difference in the lives of women and girls and primarily funds grants in the West Michigan area. However, proposals with a state or national focus, provided they include a West Michigan component, are accepted. The foundation is particularly interested in pilot programs and gives priority to organizations that do not have access to traditional funding sources. In reviewing proposals, Nokomis looks for these characteristics: evidence of innovative thinking and creative problem-solving, organizational values similar to the foundation's (e.g., respect for diversity), intent to foster collaboration among groups sharing similar goals, and intent to accomplish long-term social change (multiyear projects are welcomed). The best way to begin the process is to send the executive director a concise letter or email (no longer than two pages) that describes the proposed project and need for funding. The foundation will review the letter promptly, and indicate whether a detailed proposal may be submitted to the foundation's Board of Advisors. In some cases, more information or a site visit may be required to be able to evaluate the request. There are no deadline dates; however, the board meets quarterly to consider requests. Details are available on the website. Unsolicited proposals are not currently being accepted.
Requirements: Giving primarily in the greater Grand Rapids, MI, area; limited support for national organizations.
Restrictions: The foundation does not provide funding to individuals or to religious organizations for religious purposes, and does not normally fund scholarships, fellowships, medical research, capital requests, endowments, or attendance at conferences. Support is rarely provided for capital expenditures (e.g., building renovations, new equipment, or endowments).
Geographic Focus: All U.S. States
Samples: Abundant Life Ministries (Grand Rapids, MI)—to support Mr. B's Basketball and Reading Camp, $2000; Ctr for Women in Transition (Holland, MI)—to support an infrastructure project, $25,000; Grand Rapids Civic Theatre (MI)—for the summer stock program, The Glass Slipper, $1000; Jewish Federation of Grand Rapids (MI)—for Rachel Simmon's lecture, $2000.
Contact: Program Contact; (616) 451-0267; (616) 451-9914; info@nokomisfoundation.org
Internet: http://www.nokomisfoundation.org/whathow.htm
Sponsor: Nokomis Foundation
161 Ottawa NW, Suite 305-C
Grand Rapids, MI 49503

Norcliffe Foundation Grants **1261**

Grants are awarded to organizations in the Puget Sound Region in and around Seattle, WA, with emphasis on higher and secondary education, cultural programs, religious associations, hospitals, and historic preservation. Support is also given for medical research, youth agencies, adult basic education, vocational education, literacy, the aged, and conservation. Grants supply funds for operating budgets, capital campaigns, conferences and seminars, scholarship funds, continuing support, annual campaigns, seed money, building funds, equipment, land acquisition, research, and special projects. Application guidelines are available upon request; applications are accepted at any time.
Requirements: Washington 501(c)3 organizations may apply.
Restrictions: Grants are not awarded to individuals or for deficit financing.
Geographic Focus: Washington
Amount: 1,000 - 25,000 USD
Samples: Seattle Center Foundation (Seattle, WA)—to construct Marion Oliver McCaw Hall, $1 million.
Contact: Arline Hefferline, Foundation Manager; (206) 682-4820; (206) 682-4821; arline@thenorcliffefoundation.com
Internet: http://www.thenorcliffefoundation.com
Sponsor: Norcliffe Foundation
999 Third Avenue, First Interstate Center, Suite 1006
Seattle, WA 98104

Nord Family Foundation Grants **1262**

The foundation has focused much of its grantmaking on programs that strengthen families and serve the public and as a general purpose foundation in the fields of social service, health, education, the arts, and civic affairs. Within these fields, special interest is focused on programs that address the needs of economically or socially disadvantaged children and families. Projects that attack root causes of problems are of special interest. The foundation has no application form. One copy of a proposal is required and should contain a cover letter signed by the organization's executive director or board president, one-page abstract, detailed description of the proposed project, copy of the organization's IRS tax-exemption letter, list of current board members, and the organization's most recent financial statement. Foundation staff is available to discuss proposal ideas, assist during the application preparation process, and answer questions.
Requirements: Most of the foundation's grants are made in Ohio. Grants are also made in certain other geographic areas, including Colorado, Massachusetts, and South Carolina.
Restrictions: The foundation does not support debt reduction, research projects, and tickets or advertising for fundraising activities.
Geographic Focus: Colorado, Massachusetts, Ohio, South Carolina
Date(s) Application is Due: Apr 1; Aug 1; Dec 1
Amount: 10,000 - 50,000 USD
Samples: Oberlin Early Childhood Ctr (OH)—for an arts program for children, $76,000; Massachusetts Coalition for the Homeless (Lynn, MA)—for the First Stop Initiative, a partnership with Boston-area health centers designed to help prevent homelessness, $10,000; Step 13 (Denver, CO)—to provide shelter and support services for homeless men, $20,000; Cooperative Ministry (Columbia, SC)—for its emergency-assistance program, $20,000.
Contact: John Mullaney, Executive Director; (800) 745-8946 or (440) 984-3939; (440) 984-3934; execdir@nordff.org or info@nordff.org
Internet: http://www.nordff.org
Sponsor: Nord Family Foundation
747 Milan Avenue
Amherst, OH 44001

Nordson Corporation Foundation Grants **1263**

The corporate foundation awards grants to nonprofit organizations in geographic areas where Nordson facilities and employees are located: Cuyahoga and Lorain counties in Ohio; the Greater Atlanta, Georgia area;

California, Rhode Island and Southeastern Massachusetts. The foundation provides a source of stable funding for community programs and projects in the areas of education, human welfare, civic, and arts and culture. Educational support is generally limited to improving elementary and secondary schools and certain programs for public and private higher education. Human welfare grants focus on children and youth. The foundation considers other funding areas, including urban affairs, volunteerism, public policy, health and health organizations, and literacy. Grants are awarded for general operating support, continuing support, annual campaigns, capital campaigns, building construction/renovation, equipment acquisition, emergency funds, seed money, scholarship funds, employee matching gifts, and technical assistance. The board meets four times each year. Deadlines vary by state; contact program staff for appropriate deadlines. Application forms are available on the website and may only be submitted online.
Requirements: Private, nonprofit organizations in California, Georgia, Ohio, Rhode Island, and southeastern Massachusetts may apply.
Restrictions: Funding is not provided for organizations whose services are not provided within the foundation's geographic areas of interest; direct grants or scholarships to individuals; organizations not eligible for tax-deductible support; organizations not exempt under Section 501(c)3 of the Internal Revenue Code; political causes, candidates, organizations or campaigns; organizations that discriminate on the basis of race, sex, or religion; or special occasion, goodwill advertising, i.e., journals or dinner programs.
Geographic Focus: California, Georgia, Massachusetts, Ohio, Rhode Island
Date(s) Application is Due: Feb 15; May 15; Aug 15; Nov 15
Amount: Up to 15,000,000 USD
Samples: Ctr for Leadership in Education (Lorain, OH)—for general operating support, $250,000; Salvation Army of Lorain (Lorain, OH)—for the capital campaign, $50,000. *Contact:* Cecilia H. Render; (440) 892-1580, ext. 5172; crender@nordson.com
Internet: http://www.nordson.com/Corporate/Community/Foundation
Sponsor: Nordson Corporation Foundation
28601 Clemens Road
Westlake, OH 44145-1119

Norfolk Southern Foundation Grants 1264

The Norfolk Southern Foundation awards grants to nonprofits in the territory served by Norfolk Southern Railway Company. The foundation offers grants in four principal areas: educational programs, primarily at the post-secondary level; community enrichment focusing on cultural and artistic organizations; environmental programs; and health and human services (primarily food banks, homeless programs, and free clinics). Decision are made by December 31 for the following year's discretionary funding program, and applicants are notified early in the following calendar year.
Requirements: Applicants should include the following in their information packet: a valid 501(c)3 or 170(c)1 letter from the IRS; a short request outlining objectives of the organization, project, and intended use of funds; a listing of the applicant's board of directors; current and potential sources of funding; audited financial statements from the last three years; and the applicant's contact name, phone number, and email address.
Restrictions: Grant requests are only accepted between July 15 and September 30 for funding in the following calendar year. Applications will not be accepted from: organizations not in the NS territory (must be served by Norfolk Southern to be considered); organizations that do not have a 501(c)3 or 170(c)(1) IRS letter; individuals or organizations established to help individuals; religious, fraternal, social or veterans organizations; political or lobbying organizations; public or private elementary and secondary schools; fundraising events, telethons, races or benefits; sports or athletic organizations or activities; community or private foundations, or other organizations that merely redistribute to other eligible organizations aggregated contributions; disease-related organizations and hospitals; mentoring programs; Boys and Girls Scout programs or similar organizations; animal organizations; non-U.S. based charities; and organizations whose programs have national scope
Geographic Focus: Alabama, Connecticut, Delaware, District of Columbia, Florida, Georgia, Illinois, Indiana, Iowa, Kentucky, Louisiana, Maine, Maryland, Massachusetts, Michigan, Mississippi, Missouri, New Hampshire, New Jersey, New York, North Carolina, Ohio, Pennsylvania, Rhode Island, South Carolina, Tennessee, Texas, Vermont, Virginia, West Virginia, Wisconsin
Date(s) Application is Due: Sep 30
Amount: Up to USD
Contact: Katie Fletcher, Executive Director; (757) 629-2881; (757) 629-2361; katie.fletcher@nscorp.com
Internet: http://www.nscorp.com/nscportal/nscorp/Community/NS%20Foundation/
Sponsor: Norfolk Southern Foundation
P.O. Box 3040
Norfolk, VA 23514-3040

Norman Foundation Grants 1265

The Norman Foundation supports efforts that strengthen the ability of communities to determine their own economic, environmental and social well-being, and that help people control those forces that affect their lives. These efforts may: promote economic justice and development through community organizing, coalition building and policy reform efforts; work to prevent the disposal of toxics in communities, and to link environmental issues with economic and social justice; link community-based economic and environmental justice organizing to national and international reform efforts. The following is considered when evaluating grant proposals: does the project arise from the hopes and efforts of those whose survival, well-being and liberation are directly at stake; does it further ethnic, gender and other forms of equity; is it rooted in organized, practical undertakings; and is it likely to achieve systemic change. In pursuing systemic change, the Foundation would hope that: the proposed action may serve as a model; the spread of the model may create institutions that can survive on their own; their establishment and success may generate beneficial adaptations by other political, social and economic institutions and structures. The Foundation provides grants for general support, projects, and collaborative efforts. We also welcome innovative proposals designed to build the capacity of social change organizations working in our areas of interest. Priority is given to organizations with annual budgets of under $1 million.
Requirements: Programs must be 501(c)3 tax-exempt organizations that focused on domestic United States issues. Prospective grantees should initiate the application process by sending a short two or three page letter of inquiry to the Program Director (fax, email or regular mail). There are no set deadlines, and letters of inquiry are reviewed throughout the year. The Foundation only accepts full proposals upon positive response to the letter of inquiry. The letter of inquiry should briefly explain: the scope and significance of the problem to be addressed; the organization's proposed response and (if appropriate) how this strategy builds upon the organization's past work; the specific demonstrable effects the project would have if successful, especially its potential to effect systemic (fundamental, institutional and significant) change; how the project promotes change on a national level and is otherwise related to the foundation's guidelines; the size of the organization's budget. All inquiries will be acknowledged and, if deemed promising, the Foundation will request a full proposal.
Restrictions: The Foundation does not make grants to individuals or universities; or to support conferences, scholarships, research, films, media and arts projects; or to capital funding projects, fundraising drives or direct social service programs, such as shelters or community health programs. The Foundation's grant making is restricted to U.S.-based organizations.
Geographic Focus: All U.S. States
Amount: 5,000 - 30,000 USD
Samples: Direct Action Welfare Group, Charleston, West Virginia, $20,000 - renewed support of statewide organizing and empowerment of people living in poverty in West Virginia (2011); Interfaith Action of Southwest Florida, Immokalee, Florida, $20,000 - renewed support for joint work with Coalition of Immokalee Workers in support of low-wage farmworkers in Florida (2011); Alaska Community Action on Toxics, Anchorage, Alaska, $30,000 - renewed support for work with tribal villages and other communities to eliminate environmental contaminants (2011).
Contact: June Makela, Program Director; (212) 230-9830; (212) 230-9849; norman@normanfdn.org
Internet: http://www.normanfdn.org/
Sponsor: Norman Foundation
147 East 48th Street
New York, NY 10017

North Carolina Arts Council Folklife Public Program Grants 1266

Public programs support: exhibitions, performances and workshops, publications, and radio and television programs that promote public knowledge and appreciation of the state's traditional arts; or salary assistance to organizations that create a staff position for a professional folklorist. Grant funds also support expenses directly related to the project including production costs, stipends, honoraria, marketing, travel, supplies, telephone, and postage.
Requirements: North Carolina nonprofit organizations are eligible.

Geographic Focus: North Carolina
Date(s) Application is Due: Mar 2
Amount: Up to 10,000 USD
Contact: Sally Peterson, Folklife Specialist; (919) 807-6507; sally.peterson@ncdcr.gov
Internet: http://www.ncarts.org/grants_programs.cfm?ID=6
Sponsor: North Carolina Arts Council
Department of Cultural Resources, 109 East Jones Street, MSC #4632
Raleigh, NC 27601-2807

North Carolina Arts Council General Support Grants 1267
This category provides funds to arts organizations to support their ongoing artistic and administrative functions. Fundable expenses may include, but are not limited to, salaries, artists fees, production, travel, promotion, postage, telephone, and facility operation. This category is designed to support groups that, over time, have consistently produced strong artistic programs and demonstrated responsible administrative practices. All grant-funded activities must take place between July 1 of the current year and June 30 of the next. Application materials are available on the website.
Requirements: North Carolina dance, literary, music, theater, and visual arts organizations may apply. Grants must be matched dollar for dollar from the organization's budget. Organizations not previously funded in this category must contact the council staff to discuss eligibility before submitting applications.
Restrictions: University museums or galleries are not eligible to apply in this category.
Geographic Focus: North Carolina
Date(s) Application is Due: Mar 2
Amount: 5,000 - 70,000 USD
Contact: Linda Bamford, Arts in Education Director; (919) 807-6502; linda.bamford@ncmail.net
Internet: http://www.ncarts.org/grants_programs.cfm?ID=7
Sponsor: North Carolina Arts Council
Department of Cultural Resources, 109 East Jones Street, MSC #4632
Raleigh, NC 27601-2807

North Carolina Arts Council Outreach Program Grants 1268
The Program has two distinct categories: technical assistance to organizations that have an operating budget of at least $10,000 and that have been producing arts programs for two or more years; and funds to support the ongoing artistic and administrative functions of organizations that have operating budgets of $50,000 or higher and have been producing arts programs for three or more years.
Requirements: North Carolina nonprofit, tax-exempt arts organizations, primarily based in and focused on the African American, Asian American, Hispanic, or Native American communities, may apply. Single-discipline organizations that are not the primary constituents of other council sections are eligible for support, as well as multidisciplinary organizations that serve a wide range of art forms including the performing, visual, and literary arts in their cultures.
Geographic Focus: North Carolina
Date(s) Application is Due: Mar 2
Amount: 2,500 - 20,000 USD
Contact: Janie Wilson, Outreach Coordinator; (919) 807-6508; janie.wilson@ncmail.net
Internet: http://www.ncarts.org/freeform_scrn_template.cfm?ffscrn_id=153
Sponsor: North Carolina Arts Council
Department of Cultural Resources, 109 East Jones Street, MSC #4632
Raleigh, NC 27601-2807

North Carolina Arts Council Statewide Service Organization Grants 1269
This category provides funds to service organizations for projects and programs that serve their members, artists, arts organizations, and the arts community. Funded programs and services may include newsletters, listserv and website management, conferences, workshops, classes, consultations, research, resource publications, presentations, and the development and distribution of promotional materials. Grant funds support administrative and program expenses directly related to the proposed programs and services. Grant amounts range from $5,000 - $35,000 and must be matched dollar for dollar by the organization.
Requirements: Organizations that provide programs and services to the arts community on a regional or statewide basis may apply. First-time applicants to this category should consult with staff to determine eligibility.
Geographic Focus: North Carolina
Date(s) Application is Due: Mar 2
Amount: 5,000 - 35,000 USD
Contact: Jeff Pettus, Visual Arts Director; (919) 807-6513; jeff.pettus@ncmail.net
Internet: http://www.ncarts.org/grants_programs.cfm?ID=18
Sponsor: North Carolina Arts Council
Department of Cultural Resources, 109 East Jones Street, MSC #4632
Raleigh, NC 27601-2807

North Carolina Arts Council Technical Assistance Grants 1270
Funds are provided to organizations to: hire knowledgeable consultants to strengthen an organization's management and programs or conduct planning meetings for a specific project; sponsor workshops or conferences; develop a resource publication; develop a community-wide cultural plan; provide scholarships to send staff members to conferences, workshops or short-term programs (available on a limited basis). Examples of issues consultants may address include, but are not limited to, staff development, community relations, fund-raising, audience development, and financial management. Organizations should contact the council staff before applying in this category.
Requirements: Any North Carolina nonprofit arts organization or organization that provides arts programs, such as schools or community organizations, may apply. Grants must be matched dollar-for-dollar by the applicant, except in cases of demonstrated need.
Geographic Focus: North Carolina
Date(s) Application is Due: Mar 2
Amount: 2,500 USD
Contact: Janie Wilson, Coordinator; (919) 807-6508; janie.wilson@ncmail.net
Internet: http://www.ncarts.org/freeform_scrn_template.cfm?ffscrn_id=121
Sponsor: North Carolina Arts Council
Department of Cultural Resources, 109 East Jones Street, MSC #4632
Raleigh, NC 27601-2807

North Carolina Arts Council Visual Arts Program Support Grants 1271
The program provides funds to North Carolina nonprofit organizations that: support innovative performing (dance, music, and theater) or visual arts programming and services; provide programs or services to the state's arts community or promote awareness about the arts in the state; advance public discussion and understanding of an artist or art form; and support innovative arts programming for public public television. All grant-funded activities must take place between July 1 of the current year and June 30 of the next. Grant funds support artistic and administrative expenses directly related to the project. Both first-time and experienced applicants are encouraged to contact council staff early in the planning of their grant proposals to receive information on preparing competitive applications and to discuss proposed projects.
Requirements: North Carolina nonprofit organizations that produce literary, performing, or visual arts programs may apply. Statewide service organizations also may apply. Grants must be matched dollar-for-dollar by the organization. Organizations may apply for projects spanning more than one year; applicants must reapply each year for funding of a multiyear project.
Geographic Focus: North Carolina
Date(s) Application is Due: Mar 2
Contact: Jeff Pettus, Visual Arts Director; (919) 807-6513; jeff.pettus@ncmail.net
Internet: http://www.ncarts.org/grants_category.cfm?ID=11&CFID=4457835&CFTOKEN=61825421&jsessionid=28302898591231777988333
Sponsor: North Carolina Arts Council
Department of Cultural Resources, 109 East Jones Street, MSC #4632
Raleigh, NC 27601-2807

North Carolina Community Development Grants 1272
The foundation supports nonprofit organizations in North Carolina to enrich the quality of life in the state, with special concern for rural regions and Cabarrus County. Grants are awarded primarily for healthcare, higher education, and community service. Other more limited areas of interest are arts, culture, historic preservation, religion, and the environment. Grants generally will be awarded for capital improvements, challenge opportunities, or special purposes rather than for operating purposes. Grant requests are considered on a quarterly basis.
Requirements: IRS 501(c)3 organizations serving North Carolina communities are eligible. Churches and governmental agencies also may apply.
Restrictions: Normally, the foundation does not make multiyear grants or frequent grants to the same organization (except for select, historic

relationships); or provide operating funds, start-up funding, or lead gifts. The foundation does not make grants to individuals, to endowment funds, for loans, or for scholarships or fellowships.
Geographic Focus: North Carolina
Date(s) Application is Due: Jan 5; Apr 5; Jul 5; Oct 5
Amount: 10,000 - 30,000 USD
Samples: Lenoir-Rhyne College (Hickory, NC)—for equipment and technology upgrades, $156,000; Mars Hill College (Mars Hill, NC)—to purchase two boilers and a fire-alarm system, $150,000.
Contact: Frank Davis, Executive Director; (704) 786-8216; (704) 785-2051
Internet: http://www.thecannonfoundationinc.org/guidelines.asp
Sponsor: Cannon Foundation
P.O. Box 548
Concord, NC 28026-0548

North Carolina GlaxoSmithKline Foundation Grants 1273
The foundation supports activities primarily in North Carolina that help meet the needs of today's society and future generations by funding programs that emphasize the understanding and application of health, science, and mathematics at all educational and professional levels. Although providing seed funds for new and worthwhile educational programs is the foundation's primary focus, requests for funding of ongoing projects will also receive consideration. Types of support include operating budgets, professorships, and conferences and seminars. Proposals may be submitted for either one-year or multi-year funding with a maximum of five years' duration. The foundation's board of directors meets four times a year to consider and award grants. Completed applications must be received by the listed deadline dates. If the stated deadline falls on a weekend or holiday, the next business day serves as the official deadline. All applicants will be notified of the board's decisions within 15 days of the board meeting.
Requirements: The foundation makes grants only to North Carolina 501(c)3 tax-exempt organizations and institutions or to governmental agencies.
Restrictions: Grants are not made to individuals for construction or restoration projects, or for international programs unless specifically exempted by the board. Funds are not ordinarily provided to programs that benefit a limited geographic region.
Geographic Focus: North Carolina
Date(s) Application is Due: Jan 1; Apr 1; Jul 1; Oct 1
Amount: 25,000 - 1,000,000 USD
Samples: North Carolina Center for Public Policy Research, $446,000; The Carolina Ballet, Healthier Living Through the Arts, $650,000; Prevent Blindness North Carolina, $100,000.
Contact: Marilyn Foote-Hudson, Executive Director; (919) 483-2140; (919) 315-3015; community.partnership@gsk.com
Internet: http://us.gsk.com/html/community/community-grants-foundation.html
Sponsor: North Carolina GlaxoSmithKline Foundation
5 Moore Drive, P.O. Box 13398
Research Triangle Park, NC 27709

North Dakota Community Foundation (NDCF) Grants 1274
Unrestricted funds are awarded in North Dakota for aid to the elderly and disadvantaged. Support is also given for health services, youth agencies, parks and recreation, arts and cultural programs, and mental health. Grants support operating budgets, continuing support, annual campaigns, seed money, building funds, equipment, matching funds, scholarship funds, special projects, research, publications, conferences, and seminars. Initial contact should be by letter. If a project appears to be appropriate to NDCF guidelines, formal application materials will be sent to the inquiring organization. Students seeking scholarships should not contact the foundation directly.
Requirements: North Dakota nonprofit organizations are eligible.
Restrictions: Grants are not made to individuals.
Geographic Focus: North Dakota
Date(s) Application is Due: Aug 15
Amount: 2,000 USD
Contact: Kevin Dvorak, President; (701) 222-8349; (701) 222-8257; kdvorak@ndcf.net
Internet: http://www.ndcf.net/Grants/grantsindex.html
Sponsor: North Dakota Community Foundation
1025 N Third Street, P.O. Box 387
Bismarck, ND 58502

North Dakota Council on the Arts Community Access Grants 1275
As a community-based grant program, Community Arts Access is designed to benefit nonprofit organizations that present arts programming in small and rural communities in North Dakota. It also supports nonprofit organizations in communities of all sizes whose arts programming makes a deliberate and focused effort to serve a special constituency or an under-served audience in that community. Funds for the program are appropriated by the state of North Dakota. Some of the program goals are to strengthen existing arts organizations and art forms, provide start-up funds for new or emerging arts organizations, and expand new audiences. Examples of supported activities include general operating costs, production costs, honoraria for artistic or technical directors, musical scores/performance rights, printing costs for programs and catalogs, and artist services. Grant requests may not exceed $2,000, and $650 is the minimum request. Applicants are encouraged to submit a notice of intent to apply. While this is not a requirement, it will assist the Council on the Arts in the planning of review panels and other matters.
Requirements: Applicant must be registered as a non-profit organization with the state of North Dakota, or be a community or county government entity. Organizations may form partnerships with state agencies, for-profit businesses, and other entities, but the non-profit organization must be the applicant. A 1:1 match is required. Of this, up to half may be documented in-kind.
Restrictions: Organizations supported through the Institutional Support and Mini-Grant programs, requests for Artists in Residence or LEAP activities, reduction of a deficit, and projects completed at the time of the application are ineligible.
Geographic Focus: North Dakota
Date(s) Application is Due: Apr 1; Nov 1
Amount: 650 - 2,000 USD
Contact: Amy Schmidt, Public Information Officer; (701) 328-7594; (701) 328-7595; amschmid@nd.gov or comserv@nd.gov
Internet: http://www.nd.gov/arts/grants/CAAguidelines.html
Sponsor: North Dakota Council on the Arts
1600 E Century Avenue, Suite 6
Bismarck, ND 58503-0649

North Dakota Council on the Arts Institutional Support Grants 1276
The Institutional Support program is designed to benefit artists, arts organizations, and the general public. The program provides general support for local arts councils and other arts organizations, as well as support for performances, exhibitions, publications, classes, workshops, and special events in all arts disciplines. The program's goals are to assist arts institutions and cultural organizations in improving artistic or administrative standards; encourage arts organizations to attain financial stability by developing a diversified funding base; expand cultural opportunities to new audiences and under-served areas; and increase opportunities for local artists and others to participate in a wide range of arts activities. Examples of funded activities include general operating expenses; honoraria for artistic and technical staff/services; and production costs for performances, exhibitions, and publications. Letter of intent is due by January 15; application must be received by March 15. Application materials are available on the website.
Requirements: Applicant North Dakota-based organizations must comply with all NDCA general policy guidelines; comply with applicable state and federal laws; submit complete and accurate applications and provide at least 50 percent of the total cash cost of the project; and submit current long-range plans that include goals and measurable objectives for the organization. Applicants whose operating budgets exceed $200,000 must be tax-exempt and submit independent audits for the most recently completed fiscal year. Presentation, production, or service of the arts must be the primary activity of the applicant organization.
Restrictions: The following are ineligible: organizations supported through Access; capital architectural improvements or purchase or long-term rental of equipment or property; benefits or hospitality costs; fellowships, scholarships, or tuition fees; activities restricted to an organization's membership; and proposals which match federal funds with federal funds.
Geographic Focus: North Dakota
Date(s) Application is Due: Mar 15
Amount: 2,000 - 10,000 USD
Contact: Jan Webb, Executive Director; (701) 328-7592; (701) 328-7595; comserv@state.nd.us
Internet: http://www.nd.gov/arts/grants/ISguidelines.html
Sponsor: North Dakota Council on the Arts
1600 E Century Avenue, Suite 6
Bismarck, ND 58503-0649

North Dakota Council on the Arts Presenter Support Grants 1277

Presenter Support is designed to benefit nonprofit organizations that are not eligible for other major grant programs through the North Dakota Council on the Arts, offers financial support for arts events and programming, and supports organizations in communities with a population of 6,000 or more. Goals of the program include: to encourage existing arts organizations to build upon themselves, enhance the artistic quality of their programming, and expand their audience; to promote knowledge and appreciation of the arts in North Dakota's communities; to provide start-up funds or general operating support for new or emerging arts programs; and to provide opportunities for North Dakota artists. Grant requests may not exceed $2,000. Annual deadlines are April 1 and November 1.

Requirements: Applicants are encouraged to submit a notice of intent to apply. While this is not a requirement, it will assist the Council on the Arts in the planning of review panels and other matters.

Restrictions: Applicant must be registered as a 501(c)3 non-profit organization with the state of North Dakota, or be a community or county government entity. Organizations may form partnerships with state agencies, for-profit businesses, and other entities, but the non-profit organization must be the applicant. An applicant must be from a community with a population of 6,000 or more, according to the most recent census available. A 1:1 cash match is required. Requested funds can cover no more than half of the total expenses for the programming.

Geographic Focus: North Dakota

Date(s) Application is Due: Apr 1; Nov 1

Amount: Up to 2,000 USD

Contact: Amy Schmidt, Public Information Officer; (701) 328-7594; (701) 328-7595; amschmid@nd.gov or comserv@nd.gov

Internet: http://www.nd.gov/arts/grants/PRSguidelines.html

Sponsor: North Dakota Council on the Arts
1600 E Century Avenue, Suite 6
Bismarck, ND 58503-0649

North Dakota Council on the Arts Special Project Grants 1278

Grants provide an opportunity for organizations to initiate new projects without delay and to take advantage of possible touring events. The matching funds may be in cash or documented in-kind services and contributions. Examples of supported activities are general operating expenses; honoraria for artistic and technical staff services; and production costs for performances, exhibitions, and publications. Applications will be accepted throughout the year on a funds-available basis. Applications must be submitted no later than four weeks prior to the event. Early application is recommended since grant funds are limited. Special Project grants for a particular fiscal year (July 1 to June 30) may not be submitted after May 31 of that calendar year. Grant requests may not exceed $1,000 or 50 percent of the total project cost, which ever is less, and awards may be less based on review of the application. In-kind match can be up to 25 percent of the total project cost. Application materials are available on the website.

Requirements: Applicant organizations must comply with all NDCA general policy guidelines and be based in North Dakota.

Restrictions: The following are ineligible: organizations supported through Access or Institutional Support; capital architectural improvements or purchase or long-term rental of equipment or property; benefits or hospitality costs; fellowships, scholarships, or tuition fees; activities restricted to an organization's membership; and proposals which match federal funds with federal funds.

Geographic Focus: North Dakota

Amount: Up to 1,000 USD

Contact: Jan Webb, Executive Director; (701) 328-7592; (701) 328-7595; jwebb@state.nd.us

Internet: http://www.nd.gov/arts/grants/SPguidelines.html

Sponsor: North Dakota Council on the Arts
1600 E Century Avenue, Suite 6
Bismarck, ND 58503-0649

Northern Chautauqua Community Foundation Community Grants 1279

The foundation awards grants to nonprofit, tax-exempt organizations located in Northern Chautauqua County, New York. Priority will be given to programs representing innovative and efficient approaches to serving community needs and opportunities, projects that assist citizens whose needs are not met by existing services, projects that expect to test or demonstrate new approaches and techniques in the solutions of community problems, and projects that promote volunteer participation and citizen involvement in the community. Consideration will be given to the potential impact of the request and the number of people who will benefit. Seed grants will be awarded to initiate promising new programs in the foundation's field of interest as well as challenge grants to encourage matching gifts. Except in unusual circumstances, grants are approved for one year at a time. Contact the foundation office for an application.

Requirements: IRS 501(c)3 organizations in Northern Chautauqua County, New York, are eligible.

Restrictions: Areas generally not funded are capital campaigns to establish or add to endowment funds, general operating budgets for existing organizations, publication of books, conferences, or annual fund-raising campaigns.

Geographic Focus: New York

Date(s) Application is Due: Mar 23; Sep 21

Amount: 12,500 USD

Contact: Diane E. Hannum, Executive Director; (716) 366-4892; (716) 366-3905; dhannum@nncfoundation.org or info@nccfoundation.org

Internet: http://www.nccfoundation.org/Grantseekers/ApplyforaGrant/tabid/256/Default.aspx

Sponsor: Northern Chautauqua Community Foundation
212 Lake Shore Drive West
Dunkirk, NY 14048

Northern Trust Company Charitable Trust and Corporate Giving Grants 1280

Contributions from the Charitable Trust support program, general operating, capital, or endowment priorities. Grants usually are confined to programs and agencies that focus on advancing the well-being of disadvantaged women and children, and people with disabilities. Priority is given to programs or agencies that serve the following Chicago neighborhoods: Chatham, Englewood, Humboldt Park, Logan Square, Loop, Washington Park, and West Town. Applications, including all material specified in the checklist must be received in the Community Affairs office before 5:00 pm on the deadline date. Deadlines for requests for funding are determined by area of service, as follows: social welfare—January 13 and August 12, education—May 13; and arts and culture—May 13.

Requirements: Nonprofit organizations in Illinois are eligible. A proposal should include a short cover letter, an operating budget for the current year, a copy of the agency's most recent audited financial statement, a list of members of the agency's governing board, a list of Chicago-based corporate and foundation contributors and amounts each has contributed in the last calendar year, and a letter from the IRS indicating tax-exempt status.

Geographic Focus: Illinois

Date(s) Application is Due: Jan 13; May 13; Aug 12

Amount: 2,500 - 5,000 USD

Samples: Parents United for Responsible Education (Chicago, IL)—for operating support, $5000; Chicago Reporter (Chicago, IL)—for operating support, $3000.

Contact: Dawn McGovern, Program Contact; (312) 444-4059

Internet: http://www.northerntrust.com/aboutus/community/charitable/index.html

Sponsor: Northern Trust Company
50 S LaSalle Street, Suite L-7
Chicago, IL 60675

Northland Foundation Grants 1281

The Northland Foundation provides resources to programs that value children and families and help the next generation develop into responsible, caring adults; provide individuals and families with the tools to become self-reliant through economic and social justice; and encourage older adults to share their vitality and wisdom. Tax-exempt nonprofits located in or serving the seven-county Arrowhead Region may apply for grant funding. In order to be considered, projects must address one of the following three priority areas: Connecting Kids and Communities/Strengthening Families; Opportunities for Self-Reliance; Aging with Independence. Applicants interested in applying for grant funds are strongly encouraged to contact the Northland Foundation to discuss project ideas with program staff as the first step.

Requirements: The Northland Foundation serves 501(c)3 nonprofit organizations in the seven-county area of Aitkin, Carlton, Cook, Itasca, Koochiching, Lake, and Saint Louis Counties of Minnesota. To apply for funds, organizations are asked to submit a pre-application form (available online at the Foundation's website). If you have questions or need to request a hard copy, please call or email Erik Torch, Grants Manager. The Foundation's Board of Trustees reviews pre-applications on a monthly basis. Pre-applications must be received

by the 15th of each month for review by the board the following month. Following this initial review, applicants are notified by letter if a full proposal is requested and when it is due. On average, consideration of a full proposal takes 60 to 90 days.
Restrictions: Grants do not support individuals religious programs, endowments, fundraising campaigns, buildings or major equipment, festivals, traditional government services, or programs for which public support has been cut.
Geographic Focus: Minnesota
Date(s) Application is Due: Jan 15; Feb 15; Mar 15; Apr 15; May 15; Jun 15; Jul 15; Aug 15; Sep 15; Oct 15; Nov 15; Dec 15
Samples: The Foundation generally does not consider requests for: religious programs or activities (faith-based or religious organizations may apply for support for activities that benefit the larger community, but not for those which have religious purposes); endowment campaigns; buildings or major equipment; individuals or private foundations; fundraising campaigns or dinners, ticket sales, festivals, celebrations, and similar activities; and traditional government services or replacement of funding for which public support has been cut.
Contact: Erik Torch, Grants Manager; (800) 433-4045 or (218) 723-4040; (218) 723-4048; info@northlandfdn.org
Internet: http://www.northlandfdn.org/grants.html
Sponsor: Northland Foundation
202 West Superior Street, Suite 610
Duluth, MN 55802

Northrop Grumman Foundation Grants **1282**

Northrop Grumman's priority is to provide opportunities related to science, technology, engineering and mathematics (STEM) for students and teachers. The foundation supports diverse and sustainable NATIONAL-LEVEL programs that enhance the education experience for students and provide teachers with the training and tools they need to be successful in the classroom.
Requirements: Grant requests must be submitted online via the Foundation's website. Grant requests must include: tax exempt number; non-profit or institution contact name, title, address, phone number, fax number; brief history of the organization, mission statement, goals and objectives; type and scope of services offered, and the geographical area serviced; specific details as to how requested funds would be used; project budget and amount requested; demographic impacted; current operating budget including latest financial statement; list of other corporate funders; list of directors and/or officers, and their affiliations; Northrop Grumman employee sponsor, if applicable (name and phone number); and contact information.
Restrictions: The Foundation will not consider the following requests: individuals; fundraising events such as raffles, walk-a-thons, banquets or dinners; campus student organizations, fraternities, sororities, and honor societies; religious schools or colleges whose primary focus is to promote religious beliefs; athletic teams, support organizations; advertising or underwriting expenses; capital campaigns; endowments; tuition; choirs, bands, or drill teams.
Geographic Focus: All U.S. States
Amount: 500 - 200,000 USD
Samples: University of Nevada, Las Vegas, Nevada, $30,000 - to purchase computer equipment and software for the Transportation Research Center; California State University at Long Beach, Long Beach, Caliornia, $10,000 - for curriculum development in software engineering.
Contact: Carleen Beste, (888) 478-5478; carleen.beste@ngc.com
Internet: http://www.northropgrumman.com/corporate-responsibility/corporate-citizenship/foundation-grant-guidelines.html
Sponsor: Northrop Grumman Foundation
1840 Century Park E, MS 131/CC
Los Angeles, CA 90067

Northwestern Mutual Foundation Grants **1283**

The people of Northwestern Mutual have a long history of community involvement. To carry out its corporate contributions program, Northwestern Mutual created a private foundation, The Northwestern Mutual Foundation. The Northwestern Mutual Foundation focuses its funding in Milwaukee, where the company is headquartered. Therefore, applying for a grant from the Northwestern Mutual Foundation is limited to Milwaukee-area nonprofit organizations with programs centered on Education, Health & Human Services or Arts & Culture.
Requirements: Northwestern Mutual Foundation does not accept unsolicited grant requests. Groups new to the Foundation are asked to submit a written letter of intent, describing the organization, funding request, and provide information about the program for which you are seeking support. The Foundations team will review your letter of intent and, if they are interested in learning more about your project, you will receive an application form. Groups that have an active relationship with the Foundation and currently receive funding are allowed to apply annually for support. Once an organization submits an application, the review process takes about 90 days. The Foundation review's Milwaukee-area grants on a monthly basis.
Restrictions: Milwaukee-area nonprofits are eligible to apply. The Foundation defines the Milwaukee-area as Milwaukee County, with limited programmatic grants in Waukesha, Racine and Ozaukee Counties.
Geographic Focus: Wisconsin
Amount: 10,000 - 800,000 USD
Samples: Boys and Girls Clubs of Greater Milwaukee, Milwaukee, WI, $800,000 (2008); United Performing Arts Fund, Milwaukee, WI, $605,000 (2008); Scholarship America, Saint Peter, MN, $205,425 (2008)
Contact: Edward J. Zore , President; (414) 271-1444
Internet: http://www.nmfn.com/tn/aboutus—fd_intro
Sponsor: Northwestern Mutual Foundation
720 East Wisconsin Avenue
Milwaukee, WI 53202-4797

Northwest Fund for the Environment Grants **1284**

The fund's mission is to protect Washington's fish, native wildlife, natural forests, wetlands and shorelines; and preserve pure and free-flowing waters. Grant programs include aquatic ecosystem protection—freshwater ecosystems, saltwater ecosystems, and salmon; growth management—prevent damage to environmentally sensitive areas, limit rural growth, support the use of smart growth policies within urban growth areas, and support environmentally beneficial use of Washington State's land and natural resources; and capacity building—develop and increase the capacity of organizations to achieve their programmatic objectives in an effective, efficient, and sustainable manner. Sixteen-month grants are awarded. Guidelines are available online.
Requirements: Nonprofit organizations serving Washington state are eligible.
Restrictions: The fund does not support endowment or capital campaigns, land acquisition, structural restoration, political activities, capital projects, scholarships, purely educational activities, public conferences, youth groups, videos and publications, Web page development, museum displays, art projects, research, government agencies, or debt reduction.
Geographic Focus: Washington
Date(s) Application is Due: Feb 1
Amount: 1,000 - 40,000 USD
Samples: Friends of Gray's Harbor (WA)—for a program to protect the Westport Interdunal and Aquatic Ecosystem, $18,000; People for Puget Sound (WA)—for a program to protect and restore Puget Sound's near shore habitats, $12,000; Western Environmental Law Ctr (WA)—for general operating support, $3000.
Contact: Pam Fujita-Yuhas, (206) 386-7220; (206) 386-7223; staff@nwfund.org
Internet: http://www.nwfund.org
Sponsor: Northwest Fund for the Environment
1904 Third Avenue, Suite 615
Seattle, WA 98101

Norton Foundation Grants **1285**

The Mission of the Norton Foundation, is to make grants designed to meet the needs of children and adolescents in Louisville, Kentucky. The Foundation supports experiential and holistic education that encourages their social, emotional, intellectual, physical and ethical development. The Foundation gives priority to programs that use the arts to achieve this goal. The Foundation also supports social services benefiting children and adolescents which are protective and preventative in nature. Civic projects in Louisville and Jefferson County which enhance the lives of children and adolescents are also considered for funding. The Board of Trustees meets three times per year. Applications must precede the meeting by approximately one month. Deadlines and meeting days fluctuate. Current deadline may be learned by calling or emailing the office. Grant application is available at the Foundation's website.
Requirements: Grants are made to qualified 501(C)3 public charities (but not private foundations) that carry out activities primarily in the greater metropolitan Louisville area.
Restrictions: The Foundation does not make grants to individuals, nor may it designate funds for legislation or support activities that seek to influence the legislative process, except as allowed by the Internal Revenue Code of 1986, as amended.

Geographic Focus: Kentucky
Amount: 5,000 - 60,000 USD
Contact: Lucy Crawford, Executive Director; (502) 893-9549; (502) 896-9378; lcrawford@nortonfoundation.com
Internet: http://www.nortonfoundation.com/application.html
Sponsor: Norton Foundation
4350 Brownsboro Road, Suite 133
Louisville, KY 40207-1679

Norwin S. and Elizabeth N. Bean Foundation Grants **1286**
The Norwin S. and Elizabeth N. Bean Foundation was established in 1967 as a general purpose foundation to serve the communities of Manchester and Amherst and, consistent with the wishes of the founders, grants are made in the fields of arts and humanities, education, environment, health, human services, and public/society benefit.
Requirements: Applications are accepted from nonprofit 501(c)3 organizations and municipal and public agencies serving the communities of Manchester and Amherst, New Hampshire. Priority consideration is given to organizations operating primarily in those two communities. However, the Foundation will consider applications from statewide or regional organizations which provide a substantial and documented level of service to Manchester and Amherst.
Restrictions: The foundation does not make grants to individuals or provide scholarship aid.
Geographic Focus: New Hampshire
Date(s) Application is Due: Dec 1; Apr 1; Sep 1
Contact: Kathleen Cook, Manager; (603) 493-7257; KCook@BeanFoundation.org
Internet: http://www.beanfoundation.org/grants/bean-foundation-grant/application-criteria.aspx
Sponsor: Norwin S. and Elizabeth N. Bean Foundation
40 Stark Street
Manchester, NH 03301

NSERC Brockhouse Canada Prize for Interdisciplinary Research in Science and Engineering Grant **1287**
The Brockhouse Canada Prize for Interdisciplinary Research in Science and Engineering recognizes outstanding Canadian teams of researchers from different disciplines who have combined their expertise to produce achievements of outstanding international significance in the natural sciences and engineering. The prize, accompanied by a team research grant of $250,000, reflects NSERC's commitment to supporting Canadian research through strategic investments in people, discovery and innovation. The grant supports the direct costs of university-based research and/or the enhancement of research facilities. The grant may be distributed in one lump sum or up to five instalments, depending on the needs of the recipients.
Requirements: Research teams nominated for the Brockhouse Canada Prize must have at least two members who are independent researchers, one of whom must hold an NSERC grant. The team can be part of an international effort, but the majority of the nominated team members must be employed at a Canadian university or public or private organization. NSERC recognizes that teams may change between the time of the specific research achievements and the time of nomination. Nominations will be accepted when changes have occurred but only as long as the core of the team remains intact. Contributions must be primarily in the natural sciences and engineering, and of an interdisciplinary and collaborative nature.
Restrictions: Any Canadian citizen may nominate a research team for the Brockhouse Canada Prize. Self nominations will not be accepted. Current NSERC Council members cannot be nominated. Since the prize is for interdisciplinary research, nominators should consult NSERC's Guidelines for the Preparation and Review of Applications in Interdisciplinary Research. Nominators should also consult NSERC's Guidelines for the Preparation and Review of Applications in Engineering and the Applied Sciences. See website for deadline & hyper links to above mentioned guidelines.
Geographic Focus: Canada
Date(s) Application is Due: Jun 1
Amount: 250,000 USD
Contact: Grants Administrator; (613) 995-5829; (613) 992-5337; brockhouse@nserc-crsng.gc.ca
Internet: http://www.nserc-crsng.gc.ca/Prizes-Prix/Brockhouse-Brockhouse/Index-Index_eng.asp
Sponsor: Natural Sciences and Engineering Research Council of Canada
350 Albert Street
Ottawa, ON K1A 1H5 Canada

NSERC Gerhard Herzberg Canada Gold Medal for Science and Engineering Grants **1288**
The NSERC Herzberg Medal is awarded annually to an individual who has demonstrated sustained excellence and influence in research, for a body of work conducted in Canada that has substantially advanced the natural sciences or engineering fields. The award is meant to celebrate Canada's most outstanding scientists and engineers and to raise public awareness about the major contributions that Canada's top researchers make to international science and technology, and to bettering people's lives. In addition to the medal, the winner is guaranteed $1 million to use for personal university-based research or to direct in some related way such as the establishment of research scholarships, fellowships or chairs in his or her name at Canadian universities. The monetary award will be distributed over a five-year period.
Requirements: To be eligible, a candidate must be a scientist or engineer from a Canadian university, government lab or private firm. Candidates may be nominated by any individual or group; however, the nominators must be Canadian citizens or permanent residents of Canada. Posthumous or self nominations will not be accepted. Current NSERC Council members are not eligible for nomination.
Restrictions: An individual may win the NSERC Herzberg Medal only once.
Geographic Focus: Canada
Date(s) Application is Due: May 1
Amount: 1,000,000 USD
Contact: Grants Administrator; (613) 995-5829; (613) 995-7753; inquiries.herzberg@nserc-crsng.gc.ca
Internet: http://www.nserc-crsng.gc.ca/Prizes-Prix/Herzberg-Herzberg/About-Apropos_eng.asp
Sponsor: Natural Sciences and Engineering Research Council of Canada
350 Albert Street
Ottawa, ON K1A 1H5 Canada

NSERC Michael Smith Awards **1289**
The Michael Smith Awards for Science Promotion focus on people and groups who are inspirational in the way they promote science to the general public. The Awards are an opportunity for Canada's science community to recognize, support and encourage outstanding science promoters.
Requirements: Any individual, organization or company within Canada may be nominated for the award. Nominees will have made a successful and sustained effort to encourage public interest in and an understanding of the natural sciences and engineering (including math and technology) outside the formal education system. Science promotion activities with award potential could include activities such as: organizing science camps, fairs, clubs or programs with youth organizations; creating new learning materials; developing science and engineering related co-op programs or job shadowing initiatives; arranging demonstrations, visits and lectures; creating new learning materials;writing books and articles;creating radio or television programs and generating public involvement through multi-media programs.
Geographic Focus: Canada
Date(s) Application is Due: Sep 1
Amount: 5,000 - 10,000 USD
Contact: Grants Administrator; (613) 996-1417; (613) 992-5337; michaelsmithawards@nserc-crsng.gc.ca
Internet: http://www.nserc-crsng.gc.ca/Prizes-Prix/Smith-Smith/Index-Index_eng.asp
Sponsor: Natural Sciences and Engineering Research Council of Canada
350 Albert Street
Ottawa, ON K1A 1H5 Canada

NSF Biological Field Stations and Marine Laboratories Grants **1290**
This program supports refurbishment, rehabilitation, enhancement, and construction, including laboratory renovations, at these research resources. Sites are required to have a plan for archiving (in electronic form) and making shareable scientific databases available on the unique data they obtain. Support can be provided for necessary computer equipment, connectivity, and development of these scientific database. Deadline is the first Friday in March each year. NSF 01-59
Requirements: U.S. colleges and universities, free-standing research and education institutions, and U.S. chartered corporations with formally constituted research and education programs at field stations or marine laboratories are eligible to apply.
Geographic Focus: All U.S. States
Amount: Up to 500,000 USD

Contact: Drive Gerald Selzer, Program Director; (703) 292-8470; gselzer@nsf.gov
Internet: http://www.nsf.gov/pubs/2001/nsf0159/nsf0159.htm
Sponsor: National Science Foundation
4201 Wilson Boulevard
Arlington, VA 22230

NSF Education and Human Resources Project Grants **1291**

The ultimate goal of the program is to provide leadership and ensure the vitality of the nation's science, mathematics, engineering, and technology education from K-16, and through graduate levels. Grants support research and educational studies or activities, such as salaries and expenses, permanent equipment, expendable equipment and supplies, travel, publication costs, and other direct and indirect costs. Fellowships provide for stipends and allowances to be paid to the awardee through her/his institution.
Requirements: Public and private colleges (two-year and four-year) and universities, state and local educational agencies, nonprofit and private organizations, professional societies, science academies and centers, science museums and zoological parks, research laboratories, and other institutions with an educational mission may apply.
Geographic Focus: All U.S. States
Amount: 128,125 USD
Contact: Program Contact; (703) 292-8600; jramaley@nsf.gov
Internet: http://www.ehr.nsf.gov
Sponsor: National Science Foundation
4201 Wilson Boulevard, Room 805
Arlington, VA 22230

NSF Partnerships in Astronomy & Astrophysics Research and Education **1292**

The objective of the program is to enhance diversity in astronomy and astrophysics research and education by stimulating the development of formal, potentially long-term, collaborative research and education relationships between minority-serving colleges and universities and the NSF-supported facilities, projects or faculty members at research institutions (including private observatories). As retention of traditionally underrepresented students is key to the success of this program, a solid mentoring scheme is vital. PAARE awards are expected to help build a foundation for students at an early point in their careers and help these students make the next step in their careers. The partnerships are intended to provide education and mentoring as a form of professional development to help these students succeed long after their work on the PAARE research. Funded activities might include, but are not limited to, the development of collaborative and mutually beneficial astronomy-related research and education projects, support for graduate and undergraduate students and exchanges of faculty and students. Well-prepared high-school students may also participate. Of special interest are activities based on research and education connections between the participants, and designed to increase recruitment, retention and degree attainment by members of groups underrepresented in astronomy and astrophysics research. Proposers are encouraged to contact NSF program staff to discuss the appropriateness of the planned activities.
Requirements: Proposals may only be submitted by minority-serving colleges and universities, including Historically Black Colleges and Universities (HBCUs), Hispanic-serving institutions (HSIs), and Tribally Controlled Colleges (TCCs). Each proposal must be submitted in collaboration with (and may include a subaward to) one or more NSF-supported facilities, projects or partnering faculty members at research institutions. Colleges and universities eligible to participate in this activity must offer baccalaureate degrees in physics or astronomy and meet at least one of the following criteria: 1) Be designated by the Department of Higher Education in FY 1994 as a Hispanic-serving Institution (HSI) under Title III of the Higher Education Act of 1965, as amended [See 20 U.S. C 1059 (copyright symbol); Public Law 102-325, Section 316, July 22, 1992]. 2) Be designated by the Department of Education as a Historically Black College or University (HBCU) under Title III of the Higher Education Act of 1965, as amended (see 34 CFR 608.2). 3) Be cited as a Tribal College or University in Section 532 of the Equity in Education Land-Grant Status October of 1964; Tribally Controlled Community College Assistance Act of 1978, Public Law 95-471. 4) Be a college or university whose undergraduate enrollment consists of at least 50% one or more ethnic minorities underrepresented in science and engineering in the U.S. , and not a Doctoral/Research University-Extensive institution in the Carnegie classification (for the Carnegie classification see http://www.carnegiefoundation.org/classifications/index.asp?key=785). African American, Hispanic Americans, Native Americans or Native Alaskans and Hawaiian/Pacific islanders are ethnic minorities underrepresented in science and engineering in the U.S. . Partnering institutions or organizations may be any institution or organization eligible for NSF funding that supports a research program in astronomy and astrophysics including AST-funded facilities and also private observatories. Research groups and individual scientists at research institutions are also eligible partners, provided their institution shows evidence of commitment to the proposed program as demonstrated in a letter from the institution describing its support of the partnership. Proposals may include subawards to the partnering institution, provided it has demonstrated a commitment to the activity at least for the duration of the PAARE grant.
Geographic Focus: All U.S. States
Date(s) Application is Due: Aug 3
Contact: Tammy Bosler, AAAS Fellow; (703) 292-8248; (703) 292-9034; tbosler@nsf.gov
Internet: http://nsf.gov/funding/pgm_summ.jsp?pims_id=501046&org=NSF&sel_org=NSF&from=fund
Sponsor: National Science Foundation
4201 Wilson Boulevard
Arlington, VA 22230

NSS Foundation Hunting Heritage Partnership Grants **1293**

The program designed to build a strong partnership between the foundation, the Congressional Sportsmen's Foundation, and state wildlife agencies by providing funding to state wildlife agencies to create greater hunting opportunities and put more hunters in the field. Grants support a range of hunter-related programs—increasing hunter access, hunter retention, hunter recruitment, programs that create more opportunities to hunt, and communications programs geared toward retaining or recruiting hunters. The deadline for submitting proposals normally falls in early spring, and NSSF will notify grant recipients within two months following the deadline. Priority consideration is given to projects that will be completed by March 1st of the year following signing of the official grant documentation. Application materials and instructions are available online.
Requirements: State wildlife agencies are eligible. Eligible projects must address one or more of the following: recruitment of new hunters in the state; retention of current hunters in the state; increased hunter access; and/or communications or outreach geared toward retaining or recruiting hunters.
Restrictions: The following are ineligible: projects including activities other than hunting with a firearm; projects that include the purchase of land; projects that focus specifically on the management of wildlife habitats or ecosystems; projects that focus on the planning of meetings, symposia, conferences, etc; projects that involve building or improving existing structures; or all other projects that are not directly related to the above-stated project eligibility requirements as determined by the foundation.
Geographic Focus: All U.S. States
Amount: Up to 500,000 USD
Samples: Florida Fish and Wildlife Conservation Commission—to help fund a survey and planning efforts for the Summit on the Future of Hunting in Florida, $15,000; Kansas Big Brothers Big Sisters (Wichita, KS)—to expand nationally a mentoring program that teaches youths such outdoor sports as archery, fishing, hunting, and target shooting, $250,000.
Contact: Steve Wagner, (203) 426-1320; (203) 426-1087; swagner@nssf.org or info@nssf.org
Internet: http://www.nssf.org/grants/index.cfm?AoI=generic
Sponsor: National Shooting Sports Foundation
Flintlock Ridge Office Center, 11 Mile Hill Road
Newtown, CT 06470-2359

NYCT Health Services, Systems, and Policies Grants **1294**

The Trust supports projects that strengthen preventive health care, improve access to services, promote the efficient use of health resources, and develop the skills and independence of people with special needs. The primary goal of this program is to improve the effectiveness, responsiveness, and equity of health care in New York City. Specifically, the program makes grants: for services, policy research, advocacy, and technical assistance that promote the accessibility of basic health services, especially in minority and immigrant communities; to strengthen health service providers, especially those serving the city's poorest residents; and to promote healthy lifestyles. The grant review process takes from two to six months. Grants range from $5,000 to $100,000; an average grant is around $60,000.
Requirements: Grants are made primarily to nonprofit organizations located in the five boroughs of New York City. Grants for programs outside the area

are generally from funds designated for specific charities or have been made at the suggestion of donors.
Restrictions: The trust does not make grants to individuals, offer general or capital funding, endowments, building construction/renovation, deficit financing, films, or religion.
Geographic Focus: New York
Amount: 5,000 - 100,000 USD
Contact: Joyce M. Bove, Senior Vice President; (212) 686-0010, ext. 552; (212) 534-8528; info@nycommunitytrust.org or grants@nycommunitytrust.org
Internet: http://www.nycommunitytrust.org/ForGrantSeekers/GrantmakingGuidelines/HealthandPeoplewithSpecialNeeds/tabid/207/Default.aspx
Sponsor: New York Community Trust
909 Third Avenue, 22nd Floor
New York, NY 10022

NYFA Artists in the School Community Planning Grants **1295**
Planning grants emphasize collaborations between schools, teaching artists, and/or cultural organizations to prepare for first-time Implementation projects or to further develop existing Implementation projects. Planning Grants offer schools the opportunity to assess needs, identify resources, and explore pilot program ideas. Applicants may apply for one year of planning support with the intent to apply for an Implementation grant in the same fiscal year. Funding of Planning grants does not guarantee funding of Implementation grants. The award is not designed to support artist-student contact, though pilot activities are acceptable. Awards are matching grants and range from $500 to $2,000. NYFA contributes up to 50% of total project costs.
Requirements: Schools, school districts, BOCES, Teacher Centers, colleges and universities or on Indian nation land in New York State are eligible to apply. Applicants must provide, through in-kind resources and cash, matching support for artist fees, materials and supplies, teacher release time, teacher compensation and all other project costs. In-kind contributions cannot exceed 1/3 of the applicant's match.
Restrictions: Nonprofit cultural organizations are not eligible to apply. New York State non-profit organizations may work collaboratively with schools and artists; however the school must be the lead organization. Planning Grants can only be used for artist fees and/or artist materials and supplies.
Geographic Focus: New York
Date(s) Application is Due: Nov 5
Amount: 500 - 2,000 USD
Contact: Susan Ball, Interim Director of Programs; (212) 366-6900, ext. 321; (212) 366-1778, sball@nyfa.org or ASC_Planning@nyfa.org
Internet: http://www.nyfa.org/level3.asp?id=35&fid=2&sid=22
Sponsor: New York Foundation for the Arts
20 Jay Street, 7th Floor
Brooklyn, NY 11201

NYFA Building Up Infrastructure Levels for Dance Grants **1296**
The BUILD program sustains New York City dance companies with small- and mid-sized budgets by offering choreographers and their dancers an opportunity to access the financial support necessary to build and maintain infrastructure and longevity. BUILD identifies and awards artistic merit, fosters long-term strategies to develop and sustain organizational health, and strengthens the organizational environment so that time and resources are available to create, conceive, and advance dance companies' artistic missions. BUILD supports, but is not limited to, requests for administrative costs; consultant fees; press and/or booking agent fees; company promotional materials; studio or space rental; and computers/equipment.
Requirements: New York City 501(c)3 tax-exempt organizations (or organizations with a 501(c)3 fiscal sponsor) are eligible to apply under category 1 (have a three-year-average budget between $16,000 and $80,000 per annum; and have performed work at least twice during the past three years) and category 2 (have a three-year-average budget between $81,000 and $160,000 per annum; and have produced at least three seasons of choreography with one season produced by a presenter other than the company itself). Additionally, BUILD provides stability grants of $1,000 to $2,500.
Restrictions: BUILD will not support requests for production costs associated with the performance of work including costumes, lighting, set design, or music fees; touring or traveling costs; or compensation for dancers, musicians, choreographers, teachers, or accompanists.
Geographic Focus: New York
Date(s) Application is Due: Apr 29
Amount: 10,000 - 20,000 USD
Contact: Pter Cobb, (212) 366-6900, ext. 212; (212) 366-1778; pcobb@nyfa.org
Internet: http://www.nyfa.org/level2.asp?id=78&fid=2
Sponsor: New York Foundation for the Arts
20 Jay Street, 7th Floor
Brooklyn, NY 11201

NYSCA Architecture, Planning, and Design: General Operating Support Grants **1297**
General Operating Support grants represent an investment by NYSCA in an organization's ongoing work, rather than a specific project program in order to help organizations become more effective in fulfilling their mission. The Council examines the nature, scope, and quality of an organization's programs and activities when considering the provision and level of support. Support for this grant is awarded on a multi-year basis.
Requirements: Applicants must register with NYSCA before February 22 to be eligible for funding the following fiscal year. An applicant for general operating support must also meet the following conditions: have a primary focus in the discipline in which the organization is seeking support; have an organizational mission that is primarily devoted to arts and culture with a prior record of accomplishment in producing or presenting cultural activities; demonstrate fiscal stability as indicated by such factors as a positive fund balance, an absence of substantial, recurring organizational deficits, a realistic and balanced organizational budget, diverse revenue sources, and strong controls; one or more qualified, salaried administrative staff; a viable board of directors and officers that exercises oversight and accountability for governance, operations, programming and finances; and must have ongoing programs, exhibitions, productions or other art and cultural activities that are open to the general public. First time applicants are required to call program staff before the registration deadline. Applications are available at the website and should be submitted online.
Restrictions: General Operating Support grants will be no less than $5,000 and shall not exceed 25% of an organization's budget, based on the income and expense statement for the organization's most recently completed fiscal year. Applicants cannot apply for both General Operating Support and General Program Support. In addition, NYSCA does not fund: major expenditures for the establishment of new organizations; accumulate deficits; debt reductions; programs of public universities or New York state agencies or departments; programs of public school districts or their affiliates; activities restricted to an organization's membership; operating expenses or fellowships at professional training schools that are not open to the general public; programs that are essentially recreational, rehabilitation, or therapeutic; operating expenses of privately owned facilities, such as homes or studios; components of an organization's budget that are not directed toward programs in New York State; competitions or contests; out-of-state travel expenses; or hospitality or entertainment costs of receptions, performance or museum openings, or fundraising benefits.
Geographic Focus: New York
Date(s) Application is Due: Apr 1
Samples: Buffalo Niagra RIVERKEEPER, Buffalo, New York, $15,824 - general operating support (2011); Historic Saranac Lake, Franklin, New York, $5,934 - general operating support (2011).
Contact: Kristin Herron, Senior Program Officer; (212) 741-7848; kherron@nysca.org
Internet: http://www.nysca.org/public/guidelines/architecture/general_operating.htm
Sponsor: New York State Council on the Arts
175 Varick Street
New York, NY 10014-4604

NYSCA Architecture, Planning, and Design: General Program Support Grants **1298**
General Program Support grants fund activities of arts and cultural programs that are operated as independent entities within their own organization, or for significant arts programming within a nonprofit whose mission is not art-based. The Council examines the nature, scope, and quality of an organization's programs and activities, its managerial and fiscal competence, and its public service when considering the provision and level of support.
Requirements: Applicants must register with NYSCA before February 22 to be eligible for funding the following fiscal year. An applicant for General Program Support must also meet the following conditions: have significant ongoing activities that address a focus in architecture, planning and design; substantial commitment to arts and culture, with a prior record of accomplishment in producing or presenting cultural activities; demonstrate fiscal stability as

indicated by such factors as a positive fund balance, an absence of substantial, recurring organizational deficits, a realistic and balanced organizational budget, diverse revenue sources, and strong controls; one or more qualified, salaried administrative staff; a viable board of directors and officers that exercises oversight and accountability for governance, operations, programming and finances; and must have ongoing programs, exhibitions, productions or other art and cultural activities that are open to the general public. First time applicants are required to call program staff before the registration deadline. Applications are available at the website and should be submitted online.
Restrictions: General Program Support grants will be no less than $5,000 and shall not exceed 25% of an organization's budget, based on the income and expense statement for the organization's most recently completed fiscal year. In addition, applicants cannot apply for both General Operating Support and General Program Support. In addition, NYSCA does not fund: major expenditures for the establishment of new organizations; accumulate deficits; debt reductions; programs of public universities or New York state agencies or departments; programs of public school districts or their affiliates; activities restricted to an organization's membership; operating expenses or fellowships at professional training schools that are not ope to the general public; programs that are essentially recreational, rehabilitation, or therapeutic; operating expenses of privately owned facilities, such as homes or studios; components of an organization's budget that are not directed toward programs in New York State; competitions or contests; out-of-state travel expenses; or hospitality or entertainment costs of receptions, performance or museum openings, or fundraising benefits.
Geographic Focus: New York
Date(s) Application is Due: Apr 1
Samples: Friends of the High Line, New York, New York, $24,923 - program development and exhibitions (2011).
Contact: Kristin Herron, Senior Program Officer; (212) 741-7848; kherron@nysca.org
Internet: http://www.nysca.org/public/guidelines/architecture/general_program.htm
Sponsor: New York State Council on the Arts
175 Varick Street
New York, NY 10014-4604

NYSCA Architecture, Planning, and Design: Independent Project Grants 1299

Independent Projects allow for individuals (or a team) to creatively explore or research an issue or problem in the design, planning and/or historic preservation fields which advances that field and contributes to the public's understanding of the built environment. The category seeks projects that are innovative in nature and emphasize the artistry of design excellence.
Requirements: Applicants must register with NYSCA online before February 22 to be eligible for funding the following fiscal year. Independent Project grants must originate with the individual (or team), but applications can only be submitted through a sponsoring organization. In addition: only design planning and historic preservation professionals who are New York State residents are eligible; and individuals may be associated with only one project request per year. Applications can be found at the website, and must be submitted online.
Restrictions: Student projects are not eligible. Funds cannot be used for out-of-state travel expenses.
Geographic Focus: New York
Date(s) Application is Due: Apr 1
Amount: Up to 10,000 USD
Contact: Kristin Herron, Senior Program Officer; (212) 741-7848; kherron@nysca.org or apd@nysca.org
Internet: http://www.nysca.org/public/guidelines/architecture/independent_projects.htm
Sponsor: New York State Council on the Arts
175 Varick Street
New York, NY 10014-4604

NYSCA Arts Education: General Operating Support Grants 1300

General Operating Support grants fund an organization's ongoing work, rather than a specific project or program in order to help organizations become more effective in fulfilling their mission, especially in arts education. The Council examines the nature, scope, and quality of an organization's programs and activities, its managerial and fiscal competence, and its public service when considering the provision and level of support.
Requirements: Applicants must register before February 22 to be considered for funding that fiscal year. In addition, applicant's must meet the following conditions: have a primary focus in arts education; have an organizational mission primarily devoted to arts and culture with a prior record of accomplishment in producing or presenting cultural activities; demonstrate fiscal stability as indicated by such factors as a positive Fund Balance, have an absence of substantial and recurring organizational deficits, a realistic and balanced organizational budget, have diverse revenue sources, and strong internal controls; one or more qualified staff; a viable board of directors and officers that exercises oversight and accountability for governance, operations, programming and finances; and must have ongoing programs, exhibitions, productions, or other art and cultural activities that are open to the general public. Applications can be found at the website and must be completed online. First time applicants must contact program staff before registration deadline.
Restrictions: Applicants cannot apply for both General Operating Support and General Program Support. Grants will be no less than $5,000 and shall not exceed 25% of an organization's budget.
Geographic Focus: New York
Date(s) Application is Due: Apr 1
Contact: Kathleen Masterson, Senior Program Officer; (212) 741-2622; kmasterson@nysca.org
Internet: http://www.nysca.org/public/guidelines/arts_education/general_operating.htm
Sponsor: New York State Council on the Arts
175 Varick Street
New York, NY 10014-4604

NYSCA Arts Education: Local Capacity Building Grants 1301

Local Capacity Building grants offer support to organizations to administer regrant programs that support arts partnerships between schools and cultural organizations or individual artists. Local Capacity Building programs generally support projects that are small and represent first-time or new forays into arts in education on the part of the school applicants. Each Local Capacity Building program site serves a specific region of the state and is expected to promote the regrant program, coordinate application and panel review processes, and provide ongoing technical assistance and professional development.
Requirements: Applicants must have: a full-time, paid executive director; a designated, qualified staff member (preferably not the executive director) to serve as coordinator of the program; and resources to provide appropriate technical assistance, outreach, and professional development opportunities for constituent schools, artists, and cultural organizations in the service area. First time applicants are required to call program staff before the registration deadline. Applications are at the website and must be submitted online.
Restrictions: NYSCA does not fund: operating expenses of privately owned facilities, such as homes or studios; components of an organization's budget that are not directed toward programs in New York State; and competitions or contests.
Geographic Focus: New York
Date(s) Application is Due: Apr 1
Contact: Kathleen Masterson, Senior Program Officer; (212) 741-2622; kmasterson@nysca.org
Internet: http://www.nysca.org/public/guidelines/arts_education/local_capacity.htm
Sponsor: New York State Council on the Arts
175 Varick Street
New York, NY 10014-4604

NYSCA Dance: General Operating Support Grants 1302

General Operating Support grants sponsor an organization's ongoing work, rather than a specific project, in order to help organizations become more effective in fulfilling their mission. The Council examines the nature, scope, and quality of an organization's programs and activities, its managerial and fiscal competence, and its public service when considering the provision and level of support. Support is awarded on a multi-year basis.
Requirements: Applicants must register with the Council before February 22 to be considered for funding. In addition, all applicants must: have a primary focus in dance; have an organizational mission that is primarily devoted to arts and culture with a prior record of accomplishment in producing or presenting cultural activities; demonstrate fiscal stability as indicated by such factors as a positive Fund balance, an absence of substantial and/or recurring organizational deficits, a realistic and balanced organizational budget, diverse revenue sources, and strong internal controls; one or more qualified, salaried

administrative staff; a viable board of directors and officers that exercises oversight and accountability for governance, operations, programming and finances; have ongoing programs, exhibitions, productions or other art and cultural activities that are open to the general public; demonstrate significant services or activity in New York State, which is defined as a home season of at least 7 performances within the last three years. Applications can be found at the website and should be submitted online. First-time applicants are required to call staff before the registration deadline.
Restrictions: General Operating Support will be no less than $5,000 and shall not exceed 25% of an organization's budget. Applicants cannot apply for both General Operating Support and General Program Support.
Geographic Focus: New York
Date(s) Application is Due: Apr 1
Contact: Beverly D'Anne, Senior Program Officer; (212) 741-3232 or (212) 741-3331; bdanne@nysca.org or dlim@nysca.org
Internet: http://www.nysca.org/public/guidelines/dance/general_operating.htm
Sponsor: New York State Council on the Arts
175 Varick Street
New York, NY 10014-4604

NYSCA Electronic Media and Film: General Operating Support **1303**
General Operating Support sponsors an organization's ongoing work, rather than a specific project or program. The Council examines the nature, scope, and quality of an organization's programs and activities, its managerial and fiscal competence, and its public service when considering the provision and level of support. Support is awarded on multi-year basis.
Requirements: Applicants must register with the Council before February 22 to be considered for funding. In addition, applicants must have: a primary focus in Electronic Media and Film; an organizational mission that is primarily devoted to arts and culture with a prior record of accomplishment in producing or presenting cultural activities; demonstrated fiscal stability as indicated by such factors as a positive Fund Balance, an absence of substantial and/or recurring organizational deficits, a realistic and balanced organizational budget, diverse revenue sources, and strong internal controls; one or more qualified, salaried administrative staff; a viable board of directors and officers that exercises oversight and accountability for governance, operations, programming and finances; and ongoing programs, exhibitions, productions or other art and cultural activities that are open to the general public. First-time applicants are required to call staff before the registration deadline.
Restrictions: General Operating Support grants will be no less than $5,000 and shall NOT exceed 25% of the applicant organization's budget. Also, applicants CANNOT apply for both General Operating Support and General Program Support.
Geographic Focus: New York
Date(s) Application is Due: Apr 1
Contact: Karen Helmerson, Senior Program Officer; (212) 741-3003 or (212) 741-7847; khelmerson@nysca.org or fchiu@nysca.org
Internet: http://www.nysca.org/public/guidelines/electronic_media/general_operating.htm
Sponsor: New York State Council on the Arts
175 Varick Street
New York, NY 10014-4604

NYSCA Folk Arts: General Operating Support Grants **1304**
General Operating Support grants represent an investment by NYSCA in an organization's ongoing work, rather than a specific project or program, in order to help organizations become more effective in fulfilling their mission. The Council examines the nature, scope, and quality of an organization's programs and activities when considering the provision and level of support. Support for this grant is awarded on a multi-year basis.
Requirements: Applicants must register with NYSCA before February 22 to be eligible for funding. An applicant for general operating support must also meet the following conditions: have a primary focus in Folk Arts; have an organizational mission that is primarily devoted to arts and culture with a prior record of accomplishment in producing or presenting cultural activities; demonstrate fiscal stability as indicated by such factors as a positive fund balance, an absence of substantial, recurring organizational deficits, a realistic and balanced organizational budget, diverse revenue sources, and strong controls; one or more qualified, salaried administrative staff; a viable board of directors and officers that exercises oversight and accountability for governance, operations, programming and finances; and must have ongoing programs, exhibitions, productions or other art and cultural activities that are open to the general public. Also, projects must be developed in close consultation and collaboration with the communities and artists whose traditions are to be presented. First time applicants are required to call program staff before the registration deadline. Applications are available at the website and should be submitted online.
Restrictions: Applicants cannot apply for both General Operating Support and General Program Support. Grants will be no less than $5,000 and shall not exceed 25% of an organization's budget. Folk Arts emphasizes support for presentations grounded in the traditional modes of practicing folk art, and not programming involving choreography, theatricality, or stylization that significantly alters traditions. Support is also not available for programming involving artists who appropriate, interpret, or revive the traditions of other communities.
Geographic Focus: New York
Date(s) Application is Due: Apr 1
Contact: Robert Baron, Senior Program Officer; (212) 741-7755 or (212) 741-7143; rbaron@nysca.org or rputnam@nysca.org
Internet: http://www.nysca.org/public/guidelines/folk_arts/general_operating.htm
Sponsor: New York State Council on the Arts
175 Varick Street
New York, NY 10014-4604

NYSCA Literature: General Operating Support Grants **1305**
General Operating Support grants sponsor an organization's ongoing work, rather than a specific project, in order to help organizations become more effective in fulfilling their mission. The Council examines the nature, scope, and quality of an organization's programs and activities, its managerial and fiscal competence, and its public service when considering the provision and level of support. Support is awarded on a multi-year basis.
Requirements: Applicants must register with the Council before February 22 to be considered for funding. In addition, all applicants must: have a primary focus in Literature; have an organizational mission that is primarily devoted to arts and culture with a prior record of accomplishment in producing or presenting cultural activities; demonstrate fiscal stability as indicated by such factors as a positive Fund balance, an absence of substantial and/or recurring organizational deficits, a realistic and balanced organizational budget, diverse revenue sources, and strong internal controls; one or more qualified, salaried administrative staff; a viable board of directors and officers that exercises oversight and accountability for governance, operations, programming and finances; and have ongoing programs, exhibitions, productions or other art and cultural activities that are open to the general public. Applications can be found at the website and should be submitted online. First-time applicants are required to call staff before the registration deadline.
Restrictions: General Operating Support will be no less than $5,000 and shall not exceed 25% of an organization's budget. Applicants cannot apply for both General Operating Support and General Program Support.
Geographic Focus: New York
Date(s) Application is Due: Apr 1
Contact: Robert Zukerman, Senior Program Officer; (212) 741-7077; rzukerman@nysca.org
Internet: http://www.nysca.org/public/guidelines/literature/general_operating.htm
Sponsor: New York State Council on the Arts
175 Varick Street
New York, NY 10014-4604

NYSCA Museum: General Operating Support Grants **1306**
General Operating Support grants sponsor an organization's ongoing work, rather than a specific project, in order to help organizations become more effective in fulfilling their mission. The Council examines the nature, scope, and quality of an organization's programs and activities, its managerial and fiscal competence, and its public service when considering the provision and level of support. Support is awarded on a multi-year basis.
Requirements: Applicants must register with the Council before February 22 to be considered for funding. Museums must have been open to the public for a minimum of one year prior to the registration deadline and provide a minimum of 120 days per year. In addition, all applicants must: have a primary focus in Museums; have an organizational mission that is primarily devoted to arts and culture with a prior record of accomplishment in producing or presenting cultural activities; demonstrate fiscal stability as indicated by such factors as a positive Fund balance, an absence of substantial and/or recurring organizational deficits, a realistic and balanced organizational budget, diverse

revenue sources, and strong internal controls; one or more qualified, salaried administrative staff; a viable board of directors and officers that exercises oversight and accountability for governance, operations, programming and finances; and have ongoing programs, exhibitions, productions or other art and cultural activities that are open to the general public. Applications can be found at the website and should be submitted online. First-time applicants are required to call staff before the registration deadline.
Restrictions: General Operating Support will be no less than $5,000 and shall not exceed 25% of an organization's budget. Applicants cannot apply for both General Operating Support and General Program Support. Organizations open to the public by appointment only do not meet this requirement.
Geographic Focus: New York
Date(s) Application is Due: Apr 1
Contact: Kristin Herron, Senior Program Officer; (212) 741-7848; kherron@nysca.org
Internet: http://www.nysca.org/public/guidelines/museums/general_operating.htm
Sponsor: New York State Council on the Arts
175 Varick Street
New York, NY 10014-4604

NYSCA Music: General Operating Support Grants **1307**
General Operating Support grants represent an investment by NYSCA in an organization's ongoing work, rather than a specific project or program, in order to help organizations become more effective in fulfilling their mission. The Council examines the nature, scope, and quality of an organization's programs and activities when considering the provision and level of support. Support for this grant is awarded on a multi-year basis.
Requirements: Applicants must register with NYSCA before February 22 to be eligible for funding. An applicant for general operating support must also meet the following conditions: have a primary focus in Music; have an organizational mission that is primarily devoted to arts and culture with a prior record of accomplishment in producing or presenting cultural activities; demonstrate fiscal stability as indicated by such factors as a positive fund balance, an absence of substantial, recurring organizational deficits, a realistic and balanced organizational budget, diverse revenue sources, and strong controls; one or more qualified, salaried administrative staff; a viable board of directors and officers that exercises oversight and accountability for governance, operations, programming and finances; and must have ongoing programs, exhibitions, productions or other art and cultural activities that are open to the general public. First time applicants are required to call program staff before the registration deadline. Applications are available at the website and should be submitted online.
Restrictions: Applicants cannot apply for both General Operating Support and General Program Support. Grants will be no less than $5,000 and shall not exceed 25% of an organization's budget.
Geographic Focus: New York
Date(s) Application is Due: Apr 1
Contact: Beverly D'Anne, Senior Program Officer; (212) 741-3232; bdanne@nysca.org
Internet: http://www.nysca.org/public/guidelines/music/general_operating.htm
Sponsor: New York State Council on the Arts
175 Varick Street
New York, NY 10014-4604

NYSCA Presenting: General Operating Support Grants **1308**
General Operating Support grants sponsor an organization's ongoing work, rather than a specific project or program. The Council examines the nature, scope, and quality of an organization's programs and activities, its managerial and fiscal competence, and its public service when considering the provision and level of support.
Requirements: Applicants must register with the Council by February 22 to be considered for funding. Also, an organization must meet the following conditions: a primary focus in presenting; an organizational mission primarily devoted to arts and culture with a prior record of accomplishment in producing or presenting cultural activities; a minimum of ten discrete presentations by ten different professional performing artists; demonstrate fiscal stability as indicated by such factors as a positive Fund balance, an absence of substantial and/or recurring organizational deficits, a realistic and balanced organizational budget, diverse revenue sources and strong internal controls; one or more qualified, salaried administrative staff; a viable board of directors and officers that exercises oversight and accountability for governance, operations, programming and finances; and must have on going programs, exhibitions, productions, or other art and cultural activities that are open to the general public. Applications can be found at the website and must be submitted online. First-time applicants are required to call the Presenting staff before the registration deadline.
Restrictions: Total requested amounts may not exceed 25% of the total project budget and must be more than $5,000. Applicants may not apply for both General Operating Support and General Program Support grants. In addition, the following activities are not eligible: single- and two-day festivals (unless incorporated within a larger presenting season); competitions, contests, talent showcases or parades; poetry readings (unless incorporated within a performance context) or staged readings; magic shows or ventriloquists; lectures, in-school classroom activity, master classes, or workshops; presentations or events that include the presentation of the organization's own work or work of their staff or board members, even when the project includes guest artists; and student work.
Geographic Focus: New York
Date(s) Application is Due: Apr 1
Contact: Leanne Tintori Wells, Program Officer; (212) 741-2227; lwells@nysca.org
Internet: http://www.nysca.org/public/guidelines/presenting/general_operating.htm
Sponsor: New York State Council on the Arts
175 Varick Street
New York, NY 10014-4604

NYSCA Special Arts Services: General Operating Support Grants **1309**
General Operating Support grants sponsor an organization's ongoing work, rather than a specific project or program. The Council examines the nature, scope, and quality of an organization's programs and activities, its managerial and fiscal competence, and its public service when considering the provision and level of support. This grant specifically helps to ensure the quality, viability, and productivity of artists and institutions within communities of color and other specific cultures. Special Arts Services also welcomes requests from organizations serving the disabled community by offering professionally-directed training in an arts discipline with the goal of more advanced study or career entry.
Requirements: Applicants must register with the Council by February 22 to be considered for funding. Also, an organization must meet the following conditions: a primary focus of providing cultural programs within and for communities of color or other ethnic communities; an organizational mission primarily devoted to arts and culture with a prior record of accomplishment in producing or presenting cultural activities; demonstrate fiscal stability as indicated by such factors as a positive Fund balance, an absence of substantial and/or recurring organizational deficits, a realistic and balanced organizational budget, diverse revenue sources and strong internal controls; one or more qualified, salaried administrative staff; a viable board of directors and officers that exercises oversight and accountability for governance, operations, programming and finances; and must have on going programs, exhibitions, productions, or other art and cultural activities that are open to the general public. Applications can be found at the website and must be submitted online. First-time applicants are required to call the Presenting staff before the registration deadline.
Restrictions: Total requested amounts cannot exceed 25% of the total project budget and will be no less than $5,000. Applicants cannot apply for both General Operating Support and General Program Support. In addition, organizations whose projects are directed toward general audiences or organizations in which artists do not represent those communities previously mentioned are not eligible for support and should consult the guidelines of other areas of support.
Geographic Focus: New York
Date(s) Application is Due: Apr 1
Contact: Robert Baron, Senior Program Officer; (212) 741-7755; rbaron@nysca.org
Internet: http://www.nysca.org/public/guidelines/special_arts_services/general_operating.htm
Sponsor: New York State Council on the Arts
175 Varick Street
New York, NY 10014-4604

NYSCA State and Local Partnerships: General Operating Support Grants 1310

General Operating Support grants sponsor an organization's ongoing work, rather than a specific project or program. The Council examines the nature, scope, and quality of an organization's programs and activities, its managerial and fiscal competence, and its public service when considering the provision and level of support. Specifically, State and Local Partnerships grants seek to: strengthen the leadership role of local/regional arts organizations in encouraging local cultural development and increasing resources available for the arts; encourage greater participation in the arts through support of a wide range of local, regional, and statewide programs and services responding to assessed cultural needs and reaching the full diversity of each community served; and enhance the professional capability of multi-arts organizations operating on the local levels and arts service organizations promoting the development of the arts and providing arts services statewide.

Requirements: Applicants must register with the Council by February 22 to be considered for funding. Also, an organization must meet the following conditions: a primary focus of providing local arts and cultural initiatives; an organizational mission primarily devoted to arts and culture with a prior record of accomplishment in producing or presenting cultural activities; demonstrate fiscal stability as indicated by such factors as a positive Fund balance, an absence of substantial and/or recurring organizational deficits, a realistic and balanced organizational budget, diverse revenue sources and strong internal controls; one or more qualified, salaried administrative staff; a viable board of directors and officers that exercises oversight and accountability for governance, operations, programming and finances; and must have on going programs, exhibitions, productions, or other art and cultural activities that are open to the general public. Applications can be found at the website and must be submitted online. First-time applicants are required to call the State and Local Partnerships staff before the registration deadline.

Restrictions: Total requested amounts cannot exceed 25% of the total project budget and will be no less than $5,000. Applicants cannot apply for both General Operating Support and General Program Support.

Geographic Focus: New York

Date(s) Application is Due: Apr 1

Contact: Leanne Tintori Wells, Senior Program Officer; (212) 741-2227; lwells@nysca.org

Internet: http://www.nysca.org/public/guidelines/state_partnerships/general_operating.htm

Sponsor: New York State Council on the Arts
175 Varick Street
New York, NY 10014-4604

NYSCA Visual Arts: General Operating Support Grants 1311

General Operating Support grants sponsor an organization's ongoing work, rather than a specific project or program. The Council examines the nature, scope, and quality of an organization's programs and activities, its managerial and fiscal competence, and its public service when considering the provision and level of support. Visual Arts supports a wide range of contemporary art activity for the benefit of the public and the advancement of the field with a goal of assisting New York State artists in their efforts to create and exhibit new work, interpret the work of contemporary visual artists to the public, and encourage dialogue and critical commentary about the visual arts.

Requirements: Applicants must register with the Council by February 22 to be considered for funding. Also, an organization must meet the following conditions: a primary focus in visual arts; an organizational mission primarily devoted to arts and culture with a prior record of accomplishment in producing or presenting cultural activities; demonstrate fiscal stability as indicated by such factors as a positive Fund balance, an absence of substantial and/or recurring organizational deficits, a realistic and balanced organizational budget, diverse revenue sources and strong internal controls; one or more qualified, salaried administrative staff; a viable board of directors and officers that exercises oversight and accountability for governance, operations, programming and finances; and must have on going programs, exhibitions, productions, or other art and cultural activities that are open to the general public. Applications can be found at the website and must be submitted online. First-time applicants are required to call the Visual Arts staff before the registration deadline.

Restrictions: Total requested amounts cannot exceed 25% of the total project budget and will be no less than $5,000. Applicants cannot apply for both General Operating Support and General Program Support. In addition, organizations cannot require or request artists to pay a fee for participation in projects funded by Visual Arts, and commissions on sales of art in projects funded by NYSCA cannot exceed 25% of the sale price. Events such as festivals and open studios are not supported.

Geographic Focus: New York

Date(s) Application is Due: Apr 1

Contact: Karen Helmerson, Senior Program Officer; (212) 741-3003; khelmerson@nysca.org

Internet: http://www.nysca.org/public/guidelines/visual_arts/general_operating.htm

Sponsor: New York State Council on the Arts
175 Varick Street
New York, NY 10014-4604

OCS Social Services Block Grants 1312

Social Services Block Grant (SSBG) funds are to enable each State to furnish social services best suited to meet the needs of the individuals residing within the State. Such services may be, but are not limited to: daycare for children or adults, protective services for children or adults, special services to persons with disabilities, adoption, case management, health-related services, transportation, foster care for children or adults, substance abuse, housing, home-delivered meals, independent/transitional living, employment services or any other social services found necessary by the State for its population. Services funded by the SSBG as far as practicable under the conditions of that State are directed at one or more of five goals: achieving or maintaining economic self-support to prevent, reduce or eliminate dependency; achieving or maintaining self-sufficiency, including reduction or prevention of dependency; preventing or remedying neglect, abuse or exploitation of children and adults unable to protect their own interest, or preserving, rehabilitating or reuniting families; preventing or reducing inappropriate institutional care by providing for community-based care, home-based care or other forms of less intensive care; and/or securing referral or admission for institutional care when other forms of care are not appropriate or providing services to individuals in institutions.

Requirements: Funds are allocated to the 50 States, the District of Columbia, the Commonwealth of Puerto Rico, and the Territories of Guam, American Samoa, the Virgin Islands, and the Northern Mariana Islands.

Geographic Focus: All U.S. States

Contact: Marsha Werner, Program Specialist; (202) 401-5281; (202) 401-5718; Marsha Werner@acf.hhs.gov

Internet: http://www.acf.hhs.gov/programs/ocs/ssbg/index.html

Sponsor: Office of Community Services
370 L'Enfant Promenade SW, 5th Floor East
Washington, DC 20447

Ohio Arts Council Capacity Building Grants for Organizations and Communities 1313

Capacity building funds are designed to strengthen Ohio's nonprofit arts and cultural sector by helping applicants improve internal governance and leadership, cultivate strategic community linkages, and develop financial and human resources for long-term stability. Building organizational capacity is a long-term, evolutionary process that organizations must engage in purposefully. The program provides funding for work in three areas of capacity: (1) Organizational Governance and Leadership; (2) Strategic Community Linkages; and, (3) Assets and Resources Development. For other topics appropriate to your organization, contact and discuss with the Program Coordinator. Grants for capacity building generally range from $500 to $5,000. Organizations must show a 1:1 match, half of which may be from allowable, appropriate in-kind donations.

Requirements: All nonprofit arts, cultural and community-based organizations in Ohio that demonstrate a strong commitment to using the arts effectively and authentically in their programming may apply to this program. However, due to limited funding, small, emerging, and mid-sized arts and cultural organizations generally are given priority. Call the OAC before submitting an application. Applications must be received in OLGA (online grant application system) no later than 5 p.m. on the second Friday of any given month. Because effective capacity building activities require careful planning, applications will be accepted only through the second Friday of April (for activities occurring May 15-June 30), except in rare circumstances. Beginning June 1 of each year, applications will be accepted for the next fiscal year.

Restrictions: See the Legal Requirements page of the website for a detailed listing of funding restrictions.

Geographic Focus: Ohio

Amount: 500 - 5,000 USD

Contact: Katherine Eckstrand, Director of Community Development; (614) 728-4467 or (614) 466-2613; (614) 466-4494; katherine.eckstrand@oac.state.oh.us
Internet: http://www.oac.state.oh.us/grantsprogs/guidelines/CapacityBuilding.asp#top
Sponsor: Ohio Arts Council
727 E Main Street
Columbus, OH 43205-1796

Ohio Arts Council Sustainability Program Grants **1314**
Funding from this program supports organizations that provide essential arts programming to their community and are integral to its cultural legacy. Through direct financial support of ongoing programming by arts, non-arts and cultural organizations, the OAC sustains the vitality of Ohio economically, educationally and culturally. The program allows organizations to plan and conduct ongoing arts programs - either a full year of activities or recurring projects - in both traditional spaces (galleries, concert halls, theaters, museums) and nontraditional venues (hospitals, shopping malls, retirement centers, places of worship). Grants are based on the arts program's budget (see website for formula), not the organization's total budget. Indirect costs may be shown as in-kind but not as part of the cash match. The application deadline is for odd-numbered years only.
Requirements: This funding program provides two-year grants to organizations for annual arts programming or a recurring single project or activity. Repeated events, such as a yearly festival, are eligible. The program supports organizations that offer broad-based arts programming in any discipline (multiarts, performing arts, literature, traditional arts, visual arts) that is produced and presented by nonprofit arts and cultural organizations, other nonprofit or government entities, and colleges or universities that offer arts programming. Applicants to the Sustainability program must have received OAC funds at least twice in the past five years. This previous support must have come from an OAC funding program that evaluated and scored the application through a panel process. First-time applicants to the OAC and organizations with budgets of $25,000 or less should refer to the Arts Access Program. Applicants may be: nonprofit arts and cultural organizations; social service agencies; other nonprofit organizations that provide arts programming; educational organizations that demonstrate a commitment to arts programming in a larger community setting; non-arts organizations such as colleges and universities, government entities and social service organizations may apply to the Sustainability program only for their ongoing arts component or programming.
Restrictions: Please read Legal Requirements and Ohio Arts Council Rules and Grants Process for Organizations before applying to this program. Both documents are available for download at the website.
Geographic Focus: Ohio
Date(s) Application is Due: Feb 1
Contact: Dan Katona, Director of Organizational Services; (614) 995-1662 or (614) 466-2613; (614) 466-4494; dan.katona@oac.state.oh.us
Internet: http://www.oac.state.oh.us/grantsprogs/guidelines/Sustainability.asp
Sponsor: Ohio Arts Council
727 E Main Street
Columbus, OH 43205-1796

Oklahoma City Community Programs and Grants **1315**
The community foundation functions to enhance the quality of life in Oklahoma by awarding grants to nonprofits in its areas of interest, including arts and cultural programs, education, health care, health associations, and human services. Types of support include general operating support, continuing support, annual campaigns, building/renovation, equipment, emergency funds, program development, seed grants, fellowships, scholarship funds, research, and matching funds. The grants assist organizations with activities that provide new or expanded services to the community in response to new opportunities and changing circumstances. The community foundation views its role as a partner with other organizations and regards contributions and participation by other individuals and groups as an essential element in grant activities. Especially encouraged are programs and services that are oriented toward the entire population and are not restricted only to those people who live in a particular geographic location or who are members of a particular organization. The foundation encourages nonprofit organizations to cooperate and pool their resources to meet community needs. The use of volunteers as a significant program component is considered favorably as is active participation of the agency's board of directors and a broad base of financial support in the community. Grants are generally made for a specified time period and are nonrenewable. Applications and guidelines for each program are available on the website.
Requirements: 501(c)3 nonprofit organizations serving the greater Oklahoma City area, and programs that benefit persons living in the greater Oklahoma City metropolitan area, are eligible.
Restrictions: Grants are not awarded to individuals or to benefit specific individuals. No faxed or emailed proposals are accepted.
Geographic Focus: Oklahoma
Samples: Arts Council of Oklahoma City (OK)—to support a collaborative summer program of the Oklahoma City Parks and Recreation Department, After School Options, and four local school districts, $20,000; Mesta Park Neighborhood Assoc (OK)—to create a new median strip to reduce the volume of traffic around NW 18th Street and N Shartel Boulevard, $10,000; Neighborhood Alliance (OK)—for a computer-resource center, $22,788.
Contact: Grants Manager; (405) 235-5603; (405) 235-5612; info@occf.org
Internet: http://www.occf.org/occf/community_programs/index.php
Sponsor: Oklahoma City Community Foundation
P.O. Box 1146
Oklahoma City, OK 73103-1146

Olin Corporation Charitable Trust Grants **1316**
The charitable trust supports nonprofits in company-operating areas. Grants focus on three priority categories: education, with a science and technology emphasis; programs that include Olin employees as volunteers and that impact communities in which Olin employees work and live; and conservation, environmental education, and environmental research. Types of support include general operating budgets, continuing support, annual campaigns, seed money, emergency funds, building funds, equipment, land acquisition, special projects, research, publications, conferences and seminars, internships, scholarship funds, employee-related scholarships, fellowships, and employee matching gifts. U.S. -based nonprofits with an international focus are supported primarily through matching gifts. There are no application deadlines. Applicants should submit a letter of request. The board meets in January to consider requests.
Requirements: Support is directed primarily to communities where Olin has a major employee presence.
Restrictions: Grants are not awarded to individuals or for endowments.
Geographic Focus: All U.S. States
Amount: 50 - 50,000 USD
Samples: Thirteen communities in Olin operating areas—for education programs, with a focus on computer technology and science education, $242,137 divided.
Contact: Program Contact; (314) 480-1400
Internet: http://www.olin.com/about/charitable.asp
Sponsor: Olin Corporation Charitable Trust
190 Carondelet Plaza, Suite 1530
Clayton, MO 63105-3443

Olive B. Cole Foundation Grants **1317**
The foundation awards grants to Indiana nonprofit organizations in its areas of interest, including arts and cultural programs, higher education, hospitals, youth services, and public affairs. Types of support include general operating support, continuing support, building construction/renovation, equipment acquisition, land acquisition, seed money, scholarships to individuals, and matching funds. The board meets usually in February, May, August, and November. Applicants must obtain guidelines and application forms.
Requirements: Indiana nonprofit organizations are eligible to apply.
Geographic Focus: Indiana
Amount: 100 - 120,000 USD
Samples: Tri-State U (Angola, IN)—for its master's degree program in engineering technology, $100,000.
Contact: Program Contact
Sponsor: Olive B. Cole Foundation
6207 Constitution Drive
Fort Wayne, IN 46804

OneFamily Foundation Grants **1318**
The foundation awards grants to eligible Washington nonprofit organizations working to improve the lives of women living in poverty and at-risk youth, for support services for abused women, and for efforts to end sexual abuse against women and children. Consideration is given to programs that provide training and skills development to low-income women and services providing

basic needs such as shelter, counseling, food, and childcare; educational and mentoring projects to help prevent teen pregnancy; job-training programs for youth and school/community-based programs to help low-income youth complete their education; parenting, training, and education programs to help break the cycle of family violence; shelters and services to support abused and neglected children and women; and hands-on programs to encourage philanthropy among children and youth. Grants will support operating expenses, special projects, and minor capital costs necessary to assure the success of a funded project. For general grants, two-page preapplication letters are due on the third Friday in March, July, and November and final proposals are due the second Friday in January, May, and September. Annual deadlines may vary; contact program staff for exact dates.
Requirements: Nonprofit 501(c)3 organizations based in King County, Snohomish County, or the Olympic Peninsula of Washington State are eligible to apply for funding.
Restrictions: Grants are not made to: individuals, scholarships, schools, research, summer camps, athletic events, video or film projects, website development, book publications. No multi-year requests are considered. Groups who have been declined three times are ineligible to reapply.
Geographic Focus: Washington
Amount: 5,000 - 12,000 USD
Samples: Amara Parenting and Adoption, Seattle, Washington, $12,000 - to foster-adoption the program, training for foster parents, and support for hard-to-place children (2010); First Step Family Support Center, Port Angeles, Washington, $11,154 - Parent-Child Interaction Therapy (2010); Indian Law Resource Center, Helena, Washington. $8,000 - Safe Women/Strong Nations, breaking the cycle of violence against Native women (2010).
Contact: Therese Ogle, Foundation Advisor; (206) 781-3472; (206) 784-5987; Oglefounds@aol.com
Internet: http://fdncenter.org/grantmaker/onefamily
Sponsor: OneFamily Foundation
6723 Sycamore Avenue NW
Seattle, WA 98117

Ontario Arts Council Arts Service Organizations Grants **1319**

This program supports provincial or national membership-based Arts Service Organizations (ASOs) that provide services and programs to support their members' professional, career or organizational development and promote an awareness of the arts in Ontario. The program provides operating and project support. Potential new applicants must contact the officer well in advance of the deadline to discuss eligibility and to request an application package.
Requirements: To be eligible for this program, arts service organizations must: be not-for-profit (with the exception of book and magazine publishers); be Ontario-based; be led by qualified professional personnel; have been in operation for at least two years; have a demonstrated record of regular, ongoing programming in their communities; have proof of sound financial management; submit verification of financial results of the last completed fiscal year with their applications; and be governed by a board of directors or an advisory body responsible for the organization. ASOs that serve an ethno-racial membership that are not provincial or national in scope, but that may have a provincial or national impact, may also be eligible to apply.
Geographic Focus: Canada
Date(s) Application is Due: Mar 3
Samples: Canadian Music Centre, Toronto, Ontario, Canada, $48,000; CCI - Ontario Presenting Network, Toronto, Ontario, Canada, $55,000; FU.S. ION: The Ontario Clay and Glass Association, Toronto, Ontario, Canada, $32,081; League of Canadian Poets, Toronto, Ontario, Canada, $20,000.
Contact: Lorraine Filyer, Program Officer; (416) 969-7438 or (800) 387-0058, ext. 7438; lfilyer@arts.on.ca
Internet: http://www.arts.on.ca/Page88.aspx
Sponsor: Ontario Arts Council
151 Bloor Street West, 5th Floor
Toronto, ON M5S 1T6 Canada

Ontario Arts Council Choirs and Vocal Groups Grants **1320**

This program provides operating support to not-for-profit, professional choral organizations as well as project support to choirs and vocal groups in Ontario to assist them to produce and present art and arts services to the public and to sustain a healthy arts community. There are two types of grants available: operating grants—commit funding to the operating and programming expenses of professional choral organizations that meet the assessment criteria for ongoing support; and project grants—offer assistance toward the professional artistic costs of specific music programming (such as a concert series or individual performances) by choirs or vocal collectives.
Requirements: To be eligible for support, choral organizations must: be not-for-profit (with the exception of book and magazine publishers); be Ontario-based; be led by qualified professional personnel; have been in operation for at least two years; have a demonstrated record of regular, ongoing programming in their communities; have proof of sound financial management; submit verification of financial results of the last completed fiscal year with their applications; and be governed by a board of directors or an advisory body responsible for the organization.
Restrictions: The following are not eligible: choirs that operate under the umbrella of a parent organization that is currently funded through another Ontario Arts Council program (i.e., as part of another choir or orchestra); choirs that are attached to, or affiliated with educational or religious institutions; choirs giving performances exclusively as part of religious worship; tours and exchange programs; or recording projects.
Geographic Focus: Canada
Date(s) Application is Due: Apr 1
Samples: Amabile Choirs of London Canada, London, Ontario, Canada, $18,000; Guelph Youth Singers, Guelph, Ontario, Canada, $12,000; Toronto Children's Chorus, Toronto, Ontario, Canada, $50,000.
Contact: Georgina Braoudakis, Music Officer - French Services; (416) 969-7417 or (800) 387-0058, ext. 7417; gbraoudakis@arts.on.ca
Internet: http://www.arts.on.ca/Page101.aspx
Sponsor: Ontario Arts Council
151 Bloor Street West, 5th Floor
Toronto, ON M5S 1T6 Canada

Ontario Arts Council Community and Multi Arts Organizations Grants **1321**

The objective of the program is to provide operating and annual support to Ontario nonprofit, professional community and multi-arts organizations to assist them to produce and present art and arts services to the public and to sustain a healthy arts community. Major goals include: to support growth and sustenance of the arts in Ontario through focused investment in artists and arts organizations; and to fund and encourage opportunities for arts education, public participation, and community involvement in the arts in Ontario. Programming grants commit funding to the programming expenses of professional arts organizations that meet the assessment criteria for ongoing support. There are multi-year and annual grants. Potential new applicants must contact the officer well in advance of the deadline to discuss eligibility and to request an application package. Guidelines are available online.
Requirements: Arts organizations must be nonprofit (with the exception of book and magazine publishers) and Ontario-based; have been in operation for at least two years; have a demonstrated record of regular, ongoing activities in their community; and have proof of sound financial management and be governed by a board of directors or an advisory body responsible for the organization. In addition, to be eligible for OAC operating funding, professional multi-arts festivals must have a year-round infrastructure and artistic leadership.
Restrictions: Art classes are not eligible for funding through this program. In the block grants to book publishers category, ineligible titles are listed in the guidelines.
Geographic Focus: Canada
Date(s) Application is Due: Apr 1
Samples: Art Starts Neighbourhood Cultural Centre, Toronto, Ontario, Canada, $32,000; Atikokan Intergenerational Centre for Arts and Alternatives, Atikokan, Ontario, Canada, $25,400; Workers Arts and Heritage Centre, Hamilton, Ontario, Canada, $15,915.
Contact: Georgina Braoudakis, French Services Director; (416) 969-7417 or (800) 387-0058, ext. 7417; gbraoudakis@arts.on.ca
Internet: http://www.arts.on.ca/Page103.aspx
Sponsor: Ontario Arts Council
151 Bloor Street West, 5th Floor
Toronto, ON M5S 1T6 Canada

Ontario Arts Council Dance Organizations Grants **1322**

The Dance Organizations program provides operating support to not-for-profit, professional arts organizations in Ontario to assist them to produce and present dance and dance services to the public in order to sustain a healthy dance community. It supports: excellence in the arts, regional activity, linguistic and cultural diversity and Aboriginal and Franco-Ontarian identity;

and arts education, public participation and community involvement in the arts in Ontario.
Requirements: To be eligible for grant funding, arts organizations must: be not-for-profit (with the exception of book and magazine publishers); be Ontario-based; be led by professional personnel; have been in operation for at least two years; have a demonstrated record of regular, ongoing programming in their communities; have proof of sound financial management; submit verification of financial results of the last completed fiscal year with their applications; and be governed by a board of directors or an advisory body responsible for the organization. In addition to the above, in order to apply to the program an applicant must: have produced an annual season or have operated on a continuous basis for at least three years; have an appropriate administrative infrastructure, according to the scope and scale of the organization's mandate; and engage Ontario-resident dance artists.
Restrictions: Ineligible applicants include: membership-based provincial/national dance service organizations; and union or labor organizations that protect or establish economic rights.
Geographic Focus: Canada
Date(s) Application is Due: Mar 17
Samples: Andrea Nann Dreamwalker Dance Company, Toronto, Ontario, Canada, $10,000; Ballet Jorgen Canada, Toronto, Ontario, Canada, $165,000; The Guelph Contemporary Dance Festival, Guelph, Ontario, Canada, $16,245; MOTU.S. O Dance Theatre, Stouffville, Ontario, Canada, $20,000.
Contact: Myles Warren, Dance Officer; (416) 969-7422 or (800) 387-0058, ext. 7422; mwarren@arts.on.ca
Internet: http://www.arts.on.ca/Page123.aspx
Sponsor: Ontario Arts Council
151 Bloor Street West, 5th Floor
Toronto, ON M5S 1T6 Canada

Oppenstein Brothers Foundation Grants **1323**

Grants are awarded in the Kansas City, MO, area primarily for social services and early childhood, elementary, secondary, adult basic, vocational, and higher education; family planning and services; social services and welfare agencies; Jewish welfare organizations; and programs for youth, the handicapped, disadvantaged, mentally ill, homeless, minorities, and elderly. Additional areas of interest include arts/cultural programs, the performing arts, museums, health care and health organizations, and AIDS research. The foundation considers requests for general operating support, capital campaigns, building and renovation, emergency funds, conferences and seminars, seed money, curriculum development, consulting services, and matching funds. Proposals may be submitted at any time.
Requirements: Nonprofit organizations in the metropolitan Kansas City, MO, area may submit grant proposals.
Restrictions: Grants are not awarded to support individuals, annual campaigns, scholarships, fellowships, medical equipment, or endowment funds.
Geographic Focus: Missouri
Amount: 5,000 - 15,000 USD
Samples: Arts Partners Fund (Kansas City, MO)—for program support; Children's Mercy Hospital (Kansas City, MO)—for program support.
Contact: Sheila Rice, Program Officer; (816) 234-8671
Sponsor: Oppenstein Brothers Foundation
922 Walnut Street, Suite 200
Kansas City, MO 64106-1809

Oprah Winfrey Foundation Grants **1324**

The foundation focuses on education and on empowering children, women, and families. Grants are made in a range of interests, including art and community, children and youth, education, health, and social services. Types of support include pilot, program, and operating grants. There are no application deadlines.
Requirements: Nonprofit organizations are eligible, with preference given to Chicago.
Geographic Focus: All U.S. States
Amount: 10,000 - 100,000 USD
Contact: Grants Administrator; (312) 633-1000
Sponsor: Oprah Winfrey Foundation
110 N Carpenter Street
Chicago, IL 60607

Orchard Foundation Grants **1325**

The foundation makes grants to eligible New York and New England nonprofit organizations in its areas of interest, including environment (air quality, biodiversity, fresh and coastal waters, forests, toxic substances, and pollution prevention); children, youth, and families (child welfare systems, literacy, and pregnancy prevention); and campaign finance reform. The foundation will occasionally provide seed money, operating support, and start-up capital to smaller home-grown organizations provided that strong local support has been obtained for a project in the form of membership and contributions, and that the entire mission of the organization coincides with a field of interest to the foundation. The listed deadlines are for concept letters.
Requirements: The foundation focuses on Massachusetts, Maine, New Hampshire, New York, Vermont, Connecticut, and Rhode Island. The foundation accepts letters of inquiry from groups in those seven states as well as from national groups with regional offices or projects in the area.
Restrictions: Grants are not made to individuals or for endowments, annual or capital campaigns, religious programs, any religion-affiliated organization, conference participation/travel unrelated to current foundation grant, research efforts unrelated to advocacy interests of the foundation, scholarships, fellowships, building projects, equipment needs, film and video projects, land acquisition, animal hospitals/rehabilitation centers, or groups that focus on specific diseases or conditions. Loans are not made.
Geographic Focus: Connecticut, Maine, Massachusetts, New Hampshire, New York, Rhode Island, Vermont
Date(s) Application is Due: Mar 1; Sep 1
Amount: 3,000 - 15,000 USD
Samples: New England Forestry Foundation (Groton, MA)—to purchase the largest forestland easement in U.S. history, which will protect 762,192 acres in Maine from development, $35,000.
Contact: Executive Director; (207) 799-0686; orchard@maine.rr.com
Internet: http://home.maine.rr.com/orchard
Sponsor: Orchard Foundation
P.O. Box 2587
Portland, ME 04116

Ordean Foundation Grants **1326**

The Foundation, established in 1933, supports organizations involved with alcoholism, children/youth, services, crime/violence prevention, youth, education, family services, food services, health care, homeless, human services, housing/shelter, human services, medical care, rehabilitation, mental health/crisis services, substance abuse, services, YM/YWCAs & YM/YWHAs, aging, disabilities, economically disadvantaged. Grants will be awarded for up to three years. Applications are reviewed on an ongoing basis; the deadline is the 15th of each month.
Requirements: Non-profits in the Duluth and contiguous cities and townships in Street Louis County, Minnesota are eligible. The Foundation accepts the Minnesota Common Grant Application Form.
Restrictions: No support for direct religious purposes, or for political campaigns or lobbying activities. No grants to individuals (directly), or for endowment funds, travel, conferences, seminars or workshops, telephone solicitations, benefits, dinners, research, including biomedical research, deficit financing, national fund raising campaigns, or to supplant government funding.
Geographic Focus: Minnesota
Amount: 1,000 - 290,000 USD
Samples: Lake Superior Community Health Center, Duluth, MN, $350,000; Safe Haven Shelter for Battered Women, Duluth, MN, $80,000; YMCA, Duluth Area Family, Duluth, MN, $150,000
Contact: Stephen A. Mangan, Executive Director; (218) 726-4785; (218) 726-4848; ordean@computerpro.com
Sponsor: Ordean Foundation
501 Ordean Building
Duluth, MN 55802-4725

Oregon Community Foundation Grants **1327**

The community foundation supports nonprofit organizations in Oregon to meet educational, environmental, cultural, medical, social, and civic needs in all areas and at all levels of society throughout the state. Grants are awarded to support arts and cultural programs, adult basic education and literacy, reading education, health care and health organizations, human services, youth development, community development, and government/public administration. Types of funds include general operating support, building construction/renovation, equipment acquisition, seed money, land acquisition,

program development, scholarship funds, matching funds, and technical assistance. Contact the office for application forms.
Requirements: Oregon nonprofit organizations may apply.
Restrictions: Grants are not awarded to individuals or religious organizations for religious purposes or for endowments, annual campaigns, deficit financing, research, publications, films, or conferences.
Geographic Focus: Oregon
Date(s) Application is Due: Feb 1; Aug 1
Amount: 5,000 - 35,000 USD
Samples: School and Community Reuse Action Project (Portland, OR)—to provide information and materials to students and community members about the importance of reusing and recycling materials, $20,000; Southern Oregon Historical Society (Medford, OR)—for its fundraising campaign, $14,000; Ctr for Nonprofit Legal Services (Medford, OR)—for its campaign to purchase the center's current site and add to its endowment, $15,000; Oregon Zoo Foundation (Portland, OR)—to expand youth-volunteer opportunities at the Oregon Zoo's new family farm exhibit, $20,000.
Contact: Program Contact; (503) 227-6846, ext. 414; (503) 274-7771; info@ocfl.org
Internet: http://www.ocf1.org/grant_programs/grant_programs_fr.htm
Sponsor: Oregon Community Foundation
1221 SW Yamhill, #100
Portland, OR 97205

Oregon Youth Soccer Foundation Grants **1328**
The foundation awards grants to support soccer-related projects for youth in Oregon. Participation in the Oregon Youth Soccer program enables children to grow physically, mentally and socially, developing the invaluable tools of character, discipline, teamwork, leadership, and self-esteem. It is the goal of the Oregon Youth Soccer Foundation to foster these values for the years to come, providing children with healthy, exciting and rewarding adult-supervised activity. Areas of interest include increasing the number of participants, increasing the availability of fields and facilities, improving the quality of play, enhancing gender equity, promoting participation by minority and disadvantaged youth, and encouraging recreational soccer programs and activities for youth in economically disadvantaged families. Requests for field development projects are favored if they are collaborative and foundation funds are critical to the project's success. Proposals for hard assets receive priority over requests for operating or ongoing maintenance costs.
Geographic Focus: Oregon
Date(s) Application is Due: Dec 15
Contact: Chuck Keers, Executive Director; (800) 275-7353 or (503) 626-1625; (503) 520-0302; info@oysf.org
Internet: http://www.oregonyouthsoccer.org/service/oysfoundation.aspx
Sponsor: Oregon Youth Soccer Foundation
4840 SW Western Avenue, Suite 800
Beaverton, OR 97005

OSI Burma Project Grants **1329**
The Project is dedicated to helping Burma make the transition from a closed to an open society. To this end, the Project supports initiatives and organizations worldwide that are committed to achieving an open society in Burma. The Project supports building the capacity of individuals and civil society organizations; promoting and improving the human rights and political and social standing of ethnic and marginalized groups from Burma; increasing the quality and dissemination of information about Burma inside the country, regionally, and internationally; encouraging the international community to push for positive change in Burma; and assisting in the preparation for Burma's political transition.
Requirements: All proposals must include: a narrative describing the organization and the specific activities for which it seeks funding; and an itemized budget.
Restrictions: The Project does not make multi-year or supplemental grants. Ineligible projects include: unsolicited research projects, conference proposals, and organizational newsletters; social welfare projects, including health care, schools (outside of OSI's Burma Project Education activities), orphanages, and provision of social services; cultural projects, including those related to cultural heritage and preservation, museums, literature, and fine and performing arts unless directly connected to the protection and promotion of civil and political rights; environmental projects unless directly connected to the protection and promotion of civil and political rights; development projects (i.e., construction of buildings, well-digging); microfinance and loans.
Geographic Focus: All U.S. States
Date(s) Application is Due: Jan 15; Jul 15
SContact: Maureen Aung-Thwin, Director; (212) 548-0632; (212) 548-4655; maungthwin@sorosny.org
Internet: http://www.soros.org/initiatives/bpsai/focus_areas/burma
Sponsor: Open Society Institute
400 W 59th Street, 3rd Floor
New York, NY 10019

Ottinger-Sprong Charitable Foundation Scholarships **1330**
Established in Indiana in 2002, the Ottinger-Sprong Charitable Foundation provides scholarships to graduates of Zionsville Community High School, in Zionsville, Iindiana, attending a state accredited college, university, or technical/vocational institute. Applications are required, and should include a detailed description of the individual need and amount of funding requested. The annual deadline is March 21, and applicants should use a letter of inquiry as their initial approach.
Geographic Focus: Indiana
Date(s) Application is Due: Mar 21
Amount: 500 - 2,000 USD
Contact: Candace E. Buckmaster, (317) 873-5669 or (317) 769-5619
Sponsor: Ottinger-Sprong Charitable Foundation
P.O. Box 13
Zionsville, IN 46077-0013

Ottinger Foundation Grants **1331**
The Ottinger Foundation is a private family foundation that funds non-profit organizations that promote innovative policies and citizen activism to build a movement for change. It supports organizations that address structural or root causes of social problems and focus on systemic social change rather than direct services. Organizations and projects funded by the Ottinger Foundation include a sound strategic vision, a concrete action plan, and strong components of advocacy and grassroots organizing. Projects must have national significance. The Foundation also favor organizations that are involved in coalition building as well as building leadership and organizational infrastructure. The Foundation continues its program area focusing on economic security issues and is only accepting proposals in the form of a brief letter of intent in this area. Grants generally range from $10,000 to $50,000.
Requirements: IRS 501(c)3 tax-exempt organizations may apply. Due to the large number of proposals received, initial letters of inquiry are discouraged and will not receive a response. email proposals will also not be accepted.
Restrictions: The foundation does not make grants to organizations that traditionally enjoy popular support, such as universities, museums, hospitals, or schools. The foundation does not support individuals, academic research, film or video projects, the construction or restoration of buildings, conferences, books, or local programs that do not have national significance.
Geographic Focus: All U.S. States
Amount: 10,000 - 50,000 USD
Samples: Maine Citizen Leadership Fund, Maine - for voter education and registration activities in Maine, $10,000; Southern California Industrial Areas Foundation, California - for the Active Citizenship Campaign, $10,000; Washington Environmental Alliance for Voter Education, Washington - for general support, $10,000; Land and Water Fund - for constituency building in the Rocky Mountain and desert states, $10,000.
Contact: Michele Lord, Executive Director; (212) 764-1508; (917) 438-4639; info@ottingerfoundation.org
Internet: http://www.ottingerfoundation.org/guidelines.html
Sponsor: Ottinger Foundation
80 Broad Street, 17th Floor
New York, NY 10004

Otto Bremer Foundation Grants **1332**
The foundation concentrates its grantmaking activity in communities served by Bremer-affiliated banks and provides financial assistance to nonprofit organizations whose work contributes to the well-being of these towns. The foundation looks to support programs that promote civil and political rights, including freedom of assembly, speech, and religion; economic and social rights, including the right to education, food, health care, and shelter; and cultural and environmental rights, including the right to live in a clean environment and participate in the cultural and political events of one's community. Types of support include program development, operating support, capital (including building and equipment), matching or challenge grants, and internships. Applications are accepted throughout the year. Most grants are given for a one-year period, although some multiyear grants are awarded. The foundation

encourages initial telephone or written inquiries concerning its interest in a particular project. Applicants are also encouraged to contact foundation staff for assistance in the development of a proposal.
Requirements: Private nonprofit or public 501(c)3 tax-exempt organizations whose beneficiaries are residents of Minnesota, North Dakota, or Wisconsin with priority given to those communities or regions served by Bremer affiliates.
Restrictions: Requests for the following types of projects are discouraged: annual fund drives; benefit events; camps; commercial and business development; K-12 education; medical research; sporting activities; building endowments other than for the development of community foundations; capital requests for hospitals and nursing homes; theatrical productions, including motion pictures, books, and other artistic or media projects; municipal and government services; or historical preservation, museums, and interpretive centers.
Geographic Focus: Minnesota, North Dakota, Wisconsin
Amount: 552 - 259,235 USD
Contact: Danielle Cheslog, Grants Manager; (651) 312-3717 or (651) 227-8036; (651) 312-3665; danielle@ottobremer.org or obf@ottobremer.org
Sponsor: Otto Bremer Foundation
445 Minnesota Stret, Suite 2250
Saint Paul, MN 55101-2107

Overbrook Foundation Grants **1333**

The foundation strives to improve the lives of people by supporting projects that protect human and civil rights, advance the self-sufficiency and well being of individuals and their communities, and conserve the natural environment. The foundation's environment program supports organizations working to develop better consumption and production habits in the United States and in Latin America (currently Brazil, Mexico and Ecuador only). In Latin America the primary objective is to conserve the planet's dwindling biodiversity. The foundation's human and civil rights program is multifaceted and provides support to the following: reproductive health rights; domestic criminal system reform efforts; lesbian, gay, bisexual, and transgender rights; gun violence prevention and international human rights. An emphasis is placed on work that protects the rights of children and women. The foundation supports projects both domestically and internationally (with a particular focus in Latin America and South Africa). Generally speaking, the foundation's domestic programs support policy development, advocacy, coalition building, research, legal and other strategies likely to impact large classes of people or shape issues important to the foundation's mission. In its international funding, the foundation also supports organizations providing direct services. The first step in the application process is to Submit a letter of inquiry; full application is by invitation. Guidelines are available online.
Requirements: 501(c)3 tax-exempt organizations are eligible.
Restrictions: The foundation does not make grants to individuals and rarely for endowments, building campaigns, deficit financing, or religious purposes. Grant funds may not be used to participate in or intervene in any political campaign on behalf of or in opposition to any candidate for public office or to conduct, directly or indirectly, any voter registration drive (within 4945(d)2 of the IRS code). Grants are not made for debt reduction. Funding for conferences, publications, and media is limited to projects directly related to priorities in the foundation's program areas.
Geographic Focus: All U.S. States
Samples: Rainforest Alliance (New York, NY)—for efforts to ensure the conservation of biological diversity within the tourism industry in Ecuador, $70,000; Gender Public Advocacy Coalition (Washington, DC)—for operating or program support, $40,000; National Public Radio (Washington, DC)—to support coverage of environmental issues on its news program, $50,000; Educational Fund to Stop Gun Violence (Washington, DC)—for its work to spur congressional legislation designed to curb gun-related violence, $50,000.
Contact: Grants Administrator; (212) 661-8710; (212) 661-8664; apply@overbrookfoundation.org
Internet: http://www.overbrook.org
Sponsor: Overbrook Foundation
122 E 42nd Street, Suite 2500
New York, NY 10168

Owens Corning Foundation Grants **1334**

The Owens Corning Foundation's giving programs are made directly to non-profit organizations that most effectively provide direct service on behalf of disadvantaged children and families in the following areas: affordable housing; K-16 education; federated giving programs; arts and culture; and civic betterment. Funding emphasis is given to projects and organizations that promote diversity and social welfare, serve a broad sector of the community, and have a proven record of success.
Requirements: Applications are not accepted and there are no specific deadlines. Request for contributions (both financial and in-kind) must be made in writing on agency letterhead and include the following: description of the mission and work of the organization, including the audience and community the organization it serves; an outline of the specific request and a statement explaining how it accomplishes and measures the organization's goals; a description of the organization's anticipated outcome and benefits resulting from this grant; the amount requested; an outline of services or promotional opportunities available to the Owens Corning Foundation for contribution; proof of tax exempt status or tax exempt number; and other funding commitments to project.
Restrictions: In general, funding is not considered for the following organizations or types of activities: religious, political or discriminatory organizations; travel funds of any kind; capital campaigns and ongoing operations support; grants to individuals; special events such as conferences and sports competitions; organizations or projects in countries where the U.S. government restricts business dealings; or agencies that receive United Way support to the degree which we are already contributing. Giving is on a national basis in areas of company operations, with emphasis on Ohio.
Geographic Focus: All U.S. States
Contact: Simone Hayes, President; (419) 248-8000; (419) 325-3031; OCFoundation@owenscorning.com
Internet: http://sustainability.owenscorning.com/contents/community-alliances/oc-foundation/
Sponsor: Owens Corning Foundation
1 Owens Corning Parkway
Toledo, OH 43659

Owens Foundation Grants **1335**

The Owens Foundation, established in 1985, supports organizations involved with housing/shelter; development; human services; secondary school/education; economically disadvantaged; homelessness. Giving is primarily in Chicago, IL. area. There are no specific deadlines with which to adhere. Contact the Foundation for further application information and guidelines.
Requirements: Must be a non-profit in Chicago, IL.
Restrictions: No grants to individuals directly, or for capital campaigns, building funds, or raffles.
Geographic Focus: Illinois
Amount: 10,000 - 300,000 USD
Samples: CARA Program, Chicago, IL, $372,500 - helps homeless and at-risk individuals transform their lives through comprehensive training, permanent job placement and critical support services; The Emergency Fund, Chicago, IL, $264,600 - provides emergency funding into the hands of church and lay organizations located in very poor Chicago neighborhoods. Funds used to avoid homelessness and to provide access to long term self-sufficiency solutions
Contact: Mary M. Owens, President; (708) 361-8845
Sponsor: Owens Foundation
7804 College Drive, Suite 3SW
Palos Heights, IL 60463-1473

PacifiCare Foundation Grants **1336**

The foundation's mission is to improve the quality of life for residents of areas where PacifiCare Health Systems does business. The foundation's focus areas are: child/youth, including child care, youth activity programs, at-risk youth, and counseling programs; education, including school programs that promote self-esteem, encourage academic achievement and the development of specific skills, literacy programs, training programs, and programs that improve the effectiveness of the educational system; health, including prevention, health education, access to health care, and improved quality of health care of targeted populations; human/social services, including housing, shelters, education, protection, community development, crime prevention, food, transportation, and other social services for targeted populations; and senior, including social services, nutrition, education, volunteer, and and adult day care. Preference will be given to proposals for specific projects. Requests for operating costs will be considered if the request is very specific and clearly defined. Seed grant requests also receive consideration. Organizations funded by the foundation are welcome to reapply annually. Application forms are available on the foundation's website.

Requirements: IRS 501(c)3 nonprofit organizations serving residents of PacifiCare regions in Arizona, California, Colorado, Nevada, Oklahoma, Oregon, Texas, and Washington are eligible. The proposal must include two copies of the following: application form; checklist form; cover letter accompanying the proposal, signed by either the CEO or appointee of the organization, summarizing the proposed project, the problem addressed, the amount requested, and the name and phone number of the contact person; the written proposal, which should not exceed 2-5 pages in length and should include background information, description of the problem, need or issue being addressed, and a complete description of the proposed project; most recent audited financial statement and 990; current operating budget and line item budget for the specific project; list of major funders and amounts; list of board of directors; and one paragraph summary of previous support from the PacifiCare Foundation.
Restrictions: The foundation will not consider grants for arts/cultural programs, associations, annual campaigns, associations (professional/technical), capital campaigns, challenge/matching grants, hosting/supporting conferences, individual support, private foundations, programs that promote religious doctrine, research, scholarships, or sponsorship of special events.
Geographic Focus: Arizona, California, Colorado, Nevada, Oklahoma, Oregon, Texas, Washington
Date(s) Application is Due: Jan 1; Jul 1
Amount: 2,000 - 10,000 USD
Samples: Casa de Esperanza, Green Valley, Arizona, $10,000 - to provide inter-generational community programming for children and the elderly; Escape Family Resource Center, Houston, Texas, $10,000 - for a school-based child abuse prevention and family support program.
Contact: Riva Gebel, Director; (714) 825-5233
Internet: http://www.pacificare.com/vgn/images/portal/cit_60701/127503Guidelines_for_Charitable_Giving.pdf
Sponsor: PacifiCare Foundation
P.O. Box 25186, MS LC03-159
Santa Ana, CA 92799

Pacific Life Foundation Grants 1337

The foundation makes contributions in the areas of health and human services; education; arts and culture; environment; and civic and community services. Types of support include capital campaigns, annual operating expenses, program development, employee matching gifts, and in-kind gifts. Special attention is given to programs that provide assistance to people in great need, educational opportunities for youth, and multicultural awareness and understanding. Additionally, each year the foundation selects two or more areas of special focus (e.g., AIDS, child abuse prevention, minority needs). Most grants in the special focus areas are made later in the calendar year after considerable research and review. The foundation generally makes annual grants. Organizations may reapply for funding assistance, but grants are made to one organization for no more than three consecutive years. Applications must be received between July 15 and August 31. To ensure the application is received by the deadline, it must be postmarked by August 29.
Requirements: Contributions are made primarily in areas with large concentrations of Pacific Life employees: generally, Orange County, California, and the Greater Phoenix, Arizona area. Some California statewide and national organizations also receive support.
Restrictions: The foundation does not support individuals; political parties, candidates, and organizations; professional associations; veterans' and labor organizations; social or athletic clubs; sectarian or denominational religious organizations; or organizations receiving United Way funding.
Geographic Focus: All U.S. States
Date(s) Application is Due: Aug 31
Amount: 2,500 - 10,000 USD
Samples: U.S. Fund for UNICEF (New York, NY)—for relief efforts in South Asia and Africa, $1 million.
Contact: Brenda Hardwig, Program Contact; (949) 219-3787; (949) 219-7614; info@PacificLife.com
Internet: http://www.pacificlife.com/About+Pacific+Life/Foundation+or+Community
Sponsor: Pacific Life Foundation
700 Newport Center Drive
Newport Beach, CA 92660

Packard Foundation Children, Families, and Communities Program— Preschool and Early Education Grants 1338

The program's central focus is to achieve access to voluntary preschool for all three- and four-year-olds by funding research, analysis, leadership, and constituency-building that promote this goal. Grants are awarded to enhance and expand statewide advocacy efforts and strengthen the coalition of constituency groups in support of preschool for all; refine preschool for all policy proposals and recommendations and support further research on the benefits of preschool for all in California; and provide ongoing support to local flagship preschool for all efforts that demonstrate the promise of high-quality preschool when implemented on a large scale. Most grants will be awarded in California. Staff will solicit proposals for local flagship programs from specific applicants. A limited pool of funding will be available to respond to unsolicited letters of inquiry for innovative projects that fall within the areas listed.
Requirements: Eligible applicants are 501(c)3 nonprofit organizations.
Geographic Focus: All U.S. States
Amount: 100,000,000 USD
Samples: California Head Start Assoc (Sacramento, CA)—to mobilize Head Start parents and program employees in advocating preschool for all children, $50,000; Child Care Law Ctr (San Francisco, CA)—to provide technical assistance related to advocating preschool for all children and to the Affordable Buildings for Children's Development program, and to analyze and develop policies related to California's child-care system, $320,000; First 5 Alameda County (San Leandro, CA)—to create workforce-development models in the fields of early-childhood education, $100,000; Mexican American Legal Defense and Educational Fund (Los Angeles, CA)—to mobilize Latino parents, to advocate preschool for all children, and to identify solutions to implementation challenges, $155,000.
Contact: Program Officer; (650) 948-7658
Internet: http://www.packard.org/index.cgi?page=cfc-upe
Sponsor: David and Lucile Packard Foundation
300 Second Street, Suite 200
Los Altos, CA 94022

Pajaro Valley Community Health Health Trust Insurance/Coverage & Education on Using the System Grants 1339

The Trust provides grants for projects that advance our mission to improve the health and quality of life for all people of the greater Pajaro Valley. The primary goals of the Health Insurance/Coverage & Education on Using the System Initiative are to increase the number of Pajaro Valley residents with health insurance, increase residents understanding and appropriate use of a medical home (family practitioner), and decrease inappropriate use of the emergency department. The Trust will support programs that increase the number of Pajaro Valley residents that have health insurance, as well as programs that improve access to health care for our community's more vulnerable populations. Additionally, the Trust will look at community-wide solutions to these issues.
Requirements: Applicant organizations must provide or plan to provide programs/services benefiting the health of residents in the Trust's primary geographic service area. Communities within this service area include Watsonville, Pajaro, Freedom, and Aromas. The home office of the applicant organization need not be located in the Pajaro Valley, but the applicant organization must demonstrate that it provides or plans to provide services that directly benefit residents of the Pajaro Valley. The applicant organization must be a nonprofit, 501(c)3 tax-exempt organization; a school-based health program; or have a 501(c)3, tax-exempt organization as a fiscal sponsor.
Restrictions: In general, the Trust's Board of Directors prefers not to fund programs or projects administered by a city, county, state, or federal government with the exception of school-based health programs. In general, the Trust does not give grants to: projects that do not substantially benefit residents of the Pajaro Valley; projects and proposals unrelated to the Trust's mission, eligibility requirements, and current strategic plan funding priorities and objectives; individuals, with the exception of the Trust's scholarship programs; religious organizations for secular purposes; endowments, building campaigns, annual fund appeals, fundraising events, or celebrations; or commercial ventures.
Geographic Focus: California
Samples: La Manzana Community Resources, La Manzana, California, $12,000 - to assist low-income families in accessing public health benefits (2010); Healthy Kids of Santa Cruz County, Santa Cruz, California, $15,000 - to provide access to health insurance to children in the Pajaro Valley who have incomes at or below 300% of the federal poverty level (2010); Santa Cruz Community Counseling Center, Santa Cruz, $5,000 - to launch a health

literacy campaign focusing on low-income families with children birth to five years old (2010).
Contact: Raquel Ramirez Ruiz, Director of Programs; (831) 763-6456 or (831) 761-5639; (831) 763-6084; info@pvhealthtrust.org or raquel_dhc@pvhealthtrust.org
Internet: http://www.pvhealthtrust.org/grants_core.html
Sponsor: Pajaro Valley Community Health Trust
85 Nielson Street
Watsonville, CA 95076

Pajaro Valley Community Health Trust Diabetes and Contributing Factors Grants 1340

The Trust provides grants for projects that advance our mission to improve the health and quality of life for all people of the greater Pajaro Valley. The primary goals of the Diabetes and Contributing Factors Initiative are to reduce the risk factors associated with diabetes, reduce complications related to diabetes, and decrease the prevalence of childhood and adult obesity in the Pajaro Valley. The Trust will mobilize communities in the tri-county area to prevent the increase of type-2 diabetes in youth and young adult populations; teach diabetes self-management, and provide medical nutrition therapy to people living with diabetes thereby preventing the life-threatening complications associated with diabetes. Further, the Trust will promote "best practices" in clinical management of diabetes throughout the region. The Trust will seek to minimize factors that contribute to diabetes, including obesity, poor nutrition, and lack of physical activity.
Requirements: Applicant organizations must provide or plan to provide programs/services benefiting the health of residents in the Trust's primary geographic service area. Communities within this service area include Watsonville, Pajaro, Freedom, and Aromas. The home office of the applicant organization need not be located in the Pajaro Valley, but the applicant organization must demonstrate that it provides or plans to provide services that directly benefit residents of the Pajaro Valley. The applicant organization must be a nonprofit, 501(c)3 tax-exempt organization; a school-based health program; or have a 501(c)3, tax-exempt organization as a fiscal sponsor.
Restrictions: In general, the Trust's Board of Directors prefers not to fund programs or projects administered by a city, county, state, or federal government with the exception of school-based health programs. In general, the Trust does not give grants to: projects that do not substantially benefit residents of the Pajaro Valley; projects and proposals unrelated to the Trust's mission, eligibility requirements, and current strategic plan funding priorities and objectives; individuals, with the exception of the Trust's scholarship programs; religious organizations for secular purposes; endowments, building campaigns, annual fund appeals, fundraising events, or celebrations; or commercial ventures.
Geographic Focus: California
Amount: 5,000 - 30,000 USD
Samples: Community Action Board of Santa Cruz County, Santa Cruz, California, $10,000 - to support the REAL for Diabetes Prevention project (2010); Ecology Action, Willits, California, $9,000 - to support the Boltage program, a daily student biking and walking tracking program (2010); Mesa Verde Gardens, Mesa Verde, California, $15,000 - to support the start-up of a second Community Garden (2010).
Contact: Raquel Ramirez Ruiz, Director of Programs; (831) 763-6456 or (831) 761-5639; (831) 763-6084; info@pvhealthtrust.org or raquel_dhc@pvhealthtrust.org
Internet: http://www.pvhealthtrust.org/grants_core.html
Sponsor: Pajaro Valley Community Health Trust
85 Nielson Street
Watsonville, CA 95076

Pajaro Valley Community Health Trust Oral Health: Prevention & Access Grants 1341

The Trust provides grants for projects that advance our mission to improve the health and quality of life for all people of the greater Pajaro Valley. The primary goals of the Oral Health Initiative are to reduce the risk factors associated with oral health disease, increase the number of Pajaro Valley residents with ready access to comprehensive dental care, and decrease the prevalence of dental disease among residents of the Pajaro Valley. The Trust's goals include improving access to dental treatment and preventing dental disease. Through this initiative, the Trust will look at systematic issues facing oral health care, particularly in the areas of prevention and access to care, and work with others in the community to remove these barriers.
Requirements: Applicant organizations must provide or plan to provide programs/services benefiting the health of residents in the Trust's primary geographic service area. Communities within this service area include Watsonville, Pajaro, Freedom, and Aromas. The home office of the applicant organization need not be located in the Pajaro Valley, but the applicant organization must demonstrate that it provides or plans to provide services that directly benefit residents of the Pajaro Valley. The applicant organization must be a nonprofit, 501(c)3 tax-exempt organization; a school-based health program; or have a 501(c)3, tax-exempt organization as a fiscal sponsor.
Restrictions: In general, the Trust's Board of Directors prefers not to fund programs or projects administered by a city, county, state, or federal government with the exception of school-based health programs. In general, the Trust does not give grants to: projects that do not substantially benefit residents of the Pajaro Valley; projects and proposals unrelated to the Trust's mission, eligibility requirements, and current strategic plan funding priorities and objectives; individuals, with the exception of the Trust's scholarship programs; religious organizations for secular purposes; endowments, building campaigns, annual fund appeals, fundraising events, or celebrations; or commercial ventures.
Geographic Focus: California
Amount: 5,000 - 30,000 USD
Samples: Dientes Community Dental Care, Santa Cruz, California, $10,000 - to support the delivery of dental services to low-income, uninsured adults from the Pajaro Valley (2010); Salud Para La Gente, Watsonville, California, $10,000 - to support the delivery of dental services to low-income, uninsured adults from the Pajaro Valley (2010).
Contact: Raquel Ramirez Ruiz, Director of Programs; (831) 763-6456 or (831) 761-5639; (831) 763-6084; info@pvhealthtrust.org or raquel_dhc@pvhealthtrust.org
Internet: http://www.pvhealthtrust.org/grants_core.html
Sponsor: Pajaro Valley Community Health Trust
85 Nielson Street
Watsonville, CA 95076

Palmer Foundation Grants 1342

The foundation considers proposals that empower young people ages 0 to 25. General categories include arts and culture, education, health, and human services. In making awards, the foundation places the highest priority on applications that demonstrate a level of cooperation with other organizations, including leveraging financial and in-kind support from other groups; clearly avoids duplication of existing services; where applicable, demonstrates potential for continued funding from internal or other sources after the grant period; and offer challenge grants in order to stimulate support of the project by other organizations or individuals. The board will review Letters of Intent each month through the listed deadlines; full proposals are by invitation. Letters of intent may be submitted online. Guidelines are available online.
Requirements: 501(c)3 tax-exempt organizations are eligible. The foundation's geographical region is usually limited to the Mid West states, the Mid Atlantic states. Guatemala, and El Salvador.
Restrictions: The foundation does not usually support the following types of activities: grants to individuals or scholarships; endowment drives or capital campaigns; general operating expenses for an existing project, except to support an innovative program during the initial years of operation; grants for political activities, sectarian religious purposes, or individual medical or scientific research projects; or repeated funding to the same program or organization for the same purposes on an annual or ongoing basis.
Geographic Focus: All U.S. States
Date(s) Application is Due: Jan 31; Jul 31
Samples: Arlington Alexandria Coalition for the Homeless (VA)—$3000; Elca Urban Outreach Ctr (Kenosha, WI)—$12,000; Coastal Hospice (Salisbury, MD)—$15,000.
Contact: Diane Pavela, (262) 842-0079; (262) 842-0069; thepalmerfoundation@mcleodusa.net
Internet: http://www.thepalmerfoundation.org
Sponsor: Palmer Foundation
1025 56th Street
Kenosha, WI 53140

Parker Foundation Grants 1343

Grants are given to nonprofit organizations operating in San Diego County, CA, for purposes leading to the betterment of all aspects of life of the people of the county. Grants may be in support of adult and youth services, performing and visual arts, museums and zoos, AIDS, education, and community activities. Types of support include seed money, matching funds, operating grants, annual campaigns, emergency funds, building construction/renovation, equipment acquisition, land acquisition, research, program-

related investments, continuing support, special projects, and publications. Applications in writing are accepted at any time.
Requirements: 501(c)3 San Diego County, CA, nonprofit organizations are eligible.
Restrictions: Grants are not made to individuals nor is grant support given to religious organizations for denominational programs.
Geographic Focus: California
Amount: 5,000 - 50,000 USD
Samples: Neurosciences Institute (La Jolla, CA)—for its campaign for endowment and research operations, $50,000.
Contact: Program Contact; (858) 677-1431; (858) 677-1477
Internet: http://www.TheParkerFoundation.org
Sponsor: Parker Foundation
4365 Executive Drive, Suite 1100
San Diego, CA 92121-2133

Park Foundation Grants 1344

The foundation awards grants to nonprofit organizations in central New York and areas in the U.S. Southeast. Areas of interest include education and higher education, animal welfare, environment, television, and general charitable giving. Types of support include general operating support, program development, professorships, seed money, fellowships, scholarship funds, research grants, and matching funds. There are no application deadlines. The board meets in March, June, August, October, and December. Obtain application forms.
Requirements: 501(c)3 nonprofits in he eastern U.S. , primarily in central NY, Washington, DC, and North Carolina are eligible.
Restrictions: For-profit organizations and individuals are not eligible.
Geographic Focus: All U.S. States
Amount: 5,000 - 100,000 USD
Samples: North Carolina State University (Raleigh, NC)—for Park Scholarships, $647,710; Beach Preservation Assoc of Pine Knoll Shores (Atlantic Beach, NC)—for general operating support, $150,000; North Carolina State U (Raleigh, NC)—for the Park Scholarship program, $226,018.
Contact: Linda Madeo, Executive Director; (607) 272-9124; (607) 272-6057
Sponsor: Park Foundation
P.O. Box 550
Ithaca, NY 14851

Partnership Enhancement Program (PEP) Grants 1345

The mission of the National Tree Trust continues through the Arbor Day Foundation, a nonprofit, environmental education organization with a mission of inspiring people to plant, nurture, and celebrate trees. The Partnership Enhancement Program (PEP) makes dollar-for-dollar matching monetary grants to qualifying nonprofits involved in a wide range of tree-related projects. Grants are made in four categories: tree planting and maintenance; education and training; overhead and administration; and national and regional programs. Applications for projects usually become available in June.
Requirements: To be eligible, the applying organization must: be a currently certified 501(c)3 nonprofit organization located within the United States; have been in existence for a minimum of two years; demonstrate that tree planting, maintenance, and education are components of the organization; and be volunteer based.
Geographic Focus: All U.S. States
Amount: Up to 25,000 USD
Contact: Mark Derowitsch, Public Relations Manager; (888) 448-7337; mderowitsch@arborday.org
Internet: http://www.arborday.org/generalinfo/
Sponsor: Arbor Day Foundation
100 Arbor Avenue
Nebraska City, NE 68410

Patricia Price Peterson Foundation Grants 1346

Established in 1964, the foundation awards grants to eligible California 501(c)3 nonprofit organizations and Central American countries in its areas of interest, including environmental protection and conservation (including agricultural university scholarships, orphanages, environmental education, community development, and nature reserve-conservation), science education, and federated giving. Types of support include program grants and general operating grants. Funding can be used for emergency programs, equipment, general operations, land acquisition, management development, capacity building, professorships, program development, scholarship funds, or seed money. The application deadline is in early May; call for the specific date. the applicant's initial approach should be via email, followed by the submission of a written application. Final proposals should be submitted in Spanish.
Requirements: California nonprofit organizations serving the San Francisco Bay area or Central American organizations are eligible to apply.
Geographic Focus: California, Belize, Costa Rica, Cuba, El Salvador, Guatemala, Honduras, Jamaica, Mexico, Nicaragua, Panama
Contact: Stephen W. Bennett, President; (831) 684-0958; (415) 622-5388; epeterson@aureos.co.cr or neyastv@aol.com
Sponsor: Patricia Price Peterson Foundation
17 Aqua View Drive
Selva Beach, CA 95076-1625

Patrick and Aimee Butler Family Foundation Community Arts and Humanities Grants 1347

The Butler Family Foundation makes grants through Community Grants, the Foundation Initiative Fund, and Special Projects programs. Community Grants are competitive and primarily support the Twin Cities metropolitan area of Street Paul and Minneapolis. The Foundation has an interest in making the arts and cultural programs accessible to all communities in the Twin Cities region. Funding will be granted to organizations that emphasize artistic quality, reflect the diversity of the community, and demonstrate stable programming, within the following areas: Historical Societies, primarily in Ramsey County, Minnesota; Humanities programs or organizations; Museums, and Music Education. The Foundation is most likely to make general operating or program support grants.
Requirements: Minnesota 501(c)3 nonprofits are eligible to apply.
Restrictions: The Butler Family Foundation does not make grants to organizations through fiscal agents. The Foundation does not make loans or grants to individuals. No grants are made outside of the United States. The Foundation does not fund criminal justice, economic development or education, work or vocational programs, films or videos, health care, hospitals, medical research, elementary or secondary education, and music or dance.
Geographic Focus: Minnesota
Date(s) Application is Due: Feb 7; Jun 6
Amount: 5,000 - 30,000 USD
Contact: Kerrie Blevins, Foundation Director; (651) 222-2565; (651) 222-2566; kerrieb@butlerfamilyfoundation.org
Internet: http://www.butlerfamilyfoundation.org/guidelines2011.html
Sponsor: Patrick and Aimee Butler Family Foundation
332 Minnesota Street, Suite E-1420
Saint Paul, MN 55101-1369

Patrick and Aimee Butler Family Foundation Community Environment Grants 1348

The Butler Family Foundation makes grants through Community Grants, the Foundation Initiative Fund, and Special Projects programs. Community Grants are competitive and primarily support the entire State of Minnesota. The Foundation seeks to preserve and promote stewardship of the natural environment for present and future generations. Funding will be granted to programs that positively impact environmental quality and encourage citizen participation in environmental issues. Granting will be limited to organizations and programs operating in Minnesota, whose primary mission is to address one of these issues: Water Quality of the Upper Mississippi Watershed; Environmental Education (with a preference for programs providing in-depth learning experiences); Land Preservation and Use. The Foundation is most likely to make general operating or program support grants.
Requirements: Minnesota 501(c)3 nonprofits are eligible to apply.
Restrictions: The Butler Family Foundation does not make grants to organizations through fiscal agents. The Foundation does not make loans or grants to individuals. No grants are made outside of the United States. The Foundation does not fund criminal justice, economic development or education, work or vocational programs, films or videos, health care, hospitals, medical research, elementary or secondary education, and music or dance.
Geographic Focus: Minnesota
Date(s) Application is Due: Feb 7; Jun 6
Amount: 5,000 - 30,000 USD
Contact: Kerrie Blevins, Foundation Director; (651) 222-2565; (651) 222-2566; kerrieb@butlerfamilyfoundation.org
Internet: http://www.butlerfamilyfoundation.org/guidelines2011.html
Sponsor: Patrick and Aimee Butler Family Foundation
332 Minnesota Street, Suite E-1420
Saint Paul, MN 55101-1369

Patrick and Aimee Butler Family Foundation Community Human Services Grants 1349

The Butler Family Foundation makes grants through Community Grants, the Foundation Initiative Fund, and Special Projects programs. Community Grants are competitive and primarily support the Twin Cities metropolitan area of Street Paul and Minneapolis. The Foundation has a special concern for the condition of women and children in society, particularly those living in poverty. The Foundation seeks to foster a supportive environment for all families to ensure children's healthy development. Priority will be given to enhance the ability of individuals and families to break dependencies and achieve self-reliance in the following areas: Abuse - including domestic and family violence, pornography, and prostitution; Chemical dependency; Affordable housing - including housing and services for homeless youth; Children and Families - with an emphasis on early childhood development and parenting education. Strategies that offer both practical help to those in need and advocate for systems change will be favored. The Foundation is most likely to make general operating or program support grants.
Requirements: Minnesota 501(c)3 nonprofits are eligible to apply.
Restrictions: The Butler Family Foundation does not make grants to organizations through fiscal agents. The Foundation does not make loans or grants to individuals. No grants are made outside of the United States. The Foundation does not fund criminal justice, economic development or education, work or vocational programs, films or videos, health care, hospitals, medical research, elementary or secondary education, and music or dance.
Geographic Focus: Minnesota
Date(s) Application is Due: Feb 7; Jun 6
Amount: 5,000 - 30,000 USD
Contact: Kerrie Blevins, Foundation Director; (651) 222-2565; (651) 222-2566; kerrieb@butlerfamilyfoundation.org
Internet: http://www.butlerfamilyfoundation.org/guidelines2011.html
Sponsor: Patrick and Aimee Butler Family Foundation
332 Minnesota Street, Suite E-1420
Saint Paul, MN 55101-1369

Patrick and Aimee Butler Family Foundation Community Philanthropy & the Non-Profit Management Grants 1350

The Butler Family Foundation makes grants through Community Grants, the Foundation Initiative Fund, and Special Projects programs. Community Grants are competitive and primarily support the Twin Cities metropolitan area of Street Paul and Minneapolis. Through its Philanthropy and Non-Profit Management program, the Foundation seeks to foster a vital non-profit sector by supporting regranting through community funds committed to social change; and by supporting intermediary organizations that enhance the management capacity of non-profit organizations. The Foundation is most likely to make general operating or program support grants.
Requirements: Minnesota 501(c)3 nonprofits are eligible to apply.
Restrictions: The Butler Family Foundation does not make grants to organizations through fiscal agents. The Foundation does not make loans or grants to individuals. No grants are made outside of the United States. The Foundation does not fund criminal justice, economic development or education, work or vocational programs, films or videos, health care, hospitals, medical research, elementary or secondary education, and music or dance.
Geographic Focus: Minnesota
Date(s) Application is Due: Feb 7; Jun 6
Amount: 5,000 - 30,000 USD
Contact: Kerrie Blevins, Foundation Director; (651) 222-2565; (651) 222-2566; kerrieb@butlerfamilyfoundation.org
Internet: http://www.butlerfamilyfoundation.org/guidelines2011.html
Sponsor: Patrick and Aimee Butler Family Foundation
332 Minnesota Street, Suite E-1420
Saint Paul, MN 55101-1369

Patrick and Anna M. Cudahy Fund Grants 1351

The Patrick and Anna Cudahy Fund is a general purpose foundation which primarily supports organizations in Wisconsin and the metropolitan Chicago area. The principal areas of interest are social service, youth, and education with some giving for the arts, and other areas. Some support is also given for local and national programs concerned with public interest and environmental issues. A few grants are given for international programs but only to those which are represented by a United States based organization.
Requirements: Nonprofits organizations in Wisconsin and the metropolitan Chicago area are eligible. See Foundations website for additional guidelines and application form: http://www.cudahyfund.org/Guideliines.htm
Restrictions: Organizations may submit only one proposal during any calendar year. Requests are not considered for: organizations and projects primarily serving a local constituency outside of Wisconsin and the Chicago metropolitan area; organizations outside the United States who are not represented by a United States based 501 [c]3 organization; grants to individuals; loans or endowments.
Geographic Focus: Illinois, Wisconsin
Date(s) Application is Due: Jan 5; Apr 5; Jul 5; Oct 5
Amount: 5,000 - 25,000 USD
Samples: Angel of Hope Clinic, Milwaukee, WI, $10,000 - Angel of Hope Clinic (2008); DePaul University College of Law Chicago,IL, $22,000 - Summer Programs (2008); Helen Bader Institute, Milwaukee, WI, $10,000 - Scholarships (2008)
Contact: Janet S. Cudahy, President; (847) 866-0760; (847) 475-0679
Internet: http://www.cudahyfund.org/Guideliines.htm
Sponsor: 1609 Sherman Avenue, #207
Evanston, IL 60201

Paul and Edith Babson Foundation Grants 1352

The foundation supports nonprofit organizations in the greater Boston area with few continuing exceptions by awarding grants for unrestricted purposes, special programs, capital support, and endowment. The foundation's areas of interest include culture—historic preservation, libraries, museums, and music; education—higher education, private secondary education, and scholarship funds (no individual scholarships); environment—conservation/protection of natural resources; health—community-based health care, family services, and hospitals; social services—counseling, federated drives, and youth recreation and fitness; and entrepreneurship and economic development. An exploratory telephone call is recommended.
Requirements: IRS 501(c)3 tax-exempt organizations in Massachusetts are eligible.
Restrictions: Films, videos, conferences, and fund-raising events will not be supported.
Geographic Focus: Massachusetts
Date(s) Application is Due: Feb 6; Sep 9
Amount: 2,500 - 25,000 USD
Contact: Elizabeth Nichols, Grants Administrator; (617) 523-8368; (617) 523-8949; pebabsonfdn@babsonfoundations.org
Internet: http://www.babsonfoundations.org/P_Eguidelines.html
Sponsor: Paul and Edith Babson Foundation
50 Congress Street
Boston, MA 02109-4017

Paul and Mary Haas Foundation Contributions and Student Scholarships 1353

Grants are given to tax-exempt organizations in six areas: civic and charitable, education (including adult basic education, adult/family literacy training, curriculum development, and vocational programs), health, religion, the arts, and college scholarships. Funding is generally seed money for innovative services in the Corpus Christi, TX, area. Creative, innovative, and exploratory projects are encouraged, with less interest in building projects and areas covered by normal budgets. Additional types of support include general operating support, equipment acquisition, program development, conferences and seminars, and scholarship funds and scholarships to individuals. Requests for support are normally reviewed on a year-round basis in the order in which they are received. All grants are made for one year and are not automatically renewed. Applications for scholarships are due in August at the beginning of senior high school year; application for other grants are accepted at any time.
Requirements: Grants are made to Texas organizations with 501(c)3 status. Initial inquiries should be made in the form of a one- to two-page written proposal.
Geographic Focus: Texas
Amount: 35 - 250,000 USD
Samples: Corpus Christi Neighborhood Ctrs (TX)—for general operating support, $5000.
Contact: Karen Wesson, Administrative Director; (361) 887-6955; (361) 883-5992; haasfdn@aol.com
Sponsor: Paul and Mary Haas Foundation
P.O. Box 2928
Corpus Christi, TX 78403

Paul E. and Klare N. Reinhold Foundation Grants 1354

The foundation makes grants in Clay County, Florida, for projects in health, religion, children and youth, music appreciation and education, art appreciation and education, and public improvement. Types of support include building construction/renovation, capital campaigns, emergency funds, equipment, land acquisition, matching/challenge grants, operating grants, and seed money grants. Details are available on the website.

Requirements: 501(c)3 tax-exempt organizations in Florida's Clay County are eligible.

Restrictions: Grants do not support advertising for fund-raising campaigns, tickets, debt reduction, endowments, attempts to influence legislation, or basic operating costs.

Geographic Focus: Florida

Amount: Up to 10,000 USD

Samples: Clay County Habitat For Humanity, Inc (FL)—to supplement a Capacity Building Grant to help pay the Executive Director's salary, $20,000; Alzheimer's Assoc (FL)—to support Caregiver Education By enhancing the resource library, $3000; Christ Episcopal Church Building Fund (FL)—dedication of family/gathering room in honor of Thomas E. Camp, III, $50,000; Keystone Heights Elementary School (FL)—for additional supplies for Project Playground, $500.

Contact: Program Contact; (904) 269-5857; (904) 269-8382; lhoke@reinhold.net

Internet: http://www.reinhold.org/html/guidelines.htm

Sponsor: Paul E. and Klare N. Reinhold Foundation
1845 Town Center Boulevard, Suite 105
Orange Park, FL 32003

Paul Rapoport Foundation Grants 1355

The Paul Rapoport Foundation was established in 1987 with funds from the estate of Paul Rapoport, a founder of both New York City's LGBT Community Services Center and GMHC. For its final years of grantmaking the Foundation's focus will be on three populations of low or no income: transgender communities of color; LGTBQ youth of color, ages 24 and under; and LGTB seniors of color aged 60 and over. The Foundation will also consider funding programs of organizations not focused exclusively on the LGTB community if the number of LGTBQ clients of color served by the program is at least 50%. The foundation awards grants to nonprofits in the metropolitan area of New York, New York. Types of support include general operating support, continuing support, building construction and renovation, program development, conferences and seminars, publications, seed money, technical assistance, and matching funds. There are no application forms. The board meets in February, June, and October to consider requests. Grants of $50,000 and higher, per year are awarded.

Requirements: The Foundation funds only non-profit, charitable organizations as defined by the Internal Revenue Service Code Section 509(a). The Foundation funds primarily within the five boroughs of New York City, as well as on Long Island, in Westchester and nearby New Jersey. It will only fund national organizations when they request funding for programs specific to the New York metropolitan area.

Restrictions: The Foundation will no longer support start-up organizations. The Foundation does not support medical research, cultural and artistic activities, major building campaigns, endowments, grants or scholar-ships to individuals or to other foundations. The Foundation does not make grants for purposes of influencing elections or legislation, or for any other activity that may jeopardize the Foundation's tax-exempt status.

Geographic Focus: New York

Date(s) Application is Due: Feb 1; Jun 1; Oct 1

Samples: Ali Forney Center (AFC), New York, New York, $150,000 (1st year of 3-year grant totaling $450,000) - creation of an In-house Development Department (2011); Friends of Green Chimneys, New York, New York, $230,000 (1st year of 4-year grant totaling $665,000) - (a) Career Development Program for LGTB Foster Care and Runaway and Homeless Youth, (b) Infrastructure Development for NYC Division of Green Chimneys, (c) Engineering Study of Basement of Gramercy Building (2011).

Contact: Jane D. Schwartz, Executive Director; (212) 888-6578; (212) 980-0867; Ona M. Winet, Program Director; (212) 888-6578; (212) 980-0867

Internet: http://www.paulrapoportfoundation.org/guide.html

Sponsor: Paul Rapoport Foundation
220 E 60th Street, Suite 3H
New York, NY 10022

PDF Community Organizing Grants 1356

Peace Development Fund awards Community Organizing Grants to any organization in the United States, Haiti and/or Mexico that fit into PDF's guidelines. Specifically, this award sponsors organizations that focus on social justice, organizing to shift powers, working to build a movement, dismantling oppression, and creating new structures in these geographical areas.

Requirements: Applications are available at PDF's website and must be emailed to grants@peacefund.org by 5:00 pm Pacific Standard Time on the due date. This grant is highly competitive and the Fund will only award grants to organizations that align with PDF's guidelines.

Restrictions: PDF will not fund programs outside the U.S., Mexico or Haiti unless specified for a special initiative or Donor Advised fund. Also, PDF will not fund: individuals and/or organizations with strong leadership from only one person; conferences and other one-time events; audio-visual productions and distribution, including TV, radio, publications, films, etc; research that is NOT directly linked to an organizing strategy; academic institutions or scholarships; other grant-making organizations; or organizations with large budgets ($300,000 or more) or who have access to other sources of funding.

Geographic Focus: All U.S. States, Puerto Rico, Haiti, Mexico, Virgin Islands (U.S.)

Date(s) Application is Due: May 20

Amount: 2,000 - 5,000 USD

Samples: Ignite, San Francisco, California, $4,142 - develop semester-long curriculum in public high schools and non-profits that provide exposure to local political role models, policy experience, civic education and leadership opportunities (2011).

Contact: Kazu Haga, Program Coordinator; (415) 642-0900 or (415) 205-6776; (415) 642-8200; kazu@peacefund.org or grants@peacefund.org

Internet: http://www.peacedevelopmentfund.org/page/commorg

Sponsor: Peace Development Fund
44 N Prospect Street, P.O. Box 1280
Amherst, MA 01004

Peacock Foundation Grants 1357

Established by Henry B. Peacock, Jr. in 1947, the mission of Peacock Foundation, Inc. is to enhance and promote the good health and well being of children, families, and underprivileged persons in Southeast Florida, through contributions, gifts, and grants to eligible nonprofit organizations. The priorities of Peacock Foundation, Inc. include: making grants to human services providers that promote youth development, assist abused or neglected children, women, and the elderly, and seek to reduce abuse, prevent homelessness, and end hunger in our community; supporting educational programs in the arts and the environment, as well as special education for disabled persons; contributing to medical research, health care organizations, and hospitals.

Requirements: All applicants must be IRS recognized 501(c)3 public charities classified as not a private foundation, registered with the Department of Agriculture to solicit funds in Florida, when applicable, and located in and/or of significant benefit to residents to the Southeast Florida counties of Miami-Dade, Broward, or Monroe. In order for a proposal to be considered for funding, the applicant first must send a brief letter of inquiry. See Foundations website for letter of inquiry guidelines: http://www.peacockfoundationinc.org/review_progress.html.

Restrictions: Peacock Foundation, Inc. does not fund: capital campaigns, construction, or renovation projects; deficit financing or debt reduction; conferences or festivals; fundraising events or advertising; special events or athletic events; individuals; lobbying to influence legislation; religious organizations, unless engaged in a significant project benefiting the entire community.

Geographic Focus: Florida

Contact: Joelle Allen, Executive Director; (305) 373-1386

Internet: http://www.peacockfoundationinc.org/eligibility.html

Sponsor: Peacock Foundation
100 SE Second Street, Suite 2370
Miami, FL 33131

Pentair Foundation Education and Community Grants 1358

The Pentair Foundation focuses awards in two focus areas: education and community projects. Educational projects should focus on: supporting science and math education; providing "school-to-work" initiatives that prepare a student for the professional world; projects that offer alternative education; and programs that support art education. Community programs should focus on: water quality education, conservation and action; assistance to individuals in achieving self-sufficiency; entrepreneurial opportunities; opportunities for youth to gain life skills; services for youth in crisis; access to health care services;

and assistance, education and rehabilitation services for those suffering from mental and/or physical disabilities and life-threatening illness.
Requirements: Nonprofit organizations, including schools and school districts, in communities where Pentair has a presence may apply. Application must be completed online and is located at the Foundation's website.
Restrictions: The foundation does not support individuals; political, lobbying, or fraternal activities; religious groups for religious purposes; medical research by individuals; scholarships to individuals; fundraising events, sponsorships, or advertising support; travel or tour expenses; conferences, seminars, workshops, or symposiums; athletic or sports-related organizations; non 501(c)3 organizations or those operating under a fiscal agent.
Geographic Focus: Wisconsin
Date(s) Application is Due: Mar 1; Jun 1; Oct 1
Amount: 2,000 - 50,000 USD
Samples: Casa Pacifica Centers for Children and Families, Camarillo, California, $15,654- project support (2008); Center for Excellence in Education, McLean, Virginia, $2,268- general operating support (2008)
Contact: Susan Carter, Grants Administrator; (763) 656-5237; susan.carter@pentair.com
Internet: http://www.pentair.com/About_pentair_foundation.aspx
Sponsor: Pentair Foundation
5500 Wayzata Boulevard, Suite 800
Minneapolis, MN 55416

Percy B. Ferebee Endowment Grants **1359**

Grants from the Percy B. Ferebee Endowment are awarded to support charitable, scientific and literary projects, and in particular, governmental and civic projects designed to further the cultural, social, economic and physical well-being of residents of Cherokee, Clay, Graham, Jackson, Macon and Swain Counties of North Carolina and the Cherokee Indian Reservation. Grants are also awarded in the form of scholarships to assist worthy and talented young men and women who reside in said counties in pursuing their college/university degree education within the state of North Carolina. The deadline for the submission of a grant application is September 30. The deadline for scholarship applications is January 31. Application forms are available online. Applicants will receive notice acknowledging receipt of the grant request, and subsequently be notified of the grant declination or approval.
Requirements: 501(c)3 non-profits in the Cherokee, Clay, Graham, Jackson, Macon and Swain Counties of North Carolina are eligible to apply for grants. Proposals should be submitted in the following format: completed Common Grant Application Form; an original Proposal Statement; an audited financial report and a current year operating budget; a copy of your official IRS Letter with your tax determination; a listing of your Board of Directors. Proposal Statements (second item in the above Format) should answer these questions: what are the objectives and expected outcomes of this program/project/request; what strategies will be used to accomplish your objective; what is the timeline for completion; if this is part of an on-going program, how long has it been in operation; what criteria will you use to measure success; if the request is not fully funded, what other sources can you engage; an Itemized budget should be included; please describe any collaborative ventures. Prior to the distribution of funds, all approved grantees must sign and return a Grant Agreement Form, stating that the funds will be used for the purpose intended. Progress reports and Completion reports must also be filed as required for your specific grant. All current grantees must be in good standing with required documentation prior to submitting new proposals to any foundation. Scholarship recipients must be a resident of these areas and must attend a college or university in the state of North Carolina. Contact the Foundation for additional application requirements.
Restrictions: Grants are not made for political purposes, nor to organizations which discriminate on the basis of race, ethnic origin, sexual or religious preference, age or gender.
Geographic Focus: North Carolina
Date(s) Application is Due: Jan 31; Sep 30
Amount: 3,000 - 15,000 USD
Samples: Nantahala Regional Library, $15,000—general operating support; Macon County Historical Society, $7,500—general operating expenses; Reach, Inc. Resources Education Assistance Counseling & Housing, $4,000—general operating support.
Contact: Wachovia Bank, N.A., Trustee; grantinquiries6@wachovia.com
Internet: https://www.wachovia.com/foundation/v/index.jsp?vgnextoid=5d6852199c0aa110VgnVCM1000004b0d1872RCRD&vgnextfmt=default
Sponsor: Percy B. Ferebee Endowment
Wachovia Bank, NC6732, 100 North Main Street
Winston Salem, NC 27150

Perl 6 Microgrants **1360**

The program was established by a donation from Best Practical Solutions to help support Perl 6 development. Grants of $500 will be awarded to a range of Perl 6-related projects over the life of the grant program. Proposals will be accepted on a rolling schedule.
Requirements: Accepted grants might be for coding, documentation, testing or even writing articles about Perl 6. The program isn't tied to any one implementation of Perl 6 — they are interested in seeing proposals related to Pugs, Perl 6 on Parrot, Perl 6 on Perl 5 or any other Perl 6 implementation, and in general, projects that can be completed in 4-6 calendar weeks. To submit a grant proposal, send an email to perl6- microgrants@perl.org with the following information: a) A two to three paragraph summary of the work you intend to do; b) A quick bio; c) A brief description of what 'success' will mean for your project (How will we know you're done?); d) Where (if anywhere) you've discussed your project in the past; e) Where you'll be blogging about your progress. (Twice-weekly blog posts are a requirement for getting your grant money.)
Geographic Focus: All U.S. States
Amount: 500 USD
Contact: Jesse Vincent, Grant Manager; jesse@bestpractical.com
Internet: http://www.perlfoundation.org/patrick_michaud_awarded_perl_6_development_grant_as_a_joint_initiative_by_the_perl_foundation_and_mozilla_foundation
Sponsor: Perl Foundation
6832 Mulderstraat
Grand Ledge, MI 48837

Perl Foundation Grants **1361**

The Perl Foundation (TPF) is dedicated to the advancement of the Perl programming language through open discussion, collaboration, design, and code.
Requirements: Projects do not have to be large, complex, or lengthy. If you have a good idea and the means and ability to accomplish it, the project will be considered. As a general rule, a properly formatted grant proposal is more likely to be approved if it meets the following criteria: it has widespread benefit to the Perl community or a large segment of it; you can convince TPF that you can accomplish your goals; and, the project can be accomplished in the published funding range ($500 - $3,000). To submit a proposal see the guidelines at http://www.perlfoundation.org/how_to_write_a_proposal and TPF rules of operation at http://www.perlfoundation.org/rules_of_operation. Then send your proposal to tpf-proposals@perl-foundation.org. Note that proposals should be properly formatted accordingly with the required P.O.D template.
Geographic Focus: All U.S. States
Date(s) Application is Due: May 31
Amount: 500 - 3,000 USD
Samples: Improving learn.perl.org, by Eric Wilhelm and Tina Connolly; Web.pm - a lightweight web framework for Perl 6, by Ilya Belikin, Carl Masak and Stephen Weeks
Contact: Richard Dice, President; rdice@perlfoundation.org
Internet: http://news.perlfoundation.org/2009/04/2009q2_call_for_grant_proposal.html
Sponsor: Perl Foundation
6832 Mulderstraat
Grand Ledge, MI 48837

Peter Kiewit Foundation General Grants **1362**

The foundation supports nonprofits and individuals in designated geographic areas for arts and cultural programs, higher and other education, health care, human services, youth services, rural development, community development, and government/public administration. In the general purpose grants program, there are no limitations on the size or duration of the grants that may be requested. Any applicant may submit a total of up to two applications, for two separate projects, in any 12 month period. All Peter Kiewit Foundation grants are awarded on a matching funds basis.
Requirements: Grant application guidelines and application forms are required to submit a funding request and these materials are available through the Foundation office only. Potential applicants should contact the Foundation to establish an organization's eligibility to apply and to discuss the proposed project. Nonprofit 501(c)3 organizations in Rancho Mirage, California; western Iowa; Nebraska; and Sheridan, Wyoming are eligible for a maximum of 50% of the total project cost. Units of government (tax supported) in Rancho Mirage, California; western Iowa; Nebraska; and Sheridan, Wyoming may apply for a maximum of 25% of the total project cost.

Restrictions: Grants are not awarded to support elementary or secondary schools, churches, or religious groups. Grants are not awarded to individuals (except for scholarships), or for endowment funds or annual campaigns.
Geographic Focus: California, Iowa, Nebraska, Wyoming
Date(s) Application is Due: Jan 15; Apr 15; Jul 15; Oct 15
Amount: 10,000 - 500,000 USD
Samples: Camp Fire U.S. A, Omaha, Nebraska, $40,000 - program support (2009); Bemis Center for Contemporary Arts, Omaha, Nebraska, $450,000 - capital improvements (2010); Fremont Opera House, Fremont, Nebraska, $75,000 - capital improvements (2010).
Contact: Lynn Wallin Ziegenbein, Executive Director; (402) 344-7890; (402) 344-8099
Internet: http://www.peterkiewitfoundation.org/page.aspx?id=13&pid=3
Sponsor: Peter Kiewit Foundation
8805 Indian Hills Drive, Suite 225
Omaha, NE 68114-4096

Peter Kiewit Foundation Small Grants **1363**

The foundation supports nonprofits and individuals in designated geographic areas for arts and cultural programs, higher and other education, health care, human services, youth services, rural development, community development, and government/public administration. The small grants program allows the Trustees to assist a large number of worthy organizations with a broad array of small projects which are limited in scope but significant for the organization. Small grants are rarely awarded to large organizations. Small grants range in size from $500 to $10,000. The Trustees created this category of grants to support small, defined projects; not to contribute small amounts to much larger budgets.
Requirements: Grant application guidelines and application forms are required to submit a funding request and these materials are available through the Foundation office only. Potential applicants should contact the Foundation to establish an organization's eligibility to apply and to discuss the proposed project. Nonprofit 501(c)3 organizations in Rancho Mirage, California; western Iowa; Nebraska; and Sheridan, Wyoming are eligible for a maximum of 50% of the total project cost. Units of government (tax supported) in Rancho Mirage, California; western Iowa; Nebraska; and Sheridan, Wyoming may apply for a maximum of 25% of the total project cost.
Restrictions: Grants are not awarded to support elementary or secondary schools, churches, or religious groups. Grants are not awarded to individuals (except for scholarships), or for endowment funds or annual campaigns.
Geographic Focus: California, Iowa, Nebraska, Wyoming
Date(s) Application is Due: Jan 15; Apr 15; Jul 15; Oct 15
Amount: 500 - 10,000 USD
Samples: Bone Creek Art Museum, David City, Nebraska, $10,000 - program support (2009); Brownsville Fine Arts Association, Brownsville, Nebraska, $5,000 - program support (2009); Joslyn Art Museum, Omaha, Nebraska, $8,500 - program support (2009).
Contact: Lynn Wallin Ziegenbein, Executive Director; (402) 344-7890; (402) 344-8099
Internet: http://www.peterkiewitfoundation.org/page.aspx?id=14&pid=3
Sponsor: Peter Kiewit Foundation
8805 Indian Hills Drive, Suite 225
Omaha, NE 68114-4096

Pew Charitable Trusts Arts and Culture Grants **1364**

The Pew Charitable Trusts supports a broad spectrum of institutions, artists, projects, and cultural marketing initiatives. The Trusts also helps cultural organizations take advantage of technical assistance and professional development opportunities, which has proven to be an effective means of extending the impact of its investments. Pew's objectives in supporting arts and culture are twofold: to nurture artistic excellence and to expand public participation. its efforts have been successful in Philadelphia, where a thriving arts environment has helped raise the city's profile on the world stage and infused new life and energy into the region.
Requirements: Grants are made only to 501(c)3 tax-exempt organizations that are not private foundations.
Restrictions: Grants are not made to individuals or for endowments, capital campaigns, unsolicited construction requests, debt reduction, or scholarships or fellowships that are not part of a program initiated by the Trusts.
Geographic Focus: All U.S. States
Contact: Susan A. Magill, Managing Director; (202) 552-2129 or (202) 552-2000; (202) 552-2299; smagill@pewtrusts.org or info@pewtrusts.com
Internet: http://www.pewtrusts.org/our_work_category.aspx?id=18
Sponsor: Pew Charitable Trusts
2005 Market Street, Suite 1700
Philadelphia, PA 19103-7077

Pew Philadelphia Cultural Leadership Program Grants **1365**

The goal of The Philadelphia Cultural Leadership Program (PCLP) is to stimulate leadership and best practices within the cultural community by providing multiyear operating support to organizations that meet high standards of programmatic, fiscal, and management performance. All PCLP grants are for three years, and the use of the funds is unrestricted. Guidelines for renewing organizations and for new applicants are available online. Deadlines are September 6 for renewing organizations and September 27 for new applicants.
Requirements: 501(c)3 nonprofits operating in Bucks, Chester, Delaware, Montgomery, or Philadelphia Counties; have a minimum of $150,000 of annual operating revenue as evidenced by the organization's most recent audit; possess a board-approved strategic plan that extends through the proposed three-year grant period that is in active use by board, staff, and volunteers; be professionally managed with at least one full-time, paid professional staff member; provide programming that is available to the general public; attract a substantial local constituency; and show no working capital deficit in the most recent audited fiscal year.
Restrictions: Requests will not be considered for endowments; debt reduction; support for general operations or core programs of organizations outside the Philadelphia five-county area; museum, collection or library acquisitions; computer or multimedia hardware or software, except as part of trusts-initiated programs; grants made directly to individual artists, except as part of trusts-initiated programs; individual commissions, exhibitions, performing arts productions, or television or radio broadcasts, except as part of trusts-initiated programs; cultural exchange activities, except as part of trusts-initiated programs; arts education projects, except as part of the Philadelphia Cultural Leadership Program or other artistic initiatives; conferences or symposia, except as part of trusts-initiated programs; media and technology projects, except those that forward specific culture program interests and priorities; and programs originating outside the United States of America.
Geographic Focus: All U.S. States
Samples: Greater Philadelphia Cultural Alliance (PA)—for marketing efforts associated with its Campaign for Culture, including an online events calendar and an email program that offers half-price tickets, $2 million over three years; U of Pennsylvania, Museum of Anthropology and Archaeology (PA)—for general operating support, $608,000 over three years; U of Pennsylvania, Morris Arboretum (PA)—for general operating support, $284,000 over three years.
Contact: Marian Godfrey, Culture Program Director; (215) 575-4870; (215) 575-4939; culturemail@pewtrusts.org
Internet: http://www.pewtrusts.com/grants/index.cfm
Sponsor: Pew Charitable Trusts
2005 Market Street, Suite 1700
Philadelphia, PA 19103-7077

Pfizer Foundation Grants **1366**

The foundation's charitable giving programs provide grants through targeted initiatives focused primarily on health care and science education. Areas of interest include: global health—health literacy programs to improve the ability of low-income, low-literate populations to effectively comprehend and act on health information; HIV/AIDS—programs to provide Pfizer's antifungal medicine (Diflucan) to low-income HIV/AIDS patients in the world's least developed countries where the disease is most prevalent, the training of health-care workers in opportunistic infections related to HIV, and health-promotion programs that target those at high-risk of HIV infection living in countries where Pfizer is donating Diflucan; international trachoma initiative—programs to provide Pfizer's key antibiotic (Zithromax) to countries implementing public-health programs to combat trachoma, including community-based initiatives to provide surgery, antibiotics, promotion of clean faces, and education about the disease; disaster relief—requests for product donations following floods, earthquakes, droughts, wars, and other disasters domestically and abroad; K-12 science education—partnerships between Pfizer sites and local schools, with an emphasis on training teachers, developing curriculum, constructing science labs, and support of exhibits and educational outreach programs at science-rich institutions across the country; and community and cultural—programs in Pfizer communities, with a particular focus in the New York City for a range of organizations that address urgent community needs, seek

long-term solutions to community issues, and strengthen the cultural vitality of diverse communities.
Requirements: Nonprofit 501(c)3 organizations and schools are eligible.
Restrictions: The following types of organizations or activities are excluded from support: fundraising events or activities such as telethons, walkathons, and races; specific performances or concerts; sporting events; endowment campaigns; building fund drives and capital campaigns (except science lab renovations in partner schools and universities); film, video, television, or radio projects (except as part of a health literacy program); requests for loans or debt retirement; trips, tours, or cultural exchange programs; conferences, seminars, briefing programs, and similar activities (except in instances where the event evolves from Pfizer programs in health care and science education); organizations already supported through United Way contributions; operating expenses of United Way local agencies (except through annual United Way campaigns); grants to individuals; political causes or candidates; anti-business organizations; or organizations that practice discrimination or limit membership on the basis of race, creed, gender, age, sexual preference, or national origin.
Geographic Focus: All U.S. States
Samples: International and local relief organizations—to support relief efforts in South Asia and Africa, $25 million value in drugs and $10 million cash distributed; Western Michigan U (MI)—for unrestricted use, as part of its capital campaign, $1 million; Western Michigan U (MI)—for its life-sciences programs, $2.9 million value in scientific equipment.
Contact: Grants Administrator; (800) 733-4717 or (212) 573-2323
Internet: http://www.pfizer.com/subsites/philanthropy/caring/index.html
Sponsor: Pfizer
235 E 42nd Street
New York, NY 10017-5755

Phelps County Community Foundation Grants **1367**
The Phelps County Community Foundation's grants program provides a means by which not-for-profit charitable organizations may secure financial assistance for projects and programs which will enhance the quality of life for residents of Phelps County, Nebraska. The foundation awards grants in the areas of education, culture, human services, health and recreation, and community. Priority is given to seed grants to initiate promising new projects or programs, programs representing innovative and efficient approaches to serving community needs and opportunities, challenge grants, organizations that work cooperatively with other community agencies, projects or programs where a moderate amount of grant money can effect a significant result, and projects or programs that enlist volunteer participation and citizen involvement. Types of support include general operating grants, continuing support grants, building construction/renovation, equipment acquisition, program development, publication, seed money, scholarship funds, and matching grants. Applicants must have a plan for future funding and support from other sources.
Requirements: Grants are made to 501(c)3 nonprofit organizations in Phelps County, Nebraska, and sometimes to governmental agencies for capital expenditures and/or capital improvements within Phelps County.
Restrictions: Grants are not made to individuals, to support political activities, to support operating expenses of well-established organizations or public service agencies, to establish new endowment funds, for travel or related expenses for individuals or groups, for operating support of governmental agencies, to religious groups for religious purposes, to profit-making enterprises, or to agencies serving a populace outside of Phelps County. In addition, grants are not made to support annual fund drives or to eliminate previously incurred deficits.
Geographic Focus: Nebraska
Date(s) Application is Due: Apr 1; Oct 1
Amount: Up to 25,000 USD
Samples: American Legion Baseball, Holdrege, Nebraska, $22,000 - new concession stand (2009); Bertrand Nursing Home, Bertrand, Nebraska, $7,632 - operating expenses (2009).
Contact: Vickie Klein, Executive Director; (308) 995-6847; (308) 995-2146; vlpccf@phelpsfoundation.org
Internet: http://www.phelpsfoundation.org/grants.html
Sponsor: Phelps County Community Foundation
504 4th Avenue
Holdrege, NE 68949

Philadelphia Foundation General Operating Support Grants **1368**
General Operating Support Grants are funds that are unrestricted for use by high-performing nonprofit organizations. These funds may be used for all mission-related activities, including contributions to capital campaigns and endowments. Nonprofits that meet the basic eligibility requirements are asked to complete the General Operating Support Full Application, which includes a self-selection exercise to determine the organizational life cycle stage. The Foundation does not have application deadlines and accepts General Operating Support applications at any time.
Requirements: IRS 501(c)3 organizations located in Bucks, Chester, Delaware, Montgomery, and Philadelphia Counties of Pennsylvania are eligible.
Restrictions: Grants are rarely made to affiliates of national or international organizations, government agencies, organizations not located in Southeastern Pennsylvania, organizations with budgets of more than $1.5 million, private schools, or umbrella-funding organizations.
Geographic Focus: Pennsylvania
Contact: Libby Walsh, Program Associate; (215) 563-6417; (215) 563-6882; lwalsh@philafound.org or oeapplications@philafound.org
Internet: https://www.philafound.org/ForNonprofits/DiscretionaryGrantmaking/GeneralOperatingSupport/tabid/243/Default.aspx
Sponsor: Philadelphia Foundation
1234 Market Street, Suite 1800
Philadelphia, PA 19107

Phil Hardin Foundation Grants **1369**
The foundation targets its funding to education. Specific priorities are to strengthen the capacity of communities to nurture and educate young children; the capacity of higher education institutions to renew communities and their economies; the capacity of communities for locally initiated educational improvement and economic development; and state- and local-level policy and leadership initiatives that fit with foundation goals. Types of support include general operating support, continuing support, building construction/renovation, equipment acquisition, endowment funds, program development, conferences and seminars, professorships, publication, seed grants, fellowships, scholarship funds, research, and matching funds. The foundation also operates four K-12 fellowship programs. Deadlines vary between programs; contact program staff for specific fellowship deadlines.
Requirements: Applicants must either be based in Mississippi or the project must benefit Mississippi, depending on the program.
Geographic Focus: All U.S. States
Amount: Up to 6,000,000 USD
Samples: Meridian Foundation (MS)—to endow the Riley Education and Performing Arts Center, $2.5 million.
Contact: C. Thompson Wacaster, (601) 483-4282; (601) 483-5665; info@philhardin.org
Internet: http://www.philhardin.org
Sponsor: Phil Hardin Foundation
1921 24th Avenue
Meridian, MS 39301

Phoenix Suns Charities Grants **1370**
The Phoenix Suns Charities awards general operating grants, project grants, challenge grants, and capital building grants to Arizona nonprofit organizations. Specific areas of grantmaking interest include arts and cultural programs focusing on children; education primarily focusing on pre-K-12; health care education for youth; museums and science centers and science projects for youth; and social services focusing on children and family issues. Recipients of the Playmaker Award may use funds for building projects.
Requirements: Arizona 501(c)3 organizations, primarily in Maricopa County, may submit grant requests.
Geographic Focus: Arizona
Date(s) Application is Due: Apr 30
Amount: 1,000 - 10,000 USD
Samples: To be distributed among 87 nonprofit groups in Arizona (AZ)—to provide services to children in the areas of the arts, athletics, education, health and human services, and recreation, $468,050.
Contact: Thomas Ambrose, Executive Director; (602) 379-7767; (602) 530-2251
Internet: http://www.nba.com/suns/news/charities_index.html
Sponsor: Phoenix Suns
201 E Jefferson
Phoenix, AZ 85004

Phoenixville Community Health Foundation Grants **1371**

The foundation operates in Pennsylvania and seeks to become the champion of community health. Categories of funding include personal health, including physical/behavioral health of children, youth, adults, senior citizens, and those at risk for abuse, neglect, or violence; and community health, including environmental and civic health of the community-at-large and the promotion of educational opportunities for individuals aspiring to be in the health field. Requests must demonstrate that the program/organization is addressing a community need and not duplicating existing efforts. Types of support include program support, general operations, capital projects, and equipment acquisition. Both single- and multiyear initiatives are considered. Applicants should discuss their funding interest with foundation staff; a grant request packet will be given if the proposed initiative fits within foundation guidelines. The board meets bimonthly.

Requirements: Pennsylvania 501(c)3 tax-exempt organizations serving Chester and Montgomery Counties are eligible.

Restrictions: Grants are not awarded for direct scholarship support to individuals; purchases of tickets or advertising for benefit purposes; coverage of continuing operating deficits; document publication; pass-through grant support through a third party (except United Way); and fraternal organizations, political parties or candidates, veterans, labor or local civic groups, or groups engaged in influencing legislation.

Geographic Focus: Pennsylvania

Samples: Montgomery County Dept of Economic and Workforce Development (Norristown, PA)—to expand its CareerLink Employment Program to the Phoenixville Library, $30,800; Chester County Futures (West Chester, PA)—to establish a mentor program to help at-risk youths with the potential to attend college, $15,000; Phoenixville Area Police Athletic League (PA)—for program support, $10,000; Phoenixville Area Economic Development Corp (PA)—for general operating support, $35,000.

Contact: Carol Poinier, Grants, Operations Manager; (610) 917-9890; (610) 917-9861; pchf1@juno.com

Internet: http://www.pchf1.org/gmakeover.html

Sponsor: Phoenixville Community Health Foundation
1260 Valley Forge Road, Suite 102
Phoenixville, PA 19460

Piedmont Health Care Foundation Grants **1372**

The health care foundation serves South Carolinians in Piedmont and Greenville and awards general operating grants to local nonprofit organizations to support activities and programs in the areas of health education and research, health care, and community development.

Requirements: South Carolina nonprofit organizations may apply.

Geographic Focus: South Carolina

Date(s) Application is Due: Aug 15

Amount: 2,000 - 100,000 USD

Contact: J.P. Southerland, Executive Director; (864) 370-0212; (864) 370-0212; jsouther@bellsouth.net

Sponsor: Piedmont Health Care Foundation
P.O. Box 9303
Greenville, SC 29604

Piedmont Natural Gas Foundation Health and Human Services Grants **1373**

Piedmont Natural Gas Foundation's Health and Human Services grant focuses funding toward: organizations providing outreach services to community members with basic needs, including shelter, food and clothing; substance abuse or mental illness; organizations providing services or programs for a range of human service needs including youth engagement and mentoring, special needs and disability assistance, substance abuse or mental illnesses, transitional housing and situational homelessness support, and gang violence prevention; organizations providing emergency/disaster relief; increased access to critical healthcare services and comprehensive medical treatment including preventative care, prescription medication, medical exams, screenings, immunizations and dental care; and increased access to mental health services.

Requirements: Organizations must be a 501(c)3 non-profit organization or a qualified government entity. All grant requests must be submitted through Piedmont's online grant application form located at Piedmont's website.

Restrictions: Piedmont Natural Gas Foundation will not fund: religious, fraternal, political or athletic groups; four-year colleges and universities; private foundations; or social or veterans' organizations. In addition to these restrictions, contributions will generally not be made to or for: individuals; pre-college level private schools, except through the Employee Matching Gifts program; travel and conferences; third-party professional fundraising organizations; controversial social causes; religious organizations with programs limited to or expressly for their membership only; athletic events and programs; agencies already receiving Piedmont support through United Way or a united arts drive, with the exception of an approved capital campaign; or any proposal outside of the geographic area where Piedmont Natural Gas does business.

Geographic Focus: North Carolina, South Carolina, Tennessee

Amount: 500 - 30,000 USD

Contact: George Baldwin, President; (704) 731-4063; (704) 731-4086; george.baldwin@piedmontng.com

Internet: http://www.piedmontng.com/ourcommunity/ourfoundation.aspx#guidelines

Sponsor: Piedmont Natural Gas Foundation
4720 Piedmont Row Drive
Charlotte, NC 28210

Pinellas County Grants **1374**

The Pinellas Community Foundation was established in 1969, it distributes grants twice annually to a wide variety of non-profit agencies, organizations and programs that enhance and support the quality of life in Pinellas County, Florida. Areas of interest are: art, culture, health care, environment, community development, employment opportunities, the underserved, and social services.

Requirements: Eligibility: a non-profit, 501(c)3; be headquartered in Pinellas County; provide social services to people in Pinellas County; not have a large endowment or fund raising staff; provide recent audited financial statements. For Grant Applications call Pinellas Community Foundation: (727) 531-0058.

Geographic Focus: Florida

Date(s) Application is Due: Jun 15; Oct 1

Contact: Julie Scales, Executive Director; (727) 531-0058; (727) 531-0053; info@pinellasccf.org

Internet: http://www.pinellasccf.org/pinellas-community-foundation-pcf-clearwater-fl-our-grants-programs.htm

Sponsor: Pinellas County Community Foundation
5200 East Bay Drive, Suite 202
Clearwater, FL 33764

Pinkerton Foundation Grants **1375**

The Pinkerton Foundation is an independent grantmaking foundation established in 1966 by Robert Allan Pinkerton with the broad directive to reduce the incidence of crime and to prevent juvenile delinquency. The Foundation's principal program interests are focused on economically disadvantaged children, youth and families, and severely learning disabled children and adults of borderline intelligence. The Foundation supports efforts to strengthen and expand community-based programs for children, youth and families in New York City. The Foundation also occasionally funds research, demonstration and evaluation projects in its principal program areas. While grants for direct service projects are usually limited to New York City, those with potential for national impact or replication may go beyond this geographic limitation. The Foundation's Board of Directors have two grantmaking meetings per year, in May and in December. Letters of inquiry are welcome throughout the year. Additional guidelines are available at the Foundation's website.

Requirements: Grants are awarded primarily to New York City 501(c)3 nonprofit public charitable organizations.

Restrictions: The foundation does not grant requests for emergencies, medical research, direct provision of health care, religious education, conferences, publications, or capital projects.

Geographic Focus: All U.S. States

Date(s) Application is Due: Feb 1; Sep 1

Amount: 25,000 - 250,000 USD

Samples: Reel Works Teen Filmmaking, Brooklyn, NY, $35,000—operating support for filmmaking program that serves up to 180 high school students (2009); Madison Square Boys & Girls Club (New York, NY) $250,000—for after school and summer program operations at Madison's clubhouses (2009); New York Cares, Inc., New York, NY, $20,000—in support of their SAT Prep Program (2009).

Contact: Joan Colello, Executive Director; (212) 332-3385; (212) 332-3399; pinkfdn@pinkertonfdn.org

Internet: http://fdncenter.org/grantmaker/pinkerton

Sponsor: Pinkerton Foundation
610 Fifth Avenue, Suite 316
New York, NY 10020

Pioneer Hi-Bred Community Grants 1376

The international corporation supports community-based projects in the areas of agriculture, education, farm safety, and the environment. Priority consideration is given to projects located in Pioneer facility communities or rural agricultural regions and to organizations with active Pioneer management/employee participation and company-related expertise and interest. Types of support include capital grants, general operating grants, program development grants, and seed money grants. The company accepts proposals from nonprofit organizations nationwide but favors programs in its operating communities. Pioneer prefers to make direct contributions to organizations, rather than sponsorships, ticket or table purchases. This allows more funding to go directly toward the non-profit organization; however, we are willing to consider sponsorships when Pioneer employees are actively involved with the organization. The employee must present the request to Community Investment at least one month in advance. Due to the number of non-profit events held annually, there is a $1,000 maximum contribution level per event per year. The company favors proposals that demonstrate cooperation with other community-based programs, broad-based funding, community need, and positive results. Grant proposals are reviewed on a quarterly basis.
Requirements: Nonprofit organizations are eligible. All requests should be directed to the Pioneer Hi-Bred office within the local area. Otherwise, send to the contact listed. Pioneer does not respond favorably to verbal requests.
Restrictions: Grants are not made to individuals, religious or political organizations that promote a particular doctrine, elected officials, company marketing or advertising, or organizations where there is a conflict of interest with Pioneer Hi-Bred.
Geographic Focus: All U.S. States
Amount: Up to 5,000 USD
Contact: Grants Administrator; (800) 247-6803, ext. 3915; (515) 334-4415; community.investment@pioneer.com
Internet: http://www.pioneer.com/web/site/portal/menuitem.bb020a6d93d9d318bc0c0a03d10093a0/
Sponsor: Pioneer Hi-Bred International
6900 NW 62nd Avenue, P.O. Box 246
Johnston, IA 50131

Piper Jaffray Foundation Communities Giving Grants 1377

The foundation supports organizations and programs that enhance the lives of people living and working in communities in which the company has offices. Of primary interest is support for organizations that increase opportunities for individuals to improve their lives and help themselves. Highest priority is given to family stability programs (including housing, family violence, responsible parenting), early childhood development, job training/career development, youth development, and adult education services. The foundation will also consider requests from organizations that work to increase citizen understanding or involvement in civic affairs or that enhance the artistic and cultural life of the community. Requests for general operating support from proven nonprofit organizations will be considered. Requests for project and capital support will be considered on a very selective basis. Support for higher education and K-12 public and private schools is provided primarily through the company gift-matching program. Contact the foundation for deadline dates.
Requirements: IRS 501(c)3 organizations located in the Minneapolis/Saint Paul metropolitan area should submit requests directly to the foundation. Organizations located outside the Minneapolis/Saint Paul metropolitan area should submit requests to the nearest Piper Jaffray office for forwarding to the foundation. Offices are located in communities in Arizona, California, Colorado, Idaho, Illinois, Iowa, Kansas, Kentucky, Minnesota, Missouri, Montana, Nebraska, Nevada, North Dakota, Ohio, Oregon, South Dakota, Tennessee, Utah, Washington, Wisconsin, and Wyoming.
Restrictions: Requests will not be considered from newly formed nonprofit organizations; individuals; teams; religious, political, veterans, or fraternal organizations; or organizations working to treat or eliminate specific diseases. Support is not available for basic or applied research, travel, event sponsorship, benefits or tickets, or to eliminate an organization's operating deficit.
Geographic Focus: Arizona, Arkansas, California, Colorado, Idaho, Illinois, Iowa, Kansas, Kentucky, Minnesota, Missouri, Montana, Nebraska, Nevada, North Dakota, Ohio, Oregon, South Dakota, Tennessee, Utah, Washington, Wisconsin, Wyoming
Date(s) Application is Due: Mar 18
Amount: 1,000 - 5,000 USD
Contact: Connie McCuskey, Vice President; (612) 303-1309; (612) 342-6085; communityrelations@pjc.com
Internet: http://www.piperjaffray.com/2col_largeright.aspx?id=127
Sponsor: Piper Jaffray Foundation
800 Nicollet Mall, Suite 800
Minneapolis, MN 55402

Playboy Foundation Grants 1378

The Playboy Foundation seeks to foster social change by confining its grants and other support to projects of national impact and scope involved in fostering open communication about, and research into, human sexuality, reproductive health and rights; protecting and fostering civil rights and civil liberties in the United States for all people, including women, people affected and impacted by HIV/AIDS, gays and lesbians, racial minorities, the poor and the disadvantaged; and eliminating censorship and protecting freedom of expression and First Amendment rights. The Foundation does not accept unsolicited proposals, but welcomes letters of inquiry via post for the areas of interest noted above. Grants awarded by the Foundation are typically up to $10,000.
Restrictions: The foundation will not consider religious programs, individual needs, capital campaigns, endowments, scholarships, or fellowships; social services, including residential care, clinics, treatment, or recreation programs; national health, welfare, educational, or cultural organizations, or their state affiliates; or government agencies or projects.
Geographic Focus: All U.S. States
Amount: 5,000 - 10,000 USD
Contact: Executive Director; (312) 373-2437 or (312) 751-8000; (312) 751-2818; giving@playboy.com
Internet: http://www.playboyenterprises.com/foundation
Sponsor: Playboy Foundation
680 North Lake Shore Drive
Chicago, IL 60611

Ploughshares Fund Grants 1379

Grants address the significant proliferation risks in emerging nuclear technologies through research projects and education efforts directed to policymakers, the media, and the public. Types of support include conferences and seminars, continuing support, emergency support, general operating support, project development, publication grants, research grants, and seed grants. Specific grant programs are directed to ending the threat from nuclear, chemical, and biological weapons; stopping the spread of weapons of war; addressing the environmental legacy of the nuclear age; promoting public understanding and participation; and preventing global and regional conflict. Ploughshares has initiated media programs including radio talk shows, op-ed writing services, and seminars for reporters to inform the public and influence policymakers on related issues. In an effort to prevent conflict, the foundation supports peacekeeping efforts and research, public education, and advocacy on nuclear weapons and security issues.
Requirements: U.S. and international nonprofit organizations and individuals may apply.
Geographic Focus: All U.S. States
Date(s) Application is Due: Feb 15; Jul 15
Amount: 500 - 50,000 USD
Contact: Executive Director; (415) 775-2244; (415) 775-4529; proposals@ploughshares.org
Internet: http://www.ploughshares.org/grants.php?a=2&b=0&c=0
Sponsor: Ploughshares Fund
Fort Mason Center, Building B, Suite 330
San Francisco, CA 94123

Polk Bros. Foundation Grants 1380

The primary focus of the Foundation is programs that work with populations of need, particularly children, youth, and families in underserved Chicago communities. Very few awards are made to organizations located outside the city of Chicago. Grants are made for both new and ongoing initiatives in four program areas: social service, education, culture and health care. In all areas, proposals should address increased access to services and improvement of the quality of life for area residents. Grants are seldom made for capital support.
Requirements: Illinois 501(c)3 nonprofit organizations are eligible. Preference is given to requests from Chicago. An organization that has not previously received a grant from the Foundation should first call the Foundation office or complete the pre-application form available on the Foundation website. The Foundation will then mail an application form or contact the organization with further questions.

Restrictions: The Polk Bros. Foundation will not support: organizations that devote a substantial portion of their activities to attempting to influence legislation or to participating in campaigns on behalf of candidates for public office; religious institutions seeking support for programs whose participants are restricted by religious affiliation or whose services promote a particular creed; purchase of dinner or raffle tickets or advertising in dinner programs; medical, scientific, or academic research; grants to individuals; tax-generating entities (municipalities, school districts, etc.) for services within their normal responsibilities. The Foundation will not consider more than one request from an organization or its affiliates in a 12-month period, nor will it generally fund more than eight percent of an organization's operating budget.
Geographic Focus: Illinois
Amount: Up to 15,000 USD
Samples: Chicago High School for the Arts, $750,000 - general operating (2009); Advocate Illinois Masonic Medical Center, $90,000 - school-based health centers at Amundsen and Lake View High Schools (2009); Albany Park Theater Project, $80,000 - youth development through theater program (2009); America Scores Chicago, $25,000 - salary support for the education and soccer directors (2009)
Contact: Suzanne Doombos Kerbow, Assistant Director; (312) 527-4684; (312) 527-4681; questions@polkbrosfdn.org
Internet: http://www.polkbrosfdn.org/guidelines.htm
Sponsor: Polk Brothers Foundation
20 West Kinzie Street, Suite 1110
Chicago, IL 60611

Pollock Foundation Grants **1381**
The foundation awards grants to Texas nonprofit organizations in its areas of interest, including cultural programs, dental education and schools, health care and health organizations, Jewish organizations and temples, libraries and library science, nursing, public health education and schools, social services, and youth development. Grants support program develoment and general operating expenses. There are no application deadlines. Contact the office for application materials.
Requirements: Texas nonprofit organizations are eligible. Preference is given to requests from Dallas.
Geographic Focus: Texas
Amount: 1,000 - 300,000 USD
Samples: Reading and Radio Resource, Dallas, TX, $6,000 (2008); Dallas Symphony Association, Dallas, TX, $300,000 (2008); Temple Emanu-El, Dallas, TX, $50,000 (2008).
Contact: Robert Pollock, Trustee, (214) 871-7155, (214) 871-8158
Sponsor: Pollock Foundation
2626 Howell Street, Suite 895
Dallas, TX 75204

Porter County Community Foundation Professional Development Grants **1382**
The Porter County Community Foundation offers Professional Development Grants to support consulting work for nonprofit organizations or attendance at continuing education programs identified by nonprofit organizations that meet their individual needs and schedules. These grants can be used to cover consulting time, conference registration fees or college tuition fees. Nonprofit organizations may receive up to $1,500 per year, and each organization is limited to two grants per calendar year. The maximum grant amount for the use of a consultant is $1,500 and the maximum grant amount for the attendance of a conference or training is $750 per registration.
Requirements: In applying for a grant to hire a consultant, the applicant should submit a letter describing the consultant's mission, company, and credentials. In applying for grants to attend conferences, there are several items to be addressed in a numbered narrative that does not exceed two pages. Applicant should consult the website for the detailed information requested in a specific format.
Restrictions: Because funding is limited, grants cannot cover travel expenses, lodging costs, meals, books or supplies.
Geographic Focus: Indiana
Amount: 1,500 USD
Contact: Brenda A. Sheetz, Program Administrator; (219) 465-0294; (219) 464-2733; bsheetz@portercountyfoundation.org
Internet: http://www.portercountyfoundation.org/grantprograms.html
Sponsor: Porter County Community Foundation
57 South Franklin Street, Suite 207, P.O. Box 302
Valparaiso, IN 46384

Porter County Health and Wellness Grant **1383**
The Porter County Health and Wellness Fund awards grants to nonprofit organizations that promote, support, and/or advance health care in Porter County. Funding priorities include: increasing health care access for the underserved; improving and promoting healthy lifestyles for youth; and improving the nonprofit's operational capabilities to provide health care services. The maximum grant amount is $25,000.
Requirements: In addition to the application, all grant application packets must include the following information: a grant request cover page; a grant narrative; a project budget; a current operating budget and financial statement; the names and principal occupations of the organization's Board of Directors; the organization's grant application approval by their Board of Directors; and a copy of the organization's 501(c)3 tax exemption ruling.
Restrictions: Grants will not be made to: individuals; membership contributions; event sponsorships; programs that are sectarian or religious in nature; political organizations or candidates; contributions to endowment campaigns; campaigns to reduce previously incurred debt; and programs already completed.
Geographic Focus: Indiana
Date(s) Application is Due: Jun 15
Amount: 25,000 USD
Contact: Brenda Sheetz, Health/Wellness Fund Contact; (219) 465-0294; (219) 464-2733; bsheetz@portercountyfoundation.org
Internet: http://www.portercountyfoundation.org/grantprograms.html
Sponsor: Porter County Community Foundation
57 South Franklin Street, Suite 207, P.O. Box 302
Valparaiso, IN 46384

Portland Foundation Grants **1384**
The Portland Foundation Community Grants are particularly interested in proposals for start-up costs for new programs; one-time projects or needs; and capital needs beyond an applicant's capabilities and means. In addition, limited funding is available in the following areas: emergency service agencies; programs that benefit the elderly of Jay County; needy families; libraries; historical facilities; care and prevention of cruelty to animals; handicapped children; and education of sensory impaired children. The Foundation funds twice yearly in the summer and winter. Both applications are available on the website.
Requirements: The grant application is available on the Foundation website, and must be sent electronically. Ten complete proposal packages are then mailed to the Foundation and must include: a completed, computer-generated application (typed or handwritten applications cannot be accepted); copy of the 501(c)3 IRS determination letter, the organization's most recent financial statements, current budget reflecting year-to-date income and expenses; purchase estimates and/or project bids, if applicable; phone number where contact person can be reached; requested signatures; completed Counterterrorism Compliance form; and an explanation of why any of the above is not included.
Restrictions: The Foundation will not normally consider grants for the following purposes: individuals other than scholarships; organizations for religious or sectarian purposes; make-up of operating deficits, post-event or after-the-fact situations; endowment campaigns; or for any propaganda, political or otherwise, attempting to influence legislation or intervene in any political affairs or campaigns. The Foundation is reluctant to approve grants for the purpose of maintaining an on-going operating budget or for multi-year grants requests. However, exceptions to this may be made at the discretion of the Foundation.
Geographic Focus: Indiana
Date(s) Application is Due: Jan 6; Jul 6
Amount: 1,000 - 25,000 USD
Samples: Jay Community Center, purchase of equipment for senior citizen fitness classes, $2,000 (2010); Dunkirk Beautification Committee, underwrite three concerts in the Webster Park Depot Concert Series, $1,450 (2010); Jay County 4th of July Committee, operating support of the 4th of July celebration activities, $4,500 (2010).
Contact: Douglas Inman, Executive Director; (260) 726-4260; (260) 726-4273; tpf@portlandfoundation.org
Internet: http://www.portlandfoundation.org/winter-grants-scholarships
Sponsor: Portland Foundation
112 East Main Street
Portland, IN 47371

Powell Family Foundation Grants **1385**
The foundation awards grants to nonprofits in the Kansas City area for support of programs in the areas of environment, civic affairs, and youth. Types of support include general operating support, continuing support, annual

campaigns, capital campaigns, equipment acquisition, and program/project development. There are no application forms. Letters of intent must be received 30 days preceding board meetings. The foundation prefers written inquiries and will send guidelines if the project meets foundation criteria.
Requirements: Nonprofits in, or serving the residents of, Missouri are eligible.
Restrictions: The foundation does not support welfare or social services programs.
Geographic Focus: Missouri
Amount: 2,500 - 25,000 USD
Contact: George Powell, Jr., President; (913) 236-0003; (913) 262-0058
Sponsor: Powell Family Foundation
4350 Shawnee Mission Parkway, Suite 280
Fairway, KS 66205-2528

Powell Foundation Grants **1386**

The purpose of the Powell Foundation is to distribute funds for public charitable purposes, principally for the support, encouragement and assistance to education, health, conservation, and the arts with a direct impact within the Foundation's geographic zone of interest The Foundation places priority on organizations and programs that serve residents in Harris, Travis and Walker counties, Texas, principally in the fields of education, the arts, health and conservation. The Foundation's current emphasis is in the field of public education in the broadest sense. Other areas of interest continue to be community service projects focused on the needs of children, the disadvantaged, the urban environment, and the visual and performing arts, especially in the Greater Houston, Texas area. The Foundation operates on a calendar year and its Board meets twice a year in the spring and in the fall. Submission of proposals is required at least two months prior to a meeting for consideration at that meeting. To allow for optimum consideration and due diligence, those seeking grants are encouraged to apply to the foundation on an ongoing basis. Grants that do not make the deadline for one meeting will be carried forward to the next meeting. Each request must be in writing and should be accompanied by the proposal summary and the required list of attachments. See the foundation's website for additional guidelines.
Requirements: Texas IRS 501(c)3 tax-exempt organizations serving Harris, Walker, and Travis counties are eligible to apply.
Restrictions: Normally, the Foundation will not support: requests for building funds or grant commitments extending into successive calendar years; grants to religious organizations for religious purposes; fund raising events or advertising; grants to other private foundations; grants to cover past operating deficits or debt retirement; grants for support to individuals; grants that impose the exercise of responsibility upon the Foundation. For example: private operating foundations or certain supporting organizations.
Geographic Focus: Texas
Amount: 1,000 - 20,000 USD
Samples: Houston Ballet Foundation, Houston, TX, $10,000—support for the 2008-2009 artistic season and related educational outreach efforts (2008); Trust for Public Land, Austin, TX, $10,000—support for the Texas public parks, recreation and open spaces (2008); Christian Community Service Center, Houston, TX, $6,750—to sponsor 150 children for back to school with new uniforms and grade requested supplies (2008).
Contact: Caroline J. Sabin, Executive Director; (713) 523-7557; (713) 523-7553; info@powellfoundation.org
Internet: http://www.powellfoundation.org/powellguide.htm
Sponsor: Powell Foundation
2121 San Felipe, Suite 110
Houston, TX 77019-5600

Powell Foundation Grants **1387**

Established in Tennessee in 2000, the Powell Foundation's primary fields of interest include boy scouts, children and youth programs, Christian agencies and churches, health care, higher education, housing, and volunteer services. There are no specific application formats or deadlines with which to adhere, and applicants should submit a detailed description of their project, along with the amount of funding requested. The average range of funding is $7,500 to $25,000.
Geographic Focus: Tennessee
Samples: University of Tennessee, Knoxville, Tennessee, $7,500 - support of the veterinary school (2009); East Tennessee State University Foundation, Johnson City, Tennessee, $24,000 - Powell Choral Music Scholars Endowment (2009); Story Telling Association, Johnson City, Tennessee, $20,000 - gift to the local Story Telling Association (2009).
Contact: James J. Powell, Chairperson; (423) 282-0111
Sponsor: Powell Foundation
3622 Bristol Highway
Johnson City, TN 37601-1324

PPG Industries Foundation Grants **1388**

Funding requests for a variety of project proposals that advance the foundation's interests are eligible for consideration. These may include capital projects, operating grants and special projects. In general, the foundation gives priority to applications from organizations dedicated to enhancing the welfare of communities in which PPG is a resident. Each grant application is reviewed with regard to the: compatibility of the applicant's goals with the foundation's priorities and available resources; financial needs of the organization; past practices of the foundation with respect to that organization; capability and reputation of the applicant; funds available to the applicant from other sources; extent to which the work of the applicant duplicates that of other organizations; public scope and impact of the applicant's proposal; and the interest of other corporate foundations with respect to the applicant. Historically the foundation has supported nonprofits in the areas of human services, health and safety, civic and community affairs, education, and cultural and arts. Requests for funding are accepted year-round. Determinations are made by the foundation's screening committee and board of directors.
Requirements: Applicants must use PPG's online grant making system to apply. The link is on the website. PPG Industries Foundation will review applications on a regular basis and will contact all grantseekers with proposals of interest. Organizations located in the Pittsburgh area and organizations of national scope should direct any questions to the executive director of the foundation. Organizations serving communities where PPG facilities are located should direct any questions to the local PPG Industries Foundation agent in their area. A list of these may be found at the PPG Foundation website under the Foundation Governance link.
Restrictions: The foundation will not award grants for: advertising or sponsorships; endowments; political or religious purposes; projects which would directly benefit PPG Industries, Inc; or special events and telephone solicitations. Operating grants are not made to United Way agencies.
Geographic Focus: All U.S. States
Samples: YMCA of Metropolitan Milwaukee, South Shore Center, Milwaukee, Wisconsin, $3,000 - funding supports SPLASH swimming program for second-graders (2011); Carlisle Regional Performing Arts Center, location unspecified, $3,000 - funding supports maintenance, technology upgrade costs (2011); Robert Morris University, Moon Township, Pennsylvania, $350,000 - funding supports renovation of the Career and Leadership Development Center.
Contact: Sue Sloan, Executive Director; (412) 434-2453; (412) 434-4666; foundation@ppg.com
Internet: http://www.ppg.com/en/ppgfoundation/Pages/Grant_Policies.aspx
Sponsor: PPG Industries Foundation
One PPG Place
Pittsburgh, PA 15272

Price Chopper's Golub Foundation Grants **1389**

Price Chopper's Golub Foundation provides financial support to eligible charitable organizations with a current 501(c)3 tax exempt status. Contributions are made through planned, continued giving programs in the areas of health and human services, arts, culture, education, and youth activities, within Price Chopper marketing areas. To be considered for funding, mail a written request, on letterhead for the organization seeking the donation, six to eight weeks prior to needed support or response deadlines. The Foundation reviews capital campaign requests quarterly, so please allow three to four months for a response.
Requirements: The Foundation's six state marketing area includes a specific mile radius around its stores in New York (Albany, Broome, Cayuga, Chenango, Clinton, Columbia, Cortland, Delaware, Dutchess, Essex, Franklin, Fulton, Greene, Hamilton, Herkimer, Jefferson, Lewis, Madison, Montgomery, Oneida, Onondaga, Orange, Oswego, Otsego, Rensselaer, Street Lawrence, Saratoga, Schenectady, Schoharie, Sullivan, Tioga, Tompkins, Ulster, Warren, and Washington counties), Massachusetts (Berkshire, Hampden, Hampshire, Middlesex, and Worcester counties), Vermont (Addison, Bennington, Caledonia, Chittenden, Essex, Franklin, Grand Isle, Lamoille, Orange, Orleans, Rutland, Washington, Windham, and Windsor counties), Pennsylvania (Lackawanna, Luzerne, Pike, Susquehanna, Wayne, and Wyoming counties), Connecticut (Hartford, Litchfield, New Haven, Tolland, and Windham counties) and New Hampshire (Cheshire, Grafton, and Sullivan counties).

Restrictions: The Foundation does not support: individuals; annual meetings; endowments; film and video projects; program advertising; funding for travel; organizations or events outside of its marketing area; events to raise funds for groups outside of its local community; conferences, conventions, or symposiums; publishing; operating expenses; scholarship programs outside of its own; or capital campaigns of national, religious or political organizations.
Geographic Focus: Connecticut, Massachusetts, New Hampshire, New York, Pennsylvania, Vermont
Contact: Deborah Tanski, Administrator; (518) 356-9450 or (518) 379-1270; (518) 374-4259
Internet: http://www.pricechopper.com/GolubFoundation/GolubFoundation_S.las
Sponsor: Price Chopper's Golub Foundation
P.O. Box 1074
Schenectady, NY 12301

Price Family Charitable Fund Grants **1390**

Established in 1983, the Price Family Charitable Fund serves the San Diego, Carlsbad and, San Marcos, California region. The foundation is interested in supporting the economically disadvantaged, giving primarily for education and philanthropy purposes. The types of support include: annual campaigns; fellowships; program evaluation; scholarship funds; scholarships to individuals and; general operating support. There's no formal application to submit. Potential grantees much first submit a letter of Inquiry including: project goals, objectives and expected results (maximum of one page); project narrative (maximum of five pages); project budget (maximum of one page); a list of grants, if any, received by organization in the last 12 months for this program/project (sources and amounts); a list of the organization's current board of directors, including each member's name, profession, and office help on the board, if any.
Requirements: Non-profit organizations with 501(c)3 status or governmental units such as public schools or city departments in are available for funding. The Foundation gives primarily in the following region of: San Diego; Carlsbad; San Marcos, California.
Restrictions: Grants are not made: to organizations whose primary purpose is religious, or for propagandizing, influencing legislation and/or elections, promoting voting registration, for political candidates, political campaigns or organizations engaged in political activities; or to federal appeals or to organizations the collect funds for redistribution to other non-profit groups. Unsolicited requests for funds are not accepted.
Geographic Focus: California
Samples: George G. Glenner Alzheimer's Family Centers, Inc., San Diego, CA, $33,000—Dementia Care Training & Public Scholarships (2008); Episcopal Community Services, San Diego, CA, $60,000—general support (2008); A Reason to Survive, San Diego, CA, $100,000—capacity building (2008).
Contact: Terry Malavenda, (858) 551-2330
Sponsor: Price Family Charitable Fund
7979 Ivanhoe Avenue, Suite 520
La Jolla, CA 92037-4513

Price Gilbert, Jr. Charitable Fund Grants **1391**

The Price Gilbert, Jr. Charitable Fund was established under the will of Price Gilbert, Jr. in 1973. During his life, Gilbert made bequests to the Georgia Tech Foundation with preference for the Price Gilbert Memorial Library, the Atlanta Speech School, the University of Georgia Foundation for the Gilbert Infirmary, and Northside Methodist Church. The remainder of his estate funded the Price Gilbert, Jr. Charitable Fund. Wells Fargo Bank serves as Trustee to a portion of this successor fund. The purpose of the Price Gilbert, Jr. Charitable Fund is to distribute to such charitable and/or educational institutions in the Atlanta area as selected by said Trustee as are recognized by the Internal Revenue Service.
Requirements: All grants are made to qualified 501(c)3 organizations in the Atlanta area, taking into consideration the charitable intent of Mr. Gilbert. Consideration will be given to the Georgia Tech Foundation and the Atlanta Speech School in grantmaking decisions. Proposals should be submitted in the following format: completed Common Grant Application Form; an original Proposal Statement; an audited financial report and a current year operating budget; a copy of your official IRS Letter with your tax determination; a listing of your Board of Directors. Proposal Statements (second item in the above Format) should answer these questions: what are the objectives and expected outcomes of this program/project/request; what strategies will be used to accomplish your objective; what is the timeline for completion; if this is part of an on-going program, how long has it been in operation; what criteria will you use to measure success; if the request is not fully funded, what other sources can you engage; an Itemized budget should be included; please describe any collaborative ventures. Prior to the distribution of funds, all approved grantees must sign and return a Grant Agreement Form, stating that the funds will be used for the purpose intended. Progress reports and Completion reports must also be filed as required for your specific grant. All current grantees must be in good standing with required documentation prior to submitting new proposals to any foundation.
Restrictions: Grants are not made for political purposes, nor to organizations which discriminate on the basis of race, ethnic origin, sexual or religious preference, age or gender.
Geographic Focus: Georgia
Date(s) Application is Due: Aug 1
Amount: 2,000 - 100,000 USD
Samples: Youth Communication, Metro Atlanta, Inc., $10,000— equipment capital campaign; Metropolitan Atlanta Arts and Culture Coalition, $50,000—arts and culture funding; English for Successful Living, Inc., $2,100—database management system.
Contact: Joyce Yamaato, Wells Fargo Trustee; (888) 234-1999; (877) 746-5889; grantadministration@ wellsfargo.com
Internet: https://www.wachovia.com/foundation/v/index.jsp?vgnextoid=13d852199c0aa110VgnVCM1000004b0d1872RCRD&vgnextfmt=default
Sponsor: Price Gilbert, Jr. Charitable Fund
3280 Peachtree Road NE, Suite 400
Atlanta, GA 30305

Prince Charitable Trusts Chicago Grants **1392**

The trusts awards grants to eligible Chicago nonprofit organizations in its areas of interest: arts and culture, education, environment, health, and social services.
Requirements: The Trusts Chicago program only funds organizations within the city limits of Chicago (with the exception of grants made through the MacArthur Fund for Arts and Culture at Prince). The Trusts make grants only to charitable organizations that are exempt from federal income tax under Section 501(c)3 of the Internal Revenue Code and are classified as public charities under Sections 509(a)(1) or 509(a)(2). All grant applications must include a Prince Charitable Trusts cover sheet, see the Trusts website, http://foundationcenter.org/grantmaker/prince/chi_app.html for proper form and additional guidelines.
Restrictions: The Trusts do not fund projects that promote or proselytize any religion. While the Trusts do fund the projects of faith-based organizations, those projects must be secular in nature. The Trusts do not fund organizations that discriminate on the basis of ethnicity, race, color, creed, religion, gender, national origin, age, disability, marital status, sexual orientation, gender identity, or any veteran's status.
Geographic Focus: Illinois
Date(s) Application is Due: Jan 13; May 1; Jun 1
Contact: Sharon Robison, Grants Manager; (312) 419-8700; (312) 419-8558; srobison@prince-trusts.org
Internet: http://www.fdncenter.org/grantmaker/prince/chicago.html
Sponsor: Prince Charitable Trusts
303 West Madison Street, Suite 1900
Chicago, IL 60606

Prince Charitable Trusts District of Columbia Grants **1393**

The trusts awards grants to eligible Washington D.C. nonprofit organizations in its areas of interest: arts and culture, community, environment, health, emergency services, youth and provide a limited number of capital grants each year.
Requirements: The Trusts make grants only to charitable organizations that are exempt from federal income tax under Section 501(c)3 of the Internal Revenue Code and are classified as public charities under Sections 509(a)(1) or 509(a)(2). Electronic proposals are preferred. Attachments may be mailed separately. Proposals should include the Prince Charitable Trust Grant Application Cover Sheet and the Common Grant Application Format of Washington Grantmakers. These forms and additional guidelines may be obtained at the Trusts website, http://foundationcenter.org/grantmaker/prince/dc_app.html.
Restrictions: The Trusts do not make grants to individuals, nor does it fund projects that promote or proselytize any religion. While the Trusts do fund the projects of faith-based organizations, those projects must be secular in nature.

Geographic Focus: District of Columbia
Date(s) Application is Due: Feb 1; Sep 1; Aug 10
Amount: 10,000 - 30,000 USD
Contact: Kristin Pauly, Managing Director; (202) 728-0646; (202) 466-4726; kpauly@princetrusts.org
Internet: http://www.fdncenter.org/grantmaker/prince/dc_interest.html
Sponsor: Prince Charitable Trusts
816 Connecticut Avenue NW
Washington, DC 20006

Prince Charitable Trusts Rhode Island Grants **1394**

The trusts awards grants to eligible Rhode Island nonprofit organizations in its areas of interest: arts and culture, environment and social services. In Rhode Island, the Trusts support programs that improve the quality of life for residents of the city of Newport and Aquidneck Island. Generally, the Trusts only support programs that are regional or statewide when these programs have a direct or indirect impact on Newport or Aquidneck Island.
Requirements: The Trusts make grants only to charitable organizations that are exempt from federal income tax under Section 501(c)3 of the Internal Revenue Code and are classified as public charities under Sections 509(a)(1) or 509(a)(2). All grant applications must include a Prince Charitable Trusts cover sheet, see the Trusts website, http://foundationcenter.org/grantmaker/prince/ri_app.html for proper form and additional guidelines.
Restrictions: The Trusts do not fund organizations that discriminate on the basis of ethnicity, race, color, creed, religion, gender, national origin, age, disability, marital status, sexual orientation, gender identity, or any veteran's status. The Trusts do not fund projects that promote or proselytize any religion. While the Trusts do fund the projects of faith-based organizations, those projects must be secular in nature. The Trusts also do not make grants to individuals.
Geographic Focus: Rhode Island
Date(s) Application is Due: Jun 1
Contact: Sharon Robison, Grants Manager; (312) 419-8700; (312) 419-8558; srobison@prince-trusts.org
Internet: http://fdncenter.org/grantmaker/prince/ri.html
Sponsor: Prince Charitable Trusts
303 West Madison Street, Suite 1900
Chicago, IL 60606

Principal Financial Group Foundation Grants **1395**

The foundation addresses concerns in the areas of health and human services, education, arts and culture, environment, and recreation and tourism. The primary objective is to support, through charitable contributions, selected nonprofit organizations primarily located in the greater Des Moines, IA, area. The foundation also will consider requests from organizations located in areas where the corporation has offices, including Des Moines, Mason City and Cedar Falls, IA; Grand Island, NE; Spokane, WA; Wilmington, DE; Appleton, WI; and Phoenix, AZ. The objectives, priorities, and programs seek to reflect the needs and concerns of communities in which the corporation operates. Support is given for annual campaigns, building funds, capital campaigns, continuing support, employee matching gifts, in-kind gifts, performances and exhibitions, conferences and workshops, adult basic education, vocational programs, operating budgets, internships, demonstration grants, matching grants, and seed grants. Contribution requests are considered on a quarterly basis, in accordance with the following schedule: health and human services, March 1; education, June 1; arts and culture, September 1; and environment, recreation, and tourism, December 1.
Requirements: 501(c)3 tax-exempt organizations in company operating locations may apply.
Restrictions: Proposals for athletic groups, conferences, endowments, fellowships, festivals, fraternal organizations, health care facility fund drives, libraries, or religious groups are denied.
Geographic Focus: Delaware, Iowa, Nebraska, Washington
Date(s) Application is Due: Mar 1; Jun 1; Sep 1; Dec 1
Amount: 1,000 - 50,000 USD
Contact: Laura Sauser, Community Investment Consultant; (515) 247-7227; (515) 246-5475
Internet: http://www.principal.com/about/giving/grant.htm
Sponsor: Principal Financial Group Foundation
711 High Street
Des Moines, IA 50392-0150

Procter and Gamble Fund Grants **1396**

The fund supports nonprofit organizations in company-operating locations in the areas of education, health and social services, civic projects, cultural organizations, disaster relief, and environmental efforts. Grants are awarded to education initiatives in local communities, such as teacher training efforts, with a focus on economic teaching; and other efforts by public policy, research, and economic education organizations. Employee voluntarism is prevalent in many K-12 initiatives. Most health and human services funding supports the United Way. The Salvation Army, Red Cross, hospitals, food banks, and other social service organizations receive support. Community support is awarded through grants that bolster economic growth and enrichment, including support for a youth jobs program, libraries, zoos, and local chambers of commerce. Support is awarded to a variety of arts organizations, including theater, dance, music, and visual arts. Major environmental groups also receive support. Grant Application Cycles are July 1 through September 30 and December 1 through February 28, grant requests are only accepted during those times.
Requirements: 501(c)3 organizations in communities where Procter and Gamble Company manufacturing plants are located are eligible.
Geographic Focus: All U.S. States
Amount: Up to 25,000,000 USD
Contact: Brenda Ratliff, Administrator, Corporate Philanthropy; (513) 945-8454; (513) 945-5211; pgfund.im@pg.com
Internet: http://www.pg.com/company/our_commitment/grant_application_guidelines.shtml
Sponsor: Procter and Gamble Fund
P.O. Box 599
Cincinnati, OH 45201

Prospect Hill Foundation Grants **1397**

The foundation's national giving focuses on environmental conservation, especially in the Northeast and in Latin America; nuclear weapons control; and population growth/control in relation to natural resources, food supply, and opportunity to live a quality life. Types of support include matching funds, operating budgets, seed grants, and projects/programs. Preference goes to proposals for projects rather than for general support. Grant requests may be submitted year-round. Information and guidelines are available online.
Requirements: Giving is primarily in the northeastern United States, including New York and Rhode Island. Social service grants are limited to New York groups.
Restrictions: The foundation does not consider grants to individuals nor for basic research, sectarian religious activities, or organizations that lack tax exemption under United States law.
Geographic Focus: All U.S. States
Amount: 10,000 - 25,000 USD
Samples: Bulletin of the Atomic Scientists (Chicago, IL)—to enhance coverage of international and security issues in the Bulletin of the Atomic Scientists, $15,000; San Miguel-CASA (Guanajuato, Mexico)—toward the Professional Midwifery School, $35,000; Cunningham Dance Foundation (New York, NY)—for general support, $25,000; Fifth Avenue Presbyterian Church (New York, NY)—toward the capital campaign, $50,000.
Contact: Laura Callanan, Executive Director; (212) 370-1165; (212) 599-6282
Internet: http://fdncenter.org/grantmaker/prospecthill
Sponsor: Prospect Hill Foundation
99 Park Avenue, Suite 2220
New York, NY 10016-1601

Prudential Foundation Grants **1398**

The foundation's areas of interest are ready-to-learn programs, ready-to-work programs, and ready-to-live programs. Grants support programs in the areas of business and economic research; education; health; public affairs; conservation and ecology; cultural activities; urban and community affairs; research and professional training in long-term health care and family care; job creation, employment of the elderly, and welfare-to-work programs; building and equipment needs; programs for children and youth; and assistance to minorities. Types of support include operating support, continuing support, annual campaigns, seed money, matching funds and employee matching gifts, consulting services, technical assistance, employee-related scholarships, research, capital campaigns, conferences and seminars, and projects/programs. The foundation is especially interested in proposals that anticipate and address potential major problems. Funds are targeted to areas where Prudential has a strong presence. Applicant should make initial contact with a brief letter to

determine whether a more detailed proposal would be acceptable. Applications are available on the web site.
Requirements: Tax-exempt nonprofit organizations are eligible. Priority in order of preference goes to programs in Newark and surrounding communities; Los Angeles, CA; Jacksonville, FL; Atlanta, GA: Minneapolis, MN; Philadelphia, PA; and Houston, TX. Third priority are national programs that can be implemented or replicated in the above cities.
Geographic Focus: Arizona, California, Florida, Georgia, Minnesota, New Jersey, Pennsylvania, Texas
Amount: Up to 100,000,000 USD
Samples: National Governors Assoc (Washington, DC)—for efforts to create and implement ways to improve high school-graduation and college-preparedness rates in 13 states, $1 million; For relief efforts in South Asia and Africa, $1 million.
Contact: Foundation Director; (973) 802-4791; community.resources@prudential.com
Internet: http://www.prudential.com/view/page/public/12154
Sponsor: Prudential Foundation
751 Broad Street, 15th Floor
Newark, NJ 07102-3777

Public Welfare Foundation Grants **1399**
Grants are awarded primarily to grassroots organizations in the United States and abroad, with emphasis on the environment, disadvantaged elderly and youth, population and reproductive health, economic development, welfare reform, health, human rights and global security, criminal justice, and community development. Programs must serve low-income populations, with preference to short-term needs. Types of support include matching funds, operating budgets, seed money, continuing support, and special projects. Grant guidelines are available upon request. Proposal with cover letter should be addressed to the Steering Committee at the address listed.
Requirements: Nonprofit organizations and, in certain cases, organizations without 501(c)3 status, may apply for grant support. Eligible exceptions are listed in the guidelines (available upon request).
Restrictions: Grants will not be made to individuals or for religious purposes, building funds, capital improvements, endowments, scholarships, graduate work, foreign study, conferences, seminars, publications, research, workshops, consulting services, annual campaigns, or deficit financing.
Geographic Focus: All U.S. States
Amount: 25,000 - 50,000 USD
Samples: Fair Housing Agency of Alabama (Mobile, AL)—to provide temporary and long-term housing and other support to people in Mobile, AL, left homeless by Hurricane Katrina, $10,000; Louisiana Bucket Brigade (Baton Rouge, LA)—to train people to monitor environmental pollution in their neighborhoods, $25,000; Share Foundation (San Francisco, CA)—to provide relief and support for reconstruction efforts in El Salvador following Hurricane Stan, $25,000; Environmental Support Ctr (Washington, DC)—to provide small grants to environmental justice groups in the Gulf Coast region that are struggling to reestablish their programs in the wake of recent hurricanes, $75,000.
Contact: Grants Administrator; (202) 965-1800; (202) 265-8851; reviewcommittee@publicwelfare.org
Internet: http://www.publicwelfare.org/about/about.asp
Sponsor: Public Welfare Foundation
1200 U Street NW
Washington, DC 20009

Publix Super Markets Charities Grants **1400**
Grants support programs of Florida nonprofit organizations in the areas of community funds, disabled, higher education, social services, and youth. Types of support include general operating support and support of special projects. In addition to giving to thousands of local projects, Publix annually supports five organizations in companywide campaigns: Special Olympics, March of Dimes, Children's Miracle Network, United Way, and Food Industry Crusade Against Hunger. Contact the office for required application form. There are no application deadlines; the board meets monthly.
Requirements: Florida nonprofits are eligible.
Geographic Focus: Florida
Amount: 500 - 100,000 USD
Samples: United Way International (Alexandria, VA)—to assist tsunami-relief efforts, $250,000.
Contact: Director of Community Affairs; (863) 680-5339
Internet: http://www.publix.com/about/CommunityInvolvement.do
Sponsor: Publix Super Markets Charities
P.O. Box 407
Lakeland, FL 33802-0407

Puerto Rico Community Foundation Grants **1401**
The Foundation wishes to develop the capacities of communities in Puerto Rico so that they may achieve social transformation and economic self-sufficiency, by stimulating investment in communities and maximizing the impact and yield of each contribution. Grants are awarded in the areas of: education; community development; financial development; development of social interest housing; and philanthropy. Types of support include: general operating support; emergency funds; conferences and seminars; professorships; publications; research; technical assistance; consulting services; and matching funds. There are no application deadlines; the board meets in March, June, September, and December to consider requests.
Requirements: Organizations applying for grants must comply with the conditions below in order to demonstrate eligibility: be duly incorporated and registered as a nonprofit organization, according to the laws of the Commonwealth of Puerto Rico; be located and offer services in Puerto Rico. Present a copy of the following documents: certificate of good standing from the State Department; certificate from the Treasury Department; statement of organization's total budget for the year for which funds are solicited; financial statements; list of current members of Board of Directors. Should include each member's address and phone number; resume or curriculum vitae of the Project Director.
Restrictions: The foundation does not make grants to support individuals, annual campaigns, seed money, endowments, deficit financing, scholarships, or building funds.
Geographic Focus: Puerto Rico
Amount: 1,000 - 40,000 USD
Contact: Grants Administrator; (787) 721-1037; (787) 721-1673; fcpr@fcpr.org
Internet: http://www.fcpr.org/
Sponsor: Puerto Rico Community Foundation
P.O. Box 70362
San Juan, PR 00936-8362 Puerto Rico

Putnam County Community Foundation Grants **1402**
The Putnam County Community Foundation is a nonprofit public charity established in 1985 to administer funds, award grants and provide leadership, enriching the quality of life and strengthening community in Putnam County. The Community Foundation administers more than 174 funds for donors supporting a variety of charitable activities. Three types of grants offered include: community grants, non-profit endowment building grants, and youth philanthropy grants. Types of support include: building renovation; consulting services; income development; matching/challenge support; program-related investments/loans; program development; scholarship funds; seed money; and technical assistance. The first funding cycle has a preliminary grant application due date of February 1, with full grants due by March 9; the second funding cycle has a preliminary grant application due date of August 1, with full grants due by September 9.
Requirements: A final report is due at the time of project completion. Unless other arrangements are made, it is expected that projects will be completed within one year of the grant award.
Restrictions: In general, grants from the Community Grants will not be awarded for the following: individuals; ongoing operational expenses (salaries, rent, and utilities); projects that do not serve Putnam County citizens; projects normally fully funded by units of government; projects to build or fund an endowment; religious activities or programs that appear to serve one denomination and not the community at large; political organizations or campaigns; national and state-wide fund raising projects; projects that could be considered discriminatory; projects operated by for-profit companies; or projects requesting retroactive funding.
Geographic Focus: Indiana
Date(s) Application is Due: Feb 1; Mar 9; Aug 1; Sep 9
Contact: M. Elaine Peck, Executive Director; (765) 653-4978; (765) 653-6385; epeck@pcfoundation.org or info@pcfountation.org
Internet: http://www.pcfoundation.org/grant_what_we_fund.html
Sponsor: Putnam County Community Foundation
2 South Jackson Street, P.O. Box 514
Greencastle, IN 46135

Putnam Foundation Grants **1403**
The foundation, established in 1952, awards grants to eligible New Hampshire nonprofit organizations in its areas of interest, including civic and public affairs, cultural programs, ecology and environmental protection, education, historic preservation, public affairs and government, and youth programs. Types of support include capital campaigns (including endowments), general operating grants, and project grants. There are no application deadlines or forms.
Requirements: New Hampshire nonprofit organizations serving the Monadnock region are eligible.
Geographic Focus: New Hampshire
Amount: 30,000 - 500,000 USD
Samples: Keene State College, Keene, NH, $500,000—for distinguished chair in chemistry (2008); Historic Harrisville, Harrisville, NH, $100,000—for second of three payment pledge (2008); Apple Hill Center for Chamber Music, Sullivan, NH, $50,000—for grant to support a Playing for Peace tour (2008).
Contact: Rosamond P. Delori, Secretary; (603) 352-2448; (603) 355-9954
Sponsor: Putnam Foundation
20 Central Square, 2nd Floor, P.O. Box 323
Keene, NH 03431-0323

Quixote Foundation Grants **1404**
The foundation awards grants in its areas of interest, including restoring democracy in the United States through voter engagement and voter-verified paper ballots; safeguarding the world's natural environment through science, conservation, and advocacy; promoting sustainable energy use and technologies; and protecting civil liberties and reproductive rights in the United States. Support takes the form of operating and program grants, technical assistance, research, convening, and activism. Grants do not support endowment or capital purposes. Proposals are by invitation only. Currently letters of inquiry are accepted in the following areas: developing effective message strategies to safeguard the world's natural environment and reforming media coverage and promoting public awareness of economic inequality. Unless you are a current grant recipient, please do not telephone or email the foundation with project briefings or requests for meetings. Guidelines are available online.
Restrictions: Letters of request may not be submitted before November 15.
Geographic Focus: All U.S. States
Samples: Electronic Frontier Foundation (San Francisco, CA)—to develop litigation strategies to respond to problems that arise from computerized voting, $21,000.
Contact: Program Contact; (206) 783-5554; (206) 783-1815; lenore@quixotefoundation.org
Internet: http://www.iinet.com/~quixoteman/index.htm
Sponsor: Quixote Foundation
5703 20th Avenue NW
Seattle, WA 98107

Qwest Foundation Grants—Community **1405**
The foundation seeks to support community-based development programs that promote economic growth; support community programs that build the capacity of organizations to provide service; and support the United Way. Grants are reviewed on an invitation-only basis. Project ideas that fit the guidelines can be submitted in a brief letter of inquiry, requesting an invitation to apply.
Requirements: Eligible are 501(c)3 nonprofit organizations located in the Qwest service area.
Restrictions: The foundation is unable to fund direct grants or scholarships to individuals; political organizations; sectarian religious activities; capital campaigns, chairs, or endowments; private foundations or pass-through organizations; general operating funds for single-disease health groups; goodwill advertising; or organizations that receive 3 percent or more of funds from United Way.
Geographic Focus: All U.S. States
Date(s) Application is Due: Apr 15
Amount: Up to 10,000 USD
Contact: Qwest Foundation; (303) 896-1266; Qwest.Foundation@qwest.com
Internet: http://www.qwest.com/about/company/sponsorships/foundation/improving.html
Sponsor: Qwest Foundation
1801 California Street, 50th Floor
Denver, CO 80202

Qwest Foundation Grants—Economic Development **1406**
The foundation supports innovative programs that focus on economic development and address the following: building job-entry skills through initiatives that focus on school-to- career transition, adult learning, and workforce development. Types of support include employee matching gifts, special projects, continuing support, matching funds, seed money, and technical assistance. Applicants must demonstrate how technology will assist them in meeting their organizational mission. Questions and proposals should be directed to the appropriate regional program officer as listed in the guidelines available on the website. Check the website for availability of funding.
Requirements: Eligible are 501(c)3 nonprofit organizations located in the Qwest service areas.
Restrictions: The foundation is unable to fund: direct grants or scholarships to individuals; political organizations; sectarian religious activities; capital campaigns, chairs, or endowments; private foundations or pass-through organizations; general operating funds for single-disease health groups; goodwill advertising; or organizations that receive 3 percent or more of funds from United Way.
Geographic Focus: All U.S. States
Amount: Up to 10,000 USD
Contact: Qwest Foundation; (303) 896-1266; Qwest.Foundation@qwest.com
Internet: http://www.qwest.com/about/company/sponsorships/foundation/innovative_Uses.html
Sponsor: Qwest Foundation
1801 California Street, 50th Floor
Denver, CO 80202

Qwest Foundation Grants—Education **1407**
The foundation will support programs in K-12 education. The foundation will consider programs that support: innovative models to strengthen K-12 public school education; improve the skills and leadership of educators; and effectively use technology to improve K-12 public school instruction. Subgrants currently are available in Idaho. Project ideas that fit the guidelines can be submitted in a brief letter of inquiry, requesting an invitation to apply.
Requirements: Eligible are 501(c)3 nonprofit organizations located in the Qwest service area.
Restrictions: The foundation is unable to fund direct grants or scholarships to individuals; political organizations; sectarian religious activities; capital campaigns, chairs, or endowments; private foundations or pass-through organizations; general operating funds for single-disease health groups; goodwill advertising; or organizations that receive 3 percent or more of funds from United Way.
Geographic Focus: Idaho
Date(s) Application is Due: Nov 18
Amount: Up to 10,000 USD
Contact: Qwest Foundation; (303) 896-1266; Qwest.Foundation@qwest.com
Internet: http://www.qwest.com/about/company/sponsorships/foundation/investing.html
Sponsor: Qwest Foundation
1801 California Street, 50th Floor
Denver, CO 80202

R.C. Baker Foundation Grants **1408**
The foundation makes grants to U.S. nonprofit organizations for projects and programs that support social services for youth and the elderly, crime prevention, education, religion (Christian, Episcopal, Friends, Jewish, Methodist, and Presbyterian), scientific research, culture, and health. Support will be provided for fellowships and scholarships, general operating grants, challenge/matching grants, emergency funds, building funds, equipment, continuing support, annual campaigns, capital campaigns, renovation projects, and special projects. Submit cover letter with proposal. The board meets in June and November to consider requests.
Requirements: Nonprofit organizations are eligible. $25,000 to
Restrictions: Anaheim Memorial Medical Center, Anaheim, CA - $40,000; Harvey Mudd College, Claremont, CA - $25,000
Date(s) Application is Due: May 1; Oct 1
Amount: 1,000 - 280,000 USD
Samples: Anaheim Memorial Medical Center, Anaheim, CA - $40,000; Harvey Mudd College, Claremont, CA - $25,000
Contact: Frank Scott, Chairman; (714) 750-8987
Sponsor: R.C. Baker Foundation
P.O. Box 6150
Orange, CA 92863-6150

R.T. Vanderbilt Trust Grants 1409

The trust awards grants in its areas of interest, including the arts, education, environmental programs, health care, historic preservation and societies, hospitals, and human services. Types of support include building construction/renovation, endowments, general operating support, and program development. The board meets in April, June, September, and December.

Requirements: There are no applications to submit. Proposals should be submitted in writing.

Restrictions: Applications are not accepted. Gives primarily to Connecticut, with some giving in Maine and New York. The trust does not give grants to individuals.

Geographic Focus: Connecticut, Maine, New York

Amount: Up to USD

Samples: The Historical Society of the Town of Greenwich, Cos Cob, Connecticut - $70,000 (2008); Music for Youth, Westport, Connecticut - $20,000 (2008); Metropolitan Museum of Art, New York, New York - $15,000 (2008)

Contact: Gloria Kallas, Trustee; (908) 598-3582; (336) 732-2024/(336) 747-8722

Sponsor: R.T. Vanderbilt Trust
1525 West WT Harris Boulevard
Charlotte, NC 28288-5709

RadioShack StreetSentz Community Grants 1410

The grant program is designed to offer answers—answers that bring community impact through programs or projects conducted by local nonprofit organizations. The program currently focuses on two areas: prevention of family violence/abuse, and/or child abduction. Guidelines are available online.

Requirements: 501(c)3 tax-exempt organizations and municipalities, including local police departments, are eligible. Applicant organization must offer solutions to help prevent family violence/abuse and/or child abduction; and directly impact or benefit, through programs and/or services, a RadioShack community.

Restrictions: Grants cannot be considered for individuals; endowments or private foundations that are themselves grant-making organizations; construction or major renovation projects; to fund advertising or marketing programs; fundraising events and sponsorships (i.e., golf tournaments, dinners, auctions); multiyear grants; religious, political, and fraternal organizations; or trips, sporting events, tours, and transportation.

Geographic Focus: All U.S. States

Date(s) Application is Due: Mar 15; Jun 15; Sep 15; Dec 15

Amount: Up to 500 USD

Contact: Community Relations Manager; (817) 415-3699; (817) 415-0939; corporate.citizenship@radioshack.com

Internet: http://www.radioshackcorporation.com/cc/contributions.html

Sponsor: RadioShack Corporation
200 RadioShack Circle, MS CF3-323
Fort Worth, TX 76102-1964

Ralph and Virginia Mullin Foundation Grants 1411

The foundation provides small grants to animal welfare and shelter organizations. The foundation also gives a few gifts annually to organizations that are working to become incorporated and obtain 501(c)3 status. Those grant recipients must use funds for costs directly related to achieving these goals.

Requirements: The foundation currently does not have a website. Contact the sponsor by mail or email for any additional guidelines or questions.

Geographic Focus: All U.S. States

Date(s) Application is Due: Sep 30

Amount: Up to 2,000 USD

Contact: Rob Rauh, (520) 881-6607; (520) 881-6775; rob@hrtucson.com

Sponsor: Ralph and Virginia Mullin Foundation
2401 E Speedway Boulevard
Tucson, AZ 85719

Ralph M. Parsons Foundation Grants 1412

The foundation encourages and supports projects and programs deemed beneficial in several major areas of interest. Higher education grants will be awarded with a strong emphasis on the fields of engineering, technology, and the sciences. University-based fellowships, developmental research, and equipment and building modifications for special projects or programs will be considered. Social impact grants focus on assistance to socially or economically disadvantaged groups, including women and children, families, youth, and the elderly. Civic and cultural grants extend and enhance the cultural life of all people by providing opportunities for access to cultural experiences where few or none have existed. Health grants target services to the disadvantaged, elderly, families, AIDS victims, and youth through support of programs and medical equipment associated with these services. Special projects grants respond to emerging societal needs or projects that fall outside the foundation's established areas of interest. Types of support include seed money, equipment, matching funds, special projects, internships, renovation projects, research, scholarship funds, fellowships, and operating budgets. The foundation staff submits applications to the board of directors six times per year, in alternate months, beginning in January. The first step in the application process is to mail a brief letter to the executive director, including a description of the project to be funded, the amount requested, justification for such a request, and background information about the applying organization.

Requirements: IRS 501(c)3 tax-exempt organizations located in Los Angeles County are eligible. (Applicant higher education institutions are not limited to this geographic area.)

Restrictions: IRS 509(a) private foundations are ineligible. Funding generally is not favored for general fund-raising events, dinners, or mass mailings; direct aid to individuals; conferences, seminars, workshops, etc; sectarian, religious, or fraternal purposes; endowment; federated fund-raising appeals; programs for which substantial support from government or other sources is available; nor support of candidates for political office or to influence legislation.

Geographic Focus: All U.S. States

Samples: Pitzer College (Claremont, CA)—to develop the Science Learning Community, $250,000.

Contact: Wendy Hoppe, Executive Director; (213) 482-3185; (213) 482-8878

Internet: http://www.rmpf.org

Sponsor: Ralph M. Parsons Foundation
1055 Wilshire Boulevard, Suite 1701
Los Angeles, CA 90017

Ralphs Food 4 Less Foundation Grants 1413

The foundation supports nonprofits primarily in areas of company operations in southern California, from Santa Barbara to San Diego, for programs and activities to improve the well-being of youth through education, recreation, and health-related programs; expand cultural awareness and appreciation of the arts; strengthen neighborhoods; and assist communities in the aftermath of local disasters. Types of support include special projects and general operating expenses. There are no application deadlines. Applicants should submit a letter of application.

Requirements: To be eligible, your organization must be: a 501(3) tax exempt nonprofit; located in Southern California; working in one of the focus areas. Requests for funding must arrive eight (8) weeks prior to the event date or date of need.

Restrictions: Funding is not available to: individuals; capital campaigns; travel expenses; projects of sectarian or religious organizations whose principal benefit is for their own members or adherents; organizations that discriminate on the basis of sex, race, religion, sexual orientation or national origin; third party giving.

Geographic Focus: California

Samples: Los Angeles Rescue Mission, Los Angeles, CA - $10,000 (2008); Community Environmental Council, Santa Barbara, CA - to support its annual Earth Day Festival $1,250 (2009); The Museum of Tolerance (MOT), Los Angeles, CA - to fund the MOT's student programs $10,000 (2008)

Contact: Michelle Williams, Executive Director; (310) 884-6205 or (310) 900-3522

Internet: http://www.ralphs.com/corpnewsinfo_charitablegiving_art5.htm

Sponsor: Ralph's-Food 4 Less Foundation
P.O. Box 54143
Los Angeles, CA 90054

Raskob Foundation for Catholic Activities Grants 1414

The foundation supports Roman Catholic church organizations and missionary activities worldwide. Grants support elementary and secondary education, community action and development, missionary activities, ministries (including youth and parish), health care, social concerns, AIDS victims, finance and development, and relief services. Types of support include operating budgets, seed money, emergency funds, equipment, land acquisition, conferences and seminars, program-related investments, renovation projects, special projects, and matching funds. Deadlines are June 8 and August 8 for the fall meeting; and December 8 and February 8 for the spring meeting.

Requirements: Roman Catholic organizations listed in the Kenedy Directory of Official Catholic Organizations may apply.
Geographic Focus: All U.S. States
Date(s) Application is Due: Feb 8; Aug 8
Amount: 5,000 - 15,000 USD
Samples: Sisters of Mercy (Belize)—toward the renovations/repairs of the convent building, $3000; Church of Immaculate Conception (Andhra Pradesh, India)—to purchase milch cows as income-generating projects for Mahilda Mandel self-help women's groups in the parish, $7200; Daughters of Divine Love (Enugu, Nigeria)—toward the annual salary of a doctor and two nurses and purchase of essential drugs and medical materials for Saint Luke's Maternity Clinic in Enugu, $4000; Salpointe Catholic High School (Tucson, AZ)—to purchase class sets of graphing calculators, $1000.
Contact: Maureen Horner, Grants Management; (302) 655-4440; (302) 655-3223
Internet: http://www.rfca.org/grantinfo.htm
Sponsor: Raskob Foundation for Catholic Activities
P.O. Box 4019
Wilmington, DE 19807

Rathmann Family Foundation Grants **1415**
The foundation's main funding areas are education, with priority given to science and math; the arts; children and youth health organizations; and preservation of the environment. Types of support include general operating support, continuing support, capital campaigns, equipment acquisition, endowment funds, program development, conferences and seminars, seed grants, curriculum development, fellowships, internships, scholarship funds, research, and matching funds. There are no specific deadlines or application forms, and interested parties should begin by contacting the Foundation directly.
Requirements: Grants are awarded to organizations in the San Francisco Bay, California area; the Annapolis, Maryland area; the Seattle, Washington area; the Philadelphia, Pennsylvania area: and metropolitan Minneapolis/Saint Paul, Minnesota.
Restrictions: Grants are not awarded to/for private foundations; religious organizations for religious activities; civil rights; social action; advocacy organizations; fraternal groups; political purposes; mental health counseling; individuals; or fundraisers, media events, public relations, annual appeals, or propaganda.
Geographic Focus: California, Maryland, Minnesota, Pennsylvania, Washington
Amount: 1,000 - 100,000 USD
Contact: Rick Rathmann, (410) 349-2376; (410) 349-2377
Sponsor: Rathmann Family Foundation
1290 Bay Dale Drive, P.O. Box 352
Arnold, MD 21012

Ray Foundation Mental Health and Substance Abuse Prevention Grants **1416**
The purpose of this program is to support youth agencies with programs in mental health and substance abuse prevention, with particular interest in promoting sports and aviation as alternatives to drug abuse. Additional areas of interest include fine arts, historic preservation, higher and other education, and science and technology. Types of support include building construction/renovation, consulting services, continuing support, emergency funds, equipment acquisition, general operating grants, see grants, publications, research grants, and technical assistance.
Requirements: Youth agencies in the Pacific Northwest are eligible to apply.
Restrictions: Grants are not made to individuals or for deficit funding, and no support is given to religious organizations unless they are requesting funds for a community project.
Geographic Focus: Oregon, Washington
Contact: James Ray, President; (775) 782-8337
Sponsor: Ray Foundation
2241 Park Place, Suite A1
Minden, NV 89423

Rayonier Foundation Grants **1417**
The foundation awards grants to eligible nonprofit organizations in its areas of interest, including children and youth, community development, disadvantaged (economically), education, engineering, environmental programs, families, health care and hospitals, libraries, minorities, performing arts, recreation science, social services, technology, and volunteerism. Types of support include annual campaigns, building construction/renovation, continuing support, employee matching gifts, employee-related scholarships, endowments, equipment acquisition, general operating support, matching/challenge grants, performing arts, program development, recreation, science, research grants, scholarship funds, and seed grants.
Requirements: Nonprofit organizations in Florida, Georgia, and Washington are eligible.
Geographic Focus: Florida, Georgia, Washington
Amount: 250 - 25,000 USD
Samples: United Way of Clallam County, Port Angeles, WA - $4,243; Florida Community College at Jacksonville Foundation, Jacksonville, FL - $25,000; University of Virginia, Charlottesville, VA - $7,500
Contact: Charles H. Hood, President; (904) 357-9100; (904) 357-9101; info@rayonier.com
Sponsor: Rayonier Foundation
50 North Laura Street, Stuite 1900
Jacksonville, FL 32202

Raytheon Company Corporate Contributions Program **1418**
Raytheon's philanthropic interests are strategically focused on math and science education—math, science, engineering, or teacher development from K to college; access and opportunity—help women, minorities, the disadvantaged, or disabled develop skills to participate in the classroom or marketplace; and environmental stewardship—prevent pollution and care for natural resources. The company supplements cash gifts with in-kind donations of appliances, electronics, or other products. Types of support include building construction/renovation, capital campaigns, equipment, general operating support, project development, and technical assistance. Application and guidelines are available online.
Requirements: Nonprofit groups near company facilities may apply.
Restrictions: Funding requests should not be submitted for individuals; operating support for organizations affiliated with the United Way; religious, fraternal, political, athletic, or veterans' organizations; health and disease-specific organizations; basic research projects; sponsorships of local groups or individuals to participate in regional, national, or international competitions, conferences or events; private foundations; in-kind contributions; private elementary and secondary schools; or organizations whose activities are primarily national or international in scope.
Geographic Focus: All U.S. States
Amount: Up to 5,000,000 USD
Samples: Exploration Place (Wichita, KS)—to support the capital campaign, $300,000; Air Force Memorial Commission—to support the design, construction, and dedication of the Air Force Memorial in Washington, DC, $200,000; American Battle Monuments Commission—for the National World War II Memorial, $120,000; Youth Tech Entrepreneurs—to support operating expenses, $25,000.
Contact: Contribution Program Manager; (781) 522-3000; (781) 860-2999; corporatecontributions@raytheon.com
Internet: http://www.raytheon.com/community
Sponsor: Raytheon Company
870 Winter Street
Waltham, MA 02451

RBC Dain Rauscher Foundation Grants **1419**
The foundation awards grants to youth education efforts, social services programs, and the arts. In youth education, K-12 programs that serve students of color or disadvantaged children, and programs that help children understand the country's economic system are funded. The emphasis in social services giving is programs that foster economic independence and self-sufficiency and that help families. Types of support include general operating support, continuing support, annual campaigns, building construction/renovation, seed grants, and matching gifts.
Geographic Focus: Arizona, California, Illinois, Iowa, Kansas, Louisiana, Minnesota, Montana, Nebraska, North Dakota, Oklahoma, Oregon, South Dakota, Texas, Utah, Washington, Wyoming
Amount: Up to 20,000 USD
Contact: Sherry Koster, Program Manager; (612) 371-2765 or (612) 371-2936; (612) 371-7933; sherry.koster@rbcdain.com
Internet: http://www.rbcwm-usa.com/DRP_1.0/Public_Site/Common_Pages/DRP_1.0VSectionIndex/1,73394,4-3-2-0,00.html
Sponsor: RBC Dain Rauscher Foundation
60 South 6th Street, P2
Minneapolis, MN 55402-4422

RCF General Community Grants 1420

Six times a year, the Richland County Foundation awards General Community Grants to nonprofit organizations through a competitive process. In doing so, the Foundation looks to partner with nonprofit organizations to respond to current community needs in the following areas: education; health services; arts and culture; community services; children, youth and families; human services; environment; and employment and economic development. Application deadlines are 5:00 p.m. on the first Friday of January, March, May, July, September, and November. Applications must be at the Foundation Office by 5:00 p.m. on the due date to meet the deadline. Final decisions on all grant applications are made by the Board of Trustees approximately 6 – 8 weeks following the grant deadline.

Requirements: 501(c)3 public charities, government entities, schools, and nonprofit medical facilities serving residents of Richland County are eligible to apply. The application procedure should begin with a telephone call to the Program Officer to schedule an initial meeting to discuss the project. The Foundation typically looks for several of the following key elements in submitted applications: a one-time grant, especially for a pilot project which can serve as a model or be replicated; a project in which the Foundation is a funding partner, rather than the sole funder; a project or program which promotes volunteer involvement; an organization which can demonstrate the ability to sustain the project in the future when Foundation grant dollars end; projects or programs which are a collaborative effort(s) among nonprofit organizations in the community which eliminate duplication of services; a project which is likely to make a clear difference in the quality of life of a substantial number of people; an organization which is proposing a practical approach to a solution of a current community problem; a project or program which is focusing on prevention; and a worthy community project for which a grant from the Foundation will most likely leverage additional financial support. Applicants who have a program or project that meets these criteria are encouraged to contact the Foundation to discuss submitting an application.

Restrictions: Community grants are awarded from endowed, unrestricted and field of interest funds. Richland County Foundation typically does not provide funding from unrestricted funds for the following: sectarian activities of religious organizations; operating expenses for annual drives or to eliminate debt; medical, scientific or academic research; individuals other than for college scholarships; travel to or in support of conferences, or travel for groups such as bands, sports teams and classes (unless through special grant programs such as Summertime Kids or the Teacher Assistance Program); capital improvements to building and property not owned by the organization or covered by a long term lease; computer systems; projects that taxpayers support or expected to support; and political issues.

Geographic Focus: Ohio

Samples: Ashland University, Ashland, Ohio, $250,000 - this grant is part of a $15.5 million campaign to build a College of Nursing facility in Richland County (2011); Richland Community Development Group, Mansfield, Ohio, $50,000 - this supports phase two of a pilot project to coordinate a county-wide collaborative effort for both economic and community development (2011).

Contact: Bradford Groves, President; (419) 525-3020; (419) 525-1590; bgroves@rcfoundation.orgRebecca Smith, Program Officer; (419) 525-3020; (419) 525-1590; bsmith@rcfoundation.org

Internet: http://www.richlandcountyfoundation.org/grant-information/types-of-grants/community

Sponsor: Richland County Foundation
24 West Third Street, Suite 100
Mansfield, OH 44902-1209

Regional Arts and Cultural Council General Support Grants 1421

RACC supports the region's vital arts and culture community through a variety of grant programs. The General Support Grants aims to provide general financial support to arts organizations in Multnomah, Washington, and Clackamas Counties, based on their artistic excellence, proven service to the community, administrative and fiscal competence and RACC grant compliance. The General Support Grants seeks to fund arts organizations and provide a wide range of high quality arts programming made available to the public. The General Support application process is bi-annual. General Support grants are for arts organizations with eligible expenses between $80,000 and $500,000.

Requirements: Some of the basic eligibility requirements for General Support are: be an arts organization; have IRS 501(c)3 tax status; have been in existence for a minimum of three years or be the result of merging organizations with at least a three-year history each; have minimum eligible income of $80,000; have at least one paid professional administrative staff; and have continuous administration throughout the year. The General Support Grant program provides financial support to Multnomah, Washington and Clackamas County not-for-profit organizations and individual artists.

Geographic Focus: Oregon

Amount: 6,000 - 150,000 USD

Contact: Tonisha Toler, Grants & Outreach Coordinator; (503) 823-5866 or (503) 823-5111; (503) 823-5432; ttoler@racc.orgHelen Daltoso, Grants Officer; (503) 823-5402 or (503) 823-5111; (503) 823-5432; hdaltoso@racc.org

Internet: http://www.racc.org/grants/general-support-grants

Sponsor: Regional Arts and Cultural Council
108 NW 9th Avenue, Suite 300
Portland, OR 97209-3318

Regional Arts and Cultural Council Opportunity Grants 1422

The Opportunity Grants is funded by the City of Portland and is designed to provide grants to Portland-based nonprofit arts and cultural organizations to help meet special opportunities or assist organizations with emergencies that arise during the year and that are not part of the applicant's annual budget or regular programming. There will be multiple cycles of this grant throughout the fiscal year. It is meant to supplement but not be a substitute for any other existing RACC grant.

Requirements: Portland-based nonprofit arts and culture organizations are eligible to apply for the Opportunity Grant provided that they meet all the following *requirements:* is a nonprofit arts and culture organization that regularly presents arts and/or cultural events or arts projects; has current tax-exempt status under Section 501(c)3 of the Internal Revenue Service and regularly produces financial statements; is headquartered and has a physical address in the City of Portland; provides arts and culture programs and events that are advertised and open to the public; and is current on all RACC grant agreements and has submitted final reports for all completed RACC grants.

Restrictions: Applicants receiving funds from this program will not be eligible to apply again for a period of 24 months from the date of the final report submission to RACC.

Geographic Focus: Oregon

Date(s) Application is Due: Sep 7

Contact: Tonisha Toler, Grants & Outreach Coordinator; (503) 823-5866 or (503) 823-5111; (503) 823-5432; ttoler@racc.orgHelen Daltoso, Grants Officer; (503) 823-5402 or (503) 823-5111; (503) 823-5432; hdaltoso@racc.orgCynthia Knapp, Director of Operations; (503) 823-5403 or (503) 823-5111; (503) 823-5432; cknapp@racc.org

Internet: http://www.racc.org/grants/opportunity-grants

Sponsor: Regional Arts and Cultural Council
108 NW 9th Avenue, Suite 300
Portland, OR 97209-3318

Reinberger Foundation Grants 1423

The foundation supports medical research, colleges and universities, cultural organizations, environmental organizations, and social services agencies. Types of support include building construction/renovation, equipment acquisition, general operating support, continuing support, annual campaigns, capital campaigns, endowment funds, debt reduction, program development, publication, scholarship funds, research, and matching funds.

Requirements: Most organizations receiving assistance are in the Cleveland and Columbus, OH, areas.

Geographic Focus: Ohio

Samples: Ideastream (Cleveland, OH) and Playhouse Square Foundation (Cleveland, OH)—for the Idea Center at Playhouse Square, which will offer educational programs that incorporate the performing arts, radio, television, and other technologies, $1 million.

Contact: Robert Reinberger, President; (216) 292-2790; (216) 292-4466

Sponsor: Reinberger Foundation
27600 Chagrin Boulevard
Cleveland, OH 44122

RESIST Arthur Raymond Cohen Memorial Fund Grants 1424

RESIST, founded in 1967, was originally formed to oppose the war in Vietnam and to support draft resistance. By the 1970s, RESIST expanded its scope dramatically by making the connection between the unequal distribution of power and money at home, and a system of U.S. domination abroad. The Arthur Raymond Cohen Memorial Fund Grant is designed to support the causes to which Arthur Cohen (1918-1986) was committed: opposition to the arms race,

the cold war, and American intervention abroad; and support for civil liberties, the fight against racism; and the struggle of workers and unions at home.
Restrictions: RESIST does not fund: organizations with annual budgets over $150,000; individuals; groups that primarily provide direct services (to individuals, families or communities) that are not part of progressive organizing activities; research, litigation or legal organizations unless they are directly connected to progressive organizing campaigns; organizations located outside the United States; the development or production of films, videos or radio projects; media or cultural organizations not directly connected to progressive organizing campaigns; organizations with access to traditional sources of funding; or other foundations or grant giving organizations.
Geographic Focus: All U.S. States
Date(s) Application is Due: Feb 4; Apr 1; Jun 3; Aug 5; Sep 30; Dec 3
Contact: Robin Carton, Director of Grants; (617) 623-5110; robin@resistinc.org
Internet: http://www.resistinc.org/node/1528
Sponsor: RESIST
259 Elm Street
Somerville, MA 02144

RESIST Freda Friedman Salzman Memorial Fund Grants **1425**
RESIST, founded in 1967, was originally formed to oppose the war in Vietnam and to support draft resistance. By the 1970s, RESIST expanded its scope dramatically by making the connection between the unequal distribution of power and money at home, and a system of U.S. domination abroad. The Freda Friedman Salzman Memorial Fund is dedicated to the purpose of supporting organized resistance to the institutions and practices that rob people of their dignity as full human beings, giving a high priority to the efforts of Native American peoples to resist cultural as well as actual genocide.
Restrictions: RESIST does not fund: organizations with annual budgets over $150,000; individuals; groups that primarily provide direct services (to individuals, families or communities) that are not part of progressive organizing activities; research, litigation or legal organizations unless they are directly connected to progressive organizing campaigns; organizations located outside the United States; the development or production of films, videos or radio projects; media or cultural organizations not directly connected to progressive organizing campaigns; organizations with access to traditional sources of funding; or other foundations or grant giving organizations.
Geographic Focus: All U.S. States
Date(s) Application is Due: Feb 4; Apr 1; Jun 3; Aug 5; Sep 30; Dec 3
Contact: Robin Carton, Director of Grants; (617) 623-5110; robin@resistinc.org
Internet: http://www.resistinc.org/node/1528
Sponsor: RESIST
259 Elm Street
Somerville, MA 02144

RESIST General Support Grants **1426**
RESIST, founded in 1967, was originally formed to oppose the war in Vietnam and to support draft resistance. By the 1970s, RESIST expanded its scope dramatically by making the connection between the unequal distribution of power and money at home, and a system of U.S. domination abroad. Organizations with an annual budget of $150,000 or less may apply for a one-year grant with the maximum amount requested not to exceed $3,000. RESIST provides funds for general support as a means of enabling grantees to build infrastructure and capacity while engaged in on-going social justice activism. Up to $4,000 is given for general support as a means of building infrastructure and capacity while engaged in on-going social justice activism.
Requirements: Organizations with a budget of approximately $125,000 or less may apply for a one-year grant.
Restrictions: RESIST does not fund: organizations with annual budgets over $150,000; individuals; groups that primarily provide direct services (to individuals, families or communities) that are not part of progressive organizing activities; research, litigation or legal organizations unless they are directly connected to progressive organizing campaigns; organizations located outside the United States; the development or production of films, videos or radio projects; media or cultural organizations not directly connected to progressive organizing campaigns; organizations with access to traditional sources of funding; or other foundations or grant giving organizations.
Geographic Focus: All U.S. States
Date(s) Application is Due: Feb 4; Apr 1; Jun 3; Aug 5; Sep 30; Dec 3
Amount: 500 - 4,000 USD
Contact: Robin Carton, Director of Grants; (617) 623-5110; robin@resistinc.org
Internet: http://www.resistinc.org
Sponsor: RESIST
259 Elm Street
Somerville, MA 02144

RESIST Hell Yes! Award **1427**
RESIST, founded in 1967, was originally formed to oppose the war in Vietnam and to support draft resistance. By the 1970s, RESIST expanded its scope dramatically by making the connection between the unequal distribution of power and money at home, and a system of U.S. domination abroad. To honor the moral clarity, courage and political commitment of its founders, RESIST created a new tribute grant in 2008: the Hell Yes! Award. This grant recognizes inspiring, radical activism that cuts to the heart of RESIST's mission to challenge illegitimate authority.
Restrictions: RESIST does not fund: organizations with annual budgets over $150,000; individuals; groups that primarily provide direct services (to individuals, families or communities) that are not part of progressive organizing activities; research, litigation or legal organizations unless they are directly connected to progressive organizing campaigns; organizations located outside the United States; the development or production of films, videos or radio projects; media or cultural organizations not directly connected to progressive organizing campaigns; organizations with access to traditional sources of funding; or other foundations or grant giving organizations.
Geographic Focus: All U.S. States
Date(s) Application is Due: Feb 4; Apr 1; Jun 3; Aug 5; Sep 30; Dec 3
Contact: Robin Carton, Director of Grants; (617) 623-5110; robin@resistinc.org
Internet: http://www.resistinc.org/node/1528
Sponsor: RESIST
259 Elm Street
Somerville, MA 02144

RESIST Ken Hale Tribute Grants **1428**
RESIST, founded in 1967, was originally formed to oppose the war in Vietnam and to support draft resistance. By the 1970s, RESIST expanded its scope dramatically by making the connection between the unequal distribution of power and money at home, and a system of U.S. domination abroad. The Ken Hale Tribute Grant is given in memory of the life and work of Ken Hale (1934-2001), one of the world's foremost linguists, a RESIST founder and a passionate activist for justice. This grant is given to support organizations which ensure that the voices of those most affected are given primacy in the struggle to protect and expand civil, cultural and political rights.
Restrictions: RESIST does not fund: organizations with annual budgets over $150,000; individuals; groups that primarily provide direct services (to individuals, families or communities) that are not part of progressive organizing activities; research, litigation or legal organizations unless they are directly connected to progressive organizing campaigns; organizations located outside the United States; the development or production of films, videos or radio projects; media or cultural organizations not directly connected to progressive organizing campaigns; organizations with access to traditional sources of funding; or other foundations or grant giving organizations.
Geographic Focus: All U.S. States
Date(s) Application is Due: Feb 4; Apr 1; Jun 3; Aug 5; Sep 30; Dec 3
Contact: Robin Carton, Director of Grants; (617) 623-5110; robin@resistinc.org
Internet: http://www.resistinc.org/node/1528
Sponsor: RESIST
259 Elm Street
Somerville, MA 02144

RESIST Leslie D'Cora Holmes Memorial Fund Grants **1429**
RESIST, founded in 1967, was originally formed to oppose the war in Vietnam and to support draft resistance. By the 1970s, RESIST expanded its scope dramatically by making the connection between the unequal distribution of power and money at home, and a system of U.S. domination abroad. The Leslie D'Cora Holmes Memorial Fund Grant was established in 1999 to honor the life's work and legacy of Leslie D'Cora Holmes. This fund supports activities and organizations that embody the characteristics, values, and principles that reflect her spirit-filled mission, including: empowerment for communities and individuals; self-determination through education and community organizing; harmonization of diverse communities of interest; actualization

and recognition of individual potential; courage of conviction; and pride in culture, community and self.
Restrictions: RESIST does not fund: organizations with annual budgets over $150,000; individuals; groups that primarily provide direct services (to individuals, families or communities) that are not part of progressive organizing activities; research, litigation or legal organizations unless they are directly connected to progressive organizing campaigns; organizations located outside the United States; the development or production of films, videos or radio projects; media or cultural organizations not directly connected to progressive organizing campaigns; organizations with access to traditional sources of funding; or other foundations or grant giving organizations.
Geographic Focus: All U.S. States
Date(s) Application is Due: Feb 4; Apr 1; Jun 3; Aug 5; Sep 30; Dec 3
Contact: Robin Carton, Director of Grants; (617) 623-5110; robin@resistinc.org
Internet: http://www.resistinc.org/node/1528
Sponsor: RESIST
259 Elm Street
Somerville, MA 02144

RESIST Mike Riegle Tribute Grants **1430**
RESIST, founded in 1967, was originally formed to oppose the war in Vietnam and to support draft resistance. By the 1970s, RESIST expanded its scope dramatically by making the connection between the unequal distribution of power and money at home, and a system of U.S. domination abroad. The Mike Riegle Tribute Grant is given in memory of the life and work of Boston activist Mike Riegle, a supporter of prisoners' rights, gay and lesbian liberation, and the radical movement for justice.
Restrictions: RESIST does not fund: organizations with annual budgets over $150,000; individuals; groups that primarily provide direct services (to individuals, families or communities) that are not part of progressive organizing activities; research, litigation or legal organizations unless they are directly connected to progressive organizing campaigns; organizations located outside the United States; the development or production of films, videos or radio projects; media or cultural organizations not directly connected to progressive organizing campaigns; organizations with access to traditional sources of funding; or other foundations or grant giving organizations.
Geographic Focus: All U.S. States
Date(s) Application is Due: Feb 4; Apr 1; Jun 3; Aug 5; Sep 30; Dec 3
Contact: Robin Carton, Director of Grants; (617) 623-5110; robin@resistinc.org
Internet: http://www.resistinc.org/node/1528
Sponsor: RESIST
259 Elm Street
Somerville, MA 02144

RESIST Multi-Year Grants **1431**
RESIST, founded in 1967, was originally formed to oppose the war in Vietnam and to support draft resistance. By the 1970s, RESIST expanded its scope dramatically by making the connection between the unequal distribution of power and money at home, and a system of U.S. domination abroad. Grantees who have been funded by RESIST at least two times during the preceding five years may apply for a multi-year grant. Of the two prior grant awards, the most recent must have been for the full amount given out during that cycle. Multi-year grants will cover a three year period and are designed to provide general support to eligible grantee organizations.
Requirements: All multi-year applicants must: submit answers to the Multi-Year Grant Questionnaire; and be currently eligible to receive grant awards under RESIST's Funding Guidelines. All applicants must provide specific, measurable objectives as part of their proposal. These objectives should demonstrate the capacity to plan at least one to three years ahead. In addition, groups must submit evidence of their past performance, examples of which might include prior Progress or Annual Reports, with their proposal.
Restrictions: RESIST does not fund: organizations with annual budgets over $150,000; individuals; groups that primarily provide direct services (to individuals, families or communities) that are not part of progressive organizing activities; research, litigation or legal organizations unless they are directly connected to progressive organizing campaigns; organizations located outside the United States; the development or production of films, videos or radio projects; media or cultural organizations not directly connected to progressive organizing campaigns; organizations with access to traditional sources of funding; or other foundations or grant giving organizations.
Geographic Focus: All U.S. States
Date(s) Application is Due: Feb 4; Apr 1; Jun 3; Aug 5; Sep 30; Dec 3
Amount: 500 - 4,000 USD
Contact: Robin Carton, Director of Grants; (617) 623-5110; robin@resistinc.org
Internet: http://www.resistinc.org/node/1527
Sponsor: RESIST
259 Elm Street
Somerville, MA 02144

RESIST Sharon Kurtz Memorial Fund Grants **1432**
RESIST, founded in 1967, was originally formed to oppose the war in Vietnam and to support draft resistance. By the 1970s, RESIST expanded its scope dramatically by making the connection between the unequal distribution of power and money at home, and a system of U.S. domination abroad. In 2008, the friends and family of Sharon Kurtz chose RESIST as the home of a new fund in her name. The Sharon Kurtz Memorial Fund commemorates the life of Sharon Kurtz, a community organizer who dedicated her life to making the world a more just and humane place.
Restrictions: RESIST does not fund: organizations with annual budgets over $150,000; individuals; groups that primarily provide direct services (to individuals, families or communities) that are not part of progressive organizing activities; research, litigation or legal organizations unless they are directly connected to progressive organizing campaigns; organizations located outside the United States; the development or production of films, videos or radio projects; media or cultural organizations not directly connected to progressive organizing campaigns; organizations with access to traditional sources of funding; or other foundations or grant giving organizations.
Geographic Focus: All U.S. States
Date(s) Application is Due: Feb 4; Apr 1; Jun 3; Aug 5; Sep 30; Dec 3
Contact: Robin Carton, Director of Grants; (617) 623-5110; robin@resistinc.org
Internet: http://www.resistinc.org/node/1528
Sponsor: RESIST
259 Elm Street
Somerville, MA 02144

Reynolds Family Foundation Grants **1433**
The Foundation, established in California in support of its residents, is primarily aimed at supporting educational programs, human services, and international affairs. Funding most often comes in the form of general operating support. Although there are no specific grant applications required, applicants should contact the Foundation initially by either letter or telephone, followed by a detailed letter of application outlining the project and amount of funding requested.
Geographic Focus: California
Amount: 500 - 3,000 USD
Samples: Angel Kiss Foundation, Reno, Nevada, $300,; Saint Johns Health Center Foundation, Santa. Monica, California, $3,000.
Contact: Paula M. Golden, President; (310) 600-0598 or (310) 829-8433; (310) 556-7986; paula@paulagolden.net
Internet: http://paulagolden.net/about_us
Sponsor: Reynolds Family Foundation
2132 Century Park Lane, #209
Los Angeles, CA 90067-3312

Rhode Island Foundation Grants **1434**
The foundation seeks to promote philanthropic activities that will improve the living conditions and well-being of the inhabitants of Rhode Island. Grants for capital and operating purposes principally to agencies working in the fields of education, health care, the arts and cultural affairs, youth, the aged, social services, urban affairs, historic preservation, and the environment.
Requirements: Rhode Island nonprofits organizations may apply. See Foundations website for additional guidelines.
Restrictions: The foundation does not make grants for endowments, research, religious groups for religious purposes, hospital equipment, capital needs of health organizations, or to educational institutions for general operating expenses.
Geographic Focus: Rhode Island
Samples: Ocean State Action Fund, Cranston, RI, $50,000 - for continued funding for grassroots organizing, coalition work, and public communications in support of affordable, quality health care for all Rhode Islanders (2008); Community Housing Land Trust of Rhode Island, Providence, RI, $50,000 - for new program targeting foreclosed properties or those close to being

foreclosed upon (2008); Sakonnet Preservation Association, Little Compton, RI, $25,000 - for three-community partnership to preserve drinking water quality and open space in Newport County (2008)
Contact: Owen Heleen, Vice President for Grantss; (401) 427-4009 or (401) 274-4564; (401) 331-8085; oheleen@rifoundation.org
Internet: http://www.rifoundation.org/Nonprofits/GrantOpportunities/tabid/175/Default.aspx
Sponsor: Rhode Island Foundation
1 Union Station
Providence, RI 02903

Rice Foundation Grants **1435**
The foundation awards grants to Illinois nonprofit organizations in its areas of interest, including civic affairs, higher education, hospitals, libraries, medical education, and youth programs. Project and operating support are available. There are no application forms or deadlines.
Requirements: Applicants should submit a proposal with directly to the Foundation including the following: statement of problem project will address; copy of IRS Determination Letter; brief history of organization and description of its mission; detailed description of project and amount of funding requested.
Geographic Focus: Illinois
Amount: 25,000 - 1,000,000 USD
Contact: Peter Nolan, President; (847) 581-9999
Sponsor: Daniel F. and Ada L. Rice Foundation
8600 Gross Point Road
Skokie, IL 60077-2151

Richard and Helen DeVos Foundation Grants **1436**
The foundation supports nonprofit organizations primarily in western Michigan and central Florida in its areas of interest, including religious agencies and churches and education and outreach, social services, the arts, public policy, and health care. Types of support include general operating support, continuing support, annual campaigns, capital campaigns, building construction/renovation, program development, seed grants, and matching funds.
Requirements: Application forms are not required. Applicants should submit the following: copy of IRS Determination Letter; copy of current year's organizational budget and/or project budget. The Board meets every 3 months, submit your proposal two weeks prior to the review (contact Foundation for deadline dates). Mail applications to: 126 Ottawa Avenue, N.W., Suite 500, Grand Rapids, MI 49503
Restrictions: No grants to individuals.
Geographic Focus: Florida, Michigan
Amount: 300 - 5,000,000 USD
Samples: Michigan State University, East Lansing, Michigan, $5,000,000 - For general support, payable over 1 year); Salvation Army of West Palm Beach, West Palm Beach, Florida, $50,000 - For general support, payable over 1 year
Contact: Ginny Vander Hart, Foundation Director; (616) 643-4700; (616) 774-0116; virginiav@rdvcorp.com
Sponsor: Richard and Helen DeVos Foundation Grants
P.O. Box 230257
Grand Rapids, MI 49523-0257

Richard and Rhoda Goldman Fund Grants **1437**
The fund is interested in supporting programs that will have a significant positive impact in an array of fields, including culture, the environment, population, Jewish affairs, violence prevention, children and youth, the elderly, and social and human services. Types of support include general operating support, continuing support, capital campaigns, program development, and seed money. Funds will be allocated primarily in the San Francisco Bay area of California and to organizations benefiting this area. There are no application deadlines.
Requirements: Nonprofit organizations serving primarily the San Francisco Bay area of California are eligible.
Restrictions: The fund does not accept applications for research or award grants or scholarships for individuals, conferences, documentary films, or fund-raisers. Unsolicited proposals for support of arts organizations or institutions of primary, secondary, or higher education will not be accepted.
Geographic Focus: California
Amount: 1,000 - 500,000 USD
Samples: San Francisco Beautification (CA)—for efforts to increase green schoolyards, $10,000; American Jewish Joint Distribution Committee (New York, NY)—for relief efforts following the earthquake and tsunamis that struck Southeast Asia in 2004, $30,000; United States Public Interest Research Group Education Fund (Washington, DC)—for efforts to increase attention to the role of hard money in federal political campaigns, $20,000; Community Awareness and Treatment Services (San Francisco, CA)—for support of this 24-hour shelter and transitional-housing program for women, $25,000.
Contact: Sam Salkin, Executive Director; (415) 345-6300; (415) 345-9686; info@goldmanfund.org
Internet: http://www.goldmanfund.org
Sponsor: Richard and Rhoda Goldman Fund
211 Lincoln Boulevard, P.O. Box 29924
San Francisco, CA 94129

Richard and Susan Smith Family Foundation Grants **1438**
The foundation awards grants to Massachusetts nonprofit organizations in its areas of interest, including arts and culture, children and youth, disadvantaged (economically), education (early childhood, elementary, and higher), minorities, biomedical research, health care and social services delivery. Types of support include annual campaigns, building construction/renovation, capital campaigns, curriculum development, general operating grants, program/project support, seed grants, and service delivery programs. There are no application forms.
Requirements: Massachusetts nonprofit organizations serving the greater Boston area are eligible.
Restrictions: Grants do not support political activities; religious activities; individuals; or requests for deficit financing or endowment funds.
Geographic Focus: Massachusetts
Date(s) Application is Due: Mar 15; Aug 15
Amount: 5,000 - 238,000 USD
Samples: Compassionate Care ALS, West Falmouth, MA $25,000 - for the purchase of a cargo van to transport adaptive equipment to and from patient homes (2009); United Teen Equality Center, Lowell, MA $944,780 - funding provides violence prevention, youth development, education and community organizing programs for the youth center, the grant is payable over 5 years (2009)
Contact: David Ford, Executive Director; (617) 278-5200; (617) 278-5250; dford@smithfamilyfoundation.net
Internet: http://www.smithfamilyfoundation.net
Sponsor: Richard and Susan Smith Family Foundation
1280 Boylston Street, Suite 100
Chestnut Hill, MA 02467

Richard D. Bass Foundation Grants **1439**
The Richard D. Bass Foundation's area of interest include: arts/cultural-programs, including music and dance companies; Catholic/Protestant agencies & churches; community/economic development; education; health organizations, association. The type of support available include: annual campaigns; building/renovation; capital campaigns; general/operating support. Giving primarily in the metropolitan Dallas, Texas area. Grants range from $500 - $15,000. Application deadlines are March 31 and September 30 annually.
Requirements: IRS 501(c)3 nonprofit organizations are available to apply. The Foundations gives primarily to the Dallas, Texas region of the United States but funding is not limited to Texas. Grant proposals are available through out the U.S., contact the Foundation directly before submitting a proposal to access the likely hood of funding for your project. There is no application form required when applying for funding. Submit the proposal with one copy of the organizations IRS Determination Letter.
Restrictions: Funding is not available for: private foundations; individuals.
Geographic Focus: All U.S. States
Date(s) Application is Due: Mar 31; Sep 30
Amount: 500 - 10,000 USD
Samples: Dallas Opera, Dallas, TX, $5,000—arts grant (2008); Metro Dallas Homeless Alliance, Dallas, TX, $2,500—community grant (2008); Yale University, New haven, CT, $5,000—education grant (2008); First Baptist Church, Valley Mills, TX, $500—religious grant (2008); American Foundation for the Blind, Dallas, TX, $2,500—health grant (2008).
Contact: Barbara B. Moroney, Treasurer; (214) 351-6994
Sponsor: Richard D. Bass Foundation
4516 Wildwood Road
Dallas, TX 75209-1926

Richard H. Driehaus Foundation Grants 1440

The Richard H. Driehaus Foundation, founded in 1983 and as a family foundation in 1992, benefits individuals and communities primarily by supporting the preservation and enhancement of the built and natural environments through historic preservation, encouragement of quality architectural and landscape design, and conserving open space. The Foundation also supports the performing and visual arts and makes grants to organizations that provide opportunities for working families who remain poor. The foundation currently provides funding in the areas of the Built Environment, Economic Opportunity for the Working Poor, Government Accountability/Investigative Reporting, Small Museums and Cultural Centers. The Foundation accepts no unsolicited proposals, but welcomes letters of inquiry and phone calls. Proposals are encouraged from companies that emphasize presentation instead of education or community outreach. Guidelines and application information are available online.
Requirements: Dance and theater companies in the Chicago metropolitan area that have produced at least one show in the Chicago area and that have annual operating budgets of less than $100,000 are eligible.
Restrictions: The Foundation tends not to fund large organizations with multi-million dollar budgets; arts education or arts outreach; community theater and community dance; public, private or parochial education; or health care.
Geographic Focus: Illinois
Date(s) Application is Due: Mar 1; Jul 1; Nov 1
Amount: 5,000 - 50,000 USD
Samples: Arts & Business Council of Chicago, Illinois, $30,000 - a two-year grant for operating support (2011); Arts Work Fund for Organizational Development, Chicago, Illinois, $30,000 - operating support (2011); DuSable Museum of African American History, Chicago, Illinois, $20,000 - for an exhibit on "Geoffrey and Carmen: A memoir in four movements."
Contact: Sonia Fischer, Executive Director; (312) 641-5772; (312) 641-5736; sunnyfischer@driehausfoundation.org
Internet: http://www.driehausfoundation.org
Sponsor: Richard H. Driehaus Foundation
333 North Michigan Avenue, Suite 510
Chicago, IL 60601

Richard H. Driehaus Foundation MacArthur Fund for Arts and Culture 1441

The fund will make multiyear, general operating support grants to organizations that have budgets of $500,000 or less and that reside in, and serve, the Chicago metropolitan area (the counties of Cook, DuPage, Lake, McHenry, Kane, and Will). Most grants will be in the range of $5,000 to $15,000. Most of the grants will be for general operating support. The deadline for receipt of proposals from performing arts organizations (music, theater and dance groups) is 5 p.m. on March 1. The deadline for receipt of proposals from all other groups: literary arts, visual and media arts, interdisciplinary arts, special projects, museums as well as service, policy or advocacy groups is 5 p.m. on June 1. Letters of inquiry must be: received by the listed deadline date; limited to five pages; the first four pages should include a brief description of your organization and your request; the final page should be a summary of your organization's budgets for this year. Full proposals are by invitation only.
Requirements: The following arts and culture organizations may apply: performing arts; visual and media arts; literary arts; interdisciplinary arts; special projects; museums, and service, policy or advocacy groups.
Restrictions: This program is not intended for arts education programs. Nor is it intended, for professional theater and dance companies with operating budgets of less than $150,000; those companies should visit the MacArthur Foundation website to review the guidelines for the Small Theater and Dance Group Funding Program.
Geographic Focus: Illinois
Date(s) Application is Due: Mar 1; Jun 1
Amount: 5,000 - 15,000 USD
Samples: Fear No Arts, Chicago, IL, $8,500—matching grant for the production of a 30-minute program for WTTW that will take viewers into the studios of Chicago artists (2010); I Am Chicago, Chicago, Il, $5,000—for a photo project that will document the appearance of typical Chicago residents around the city (2010).
Contact: Richard Cahan, Program Oficer; (312) 641-5772 or (847) 722-9244; (312) 641-5736; RichardCahan@aol.com
Internet: http://www.driehausfoundation.org/support
Sponsor: Richard H. Driehaus Foundation
333 North Michigan Avenue, Suite 510
Chicago, IL 60601

Richard H. Driehaus Foundation Small Theater and Dance Grants 1442

The Richard H. Driehaus Foundation, founded in 1983 and as a family foundation in 1992, benefits individuals and communities primarily by supporting the preservation and enhancement of the built and natural environments through historic preservation, encouragement of quality architectural and landscape design, and conserving open space. This program addresses the needs of small theater and dance companies in the Chicago area. Companies that emphasize professional presentation instead of education or community outreach are encouraged to apply. Use of grants may be unrestricted.
Requirements: Dance and theater companies that reside in the Chicago metropolitan area, have produced at least one show in the Chicago area, and have annual operating budgets of less than $150,000 are eligible.
Geographic Focus: Illinois
Date(s) Application is Due: Apr 25; Sep 12
Amount: 2,500 - 10,000 USD
Contact: Peter Handler, Program Officer; (312) 641-5772; (312) 641-5736; peterhandler@driehausfoundation.org
Internet: http://www.driehausfoundation.org/support
Sponsor: Richard H. Driehaus Foundation
333 North Michigan Avenue, Suite 510
Chicago, IL 60601

Richard King Mellon Foundation Grants 1443

On a national basis, the foundation makes grants to acquire and preserve key tracts of land in danger of being lost to urban growth and environmentally insensitive development. Mellon gives to nonprofits in Pittsburgh and throughout southwestern Pennsylvania to improve human services, education, medical care, civic affairs, and cultural activities. Types of support include capital grants, challenge/matching grants, general operating grants, project grants, and seed money grants. Application and guidelines are available online.
Requirements: Projects originating in Pittsburgh and southwestern Pennsylvania are given special priority.
Restrictions: The Foundation gives priority to projects and programs that have clearly defined outcomes and an evaluation component. It does not consider requests on behalf of individuals, or from outside the Untied States. The Foundation does not encourage requests from outside Pennsylvania.
Geographic Focus: Pennsylvania
Samples: Saint Vincent College (LaTrobe, PA)—for a business and conference center, $5 million; Westminster College (New Wilmington, PA)—to renovate an academic and administration building, $300,000; Carnegie Museums of Pittsburgh (PA)—to renovate and expand dinosaur exhibits at the Carnegie Museum of Natural History, $3 million; Direct Relief International (Santa Barbara, CA)—to assist tsunami-relief efforts, $500,000.
Contact: Michael Watson, Senior Vice President; (412) 392-2800; (412) 392-2837
Internet: http://foundationcenter.org/grantmaker/rkmellon/
Sponsor: Richard King Mellon Foundation
500 Grant Street, Suite 4106
Pittsburgh, PA 15219-2502

Richard M. Fairbanks Foundation Grants 1444

The Richard M. Fairbanks Foundation, Inc. was established in 1986 by Richard M. Fairbanks, founder and owner of Fairbanks Communications. An independent private foundation granting funds to qualifying nonprofit organizations, programs, and projects in the greater Indianapolis, Indiana area. Exceptions to this geographic limitation are normally made only for organizations historically supported by the Fairbanks family or for national disasters. If you are interested in learning if your organization and project/program matches the Richard M. Fairbanks Foundation's areas of interest and funding guidelines, you may contact the foundation by telephone, email or brief written letter of inquiry. Please note that the Fairbanks Foundation does not accept unsolicited proposals.
Requirements: The Foundation: makes grants only to tax exempt public charities as defined in Sections 501(c)3 & 509(a)(1)(2)(3) of the Internal Revenue Code, except as prohibited for 509(a)(3) Type III organizations; will not consider requests for loans and grants to individuals; does not make grants or give support to conferences, seminars, media events, or workshops unless they are an integral part of a broader program; ordinarily considers grant requests only from organizations located in Greater Indianapolis, Indiana.
Geographic Focus: Indiana

Samples: Prevent Blindness Indiana - in support of General Operations, $15,000 (2008); Indiana University School of Nursing - in support of School of Nursing Learning Consortium for Faculty Development in Simulation Technology, $167,887 (2008).
Contact: Claire Fiddian-Green, Grants Officer; (317) 663-4189 or (317) 846-7111; (317) 844-0167; Fiddiangreen@rmfairbanksfoundation.org
Internet: http://www.rmfairbanksfoundation.org/default.asp?p=3
Sponsor: Richard M. Fairbanks Foundation
9292 North Meridian Street, Suite 304
Indianapolis, IN 46260

Rich Foundation Grants **1445**
The foundation awards grants to nonprofit organizations in Atlanta, GA, to support community funds, performing arts, cultural programs, higher education, social services, homeless, youth, hospitals, heart disease, theater, and AIDS. Types of support include annual campaigns, building funds, continuing support, equipment acquisition, operating budgets, technical assistance, and research. Contact the office for application forms. The board meets quarterly to review requests.
Requirements: Nonprofit organizations in the Atlanta, GA, area are eligible for grant support.
Geographic Focus: Georgia
Date(s) Application is Due: Mar 15; Jun 15; Sep 15; Dec 15
Amount: 5,000 - 100,000 USD
Contact: Anne Poland Berg, Grant Consultant; (404) 262-2266
Sponsor: Rich Foundation
11 Piedmont Center, Suite 204
Atlanta, GA 30305

Righteous Persons Foundation Grants **1446**
The foundation, established by Steven Spielberg, makes grants nationally for projects to revitalize Jewish life, help young people learn about Judaism, and promote tolerance among people of all faiths and ethnicities. Many of the awards are for projects that explore new ideas and opportunities with a special emphasis on young people and that include many projects that may have otherwise had a difficult time obtaining funding. Projects that are national in scope or can serve as models for other communities will receive preference.
Requirements: U.S. 501(c)3 nonprofits are eligible.
Restrictions: Grants are not awarded to support endowments, capital campaigns, building funds, university faculty chairs, individual synagogues or day schools, research, or the publication of books or magazines.
Geographic Focus: All U.S. States
Amount: 5,000 - 400,000 USD
Samples: Raoul Wallenberg Committee of the United States (New York, NY)—to help bring its A Study of Heroes curriculum to additional U.S. schools and communities, $20,000 matching grant over two years; Anti-Defamation League (Los Angeles, CA)—for its Stop the Hate Program, $50,000 matching grant; Clark U (Worcester, MA)—to support a doctoral fellow in its program on the history of the Holocaust, $60,000; Jewish Television Network (Los Angeles, CA)—to produce a television program on Jewish art and culture, $50,000.
Contact: Rachel Levin, Program Officer; (310) 314-8393; (310) 314-8396
Sponsor: Righteous Persons Foundation
2800 28th Street, Suite 105
Santa Monica, CA 90405

RISCA General Operating Support Grants **1447**
Rhode Island State Council of the Arts (RISCA) awards General Operating Support (GOS) to Rhode Island's major arts presenting and producing institutions. Interested applicants who meet the eligibility requirements below should contact RISCA's organization support program coordinator for more information.
Requirements: Organizations are eligible for General Operating Support if, at the time of application, they: are a nonprofit corporation, incorporated in and conducting business in the State of Rhode Island; have 501(c)3 tax exempt status; have a primary mission that is clearly arts or arts-related; have a record of receiving grant support for at least the past three consecutive years from the Rhode Island State Council on the Arts; can provide a planning document, approved by their board of directors, which addresses artistic and administrative issues; have an operating budget in excess of $50,000 at the time of application, as shown by an certified independent audit, review, or accountant's compilation; and perform or exhibit work in a space that is physically accessible to people with disabilities, as required by law. Applicants must be governed by a revolving board of directors, trustees or an advisory board drawn from the community at large and shown to be actively involved in the activities of the organization. Organizations with budgets of $100,000 or less must have at least one part-time (minimum of 20 hours per week), year-round, paid staff member who is responsible for the oversight of the organization. Organizations with budgets from $100,000 to $1,000,000 must have both a paid professional business manager and a paid artistic director (or individuals with these functions if titles differ). The minimum combined hours for these two jobs must equal one and one-half full time positions. Organizations with budgets greater than $1,000,000 must have both a full-time, paid business manager and full-time, paid artistic director.
Geographic Focus: Rhode Island
Samples: Rhode Island School of Design, Providence, Rhode Island, $87,550 (2010); Rhode Island Philharmonic Orchestra & Music School, East Providence, Rhode Island, $89,471 (2010); South County Center for the Arts, West Kingston, Rhode Island, $9,256 (2010)
Contact: Randall Rosenbaum, Executive Director; (401) 222-3883; (401) 222-3018; randy@arts.ri.gov
Internet: http://www.arts.ri.gov/grants/gos.php
Sponsor: Rhode Island State Council on the Arts
One Capitol Hill, Third Floor
Providence, RI 02908

Robert and Polly Dunn Foundation Grants **1448**
The foundation awards grants in the U.S. Southeast, with emphasis on the Atlanta, GA, area, for projects in the area of youth, child development, and higher education. Types of support include capital campaigns, general operating support, and scholarship funds. There are no application forms. The board meets in June and December to consider requests.
Restrictions: Grants do not support individuals and not awarded to support endowment funds, loans, or program-related investments
Geographic Focus: Georgia
Date(s) Application is Due: Apr 30; Sep 30
Amount: Up to 587,925 USD
Contact: Karen Wilbanks, Executive Director; (404) 816-2883; (404) 816-2883
Sponsor: Robert and Polly Dunn Foundation
P.O. Box 723194
Atlanta, GA 31139

Robert G. Cabell III and Maude Morgan Cabell Foundation Grants **1449**
The foundation supports capital projects of Virginia nonprofit organizations in the areas of arts and culture, community development, higher education, historic preservation, the arts and culture, religion (Christian, Episcopal, Protestant, and Roman Catholic), social services, and community welfare. Preference will be given to the Richmond, Virginia, area. There are no application forms. Applicants may submit a written proposal that includes a brief description of the overall mission of the organization, a brief description of how the specific project supports the overall mission, a project budget, the level and type of support for the project from the local area, applicant's current operating budget and most recent budget, list of governing board and its officers, evidence of 501(c)3 status, and cover letter. Proposals are considered at grant review meetings each spring and fall.
Requirements: Virginia 501(c)3 tax-exempt organizations that are not classified as private foundations or private operating foundations are eligible.
Restrictions: The foundation does not make grants to individuals, primary or secondary schools, or state-supported organizations; nor will grants be made for debt reduction, endowments (except for faculty development), general operating expenses, research, or scholarships.
Geographic Focus: District of Columbia, Maryland, Virginia
Date(s) Application is Due: Apr 1; Oct 1
Amount: 25,000 - 500,000 USD
Samples: Nature Conservancy, Richmond, Virginia, $500,000 - for marine protection conservancy (2008); Chesapeake Bay Foundation, Annapolis, Maryland, $400,000 - for construction of two offshore breakwaters (2009); Randolph-Macon College, Ashland, Virginia, $200,000 - for Cabell research professorship endowment (2008).
Contact: Jill A. McCormick, Executive Director; (804) 780-2050; (804) 780-2198; Cabell.foundation@gmail.com
Sponsor: Robert G. Cabell III and Maude Morgan Cabell Foundation
901 E Cary Street, Suite 1402
Richmond, VA 23219-4037

Robert R. McCormick Tribune Foundation Grantss 1450

The foundation funds programs in the areas of community development, citizenship, journalism, and education. The communities program is designed to combine the efforts of the foundation and various corporate entities to increase local philanthropy and improve the social and economic conditions of communities. The citizenship program awards grants to promote patriotism, service, and volunteerism; encourage effective philanthropy; and honor the U.S. armed forces. The journalism program supports research, development, and education to assist and inform journalism's leaders, encourage informed coverage of national security issues, and support freedom of expression. The education program is designed to focus on the quality of early childhood education, increase the number of accredited preschool programs, strengthen the skills of preschool program directors, improve the professional development system for preschool teachers, and heighten public understanding of the importance of early childhood education. Types of support include building/renovation funds, equipment, capital campaigns, operating budgets, technical assistance, land acquisition, matching funds, program-related investments, and special projects. Preproposal discussion with staff is encouraged. Applications are accepted at any time.
Requirements: The foundation funds education programs in the Chicago metropolitan area only. Community programs are funded in Anaheim; Atlanta; Chicago; Cleveland; Denver; El Paso; Escondido; Fort Lauderdale; Los Angeles; Manhattan, KS; New York; Newport News, VA; Orlando; and Phoenix.
Geographic Focus: Arizona, California, Colorado, Connecticut, Florida, Georgia, Illinois, Kansas, Louisiana, Massachusetts, New York, Ohio, Texas, Virginia, Washington
Date(s) Application is Due: Jun 1; Sep 1; Oct 1
Samples: Gettysburg National Battlefield Museum Foundation (York, PA)—for a gallery that will showcase the contributions of Illinois troops during the Civil War's Battle of Gettysburg, $1 million; National-Louis U, Ctr for Early Childhood Leadership (Chicago, IL)—for new programs for early-childhood administrators, a national public-awareness campaign on early-childhood issues, and an endowment that will support research, scholarships, and special projects, $2.1 million; Rush U Medical Ctr (Chicago, IL)—for a state-of-the-art emergency-services facility, $7.5 million.
Contact: Mark Hallett, Senior Program Officer; (312) 222-3512; (312) 222-3523; mhallett@tribune.com
Internet: http://www.rrmtf.org/mtf/mtfinfo.htm
Sponsor: Robert R. McCormick Tribune Foundation
435 N Michigan Avenue, Suite 770
Chicago, IL 60611

Robert W. Deutsch Foundation Grants 1451

The foundation provides support to technology programs in institutions of higher education in Maryland. Types of support include: continuing support, curriculum development, fellowships, general operating support, internship funds, organizational development, program development, research, and seed grants. There are no application deadlines or forms; submit initial inquiries by email or postal mail.
Restrictions: No support for religious or political organizations.
Geographic Focus: Maryland
Amount: 5,000 - 210,000 USD
Samples: University of Maryland-College Park, College Park, MD. $250,000 - For nanotechnology research, payable over 1 year.
Contact: Jane Brown, Executive Director; (410) 252-9244; (410) 252-0997; rdeutsch@rwd.com
Sponsor: Robert W. Deutsch Foundation
5521 Research Park Drive
Baltimore, MD 21228-4664

Robins Foundation Grants 1452

The foundation awards grants to nonprofit organizations in the Richmond, VA, area. Areas of interest include general grants—including cultural, charitable, scientific, environmental, and educational programs, and at-risk youth; and early childhood/quality improvement grants— for organizations that devote a major portion of their resources to young children and their families. The goal is to help improve the quality of services by providing funding for accreditation, staff training, facilities improvements, and similar initiatives. The foundation seeks projects that meet well-defined community needs, use effective approaches that build on proven programs, develop models with potential for wider application, foster self-reliance and/or end dependency, and focus on prevention as well as treatment. Types of support include capital grants and endowments.
Requirements: 501(c)3 organizations based in Virginia are eligible. Organizations based in Virginia that have or support programs outside Virginia or the United States also are eligible.
Restrictions: In general, the foundation does not make grants to support annual operating funds or budgets, special events or fundraising benefits, or religious purposes unless they are otherwise compatible with the objectives of the foundation.
Geographic Focus: Virginia
Amount: 10,000 - 100,000 USD
Contact: William Roberts Jr., Executive Director; (804) 697-6917; (804) 697-6797; wlrjr@robins-foundation.org
Internet: http://www.robins-foundation.org
Sponsor: Robins Foundation
Capitol Station, P.O. Box 1124
Richmond, VA 23218-1124

Rochester Area Community Foundation Grants 1453

The foundation seeks to improve the quality of life in the community and awards grants in the areas of child development, education, the environment, arts and cultural programs, health services, community development, and social services and general charitable giving. Types of support include general operating support, building construction/renovation, equipment acquisition, program development, conferences and seminars, publication, seed grants, scholarship funds, technical assistance, consulting services, and scholarships to individuals. There are no application deadlines. The board meets in January, February, March, May, June, July, October, and November.
Requirements: Nonprofits in Monroe, Livingston, Ontario, Orleans, Genessee, and Wayne Counties, NY, are eligible.
Restrictions: Grants do not support partisan political organizations or religious projects, individuals, annual campaigns, deficit financing, land acquisition, endowments, or emergency funds.
Geographic Focus: New York
Samples: Heritage Christian Services, $5,000—to support the annual Sheep Shearing Festival at Springdale Farm (2009); Step by Step of Rochester, $12,000—to support the merger of Step by Step and Samaritan Women. Both organizations provide support to incarcerated women and their children (2009); Arts & Cultural Council for Greater Rochester, $42,500—for Community Arts Grants, which are administered by the Arts & Cultural Council, have a capacity-building focus, and are aimed at smaller arts organizations (2009); Lifespan of Greater Rochester, $10,000—for a financial management program which trains volunteers to provide in-home assistance with bill paying, budgeting, government benefits (such as Medicare and Medicaid), and other financial tasks for physically and/or mentally frail older adults (2009).
Contact: Marlene Cole, Administrative Assistant; (585) 341-4333; (585) 271-4292; mcole@racf.org
Internet: http://www.racf.org/page10000903.cfm
Sponsor: Rochester Area Community Foundation
500 East Avenue
Rochester, NY 14607-1912

Rockefeller Brothers Fund Charles E. Culpeper Arts and Culture Grants in New York City 1454

The Fund seeks to foster an environment in which artists and the creative process can flourish by supporting organizations that assist individual artists and the creative process, provide infrastructure to sustain the artistic life, and offer additional opportunities to artists for developing skills complementary to their creative talents. In addition, the Fund seeks to sustain and advance small and mid-size cultural organizations, particularly those that are community based and/or culturally specific through the following strategies: supporting core operations by providing non-renewable, two-year capacity-building grants of up to $50,000 per year; strengthening long-term financial viability by providing endowment grants and cash reserve grants of up to $250,000 to cultural and arts organizations that demonstrate the potential for long-term leadership and excellence in the presentation of creative work to the broadest possible audiences; enhancing institutional leadership through competitive awards to arts and cultural organizations for innovative, team-based leadership conferences designed to strengthen long-range organizational management and governance; and offering grants of up to $15,000 to cover the costs of the leadership conference, including the participation of professional consultants, advisors, or facilitators (following completion of a leadership conference, the Fund may make an additional award of up to $25,000 to support the

participating organization's efforts to implement some aspects of what was learned through the conference.
Requirements: A prospective grantee must be located in New York City, and must be either a tax-exempt organization or an organization seeking support for a project that would qualify as educational or charitable.
Restrictions: The fund does not make grants to individuals, nor does it as a general rule support research, graduate study, or the writing of books or dissertations by individuals.
Geographic Focus: New York
Amount: Up to 250,000 USD
Contact: Ben Rodriguez-Cubenas, Program Director; (212) 812-4200; (212) 812-4299; info@rbf.org
Internet: http://www.rbf.org/programs/
Sponsor: Rockefeller Brothers Fund
437 Madison Avenue, 37th Floor
New York, NY 10022-7001

Rockefeller Brothers Fund Democratic Practice Grants **1455**
The Fund's Democratic Practice program has two parts: the health of democracy in the United States and the strength of democracy in global governance. Each focus has two distinct goals. Based on a careful assessment of local needs and priorities, the Fund may also pursue one or more of these goals in a limited number of its pivotal places. Recognizing that there is no single model of effective democratic practice, the Fund emphasizes flexibility and adaptability to different contexts in these pivotal places.
Requirements: A prospective grantee in the United States or foreign counterpart must be either a tax-exempt organization or an organization seeking support for a project that would qualify as educational or charitable.
Restrictions: The fund does not make grants to individuals, nor does it as a general rule support research, graduate study, or the writing of books or dissertations by individuals.
Geographic Focus: All U.S. States
Amount: 25,000 - 300,000 USD
Contact: Benjamin R. Shute, Secretary; (212) 812-4200; (212) 812-4299; info@rbf.org
Internet: http://www.rbf.org/programs/
Sponsor: Rockefeller Brothers Fund
437 Madison Avenue, 37th Floor
New York, NY 10022-7001

Rockefeller Brothers Fund Sustainable Development Grants **1456**
The Fund's sustainable development grant making endeavors to address global challenges by supporting environmental stewardship that is ecologically based, economically sound, socially just, culturally appropriate, and consistent with intergenerational equity. The Fund encourages government, business, and civil society to work collaboratively on environmental conservation and to make it an integral part of all development planning and activity. Recognizing the global nature of many environmental problems, the Fund also promotes international cooperation in addressing these challenges. Some of the Fund's sustainable development strategies are pursued at the global level, while others are pursued primarily in North America. The Russian Far East is the focus of a modest program of grant making. Major goals include: combating global warming; protecting ecosystems; and conserving biodiversity. In all regions where the RBF is engaged in sustainable development grant making, it monitors the social and environmental effects of development programs and fiscal policies that are associated with global economic integration and seeks to integrate activities across geographic areas to promote maximum impact.
Requirements: A prospective grantee in the United States or foreign counterpart must be either a tax-exempt organization or an organization seeking support for a project that would qualify as educational or charitable.
Restrictions: The fund does not make grants to individuals, nor does it as a general rule support research, graduate study, or the writing of books or dissertations by individuals.
Geographic Focus: All U.S. States
Amount: 25,000 - 300,000 USD
Contact: Michael Northrop, Program Director; (212) 812-4200; (212) 812-4299; info@rbf.org
Internet: http://www.rbf.org/programs/
Sponsor: Rockefeller Brothers Fund
437 Madison Avenue, 37th Floor
New York, NY 10022-7001

Rockwell Fund Inc Grants **1457**
The fund's special emphases are education, human services, and public health. Other fields of interest are arts/humanities, civic/environment, and historic preservation. While the fund traditionally has contributed to buildings and endowments, its current emphasis is on programs or projects and general operating support. The fund is open to allocating a portion of a program or project budget to general and administrative expenses. Complete grant proposals will be accepted anytime throughout the year and will be considered at grant decision meetings in January, April, July, and October. If an organization has applied for funding in the past the request must be dated at least one year from the previous submission. Application and guidelines are available online.
Requirements: Grants are made only to nonprofit, tax-exempt organizations in Texas, unless the purpose of the grant is to benefit a Texas project. Limited grants are made outside of Houston, and applications for such grants are discouraged.
Restrictions: The fund does not participate in feasibility studies and generally does not make grants for the following: individuals; underwriting for benefits, dinners, galas, or other fundraising events; mass solicitations; medical or scientific research projects; parochial schools; organizations outside of Texas; or government agencies.
Geographic Focus: Texas
Amount: 3,000 - 125,000 USD
Samples: Gladney Fund (Fort Worth, TX)—to support the adoption and maternity services organization's Houston regional office, $10,000.
Contact: Carolyn Watson, Program Officer; (713) 629-9022; (713) 629-7702; cwatson@rockfund.org
Internet: http://www.rockfund.org
Sponsor: Rockwell Fund
1330 Post Oak Boulevard, Suite 1825
Houston, TX 77056

Rockwell International Corporate Trust Grants **1458**
Grants are awarded in the areas of education and youth development, with emphasis in math, science, and engineering; and culture and the arts, with emphasis on youth educational programs. Rockwell also contributes to health, human services, and civic organizations and also gives special consideration to qualifying organizations in which employees are involved as volunteers. Types of support include capital grants, challenge/matching grants, conferences and seminars, development grants, endowments, research grants, scholarship funds, and general operating grants. Awards include single-year, multiple-year, and provisional continuing support of specific programs. Applicants should submit full, detailed proposals. Proposals are accepted at any time. At the website, click on About Us, then Corporate Citizenship, and then Rockwell Automation Corporation Trust.
Restrictions: Organizations are not eligible if they have not received a permanent, tax-exempt ruling determination from the federal government; if they cannot provide current full, certified, audited financial statements; or if they are private foundations. Funding will not be considered for the following purposes: general endowments, deficit reduction, grants to individuals, federated campaigns, organizations or projects outside the United States, religious organizations for religious purposes, or fraternal or social organizations.
Geographic Focus: All U.S. States
Amount: 1,000 - 50,000 USD
Contact: Rockwell International Corporation General Information; (562) 797-3311
Internet: http://www.rockwell.com
Sponsor: Rockwell International Corporate Trust
1201 S Second Street
Milwaukee, WI 53204

Roger L. and Agnes C. Dell Charitable Trust II Grants **1459**
The trust's major purpose is to assist education, the arts, and human service programs. The trust awards grants to eligible Minnesota nonprofit organizations in its areas of interest, including arts and culture, education, human services, Jewish agencies and temples, YMCAs, YWCAs, youth, and service programs. Types of support include funding for general operations and for specific project proposals.
Requirements: Minnesota 501(c)3 tax-exempt organizations in Fergus Falls and the surrounding area are eligible.
Restrictions: Individuals are not eligible for grants.
Geographic Focus: Minnesota
Date(s) Application is Due: Jun 15; Oct 15
Amount: 100 - 50,000 USD

Contact: Richard C. Hefte, Trust Manager; (218) 998-3355; (218) 736-3950; dell@prtel.com
Sponsor: Roger L. and Agnes C. Dell Charitable Trust II
110 North Mill Street
Fergus Falls, MN 56537

Rogers Family Foundation Grants 1460

The Rogers Family Foundation funds nonprofit organizations that provide educational, medical, artistic, and religious services within Massachusetts' Merrimack Valley and North Shore and southeastern New Hampshire. See website for specific areas served.
Requirements: Applicants must be tax exempt under section 501(c)3 of the Internal Revenue Code and classified as "not a private foundation" under Section 509(a) of the Code. All applications are submitted on-line. The online application follows the Common Proposal designed and published by Associated Grant Makers, Inc. See website for detailed online application and instructions.
Restrictions: Traditionally the Foundation awards grants to organizations located in Massachusetts' Merrimack Valley and North Shore and southeastern New Hampshire. From time to time grants may be made outside of this normal geographic area.
Geographic Focus: Massachusetts, New Hampshire
Date(s) Application is Due: Mar 1; Sep 1
Amount: 25,000 USD
Samples: Anna Jaques Community Health Foundation, Newburyport, Massachusetts, $10,000 - general operating (2008); Asian Center of Merrimack Valley, Lawrence, Massachusetts, $10,000 - general operating (2008); Bellesini Academy, Lawrence, Massachusetts, $10,000 - general operating (2008).
Contact: Susan Haff, (617) 426-7080; (617) 426-7087
Internet: http://www.rogersfamilyfoundation.com/app/
Sponsor: Rogers Family Foundation
c/o GMA Foundations
Boston, MA 02110

Rollins-Luetkemeyer Foundation Grants 1461

The foundation awards grants to eligible Maryland nonprofit organizations in its areas of interest, including education (early childhood, elementary school, and higher education), health care and health organizations, historic preservation, Protestant churches and organizations, and social services. Types of support include annual campaigns, building construction/renovation, general operating support, and project support.
Requirements: The Foundation gives funding mainly for building funds for early childhood, elementary and secondary schools. They also support certain health organizations and historical preservation. There is no deadline or application form, so the applicant should submit a letter of intent.
Restrictions: Maryland nonprofit organizations, with preference given to the Baltimore area, are eligible. No grants to individuals.
Geographic Focus: Maryland
Contact: John A. Luetkemeyer, Jr., President; (443) 921-4358
Sponsor: Rollins-Luetkemeyer Foundation
1427 Clarkview Road, Suite 500
Baltimore, MD 21209

RosaMary Foundation Grants 1462

The foundation supports grantseekers within the greater New Orleans area. Highest priority is given to grants in the following categories: education, with emphasis on private institutions; human service organizations; arts, both performing and applied; community development activities; and governmental oversight activities. Types of support include capital, program, and short-term operating grants. Guidelines are available online.
Requirements: Nonprofit organizations serving the greater New Orleans, LA, area may submit grant proposals.
Restrictions: Grants are not awarded to support ticket purchases or to back fund-raising events.
Geographic Focus: Louisiana
Date(s) Application is Due: Feb 1; Sep 1
Amount: 5,000 - 150,000 USD
Contact: Toni Myers, Executive Administrator; (504) 895-1984; (504) 895-1988; info@rosamary.org
Internet: http://www.rosamary.org
Sponsor: RosaMary Foundation
P.O. Box 13218
New Orleans, LA 70185

Rose Community Foundation Aging Grants 1463

In its Aging program area, Rose Community Foundation promotes change in how communities organize care and support for both seniors and caregivers, with particular attention to the needs of low- and moderate-income seniors. In addition to funding community-based programs, the Foundation plays a leadership role in strengthening the existing network of aging resources, including initiatives that bring together community and government partners to address key issues in aging. The Foundation is especially interested in projects that address the following priorities: direct in-home and community-based services; transportation; and end-of-life care.
Requirements: Colorado 501(c)3 tax-exempt organizations serving the residents of Adams, Arapahoe, Boulder, Denver, Douglas, and Jefferson Counties are eligible.
Geographic Focus: Colorado
Contact: Therese Ellery, Senior Program Officer; (303) 398-7413 or (303) 398-7400; (303) 398-7430; tellery@rcfdenver.org
Internet: http://www.rcfdenver.org/programs_aging.htm
Sponsor: Rose Community Foundation
600 South Cherry Street, Suite 1200
Denver, CO 80246-1712

Rose Community Foundation Education Grants 1464

The Foundation's grantmaking in education reflects the principle that school programs, policies and practices should ensure the highest possible quality teaching in a community's classrooms. While the Foundation focuses its resources on efforts that lead to improved student achievement, it places greatest emphasis on two priorities in prekindergarten through grade 12. The first is quality teaching. Research consistently shows that more than any other factor in school, the quality of a student's teacher has the greatest impact on his or her performance. As a result, Rose Community Foundation values efforts to recruit, develop and retain great educators. The second priority is systemic change in individual schools and in public education. While the root causes of low student performance are many, schools and school districts do not always have the systems in place to advance learning and close persistent learning gaps between high-achieving and low-achieving students.
Requirements: Colorado 501(c)3 tax-exempt organizations serving the students of Adams, Arapahoe, Boulder, Denver, Douglas, and Jefferson Counties are eligible.
Geographic Focus: Colorado
Contact: Phil Gonring, Senior Program Officer; (303) 398-7415 or (303) 398-7400; (303) 398-7430; pgonring@rcfdenver.org
Internet: http://www.rcfdenver.org/programs_education.htm
Sponsor: Rose Community Foundation
600 South Cherry Street, Suite 1200
Denver, CO 80246-1712

Rose Foundation For Communities and the Environment Consumer Privacy Rights Grants 1465

The Rose Foundation supports grassroots initiatives to inspire community action to protect the environment, consumers and public health. The purpose of the Consumer Privacy Rights Fund is to support projects that relate to the preservation or promotion of privacy rights of California consumers or residents, among others. This includes, but is not limited to, grants to strengthen the organizational capacity of groups whose core mission is privacy rights.
Requirements: The applicant must demonstrate that it has the experience and expertise to promote the goals of the fund, and the capability to carry out the proposed project. The applicant must have 501(c)3 non-profit status, or a fiscal sponsor. Funds may not be used for litigation or lobbying purposes. All applicants must submit a letter of inquiry (2-pages maximum) before submitting a full proposal. Letters of inquiry are due August 31. This allows the Foundation to determine if the project will fit within the guidelines of any currently-available restitution fund. Letters of inquiry may be sent by either regular mail or email. Letters should be addressed to Karla James, Managing Director. Rose Foundation staff will contact you either by phone or email within one week of receiving your letter. At that time, the Foundation will either invite a proposal, or decline a proposal. If invited to, submit a full proposal which explains your project in detail. Full proposals are due on October 1.
Geographic Focus: California
Date(s) Application is Due: Aug 31; Oct 1
Contact: Tim Little, Executive Director; (510) 658-0702; (510) 658-0732; tlittle@rosefdn.org

Internet: http://rosefdn.org/article.php?list=type&type=76
Sponsor: Rose Foundation For Communities and the Environment
6008 College Avenue, Suite 10
Oakland, CA 94618

Rose Foundation For Communities and the Environment Northern California Environmental Grassroots Grants 1466

The Rose Foundation supports grassroots initiatives to inspire community action to protect the environment, consumers and public health. The Grassroots Fund supports small groups throughout greater northern California that are tackling tough environmental problems including toxic pollution, urban sprawl, environmental degradation of rivers, wild places, as well as the communities health. Most grant are for a one year period. Grassroots Fund grantees are also eligible to receive up to $200 of training scholarships per year. The scholarships cover 80% of the registration cost of training. Grantees traveling more than 75 miles round trip will also receive a travel stipend. See Foundations website for further guidelines.
Requirements: To be eligible for a grassroots grant, the applicant must meet the following criteria: geographic scope - project impact must be in Northern California (includes the entire Sierra Nevada Mountains, Bay Area, Central Valley, Central Coast, and North Coast); organization size - annual income or expenses of $100,000 or less; issues supported - include, but are not limited to; environmental health and justice, land management and urban sprawl, habitat and wilderness protection, sustainable forestry, water resources, agriculture, sustainability, and pollution; strategies supported - general support for organizations with an environmental mission, or project support for strategies such as community-based advocacy, technical assistance, litigation, restoration projects, organizing expenses, grassroots campaigns, and environmental education; tax status - applicants may be a nonprofit, be fiscally sponsored by another nonprofit, or ask for fiscal sponsorship from the fund. An application form is available for download on the Foundations website. Mail application in by deadline, emailed or faxed applications will not be accepted.
Restrictions: Not eligible for support: capital campaigns, annual fundraising appeals, government agencies, colleges or universities and individuals.
Geographic Focus: California
Date(s) Application is Due: Feb 1; May 1; Aug 1; Nov 1
Amount: Up to 5,000 USD
Contact: Tim Little, Executive Director; (510) 658-0702; (510) 658-0732; tlittle@rosefdn.org
Internet: http://rosefdn.org/article.php?list=type&type=36
Sponsor: Rose Foundation For Communities and the Environment
6008 College Avenue, Suite 10
Oakland, CA 94618

Rose Foundation For Communities and the Environment Southeast Madera County Responsible Growth Grants 1467

The Rose Foundation supports grassroots initiatives to inspire community action to protect the environment, consumers and public health. The Southeast Madera County Responsible Growth Fund was created to advocate for responsible growth in Madera County through adherence to California land use laws and Madera County General Plan policies, to promote comprehensive and integrated planning, and to ensure full compliance with the requirements of the California Environmental Quality Act, within, or pertaining to, the southeastern portion of Madera County. This Target Area is bounded on the West by State Route 99, on the North by SR 145 and on the East and South by the Millerton Reservoir and the San Joaquin River.
Requirements: Eligible applicants include governmental, public agency, quasi-governmental, or non-profit entities qualified pursuant to the requirements of the California Franchise Tax Board and the Internal Revenue Code whose purposes include advocating for or engaging in comprehensive planning within, or for the benefit of, Madera County. Initial contact should be through a Letter of Inquiry, no more than three pages concisely describing each of the following: proposed project; project goals; explain your strategy and why this project is important; time frame; funding need; other anticipated sources of support; and a brief description of the organization requesting funds. If invited to submit a full proposal include the following: 1 page cover sheet consisting of: applicant's name, address, telephone number and website; primary contact person's name, address, telephone number, and email; amount of funds requested; EIN number; 1 - 2 paragraph short description of the proposed project; proposed start date for the project; specific statement of authorization of the application by the applicant's executive officer, including executive officer's signature. Narrative project description, not more than 5 pages long. The narrative description should describe the applicant, proposed project, overall strategic considerations, specific project workplan, key deliverables, and any other factors for consideration, such as urgency of need for support. Required Attachments: project budget; identification of other potential sources of project funding; organizational budget for the current year; balance sheet and profit/loss statement for the most recently completed year; description of lead project staff; Board of directors roster; timetable of activities; description of how the applicant will evaluate progress and any key metrics that will be used to measure performance towards grant objectives; IRS 501(c)3 determination letter or other acceptable documentation of nonprofit purpose or fiscal sponsorship. Optional Attachments: press clippings or other material describing the organization and key past accomplishments (limit 3); Letters of Reference (limit 3); submit the original application, plus 5 copies, by U.S. mail or delivery service to the Foundation.
Geographic Focus: California
Amount: 12,000 - 100,000 USD
Contact: Tim Little, Executive Director; (510) 658-0702; (510) 658-0732; tlittle@rosefdn.org
Internet: http://rosefdn.org/article.php?list=type&type=114
Sponsor: Rose Foundation For Communities and the Environment
6008 College Avenue, Suite 10
Oakland, CA 94618

Roy A. Hunt Foundation Grants 1468

The foundation awards general grants in the areas of arts and culture; education; environmental conservation; health; human services; international affairs, development, and peace; public/safety benefit; and religion. Most grants are awarded for general operating support. The foundation also funds special initiatives in the areas of community development, environment, and youth violence prevention. Special initiative grants are administered according to specific guidelines and have earlier application deadlines. Guidelines for both categories are available online. First-time applicants are advised to submit a preliminary letter of inquiry. Proposals for general grants from previously funded organizations are considered only in November and do not require a preliminary letter of inquiry. Deadlines are April 15 and September 15 for general grants; and March 1 and August 1 for special initiatives.
Requirements: Tax-exempt organizations are eligible.
Geographic Focus: Massachusetts, Pennsylvania
Amount: 100 - 25,000 USD
Samples: Peace Development Fund (Amherst, MA)—general operating support, $4000; Shadyside Hospital Foundation (Pittsburgh, PA)—for the Hillman Cancer Ctr capital campaign, $10,000; Buddhist Ray (New York, NY)—for the Tricycle magazine, $5000; Ligonier Valley Library (PA)—for general operating support, $4000.
Contact: Grants Administrator; (412) 281-8734; (412) 255-0522; info@rahuntfdn.org
Internet: http://www.rahuntfdn.org/programs.shtml
Sponsor: Roy A. Hunt Foundation
1 Bigelow Square, Suite 630
Pittsburgh, PA 15219-3030

Roy J. Carver Charitable Trust Public Library Grants 1469

The Trust offers directed support for the establishment, expansion and enhancement of community-based library facilities and services. Grants of up to $60,000 are generally awarded for construction, renovation and/or furnishings and equipment needs, including technology-based initiatives that link libraries across multiple sites. Projects emphasizing library patronage among youth are especially encouraged.
Requirements: Grants are made to 501(c)3 tax-exempt public libraries in Iowa and western Illinois.
Restrictions: The Trust does not provide grants specifically targeted to making libraries handicapped accessible. In addition, the Trust has traditionally avoided awarding grants to support the creation of Iowa Communications Network (ICN) classrooms within new or existing library facilities. Also, the Trust does not provide funding for joint school/community library projects or facilities. Once a facility has successfully secured a grant award from the Carver Trust, no additional applications for funding will be considered for a period of at least five years.
Geographic Focus: Illinois, Iowa
Amount: Up to 60,000 USD
Samples: Crew Public Library, Salem, IA, $60,000—new library construction (2009); Fontanelle Public Library, Fontanelle, IA, $45,000—library expansion (2009); Red Oak Public Library, Red Oak, IA , $60,000—library renovation and expansion (2009).

Contact: Drive Troy Ross, Executive Administrator; (563) 263-4010; (563) 263-1547; info@carvertrust.org
Internet: https://www.carvertrust.org/index.php?page=45
Sponsor: Roy J. Carver Charitable Trust
202 Iowa Avenue
Muscatine, IA 52761-3733

RRF General Program Grants 1470

The program funds service, education, research, and advocacy projects. The foundation is particularly interested in innovative projects that have the potential to change practice, policy, or delivery systems. The foundation's programs seek to improve the availability and quality of community-based and institutional long-term care programs; expand opportunities for older persons to play meaningful roles in society; support selected basic, applied, and policy research into the causes and solutions of significant problems of the aged; and increase the number of professionals and paraprofessionals adequately prepared to serve the elderly. Proposals fall into three general categories: research, model projects and service, and education and training. Guidelines are available online.
Requirements: Direct service projects that seek to improve the availability and quality of community-based and institutional long-term care programs; expand opportunities for older persons to play meaningful roles in society; support selected applied and policy research into the causes and solutions of significant problems of the aged; increase the number of professionals and paraprofessionals adequately prepared to serve the elderly.
Restrictions: The foundation will only consider proposals from applicants in Illinois, Indiana, Iowa, Kentucky, Missouri, Wisconsin, and Florida. Priority is given to nonprofit organizations serving the Chicago metropolitan area.
Geographic Focus: Florida, Illinois, Indiana, Iowa, Kentucky, Missouri, Wisconsin
Date(s) Application is Due: Feb 1; May 1; Aug 1
Amount: Up to 15,000,000 USD
Contact: Marilyn Hennessy, President; (773) 714-8080; (773) 714-8089; info@rrf.org
Internet: http://www.rrf.org/generalProgram.htm
Sponsor: Retirement Research Foundation
8765 W Higgins Road, Suite 430
Chicago, IL 60631-4170

RRF Organizational Capacity Building Grants 1471

The foundation provides grants for capacity-building activities that will help a nonprofit organization improve its management or governance to better serve the elderly. The following are examples of activities that will be supported but are not meant to exclude other ideas: planning (strategic, business, and financial plans) to steer an organization through changes; organizational assessments to identify problem areas that need to be strengthened; evaluation to develop outcome measures and determine progress in order to strengthen accountability to constituents and funding sources; public relations, communications, and marketing to increase awareness and utilization of services; financial management and resource development to improve financial systems, explore revenue options, and develop a stronger funding base; human resources management to enhance professional development, do team building, and improve the working environment; information systems management to identify and incorporate technology to improve efficiency; restructuring and building relations among organizations to strengthen service delivery, reduce costs, share resources, develop joint evaluations, or achieve other benefits; and board assessment, recruitment, training and structuring to strengthen the governance of the organization. All organizations that receive a grant are eligible for additional funding over the course of the grant, to be used flexibly for technical assistance opportunities that arise during the course of the grant. These may include seminars, workshops, short-term courses, publications, or other training opportunities related to organizational capacity building.
Requirements: For an organization to be eligible, it must meet the following criteria: be a nonprofit organization, but not a unit of government; be located in Cook, DuPage Kane, Kendall, Lake, or McHenry County, IL; provide services to the elderly; and intentionally give a high priority to the elderly.
Restrictions: The foundation will not fund building, renovation or capital improvements; emergency needs; deficits; or one-time events that do not build long-term capacity, i.e. fundraising events or one-time conferences.
Geographic Focus: Illinois
Date(s) Application is Due: Feb 1; May 1; Aug 1
Amount: 30,000 - 75,000 USD
Contact: Mary O'Donnell, Coordinator; (773) 714-8080; info@rrf.org
Internet: http://www.rrf.org/organizationalCapacityBuildingProgram.htm
Sponsor: Retirement Research Foundation
8765 W Higgins Road, Suite 430
Chicago, IL 60631-4170

Rucker-Donnell Foundation Grants 1472

The Foundation, established in 2001, is involved with the support of community expansion and development throughout the Murfreesboro, Tennessee, region. It would appear that, in the past, the Foundation's primary fields of interest include: community development/expansion, the arts, and the environment. Specific support is given for general operations. There are no particular deadlines or guidelines, and potential applicants should contact the office before proceeding.
Geographic Focus: Tennessee
Contact: Rick G. Mansfield, Trustee; (615) 890-5700
Internet: http://ruckerdonnellfoundation.org/templates/System/default.asp?id=37512
Sponsor: Rucker-Donnell Foundation
110 S Maple Street
Murfreesboro, TN 37130-3530

Russell Berrie Foundation Grants 1473

The foundation supports nonprofit organizations primarily in Israel and the New York and New Jersey metropolitan areas. Grants are awarded for education (colleges and universities, Jewish education, divinity schools, parochial elementary and secondary schools, and religious higher education), health care (hospitals and respite homes), international programs (development programs, ministries, and missions), religious organizations (religious welfare, synagogues, and temples), social issues, and youth welfare. Types of support include capital support and general operating support. Applicants should submit a brief letter of inquiry and include a description of the program and the organization, including a financial statement. There are no application deadlines.
Requirements: Christian, Jewish, and Roman Catholic organizations in New York, New Jersey, and Israel are eligible.
Geographic Focus: New Jersey, New York, Israel
Amount: 5,000 - 20,000 USD
Samples: Pave the Way Foundation (New York, NY)—for unrestricted support of this organization that promotes good will and reconciliation between different religions, $100,000; American Technion Society (New York, NY)—to establish a nanotechnology institute at the Technion-Israel Institute of Technology, in Haifa, $26 million.
Contact: Susan Strunk, Administrative Director; (201) 928-1880
Internet: http://www.russberrie.com/foundation.html
Sponsor: Russell Berrie Foundation
300 Frank Burr Boulevard, Building E, 7th Floor
Teaneck, NJ 07666-6704

Russell Family Foundation Environmental Sustainability Grants 1474

The foundation is committed to improving protection of the environment in western Washington, with an emphasis on the waters of Puget Sound. The foundation focuses its grantmaking in this program on Puget Sound, Environmental Education and Green Business and supports systemic and community-centered strategies that encourage collaboration across sectors and, where possible, leverage other support, build partnerships and reach new audiences. Though not a requirement for funding, they welcome projects that effectively address and connect several of the above-mentioned areas of interest.
Requirements: A Letter of Inquiry is required prior to any formal application. If the foundation is interested in considering a grant request, they will ask for a more detailed proposal. Full proposals are accepted by invitation only.
Restrictions: Requests are accepted from 501(c)3 organizations. Nonprofit entities such as public schools and school districts also may apply. Organizations must be located in and/or provide services within the Puget Sound region. The region includes 12 counties: Clallam, Jefferson, Kitsap, Mason, Thurston, Pierce, King, Snohomish, Skagit, Whatcom, Island, and San Juan.
Geographic Focus: Washington
Date(s) Application is Due: Jan 8; Jul 16
Amount: 1,000 - 35,000 USD
Contact: Grant Administrator; info@trff.org
Internet: http://www.trff.org/grant_programs/env_education.asp
Sponsor: Russell Family Foundation
P.O. Box 2567
Gig Harbor, WA 98335

Ruth Anderson Foundation Grants 1475

The Ruth Anderson Foundation awards grants to Florida nonprofit organizations in Dade County. The Foundation's funding interests include AIDS research; children and youth services; homeless/housing shelters; human services; and substance abuse services. There are no application forms or deadlines. The initial approach should consist of a brief exploratory letter; full proposals will be by invitation only. The board meets throughout the year to consider requests for funding.
Requirements: Miami Dade County 501(c)3 tax-exempt organizations are eligible.
Restrictions: Grants are not awarded to individuals. Funding is limited to the Miami area.
Geographic Focus: Florida
Amount: 1,000 - 10,000 USD
Contact: Funding Contact; (305) 789-4929
Sponsor: Ruth Anderson Foundation
1525 W. W.T. Harris Boulevard, D1114-044
Charlotte, NC 28288-1161

Ruth and Vernon Taylor Foundation Grants 1476

The foundation awards grants to nonprofit organizations in the areas of arts and humanities, civic and public affairs, secondary schools, higher education, environment, hospitals, human services, health, youth services, and social services. Types of support include general operating support, building construction and renovation, endowment funds, and research. The foundation suggests that initial contact be made in writing, since unsolicited requests for funds are not accepted. The Board meets in May and September.
Requirements: Organizations located in Colorado, Illinois, Montana, New Jersey, New York, Pennsylvania, Texas, or Wyoming are eligible.
Restrictions: Grants are not awarded to individuals.
Geographic Focus: Colorado, Illinois, Montana, New Jersey, New York, Pennsylvania, Texas, Wyoming
Amount: 1,000 - 20,000 USD
Contact: Douglas Taylor, Trustee; (303) 893-5284; (303)893-8263
Sponsor: Ruth and Vernon Taylor Foundation
518 17th Street, Suite 1670
Denver, CO 80202

Ruth Eleanor Bamberger and John Ernest Bamberger Memorial Foundation Grants 1477

The Foundation is dedicated to fulfilling the Founders' desires to help people reach their individual potential. The Foundation assists people of all ages, but especially children and young people through educational opportunities and scholarships, supporting crisis care and protective services, dental aid, after school programs, etc.
Requirements: Only residents of Utah may apply.
Restrictions: Grants and scholarships are given only to organizations, not to individuals personally.
Geographic Focus: Utah
Date(s) Application is Due: Mar 16; Sep 28
Amount: 1,000 - 20,000 USD
Contact: Eleanor Roser, Treasurer; (801) 364-2045; bambergermemfdn@qwestoffice.net
Internet: http://www.ruthandjohnbambergermemorialfdn.org/
Sponsor: Ruth Eleanor Bamberger and John Ernest Bamberger Memorial Foundation
136 S Main, Suite 418
Salt Lake City, UT 84101-1690

Ruth H. and Warren A. Ellsworth Foundation Grants 1478

The foundation awards grants to nonprofits in Massachusetts in support of the arts, children and youth, community development, education and higher education, and health care and hospitals. Types of support include general operating support, continuing support, annual campaigns, building construction/renovation, equipment acquisition, emergency funds, and seed grants. There are no application forms.
Requirements: Nonprofits in the Worcester, MA, area are eligible.
Restrictions: Grants are not awarded to individuals or for endowment funds, scholarships, fellowships, research, publications, conferences, matching gifts, or loans.
Geographic Focus: Massachusetts
Amount: 500 - 100,000 USD
Samples: Bancroft School, Worcester, MA, $125,000; UMass Memorial Foundation, Worcester, MA, $50,000
Contact: Sumner Tilton Jr., Trustee; (508) 798-8621
Sponsor: Ruth H. and Warren A. Ellsworth Foundation
370 Main Street, 12th Floor, Suite 1250
Worcester, MA 01608-1723

Ruth Mott Foundation Grants 1479

The community is invited to submit grant requests for the program areas of arts—culture, music, theater, dance, media, graphics, photography, storytelling, and crafts; beautification—enhance neighborhoods and quality of life in the greater Flint area; and health promotion—healthy and active lifestyles and environments such as physical activity, proper nutrition, responsible sexual behavior, and overall well-being. Types of support include special projects, capacity building (planning, technical assistance, and resource development), evaluation, and general purposes. Priority is given to requests that bring diverse segments of the community together to share ideas and common interests and to respectfully address and resolve differences; enable the engagement of citizens in civic life, community service and leadership; ensure that all stakeholders are informed and involved in decisions affecting them; promote life-long learning and involvement; share and celebrate community members' unique talents, histories, cultures, and contributions; and benefit low-income segments of the community and reduce social, economic, and racial disparities. Concept papers may be submitted at any time throughout the year; full proposals are by invitation.
Requirements: Michigan nonprofit organizations are eligible. Preference is given to requests from Flint, MI.
Geographic Focus: All U.S. States
Amount: Up to 65,000,000 USD
Samples: Flint Institute of Music (MI)—for the Bradley's Tap Festival for Youth, $72,000; Genesis Pentecostal Church of God (MI)—for the Peace Garden, $57,800; F.A.C.E.D. (MI)—to build organizational capacity, $25,000; American Arab Heritage Council (MI)—to support the Family Health and Art Fair, $28,000.
Contact: Grants Administrator; (810) 233-0170
Internet: http://www.ruthmottfoundation.org
Sponsor: Ruth Mott Foundation
111 E Court Street, Suite 3C
Flint, MI 48502-1649

RWJF Partners Investing in Nursing's Future Grants 1480

The program is a collaborative initiative of the Robert Wood Johnson Foundation (RWJF) and the Northwest Health Foundation (NWHF), with the intention of addressing nursing issues at the community level through funding partnerships with local and regional foundations. Up to 10 awards of up to $250,000 each will be made for projects lasting up to 24 months. Local foundations, with other partners (such as state workforce investment boards, hospital and long-term-care associations, foundations and other funding sources) will match these awards with at least $1 for every $2 provided by the program. Funding will be commensurate with the size and scope of the proposed activity and the foundation's experience with nursing issues. Funding is not intended to support the continuation of ongoing projects, but it may support new programs led by foundations that are already working in the field of nursing. October 29 is the deadline for receipt of brief proposals, and January 5 is the deadline for receipt of invited full proposals.
Requirements: Eligible institutions include local or regional private, family or community foundations and public charities. Eligible foundations are those classified as tax-exempt under Section 501(c)3 as a public charity or private foundation, a nonexempt charitable trust treated as a private foundation under Section 4947(a)(1), or organizations that claim status as private operating foundations under Section 4942(j)(3) or (5) of the Internal Revenue Code. Government entities, corporate grantmakers and others may participate as part of funding collaboratives; however, they may not serve as the applicant institution. All proposals to this program must address one or more of these topics: (1) Diversity; (2) Educational Infrastructure and Faculty Development; (3) Public Health; (4) Long-Term Care; and/or (5) Mid-Level Management. Proposals for planning as well as implementation projects will be considered. Deadline for receipt of brief proposals - November 9. Deadline for receipt of invited full proposals - February 1.
Restrictions: This program accepts only proposals submitted through the RWJF Grantmaking Online system at http://grantmaking.rwjf.org/pin2.
Geographic Focus: All U.S. States
Date(s) Application is Due: Oct 29; Jan 5

Amount: Up to 250,000 USD
Contact: Judith L. Woodruff, Program Director; (971) 230-0093; judith@nwhf.org
Internet: http://www.rwjf.org/applications/solicited/cfp.jsp?ID=20903
Sponsor: Robert Wood Johnson Foundation
College Road E and Route 1, P.O. Box 2316
Princeton, NJ 08543-2316

Ryder System Charitable Foundation Grants **1481**

The Ryder System Charitable Foundation was established in 1984 in Florida. The Foundation supports zoological societies and organizations involved with arts and culture, education, animal welfare, health, cystic fibrosis, and human services. Giving is limited to Los Angeles, CA, southern FL, Atlanta, GA, Street Louis, MO, Cincinnati, OH, and Dallas, TX.
Requirements: Organizations in California, Florida, Georgia, Missouri, Ohio, and Texas are eligible to apply. There is no application form, Applicants should submit the following: brief history of organization and description of its mission; copy of most recent annual report/audited financial statement/990; explanation of why grantmaker is considered an appropriate donor for project; listing of board of directors, trustees, officers and other key people and their affiliations; detailed description of project and amount of funding requested; copy of IRS Determination Letter.
Geographic Focus: California, Florida, Georgia, Missouri, Ohio, Texas
Amount: 100 - 100,000 USD
Samples: Scholarship America, Saint Peter, MN, $10,000
Contact: Grants Administrator c/o Corp. Tax; (305) 500-3031; (305) 500-4579; foundation@ryder.com
Sponsor: Ryder System Charitable Foundation
11690 NW 105th Street
Miami, FL 33178-1103

S. D. Bechtel, Jr. Foundation / Stephen Bechtel Fund Character and Citizenship Development Grants **1482**

The Foundation/Fund believe that all people are capable of making positive choices and ethical decisions, and of becoming active citizens. For young people, it is critical that they are provided with consistent and sound mentoring, and the encouragement to participate in new learning opportunities to realize their full potential and become responsible and active citizens. The directors have a strong interest in programs for young people that build character and programs for the broader public that advance an understanding of, and commitment to, the practice of citizenship. The Foundation/Fund support organizations working to achieve the following objectives: increasing opportunities for youth in the San Francisco Bay Area to interact with exemplary role models and participate in a variety of worthwhile learning opportunities so that they are able to develop a framework for ethical living; and advancing a vibrant and productive national conversation about why active citizenship matters and how Americans can cultivate and sustain these values.
Requirements: The primary geographic focus of the Foundation/Fund is the San Francisco Bay area. The Foundation/Fund: support non-profit organizations providing quality programs in science, technology, engineering and math (STEM) education, environment, environmental education, character and citizenship development and preventive healthcare and selected research; provide capital support; provide operational support; and provide project support.
Restrictions: The Foundation/Fund do not provide endowment funding, international grants, or grants for individuals.
Geographic Focus: California
Date(s) Application is Due: Oct 1
Amount: 5,000 - 25,000 USD
Contact: Program Coordinator; (415) 284-8675; (415) 284-8571; sdbjr@sdbjrfoundation.org
Internet: http://www.sdbjrfoundation.org/program_areas.htm#Char_citiz
Sponsor: S. D. Bechtel, Jr. Foundation / Stephen Bechtel Fund
P.O. Box 193809
San Francisco, CA 94119-3809

S. D. Bechtel, Jr. Foundation / Stephen Bechtel Fund Environmental Education Grants **1483**

The Foundations believe that environmental education is vital to the development of a knowledgeable, skilled, and responsible California population that takes individual and collective actions to protect and improve the environment, human health, and economic prosperity. The Directors have a particular interest in supporting environmental education in order to further the goals of the STEM education, environment, character and citizenship development, and preventive healthcare program areas by improving access to high-quality programs and engaging all Californians in environmental learning and behavior. The Foundation supports organizations working to achieve the following objectives: building the research base to advance environmental education teaching and learning; expanding support for environmental education and promote environmental behavior; inspiring personal connections to the natural world and interest in STEM learning by strengthening systems that serve students in the San Francisco Bay Area; and encouraging local stewardship and develop new environmental leaders from urban communities in the San Francisco Bay Area.
Requirements: The primary geographic focus of the Foundation/Fund is the San Francisco Bay area. The Foundation/Fund: support non-profit organizations providing quality programs in science, technology, engineering and math (STEM) education, environment, environmental education, character and citizenship development and preventive healthcare and selected research; provide capital support; provide operational support; and provide project support.
Restrictions: The Foundation/Fund do not provide endowment funding, international grants, or grants for individuals.
Geographic Focus: California
Date(s) Application is Due: Oct 1
Amount: 5,000 - 25,000 USD
Contact: Program Coordinator; (415) 284-8675; (415) 284-8571; sdbjr@sdbjrfoundation.org
Internet: http://www.sdbjrfoundation.org/program_areas.htm#enviro_ed
Sponsor: S. D. Bechtel, Jr. Foundation / Stephen Bechtel Fund
P.O. Box 193809
San Francisco, CA 94119-3809

S. D. Bechtel, Jr. Foundation / Stephen Bechtel Fund Environment Grants **1484**

The Foundation/Fund believe that the sustainable management of natural resources is vital to California's quality of life and economic well-being. The directors have a particular interest in supporting well-managed organizations and networks that promote lasting environmental benefits for California. The Foundation/Fund support organizations working to achieve the following objectives: advance the institutions and infrastructure necessary for California to manage its water resources to support a healthy economy while protecting public health, safety and critical ecosystem services; protect and enhance the network of lands, waters, and organizations sustaining the migratory birds of the Pacific Flyway; secure sustained investment in parks and build capacity of park managers and park supporting organizations; and support selected science and policy research to illuminate the path to a more secure and sustainable energy future.
Requirements: The primary geographic focus of the Foundation/Fund is the San Francisco Bay area. The Foundation/Fund: support non-profit organizations providing quality programs in science, technology, engineering and math (STEM) education, environment, environmental education, character and citizenship development and preventive healthcare and selected research; provide capital support; provide operational support; and provide project support.
Restrictions: The Foundation/Fund do not provide endowment funding, international grants, or grants for individuals.
Geographic Focus: California
Date(s) Application is Due: Oct 1
Amount: 5,000 - 25,000 USD
Contact: Coordinator; (415) 284-8675; (415) 284-8571; sdbjr@sdbjrfoundation.org
Internet: http://www.sdbjrfoundation.org/program_areas.htm
Sponsor: S. D. Bechtel, Jr. Foundation / Stephen Bechtel Fund
P.O. Box 193809
San Francisco, CA 94119-3809

S. D. Bechtel, Jr. Foundation / Stephen Bechtel Fund Preventive Healthcare and Selected Research Grants **1485**

The Foundation?fund believe that access to quality care, preventive health care and research programs can help individuals of all ages increase life expectancy and improve their quality of life. The directors have a particular interest in promoting nutritional health, fitness, and wellness in order to increase positive health outcomes. The Foundation/Fund support organizations working to achieve the following objectives: enabling San Francisco Bay Area community clinics and school-based health centers to improve the quality and delivery of medical care; enhancing and expand school-based efforts in the San Francisco

Bay Area that improve the nutritional health and fitness of children; and advancing research related to Alzheimer's, aging, nutrition or other Board-determined specific research initiatives.
Requirements: The primary geographic focus of the Foundation/Fund is the San Francisco Bay area. The Foundation/Fund: support non-profit organizations providing quality programs in science, technology, engineering and math (STEM) education, environment, environmental education, character and citizenship development and preventive healthcare and selected research; provide capital support; provide operational support; and provide project support.
Restrictions: The Foundation/Fund do not provide endowment funding, international grants, or grants for individuals.
Geographic Focus: California
Date(s) Application is Due: Oct 1
Amount: 5,000 - 25,000 USD
Contact: Program Coordinator; (415) 284-8675; (415) 284-8571; sdbjr@sdbjrfoundation.org
Internet: http://www.sdbjrfoundation.org/program_areas.htm#health
Sponsor: S. D. Bechtel, Jr. Foundation / Stephen Bechtel Fund
P.O. Box 193809
San Francisco, CA 94119-3809

S. D. Bechtel, Jr. Foundation / Stephen Bechtel Fund Science, Technology, Engineering and Math (STEM) Education Grants 1486
The Foundation/Fund believe that America's strength in the STEM fields enables its capacity to compete globally, enhances its opportunities for innovation, and leads to economic prosperity and a better quality of life for society as a whole. The directors have a particular interest in supporting science, technology, engineering, and math education in order to foster a robust and competitive workforce and to develop a STEM-literate populace that understands and appreciates the contributions made by engineering and science to society's welfare. The Foundation/Fund support organizations to achieve the following objectives: engaging students at an early age (K-8) in STEM learning both in-school and out-of-school, particularly in the San Francisco Bay Area; enable and strengthen STEM pathways at key transition points along California's K-14 public educational system; developing regional and state infrastructure, capacity and networks to advance STEM teaching and learning in California; and supporting public awareness and advocacy efforts to build demand for STEM education.
Requirements: The primary geographic focus of the Foundation/Fund is the San Francisco Bay area. The Foundation/Fund do: support non-profit organizations providing quality programs in science, technology, engineering and math (STEM) education, environment, environmental education, character and citizenship development and preventive healthcare and selected research; provide capital support; provide operational support; and provide project support.
Restrictions: The Foundation does not provide endowment funding, international grants, or grants for individuals.
Geographic Focus: California
Date(s) Application is Due: Oct 1
Amount: 5,000 - 25,000 USD
Contact: Coordinator; (415) 284-8675; (415) 284-8571; sdbjr@sdbjrfoundation.org
Internet: http://www.sdbjrfoundation.org/program_areas.htm
Sponsor: S. D. Bechtel, Jr. Foundation / Stephen Bechtel Fund
P.O. Box 193809
San Francisco, CA 94119-3809

S.H. Cowell Foundation Grants 1487
The foundation awards grants for a wide variety of causes to nonprofit organizations in northern California. Projects of interest include those that support children, youth, and families; education; housing; alcohol abuse prevention; religious organizations, education, and welfare; school-to-work employment training; population and environment; family planning; and conventional arms control. Applicants are encouraged to obtain most of their operating and project funding from other sources. Matching and challenge grants will be awarded under appropriate circumstances. The foundation prefers to award grants for one-time capital needs or for specific projects that are time-definite in nature and likely to become self-sufficient within several years. The application process should begin with a phone call. If interested, the foundation will request a short letter and then a formal proposal.
Requirements: Grants are made only to 501(c)3 tax-exempt organizations primarily in northern California.
Restrictions: The foundation does not normally make grants to individuals, for start-up of new organizations, for academic or other research, for general support, for annual fund-raising, to governmental agencies, to churches for religious support, to hospitals for medical research or treatment, for conferences, for media projects, or for political lobbying.
Geographic Focus: California
Amount: Up to 500,000 USD
Samples: Adventure Risk Challenge, Truckee, CA, $25,000 - to launch year-round expansion of the Adventure Risk Challenge (ARC) summer program (2008); Boys & Girls Clubs of the North Valley Chico, CA, $500,000 - to launch a Boys & Girls Club in South Oroville (2008); East Bay Asian Local Development Corporation Oakland, CA, $375,000 - to complete the budget to install a park at Lion Creek Crossings (2008)
Contact: Susan Vandiver, Program Contact; (415) 397-0285; (415) 986-6786; info@shcowell.org
Internet: http://www.shcowell.org/grant/grant.php
Sponsor: S.H. Cowell Foundation
120 Montgomery Street, Suite 2570
San Francisco, CA 94104

S. Livingston Mather Charitable Trust Grants 1488
The S. Livingston Mather Charitable Trust was established in 1953 in Ohio by Cleveland-Cliffs vice-president Samuel Livingston Mather. The Trust's primary areas of interest include cultural programs, education, child welfare, and social services. Support is also available for youth programs, the environment, and natural resources. Giving is primarily restricted to the northeastern Ohio area. Applicants should contact the Trust prior to submitting an application.
Requirements: Unsolicited requests for funds not accepted, contact the Trust before sending a proposal.
Restrictions: No support is available for: endowments; science; medical research programs; in areas appropriately supported by the government and/or the United Way; individuals; or deficit financing.
Geographic Focus: Ohio
Amount: 100 - 100,000 USD
Samples: Cleveland Museum of Art, Cleveland, OH, $20,000; Cuyahoga Valley Countryside Conservancy, Peninsula, OH, $7,500.
Contact: Janet W. Havener, Director, c/o Glenmede Trust Company; (215) 419-6000
Sponsor: S. Livingston Mather Charitable Trust
1 Corporate Exchange, 25825 Science Park Drive, Suite 110
Beachwood, OH 44122

S. Mark Taper Foundation Grants 1489
The S. Mark Taper Foundation, founded in 1989, is a private family foundation dedicated to enhancing the quality of people's lives by supporting nonprofit organizations and their work in the Los Angeles, Long Beach, Santa Ana, California communities. Areas of interest are broad and include but are not limited to education, the environment, independent living for the disabled, abused women, immigrant health care, children, hunger, housing, AIDS, teenage pregnancy prevention, job creation and economic revitalization, individuals with visual impairments, and the arts. Types of support include capital grants, challenge/matching grants, general operating grants, research grants, program/project grants, seed money grants, and scholarships. Grants are made generally for one year.
Requirements: 501(c)3 nonprofit organizations in California are eligible for grant support. Application forms are required therefore your initial approach should be a Letter of Inquiry containing one copy of the proposal and the following: brief history of organization and description of its mission; copy of most recent annual report/audited financial statement/990; detailed description of project and amount of funding requested; list of source(s) of last three years of funding for the specific project (if any) and, the organization.
Geographic Focus: California
Date(s) Application is Due: Dec 1
Amount: 5,000 - 500,000 USD
Samples: Korean Health Education Information and Research Center, Los Angeles, CA - $500,000; Santa Clarita Child and Family Development Center, Santa Clarita, CA - $100,000; Los Angeles Unified School District Education Foundation, Los Angeles, CA - $200,000
Contact: Raymond Reister, Executive Director; (310) 476-5413; (310) 471-4993; rreisler@smtfoundation.org or info@smtfoundation.org
Internet: http://www.smtfoundation.org/
Sponsor: S. Mark Taper Foundation
12011 San Vicente Boulavard, Suite 400
Los Angeles, CA 90049

Sage Foundation Grants 1490

The foundation awards grants nationwide, with emphasis on the Midwest, to nonprofit organizations in support of higher education, legal education, and secondary education; seniors; hospitals; disabled; Catholic giving and welfare; youth; child welfare; social services; and cultural programs. Types of support include annual campaigns, building construction/renovation, capital campaigns, challenge grants, endowments, equipment acquisition, general operating grants, multi-year support, project development, research, and scholarship funds. There are no application deadlines or forms; submit a letter of inquiry. The board meets quarterly.

Geographic Focus: All U.S. States
Amount: 1,000 - 250,000 USD
Contact: Melissa Sage Fadim, Grants Administrator; (810) 227-7660 or (212) 737-7311
Sponsor: Sage Foundation
P.O. Box 1919
Brighton, MI 48116

Saint Ann Foundation Grants 1491

The foundation extends the mission of Jesus Christ through the ministry of the Sisters of Charity of Saint Augustine in the area of human services. It provides financial support for the development and implementation of programs that address the fundamental causes of human suffering and directly serve the basic human needs of the socially and economically disadvantaged. The foundation uses a variety of approaches to grantmaking in striving to fulfill its mission, including responsive grants—designed to elicit creative responses to the concerns reflected in the foundation's goals and priorities; kinship care initiative—a significant commitment to document the nature and extent of kinship care, and to increase the public's awareness of this growing phenomenon; and religious communities initiative—created to support collaborative efforts of religious communities located in Region VI of the Leadership Conference of Women Religious (Ohio, Kentucky and Tennessee), as well as in South Carolina. Contact the office or submit a brief letter of inquiry prior to submitting a complete proposal. Guidelines are available online.

Requirements: The mission, programs, and services of the grant applicant should be consistent with the mission and values of the foundation. The applicant organization must be tax-exempt and nonprofit as defined by the IRS. Proposals will be considered from organizations located in the following counties in Ohio: Ashland, Cuyahoga, Geauga, Lake, Lorain, Medine, Summit and Wayne. Projects of religious communities will be considered from LCWR Region VI (Ohio, Kentucky, Tennessee) and South Carolina.
Restrictions: The foundation does not fund: annual appeals or membership drives; capital construction; endowment funds; debt retirement; grants to individuals; or fund-raising campaigns.
Geographic Focus: Kentucky, Ohio, South Carolina, Tennessee
Date(s) Application is Due: Apr 1
Amount: Up to 30,000 USD
Samples: Boy Scouts of America, Heart of Ohio Council (Ashland, OH)—for its scouting program for urban boys, $10,000; Hispanic Urban Minority Alcohol and Drug Abuse Program (Cleveland, OH)—for its Hispanic Youth Center, $25,000; West Side Catholic Ctr (Cleveland, OH)—for its women's shelter, $15,000; Cleveland Public Theatre (Cleveland, OH)—for a theater for youths living in public housing, $20,000.
Contact: Kathy Csank, Program Contact; (216) 241-9300; (216) 241-9345; kcsank@socstannfdn.org or mail@socstannfdn.org
Internet: http://www.socstannfdn.org/StA/StAMission.html
Sponsor: Saint Ann Foundation
1422 Euclid Avenue, Suite 425
Cleveland, OH 44115-1901

Saint Louis Rams Foundation Community Donations 1492

The foundation supports nonprofits that help inspire positive change for youth in the Saint Louis area. Programs that impact youth in the general fields of education, literacy, health, and recreation will be considered. Annually, the Rams provide to charitable groups more than 3,500 items, helping recipient organizations raise thousands of dollars through raffles, auctions and other fundraising endeavors. Other types of financial support include program development grants and general operating grants. The foundation does not accept unsolicited requests, but initial information may be sent for the office to keep on file for future opportunities.

Requirements: Nonprofits in the metropolitan Saint Louis, Missouri, area, including southern Illinois and eastern Missouri, are eligible. Preference is given to organizations that partner with other local nonprofits and offer creative approaches for more than grants (i.e., personnel involvement or in-kind support) and ways the Rams can participate.
Restrictions: The Rams do not provide monetary contributions or merchandise donations for the following: businesses, retail and otherwise; capital campaigns/start-up funding for new businesses; on-line auctions; chamber of commerce/city/neighborhood festivals such as homecoming celebrations and carnivals that do not directly benefit a charitable organization; class reunions; family reunions; pageant contestants (beauty and otherwise); student ambassador/exchange programs; or non-charity events and organizations such as company picnics, employee golf tournaments, employee recognition/incentive programs, card clubs, car shows, "poker runs", and organized adult leisure sports teams.
Geographic Focus: Missouri
Date(s) Application is Due: Jan 1; Jul 1
Contact: Donations Coordinator; (314) 516-8788 or (314) 982-7267; (314) 770-0392
Internet: http://www.stlouisrams.com/community/donations.html
Sponsor: Saint Louis Rams Foundation
1 Rams Way
Saint Louis, MO 63045

Saint Paul Companies Foundation Grants 1493

Saint Paul Companies is dedicated to strengthening the communities in which its employees live and work. Grants are considered for programs that fall under one or more of the following focus areas: enrich lives and celebrate diversity through arts and culture; revitalize communities; and educate underserved populations to create social and economic opportunities. Grants are made for operating,support, program/project support, capital support, start-up funding, and transitional support. Grantmaking is restricted to the Twin Cities (primarily Saint Paul), the Baltimore area, the United Kingdom, and selected locations where the corporation has a significant business presence. An organization seeking funds for new programs should begin the application process by submitting a one-page letter describing the request. The foundation no longer accepts paper applications; all applications must be made online. Application guidelines at the Travelers website.

Geographic Focus: Minnesota, United Kingdom
Date(s) Application is Due: Sep 1
Amount: 15,000 - 250,000 USD
Contact: Ronald McKinley, Community Affairs; (651) 310-2623 or (800) 328-2189
Internet: http://www.travelers.com/corporate-info/about/community/foundation.aspx
Sponsor: Saint Paul Companies
385 Washington Street
Saint Paul, MN 55102-1396

Saint Paul Foundation Grants 1494

The community foundation serves the greater Saint Paul, Minnesota, area and makes grants to support educational (including adult basic education and literacy programs), charitable, or cultural programs/projects that benefit residents of Ramsey, Washington, and Dakota Counties. The foundation's grantmaking vehicles include project/program, start-up costs, general operating support, capital projects, and matching funds. Support will ordinarily not exceed three years. There are no application deadlines; however, full proposals must be received approximately three and one-half months prior to the meeting date. The board meets in April, August, and December.

Requirements: Minnesota 501(c)3 tax-exempt organizations are eligible.
Restrictions: The foundation will not consider requests for ongoing annual operating expenses; sectarian religious programs; grants to individuals; capital projects located outside Ramsey, Dakota, and Washington Counties; or programs not serving residents of Ramsey, Dakota, and Washington Counties.
Geographic Focus: Minnesota
Amount: 250 - 500,000 USD
Contact: John G. Couchman, Vice-President; (651) 224-5463; (651) 224-8123; jgc@saintpaulfoundation.org or inbox@saintpaulfoundation.org
Internet: http://www.saintpaulfoundation.org/grants/apply_for_a_foundation_grant/
Sponsor: Saint Paul Foundation
55 Fifth Street E, Suite 600
Saint Paul, MN 55101-1797

Saint Paul Travelers Foundation Grants **1495**

Saint Paul Travelers partners with employees, communities, and business partners to help build a civil society by investing in people and institutions for long-term success. The foundation supports initiatives that: revitalize communities; educate underserved populations to create social and economic opportunities; and enrich lives and celebrate diversity through arts and culture. Contributions will be designated for operating support, program/ project support, capital support, start-up funding, or transitional support. The foundation will accept online grant applications at any time during the year. Guidelines are available online.

Requirements: Grantmaking will be restricted to nonprofit organizations in the Twin Cities (primarily Saint Paul), the Baltimore area, the United Kingdom, and selected locations where Saint Paul Travelers has a significant business presence. National organizations may receive support for specific initiatives that fit within the foundation's funding priorities.

Restrictions: Contributions will not be used for organizations that discriminate on the basis of race, gender, religion, culture, age, physical disability, sexual orientation, or status as a military veteran; sectarian religious organizations, unless it can be shown that the organization is seeking charitable funds in the direct interest of the whole community; veterans' and fraternal organizations; political or lobbying organizations; benefits, fundraisers, walk-a-thons, telethons, galas, or other revenue-generating events; advertising; scholarships to individuals; health or disease-specific organizations, health care or other emergency assistance for individuals, or hospitals and other health services generally supported by third-party reimbursement mechanisms; replacement of government funding; start-up, capital, or operations of public or charter schools; human services such as counseling, chemical abuse, or family programs; environmental programs; special events, except when the event is a key strategy in a continuum of efforts to achieve community goals in the foundation's priority areas; or nonacademic job placement programs.

Geographic Focus: All U.S. States

Date(s) Application is Due: Sep 15

Samples: Approximately 100 nonprofit groups in Minneapolis-Saint Paul, and Hartford, CT (MN, CT)—to support work in the areas of arts and culture, community development, and education, $2.619 million divided; Nonprofit groups in Minneapolis-Saint Paul, MN; Hartford, CT; and elsewhere—for support of arts and cultural organizations, in conjunction with the Saint Paul Travelers Foundation and the Saint Paul Travelers Connecticut Foundation, $1,871,750 distributed.

Contact: Grants Administrator; (651) 310-7911

Internet: http://www.stpaultravelers.com/about/community/stpaul/index.html

Sponsor: Saint Paul Travelers Foundation
385 Washington Street
Saint Paul, MN 55102

Salem Foundation Grants **1496**

The primary purpose of the Foundation is support of higher education, cultural activities, health services, hospital building funds, and Christian giving. Its fields of interest include: arts; Christian agencies and churches; the disabled; education (secondary and higher); the environment; family services; federated giving programs; health care (particularly heart and circulatory disease research); hospitals; human services; museums; and Protestant federated giving programs. Types of support include: annual campaigns, building/renovation projects, capital campaigns, general operating support, and program development. There is no formal application process and no deadlines. Please contact via letter.

Restrictions: Giving primarily in Florida, Maine and Minnesota. No grants to individuals.

Geographic Focus: Florida, Maine, Minnesota

Amount: Up to 10,000 USD

Contact: Robert S. Parish, President; (952) 476-6292

Sponsor: Salem Foundation
2181 Springwood Road
Wayzata, MN 55391-2254

Salt River Project Grants **1497**

The energy/utilities company awards grants in Arizona to nonprofit organizations that address critical needs within its service communities. Project grants, general support, in-kind services, and volunteer support are awarded in general areas of interest, which include arts and culture, civic affairs, education, health, science, and social services delivery. Specific areas of interest include major professional arts organizations and youth and adult arts activities; minority/community leadership and strategic planning; engineering education, math and science education, vocational skills development, and education of women and minorities; health; environmental quality and water/electrical resources; food, shelter, self-sufficiency, youth, and housing development; and funding for teachers and schools. Guidelines are available on the website.

Requirements: Arizona nonprofits in SRP service communities may apply.

Restrictions: SRP does not donate services, including water or electricity, or equipment for which a fee is normally charged.

Geographic Focus: Arizona

Samples: Globe-Miami Community Concert Assoc (Globe-Miami, AZ)—for program support; City of Peoria Parks and Recreation Festival of Lights (Peoria, AZ)—for program support; Queen Creek Elementary School (Queen Creek, AZ)—for operating support.

Contact: Program Contact; (602) 236-2573; contrib@srpnet.com

Internet: http://www.srpnet.com/community/contributions

Sponsor: Salt River Project
P.O. Box 52025
Phoenix, AZ 85072-2025

Samuel Freeman Charitable Trust Grants **1498**

The trust has broad funding interests in supporting U.S. charitable, scientific, literary, and education programs. The trust awards grants to support cancer research and treatment; the preservation, exhibition, and operation of historical railway equipment; and secondary schools and universities. Types of support include general operating support, continuing support, annual campaigns, and seed money. There are no application deadlines; proposals are reviewed throughout the year.

Requirements: U.S. nonprofit organizations may apply.

Geographic Focus: All U.S. States

Amount: 1,000 - 150,000 USD

Contact: Linda Franciscovich, c/o U.S. Trust Company, (212) 852-3683; (212) 852-3377

Sponsor: Samuel Freeman Charitable Trust
114 W 47th Street
New York, NY 10036-1532

Samuel N. and Mary Castle Foundation Grants **1499**

The foundation supports Hawaii nonprofit organizations by awarding grants to support a broad area of programs/projects, including the arts, education, environment, religion, health, children, and families. Types of support include building and renovation funds, challenge grants, project development, operating budgets, equipment acquisition, seed money, land acquisition, and capital campaigns. There are no application deadlines. The board meets in March, June, September, and December to consider requests.

Requirements: Hawaii nonprofit organizations may apply.

Geographic Focus: Hawaii

Date(s) Application is Due: Feb 1; Jun 1; Oct 1

Amount: 5,000 - 25,000 USD

Samples: Hawaii Theater Ctr (Honolulu, HI)—for operating support, $10,000; Kauai Children's Discovery Museum (Kapaa, HI)—for its early-childhood program, $15,000; Trinity Lutheran Church and School (Wahi-awa, HI)—to renovate its sports facilities, $10,000; Castle Medical Ctr (Kailua, HI)—to construct a new wing for this hospital, $10,000.

Contact: Alfred Castle, Executive Director; (808) 522-1101; (808) 522-1103; acastle@aloha.net

Internet: http://www.fdncenter.org/grantmaker/castle

Sponsor: Samuel N. and Mary Castle Foundation
733 Bishop Street, Suite 1275
Honolulu, HI 96813

Samuel Rubin Foundation Grants **1500**

The foundation is dedicated to the pursuit of peace and justice and the search for an equitable reallocation of the world's resources and believes these objectives can be achieved only through the fullest implementation of social, economic, political, civil, and cultural rights for all the world's people. Grants are awarded to support projects that reach toward the solutions to bring about this state. Types of support include general operating support and seed money. Applications should be in the form of a letter and include a budget and tax determination letter. The Board of Directors normally meets three times a year. Application deadlines are the first Friday in January, September, and May. Application will not be accepted through fax transmission or email.

Restrictions: Funds are not granted to individuals or for buildings, endowments, or scholarships.

Geographic Focus: All U.S. States
Amount: 5,000 - 10,000 USD
Contact: Cora Weiss, President; (212) 697-8945; (212) 682-0886; info@samuelrubinfoundation.org
Internet: http://www.samuelrubinfoundation.org
Sponsor: Samuel Rubin Foundation
777 United Nations Plaza
New York, NY 10017-3521

Samuel S. Fels Fund Grants **1501**

Since the Fels Fund has a small budget - approximately $2.5 million in the next few years - it could not possibly provide ongoing operating support to hundreds of organizations. Instead, the Fund tries to make grants at critical junctures. Critical junctures are points in an organization's life when there is a need to change methodologies. This could mean growing, shrinking, trying a new type of programming, experimenting with staffing, piloting a project that might support itself eventually, opening a satellite, seeking new accreditation, retraining staff or board or rethinking the physical plant. The fund supports activities or projects in the fields of education, the arts, and community services, which are intended to improve the quality of life in Philadelphia, Pennsylvania. Applicant organizations also must be located in Philadelphia. Types of support include general operating support, continuing support, program development, seed funding, curriculum development, internships, matching funds, and technical assistance. Grants at Fels range in size from $3,000 to $30,000. Occasionally, the Fund will make a larger grant in an exceptional situation. Applications are accepted at any time (with the exception of Arts and Humanities projects which are due by 5 p.m. on January 15th or May 15th).
Requirements: Philadelphia nonprofits may apply.
Restrictions: Grants are not awarded to support multi-year projects, umbrella-funding groups, scholarships, travel, research, capital funds, major equipment, endowments, deficit financing, ticket purchases, ads, fund-raising events, or emergency aid.
Geographic Focus: Pennsylvania
Amount: 3,000 - 30,000 USD
Samples: 11th Hour Theatre Company, Philadelphia, Pennsylvania, $3,000 - General support (2009); 1812 Productions, Philadelphia, Pennsylvania, $5,000 - General support (2009); Community Women's Education Project, Philadelphia, Pennsylvania, $15,000 - Capacity building (2009).
Contact: Helen Cunningham, Executive Director; (215) 731-9455; (215) 731-9457; helenc@samfels.org
Internet: http://www.samfels.org/apps.html
Sponsor: Samuel S. Fels Fund
1616 Walnut Street, Suite 800
Philadelphia, PA 19103-5313

Samuel S. Johnson Foundation Grants **1502**

The Samuel S. Johnson Foundation was incorporated in 1948 and supports organizations primarily in Oregon and Clark County, Washington region. The Foundation gives to: formal education programs leading to an R.N. status or baccalaureate or higher college/university degree in nursing; vocational education programs targeting high school drop-outs and high school grads who are not able to pursue junior college or higher formal education and which offer them job-specific technical training, mentoring or coaching; emergency food assistance programs; rural mobile health screening/care projects benefiting the uninsured medically needy; environmental programs, coastal & marine ecosystems, sustainable agriculture and communities.
Requirements: Grants are awarded to non-profit organizations in Oregon and Clark County, Washington. Contact the Foundation for current focus and guidelines with a phone call before submitting a proposal. No Application form is required, however you must include the following in your proposal: copy of IRS Determination Letter; brief history of organization and description of its mission; copy of most recent annual report/audited financial statement/990; listing of board of directors, trustees, officers and other key people and their affiliations; detailed description of project and amount of funding requested; contact person; copy of current year's organizational budget and/or project budget; listing of additional sources and amount of support. Include one copy of the proposal. The board meets twice a year, in May and October, with no deadline date for the submitting of proposals. If your proposal is accepted, you will receive notification within 2 - 3 weeks after the board meets.
Restrictions: No support for foreign organizations. No grants or scholarships to individuals, or for leadership training or staff development, campaigns to retire debt, annual campaigns, deficit financing, construction, sole underwriting of major proposals or projects, demolition or endowments.
Geographic Focus: Oregon, Washington
Amount: 400 - 100,000 USD
Contact: Mary A. Krenowicz, Secretary; (541) 548-8104; (541) 548-2014; mary@tssjf.org
Sponsor: Samuel S. Johnson Foundation
P.O. Box 356
Redmond, OR 97756-0079

San Antonio Area Foundation Grants **1503**

Grants are usually awarded in the areas of health care and biomedical research, community and social services, arts and culture, education (early childhood education, higher education, medical schools, nursing schools, adult basic education and literacy), and animal services. Types of support include operating budgets, continuing support, annual campaigns, seed grants, emergency funds, equipment acquisition, matching funds, scholarship funds, research, lectureships, professorships, and building renovations. Applicants must submit a letter of intent to apply; if the letter is approved, the foundation will send a request for a proposal to the applicant. The foundation only reviews full proposals from applicants whose letters of intent have been approved. If asked to submit a proposal, the applicant will be sent an application package with a letter of notification in early February.
Requirements: Grants are made to organizations in the San Antonio, Texas, area.
Geographic Focus: Texas
Date(s) Application is Due: Nov 15
Amount: 250 - 250,000 USD
Samples: San Antonio Symphony (TX)—for the Young People's Concert series, $25,000; Southwest Foundation for Biomedical Research (San Antonio, TX)—to purchase equipment, $15,000.
Contact: Lydia R. Saldana, Program Officer; (210) 228-3753 or (210) 225-2243; (210) 225-1980; lsaldana@saafdn.org or info@saafdn.org
Internet: http://www.saafdn.org/NetCommunity/Page.aspx?pid=254
Sponsor: San Antonio Area Foundation
110 Broadway Street, Suite 230
San Antonio, TX 78205-1948

San Diego Foundation Arts & Culture Grants **1504**

The Foundation's grant-making process in the area of arts and culture will distribute funds to organizations working collaboratively to create innovative new works and/or processes. It anticipates making six to eight high-impact grants in the community in this grant cycle, with grants between $10,000 and $50,000. This Art Works for San Diego program supports projects that can achieve the following results: provide San Diego residents and visitors with high quality arts and culture experiences; incorporate arts and culture into community problem solving; enable people to come together and connect with each other; build bridges between the arts and culture community and the community at large; and increase cultural patronage including hands-on involvement, audience participation and philanthropy.
Requirements: To be eligible, organizations must be providing services in San Diego County. The organizations must have a 501(c)3 IRS tax exempt status. An organization may serve as a fiscal sponsor for a charitable organization that does not have a 501(c)3 status if a cooperative relationship between the two can clearly be demonstrated. The fiscal sponsor must be willing to administer the grant if awarded.
Restrictions: Generally, the Foundation does not make grants for: organizations that have previously received funding from the Foundation but have not submitted required final reports; major building/capital campaigns; scholarships; endowments; for-profit organizations; projects that promote religious doctrine; individuals; organizations outside San Diego County; marketing and/or promotional materials (annual reports, brochures, video productions); re-granting dollars to other nonprofit organizations or individuals; short-term, annual or one time events, including festivals, performances and conferences; travel outside of the San Diego region, or; existing obligations or debt.
Geographic Focus: California
Date(s) Application is Due: Jan 16
Contact: Kerri Favela, (619) 235-2300, ext. 1329; kerri@sdfoundation.org
Internet: http://www.sdfoundation.org/communityimpact/cycle2006.html#ac
Sponsor: San Diego Foundation
2508 Historic Decatur Road, Suite 200
San Diego, CA 92106

San Diego Foundation Civil Society Grants **1505**

The San Diego Foundation's Civil Society Working Group was established with the mission to foster civic engagement in community problem solving leading to an improved quality of life for all residents. The San Diego region requires a shared vision to enable effective and inclusive dialogue for the purpose of planning for balanced and equitable future growth. The goal of this initiative is to establish a framework to address the need for housing across the San Diego region resulting in livable communities with choices for all. Preference will be given to applicants with strategic partnerships that demonstrate the experience, skills, and capacity to achieve stated results and commit to sharing best practices and lessons learned to advance initiative goals. Applicants are encouraged to apply for grants generally between $25,000 and $50,000.

Requirements: To be eligible, organizations must be providing services in San Diego County. The organizations must have a 501(c)3 IRS tax exempt status. An organization may serve as a fiscal sponsor for a charitable organization that does not have a 501(c)3 status if a cooperative relationship between the two can clearly be demonstrated. The fiscal sponsor must be willing to administer the grant if awarded.

Restrictions: Generally, the Foundation does not make grants for: organizations that have previously received funding from the Foundation but have not submitted required final reports; major building/capital campaigns; scholarships; endowments; for-profit organizations; projects that promote religious doctrine; individuals; organizations outside San Diego County; marketing and/or promotional materials (annual reports, brochures, video productions); re-granting dollars to other nonprofit organizations or individuals; short-term, annual or one time events, including festivals, performances and conferences; travel outside of the San Diego region, or; existing obligations or debt.

Geographic Focus: California

Date(s) Application is Due: Jan 16

Amount: 25,000 - 50,000 USD

Contact: Shelley Lyford, Research & Development Manager; (619) 235-2300; Shelley@sdfoundation.org

Internet: http://www.sdfoundation.org/communityimpact/cycle2006.html#ac

Sponsor: San Diego Foundation
2508 Historic Decatur Road, Suite 200
San Diego, CA 92106

San Diego Women's Foundation Grants **1506**

The San Diego Women's Foundation (SDWF) strengthens and improves women's capacities to engage in significant philanthropy in the San Diego region. The foundation chooses one focus area of grant making each year. Its primary focus areas include: education, arts and culture, environment, employment and economic development, civil society, and health and human services. Check the web site each September for that year's focus guidelines.

Requirements: Only 501(c)3 organization within San Diego County should apply.

Geographic Focus: California

Date(s) Application is Due: Dec 6

Amount: 25,000 USD

Contact: Tracy Johnson, Director; (619) 814-1374 or (619) 235-2300; (619) 239-1710; tracy@sdfoundation.org

Internet: http://www.sdwomensfoundation.org/

Sponsor: San Diego Women's Foundation
2508 Historic Decatur Road, Suite 200
San Diego, CA 92106

Sands Foundation Grants **1507**

The Venetian Foundation (now the Sands Foundation) was formed December 7, 2000, by the Venetian Casino Resort. Today, the Las Vegas Sands Corporation's primary philanthropic initiative is pursued through Sands Foundation, a non-profit 501(c)3 organization. Sands Foundation pursues a mission of supporting charitable organizations and endeavors that concentrate on assisting youth, promoting health, and expanding educational opportunities within the local communities. The Foundation also supports causes that empower minority communities and improve underprivileged areas, as well as other valuable charitable and philanthropic activities permitted under relevant tax-exempt laws. Sands Foundation pursues a mission of supporting charitable organizations and endeavors that concentrate on assisting youth, promoting health, and expanding educational opportunities within our local communities. The Foundation also supports causes that empower minority communities and improve underprivileged areas, as well as other valuable charitable and philanthropic activities permitted under relevant tax-exempt laws. Charitable requests along with supporting documents may either be faxed or mailed.

Requirements: All charitable requests must be submitted in writing. Written requests should include the following: agency/organization information (brochures, information packet, list of the board of directors, history, background, or other helpful information); 501(c)3 tax identification number; contact person; mailing address and telephone number; overview of project or event at hand; date, time, location for event requests; purpose of request; very specific information about the amount/item(s) requested; and target population which will benefit from support.

Geographic Focus: Nevada, Pennsylvania, Macau, Singapore

Amount: 5,000 - 100,000 USD

Samples: Keep Memory Alive, Las Vegas, Nevada, $25,000 (2009); Landmark Media Enterprises, Norfolk, Virginia, $37,500 (2009); Emeril Lagasse Foundation, New Orleans, Louisiana, $5,000 (2009).

Contact: Community Development Department; (702) 607-1677; (702) 607-1044; foundation@venetian.com

Internet: http://www.lasvegassands.com/LasVegasSands/Sands_Foundation/Donation_Request.aspx

Sponsor: Sands Foundation
3355 Las Vegas Boulevard South
Las Vegas, NV 89109-8941

Sands Memorial Foundation Grants **1508**

The foundation awards grants to Montana nonprofits in the area of companion animal protection and care, including spay/neuter programs and cruelty-prevention programs. Types of support include general operating support, continuing support, building construction/renovation, equipment acquisition, emergency funds, and seed grants. Application forms are required.

Requirements: Montana nonprofit organizations may apply.

Restrictions: Individuals are ineligible.

Geographic Focus: Montana

Date(s) Application is Due: Oct 30

Contact: Cynthia Bryson, President; (406) 265-4271; (406) 265-4271; smf@hi-line.net

Sponsor: Sands Memorial Foundation
P.O. Box 1450
Havre, MT 59501-1450

Sands Point Fund Grants **1509**

Established by Howard and Roslyn Zuckerman in Monsey, New York, in 2007, the Sands Point Fund is primarily interested in offering support to educational programs and Jewish agencies/synagogues. Amounts range up to a maximum of $2,500. There are no specific guidelines, application formats, or deadlines with which to adhere, and applicants should begin by contacting the Trust directly.

Geographic Focus: New York

Amount: Up to 2,500 USD

Samples: Ohr Somayach Educational Program, Monsey, New York, $2,500 (2010); Mesivta Tifereth Jerusalem Project, New York, New York, $2,500 (2010).

Contact: Howard Zuckerman, Trustee; (212) 972-3600

Sponsor: Sands Point Fund
6 Sand Point Road
Monsey, NY 10952-2110

Sandy Hill Foundation Grants **1510**

The Sandy Hill Foundation offers awards to eligible nonprofit organizations in the areas of education, health care, and social services. The foundation gives primarily to the arts and culture, higher education, hospitals, health associations, social services, and federated giving programs. Their areas of interest include the arts; child and youth services; community and economic development; health organizations and associations; higher education; hospitals; human services; Protestant agencies and churches; recreation camps; and United Way and Federated Giving Programs. It also offers college scholarships for designated local area schools.

Requirements: There is no application or specific deadline for nonprofit giving. See contact information for current scholarship application due April 1.

Restrictions: The foundation gives primarily to the greater Hudson Falls, NY area. No grants are given to individuals.

Geographic Focus: New York

Date(s) Application is Due: Apr 1

Amount: Up to USD
Samples: Glens Falls Hospital Foundation, Glens Falls, New York - $65,000 (2009); World Awareness Childrens Museum, Glens Falls, New York - $22,500 (2009)
Contact: Nancy Juckett Brown, Trustee; (518) 791-3490
Sponsor: Sandy Hill Foundation
P.O. Box 30
Hudson Falls, NY 12839-0030

Santa Fe Community Foundation Grants 1511
The mission of the community foundation is to provide leadership in helping meet the needs of the people of Santa Fe and northern New Mexico. Grants are awarded in three categories. General Grants address community concerns and help generate solutions in the areas of arts, civic affairs, education, environment, and health and human services. Technical Assistance Connector grants assist organizations to obtain professional expertise in board/staff development, fundraising, strategic planning, program evaluation, budgeting and financial management, public relations and marketing, volunteer management, and mergers. Lesbian and Gay Community Funding Partnership grants assist organizations serving lesbian, gay, and bisexual populations. Types of support include multiyear grants, general operating support, matching grants, and technical assistance grants. The foundation is particularly interested in funding initiatives that are collaborative, inclusive, respond to major gaps in service, and are rooted in the community. Listed deadline is for LGBT grants. Annual deadline dates may vary; contact program staff for exact dates.
Requirements: IRS 501(c)3 tax-exempt organizations serving residents of Santa Fe, Los Alamos, Rio Arriba, Taos, San Miguel, and Moro Counties in New Mexico are eligible.
Restrictions: The foundation does not award grants to individuals or for religious purposes, political purposes, capital outlay or capital campaigns, endowment, or governmental agencies experiencing operational budget cuts.
Geographic Focus: New Mexico
Date(s) Application is Due: Jul 1
Amount: 2,000 - 10,000 USD
Samples: Santa Fe Children's Museum (Santa Fe, NM)—for a comprehensive three-year summer program for children aged five to seven from low-income Santa Fe families, $130,000; El Bien Estar de Familias Daycare Ctr (Tierra Amarilla, NM)—operating support for this child care center that serves the rural Chama/Tierra Amarilla area of New Mexico, $10,000.
Contact: Dolores Roybal, Program Officer; (505) 988-9715; (505) 988-1829; droybal@santafecf.org
Internet: http://www.santafecf.org/grants/general.php
Sponsor: Santa Fe Community Foundation
P.O. Box 1827
Santa Fe, NM 87504-1827

Santa Maria Foundation Grants 1512
Established in New York in 1978, the foundation awards grants primarily to Catholic organizations to provide spiritual and religious renewal shelters for the homeless and unwed mothers. Types of support include continuing support and general operating grants. There are no application forms or deadlines with which to adhere. Initial approach should be by letter.
Geographic Focus: All U.S. States
Date(s) Application is Due: Sep 1
Amount: Up to 400,000 USD
Samples: College of Mount Saint Vincent, Riverdale, New York, $400,000; Grace Outreach, Bronx, New York, $85,000; Diocese of Portland, Portland, Maine, $80,000.
Contact: Patrick P. Grace, President and Director; (914) 395-1830
Sponsor: Santa Maria Foundation
19 Mountain Avenue
Mount Kisco, NY 10549-1321

Sapelo Foundation Environmental Protection Grants 1513
The Sapelo Foundation is a private family foundation focusing its funding within the State of Georgia. The Foundation is particularly interested in projects that involve multiple groups that work cooperatively toward common goals, accomplish systemic reform, and have a statewide impact. In addition, the Foundation gives special attention to low-resource regions in the state and innovative, community-based projects within the Foundation's focus areas. The Foundation believes that the preservation of Georgia's finite natural resources benefits all species of life and is essential to their health and long-term survival. Currently, the Foundation's primary focus is a strategic campaign addressing water resource management and policy in Georgia. The Foundation was instrumental in the creation of the Georgia Water Coalition and its active members currently receive priority for funding. Grants range from $1,000 to $60,000, and the average award is between $5,000 and $25,000.
Requirements: Georgia 501(c)3 nonprofit organizations are eligible.
Restrictions: The Foundation does not give priority to: academic research; land acquisition; environmental education centers and nature centers; wildlife parks or animal rehabilitation center; or museums. The Foundation does not support projects operating solely within the Metro Atlanta Area. The Foundation does not fund the following: brick-and-mortar, building projects or renovations, including construction materials and labor costs; endowment funds; fraternal groups or civic clubs; health care initiatives or medical research; individuals; national or regional organizations, unless their programs specifically benefit Georgia and all funds are spent within the state; organizations that are not tax-exempt; or payment of debts.
Geographic Focus: Georgia
Date(s) Application is Due: Mar 1; Sep 1
Amount: 1,000 - 60,000 USD
Contact: Phyllis Bowen, Executive Director; (912) 265-0520; (912) 254-1888; info@sapelofoundation.org or sapelofoundation@mindspring.com
Internet: http://www.sapelofoundation.org/index.html
Sponsor: Sapelo Foundation
1712 Ellis Street, 2nd Floor
Brunswick, GA 31520

Sapelo Foundation Social Justice Grants 1514
The Sapelo Foundation is a private family foundation focusing its funding within the State of Georgia. The Foundation is particularly interested in projects that involve multiple groups that work cooperatively toward common goals, accomplish systemic reform, and have a statewide impact. In addition, the Foundation gives special attention to low-resource regions in the state and innovative, community-based projects within the Foundation's focus areas. The Foundation believes that the development of sound public policy is crucial to effective government and the empowerment of the citizenry. Therefore, it is the aim of the Foundation to strengthen representative democracy in Georgia through efforts that educate the public about government institutions and policies, promote civic engagement and responsibility, and monitor government performance. Currently, the Foundation's primary focus is a strategic campaign advocating for fairness for children in the state's justice system. Grants range from $1,000 to $60,000, and the average award is between $5,000 and $25,000.
Requirements: Georgia 501(c)3 nonprofit organizations are eligible.
Restrictions: The Foundation does not give priority to: academic research; local government entities; human services programs; criminal justice programs designed to rehabilitate and/or punish individuals; senior citizen's programs; after-school mentoring/tutoring programs; single-site day care facilities; homeless shelters or programs; affordable housing; or programs serving the physically or developmentally disabled. The Foundation does not support projects operating solely within the Metro Atlanta Area. The Foundation does not fund the following: brick-and-mortar, building projects or renovations, including construction materials and labor costs; endowment funds; fraternal groups or civic clubs; health care initiatives or medical research; individuals; national or regional organizations, unless their programs specifically benefit Georgia and all funds are spent within the state; organizations that are not tax-exempt; or payment of debts.
Geographic Focus: Georgia
Date(s) Application is Due: Mar 1; Sep 1
Amount: 1,000 - 60,000 USD
Contact: Phyllis Bowen, Executive Director; (912) 265-0520; (912) 254-1888; info@sapelofoundation.org or sapelofoundation@mindspring.com
Internet: http://www.sapelofoundation.org/index.html
Sponsor: Sapelo Foundation
1712 Ellis Street, 2nd Floor
Brunswick, GA 31520

Sarah Scaife Foundation Grants 1515
Approximately 80 percent of the annual grants are made to public policy programs that address major domestic and international issues. There are no geographic restrictions. Other grants are made in the fields of education and culture, health and medicine, scientific research, public affairs, and recreation and equipment in all geographic areas, but primarily in western Pennsylvania. Types of support include general operating support, continuing support, program development, conferences and seminars, publication, seed grants,

fellowships, research, and matching funds. Applications are accepted at any time. Foundation staff considers requests in February, May, September, and November.
Restrictions: Grants are not made to individuals or to national organizations for general fund-raising purposes.
Geographic Focus: All U.S. States
Amount: 25,000 - 200,000 USD
Samples: U of Pittsburgh (Pittsburgh, PA)—to construct facilities for the planned Pittsburgh Institute for Neurodegenerative Diseases, $5.4 million.
Contact: Michael Gleba, Vice President of Programs; (412) 392-2900
Internet: http://www.scaife.com/sarah.html
Sponsor: Sarah Scaife Foundation
1 Oxford Center, 301 Grant Street, Suite 3900
Pittsburgh, PA 15219

Sara Lee Foundation Grants **1516**
The foundation's cash grants program concentrates on the Chicago metropolitan area. Special interests include organizations that serve the disadvantaged with emphasis on programs concerning hunger and homelessness, job placement, housing, and women's issues; education, including child development education, adult basic education, and literacy skills; and arts and cultural institutions including libraries. The foundation also funds a scholarship program and youth ambassador program for employees of the Sara Lee Corporation and its subsidiaries. Additional types of support include employee matching gifts, special projects, operating budgets, annual campaigns, and continuing support. The annual leadership awards recognize and support nonprofit organizations that demonstrate innovative leadership in improving life for the disadvantaged in communities where Sara Lee Corporation divisions have facilities; two to four awards are presented each year. Leadership awards are not restricted to Illinois nonprofits. Annual deadline may vary; contact program officer for exact date.
Requirements: IRS 501(c)3 nonprofit organizations in Illinois that have been in existence for at least two years at the time of application and that are located in a community where a Sara Lee Corporation division has facilities are eligible.
Restrictions: Grants do not support individuals; organizations with a limited constituency, such as fraternities or veterans groups; organizations that limit their services to members of one religious group, or those whose services propagate religious faith or creed, including churches, seminaries, bible colleges, and theological institutions; political organizations or those having the primary purpose of influencing legislation or promoting a particular ideological point of view; elementary and secondary schools, either private or public; units of government or quasi-governmental agencies; or hospitals and health organizations concentrating their research and/or treatment in one area of human disease.
Geographic Focus: Illinois
Date(s) Application is Due: Jan 10; Jul 10
Amount: Up to 15,000 USD
Samples: Steppenwolf Theatre Co (Chicago, IL)—for its campaign to build endowment and to support key programs, $1 million.
Contact: Robin Tryloff, Executive Director; (312) 558-8448; (312) 419-3192
Internet: http://www.saraleefoundation.org/funding/focus.cfm
Sponsor: Sara Lee Foundation
3 First National Plaza
Chicago, IL 60602-4260

Sartain Lanier Family Foundation Grants **1517**
The foundation awards grants to Georgia nonprofits in support of education, health and human services, arts, environment, and community development. Types of support include building and renovation; capital campaigns; endowments; general operating support; program development; and program-related investments and loans. The foundation's board meets in May and November of each year to consider grant requests. Prior to submitting a full proposal, applicants should submit a letter limited to two pages summarizing the request. The letter should include a brief description of the organization and its purpose, the project for which funding is requested, the total cost of the project, and the amount being requested.
Requirements: Nonprofit organizations in the southeastern United States are eligible to apply, however, the majority of recipients are located in Georgia and specifically the Atlanta metro area.
Restrictions: The foundation does not make grants for individuals; churches or religious organizations for projects that primarily benefit their own members; partisan political purposes; tickets to charitable events or dinners, or to sponsor special events or fundraisers.
Geographic Focus: Georgia
Contact: Patricia Lummus, Assistant Director; (404) 564-1259; (404) 564-1251; plummus@lanierfamilyfoundation.org
Internet: http://www.lanierfamilyfoundation.org/grant.html
Sponsor: Sartain Lanier Family Foundation
25 Puritan Mill, 950 Lowery Boulevard
Atlanta, GA 30318

SAS Community Relations Grants **1518**
SAS's financial grants program focuses primarily on K-12 education, particularly the integration of technology and education as a means of improving the educational process. Grants are awarded for programs or operations, with a minimal portion applied to overhead. The program also supports product donations, and employee-volunteer opportunities. There are no application deadlines.
Requirements: North Carolina 501(c)3 tax-exempt organizations are eligible.
Restrictions: The program does not consider funding for professional athletic sponsorships; benefit/yearbook advertising; religious causes; political parties, candidates, or issues; organizations that are in any way exclusive; trips, tours; independent film/video productions; or requests from individuals.
Geographic Focus: All U.S. States
Contact: Grants Administrator; (919) 677-8000; (919) 677-4444; communityrelations@sas.com
Internet: http://www.sas.com/corporate/community/index.html
Sponsor: SAS Institute
100 SAS Campus Drive
Cary, NC 27513-2414

Schering-Plough Foundation Community Initiatives Grants **1519**
The Schering-Plough Foundation, a non-profit membership corporation established in 1955, is dedicated to working with the citizens of our communities to help them realize their full potential and enhance their quality of life. Support for community development takes many forms and allows the Foundation to reach out to numerous, highly diverse groups within its communities. The Foundation continues to support organizations that promote culture and the arts, environmental issues, legal services, etc. and are always seeking out new and innovative ways to serve the citizens of its communities.
Requirements: The Foundation considers requests from tax-exempt, 501(c)3 non-profit organizations located in the United States, or its possessions, whose goals and activities fall within its stated objectives and areas of interest. All requests for funding must be made online. National organizations are eligible to apply.
Restrictions: Grants are not made to individuals.
Geographic Focus: All U.S. States
Amount: 5,000 - 200,000 USD
Contact: Christine Fahey, Assistant Secretary; (908) 298-7232; (908) 298-7349
Internet: http://www.schering-plough.com/company/foundation.aspx
Sponsor: Schering-Plough Foundation
2000 Galloping Hill Road
Kennilworth, NJ 07033-0530

Scherman Foundation Grants **1520**
The main areas of interest for the foundation are the environment, peace and security, reproductive rights and services, human rights and liberties, the arts, and social welfare. Priority is given to organizations in New York City in the areas of the arts and social welfare. Requests for support should be made in a brief letter addressed to the President (Mike Pratt) outlining the purpose for the funds being sought; program description; budget; list of directors and staff; audited financial statement; sources of support; and evidence of tax status. The board meets four times a year to consider applications.
Requirements: Organizations must be tax-exempt 501(c)3. Requests for support may be submitted online at submissions@scherman.org, clearly marked as PROP.O.SAL in the subject line.
Restrictions: The foundation does not accept applications through fax. Funding is not given to: individuals; colleges, universities, or professional schools; medical, science, or engineering research; capital campaigns; conferences; or specific media or arts productions. Do not submit video or audio cassettes or CD's, unless requested to do so.
Geographic Focus: All U.S. States

Amount: 1,000 - 60,000 USD
Samples: Center for Community Change, Washington, D.C., $50,000 (2010); Green Guerillas, New York, New York, $25,000 (2010)
Contact: Mike Pratt, Program Officer; (212) 832-3086; (212) 838-0154; mpratt@scherman.org
Internet: http://www.scherman.org/html2/approc.html
Sponsor: Scherman Foundation
16 East 52nd Street, Suite 601
New York, NY 10022-5306

Schlessman Family Foundation Grants **1521**
The foundation awards grants to Colorado nonprofits in its areas of interest, including higher and other education, cultural programs, youth, disabled, and social services. Types of support include general operating support, continuing support, annual campaigns, capital campaigns, equipment acquisition, endowment funds, program development, curriculum development, scholarship funds, and matching grants. Emphasis will be given to programs in Front Range, CO. Applicants should submit a letter of request.
Requirements: Colorado nonprofits in the greater Denver area are eligible to receive grant support.
Geographic Focus: Colorado
Date(s) Application is Due: Dec 31
Amount: Up to 21,000,000 USD
Samples: Urban Ministries (CO)—for operating support, $6000; Adult Learning Source (CO)—for operating support, $7500; Greeley Meals on Wheels (CO)—for operating support, $2000; Hospice of Metro Denver (CO)—for operating support, $3000.
Contact: Patricia Middendorf, Treasurer; (303) 831-5683; (303) 831-5676; pamiddendorf@qwest.net
Internet: http://www.schlessmanfoundation.org
Sponsor: Schlessman Family Foundation
1301 Pennsylvania Street, Suite 800
Denver, CO 80203-5015

Schramm Foundation Grants **1522**
The foundation awards grants to Colorado nonprofit organizations in its areas of interest, including arts and culture, civic affairs, community development, education (elementary, secondary, and higher), healthcare, housing, humanities, medical research, science, social services delivery, technology, women's issues, and youth. Types of support include building construction/renovation, continuing support, equipment acquisition, general operating support, matching/challenge grants, program development, and scholarship funds. Applications are accepted from July 1 through the listed application deadline.
Requirements: Colorado 501(c)3 nonprofit organizations are eligible. Preference is given to requests from the Denver area.
Restrictions: Grants do not support advertising, advocacy organizations, individuals, international organizations, political organizations, religious organizations, school districts, special events, or veterans organizations.
Geographic Focus: Colorado
Date(s) Application is Due: Aug 31
Amount: 500 - 26,500 USD
Samples: U of Denver (CO)—to renovate Spruce Hall of the Graduate School of Social Work, $100,000.
Contact: Gary Kring, President; (303) 797-6718
Sponsor: Schramm Foundation
800 Grant Street, Suite 404
Denver, CO 80203

Schumann Fund for New Jersey Grants **1523**
The Schumann Fund for New Jersey is a tax exempt, private foundation, incorporated as a corporation not for pecuniary profit under the laws of the State of New Jersey. Schumann Fund program priorities fall into four categories: Early Childhood Development; Environmental Protection; Essex County; and Public Policy.
Requirements: There is no standard application form to be used in presenting a request to the Schumann Fund for New Jersey, but organizations may use the New York/New Jersey Common Application Form if they choose. The Foundation asks that a written proposal be submitted which includes a clear description of the purpose of the grant, the need or problem that will be addressed, the work to be undertaken, the staffing plan for project implementation, any collaborative efforts underway or contemplated, and the means of evaluating progress. The proposal must include the following items: a copy of the organization's latest audited financial statement; current organizational and project budgets identifying all sources of revenue and categories and amounts of expenditures; brief resumes of key organization and project staff; the project time frame and projected sources of future funding; a list of the organization's board of directors; Internal Revenue Service documents confirming the organization's status as a 501(C)3 organization. The Schumann Fund Board of Trustees meets quarterly.
Restrictions: In general, the Schumann Fund for New Jersey does not accept applications for capital campaigns, annual giving, endowment, direct support of individuals, or local programs in counties other than Essex. Projects in the arts, health care, and housing development normally fall outside the fund's priority areas.
Geographic Focus: New Jersey
Date(s) Application is Due: Jan 15; Apr 15; Jul 15; Oct 15
Amount: 15,000 - 100,000 USD
Samples: New Jersey Association of Child Care Resource and Referral Agencies, Trenton, New Jersey, $15,000 - for using new data to develop an advocacy agenda to improve family child care; Rutgers, the State University of New Jersey, Camden, New Jersey, $80,000 - for campaign for Children's Literacy, comprehensive effort that provides professional development and certification to early childhood teachers, monthly seminars for parents, and library outreach initiative to encourage parents to read to their children.
Contact: Barbara Reisman, Executive Director; (973) 509-9883; (973) 509-1149
Internet: http://foundationcenter.org/grantmaker/schumann/program_guidelines.html
Sponsor: Schumann Fund for New Jersey
21 Van Vleck Street
Montclair, NJ 07042

Scott B. and Annie P. Appleby Trust Grants **1524**
The trust supports programs and projects of nonprofit organizations in the categories of higher education, cultural programs, and child welfare. Types of support include general operating support, continuing support, capital campaigns, building construction/renovation, and scholarship funds. Interested applicants are encouraged to submit a letter describing the intent and purpose of the organization with a specific proposal for allocation of funds.
Requirements: The foundation funds those in the District of Columbia, Florida, and Georgia.
Geographic Focus: District of Columbia, Florida, Georgia
Amount: 2,000 - 50,000 USD
Contact: Program Contact, c/o SunTrust Banks
Sponsor: Scott B. and Annie P. Appleby Trust
P.O. Box 2018
Sarasota, FL 34230

Seattle Foundation Grants **1525**
The foundation awards grants to nonprofits in all fields that improve the quality of life for King County residents. While grants are made across all fields, principal funding areas include arts, culture, and humanities; education; environment/animals; health; human services; and public/society benefit. Types of support include capital, equipment, and operating support grants to increase organizations' capacities to serve their constituents. Grants to any one organization will generally not be approved more often than once every three years. Application and guidelines are available online.
Requirements: IRS 501(c)3 tax-exempt organizations located in King County, Washington, are eligible.
Restrictions: Grants are not made to individuals or to religious organizations for religious purposes. Grants will not be awarded for endowment; general purposes; funding of conferences or seminars; discriminatory purposes on the basis of race or creed; or the production of books, films, or videos.
Geographic Focus: Washington
Date(s) Application is Due: Jan 1; Apr 1; Jul 1; Oct 1
Amount: 10,000 - 25,000 USD
Samples: The Japanese Legacy Project (Seattle, WA)—to purchase equipment to gather video interviews and historical photographs and documents for an online digital archive depicting the incarceration of Japanese-Americans during World War II and other facets of Japanese-American history, $20,000; Harborview Medical Ctr (Seattle, WA)—for a project that seeks to increase over a two-year period the number of foster children up to age five enrolled in Head Start in King County, WA, $100,000.

Contact: Program Contact; (206) 622-2294; (206) 622-7673; grantmaking@seattlefoundation.org
Internet: http://www.seafound.org/grantseekers/index.html
Sponsor: Seattle Foundation
1200 Fifth Avenue, Suite 1300
Seattle, WA 98101-3151

SecurianFoundation Grants **1526**

The program mission is to enhance the quality of life and vitality of the communities in which it does business. Areas of priority include economic independence—programs that promote economic independence, including job-training and -placement services, work readiness, and career development programs for unemployed/underemployed and disadvantaged individuals; higher education—support to private colleges and universities (and tax-supported colleges and universities under certain conditions), with priority given to math, economics, and business and youth development intervention programs that encourage the pursuit of higher education; human services and special community needs—major operating support to the United Way and to non-United Way human services organizations that are demonstrating a service in an area of unmet need; and the arts—major arts and cultural organizations that provide services to a broad audience and stimulate the cultural vitality of the community. The company also has an employee matching gifts program for K-12 and higher education, vocational and specialized schools, hospitals, and arts and cultural organizations.
Requirements: IRS 501(c)3 nonprofit organizations primarily in the twin cities of Saint Paul and Minneapolis, MN, where the company and foundation are headquartered, are eligible.
Restrictions: Grants are not awarded to individuals or for benefits, trips, tours, political activities, or religious services/groups.
Geographic Focus: Minnesota
Date(s) Application is Due: Feb 15; May 15; Aug 15; Nov 15
Amount: 1,000 - 50,000 USD
Samples: United Way, Greater Twin Cities, (Minneapolis, MN)—for annual support, $355,000; University of Minnesota (Minneapolis, MN)—for leadership course and speaker series, $200,000.
Contact: Lori Koutsky, Manager; (651) 665-3501; (651) 665-3551; Lori.Koutsky@minnesotamutual.com
Internet: http://www.securian.com/About/giveguide.asp
Sponsor: Securian Foundation
400 Robert Street N
Saint Paul, MN 55101-2098

Sensient Technologies Foundation Grants **1527**

The foundation supports organizations involved with arts and culture; children/youth, services; community/economic development; education; education, fund raising/fund distribution; education, research; family services; food services; general charitable giving; health care; higher education; homeless, human services; hospitals (general); human services; medical research, institute; mental health/crisis services; nutrition; performing arts; residential/custodial care, hospices; United Ways and Federated Giving Programs; Urban/community development; and voluntarism promotion. The foundation's types of support include: annual campaigns; capital campaigns; emergency funds; endowments; general operating support; matching/challenge support; program development; research; and scholarship funds.
Requirements: An application form is not required. Submit a letter of inquiry as an initial approach. The advisory board meets in January and June/July or as needed, with deadline for proposal review one month prior to board meetings.
Restrictions: The foundation gives primarily to its areas of interest in Indianapolis, Indiana; Street Louis, Missouri; and Milwaukee, Wisconsin. It does not support sectarian religious, fraternal, or partisan political organizations. It does not give grants to individuals.
Geographic Focus: Indiana, Missouri, Wisconsin
Contact: Douglas L. Arnold, (414) 271-6755; (414) 347-4783
Sponsor: Sensient Technologies Foundation
777 E Wisconsin Avenue
Milwaukee, WI 53202-5304

Seventh Generation Fund Grants **1528**

The fund works directly with grassroots Native American communities and traditional indigenous societies throughout the Americas in support of Native peoples' community organizing, issue advocacy, economic renewal, cultural revitalization, environmental justice, and related restorative development efforts. Grants support projects in the areas of arts and cultural expression, environmental health and justice, indigenous people of the Americas, sacred Earth, and sustainable communities. Types of support include small grants—seed money, general operating support; technical assistance grants—training and capacity building; and mini grants—community-based projects. Application and guidelines are available online.
Requirements: 501(c)3 (and organizations with 501(c)3 fiscal sponsors) focused in the Native American community are eligible. Mini-grant applicants need not have 501(c)3 status.
Geographic Focus: All U.S. States
Date(s) Application is Due: Mar 1; Jun 1; Sep 1; Dec 1
Amount: 50 - 10,000 USD
Contact: Elaine Quitiquit, Program Associate; (707) 825-7640; (707) 825-7639; eq7gen@pacbell.net
Internet: http://www.7genfund.org/we_help.html
Sponsor: Seventh Generation Fund
P.O. Box 4569
Arcata, CA 95518

Seybert Institution for Poor Boys and Girls Grants **1529**

The charitable foundation supports nonprofit organizations providing services for disadvantaged youth in Philadelphia. The foundation is interested in projects for abused, deprived children and youth counseling services. The institute also supports special projects that encourage disadvantaged children in Philadelphia public elementary schools to develop leadership and academic skills. Generally grants range up to $7,500 and are made on a one-year basis. Recipients must provide a detailed narrative and financial report on how the funds were spent. The deadline for requests for after school and summer programs is March 17. The deadlines for other grant requests are January 2 and October 1.
Requirements: IRS 501(c)3 tax-exempt nonprofit organizations operating to benefit poor boys and girls in Philadelphia, PA, are eligible.
Geographic Focus: Pennsylvania
Date(s) Application is Due: Jan 2; Mar 17; Oct 1
Amount: Up to 7,500 USD
Samples: Center for Grieving Children & Families, Philadelphia, PA, $5,000—operating support (2008); Wagner Free Institute of Science, Philadelphia, PA, $5,000—children's and family outreach programs (2008); Art-Reach, Philadelphia, PA, $7,000—supplementary arts education project (2008).
Contact: Judith L. Bardes, Manager; (610) 828-8145; (610) 834-8175; judy1@aol.com
Internet: http://www.grants-info.org/seybert/guidelines.htm
Sponsor: Adam and Maria Sarah Seybert Institution for Poor Boys and Girls
P.O. Box 540
Plymouth Meeting, PA 19462-0540

Shared Earth Foundation Grants **1530**

The foundation is committed to the tenet that all creatures have an enduring claim to sustainable space on this planet. The foundation will fund organizations that promote protection and restoration of habitat for the broadest possible biodiversity, that foster respect for other species and individual creatures, that work to limit detrimental human impact on the planet, and that further the inherent right of all creatures to share the Earth. The foundation looks to fund primarily, though not exclusively, small organizations. It will provide administrative as well as project funds, with possibility for renewal or continuation, in the United States and abroad, to groups working in the natural and political worlds. Guidelines and application are available online.
Geographic Focus: All U.S. States
Date(s) Application is Due: Dec 15
Amount: 5,000 - 10,000 USD
Samples: Environmental Film Festival (Washington, DC)—to support the Environmental Film Festival 2004, $10,000; African Wildlife Foundation (Washington, DC)—to help create the Great Limpopo Transfrontier Park, and Conservation Area in South Africa, Zimbabwe, and Mozambique, to minimize threats to sustainable livelihoods while achieving important conservation goals, $20,000; Rachel's Network (Washington, DC)—general support for a women's environmental network working to make the environment an important part of the national agenda, $25,000.
Contact: Caroline Gabel, (410) 778-6868; sharedearth@aol.com
Internet: http://www.sharedearth.org
Sponsor: Shared Earth Foundation
113 Hoffman Lane
Chestertown, MD 21620

Shubert Foundation Grants 1531

The grants build and perpetuate the live performing arts, particularly the professional theater, in the United States by supporting theatrical organizations, dance companies, and arts-related institutions that maintain and support the theater. Professional resident theaters are major recipients of financial support. Artistic achievement, administrative strength, and fiscal stability are factored into each evaluation, as is the company's development of new work and other significant contributions to the field of professional theater in the United States. Applications from dance companies will be accorded consideration in the same manner and under the same criteria as theater companies. Support is also provided for nonperforming arts-related organizations, such as those that coordinate and/or assist in the development of the performing arts. A limited number of grants are made to graduate drama departments of private universities. These departments are evaluated principally in terms of their ability to train and develop theater artists. A limited number of human services grants are made to exceptional institutions that are dedicated to improving the quality of life, both in and beyond their own communities. Applications are October 17, for dance, arts related, education, and human services applications; and December 1, for theater applications. Application and guidelines are available online.

Requirements: Tax-exempt 501(c)3 organizations may apply for grant support.

Restrictions: Grants are not awarded to individuals or for capital or endowment funds, seed money, research, conduit organizations, renovation projects, audience development, productions for specialized audiences, scholarships, fellowships, or matching gifts.

Geographic Focus: All U.S. States

Date(s) Application is Due: Oct 17; Dec 1

Amount: 5,000 - 35,000 USD

Samples: Vivian Beaumont Theater (New York, NY)—for general operating support, $275,000; Crossroads Theatre Comp (New Brunswick, NJ)—for operating support, $25,000; Alvin Ailey American Dance Theater (New York, NY)—for operating support, $85,000.

Contact: Vicki Reiss, Executive Director; (212) 944-3777; (212) 944-3707

Internet: http://www.shubertfoundation.org/grantprograms/default.asp

Sponsor: Shubert Foundation

234 W 44th Street

New York, NY 10036

Sidgmore Family Foundation Grants 1532

The foundation supports programs that ensure the health, education, and general well-being of children, youth, and young adults. The foundation is interested in funding organizations with programs, projects, and research that utilize sports to promote the physical, mental, and spiritual development of young people; recognize that an impoverished environment limits the possibilities for children to develop and thrive; improve the quality of education available to youth, with special emphasis on programs designed to improve teacher training and teaching methods; and further advance knowledge and research in the medical fields of vision, hearing, and allergies. There are no application deadlines. Guidelines are available online.

Requirements: Nonprofit organizations are eligible. Preference is given to organizations that serve residents in the Washington metropolitan area, Maryland, and Virginia.

Restrictions: Grants do not support government agencies, national health organizations, political activities, or public policy advocacy groups.

Geographic Focus: All U.S. States

Contact: Administrator; (516) 541-2713; (516) 541-2803; SidgmoreFound@aol.com

Internet: http://fdncenter.org/grantmaker/sidgmore/prior.html

Sponsor: Sidgmore Family Foundation

71 Leewater Avenue

Massapequa, NY 11758

Sidney Stern Memorial Trust Grants 1533

The foundation awards grants to nonprofit organizations in its areas of interest, including civil rights, children and youth, community development, disabled, education, health and science, social services, and Native Americans. Types of support include annual campaigns, building construction/renovation, deficit financing, emergency funds, endowment funds, equipment acquisition, land acquisition, scholarship funds, seed grants, special projects, and research. Requests from California receive preference. There are no application deadlines. The board meets monthly, except August.

Geographic Focus: All U.S. States

Amount: 2,500 - 8,000 USD

Contact: Program Contact; (310) 459-2117

Sponsor: Sidney Suitern Memorial Trust

P.O. Box 893

Pacific Palisades, CA 90272

Sid W. Richardson Foundation Grants 1534

Grants are provided to tax-exempt organizations in Texas in the areas of education (museums, learning centers, day schools, K-12 schools, higher education institutions, and business and economic education), health (medical schools, organ donor registries, hospitals, disease prevention, health science centers, and nursing associations), arts (arts councils, visual and performing arts festivals, museums, ballet, symphony orchestra, and arts education programs), and human services (boys' and girls' clubs, united funds, the elderly, crime prevention, the disabled, housing opportunities, food programs, and drug and alcohol abuse prevention); specific goals within these larger areas change periodically. Types of support include operating budgets, seed grants, building construction funds, equipment acquisition, endowment funds, research, publications, conferences and seminars, matching funds, continuing support, and projects/programs. Award amounts vary depending on proposed projects.

Requirements: Proposals must cover programs and projects within Texas.

Restrictions: Grants are not made to individuals.

Geographic Focus: Texas

Date(s) Application is Due: Jan 15

Amount: 10,000 - 100,000 USD

Samples: All Saints Episcopal School (Fort Worth, TX)—for its capital campaign, $1 million.

Contact: Valleau Wilkie Jr., Director; (817) 336-0494; (817) 332-2176

Internet: http://www.sidrichardson.org/GrantInfo.html

Sponsor: Sid W. Richardson Foundation

309 Main Street

Fort Worth, TX 76102

Simmons Foundation Grants 1535

The foundation awards grants to Maine nonprofits in its areas of interest, including arts, higher education, family services, health care, food services, health organizations, human services, children and youth, services and women. Types of support include general operating support, building construction/renovation, equipment acquisition, and scholarship funds.

Requirements: There are no application forms or deadlines however your initial approach should be in the form of a letter. Applicants should submit the following: detailed description of project and amount of funding requested; brief history of organization and description of its mission; descriptive literature about organization; copy of IRS Determination Letter.

Geographic Focus: Maine

Contact: Suzanne McGuffey, Treasurer; (207) 774-2635

Sponsor: Simmons Foundation

1 Canal Plaza

Portland, ME 04101-4098

Simpson Fund Grants 1536

The fund serves a broad range of organizations in its operating communities that address key community needs such as education, health services, economic development, the arts, and more. Simpson also provides support to environmental and conservation projects, such as environmental education, habitat restoration, research relevant to the timber industry, as well as other projects that impact the timber business. The fund makes an extra effort to support organizations of interest to, or recommended by, Simpson employees. Support is generally committed for one year at a time. Capital projects are given priority over requests for contributions to operating funds. The fund supports the United Way in all of its operating communities. Guidelines are available online.

Requirements: Contributions are limited to Simpson communities: Washington—Pierce, Mason, Thurston and Grays Harbor Counties; Oregon—Lincoln and Tillamook Counties; and California—Del Norte and Humboldt Counties.

Geographic Focus: California, Oregon, Washington

Amount: 1,000 - 10,000 USD

Contact: Grants Administrator; (206) 224-5198; cmusgra@simpson.com

Internet: http://www.simpson.com/communitycontribute.cfm

Sponsor: Simpson Fund

1301 Fifth Avenue, Suite 2800

Seattle, WA 98101-2613

Sister Fund Grants for Women's Organizations 1537

The Sister Fund supports justice and fullness of life for women and girls in society. The fund seeks to identify and support programs that foster women's full development through the promotion of social, economic, political, and spiritual growth. Priority is given to: community programs, including those that are faith-based, that empower women and girls with the ways and means to bring about necessary changes in their lives and communities; programs and organizations that seek to radically transform social, economic, political, and religious institutions and dogma that oppress women and girls; efforts to develop liberative women's theologies that encompass our diversity, including feminist, womanist, mujerista, Asian, and Native American theologies and that reflect on the religious understandings and practices of grassroots women; and activities that encourage dialogue and collaboration between women's movements and expressions of women's spiritualities that seek justice.
Requirements: Nonprofit organizations are eligible to apply.
Restrictions: Funding will not be given to: groups which do not have their own 501(c)3 or a fiscal sponsor with 501(c)3 IRS tax determination; individuals; state, county or municipal agencies; capital/building acquisition or improvements; scholarship funds or student aid; or deficit financing.
Geographic Focus: All U.S. States
Amount: 5,000 - 30,000 USD
Samples: Catholics for Free Choice (Washington, DC)—for the Women, Religion, and Public Policy Project, $10,000; Assistance to Iranian Refugees (New York, NY)—to aid female Iranian asylum seekers through case management, advocacy, education, and organizing services, $10,000; Iris House (New York, NY)—to renovate a new facility to provide services to HIV-positive women, $25,000.
Contact: Sunita Mehta, Director of Grants and Programs; (212) 260-4446; (212) 260-4633; info@sisterfund.org
Internet: http://www.sisterfund.org/about_mission.php
Sponsor: Sister Fund
116 E 16th Street, 7th Floor
New York, NY 10003

Sisters of Charity Foundation of Canton Grants 1538

The foundation's interests encompass the broad areas of health, education, and social services. Within these areas, the foundation strives to fund innovative and effective programs that address the root causes of poverty, reach out to youth and families, and enhance organizational capacity.
Requirements: Ohio tax-exempt, nonprofit organizations in the Stark County area are eligible. Proposals from surrounding counties including Carroll, Holmes, Tuscarawas, and Wayne may be considered.
Restrictions: Grants normally are not awarded to fund requests for capital campaigns, or operating expenses/debt reduction of established organizations, unless it can be demonstrated that the program services will have significant impact on addressing the root causes of poverty. Grants do not support annual appeals or membership drives, endowment funds, or individuals.
Geographic Focus: All U.S. States
Samples: Stark Community Foundation, Fund for Our Economic Future (Canton, OH)—for a regional, philanthropic economic-development program, $50,000; Saint Mark Baptist Church (Canton, OH)—for an after-school and summer enrichment program, $10,000; American Heart Assoc (Canton, OH)—for a minority-outreach program, $30,000 (maximum) challenge grant; Pathway Caring for Children (Canton, OH)—to provide respite care and support to parents in an effort to prevent disrupted adoptions, $38,000 over two years.
Contact: Rebecca Huff, Grants Manager; (330) 454-5800; (330) 454-5909; bhuff@scfcanton.org
Internet: http://www.scfcanton.org/grant.html
Sponsor: Sisters of Charity Foundation of Canton
400 Market Avenue North, Suite 300
Canton, OH 44702-1556

Sisters of Mercy of North Carolina Foundation Grants 1539

The foundation provides grants to tax-exempt health care, educational, and social service organizations that assist women, children, the elderly, and the poor to improve the quality of their lives. Types of support include start-up grants for new organizations or programs, ongoing operating expenses for individual organizations, program or project expenses, building renovation, and equipment acquisition. Preference will be given to organizations whose efforts are collaborative, ecumenical, and multicultural. Particular attention will be given to organizations that serve the unserved or underserved. Annual deadline dates may vary; contact program staff for exact dates.
Requirements: Tax-exempt health care, education, and social service organizations in North and South Carolina are eligible to apply.
Restrictions: The foundation does not ordinarily support projects, programs, or organizations that serve a limited audience; biomedical or clinical research; units of the federal government; political activities; publication of newsletters, magazines, books and the production of videos; conferences and travel; endowment funds; capital fundraising campaigns; annual giving campaigns; or social events or similar fundraising activities.
Geographic Focus: North Carolina, South Carolina
Date(s) Application is Due: Apr 1; Aug 1; Dec 1
Amount: 25,000 - 150,000 USD
Samples: Greater Carolinas Chapter of the American Red Cross (Charlotte, NC)—to provide free transportation to and from medical appointments, $50,000.
Contact: Grants Administrator; (704) 366-0087; (704) 366-8850; contact@somncfdn.org
Internet: http://www.somncfdn.org/grantseekers.html
Sponsor: Sisters of Mercy of North Carolina Foundation
2115 Rexford Road, Suite 401
Charlotte, NC 28211

Sisters of Street Joseph Healthcare Foundation Grants 1540

The Sisters of Street Joseph Healthcare Foundation is a non-profit, public benefit corporation, which addresses the needs of the working and indigent poor in: Southern California; San Francisco Bay Area; Humboldt County; Fresno County. The Sisters of Street Joseph Healthcare Foundation funds programs which directly serve the needs of the underserved, especially families and children at risk. The Foundation sponsors or supports long-term efforts which are closely identified with the Sisters of Street Joseph of Orange and their mission of bringing unity and healing where divisiveness and oppression exist. The foundation supports the concept of Healthy Communities and desire to fund programs and organizations that: provide direct health-related services; support and transform the individual, social, economic, institutional, and cultural aspects of communities; provide change within larger societal systems to benefit low-income and at-risk populations; and develop the leadership and capacity for self-determination of those served by our funding. The Sisters of Street Joseph Healthcare Foundation is particularly interested in proposals which fall into these funding categories: mental health services; health services; homeless services; violence prevention.
Requirements: Southern California, Humbolt County, Fresno County and San Francisco bay area nonprofits are eligible.
Restrictions: The Foundation does not fund direct support to individuals, annual fund drives, or capital campaigns.
Geographic Focus: California
Amount: 1,000 - 50,000 USD
Samples: Access OC, Irvine, CA $50,000 - to improve access to specialty care for the safety net population (2008); Boys & Girls Clubs, Garden Grove, CA $30,000 - to fund transportation to improve access to healthcare for low-income families (2008); Casa Teresa, Orange, CA $40,000 - to assist homeless pregnant women with services to help them move from a low-income situation to self-sufficiency (2008)
Contact: Sister Regina Fox, Program Director; (714) 633-8121, ext. 7109; rfox@csjorange.org
Sponsor: Sisters of Street Joseph Healthcare Foundation
440 South Batavia Street
Orange, CA 92868-3998

Skaggs Foundation Grants 1541

The Skaggs Foundation was established in 1962 in California, and currently provides funding in Alaska. The foundations area of interest include: animals/wildlife; preservation/protection; children services; special education; environmental education; environment; natural resources; marine science. Types of support available with these funds include: continuing support; endowments; equipment; general/operating support; internship funds; land acquisition; matching/challenge support; program evaluation; research; technical assistance.
Requirements: Nonprofit organizations are eligible, preference is given to requests from Alaska. The initial approach should be a one or two page letter of inquiry. There is no formal application form. Applicants should submit the following: copy of IRS Determination Letter; copy of current year's organizational budget and/or project budget; one copy of the proposal.
Restrictions: No grants to individuals.
Geographic Focus: Alaska

Date(s) Application is Due: May 1; Oct 1
Contact: Samuel D. Skaggs Jr., President; (907) 463-4843
Sponsor: Skaggs Foundation
P.O. Box 20510
Juneau, AK 99802-0510

Skillman Foundation Good Neighborhoods Grants **1542**
The Good Neighborhoods program encourages the creation of safe, healthy, and vibrant neighborhoods where children with the support of caring adults, programs, and experiences can develop fully. Launched in January 2006, the program provides full-scale support to six Detroit neighborhoods where more than 65,000 children live, roughly 30% of the city's child population. Half of the children in these neighborhoods live in poverty. This program encourages the creation of safe, healthy and vibrant neighborhoods where children, with support of caring adults, programs and experiences, can develop fully. The six neighborhoods are: Brightmoor; Cody/Rouge; Northend (also known as Central); Osborn; Chadsey/Condon, in Southwest Detroit; and Vernor, in Southwest Detroit. The goal of the Good Neighborhoods program is to ensure that children experience safe, healthy and high-quality environments where they can thrive: neighborhoods with resources, opportunities and assets for children to develop fully and pursue prosperity.
Requirements: The applicant organizations must be tax exempt and may not be a 509(a) private foundation. The foundation's primary geographic area of focus is the Detroit metropolitan area.
Restrictions: The foundation does not award grants directly to individuals or provide loans of any kind; nor does it support sectarian religious activities, political lobbying, political advocacy, legislative activities, endowments, annual fund drives, basic research, or support of past operating deficits.
Geographic Focus: Michigan
Amount: 10,000 - 2,000,000 USD
Contact: Tonya Allen, Vice President of Programs; (313) 393-1185; (313) 393-1187; info@skillman.org
Internet: http://www.skillman.org/good-neighborhoods/
Sponsor: Skillman Foundation
100 Talon Centre Drive, Suite 100
Detroit, MI 48207

Skoll Foundation Grants **1543**
The foundation's priorities are advancing systemic change that benefits communities and investing in social entrepreneurs. The foundation makes Skoll Awards for Social Entrepreneurship, which support organizations around the world; and the Skoll Awards for Innovation in Silicon Valley, which are made annually to nonprofit organizations demonstrating exceptional creativity, sustained commitment, and a clear record of accomplishment in addressing Silicon Valley's most significant challenges. Letters of intent are accepted throughout the year. Guidelines are available online.
Requirements: Nonprofits worldwide, with special interest in California and America, are eligible.
Geographic Focus: All U.S. States
Samples: Rugmark Foundation (Washington, DC)—recipient of the Skoll Award for Social Entrepreneurship, $440,000 over three years; Tides Ctr (San Francisco, CA)—to expand its services that assist individuals and nonprofit organizations working in such areas as economic development, the environment, and social justice, $225,000; Lenders for Community Development (San Jose, CA)—award recipient, for renewed operating support, $340,000 over two years; Silicon Valley Council of Nonprofits (San Jose, CA)—award recipient, for first-time operating support, $60,000.
Contact: Grants Administrator; (650) 331-1031; grants@skollfund.org
Internet: http://www.skollfoundation.org
Sponsor: Skoll Foundation
250 University Avenue, Suite 200
Palo Alto, CA 94301

Smith Richardson Foundation International Security and Foreign Policy Grants **1544**
The objective of the International Security and Foreign Policy Program is to assist the U.S. policy community in developing effective national security strategies and foreign policies. The Foundation is committed to supporting projects that help the policy community face the fundamental challenge of ensuring the security of the United States, protecting and advancing American interests and values abroad, and enhancing international order. The International Security and Foreign Policy Program has a number of priority areas of interest. In recent years, the Foundation has sought to assist the policy community's efforts to combat global terrorism by supporting projects on critical issues, such as improving intelligence gathering. Because the battle against terrorism will also be fought on the ideological front, the Foundation has supported projects on improving U.S. public diplomacy in order to promote democracy and to give foreign publics a better understanding of U.S. policies.
Requirements: The Smith Richardson Foundation has a rigorous proposal review process. The first step in the process is the submission of a concept paper. Concept papers should not exceed five pages, follow concept paper template (see website) when preparing a submission. Upon receipt of a grant application, the Foundation will either mail or email a confirmation of receipt to the grant applicant. Requests for grants of $50,000 or less are reviewed on an ongoing basis and are handled as promptly as possible. Requests for grants greater than $50,000 and for multi-year grant support are made at one of the regular board meetings. If the staff determines that a project warrants further consideration under the Foundation's guidelines, an applicant will be asked to submit a full proposal that conforms to a proposal template provided by the Foundation.
Geographic Focus: All U.S. States
Contact: Drive Nadia Schadlow, Senior Program Officer; (203) 222-6222; (203) 222-6282; Schadlow@srf.org
Internet: http://www.srf.org/grants/international.php
Sponsor: Smith Richardson Foundation
60 Jesup Road
Westport, CT 06880

SOCFOC Catholic Ministries Grants **1545**
The Sisters of Charity Foundation of Cleveland belongs to a community of Catholic health and social service organizations inspired to service by the healing ministry of Jesus Christ. As a supporting foundation to the congregation of the Sisters of Charity of Street Augustine, the Foundation gives priority to the ministries of the Sisters of Charity Health System. A limited amount of remaining funds may be available to other Catholic ministries in health and human services in Cuyahoga County. Funding is limited to Invited Proposals.
Requirements: Each proposal to the Foundation must include a completed application form, proposal narrative, budget, and Budget Narrative. The application form and guidelines for the proposal narrative may be found on this website under the specific program area. Eligible organizations are 501(c)3 organizations or governmental agencies or units.
Restrictions: The Foundation does not make grants to individuals.
Geographic Focus: Ohio
Amount: 10,000 - 150,000 USD
Samples: Secretariat for Parish Life & Development, OH, $10,000;2008; Street Vincent Charity Hospital, OH, $151,600;2008
Contact: Lynn Berner, Program Officer; (216) 241-9300; (216) 241-9345; lberner@socfdncleveland.org
Internet: http://www.socfdncleveland.org/RespondingToOurCommunity/CatholicMinistries/tabid/313/Default.aspx
Sponsor: Sisters of Charity Foundation of Cleveland
The Halle Building, 1228 Euclid Avenue, Suite 330
Cleveland, OH 44115-1834

SOCFOC Good Samaritan Grants **1546**
The Sisters of Charity Foundation of Cleveland provides support each year to organizations meeting the basic needs such as food, clothing, shelter, and transportation of those living in poverty in Cuyahoga County. The Good Samaritan Grants are intended for programs that provide direct goods and services for individuals living in poverty.
Requirements: Organizations must be tax-exempt, nonprofit organizations that primarily serve the Cuyahoga County.
Geographic Focus: Ohio
Date(s) Application is Due: Jun 2
Amount: Up to 10,000 USD
Samples: 2100 Lakeside Mens Shelter, Emergency Assistance Program, Cleveland, OH, $10,000;2008; Interfaith Hospitality Network of Greater Cleveland, Homeless Family Day Center Project, Shaker Heights, OH, $7,500;2008
Contact: Ursula Craig, Grants Coordinator; (216) 241-9300; (216) 241-9345; ucraig@socfdncleveland.org
Internet: http://www.socfdncleveland.org/RespondingToOurCommunity/GoodSamaritanGrantProgram/tabid/148/Default.aspx
Sponsor: Sisters of Charity Foundation of Cleveland
The Halle Building, 1228 Euclid Avenue, Suite 330
Cleveland, OH 44115-1834

SOCFOC Reducing Health & Educational Disparities in the Central Neighborhood Grants 1547

The Sisters of Charity Foundation of Cleveland is committed to helping families and individuals overcome the challenges of poverty. In this grant opportunity the Foundation focuses on health, housing and education as key components to building stronger families and stable neighborhoods. The Foundation seeks to reduce both health and educational disparities in the Cuyahoga County.

Requirements: Applicants must be 501(c)3 organizations or governmental units or agencies (such as schools) that primarily serve the Cuyahoga County.

Geographic Focus: Ohio

Date(s) Application is Due: Apr 7

Amount: 40,000 - 150,000 USD

Contact: Ursula Craig, Grants Coordinator; (216) 241-9300; (216) 241-9345; ucraig@socfdncleveland.org

Internet: http://www.socfdncleveland.org/sistersofcharity/OurFocusAreas/HealthDisparities/HealthintheCentralNeighborhood/tabid/344/Default.aspx

Sponsor: Sisters of Charity Foundation of Cleveland
The Halle Building, 1228 Euclid Avenue, Suite 330
Cleveland, OH 44115-1834

SOCFOC Saint Ann Legacy Grants 1548

The Sisters of Charity Foundation of Cleveland awards grants to support the ministries of women religious as they devote themselves to living he Gospel. In support of ongoing work, planning and capacity-building of women religious is focused primarily in Ohio, but could also include Kentucky and Tennessee (which constitute Region VI of the Leadership Conference of Women Religious.)

Requirements: Organizations must have a tax-exempt status as nonprofit organizations, as identified bby the Internal Revenue Service Code. Grants are not made to individuals.

Geographic Focus: Kentucky, Ohio, Tennessee

Date(s) Application is Due: Jun 16

Amount: 20,000 USD

Contact: Ursula Craig, Grants Coordinator; (216) 241-9300; (216) 241-9345; ucraig@socfdncleveland.org

Internet: http://www.socfdncleveland.org/sistersofcharity/OurFocusAreas/ReligiousCommunities/SaintAnnLegacy/tabid/328/Default.aspx

Sponsor: Sisters of Charity Foundation of Cleveland
The Halle Building, 1228 Euclid Avenue, Suite 330
Cleveland, OH 44115-1834

Solo Cup Foundation Grants 1549

The foundation awards grants to Illinois nonprofit organizations in its areas of interest, including higher education, health, social services, and Christian organizations and churches. Types of support include capital campaigns, general operating support, and scholarship funds. There are no application deadlines or forms.

Requirements: Illinois nonprofit organizations are eligible.

Geographic Focus: Illinois

Amount: 5,000 - 85,000 USD

Samples: La Rashida Children's Hospital (Chicago, IL)—for a capital campaign to modernize and upgrade its inpatient facility, $1 million; Immaculate Conception Church (Chicago, IL)—for restoration project, $85,000; Congregation of the Passion (Chicago, IL)—for general support, $50,000.

Contact: Robert M. Korzenski, President and CEO; (847) 831-4800; (847) 579-3245; info@solocup.com

Sponsor: Solo Cup Foundation
1700 Old Deerfield Road
Highland Park, IL 60035

Sony Electronics Charitable Contributions Program Grants 1550

The core of Sony Electronics' corporate community affairs efforts is its contributions to the communities of which it is a part. The corporation's primary focus is strengthening education at the primary and secondary school levels, with consideration also given to selected higher education initiatives. While positive consideration is given to efforts that promote literacy and basic educational competency, the company also seeks to apply its financial, technological, and human resources to the encouragement of the technical scientific skills required of tomorrow's workforce. Other areas for funding consideration at both the local and corporate levels include health and welfare, minority affairs, civic efforts, and arts and culture. Types of support include general operating budgets, continuing support, annual campaigns, seed grants, building construction, equipment acquisition, endowment funds, employee matching gifts, internships, and employee-related scholarships. Requests are accepted throughout the year. There is no grant application form, but the company requires a brief written description of the organization, including its legal name, history, activities, purpose, and proof of 501(c)3 status; history of previous support from Sony Electronics Inc, the Sony U.S. A Foundation, or a Sony business unit; amount of request; and a description of the purpose for which the grant is requested.

Requirements: U.S. nonprofits, including schools and districts, are eligible.

Restrictions: Sony does not award grants to organizations that practice discrimination, partisan political organizations, religious organizations, labor unions, endowment or capital campaigns of national organizations, organizations whose primary purpose is to influence legislation, testimonial dinners in general, for-profit publications seeking advertisements, individuals seeking self-advancement, or foreign or non-U.S. organizations.

Geographic Focus: All U.S. States

Amount: 1,000 - 100,000 USD

Contact: Ann Morfogen, (212) 833-6873; (212) 833-6862; Ann_Morfogen@sonyusa.com

Internet: http://www.sony.com/SCA/philanthropy/guidelines.shtml

Sponsor: Sony Corporation of America
550 Madison Avenue, 33rd Floor
New York, NY 10022-3211

Sorenson Legacy Foundation Grants 1551

The foundation has a broad spectrum of philanthropic interests and supports endeavors that: encourage and support the long-term preservation and enhancement of the quality of life of all humankind, especially of families and children; assist the disenfranchised of society, such as but not limited to, abused spouses and children, in order that they receive the full benefits of membership in society and fulfill their potential as human beings; promote medical research and the development of innovative medical technologies for saving lives and alleviating pain and suffering; promote the development of the arts, including art education in schools, assistance of promising young artists, and support of performing arts organizations; promote community development and security, adequate and affordable housing, and education and job training; promote law and order generally and provide youth with alternatives to gangs, crime and socially nonproductive behavior; protect and enhance the environment, preserve wild and open spaces, and promote development of parks and green spaces; promote the development of science, culture and recreation; promote world peace and unity through a greater understanding, tolerance and harmony among religious, national and ethnic groups; advance the programs at private and state universities and colleges that are consistent with the foundation's charter; and, advance the mission of the Church of Jesus Christ of Latter-day Saints in all its places.

Geographic Focus: All U.S. States

Contact: Executive Director, (801) 461-9700; (801) 461-9722

Internet: http://www.sorensoncompanies.com/giving_back.html

Sponsor: Sorenson Foundation
2511 South West Temple Street
Salt Lake City, UT 84115

Sosland Foundation Grants 1552

The foundation awards grants to nonprofit organizations in the metropolitan bistate Kansas City area. Areas of interest include arts and culture, higher education, health care, Jewish services, and social services. Types of support include program development, building construction/renovation, equipment acquisition, development grants, endowments, general operating grants, and matching gifts. There are no application forms or deadlines. Applicants should send a letter including a description of the program and the organization, a list of board and staff, and proof of tax-exempt status.

Requirements: Metropolitan bistate Kansas City 501(c)3 nonprofit organizations are eligible.

Restrictions: Individuals and publications or conferences are ineligible.

Geographic Focus: Kansas, Missouri

Amount: 1,000 - 5,000 USD

Samples: William Jewell College (Liberty, MO)—to renovate Jewell Hall, $50,000.

Contact: Program Contact; (816) 756-1000; (816) 756-0494

Internet: http://www.soslandfoundation.org

Sponsor: Sosland Foundation
4800 Main Street, Suite 100
Kansas City, MO 64112

South Carolina Arts Commission Annual Operating Support for Organizations Grants 1553

This program provides twelve-month operational support to SC arts organizations with primary missions involving these artistic functions: Producing, Service, Presenting, Education. Support is broad in scope and can be used for a variety of arts programs, salaries, artist fees, supplies, and other operating expenses at the discretion of the organization within the eligibility and legal requirements defined in these guidelines. There is no pre-set funding range. Awards will be based on organizational budgets, application reviews, and the availability of funds.

Requirements: Organizations requesting Annual Operating Support must have completed one fiscal year of programming in order to be eligible to apply. Applicant must be a SC organization with primary mission focused on the arts (or an organization that serves as the primary arts provider in its community). Applicant must also be (1) a charitable organization currently registered with the Office of the Secretary of State that has its own federal tax exempt status with the Internal Revenue Service; or, (2) a charitable organization currently registered with the Office of the Secretary of State applying through a tax exempt fiscal agent organization; or, (3) a unit of local government. Applicant must have a valid DUNS number. A minimum of 2:1 cash match is required. No in-kind expenses are allowed as part of applicant's match in this category. Applications must be submitted via the Online SC Arts Resources (OSCAR) application process by 5:00 PM on the posted deadline date. NOTE: This grant requires a filing fee of $15.00, payable by check made out to South Carolina Arts Commission OR online credit card payment.

Restrictions: No in-kind expenses are allowed as part of applicant's match in this category. Payment will be on a reimbursement basis only. Organizations requesting Annual Operating Support may not apply for Long Term or Quarterly Support (except for requests for staff professional development under Quarterly Support grants).

Geographic Focus: South Carolina

Date(s) Application is Due: Feb 15

Contact: Rusty Sox, Coordinator; (803) 734-8696; rsox@arts.sc.gov

Internet: http://www.southcarolinaarts.com/grants/organizations/annual.shtml

Sponsor: South Carolina Arts Commission
1800 Gervais Street
Columbia, SC 29201

South Carolina Arts Commission Incentive Grants for Employer Sponsored Benefits (ESB) 1554

Many arts organizations are facing difficulties recruiting and retaining qualified staff because they lack the capacity to compete with larger organizations when it comes to benefits packages. Competitive salaries or bonuses are no longer enough to recruit and retain staff. Today's market requires an attractive package which includes employer sponsored benefits which are a direct cost to the organization. The bottom line for many organizations looking to build organizational capacity through staff recruitment and retention is whether or not the organization is able to afford basic health insurance coverage as an employee benefit. And, for organizations that do offer benefits, there is need to control the costs. In an effort to assist organizations, SCAC is offering a grant program to encourage employer sponsored benefits.

Requirements: Applicant must be a SC organization with primary mission focused on the arts (or an organization that serves as the primary arts provider in its community). Applicant must also be: (1) a charitable organization currently registered with the Office of the Secretary of State that has its own federal tax exempt status with the Internal Revenue Service; (2) a charitable organization currently registered with the Office of the Secretary of State applying through a tax exempt fiscal agent organization; or, (3) a unit of local government with primary mission focused on the arts. This program requires a match: 1:1 - up to 50% of benefits for year 1; 2:1 - up to 33% of benefits for year 2.

Restrictions: Applicant may not be a unit of state or federal government, college, university, or K-12 public or private school. Funds may not be used for employee bonuses or salary increases. Payment will be on an expense reimbursement basis only.

Geographic Focus: South Carolina

Amount: Up to 2,000 USD

Contact: Rusty Sox, Coordinator; (803) 734-8696; rsox@arts.sc.gov

Internet: http://www.southcarolinaarts.com/grants/organizations/benefits.shtml

Sponsor: South Carolina Arts Commission
1800 Gervais Street
Columbia, SC 29201

South Carolina Arts Commission Leadership and Organizational Development Grants 1555

The program was established to support arts leaders' (professional administrators and board members) acquisition of skills and practical tools which hone their ability to lead, develop, and sustain the overall health and vitality of South Carolina's arts organizations. Funding is targeted to professional arts administrators and board members of arts organizations. Grantees will identify a set of critical individual or operational capacity-building issues toward which the funds will be used. For the purpose of this initiative, capacity-building is defined as activities that either strengthen individual ability to lead or improve organizational functioning and sustainability. Leadership Development funding includes: costs for individuals to receive professional development; costs involved in coordinating and/or conducting professionally facilitated learning for individuals or groups across position or discipline. Organizational Development funding includes: costs for professional consultant/consulting firms providing services in areas such as fundraising, financial management, marketing, executive transition, public relations, board development, strategic planning, program development, technology, etc; costs involved with coordinating and/or conducting professionally facilitated learning for individuals or groups across position or discipline.

Requirements: Before applying, you are strongly advised to discuss the project with your county coordinator to determine whether your project meets the guidelines. Applicants must: (1) be a nonprofit, charitable arts organization that is currently registered with the Office of the Secretary of State of South Carolina, and that either has its own federal tax-exempt status with the IRS or applies through a fiscal agent; (2) have the production or presentation of arts events or service to the arts as its primary organizational mission; OR be the primary provider of general, multidisciplinary arts programs and/or services within a particular community or region; and, (3) have completed at least one full fiscal year in operation prior to application. Applications must be received at least six weeks before the start of the project or activity. Projects must be completed by June 30. Applications received after May 15 must be for projects beginning after July 1. A 1:1 match is required - 50% of the applicant's match must be cash.

Restrictions: Applicants may not be a unit of SC State government. Individual artists are not eligible to apply to this program. Applicants may submit only one application per project per year. This category is not intended to fund annual or recurring projects. However, organizations/individuals previously funded under this category and intending to apply for funds to support the same or a similar project must demonstrate how receiving additional funds will substantially improve organizational functioning and sustainability or strengthen an individual's ability to lead the organization.

Geographic Focus: South Carolina

Contact: Joy Young, Program Director; (803) 734-8203; jyoung@arts.sc.gov

Internet: http://www.southcarolinaarts.com/grants/organizations/leadershiporgdev.shtml

Sponsor: South Carolina Arts Commission
1800 Gervais Street
Columbia, SC 29201

Southwest Florida Community Foundation Arts & Attractions Grants 1556

The program was established to use existing resources in Lee County to assist arts and attractions agencies, especially to encourage repeat visits, strengthen a need in the arts, provide the financial foundation that will encourage additional and create greater resources for growth, and partner with motivated professionals to maximize the expenditure and ensure a quality return on investments. Two types of grants will be offered: Marketing & Visitor Enhancement Grants and Basic Operating Grants.

Requirements: Marketing and Visitor Enhancement Grants: All Tourist Development Council funds will be granted to this grant category. Only Lee County 501(c)3 agencies will be eligible. Basic Operating Grants: These grants provide unrestricted funds for the general administration, operations and programs of arts and attractions organizations located in Lee County. These grants can be allocated for capital improvement purchases.

Geographic Focus: Florida

Date(s) Application is Due: Jun 12

Amount: Up to 25,000 USD

Contact: Carol McLaughlin, Chief Program Officer; (239) 274-5900, ext. 225; (239) 274-5930; cmclaughlin@floridacommunity.com

Internet: http://www.floridacommunity.com/grantseekers/applications/

Sponsor: Southwest Florida Community Foundation
8260 College Parkway, Suite 101
Fort Myers, FL 33919

Southwest Gas Corporation Foundation Grants 1557

The corporate foundation supports nonprofit organizations in its service communities. General support grants and employee matching gifts are made in the areas of education (universities, colleges, and literacy programs) and social services (United Way organizations, youth groups, community service, and volunteer organizations). Additional areas of interest are arts/culture and health. Types of support include general operating grants, projects grants, conferences and seminars, building construction/renovation, capital campaigns, emergency funds, employee matching gifts,research grants, donated equipment, and in-kind services. In southern Arizona, contact Marty Looney, P.O. Box 26500, Tucson, AZ 85726-6500; (520) 794-6416.
Requirements: Nonprofit organizations in Arizona; San Bernardino County, CA; and Nevada may apply.
Geographic Focus: Arizona, California, Nevada
Amount: Up to 620,567 USD
Samples: Phoenix Art Museum (Phoenix, AZ)—for general support, $3000; Boys and Girls Clubs (Tucson, AZ)—for general support, $1000; Community Food Bank (Phoenix, AZ)—for general support, $3500.
Contact: Suzanne Farinas, (702) 876-7247; (702) 876-7037
Internet: http://www.swgas.com
Sponsor: Southwest Gas Corporation
P.O. Box 98510
Las Vegas, NV 89193-8510

Speckhard-Knight Charitable Foundation Grants 1558

The foundation is dedicated to improving the quality of life in Jackson and Washtenaw counties in Michigan, and aiding environmental efforts in the third world. Grants support nonprofit organizations that work in the areas of adoption, foster care, at-risk families, and the environment. Types of support include start-up grants, salaries, and operating support. To apply for a grant, download and print out the Common Grant Application Form from the Council of Michigan Foundations.
Requirements: Michigan nonprofit organizations serving Jackson and Washtenaw Counties are eligible.
Restrictions: Grants do not support construction costs.
Geographic Focus: Michigan
Date(s) Application is Due: Mar 20; Jun 6; Oct 17
Amount: 2,000 - 20,000 USD
Contact: Gerald Knight, (734) 761-8752 or (734) 355-9926; (734) 827-0091; zmjk@comcast.net
Internet: http://www.skcf.org
Sponsor: Speckhard-Knight Charitable Foundation
771 Bogey Court
Ann Arbor, MI 48103

Sport Manitoba Women to Watch Grants 1559

A major initiative is the Women to Watch Grants. Working in partnership with Provincial Sport Organizations and Coaching Manitoba, Sport Manitoba provides a monthly grant of $500 to a female athlete, team, official or volunteer to assist them in enhancing their women in sport career. A $500 monthly grant is also awarded to a female coach to assist them in further developing the skills necessary to attain a higher level of coaching or increased level of coaching experience. Grants may be used to offset costs such as training, travel, certification, sport equipment, competitions/tournaments, camps, leadership development, professional development and child care costs related to future development in their sport.
Requirements: Applicants must be female and a member of their provincial sport organization in good standing as an athlete, coach, official or in a leadership position either as a volunteer or paid staff. The application must be endorsed by the PSO with a commitment to matching the $250 grant from Sport Manitoba/Coaching Manitoba.
Geographic Focus: Canada
Date(s) Application is Due: Mar 15; Jul 15; Nov 30
Amount: 1,000 USD
Contact: Shawnee Scatliff, Program Coordinator; (204) 885-7400; (204) 925-5916; sscatliff@mts.net
Internet: http://sportmanitoba.ca/programs/womensport.php
Sponsor: Sport Manitoba
200 Main Street
Winnipeg, MB R3C 4M2 Canada

Sprague Foundation Grants 1560

Grants are made to hospitals, arts and cultural organizations, civic and community affairs, educational institutions, and health and human service organizations and charities located in New York and Massachusetts. Types of support include general operating support, matching and challenge funds, and program development. The initial approach should be a letter requesting the foundation's guidelines. Grants are awarded at the June and December board meetings.
Requirements: Only residents of New York and Massachusetts may apply.
Restrictions: No grants are provided to individuals, for building funds, or for loans.
Geographic Focus: Massachusetts, New York
Date(s) Application is Due: Apr 15; Oct 1
Amount: 1,000 - 55,000 USD
Contact: Linda Franciscovich, c/o U.S. Trust Company of New York, (212) 852-3377
Sponsor: Seth Sprague Educational and Charitable Foundation
114 W 47th Street
New York, NY 10036-1532

Springs Close Foundation Grants 1561

Since it was chartered in 1942, the Springs Close Foundation has contributed over $85 million to a wide variety of charitable and educational causes designed to improve the quality of life and well-being of the people in Chester, Lancaster and York Counties. Support includes, but is not limited to, food, shelter and medical assistance. This temporary change in focus is in response to high levels of unemployment and economic distress in the Foundation's service areas. The Foundation also makes occasional statewide grants in South Carolina. There are three major areas of program interest: Recreation and Environment, Public Education and Early Childhood Development, Community Service and Health
Requirements: Grants are made only to organizations that are tax-exempt under Section 501(c)3 of the Internal Revenue Code. No grants are made to individuals.
Restrictions: The Foundation will only consider grant requests from eligible nonprofit organizations that can effectively deliver emergency and basic support to citizens in Chester and Lancaster counties and a portion of York County.
Geographic Focus: South Carolina
Date(s) Application is Due: Mar 1; Oct 1
Amount: 5,000 - 50,000 USD
Contact: Angela McCrae, President; (803) 548-2002; (803) 548-1797
Internet: http://www.thespringsclosefoundation.org/grants.htm
Sponsor: Springs Close Foundation
1826 Second Baxter Crossing
Fort Mill, SC 29708

Sprint Foundation Grants 1562

The foundation's charitable giving program emphasizes support of nonprofit local and regional organizations in those communities in which the corporation has a major presence. The foundation focuses its contributions in four major areas of interest. Education—programs that increase and improve student achievement, family engagement and professional development for educators; K-12 education; and higher education through its Matching Gift program, as well as through partnerships with the United Negro College Fund, the Hispanic College Fund, and targeted MBA programs and undergraduate institutions to provide financial assistance and employment opportunities for students pursuing degrees in business and technology-related fields. Unsolicited scholarship requests will not be considered for funding. Arts and Culture—visual and performing arts organizations, theater, symphonies, museums, and other cultural organizations and activities that contribute to a thriving and diverse community. Youth Development—mentoring programs, minority youth endeavors, broad-scale community youth activities focused on building leadership and social skills, and programs that support business and economic education for youth. Community Development—regional initiatives that contribute to a strong civic infrastructure and a vibrant, healthy community; and, on a national level, the foundation matches funds raised for its national food drive and United Way pledges made by Sprint employees who participate in the corporation's national campaign. Types of support include general operating support, continuing support, annual campaigns, capital campaigns, program development, and employee matching gifts. The foundation accepts proposals throughout the year.

Requirements: 501(c)3 organizations in Atlanta, Boston, Chicago, Dallas, Kansas City, Las Vegas, Los Angeles, New York City, Orlando, San Francisco and the District of Columbia are eligible; however, these areas are subject to change. Support of national organizations with a broad sphere of interests will be considered on a case-by-case basis. The foundation's geographic focus is primarily domestic.
Restrictions: Organizations generally excluded from the foundation's grantmaking activities include political, religious, fraternal, labor, and veterans organizations; hospitals; and neighborhood associations. No grants are made to individuals.
Geographic Focus: All U.S. States
Amount: Up to 52,000,000 USD
Samples: American Red Cross, National Disaster Relief Fund (Washington, DC)—to provide support services to victims of the September 11 terrorist attacks, $500,000; Prairie View A&M U (TX)—to build a Broadband Data laboratory and supporting curriculum, $600,000.
Contact: David Thomas, Executive Director; (913) 624-3343; (913) 624-3490
Internet: http://www.sprint.com/community/sprint_foundation/index.html
Sponsor: Sprint Foundation
2330 Shawnee Mission Parkway
Westwood, KS 66205

Square D Foundation Grants **1563**
The foundation makes donations for operating support, capital development needs, and special projects to nonprofit organizations in the areas of education, social welfare, arts and cultural and civic affairs, and health. Each year the foundation supports United Way in communities where the company and its domestic subsidiaries have significant operations. Donations are not normally made to organizations already receiving support through United Way. Support of higher education is achieved through scholarships, endowments for faculty and acquisition or expansion of equipment or facilities, unrestricted operating support, and the matching gift program. Submit letters of application between June and August.
Requirements: Giving primarily to 501(c)3 tax-exempt organizations in areas of company operations, with emphasis on: Illinois; Indiana; Iowa; Kentucky; Missouri; Nebraska; North Carolina; Ohio; South Carolina; Tennessee; and Wisconsin.
Restrictions: Grants are not made to religious organizations for religious purposes, political groups and organizations, labor unions and organizations, organizations making requests by telephone, organizations listed by the U.S. attorney general as subversive, or to individuals.
Geographic Focus: Illinois, Indiana, Iowa, Kentucky, Nebraska, North Carolina, Tennessee, Texas, Wisconsin
Date(s) Application is Due: Aug 31
Amount: Up to 27,000,000 USD
Contact: Harry Wilson, Secretary; (847) 397-2600
Internet: http://www.squared.com
Sponsor: Square D Foundation
1415 South Roselle Road
Palatine, IL 60067

SSA Work Incentives Planning and Assistance (WIPA) Projects **1564**
The overall goal of the Work Incentives Planning and Assistance (WIPA) Program is to better enable SSA's beneficiaries with disabilities to make informed choices about work. The major purpose of these projects is to disseminate accurate information to beneficiaries with disabilities (including transition-to-work aged youth) about work incentives programs and issues related to such programs, to enable them to make informed choices about working and whether or when to assign their Ticket to Work, as well as how available work incentives can facilitate their transition into the workforce. Subject to the availability of funds, SSA anticipates minimum awards of $100,000 for individual state WIPA projects (minimum awards for territories will remain at $50,000) and a maximum of $300,000 will be available to fund specific WIPA projects annually. Awardees are required to contribute a non-Federal match of project costs of at least 5% of the total project cost. The non-Federal share may be cash or in-kind (property or services). Awards made under this announcement may be renewed annually through FY 2009. A cooperative agreement may be awarded to any State or local government (excluding any State administering the State Medicaid program), public or private organization, or nonprofit or for-profit organization (for profit organizations may apply with the understanding that no cooperative agreement funds may be paid as profit to any awardee), as well as Native American tribal organizations that the Commissioner determines is qualified to provide work incentives planning, assistance and outreach services to all SSDI and SSI beneficiaries with disabilities, within the targeted geographic area. The deadline is July 1, with Letters of Intent due by May 30.
Requirements: States, local governments, the District of Columbia, Puerto Rico, U.S. territories, and nonprofit and for-profit organizations are eligible to apply.
Geographic Focus: All U.S. States
Date(s) Application is Due: Jul 1
Amount: 50,000 - 300,000 USD
Contact: Regina Bowden, Project Officer, Office of Employment Support Programs; (410) 965-7145 or (800) 772-1213; regina.bowden@ssa.gov
Internet: http://www.socialsecurity.gov/work/ServiceProviders/wipafactsheet.html
Sponsor: Social Security Administration
6401 Security Boulevard, 107 Altmeyer Building
Baltimore, MD 21235-6401

Street Joseph Community Health Foundation Improving Healthcare Access Grants **1565**
The Street Joseph Community Health Foundation was established in 1998 when the Poor Handmaids of Jesus Christ sold the Street Joseph Medical Center and reorganized the Street Joseph Community Health Foundation with a significant share of the proceeds. Proceeds from the Foundation's endowment are redistributed as grants typically ranging from $5,000 to $35,000 to advance programs, projects and partnerships that improve the access to quality health care and the health of the poor and powerless of Allen County, Indiana. Typically, only programs that can demonstrate that greater than 51 percent of their clients are very low income with health issues are considered for these grants. The Foundation also considers these values of the Poor Handmaids as a part of its grant review process: respecting and valuing each person; standing with the poor and powerless; using our talents and resources to respond to the emerging needs of society; nurturing leadership in our efforts to bring peace to the world. The Foundation will consider requests for program support, operations, seed monies, program-related equipment, staff continuing education, technical assistance, and matching funds. The Foundation will commit support on an annual basis only. Additional funding will be contingent upon program performance.
Requirements: Applicants should have a demonstrated history of serving poor and powerless populations with medical, dental, mental, and/or spiritual health care and wellness services. Applicants should be not-for-profit entities classified as 501(C)(3) by the Internal Revenue Service. Partnerships between not-for-profits are encouraged. The proposed grant must be operated for the benefit of residents of Allen County, Indiana.
Restrictions: Grant applications will not be accepted for building projects, elimination of deficits, support of political activities, individuals, or projects already completed.
Geographic Focus: Indiana
Date(s) Application is Due: Mar 1; Sep 1
Amount: 5,000 - 35,000 USD
Samples: AIDS Task Force, Inc., $9,000 - support for emergency medical assistance to people living with HIV and AIDS in Allen County; Boys & Girls Clubs of Fort Wayne, $7,000 - support for the Cavity-Free Zone program promoting dental health and hygiene in low-income children; Cedars H.O.P.E., Inc., $5,000 - matching grant to support the program staff who house mentally ill women suffering from complex psychiatric and medical conditions.
Contact: Meg Distler, Executive Director; (260) 969-2001, ext. 201; (260) 969-2004; mdistler@sjchf.org
Internet: http://www.stjosephhealthfdn.org/index.php?option=com_content&view=article&id=79&Itemid=70
Sponsor: Street Joseph Community Health Foundation
2826 South Calhoun Street
Fort Wayne, IN 46807

Stackner Family Foundation Grants **1566**
The foundation awards grants concentrated in the Milwaukee metropolitan area for building programs and equipment acquisition, medical research, programs at all levels of education, social welfare, child welfare, and programs that assist the physically disabled. Additional categories of support include general operating support, continuing support, annual campaigns, capital campaigns, and program development. The board meets each year in January, April, July, and October. Application forms are not required.

Requirements: Nonprofit organizations in the greater Milwaukee, WI, area may request grant support.
Geographic Focus: Wisconsin
Date(s) Application is Due: Mar 15; Jun 15; Sep 15; Dec 15
Amount: 25 - 25,000 USD
Samples: Horizon House (Milwaukee, WI)—for an outpatient program, $4000;Penfield Childrens Ctr (Milwaukee, WI)—for the capital campaign, $10,000.
Contact: Paul Tillman, (414) 646-5409; Stackner@MSH.com
Sponsor: Stackner Family Foundation
411 E Wisconsin Avenue
Milwaukee, WI 53202-4497

Stan and Sandy Checketts Foundation **1567**
Established by Stan and Sandy Checketts in 1998, the Foundation's primary focus is on human services and helping individuals defray medical expenses. Primary fields of interest include: children and youth programs, health care, housing and shelter programs, human services, and recreation. Types of support are general operating funds and grants to individuals. Applicants should submit a detailed description of the project, along with the amount of funding requested. There are no deadlines, and the primary geographic focus is Utah.
Geographic Focus: Utah
Contact: Stan Checketts, President; (435) 752-1987; (435) 752-1948
Sponsor: Stan and Sandy Checketts Foundation
350 West 2500 North
Logan, UT 84341-1734

Starr Foundation Grants **1568**
The foundation awards grants to nonprofit organizations in the areas of education, medicine and health care, human needs, public policy, and culture. Education grants support scholarships for deserving students, groups that offer need-based financial aid, and international-exchange programs. Human needs grants support food programs for the poor, job training, literacy, adequate housing, and programs for the disabled. Medicine and health care grants include capital grants to hospitals, significant research grants, and grants to assist in the provision of health care to underserved communities. Public policy grants support international relations and democratic institutions around the world. Culture grants go to exchange programs and provide services to the elderly and/or disabled. The foundation rarely funds local charities outside of New York City but may fund national organizations that serve communities outside of New York. Types of support include multiyear grants, general operating grants, and capacity-building grants. There are no application deadlines. The board meets throughout the year.
Geographic Focus: All U.S. States
Amount: Up to 70,000,000 USD
Samples: World Trade Ctr Memorial Foundation (New York, NY)—to build the World Trade Center Memorial and a museum to remember the September 11, 2001, and February 26, 1993, terrorist attacks, $25 million; Johns Hopkins U (Baltimore, MD)—to endow a professorship and support other needs at the South Asia Studies program of the university's Nitze School of Advanced International Studies, $3 million; Dickinson College (Carlisle, PA)—to augment a scholarship endowment, $1 million; For relief efforts in South Asia and Africa—$2.5 million distributed.
Contact: Florence Davis, President; (212) 770-6882; florence.davis@starrfdn.org or grants@starrfoundation.org
Internet: http://fdncenter.org/grantmaker/starr
Sponsor: Starr Foundation
70 Pine Street, 14th Floor
New York, NY 10270

Star Tribune Foundation Grants **1569**
The foundation supports programs and organizations that strengthen and enhance the quality of life in its operating communities and awards grants in three focus areas: programs that enable people to move from dependency to self-reliance; the cultural community with emphasis on preeminent institutions and writing-related programs that also enlighten social consciousness; and programs that foster civic involvement and that strengthen the place of the media in society. Priority will be given to programs that support family planning, responsible parenting, and family stability; programs to aid self-reliance, including job training, career development, and youth development intervention; programs that strengthen Minneapolis and Saint Paul as vital central cities; cultural institutions that provide the base and stimulate the cultural vitality of the community; writing, publishing, and theater programs that stimulate creativity, diversity, and expression of societal values; programs and organizations that help people understand the world and important civic issues; and media-related programs directed at preserving First Amendment rights and a free press. Applications for major or one-time grants are generally considered on a calendar-quarter basis. Proposals for annual operating grants should be submitted in January.
Requirements: 501(c)3 tax-exempt organizations in Minneapolis, Minnesota, are eligible to apply.
Restrictions: As a general rule, support will not be made to/for organizations whose objectives are principally related to health and medicine, substance abuse, rehabilitation, and research; religious programs; international programs; political programs; individuals; subsidized publications or films; conferences; travel; advertising; fund-raising events; or general operating support.
Geographic Focus: Minnesota
Amount: 5,000 - 10,000 USD
Samples: Big Brothers/Big Sisters of Greater Minneapolis (Minneapolis, MN)—to support a capital campaign for a new headquarters building, $10,000; Club Fed (Minneapolis, MN)—to create positive alternative activities for youth in northern Minneapolis, $5000; Old Highland Neighborhood Assoc (MN)—to support neighborhood and community development, $500.
Contact: Sandra Fleitman, Foundation Coordinator; (612) 673-7051; (612) 673-7307; sfleitman@startribune.com
Internet: http://www.startribunecompany.com/140
Sponsor: Star Tribune Foundation
425 Portland Avenue S
Minneapolis, MN 55488-0002

State Farm Companies Strong Neighborhoods Grants **1570**
State Farm is committed to helping maintain the vibrancy and culture of neighborhoods in various communities throughout the U.S. and Canada. They demonstrate this commitment by supporting nonprofit organization programs that: make housing affordable; promote first-time homeownership; eliminate barriers to homeownership; educate homebuyers about insurance, loss mitigation, and homeownership; foster sustainable communities, and; rehabilitate neighborhoods or communities.
Restrictions: The company does not fund: organizations that are not a governmental entity, a stable nonprofit 501(c)3 organization with a diverse funding base, an educational institution, or a Canadian charitable organization; individuals seeking personal help or scholarships; religious programs; politically partisan programs, or; organizations outside the U.S. and Canada.
Geographic Focus: All U.S. States
Contact: Strong Neighborhoods Grants Coordinator; (309) 766-2161; (309) 766-2314; home.sf-foundation.494b00@statefarm.co
Internet: http://www.statefarm.com/about/part_spos/grants/cogrants.asp
Sponsor: State Farm Insurance Company
1 State Farm Plaza, B-4
Bloomington, IL 61710-0001

State Strategies Fund Grants **1571**
The program supports state-based strategies to increase civic participation in political life, empower disadvantaged constituencies, and promote political reform. Areas of interest include campaign finance reform, fair tax policy, affordable health care, and the environment. Permanent state-based coalitions that have a long-term strategy for uniting diverse constituencies with a grassroots base and that have a common vision and policy agenda for economic and social justice receive grants. The grant program supports organizations with the following goals: to build strong and effective relationships and collaboration among diverse groups; to integrate a broad array of issues into a common progressive agenda; to develop the collective power of constituents to implement this common agenda; to increase the capacity of underrepresented constituencies to have greater impact on public policy and governance at the state level; to enhance the capacity of grassroots organizations to mobilize their members; and to develop new public leaders representing and accountable to disadvantaged constituencies. Applications should be submitted by email. Attachments and/or mailed applications must be postmarked by the listed application deadline.
Geographic Focus: All U.S. States
Date(s) Application is Due: Aug 25
Samples: Alabama Organizing Project (AL)—to support Greater Birmingham Ministries, $35,000; Citizen Action Illinois (IL)—to support the Public

Action Foundation, $40,000; New York Community Leadership Institute (NY)—$30,000; Wisconsin Citizen Action (WI)—$50,000.
Contact: Amy Clough, Grants Manager; (413) 256-0349, ext. 12; (413) 256-3536; aclough@proteusfund.org
Internet: http://www.proteusfund.org/grantmaking/ssf
Sponsor: State Strategies Fund
264 N Pleasant Street
Amherst, MA 01002

State Street Foundation Grants **1572**

The foundation focuses grantmaking worldwide on three areas: neighborhood revitalization, education and job training and development, and youth programs. Of special interest are projects that strengthen organizations' capacity to address community needs. In addition, the foundation provides funding for health and human needs and civic improvement projects that support its areas of focus. Types of support include annual campaigns, employee matching gifts, general operating budgets, matching funds, special projects, affordable housing rehabilitation projects, and technical assistance to achieve nonprofit performance improvement. Creative partnerships are encouraged between the public and private sectors. Contact the office for proposal guidelines.
Requirements: 501(c)3 organizations that are not private foundations and are located in Alameda, Los Angeles, and San Francisco, CA; Connecticut; Florida; Atlanta, GA; Illinois; Boston and the Cape Cod, MA, area; Saint Louis and Kansas City, MO; New Hampshire; New Jersey; and New York are eligible.
Restrictions: The foundation does not make grants for scholarships or fellowships; research projects; emergency cash flow, deficit spending, or debt liquidation situations; seed money/start-up programs; trips, tours, and transportation expenses; or films or videos.
Geographic Focus: California, Connecticut, Florida, Georgia, Illinois, Massachusetts, Missouri, New Hampshire, New Jersey, New York
Amount: 3,000 - 25,000 USD
Samples: Volunteer Florida Foundation (Tallahassee, FL)—for the Hurricane Charley Disaster Relief Fund, $150,000.
Contact: Grants Administrator; (617) 664-1937; gabowman@statestreet.com
Internet: http://www.statestreet.com/company/community_affairs/global_philanthropy/overview.html
Sponsor: State Street Foundation
225 Franklin Street, 12th Floor
Boston, MA 02110

Staunton Farm Foundation Grants **1573**

The foundation awards grants in the field of mental health in southwestern Pennsylvania. Projects that represent new and different approaches for organizations and ultimately affect patient care are encouraged. Support may be for more than one year, but the project must become self-sustaining following the grant period. Applicants should submit a letter of intent; full proposals are by invitation.
Requirements: Nonprofit organizations in the 10-county area in southwestern Pennsylvania including Washington, Greene, Fayette, Westmoreland, Armstrong, Butler, Lawrence, Beaver, Indiana, and Allegheny are eligible.
Geographic Focus: Pennsylvania
Date(s) Application is Due: Jun 1; Dec 1
Samples: Squirrel Hill Health Center, Pittsburgh, PA, $172,000 - for Comprehensive Mental Health Care and Collaborative Wellness Program; Hill House Association, Pittsburgh, PA, $77,500 - for Ex-Offenders and Non-Custodial Parents Employment Program; Allegheny County Department of Human Services, Pittsburgh, PA, $69,000 - for Community Reintegration Project
Contact: Joni Schwager, Executive Director; (412) 281-8020; (412) 232-3115; jschwager@stauntonfarm.org
Internet: http://www.stauntonfarm.org
Sponsor: Staunton Farm Foundation
650 Smithfield Street, Centre City Tower, Suite 210
Pittsburgh, PA 15222

Steelcase Foundation Grants **1574**

The foundation make grants to nonprofit organizations, projects, and programs in corporate communities. Grants are awarded in the areas of human service, health, education, community development, the arts, and the environment. Preference is given to programs designed to improve the quality life for disadvantaged, disabled, young, and elderly people. Matching gifts are made to educational, arts, and environment programs supported by Steelcase employees, retirees, and directors. To obtain a grant application, send a letter on letterhead, signed by the organization's chief executive officer. Include the following items in the letter: description of the organization or project; expected results of the project; amount of grant funds requested; and a copy of 501(c)3 nonprofit certification. Guidelines are available online.
Requirements: The foundation makes grants to IRS-certified nonprofit organizations in areas where Steelcase manufacturing plants are located (Grand Rapids, MI; Fletcher, NC; City of Industry, CA; Athens, AL; Toronto, Canada; and Tijuana, Mexico.)
Restrictions: The foundation does not provide grants to individuals or to organizations that discriminate on the basis of race, religion, sex, disability, or national origin; have received a Steelcase foundation grant within the past 12 months; request support for a conference or seminar; or request support for religious programs (nonsectarian programs for humanitarian purposes are eligible for consideration.)
Geographic Focus: Alabama, California, Michigan, Canada, Mexico
Amount: 2,000 - 673,000 USD
Samples: Aquinas College (Grand Rapids, MI)—for its Sustainable Business Program, $1 million.
Contact: Executive Director; (616) 475-2009; (616) 475-2200; sbroman@steelcase.com
Internet: http://www.steelcase.com/na/ourcompany.aspx?f=10042&c=10022
Sponsor: Steelcase Foundation
P.O. Box 1967, CH4E
Grand Rapids, MI 49501

Steele-Reese Foundation Grants **1575**

The foundation's available income is divided equally for grants to operating charities in southern Appalachia (particularly Kentucky) and in the Northwest (particularly Idaho). In both areas the funds are devoted to education, health, welfare, and the humanities. Types of support include general operating support, equipment, endowment funds, matching funds, professorships, scholarship funds, and capital campaigns. The foundation gives preference to projects that have, among others, the following characteristics: rural, modest in ambition, narrow in function, unglamorous, based on experience, enjoying community financial support, and essential rather than merely desirable. While the foundation considers southern Kentucky and Idaho to be its territories of primary concern, it makes grants to organizations operating throughout southern Appalachia and in Oregon, Montana, and Wyoming.
Requirements: Applicant should submit a letter requesting guidelines. Only residents of Georgia, Idaho, Kentucky, Montana, North Carolina, Texas, and Wyoming are eligible to apply. Personal and telephone inquiries are not encouraged.
Restrictions: The foundation does not make grants to individuals, to community chest or similar drives, for conferences or workshops, for efforts to influence elections or legislation, for planning purposes or experimental projects, for emergencies, or for permanent support except for occasional endowment grants to organizations where stability is critically important.
Geographic Focus: Georgia, Idaho, Kentucky, Montana, North Carolina, Texas, Wyoming
Date(s) Application is Due: Mar 1
Amount: 10,000 - 50,000 USD
Samples: Frontier Nursing Service, Wendover, KY, $40,000 - to purchase a new phone system for the Mary Breckenridge Hospital; Mountain Home Montana, Missoula, MT, $28,000 - salary support for the director of a teen-mother residency program; West Central Highlands Resource Conservation and Development Council, Emmett, ID, $10,000 - for upgrades and renovations of the Indian Valley Community Hall.
Contact: Charles U. Buice, (212) 505-2696; charlesbuice@hotmail.com
Internet: http://www.steele-reese.org/what.html
Sponsor: Steele-Reese Foundation
32 Washington Square West
New York, NY 10011

Stella and Charles Guttman Foundation Grants **1576**

The majority of grants are made to organizations providing services to people in the New York City metropolitan area. Contributions also are made to organizations performing scientific research or research relating to the delivery of social services without geographical limitations. The foundation supports programs that address the educational and social service needs of at-risk children and youth, including arts and cultural programs, drug prevention programs, family planning services, health and mental health services,

intergenerational programs, programs for the physically disabled, and youth employment programs. The foundation also supports programs that promote the general welfare of the elderly and enhance their quality of life. Charities that conduct activities in Israel, including programs that foster improved relations between Jews and Arabs, also receive support. The foundation maintains a special grant category through which it can respond to special projects and address critical needs outside its principal program areas. Types of support include general operating support, continuing support, program development, and matching funds.
Requirements: Charitable 501(c)3 or 170(b)1 organizations are eligible with a strong emphasis on New York City and Israel.
Restrictions: The foundation does not make grants directly to individuals or to organizations not qualified as charitable, for foreign travel or study, to initiate or defend public interest litigation, to support anti-vivisectionist causes, or to religious organizations for religious observances.
Geographic Focus: New York
Amount: 5,000 - 30,000 USD
Samples: Educational Alliance (New York, NY)—for general support, $25,000; Creative Ctr for Women with Cancer (New York, NY)—for general support, $25,000; Givat Haviva Educational Foundation (New York, NY)—for the Children Teaching Children program and Ibn Rouchd School in Jat, Israel, $16,000.
Contact: Elizabeth Olofson, Executive Director; (212) 371-7082; (212) 371-8936; info@guttmanfoundation.org
Internet: http://www.guttmanfoundation.org
Sponsor: Stella and Charles Guttman Foundation
122 E 42nd Street, Suite 2010
New York, NY 10168

Stella B. Gross Charitable Trust Grants **1577**
The charitable trust supports Santa Clara County, CA, tax-exempt charitable organizations in its areas of interest, including arts and culture, child development, education and higher education, hospitals and health care organizations, medical research, human services, Roman Catholic federated giving programs, and government/public administration. Programs should be unique, have measurable outcome objectives, and organizations should have a plan to sustain the program. Types of support include general operating support, continuing support, program development, and seed money grants.
Requirements: Santa Clara County, CA, nonprofits may apply.
Geographic Focus: California
Date(s) Application is Due: May 31; Nov 30
Amount: 1,000 - 23,000 USD
Samples: Fremont Union High School District (Fremont, CA)—for the teen parenting program, $4000; Catholic Charities, Diocese of San Jose (San Jose, CA)—general support, $10,000.
Contact: Fatima Mendoza, Trust Associate; (800) 232-2430 or (408) 947-5160; fmendoza@bankofthewest.com
Sponsor: Stella B. Gross Charitable Trust
P.O. Box 1121
San Jose, CA 95108

Sterling-Turner Charitable Foundation Grants **1578**
The charitable foundation awards grants to Texas organizations, primarily for higher and secondary education, adult basic education and literacy, social services, youth, the elderly, fine and performing arts groups and other cultural programs, church support and religious programs (Catholic, Jewish, and Protestant), hospitals and health services, hospices, research, conservation, and civic and urban affairs. Grants are awarded for general operating support, annual campaigns, capital campaigns, continuing support, building construction/renovation, equipment acquisition, endowment funds, program and project development, conferences and seminars, curriculum development, fellowships, scholarship funds, research, and matching funds. The board meets in April.
Requirements: Nonprofit Texas organizations in Tom Green, Kerr, Fort Bend, Harris and Travis County, may submit written requests for grants.
Restrictions: Individuals are ineligible.
Geographic Focus: Texas
Date(s) Application is Due: Mar 1
Amount: 5,000 - 25,000 USD
Samples: Kinkaid School (Houston, TX)—for program support, $10,000; Houston Baptist U (Houston, TX)—for program support, $25,000; Museum of Fine Arts of Houston (Houston, TX)—for operating support, $166,667.
Contact: Patricia Moser, Executive Assistant; (713) 237-1117; (713) 223-4638; patricia@sterlingturnerfoundation.org
Internet: http://sterlingturnerfoundation.org
Sponsor: Sterling-Turner Charitable Foundation
815 Walker Street, Suite 1543
Houston, TX 77002-5724

Steve Young Family Foundation Grants **1579**
The major fields of interest of the foundation include philanthropy, voluntarism, and recreation programs. Areas of most recent giving has concentrated its efforts on assisting children in need, focusing on family togetherness and welfare, as well as major health issues. The foundation's geographic focus is of a national scope.
Restrictions: 501(c)3 organizations that have a national appeal.
Geographic Focus: All U.S. States
Samples: $10,000, Twin Towers Orphan Fund, Bakersfield, CA; National Brain Tumor Foundation, San Francisco, CA
Contact: Jon Steven Young, (800) 994-3837
Sponsor: Steve Young Family Foundation
559 W 500th Street South
Bountiful, UT 84010

Stewart Huston Charitable Trust Grants **1580**
The purpose of the Trust is to provide funds, technical assistance and collaboration on behalf of non-profit organizations engaged exclusively in religious, charitable or educational work; to extend opportunities to deserving needy persons. Giving primarily in the Savannah, GA, area and Coatesville, Pennsylvania.
Requirements: 501(c)3 nonprofit organizations are eligible.
Restrictions: Grants are not awarded for scholarship support to individuals, endowment purposes, purchases of tickets or advertising for benefit purposes, coverage of continuing operating deficits, or document publication costs. Support is not provided to intermediate or pass-through organizations (other than United Way) that in turn allocate funds to beneficiaries or to fraternal organizations, political parties or candidates, veterans, labor or local civic groups, volunteer fire companies, or groups engaged in influencing legislation.
Geographic Focus: Georgia, Pennsylvania
Date(s) Application is Due: Jan 15; Mar 1; Sep 1
Amount: 1,000 - 15,000 USD
Contact: Scott Huston, Program Director; (610) 384-2666; (610) 384-3396; admin@stewarthuston.org
Internet: http://www.stewarthuston.org
Sponsor: Stewart Huston Charitable Trust
50 South First Avenue
Coatesville, PA 19320

Stocker Foundation Grants **1581**
The foundation supports creative initiatives that can be catalysts for constructive change. Preference is given to programs that have the promise of solution, with emphasis on education, the arts, women's issues, youth leadership, the disadvantaged, the physically challenged, and community needs. Specific areas of interest are arts education; community/grassroots partnerships; leadership; primary and secondary education enrichment programs; health care for the underserved; community involvement; and social services. Grants are awarded for general support, building funds, curriculum development, publications, equipment, endowments, projects, challenge/matching, and seed money. This award is considered three times throughout the year.
Requirements: Funds are made to organizations in Lorain County, Ohio; Pima County, Arizona; San Francisco County, California; Bernalillo and Dona Ana Counties, New Mexico; and King County, Washington.
Restrictions: Grants do not support annual campaigns, conferences, deficit financing, government services, public school services required by law, or research projects.
Geographic Focus: Arizona, California, New Mexico, Ohio, Washington
Date(s) Application is Due: May 15; Aug 15; Dec 15
Amount: 2,000 - 15,000 USD
Samples: Douglas Ctr for Performing Arts (Douglas, AZ)—to support the youth theater program, $3500.
Contact: Patricia O'Brien, Executive Director; (440) 246-5719; (440) 246-5720; pobrien@stockerfoundation.org
Internet: http://www.stockerfoundation.org/fund.html
Sponsor: Stocker Foundation
401 Broadway Avenue, Suite 101
Lorain, OH 44052

Strake Foundation Grants 1582

The purpose of the foundation's grant program is to fund primarily Roman Catholic-affiliated associations, including hospitals and higher and secondary educational institutions. Additional areas of interest include adult basic education and literacy, museums, and arts and culture. Support is provided for operating budgets, continuing support, annual campaigns, special projects, matching funds, scholarship funds, building construction/renovation, and research.

Requirements: Awards are made to organizations located only in the United States, primarily in Texas.

Restrictions: Awards are not made to support elementary schools or individuals, nor for deficit financing, consulting services, technical assistance, publications, or loans.

Geographic Focus: Texas

Date(s) Application is Due: Apr 1; Oct 1

Amount: 1,000 - 20,000 USD

Samples: College of Saint Thomas More (Fort Worth, TX)—to support courses and materials related to the college's new bachelor of arts degree, $10,000.

Contact: George Strake Jr., President; (713) 216-2400; (713) 216-2401; foundation@strake.org

Sponsor: Strake Foundation
712 Main Street, Suite 3300
Houston, TX 77002

Stranahan Foundation Grants 1583

Giving is largely for higher education but there is also support given for community foundations and community funds, youth, social service, health agencies, and cultural organizations, including a fine arts museum and performing arts groups.

Requirements: Nonprofit organizations in Ohio are eligible to apply.

Restrictions: Grants are not made to individuals.

Geographic Focus: Ohio

Date(s) Application is Due: Mar 1; Jul 1; Nov 1

Amount: 1,000 - 300,000 USD

Contact: Pam Roberts, (419) 882-5575; (419) 882-2072; proberts@stranahanfoundation.org

Internet: http://www.stranahanfoundation.org

Sponsor: Stranahan Foundation
4159 Holland-Sylvania Road, Suite 206
Toledo, OH 43623-2590

Streisand Foundation Grants 1584

The foundation awards grants for national programs affecting women and at-risk youth. Areas of support include programs for children and youth, with a focus on the economically disadvantaged; civil rights, with emphasis on race relations between African Americans and Jews; AIDS research, advocacy, service, and litigation; nuclear disarmament; and environmental preservation. Types of support include general operating grants, technical assistance, and project-specific support. Applicants are asked to submit one-to two-page letters of inquiry along with a copy of the 501(c)3 determination letter. Applications are accepted between September 1 and the listed deadline. Guidelines are available online.

Requirements: 501(c)3 nonprofits and California projects in the Los Angeles area are eligible.

Restrictions: Grants are not made to individuals nor do they support start-up organizations, endowments, or capital campaigns.

Geographic Focus: All U.S. States

Date(s) Application is Due: Dec 1

Amount: 10,000 - 20,000 USD

Samples: Crossroads Community Foundation (Santa Monica, CA)—to support free quality arts and enrichment programming for children at Walgrove Elementary School in Venice, CA, $5000; Women Against Gun Violence (Culver City, CA)—to galvanize support for the reduction and prevention of gun violence, $5000; League of Conservation Voters Education Fund (Washington, DC)—to help grassroots environmental organizations motivate their members to be involved in the decision-making process, $20,000.

Contact: Program Contact; (310) 535-3767; (310) 314-8396; stfnd@aol.com

Internet: http://www.barbrastreisand.com/bio_streisand_foundation.html

Sponsor: Streisand Foundation
2800 28th Street, Suite 105
Santa Monica, CA 90405

Strengthening Families - Strengthening Communities Grants 1585

The foundation is committed to improving the quality of life for residents of metropolitan Richmond. Competitive grantmaking focuses on building or enhancing the resources of the charitable sector to address: basic human needs for children and families who are impoverished; child and youth development, with an emphasis on young people who are at moderate or high risk of experiencing problems in school, in their social interactions, or with lifestyle choices; community development that promotes affordable housing and safe neighborhoods; opportunities to broadly enrich family and community life; and collaborative models of service, volunteerism, and community leadership development. Generally, projects undertaken in collaboration with other nonprofits receive a higher priority. These may include requests that address unmet or emerging community needs or allow for program expansion or enhancement. Collaboratives that include current recipient organizations or that minimize duplication of services will be considered. The foundation will give preference to those organizations that seek to develop or enhance their work through a cohesive regional strategy. Guidelines are available online.

Requirements: Proposals will be accepted from charitable organizations that serve the residents of metropolitan Richmond and Central Virginia. Generally, projects undertaken in collaboration with other nonprofits receive a higher priority. These may include requests that address unmet or emerging community needs or allow for program expansion or enhancement. Collaboratives that include current recipient organizations or that minimize duplication of services will be considered. The foundation will give preference to those organizations that seek to develop or enhance their work through a cohesive regional strategy.

Geographic Focus: Virginia

Date(s) Application is Due: May 5; Nov 5

Amount: 5,000 - 100,000 USD

Samples: Daily Planet, Inc (VA)—to provide operating support for the Health Care Clinic, which serves homeless men and women, $25,000; Richmond SCORE (VA)—to equip the agency, whose retired business owners and managers volunteer to provide assistance to nonprofit and for-profit organizations, with technology to track and evaluate its work, $10,000; ElderHomes Corp (VA)—to provide program support for the Volunteer Services Program, which provides home repairs for low-income elderly and/or disabled, $35,000; Assisting Families of Inmates, Inc (VA)—to support the Milk and Cookies Children's Program, designed to address the physical, emotional, and social needs of children with incarcerated parents and their caregivers, $15,000.

Contact: Susan Hallett, Program Officer; (804) 330-7400; (804) 330-5992; shallett@tcfrichmond.org

Internet: http://www.tcfrichmond.org/page2954.cfm#CF

Sponsor: Community Foundation Serving Richmond and Central Virginia
7501 Boulders View Drive, Suite 110
Richmond, VA 23225

Strowd Roses Grants 1586

Strowd Roses, Inc. is a private charitable foundation which was established in 2001 under the will of Mrs. Irene Harrison Strowd of Chapel Hill, North Carolina. The Board of Directors of Strowd Roses, Inc. makes grants to qualified tax-exempt charitable, educational, religious and public organizations that are based in Chapel Hill or Carrboro, or are devoted primarily to benefiting the citizens of those communities. Grants may also be made to individuals engaged in projects designed to enhance the Chapel Hill/Carrboro community. Grants may, at the Board's discretion, include support for operating as well as capital expenditures, seed money and matching grants. Grants to individuals may be used for scholarships or fellowships; to produce a report or similar product; or to improve or enhance a literary, artistic, musical, scientific, teaching or similar capacity, skill or talent which will be used to benefit the life of the community. Particular consideration is given to those projects and purposes which further the interests of Mr. and Mrs. Strowd, including the welfare of children and youth, the enhancement of the environment, and the promotion of a sense of civic duty.

Requirements: Applicants should submit the appropriate application form (see foundations website), along with a proposed budget and evidence of their tax-exempt status (IRS determination letter or comparable documentation) to: Board of Directors, Strowd Roses, Inc., P.O. Box 3558, Chapel Hill, NC, 27515-3558.

Geographic Focus: North Carolina

Date(s) Application is Due: Jan 31; Apr 30; Jul 31; Oct 31

Amount: 10,000 USD

Contact: Jennifer Boger, Grant Coordinator; (919) 929-1984; (919) 929-1990; jboger@strowdroses.org
Internet: http://www.strowdroses.org/grantApp.htm
Sponsor: Strowd Roses
P.O. Box 3558
Chapel Hill, NC 27515-3558

Stuart Foundation Grants **1587**

The foundation's mission is to help children and youth in California and the state of Washington become capable, responsible citizens. Areas of interest include strengthening communities that serve families (community building, service integration, institutional and community partnerships, professional development, and technical assistance), strengthening the child welfare system (permanency, supportive services for youth, comprehensive assessment and services, prevention, or volunteering), strengthening public schools (teacher development, public policy, early learning, systemic school reform, and other opportunities), and policy analysis and advocacy. The foundation is interested in funding programs that promote collaboration and integrated services to improve children's outcomes. Grants also include assistance with community engagement, conflict resolution, research, technology, and training. Types of support include seed money, operating support, and special projects. Programs receive funding each year; renewal is subject to board and staff decisions. Obtain a guidelines brochure from the office.
Requirements: The foundation supports programs serving California and Washington.
Restrictions: The foundation does not make grants to support political activities, endowments, building campaigns, fundraising events, material acquisition, or operating funds.
Geographic Focus: California, Washington
Date(s) Application is Due: Mar 1; Jun 1; Sep 1; Dec 1
Amount: 5,000 - 100,000 USD
Samples: Washington Education Foundation (Issaquah, WA)—for the Foster Care to College Partnership, which seeks to expand access to college for children in Washington State who are in foster care, $234,751; Partnership for Learning (Seattle, WA)—for its efforts to increase public understanding of, and support for, standards-based education reforms in Washington State, $100,000; Parent Services Project (San Rafael, CA)—for an institute that works to build the leadership skills of parents in Marin County, CA, $25,000; Foundation Consortium/San Francisco Foundation Community Initiative Funds (San Francisco, CA)—for general support as this organization ceases operations, documents its work, and transitions its projects to other entities, $160,000.
Contact: Stephanie Titus, Grants Manager; (415) 393-1551; (415) 393-1552
Internet: http://www.stuartfoundation.org/how.html
Sponsor: Stuart Foundation
50 California Street, Suite 3350
San Francisco, CA 94111-4735

Sulzberger Foundation Grants **1588**

The foundation awards grants to eligible nonprofit organizations in its areas of interest, including arts and culture, education, environmental protection and natural resource conservation, hospitals, and social services delivery. Types of support include annual campaigns, building construction/renovation, endowments, general operating support, multiyear grants, programs and projects, and scholarship funds. There are no application forms or deadlines. Preference is given to requests from New York City and Chatanooga.
Restrictions: Individuals are not eligible. Loans and matching grants are not awarded.
Geographic Focus: All U.S. States
Amount: 100 - 255,000 USD
Samples: New York Times Company Foundation (New York, NY)—for the Neediest Cases Fund, $100,000.
Contact: Marian Heiskell, President; (212) 556-1400
Sponsor: Sulzberger Foundation
229 W 43rd Street, Suite 1031
New York, NY 10036

Sunflower Foundation Capacity Building Grants **1589**

The Foundation funds two types of Capacity Building grants: Assessment (grant limit is based on scope of work) —the first step of any effort to build capacity within an organization is an assessment of present capacity to identify what is working well and what needs to be strengthened (the Foundation will fund technical assistance, consulting, and other expenses related to conducting a formal assessment of current organizational capacity); and Implementation ($20,000 grant limit)—the Foundation will fund the implementation of capacity building strategies. Allowable expenses typically include such items as technical assistance/consulting, technology (hardware and/or software), limited equipment (e.g. telephone systems), training and assessment/evaluation.
Requirements: Proposals are invited from private nonprofit or public organizations that have a mission to improve health status or access to quality, affordable health care for Kansans.
Restrictions: The foundation will not fund ongoing general operating expenses or existing deficits; capital, endowment or specific fund-raising campaigns; fund raising events; routine continuing education; travel to conferences not directly related to the project; programs that are not Kansas-based; programs that require additional staff but demonstrate no clear means of sustainability after foundation funding; individual medical care or support; medical equipment; capital equipment (except for allowable technology); political purposes; or support of organizations that practice discrimination. Additional exclusions include: program expenses; existing staff salaries/benefits; Electronic Medical Records (EMR) technology; medical equipment; capital equipment (except for allowable technology); routine continuing education; and travel to conferences not directly related to the project.
Geographic Focus: Kansas
Date(s) Application is Due: Jun 19
Amount: Up to 20,000 USD
Contact: Grants Administrator; (785) 232-3000 or (866) 232-3020; info@sunflowerfoundation.org
Internet: http://www.sunflowerfoundation.org/flash/request.html
Sponsor: Sunflower Foundation: Health Care for Kansans
1200 SW Executive Drive, Suite 100
Topeka, KS 66615-3850

SuperValu Foundation Grants **1590**

Super Valu Stores is a wholesale food supplier. Super Valu does all of its giving directly, some through its headquarters and some through certain local plants which have their own funds. Broad areas of interest are those concerned with education and hunger. The company focuses giving in five categories, hunger relief, product and financial donations to comprehensive hunger relief organizations and non-profit food distribution centers, education, K-12 and post-secondary educational programs with a special interest in leadership development, school-to-work readiness, and after-school programs for children, workforce development, job training and self-sufficiency programs for minority, physically challenged, disabled and disadvantaged persons, fine arts, arts education programs in the corporate headquarters community, and social services, which are generally addressed through significant grants allocated to the United Way in the corporate headquarters communities.
Requirements: Organizations must be tax-exempt under Section 501(c)3 of the Internal Revenue Code.
Restrictions: Grants generally do not support: individuals; travel or research expenses; fees for participation in competitive programs; organizations that receive more than 30 percent of their funding from the United Way; capital campaigns; veteran, fraternal or labor organizations; lobbying, political, or religious programs; or organizations that are not tax-exempt under section 501(c)3 of the IRS tax code.
Geographic Focus: All U.S. States
Date(s) Application is Due: Feb 15; May 15; Aug 15; Nov 15
Amount: 250 - 300,000 USD
Contact: Jesse Benson, Director; (864) 597-4403; (612) 828-8955
Internet: http://www.supervalu.com/community/comm_application.html
Sponsor: SuperValu Foundation
P.O. Box 990
Minneapolis, MN 55440

Surdna Foundation Arts Teachers Fellowships **1591**

The foundation invites arts teachers from specialized, public arts high schools to apply for funding for artistic development through its arts teachers fellowship program. The program offers teachers the opportunity to immerse themselves in their own creative work, interact with other professional artists, and stay current with new practices. Download complete program information, guidelines, and application material, which are available online.
Requirements: Permanently assigned full- and part-time arts teachers in specialized, public arts high schools who have been teaching for at least five years are eligible. Dance, music, theater-arts, and visual-arts teachers are eligible.

Geographic Focus: All U.S. States
Date(s) Application is Due: Nov 18
Amount: Up to 6,500 USD
Contact: Edward Skloot, Executive Director; (212) 557-0010; (212) 557-0003; artsfellowship@surdna.org
Internet: http://www.surdna.org/programs/artsteachersfellowships.html
Sponsor: Surdna Foundation
330 Madison Avenue, 30th Floor
New York, NY 10017-5001

Surdna Foundation Grants **1592**

The foundation makes grants in five program areas: the environment, community revitalization, effective citizenry, the arts, and nonprofit-sector support. The environmental program emphasizes projects in four areas: biological diversity and the human communities that depend on it, human systems, transportation and urban/suburban land use, and energy. The citizenry program focuses on dispute resolution and mediation programs, youth development, encouraging community participation, and helping people work together to solve serious social and civic problems. Grants in the community revitalization field focus on access to low-cost housing, helping low-income people become more self-sufficient, and strengthening families and early-childhood education. Funding in the arts focuses on education grants to support general curriculum and professional development tailored to assist students ages 11 through 18. Nonprofit-sector grants concentrate on strengthening the sector's role in American public life and in public-policy creation; promoting the study of overlapping issues such as tax exemption and public funding; galvanizing philanthropic activity; and enhancing nonprofits' management, finance, leadership, and use of technology. The foundation makes both project and general support grants. The foundation recommends potential applicants to submit a letter of inquiry before submitting proposals. Grants are approved in February, May, and September.
Requirements: 501(c)3 organizations may apply. The foundation urges applicants to send two-to three-page letters of intent before sending proposals. IRS nonprofit status certification, recent audited financial statements, and project budget should also be included.
Restrictions: Grants are not made to individuals or given to organizations outside the United States. The foundation generally does not fund capital campaigns or building construction. Unsolicited proposals are not accepted in the arts program.
Geographic Focus: All U.S. States
Samples: National 4-H Council (Chevy Chase, MD)—to start up the Youth in Governance Initiative, which will prepare and place young people in decision-making bodies within the state and local structures of the initiative's three pilot states, $110,000; Maryland Assoc of Nonprofit Organizations (Baltimore, MA)—for its Standards for Excellence project, which details ethical practices and policies that nonprofit groups should adhere to, $100,000 over two years.
Contact: Edward Skloot, Executive Director; (212) 557-0010; (212) 557-0003; request@surdna.org
Internet: http://www.surdna.org
Sponsor: Surdna Foundation
330 Madison Avenue, 30th Floor
New York, NY 10017-5001

Susan Mott Webb Charitable Trust Grants **1593**

The trust awards grants to eligible Alabama nonprofit organizations in its areas of interest, including the arts, civic and public affairs, animals/wildlife, community development, education, health care, religion, social services, youth programs and homelessness. Types of support include annual campaigns, building construction/renovation, capital campaigns, continuing support, curriculum development, emergency funds, endowments, equipment, general/operating support, internship funds, program development, publication, and technical assistance. Contact the Foundation for further application information and guidelines.
Requirements: Giving limited to the greater Birmingham, AL, area.
Restrictions: Grants do not support advertising, individuals, international organizations, or political organizations.
Geographic Focus: Alabama
Date(s) Application is Due: Apr 1; Oct 1
Amount: 2,000 - 100,000 USD
Samples: Alabama Symphonic Association, Birmingham, AL, $40,000; Crisis Resource Center of Southeast Kansas, Pittsburg, KS, $25,000
Contact: Laura Wainwright, Vice President, c/o Regions Bank; (205) 801-0380; (205) 581-7433; laura.wainwright@regions.com
Sponsor: Susan Mott Webb Charitable Trust
P.O. Box 11426
Birmingham, AL 35202-1426

Susan Vaughan Foundation Grants **1594**

The Susan Vaughan Foundation established in 1952, supports non-profits involved with: education, particularly to a library; arts; environment, natural resources; higher education; human services. The Foundation gives primarily in Houston and Austin Texas area with support in the form of: annual campaigns; building/renovation; capital campaigns; general/operating support; matching/challenge support.
Requirements: There is no formal application form required, applicant must be a non-profit in the Houston and Austin, Texas region. Initial contact should be made through a Letter of Inquiry.
Geographic Focus: Texas
Amount: 2,500 - 630,000 USD
Samples: Clayton Library Friends, Houston, TX, $630,000; Houston Downtown Park Conservancy, Houston, TX, $50,000; Trees for Houston, Houston, TX, $30,000
Contact: Jennifer Grosvenor, Grant Coordinator c/o Legacy Trust Co; (713) 651-8980; jgrosvenor@legacytrust.com
Sponsor: Susan Vaughan Foundation
600 Jefferson Street, Suite 300
Houston, TX 77002-7377

SVP Early Childhood Development and Parenting Grants **1595**

The foundation has established education and children's issues as grantmaking priorities and awards grants to Puget Sound nonprofits to support positive outcomes for children (prenatal through 18 years old). There are two grant cycles: a fall children's grant cycle and a spring education grant cycle. Types of support include curriculum development/teacher training, institutional development, education programs, general operating support, materials/equipment acquisition, seed grants, service delivery programs, and technical assistance. Letters of inquiry are invited. The letter of inquiry should not exceed two pages in length and have no attachments, with the following information: one paragraph summarizing the organization's mission, history, and goals; a summary of goals and specific activities to be supported by the grant (include population served); a description of how success will be measured; a description of how SVP volunteer or professional services will be used; and budget figures, including the amount requested, the total budget for the project, and the organization's operating budget for the current year. Letters of inquiry may be sent by fax, email as a Word attachment, and mail. Full proposals will be invited.
Requirements: Programs must serve King County in Washington. Applicants must be classified as nonprofit 501(c)3 public charities or public schools or school districts qualifying under section 170(c) of the IRS code.
Restrictions: The foundation does not consider requests from individuals, organizations that discriminate, religious organizations for sectarian purposes, sports teams, and political or lobbying organizations. The foundation does not consider requests for auctions or fund-raising events, debt reduction, endowment funds or capital campaigns, litigation or legal expenses, land acquisition, productions, or performances.
Geographic Focus: Washington
Date(s) Application is Due: Dec 2
Amount: 40,000 USD
Samples: Kimball Elementary School (WA)—to continue funding for the counselor and coordinator positions as well as start-up funds for an extended learning program, $45,000; Youth Eastside Services (WA)—to hire program evaluation and research staff, a parenting volunteer coordinator, and to network the YES agency, $60,000.
Contact: Paul Shoemaker, Executive Director; (206) 374-8757; (206) 728-0552; paulshoe@svpseattle.org or info@svpseattle.org
Internet: http://www.svpseattle.org/grant_guidelines/early_childhood.htm
Sponsor: Social Venture Partners
1601 Second Avenue, Suite 605
Seattle, WA 98101-1541

Swaim-Gause-Rucker Foundation Grants **1596**

The Foundation, established in May of 1979, offers general charitable giving throughout the Mart, Texas, region. Funding comes in the form of gifts, grants, and general loans that support 501(c)3 organizations' general operations and new projects. There are no specific application forms or deadlines with

which to adhere. Applicants seeking support should submit: a copy of their IRS determination letter; a detailed description of the project; and a budgeted amount of funding requested.
Geographic Focus: Texas
Contact: Wells Fargo Private Client Services; (254) 714-6160
Sponsor: Swaim-Gause-Rucker Foundation
P.O. Box 2626
Waco, TX 76702-2626

T. James Kavanagh Foundation Grants **1597**
A large percentage of funding supports the Catholic church and religious associations, along with support for U.S. Roman Catholic schools, with emphasis on Pennsylvania and southern New Jersey. The foundation also makes music awards. Types of support include annual campaigns, continuing support, equipment, general operating support, program development, research, and scholarship funds. Proposals should be submitted preferably by the end of February, July, or October. The board meets in March, August, and November to consider requests.
Requirements: Giving is strictly limited to the U.S. , with emphasis on southern NJ and PA. Any Roman Catholic affiliate, church, school, college, or hospital will be considered.
Restrictions: Grants will not be awarded outside of the United States, not even to U.S. missions or to help their agencies abroad. No funding will be given for individuals; endowment funds; seed money; deficit financing; land acquisition; publications; conferences; scholarships or fellowships; matching gifts; or loans.
Geographic Focus: All U.S. States
Amount: 2,000 - 10,000 USD
Samples: Saint Joseph's R.C. School (Sharon, PA)—for the learning assistance program, $10,000; Opera Company of Philadelphia (Philadelphia, PA)—$10,000; Merion Mercy Academy (Merion Station, PA)—$5000.
Contact: Thomas Kavanagh, Trustee; (610) 356-4606
Sponsor: T. James Kavanagh Foundation
234 E State Street
Sharon, PA 16146

T.L.L. Temple Foundation Grants **1598**
The foundation awards grants to Texas nonprofit organizations in its areas of interest, including health, community and social services, civic affairs, cultural activities, and education. Types of support include general operating support, capital campaigns, building construction and renovation, equipment acquisition, program development, scholarship funds, research grants, matching funds, and emergency funds. There are no application deadlines.
Requirements: Nonprofit organizations in Texas counties constituting the East Texas Pine Timber Belt are eligible.
Restrictions: Grants do not support private foundations or individuals, nor are grants made in support of deficit financing.
Geographic Focus: Texas
Amount: 5,000 - 60,000 USD
Samples: Methodist Retirement Communities (Lufkin, TX)—for George Henderson, Jr. Special Care Unit, $1.9 million; Angelina College (Lufkin, TX)—for land purchase, $1 million; Alzheimer's Disease and Related Disorders Assoc (Chicago, IL)—for the Temple Foundation Discovery Awards for Alzheimer's Disease Research, $2.5 million.
Contact: A. Wayne Corely, Executive Director; (936) 639-5197
Sponsor: T.L.L. Temple Foundation
109 Temple Boulevard, Suite 300
Lufkin, TX 75901

T. Raymond Gregory Family Foundation Grants **1599**
The Foundation, established in 1991, is supported by Gregory Galvanizing & Metal Processing and Gregory Industries. Offering general operating support primarily in the Canton, Ohio, Region, the Foundation supports service clubs and organizations involved with nursing education and human services. Fields of interest include: child and youth services; community development; service clubs; family and human services; nursing school programs; and service delivery programs. A formal application is not required, and an applicant should contact the Foundation initially with a letter of inquiry. There are no specific deadlines.
Geographic Focus: Ohio
Amount: 1,800 - 12,000 USD
Samples: Aultman College of Nursing, Canton, OH, $17,320 (2008); Pathway Caring for Children, Canton, OH, $12,000 (2008); Pegasus Farm & Equestrian Center for the Disabled, Canton, OH, $1,000 (2008).
Contact: T. Raymond Gregory, (330) 477-4800; (330) 453-9691
Sponsor: T. Raymond Gregory Family Foundation
1723 Cleveland Avenue SE
Canton, OH 44707

T. Rowe Price Associates Foundation Grants **1600**
T. Rowe Price has a long tradition of philanthropy and investment in the communities where our associates live and work. Central to this tradition is the T. Rowe Price Foundation. Launched in 1981, the Foundation provides direct grants to U.S.-based nonprofit organizations that enhance community life through education, arts and culture, human services, and civic and community initiatives. Globally, nonprofit organizations receive support from the Foundation's associates through a Matching Gift Program. The Foundation's history of giving in its communities is strong—and consistent with the firm's goals and values.
Requirements: Although not limited to, giving is primarily made in the metropolitan Baltimore, Maryland, area.
Restrictions: No support provided for religious or political organizations; hospitals or health care providers; recreational sports leagues and sports related fundraisers; private foundations; or grants to individuals.
Geographic Focus: Maryland
Amount: 25 - 275,000 USD
Samples: Maryland Institute College of Art, Baltimore, Maryland - for unrestricted support, $30,000; Baltimore Symphony Orchestra, Baltimore, Maryland - for unrestricted support, $30,640; YMCA of Metropolitan Phoenix, Phoenix, Arizona - for civic and community purposes, $5000.
Contact: Christine Stein, Program Director; (410) 345-3603; (410) 345-2848
Internet: http://corporate.troweprice.com/ccw/home/ourCompany/aboutUs/communityInvolvement.do
Sponsor: T. Rowe Price Associates Foundation
100 E Pratt Street, 8th Floor
Baltimore, MD 21202

TAC Arts Projects Grants **1601**
The Tennessee Arts Commission (TAC) Arts Project Support (APS) grants supply funding to organizations which are located in urban areas of Tennessee and which provide a wide variety of public-value arts projects and programs such as: projects that involve and promote professional Tennessee artists; visiting artists conducting master classes; specific aspects of workshops, festivals, and conferences; public performances, productions, and exhibitions produced by the applicant; exhibitions of art by Tennessee artists and artists from outside Tennessee; promotion, publicity, and newsletters; administrative and artistic staff support; research and documentation as part of an arts project or program development; consultancies and residencies for administrative and artistic activities; the development of long-range planning documents; touring projects that bring professional performers to communities across the state; improved program accessibility for underserved constituencies, e.g., children, people living in rural communities or isolated settings, people with disabilities, people of color and senior citizens; art in public places (additional information available from the Director of Visual Arts); extensions of literary projects, journals with continuing publication or juried anthologies; apprenticeship programs; computer software/training; technical/production support; and technical assistance projects. APS grant amounts range from $500 to $7,000 for non-arts organizations and $500 to $9,000 for arts-focused groups. Arts organizations serving a statewide audience may apply for up to $10,000. Applicants should contact the Tennessee Arts Commission to verify current submission dates and requirements.
Requirements: The following entities are eligible to apply for APS grants: 501(c)3 not-for-profit organizations in urban areas of and chartered in Tennessee; and Tennessee colleges and universities who meet the tax-exempt requirements just described for not-for-profit organizations. Entities bordering Tennessee (and serving urban areas in Tennessee) are also eligible to apply if they meet the criteria described for instate applicants. First time applicants must contact the TAC prior to submitting an application to verify eligibility. All first time 501(c)3 applicants must provide the TAC with copies of all of the basic nonprofit status documentation, which includes a copy of the organization's Tennessee State Charter, the IRS 501(c)3 Determination Letter and a recent copy of the by-laws of the organization. Proposed projects must involve one or more TAC recognized classical art forms, including visual art, crafts, media, music, theater, dance, folk and ethnic art, or literary arts. Applicants who apply in more than

one TAC grant category in a single fiscal year must submit entirely unrelated projects for each proposal. All APS applicants must submit an online eGRANT application by January 18 at 4:30 pm. The link to the eGRANT form is available at the grant website. Additionally, hard copies and required supporting documents described in the guidelines at the grant website must be mailed or hand-delivered to the TAC by Jan 18 at 4:30 pm to complete the application process. Applications must contain a clear, single- project focus. Requested funds should be listed under one expense category on the budget page (and should correspond with the Activity Code indicated on the application). Grant funds must be matched one-to-one (1:1). A project may start no earlier than July 1 and must end no later than June 15. For more requirements, applicants should read the guidelines at the grant website. Additionally applicants should read the legal requirements page at http://www.tn.gov/arts/legal.htm.
Restrictions: An APS application may be submitted only by an organization chartered in Tennessee and located in an urban county (for a list of TAC's urban and rural designations, see the downloadable guidelines at the grant website). K-12 schools are not eligible to apply. Colleges and universities are eligible only for activities that clearly serve the needs of surrounding communities or the state and are designed to involve a broad audience. Activities that are credit-producing or are oriented primarily to students and the academic community are not eligible. An eligible organization may submit only one APS application for the current fiscal year. APS applicants may not apply for a Partnership Support, Cultural Education Partnership or Major Cultural Institution grant. Additional restrictions on funding are listed on the legal requirements page at http://www.tn.gov/arts/legal.htm.
Geographic Focus: Alabama, Arkansas, Georgia, Kentucky, Mississippi, Missouri, North Carolina, Tennessee, Virginia
Date(s) Application is Due: Jan 18
Amount: 500 - 10,000 USD
Contact: Kim Leavitt, Director of Arts Education; (615) 532-5934; (615) 741-8559; kim.leavitt@tn.gov
Internet: http://www.tn.gov/arts/grant_categories.htm
Sponsor: Tennessee Arts Commission
401 Charlotte Avenue, Citizens Plaza Building
Nashville, TN 37243-0780

TAC Cultural Education Partnership **1602**

The Cultural Education Partnership (CEP) category offers general, non-project support to well-established, free-standing 501(c)3 college/university level arts educational institutions. Only academic institutions which have as their mission training and/or accreditation in one or more arts disciplines and represent the highest level of quality art education and administration are eligible in this category. CEP applicants must also have an annual cash operating income (excluding in-kind contributions) of at least $1 million per year. The maximum grant amount is 10 percent of the total operating expenses of the most recently completed, audited year, up to $60,000. The total cash operating expenses (less any capital expenditures, loan payments or penalties, endowment funds, cash reserves, furniture or fixtures exceeding $2,500.00) will be determined by adding together the personnel, outside fees and services, space rental, travel, marketing, and remaining operating expenses. Annual deadline dates may vary; contact Tennessee Arts Commission (TAC) staff or check the TAC website for exact dates.
Requirements: Applicants must read the legal requirements section at the TAC website (under the Grants tab) for further requirements before making application. In addition to satisfying all "General Requirements," eligible applicants must be a freestanding academic arts institution which has as its mission training and/or accreditation in one or more arts disciplines and which demonstrates significant community involvement in the grant application. Applicants must also comply with all of the following conditions to qualify in the CEP category: have one or more full time and adequately compensated personnel (president, academic dean, teaching staff, and other administrative staff); have existed as an academic arts institution for a minimum of five (5) years prior to the date of application; be an accredited institution or recognized nationally for the quality of specialized training or academic instruction offered; have received, for three (3) of the past five (5) years, funding from the TAC through the Arts Access, Arts Project Support, Rural Arts Project Support, Partnership Support, or Major Cultural Institution grants; demonstrate proof of arts advocacy; demonstrate ongoing fiscal responsibility through an audit conducted externally by a certified public accountant for its most recently completed fiscal year; use an accrual accounting system; and have evidence of significant service to the community (because of public dollars awarded by the TAC). Public service is defined as programming and activities that add value to the community being served by the applicant institution. These activities can be, but are not exclusive to: providing needed services to under-served populations; neighborhood outreach classes and workshops; and concerts, performances, and exhibitions that are of interest to the community. Institutions must submit an audit of their most recently completed fiscal year at the time of application. If a more recent audit is in process, applicants may include a letter from the institution's CPA explaining when it will be completed and available. However, no audits will be accepted after March 1, 2011. First time applicants must include an audit of their most recently completed fiscal year at the time of application. All CEP applicants must submit an online eGRANT application (the link to which can be found at the grant website) by 4:30 p.m. (CST) on the due date. In addition, the correct number of printed eGrant applications along with any required documents must be postmarked or hand-delivered to the TAC by 4:30 p.m. (CST) on the due date. Applicants who apply every year are reviewed every third year by an out-of-state reviewer with knowledge of academic arts institutions. Organizations being reviewed must submit 8 (eight) printed sets of applications and accompanying documents. Organizations not being reviewed submit only 3 (three) printed sets.
Restrictions: CEP funds may not be used for: capital improvements (building or construction); elimination of an accumulated debt; planned fundraising activities; projects that have implicit religious content, express a particular religious view or advance a religious purpose; "seed money" for starting new organizations; out-of-state travel expenses; any type of endowment campaign or program; insurance premiums; office space rental; janitorial service and general physical plant maintenance; food and hospitality; vanity publications; scholarly arts-related research and writing; cash awards; legal fees; and payments to members of the organization's board. Previous applicants who fail to meet the $1 million base operating figure will have a one-year "grace period" before losing eligibility in the CEP category; however, the applicants must maintain the $1 million base operating figure for a minimum of two consecutive years before another request for a one year grace period may be made. The TAC will not make grants to an organization with a standing deficit unless a plan to reduce that deficit is submitted with the application.
Geographic Focus: Tennessee
Date(s) Application is Due: Jan 4
Amount: Up to 60,000 USD
Contact: Rod Reiner, Deputy Director; (615) 741-2093; (615) 741-8559; rod.reiner@tn.gov
Internet: http://www.tn.gov/arts/grant_categories.htm
Sponsor: Tennessee Arts Commission
401 Charlotte Avenue, Citizens Plaza Building
Nashville, TN 37243-0780

TAC Major Cultural Institutions Grants **1603**

The major cultural institution (MCI) grants from the Tennessee Arts Commission (TAC) offer general, nonproject-oriented support to those well-established Tennessee arts organizations that represent the highest level of quality programming and administration and have annual operating incomes (excluding in-kind contributions) of $1 million per year. The maximum grant amount is 10 percent of the total operating expenses of the most recently completed, audited year, up to $100,000. The total cash operating expenses will be determined by adding together the personnel, outside fees and services, space rental, travel, marketing, and remaining operating expenses. Annual deadline dates may vary; contact program staff for exact dates.
Requirements: The following presentations of requirements and restrictions are not all-inclusive. Before applying for a grant, applicants are responsible for reading TAC's Legal Requirements found on the web site at: http://www.arts.state.tn.us/legal.htm. An applicant must be a 501(c)3 organization with an artistic mission chartered in the state of Tennessee; be either a single-entity agency responsible for its own programming and primarily dedicated to one art discipline, or an arts council which serves a broad population and interacts with local arts organizations; have existed as an arts institution or arts council for a minimum of five (5) years prior to the date of application; have received funding from the TAC Arts Access, Arts Project Support, Rural Arts Project Support, or Partnership/General Operating Support grants for three (3) of the past five (5) years; have a full-time, paid professional business staff and/or full-time paid artistic director; have a demonstrated commitment to compensate (in salaries, wages, fees, and/or benefits) the administrative, artistic, and technical/production personnel whose services contribute directly to the organization applying for matching funds; have a significant amount of year-round public activity; and demonstrate ongoing fiscal responsibility through an audit conducted externally by a certified public accountant for its most recently completed fiscal year. Applicants should use an accrual accounting

system. Organizations must submit an audit of their most recently completed fiscal year at the time of application. If a more recent audit is in process, include a letter from the organization's CPA explaining when the audit will be completed and available. However, the most recent audit must be submitted no later than March 1. Under no circumstances will a MCI grant contract be issued without receipt of the grantee's audit covering the required time period. First time applicants must include an audit at the time of application. All MCI applicants must submit an online eGRANT application (the link to which can be found at the grant website) by 4:30 p.m. (CST) on the due date. In addition, applicants must print the required number of copies of the completed eGRANT application, attach the required accompanying documents to each copy and mail or hand carry these sets to the TAC by 4:30 p.m. (CST) on the due date. Applicant organizations are reviewed every other year by out-of-state evaluators. Organizations must submit a completed application with the required attachments every year. Organizations being reviewed must submit 8 (eight) sets. Organizations not being reviewed submit only 3 (three) sets.
Restrictions: MCI funds may not be used for capital expenditures; loan payments or penalties; endowment funds; cash reserves; furniture or fixtures exceeding $2,500; out-of-state travel expenses; or in-school, curriculum-based projects. Previous applicants who fail to meet the $1 million base operating figure will have a one-year "grace period" before losing eligibility in the MCI category; however, the applicants must maintain the $1 million base operating figure for a minimum of two consecutive years before another request for a one year grace period may be made. Freestanding academic institutions, which have as their mission training and accreditation in one or more arts disciplines, are not eligible in this category. (These organizations currently include: Arrowmont School of Arts and Crafts, Memphis College of Art, O'More College of Design, and Watkins College of Art and Design.) These and eligible organizations may submit an application under TAC's Cultural Education Partnership grant category.
Geographic Focus: Tennessee
Date(s) Application is Due: Jan 4
Amount: Up to 100,000 USD
Samples: Memphis Orchestral Society, Inc., Memphis, Tennessee, $79,800 (2009); Memphis Arts Council, Memphis, Tennessee, $71,300 (2009)
Contact: Diane Williams, Director of Grants Management; (615) 741-6395; (615) 741-8559; diane.williams@tn.gov
Internet: http://www.tn.gov/arts/grant_categories.htm
Sponsor: Tennessee Arts Commission
401 Charlotte Avenue, Citizens Plaza Building
Nashville, TN 37243-0780

TAC Partnership Support Grants **1604**

The Partnership Support (PS) grants provide annual general (non-project) support toward ongoing administrative costs to established Tennessee arts organizations. An organization may receive up to 12 percent of its total cash operating expenses in its most recently completed and audited fiscal year. An organization's total day-to-day operating expenses will be determined by adding together personnel, outside fees and services, space rental, travel, marketing, and remaining operating expenses as verified within the submitted audit. The applicant may request no more than $40,000. The actual amount of an applicant organization's grant for PS will depend upon its rating in the review process and upon the total amount of funds available to the Tennessee Arts Commission (TAC). Renewing applicant organizations are reviewed every other year by a peer advisory panel. New applicants must be reviewed for two consecutive years by a peer advisory panel before they may begin the review rotation process. The staff of the TAC will contact all current PS applicants and inform them of the review schedule. Annual application deadline dates vary; contact program staff for exact dates. First time applicants in the PS category MU.S. T consult with TAC staff before applying.
Requirements: An applicant must be a free-standing 501(c)3 arts group independent of any other organization and chartered in the state of Tennessee; be an established arts organization responsible for its own programming; have a mission statement that is solely arts-focused; and be either a single-entity group dedicated to one arts discipline or a cross-disciplinary group such as an arts council, arts festival, or arts center. Additionally an applicant must comply with all of the following conditions: that the organization has received previous funding from TAC for three (3) of the past five (5) years through TAC's Arts Access, Arts Project Support or Rural Arts Project Support grants; that the organization has year-round paid professional managerial leadership; that the organization directly employs at least one (1) full-time paid administrator (as opposed to using a subsidiary) and that any other full or part time staff are directly employed as well; that the organization demonstrates ongoing fiscal responsibility through a single entity audit conducted externally by a Certified Public Accountant (CPA) for its most recently completed fiscal year; and that the organization has a board-approved long-range plan covering at least the current fiscal year and the next fiscal year. All these conditions must be met at time of application. Please note that in general "full-time" means an employee is paid for approximately 40 hours of work per week and the salary is his or her primary source of income. Arts organizations in neighboring states which are located within five (5) miles of the Tennessee state border, significantly serve Tennesseans and meet all eligibility requirements may also apply for a PS grant. For additional requirements, applicants should review http://www.tn.gov/arts/legal.htm at the TAC website. All PS applicants must submit an online eGRANT application by 4:30 p.m. (CST) on the due date. The link to the eGRANT is available at the grant website. In addition, applicants MU.S. T print the required number of copies of the completed eGRANT application to submit by mail along with all required accompanying documents. The printed applications and documents must also be postmarked or hand-delivered to the TAC by 4:30 p.m. (CST) on the due date. Organizations must complete a full application every year and include required accompanying documents; however, organizations being reviewed must submit sixteen (16) sets while organizations not being reviewed submit only three. Organizations with budgets over $100,000 annually should use an accrual accounting system. Organizations with annual budgets under $100,000 may use a cash accounting system and may submit a one-year audit and management letter every two years, e.g., for Fiscal Year 2012, an audit for either the organization's Fiscal Year 2009 or 2010. Failure to submit a single entity audit by the time of application requires a letter by the organization's CPA explaining why the audit is unavailable and when it will be completed.
Restrictions: Most PS recipients are organizations operating with an annual budget below $1 million. However, the category is open to arts organizations with budgets in excess of this level, but who do not qualify for TAC's Major Cultural Institution (MCI) or Cultural Education Partnership (CEP) grant categories (see guidelines for these categories at the TAC website for further information). Capital expenses, cash reserves, endowment funds, loan repayments or penalties, in-kind, depreciation, bank fees or furniture and fixture expenditures exceeding $2,500 are not allowable as operating expenses. Colleges, universities, and government units are not eligible for PS unless the unit is an official arts agency. An applicant's audit must be submitted by the date of the application's scheduled panel review and cannot be submitted as a subsidiary of another organization. If the required audit is NOT submitted by that date, the applicant's eligible funding request will be established using the organization's operating expenses from their most recent audit on file at the TAC. Under no circumstances will a PS grant contract be issued without receipt of the grantee's audit covering the required time frame.
Geographic Focus: Alabama, Arkansas, Georgia, Kentucky, Mississippi, Missouri, North Carolina, Tennessee, Virginia
Date(s) Application is Due: Jan 18
Amount: Up to 40,000 USD
Samples: Children's Museum of Oak Ridge, Anderson, Tennessee, $28,800 (2009); Tullahoma Fine Arts Center, Inc., Tullahoma, Tennessee, $5,000 (2009); Tennessee Philharmonic Symphony Orchestra, Murfreesboro, Tennessee, $9,800 (2009)
Contact: Rod Reiner, Deputy Director, Arts Program Division; (615) 741-2093; (615) 741-8559; rod.reiner@tn.gov
Internet: http://www.tn.gov/arts/grant_categories.htm
Sponsor: Tennessee Arts Commission
401 Charlotte Avenue, Citizens Plaza Building
Nashville, TN 37243-0780

TAC Rural Arts Project Support Grants **1605**

The Tennessee Arts Commission (TAC) Rural Arts Project Support (RAPS) grants supply funding to organizations which are located in rural areas of Tennessee and which provide a wide variety of public-value arts projects and programs such as: projects that involve and promote professional Tennessee artists; visiting artists conducting master classes; specific aspects of workshops, festivals, and conferences; public performances, productions, and exhibitions produced by the applicant; exhibitions of art by Tennessee artists and artists from outside Tennessee; promotion, publicity, and newsletters; administrative and artistic staff support; research and documentation as part of an arts project or program development; consultancies and residencies for administrative and artistic activities; the development of long-range planning documents; touring projects that bring professional performers to communities across the state; improved program accessibility for underserved constituencies, e.g., children, people living in rural communities or isolated settings, people with disabilities,

people of color and senior citizens; art in public places (additional information available from the Director of Visual Arts); extensions of literary projects, journals with continuing publication or juried anthologies; apprenticeship programs; computer software/training; technical/production support; and technical assistance projects. RAPS grant amounts range from $500 to $7,000 for non-arts organizations and $500 to $9,000 for arts-focused groups. Applicants should contact the Tennessee Arts Commission to verify current submission dates and requirements.
Requirements: The following entities are eligible to apply for RAPS grants: 501(c)3 not-for-profit organizations in rural areas of and chartered in Tennessee; and Tennessee colleges and universities who meet the tax-exempt requirements just described for not-for-profit organizations. Entities bordering Tennessee (and serving rural areas in Tennessee) are also eligible to apply if they meet the criteria described for instate applicants. First time applicants must contact the TAC prior to submitting an application to verify eligibility. All first time 501(c)3 applicants must provide the TAC with copies of all of the basic nonprofit status documentation, which includes a copy of the organization's Tennessee State Charter, the IRS 501(c)3 Determination Letter and a recent copy of the by-laws of the organization. Proposed projects must involve one or more TAC recognized classical art forms, including visual art, crafts, media, music, theater, dance, folk and ethnic art, or literary arts. Applicants who apply in more than one TAC grant category in a single fiscal year must submit entirely unrelated projects for each proposal. All RAPS applicants must submit an online eGRANT application by January 18 at 4:30 pm. The link to the eGRANT form is available at the grant website. Additionally, hard copies and required supporting documents described in the guidelines at the grant website must be mailed or hand-delivered to the TAC by Jan 18 at 4:30 pm to complete the application process. Applications must contain a clear, single- project focus. Requested funds should be listed under one expense category on the budget page (and should correspond with the Activity Code indicated on the application). Grant funds must be matched one-to-one (1:1). A project may start no earlier than July 1 and must end no later than June 15. For more requirements, applicants should read the guidelines at the grant website. Additionally applicants should read the legal requirements page at http://www.tn.gov/arts/legal.htm.
Restrictions: A RAPS application may be submitted only by an organization chartered in Tennessee and located in a rural county (for a list of TAC's urban and rural designations, see the downloadable guidelines at the grant website). K-12 schools are not eligible to apply. Colleges and universities are eligible only for activities that clearly serve the needs of surrounding communities or the state and are designed to involve a broad audience. Activities that are credit-producing or are oriented primarily to students and the academic community are not eligible. An eligible organization may submit only one RAPS application for the current fiscal year. RAPS applicants may not apply for a Partnership Support, Cultural Education Partnership or Major Cultural Institution grant. Additional restrictions on funding are listed on the legal requirements page at http://www.tn.gov/arts/legal.htm.
Geographic Focus: Alabama, Arkansas, Georgia, Kentucky, Mississippi, Missouri, North Carolina, Tennessee, Virginia
Date(s) Application is Due: Jan 18
Amount: 500 - 9,000 USD
Contact: Rich Boyd, Executive Director; (615) 532-9797; (615) 741-8559; rich.boyd@tn.gov
Internet: http://www.tn.gov/arts/grant_categories.htm
Sponsor: Tennessee Arts Commission
401 Charlotte Avenue, Citizens Plaza Building
Nashville, TN 37243-0780

Target Foundation Grants **1606**
The foundation welcomes applications from nonprofit organizations in the Minneapolis/Saint Paul metropolitan area. Types of support include operating, project, and capital grants. The foundation is specifically interested in partnering with arts and cultural institutions to make special exhibitions, performances, and events visible and accessible to the community; and supporting direct service organizations that sustain the basic shelter, food, and clothing needs of individuals or families at risk. Proposals are accepted throughout the year; the preferred submission time is February through November. Organizations that fit foundation guidelines may apply for funding by submitting a grant request via U.S. postal mail.
Requirements: 501(c)3 nonprofit organizations in the Minneapolis/Saint Paul metropolitan area are eligible.
Restrictions: The foundation does not make grants to individuals or to religious groups for religious purposes; usually support national ceremonies, memorials, conferences, fundraising dinners, testimonials, or other similar events; usually support health, recreation, therapeutic programs; living subsidies; or care of disabled persons.
Geographic Focus: Minnesota
Date(s) Application is Due: Oct 1
Amount: 10,000 - 50,000 USD
Contact: Bridget McGinnis, Grants Administrator; (612) 696-6098; (612) 696-5088; guidelines@target.com
Internet: http://sites.target.com/site/en/corporate/page.jsp?contentId=PRD03-001819
Sponsor: Target Foundation
1000 Nicollet Mall, TPS-3080
Minneapolis, MN 55403

Taubman Endowment for the Arts **1607**
The endowment was formed to support the arts through grants awards. Grants are awarded primarily in Detroit, MI. Applications are accepted at any time.
Restrictions: Grants are not made to individuals.
Geographic Focus: Michigan
Samples: Smithsonian Institute (Washington, DC)—for general operating support, $12,000; Detroit Symphony Orchestra Hall (Detroit, MI)—for general operating support, $2000.
Contact: Fred Henshaw, Director; (248) 258-7207; (248) 258-7476
Sponsor: Taubman Endowment for the Arts
200 E Long Lake Road, Suite 300
Bloomfield Hills, MI 48304

Taubman Foundation Grants **1608**
Grants awarded by the foundation cover projects in the fields of higher education and medical research. Applications are accepted at any time.
Requirements: 501(c)3 tax-exempt organizations are eligible. Giving is primarily made in Michigan.
Restrictions: Grants are not made to individuals.
Geographic Focus: Michigan
Amount: Up to 5,000,000 USD
Samples: Brown U (Providence, RI)—program support, $200,000; Michigan Partnership for New Education (East Lansing, MI)—program support, $97,000; United States Department of Education (Washington, DC)—program support, $10,000.
Contact: Fred Henshaw, Executive Director; (248) 258-7207; (248) 258-7476
Sponsor: Taubman Foundation
200 E Long Lake Road, Suite 300
Bloomfield Hills, MI 48304

Ted Arison Family Foundation Grants **1609**
The foundation awards general support grants to foreign and U.S. -based nonprofits in its areas of interest, including arts and culture, international studies and education, foreign educational institutions, and Jewish organizations. Preference will be given to support for Middle East relations and Jewish organizations. Lesser consideration will be given to U.S. based nonprofits with an international focus. An applicant should submit a brief proposal that describes the organization, amount requested, purpose of request, recently audited financial statement, and proof of tax exemption. There are no application deadlines.
Requirements: Funding is primarily for New York nonprofits.
Geographic Focus: New York
Amount: 10,000 - 100,000 USD
Samples: Performing Arts Center Foundation of Greater Miami (Miami, FL)—for operating support, $3,33; American Committee for Tel Aviv Foundation (New York, NY)—for Tel Aviv Foundation Israel Arison Art Campus, $123,500; Kartemquin Educational Films (Chicago, IL)—for film, Is Jerusalem Burning, $90,000; American Friends of Keshet Eilon (New York, NY)—for scholarships for Violin Master Course, $40,000.
Contact: Maddy Rosenburg, (305) 599-2600
Sponsor: Ted Arison Family Foundation U.S. A
3655 NW 87th Avenue
Miami, FL 33178-2428

Telluride Foundation Community Grants **1610**
The foundation offers an annual granting cycle for nonprofit organizations that serve people living and/or working in Colorado's San Miguel County. Grants are awarded to enhance the quality of life for the region. Types of

support include general/operating support, existing and new programs, annual campaigns, conferences and seminars, consulting services, matching funds, technical assistance, and seed money or start-up funds. Guidelines and application are available online.
Requirements: 501(c) tax-exempt organizations (and organizations with 501(c)3 fiscal sponsors) serving San Miguel County are eligible.
Restrictions: Grants will not be awarded for building/renovation, capital campaigns, debt reduction or retiring past operating deficits, fellowships or other grants to individuals, loans, publications (i.e., annual reports), litigation, political campaigns, economic development, or endowment funds.
Geographic Focus: Colorado
Date(s) Application is Due: Oct 21
Amount: 500 USD
Samples: MountainFilm (Telluride, CO)—for programs for high-school students, $10,000; Ucompahgre Medical Ctr (Norwood, CO)—to purchase an X-ray machine, $25,000; Telluride Ski and Snowboard Club (CO)—for operating support, $12,500; Telluride Historical Museum (CO)—for operating support, $10,000.
Contact: Lorrie Mahoney, Programs Director; (970) 728-8717; (970) 728-9007; lorrie@telluridefoundation.org
Internet: http://www.telluridefoundation.org/communitygrants.html
Sponsor: Telluride Foundation
620 Mountain Village Boulevard, Suite 2B
Telluride, CO 81435

Temple-Inland Foundation Grants **1611**
The foundation makes grants to IRS 501(c)3 tax-exempt organizations located in geographic operating areas of Temple-Inland Inc's subsidiary companies. Areas of interest include services for children and youth, Christian churches and organizations, education at all levels, health care and organizations, human services, and arts and culture. Types of support include general operating support, research, employee matching gifts, and employee-related scholarships. Requests should be received two weeks prior to quarterly board meetings. Submit a written request for guidelines and specific application deadlines. The listed deadline date is for scholarships.
Restrictions: Ineligible applicants include fraternal, veterans, political, local social, and service organizations.
Geographic Focus: All U.S. States
Date(s) Application is Due: Mar 15
Amount: 1,000 - 30,000 USD
Contact: Richard Warner, (936) 829-1721; (936) 829-7727
Internet: http://www.templeinland.com
Sponsor: Temple-Inland Foundation
1300 S Mopac
Austin, TX 78749

Temple Hoyne Buell Foundation Grants **1612**
The foundation awards grants to nonprofits in Colorado for programs that help underserved children in three areas: early childhood education and development (preschools, home visitation, service provider's professional development, parenting skills, and literacy); social and emotional development of children (mentoring, intergenerational, and after-school activities); and family stability for children (teen pregnancy prevention, counseling services, and family centers). Types of support include operating budgets, continuing support, equipment acquisition, curriculum development, scholarship funds, technical assistance, program development, and matching funds. Contact the office for application materials. Applications are due the 1st business day of January, May, and September.
Requirements: Nonprofit organizations in Colorado may apply.
Restrictions: Grants do not support advertising, athletic groups, individuals, international organizations, religious or political projects, special events, past operating deficits, debt retirement, litigation, medical programs, multiyear awards, testimonial events, annual campaigns, endowments, membership drives, or conferences.
Geographic Focus: Colorado
Date(s) Application is Due: Jan 2; May 1; Sep 1
Amount: 10,000 - 50,000 USD
Contact: Susan Steele, Executive Director; (303) 744-1688; (303) 744-1601; info@buellfoundation.org
Internet: http://www.buellfoundation.org/granttypes.htm
Sponsor: Temple Hoyne Buell Foundation
1666 S University Boulevard, Suite B
Denver, CO 80210

Texas Commission on the Arts Arts Respond Project Grants **1613**
This program provides project assistance grants on a short-term basis and may include administrative costs directly related to the project. Projects must address one of the following priority areas: education, health and human services, economic development, public safety, criminal justice, natural resources, or agriculture. Organizations that are eligible are: Arts Organizations, Established Arts Organizations, Minority Arts Organizations, Rural Arts Providers.
Requirements: To be eligible for TCA grants, an organization must: be a tax-exempt nonprofit organization as designated by the Internal Revenue Service and/or must be an entity of government; be incorporated in Texas; have fulfilled all its outstanding contractual obligations to the State of Texas (i.e. student loans, child support, taxes, etc.); and comply with regulations pertaining to federal grant recipients including Title VI of the Civil Rights Act of 1964, Section 504 of the Rehabilitation Act of 1973, the Age Discrimination Act of 1975, the Education Amendments of 1972, the Americans with Disabilities Act of 1990, and the Drug Free Workplace Act of 1988.
Geographic Focus: Texas
Amount: Up to 45,000 USD
Contact: Director of Programs; (512) 463-5535 or (800) 252-9415; (512) 475-2699; front.desk@arts.state.tx.us
Internet: http://www.arts.state.tx.us/index.php?option=com_wrapper&view=wrapper&Itemid=86
Sponsor: Texas Commission on the Arts
P.O. Box 13406
Austin, TX 78711-3406

Texas Commission on the Arts Create-5 Program Grants **1614**
The intent of this grant is to advance the creative economy of Texas by investing in arts organizations. This program provides multi-year operational support. Applicants write their grant for a one year period, and if funded, will provide an update for the second year. Depending on the availability of funds, the organization's award amount will be the same for two fiscal years. New organizations may only apply in odd numbered years.
Requirements: To be eligible for TCA grants, an organization must: Be a tax-exempt nonprofit organization as designated by the Internal Revenue Service and/or must be an entity of government Be incorporated in Texas Have fulfilled all its outstanding contractual obligations to the State of Texas (i.e. student loans, child support, taxes, etc.) Comply with regulations pertaining to federal grant recipients including Title VI of the Civil Rights Act of 1964, Section 504 of the Rehabilitation Act of 1973, the Age Discrimination Act of 1975, the Education Amendments of 1972, the Americans with Disabilities Act of 1990, and the Drug Free Workplace Act of 1988.
Geographic Focus: Texas
Date(s) Application is Due: Mar 15
Amount: 3,000 - 50,000 USD
Contact: Director of Programs; (512) 463-5535 or (800) 252-9415; (512) 475-2699; front.desk@arts.state.tx.us
Internet: http://www.arts.state.tx.us/index.php?option=com_wrapper&view=wrapper&Itemid=86
Sponsor: Texas Commission on the Arts
P.O. Box 13406
Austin, TX 78711-3406

Textron Corporate Contributions Grants **1615**
Textron focuses philanthropic giving in the following areas: workforce development and education—education at all levels, job training and employment development, and college/university support; and healthy families/vibrant communities—arts and culture, community revitalization, and health and human services organizations. Types of support include general operating grants, capital campaigns, building construction/renovation, equipment acquisition, program development, conferences and seminars, publication, seed money, fellowships, scholarship funds, research, technical assistance, consulting services, and matching funds. Guidelines and application are available online.
Requirements: Textron targets its giving to nonprofit agencies located in its headquarters state of Rhode Island and those locations where the company has divisional operations. Organizations outside of Rhode Island should contact the local Textron company.
Restrictions: Grants do not support organizations without 501(c)3 tax-exempt status; individuals, including political candidates; churches, seminaries, or other religious organizations for religious activities; political causes and organizations representing fraternal or self-segregated populations; or

organizations that discriminate by race, color, creed, gender, sexual preference, or national origin.
Geographic Focus: All U.S. States
Date(s) Application is Due: Mar 1; Sep 1
Samples: U of Rhode Island (RI)—for its campaign to rebuild the College of Business Administration, $300,000.
Contact: Cate Roberts, Director of Community Affairs; (401) 457-3172; (401) 457-2225
Internet: http://www.textron.com/about/commitment/corp_giving/apply_for_grant.jsp
Sponsor: Textron Charitable Trust
40 Westminster Street
Providence, RI 02903

Thelma Doelger Charitable Trust Grants **1616**
The trust awards grants in the San Francisco Bay area to zoos, hospitals, and organizations supporting animal welfare and senior citizens. Grants are awarded for general purposes and to support operating budgets. There are no application deadlines. Application forms are required.
Requirements: Nonprofit organizations in the San Francisco Bay area of northern California may submit grant requests.
Restrictions: Individuals are not eligible.
Geographic Focus: California
Amount: 2,000 - 75,000 USD
Samples: San Francisco Zoo (CA)—for operating support, $100,000; Marin Humane Society (Novato, CA)—for operating support, $70,000.
Contact: D. Eugene Richard, Trustee; (650) 755-2333
Sponsor: Thelma Doelger Charitable Trust
950 Daly Boulevard, Suite 300
Daly City, CA 94015-3004

Third Wave Foundation Lela Breitbart Memorial Fund Grants **1617**
Third Wave Foundation will use this endowed fund to offer an annual grant of $3,000 in memory of Lela Breitbart to innovative organizations working on issues of reproductive justice around the country. This grant will be given to programs that are developed and led by women and transgender people between the ages of 15 and 30, with an emphasis on supporting and strengthening young women, transgender youth and their allies working for gender, racial, social, and economic justice.
Requirements: Applicant organizations and/or programs must be based in the United States.
Geographic Focus: All U.S. States
Amount: 3,000 USD
Contact: Program Director; (212) 228-8311; (212) 780-9181; info@thirdwavefoundation.org
Internet: http://www.thirdwavefoundation.org/grant-making/breitbart
Sponsor: Third Wave Foundation
25 East 21st Street
New York, NY 10010

Third Wave Foundation Organizing and Advocacy Grants **1618**
Third Wave is a feminist, activist foundation that works nationally to support young women and transgender youth ages 15 to 30. Through strategic grantmaking, leadership development, and philanthropic advocacy, it supports groups and individuals working towards gender, racial, economic, and social justice. The Organizing and Advocacy (O&A) Fund supports work that challenges sexism, racism, homophobia, transphobia, economic injustice, and other forms of oppression in interesting ways. Grants are provided for both specific projects and general operating support.
Requirements: Applicant organizations and/or programs must be based in the United States.
Geographic Focus: All U.S. States
Date(s) Application is Due: Apr 1; Oct 1
Amount: 1,000 - 10,000 USD
Contact: Monique Mehta, Executive Director; (212) 228-8311; (212) 780-9181; info@thirdwavefoundation.org
Internet: http://www.thirdwavefoundation.org/grant-making/organizing-and-advocacy
Sponsor: Third Wave Foundation
25 East 21st Street
New York, NY 10010

Third Wave Foundation Reproductive Health and Justice Grants **1619**
The foundation supports work, organizing, and activism that exists to challenge sexism, racism, homophobia, economic injustice, and other forms of oppression. The Reproductive Health and Justice Initiative is grounded in the view that reproductive rights are a fundamental human right, and that these rights cannot be fully expressed or enjoyed unless people have access to the means to fulfill them. The initiative works to help build solidarity and movement between young people, particularly young women of color and transgender youth, who have been overlooked, unheard, or tokenized within the larger movement. Proposed projects should benefit, focus on, and be developed and led by women between the ages of 15 and 30, with an emphasis on low-income women, differently abled women, women of color, and lesbian and bisexual women. Grants are made for project support and for general operating support. One grant proposal per organization will be accepted each year.
Requirements: Applicants and/or programs must be based in the United States.
Geographic Focus: All U.S. States
Date(s) Application is Due: Apr 1; Oct 1
Amount: 1,000 - 10,000 USD
Contact: Monique Mehta, Executive Director; (212) 228-8311; (212) 780-9181; info@thirdwavefoundation.org
Internet: http://www.thirdwavefoundation.org/grant-making/reproductive-health-and-justice
Sponsor: Third Wave Foundation
25 East 21st Street
New York, NY 10010

Thomas and Agnes Carvel Foundation Grants **1620**
This foundation awards support for general charitable purposes as well as for nutrition research and youth programs to nonprofit organizations in the tri-state area comprising New York, New Jersey, and Connecticut. Types of support include general operations grants, capital grants, grants in aid, program/project grants, matching gifts, and research grants. Application should be by letter and should outline the project, budget, and staffing of the project for which funding is being requested.
Requirements: IRS 501(c)3 organizations in New York, New Jersey, and Connecticut are eligible.
Restrictions: Grants are not made to individuals.
Geographic Focus: Connecticut, New Jersey, New York
Date(s) Application is Due: Oct 1
Amount: 2,000 - 200,000 USD
Samples: Seton Hall (South Orange, NJ)—to provide full scholarships to 10 high-school students from Newark, NJ, who commit to a year of volunteer service in Newark upon graduation, $50,000.
Contact: Ann McHugh, Vice President; (914) 793-7300
Sponsor: Thomas and Agnes Carvel Foundation
35 E Grassy Sprain Road
Yonkers, NY 10710

Thomas and Dorothy Leavey Foundation Grants **1621**
Thomas Leavey and partner John C. Tyler began the Farmer's Insurance Company in 1928. The foundation was begun in 1952 by Leavey and his wife, Dorothy. Thomas Leavey died in 1980 and Dorothy actively led the foundation until her death in 1998. Giving primarily in southern California, the Foundation offers support for: hospitals, medical research, higher and secondary education, Catholic church groups; and provides scholarships to children of employees of Farmers Group.
Requirements: The foundation gives primarily in southern California.
Geographic Focus: California
Amount: 10,000 - 2,000,000 USD
Samples: Childrens Museum of Los Angeles, Lake View Terrace, CA, $250,000; Santa Clara University, Santa Clara, CA, $2,000,000; Orthopaedic Hospital, Los Angeles, CA, $100,000.
Contact: Kathleen Leavey McCarthy, Chair; (310) 551-9936
Sponsor: Thomas and Dorothy Leavey Foundation
10100 Santa Monica Boulevard, Suite 610
Los Angeles, CA 90067-4110

Thomas Austin Finch, Sr. Foundation Grants **1622**
The purpose of the Finch Foundation is the improvement of the mental, moral and physical well-being of the inhabitants of Thomasville, North Carolina, with emphasis on improving education, improving health related facilities and attracting new business to the community. However, grants are made for a wide

variety of charitable causes throughout the greater Thomasville area. In general, grants are awarded for seed money, matching funds and general purposes. Primary consideration is given to projects of a non-recurring nature or to start up funding of limited duration. The foundation meets twice a year to review grant requests. Requests must be submitted by February 15th for the Spring Meeting and October 15th for the Fall Meeting. Application forms are available online. Applicants will receive notice acknowledging receipt of the grant request, and subsequently be notified of the grant declination or approval.
Requirements: Eligible applicants are IRS 501(c)3 non-profit organizations located within the corporate limits of the City of Thomasville, North Carolina or, organizations where the benefits of the grant will inure primarily to the residents of Thomasville. Proposals should be submitted in the following format: completed Common Grant Application Form; an original Proposal Statement; an audited financial report and a current year operating budget; a copy of your official IRS Letter with your tax determination; a listing of your Board of Directors. Proposal Statements (second item in the above Format) should answer these questions: what are the objectives and expected outcomes of this program/project/request; what strategies will be used to accomplish your objective; what is the timeline for completion; if this is part of an on-going program, how long has it been in operation; what criteria will you use to measure success; if the request is not fully funded, what other sources can you engage; an Itemized budget should be included; please describe any collaborative ventures. Prior to the distribution of funds, all approved grantees must sign and return a Grant Agreement Form, stating that the funds will be used for the purpose intended. Progress reports and Completion reports must also be filed as required for your specific grant. All current grantees must be in good standing with required documentation prior to submitting new proposals to any foundation.
Restrictions: Grants are generally not made for typical operational or maintenance-oriented purposes, political purposes, nor to organizations which discriminate on the basis of race, ethnic origin, sexual or religious preference, age or gender.
Geographic Focus: North Carolina
Date(s) Application is Due: Feb 15; Oct 15
Amount: 1,500 - 100,000 USD
Samples: Memorial United Methodist Church, $30,000—general operating funds; Hospice of Davidson County, Inc., $60,000—construction of inpatient facility; Thomasville City Schools, $24,400—active classroom project.
Contact: Wachovia Bank, N.A., Trustee; grantinquiries6@wachovia.com
Sponsor: Thomas Austin Finch, Sr. Foundation
Wachovia Bank, NC6732, 100 North Main Street
Winston Salem, NC 27150

Thomas B. and Elizabeth M. Sheridan Foundation Grants **1623**
The foundation awards grants to Maryland nonprofits in support of arts and culture and private secondary education. Types of support include general operating support, continuing support, annual campaigns, capital campaigns, building construction and renovation, equipment acquisition, endowment funds, program development, scholarship funds, and matching funds. Contact the office for application forms. There are no application deadlines. The board meets in March, June, September, and December.
Requirements: Nonprofit organizations in the greater Baltimore, MD, area are eligible.
Restrictions: Grants are not awarded to individuals, for employee matching gifts, or for loans.
Geographic Focus: Maryland
Amount: 500 - 126,000 USD
Samples: Notre Dame Preparatory School (Towson, MD)—to renovate its biology, chemistry, and physics laboratories, as part of its capital campaign, $50,000; Baltimore Symphony Orchestra (Baltimore, MD)—$126,000; Gilman School (Baltimore, MD)—$103,000; Contemporary Museum (Baltimore, MD)—$10,000.
Contact: James Sinclair, President; (410) 771-0475
Sponsor: Thomas B. and Elizabeth M. Sheridan Foundation
11350 McCormick Road, Executive Plaza II, Suite 704
Hunt Valley, MD 21031

Thomas C. Ackerman Foundation Grants **1624**
The foundation awards grants to California nonprofits in its areas of interest, including arts and culture, community development, education, and health and human services. Types of support include general operating support, emergency grants, seed grants, scholarship funds, and matching grants. Contact the office for application forms. Deadlines listed are for letters of intent. Annual deadline dates may vary; contact program staff for exact dates.
Requirements: California nonprofits, primarily in San Diego County, are eligible.
Restrictions: The foundation does not award grants to religious organizations for religious purposes; individuals; or for brick-and-mortar projects, conferences, symposia, or human medical or biological research.
Geographic Focus: California
Date(s) Application is Due: Jan 31; Apr 29; Jul 29; Oct 31
Amount: 300 - 25,000 USD
Samples: San Diego Senior Olympics (San Diego, CA)—for Website Online Registration Development, $3500; San ElderHelp of San Diego (San Diego, CA)—for Shared Housing Program, $10,000; Museum of Contemporary Art (San Diego, CA)—for the program Off Broadway: Emerging Artists in Downtown San Diego, $7500.
Contact: Program Contact; (619) 699-5411; (619) 232-8311; Info@AckermanFoundation.org or pgarcia@luce.com
Internet: http://www.ackermanfoundation.org
Sponsor: Thomas C. Ackerman Foundation
600 W Broadway, Suite 2600
San Diego, CA 92101-3391

Thomas Sill Foundation Grants **1625**
The foundation provides encouragement and financial support to qualifying Manitoba organizations that strive to improve the quality of life in the province. Areas of interest include the performing and visual arts, historic preservation and historic sites, museums and libraries, adult and continuing education, literacy, universities, health, the environment, social sciences, community legal issues, special education, children and abused women, the visually and hearing disabled, physically disabled children, the mentally and learning disabled, sheltered workshops, and camps and day care programs. Funding priority is capital grants, pilot projects, and demonstration projects. Operating grants are rarely issued, and when awarded are usually for start-up purposes. Decisions are made monthly. Application forms and guidelines are available upon request.
Requirements: Charitable organizations may apply for grant support.
Geographic Focus: All U.S. States, Canada
Amount: 1,000 - 50,000 CAD
Samples: Misericordia General Hospital Foundation (Winnipeg, Manitoba)—for computer software, $C13,000; Gifts for Kids (Manitoba)—for Christmas gifts for needy children in remote locations, $C5000; Manitoba Theatre Centre (Manitoba)—for a new lighting system, $C10,000.
Contact: Program Contact; (204) 947-3782; (204) 956-4702
Internet: http://www.thomassillfoundation.com
Sponsor: Thomas Sill Foundation
600-175 Hargrave Street
Winnipeg, MB R3C 3R8 Canada

Thomas Thompson Trust Grants **1626**
The Thompson Trust limits its distribution of funds to organizations located in Windham County, Vermont, (primarily the Town of Brattleboro) or in Dutchess County, New York (primarily the Town of Rhinebeck) which predominately serve residents located in those areas. The Will of Thomas Thompson was executed in 1867 and defined his charitable purposes rather narrowly as was the practice with 19th Century philanthropy. By successive court decrees in the 20th Century, the Trustees are now authorized to make grants to charitable organizations whose work and purposes promote health, education or the general social or civic betterment in the stated geographical areas; but the Trustees will continue to place particular emphasis on healthcare and other social services. The Trustees generally meet on the fourth Thursday in January, April, July and October. Applications are due by the first day of the month of the meeting.
Requirements: Organizations must have operated for three consecutive years before applying and be located in Windham County, VT, with preference given to Brattleboro; or Duchess County, New York, with preference given to Rhinebeck.
Restrictions: Grants are not made for general operating support, seed money, endowment purposes, or loans.
Geographic Focus: New York, Vermont
Date(s) Application is Due: Jan 1; Apr 1; Jul 1; Oct 1
Amount: 1,000 - 20,000 USD
Contact: Susan T. Monahan, Program Contact; (617) 951-1108; (617) 542-7437; smonahan@rackemann.com

Internet: http://www.cybergrants.com/thompson/grant.html
Sponsor: Thomas Thompson Trust
160 Federal Street, 13th Floor
Boston, MA 02110-1700

Thomas W. Briggs Foundation Grants **1627**
The Foundation provides gifts that help serve the needs of thousands in the Memphis area. The focus of the funding includes youth projects and programs, education, social services, arts and cultural organizations and civic organizations that promote quality of life. Although some grants are multi-year pledges, many fall in the one-year $5,000 to $25,000 range.
Requirements: Applicants are asked to submit a proposal letter of not more than two pages, giving a brief history of the organization, stating goals and services provided and a list of present sources of funding. Tennessee nonprofit organizations are eligible to apply.
Restrictions: The Foundation does not support public and private schools, churches and synagogues, nationally affiliated organizations and seminars as well as special events. New applicants are required to set up an appointment before applying for a grant.
Geographic Focus: Tennessee
Date(s) Application is Due: Feb 1; Aug 1
Amount: 5,000 - 25,000 USD
Samples: Agape, Nashville, TN, $10,000—program support (2008); Fire Museum of Memphis, Memphis, TN, $10,000—program support (2008); Memphis Literacy Council, Memphis, TN, $10,000—program support (2008).
Contact: Joanne Tilley, Executive Director; (901) 680-0276; (901) 767-1135
Internet: http://www.thomaswbriggsfoundation.com/funding.html
Sponsor: Thomas W. Briggs Foundation
6075 Poplar Avenue, Suite 330
Memphis, TN 38119

Thompson Charitable Foundation Grants **1628**
Established in 1987, the Foundation supports organizations involved with education, Christian organizations, Autism research, health, human services, youth, including funding for capital and building improvements for human service organizations and educational institutions. Giving is limited to Bell, Clay, Laurel, and Leslie counties, Kentucky; Anderson, Blount, Knox, and Scott counties, Tennessee; and Buchanan and Tazewell counties, Virginia.
Requirements: Nonprofits operating in Bell, Clay, Laurel, and Leslie counties, Kentucky; Anderson, Blount, Knox, and Scott counties, Tennessee; and Buchanan and Tazewell counties, Virginia are eligible to apply. Initial contact should be a letter, no more then 2 pages long. The letter should include: a statement of the problem, the project will address; a detailed description of project, and amount of funding requested.
Restrictions: No support for religious or political organizations, budget deficits or endowments.
Geographic Focus: Kentucky, Tennessee, Virginia
Date(s) Application is Due: Mar 31; Sep 1
Amount: 2,000 - 500,000 USD
Contact: Debbie Black, Executive Director; (865) 588-0491; (865) 588-4496; debbie@cf.org
Sponsor: Thompson Charitable Foundation
800 South Gay Street, Suite 2021
Knoxville, TN 37929-9710

Thompson Foundation Grants **1629**
With $3,500 in savings, Bob and Ellen Thompson - along with Thompson's uncle, Wilford McCully - started the Thompson-McCully Company, a contract road paving company, in 1959. The Thompson Foundation's mission is to help low-income people rise out of poverty and become self-sufficient. The foundation awards grants to eligible Michigan nonprofit organizations that support economically disadvantaged residents and help them rise out of poverty. Types of support include emergency funds, general operating grants, program development, scholarship funds, and seed grants. There are no application forms. The board meets in February, April, June, August, October, and December.
Requirements: Although the Foundation serves a seven-county region (Wayne, Oakland, Macomb, Street Clair, Livingston, Washtenaw, and Monroe), the vast majority of its funds are used to serve those who live in Detroit, Highland Park and Hamtramck.
Geographic Focus: Michigan
Contact: John Ziraldo, Executive Director; (734) 453-6412; (734) 453-6475; cebejer@thompsonfdn.org
Internet: http://www.thompsonfdn.org/
Sponsor: Thompson Foundation
P.O. Box 6349
Plymouth, MI 48170

Thornton Foundation Grants **1630**
The foundation awards grants to Calilfornia nonprofit organizations in its areas of interest, including arts/ and culture and higher/secondary education. Types of support include annual campaigns, building construction/renovation, continuing support, endowment funds, and research. There are no application deadlines.
Requirements: California nonprofit organizations are eligible.
Geographic Focus: California
Amount: 1,000 - 200,000 USD
Contact: Charles Thornton Jr., President; (213) 629-3867
Sponsor: Thornton Foundation
523 W Sixth Street, Suite 636
Los Angeles, CA 90014

Three Guineas Fund Grants **1631**
In 2009, Three Guineas Fund restructured as a private foundation. The fund makes grants in education and the environment consistent with the foundation's bylaws, while keeping its core commitment to women and girls. Currently, the fund welcomes projects that create access to opportunity for women and girls, especially in education and the economy. Grantmaking includes projects that advance and support girls and women in the areas of entrepreneurship; science, math, and technology; leadership; sports; access to education and the economy; and dissemination and distribution of strategies, research, or documentation of women's and girls' issues. Types of support include start-up projects and general operating grants for established programs. The fund is open to multi-year grants. Submit a letter of inquiry; full proposals are by request only.
Requirements: 501(c)3 tax-exempt organizations and organizations with a fiscal agent with that status are eligible.
Restrictions: The fund does not make grants to support direct service projects, unless they are of strategic interest as potentially scalable models; scholarship programs; film production; fundraising events; conferences; or individuals.
Geographic Focus: All U.S. States
Date(s) Application is Due: Jun 15
Contact: Grants Administrator; (415) 348-1581; (415) 348-1584; info@3gf.org
Internet: http://www.3gf.org/index.html
Sponsor: Three Guineas Fund
153 Upper Terrace
San Francisco, CA 94117

Threshold Foundation Grants **1632**
The foundation serves the social-change movement through collaborating with and funding innovative American and international nonprofit organizations and individuals working toward social justice, environmental sustainability, humane economic systems, and peaceful coexistence. The foundation has three grant review committees: policy and systemic change, coexistence and community, and new visions for culture and society. Grants fund general operating expenses and special projects. Complete guidelines and forms are available online. Annual deadline dates vary; contact program staff for exact dates.
Requirements: Organizations with 501(c)3 tax exempt status are eligible. Occasionally, 501(c)4 lobbying organizations are funded.
Restrictions: Grants do not support emergency or discretionary funding.
Geographic Focus: All U.S. States
Amount: 5,000 - 25,000 USD
Samples: Lambi Fund of Haiti (Haiti)—for field support and training to small economic development project that are conceived and implemented by peasant, women's, or community associations and are designed to become self-sustaining within 18 months, $20,000; About Face Theatre Collective—general support for this collective of artists who, regardless of their sexuality, are committed to the creation of performances that examine and participate in the development of gay and lesbian lives, histories and experiences, $5000.
Contact: Foundation Administrator; tholdgrants@tides.org
Internet: http://www.thresholdfoundation.org
Sponsor: Threshold Foundation
P.O. Box 29903
San Francisco, CA 94129-0903

Tides Foundation Grants 1633

The foundation actively promotes change toward a healthy society and channels its grantmaking to the following issue areas: arts, culture and alternative media; civic participation; death penalty abolishment; drug policy reform; economic development; economic and racial justice; environmental justice; gay, lesbian, bisexual, and transgender issues; HIV/AIDS; Native communities; peace strategies; women's empowerment and reproductive health; youth development and organizing; and violence prevention. The foundation prefers to fund creative, effective solutions to problems.
Requirements: Nonprofit organizations are eligible. Preference is given to nonprofits engaged in grassroots organizing.
Restrictions: Tides does not accept requests from universities, schools, individuals, or corporations; nor for capital campaigns, endowments, or film production.
Geographic Focus: All U.S. States
Amount: 1,000 - 7,000,000 USD
Contact: Idelise Malave, Executive Director; (415) 561-6366; (415) 561-6401; imalave@tides.org
Internet: http://www.tidesfoundation.org/index_tf.cfm
Sponsor: Tides Foundation
P.O. Box 29903
San Francisco, CA 94129-0903

Times Mirror Foundation Grants 1634

The foundation makes grants to nonprofit organizations in operating communities in its areas of interest, including journalism, education, literacy, community enrichment, and art and culture. The foundation focuses its support on programs that improve the quality of journalism, education and literacy, strengthen the fabric of the community, and enhance cultural appreciation and understanding. In addition, the foundation approves grants for unrestricted operating support, capital campaigns, seed grants, and special projects. Qualified organizations seeking grant support should send a two- to three-page letter briefly describing the organization, its purpose, programs, any special project to be considered, and its governing boards. Proof of tax-exempt status, list of current supporting organizations and amount of support, an organizational budget for current and upcoming fiscal years, and a copy of the most recent financial statements should be included.
Requirements: The foundation's geographical area is restricted to Southern California (Los Angeles, Orange, Ventura, San Bernardino and Riverside counties); Stamford, Greenwich and Hartford, Connecticut; and Allentown, Pennsylvania, and Queens and Long Island, New York. An applicant organization must include evidence of 501(c)3 status when requesting funds.
Restrictions: The foundation will not consider grants for production costs of films, videos, or television programs; religious or fraternal purposes; publications; conferences; or to individuals.
Geographic Focus: California, Connecticut, New York, Pennsylvania
Date(s) Application is Due: Apr 15; Oct 15
Amount: 1,000 - 25,000 USD
Samples: Maryland African American Museum (Baltimore, MD)—for its capital campaign, $80,000; Archdiocese of Baltimore Chancery (Baltimore, MD)—for its Reading Scholars program, $25,000; Ctr for Nonprofit Management (Los Angeles, CA)—for its resource library of nonprofit-related materials, $15,000.
Contact: Michelle Williams, Executive Director; (213) 237-3945; (213) 237-2116
Internet: http://www.timesmirrorfoundation.org
Sponsor: Times Mirror Foundation
202 W First Street
Los Angeles, CA 90053

TJX Foundation Grants 1635

The primary mission of the contribution program is to help needy families and children. The foundation also supports services in communities where the companies do business that promote sound mental and physical health, provide shelter, enhance education and job readiness, and build community ties. Contributions will be made in the areas of education, social services, health, civic and community affairs, and art and culture. Types of support include continuing support, general operating support, and program development.
Requirements: IRS 501(c)3 tax-exempt organizations are eligible.
Restrictions: The foundation will not fund individuals, political organizations, publications, cash reserves, seed money/start-up projects, endowments, religious groups, public policy research, travel grants, environmental issues, education loans, international organizations, film/photography, conferences/seminars, unrestricted grants, fellowships, or advocacy.
Geographic Focus: All U.S. States
Amount: 5,000 - 25,000 USD
Contact: Christine Strickland, Foundation Manager; (508) 390-3199; (508) 390-2091; Christy_Strickland@TJX.com
Internet: http://www.tjx.com/corprespons/commsupp.html
Sponsor: TJX Foundation
770 Cochituate Road, Route 1E
Framingham, MA 01701

Topeka Community Foundation Grants 1636

The foundation awards grants to Kansas nonprofits in its areas of interest, including arts and culture, early childhood education, education, environment, substance abuse services, children and youth services, family services, community development, and public affairs. Types of support include general operating support, continuing support, annual campaigns, capital campaigns, building construction/renovation, emergency funds, program development, seed money, scholarship funds and scholarships to individuals, and matching funds. The board meets bimonthly to consider requests.
Requirements: Grants are awarded to Topeka and Shawnee County, Kansas, nonprofit organizations.
Restrictions: Grants are not awarded to religious organizations for religious purposes or for scientific, medical, or academic research.
Geographic Focus: Kansas
Contact: Roger K. Viola, President; (785) 272-4804; (785) 272-4644; viola@topekacommunityfoundation.org
Internet: http://www.topekacommunityfoundation.org/page31525.cfm
Sponsor: Topeka Community Foundation
5431 SW 29th Street, Suite 300
Topeka, KS 66614

Town Creek Foundation Grants 1637

The foundation awards grants in four general areas: preservation and enhancement of the nation's environment and the monitoring of federal, state, and local officials and bodies responsible for the enforcement of legislation enacted to protect the environment; the dissemination, via public radio and television, of news and commentary; the search for ways to secure a peaceful and democratic society, supporting projects that challenge and redirect the military economy, reduce the risk of war, and promote a government responsive and accountable to its citizens; and the improvement of the quality of life and the opportunity for advancement for the people of Talbot County, MD, where such opportunities have been adversely affected by economic and social conditions. Types of support include continuing support, operating support, program development, seed money, and matching funds. The foundation will consider proposals at any time during the year. The foundation can be reached, customarily, on Mondays and Wednesdays.
Requirements: IRS 501(c)3 tax-exempt organizations are eligible. Social service grants are limited to nonprofits in Talbot County, Maryland.
Restrictions: The Foundation does not provide grants for the following: programs or organizations outside of the United States; individuals; primary and secondary schools; colleges or universities, except when some aspect of their work is an integral part of a program supported by the Foundation; hospitals or health care institutions; ministry or religious programs; endowment, capital or building fund campaigns, or the purchase of land and/or buildings; research or scholarship programs; conferences not part of a program supported by the Foundation; publication of books and periodicals; or visual or performing arts projects.
Geographic Focus: All U.S. States
Amount: 10,000 - 250,000 USD
Samples: American Rivers, Durham, North Carolina, $50,000 - renewal of "The Chesapeake Federal Policy Project" (2011); Living on Earth / World Media Foundation, Somerville, Massachusetts, $125,000 - to produce, broadcast and distribute programming focusing on past, present and future efforts to restore the Chesapeake Bay (2011); Wicomico Environmental Trust, Salisbury, Maryland, $50,000 - general support to continue to develop into a strong, sustainable organization that will have an effective, long-term impact on increasing public awareness of and advocacy for environmental protection of the natural resources of Wicomico County (2011).
Contact: Stuart Alan Clarke, Executive Director; (410) 763-8171; (410) 763-8172; info@towncreekfdn.org or sclarke@towncreekfdn.org
Internet: http://www.towncreekfdn.org/tcfsite/tguides.html
Sponsor: Town Creek Foundation
121 N. West Street
Easton, MD 21601

Transamerica Foundation Grants 1638

The foundation will consider favorably grants to established organizations with reputations for excellence and cost-effectiveness. Particular emphasis will be given to innovative programs that address root causes and develop preventive strategies and solutions to society's problems in the areas of homelessness, affordable housing, and health and wellness, especially where the contribution will achieve positive public recognition and will stimulate others to provide long-range support. Types of support include continuing support, matching funds, operating budgets, employee-related scholarships, and special projects. Contributions are normally made on a year-to-year basis with no assurance of renewal of support. Pledges may be considered for periods not exceeding three years. Most grants will be awarded in the San Francisco Bay area.
Requirements: Nonprofit organizations are eligible.
Restrictions: The foundation will not make contributions to organizations that are exclusively religious.
Geographic Focus: All U.S. States
Amount: 1,000 - 50,000 USD
Contact: Program Director; (319) 398-8852
Internet: http://www.transamerica.com
Sponsor: AEGON Transamerica Foundation
4333 Edgewood Road, NE
Cedar Rapids, IA 52499-3210

Trinity Conference Center Meeting Spirit Grants 1639

The mission of the center, part of the Trinity Grants of Trinity Church Wall Street, is to provide a private setting where nonprofit organizations (religious or secular) and public sector institutions can retreat to do their important work. Applicants must be involved in the areas consistent with the program, such as the religion/spirituality, education, family services, environment, or the arts. Applications are available on the website.
Requirements: 501(c)3 nonprofit organizations are eligible.
Geographic Focus: All U.S. States
Contact: Jon Denn; (860) 672-1000; (860) 672-6968; triconfcen@aol.com
Internet: http://www.trinitywallstreet.org/center/sgrants/index.html
Sponsor: Trinity Conference Center
79 Lower River Road
West Cornwall, CT 06796

Turner B. Bunn, Jr. and Catherine E. Bunn Foundation Grants 1640

The Foundation, established in North Carolina in 2000, gives primarily to children and youth services, Christian agencies and churches, educational programs, and human services supporting residents of North Carolina. An application form is not required, and applicants should submit the following: brief history of organization and description of its mission; copy of IRS Determination Letter; and a detailed description of project and amount of funding requested. There are no annual deadlines, and applicants should submit the entire proposal via mail.
Geographic Focus: North Carolina
Samples: Barton College Scholarship Fund, Wilson, North Carolina, $8,600 (2010); Boys and Girls Club of Coastal Carolina, Morehead City, North Carolina, $3,800 (2010); Hope Station Renovation, Wilson, North Carolina
Contact: Turner B. Bunn III, Director; (252) 243-3136; (252) 243-8293; tbb3@nc.rr.com
Sponsor: Turner B. Bunn, Jr. and Catherine E. Bunn Foundation
P.O. Box 3299
Wilson, NC 27895-3299

TWS Foundation Grants 1641

The foundation awards grants to eligible nonprofit organizations in its areas of interest, including community development, arts, health care, public policy, research, and human services. Types of support include general operating support and scholarship funds. There are no application forms or deadlines.
Requirements: Nonprofit organizations, primarily in Connecticut, New York, Rhode Island, and Texas, are eligible.
Geographic Focus: Connecticut, New York, Rhode Island, Texas
Amount: 100 - 230,000 USD
Samples: National Center for Policy Analysis (Dallas, TX)—$200,000; Westerly Hospital Foundation (Westerly, RI)—$100,000; Philharmonic-Symphony Society of New York (New York, NY)—$10,000.
Contact: Thomas Smith, Trustee
Sponsor: TWS Foundation
323 Railroad Avenue
Greenwich, CT 06830-6306

Tyco Electronics Foundation Grants 1642

The foundation provides grants to nonprofit organizations in geographic areas where Tyco Electronics Corp has a significant employee population and for specific projects or programs in broad categories, including education (with an emphasis on math and science), community impact, and arts and culture. In addition to a matching gifts program for employee contributions to accredited high schools, colleges, and universities, the foundation makes direct grants for programs that address a business or community concern of Tyco Electronics. Organizations that support precollege math and science education receive special attention. Agencies that promote personal growth, career opportunities, and economic self-sufficiency are encouraged to apply, as are local chapters of health- and civic-related organizations. Local United Way chapters benefit from donations that have a correlation to the level of employee giving. Organizations working to conserve or improve the environment through education may also receive funds. Special attention is given to communitywide arts organizations that solicit and allocate funds for a number of arts groups and institutions. Local public television and radio stations are encouraged to apply for funding of specific education initiatives. Capital campaigns of significant arts and cultural organizations serving communities in which the corporation has a major presence also will receive consideration. Grants also are awarded to support general operations, program development, and employee matching gifts. Applications are accepted throughout the year but are considered on the listed application deadlines.
Requirements: Organizations receiving funding must have IRS tax-exempt status and be located in company-operating areas (Roanoke, VA; the Triangle area of North Carolina; Rock Hill, SC; and central Pennsylvania).
Restrictions: The foundation generally will not support organizations in geographic areas where Tyco Electronics has few or no employees; individuals, private foundations, national organizations, or service clubs; fraternal, social, labor, or veterans organizations; organizations that discriminate on the basis of race, religion, color, national origin, physical or mental conditions, veteran or marital status, age, or sex; churches or religious organizations in general; political campaigns; general operating needs of United Way agencies; loans or investments; or programs that pose a potential conflict of interest.
Geographic Focus: California, Massachusetts, Michigan, North Carolina, Pennsylvania, South Carolina, Texas, Virginia
Date(s) Application is Due: Mar 15; Jun 15; Sep 15; Dec 15
Amount: 250 - 25,000 USD
Contact: Mary Rakoczy, (717) 592-4869; (717) 592-4022; mjrakocz@tycoelectronics.com
Internet: http://www.tycoelectronics.com/about/foundation/vision.stm
Sponsor: Tyco Electronics Foundation
P.O. Box 3608, MS 140-10
Harrisburg, PA 17105-3608

U.S. Department of Education American Overseas Research Centers 1643

This program provides grants to establish or operate overseas research centers that promote postgraduate research, exchanges, and area studies. Grants may be used to pay for all or a portion of the cost of establishing or operating a center or program. Costs may include faculty and staff stipends and salaries; faculty, staff, and student travel; operation and maintenance of overseas facilities; teaching and research materials; the acquisition, maintenance, and preservation of library collections; travel for visiting scholars and faculty members who are teaching or conducting research; preparation for and management of conferences; and the publication and dissemination of material for the scholars and general public.
Requirements: Eligible Applicants are Consortia of institutions of higher education that: receive more than 50 percent of their funding from public or private U.S. sources; have a permanent presence in the country in which the center is located; and, are tax-exempt nonprofit organizations described in Section 501(c)3 of the Internal Revenue Code. *Geographic Focus:* All U.S. States
Date(s) Application is Due: Mar 15
Amount: 80,000 - 100,000 USD
Samples: FY 2007 - FY 2010: American Institute for Sri Lankan Studies, $60,511; American Research Center in Egypt, $72,582; American School of Classical Studies at Athens, $91,598; Center for Khmer Studies, $82,909; American Institute for Maghrib Studies, $109,406; American Institute of Indian Studies, $109,650; American Research Center in Turkey, $109,406; West Africa Research Association, $106,195; Palestinian American Research Center, $88,181; American Institute of Pakistan Studies, $63,893; American Center for Mongolian Studies, $105,669.

Contact: Cheryl Gibbs, (202) 502-7634; (202) 502-7859; cheryl.gibbs@ed.gov
Internet: http://www.ed.gov/programs/iegpsaorc/index.html
Sponsor: U.S. Department of Education
1990 K Street NW, 6th Floor
Washington, DC 20006-8521

Unilever U.S. Grants **1644**
The foundation awards grants to nonprofit organizations nationwide in company-operating locations in the areas of civic affairs, education, environment, health care, and social services. Capital grants are awarded only to hospitals in plant communities. Types of support include general operating grants and matching gifts. Applicants must submit a written proposal; proposals are accepted throughout the year.
Requirements: 501(c)3 nonprofit organizations in company-operating areas are eligible to apply.
Restrictions: Grants do not support religious, labor, political, or veterans' organizations; individuals (except for employee-related scholarships); goodwill advertising, fundraising events, or capital campaigns; or loans.
Geographic Focus: All U.S. States
Amount: 500 - 200,000 USD
Samples: National Park Foundation (Washington, DC)—for the National Parks Junior Ranger Program and recreation, recycling, and volunteer programs, $22 million value in grants and noncash donations over four years.
Contact: Grants Administrator; (212) 894-2236; (212) 318-3600
Internet: http://www.unilever.com
Sponsor: Unilever United States Foundation
700 Sylvan Avenue
Englewood Cliffs, NJ 07632

Union Bank of California Foundation Grants **1645**
The foundation supports nonprofit organizations in company-operating locations to improve the quality of life for residents and employees. Areas of support include community economic development; health and social services; housing; preschool, elementary, secondary, and higher education; culture and performing arts; and disadvantaged and homeless youth and minorities. Grants are awarded for general purposes, operating budgets, continuing support, annual campaigns, emergency funds, building funds, equipment, and employee matching gifts. There are no application deadlines. The board meets monthly.
Requirements: Nonprofits in company-operating areas are eligible, including San Diego, San Francisco, Los Angeles, Anaheim, Berkeley, Del Mar, Fresno, Irvine, Mission Grove, Pasadena, Sacramento, Salinas, San Jose, Santa Ana, and Torrance, CA.
Restrictions: The foundation does not support individuals, political groups, organizations receiving a majority of funding from United Way, or groups with limited membership. Grants do not support advertising.
Geographic Focus: California
Amount: 5,000 - 25,000 USD
Samples: U of the Pacific (Stockton, CA)—to purchase books and teaching materials on Japanese-American relations, $21,000; American Red Cross-San Diego/Imperial Counties Chapter (San Diego, CA)—for relief efforts related to the recent widespread wildfires in California, $75,000; Eden Housing (Hayward, CA)—for summer youth-enrichment programs at low-cost housing complexes in the San Francisco Bay area, $20,000.
Contact: Grants Administrator; (619) 230-4501
Internet: http://www.uboc.com/about/main/0,,2485_3457,00.html
Sponsor: Union Bank of California Foundation
530 B Street, S-650
San Diego, CA 92101

Union Carbide Foundation Grants **1646**
The foundation supports nonprofits in areas of company operations, including Danbury, CT; Kanawha Valley, WV; central New Jersey; Taft, LA; and Texas City and Seadrift, TX. Grants also are awarded outside of the United States. The majority of grant supports goes for restructuring elementary and secondary education: developing math and science programs, advancing technology through research, preparing women and minorities for technical careers, and environmental protection. Additional areas of consideration include health and social services, civic affairs, the environment, and higher education. Grants are awarded for general operations, emergency funds, in-kind gifts, and programs/projects. The board meets in the spring and fall to consider grant proposals.
Requirements: Nonprofits in company-operating areas in Connecticut, West Virginia, New Jersey, Louisiana, and Texas may apply.
Geographic Focus: Connecticut, Louisiana, New Jersey, Texas, West Virginia
Amount: 5,000 - 45,000 USD
Contact: Grants Administrator; (203) 794-2000
Internet: http://www.dow.com/facilities/namerica/texops/community/grants.htm
Sponsor: Union Carbide Foundation
39 Old Ridgebury Road, L-4
Danbury, CT 06817-0001

Union Pacific Foundation Grants **1647**
The foundation has a strong interest in promoting organizational effectiveness among nonprofits. To that end, this foundation dedicates the majority of their grants to help nonprofit organizations build their capacity, increase their impact, and operate more efficiently and effectively. Grants are made primarily to proposals that fall within three categories: community and civic, fine arts, and health and human services. The community and civic category focuses on assisting community-based organizations and related activities that improve and enrich the general quality of life in the community. This category includes organizations such as aquariums, botanical gardens, children's museums, history/science museums, public libraries, public television and radio, and zoos. The fine arts category seeks to create a wider opportunity for the enjoyment of and participation in the visual and performing arts. A limited amount of funding is available for this category. Preference will be given to those organizations with whom the foundation has an established relationship. The health and human services category assists organizations dedicated to improving the level of health care or providing human services in the community. Types of support include general operating support, continuing support, capital campaigns, building construction/renovation, curriculum development, equipment acquisition, program development, and matching funds.
Requirements: The foundation will accept only online applications; printed copies of the application are not available and will not be accepted. Grants are made to institutions located in communities served by Union Pacific Corporation and its operating company Union Pacific Railroad Company.
Restrictions: Grants will not be given to organizations that are not tax-exempt; specialized national health organizations; political organizations; organizations engaged in influencing legislation; religious organizations that are sectarian or denominational in purpose; veterans organizations; labor groups, social clubs, fraternal organizations, or individuals. United Way-affiliated organizations may apply only for capital projects that have received written approval from United Way.
Geographic Focus: All U.S. States
Date(s) Application is Due: Aug 15
Amount: 5,000 - 10,000 USD
Contact: Union Pacific Foundation; (402) 271-5600; (402) 271-5477; upf@up.com
Internet: http://www.up.com/found/grants.shtml
Sponsor: Union Pacific Corporation
1400 Douglas Street, Stop 1560
Omaha, NE 68179

United Airlines Foundation Education Grants **1648**
The foundation's primary mission is to help elementary, middle, and high school students prepare for challenging and rewarding careers. The foundation invites proposals year-round for projects that enhance education opportunities beyond the classroom, including programs involving museums and other cultural entities. Other major education focus areas include mentoring and tutoring; and adopt-a-school and school-to-work programs, which support students via job shadowing, mentoring, internships, and apprenticeships. Cultural and civic institutions receive consideration for funding of programs with a school outreach component. Grants support specific projects, annual campaigns, general operating budgets, research grants, employee-related scholarships, and employee matching gifts. The board meets in March, June, September, and December. Applicants should call for availability and deadlines.
Requirements: Nonprofits and school districts in Boston, MA; Chicago, IL; Denver, CO; Los Angeles and San Francisco, CA; New York, NY; Miami, FL; and Seattle, WA are eligible.
Restrictions: The foundation does not support capital grants, in-kind donations, or development campaigns.
Geographic Focus: California, Colorado, Florida, Illinois, Massachusetts, New York, Washington
Amount: 1,000 - 50,000 USD

Contact: Grants Administrator; (708) 700-7345; uafoundation@ual.com
Internet: http://www.united.com/page/article/0,,1367,00.html
Sponsor: United Airlines Foundation
P.O. Box 66100
Chicago, IL 60666

Until There's a Cure Foundation Grants **1649**

The foundation supports HIV/AIDS organizations throughout the United States. Grants focus on four priorities: care and services to meet the immediate needs of people living with HIV/AIDS, prevention education, vaccine development and research, and policy development and research. Types of support include capital campaigns, equipment acquisition, program development, and general operating support.
Requirements: 501(c)3 nonprofit U.S. organizations are eligible for grant support.
Restrictions: The foundation does not make grants for: for walk-a-thons, tournaments, or special events; to organizations with religious affiliations, unless the program is open to the entire community without regard to religious beliefs; for costs already incurred by an organization; or to fund general administration expenses of an organization rather than for specific projects and programs
Geographic Focus: All U.S. States
Date(s) Application is Due: Apr 29
Amount: 1,000 - 40,000 USD
Samples: AIDS Service Agency of North Carolina (NC)—$9000; AIDS Task Force Greater Cleveland (Cleveland, OH)—$41,818; AIDS Walk Atlanta (Atlanta, GA)—$15,000; Wisconsin AIDS Fund (WI)—$40,000.
Contact: Grants Administrator; (800) 888-6845 or (650) 332-3200; (650) 332-3210; grants@utac.org
Internet: http://www.utac.org
Sponsor: Until There's a Cure Foundation
560 Mountain Home Road
Redwood City, CA 94062

UPS Foundation Nonprofit Effectiveness Grants **1650**

Since the launch of its Volunteer Impact Initiative in 1999, the UPS Foundation has focused on helping nonprofit organizations operate more effectively and efficiently. Widely regarded as a well-run company, UPS provides non-profits a variety of management and operational expertise in areas such as human resources management, technology, and other knowledge resources. This provides a robust hands on component that supports the foundation's philanthropy. It's the perfect example of taking the core assets of the corporation and applying them in a way that helps the independent sector address society's many challenges. Most nonprofit agencies face daunting tasks in raising funds, analyzing needs, managing volunteers and measuring results. With its employees and families volunteering more than 1.2 million hours of their time each year, UPS understands these challenges first hand. Helping nonprofit agencies more effectively manage them can further the impact of the services they provide to local communities. The UPS Foundation is currently focusing its resources on such areas as volunteer management, leadership development, social enterprise, and capacity building through new technology.
Requirements: IRS 501(c)3 tax-exempt organizations are eligible to apply.
Restrictions: The foundation does not award grants to individuals, religious organizations or theological functions, or church-sponsored programs limited to church members. Grants supporting capital campaigns, endowments, or operating expenses are seldom approved.
Geographic Focus: All U.S. States
Amount: 1,000 - 200,000 USD
Contact: Ken Sternad, President; (404) 828-6374; (404) 828-7435
Internet: http://responsibility.ups.com/UPS+Foundation/Focus+On+Giving/Nonprofit+Effectiveness
Sponsor: United Parcel Service (UPS) Foundation
55 Glenlake Parkway NE
Atlanta, GA 30328

U.S. Bank Foundation Grants **1651**

The foundation seeks to build strong partnerships and lasting value in operating communities by supporting organizations that improve the educational and economic opportunities of low- and moderate-income individuals and families; and enhance the cultural and artistic life of the communities in which employees live and work. Areas of support include human services; economic opportunity and neighborhood housing development; elementary and secondary education; and arts and culture. Types of support include general operating budgets, capital support, equipment acquisition, employee matching gifts, employee-related scholarships, special projects, renovation projects, and matching funds. Application deadlines vary by state. Guidelines are available online.
Requirements: Nonprofit organizations in company-operating locations are eligible, including Colorado, Illinois, Iowa, Kansas, Minnesota, Montana, Nebraska, North Dakota, South Dakota, Wisconsin, and Wyoming.
Restrictions: The foundation does not award grants to fraternal organizations, merchant associations, chamber memberships or programs, or 501(c)(4) or (6) organizations; fundraising events or sponsorships; private foundations; organizations outside U.S. Bancorp communities; programs operated by religious organizations for religious purposes; political organizations; individuals; travel and related expenses; endowment campaigns; deficit reduction; or organizations receiving primary funding from United Way.
Geographic Focus: Colorado, Illinois, Iowa, Kansas, Minnesota, Montana, Nebraska, North Dakota, South Dakota, Wisconsin, Wyoming
Contact: Teresa Bonner, Charitable Giving; (612) 303-0737
Internet: http://www.usbank.com/cgi_w/cfm/about/community_relations/charit_giving.cfm
Sponsor: U.S. Bank Foundation
800 Nicollet Mall, 23rd Floor
Minneapolis, MN 55402

U.S. G Foundation Grants **1652**

The foundation supports nonprofits in company-operating areas in the categories of arts/culture, higher education, hospitals and health care, social welfare, youth agencies, federated giving, public policy research, and government/public administration. Types of support include general operating support, continuing support, annual campaigns, capital campaigns, building construction/renovation, equipment acquisition, scholarship funds, research, technical assistance, employee matching gifts and employee-related scholarships, and matching grants. There are no required application forms or deadlines. The board meets quarterly to consider requests. Giving primarily in areas of company operations.
Restrictions: Grants are not made to individuals.
Geographic Focus: All U.S. States
Amount: 1,000 - 40,000 USD
Samples: Child Welfare League of America (Washington, DC)—to conduct the Positive Parenting for Homeless Families of Young Children program, $100,000.
Contact: Harold Pendexter, Program Contact; (312) 606-4297; (312) 606-5316
Sponsor: U.S. G Foundation
125 S Franklin Street
Chicago, IL 60606

U.S. Trust Corporation Foundation Grants **1653**

The foundation supports worthy, nonprofit organizations in the communities in which U.S. Trust does business. Funded organizations include cultural and arts institutions and community services organizations that assist low-to moderate-income residents. The corporate contributions committee reviews proposals continuously throughout the year, and meets formally twice per year to award grants. Types of support include general operating support, continuing support, annual campaigns, capital campaigns, building construction/renovation, endowment funds, program development, and matching funds. Preference is given to organizations that demonstrate an ability to solve problems and provide direct services, innovative programs with broad-based community support and community development impact, organizations in which U.S. Trust employees are active, privately supported rather than tax-supported organizations, and programs that encourage self-sufficiency of participants. Proposals are reviewed year round. Proposal deadlines are March 1 for culture and arts grants and September 1 for community services grants.
Requirements: Grant giving is concentrated in the communities in which U.S. Trust does business, and is directed to 501(c)3 nonprofit organizations.
Restrictions: Grants are not made to individuals for education or other purposes; educational, religious, veterans, fraternal, or labor organizations unless engaged in a significant project benefiting the entire community; organizations, projects, or programs outside the United States; political organizations or candidates; organizations requesting support for advertising; organizations supported by umbrella organizations; or organizations with operating budgets of $150,000 or less.
Geographic Focus: California, Connecticut, Delaware, District of Columbia, Florida, Minnesota, New Jersey, New York, North Carolina, Oregon, Pennsylvania, Texas, Virginia

Date(s) Application is Due: Mar 1; Sep 1
Amount: 10,000 - 30,000 USD
Contact: Carol Strickland, Chairman of the Corporate Contributions Committee; (212) 852-1330; (212) 852-1341; cstrickland@ustrust.com or foundation@ustrust.com
Internet: http://www.ustrust.com/public/ustrust/our_firm/community_contributions?cmsid=P-564113&lvl1=our_firm&lvl2=community_contributions
Sponsor: U.S. Trust Corporation Foundation
114 W 47th Street
New York, NY 10036

Utah Arts Council General Support Grants **1654**
These grants offer general, nonproject-oriented support to Utah's arts organizations that have already developed a full range of programming and staffs appropriate to their discipline. Support will permit organizations whose primary purpose and activities are the production and/or coordination of programs in the performing, visual, or literary arts to continue, strengthen, and expand current programs. Applicants are limited to requests of no more than 20 percent of their preceding year's actual income. Applicants for general support should not assume that this grants program will be ongoing or that funding is renewable if awarded one time.
Requirements: Established Utah arts organizations are eligible. Applicants must have a paid staff for administrative, technical, and artistic duties. Grants must be matched with at least an equal amount of cash. Applicants must submit a copy of an audit by an independent accounting firm for the preceding fiscal year.
Geographic Focus: Utah
Date(s) Application is Due: Oct 1
Contact: Sherry Waddingham, Grants Officer; (801) 236-7550 or (801) 236-7555; (801) 236-7556; swaddingham@utah.gov
Internet: http://www.arts.utah.org/grants
Sponsor: Utah Arts Council
617 E South Temple
Salt Lake City, UT 84102-1177

V.V. Cooke Foundation Grants **1655**
The foundation awards grants to nonprofits in Kentucky, with an emphasis on support of the Baptist Church and religious organizations, schools and higher education institutions, and medical education. Children and youth organizations also receive support. Types of funding include: general operating support; continuing support; annual campaigns; capital campaigns; building construction and renovation; equipment acquisition; program development; and professorships. Application deadlines are January 15, April 15, July 15, and October 15.
Requirements: Grants are awarded to nonprofit organizations in Kentucky.
Restrictions: Grants are not awarded to individuals or for general endowment funds, scholarships, fellowships, or loans.
Geographic Focus: Kentucky
Date(s) Application is Due: Jan 15; Apr 15; Jul 15; Oct 15
Amount: 100 - 50,000 USD
Samples: Campbellsville U (Campbellsville, KY), Cumberland College (Williamsburg, KY), and Georgetown College (Georgetown, KY)—to raise funds for student financial aid and for capital projects, $90,000 jointly.
Contact: Theodore L. Merhoff, Executive Director; (502) 241-0303; merhoff@bellsouth.net or cookefdn@bellsouth.net
Sponsor: V.V. Cooke Foundation
P.O. Box 202
Pewee Valley, KY 40056-0202

Valentine Foundation Grants **1656**
The foundation supports organizations and programs that empower women and girls to recognize and develop their full potential or that are making efforts to change established attitudes that discourage women and girls from realizing their potential. Grants are made to support effective fundamental change, including efforts to change attitudes, policies, and social patterns. Funding is generally split to offer equal support to programs for girls and programs for women. Programs for women must include advocacy for social change. A two-page descriptive letter must meet the listed application deadline date; if interested, the foundation will invite a full proposal.
Requirements: The foundation primarily funds nonprofits serving the greater Philadelphia area or that have a national focus.
Restrictions: The foundation will not fund scholarships, endowments, or capital.
Geographic Focus: All U.S. States
Date(s) Application is Due: Jun 30
Amount: 5,000 - 15,000 USD
Samples: Women's Campaign Internatational, Philadelphia, PA, $10,000—Global Awareness and Girl's Leadership Initiative pilot program (2009); Women Thrive, Washington, DC, $5,000—general operating (2009); Women's Way, Philadelphia, PA, $39,000—Education and Advocacy Initiative (2009).
Contact: Alexandra Frazier, Director; (610) 642-4887; (610) 642-4887; info@valentinefoundation.org
Internet: http://www.valentinefoundation.org/guidelines.html
Sponsor: Valentine Foundation
300 Quarry Lane
Haverford, PA 19041

Valley Foundation Grants **1657**
The foundation makes grants to nonprofit Santa Clara County, CA, organizations for programs and projects in the areas of medical services and health care for lower income households, the arts, seniors, and education. Types of support include research, general operating budgets, endowment, and matching funds. Applicants are required to submit a one- or two-page letter of intent describing the organization, need to be addressed, goals of the project, and total project budget. A full proposal will be requested if the project falls within the foundation's areas of interest. The board meets four times each year to consider requests. Letters of intent must be submitted electronically by the listed application deadlines.
Requirements: Nonprofit organizations in Santa Clara County, CA, may submit applications.
Restrictions: The foundation avoids grants that provide more than one-fourth of an organization's total budget in a 12-month period, usually expecting community and applicant commitment to a project through cost sharing. Applications cannot be accepted for the benefit of individuals, political purposes, or religious purposes.
Geographic Focus: California
Date(s) Application is Due: Feb 1; May 1; Jul 1; Nov 1
Amount: 10,000 - 100,000 USD
Samples: San Jose State U (CA)—to endow a chair in the School of Nursing, $1 million; Tapestry Arts (San Jose, CA)—for a multicultural dance program at five elementary schools, $10,000.
Contact: Program Contact; (408) 358-4545; (408) 358-4548; admin@valley.org
Internet: http://www.valley.org
Sponsor: Valley Foundation
16450 Los Gatos Boulevard, Suite 210
Los Gatos, CA 95032-5594

van Beuren Charitable Foundation Grants **1658**
The foundation awards grants to eligible Rhode Island nonprofit organizations in its areas of interest, including environment, land resources, history/archeology, and human services. Types of support include building construction/renovation, capital campaigns, general operating grants, land acquisition, and program development. Proposal requirements and application are available on the website.
Requirements: Rhode Island nonprofit organizations serving Newport County are eligible.
Geographic Focus: Rhode Island
Date(s) Application is Due: Jun 15
Amount: 2,000 - 250,000 USD
Contact: John van Beuren, President; (401) 846-8167; (401) 849-6859; vbcfnd@aol.com
Internet: http://www.vbcf.net
Sponsor: Van Beuren Charitable Foundation
P.O. Box 4098
Middletown, RI 02842

Vancouver Foundation Disability Supports for Employment Grants **1659**
The purpose of the Disability Supports for Employment Fund (DSEF) is to support new approaches to employment for people with disabilities that may complement or augment existing programs in the community. The intent of the program is to support initiatives by non-profit, charitable organizations that will promote the social and economic independence of individuals with disabilities.

Requirements: Grants are available to assist eligible organizations throughout B.C. who are working to increase employment opportunities and ultimately the rate of employment for persons with disabilities in their communities. Projects must demonstrate that they do not duplicate or replicate existing government-funded programs, supports and services for persons with disabilities. There is a two-stage application process. The first stage, submit a Letter of Inquiry, consisting of an informal proposal to determine basic suitability and eligibility. The second stage is a full application. If your Letter of Inquiry fits within the funding guidelines you will be sent a grant application form with specific instructions for completion. The deadline dates are June 18 for the Letter of Inquiry and August 13 for the grant application. Applicant will receives final decision approximately 12 weeks after deadline.
Geographic Focus: Canada
Date(s) Application is Due: Jun 18
Contact: Andria Teather, Director; (604) 688-2204; (604) 688-4170; info@vancouverfoundation.ca
Internet: http://www.vancouverfoundation.ca/grants/specialprograms.htm
Sponsor: Vancouver Foundation
555 West Hastings Street, Suite 1200
Vancouver, BC V6B 4N6 Canada

Vanguard Public Foundation Grant Funds **1660**
Vanguard provides funding to groups in northern California under four categories; the Social Justice Fund, the Community Institution Building Program, the Technical Assistance and Capacity Building Program, and the Social Justice Sabbatical Fund. Types of support include seed money, technical assistance, and operating expenses. Priority is given to projects without access to traditional funding sources because they may be thought to be risky, controversial, or of low priority. Vanguard strongly encourages coalitions that emphasize joint strategies and projects. Visit the web site for application guidelines. The next deadline to submit a proposal for the Social Justice Fund is October 14 and for a Social Justice Sabbatical is December 15. Annual deadline dates may vary; contact program staff for exact dates.
Requirements: Vanguard funds new or existing organizations involved in direct organizing or advocacy that are based in northern California (i.e., all counties north of Monterey). At the time a grant is made, an organization must either be tax-exempt or have a fiscal sponsor.
Restrictions: Vanguard does not fund capital campaigns or equipment purchase; organizations involved in direct services, research, or education, unless the proposed project clearly has an organizing component and cannot be supported within the general program budget; production costs for film; out-of-state travel, one-time conferences or events not integrally related to ongoing organizing; organizations with access to traditional funding sources and budgets of over $200,000 (unless the project for which funds are requested is unlikely to attract support because of its risky or controversial character); and costs already incurred.
Geographic Focus: California
Date(s) Application is Due: Oct 14; Dec 15
Samples: Global Fund for Women (CA)—for general operating support, $11,000; Cannery Workers' Assoc (CA)—for community development, $8000; National Coalition of Education Activists (CA)—for general operating support, $8075.
Contact: Grants Director; (415) 487-2111; (415) 487-2124; danielle@vanguardsf.org or vpf@vanguardsf.org
Internet: http://www.vanguardsf.org
Sponsor: Vanguard Public Foundation
383 Rhode Island Street, Suite 301
San Francisco, CA 94103

VDH Rescue Squad Assistance Fund Grants **1661**
The Financial Assistance for Emergency Medical Services Grants, known as the Rescue Squad Assistance Fund (RSAF) Grants is a multi-million dollar matching grant program for Virginia governmental, non-profit EMS agencies and organizations to provide financial assistance based on a demonstrated need. Items eligible for funding include EMS equipment and vehicles, computers, EMS management programs, courses/classes and projects benefiting the recruitment and retention of EMS members. RSAF is primarily a reimbursement grant that requires the grantee to make the purchase for the awarded item(s) and then submit an invoice for reimbursement.
Requirements: Applicant must be a Virginia non-profit agency/organization or governmental organization involved in emergency medical service (ems); applicant must submit verification of its FIN. Verification can be provided in the following formats: copy of the original letter from the IRS issuing FIN, copy of the latest tax returns (1st page only), statement from the County Administrator or City Manager of the municipality stating that the application is non-profit or a government agency and verifies their FIN; applicant must submit a copy (1st page only) of the most recent Federal Tax Return from the IRS (Form 990); applicant must submit the Virginia Office of EMS Affirmation Page in its entirety including the original signature of the Authorized Agent, the Fiscal Officer (Treasurer) and the Operational Medical Director (OMD). All Grant Applications must be submitted via the Internet. The Affirmation page is due by September 15 with original signatures. Faxed Applications will not be accepted. Submit all grant information to: Office of Emergency Medical Services, Attn: Amanda Davis - Grant Manager, 109 Governor Street, Suite UB-55, Richmond, VA 23219.
Restrictions: Applications submitted with line items less then $500.00 will be disqualified.
Geographic Focus: Virginia
Date(s) Application is Due: Sep 15
Contact: Amanda Davis, Grant Manager; (804) 864-7600; (804) 864-7580
Internet: http://www.vdh.virginia.gov/OEMS/Grants/index.htm
Sponsor: Virginia Department of Health
P.O. Box 2448
Richmond, VA 23218

Vernon K. Krieble Foundation Grants **1662**
The foundation awards grants worldwide in its areas of interest, including arts and performing arts, Canada, civil rights, education and higher education, government/public administration and public affairs, hospitals, leadership development, and youth programs. Limited funds are available to applying organizations; most grants are awarded to preselected organizations.
Requirements: Nonprofit organizations are eligible.
Geographic Focus: All U.S. States
Date(s) Application is Due: Jun 1; Dec 1
Amount: 1,000 - 5,000 USD
Samples: American Foreign Policy Council, (Washington, DC)—for general support, $10,000; Connecticut Childrens Medical Ctr (Hartford, CT)—for general support, $5000; U of Hartford, Hartford Art School (West Hartford, CT)—for general support, $2000; American Enterprise Institute for Public Policy Research (Washington, DC)—for general support, $1000.
Contact: Helen Krieble, President; (303) 758-3956; (303) 488-0068
Sponsor: Vernon K. Krieble Foundation
1777 S Harrison Street, Suite 807
Denver, CO 80210

Viacom Foundation Grants (Formerly CBS Foundation) **1663**
The purpose of the foundation is to strengthen the communities in which Viacom employees and audiences live and work. Grants are awarded to nonprofit organizations in the areas of arts & culture, children/youth/family, diversity, education, environment, health/medical, industry, social/civic/human services. Types of support include general operating grants, matching gifts, continuing support, annual campaigns, capital campaigns, curriculum development, program grants, and scholarships to children of Viacom employees only. Grants are made through corporate contributions and employee matching gifts to selected nonprofit organizations on a one-to-one basis.
Requirements: To submit an application send a proposal outlining project and expected benefit(s), copy of IRS 501(c)3 determination letter, financial plan, list of board of directors and officers, and a copy of latest audited financial statements.
Restrictions: The program does not make loans or grants for advertising, endowments, or for capital costs including construction and renovation. Individuals are not eligible.
Geographic Focus: All U.S. States
Contact: Karen Zatorski, Vice President, Public Affairs; (212) 975-8552
Internet: http://www.viacom.com/fundingoverview.jhtml
Sponsor: Viacom Foundation
51 West 52nd Street
New York, NY 10019

Victoria Foundation Grants **1664**
The foundation concentrates on addressing the educational and socioeconomic challenges within the city of Newark and pressing environmental concerns throughout New Jersey. Five major goals of the foundation are to foster community and professional leadership, support capacity-building efforts of nonprofits, enhance the effectiveness of community institutions, encourage

community collaborations, and achieve racial and ethnic equity. Victoria's grantmaking activities are concentrated in the areas of education, environment, neighborhood development and urban revitalization, and youth and families. Types of support include general operating support, continuing support, seed money grants, building and renovations, matching funds, scholarship funds, projects/programs, research, consulting services, and technical assistance. Grants generally are for one year, with possible renewal. The foundation's trustees meet in June and November to review grant applications. Elementary and secondary schools are asked to submit proposals by March 1 for funding for the next school year. Specific guidelines for elementary and secondary schools are available upon request. Receipt of proposals will be acknowledged within two weeks.
Requirements: The foundation funds 501(c)3 tax-exempt organizations in New Jersey.
Geographic Focus: New Jersey
Date(s) Application is Due: Feb 1; Mar 1; Aug 1
Amount: 5,000 - 200,000 USD
Samples: Bank Street College of Education (New York, NY)—to develop two New Beginnings demonstration schools and at least six demonstration classrooms in two primary schools in Newark, NJ, $350,000.
Contact: Catherine McFarland, Executive Officer; (973) 748-5300; (973) 748-0016; CatherineMcFarland@victoriafoundation.org
Internet: http://www.victoriafoundation.org/how_guidelines.html
Sponsor: Victoria Foundation
946 Bloomfield Avenue, 2nd Floor
Glen Ridge, NJ 07028

Vigran Family Foundation Grants **1665**
Lifelong Richmond, Indiana, resident Stanley Vigran considered forming a private foundation as a way to support causes that were important to him and his family including education, religion, and the arts. The Vigran family remains actively involved through a separate board which oversees the operations of the organization. Today, Stan's sons carry on the family tradition of giving in the Whitewater Valley and remain involved in the causes that were so much a part of their father's work. Contact the Foundation for further application guidelines.
Requirements: IRS 501(c)3 tax-exempt organizations serving Wayne County, Indiana, and its residents are eligible to apply.
Geographic Focus: Indiana
Contact: Stephen C. Borchers, Executive Director; (765) 962-1638; (765) 966-0882; steve@waynecountyfoundation.org
Internet: http://www.waynecountyfoundation.org/grant_center/vigran.html
Sponsor: Vigran Family Foundation / Wayne County Foundation
33 South 7th Street, Suite 1
Richmond, IN 47374

Virginia Commission for the Arts General Operating Grants **1666**
The commission awards grants for general operating support to assist organizations of artistic merit in fulfilling their missions by providing funds to maintain their stability and encourage their advancement. Funds may be awarded to cover general operating expenses, special projects, construction or renovation costs, and reserve funds. Most general operating support grants are awarded for a two-year period. Organizations may apply for 10 percent of their previous year's cash income for each year of the grant period. Application materials are available on the website.
Requirements: Virginia organizations whose primary purpose is the arts (excluding units of government and educational institutions and their private companion foundations), that have an independent governing board, and that are exempt from federal income tax under Section 501(c)3 of the Internal Revenue Code are eligible to apply. Organizations must be incorporated for at least a year before applying for General Operating Support and must have completed a season of programs.
Geographic Focus: Virginia
Date(s) Application is Due: Mar 1
Amount: 500 - 150,000 USD
Contact: Cathy Welborn, Program Coordinator; (804) 225-3132; (804) 225-4327; catherine.welborn@arts.virginia.gov
Internet: http://www.arts.virginia.gov/grants/infrastructure/support_artorg.html
Sponsor: Virginia Commission for the Arts
223 Governor Street, 2nd Floor
Richmond, VA 23219-2010

Virginia Commission for the Arts Project Grants **1667**
The primary purposes of Virginia Commission for the Arts Project Grants are: to increase access to high quality arts for all Virginians; to increase opportunities for artists to create and present their work; and to expand arts education opportunities for young people. This grant program supports a wide variety of arts activities and is open to any not-for-profit organization presenting the arts. It is one of the Commission's most competitive grant programs. Generally, the Commission will not support the same project for more than three years. The Commission will favor applications for the creation and/or production of new works by Virginia artists. Eligible activities include: commissions of new works of art; performances, exhibitions, film or video screenings, readings, and publication of literature; operating support for new and emerging arts organizations (organizations whose primary purpose is the arts, that are three years old or less, and that had a previous year's income of less than $50,000); artist residencies; workshops, seminars, classes; guest artists; educational programs of arts organizations; classes or other training in all disciplines of the arts; summer arts camps; scholarships for young people for arts instruction; arts festivals; architectural feasibility studies; surveys and planning; conferences; information and advisory services to artists and arts organizations; space and equipment for artists; touring events from out of state; and transportation for school children, older adults, and other special groups to attend arts events.
Requirements: Virginia not-for-profit organizations, units of government, or educational institutions that meet the basic eligibility criteria are eligible. Each department of a college or university is considered to be a separate applicant. Organizations receiving general operating support grants will not be eligible for Project Grants.
Geographic Focus: Virginia
Date(s) Application is Due: Mar 1
Contact: Cathy Welborn, Program Coordinator; (804) 225-3132; (804) 225-4327; catherine.welborn@arts.virginia.gov
Internet: http://www.arts.virginia.gov/grants/accessible/project_grants.html
Sponsor: Virginia Commission for the Arts
223 Governor Street, 2nd Floor
Richmond, VA 23219-2010

Virginia Environmental Endowment Kanawha and Ohio River Valleys Grants **1668**
Currently limited to the Kanawha and Ohio River Valleys of Kentucky and West Virginia, this program supports research, education, and community action on water quality and the effects of water pollution on public health and the environment. Emphasis is given to collaboration by citizens, government, and industry to develop effective public policies and to increasing public participation in water quality monitoring and watershed management.
Requirements: Constructive, result-oriented projects that are conducted by existing nonprofit organizations are funded. Activities that unite business, government, and civic interests for environmental improvement are encouraged, as are projects that serve as models for other communities. Organizations must be in Kentucky or West Virginia.
Geographic Focus: Kentucky, West Virginia
Date(s) Application is Due: Jun 15
Samples: Kentucky Waterways Alliance (Munfordville, KY)—for a statewide citizens' group that works to monitor and protect water quality and to raise public awareness about related issues, $40,000 over two years; West Virginia Rivers Coalition (Elkins, WV)—to develop scientifically sound criteria for determining the level of nutrients in West Virginia rivers, $17,200.
Contact: Gerald McCarthy, Executive Director; (804) 644-5000; (804) 644-0603; info@vee.org
Internet: http://www.vee.org/programs.cfm
Sponsor: Virginia Environmental Endowment
1051 E Cary Street, 3 James Center, Suite 1400, P.O. Box 790
Richmond, VA 23218-0790

Virginia Environmental Endowment Mini Grants **1669**
Mini grants are awarded in the areas of environmental education, and water protection quality. The focus of environmental education grants is to increase training in environmental education for educators and school administrators and to expand the use of existing educational resources (curricula, multi-media programs, publications, field studies) in schools and community programs. Projects must focus on water quality, land use, and/or sustainable communities; and must include training for teachers/project leaders and service learning activities that engage students and community members in research to solve environmental problems. Water quality protection grants are awarded to

increase public involvement in the restoration and protection of Virginia's water resources through water quality testing and monitoring, pollution prevention, and public education. Matching funds from other sources are usually required. Mini grants may include support for training, research, data collection and analysis, monitoring equipment, supplies, curriculum materials, publications, printing, and promotion. Requests for computer and multi-media equipment and instructional software must be accompanied by specific plans for related teacher training, curriculum integration, and long-term maintenance. Guidelines are available online.
Requirements: Primary, intermediate, and secondary schools (public and private), as well as nongovernmental, nonprofit community organizations in Virginia, are eligible to apply.
Restrictions: Local, state, and federal government agencies and programs are not eligible. Grants will not be provided for salaries or benefits of school personnel or for field trips outside Virginia. Grants will not be awarded for political action programs, capital drives and building funds, boats, scholarships, endowments, lawsuits and litigation, or overhead costs.
Geographic Focus: Virginia
Date(s) Application is Due: Jun 15; Dec 1
Amount: 1,000 - 5,000 USD
Samples: Fishburn Park Elementary School (Roanoke, VA)—for curriculum programs, teacher training, and habitat design in wetlands and water protection, $4425 matched by $3955; Turner Ashby High School (Bridgewater, VA)—for water quality education programs, $3483 matched by $4347.
Contact: Gerald McCarthy, Executive Director; (804) 644-5000; (804) 644-0603; info@vee.org
Internet: http://www.vee.org/programs.cfm
Sponsor: Virginia Environmental Endowment
1051 E Cary Street, 3 James Center, Suite 1400, P.O. Box 790
Richmond, VA 23218-0790

Virginia Environmental Endowment Virginia Program Grants **1670**
The program focuses specifically on improving the quality of the environment for the direct benefit of the citizens of the Commonwealth of Virginia. Emphasis is given to the following programs: pollution prevention, natural resources conservation, sustainable communities, and environmental education; to enable citizens to identify local environmental problems, develop creative solutions, and share results with other communities; and to support legal research and education on other policies and laws that affect Virginia's environment. Types of support include operating budgets, continuing support, seed grants, matching funds, scholarship funds, project development, research, conferences and seminars, and publications. Applicants must submit four copies of full proposals for consideration. A copy of the annual report may be requested, wherein explicit application instructions are listed.
Requirements: Eligible for funding are constructive, result-oriented projects that are conducted by existing Virginia nonprofit organizations. Activities that unite business, government, and civic interests for environmental improvement are encouraged, as are projects that serve as models for other communities.
Geographic Focus: Virginia
Date(s) Application is Due: Jun 15; Dec 1
Samples: Nature Conservancy-Virginia Program Office (Charlottesville, VA)—for its campaign to increase financing for Virginia's natural resources, $90,000; Shenandoah Valley Pure Water Forum (Harrisonburg, VA)—to help implement a user-friendly resource on technical and scientific data related to water quality and quantity in the Shenandoah Valley, $24,344.
Contact: Gerald McCarthy, Executive Director; (804) 644-5000; (804) 644-0603; info@vee.org
Internet: http://www.vee.org/programs.cfm
Sponsor: Virginia Environmental Endowment
1051 E Cary Street, 3 James Center, Suite 1400, P.O. Box 790
Richmond, VA 23218-0790

Virginia G. Piper Charitable Trust Grants **1671**
The trust awards grants to nonprofit organizations, primarily serving residents of Maricopa County, AZ, that have actively operated as a Section 501(c)3 organization for at least three years, in its areas of interest, including early childhood, youth, and arts and culture. The trust seeks proposals that link health, medical research and/or educational programs specifically to the needs of children, youth, and the elderly, as well as faith-based organizations that can use their considerable capacity and presence to address needs in these areas. Types of funding support include program grants, capital grants, endowment grants, challenge grants, and single- and multi-year grants. There are no application forms. Letters of inquiry can be submitted at any time.
Requirements: Arizona nonprofit organizations, primarily in Maricopa County, are eligible.
Restrictions: Individuals are not eligible.
Geographic Focus: Arizona
Amount: 5,000 - 2,000,000 USD
Samples: East Valley Children's Theatre (Mesa, AZ)—for marketing activities related to the theater's move to the new Mesa Arts Center, $12,000; Saint Mary's Food Bank (Phoenix, AZ)—to enable three local food banks to gather and distribute food donated by a chain of grocery stores, $225,000; Mount Claret Retreat Ctr (Phoenix, AZ)—to renovate and construct facilities at this small retreat and conference center owned by the Diocese of Phoenix, $250,000; Mesa Community College (AZ) and Scottsdale Community College (AZ)—to establish centers at which older adults can learn about health and physical fitness, as well as educational, paid, and volunteer opportunities, $533,946 over three years, and $347,010 over two years, respectively.
Contact: Karin Bishop, Grants Manager; (480) 948-5853; (408) 348-1316; info@pipertrust.org
Internet: http://www.pipertrust.org
Sponsor: Virginia G. Piper Charitable Trust
6720 N Scottsdale Road, Suite 350
Scottsdale, AZ 85253

Visiting Nurse Foundation Grants **1672**
The foundation awards grants in support of home- and community-based health care for the medically underserved in Cook and the collar counties of Lake, McHenry, DuPage, Kane and Will, with a focus on Chicago. Priority areas are home health care services; prevention and health promotion; and early intervention. Preference is given to programs using nurses to provide the care. Types of support include program, capital, and general operating grants. Letters of intent should be submitted by deadline dates listed, and full proposals will be by invitation only.
Requirements: Nonprofit organizations in Cook, Lake, McHenry, DuPage, Kane, and Will counties of Illinois are eligible.
Restrictions: No grants are made to individuals.
Geographic Focus: Illinois
Date(s) Application is Due: Jan 19; Apr 19; Oct 20
Amount: 15,000 - 80,000 USD
Contact: Robert N. DiLeonardi, Executive Director; (312) 214-1521; (312) 214-1529; info@vnafoundation.net
Internet: http://www.vnafoundation.net
Sponsor: Visiting Nurse Association Foundation
20 N Wacker Drive, Suite 3118
Chicago, IL 60606

Vulcan Materials Company Foundation Grants **1673**
The company foundation supports nonprofit organizations in company-operating areas. Grants support a broad array of programs and projects in the areas of health and welfare, community and economic development, education (including an employee matching grants program), the environment, law and justice, women and children, arts and humanities, minorities, and literacy. Requests will be considered for support of general operating expenses, capital and annual campaigns, scholarship funds, research, continuing support, and seed money. There are no application deadlines.
Requirements: The foundation awards grants only to public charities and units of government, such as public schools and parks. A public charity is any Section 501(c)3 charitable organization that is not a private foundation because it meets one of the three internal Revenue Code definitions: 509(a)1, 509(a)2 or 509(a)3.
Restrictions: The foundation does not fund individuals; organizations outside the United States; telephone or mass-mail appeals, political organizations; testimonial dinners; sectarian religious activities; organizations which have discriminatory practices; or athletic, labor, fraternal and veterans associations. The Foundation generally will not consider requests from organizations located in communities where Vulcan has no operations, offices or employees.
Geographic Focus: Alabama, Arizona, Arkansas, California, Florida, Georgia, Illinois, Indiana, Iowa, Kansas, Kentucky, Louisiana, Maryland, Mississippi, Missouri, New Mexico, North Carolina, Pennsylvania, South Carolina, Tennessee, Texas, Virginia, Wisconsin
Amount: Up to 28,000,000 USD
Samples: Auburn U Foundation (Auburn U, AL)—for scholarships and fellowships, $45,000; Family and Child Services (Birmingham, AL)—for youth programs, $20,000; Metropolitan Arts Council (Birmingham, AL)—for general support, $79,233.

Contact: Program Contact; (205) 298-3222; giving@vmcmail.com
Internet: http://www.vulcanmaterials.com/social.asp?content=guidelines
Sponsor: Vulcan Materials Company Foundation
P.O. Box 385014
Birmingham, AL 35238-5014

W.M. Keck Foundation Grants **1674**

The foundation concentrates on strengthening studies and programs in accredited universities and colleges and major, independent medical research institutions in the areas of science, engineering, and medicine. Consideration also is given to liberal arts education and elementary and secondary education. Additionally, some consideration, focused in southern California, is given to organizations in the categories of arts and culture, civic and community, health care, early education (0 to five years old) and precollegiate education. Grants have been awarded to support medical research, purchase needed equipment, and renovate laboratory space at premier institutions of higher education and research across the country. The foundation considers applications that reflect institutional priorities as identified by the applicant's CEO. Grants are awarded twice each year, in June and December. Initial application must be by letter of inquiry, not to exceed three pages, accompanied by evidence of tax-exemption; and most recent, full, certified, audited financial statements. Letters of inquiry are accepted year-round. Submission of full proposal is upon invitation of the foundation only after review of the inquiry letter; unsolicited proposals are not accepted at any time.
Requirements: U.S. four-year colleges and universities, medical schools, and major independent research institutions are eligible. Applicant organizations must be classified 501(c)3 and not as a private foundation under 509(a) of the IRS code.
Restrictions: Grants are not considered for individuals, routine expenses, deficit reduction, fund-raising events, dinners or mass mailings, conferences or seminars, publications or films, or public policy research. Support is not given to conduit organizations or organizations lacking permanent tax-exempt ruling determination from the federal government and state of California (for California-based applicants). Electronic applications are not accepted.
Geographic Focus: All U.S. States
Date(s) Application is Due: May 15; Nov 15
Amount: Up to 100,000,000 USD
Samples: U of Wisconsin at Madison (WI)—for a three-year project involving stem-cell research, $1.25 million; Carnegie Mellon U (Pittsburgh, PA)—for research into the ways in which the brain deciphers language, which may yield advances in the treatment of such neurological disorders as autism and dyslexia, $750,000; Keck Graduate Institute of Applied Life Sciences (Claremont, CA)—to increase its endowment and augment its general operating fund, $20,000 over seven years.
Contact: Drive Sandra Glass, Program Vice President; (213) 680-3833; (213) 614-0934; info@wmkeck.org
Internet: http://www.wmkeck.org
Sponsor: W.M. Keck Foundation
550 S Hope Street, Suite 2500
Los Angeles, CA 90071

W.P. and H.B. White Foundation Grants **1675**

The foundation awards grants to nonprofits in the metropolitan area of Chicago, IL, for social services; early-childhood, elementary, higher, and adult education; and health. Types of support include general operating budgets, continuing support, annual campaigns, building funds, capital campaigns, and special projects. The board meets in March, June, September, and December to consider requests.
Requirements: Only Illinois organizations are eligible to apply.
Geographic Focus: Illinois
Date(s) Application is Due: Feb 1; May 1; Aug 1; Nov 1
Amount: 10,000 - 30,000 USD
Samples: Austin Career Education Ctr (Chicago, IL)—for operating support, $12,000; Greater Chicago Food Depository (Chicago, IL)—for operating support, $20,000; Roosevelt U (Chicago, IL)—for program support, $10,000.
Contact: M. Margaret Blandford, Executive Director; (847) 446-1441
Sponsor: W.P. and H.B. White Foundation
540 Frontage Road, Suite 3240
Northfield, IL 60093

W.W. Smith Charitable Trust Grants **1676**

The trust awards grants regionally in its areas of interest, including basic medical research dealing with cancer, AIDS, and heart disease; scholarship programs for undergraduate students at four-year universities and colleges; and proposals that address specifically food, clothing, and shelter for children and the aged. Resources are concentrated in areas where the most need can be discerned and where government or private assistance has not been available. Types of support include capital projects, challenge/matching grants, general operating grants, program grants, and research grants. Requests for grants for food, clothing, and shelter for children and the aged are considered throughout the year. Application deadlines are June 15 for cancer and AIDS research; and September 15 for heart research. Grants may be for more than one year but not for more than three years.
Requirements: Grant recipients are limited to organizations within the five-county area of Pennsylvania including Buck, Chester, Delaware, Montgomery, and Philadelphia Counties. Organizations must be tax-exempt and not classified as private foundations or private operating foundations.
Restrictions: After three consecutive years of funding, at least two years must elapse before further applications from the organization may be considered.
Geographic Focus: Pennsylvania
Date(s) Application is Due: Jun 15; Sep 15
Amount: 15,000 - 84,000 USD
Samples: La Salle U (Philadelphia, PA)—for financial aid for students, $98,000; Philadelphia College of Bible (Langhorne, PA)—for financial aid for students, $58,000.
Contact: Frances Pemberton, Trust Administrator; (610) 397-1844; (610) 397-1680
Internet: http://www.wwsmithcharitabletrust.org
Sponsor: W.W. Smith Charitable Trust
200 Four Falls Corporate Center, Suite 300
West Conshohocken, PA 19428

Wachovia Foundation Grants **1677**

The foundation awards grants to eligible tax-exempt organizations in four primary areas: education, community and economic development, arts and culture, and health and human services. Its mission is to build strong and vibrant communities, improve the quality of life, and make a positive difference in Wachovia communities. Contributions are coordinated through regional Wachovia Community Affairs offices (list available online), in Florida; Georgia; New Jersey, New York, and Connecticut; North and South Carolina (except for Charlotte); North Carolina—Charlotte); Pennsylvania and Delaware; Virginia, Maryland, and Washington, DC; Wachovia Securities; and national requests. Guidelines and application are available online.
Requirements: Applicant organizations must have a 501(c)3 nonprofit tax-exempt classification, be located or provide service in Wachovia's markets, have broad community support and address specific community needs; and demonstrate fiscal and administrative stability.
Restrictions: Grants are not made to support individuals; travel or conferences; political causes or candidates; organizations whose primary purpose is to influence legislation; religious, veteran, or fraternal organizations for programs limited to specific groups; retirement homes or communities; precollege-level private schools; or organizations already receiving support through United Way or a United Arts drive, except for approved capital campaigns.
Geographic Focus: All U.S. States
Amount: 5,000 - 100,000 USD
Samples: Virginia Commonwealth U (VA)—for the schools of business and engineering, $400,000; Rowan Regional Medical Ctr Foundation (Salisbury, NC)—for its capital campaign for a new emergency department, patient-care facility, and community-education center, $150,000.
Contact: Grants Administrator; (704) 374-4085; (704) 374-2484
Internet: http://www.wachovia.com/inside/page/0,,139_414_430,00.html
Sponsor: Wachovia Foundation
301 S College Street, Suite 4000, One Wachovia Center
Charlotte, NC 28288-0013

Wallace Global Fund Grants **1678**

The foundation awards grants to programs that support global sustainable development by the stabilization of growth of human populations; participatory and accountable economic, social and environmental governance; and significant changes in global patterns of production and consumption. Preference is given to projects that involve policy research and action on a global or regional level; public and private sector partnerships; collaboration among non-governmental organizations; utilization of market mechanisms; and innovative and cross-

cutting projects. Types of support include general operating expenses, multi-year support, and the cultivation of public intellectuals and policy leaders. Applications are reviewed on an ongoing basis.
Requirements: Interested applicants are encouraged to submit a concept paper of three pages or less before submitting a full proposal.
Restrictions: Grants are not made to: individuals; universities; for-profit organizations; endowments; capital fund projects; scholarships; conferences; books or magazines; building construction; or travel (not including project-related travel). The fund does not support film or video projects, the acquisition of land, or grants intended to support candidates for political office.
Geographic Focus: All U.S. States
Amount: 2,000 - 400,000 USD
Samples: Rainforest Action Network—for the Old Growth Campaign, aimed at shifting the forest products industry away from old growth wood and toward sustainable alternatives, $40,000; Advocates for Youth—support for Standing Up for Research-Based Approaches to Adolescent Sexual Health, $30,000 over six months.
Contact: Catherine Cameron, Executive Director; (202) 452-1530; (202) 452-0922; tkroll@wgf.org
Internet: http://www.wgf.org/grants_finances.html
Sponsor: Wallace Global Fund
1990 M Street NW, Suite 250
Washington, DC 20036

Walt Disney Company Foundation Grants **1679**
The foundation funds medical and health services, health and welfare of children, youth activities, higher education, community funds, music, and cultural arts in Los Angeles and Orange Counties in California and Orange and Osceola Counties in Florida. Types of support include general operating support, continuing support, annual campaigns, capital campaigns, program development, scholarship funds, fellowships, and employee-related scholarships. Previous grants have supported downtown revitalization in both New York City, where Disney redeveloped an old Times Square theater, and Los Angeles, where support has been given for a new music hall that will be home to the Los Angeles Philharmonic Orchestra.
Requirements: 501(c)3 tax-exempt organizations in California and Florida may apply.
Restrictions: Disney will not make grants for scholarships, religious organizations, building campaigns, start-up campaigns, seed purposes, research, loans, conferences, general fund drives, annual charitable appeals, and political purposes.
Geographic Focus: California, Florida, New York
Amount: 1,000 USD
Samples: Boys and Girls Clubs of America (Atlanta, GA)—for the group's 2006 Centennial Celebration and to support clubs in Southern California and central Florida, $3 million.
Contact: Tillie Baptie, Executive Director; (818) 560-1006; (818) 563-5271
Internet: http://disney.go.com/disneyhand/contributions/wdcfoundation.html
Sponsor: Walt Disney Company Foundation
500 S Buena Vista Street
Burbank, CA 91521-0987

Walter and Elise Haas Fund Grants **1680**
The mission of the fund is to help build a healthy, just, and vibrant society in which people feel connected to and responsible for their community. The fund supports nonprofit organizations in its areas of interest, including the arts—arts education, preservation of cultural heritage, cultural commons, and the Creative Fund; economic security—incomes, assets, and economic development; Jewish life—promoting diversity, creative expression, building partnerships, and new leadership; education—youth leadership, parent organizing, community partnerships, and school partnerships with the community; and other grantmaking interests. Types of support include operating budgets, technical assistance, continuing support, seed money, land acquisition, emergency funds, capital campaigns, building funds, special projects, equipment, matching funds, and endowment funds. There are no application deadlines. Submit an application cover sheet with the proposal.
Requirements: 501(c)3 tax-exempt organizations that are not classified as 509(a) private foundations, fiscal sponsors meeting these classifications, and governmental entities are eligible. Applicant organization must be based in or managing significant activities in San Francisco or Alameda County. Within Alameda County, the fund places the highest priority on projects in Oakland and Berkeley. The Jewish Life program area's geographic focus extends to the broader Bay Area. At present, the Creative Work Fund considers applications from Alameda, Contra Costa, San Francisco, and Solano counties.
Restrictions: As a general rule, the fund does not provide grants to individuals or to for-profit entities; for general fundraising benefits and events; for endowment campaigns (Rare exceptions may be made for organizations that have a long-standing relationship to the fund's legacy or when endowment goals are incorporated into a larger capital campaign.); for the creation of a film or video, or of original creative art work, except through the Creative Work Fund; or for scholarships or fellowships.
Geographic Focus: California
Contact: Pamela David, Executive Director; (415) 398-4474
Internet: http://www.haassr.org/html/current_programs/index.cfm
Sponsor: Walter and Elise Haas Fund
1 Lombard Street, Suite 305
San Francisco, CA 94111-1130

Walter L. Gross III Family Foundation Grants **1681**
The foundation awards grants to eligible Ohio and Kentucky nonprofit organizations in its areas of interest, including animals and wildlife, Christian churches and organizations, community outreach programs, education, environment, health care and medical, and social services. Grants are considered on a case-by-case basis and have been awarded to support building construction/renovation and general operating support. There are no application forms or deadlines with which to adhere, and applicants should begin by contacting the office directly.
Requirements: Ohio and Kentucky 501(c)3 nonprofit organizations are eligible to apply.
Geographic Focus: Kentucky, Ohio
Amount: 1,000 - 20,000 USD
Samples: Habitat for Humanity, Cincinnati, Ohio—for general support, $10,000; Miami Uuniversity Foundation, Oxford, Ohio—for general support, $300,000; Our Daily Bread, Cincinnati, Ohio—for general support, $2,000.
Contact: Walter L. Gross III, President; (513) 785-6060 or (513) 785-6072; (513) 683-9467
Sponsor: Walter L. Gross III Family Foundation
9435 Waterstone Boulevard, Suite 390
Cincinnati, OH 45249-8227

Walter S. Johnson Foundation Grants **1682**
The foundation invests in programs to help children and youth throughout northern California, with particular interest in the San Francisco Bay area and in Washoe County, Nevada. The foundation's grants reflect one or more of three goals: ensure the well-being of children and youth, strengthen public education, and assist young people in the transition to adulthood. To strengthen public education, grants are made for the professional development of educators—especially recruitment, preparation, and support of new teachers. It also helps reform how schools prepare students for college. In supporting youth in their transition to adulthood, grants are made for school-to-career training, teaching, and support activities. The foundation helps nonprofits focusing on positive youth attributes and explores opportunities to work with adjudicated youth. Additional funding interests include improving support services in low-income neighborhoods and helping families in crises, such as homelessness, divorce, or domestic violence situations. From time to time, the foundation makes grants that are outside the regular guidelines. Some reflect special board interests, others may respond to major natural disasters, and still others provide an opportunity to explore potential new areas for future grant making. Types of support include general operating grants, research grants, and special projects. Potential applicants are encouraged to call before submitting an application.
Requirements: Proposals are accepted from non-profit organizations throughout Northern California and Washoe County, Nevada.
Restrictions: The foundation does not consider proposals for grants to individuals or to religious organizations for sectarian purposes. Funds are not provided for capital projects, organizational deficits, or general operating support.
Geographic Focus: California, Nevada
Amount: 3,000 - 50,000 USD
Samples: Forum for Youth Investment Impact Strategies (Washington, DC)—to provide technical assistance to 11 district-community partnerships of a high school reform initiative, $100,000; Markkula Center/Character Based Literacy Project, Santa Clara University (Santa Clara, CA)—to continue implementing the Character Based Literacy curriculum, document student gains, and develop and implement a business plan, $200,000; Berkeley Biotechnology

Education (CA)— for continuing support of its school-to-career program, $60,000; Catholic Charities of the East Bay (Oakland, CA)—to create a coordinated continuum of services for youth who are leaving the foster care system, $75,000; YouthBuild U.S. A (Somerville, MA)—to strengthen its youth-development programs in California, $200,000.
Contact: Donna Takasuka, Grants Administrator; (650) 326-0485; (650) 326-4320; dtakasuka@wsjf.org
Internet: http://www.wsjf.org
Sponsor: Walter S. Johnson Foundation
525 Middlefield Road, Suite 160
Menlo Park, CA 94025

Warsh-Mott Legacy Grants **1683**
The foundation awards grants in its areas of interest, including biotechnology, economic globalization— balancing short-term efforts that oppose the NAFTA/WTO/FTAA trade regimes with long-term efforts to develop alternative economic models; and food sovereignty—seed saving, soil building, protecting pollinators, and preserving traditional knowledge of how food is grown. Types of support include continuing support, equipment acquisition, matching grants, general operating grants, publications, research, special projects, and technical assistance. Submit a letter of inquiry; full proposals are by invitation.
Requirements: Applicant organizations must be classified as a 501(c)3 by the U.S. Internal Revenue Service. Foreign applicants should note that the foundations make a very limited number of grants abroad.
Restrictions: Grants do not support endowments, capital funds, or film/video projects.
Geographic Focus: All U.S. States
Amount: 15,000 - 30,000 USD
Samples: U of Texas, School of Public Health (Houston, TX)—for study of dioxins and effects on public health, $20,000. Council for Responsible Genetic (Boston, MA)—for general support, $30,000. Nevada Outdoor Recreation Assoc (Carson City, NV)—to purchase equipment), $20,000.
Contact: Program Contact; (707) 874-2942; (707) 874-1734; inquiries@csfund.org
Internet: http://www.csfund.org/procedures.html
Sponsor: Warsh-Mott Legacy Foundation
469 Bohemian Highway
Freestone, CA 95472

Washington Post Contributions Program Grants **1684**
The contributions program supports qualified nonprofit organizations of the Washington, DC, metropolitan community whose ongoing programs directly benefit those in the community who are in need and that focus on key issues in the areas of education, health and human services, the arts, civic betterment, and community service. Special interest is given to organizations whose programs serve the most needy and least able citizens; seek to fill unmet societal needs or solve long-standing community problems; and address key community issues and concerns in collaborative and imaginative ways. Grants are awarded to support specific programs or for general operating support. Funding rarely is available for capital campaigns. Applications for capital campaigns that meet the Post's general guidelines are held until December and will be funded only if resources are available at the time of review. There are no application forms. Proposals should include a one-page cover sheet; a three- to five-page application letter; supporting documents; list of board of directors and officers; a copy of the most recent annual report; and several relevant articles, reviews, brochures, etc., about the project or organization. Deadlines are the first Tuesday in March, June, September, and December.
Requirements: Organizations that are tax-exempt under section 501(c)3 of the Internal Revenue Code that operate in the Washington, DC, metropolitan area are eligible.
Restrictions: Funding is not available for individuals; national or other organizations whose programs do not directly serve Washington-area needs; religious organizations for religious purposes; fraternal, membership, or veterans organizations or athletic teams, volunteer fire/emergency services, or similar groups; political action or advocacy groups; multiyear grants; challenge grants; third-party fund-raising efforts; conferences; research; or start-up projects. Applications are not accepted.
Geographic Focus: All U.S. States
Contact: Eric Grant, Director; (202) 334-6834; (202) 334-5609
Internet: http://washpost.com/community/charities/contributions.shtml
Sponsor: Washington Post Educational Foundation
1150 15th Street NW
Washington, DC 20071

Wayne and Gladys Valley Foundation Grants **1685**
The foundation awards grants to California nonprofits in its primary areas of interest, including education at all levels, health care and medical research, youth and families, human services, sciences and engineering, and religion. Types of support include general operating support, building construction/renovation, program development, professorships, research, and matching funds. There are no application forms or deadlines. The board meets in February, May, September, and November to consider requests.
Requirements: California nonprofits in Alameda, Contra Costa, and Santa Clara Counties are eligible.
Geographic Focus: California
Samples: U of the Pacific (Stockton, CA)—for its new biological-sciences center, $2.5 million; Santa Clara U (CA)—to construct a new library, $15 million; Dominican U of California (San Rafael, CA)—for a new science and technology center, $2.25 million.
Contact: Michael Desler, Executive Director; (510) 466-6060; (510) 466-6067; info@wgvalley.org
Sponsor: Wayne and Gladys Valley Foundation
1939 Harrison Street, Suite 510
Oakland, CA 94612-3532

Weatherwax Foundation Grants **1686**
The foundation awards grants in Michigan to projects that promote and support education, civic and social programs, culture, science, and the arts, primarily in the greater Jackson area and, to a lesser extent, in the adjacent counties. Types of support include building construction and renovation; matching and challenge grants; general operating grants; program development; scholarships; annual and capital campaigns; and emergency funds. The initial approach is a two-page grant proposal that may be submitted at any time. Granting decisions are made in January, May, and August.
Requirements: Giving primarily in Hillsdale, Lenawee, and Jackson counties, MI.
Restrictions: No grants to individuals; or for computer purchases.
Geographic Focus: Michigan
Amount: 1,000 - 200,000 USD
Samples: Albion College (MI)—for music facility renovation, $125,000; Michigan Theatre (MI)—for restoration, strategic planning, and executive search, $27,500; Family Service and Children's Aid (MI)—for general operating support and neighborhood outreach activities, $45,491.
Contact: Program Contact; (517) 787-2117; (517) 787-2118
Internet: http://www.lib.msu.edu/harris23/grants/wfbrochu.htm
Sponsor: Weatherwax Foundation
P.O. Box 1111
Jackson, MI 49204

Weaver Foundation Grants **1687**
The mission of the foundation is to help the Greater Greensboro community enhance and improve the quality of life and the economic environment for its citizens while developing a sense of philanthropy, civic education, and commitment in current and future generations of the founders' families. The focus areas include support for education; programs for children and youth; protection of the environment; efforts to reduce poverty and improve the lives of the disadvantaged and the needy; advancement of human and civil rights, racial tolerance, and diversity; enhancement of parks, recreation, and the quality of life; and economic development. Inquiries are welcomed via letter, telephone, or email; full proposals are by invitation. Grants are generally made quarterly.
Requirements: 501(c)3 nonprofits serving the greater Greensboro, NC, community are eligible.
Restrictions: The foundation does not support political programs or voter registration efforts, conferences, travel, video production, fraternal groups, individuals, or religious organizations.
Geographic Focus: North Carolina
Amount: 5,000 - 50,000 USD
Contact: Tara Sandercock, Vice President for Programs; (336) 378-7910; (336) 275-9602; rlm@weaverfoundation.com
Internet: http://www.weaverfoundation.com
Sponsor: Weaver Foundation
P.O. Box 26040
Greensboro, NC 27420-0640

WebMethods Foundation Grants 1688

The foundation awards grants to nonprofit organizations in the greater District of Columbia area focused on low-income and affordable housing and on issues surrounding homeless families, single mothers, and youth. Types of support include grants for new initiatives, general operations, and capacity building. Guidelines are available online.
Requirements: 501(c)3 charitable organizations within a 100-mile radius of Washington, DC, are eligible.
Geographic Focus: District of Columbia
Contact: Grants Administrator; (703) 460-6080; (703) 460-2599; foundation@webMethods.org
Internet: http://www.webMethods.org
Sponsor: WebMethods Foundation
3930 Pender Drive
Fairfax, VA 22030

Weeden Foundation Grants 1689

The purpose of the foundation is to address the adverse impact of the growing human population and overuse of natural resources on the biological fabric of the planet. The main priority of the foundation is biodiversity. Population growth and overconsumption have also evolved into major program interests. Proposed projects should protect ecosystems and wildlife or raise the status of women and increase awareness about family planning. The foundation awards general operating, seed money, and project/program grants. Applicants may submit a letter of inquiry. If interested, the foundation will request a full proposal. Send requests six weeks prior to the board meetings in March, June, and October.
Requirements: 501(c)3 nonprofit organizations are eligible.
Restrictions: The foundation does not: award grants for endowment or capital fund projects; support large organizations with well-established funding sources, except to assist them in launching promising, new projects for which funding is not readily available; allow any portion of a grant to be used for university overhead or indirect costs; award general support grants, except to small organizations with entire missions that coincide with an area of interest to the foundation; or award grants to individuals, but does provide support for an individual's project if it is sponsored by a domestic or foreign educational, scientific, or charitable organization.
Geographic Focus: All U.S. States
Amount: 10,000 - 30,000 USD
Samples: Alaska Conservation Foundation (AK)—$15,000; Alternatives to Growth Oregon (OR)—$50,000; Population Coalition—$25,000.
Contact: Program Contact; (212) 888-1672; (212) 888-1354; weedenfdn@weedenfdn.org
Internet: http://www.weedenfdn.org
Sponsor: Weeden Foundation
747 3rd Avenue, 34th Floor
New York, NY 10017

Westar Energy Foundation Grants 1690

The foundation awards grants to nonprofit organizations in company operating areas in Kansas. Areas of interest include children and youth, particularly educational programs related to enhancing employment opportunities; health programs related to the general well-being of the community; seniors, particularly with energy assistance programs; and environmental programs, particularly programs cooperating with federal, state, and local government units in nonpartisan efforts to improve the environment or educate the public about environmental issues. Types of support include building funds, capital campaigns, continuing support, emergency funds, equipment, fellowships, in-kind gifts, general operating budgets, renovation projects, research, scholarship funds, and seed money. There are no application deadlines; the board meets quarterly to consider requests.
Requirements: Nonprofit organizations in company-operating areas of Kansas are eligible to apply.
Geographic Focus: Kansas
Amount: 300 - 10,000 USD
Samples: Exploration Place (Wichita, KS)—for its capital campaign, and for the Season of Creativity exhibit, $100,000 and $40,000, respectively.
Contact: Cynthia McCarvel, President; (785) 575-1544; (785) 785-6399
Internet: http://www.wstnres.com/corp_com/contentmgt.nsf/publishedpages/foundation?opendocument&menu=5
Sponsor: Westar Energy Foundation
P.O. Box 889
Topeka, KS 66601-0089

West Virginia Commission on the Arts Major Institutions Support Grants 1691

The purpose of the grants is to support and stabilize existing organizations that contribute to the development of West Virginia's culture by providing financial assistance toward their overall programming budget. The criteria with which proposals will be judged include artistic excellence, effective management, service to community, and year-round programming. Applications must be submitted with an overall budget and separate individual project forms, each of which will request a bottom-line figure of the project's total costs and the organization's general operating expenses and its project match. In addition to the application, proposals must include a certified independent audit; total estimated upcoming budget showing all revenue and expenditures anticipated; a three-year organizational plan; proof of efforts to comply with 504 regulations; the organization's entire operating budget, less federal funds and building costs; and not more than one copy of each support sample(posters, brochures, catalogs, etc.). A list of eligible items of support to museums, arts institutions, and symphonies may be obtained from the office.
Requirements: Applicant organizations must have a minimum operating base of at least $500,000; be in existence for five years as a West Virginia nonprofit organization, during which time a permanent, paid, professional staff has administered the organization's programming on an annual basis; serve a large audience that represents a broad cross section of citizens, including people who are disabled or institutionalized, senior citizens, lower income groups, and culturally diverse audiences; demonstrate compliance with Section 504 of the Rehabilitation Act; and contribute to the development of West Virginia's culture.
Restrictions: Organizations whose primary thrust is education and that award academic credits; organizations whose main purpose is not the arts; divisions or departments of larger institutions; national service organizations; and organizations receiving funds from other state agencies are ineligible.
Geographic Focus: West Virginia
Date(s) Application is Due: Mar 1
Amount: 65,000 - 125,000 USD
Contact: Barbara Anderson, Grants Coordinator; (304) 558-0220; (304) 558-2779; barbie.anderson@wvculture.org
Internet: http://www.wvculture.org/arts/grantsbk.html#programs
Sponsor: West Virginia Commission on the Arts
1900 Kanawha Boulevard E
Charleston, WV 25305-0300

West Virginia Commission on the Arts Planning and Organizational Development Grants 1692

This project was created to encourage individual West Virginia arts organizations and communities to develop long-range plans needed to strengthen and advance their administrative and technical development and their artistic programs. The program involves intensive planning and technical assistance that should begin with an assessment of the current status of the organization or community. The assessment is used to structure a plan to develop the future directions for the arts organization and/or the cultural life of a community.
Requirements: Only residents of West Virginia may apply.
Geographic Focus: West Virginia
Date(s) Application is Due: Mar 1
Contact: Barbara Anderson, Grants Coordinator; (304) 558-0220; (304) 558-2779; barbie.anderson@wvculture.org
Internet: http://www.wvculture.org/arts/grantsbk.html#programs
Sponsor: West Virginia Commission on the Arts
1900 Kanawha Boulevard E
Charleston, WV 25305-0300

Weyerhaeuser Company Foundation Grants 1693

The foundation's mission is to improve the quality of life in communities where Weyerhaeuser has a major presence and to provide leadership that increases public understanding of issues where society's needs intersect with the interests of the forest products industry. Community service grants include awards in the fields of education and youth, health and welfare, civic and community improvement, and culture and the arts. In addition to community grants, industry-related awards are made to educational institutions, environmental groups, and professional organizations that promote further understanding of how the forest products industry responds to a changing society. Types of support include seed money, building construction/renovation, equipment acquisition, employee-related scholarships, publication, conferences and seminars, fellowships, lectureships, operating budgets, research, program

development, employee matching gifts, and technical assistance. Applicants should send a short letter that introduces the project and sponsoring organization and provide tax-exempt status evidence. If further consideration is warranted, the foundation may ask for additional information or a formal proposal. Proposals may be submitted at any time.
Requirements: Applying organizations must have nonprofit, tax-exempt status. To be considered for funding, an organization must: serve a community within a 50-mile radius of a major Weyerhaeuser facility; support a state-wide issue of interest to the Foundation and Weyerhaeuser in the key states of Alabama, Arkansas, Louisiana, Mississippi, North Carolina, Oklahoma, Oregon or Washington; or support a selected, high-priority national or international initiative directly related to the sustainability and importance of working forests. A limited number of smaller awards are also made to other locales where fewer employees are based.
Restrictions: Grants are not awarded to individuals or for political campaigns, activities that influence legislation, religious organizations seeking funds for theological purposes, or funds to purchase tickets or tables at fundraising benefits.
Geographic Focus: Alabama, Arizona, Arkansas, California, Colorado, District of Columbia, Georgia, Idaho, Illinois, Kentucky, Louisiana, Maryland, Michigan, Minnesota, Mississippi, Missouri, New Hampshire, New Jersey, New Mexico, North Carolina, Ohio, Oklahoma, Oregon, Pennsylvania, South Carolina, Texas, Utah, Virginia, Washington, West Virginia, Wisconsin
Date(s) Application is Due: Aug 31
Contact: Anne Levya, Team Coordinator; (253) 924-3159; (253) 924-3658; foundation@weyerhaeuser.com or anne.leyva@weyerhaeuser.com
Internet: http://www.weyerhaeuser.com/Sustainability/Foundation
Sponsor: Weyerhaeuser Company Foundation
P.O. Box 9777
Federal Way, WA 98063-9777

Whatcom Community Foundation Grants **1694**
The foundation awards grants to eligible Washington nonprofit organizations for programs and projects that build community capacity and community connections. Priority is placed on applications that show the greatest promise of leveraging additional support from the community. The foundation is interested in supporting activities and organizations that improve the ability of people to help themselves, increase nourishing connections among people, take cooperative approaches to community issues, and enable community institutions to be responsive to all citizens. Successful proposals describe not only what an organization proposes to do, but also how it involves others in the community toward problem-solving and long-term planning for Whatcom County's future. Effective proposals are likely to involve and affect youth and will take a long-term view of living in concert with the natural environment that makes Whatcom County a desirable place to live.
Requirements: Washington tax-exempt nonprofit organizations serving Whatcom County are eligible.
Restrictions: Grants do not support capital requests (bricks and mortar); endowment funds; debt retirement; political campaigns; religious activities; memberships in civic organizations or trade associations; courtesy advertising; tickets for benefits; fundraising events, individuals; for-profit organizations; or organizations that discriminate on the basis of gender, religion, sexual orientation, ethnicity, national origin, or physical ability.
Geographic Focus: Washington
Date(s) Application is Due: Feb 1
Amount: 1,000 - 10,000 USD
Samples: Safe Start Consortium (WA)—for a staff position to coordinate multi-agency strategic planning and fund development for reducing the exposure of young children to violence, $10,000; National Information Center for Ecology (WA)—for a project involving children in wildlife habitat enhancement along Fever Creek in Bellingham, $5000; Cornwall Park Church of God (WA)—for a summer program for children in first through fifth grades who have endured high-stress experiences, $4000; Lynden Pioneer Museum (WA)—for the museums' elementary educational workshops, $400.
Contact: Grants Administrator; (360) 671-6463; (360) 671-6437; wcf@whatcomcf.org
Internet: http://www.nas.com/~wcf
Sponsor: Whatcom Community Foundation
119 Grand Avenue, Suite A
Bellingham, WA 98225

Whirlpool Foundation Grants **1695**
Building on its history of concern for the communities in which Whirlpool operates, the foundation gives priority to projects addressing three strategic issues: lifelong learning, comprising programs addressing basic education, job training or retraining, and continuing education; cultural diversity, which includes support of programs that enable communities to appreciate diversity and promote better understanding among people through the study of language, customs, and traditions, and innovative cultural exchanges; and quality family life, which supports innovative community-based responses designed to strengthen families, improve parenting capabilities, and address the balance between parenting and job performance. Foundation resources are allocated across three programs—foundation grants; employee-directed programs, such as matching gifts and Dollars for Doers programs; and scholarships for employees' dependents. Additional types of support include matching funds, operating budgets, annual campaigns, emergency funds, building funds, equipment, and research. Applications are reviewed four times annually. Applicants are encouraged to contact the office for company operating areas and for additional information including where to submit applications.
Requirements: Tax-exempt organizations worldwide in Whirlpool communities are eligible.
Restrictions: Grants will not be made to individuals; for-profit organizations; political causes; religious-related organizations; social, labor, veterans, or fraternal organizations; athletic associations and events; fund-raising benefits; United Way agencies seeking general operating support; or national groups whose local chapters have already received support.
Geographic Focus: All U.S. States
Amount: 1,000 - 5,000 USD
Samples: Lake Michigan College (MI)—for the center for technical training, $1 million over four years; Gilda's Club (New York, NY)—to educate families about the value of social and emotional support when family members are living with cancer, $200,000 over two years.
Contact: Pamela Silcox, Operations Manager; (269) 923-5584; (269) 925-0154; pamela_j_silcox@whirlpool.com
Internet: http://www.whirlpoolcorp.com/responsibility/building_communities/whirlpool_foundation.aspx
Sponsor: Whirlpool Foundation
2000 North M-63
Benton Harbor, MI 49022-2692

Whitehall Foundation Neurobiology Research Grants **1696**
Through its program of grants and grants in aid, the foundation assists scholarly research in the life sciences. The foundation is currently interested in basic research in invertebrate and vertebrate (excluding clinical) neurobiology, specifically investigations of neural mechanisms involved in sensory, motor, and other complex functions of the whole organism as these relate to behavior. Research grants are available to established scientists of all ages working at accredited institutions and will be awarded for up to three years, with possible renewal on a competitive basis for a maximum of two years. Grants in aid are designed for researchers at the assistant professor level who experience difficulty in competing for research funds because they have not yet become firmly established. Grants in aid will also be made to senior scientists. The foundation's policy is to assist those dynamic areas of basic biological research that are not heavily supported by federal agencies or other foundations with specialized missions. Types of support include personnel (salary support for students and technicians); permanent equipment, materials, and supplies needed to complete the project; travel for research; publication costs; and overhead (no more than 25 percent or supplies). Applicant should initiate the proposal process by submitting a one-page letter written in technical language identifying the nature of the research proposal and indicating whether the request is for a grant or grant in aid. Grant application forms will be sent to those applicants whose proposed project matches the foundation's current funding interests. Deadlines listed are for letters of intent.
Requirements: Accredited U.S. institutions are eligible. The foundation prefers to support scientists at the beginning of their career and those senior scientists who have maintained productivity. The principal investigator must hold no less than the position of assistant professor or the equivalent.
Geographic Focus: All U.S. States
Date(s) Application is Due: Jan 15; Apr 15; Oct 1
Amount: Up to 30,000 USD
Samples: Daniel Pollen, U of Massachusetts (MA)—for research on the cerebral integration in the primate visual system, $40,000 of three-year grant; Richard Ivry, U of California (CA)—for research on the role of the cerebellum in temporal processing, $24,000 final payment on three-year grant; Paul

Black, Boston U (Boston, MA)—to support research on brain-immune system interactions, $130,020 final payment on three-year grant.
Contact: Program Director; (561) 655-4474; (561) 655-4978; email@whitehall.org
Internet: http://www.whitehall.org
Sponsor: Whitehall Foundation
P.O. Box 3423
Palm Beach, FL 33480

Whiting Foundation Grants **1697**
The grant program awards funds for broad purposes: in Michigan, to further secular and religious education and research of all kinds; to aid and improve the physical, financial, mental, and moral condition of the poor, the sick, the young, the aged, and the disabled among all classes; and nationally for cancer research. Types of support include general operating support and program development. Although funding is on a national scale the majority of funding is primarily made in the greater Flint, MI, area. Application forms are not required.
Geographic Focus: All U.S. States
Date(s) Application is Due: Apr 30
Amount: 500 - 500,000 USD
Samples: Cancer Research Institute (New York, NY)—$10,000; Insight Inc (Flint, MI)—$10,000; Christ Episcopal Ctr (Flint, MI)—$7500; Whaley Childrens Ctr (Flint, MI)—$30,000.
Contact: Donald Johnson, Jr., President; (810) 767-3600
Sponsor: Whiting Foundation
901 Citizens Bank Building
Flint, MI 48502

Widgeon Point Charitable Foundation Grants **1698**
The foundation supports nonprofits in New York and Connecticut in its areas of interest, including secondary, higher, legal, and medical education; youth; zoos; museums; arts and culture; conservation and environment; historic preservation; family planning; libraries; and religion. Types of support include general operating budgets, capital campaigns, building funds, endowment funds, equipment acquisition, conferences and seminars, publications, and renovation projects. There are no application deadlines. Applicants should submit a two-page letter of application.
Requirements: Nonprofits in New York and Connecticut are eligible.
Restrictions: Grants are not awarded to individuals or for endowments, capital costs, renovation, equipment, conferences, publications, and media projects.
Geographic Focus: Connecticut, New York
Amount: 1,000 - 25,000 USD
Samples: Connecticut Fund for the Environment (CT)—for operating support, $5000;Boys Club of New York (NY)—for operating support, $2000.
Contact: John Robinson, President; (203) 861-7314
Sponsor: Widgeon Point Charitable Foundation
3000 Marcus Avenue
Lake Success, NY 11042-1066

Wieboldt Foundation Grants **1699**
The Wieboldt Foundation limits its grant making to the Chicago metropolitan area. The foundation supports multi-issue community organizing groups that work in low-income neighborhoods, that are accountable to neighborhood residents, and through which people are empowered to have a major voice in shaping decisions that affect their lives.
Requirements: The Wieboldt Foundation supports organizations that: organize by enlisting and nurturing participation of a large number of neighborhood residents, organizations and institutions; recruit, develop, and formally train local leadership; enable local residents to develop an agenda, to devise strategies, and to carry out action effectively to address issues; demonstrate innovative strategies or create new local institutions that strengthen local community capacity; broaden their impact by working with other groups, whenever possible; are led by a board of directors that is representative of and accountable to community residents; show evidence of significant local fundraising. To be considered for financial support, send us a Letter of Inquiry to awards@wieboldt.org outlining the nature of your organization and rationale for funding from the Wieboldt Foundation. Letters of Inquiry will be reviewed by staff and a committee of the board who will make a determination on whether to invite your organization to submit a full proposal.
Restrictions: The Wieboldt Foundation generally does not fund individuals, studies and research, conferences, capital development, or direct or social service programs.
Geographic Focus: Illinois
Date(s) Application is Due: Jun 1; Aug 3; Oct 5; Nov 30
Amount: 3,000 - 40,000 USD
Samples: Woods Fund of Chicago, Chicago, IL, $5,000 - for support of Saul Alinsky Centennial Symposium (2009); Midwest Academy, Chicago, IL, $15,000 - Summer Internship Program (2009); Women & Girls Collective Action Network, Chicago, IL, $10,000 - for general operating support (2009)
Contact: Regina McGraw, Executive Director; (312) 786-9377, ext. 1; (312) 786-9232; reginam@wieboldt.org
Internet: http://wieboldt.org/grant-guidelines/
Sponsor: Wieboldt Foundation
53 West Jackson Boulivard, Suite 838
Chicago, IL 60604

Wilbur Foundation Grants **1700**
The Wilbur Foundation concentrates its funding in the field of humanities, especially history, literature, religion and philosophy. It seeks to support institutions and projects that are calculated to uphold or carry on the traditions of society. Applications are accepted between September 1 and December 31.
Requirements: Tax-exempt nonprofit organizations that reflect a concern for historical continuity and studies of a traditional nature may apply.
Restrictions: Except for resident fellowships, no grants are made to individuals, and the foundation does not consider grants for general building purposes.
Geographic Focus: All U.S. States
Date(s) Application is Due: Dec 31
Contact: Gary Ricks, President; (805) 563-1082; grants@wilburfoundation.org
Internet: http://www.wilburfoundation.org/grant.htm
Sponsor: Wilbur Foundation
P.O. Box 3370
Santa Barbara, CA 93130-3370

WILD Foundation Grants **1701**
Founded in 1974, WILD is the only international organization dedicated entirely and explicitly to wilderness protection around the world. WILD works to protect the planet's last wild places and the wildlife and people who depend upon them, because wilderness areas provide essential social, spiritual, biological and economic benefits. The WILD Foundation focuses on four main program areas: World Wilderness Congress, wilderness policy and research, communications and field projects. Refer to the Foundations website for more detailed information on each program of interest. There are no specific deadlines with which to adhere. Contact the Foundation for further application information and guidelines.
Geographic Focus: All U.S. States
Contact: Charlotte Baron, Chairperson; (303) 442-8811; (303) 442-8877; info@wild.org
Internet: http://www.wild.org/main/about/
Sponsor: WILD Foundation
717 Poplar Avenue
Boulder, CO 80304

Willard and Pat Walker Charitable Foundation Grants **1702**
The foundation awards grants to Arkansas nonprofit organizations in its areas of interest, including arts, health organizations, higher education, and social services. Types of support include building construction/renovation, general operating grants, and program development. There are no application forms or deadlines.
Requirements: Arkansas nonprofit organizations are eligible.
Restrictions: Individuals are not eligible.
Geographic Focus: Arkansas
Samples: Ouachita Baptist (Arkadelphia, AR)—for its capital campaign, $2.5 million; U of Arkansas for Medical Sciences (Little Rock, AR)—to expand research and patient care in the areas of Alzheimer's disease, eye diseases, and mental illness, $21.5 million; U of Arkansas (Fayetteville, AR)—to construct a building as part of the College of Business, $8 million.
Contact: Tommy Karr, (501) 756-7031
Sponsor: Willard and Pat Walker Charitable Foundation
P.O. Box 5000
Springdale, AR 72765-5000

William A. Badger Foundation Grants 1703

The Nabors to Neighbors Foundation was created in 2007 to assist charitable organizations focusing on need based projects for direct programming, capital and operating initiatives. This is a family foundation dedicated to organizations that deliver measurable results, seek partnerships and collaborations, utilize their resources within their respective communities while working to increase equity for those most in need. The Foundation encourages nonprofit organizations to apply who specialize in, though not limited to, improving the lives of children, education and medical initiatives. The Foundation makes no geographic restrictions on distributions. However, it has been the practice of the Trustees to make grants within Whitfield County, specifically Dalton, located in north Georgia. Requests must be postmarked by February 1, July 9 or October 1 in order to be considered.

Requirements: The Nabors to Neighbors Foundation makes grants to qualified 501(c)3 organizations. All requests must include: background information on the organization, including a brief history, the organization's current address and phone number and the name and title or the primary contact; the goals, objectives, and budget for the one project or program for which funds are being requested; the amount of the grant requested; summary of how the funds will be used; supporting financial information on the organization, to include current financial status and listing of Board of Trustees; copy of organization's tax exemption letter from the Internal Revenue Service. Application form is available online and all requests must be postmarked by February 1, July 9 or October 1 in order to be considered.

Restrictions: Grants are not made to: individuals; an organization to be used as pass-through funds for an ineligible organization Faith-based organizations without a 501(c)3 exemption; organizations with political purposes, nor to organizations which discriminate on the basis of race, ethnic origin, sexual or religious preference, age or gender.

Geographic Focus: All U.S. States

Date(s) Application is Due: Feb 1; Jul 9; Oct 1

Contact: Trustee, c/o Wachovia Bank; grantinquiries8@wachovia.com

Internet: https://www.wachovia.com/foundation/v/index.jsp?vgnextoid=108bf296ac212210VgnVCM100000617d6fa2RCRD&vgnextfmt=default

Sponsor: Nabors to Neighbors Foundation
3280 Peachtree Road NE, Suite 400, MC G0141-041
Atlanta, GA 30305

William and Charlotte Parks Foundation for Animal Welfare Grants 1704

The foundation awards grants to support animal protection to both animal protection organizations and to individual scholars who are pursuing a course of study that might advance the goals of the trust founders. Organizations may receive funds for capital projects, for general operating expenses, or for specific projects. Doctoral or post-doctoral candidates may receive funds to support a specific research project. These funds must be distributed through an organization with 501(c)3 status. Deadlines are May 1 for project, operating, and capital grants; and December 1 for PhD/veterinary fellowships. Application and guidelines are available online.

Requirements: 501(c)3 tax-exempt organizations are eligible. A non-U.S. applicant must be registered as a charitable organization in the home country.

Restrictions: Grants will not normally be awarded to improve animal health, for local spay/neuter assistance, to save endangered species, to rehabilitate wildlife, or to support political candidates. Grants focused on the conservation or protection of wild animal populations will not be funded. Grants will not ordinarily be made to organizations with an annual income of more than $1 million or a large asset base, with the exception of institutions of higher learning.

Geographic Focus: All U.S. States

Date(s) Application is Due: May 1; Dec 1

Amount: 10,000 - 30,000 USD

Contact: Donna Pease, (301) 548-7726; info@parksfoundation.org

Internet: http://www.parksfoundation.org

Sponsor: William and Charlotte Parks Foundation
700 Professional Drive
Gaithersburg, MD 20879

William and Flora Hewlett Foundation Education Grants 1705

The Hewlett Foundation concentrates its grantmaking around its core program areas: education, environment, global development, performing arts, philanthropy, and population. In addition, the Foundation makes grants to support disadvantaged communities in the California, Bay Area region.

Requirements: Initial contact should be by letter of inquiry addressed to the president providing a straightforward statement of needs and aspirations for support. Applicants who receive favorable responses will be invited to submit formal proposals.

Restrictions: Requests will not be considered to fund student aid, construction, equipment and computer purchases, education research, basic scientific research, health research, or health education programs.

Geographic Focus: California

Samples: Los Angeles Alliance for a New Economy, $90,000—environmental grant (2010); American Conservatory Theater, $40,000—performing arts grant (2010); International Planned Parenthood Federation, Western Hemisphere Region, $500,000—population grant (2010).

Contact: Paul Brest, President; (650) 234-4500; (650) 234-4501; info@hewlett.org

Internet: http://www.hewlett.org/Grantseekers

Sponsor: William and Flora Hewlett Foundation
2121 Sand Hill Road
Menlo Park, CA 94025

William and Flora Hewlett Foundation Environmental Grants 1706

The program has three goals: to save the great ecosystems of the North American West; to reduce the environmental impacts of fossil-fuel energy systems by promoting energy efficiency and renewable energy sources; and to build an infrastructure for environmental concerns among California's growing but still underrepresented populations in the LA basin and the Central Valley. Types of support include general operating funds, seed money, continuing support, emergency funds, land acquisition, special projects, matching funds, employee matching gifts, and endowment funds. Grants must be approved by the board of directors, which meets quarterly. Meeting dates are available upon request. The foundation does not accept proposals via fax or email.

Requirements: Initial contact should be by letter of inquiry addressed to the president providing a straightforward statement of needs and aspirations for support. Applicants who receive favorable responses will be invited to submit formal proposals.

Restrictions: The foundation usually does not support proposals in the areas of basic research; capital construction; conferences, symposia, or workshops; environmental education (K-12 or adult); museum facilities, exhibits, or programs; or specific media projects. The foundation does not make awards to individuals, organizations outside the United States, or local land trusts, nor does it support community organizing, advocacy, or litigation.

Geographic Focus: All U.S. States

Samples: Centro Interdisciplinario de Biodiversidad y Ambiente (Mexico)—to design and implement a rapid-transit bus corridor in Mexico City, $400,000; David Suzuki Foundation (Vancouver, Canada)—for the Turning Point Initiative, which works on land-use issues on the North Pacific Coast, $750,000; Nature Conservancy (Arlington, VA)—to raise money for the protection of Great Bear Rainforest, in western Canada, $345,000; Relational Culture Institute (Fresno, CA)—for an air-quality project in California's San Joaquin Valley, $90,000.

Contact: Hal Harvey, Program Director; (650) 234-4500, ext. 5647; (650) 234-4501; info@hewlett.org

Internet: http://www.hewlett.org/Programs/Environment/envHome.htm

Sponsor: William and Flora Hewlett Foundation
2121 Sand Hill Road
Menlo Park, CA 94025

William and Flora Hewlett Foundation Performing Arts Grants 1707

The program's mission is to support artistic expression and its enjoyment through grantmaking aimed at the sustainability of high-quality Bay Area organizations. Organizations working in dance, music, musical theater, opera, and theater are eligible for consideration. The program supports the following types of organizations: performing companies, presenting organizations, service organizations, arts councils, training and participation programs, and national and nonresident organizations that serve Bay Area artists and audiences. The program also makes grants to film and media service organizations. The focus of support is on long-term artistic development and managerial stability achieved primarily through a strategy of multiyear general operating support to organizations of programmatic merit that operate without incurring annual deficits. The foundation gives preference to independent nonprofit Bay Area organizations with an established record of artistic achievement, administrative capacity, audience support, and realistic planning and implementation for artistic and organizational development. Artistic training programs, particularly those focused on young people, continue to be of interest.

Requirements: The program's geographic focus is the nine California counties that border the San Francisco Bay, with additional limited funding in Santa

Cruz and Monterey counties. Letters of inquiry addressed to the president providing a statement of needs and aspirations for support should precede formal applications.
Restrictions: Grants are not made for visual or literary arts; humanities; elementary and secondary school programs; college or university proposals; community art classes; folk arts, including crafts and popular music; recreational, therapeutic, and social service arts programs; nor to individuals. The foundation also does not support one-time events such as seminars, conferences, festivals, or cultural foreign exchange programs, nor provide assistance with touring costs for performing companies.
Geographic Focus: California
Date(s) Application is Due: Apr 1; Aug 31; Dec 1
Samples: Bay Area Video Coalition (San Francisco, CA)—for general support, $300,000; Dancers Group (San Francisco, CA)—for Bay Area Celebrates National Dance Week, $60,000; Oakland Ballet (Oakland, CA)—for organizational assessment and strategic planning, $35,000; Wallace Alexander Gerbode Foundation (San Francisco, CA)—to make grants to young California performing artists, $450,000.
Contact: Moy Eng, Program Director; (650) 234-4500; (650) 234-4501; info@hewlett.org
Internet: http://www.hewlett.org
Sponsor: William and Flora Hewlett Foundation
2121 Sand Hill Road
Menlo Park, CA 94025

William B. Dietrich Foundation Grants **1708**
The foundation awards grants to nonprofits in Pennsylvania in its areas of interest, including elderly services; AIDS and AIDS research; children and youth services; education and higher education; historic preservation; human services; museums; and secondary education. Types of support include general operating support, capital campaigns, building construction/renovation, program development, research, and matching funds. There are no application forms or deadlines.
Requirements: Pennsylvania nonprofits are eligible to apply.
Restrictions: No grants are provided for individuals.
Geographic Focus: Pennsylvania
Samples: Woodmere Art Museum (Philadelphia, PA)—to expand its administrative offices, $200,000; Wellness Community of Philadelphia (PA)—to restore and renovate an 18th-century barn that will serve as a new facility for this group that offers programs and services for people with cancer and their families, $350,000.
Contact: William Dietrich, President; (215) 979-1919
Sponsor: William B. Dietrich Foundation
P.O. Box 58177
Philadelphia, PA 19102-8177

William B. Stokely Jr. Foundation Grants **1709**
The foundation participates in scholarship funds at various colleges and universities mainly in the east Tennessee area. Grants are made to the educational institutions, which then distribute funds through their scholarship programs. Consideration also will be given to the requests of arts, health service, civic organizations, and youth services. Grants support general operations, continuing support, annual campaigns, capital campaigns, endowment funds, and scholarship funds. The foundation does not require completion of a formal application, nor are there established deadline dates. All proposals must be submitted in writing and addressed to the foundation president. The board meets in February, May, August, and November.
Requirements: Tennessee organizations with 501(c)3 tax-exempt status are eligible.
Restrictions: The foundation does not donate funds to individuals.
Geographic Focus: Tennessee
Amount: 100 - 100,000 USD
Contact: William Stokely III, President; (865) 966-4878
Sponsor: William B. Stokely Jr. Foundation
620 Campbell Station Road, Suite 27
Knoxville, TN 37922-1636

William Blair and Company Foundation Grants **1710**
The foundation awards grants to Illinois nonprofit organizations in its areas of interest, including arts and culture, civic and public affairs, community development, elementary education, health care, higher education, Jewish and Catholic giving, secondary education, social services, and youth programs. Types of support include annual campaigns, building construction/renovation, capital campaigns, fellowships, general operating support, multiyear funds, continuing support, scholarship funds and scholarships to individuals, sponsorships, internships, and United Way. Preference is given to requests from the greater Chicago metropolitan area.There are no application deadlines or forms. Submit a letter of request.
Requirements: Illinois nonprofit organizations are eligible.
Geographic Focus: Illinois
Amount: 100 - 25,000 USD
Samples: Chicago Botanic Garden (Glencoe, IL)—for general support, $10,000; Commercial Club Foundation (Chicago, IL)—for general support, $25,000.
Contact: David Coolidge III, Vice President; (312) 236-1600
Sponsor: William Blair and Company Foundation
222 W Adams Street, 28th Floor
Chicago, IL 60606

William Boss Foundation Grants **1711**
The Foundation supports the arts, higher education, human service programs, libraries/library science, museums, performing arts, and youth programs. Types of support include general operating and program specific.
Requirements: Applicants should submit the following: copy of IRS determination letter, detailed description of project and amount of funding requested, and additional materials and supporting documentation.
Restrictions: Giving is primarily restricted to Minnesota. No grants for individuals.
Geographic Focus: Minnesota
Date(s) Application is Due: Jun 15
Contact: Dan McKeown, Treasurer; (651) 653-0599
Sponsor: William Boss Foundation
5858 Centerville Road
Street Paul, MN 55127-6804

William C. Woolf Foundation Grants **1712**
The foundation exists to enhance the quality of life for citizens of Shreveport, LA, and awards one-year grants to eligible Louisiana nonprofit organizations for a variety of programs and activities. Proposals must meet the listed application deadline and include a copy of the IRS tax-determination letter.
Requirements: 501(c)3 tax-exempt organizations located in northwestern Louisiana are eligible.
Restrictions: Grants are not made to individuals.
Geographic Focus: Louisiana
Amount: 300 - 50,000 USD
Contact: Barbara York, Chair
Sponsor: William C. Woolf Foundation
333 Texas Street, SH 2069
Shreveport, LA 71101

William E. and Bertha E. Schrafft Charitable Trust Grants **1713**
The trust makes grants to charitable institutions in the greater Boston, MA, metropolitan area that are involved with education of indigent or otherwise disadvantaged youth. Grants are awarded for programs or projects, continuing support, annual campaigns, general operating support, and scholarship funds. The trustees meet approximately six times each year to consider requests; there are no application deadlines.
Requirements: Grants are awarded to nonprofit organizations in Massachusetts, with emphasis on the Boston area.
Restrictions: Grants are not awarded to individuals or for matching gifts, seed money, emergency funds, or deficit financing.
Geographic Focus: Massachusetts
Amount: 5,000 - 25,000 USD
Samples: Mother Caroline Academy and Education Ctr (MA)—for general operating support, $15,000; Institute of Contemporary Art (MA)—for a teen education program, $10,000; Gordon College (MA)—for scholarship support, $45,000; Catholic Schools Foundation (MA)—for the inner-city scholarship fund, $15,000.
Contact: Karen Faulkner, Executive Director; (617) 457-7327; funding@schrafftcharitable.org
Internet: http://www.schrafftcharitable.org
Sponsor: William E. and Bertha E. Schrafft Charitable Trust
One Boston Place, 34th Floor
Boston, MA 0002108-4408

William G. and Helen C. Hoffman Foundation Grants 1714

Helen C. Hoffman resided in the Village of South Orange, New Jersey. Her foundation was established in 1998 in memory of herself and her husband after the death of their daughter Corinne Blair. Her testamentary wish was to establish this foundation for charitable, religious, scientific, literary, and educational purposes. Her preference was to support blindness and its cure. Approximately 90% of the grants will provide support to the blind and, to medical research for the prevention of blindness. The remaining 10% will fund annual grants in the following areas of interest: education, the arts, environment and, social/civic causes. Requests must be received by January 15 for the March meeting and, August 22 for the October meeting. Application forms are available online. Applicants will receive notice acknowledging receipt of the grant request, and subsequently be notified of the grant declination or approval.

Requirements: Any U.S. 501(c)3 non-profit organizations may apply. Proposals should be submitted in the following format: completed Common Grant Application Form; an original Proposal Statement; an audited financial report and a current year operating budget; a copy of your official IRS Letter with your tax determination; a listing of your Board of Directors. Proposal Statements (second item in the above Format) should answer these questions: what are the objectives and expected outcomes of this program/project/request; what strategies will be used to accomplish your objective; what is the timeline for completion; if this is part of an on-going program, how long has it been in operation; what criteria will you use to measure success; if the request is not fully funded, what other sources can you engage; an Itemized budget should be included; please describe any collaborative ventures. Prior to the distribution of funds, all approved grantees must sign and return a Grant Agreement Form, stating that the funds will be used for the purpose intended. Progress reports and Completion reports must also be filed as required for your specific grant. All current grantees must be in good standing with required documentation prior to submitting new proposals to any foundation.

Restrictions: Grants are not made for political purposes, nor to organizations which discriminate on the basis of race, ethnic origin, sexual or religious preference, age or gender.

Geographic Focus: All U.S. States

Date(s) Application is Due: Jan 15; Aug 22

Amount: 5,000 - 15,000 USD

Samples: Tri-County Scholarship Fund, $5,000—scholarships for economically disadvantaged students to receive a private elementary/secondary education; New Eyes for the Needy, Inc., $20,000— eyeglasses for poor Kentuckians; Christian Health Care Center Foundation, $10,000— support senior subsidies for adult day services.

Contact: Wachovia Bank, N.A., Trustee; grantinquiries2@wachovia.com

Internet: https://www.wachovia.com/foundation/v/index.jsp?vgnextoid=522852199c0aa110VgnVCM1000004b0d1872RCRD&vgnextfmt=default

Sponsor: William G. and Helen C. Hoffman Foundation
190 River Road, NJ3132
Summit, NJ 07901

William G. Baker, Jr. Memorial Fund Grants 1715

The William G. Baker, Jr. Memorial Fund was established in 1964 by Mary S. Baker in memory of her husband. The fund continues the Baker's civic-minded philanthropic tradition, offering grants that range from $1,000 to $40,000. Its grant making program primarily benefits the residents of the greater Baltimore area. The Fund commits its resources to enhance the region's economy and quality of life through investments in a broadly defined cultural sector in which all residents may participate and thrive. Its grants will support artistic and cultural organizations and their partners that enhance an individual's sense of self and pleasure and make Baltimore a more attractive place to live, work and play.

Requirements: Organizations (or their fiscal agents) serving the Baltimore area that qualify as public charities under section 501(c)3 of the Internal Revenue Code and do not discriminate on the basis of race, creed, national origin, color, physical handicap, gender or sexual orientation are eligible to apply.

Restrictions: No grants will be made to individuals, or for religious/sectarian purposes or deficit financing.

Geographic Focus: Maryland

Date(s) Application is Due: Jan 1; Mar 3; Jul 7; Sep 26

Amount: 1,000 - 40,000 USD

Contact: Odessa Hampton; (410) 332-4171; ohampton@bcf.org

Internet: http://www.bcf.org/ourgrants/ourgrantsdetail.aspx?grid=1

Sponsor: William G. Baker, Jr. Memorial Fund
2 East Read Street, 9th Floor
Baltimore, MD 21202

William G. Gilmore Foundation Grants 1716

The foundation supports nonprofits primarily in the San Francisco Bay Area, CA; some funding also in Pueblo, CO and Portland, OR. Giving primarily for the arts, health, and children, youth, and social services.

Requirements: California, Colorado, and Oregon nonprofits are eligible to apply. Contact the Foundation for additional application information.

Restrictions: No grants to individuals.

Geographic Focus: California, Colorado, Oregon

Amount: 1,000 - 50,000 USD

Contact: Faye Wilson, Executive Director; (415) 546-1400; (415) 391-8732

Sponsor: William G. Gilmore Foundation
120 Montgomery Street, Suite 1880
San Francisco, CA 94104-4317

William G. McGowan Charitable Fund Grants 1717

The fund awards grants to eligible nonprofit organizations that are devoted to three specific philanthropic goals: developing the talents and gifts of the very young, especially those who have been disenfranchised by virtue of low income status, inner-city conditions or family situations; funding for selected areas of medical research directed toward finding cures for, or relieving the pain and suffering of, those afflicted with debilitating conditions or diseases; and the McGowan Scholars program, which provides financial assistance to selected college and university students interested in pursuing an undergraduate or graduate degree at a college or university business school accredited by the International Association for Management Education or Association of Collegiate Business Schools and Programs.

Requirements: Nonprofit organizations in the following states and cities are eligible: Chicago, IL; District of Columbia and its Virginia suburbs; metropolitan Kansas City, western New York; and northeast Pennsylvania.

Restrictions: The fund does not support multiyear grants; accept requests online; or fund art or theatrical activities, building funds, church renovation campaigns, or endowments.

Geographic Focus: California, District of Columbia, Illinois, Missouri, New York, Pennsylvania, Virginia

Date(s) Application is Due: Jan 2; May 1; Sep 1

Amount: 10,000 - 100,000 USD

Samples: Rochester Institute of Technology, College of Applied Science (NY)—to construct the Center for Telecommunications, $2 million; U of the Pacific (Stockton, CA)—for a scholarship for a business student, $18,000; Foundation for the National Archives (Washington, DC)—for the National Archives Experience, which will make important American documents accessible to the public and teach visitors about the value of archives, $5 million.

Contact: Bernard Goodrich, Executive Director; (301) 320-8570; (301) 320-8627; goodric@aol.com or info@mcgowanfund.org

Internet: http://www.mcgowanfund.org/guidelines.html

Sponsor: William G. McGowan Charitable Fund
P.O. Box 40515
Washington, DC 20016-0515

William G. Selby and Marie Selby Foundation Innovative Partnership Grants 1718

The goal of this Program is to encourage human services and arts organizations to work in collaboration. Innovative Partnerships will continue to be based on joint efforts of arts and human service providers to develop programs and deliver services together which could not be accomplished separately. A collaborative planning process should identify needs, clarify objectives of both partners and identify the resources and strengths each partner can bring to the project. The results of engaging in such a process will be sustained benefits for both organizations, as well as meaningful outcomes for the program participants. Peripheral benefits will evolve for both organizations as a true partnerships takes hold and develops overtime. The Foundation will accept joint applications from arts and human services organizations for grants up to $10,000. Applications must be in the Foundation office by 5:00 p.m. on December 1st.

Requirements: Nonprofit organizations from Sarasota and Manatee counties, Florida, are eligible.

Restrictions: Schools and/or day care facilities Pre-K through 12 are not eligible.

Geographic Focus: Florida

Date(s) Application is Due: Dec 1

Amount: Up to 10,000 USD

Samples: Circus Sarasota, $10,000 (each)—to build a sustaining partnership with Laughter Unlimited; Sarasota Coalition on Substance Abuse, $6,620 (each)—to build a sustaining partnership with Poetry in Motion.
Contact: Janet D. Noah, Grants Manager; (941) 957-0442; (941) 957-3135; jnoah@selbyfdn.org
Internet: http://www.selbyfdn.org/applyInnovative.html
Sponsor: William G. Selby and Marie Selby Foundation
1800 Second Street, Suite 750
Sarasota, FL 34236

William J. and Dorothy K. O'Neill Foundation Grants 1719
Foundation grantmaking activities include family, health, arts and culture, community, animals, education, environment, employment, fatherhood, recreation, religion, law enforcement/crime, human services, and housing. Types of support include general operating support, program development, seed grants, and matching funds. The foundation has no formal application form; requests should be made in writing. Grants are awarded for capacity building activities that develop or improve the effectiveness, impact and strength of: the organization's Board of Trustees and/or its Board leadership; the organization's strategic plan; the organization's staff; and the organization's programs. Grant requests should include the amount requested; specific project including goals, objectives, approach, and methods; project budget and timeline; other sources of funding; evaluation plan; qualifications and experience of key personnel; description of organization; most recent annual report; and copy of IRS classification letter. Requests may be submitted at any time but will be considered four times each year when the grantmaking committee meets. Annual deadline dates may vary; contact program staff for exact dates.
Requirements: 501(c)3 organizations in metropolitan areas where O'Neill family members currently live are eligible, including Washington, DC; Naples, FL, area; Big Island, HI; Baltimore/Annapolis, MD; New York, NY area; Cincinnati/Cleveland, OH; Columbus and Licking County, OH; Richmond/Virginia Beach, VA; and Houston, TX.
Restrictions: The foundation does not make grants to individuals, to organizations that are wholly outside the United States, or in response to form letters for annual appeals.
Geographic Focus: District of Columbia, Florida, Hawaii, Maryland, New York, Ohio, Texas, Virginia
Date(s) Application is Due: Jan 24; Apr 25; Jul 18; Oct 10
Amount: 35,000 - 620,000 USD
Samples: Children's Museum of Manhattan (New York, NY)—for new program development, $20,000; Virginia Supportive Housing (Richmond, VA)—for administrative structure changes, $20,000; Highbridge Community Life Ctr (Bronx, NY)—for CFO position, $20,000; North Union Farmers Market (Cleveland, OH)—for field worker consultant, $20,912.
Contact: Program Contact; (216) 831-4134, (216) 831-3779; oneillfdn@aol.com
Internet: http://www.oneillfdn.org/application.htm
Sponsor: William J. and Dorothy K. O'Neill Foundation
30195 Chagrin Boulevard, Suite 250
Cleveland, OH 44124

William K. Warren Foundation Grants 1720
The foundation awards grants to eligible nonprofit organizations in its areas of interest, including Catholic healthcare facilities, Catholic social services, education, and medical research. Types of support include building construction/renovation, endowment campaigns, general operating support, program development, and research grants. Grants are awarded primarily in Oklahoma. There are no application forms or deadlines. The board meets semiannually.
Geographic Focus: Oklahoma
Amount: 1,000 - 50,000 USD
Samples: Salvation Army of Tulsa (OK)—for general operating support, $135,000; Saint Anthony Hospital Foundation (Oklahoma City, OK)—for general support, $100,000.
Contact: Grants Administrator; (918) 492-8100
Sponsor: William K. Warren Foundation
P.O. Box 470372
Tulsa, OK 74147-0372

William N. and Myriam Pennington Foundation Grants 1721
The foundation supports education, health, and medical research in Nevada. Funding priority is given to organizations serving children and youth, the elderly, and the economically disadvantaged. Types of support include general operating support, building construction/renovation, equipment acquisition, and scholarships to individuals.
Requirements: Nevada nonprofits may apply for grant support.
Geographic Focus: Nevada
Amount: 2,500 - 200,000 USD
Samples: Assistance League of Reno-Sparks (Reno, NV)—for general support, $15,000; U of Nevada, Department of Speech Pathology (Reno, NV)—for equipment, $17,500.
Contact: Kent Green, Foundation Manager; (775) 333-9100
Sponsor: William N. and Myriam Pennington Foundation
441 W Plumb Lane
Reno, NV 89509

William Penn Foundation Grants 1722
The principal mission of the foundation is to help improve the quality of life in the Delaware Valley. Grants are made in the categories of children, youth, and families; arts and culture; and environment and communities. Under the category of children, youth, and families, grants are made to promote the full development of children and youth to become capable adults and productive citizens, with special emphasis on key transitions in their lives. Preference is given to programs that promote healthy birth outcomes and early childhood health; school readiness—facilitating a successful transition to school, and K-12 arts education; youth development—making an effective transition to higher education or work; and violence reduction—concern for vulnerable youth. In the area of environment and communities, grants are awarded to promote vital communities within a healthy regional ecosystem. Funding priorities include watersheds and ecosystems—protecting lands, enhancing stewardship; revitalize communities—strengthening of core urban centers; and smart growth—enhancing prosperity and livability of the region. In the area of arts and culture, preference will be given to projects that enable the creation and presentation of high-quality artistic work; provide support for artists in advancing their careers; encourage active participation in the cultural life of the region; preserve and promote the region's cultural assets; create new cultural opportunities in and for a particular neighborhood or community; and strengthen arts and cultural organizations in their core programs and administration. Written requests are accepted throughout the year; there are no formal deadlines.
Requirements: Grants are awarded to IRS 501(c)3 tax-exempt organizations in the Pennsylvania counties of Montgomery, Chester, Bucks, and Delaware; and Camden County, NJ. Environmental grants are made in a larger region, approximately a 100-mile radius from Philadelphia. In some instances, government agencies may be eligible if no nonprofit organization can conduct the equivalent activity.
Restrictions: Grants do not support individuals, nonpublic or charter schools, rehabilitation treatments, debt reduction, religious or political activities, hospital capital projects, housing construction, projects for the elderly, medical research, or replacement of government support.
Geographic Focus: New Jersey, Pennsylvania
Amount: 100,000,000 USD
Samples: Committee of Seventy (Philadelphia, PA)—for its strategic plan to advance good government in the metropolitan Philadelphia region, including through ethics legislation, an enforceable code of conduct for city employees, campaign-finance requirements for local candidates, oversight of the state's new gaming industry, and more transparent government contracts, $500,000 over two years.
Contact: Janet Haas, President; (215) 988-1830; (215) 988-1823; moreinfo@williampennfdn.org
Internet: http://www.williampennfoundation.org/info-url3564/info-url.htm
Sponsor: William Penn Foundation
100 N 18th Street, 11th Floor
Philadelphia, PA 19103

William Robert Baird Charitable Trust Grants 1723
The trust awards grants to Louisiana and Mississippi nonprofits in its areas of interest, including food banks, social services, children and youth services, and economically disadvantaged. Types of support include general operating support, program development, emergency fund, capital campaigns, endowment funds, and matching funds. There are no application forms or deadlines.
Requirements: Louisiana and Mississippi nonprofits may apply.
Restrictions: Individuals are ineligible.
Geographic Focus: Louisiana, Mississippi
Amount: 2,000 - 40,000 USD

Samples: Care Lodge Domestic Violence Shelter, Meridian, MS, $14,800 (2008); Wesley House Community Center, Meridian, MS, $39,500 (2008); Special Olympics Mississippi, Meridian, MS, $5,400 (2008).
Contact: John David Barr, Trust Administrator c/o Citizens National Bank; (601) 484-5887; jdbarr@ecitizensnationalbank.com
Sponsor: William Robert Baird Charitable Trust
512 22nd Avenue, P.O. Box 911
Meridian, MS 39302-5853

William T. Grant Foundation Youth Service Improvement Grants 1724
The program supports activities conducted by community-based organizations in the New York metropolitan area to improve the quality of services for young people (8-25 years of age). The program is designed to help good programs get better. Organizations should identify aspects of their current services that require improvement and propose a project with two main elements: (1) a plan of activities to improve the program services, and (2) an assessment plan to track the implementation of the improvement plan and its short-term results. Applications are accepted in the spring and the fall.
Requirements: To be eligible for consideration, organizations musthave 501(c)3 tax-exemption; provide services to youth located in the New York metropolitan area, defined as the following counties: (in New York) Bronx, Kings, Nassau, New York, Putnam, Queens, Richmond, Rockland, Suffolk, and Westchester counties; (in New Jersey) Bergen, Essex, Hudson, Hunterdon, Mercer, Middlesex, Monmouth, Morris, Ocean, Passaic, Somerset, Sussex, and Union counties; and (in Connecticut) Fairfield, New Haven, and Litchfield counties; serve youth aged 8-25 years; and have an operating budget between $250,000 and $5.0 million. In the case of organizations that serve youth only, this is the total organizational budget. In the case of multipurpose organizations (i.e., those not exclusively focused on youth), the organizational operating budget must be less than $20 million, and the budget for services to youth (direct and indirect costs) must be between $250,000 and $5.0 million.
Restrictions: The program program does not award grants to organizations that do not serve youth directly; staff from applicant organizations must have direct contact with youth at the point-of-service. The program does not support ongoing service delivery, general operating support, organizational development activities not directly related to improving the quality of youth services, service expansion or program growth, building campaigns, scholarships, endowments, lobbying, or awards to individuals.
Geographic Focus: Connecticut, New Jersey, New York
Amount: Up to 25,000 USD
Samples: Mental Health Association of New York - ($25,000) Adolescent Skills Center Internship-to-Work Program; Opportunities for a Better Tomorrow - ($25,000) Curriculum Development and Outcomes-Based Lesson Planning; Youth Communication New York - ($25,000) Improving Youth Services Through Enhanced Staff Training; Family ReEntry - ($25,000) Transitions Mentoring Program for Incarcerated Youth: Post-Release Improvement Project.
Contact: Sharon Brewster, ODF Grants Coordinator; (212) 752-0071; (212) 752-1398; sbrewster@wtgrantfdn.org
Internet: http://www.wtgrantfoundation.org/funding_opportunities/service-improvement-grants/youth_service_improvement/youth_service_improvement_grants
Sponsor: William T. Grant Foundation
570 Lexington Avenue, 18th Floor
New York, NY 10022-6837

Wilson-Wood Foundation Grants 1725
The Wilson-Wood Foundation established in 1983, supports organizations involved with: adult education; aging, centers/services; children/youth, services; education; health care; housing/shelter, development; human services; nutrition; women, centers/services. Giving is limited to the Manatee-Sarasota, Florida area, for for the underprivileged and the less fortunate in the community.
Requirements: Non-profits in the Manatee-Sarasota, Florida area are eligible to apply. Initial approach should be a phone call to the Foundation prior to submitting a the letter of inquiry (must be received by June 1). There is no application form required. Applicants must submit two copies of the proposal. Application must include the following information: timetable for implementation and evaluation of project; qualifications of key personnel; name, address and phone number of organization; copy of IRS Determination Letter, must be dated within the past 10 years; brief history of organization and description of its mission; copy of most recent annual report/audited financial statement/990; descriptive literature about organization; listing of board of directors, trustees, officers and other key people and their affiliations; detailed description of project and amount of funding requested; copy of current year's organizational budget and/or project budget; listing of additional sources and amount of support.
Restrictions: No support for foreign organizations, supporting organizations, or private foundations. No grants to individuals, or for endowment funds, deficit financing, travel projects, research, fundraising costs, multi-year projects, conferences, emergency funding or start up costs.
Geographic Focus: Florida
Date(s) Application is Due: Jun 1
Amount: 8,000 - 30,000 USD
Samples: Childrens Academy of Southwest Florida, Bradenton, FL, $30,000; Meals on Wheels Plus of Manatee, Bradenton, FL, $20,000; Habitat for Humanity, Venice Area, Venice, FL, $25,000
Contact: Susan Wood, Executive Director; (941) 966-3635
Sponsor: Wilson-Wood Foundation
930 Scherer Way
Osprey, FL 34229-6867

Wisconsin Arts Board Artistic Program I Support Grants 1726
Artistic Program Support I (APS I) provides artistic, program, and operational support to established nonprofit arts institutions of the highest artistic level, whose primary mission is to create and produce arts programming of significant statewide impact on the cultural life of Wisconsin. The goals of the program are to sustain organizational and financial stability and high-quality arts programming; ensure long-range planning as an approach to increasing the effectiveness of arts organizations; and increase local, statewide, and regional leadership in the arts among arts organizations in Wisconsin. Types of activities funded include general operating expenses; artistic and technical/production personnel expenses; outside artistic fees and services; artistic space rental/expenditures; production/exhibition expenses; and acquisition of artwork. Applicants are required to use the electronic application process in addition to mailing paper copies and originals to the Arts Board. Guidelines are available online.
Requirements: 501(c)3 tax-exempt arts organizations that qualify as a charitable organization under 170(c) of the Internal Revenue Code of 1954 as amended are eligible. Applicants must have a minimum annual operating budget of $698,000 in their most recently completed fiscal year to be eligible.
Restrictions: Arts Board policy does not allow applicants to apply for APS I if they receive funding through other Wisconsin Arts Board programs, excluding the Arts Challenge Initiative.
Geographic Focus: Wisconsin
Date(s) Application is Due: Nov 15
Contact: Program Manager; (608) 266-0190; (608) 267-0380; artsboard@arts.state.wi.us
Internet: http://arts.state.wi.us/static/aps1.htm
Sponsor: Wisconsin Arts Board
101 E Wilson Street, 1st Floor
Madison, WI 53702

Wisconsin Arts Board Arts Challenge Initiative Grants 1727
The Arts Challenge Initiative helps Wisconsin nonprofit arts organizations leverage income from private sources. The program is intended to spur the fund-raising efforts of arts organizations by providing state funds to organizations whose fund-raising efforts meet or exceed the total amount of eligible income raised in the previous year. The program includes three categories: minority organizations, organizations with budgets over $100,000, and organizations with budgets under $100,000. Guidelines and applications are available on the website.
Requirements: Only nonprofit arts organizations in Wisconsin are eligible.
Geographic Focus: Wisconsin
Date(s) Application is Due: Aug 1
Contact: Mark Fraire, Grantss and Services Specialist; (608) 264-8191; (608) 267-0380; mark.fraire@arts.state.wi.us
Internet: http://arts.state.wi.us/static/aci.htm
Sponsor: Wisconsin Arts Board
101 E Wilson Street, 1st Floor
Madison, WI 53702

Wolfe Associates Grants 1728
The grants program supports medical research, hospitals, all levels of education, arts and culture, youth and social service, community development, and environment. Types of support include building programs, equipment, operating budgets, continuing support, annual campaigns, matching funds,

professorships, employee matching gifts, and scholarship funds. Application guidelines should be obtained from Wolfe Associates Inc before presenting a formal application. Applications are accepted on an ongoing basis; renewal is not automatic.
Requirements: Organizations must be nonprofit with 501(c)3 status. Funding is kept almost exclusively to the Columbus and central Ohio area.
Restrictions: No grants are awarded to individuals, or for research, demonstration projects, publications, or conferences.
Geographic Focus: Ohio
Amount: 1,000 - 225,000 USD
Samples: YMCA of Central Ohio (Columbus, OH)—for operating support, $30,000; Columbus Jewish Foundation (Columbus, OH)—for operating support, $8000.
Contact: Rita Wolfe Hoag, (614) 460-3782
Sponsor: Wolfe Associates
34 S Third Street
Columbus, OH 43215

Women's Foundation of California Community Action Fund **1729**
The foundation awards grants to support projects of organizations working to improve the lives of women and girls in California. Requests will only be considered in one of the following issue areas: economic rights and justice; environmental health and justice; and reproductive rights and justice. Types of support include general operating support, project/program-specific grants, and planning grants. Serious consideration will be given to cross-sector collaborations as well as to emerging organizations, especially in rural and non-urban areas. Funding for publications and one-time events will only be considered if they are integrated within a larger strategy for social change. Application and guidelines are available online.
Requirements: California organizations that work with low-income women and girls are eligible. Priority is given to projects serving women and girls of color; immigrant, undocumented, and refugees women and girls; lesbian, bisexual, transgender, intersex, and questioning women and girls; women and girls with disabilities; women over 50; indigenous women and girls; young and/or single mothers; and women and girls in rural and non-urban communities.
Restrictions: The program does not fund capital improvements, endowments, loans, individuals, debt reduction, expenses that accrued prior to the date of the grant award, or fundraising events.
Geographic Focus: California
Date(s) Application is Due: Dec 16
Amount: Up to 35,000 USD
Contact: Grants Administrator; (415) 837-1113; (415) 837-1144
Internet: http://www.womensfoundca.org
Sponsor: Women's Foundation of California
340 Pine Street, Suite 302
San Francisco, CA 94104

Women's Foundation of California Grants **1730**
The Women's Foundation of California envisions a future where communities in California are healthy, safe and economically prosperous. The Foundation achieve's this vision by focusing on women and girls as change agents through their central role in families and communities. The Foundation supports organizations that meet the following objectives: organizations mobilizing communities to change policies and systems; to improve the lives of women and girls; developing the leadership of women and girls working to change policies and systems and create stronger movements for social justice; promoting the human rights of women and girls in all sectors of society, including economic, political, social, environmental, sexual, cultural and civil rights.
Requirements: The foundation awards grants to: California 501(c)3 nonprofit corporations or California nonprofit groups with a 501(c)3 fiscal sponsor; organization/program prioritize low-income women and girls in California; health and safety: this includes reproductive health and justice, environmental health and justice and gender-based violence; economic prosperity: this includes efforts towards economic security and economic development. Organizations or programs that utilize one or more of the following strategies to bring about measurable and sustainable change: policy advocacy; community organizing; leadership development; media and/or public education; civic participation; participatory action research; youth-led programs and initiatives. Contact the Foundation for further application information and guidelines.
Restrictions: The Women's Foundation of California does not make grants to or for the following: individuals; for-profit organizations or small businesses; start-up loans; capital projects; direct services; fundraising events; shelters; scholarships; capital improvements; endowments; loans; debt reduction; expenses that accrued prior to the date of the grant award. Funding for publications and one-time events such as retreats and conferences will only be considered if they are integrated within a larger strategy for social change.
Geographic Focus: California
Amount: 10,000 - 40,000 USD
Contact: Maya Thornell-Sandifor, Senior Program Officer; (415) 837-1113; (415) 837-1144; mayat@womensfoundca.org
Internet: http://www.womensfoundca.org/grantmaking.html
Sponsor: Women's Foundation of California
340 Pine Street, Suite 302
San Francisco, CA 94104

Women's Foundation of Minnesota Grants **1731**
The fund supports women and girls organizing for economic, political, and social change. Foundation grants are made in the following areas: social change/systems change—projects by and for women and/or girls that are designed to have a significant impact on societal attitudes and behaviors, or result in needed systemic change benefiting women and girls; grassroots empowerment—projects that bring together previously unorganized, traditionally underserved groups of women and/or girls as an initial organizing step in the process of social/systems change; and women, money, and social change—funding for new and innovative efforts that will stimulate giving and increase support for organizations, projects, and efforts benefiting women and/or girls. Types of support include start-up costs, program support, general operating support, technical assistance, and one- to two-year grants.
Requirements: Minnesota grassroots and established organizations operated by and for women and/or girls are eligible.
Restrictions: Grants do not support individuals, capital or endowment campaigns, political campaigns, or religious programs or activities.
Geographic Focus: Minnesota
Date(s) Application is Due: Jul 1
Samples: Assoc for the Advancement of Hmong Women (Minneapolis, MN)—for the Hmong Women's Health Education and Cancer Prevention Program, $12,000; Casa de Esperanza (Saint Paul, MN)—for the Fuerza Unida program, which mobilizes Latinas to help end domestic violence that affects them, $15,000; Council on Crime and Justice (Minneapolis, MN)—to disseminate research conducted by the Battered Women's Justice Project that highlights differences in levels of services provided to victims of domestic violence in Hennepin County, $10,000; Pro-Choice Resources/Naral (Minneapolis, MN)—for an effort to expand medical and surgical abortion services, especially to low-income women, by educating and training medical students and residents about the need to increase the pool of abortion providers in Minnesota, $15,000.
Contact: Pamela Moore, Program Officer; (888) 337-5010 or (612) 337-5010, ext. 23; (612) 337-0404; Pamela@wfmn.org
Internet: http://www.wfmn.org
Sponsor: Women's Foundation of Minnesota
155 Fifth Avenue S, Suite 900
Minneapolis, MN 55401

Women's Foundation of Southern Arizona Go Girls! Sports Grants **1732**
The foundation is a social change organization committed to helping women and girls overcome economic, political, gender, and social barriers. Grant categories include health, safety, and well-being for women and girls; economic justice for women and girls; and innovative programs that improve the status of women and girls. Types of support include project specific support, general operating support, and planning or start-up support. Applicants must submit an electronic letter of intent by the listed application deadline. Guidelines are available online.
Requirements: Southern Arizona nonprofit organizations are eligible.
Restrictions: The foundation does not provide funds for individuals; campaigns to elect candidates to public office; capital fund drives; debt reduction; endowments; fundraising events or one-time conferences; scholarships, fellowships, and tuition reimbursement; programs inconsistent with federal, state, and local non-discrimination statutes regarding equal employment opportunity; programs that promote religious activities; programs outside of Pima, Cochise, and Santa Cruz counties in southern Arizona; or individual classrooms or schools.
Geographic Focus: Arizona
Date(s) Application is Due: Oct 1
Amount: Up to 10,000 USD
Contact: Laura Penny, Program Officer; (520) 622-8886; (520) 770-1500; lpenny@womengiving.org

Internet: http://www.womengiving.org/programs/gogirl.php
Sponsor: Women's Foundation of Southern Arizona
2250 E Broadway Boulevard
Tucson, AZ 85719

Women's Foundation of Southern Arizona Grants 1733

Grants support projects that focus on the underlying root causes of problems faced by women and girls and create fundamental, long-term change; are community based and involve the target population in the design, development, and evaluation of the program; and foster collaboration among groups sharing similar interest areas. Preference will be given to issues such as health insurance coverage for nonelderly women, suicide among women, and the number of women living in poverty. Grants are awarded for project-specific support, general operating support, and planning or start-up support.
Requirements: Nonprofit organizations with 501(c)3 status, or emerging grassroots organizations or informal groups who have come together for a program that is consistent with the fund's mission may apply. Groups without tax-exempt status must consist of more than five women and have some type of governing body.
Restrictions: The fund does not provide funds for individuals, capital fund drives, endowments, campaigns to elect candidates to public office, programs that promote religious activities, programs outside the southern Arizona area, programs that are inconsistent with nondiscrimination ordinances regarding equal employment opportunity, and agencies that have been funded by SAWF for the last three consecutive years.
Geographic Focus: Arizona
Date(s) Application is Due: Oct 1
Amount: 600 - 10,000 USD
Samples: Boys and Girls Club of Tucson (AZ)—for the SMART Girls program, a health, fitness, prevention/education, and self-esteem enhancement program for girls ages 10 to 15, $3000; Planned Parenthood (AZ)—for TAG, an active group of young women providing peer-to-peer outreach, education, and traning and support to young women in southern Arizona as it relates to holistic sexuality and prevention, $4000.
Contact: Laura Penny, Program Officer; (520) 622-8886; (520) 770-1500; lpenny@womengiving.org
Internet: http://www.womengiving.org/grantmaking
Sponsor: Women's Foundation of Southern Arizona
2250 E Broadway Boulevard
Tucson, AZ 85719

Women's Funding Alliance Grants 1734

The alliance supports nonprofits in Washington for programs and projects supporting women and children in its areas of interest, including poverty, sexual assault, discrimination, domestic violence, education, and reproductive rights. Preference will be given to organizations that have women in leadership positions and who incorporate diversity in their projects and agencies. Grants are awarded once a year in the following areas: general operating support, capacity building, project specific and population specific. Nonprofits interested in being included on the request-for-proposal list can email the alliance. All Letters of Inquiry are due on May 31st. Applicants invited to submit a full proposal will be notified the third week of June. Full proposals are due in the Women's Funding Alliance office by 5:00 PM on July 23rd.
Requirements: Washington nonprofits are eligible.
Geographic Focus: Washington
Amount: 1,000 - 15,000 USD
Samples: Parents Organizing for Welfare and Economic Rights (P.O.WER), Olympia, WA, $15,000—P.O.WER will lead civic engagement efforts to educate and register new women voters and develop low-income, politically involved female leaders within WA State (2008); Statewide Poverty Action Network, Seattle, WA, $10,000— to fund their Vote for a Change campaign in order to increase voter turnout and participation among low-income citizens in Washington State, nearly 60% of which are women (2008); Equal Rights Washington, Seattle, WA, $25,000—funding to build leadership and civic engagement skills in lesbian, bisexual, transgender and queer (LBTQ) women in order to create social change and eliminate heterosexism and homophobia throughout health care and public health systems (2008).
Contact: Sara Reyerson, (206) 467-6733; (206) 467-7537; sara@wfalliance.org or wfa@wfalliance.org
Internet: http://www.wfalliance.org/apply_for_funding.htm
Sponsor: Women's Funding Alliance
603 Stewart Street, Suite 207
Seattle, WA 98101-1229

Women's Fund of Rhode Island Grants 1735

The fund awards grants to eligible Rhode Island nonprofit organizations for projects designed to help level the playing field for women and girls. The fund is particularly interested in the following issues: leadership—including political participation and leadership, professional development opportunities, developing leadership in girls and women, and preteen prevention strategies to address self-esteem and self-advocacy issues; health, education, and well-being—including poverty, violence, teen pregnancy, self-esteem, health education and disease prevention, and K-16 education and adult literacy; economic autonomy—including women-owned enterprise, employment readiness and opportunity, and equal and livable wage; rights—including self-determination, public policy, and government action that assures the well-being of women and girls including immigrants. Types of support include project specific support, general operating support, planning, and start-up support. The fund considers funding on a year-to-year basis and does not make multiyear commitments. Application guidelines and forms are available online. The application deadline is for letters of intent.
Requirements: 501(c)3 nonprofits that serve women and girls who reside in Rhode Island and organizations applying through 501(c)3 fiscal agents that serve the target populations and area are eligible. The fund prefers to support organizations that have limited access to other donors.
Restrictions: The fund will not support projects that discriminate on the basis of ethnicity, race, color, creed, religion, gender, national origin, age, disability, marital status, sexual orientation, gender identity, or any veteran's status; or projects that present or incorporate religion in any manner. Grants do not support individuals or scholarships, capital or endowment, biomedical research or debt reduction, fundraising events or campaigns to elect candidates to public office.
Geographic Focus: Rhode Island
Date(s) Application is Due: Feb 18
Amount: 2,500 - 25,000 USD
Contact: Marcia Conee-Tighe, (401) 274-4564; (401) 331-8085
Internet: http://www.rifoundation.org/wfri/html/index.htm
Sponsor: Rhode Island Foundation
1 Union Station
Providence, RI 02903

Wood-Claeyssens Foundation Grants 1736

The foundation awards grants to eligible California nonprofit organizations in its areas of interest, including hospitals, theater, health, music, social services, youth, visual and performing arts, disabled, civil rights, and family services. Types of support include annual campaigns, capital campaigns, continuing support, and general operating support.
Requirements: California nonprofit organizations serving Santa Barbara and Ventura Counties are eligible.
Restrictions: Grants do not support tax-supported educational institutions; government-funded organizations; religious organizations, or political organizations; individuals; or medical research.
Geographic Focus: California
Date(s) Application is Due: Jun 30
Amount: 5,000 - 25,000 USD
Contact: Noelle Claeyssens Burkey, (805) 966-0543; (805) 966-1415
Sponsor: Wood-Claeyssens Foundation
P.O. Box 30586
Santa Barbara, CA 93130-0586

Woods Charitable Fund Grants 1737

This program seeks to strengthen the community by improving opportunities and life outcomes for all people in Lincoln, NE. Areas of interest include human services, arts and culture, education, and civic and community. A small number of grants are awarded outside of these categories. Woods supports members of the nonprofit sector who are exploring creative alternatives and promoting more just, effective approaches to meet community needs. They are interested in reviewing plans for pilot projects and innovative programs as well as sustained growth for organizations whose work coincides with the purposes of the foundation. The foundation funds both direct services and policy programs. The fund gives special consideration to programs and initiatives designed to prevent youth and family violence; and to groups that have not traditionally served refugees or immigrants but are trying to integrate them into their client bases, English language education for new Americans, and efforts to develop community acceptance for immigrants and refugees. Proposals are accepted March 1 through 15, June 1 through 15, and September 1 through 15 for board meetings in June, September, and December.

Requirements: Eligible applicants are 501(c)3 organizations that serve Lincoln, Nebraska.
Restrictions: Grants are not awarded to support individual needs, endowments, scholarships or fellowships, fund-raising benefits or program advertising, religious organizations for religious programs, capital projects in health care institutions, or medical and scientific research.
Geographic Focus: Nebraska
Date(s) Application is Due: Mar 15; Jun 15; Sep 15
Amount: 10,000 - 25,000 USD
Samples: Cedar Youth Services (Lincoln, NE)—for salary support and education incentives for teachers at six of its childhood-development centers, to evaluate the effects on staff retention, and to advocate an increase in child-care reimbursement rates paid by Nebraska Health and Human Services, $120,000 over two years; Matt Talbot Kitchen and Outreach (Lincoln, NE)—to expand its offices and storage space, $22,000 maximum; Folsom Children's Zoo and Botanical Gardens (Lincoln, NE)—for a program that seeks to attract nontraditional visitors, including immigrants and refugees, and to improve their visit through special outreach and education programs, $10,000; Oasis (Lincoln, NE)—for support groups, a website, and workshops for its restorative-justice programs, $20,000.
Contact: Pam Baker, (402) 436-5971; (402) 436-4128; pbaker@woodscharitable.org
Internet: http://www.woodscharitable.org/grants.html
Sponsor: Woods Charitable Fund
P.O. Box 81309
Lincoln, NE 68501

Woods Fund of Chicago Grants **1738**
In metropolitan Chicago the fund supports a wide range of nonprofit activities that include issue analysis, public policy development, advocacy, and citizen participation in efforts to improve the functioning of the city and neighborhoods. Funding priorities are community organization, public policies affecting families, and arts and culture. Proposals are welcomed from all types of community organizing groups. New, emerging, and well-established organizations are invited to request special community organizing guidelines before submitting a proposal. Guidelines and inquiry form are available online.
Requirements: The fund makes grants to tax-exempt organizations working to enhance life for all people in the metropolitan Chicago area and to improve opportunities for its least advantaged residents.
Restrictions: Areas not eligible for grant review include business or economic development, capital campaigns, endowments, fundraising, advertising, health care organizations, housing construction/rehabilitation, medical and scientific research, individual public and private schools, religious programs, residential care, counseling, clinics, recreational programs, social welfare agencies, and scholarships.
Geographic Focus: Illinois
Date(s) Application is Due: Jan 30; Jul 30
Amount: 10,000 - 25,000 USD
Samples: Bailiwick Repertory (Chicago, IL)—for general operating support, $30,000; Chicago Theatre Company (Chicago, IL)—for general operating support, $30,000; North Lawndale Employment Network (Chicago, IL)—for advocacy and policy work in behalf of ex-inmates and development of job-training programs and a booklet that directs ex-prisoners to government and nonprofit services, $103,000 over two years.
Contact: Deborah Clark, Grants and Operations Manager; (312) 782-2698; (312) 782-4155; dclark@woodsfund.org or info@woodsfund.org
Internet: http://www.woodsfund.org
Sponsor: Woods Fund of Chicago
360 N Michigan Avenue, Suite 1600
Chicago, IL 60601

Woodward Governor Company Charitable Trust Grants **1739**
The company-sponsored trust supports nonprofits in areas of company operations, including Rockford, IL; Fort Collins, CO; and Stevens Point, WI. Areas of interest include vocational education, adult basic education, and literacy programs; health care, health organizations, and hospices; delinquency prevention programs and services; services for minorities and immigrants; human services for the homeless, community and economic development; and arts/culture, including museums. Types of support include general operations, annual campaigns, capital campaigns, continuing support, equipment acquisition, seed funding, and emergency funding. There are no application deadline dates; receipt of proposals is preferred in March and July. Applications forms are not required.
Requirements: Only Colorado, Illinois, and Wisconsin organizations are eligible to apply.
Restrictions: Grants are not awarded to individuals or for endowment funds, research, scholarships, fellowships, special projects, publications, conferences, loans, or matching gifts.
Geographic Focus: Colorado, Illinois, Wisconsin
Amount: 500 - 200,000 USD
Contact: Pam Johnson, Chair, Contributions Committee
Sponsor: Woodward Governor Company Charitable Trust
5001 N Second Street
Rockford, IL 61125-7001

Wortham Foundation Grants **1740**
The foundation awards grants to nonprofits in Harris County, TX, in its areas of interest, including arts, performing arts, museums, community improvement, and civic beautification projects. Types of support include general operating support, continuing support, annual campaigns, capital campaigns, endowment funds, emergency funds, seed money, and matching funds. Proposals should be submitted preferably by the second week of January, April, July, and October for board meetings in February, May, August, and November. Obtain application forms from the office.
Requirements: Houston nonprofit organizations in Harris County, TX, are eligible.
Restrictions: Grants are generally not awarded to colleges, universities, hospitals, or individuals.
Geographic Focus: Texas
Amount: 10,000 - 100,000 USD
Samples: Houston Grand Opera (Houston, TX)—for a multiple-year program to record, preserve, and disseminate the company's opera productions, $300,000; Museum of Fine Arts (Houston, TX)—for capital support, $1.5 million.
Contact: Barbara Snyder, Grants Administrator; (713) 526-8849; (713) 526-7222; bsnyder@wortham.org
Sponsor: Wortham Foundation
2727 Allen Parkway, Suite 1570
Houston, TX 77019

WWF Russell E. Train EFN Alumni Grants **1741**
EFN Alumni Grants support ongoing education and training for former Russell E. Train Fellows or Scholars who have earned a degree through EFN. There is no deadline for Alumni grants; they are awarded on a first-come, first-served basis. Funds may be used to attend conferences, workshops, and short-term training courses offered by universities and other institutions or to conduct research within a WWF priority place.
Requirements: To be eligible for an EFN Alumni Grant, applicants must: be a former Russell E. Train Fellow or Scholar; have submitted all reports required by their grant contracts; have completed their two-year work requirement in their home country; have a bank account in their own name that can receive U.S. dollars; not have received an EFN Alumni Grant from EFN in the past three years. To apply go to: http://www.wwfapply.com. EFN alumni from any country are eligible to apply.
Restrictions: Grant requests may not exceed U.S. $3,500 and alumni must observe a three year waiting period before requesting another grant.
Geographic Focus: All U.S. States
Amount: Up to 3,500 USD
Contact: Mercedes Gonzalez, Program Officer; (202) 778-9612; mercedes.gonzalez@wwfus.org
Internet: http://www.worldwildlife.org/science/fellowships/train/item1829.html
Sponsor: World Wildlife Fund
1250 24th Street NW, P.O. Box 97180
Washington, DC 20090-7180

WWF Russell E. Train EFN Conservation Workshop Grants **1742**
EFN Conservation Workshop Grants support non-governmental organizations, community groups, government agencies, and educational institutions. Costs covered include travel expenses, meals and accommodations, room rentals, materials, and other related costs. Administrative costs should be no more than 15 percent of the requested amount. Typical grants are between $1,500 and $7,500.
Requirements: To be eligible for an EFN Conservation Workshop Grant, the following criteria must be met: your organization must have an established presence in the following countries: Belize; Bhutan; Bolivia; Brazil; Cambodia;

Cameroon; Central African Republic; Colombia; Dem. Republic of Congo; Ecuador; Gabon; Guatemala; Guyana; Honduras; Indonesia; Kenya; Laos; Malaysia; Mexico; Mozambique; Namibia; Nepal; Peru; Philippines; Republic of Congo; Suriname; Tanzania; Vietnam; proposed training and capacity building activities must provide skills and knowledge to groups that will help advance conservation in that country; training must take place within six months of submission of the application. To apply, download the EFN Conservation Workshop Grant Application at: www.worldwildlife.org/science/fellowships/trai/WWFBinaryitem9134.doc. An application will be considered for funding only when the following information is provided: name and mission of the organization; complete contact information of the person managing the training activity; a narrative description of the activity, its objectives, and expected outcomes; start and end dates, location, and expected number of participants; a detailed budget; complete bank account information (bank accounts must be in the name of your organization and must be able to receive U.S. dollars); completed applications may be submitted to EFN by email to efn@wwfus.org. There is no application deadline. Grants are awarded to deserving proposals on a first-come, first-served basis.
Restrictions: Organizations that require funds in less than 90 days of submitting an application will not be considered for funding. Organizations are limited to one EFN Conservation Workshop Grant every two years. Priority is given to organizations that have not yet benefited from this opportunity.
Geographic Focus: All U.S. States, Brazil, Colombia, Ecuador, Mexico, Peru, Philippines
Amount: 1,500 - 7,500 USD
Contact: WWF Member Services; (800) 960-0993
Internet: http://www.worldwildlife.org/science/fellowships/train/item8955.html
Sponsor: World Wildlife Fund
1250 24th Street NW, P.O. Box 97180
Washington, DC 20090-7180

Wyoming Arts Council Community Services Grants **1743**
Two grant categories exist within this program: Project and Multiple Project. Project grants are for a specific, one-time arts project or event. Multiple Project grants are for two or more projects or events in the performing, visual, literary, media, folk, or multidisciplinary arts. Annual deadline dates may vary; contact program staff for exact dates.
Requirements: Wyoming nonprofit tax-exempt organizations are eligible to apply.
Geographic Focus: Wyoming
Date(s) Application is Due: Mar 15
Amount: Up to 5,000 USD
Contact: Rita Basom, Community Services Program Manager; (307) 777-7109; (307) 777-5499; rbasom@state.wy.us
Internet: http://wyoarts.state.wy.us/gto.html
Sponsor: Wyoming Arts Council
2320 Capitol Avenue
Cheyenne, WY 82002

Xerox Foundation Grants **1744**
The foundation's goals are to preserve and invigorate its communities, to help educate and prepare tomorrow's workers and leaders (including enhancing learning opportunities for minorities and disadvantaged), to promote volunteerism among Xerox people, and to give the company a dimension of difference. Giving is broad in scope, encompassing education/work force preparedness, science/technology, employee/community affairs, culture, and national affairs. Xerox grants tend to complement the corporation's overall business goals, i.e., to support research and education in fields of science and technology directly applicable to the business; focus on geographical areas where large numbers of Xerox people live or where there are major facilities; involve a partnership among private, government, and nonprofit organizations; address current and relevant issues; offer creative approaches to long-standing problems; and support well-defined goals. Applications are reviewed on a monthly basis.
Requirements: Grants are made only to 501(c)3 and 509(a) organizations.
Restrictions: The foundation declines requests to support individuals; capital grants (new construction or renovation); endowments or endowed chairs; organizations supported by United Way, unless permission has been granted by United Way to a member agency to conduct a capital fund drive or a special benefit; political organizations or candidates; religious or sectarian groups; or municipal, county, state, federal, or quasi-government agencies.
Geographic Focus: All U.S. States
Amount: 500 - 50,000 USD
Samples: National Underground Railroad Freedom Ctr (Cincinnati, OH)—to establish the John Parker Library, which will house a variety of research material, including a digital archive of material related to the Underground Railroad and a genealogy-research area, $1 million.
Contact: Joseph Cahalan, Vice President; (203) 968-3445; (203) 968-3330
Internet: http://www.xerox.com/foundation
Sponsor: Xerox Foundation
800 Long Ridge Road, P.O. Box 1600
Stamford, CT 06904

Yampa Valley Community Foundation Grants **1745**
The foundation will consider proposals from organizations engaged in nonprofit activities in Routt County that benefit Routt County citizens. The foundation will make grants for general operations. An online request form and an application form are available on the website. Applications are generally accepted in the spring, and recipients are notified in the early summer. Call for specific dates. Application forms are available on the website.
Requirements: Nonprofit organizations in Steamboat Springs, Colorado, may apply.
Restrictions: The foundation does not make grants for debt reduction, endowments, political, or religious purposes.
Geographic Focus: Colorado
Date(s) Application is Due: Mar 1; Jun 1; Aug 1; Nov 1
Amount: 500 - 2,500 USD
Contact: Brooke Sanchez, Program Director; (970) 879-8632; (970) 871-0431; brooke@yvcf.org
Internet: http://www.yvcf.org
Sponsor: Yampa Valley Community Foundation
465 Anglers Drive, P.O. Box 881869
Steamboat Springs, CO 80488

Yellow Corporate Foundation Grants **1746**
The corporate foundation supports nonprofit organizations in the Kansas City, MO, area. Categories of support include cultural programs and entertainment, education, community development, and health programs. United Way agencies in communities in which the company does business receive 80 percent of the foundation's giving. Education support goes to colleges and universities. Community development support includes economic development, urban leagues, and chambers of commerce. Health and social service support includes programs assisting the visually impaired; disabled children, including psychological disabilities; and groups that aid battered women.
Requirements: IRS 501(c)3 tax-exempt nonprofit organizations in Missouri are eligible.
Restrictions: Grants are not made to individuals, nor to political, religious, or national health organizations.
Geographic Focus: Missouri
Contact: Daniel J. Churay, Director; (913) 696-6170
Sponsor: Yellow Corporate Foundation
10990 Roe Avenue, M.S. A515
Overland Park, KS 66211-1213

Youngstown Foundation Grants **1747**
The foundation makes grants to nonprofit organizations in Mahoning County, OH. Organizations wishing to apply should submit a dated cover letter that includes several sentences about the organization, a paragraph or two explaining the proposed project or program (including goals, objectives, and strategies for implementation as applicable), amount requested, and IRS tax-exemption determination letter. Submit the original and nine copies of the proposal. Applications are accepted at any time.
Requirements: Nonprofits in Mahoning County, Ohio, are eligible to apply.
Restrictions: Grants are not made to individuals.
Geographic Focus: Ohio
Contact: G.M. Walsh, Executive Director; (216) 744-0320; (330) 744-0344
Sponsor: Youngstown Foundation
P.O. Box 1162
Youngstown, OH 44501

Youth Philanthropy Project **1748**
The program encourages young people from across the region to participate in community service and to develop leadership skills, and especially encourages student volunteerism and philanthropy by engaging young people in decision-making about the distribution of grant dollars.

Requirements: Any youth-run organization that impacts the City of Richmond, Henrico, Hanover and Chesterfield Counties that is in need of funding for programs that benefit the community. Applicants may include, but are not limited to, church youth groups, school clubs or volunteer organizations that involve youth in the planning, implementation and evaluation of the proposed program. Consideration is given to youth-driven organizations that provide programs or services relating to one or more of the following focus areas - [1] Creating Safe Neighborhoods: Supporting a community where neighbors share an interest in protecting their communities and providing residents with the tools to identify and address their assets and needs; [2] Strengthening Families: Encouraging families to build stronger, healthier, and more productive environments for themselves, their community and their children; and [3] Achieving Academic Success: Supporting programs that promote literacy, improve test scores, increase school attendance, and encourage parental involvement.
Restrictions: Applications sent by facsimile or email will not be accepted.
Geographic Focus: Virginia
Date(s) Application is Due: Apr 12; Oct 12
Amount: 500 - 10,000 USD
Contact: Susan Hallett, Program Officer; (804) 330-7400, ext. 124; (804) 330-5992; shallett@tcfrichmond.org
Internet: http://www.tcfrichmond.org/page2479.cfm
Sponsor: Community Foundation Serving Richmond and Central Virginia
7501 Boulders View Drive, Suite 110
Richmond, VA 23225

YSA Get Ur Good On Grants **1749**

Get Ur Good On Grants are available for youth-led service initiatives on Global Youth Service Day, April 23-25. Available to children and youth around the world, YSA's Get Ur Good On Grants will award 100 $500 grants to support projects addressing critical community needs such as poverty, education, and environmental sustainability. Grant applications are due February 22. Additional guidelines are available at: www.YSA.org/grants.
Geographic Focus: All U.S. States
Date(s) Application is Due: Feb 22
Amount: 500 USD
Contact: Megan Brudney, Grants Manager; (202) 296-2992; (202) 296-4030; Brudney@ysa.org
Internet: http://www.ysa.org/grants/programs/get-ur-good-grants
Sponsor: Youth Service America
1101 15th Street NW, Suite 200
Washington, DC 20005

YSA Lead Agency for Global Youth Service Day Grants **1750**

Youth Service America and State Farm are support up to 100 Global Youth Service Day (GYSD) and Semester of Service Lead Agencies for Global Youth Service Day (mid-April). Lead Agencies are local, regional, or statewide organizations across the United States, and the Canadian provinces of Alberta, Ontario, or New Brunswick that increase the scale, visibility, and impact of Global Youth Service Day by taking a lead role in their city, region, or state. These Lead Agencies convene a planning coalition of at least 10 partner organizations that collectively engage at least 600 youth volunteers in service on GYSD, engage local media and elected officials, and plan a high profile signature project or celebration of service. The Agencies receive a $2,000 GYSD planning grant sponsored by State Farm, travel support to attend the Youth Service Institute, and ongoing training and technical assistance from Youth Service America to ensure a successful Global Youth Service Day or Semester of Service. Past Lead Agencies have leveraged their position as a GYSD Lead Agency to strengthen their programs, form new partnerships, expand their volunteer base, garner media attention, gain support from local public officials, and secure additional funding.
Requirements: Lead agencies must be located in one of the 50 states, the District of Columbia, or the Canadian provinces of Alberta, Ontario, or New Brunswick; demonstrate the organizational capacity to fulfill the responsibilities of a lead agency; have the ability to engage a variety of community groups; have the ability to plan to mobilize a citywide, regional, or statewide National Youth Service Day celebration involving more than 500 youth volunteers in service over the weekend of the event; and respond to quick deadline press opportunities.
Geographic Focus: All U.S. States, Canada
Date(s) Application is Due: Jul 22
Amount: 2,000 USD
Contact: Mike Man, Manager of Outreach; (202) 296-2992; (202) 296-4030; mman@ysa.org or info@ysa.org
Internet: http://www.ysa.org/grants/leadagency
Sponsor: Youth Service America
1101 15th Street NW, Suite 200
Washington, DC 20005

Z. Smith Reynolds Foundation Community Economic Development Grants **1751**

The Foundation seeks to foster economic well-being for all families and to build economic vitality and sustainability for all communities. The Foundation invests in organizations and projects that achieve the following: protects and increases the incomes and assets of low-income families and individuals; and increases community control of economic assets and economic independence for the benefit of rural or low-income residents. New programs, rather than those that are well-established and well-funded, receive priority consideration. Types of support include operating budgets, continuing support, annual campaigns, seed grants, matching funds, projects/programs, conferences and seminars, and technical assistance.
Requirements: The foundation makes grants only to nonprofit, tax-exempt, charitable organizations and institutions in North Carolina.
Restrictions: The foundation does not give priority to: the arts; capital campaigns; computer hardware or software purchases; conferences, seminars, or symposiums; crisis intervention programs; fund raising events; historic preservation; local food banks; or substance abuse treatment programs.
Geographic Focus: North Carolina
Date(s) Application is Due: Feb 1; Aug 1
Amount: 5,000 - 14,000,000 USD
Contact: Mary Fant Donnan, (800) 443-8319, ext. 101 or (336) 725-7541, ext. 101; (336) 725-6069; maryd@zsr.org or info@zsr.org
Internet: http://www.zsr.org/community.htm
Sponsor: Z. Smith Reynolds Foundation
147 South Cherry Street, Suite 200
Winston-Salem, NC 27101-5287

Z. Smith Reynolds Foundation Democracy and Civic Engagement Grants **1752**

The Foundation seeks to foster a government that is accountable to the needs of the people; a media that provides fair and substantial information on issues facing the state and its people; a citizenry that is engaged, well-informed and participates in the life of the state; and sound public policy that is built upon comprehensive and balanced research. New programs, rather than those that are well-established and well-funded, receive priority consideration. Types of support include operating budgets, continuing support, annual campaigns, seed grants, matching funds, projects/programs, conferences and seminars, and technical assistance.
Requirements: The foundation makes grants only to nonprofit, tax-exempt, charitable organizations and institutions in North Carolina.
Restrictions: The foundation does not give priority to: the arts; capital campaigns; computer hardware or software purchases; conferences, seminars, or symposiums; crisis intervention programs; fund raising events; historic preservation; local food banks; or substance abuse treatment programs.
Geographic Focus: North Carolina
Date(s) Application is Due: Feb 1; Aug 1
Amount: 5,000 - 14,000,000 USD
Contact: Joy Vermillion Heinsohn, (800) 443-8319, ext. 106 or (336) 725-7541, ext. 106; (336) 725-6069; joyv@zsr.org or info@zsr.org
Internet: http://www.zsr.org/democracy.htm
Sponsor: Z. Smith Reynolds Foundation
147 South Cherry Street, Suite 200
Winston-Salem, NC 27101-5287

Z. Smith Reynolds Foundation Environment Grants **1753**

The Foundation seeks to conserve, protect, improve and restore the state's natural areas; to ensure clean air and water for all North Carolinians; and to minimize the burden of the state's environmental hazards, particularly on marginalized communities. The Foundation invests in organizations and projects that: prevent poor communities and communities of color from bearing a disproportionately high or adverse burden of environmental hazards; guarantee clean water for all; guarantee clean air for all; conserve green space; and guarantee a healthy coastal ecosystem. New programs, rather than those that are well-established and well-funded, receive priority consideration. Types of support include operating budgets, continuing support, annual campaigns,

seed grants, matching funds, projects/programs, conferences and seminars, and technical assistance.
Requirements: The foundation makes grants only to nonprofit, tax-exempt, charitable organizations and institutions in North Carolina.
Restrictions: The foundation does not give priority to: the arts; capital campaigns; computer hardware or software purchases; conferences, seminars, or symposiums; crisis intervention programs; fund raising events; historic preservation; local food banks; or substance abuse treatment programs.
Geographic Focus: North Carolina
Date(s) Application is Due: Feb 1; Aug 1
Amount: 5,000 - 14,000,000 USD
Contact: Hawley Truax, (800) 443-8319, ext. 120 or (336) 725-7541, ext. 120; (336) 725-6069; hawleyt@zsr.org or info@zsr.org
Internet: http://www.zsr.org/environment.htm
Sponsor: Z. Smith Reynolds Foundation
147 South Cherry Street, Suite 200
Winston-Salem, NC 27101-5287

Z. Smith Reynolds Foundation Pre-Collegiate Education Grants 1754
The Foundation seeks to foster an educational system that provides each student in North Carolina the constitutionally guaranteed right of a sound, basic education regardless of race, socio-economic status, gender, geography or other discriminating factors. The Foundation invests in organizations and projects that: train, place and retain highly-qualified teachers for every child and skilled administrators for every school, with particular emphasis on increasing the number of people of color in those positions; and improve educational achievement through equity in education. New programs, rather than those that are well-established and well-funded, receive priority consideration. Types of support include operating budgets, continuing support, annual campaigns, seed grants, matching funds, projects/programs, conferences and seminars, and technical assistance.
Requirements: The foundation makes grants only to nonprofit, tax-exempt, charitable organizations and institutions in North Carolina.
Restrictions: The foundation does not give priority to: the arts; capital campaigns; computer hardware or software purchases; conferences, seminars, or symposiums; crisis intervention programs; fund raising events; historic preservation; local food banks; or substance abuse treatment programs.
Geographic Focus: North Carolina
Date(s) Application is Due: Feb 1; Aug 1
Amount: 5,000 - 14,000,000 USD
Contact: Leslie Winner, Executive Director; (800) 443-8319, ext. 105 or (336) 725-7541, ext. 105; (336) 725-6069; lwinner@zsr.org or info@zsr.org
Internet: http://www.zsr.org/precollegiate_edu.htm
Sponsor: Z. Smith Reynolds Foundation
147 South Cherry Street, Suite 200
Winston-Salem, NC 27101-5287

Z. Smith Reynolds Foundation Small Grants 1755
The Z. Smith Reynolds Foundation now offers a Small Grants Process for grant requests of up to $35,000 per year for up to two years. Small grants are made in the areas of community building and economic development, the environment, governance, public policy and civic engagement, pre-collegiate education, and social justice or equity. In addition to funding projects that achieve the goals of each focus area, the foundation has an interest in building the capacity of organizations and in promoting organizational development. New programs, rather than those that are well-established and well-funded, receive priority consideration. Types of support include operating budgets, continuing support, annual campaigns, seed grants, matching funds, projects/programs, conferences and seminars, and technical assistance.
Requirements: The foundation makes grants only to nonprofit, tax-exempt, charitable organizations and institutions in North Carolina.
Restrictions: The foundation does not give priority to: the arts; capital campaigns; computer hardware or software purchases; conferences, seminars, or symposiums; crisis intervention programs; fund raising events; historic preservation; local food banks; or substance abuse treatment programs.
Geographic Focus: North Carolina
Date(s) Application is Due: Aug 3
Contact: Leslie Winner, Executive Director; (800) 443-8319, ext. 105 or (336) 725-7541, ext. 105; (336) 725-6069; lwinner@zsr.org or info@zsr.org
Internet: http://www.zsr.org/small_grants.htm
Sponsor: Z. Smith Reynolds Foundation
147 South Cherry Street, Suite 200
Winston-Salem, NC 27101-5287

Z. Smith Reynolds Foundation Social Justice & Equity Grants 1756
The Foundation seeks to eliminate the unjust and unequal treatment of people of color, immigrants and those who are economically disadvantaged; eradicate the physical and sexual violence that threatens the lives and well-being of women; protect the rights of women to make choices about their reproductive health; and provide adolescents with information and choices that encourage them to avoid pregnancy. The Foundation invests in organizations and projects that: are non-discriminatory, just communities; and protect reproductive choice and reduce domestic violence and sexual assault. New programs, rather than those that are well-established and well-funded, receive priority consideration. Types of support include operating budgets, continuing support, annual campaigns, seed grants, matching funds, projects/programs, conferences and seminars, and technical assistance.
Requirements: The foundation makes grants only to nonprofit, tax-exempt, charitable organizations and institutions in North Carolina.
Restrictions: The foundation does not give priority to: the arts; capital campaigns; computer hardware or software purchases; conferences, seminars, or symposiums; crisis intervention programs; fund raising events; historic preservation; local food banks; or substance abuse treatment programs.
Geographic Focus: North Carolina
Date(s) Application is Due: Feb 1; Aug 1
Amount: 5,000 - 14,000,000 USD
Contact: James Gore, (800) 443-8319, ext. 124 or (336) 725-7541, ext. 124; (336) 725-6069; jamesg@zsr.org or info@zsr.org
Internet: http://www.zsr.org/social_justice.htm
Sponsor: Z. Smith Reynolds Foundation
147 South Cherry Street, Suite 200
Winston-Salem, NC 27101-5287

Subject Index

Adults

Advertising

Africa

African American Students

African American Studies

African Americans

African Art

After-School Programs

Age Discrimination

Aging/Gerontology

Asia

Asia, East (Far East)

Asian Americans

Asian Arts

Assisted-Living Programs

Assistive Technology

Asthma

Astronomy

Astrophysics

At-Risk Students

Children and Youth

Civic Engagement

Civics

Civics Education

Civil Law

Civil Service

Civil Society

Civil/Human Rights

Classroom Instruction

Climatology

Community Education

Community Outreach

Community Services

Community and School Relations

Cultural Diversity

Disabled (Target Groups)

Disabled Student Support

Disabled, Accessibility for

Disabled, Education

Disadvantaged, Economically

Disaster Preparedness

Economic Justice

Economic Opportunities

Economic Self-Sufficiency

Economic Stimulus

Economic Theory

Economics

Economics Education

Education Reform

Environmental Effects

Environmental Health

Environmental Law

Environmental Planning/Policy

Environmental Programs

Environmental Protection

Environmental Research

Environmental Services

Environmental Studies

Epilepsy

Episcopal Church

Equal Opportunity

Equipment/Instrumentation

Family Planning

Family/Marriage Counseling

Farm and Ranch Management

Fellowship Programs, General

Jewish Studies

Job Training Programs

Journalism

Journalism Education

Junior High School Education

Junior and Community Colleges

Justice

Juvenile Correctional Facilities

Refugees

Regional Planning/Policy

Regional/Urban Design

Rehabilitation/Therapy

Rehabilitation/Therapy, Emotional/Social

Rehabilitation/Therapy, Occupational/Vocational

Religion

Youth Services

Youth Violence

Zoology

Zoos

Program Type Index

NOTE: Numbers refer to entry numbers

Awards/Prizes

Basic Research

Building Construction and/or Renovation

Capital Campaigns

Centers: Research/Demonstration/Service

Citizenship Instruction

Community Development

Consulting/Visiting Personnel

Cultural Outreach

Curriculum Development/Teacher Training

Exhibitions, Collections, Performances, Video/Film Production

Faculty/Professional Development

Fellowships

General Operating Support

Graduate Assistantships

Grants to Individuals

International Exchange Programs

International Grants

Job Training/Adult Vocational Programs

Matching/Challenge Funds

Materials/Equipment Acquisition (Computers, Books, Videos, etc.)

Preservation/Restoration

Professorships

Publishing/Editing/Translating

Religious Programs

Scholarships

Seed Grants

Service Delivery Programs

Symposiums, Conferences, Workshops, Seminars

Technical Assistance

Training Programs/Internships

Travel Grants

Vocational Education

Geographic Index

Note: This index lists grants for which applicants must be residents of or located in a specific geographic area. Numbers refer to entry numbers.

United States

All States

Alabama

Alaska

Arizona

Michigan

Minnesota

New Mexico

New York

North Carolina

North Dakota

Ohio

Utah

Vermont

Virginia

Washington

West Virginia

Wisconsin

Wyoming

End Index by state

Canada

www.ingramcontent.com/pod-product-compliance
Lightning Source LLC
LaVergne TN
LVHW082015200926
848481LV00010B/2865
9780983762218